UNIVERSITY CASEBOOK SERIES®

AMES, CHAFEE, AND RE ON

REMEDIES

CASES AND MATERIALS

SECOND EDITION

EMILY SHERWIN
Professor of Law
Cornell Law School

SAMUEL L. BRAY
Professor of Law
UCLA School of Law

FOUNDATION PRESS

444 Cedar Street, Suite 700
St. Paul, MN 55101
1-877-888-1330

Printed in the United States of America

ISBN: 978-1-62810-025-9

To B.B.
To A., ὡς ἄμπελος

PREFACE

This book is a teaching text, designed to introduce students to the remedies they must understand to be successful in any field of practice. These remedies are, for the most part, products of the common law. They are not the result of a grand plan or central organization, but instead grew out of the old writs and the decrees of the Chancellor. Understanding these remedies therefore requires a sense of history. To that end, this book includes not only leading cases but also historical introductions to each of the three main sections: damages, equity, and restitution.

This book treats equity as a vital part of modern law. Although equity has been procedurally retired, it continues to influence judicial decisionmaking. In particular, the division between legal and equitable remedies has proved stubbornly persistent. Accordingly, this book devotes significant space to discussion of equitable concepts and terminology.

The primary method of the book is not to catalogue rules and their exceptions, but to present leading principles of remedies law and then illustrate how these principles work across substantive areas. Often, the illustrations are a tort case and a contract case, to show how a principle has been adapted to context. A remedies course is especially suited to this approach. On many of the central questions about remedies—such as whether a court will award damages or instead issue an injunction—a student will attain mastery not through knowing propositions so much as through recognizing patterns.

Another distinguishing feature of the book is the attention given to restitutionary remedies. Restitution is enjoying a resurgence of attention among scholars and lawyers, in light of the excellent Restatement (Third) of Restitution and Unjust Enrichment (2011). The previous edition of this book expanded and modernized the discussion of restitutionary remedies, and that expansive consideration is maintained in this edition.

The most significant change is a new chapter on Remedies Against the Government. This chapter builds on the existing chapters on equity and adds more substantial coverage of topics such as federal-state relations and civil rights. Nevertheless, the book largely retains the private-law orientation that has characterized it through much of its history.

That history is long. The original materials on equity date to Dean James Barr Ames's CASES IN EQUITY JURISDICTION, first published in 1902. In 1934, Professors Zechariah Chafee, Jr., and Sidney Post Simpson assembled CASES ON EQUITY, which incorporated many of Dean Ames's materials. In the preface to the first edition of their casebook, Chafee and Simpson noted their reliance on the lecture notes of Dean Roscoe Pound, as well as contemporary writings by Professor Walter Wheeler Cook. Chafee and Simpson were later joined as editors by Professor John Philip Maloney. In 1958, Professor (later Judge) Edward

D. Re was added as an editor, and the book was retitled EQUITY: CASES AND MATERIALS. In 1982, Judge Re redesigned the book as CASES AND MATERIALS ON REMEDIES, adding discussion of damages and restitution. With the last edition, edited by Professors Emily Sherwin and Theodore Eisenberg and Joseph Re, Esquire, the book was retitled in acknowledgment of its principal past contributors, becoming AMES, CHAFEE, AND RE ON REMEDIES. We record here our great sadness at the loss of Professor Eisenberg and our gratitude to him for his many contributions to this book.

EMILY SHERWIN
SAMUEL L. BRAY

October 26, 2017

SUMMARY OF CONTENTS

PART V. ADDITIONAL TOPICS

TABLE OF CONTENTS

PART III. EQUITY

TABLE OF CASES

The principal cases are in bold type.

UNIVERSITY CASEBOOK SERIES®

AMES, CHAFEE, AND RE ON

REMEDIES

CASES AND MATERIALS

SECOND EDITION

PART I

INTRODUCTION TO REMEDIES

CHAPTER 1

INTRODUCTION

A. STUDYING JUDICIAL REMEDIES

The subject of remedies granted by courts is of immense practical importance. A classic legal maxim holds that where there is a right there is a remedy (*ubi jus ibi remedium*). This maxim, however, is not invariably true. Moreover, the judicial remedies that accompany rights can vary enormously, from nominal sums of money to billion-dollar judgments, and from orders that prevent wrongs before they occur to orders that require the defendant to undertake large-scale reparative projects. Thus, to say that a plaintiff has a legal right provides little information. To understand the meaning of the plaintiff's right, one must also determine what the plaintiff can recover through the mechanism of a lawsuit. Remedies are important to out-of-court settlement as well: the starting point for negotiation is the plaintiff's potential recovery, not the plaintiff's abstract legal right. Lawyers must also anticipate judicial remedies when they structure transactions.

The objective of a course on remedies is to teach the judicial remedies available for violations of legal rights, and more generally to make the student "remedies conscious." Prospective lawyers should be aware of the remedial choices available to plaintiffs, the defenses defendants may raise against particular remedies, the vocabulary courts use in discussing remedies, the purposes that shape judicial remedies, the sources of law that courts draw on in designing remedies, and the attitudes courts take toward their own remedial powers. To understand the field and acquire the remedial proficiency needed to provide competent legal advice, the student must approach remedies from a number of angles. The arsenal of judicial remedies and the terms in which courts discuss remedies developed over many centuries; therefore the student needs some background in the history of equity and the common law. The student must also grasp both the mechanics of remedies and the policies that influence remedial choice. Finally, the student should have a sense of how courts use legal remedies in the practical world of adjudication. To this end, the materials that follow include historical materials; a sampling of cases, old and new, that illustrate remedial doctrine and raise questions about remedial decisionmaking by courts; and data on judicial application of remedies.

The course of study laid out here addresses civil remedies, particularly as they apply to disputes between private parties—disputes based on contracts, torts, and transactions that result in unjust enrichment. At least in the private law context, the basic purpose of judicial remedies is to place a party who has been wronged, as nearly as possible, in the position that party would have been in if no wrong had occurred. The materials that follow also include discussion of public litigation, most often between an individual and a government, in which remedies may be shaped by broader social objectives.

In a legal system in which judicial decisions are open and available to the public and serve as precedents for future courts, judicial decisions can have implications beyond the parties involved in litigation. The outcome of a particular lawsuit is sure to affect the behavior of future actors who find themselves in similar circumstances, which may in turn have significant social and economic consequences. This is true of the law of remedies as well as the law defining substantive rights, and it is true in the context of private disputes as well as public litigation. Yet because remedies are distinct from rights, and because the remedy in a given case represents the final, particularized resolution of the parties' dispute, courts may take a different approach to remedial decisions than they would to decisions about substantive rights. They may exercise a greater degree of discretion and strike a different balance between general rules and individualized justice.

The discretion courts sometimes exercise in granting remedies is not (or should not be) equivalent to decision according to sentiment or whim. Since the days of the English Chancellors, judicial discretion has been understood to require an exercise of impartial judgment, guided by moral reasoning and taking into account the body of past decisions by judges. At the same time, it implies a heightened degree of attention to facts and context, even as courts are applying pre-established rules. The extent of remedial discretion is a central theme in the law of remedies.

B. TYPES OF REMEDIES

Remedies can be categorized in various ways. One classification divides remedies into specific and substitutional relief. Specific relief transfers a particular thing to the plaintiff, or brings about a particular state of affairs. Substitutional relief provides a substitute for the plaintiff's right, usually a monetary substitute.

To some extent, specific remedies and substitutional remedies run parallel to the remedies historically associated with equity and law. The division between equity and law dates to the late medieval period, when the English Chancellor, an officer of the king, began to give relief in extraordinary cases in which, for one reason or another, no remedy was available in the courts of law. From the outset, the Chancellor's remedies took the form of *in personam* decrees, which provided specific relief by ordering the defendant to act or refrain from acting in some way. The Chancellor's decrees were the precursors of modern injunctions. Meanwhile, the most prevalent remedy at law was (and is) damages, which substitute monetary compensation for what the plaintiff lost as a the result of a legal wrong. The correspondence between legal remedies and substitutional relief, however, is not perfect: courts of law also granted specific remedies for claims such as ejectment (for recovery of possession of land) and replevin (for recovery of possession of chattels).

Remedies can also be categorized according to the functions they serve. Compensatory remedies are designed to provide the plaintiff with a sum of money that will make up for the consequences of the wrong (*e.g.*, damages). Restitutionary remedies are designed to capture gains that the defendant obtained at the plaintiff's expense and cannot justly keep (*e.g.*, recovery in quasi-contract). Other remedies, especially equitable remedies, will require the defendant to do or refrain from doing some act, in order to prevent a wrong from occurring or to limit the consequences of a wrong that has already occurred (*e.g.*, injunction).

C. OBJECTIVES OF REMEDIES

Valco Cincinnati, Inc. v. N & D Machining Service, Inc.

Supreme Court of Ohio, 1986.
24 Ohio St. 3d 41.

This matter involves an action brought by Valco Cincinnati, Inc. ("Valco"), appellee, against N & D Machining Service, Inc. (d.b.a. Superior Adhesive Equipment Co.), and James E. Draginoff, appellants, alleging a wrongful appropriation of trade secrets and seeking an order that appellants be preliminarily and permanently enjoined from disclosing and using those trade secrets which in effect would prevent appellants from manufacturing certain replacement parts for Valco's products. . . .

The facts necessary to the understanding of the legal issues presented are in essence as follows. The cardboard and similar boxes in which products are packaged for shipment for consumer or industrial consumption are commonly fastened together with some type of industrial glue. The glue is generally dispensed at high speed to the containers moving on conveyors. The glue is dispensed through an applicator head within which there is a valve, activated by air pressure and controlled electronically to regulate the flow of cold glue onto the containers.

The equipment and parts manufactured by Valco include the applicator heads which extrude the glue in thin strips, the air pressure valves which control the flow of glue to the head, and the electronic controls which control the operation of the valve. The evidence advanced by Valco was to the effect that each of these components is critically designed to insure that the glue begins, and then ceases, to flow through the applicator head at precisely the right moment, in a fixed volume, without "trailing" onto surfaces where it is not desired.

Valco adduced evidence to show that it had its own engineering division in order to develop and test, in a field operation method, the heads and valves that it designed. Also, the facts were that over a period of more than twenty-four years in the business, Valco had developed a standardization of materials, processes, dimensions, and tolerances of its products. This information, gathered through its engineering, experimentation and expertise, was what Valco claimed to be its trade secret.

Appellant Draginoff was initially hired by Valco in 1976 as a machinist to be in charge of Valco's machine shop. The facts show that prior to coming to Valco, Draginoff had no experience in the commercial glue application field. Later he progressed to production manager and, as production manager, he had access to, and became familiar with, Valco's engineering drawings of its products, Valco's manufacturing processes, materials, manufacturing techniques, and also Valco's supplier and customer information. Further, the record indicates that appellant was well aware of Valco's policy pertaining to each of the above, and that he was expected, as a condition of employment, promotion and continued trust, to keep all such information confidential.

Shortly after he started with Valco, James Draginoff approached Buford L. Thomas, Valco's president, and asked if there were any objections to his setting up a machine shop in his brother's garage in order that he and his brother, Nicholas, might procure some outside machine shop work. It appears that they were given approval with the provision that such work did not interfere with James' job. The brothers were joined in this venture by a third brother, Carl, and together they incorporated a business under the name of N & D Machining Service, Inc. ("N & D"), one of the appellants herein. Neither of James' brothers had any prior experience in the commercial glue application equipment field.

Soon after starting in business, N & D contracted to make certain glue application parts for Valco, principally the applicator heads and related parts. In order to make these parts, Valco supplied N & D with its drawings, sketches and specifications, including detailed dimensions and tolerances. Valco also loaned N & D a special "jig" to make the applicator heads to Valco's strict specifications. The record shows that the jig was never returned to Valco.

In 1980, James resigned from Valco. Thereafter, it was learned that N & D had been manufacturing glue application equipment for a Valco competitor, using Valco's process, and that such equipment was offered at prices below those of Valco.

The trial court found that Valco's techniques and processes constituted protected trade secrets, that the defendants had not engineered and produced the questioned products independent of the acquired trade secret information, and that Valco had reasonably provided for measures to maintain security for its trade secrets. Accordingly, the court entered an order permanently enjoining the appellants from the reproduction of Valco replacement parts. . . .

■ HOLMES, JUSTICE. There are two issues presented upon appeal. The first is whether the trial court had sufficient evidence to support its findings that Valco's plans, materials, designs, processes, customer and pricing lists were all protected trade secrets. The second inquiry is whether the trial court abused its discretion by, in effect, *permanently* enjoining appellants from the manufacture of any valve components which might be interchanged or substituted for a Valco part. For the following reasons, we affirm the courts below.

Initially, the legal nature of the term "trade secret" must be analyzed. Ohio's courts have adopted the definition of "trade secret" found in IV Restatement of Torts (1939) 1, Section 757. Accordingly, R.C. 1333.51(A)(3) states that:

> "Trade secret' means the whole or any portion or phase of any scientific or technical information, design, process, procedure, formula, or improvement, or any business plans, financial information, or listing of names, addresses, or telephone numbers, which has not been published or disseminated, or otherwise become a matter of general public knowledge. Such . . . is presumed to be secret when the owner thereof takes measures designed to prevent it, in the ordinary course of business, from being available to persons other than those selected by the owner to have access thereto for limited purposes."

. . . Ohio has statutorily prohibited employees, in broadest terms, from disseminating or disclosing confidential matters of the employer without the knowledge and consent of the latter. . . .

Generally, under trade secret statutes, that which is proscribed is the misappropriation of the information obtained from the person holding the trade secret, whether such secret is obtained without the owner's consent, or originally with the owner's consent, and later converted to the use and gain of the one obtaining the secret. . . .

In contrast, a proper means of obtaining the information contained within a trade secret may be by way of (1) discovery by independent invention; (2) discovery by "reverse engineering," that is, by starting with the known product and working backward to find the method by which it was developed, the acquisition of the product having been by a fair and honest means, such as purchase of the item on the open market; (3) discovery under a license from the owner of the trade secret; (4) observation of the item in public use or on display; or by (5) obtaining the trade secret from published literature. . . .

[The court first affirmed the trial court's findings that Valco's designs for glue applicator parts and the processes it used to manufacture them were trade secrets, that Valco had taken reasonable steps to protect their secrecy, and that the defendants had misappropriated Valco's secrets.]

Although Ohio's trade secret statutes do not contain any specific provisions for providing injunctive relief to protect against the conversion or misappropriation of trade secrets, injunctions are, of course, the appropriate remedy to restrain the continued and future use, or threatened use, of misappropriated trade secrets.[2] The injunctive order may, in order to do equity, be as broad as reasonably thought necessary to place the injured party in the position that he would have been in had the misappropriation not taken place. Although punitive, perpetual injunctions have previously been granted. The law in the field would tend to indicate that the duration of the orders is generally limited to the extent of the time advantage gained by the misappropriator over good faith competitors, who could have gained knowledge of the trade secret by lawful and good faith means.

The trial court in this case issued an order which prohibited not only the production of parts interchangeable with Valco's parts, but also the buying or selling of any such parts made by others. Such an order may be considered punitive in nature, but we hold such not to be unreasonable as a sanction for this particular misappropriation. The appellants were not prohibited from manufacturing or dealing in parts that could be used interchangeably with other commercial glue applicators manufactured by other competitors. Therefore, the appellants are not foreclosed from doing business generally within this commercial field. . . .

As noted hereinabove, it is well-established that the trade secret policies in Ohio are to maintain standards of commercial ethics and the encouragement of invention, as well as the protection of the substantial investment of employers in their proprietary information. The underlying purposes of the injunction in this case are: to prevent appellants from being unjustly enriched, to prevent Valco's secrets from being disclosed to the public without its consent, to penalize appellants for their unethical and unlawful behavior, and to protect Valco's investment in its proprietary information. These are all legitimate state goals and are neither arbitrary nor capricious.

As to the duration of injunctive orders, such should generally terminate when a former trade secret becomes either known to good faith competitors, or is obtained by them because of the lawful availability of products that can be reverse engineered to reveal such trade secrets, subject to any additional period of restraint necessary to negate lead time acquired by the misappropriator. The trial court, in its analysis of the particular facts of the case, may determine that the circumstances were so egregious and violative of the relationship of the parties involved

---

[2] See, *e.g.*, Uniform Trade Secrets Act, Injunctive Relief (1980), 14 U.L.A. 541, 544, Section 2, which provides in part:

> "(a) Actual or threatened misappropriation may be *enjoined*. Upon application to the court, an injunction shall be terminated when the trade secret has ceased to exist, but the injunction may be continued for an additional reasonable period of time in order to eliminate commercial advantage that otherwise would be derived from the misappropriation." (Emphasis added.)

within the misappropriation that the ultimate sanction of a permanent injunction prohibiting the use of such unlawfully obtained commercial information might well be in order.

In the case here, there was evidence adduced to show the close relationship of the appellee company and the appellant James Draginoff who had worked his way into a position of confidentiality and management with the employer company. He had been granted the opportunity to form another company to produce certain products which would serve the needs of his employer, and he had been entrusted with confidential information and technical tools so as to provide assistance to that company. These confidences were violated in the guise of carrying out the agreed-upon relationship. This we hold to be a sufficiently egregious circumstance to provide the trial court with the basis for its permanent order. We conclude that the trial court did not abuse its discretion in this regard. . . .

■ WRIGHT, J., concurring in part and dissenting in part. I concur with the majority holding that sufficient evidence supported a finding of a misappropriation of trade secrets. I would limit this court's holding, however, to the first paragraph of the syllabus. As Justice Holmes points out, injunctive relief is awarded in trade secret cases in order to place the injured party in the position he would have been in but for the misappropriation. In my view a perpetual, punitive injunction does not serve this laudable purpose. Further, this type of injunctive relief conflicts with the public interest in promoting competition and in allowing employees to benefit from their knowledge and abilities.

Injunctive relief is generally limited to the period of time required for independent development by good faith competitors. The injunction would terminate once the trade secret becomes either generally known to good faith competitors or generally knowable to them because of the lawful availability of products subject to reverse engineering. The standard for injunctive relief I advocate eliminates the commercial advantage or "headstart" obtained by the misappropriator and places the injured party in the position he would have been in had the misappropriation not occurred. If a punitive measure is appropriate in a particular case, the owner of a trade secret has an adequate remedy by seeking money damages in place of or in addition to injunctive relief.

To the extent that the majority approved the granting of a perpetual injunction, I respectfully dissent.

NOTE ON THE OBJECTIVES OF REMEDIES

Shortly after graduating from law school, Learned Hand described the main purpose of a remedy this way, carefully distinguishing between cases in which the plaintiff needs to be moved forward or backward to the rightful position:

> "A remedy is an obligation destined to stand in the place of the plaintiff's rights, and be, as nearly as possible, an equivalent to him for his rights. Wherever the plaintiff has the right to the performance of some act by the defendant, that only can be a remedy to him for the defendant's failure to perform which is an equivalent to such a performance. But, obviously, to replace the plaintiff in his position before the defendant incurred his obligation is no equivalent to the plaintiff for the performance to which he had a right. It is not his former position which should be restored, but his future position which should be realized. It is only when the infraction of the plaintiff's right consists in a change from his former position that restitution can be a remedy, that is, when there has been a tort or the breach of a negative obligation; but where the infraction consists in a failure to act at all, the only remedy possible is a change in the plaintiff's former position, not a renewal of it."

Learned Hand, Restitution or Unjust Enrichment, 11 Harv. L. Rev. 249, 256 (1897).

D. THE PROBLEM OF INDIVIDUALIZED JUSTICE

Judgment According to Law

Patrick Devlin, THE JUDGE 84 (1979).

Judgment according to law is *not* invariably the same thing as judgment according to the merits of the particular case from which the judgment flows. The hallmark of judgment according to law is conformity with a set of rules. The rules should be designed so as to ensure justice in the normal case and also in any foreseeable exceptions, at least to the extent that provision for the exceptions does not make the rule intolerably cumbersome. But to frame a set of rules that would do justice in every case which could be brought within them would be, if not theoretically impossible, at any rate practically unattainable. So lawyers perforce accept the distinction between justice according to law and justice on the merits, or *ex aequo et bono* [in equity and good conscience] as they call it.

NOTE ON EQUITY

Aristotle gave the following description of equity:

> "So when the law speaks universally, and a particular case arises as an exception to the universal rule, then it is right—where the lawgiver fails us and has made an error by speaking without qualification—to correct the omission. This will be by saying what the lawgiver would himself have said had he been present, and would have included within the law had he known. What is equitable, therefore, is just, and better than one kind of justice. But it is not better than unqualified justice, only better than the error

> that results from its lacking qualification. And this is in the very nature of what is equitable—a correction of law, where it is deficient on account of its universality."

Aristotle, NICOMACHEAN ETHICS Bk. V, Ch. 11, 1137b (Roger Crisp, ed. 2000).

The word *equity* has other senses. It can refer to a moral reading of the law and its demands. Or, in a more technical sense, the word can refer to the doctrines and remedies developed by the English courts of equity. There are thus at least three main senses in which *equity* is used in this casebook and in other legal sources: (1) correcting an error that results from a general rule, often in an unanticipated case; (2) a moral reading of the law, one that may not be required by or may even be inconsistent with the positive law; and (3) the doctrines and remedies of English courts of equity, especially Chancery. These senses are not mutually exclusive, for as courts of equity decided cases (*equity* in sense three), they were influenced by the idea of correcting errors from general rules and the idea of preventing opportunistic abuse of legal rights (*equity* in senses one and two).

The remaining cases in this chapter illustrate the different senses in which *equity* may be used. In Riggs *v.* Palmer, the word has its second sense: a moral reading of the law. In Chief Judge Cardozo's dissent in Graf *v.* Hope Building Corp., the first and third senses predominate: a court of equity may correct an error resulting from a general rule. In Weinberger *v.* Romero-Barcelo, it has its third sense: the injunction is a remedy developed by the courts of equity, and to this day it remains shaped by its equitable history.

Riggs v. Palmer

Court of Appeals of New York, 1889.
115 N.Y. 506.

■ EARL, J. On the 13th day of August 1880, Francis B. Palmer made his last will and testament, in which he gave small legacies to his two daughters, . . . the plaintiffs in this action, and the remainder of his estate to his grandson, the defendant, Elmer E. Palmer . . . . The testator at the date of his will owned a farm and considerable personal property. . . . At the date of the will, and, subsequently, to the death of the testator, Elmer lived with him as a member of his family, and at his death was sixteen years old. He knew of the provisions made in his favor in the will, and, that he might prevent his grandfather from revoking such provisions, which he had manifested some intention to do, and to obtain the speedy enjoyment and immediate possession of his property, he willfully murdered him by poisoning him. [When this suit was filed, Elmer had already been convicted of murdering Francis and was serving time in a reformatory.] He now claims the property, and the sole question for our determination is, can he have it?

The defendants say that the testator is dead; that his will was made in due form and has been admitted to probate, and that, therefore, it must have effect according to the letter of the law. It is quite true that statutes regulating the making, proof and effect of wills, and the devolution of property, if literally construed, and if their force and effect can in no way and under no circumstances be controlled or modified, give this property to the murderer. . . .

Such a construction ought to be put upon a statute as will best answer the intention which the makers had in view, for [one who considers merely the letter of an instrument goes but skin deep into its meaning]. . . . In some cases the letter of a legislative act is restrained by an equitable construction; in others it is enlarged; in others the construction is contrary to the letter. . . . If the law-makers could, as to this case, be consulted, would they say that they intended by their general language that the property of a testator or of an ancestor should pass to one who had taken his life for the express purpose of getting his property? In 1 BLACKSTONE'S COMMENTARIES (91) the learned author, speaking of the construction of statutes, says: "If there arise out of them any absurd consequences manifestly contradictory to common reason, they are, with regard to those collateral consequences, void. . . . When some collateral matter arises out of the general words, and happen to be unreasonable, then the judges are in decency to conclude that the consequence was not foreseen by the parliament, and, therefore, they are at liberty to expound the statute by equity and only [as to this] disregard it;" and he gives as an illustration, if an act of parliament gives a man power to try all causes that arise within his manor of Dale, yet, if a cause should arise in which he himself is party, the act is construed not to extend to that because it is unreasonable that any man should determine his own quarrel. . . .

What could be more unreasonable than to suppose that it was the legislative intention in the general laws passed for the orderly, peaceable and just devolution of property, that they should have operation in favor of one who murdered his ancestor that he might speedily come into the possession of his estate? Such an intention is inconceivable. . . .

Besides, all laws as well as all contracts may be controlled in their operation and effect by general, fundamental maxims of the common law. No one shall be permitted to profit by his own fraud, or to take advantage of his own wrong, or to found any claim upon his own iniquity, or to acquire property by his own crime. These maxims are dictated by public policy, have their foundation in universal law administered in all civilized countries, and have nowhere been superseded by statutes. . . .

These maxims, without any statute giving them force or operation, frequently control the effect and nullify the language of wills. A will procured by fraud and deception, like any other instrument, may be decreed void and set aside, and so a particular portion of a will may be excluded from probate or held inoperative if induced by the fraud or undue influence of the person in whose favor it is. So a will may contain provisions which are immoral, irreligious or against public policy, and they will be held void.

Here there was no certainty that this murderer would survive the testator, or that the testator would not change his will, and there was no certainty that he would get this property if nature was allowed to take its course. He, therefore, murdered the testator expressly to vest himself with an estate. Under such circumstances, what law, human or divine, will allow him to take the estate and enjoy the fruits of his crime? The will spoke and became operative at the death of the testator. He caused that death, and thus by his crime made it speak and have operation. Shall it speak and operate in his favor? If he had met the testator and taken his property by force, he would have had no title to it. Shall he acquire title by murdering him? If he had gone to the testator's house and by force compelled him, or by fraud or undue influence had induced him to will him his property, the law would not allow him to hold it. But can he give effect and operation to a will by murder, and yet take the property? To answer these questions in the affirmative, it seems to me, would be a reproach to the jurisprudence of our state, and an offense against public policy.

Under the civil law evolved from the general principles of natural law and justice by many generations of jurisconsults, philosophers and statesmen, one cannot take property by inheritance or will from an ancestor or benefactor whom he has murdered. In the Civil Code of Lower Canada the provisions on the subject in the Code Napoleon have been substantially copied. But, so far as I can find, in no country where the common law prevails has it been deemed important to enact a law to provide for such a case. Our revisers and law-makers were familiar with the civil law, and they did not deem it important to incorporate into our statutes its provisions upon this subject. This is not a *casus omissus* [a case or event for which no provision has been made]. It was evidently supposed that the maxims of the common law were sufficient to regulate such a case and that a specific enactment for that purpose was not needed.

For the same reasons the defendant Palmer cannot take any of this property as heir. Just before the murder he was not an heir, and it was not certain that he ever would be. He might have died before his grandfather, or might have been disinherited by him. He made himself an heir by the murder, and he seeks to take property as the fruit of his crime. What has before been said as to him as legatee applies to him with equal force as an heir. He cannot vest himself with title by crime.

My view of this case does not inflict upon Elmer any greater or other punishment for his crime than the law specifies. It takes from him no property, but simply holds that he shall not acquire property by his crime, and thus be rewarded for its commission. . . .

The judgment of the General Term and that entered upon the report of the referee should, therefore, be reversed and judgment should be entered as follows: That Elmer E. Palmer and the administrator be enjoined from using any of the personalty or real estate left by the testator for Elmer's benefit; that the devise and bequest in the will to Elmer be declared ineffective to pass the title to him; that by reason of the crime of murder committed upon the grandfather he is deprived of any interest in the estate left by him; that the plaintiffs are the true owners of the real and personal estate left by the testator, subject to the charge in favor of Elmer's mother and the widow of the testator, under the ante-nuptial agreement, and that the plaintiffs have costs in all the courts against Elmer.

■ GRAY, J. (dissenting). . . . To sustain their position the appellants' counsel has submitted an able and elaborate brief, and, if I believed that the decision of the question could be affected by considerations of an equitable nature, I should not hesitate to assent to views which commend themselves to the conscience. But the matter does not lie within the domain of conscience. We are bound by the rigid rules of law, which have been established by the legislature, and within the limits of which the determination of this question is confined. The question we are dealing with is, whether a testamentary disposition can be altered, or a will revoked, after the testator's death, through an appeal to the courts, when the legislature has, by its enactments, prescribed exactly when and how wills may be made, altered and revoked, and, apparently, as it seems to me, when they have been fully complied with, has left no room for the exercise of an equitable jurisdiction by courts over such matters. Modern jurisprudence, in recognizing the right of the individual, under more or less restrictions, to dispose of his property after his death, subjects it to legislative control, both as to extent and as to mode of exercise. Complete freedom of testamentary disposition of one's property has not been and is not the universal rule; as we see from the provisions of the Napoleonic Code, from those systems of jurisprudence in other countries which are modeled upon the Roman law, and from the statutes of many of our states. To the statutory restraints, which are imposed upon the disposition of one's property by will, are added strict and systematic statutory rules for the execution, alteration and revocation of the will; which must be, at least, substantially, if not exactly, followed to insure validity and performance. The reason for the establishment of such rules, we may naturally assume, consists in the purpose to create those safeguards about these grave and important acts, which experience has demonstrated to be the wisest and surest. That freedom, which is permitted to be exercised in the testamentary disposition of one's estate by the laws of the state, is subject to its being exercised in conformity with the regulations of the statutes. The capacity and the power of the individual to dispose of his property after death, and the mode by which that power can be exercised, are matters of which the legislature has assumed the entire control, and has undertaken to regulate with comprehensive particularity.

The appellants' argument is not helped by reference to those rules of the civil law, or to those laws of other governments, by which the heir or legatee is excluded from benefit under the testament, if he has been convicted of killing, or attempting to kill, the testator. In the absence of such legislation here, the courts are not empowered to institute such a system of remedial justice. The deprivation of the heir of his testamentary succession by the Roman law, when guilty of such a crime, plainly, was intended to be in the nature of a punishment imposed upon him. The succession, in such a case of guilt, escheated to the exchequer. . . .

■ All concur with EARL, J., except GRAY, J., who reads dissenting opinion, and DANFORTH, J., concurring.

Graf v. Hope Building Corp.

Court of Appeals of New York, 1930.
254 N.Y. 1.

■ O'BRIEN, J. Plaintiffs, as executors of Joseph L. Graf, are the holders of two consolidated mortgages forming a single lien on real property the title to which is vested in defendant Hope Building Corporation. According to the terms of the agreement consolidating the mortgages the principal sum is made payable January 1, 1935. Nevertheless, a clause provides that the whole shall become due after default for twenty days in the payment of any installment of interest. David Herstein is the controlling stockholder and also president and treasurer of defendant. He alone was authorized to sign checks in its behalf. Early in June, 1927, he went to Europe. Before his departure a clerical assistant who was also the nominal secretary of the corporation computed the interest due July 1, and through an error in arithmetic incorrectly calculated it. Mr. Herstein signed the check for the erroneous amount but before the date upon which the interest became due, the secretary discovered the error, notified the mortgagee of the shortage of $401.87, stated that on the president's return from Europe the balance would be paid and on June 30 forwarded to the mortgagee the check as drawn. It was deposited by the mortgagee and paid by defendant. On July 5 Mr. Herstein returned, but, through an omission in his office, he was not informed of the default in the payment of interest. At the expiration of twenty-one days this action of foreclosure was begun. Defendant made tender of the deficiency but the mortgagee, strictly insisting on his contract rights, refused the tender and elected to assert the power created by the acceleration clause in the consolidation agreement.

On the undisputed facts as found, we are unable to perceive any defense to the action, and are therefore constrained to reverse the judgment dismissing the complaint. Plaintiffs may be ungenerous, but generosity is a voluntary attribute and cannot be enforced even by a chancellor. Forbearance is a quality which under the circumstances of this case is likewise free from coercion. Here there is no penalty, no forfeiture, nothing except a covenant fair on its face to which both parties willingly consented. It is neither oppressive nor unconscionable. In the absence of some act by the mortgagee which a court of equity would be justified in considering unconscionable, he is entitled to the benefit of the covenant. The contract is definite and no reason appears for its reformation by the courts. We are not at liberty to revise while professing to construe. Defendant's mishap, caused by a succession of its errors and negligent omissions, is not of the nature requiring relief from its default. Rejection of plaintiffs' legal right could rest only on compassion for defendant's negligence. Such a tender emotion must be exerted, if at all, by the parties rather than by the court. . . .

■ CARDOZO, C.J. (dissenting). . . . There is no undeviating principle that equity shall enforce the covenants of a mortgage, unmoved by an appeal *ad misericordiam* [to mercy], however urgent or affecting. The development of the jurisdiction of the chancery is lined with historic monuments that point another course. Equity declines to treat a mortgage upon realty as a conveyance subject to a condition, but views it as a lien irrespective of its form. Equity declines to give effect to a covenant, however formal, whereby in the making of a mortgage, the mortgagor abjures and surrenders the privilege of redemption. Equity declines in the same spirit, to give effect to a covenant, improvident in its terms, for the sale of an inheritance, but compels the buyer to exhibit an involuntary charity if he is found to have taken advantage of the necessities of the seller. Equity declines to give effect to a covenant for liquidated damages if it is so unconscionable in amount as to be equivalent in its substance to a provision for a penalty. One could give many illustrations of the traditional and unchallenged exercise of a like dispensing power. It runs through the whole rubric of accident and mistake. Equity follows the law, but not slavishly nor always. If it did, there could never be occasion for the enforcement of equitable doctrine.

To all this, acceleration clauses in mortgages do not constitute an exception. . . . In general, it is true, they will be enforced as they are written. In particular this has been held of a covenant in a mortgage accelerating the maturity of the principal in default of punctual payment of an installment of the interest. If the quality of penalty inheres in such a covenant at all, it is not there to such a degree as to call, in ordinary circumstances, for mitigation or repression. Less favor has been shown to a provision for acceleration of a mortgage in default of punctual payment of taxes or assessments. We have held that such a provision, though not a penalty in a strict or proper sense, is yet so closely akin thereto in view of the forfeiture of credit that equity will relieve against it if default has been due to mere venial inattention and if relief can be granted without damage to the lender. . . .

There is neither purpose nor desire to impair the stability of the rule, which is still to be enforced as one of general application, that nonpayment of interest will accelerate the debt if the mortgage so provides. The rule is well understood, and is fair to borrower and lender in its normal operation. Especially is it fair if there is a period of grace (in this case twenty days) whereby a reasonable leeway is afforded to inadvertence and improvidence. In such circumstances, with one period of grace established by the covenant, only the most appealing equity will justify a court in transcending the allotted period and substituting another. There is a difference, however, between a denial of power, without heed to the hardship calling for its use, and a definition of hardship that will limit the occasions upon which power shall be exercised. . . . However fixed the general rule and the policy of preserving it, there may be extraordinary conditions in which the enforcement of such a clause according to the letter of the covenant will be disloyalty to the basic principles for which equity exists. . . . The exercise of a dispensing power was deemed to be a branch of the jurisdiction of equity to relieve against the consequences of accident or mistake. "This does not mean that such provisions for accelerating payments are provisions for forfeitures. Fairly made and fairly enforced they are not." Even so, "a court of equity may intervene to prevent the creditor from taking an unconscionable advantage of the letter of his bargain."

When an advantage is unconscionable depends upon the circumstances. It is not unconscionable generally to insist that payment shall be made according to the letter of a contract. It may be unconscionable to insist upon adherence to the letter where the default is limited to a trifling balance, where the failure to pay the balance is the product of mistake, and where the mortgagee indicates by his conduct that he appreciates the mistake and has attempted by silence and inaction to turn it to his own advantage. The holder of this mortgage must have understood that he could have his money for the asking. His silence, followed, as it was, by immediate suit at the first available opportunity, brings conviction to the mind that he was avoiding any act that would spur the mortgagor to payment. What he did was almost as suggestive of that purpose as if he had kept out of the way in order to avoid a tender. Demand was, indeed, unnecessary to bring the debt to maturity at law. There is not a technical estoppel. The consequence does not follow that, in conditions so peculiar, the omission to make demand is without significance in equity. Significant it may then be in helping the court to a determination whether the conduct of a suitor in taking advantage of a default, so easily averted and so plainly unintentional, is consistent with good conscience. True, indeed, it is that accident and mistake will often be inadequate to supply a basis for the granting or withholding of equitable remedies where the consequences to be corrected might have been avoided if the victim of the misfortune had ordered his affairs with reasonable diligence. The restriction, however, is not obdurate, for always the gravity of the fault must be compared with the gravity of the hardship. Let the hardship be strong enough, and equity will find a way, though many a formula of inaction may seem to bar the path.

Cases such as Klein *v.* New York Life Ins. Co. (104 U.S. 88); Wheeler *v.* Connecticut Mutual Life Insurance Co. (82 N.Y. 543), and Whiteside *v.* North American Accident Insurance Co. (200 N.Y. 320) do not derogate from the doctrine that a postulant in equity for affirmative relief may be dismissed without a remedy where he is attempting as an actor in the lawsuit to make himself the beneficiary of accident or error. In those cases and in others like them there was an attempt to charge a defendant with a contractual liability in disregard of the conditions limiting its creation. The party insisting on the condition was before the court as a defendant resisting a liability which could only arise if the condition was a nullity. Here, on the other hand, there is no endeavor by the owner of the property to charge the mortgagee with an obligation to do anything affirmative. The operation of the decree will be negative altogether. There is nothing more than a refusal to give active aid and countenance to one who seeks the aid of equity and is unwilling as a price to do equity himself. In equity as in mechanics action and reaction are equal and opposite. The equity that one asks one must be ready to concede. The maxim applies "whatever be the nature of the controversy between two definite parties, and whatever be the nature of the remedy" (Pomeroy, EQUITY JURISPRUDENCE, vol. 1, § 385). The court will stand aside when by intervening it will make itself an instrument of injustice. . . .

In this case, the hardship is so flagrant, the misadventure so undoubted, the oppression so apparent, as to justify a holding that only through an acceptance of the tender will equity be done. The omission to pay in full had its origin in a clerical or arithmetical error that accompanied the act of payment, the very act to be performed. The error was not known to the debtor except in a constructive sense, for the secretary, a subordinate clerk, omitted to do her duty and report it to her principal. The deficiency, though not so small as to be negligible within the doctrine of *de minimis,* was still slight and unimportant when compared with the payment duly made. The possibility of bad faith is overcome by many circumstances, of which not the least is the one that instantly upon the discovery of the error, the deficiency was paid, and this only a single day after the term of grace was at an end. Finally, there is no pretense of damage or even inconvenience ensuing to the lender. On the contrary, and this is the vital point, the inference is inevitable that the lender appreciated the blunder and was unwilling to avert it. From his conduct on the day immediately succeeding the default, we can infer his state of mind as it existed the day before. When all these circumstances are viewed in their cumulative significance, the enforcement of the covenant according to its letter is seen to approach in hardship the oppression of a penalty, just as truly as in Noyes *v.* Anderson there was unconscionable hardship in an insistence upon a default in the discharge of an assessment. Ninety-one per cent of the interest had been paid when it matured. The other nine per cent was paid as soon as the underpayment became known to an agent competent to act, and only a day too late. Equity declines to intervene at the instance of a suitor who after fostering the default would make the court his ally in an endeavor to turn it to his benefit. . . .

■ POUND, CRANE and HUBBS, JJ., concur with O'BRIEN, J.; CARDOZO, C.J., dissents in opinion in which LEHMAN and KELLOGG, JJ., concur.

Weinberger v. Romero-Barcelo

Supreme Court of the United States, 1982.
456 U.S. 305.

■ JUSTICE WHITE delivered the opinion of the Court. . . .

[The Navy, in the course of using an island off the Puerto Rico coast for air-to-ground weapons training, discharged ammunition into the waters surrounding the island. Romero-Barcelo brought an action in United States district court to enjoin the Navy's operation, alleging a violation of the Federal Water Pollution Control Act (FWPCA). Although the district court found that the discharges did not harm the quality of the water, it held that the Navy had violated the FWPCA by discharging ordnance into the water without first obtaining a permit from the Environmental Protection Agency. It ordered the Navy to apply for a permit but refused to enjoin the operation pending consideration of the permit application. In doing so, it quoted the Supreme Court's decision in Hecht Co. *v.* Bowles, 321 U.S. 321, 329–330 (1944): "The historic injunctive process was designed to deter, not to punish."

[On appeal, the United States Court of Appeals for the First Circuit vacated the district court's order and remanded with instructions that the district court order the Navy to cease the violations until a permit was obtained. Relying on TVA *v.* Hill, 437 U.S. 153 (1978), a case in which the Supreme Court held that an imminent violation of the Endangered Species Act required injunctive relief, the court of appeals concluded that the district court erred in undertaking a traditional balancing of the parties' competing interests.]

It goes without saying that an injunction is an equitable remedy. It "is not a remedy which issues as of course," or "to restrain an act the injurious consequences of which are merely trifling." An injunction should issue only where the intervention of a court of equity "is essential in order effectually to protect property rights against injuries otherwise irremediable." Cavanaugh *v.* Looney, 248 U.S. 453, 456 (1919). The Court has repeatedly held that the basis for injunctive relief in the federal courts has always been irreparable injury and the inadequacy of legal remedies.

Where plaintiff and defendant present competing claims of injury, the traditional function of equity has been to arrive at a "nice adjustment and reconciliation" between the competing claims. In such cases, the court "balances the conveniences of the parties and possible injuries to them according as they may be affected by the granting or withholding of the injunction." Yakus *v.* United States, 321 U.S. 414, 440 (1944). "The essence of equity jurisdiction has been the power of the Chancellor to do equity and to mould each decree to the necessities of the particular case. Flexibility rather than rigidity has distinguished it." Hecht Co. *v.* Bowles, 321 U.S. 321, 329 (1944).

In exercising their sound discretion, courts of equity should pay particular regard for the public consequences in employing the extraordinary remedy of injunction. Thus, the Court has noted that "[the] award of an interlocutory injunction by courts of equity has never been regarded as strictly a matter of right, even though irreparable injury may otherwise result to the plaintiff," and that "where an injunction is asked which will adversely affect a public interest for whose impairment, even temporarily, an injunction bond cannot compensate, the court may in the public interest withhold relief until a final determination of the rights of the parties, though postponement may be burdensome to the plaintiff." Yakus *v.* United States, *supra*, at 440. The grant of jurisdiction to ensure compliance with a statute hardly suggests an absolute duty to do so under any and all circumstances, and a federal judge sitting as chancellor is not mechanically obligated to grant an injunction for every violation of law.

These commonplace considerations applicable to cases in which injunctions are sought in the federal courts reflect a "practice with a background of several hundred years of history," Hecht Co. *v.* Bowles, *supra*, at 329, a practice of which Congress is assuredly well aware. Of course, Congress may intervene and guide or control the exercise of the courts' discretion, but we do not lightly assume that Congress has intended to depart from established principles. As the Court said in Porter *v.* Warner Holding Co., 328 U.S. 395, 398 (1946):

> "Moreover, the comprehensiveness of this equitable jurisdiction is not to be denied or limited in the absence of a clear and valid legislative command. Unless a statute in so many words, or by a necessary and inescapable inference, restricts the court's jurisdiction in equity, the full scope of that jurisdiction is to be recognized and applied. 'The great principles of equity, securing complete justice, should not be yielded to light inferences, or doubtful construction.'. . ."

In TVA *v.* Hill, we held that Congress had foreclosed the exercise of the usual discretion possessed by a court of equity. There, we thought that "[one] would be hard pressed to find a statutory provision whose terms were any plainer" than that before us. The statute involved, the Endangered Species Act, required the District Court to enjoin completion of the Tellico Dam in order to preserve the snail darter, a species of perch. The purpose and language of the statute under consideration in *Hill,* not the bare fact of a statutory violation, compelled that conclusion. Section 7 of the Act requires federal agencies to "insure that actions authorized, funded, or carried out by them do not jeopardize the continued existence of [any] endangered species . . . or result in the destruction or modification of habitat of such species which is determined . . . to be critical." The statute thus contains a flat ban on the destruction of critical habitats.

It was conceded in *Hill* that completion of the dam would eliminate an endangered species by destroying its critical habitat. Refusal to enjoin the action would have ignored the "explicit provisions of the Endangered Species Act." Congress, it appeared to us, had chosen the snail darter over the dam. The purpose and language of the statute limited the remedies available to the District Court; only an injunction could vindicate the objectives of the Act.

That is not the case here. An injunction is not the only means of ensuring compliance. The FWPCA itself, for example, provides for fines and criminal penalties. Respondents suggest that failure to enjoin the Navy will undermine the integrity of the permit process by allowing the statutory violation to continue. The integrity of the nation's waters, however, not the permit process, is the purpose of the FWPCA. As Congress explained, the objective of the FWPCA is to "restore and maintain the chemical, physical, and biological integrity of the Nation's waters."

This purpose is to be achieved by compliance with the Act, including compliance with the permit requirements. Here, however, the discharge of ordnance had not polluted the waters, and, although the District Court declined to enjoin the discharges, it neither ignored the statutory violation nor undercut the purpose and function of the permit system. The court ordered the Navy to apply for a permit. It temporarily, not permanently, allowed the Navy to continue its activities without a permit.

In *Hill,* we also noted that none of the limited "hardship exemptions" of the Endangered Species Act would "even remotely apply to the Tellico Project." The prohibition of the FWPCA against discharge of pollutants, in contrast, can be overcome by the very permit the Navy was ordered to seek. The Senate Report to the 1972 Amendments explains that the permit program would be enacted because "the Committee recognizes the impracticality of any effort to halt all pollution immediately." S. Rep. 92–414, p. 43 (1971). That the scheme as a whole contemplates the exercise of discretion and balancing of equities militates against the conclusion that Congress intended to deny courts their traditional equitable discretion in enforcing the statute.

Other aspects of the statutory scheme also suggest that Congress did not intend to deny courts the discretion to rely on remedies other than an immediate prohibitory injunction. Although the ultimate objective of the FWPCA is to eliminate all discharges of pollutants into the navigable waters by 1985, the statute sets forth a scheme of phased compliance. As enacted, it called for the achievement of the "best practicable control technology currently available" by July 1, 1977 and the "best available technology economically achievable" by July 1, 1983. 33 U.S.C. § 1311(b).

This scheme of phased compliance further suggests that this is a statute in which Congress envisioned, rather than curtailed, the exercise of discretion. . . .

This Court explained in Hecht Co. *v.* Bowles, 321 U.S. 321 (1944), that a major departure from the long tradition of equity practice should not be lightly implied. As we did there, we construe the statute at issue "in favor of that interpretation which affords a full opportunity for equity courts to treat enforcement proceedings . . . in accordance with their traditional practices, as conditioned by the necessities of the public interest which Congress has sought to protect." *Id.*, at 330. We do not read the FWPCA as foreclosing completely the exercise of the court's discretion. Rather than requiring a district court to issue an injunction for any and all statutory violations, the FWPCA permits the district court to order that relief it considers necessary to secure prompt compliance with the Act. That relief can include, but is not limited to, an order of immediate cessation.

The exercise of equitable discretion, which must include the ability to deny as well as grant injunctive relief, can fully protect the range of public interests at issue at this stage in the proceedings. The District Court did not face a situation in which a permit would very likely not issue, and the requirements and objective of the statute could therefore not be vindicated if discharges were permitted to continue. Should it become clear that no permit will be issued and that compliance with the FWPCA will not be forthcoming, the statutory scheme and purpose would require the court to reconsider the balance it has struck.

Because Congress, in enacting the FWPCA, has not foreclosed the exercise of equitable discretion, the proper standard for appellate review is whether the district court abused its discretion in denying an immediate cessation order while the Navy applied for a permit. We reverse and remand to Court of Appeals for proceedings consistent with this opinion. . . .

■ [The concurring opinion of JUSTICE POWELL and dissenting opinion of JUSTICE STEVENS are omitted.]

PART II

DAMAGES

CHAPTER 2

THE HISTORY OF DAMAGES

A. EARLY MONEY REMEDIES

The primary purpose of judicial remedies is to place the plaintiff in the position he or she would have been in if the wrong complained of had not occurred. In modern courts, the remedy of damages pursues this goal by compensating the plaintiff in money for past and future losses resulting from the wrong.

Compensation is not the only possible objective of money-based legal remedies. They can be calibrated to deter future violations of the law. They can be used to recover gains the defendant obtained at the plaintiff's expense, in order to avoid unjust enrichment. (That is the objective of the restitutionary remedies discussed in later chapters.) Yet another possible function of money remedies is to provide an alternative to private revenge. For example, consider the following laws issued by Alfred the Great, the English king who reigned from AD 871 to AD 899.

The Laws of Alfred[i]

Cir. 886–87.

12. If someone burns or cuts down another person's trees without permission, let him pay over 5 shillings for each substantial tree and thereafter, no matter how many there are five pence for each tree and thirty shillings as a fine. . . .

15. If someone fights or draws his weapon in the presence of an archbishop, let him make compensation with 150 shillings. If this occurs before another bishop or royal official let him make compensation with 100 shillings. . . .

29. If anyone in a group kills a 200 *shilling wergeld* man[ii] who is guiltless, let him that acknowledges the blow pay over wergeld and fine,

---

[i] Reprinted from Bill Griffiths, EARLY ENGLISH LAW: AN INTRODUCTION 63–79 (1995). Old English terms are omitted from the text. Italicized terms are additions or explanations by the translator. Cf. PLUTARCH'S LIVES OF THEMISTOCLES, PERICLES, ARISTIDES, ALCIBIADES, AND CORIOLANUS, DEMOSTHENES AND CICERO, CAESAR AND ANTONY 25–26 (trans. John Dryden, rev. Arthur Hugh Clough, 1909): "For the ostracism was instituted [in ancient Athens], not so much to punish the offender, as to mitigate and pacify the violence of the envious, who delighted to humble eminent men, and who, by fixing this disgrace upon them, might vent some part of their rancor."

[ii] [A wergeld was the value of a person, based on social status. It could be revised upward or downward during a person's life. The wergeld fixed the basic compensation for causing the person's death. The payment of the wergeld was enforced not by a system of courts but rather by the credible threat that, if the wergeld were not paid, the kin of the dead or wounded person would exact revenge. See generally William Ian Miller, EYE FOR AN EYE (2006); A. W. B. Simpson, The Laws of Ethelbert, in LEGAL THEORY AND LEGAL HISTORY: ESSAYS ON THE COMMON LAW (1987).]

and let every man who was of the party hand over 30 shillings in token of his complicity.

30. If it is *a case of* a 600 *shilling wergeld man, let* each of them *pay* 60 shillings as a token of their complicity, and let him that struck [the] *fatal* blow *pay* wergeld . . . .

31. If he *that is killed* is a 1200 *shilling wergeld man*, let each of them *pay* 120 shillings, and *let* the one who struck the *fatal* blow *pay* wergeld . . . .

35. If someone restrains a free man *who is* innocent, let him pay compensation of ten shillings. If he flogs him, *compensation of* twenty shillings. If he put him to tortures, *compensation of* thirty shillings. . . . If he shaves off his beard let him pay compensation of twenty shillings. . . .

40. For breaking into a royal residence, *the penalty* shall be 120 shillings. . . . *Into* a 1200 *shilling wergeld* man's, thirty shillings. *Into* a 600 *shilling wergeld* man's, fifteen shillings. . . .

44. As compensation for a head-wound: if both bones (of the head) be pierced, let *the aggressor* pay him thirty shillings. If the outer bone *only* be pierced, fifteen shillings compensation. . . .

47. If someone put out another man's eye, let him pay in compensation 60 shillings and 6 pennies and a third of a penny. If it *i.e. the eye* staye in the head but he can see nothing with it, let a third part of the compensation be remitted. . . .

52. If someone's tongue is removed from his head by another's actions, let that be the same as compensation for an eye. . . .

56. If the thumb is struck off, for that must 30 shillings *be paid* in compensation.

57. If the fore finger is struck off, let the compensation be 15 shillings; for the nail let it be 4 shillings.

58. If the middle finger be struck off, the compensation shall be 12 shillings . . . .

59. If the ring finger be struck off, for that 17 shillings . . . .

60. If the little finger is struck off, for that he must *pay* 9 shillings . . . .

77. If someone sever the muscles up by the neck, and damage them so severely that he *i.e. the victim* has no control over them, and however lives on thus maimed, let *the aggressor* give him 100 shillings, unless the Witan[iii] appoint him a juster and greater *sum*.

iii [This was an assembly of Lords.]

B. THE EMERGENCE OF JURIES AND COMPENSATORY DAMAGES

In Anglo-Saxon England, there was not yet a secure enough notion of governmental authority in place to support the type of deliberative decisionmaking that judges engage in today. As a result, procedures often appealed to external sources to determine the outcome of cases. Plaintiffs made accusations, defendants swore their innocence, and their oaths were then tested in ways that avoided the appearance of mere human judgment.[iv]

One such procedure was the ordeal. The defendant might be made to walk on hot coals, or to grasp a hot iron, in the presence of a priest. If the burn festered, the defendant's oath was untrue. Alternatively, the defendant might be thrown into a body of water. If the water received the defendant (the defendant sank), the oath was true, but if the defendant was rejected by the water (the defendant floated), the oath was false and the defendant was guilty.

Trial by ordeal effectively ended in the year 1215, when the Church forbade priests to participate. A somewhat less onerous procedure was trial by oath, also known as "wager of law," in which the defendant was required to produce twelve oath-helpers to swear on the defendant's behalf. If the oath-helpers refused to swear, the defendant was guilty of the charge. The procedure of trial by oath endured much longer than trial by ordeal, and was not formally abolished until 1833.

With the development of trespass actions in the thirteenth and fourteenth centuries, jury trials became the dominant procedure for resolving civil disputes. Importantly for the subject of remedies, juries not only decided whose claim was true, but awarded money *damages* for losses resulting from a wrong. Consider the following well-known case, in which a jury awarded £100 for losses consequent to a wrong.

Scott, an Infant, by His next Friend v. Shepherd, an Infant, by Guardian

Court of Common Pleas, 1773.
96 Eng. Rep. 525.

Trespass and assault will lie for originally throwing a squib, which after having been thrown about in self-defence by other persons, at last put out the plaintiff's eye.

Trespass and assault for throwing, casting, and tossing a lighted squib at and against the plaintiff, and striking him therewith on the face, and so burning one of his eyes, that he lost the sight of it, whereby, &c. On not guilty pleaded, the cause came on to be tried before Nares, J., last Summer Assizes, at Bridgwater, when the jury found a verdict for the plaintiff with 100l. damages, subject to the opinion of the Court on this

[iv] See J.H. Baker, AN INTRODUCTION TO ENGLISH LEGAL HISTORY 72–74 (4th ed. 2002).

case:—On the evening of the fair-day at Milborne Port, 28th October, 1770, the defendant threw a lighted squib, made of gun-powder, &c. from the street into the market-house, which is a covered building, supported by arches, and enclosed at one end, but open at the other and both the sides, where a large concourse of people were assembled; which lighted squib, so thrown by the defendant, fell upon the standing of one Yates, who sold gingerbread, &c. That one Willis instantly, and to prevent injury to himself and the said wares of the said Yates, took up the said lighted squib from off the said standing, and then threw it *across* the said market house, when it fell upon another standing there of one Ryal, who sold the same sort of wares, who instantly, and to save his own goods from being injured, took up the said lighted squib from off the said standing, and then threw it to another part of the said market-house, and, in so throwing it, struck the plaintiff then in the said market-house in the face therewith, and the combustible matter then bursting, put out one of the plaintiff's eyes. Qu[are:] If this action be maintainable?

This case was argued last term by Glyn, for the plaintiff, and Burland, for the defendant: and this term, the Court, being divided in their judgment, delivered their opinions seriatim.

NARES, J., was of opinion, that trespass would well lie in the present case. That the natural and probable consequence of the act done by the defendant was injury to somebody, and therefore the act was illegal at common law. And the throwing of squibs has by [statute] been since made a nuisance. Being therefore unlawful, the defendant was liable to answer for the consequences, be the injury mediate or immediate .... The principle I go upon is what is laid down in Reynolds and Clark, Stra. 634, that if the act in the first instance be unlawful, trespass will lie ... for the consequences of it.... I do not think it necessary, to maintain trespass, that the defendant should personally touch the plaintiff; if he does it by a mean it is sufficient.... He is the person, who, in the present case, gave the mischievous faculty to the squib. That mischievous faculty remained in it till the explosion. No new power of doing mischief was communicated to it by Willis or Ryal. It is like the case of a mad ox turned loose in a crowd. The person who turns him loose is answerable in trespass for whatever mischief he may do.... [H]e who does the first wrong is answerable for all the consequential damages....

BLACKSTONE, J., was of opinion, that an action of trespass did not lie for Scott against Shepherd upon this case. He took the settled distinction to be, that where the injury is immediate, an action of trespass will lie; where it is only consequential, it must be an action on the case. The lawfulness or unlawfulness of the original act is not the criterion .... [I]f I throw a log of timber into the highway, (which is an unlawful act), and another man tumbles over it, and is hurt, an action on the case only lies, it being a consequential damage; but if in throwing it I hit another man, he may bring trespass, because it is an immediate wrong.... So that lawful or unlawful is quite out of the case; the solid distinction is between direct or immediate injuries on the one hand, and mediate or consequential on the other. And trespass never lay for the latter. If this be so, the only question will be, whether the injury which the plaintiff suffered was immediate, or consequential only; and I hold it to be the latter. The original act was, as against Yates, a trespass; not as against Ryal, or Scott. The tortious act was complete when the squib lay at rest upon Yates's stall. He, or any bystander, had, I allow, a right to protect themselves by removing the squib, but should have taken care to do it in such a manner as not to endamage others. But Shepherd, I think, is not answerable in an action of trespass and assault for the mischief done by the squib in the new motion impressed upon it, and the new direction given it, by either Willis or Ryal; who both were free agents, and acted upon their own judgment. This differs it from the cases put of turning loose a wild beast or a madman. They are only instruments in the hand of the first agent. . . . I give no opinion whether *case* would lie against Shepherd for the consequential damage; though, as at present advised, I think, upon the circumstances, it would. . . . The same evidence that will maintain trespass, may also frequently maintain case [*i.e.*, trespass on the case], but not e converso. Every action of trespass with a "per quoad" [*i.e.*, requiring reference to additional facts or proof of special damages] includes an action on the case. I may bring trespass for the immediate injury, and subjoin a "per quod" for the consequential damages;—or may bring case for the consequential damages, and pass over the immediate injury . . . . But if I bring trespass for an immediate injury, and prove at most only a consequential damage, judgment must be for the defendant. . . .

GOULD, J., was of the same opinion with Nares, J., that this action was well maintainable. . . . The line is very nice between case and trespass upon these occasions: I am persuaded there are many instances wherein both or either will lie. . . .

DE GREY, C.J. . . . Trespass is an injury accompanied with force, for which an action of trespass *vi et armis* [with force and arms] lies against the person from whom it is received. The question here is, whether the injury received by the plaintiff arises from the force of the original act of the defendant, or from a new force by a third person. I agree with my brother Blackstone as to the principles he has laid down, but not in his application of those principles to the present case. The real question certainly does not turn upon the lawfulness or unlawfulness of the original act . . . . But the true question is, whether the injury is the direct and immediate act of the defendant; and I am of opinion, that in this case it is. The throwing the squib was an act unlawful and tending to affright the bystanders. So far, mischief was originally intended; not any particular mischief, but mischief indiscriminate and wanton. Whatever mischief therefore follows, he is the author of it . . . . [T]he immediate act need not be instantaneous, but . . . a chain of effects connected together will be sufficient. It has been urged, that the intervention of a free agent will make a difference: but I do not consider Willis and Ryal as free agents in the present case, but acting under a compulsive necessity for their own safety and self-preservation. On these reasons I concur with Brothers Gould and Nares, that the present action is maintainable.

[Judgment] to the plaintiff.

NOTE

The guiding principle of damages in civil cases was stated by Chief Justice Holt in Ferrer *v.* Beale, 1 Lord Raym. 692 (1707): "Every one shall recover damages in proportion to the prejudice which he hath sustained." Over time, the common law developed rules of damages that further specified this basic principle, and these rules will be the focus of the next chapter.

Judicial Control of Juries and Damages

Charles T. McCormick, LAW OF DAMAGES 24–28 (1935).

The amount of damages, . . . from the beginning of trial by jury, was a "fact" to be found by the jurors. The findings of the jury, at the earliest period, were based on their personal knowledge. These "petty" jurors were selected from the yeomen of the neighborhood where the transaction in suit occurred, so that they might furnish that knowledge. Obviously the trial justice, usually a stranger sent out from London, with no knowledge of the affair in controversy except from the pleadings, could seldom feel justified in correcting or overturning the findings of the neighbor witnesses, so that, if injustice were done by the verdict, another method of relief must be sought. . . .

By the early fourteen hundreds, the judges made a clearer inroad upon the jurors' province of damages. They began simply to change the amount of the jury's award in clear cases. The danger of this was so apparent, if the jury's sense of responsibility were to be preserved, that bounds were soon put upon this interference. The value of trees cut down by the defendant will be known best by the jurors who have seen them, and the judges will not interfere, but, in an action for mayhem where the plaintiff comes before the bench, the judges can see the wound as well as the jurors, and so they are willing to take the responsibility of increasing or reducing the damages. So also in cases of debt, where the judges feel that the damages for the detention of the money should be kept within bounds. But it is the assembled judges in London who thus change the award, not the single judge face to face with the jury on the circuit. At best, this is uneasy stepping for the judges, and they insist that the case must be one where the extent of the injury is within their "conusans"—cognizance—meaning sometimes knowledge, sometimes jurisdiction. Finally, by the seventeen hundreds, when a more indirect means of control has been devised, this uncomfortable frontal method is dropped, and judges to-day no longer reduce or increase damages straight-out.

The real successor . . . was the device of setting aside the first verdict and granting a *new trial* of the case before a second petty jury. This was late in coming, and, when it came, was forced upon the common-law courts, by the intervention of equity in the early sixteen hundreds. In 1655 a law court in a slander case for the first time set aside a verdict on the ground of excessiveness of amount, but it was claimed to have been a "packed business," and the court's emphasis was on the misconduct. Still, in 1677, an outrageous verdict of £4,000 for scandalizing a politician was held to be beyond the court's touching, "since by the law the jury are the judges of the damages." The political implications of interference by judges with jury verdicts make the growth of the practice slow and halting, especially where the ground is amount. At first, only where there has been misconduct by the jury will the judges act. Excessiveness is a ground, but not inadequacy. . . . In 1695, however, in the King's Bench, when an indignant jury gives a lady £2,000 for two hours' imprisonment by her mother, Holt, C. J., demands their reasons, and, when they are "shy of giving a reason," bluntly tells them that they do not have "an absolute despotic power," and the full bench grants a new trial. . . . By the end of the century it was clear that in England the courts would grant a new trial if the award violated some rule of damages—such rules were still few and still chiefly confined to contracts—or if even in tort cases the court, in its discretion, considered the amount unreasonable.

Parallel with the widening of the court's power to set aside the award was the growth of the practice by the judges of guiding the jury in advance toward a finding of damages in accordance with consistent standards. This is a chapter in legal history which has not as yet been written, but we know that the charge or instruction of the jury was a feature of jury trials from the first. The amount of damages was a "fact," as to which the judge would at first presumably have offered suggestions merely; but, as standards of damages are gradually worked out for the different forms of action, particularly the contract actions, the advice takes on the tone of instruction. We may be sure that this practice of advising the jury upon the measure of their award, even more than the exercise of the power to change or set it aside, provided the main vehicle for the formulation of the rules and standards of damages. Nevertheless, it is only in the eighteen hundreds that the doctrine begins to find its way into the books that the judge is required to instruct the jury upon the measure of damages and that a misdirection on damages is ground for a new trial.

CHAPTER 3

GENERAL PRINCIPLES GOVERNING DAMAGES

A. COMPENSATION

Harris v. Peters

Appellate Court of Illinois, 1995.
274 Ill. App. 3d 206.

■ JUSTICE TULLY delivered the opinion of the court. . . .

On October 8, 1988, Harris entered into a lease agreement with U.B. Vehicle Leasing, Inc. (hereinafter UB) whereby Harris leased a 1988 Audi from UB. On September 6, 1991, the Audi was totaled in a collision with Peters' vehicle. Peters' insurer tendered Harris a check for the fair market value of the Audi. Harris endorsed the check over to UB, which under the terms of the leasing agreement applied the funds toward paying the balance due it under the agreement's terms.

On February 20, 1992, UB filed a complaint against Harris, seeking $5,560.48, the balance remaining on the lease. On April 2, 1992, Harris filed his answer to UB's complaint and a two-count third-party complaint against Peters and his insurer seeking judgment in an amount equivalent to any judgment which might be entered against Harris in the underlying UB action. In essence, Harris was seeking the difference between the Audi's fair market value and the total amount due over the term of the vehicle lease. . . . Compensatory damages are those which are awarded to a person as compensation . . . for a wrong or injury sustained by him. The purpose of awarding compensatory damages is to make the injured party whole and restore him to the position he was in before the loss, but not to enable him to make a profit or windfall on the transaction. Accordingly, when personal property is destroyed or rendered useless, the measure of damages is the fair market value of the thing in question immediately prior to its destruction. Applying these principles to the case *sub judice,* it is clear to us that the trial court did not err in dismissing Harris' complaint.

Harris urges that the only way that he can be made whole is if he is awarded the difference between the Audi's fair market value and the total amount due over the term of the vehicle lease. We disagree. We believe that Harris was made whole when he was given the fair market value of the car, which necessarily compensates for loss of use and enjoyment; Peters took a car from Harris and Harris was given back the car in the form of its cash equivalent. However, if Peters is then required to pay Harris' lease obligation in full, then Harris' economic position is enriched.

Immediately before the accident Harris had the car and an obligation to pay UB an amount of money in excess of the fair market value of the car. In other words, a negative net on the transaction. As things stand now Harris has the car (in the form of the cash payment) and the obligation to pay UB. However, if Peters is forced to pay off Harris' lease, Harris will be enriched to the extent that he has rid himself of the negative net-the obligation to pay UB which he had before the accident.

This economic or compensatory analysis holds true also if one examines this case from the standpoint of causation. The negative net is the "benefit of the bargain" Harris negotiated with UB and was in no way under the control of Peters and, consequently, [is] a loss which does not flow directly from the tort committed by Peters and therefore not recoverable.

In light of the foregoing, the judgment of the circuit court of Cook County is affirmed.

B. DIRECT AND CONSEQUENTIAL DAMAGES

New Valley Corp. v. United States

United States Court of Federal Claims, 2006.
72 Fed. Cl. 411.

■ WIESE, JUDGE. In an earlier opinion issued in this case, the court resolved in plaintiff's favor the question of whether Western Union Telegraph Company ("Western Union"), New Valley's principal subsidiary, was entitled to recover contract damages as a result of the National Aeronautics and Space Administration's ("NASA") anticipatory repudiation of a contract promising NASA's "best efforts" to launch Western Union's communications satellite, the Westar VI–S, into earth orbit. Notwithstanding this ruling, . . . defendant has moved for summary judgment asserting that the damages identified in the court's opinion do not qualify as direct damages but instead constitute consequential damages and lost profits and therefore are not recoverable under the terms of the parties' contract. Plaintiff has cross-moved for summary judgment claiming that it is entitled on the basis of the stipulated facts to recover $43.3 million pursuant to the court's earlier opinion. For the reasons set forth below, the parties' cross-motions are denied.

During the period relevant to this action (1984–1991), Western Union was a corporation in financial distress—a condition brought on by an ever-increasing interest burden arising out of indebtedness undertaken to finance capital expenditures that ultimately failed to produce their expected revenue flow. In an effort to arrest the decline in the company's fortunes, Western Union began to sell off assets, including those comprising the company's communications satellite division, the Westar Division. Included in the Westar Division assets was the Westar VI–S, a communications satellite built by Western Union at a cost of $32.2 million and acquired by Hughes Communications, Inc., in January 1989 for $20.5 million.[1] At the time Western Union contracted for the construction of the Westar VI–S, it expected to launch that satellite aboard the Space Shuttle pursuant to a contract executed with NASA in 1984. This contract, however, was later disavowed by NASA due in the main to a reevaluation of the nation's launch program precipitated by the loss of the Space Shuttle Challenger in January 1986 and the subsequent decision by President Reagan to forego commercial launches in favor of payloads that either were shuttle-unique or had national security and foreign policy implications.

Western Union eventually went into bankruptcy and following its reemergence from that process brought suit in this court seeking, *inter alia,* damages for NASA's breach of contract. . . .

[W]e ruled that . . . "the breach must be seen as the proximate cause of injury to plaintiff." We left for later consideration the question of how much more Hughes Communications would have paid for the Westar Division assets had they included a NASA launch contract. . . .

[U]nder the heading "Limitation of United States Government and Customer Liability," the launch services contract provided:

> "[T]he United States Government's liability to the Customer . . . whether or not arising as a result of an alleged breach of this Agreement, shall be limited to direct damages only and shall not include any loss of revenue, profits or other indirect or consequential damages."

Defendant maintains that the damages contemplated in the court's earlier opinion constitute consequential damages and lost profits and therefore, based on the language quoted above, are not recoverable under the parties' contract.

In support of this argument, defendant asserts that Western Union did not sell the Westar Division assets because of the breach but rather because it was confronting a liquidity crisis that left it without sufficient funds to satisfy its day-to-day operations and also meet its debt service obligations. Defendant thus maintains that plaintiff's damages cannot be said to flow directly from the breach but are instead the result of a collateral undertaking and therefore constitute consequential damages. More particularly, defendant identifies plaintiff's damages claim as a claim for lost profits, *i.e.,* monies that Western Union claims it would

---

[1] Hughes Communications acquired all of the Westar Division assets, which included three orbiting satellites as well as the Westar VI–S, for approximately $40 million. The portion of the sale price allocated to the Westar VI–S was $20.5 million.

have realized had it been able to sell its favorably priced NASA launch contract for its much higher market value.

We cannot accept this argument. Direct damages, or what are more often referred to as "general damages," are damages measured by the loss of the value of the performance promised by the breaching party. In other words, such damages are "based on the value of the very thing to which the plaintiff was entitled . . . , they encompass paper losses or unrealized losses, and . . . they are determined as of a particular date, usually by market measures." 1 Dan B. Dobbs, LAW OF REMEDIES § 2.2(3), at 40–41 (2d ed. 1993). Consequential damages (also called "special damages"), on the other hand, are those damages that "result as a secondary consequence of the defendant's non-performance," *id.* § 12:4(1), at 62, *i.e.*, they "arise from the interposition of an additional cause, without which the act done would have produced no harmful result," United States *v.* Chicago B. & Q.R. Co., 82 F.2d 131, 136 (8th Cir. 1936). Consequential damages are thus distinguishable from general damages in that rather than being based on the value of the promised performance itself, they are based on the value of some consequence that that performance may produce. Dobbs, *supra* § 12.4(1), at 62.

Consistent with these definitions, we believe that the damages identified in our earlier decision are direct damages rather than consequential damages. Specifically, we described those damages as the additional amount that Hughes Communications "would have paid for the Westar Division assets had they included a NASA launch contract." In so ruling, we had in mind only one component of the Westar Division assets, namely, the value of the launch contract. As the balance of our opinion makes clear, we expected that value to fall somewhere between the market value of a substitute launch contract (stipulated by the parties to be $31.6 million [based on negotiations between Western Union and alternative providers]) and the sale price Western Union reasonably might have expected to receive [for the NASA launch contract] given its distressed financial position and Hughes Communications' awareness of that condition.

Defendant's assertion that the sale of the Westar Division assets was a collateral undertaking and hence rendered any loss identified with that sale a consequential damage is not correct. The sale of the Westar Division assets was not the cause of the loss claimed. Rather, the cause of that loss was defendant's breach—an event that preceded the sale of the assets by many months. As we noted in our earlier opinion, the sale was simply the focal point of the loss, *i.e.*, the occasion when the market value of the launch contract could have been realized by Western Union had there in fact been no breach.

Nor is defendant correct in describing as lost profits the gain that Western Union could have expected to realize from the sale of the launch contract. That gain—the difference between the contract price and the market price (or more specifically, the price Hughes Communications would have been willing to pay)—is synonymous with the very value of the performance for which Western Union had bargained. Such a value, by definition, constitutes general damages rather than lost profits. Accordingly, defendant's motion for summary judgment must fail.

[The court then clarified that the plaintiff's direct damages should be based on the sale price Western Union would have received for the NASA launch contract, rather than either the difference between the cost of building the Westar satellite and the price paid by Hughes for the satellite, or the cost of a substitute launch.]

For the reasons set forth above and consistent with the court's earlier decision, the parties' cross-motions for summary judgment are denied. The damages issue shall proceed to trial.

NOTE

Section 2–719 of the Uniform Commercial Code provides as follows:

> "(1) Subject to the provisions of subsections (2) and (3) of this section and of the preceding section on liquidation and limitation of damages,
>
> > "(a) the agreement may provide for remedies in addition to or in substitution for those provided in this Article and may limit or alter the measure of damages recoverable under this Article, as by limiting the buyer's remedies to return of the goods and repayment of the price or to repair and replacement of non-conforming goods or parts; and
> >
> > "(b) resort to a remedy as provided is optional unless the remedy is expressly agreed to be exclusive, in which case it is the sole remedy.
>
> "(2) Where circumstances cause an exclusive or limited remedy to fail of its essential purpose, remedy may be had as provided in this Act.
>
> "(3) Consequential damages may be limited or excluded unless the limitation or exclusion is unconscionable. Limitation of consequential damages for injury to the person in the case of consumer goods is prima facie unconscionable but limitation of damages where the loss is commercial is not."

C. CERTAINTY

Kenford Co. v. County of Erie

Court of Appeals of New York, 1986.
67 N.Y.2d 257.

■ PER CURIAM. The issue in this appeal is whether a plaintiff, in an action for breach of contract, may recover loss of prospective profits for its contemplated 20-year operation of a domed stadium which was to be constructed by defendant County of Erie (County).

On August 8, 1969, pursuant to a duly adopted resolution of its legislature, the County of Erie entered into a contract with Kenford Company, Inc. (Kenford) and Dome Stadium, Inc. (DSI) for the construction and operation of a domed stadium facility near the City of Buffalo. The contract provided that construction of the facility by the County would commence within 12 months of the contract date and that a mutually acceptable 40-year lease between the County and DSI for the operation of said facility would be negotiated by the parties and agreed upon within three months of the receipt by the County of preliminary plans, drawings and cost estimates. It was further provided that in the event a mutually acceptable lease could not be agreed upon within the three-month period, a separate management contract between the County and DSI, as appended to the basic agreement, would be executed by the parties, providing for the operation of the stadium facility by DSI for a period of 20 years from the completion of the stadium and its availability for use.

Although strenuous and extensive negotiations followed, the parties never agreed upon the terms of a lease, nor did construction of a domed facility begin within the one-year period or at any time thereafter. A breach of the contract thus occurred and this action was commenced in June 1971 by Kenford and DSI.

Prolonged and extensive pretrial and preliminary proceedings transpired throughout the next 10 years, culminating with the entry of an order which affirmed the grant of summary judgment against the County on the issue of liability and directed a trial limited to the issue of damages. The ensuing trial ended some nine months later with a multimillion dollar jury verdict in plaintiffs' favor. An appeal to the Appellate Division resulted in a modification of the judgment. That court reversed portions of the judgment awarding damages for loss of profits and for certain out-of-pocket expenses incurred, and directed a new trial upon other issues. On appeal to this court, we are concerned only with that portion of the verdict which awarded DSI money damages for loss of prospective profits during the 20-year period of the proposed management contract, as appended to the basic contract. That portion of the verdict was set aside by the Appellate Division and the cause of action dismissed. The court concluded that the use of expert opinion to present statistical projections of future business operations involved the use of too many variables to provide a rational basis upon which lost profits could be calculated and, therefore, such projections were insufficient as a matter of law to support an award of lost profits. We agree with this ultimate conclusion, but upon different grounds.

Loss of future profits as damages for breach of contract have been permitted in New York under long-established and precise rules of law. First, it must be demonstrated with certainty that such damages have been caused by the breach and, second, the alleged loss must be capable of proof with reasonable certainty. In other words, the damages may not be merely speculative, possible or imaginary, but must be reasonably certain and directly traceable to the breach, not remote or the result of other intervening causes. In addition, there must be a showing that the particular damages were fairly within the contemplation of the parties to the contract at the time it was made. If it is a new business seeking to recover for loss of future profits, a stricter standard is imposed for the obvious reason that there does not exist a reasonable basis of experience upon which to estimate lost profits with the requisite degree of reasonable certainty.

These rules must be applied to the proof presented by DSI in this case. We note the procedure for computing damages selected by DSI was in accord with contemporary economic theory and was presented through the testimony of recognized experts. Such a procedure has been accepted in this State and many other jurisdictions. DSI's economic analysis employed historical data, obtained from the operation of other domed stadiums and related facilities throughout the country, which was then applied to the results of a comprehensive study of the marketing prospects for the proposed facility in the Buffalo area. The quantity of proof is massive and, unquestionably, represents business and industry's most advanced and sophisticated method for predicting the probable results of contemplated projects. Indeed, it is difficult to conclude what additional relevant proof could have been submitted by DSI in support of its attempt to establish, with reasonable certainty, loss of prospective profits. Nevertheless, DSI's proof is insufficient to meet the required standard. . . .

[W]e note that despite the massive quantity of expert proof submitted by DSI, the ultimate conclusions are still projections, and as employed in the present day commercial world, subject to adjustment and modification. We of course recognize that any projection cannot be absolute, nor is there any such requirement, but it is axiomatic that the degree of certainty is dependent upon known or unknown factors which form the basis of the ultimate conclusion. Here, the foundations upon which the economic model was created undermine the certainty of the projections. DSI assumed that the facility was completed, available for use and successfully operated by it for 20 years, providing professional sporting events and other forms of entertainment, as well as hosting meetings, conventions and related commercial gatherings. At the time of the breach, there was only one other facility in this country to use as a basis of comparison, the Astrodome in Houston. Quite simply, the multitude of assumptions required to establish projections of profitability over the life of this contract require speculation and conjecture, making it beyond the capability of even the most sophisticated procedures to satisfy the legal requirements of proof with reasonable certainty.

The economic facts of life, the whim of the general public and the fickle nature of popular support for professional athletic endeavors must be given great weight in attempting to ascertain damages 20 years in the future. New York has long recognized the inherent uncertainties of predicting profits in the entertainment field in general and, in this case, we are dealing, in large part, with a new facility furnishing entertainment for the public. It is our view that the record in this case demonstrates the efficacy of the principles set forth by this court in Cramer *v.* Grand Rapids Show Case Co. (223 N.Y. 63), principles to which we continue to adhere. In so doing, we specifically reject the "rational basis" test . . . adopted by the Appellate Division. . . .

NOTES

1. Cramer *v.* Grand Rapids Show Case Co., cited with approval in the opinion above, held that evidence of lost profits from a new business is not admissible. Compare, *e.g.*, Beverly Hills Concepts, Inc. *v.* Schatz & Schatz, Ribicoff & Kotkin, 247 Conn. 48 (1998), in which the Connecticut Supreme Court allowed evidence of lost profits from a new business but held that the evidence of profits presented was insufficient as a matter of law. On the question of admissibility, *Beverly Hills Concepts* represents the trend of modern decisions.

2. As an additional reason for reversing the award of damages for lost profits, the court in *Kenford* determined that lost profits over a period of 20 years were not within the contemplation of the parties as required by the rule of Hadley *v.* Baxendale, 156 Eng. Rep. 145 (1854). That rule is discussed in Section G(1) (Forseeability), below.

3. Meinrath was an entrepreneur in the nascent computer business of the 1970s. Singer employed Meinrath to market a line of computers in Europe and agreed to pay "bonus compensation" contingent on sales. In a suit against Singer for breach of contract, Meinrath alleged that Singer owed him $300,000 in unpaid bonus compensation. Singer disputed the sum due. As damages, Meinrath claimed the $300,000 shortfall, plus $770,000 in consequential damages for losses suffered by several Meinrath business ventures as a result of lack of capital. Singer conceded that it had actual knowledge of Meinrath's other ventures and knew that Meinrath needed the disputed funds to keep them afloat. The court nevertheless granted summary judgment for Singer on the question of consequential damages, citing a common law rule to the effect that damages for breach of a contract to pay money are limited to the sum due plus interest:

> "Plaintiff's argument that his injury was foreseeable to Singer at the time of the contract is unavailing; if he wanted to impose liability upon Singer for the failure of his business empire because of non-payment of amounts allegedly due under their contract, he could have bargained for that result by fixing liquidated damages for a breach. Accordingly, we hold that as a matter of law plaintiff's consequential loss is too remote from the main injury to be

> compensable and too speculative to be ascertainable; plaintiff is barred from recovering such damages."

Meinrath *v.* Singer, 87 F.R.D. 422, 427 (S.D.N.Y. 1980).

A number of courts have followed this rule. See, *e.g.*, United Cable Television of Baltimore Limited Partnership *v.* Burch, 354 Md. 658 (1999) (tracing the history of the rule and invoking it to hold a late fee provision in a cable television contract invalid as a penalty).

4. In 1970, acting on information from several sources, Roger Roxas, a Philippine locksmith and treasure hunter, discovered a golden Buddha, various artifacts, a skeleton wearing a Japanese military uniform, and a large cache of gold bullion in a system of underground tunnels in the Philippines. This was believed to be the Yamashita Treasure, consisting of booty plundered from various Asian countries by a Japanese general during World War II. Roxas took the Buddha and a sample of gold to his home and blasted the tunnel shut, intending to return. Shortly after the find, Philippine national security agents arrived at Roxas's house, threatened him and his family, and took the treasures stored there (along with "a piggy bank belonging to Roxas's children"). Roxas was then contacted by agents of the Philippine president, Ferdinand Marcos, who sought to discover the location of the remaining gold. In the years that followed, Roxas was repeatedly approached by agents of Marcos, threatened, tortured, and imprisoned on false charges.

In 1974 and 1975, the Philippine military conducted excavations in the area of Roxas's find. Various witnesses testified that they were contacted by Marcos or his agents for help in marketing a large quantity of gold bullion. One of these witnesses reported being taken to a room in one of Marcos's palaces, measuring "about roughly 40 by 40" and filled to the ceiling with bars of gold. Another was blindfolded, taken to a warehouse, and shown "a stack of approximately three hundred to four hundred boxes, each the size of a six-pack of beer," containing gold.

In 1986, Marcos was overthrown in a popular uprising. The United States government transported Marcos and his wife Imelda to Hawai'i. Roxas and the Golden Buddha Corporation (a corporate entity to which Roxas had assigned his rights to the treasure) sued the Marcoses for, among other things, conversion of the gold. The jury awarded damages to Roxas and Golden Buddha in the amounts of $1,400,000 for conversion of the Buddha and gold from Roxas's home and $22,000,000,000 for conversion of the gold Roxas had left underground. The Hawai'i Supreme Court reversed the verdict for $22 billion on the ground that Roxas's proof of the value of the gold was too speculative.

> "The range, for example, between O'Brien's estimate of 300 to 400 boxes of gold yields an enormous difference in value. Moreover, O'Brien testified that he actually opened only one box, which was not filled with gold, but only contained three bars. Similarly, Jonsson's vacillation among his various estimates of the dimensions of the room in which he had observed gold generates a margin of error comprising thousands of tons."

Roxas *v.* Marcos, 89 Hawai'i 91,142 (1999). In the circumstances, the court said, the witnesses' estimates of value were "little more than a guess."

Fairfax County Redevelopment and Housing Authority v. Worcester Bros. Co.

Supreme Court of Virginia, 1999.
257 Va. 382.

■ KOONTZ, JUSTICE. In this appeal, we consider whether the trial court's award of unabsorbed home office expenses to the contractor on a public construction project following an unreasonable delay by the contracting government agency was based upon sufficient proof of the existence and amount of those damages. . . .

On September 14, 1995, the Fairfax County Redevelopment and Housing Authority (the Authority) entered into a contract with Worcester Brothers Company, Inc. (Worcester Brothers), a general construction contractor, for site renovations and improvements of Washington Plaza in Lake Anne Village (the project) in Reston.

The Authority had originally solicited bids for the project based on a projected start date in July 1995, with completion of the work in 150 calendar days from the notice to proceed. Thus, the proposed date of substantial completion at the time bids were solicited was mid-December 1995. Worcester Brothers based its bid on these conditions. However, because the Authority did not award the contract to Worcester Brothers until September 14, 1995, the substantial completion date for the project was moved back to mid-February 1996.

It is not disputed that at the time Worcester Brothers commenced work on the project, the Authority had not yet obtained the necessary clearances from an adjoining property owner to allow work to proceed on a portion of the project site. The Authority did not obtain the clearances until March 6, 1996. . . .

At trial, Worcester Brothers contended that during the delay it incurred both additional field office expenses as a result of having to maintain its personnel at the job site and unabsorbed home office expenses. It presented evidence of its actual field office expenses related to the delay in the amount of $46,359.11. Worcester Brothers' accounting system did not allocate its home office expenses to particular contracts. However, Joseph P. Noonan, Worcester Brothers' president, testified that the unabsorbed home office expenses attributable to the delay amounted to $34,495.89. According to Noonan, that figure was calculated from statements prepared by Worcester Brothers' accountants reflecting the total general and administrative expenses of the company during the relevant contract period and the application of the *Eichleay* formula to those expenses. [This is an accepted formula for calculating overhead expenses attributable to government contracts, see Appeal of Eichleay Corp., 1960 WL 538 (1960).]. . .

At the conclusion of the evidence, the trial court . . . found that the Authority's delay was "manifest on this record" and was "egregious" and "frankly inexcusable." The trial court further found that Worcester Brothers' workforce had been on "standby" because the Authority "never could advise the contractor that the area would not be available until a particular date. Instead it was a rolling deadline." Finally, the trial court found that the "rolling deadline" also inhibited Worcester Brothers from seeking other contracts, and thereby minimizing the damage caused by the delay, since it could not be assured of the availability of its workforce for another project.

Having found that Worcester Brothers had satisfied its initial "burden of proving [home office] damages with reasonable certainty," the trial court turned to the question whether the *Eichleay* formula could be used to calculate the amount of those damages. Recognizing that other courts had found the *Eichleay* formula to be "a fair way of approximating" such damages, the trial court noted that after auditing Worcester Brothers' books, the Authority did not contend that any of the specific expenses were inappropriately claimed and that the Authority's witnesses failed "to present any reasoned analysis of why *Eichleay* is inappropriate." Accordingly, the trial court entered judgment for Worcester Brothers for both the field office expenses ($46,359.11) and the unabsorbed home office expenses as calculated by the *Eichleay* formula ($34,495.89). The trial court granted the Authority's motion to reconsider, and, after receiving briefs from the parties, sustained its original ruling. We awarded the Authority this appeal. . . .

[T]he resolution of this issue requires that we first consider whether Worcester Brothers established that it suffered damages in the form of unabsorbed home office expenses attributable to the Authority's delay, and, [then consider] whether there was adequate proof of the amount of those damages.

Home office expenses, commonly called overhead, include those costs that a contractor must expend for the benefit of its business as a whole. These expenses include, for example, the salaries of office staff, accounting expenses, dues and subscriptions, equipment costs, and utility services. Unabsorbed home office expenses comprise "those overhead costs needlessly consumed by a partially or totally idle contractor. A contractor continues to incur overhead costs during periods of reduced activity or delay on a particular contract. When this occurs, the 'reduced activity' contract no longer 'absorbs' its share of overhead costs." Michael W. Kauffman and Craig A. Holman, The *Eichleay* Formula: A Resilient Means for Recovering Unabsorbed Overhead, 24 Public Contract L.J. 319, 321 (1995).

When a breach by one party imposes a delay on the ability of the other party to perform its obligations under a contract, "the damages are to be measured by the direct cost of all labor and material . . . *plus fair and reasonable overhead expenses* properly chargeable . . . during the reasonable time required" to complete performance. E.I. duPont deNemours & Co. *v.* Universal Moulded Prod., 191 Va. 525, 581 (1950). In such cases, while the plaintiff must prove its damages with reasonable certainty, "[a]n absolute certainty as to the amount of the damages is not essential when the existence of a loss has been established. The quantum may be fixed when the facts and circumstances are such as to permit . . . an intelligent and probable estimate thereof." Pebble Building Co. *v.* G.J. Hopkins, Inc., 223 Va. 188, 191 (1982).

We recognize that not every instance of a delay caused by the other party to a contract will result in a contractor incurring either direct or overhead damages. However, where the evidence shows that a contractor has incurred direct damages as a result of the delay such as additional cost of labor and material, the question whether the contractor also suffered unabsorbed overhead damages necessarily must be determined from the facts and circumstances of the individual case. It is not necessary for the contractor to show that its overhead was increased as a result of the delay, but only that it could not otherwise reasonably recoup its pro rata home office expenses incurred while its workforce was idled by the delay.

Here, the evidence showed that Worcester Brothers incurred actual direct damages as a result of having to maintain its personnel on the job site far beyond the anticipated date of substantial completion. The record supports the trial court's finding that the Authority was responsible for a delay that caused Worcester Brothers' workforce to be "on standby" and this further prohibited Worcester Brothers from recouping its unabsorbed home office expenses by seeking other contracts during the delay period. Accordingly, we agree with the trial court's ruling that Worcester Brothers met its burden of proof with respect to the existence of unabsorbed home office expenses attributable to the Authority's delay.

The Authority contends, however, that even if Worcester Brothers proved that it incurred unabsorbed home office expenses as a result of the Authority's delay, the trial court erred in accepting the *Eichleay* formula as the method for determining the amount of these expenses. The Authority asserts that the contract provides that disputes between the parties will be governed by Virginia law and, since no legislative act, administrative rule, or case law in Virginia has "adopt[ed] the use of the *Eichleay* formula in claims against public bodies in Virginia," the use of the formula "was not within the parties' contemplation at the time the contract was executed." . . .

The *Eichleay* formula . . . is merely a mathematical method of prorating a contractor's total overhead expenses for a particular contract.[5]

[5] To make that proration, the total amount billed on the particular contract by the contractor . . . is divided by the contractor's total billings during the contract period . . . and this quotient is then multiplied by the contractor's home office expenses attributable to the contract period . . . to determine the amount of home office expenses allocable to the contract. Next, the

As an abstract proposition, the *Eichleay* formula has been criticized as an inadequate substitute for direct evidence of the actual amount of damages and "no less speculative" than other unsupported opinion evidence simply "because it was cast in a mathematical milieu." Berley Industries, Inc. *v.* City of New York, 45 N.Y.2d 683 (1978). In *Berley,* the New York Court of Appeals rejected the use of the *Eichleay* formula as an "administrative convenience," where there was no supporting evidence that any of the home office expenses were attributable to the delay. . . .

We are of opinion that the rationale of the latter cases is in accord with the general principles of law applicable to proving damages for delay . . . . Accordingly, where, as here, there is evidence that a contractor has suffered actual damages as a result of an unreasonable owner-caused delay, the *Eichleay* formula is an acceptable method, though not the only possible method, of calculating the portion of home office expenses attributable to delay.

In recognizing the adequacy of the evidence in this case to support the use of the *Eichleay* formula to determine unabsorbed overhead damages for the delay in this contract, we do not adopt it as the standard for determining such damages generally. Rather, as with any fact-specific question, the individual circumstances of a given case will determine whether "an intelligent and probable estimate" of such damages has been proven. *Pebble*, 223 Va. at 191. . . .

Raishevich v. Foster

United States Court of Appeals, Second Circuit, 2001.
247 F.3d 337.

■ STRAUB, CIRCUIT JUDGE. . . . For approximately fifteen years, Raishevich assembled a collection of photographic transparencies of cannabis, or marijuana, plants. In November 1993, officers of the New York State Police arrested Raishevich and seized numerous items from his home, including 347 transparencies from his cannabis collection. Although he requested that the police return his transparencies, they were destroyed by Foster, an evidence custodian for the New York State Police. On May 2, 1995, Raishevich brought suit [against Foster] pursuant to 42 U.S.C. § 1983 seeking compensatory damages for the destruction of these transparencies . . . .

During a two-day bench trial solely on the issue of damages, Raishevich produced little evidence of his past earnings from his now-destroyed transparencies. The District Court's evaluation of the evidence reveals that it found much of Raishevich's proof regarding his past

amount of home office expenses allocable to the contract is divided by the total number of days of the contractor's performance under the contract . . . to determine a daily contract home office expense rate. Finally, the daily contract home office expense rate is multiplied by the number of days of delay . . . to determine the amount of damages . . . .

earnings—findings not directly challenged on appeal—either unsubstantiated or unconvincing. The District Court discredited Raishevich's expert witness's testimony that the value of a one-time use of a transparency was $1500, seemingly finding her testimony to be both flawed and largely irrelevant. After receiving conflicting evidence regarding the value of Raishevich's transparencies, the District Court found that $200 was the proper measure of the actual value of each transparency. The District Court then examined how many prints from his transparencies Raishevich could have sold over a thirty-year period. Despite finding that evidence of his past earnings and productions was "scant," the District Court provided Raishevich with "the benefit of every doubt" and concluded that Raishevich's peak publication rate was two prints per year. This yielded sixty uses of his destroyed transparencies over a thirty-year period. At $200 per use, the damages amounted to $12,000. The District Court then doubled the award of $12,000 to $24,000 because Foster's destruction of the transparencies may have hindered Raishevich's ability to prove his damages with greater specificity. . . .

Foster then sought an order amending the District Court's findings of fact and judgment in order to reduce the damage award . . . . [T]he District Court granted Foster's motion and reduced the amount of compensatory damages to $12,000. . . . In halving the damage award, the District Court explained that it had improperly taken the "*Bigelow* principle"[2] into account twice in its initial decision, both in determining the publication rate of a Raishevich transparency and in supplementing the resulting damage figure at the end. . . .

Raishevich objects to the District Court's reduction of his compensatory damage award, arguing that the District Court did not include a duplicative consideration of the *Bigelow* principle in its initial judgment. . . .

Although Raishevich bore the burden of persuasion with regard to his entitlement to compensatory relief, he had no obligation to offer a mathematically precise formula as to the amount of damages. If the plaintiff's inability to prove an exact amount of damages arises from actions of the defendant, a factfinder "has some latitude to 'make a just and reasonable estimate of damages based on relevant data.' " Electro-Miniatures Corp. *v.* Wendon Co., 771 F.2d 23, 27 (2d Cir. 1985) (quoting Bigelow *v.* RKO Radio Pictures, Inc., 327 U.S. 251, 264 (1946)). The factfinder, however, may not base its award on speculation or guesswork. When "damages are at some unascertainable amount below an upper

[2] The "*Bigelow* principle" traces its origin to the case of Bigelow *v.* RKO Radio Pictures, Inc., 327 U.S. 251 (1946). There, the Supreme Court established that in cases in which the defendant's wrongdoing prevented the plaintiff from demonstrating the exact measure of the damages suffered, the factfinder may make a "just and reasonable estimate" of the damage caused. Although *Bigelow* involved an antitrust action and was motivated in part by the difficulty in ascertaining business damages, it also relied upon the principle that "it does not come with very good grace for the wrongdoer to insist upon specific and certain proof of the injury which it has itself inflicted."

limit and when the uncertainty arises from the defendant's wrong, the upper limit will be taken as the proper amount." Gratz *v.* Claughton, 187 F.2d 46, 51–52 (2d Cir. 1951). The *Bigelow* principle thus applies to situations in which the amount of damages, although not specifically ascertainable because of misconduct by the defendant, falls within a certain range. It provides the plaintiff with the benefit of a more liberalized standard of proof and prevents the defendant from "profit[ing] by his wrongdoing at the expense of his victim." Bigelow, 327 U.S. at 264.

In this case, the District Court reduced its initial damage award because it concluded that it had applied the *Bigelow* principle twice. Although Raishevich takes issue with this conclusion, we find that the District Court did not err in reducing the award to correct its previous double counting. While the District Court did not discuss the *Bigelow* principle in its initial opinion, it is clear that it applied *Bigelow*'s principles in determining Raishevich's peak publication rate of two prints per year. Raishevich provided little to no evidence indicating the uniqueness of his work, his exploitation of the market demand for cannabis photography or the market value of one of his transparencies. Moreover, the District Court found that, during a ten-year period, Raishevich published no more than ten prints. For some of these publications, Raishevich received no compensation or the compensation he allegedly received was deemed questionable by the District Court. The District Court also noted that in the two-year period immediately preceding the seizure, Raishevich failed to publish at all. Thus, it is clear from the initial opinion that the District Court's selection of a rate of two uses per year was a choice to use the upper limit and therefore to apply the *Bigelow* principle. That principle thus directly contributed to the $12,000 damage calculation. The District Court applied *Bigelow* again in doubling the resulting $12,000 figure to $24,000.

Raishevich points to no precedent requiring a District Court to factor the *Bigelow* principle in each point of its analysis; to do so would be to multiply the *Bigelow* factor exponentially. Our precedent suggests the opposite: *Bigelow* provides only that the factfinder is given some latitude in making a reasonable assessment of the damages, but it does not authorize the assessment of an additional penalty beyond permitting the plaintiff a more liberalized standard of proof. Although the *Bigelow* principle should be applied, it should not be applied twice. . . .

D. AVOIDABLE CONSEQUENCES

Clark v. Marsiglia

Supreme Court of New York, 1845.
1 Denio 317.

The plaintiff proved that a number of paintings were delivered to him by the defendant to clean and repair, at certain prices for each. They were delivered upon two occasions. As to the first parcel, for the repairing of which the price was $75, no defense was offered. In respect to the other, for which the plaintiff charged $156, the defendant gave evidence tending to show that after the plaintiff had commenced work upon them, he desired him not to go on, as he had concluded not to have the work done. The plaintiff, notwithstanding, finished the cleaning and repairing of the pictures, and claimed to recover for doing the whole, and for the materials furnished, insisting that the defendant had no right to countermand the order which he had given. The defendant's counsel requested the court to charge that he had the right to countermand his instructions for the work, and that the plaintiff could not recover for any work done after such countermand.

The court declined to charge as requested, but, on the contrary, instructed the jury that inasmuch as the plaintiff had commenced the work before the order was revoked, he had a right to finish it, and to recover the whole value of his labor and for the materials furnished. The jury found their verdict accordingly, and the defendant's counsel excepted. Judgment was rendered upon the verdict. . . .

■ PER CURIAM. . . . The defendant, by requiring the plaintiff to stop work upon the paintings, violated his contract, and thereby incurred a liability to pay such damages as the plaintiff should sustain. Such damages would include a recompense for the labor done and materials used, and such further sum in damages as might, upon legal principles, be assessed for the breach of the contract; but the plaintiff had no right, by obstinately persisting in the work, to make the penalty upon the defendant greater than it would otherwise have been.

To hold that one who employs another to do a piece of work is bound to suffer it to be done at all events, would sometimes lead to great injustice. A man may hire another to labor for a year, and within the year his situation may be such as to render the work entirely useless to him. The party employed cannot persist in working, though he is entitled to the damages consequent upon his disappointment. So if one hires another to build a house, and subsequent events put it out of his power to pay for it, it is commendable in him to stop the work, and pay for what has been done and the damages sustained by the contractor. He may be under a necessity to change his residence, but upon the rule contended for, he would be obliged to have a house which he did not need and could not use. In all such cases the just claims of the party employed are satisfied when he is fully recompensed for his part performance and indemnified for his loss in respect to the part left unexecuted; and to persist in accumulating a larger demand is not consistent with good faith towards the employer. The judgment must be reversed, and a *venire de novo* awarded. . . .

NOTES

1. Owners contracted with Builder for construction of a house. Upon completion, Owners rejected the house as defective. Builder offered to correct the defects but the Owners refused, maintaining that the house was beyond repair. Builder proceeded to make repairs, and ultimately tendered a building that was found to meet contract specifications. The court allowed Builder to recover the contract price:

> "Undoubtedly it is the settled general rule that, when the owner notifies a building contractor that the owner repudiates or renounces the contract and explicitly directs the contractor not to do anything further under it, the contractor cannot go on and complete the work and sue for the full contract price. . . .
>
> "But the rule runs only so far as run the reasons which give it existence. When the work has already been entered upon and has progressed to the extent that to stop will leave a situation wherein it will be impracticable to attempt a dependable estimate of the contractor's damages, or where to complete the work will diminish the damages to the owner, or at least will not enhance his damages, the contractor may go forward and complete the work. . . .
>
> "In the case before us, admitting every defect claimed by appellants when the house was tendered in June, nevertheless, the work was then at least 75 per cent. complete; and of that part incomplete the principal defects were in the fact that there was not a sufficient number of piers under the house, the piers were not located under the partition walls, the sills were insufficient both in location and in strength, and some of the windows allowed water to enter the structure. This defect in the piers and sills caused the floor to sag and to become unlevel. Applying common knowledge, we know that not to correct this situation, to do no further work, would cause the floors and the entire inside superstructure to sag further day by day and to become generally more and more out of level, and not to correct the windows promptly would cause water damage. To correct the work and to complete it, under the facts here presented, did not enhance damages, but prevented damages . . . ."

Dowling *v.* Whites Lumber & Supply Co., 170 Miss. 267, 273–75 (1934).

2. UCC § 2–704(2) provides that:

> "If the goods are unfinished, an aggrieved seller may in the exercise of reasonable commercial judgment for the purposes of avoiding loss and of effective realization either complete the manufacture and wholly identify the goods to the contract or cease manufacture and resell for scrap or salvage value or proceed in any other reasonable manner."

Comment 2 explains that:

> "the seller is given express power to complete manufacture or procurement of goods for the contract unless the exercise of

reasonable commercial judgment as to the facts as they appear at the time he learns of the breach makes it clear that such action will result in a material increase in damages. The burden is on the buyer to show the commercially unreasonable nature of the seller's action in completing manufacture."

Roberts v. Pilot Freight Carriers, Inc.

Supreme Court of North Carolina, 1968.
273 N.C. 600.

This action for property damage arises out of a collision between plaintiff's 1957 Ford dump truck and defendant's tractor-trailer. The accident occurred at approximately 4:30 p.m. on 9 December 1965 in the heavily graveled, 35-foot driveway, which connects the premises of Carolina Machinery and Supply Company (M. & S. Co.) with US Highway No. 70. M. & S. Co. is located on the north side of No. 70 a few miles west of Raleigh. In this area, No. 70 is a four-lane highway for east/west traffic with a median dividing the two lanes for opposing traffic. Both vehicles were proceeding west. Plaintiff's employee, C. G. Goldston, was hauling a load of gravel in the dump truck. Defendant's employee, H. H. Bost, was taking the tractor-trailer to the M. & S. Co. From a hillcrest 1500–1800 feet east of the M. & S. Co.'s building, the highway runs slightly downgrade until it "flattens out" several hundred feet from the driveway. At the time of the accident, the weather was clear and the road dry. The posted speed limit for the area was 60 MPH for automobiles and 50 MPH for trucks.

Evidence for plaintiff tended to show: Goldston first saw the tractor-trailer when it approached from his rear in the left or passing lane east of the hillcrest. Goldston was driving in the right lane for westbound traffic at a speed of about 45 MPH. The tractor-trailer passed him at a speed of 50 MPH. Immediately thereafter Goldston saw its right-turn signal come on, and he responded by blinking his lights—his signal to Bost that he could safely return to the right lane. Bost then applied his brakes and Goldston realized that he was stopping. Goldston applied his brakes also and—because there was a car in the left lane—pulled to the right shoulder. At the time the tractor-trailer started back into the right lane, it was about 25–30 feet, or the length of the dump truck, in front of Goldston. It turned into M. & S. Co.'s driveway, and the left front of the dump truck collided with the right rear wheels of the trailer in the driveway directly in front of the M. & S. Co.'s building. Both vehicles at once came to a complete stop. From the time Bost first turned on his right-turn signal, Goldston never saw it go off. It was blinking at the time the accident occurred. . . .

With reference to his damages, plaintiff's evidence tended to show: The cost of putting the truck in "A–1 order" after the collision would have been $1,293.47; the cost of repairing the damage caused by the accident, $991.38. Including the time required to get the parts, 3–4 weeks would have been required to make the repairs, but the work itself could have been done in 1 1/2 weeks. The dump body, the power take-off, and the body hoist were not damaged, and these could have been transferred to another chassis in two days.

Plaintiff had been using the dump truck five days a week to haul gravel from the Nello Teer Quarry near Raleigh to the Research Triangle. In his opinion, the value of the truck immediately before the collision was $2,500.00; immediately after, $1,000.00. He made no effort to buy another truck. He tried to rent a dump truck from Greensboro Ford Company but was unable to obtain one there. The dump truck has not been repaired.

Over defendant's objection and exception, plaintiff testified that after the collision, he hauled 1/3 less gravel each day and that, prior to the collision, his "approximate net earnings" from the damaged truck had been $50.00 a day. On cross-examination, he conceded that this figure was not based on any cost accounting, and that he had not considered the cost of oil, depreciation, repairs, insurance, or license fees in arriving at the truck's net earnings. . . .

J. C. Jeffries, an independent automotive damage appraiser, who examined plaintiff's 9-year-old dump truck after the collision, testified that, in his opinion, it could not be economically repaired. Repairs would have cost $991.38, and the truck, exclusive of the dump body, was worth only about $300.00 for salvage. There was, however, no damage to the dump body and power hoist, and these could have been easily transferred to another chassis in two-days' time at a cost of only $75.00. To purchase a 1957 Ford truck body on which the dump body could have been installed would have cost about $1,000.00. Subtracting the $300.00-salvage figure, the net cost of this acquisition and transfer, would have been about $775.00.

Issues were submitted to the jury and answered as follows: "1. Was the property of the plaintiff damaged by the negligence of the defendant's agent as alleged in the complaint? ANSWER: Yes. 2. If so, did the plaintiff's agent by his negligence contribute to the damages of the plaintiff as alleged in the answer? ANSWER: No. 3. What amount, if any, is the plaintiff entitled to recover of the defendant for damages to his truck? ANSWER: $1,500.00. 4. What amount if any, is the plaintiff entitled to recover by reason of his loss of use of his truck? ANSWER: $1,200.00."

■ SHARP, JUSTICE. Plaintiff's evidence, viewed in the light most favorable to him, was sufficient to substantiate his allegations that defendant's violation of G.S. § 20–154(a) and (b) was the proximate cause of the collision which damaged his dump truck.

[Defendant assigned as error the admission of evidence tending to show profits lost as a result of his deprivation of the truck, and an instruction allowing the jury to award the plaintiff damages for loss of use of the dump truck.]

When a plaintiff's vehicle is damaged by the negligence of a defendant, the plaintiff is entitled to recover the difference between the fair market value of the vehicle before and after the damage. Evidence of the cost of repairs or estimates thereof are competent to aid the jury in determining that difference. When a vehicle is negligently damaged, if it can be economically repaired, the plaintiff will also be entitled to recover such special damages as he has properly pleaded and proven for the loss of its use during the time he was necessarily deprived of it. . . .

In general, the right to recover for loss of use is limited to situations in which the damage to the vehicle can be repaired at a reasonable cost and within a reasonable time. If the vehicle is totally destroyed as an instrument of conveyance or if, because parts are unavailable or for some other special reason, repairs would be so long delayed as to be improvident, the plaintiff must purchase another vehicle. In this situation, he would be entitled to damages for loss of use only if another vehicle was not immediately obtainable and, in consequence, he suffered loss of earnings during the interval between the accident and the acquisition of another vehicle. The interval would be limited to the period reasonably necessary to acquire the new vehicle.

The fact that an owner, in lieu of repairing a vehicle which could have been economically repaired, "trades it in" on new equipment, will not preclude him from recovering damages for loss of its use during the time reasonably required to purchase new equipment or to make the repairs, whichever is shorter.

Ordinarily the measure of damages for loss of use of a business vehicle is not the profits which the owner would have earned from its use during the time he was deprived of it; it is the cost of renting a similar vehicle during a reasonable period for repairs. This limitation is an application of the rule that one who seeks to hold another liable for damages must use reasonable diligence to avoid or mitigate them. Thus, before a plaintiff may recover lost profits resulting from the deprivation of his vehicle, he must show (1) that he made a reasonable effort to obtain a substitute vehicle for the time required to repair or replace the damaged one, and (2) that he was unable to obtain one in the area reasonably related to his business. In the absence of such a showing, he may not recover lost profits. When, however, he has carried the burden of proving that no substitute vehicle could be rented, a plaintiff may recover lost profits if he can establish the amount of the loss with reasonable certainty. If a plaintiff could have rented a substitute vehicle, the cost of hiring it during the time reasonably necessary to acquire a new one or to repair the old one is the measure of his damage even though no other vehicle was rented. The burden is on the plaintiff to establish the cost of such hire. . . .

According to plaintiff's evidence, the truck was worth $2,500.00 before the collision, $1,000.00 thereafter, and the damage could have been repaired for $991.38 within 3–4 weeks. Thus, the jury might have found that repairs could have been economically made. Upon this finding, plaintiff would have been entitled to recover as damages for loss of use the reasonable cost of hiring a substitute vehicle during the time required to repair the truck with reasonable promptness. Plaintiff, however, sought only to recover lost profits, and the court permitted him to do this without showing that a substitute vehicle was unavailable in the area. His statement that he was unable to rent one from Greensboro Ford Company fell far short of proving his inability to hire a similar truck in the Research Triangle area, where he was conducting his hauling operations. Plaintiff likewise offered no evidence tending to show the cost of hiring a substitute vehicle. He made no effort to purchase another truck or to acquire a chassis on which (according to defendant's uncontradicted evidence) he could have mounted the undamaged dump body and power hoist in two days at a cost of $75.00. At the time of the trial, plaintiff still had the wrecked truck and, although twenty months had elapsed since the collision, it had not been repaired.

Thus, plaintiff, who had the burden of proof, laid no foundation to recover either lost profits or the cost of hiring a substitute vehicle for the three or four weeks in which his evidence tended to show repairs could have been made. . . .

In re WorldCom, Inc.[i]

United States Bankruptcy Court, S.D.N.Y, 2007.
361 B.R. 675.

■ ARTHUR J. GONZOLEZ, BANKRUPTCY JUDGE. Before the Court are cross-motions for summary judgment separately brought by Michael Jordan ("Jordan") and WorldCom, Inc. (hereafter referred to as the "Debtors" or "MCI").

On or about July 10, 1995, Jordan and the Debtors entered into an endorsement agreement (the "Agreement"). At that time, Jordan was considered to be one of the most popular athletes in the world. The Agreement granted MCI a ten-year license to use Jordan's name, likeness, "other attributes," and personal services to advertise and promote MCI's telecommunications products and services beginning in September 1995 and ending in August 2005. The Agreement did not prevent Jordan from endorsing most other products or services, although he could not endorse the same products or services that MCI produced. In addition to a $5 million signing bonus, the Agreement provided an annual base compensation of $2 million for Jordan. The Agreement provided that Jordan would be treated as an independent contractor and that MCI would not withhold any amount from Jordan's compensation for tax purposes. The Agreement provided that Jordan was to make himself available for four days, not to exceed four hours per day, during each contract year to produce television commercials and print

[i] Additional sections of this opinion appear in Chapter Four, below.

advertising and for promotional appearances. The parties agreed that the advertising and promotional materials would be submitted to Jordan for his approval, which could not be unreasonably withheld, fourteen days prior to their release to the general public. From 1995 to 2000, Jordan appeared in several television commercials and a large number of print ads for MCI.

On July 1, 2002, MCI commenced a case under chapter 11 of title 11 of the United States Code (the "Bankruptcy Code") in the Bankruptcy Court for the Southern District of New York. [Under the Bankruptcy Code, a debtor can choose either to reject an executory contract or to assume the contract and cure any defaults. If the debtor rejects the contract, the contract is treated as breached and the debtor is liable for damages according to applicable state law. On July 18, 2003, MCI elected to reject the Agreement with Jordan.] Following that rejection of the Agreement, Jordan filed Claim No. 36077 (the "Claim") in the amount of $8 million—seeking $2 million for each of the payments that were due in June of 2002, 2003, 2004, and 2005. MCI does not object to the Claim to the extent Jordan seeks $4 million for the 2002 and 2003 payments under the Agreement. As of the rejection in July 2003, two years remained under the Agreement.

[MCI asserted two bases for disallowance of the Claim. The first referred to a provision of the Bankruptcy Code limiting contract claims by "employees" to one year's compensation. The court concluded that Jordan was not an employee of MCI, but an independent contractor; therefore the statutory limitation did not apply. Second, MCI argued that Jordan's Claim should be reduced because he did not take reasonable steps to minimized damages. On this point, the court first concluded that Jordan was not a "lost volume seller," and therefore was not excused on this ground from the obligation to minimize damages. This portion of the opinion is reprinted in Chapter 4.]

2. *Whether Jordan Made Reasonable Efforts to Mitigate*

Jordan argues at length that MCI must show that Jordan could have entered a "substantially similar" endorsement contract in order to mitigate damages. . . . This language stems from federal employment cases concerning back pay and mitigation, which this case, while similar in many respects, is not.

Several of the justifications for the "substantially similar or equivalent" standard of employment law, aside from the general remedial policy of making the non-breaching party whole for losses caused by the breaching party, show why there is less concern here regarding a "substantially equivalent" opportunity as Jordan was not an employee of MCI. For one, the standard exists in part to ensure the employee's future advancement by mandating that the employee's promotional opportunities and status should be virtually identical to the prior position. Since Jordan was never an employee of MCI, this is not relevant. Second, to require acceptance of inferior employment can mean "that one who has been discriminated against would be obliged, in order to mitigate damages, to submit to the very discrimination of which he complains." This, obviously, has no application here. . . .

The main case relied on by Jordan for this argument regarding a "substantially similar" opportunity is a case analyzed under employment law and one that presented a completely different factual and procedural background. See Parker *v.* Twentieth Century-Fox Film Corp., 3 Cal.3d 176 (1970). In *Parker,* the plaintiff, a leading movie actress, agreed to perform in a musical-type film in California. The employer studio later decided not to make the movie and offered to the plaintiff as a substitute the leading role in a dramatic "western type" movie set in an opal mine and to be filmed in Australia. The plaintiff turned down that offer, sued for damages on the original agreement, and the trial court ruled on a summary judgment motion that the earnings from this substitute employment that the plaintiff refused could not be applied in mitigation because the second offer was "different" and "inferior.". . .

[In this case,] MCI must show the absence of reasonable efforts by Jordan to avoid consequences or minimize his damages. . . .

Since "reasonable efforts in the form of *affirmative steps* are required to mitigate damages," MCI carries its [initial] burden by showing that Jordan has not taken affirmative steps to mitigate damages. Jordan admits in his brief that at the time of the rejection of the Agreement, "Jordan had already implemented a business strategy of not accepting new endorsements." [Jordan's agent] testified that a replacement telecommunications company was not approached. [His financial advisor] testified that Jordan did not return to the endorsement marketplace to try and replace the revenue he was to be paid under the Agreement. [The financial advisor] explained that Jordan did not wish to expand his "pitchman efforts with new relationships" because of his primary goal of becoming the owner of an NBA team. Although Jordan points to his discussions with another company, Nextel, as showing that he was willing to listen to endorsement agreements after MCI's bankruptcy, MCI effectively responds that responding to an inquiry by giving them contact information and indicating a willingness to respond to another call "is not trying to find an alternative" agreement—it is, in effect, "doing nothing." Based on the foregoing, and drawing all permissible factual inferences in favor of Jordan, the Court determines that MCI has established that Jordan did not take affirmative steps to mitigate damages.

3. *Whether Jordan's Beliefs that Another Endorsement Would Dilute His Impact as an Endorser or Harm His Reputation Were Reasonable Justifications for not Mitigating Damages*

. . . .

a. *Dilution*

Jordan's dilution argument is not convincing. Jordan's agent . . . testified that although there were no "fixed numbers" for the amount of endorsements, Jordan and his representatives were wary about dilution and sensitive about "protecting the brand" of Jordan. Jordan does not set forth any facts showing that Jordan's image was at risk of dilution. MCI convincingly responds that adding an agreement to replace a lost one is merely maintaining the status quo, not a dilution of Jordan's impact by addition. MCI's expert stated that Jordan had previously had sixteen endorsement agreements in place, which further weakens Jordan's dilution argument and casts doubt on [Jordan's agent's] statement that Jordan and his advisors "always felt that less is more" in terms of endorsements. While the Court recognizes that Jordan's image is the true commodity here and its market value could be diluted from overexposure, MCI has shown that Jordan's image was not at risk of dilution by replacing the MCI endorsement agreement with another one. . . .

b. *Risk to Reputation*

Under the risk to reputation theory Jordan cites, an injured party is not allowed to recover from a wrongdoer those damages that the injured party "could have avoided without undue risk, burden or humiliation." See Restatement (2d), § 350(1). Jordan's "harm to reputation" argument is flawed because the envisioned harm to Jordan's reputation does not rise to the level of harm found in the cited case law. . . .

In Eastman Kodak Co. *v.* Westway Motor Freight, Inc., 949 F.2d 317 (10th Cir. 1991), Kodak shipped a load of sensitized photographic material on a truck operated by the defendant. Most of the material was destroyed in transit because of the defendant's mishandling. The Tenth Circuit held that Kodak was not required to sell the damaged merchandise to mitigate damages, stating that the record revealed that Kodak's reputation, which it spent considerable resources in developing, "could be harmed if it was required to sell damaged merchandise in order to mitigate damages." . . .

[A] plaintiff faced with the choice of (1) selling a sub-standard product to the public to mitigate damages caused by the breach of another and (2) doing nothing—can choose to do nothing, but Jordan was not confronted with those circumstances. While Jordan's reputation is considerable and obviously the result of careful development, there are no factual assertions that support the proposition that Jordan's choosing another endorsement opportunity is akin to being forced to sell damaged goods, as was the case in *Eastman Kodak* . . . .

4. *Whether Focusing on NBA Ownership Was a Reasonable Decision*

Jordan cites his goal of owning an NBA team as a reasonable justification for his decision not to enter additional endorsement agreements.

In support, Jordan cites cases that hold if a non-breaching plaintiff chooses a reasonable course of action despite the existence of another course of action that, in hindsight, would have been better at lessening harm, the plaintiff's damages are not reduced. A closer examination at such cases reveals that they are not applicable to Jordan's situation. Cases that Jordan cites . . . share a common theme not present in the instant matter: the non-breaching party faced a choice between two reasonable courses of action right after the breach or tort that inflicted the damage, and made a choice to lessen the damage that appeared reasonable at the time. Jordan's choice to focus on NBA team ownership, in contrast, *was not done to lessen the damage from MCI's rejection,* but was done for other, unrelated business reasons. . . .

Furthermore, Jordan did not have to pursue *any* endorsement, such as one that would be beneath a celebrity of Jordan's stature, *e.g.*, endorsing a product likely to be distasteful to Jordan or his fans. Jordan had the duty to take reasonable efforts to mitigate, such as by seeking another endorsement for an established, reputable company for compensation near to what he received from MCI. MCI has established that there is no genuine issue as to whether Jordan made reasonable efforts to do so. The Court finds that as a matter of law Jordan has failed to mitigate damages.

D. *The Need for a Further Determination of Damages*

A case cited by MCI shows the correct path for further resolution of this matter. Wisconsin Ave. Nursing Home *v.* D.C. Human Rights Commission, 527 A.2d 282 (D.C. 1987), did not, as MCI asserts, hold that the plaintiff's failure to mitigate damages *barred* any recovery. After finding that the discharged employee had not exercised reasonable diligence in seeking substitute employment, the court remanded the case for the factual determination, with the burden of proof on the defendant, of the wages the plaintiff could have earned had she diligently sought substitute employment. . . .

[T]here has been no determination and no evidence presented of what Jordan could have reasonably earned had he fulfilled his obligation to mitigate damages by entering the endorsement marketplace following MCI's rejection of the Agreement. It is not clear that Jordan could have found an endorsement agreement in 2003 that paid him $2 million a year for the contract years 2004 and 2005. It is also unlikely that Jordan would have been obligated to accept a large number of endorsements of smaller value to make up the $2 million, due to the dilution effect such a number would have, because such efforts would likely be unreasonable. However, the facts may reveal that one or more endorsements could have been found without "diluting" his image and partially or completely mitigating the damages. Although MCI's expert stated that he believed that Jordan could have easily earned $2 million from an additional endorsement in 2003, that opinion was not presented with any objective evidence of the marketplace, such as what other celebrity endorsers of Jordan's stature earned that year and which companies were in the market for an endorser of Jordan's stature. Although the Court finds that as a matter of law Jordan has not mitigated damages, there must be an evidentiary hearing on how much his claim should be reduced to reflect what portion would have been mitigated had he used reasonable efforts to do so. . . .

The Debtors are to settle an order consistent with this opinion.

NOTE

Traditionally, a lease was viewed as a transfer of property from the landlord to the tenant for the agreed term, rather than a contract by the landlord to provide space. It followed that a landlord whose tenant vacated the leased premises before the end of the lease was entitled to collect rent for the balance of the lease term, with no duty to relet. If, however, the landlord chose to relet, courts were likely to find that the lease was terminated and the tenant owed, at most, damages measured by the difference between agreed rent and fair rental value.

Modern cases have tended to reverse the common law rule. A typical example is Frenchtown Square Partnership *v.* Lemstone, Inc., 99 Ohio St.3d 254 (2003):

> "A certain duality inheres to leases. Specifically, because they are contractual instruments by which parties convey interests in real property, they are arguably susceptible of both contract law and property law principles. . . .
>
> "[U]nder the common law of contracts, mitigation is a fundamental tenet of a damage calculus. . . . [M]itigation, otherwise known as the doctrine of avoidable consequences, . . . justly place[s] an injured party in as good a position had the contract not been breached at the least cost to the defaulting party." . . .
>
> In an attempt to distinguish commercial leases from other types of leases, Frenchtown [the landlord] argues that the overall mix of shopping-center tenants is a material aspect of the bargained-for performance in a shopping-center lease. Essentially, by employing contract-law principles, Frenchtown argues that a proper mix of tenants creates a synergistic effect, and a rule that encourages abandonment will detrimentally affect not only the lessor, but also the other tenants. While we acknowledge that where two or more shops adjoin, a symbiotic relationship may exist, we decline to create a rule of law that distinguishes between single- and multishop commercial settings. The duty to mitigate arises in

all commercial leases of real property, just as it exists in all other contracts.

We emphasize that our holding does not require a lessor to accept just any available lessee. The duty to mitigate requires only reasonable efforts. Thus, the tenant mix may reasonably factor into a lessor's decisions to relet. Finally, . . . [o]ur holding that contract principles apply to the calculation of damages extends to all damages provable by the lessor. If the breaching tenant caused harm such that the lessor's profitability is affected, then that harm is compensable to the extent it is proved. This, as well as the reasonableness of introducing a replacement lessee, is a question for the trier of fact. . . .

[L]andlords owe a duty to mitigate their damages caused by a breaching tenant. That rule flows from the premise that modern leases are more than simply property-interest transfers; rather, leases possess contractual qualities that often include myriad covenants and duties and arise from a bargained-for relationship. In a practical sense, lessors and lessees contract for the use of property. Accordingly, barring contrary contract provisions, a duty to mitigate damages applies to all leases."

Id. at 256–259. *Cf.* United States National Bank of Oregon *v.* Homeland, Inc., 291 Or. 374 (1981) (holding that, as long as the landlord makes reasonable efforts to relet the property, the tenant remains liable for the difference between the agreed rent and the rent actually collected over the term of the original lease).

E. OFFSETTING BENEFITS

Indiana State Symphony Society, Inc. v. Ziedonis

Court of Appeals of Indiana, 1976.
171 Ind. App. 292.

■ WHITE, JUDGE. Plaintiff-appellee (Ziedonis), formerly employed by defendant-appellant (Symphony) as a violinist in the Indianapolis Symphony Orchestra, recovered a verdict and judgment of $6,335.00 as damages for his discharge in alleged violation of his written employment contract. Symphony's appeal charges error . . . in the amount of damages. . . .

Symphony contends that the verdict is too large by at least $3,430, which is the amount Ziedonis testified in his own case-in-chief he was paid for playing with two out-of-town orchestras during the period for which the verdict awards him the full amount of his Symphony salary. Ziedonis counters with argument to the effect that Symphony has failed to sustain its burden of proving mitigation in that it has failed to prove that the $3,430 is profit and that, inasmuch as his Symphony employment was only part-time, Symphony has failed to prove that he could not have earned this income had he not been discharged.

As to the last point, Symphony says that it is obvious that Ziedonis could not have played for those orchestras had he also been employed by Symphony. Since neither orchestra appears to have played in or near Indianapolis that proposition is irrefutable.

A majority of this court is of the opinion, for the reasons stated in Presiding Judge Buchanan's concurring opinion, that the entire $3,430 should have been deducted in mitigation of Ziedonis' damages. Therefore a remittitur will be ordered.

It is the writer's opinion, however, that the burden of proving mitigation, if any, rested on Symphony, and that it failed to prove that his earning this $3,430 actually reduced his loss. It was Ziedonis' duty to use reasonable efforts to avoid loss by securing employment elsewhere and, although it was not his burden to do so, he did prove that he had discharged that duty. The fact that in so doing he also proved that he earned a gross sum for out-of-town work in which he incurred expenses does not shift to him the burden of proving whether or not his earnings exceeded his expenses. . . .

■ BUCHANAN, PRESIDING JUDGE (concurring). I concur in the result reached by the majority, but solely on the basis that once it was proved that Ziedonis had incurred mitigating damages, the burden was on him (not the Defendant) to prove that he also had expenses which otherwise would not have been incurred.

It has long been the rule in Indiana that one wrongfully discharged must attempt to seek alternate employment in order to mitigate damages.

> . . . [I]t is the duty of a person, when unlawfully discharged, to make reasonable effort to obtain work elsewhere, and that in no event could he recover more than what his actual loss might have been had he made such reasonable effort to obtain employment. . . .

Inland Steel Co. *v.* Harris, 49 Ind. App. 157, 163 (1911). When a discharged employee obtains alternate employment there is no question that the proper measure of his damages is the amount of compensation agreed upon for the remainder of the contract period involved, less the amount which he earns from other employment. Thus, the jury should have reduced Ziedonis's award by Three Thousand Four Hundred and Thirty ($3,430.00) Dollars, the amount he earned in alternate employment.

The majority rightfully place the burden on the Defendant Symphony of showing that other employment was available to plaintiff or that the plaintiff did not use diligence in seeking other employment. This is the rule in Indiana.

In this case it was unnecessary for the Symphony to carry this burden because Ziedonis testified that he had earned Three Thousand Four Hundred and Thirty ($3,430.00) Dollars in other employment during the remainder of the contract period. However, I am aware of no Indiana cases which would require the Symphony to show that this employment was profitable to Ziedonis, *i.e.*[,] because Ziedonis had certain expenses of an unspecified amount during the time he earned the Three Thousand Four Hundred and Thirty ($3,430.00) Dollars the Symphony has failed to show that such employment was profitable.

The defendant is in no position to know plaintiff's expenses and should not reasonably be saddled with the burden of proving them. As expenses are peculiarly within the cognizance of plaintiff, he should prove them.

Presumably, something more than love of music led Ziedonis to seek employment with out-of-town symphony orchestras. He certainly had income from this employment. If he had expenses which reduced his income, he should have proved them.

Hartke v. McKelway

United States Court of Appeals, District of Columbia Circuit, 1983.
707 F.2d 1544.

■ MCGOWAN, SENIOR CIRCUIT JUDGE. . . . [Hartke, who had suffered a number of pregnancy-related health problems, decided to undergo a sterilization procedure. McKelway, her doctor, recommended a laparoscopic tubal cauterization, but failed to disclose that there remained a small risk of pregnancy. This risk was material to Hartke, who feared she might die from a further pregnancy. In fact she survived and gave birth to a healthy baby. Hartke then sued McKelway for damages for wrongful birth. The trial court allowed damages for expenses incurred and pain suffered during pregnancy and childbirth, but not for the expenses of raising the child.]

[A] major issue raised by this appeal [is] whether Hartke may recover some portion of the costs of raising to majority the child born after the failed sterilization. . . . [A]s the District Court noted, the case law from other jurisdictions is almost evenly divided. . . .

In large part, the differences appear to revolve around whether the child can be considered a kind of damage to the parents. A number of courts have ruled that as a matter of law no healthy child can ever be considered an injury to its parents, because, as one court put it, "it is a matter of universally-shared emotion and sentiment that the intangible but all-important, incalculable but invaluable 'benefits' of parenthood far outweigh any of the mere monetary burdens involved." Other courts have found that there are some cases in which the addition of a child constitutes an injury to the family. One court provided the following explanation:

> "To say that for reasons of public policy contraceptive failure can result in no damage as a matter of law ignores the fact that tens of millions of persons use contraceptives daily to

> avoid the very result which the defendant would have us say is always a benefit, never a detriment. Those tens of millions of persons, by their conduct, express the sense of the community."

Troppi *v.* Scarf, 31 Mich. App. 240, 253 (1971).

Though we need not finally decide the question given our ultimate result, we suspect that allowing the plaintiff to prove that raising a child constitutes damage is the course of greater justice. . . . Usually, of course, it is true that the birth of a healthy child confers so substantial a benefit on its parents as to outweigh the physical, emotional, and financial burdens of bearing and raising it; "else, presumably, people would not choose to multiply so freely." But when a couple has chosen not to have children, or not to have any more children, the suggestion arises that for them, at least, the birth of a child would not be a net benefit. That is their choice and the courts are required to respect it.

Nevertheless, courts have recognized that there is an unusual difficulty in wrongful conception cases in setting the amount of compensation, because the extent, if any, to which the birth of a child is an injury to particular parents is not obvious but will vary depending on their circumstances and aspirations. The parents may in fact have ended up with a child that they adore and that they privately consider to be, on balance, an overwhelming benefit to their lives.[9] This is because the parents may have sought to avoid conception for any of a number of reasons. They may have done so for socio-economic reasons, seeking to avoid disruption of their careers or lifestyle, or to conserve family resources; for eugenic reasons, seeking to avoid the birth of a handicapped child; or for therapeutic reasons, seeking to avoid the dangers to the mother's health of pregnancy and childbirth.

When a couple chooses sterilization solely for therapeutic or eugenic reasons, it seems especially likely that the birth of a healthy child,

---

[9] It has been said that courts should not allow defendants in wrongful conception cases to thrust upon the plaintiff an unwanted benefit, and that therefore a plaintiff's recovery should not be reduced by any benefits conferred by the defendant's tort. . . .

Nevertheless, the courts that allow any recovery of childrearing damages have, with apparently only two exceptions, always required that the detriments of childrearing be offset against the benefits.

It may be, as one court has said, that allowing the benefits of childrearing to reduce the damages recoverable "is nothing more nor less than the application of an offset to reduce the magnitude of verdicts and lessen the monetary shock to the medical tortfeasor and his insurer." If this is so, it is nonetheless true that this desire to reduce the verdict is widely shared, and reflects deeply felt values. The desire may perhaps be based on a sense that, "even in this day of sophisticated contraception and family planning," couples are commonly faced with unanticipated pregnancies. Thus, the sense of wrong that may arise in cases where the defendant usurps the plaintiffs' right to use their property as they please, is tempered by the knowledge that the ability to be free of unwanted pregnancy has never been all that secure. The benefits that the parents of an unplanned child derive from parenthood are nonetheless real. The feeling in wrongful conception cases may be that, especially in view of the parents' concerted efforts to avoid pregnancy, they should recover something in addition to medical expenses and pain and suffering for the disruption of their planning and of their lifestyles. But to refuse to recognize the benefits of childrearing would be contrary to all the humanistic impulses that the law should seek to reinforce and would give plaintiffs a windfall with which to deal with a problem that many couples face without compensation. . . .

although unplanned, may be, as it is for most parents, a great benefit to them. In such cases, a court will tend to feel that it is unjust to impose on the defendant doctor the often huge costs of raising the child, and will fear that a jury that did so was motivated by passion or anti-doctor prejudice. Thus, in considering the question of whether childrearing expenses may be recoverable, many courts and commentators have placed great emphasis on the couple's reasons for undergoing sterilization. . . .

[A] factfinder should place great weight on a couple's reason for undergoing sterilization in deciding whether the subsequent birth of a child, on balance, constitutes damage to the parents. Their reason for departing from the usual view that childrearing is a positive experience is in effect a calculation of the way in which they anticipate the costs of childbirth to outweigh the benefits. That calculation, untainted by bitterness and greed, or by a sense of duty to a child the parents have brought into the world, is usually the best available evidence of the extent to which the birth of the child has in fact been an injury to them. Thus, for example, where a couple sought sterilization solely for therapeutic or eugenic reasons, there is a presumption raised that the uneventful birth of a healthy child constitutes damage to the parents only to the extent that they experienced abnormal fear of harm to the mother or of the birth of a handicapped child. Courts and juries may assume that the parents treasure the child and that the usual expenses of raising it will be outweighed by the benefits derived.

The presumption raised by the evidence of the parents' reason for seeking sterilization is, however, rebuttable. If it can be shown that the parents' situation has somehow significantly changed since the sterilization—by reliance on presumed infertility in making an income-reducing career change, for example, or by a sudden increase in wealth—it may be that the original calculation of anticipated injury has changed for better or worse. Generally, however, the plaintiff's recovery will most accurately reflect the amount of injury incurred if it is limited to paying for those risks that the plaintiff specifically sought to avoid and that came to pass. . . .

It seems clear, then, that once the extraordinary dangers of childbirth for her were passed, Hartke shared the general view that having a child would, on balance, be a positive experience.

In these circumstances, we agree that the jury could not rationally have found that the birth of this child was an injury to this plaintiff. Awarding childrearing expenses would only give Hartke a windfall. . . .

NOTE ON OFFSETTING BENEFITS

Professors Ariel Porat and Eric Posner have considered the "puzzle" of why the law does not more frequently reduce a recovery because there are offsetting benefits (either for the victim or to third-parties). On that particular question, they conclude:

> "Numerous factors provide reasons for denying either the offset or the recovery of the benefits from the beneficiary. These include: (1) The law often aims at fully compensating the victim and there are factual or legal limitations to recovering from the beneficiary; (2) there are residual harms, so that deduction of private benefits would lead to underdeterrence of wrongdoing; (3) the private benefit would have been supplied more efficiently by the market or the government; (4) deduction of the private benefit or allowing recovery from the beneficiary would give victims and beneficiaries perverse incentives; (5) private benefits can be hard to measure; (6) the benefit might be offset by a hard-to-measure harm to the victim; and (7) deduction of private benefits or allowing recovery from the beneficiary can lead to activity-level distortions."

Ariel Porat and Eric Posner, Offsetting Benefits, 100 Va. L. Rev. 1165, 1205–1206 (2014).

F. THE COLLATERAL SOURCE RULE

Helfend v. Southern California Rapid Transit District

Supreme Court of California, 1970.
2 Cal.3d 1.

■ TOBRINER, ACTING C. J. Defendants appeal from a judgment of the Los Angeles Superior Court entered on a verdict in favor of plaintiff, Julius J. Helfend, for $16,400 in general and special damages for injuries sustained in a bus-auto collision that occurred on July 19, 1965, in the City of Los Angeles.

We have concluded that the judgment for plaintiff in this tort action against the defendant governmental entity should be affirmed. The trial court properly followed the collateral source rule in excluding evidence that a portion of plaintiff's medical bills had been paid through a medical insurance plan that requires the refund of benefits from tort recoveries. . . .

Plaintiff filed a tort action against the Southern California Rapid Transit District, a public entity, and Mitchell, an employee of the transit district. At trial plaintiff claimed slightly more than $2,700 in special damages, including $921 in doctor's bills, a $336.99 hospital bill, and about $45 for medicines. Defendant requested permission to show that about 80 percent of the plaintiff's hospital bill had been paid by plaintiff's Blue Cross insurance carrier and that some of his other medical expenses may have been paid by other insurance. The superior court thoroughly considered the then very recent case of City of Salinas *v.* Souza & McCue Construction Company, 66 Cal.2d 217 (1967), distinguished the *Souza* case on the ground that *Souza* involved a contract setting, and concluded that the judgment should not be reduced to the extent of the amount of insurance payments which plaintiff received. The court ruled that defendants should not be permitted to show that plaintiff had received medical coverage from any collateral source. . . .

We must decide whether the collateral source rule applies to tort actions involving public entities and public employees in which the plaintiff has received benefits from his medical insurance coverage.

The Supreme Court of California has long adhered to the doctrine that if an injured party receives some compensation for his injuries from a source wholly independent of the tortfeasor, such payment should not be deducted from the damages which the plaintiff would otherwise collect from the tortfeasor. As recently as August 1968 we unanimously reaffirmed our adherence to this doctrine, which is known as the "collateral source rule."

Although the collateral source rule remains generally accepted in the United States, nevertheless many other jurisdictions have restricted or repealed it. In this country most commentators have criticized the rule and called for its early demise. In *Souza* we took note of the academic criticism of the rule, characterized the rule as "punitive," and held it inapplicable to the governmental entity involved in that case.

We must, however, review the particular facts of *Souza* in order to determine whether it applies to the present case. The City of Salinas brought suit against Souza & McCue Construction Company, a public works contractor, and its pipe supplier for breach of a contract to construct a sewer pipe line. Souza cross-complained against the city, alleging fraudulent misrepresentation and breach of implied warranty of site conditions; and against the pipe supplier, alleging a guarantee of performance of the piping and a promise to indemnify Souza for any losses. The trial court found that the city materially misrepresented soil conditions by failing to inform Souza of unstable conditions known to the city, that with the city's knowledge Souza relied upon the misrepresentations in bidding, and that Souza should recover damages proximately caused by the city's fraudulent breach.

We held that the trial court improperly determined damages against the city by refusing to allow the city to show that the supplier had recompensed Souza for some of the damages caused by the city's breach. In this contract setting in which the supplier did not constitute a wholly independent collateral source,[7] we held that the collateral source rule cannot be applied against public entities because the collateral source

[7] In Laurenzi *v.* Vranizan, 25 Cal.2d 806 (1945), this court held that "payments by one tortfeasor on account of a harm for which he and another are each liable, diminish the amount of the claim against the other whether or not it was so agreed at the time of payment and whether the payment was made before or after judgment. Since the plaintiff can have but one satisfaction, evidence of such payments is admissible for the purpose of reducing *pro tanto* the amount of the damages he may be entitled to recover." Hence, the rule applies only to payments that come from a source entirely independent of the tortfeasor and does not apply to payments by joint tortfeasors or to benefits the plaintiff receives from a tortfeasor's insurance coverage.

rule appears punitive in nature and punitive damages cannot be imposed on public entities.

Although *Souza's* reasoning as to punitive damages might appear to apply to private tortfeasors as well as public entities and to torts as well as contract actions, we did not there consider the collateral source rule in contexts different from the specific contractual setting and particular relationship of the parties involved. We distinguish the present case from *Souza* on the ground that in *Souza* the plaintiff received payments from his subcontractor which, in the contractual setting of that case, did not constitute a truly independent source. Obviously, such a "source" differs entirely from the instant one, which derives from plaintiff's payment of insurance premiums. Here plaintiff received benefits from his medical insurance coverage only because he had long paid premiums to obtain them. Such an origin does constitute a completely independent source. Hence, although we reaffirm the holding in *Souza,* we do not believe that its reasoning either compels the abolition of the collateral source rule in all cases or requires an unwarranted exemption from the rule of public entities and their employees involved in tort actions. . . .

The collateral source rule as applied here embodies the venerable concept that a person who has invested years of insurance premiums to assure his medical care should receive the benefits of his thrift. The tortfeasor should not garner the benefits of his victim's providence.

The collateral source rule expresses a policy judgment in favor of encouraging citizens to purchase and maintain insurance for personal injuries and for other eventualities. Courts consider insurance a form of investment, the benefits of which become payable without respect to any other possible source of funds. If we were to permit a tortfeasor to mitigate damages with payments from plaintiff's insurance, plaintiff would be in a position inferior to that of having bought no insurance, because his payment of premiums would have earned no benefit. Defendant should not be able to avoid payment of full compensation for the injury inflicted merely because the victim has had the foresight to provide himself with insurance.

Some commentators object that the above approach to the collateral source rule provides plaintiff with a "double recovery," rewards him for the injury, and defeats the principle that damages should compensate the victim but not punish the tortfeasor. We agree with Professor Fleming's observation, however, that "double recovery is justified only in the face of some exceptional, supervening reason, as in the case of accident or life insurance, where it is felt unjust that the tortfeasor should take advantage of the thrift and prescience of the victim in having paid the premiums." (Fleming, INTRODUCTION TO THE LAW OF TORTS (1967) p. 131.) As we point out *infra,* recovery in a wrongful death action is not defeated by the payment of the benefit on a life insurance policy.

Furthermore, insurance policies increasingly provide for either subrogation or refund of benefits upon a tort recovery, and such refund is indeed called for in the present case. Hence, the plaintiff receives no double recovery; the collateral source rule simply serves as a means of by-passing the antiquated doctrine of non-assignment of tortious actions and permits a proper transfer of risk from the plaintiff's insurer to the tortfeasor by way of the victim's tort recovery. The double shift from the tortfeasor to the victim and then from the victim to his insurance carrier can normally occur with little cost in that the insurance carrier is often intimately involved in the initial litigation and quite automatically receives its part of the tort settlement or verdict.

Even in cases in which the contract or the law precludes subrogation or refund of benefits,[17] or in situations in which the collateral source waives such subrogation or refund, the rule performs entirely necessary functions in the computation of damages. For example, the cost of medical care often provides both attorneys and juries in tort cases with an important measure for assessing the plaintiff's general damages. To permit the defendant to tell the jury that the plaintiff has been recompensed by a collateral source for his medical costs might irretrievably upset the complex, delicate, and somewhat indefinable calculations which result in the normal jury verdict.

We also note that generally the jury is not informed that plaintiff's attorney will receive a large portion of the plaintiff's recovery in contingent fees or that personal injury damages are not taxable to the plaintiff and are normally deductible by the defendant. Hence, the plaintiff rarely actually receives full compensation for his injuries as computed by the jury. The collateral source rule partially serves to compensate for the attorney's share and does not actually render "double recovery" for the plaintiff. Indeed, many jurisdictions that have abolished or limited the collateral source rule have also established a means for assessing the plaintiff's costs for counsel directly against the defendant rather than imposing the contingent fee system. In sum, the plaintiff's recovery for his medical expenses from both the tortfeasor and his medical insurance program will not usually give him "double recovery," but partially provides a somewhat closer approximation to full compensation for his injuries.

---

[17] "Certain insurance benefits are regarded as the proceeds of an investment rather than as an indemnity for damages. Thus it has been held that the proceeds of a life insurance contract made for a fixed sum rather than for the damages caused by the death of the insured are proceeds of an investment and can be received independently of the claim for damages against the person who caused the death of the insured. The same rule has been held applicable to accident insurance contracts. As to both kinds of insurance it has been stated: 'Such a policy is an investment contract giving the owner or beneficiary an absolute right, independent of the right against any third person responsible for the injury covered by the policy.' . . . An insurer who fully compensates the insured, however, is subrogated to the rights of the insured against [or may receive a refund of benefits from] one who insured his property if the insurance was for the protection of the property of the insured, and was therefore an indemnity contract. In such cases subrogation [or refund of benefits] is the means by which double recovery by the owner is prevented and the ultimate burden shifted to the wrongdoer where it belongs. . . ." (Anheuser-Busch, Inc. *v.* Starley, 28 Cal.2d 347, 355 (dissenting opn. of Traynor, J.).) . . .

If we consider the collateral source rule as applied here in the context of the entire American approach to the law of torts and damages, we find that the rule presently performs a number of legitimate and even indispensible functions. Without a thorough revolution in the American approach to torts and the consequent damages, the rule at least with respect to medical insurance benefits has become so integrated within our present system that its precipitous judicial nullification would work hardship. In this case the collateral source rule lies between two systems for the compensation of accident victims: the traditional tort recovery based on fault and the increasingly prevalent coverage based on non-fault insurance. Neither system possesses such universality of coverage or completeness of compensation that we can easily dispense with the collateral source rule's approach to meshing the two systems. The reforms which many academicians propose cannot easily be achieved through piecemeal common law development; the proposed changes, if desirable, would be more effectively accomplished through legislative reform. In any case, we cannot believe that the judicial repeal of the collateral source rule, as applied in the present case, would be the place to begin the needed changes.

Although in the special circumstances of *Souza* we characterized the collateral source rule as "punitive" in nature, we have pointed out the several legitimate and fully justified compensatory functions of the rule. In fact, if the collateral source rule were actually punitive, it could apply only in cases of oppression, fraud, or malice and would be inapplicable to most tort, and almost all negligence, cases regardless of whether a governmental entity were involved. We therefore reaffirm our adherence to the collateral source rule in tort cases in which the plaintiff has been compensated by an independent collateral source—such as insurance, pension, continued wages, or disability payments—for which he had actually or constructively paid or in cases in which the collateral source would be recompensed from the tort recovery through subrogation, refund of benefits, or some other arrangement. Hence, we conclude that in a case in which a tort victim has received partial compensation from medical insurance coverage entirely independent of the tortfeasor the trial court properly followed the collateral source rule and foreclosed defendant from mitigating damages by means of the collateral payments.

Having concluded that the collateral source rule is not simply punitive in nature, we hold, for the reasons set out *infra*, that the rule as delineated here applies to governmental entities as well as to all other tortfeasors. We must therefore disapprove of any indications to the contrary in City of Salinas *v.* Souza & McCue Constr. Co.

Defendants would have this court create a special form of sovereign immunity as a novel exception to the collateral source rule for tortfeasors who are public entities or public employees. We see no justification for such special treatment. In the present case the nullification of the collateral source rule would simply frustrate the transfer of the medical costs from the medical insurance carrier, Blue Cross, to the public entity. The public entity or its insurance carrier is in at least as advantageous a position to spread the risk of loss as is the plaintiff's medical insurance carrier. To deprive Blue Cross of repayment for its expenditures on plaintiff's behalf merely because he was injured by a public entity rather than a private individual would constitute an unwarranted and arbitrary discrimination.

Furthermore, if we were to follow without careful analysis the *Souza* characterization of the collateral source rule as punitive in nature, we would immediately face a dilemma as to the proper treatment of the public employee's liability. In order to encourage public employees to perform their duties without the threat of untoward personal liability, we held in Johnson *v.* State of California, 69 Cal.2d 782 (1968), that a public entity must . . . indemnify and defend its employees against civil liability, except in cases of conduct outside the scope of employment or acts performed with actual fraud, corruption, or malice.

If we were to conclude that the collateral source rule cannot apply to public entities, we would be forced to reach one of three equally implausible results: (1) Since the public entity is immune from the rule and enjoys a deduction in damages, but the driver possesses no such immunity, the driver must bear the cost of the extra damages equivalent to the collateral source increment, despite our rule in *Johnson.* (2) Since the public entity is immune from the rule and enjoys a deduction in damages, the driver would initially bear the cost of the extra damages equivalent to the collateral source increment, but under *Johnson* he would be indemnified by the public entity for all the plaintiff's tort recovery. Hence, by suing both the public entity and the public employee the plaintiff can bypass the purported *Souza* rule through the *Johnson* decision. (3) Finally, since the public entity is immune from the rule and enjoys a deduction in damages, the only way to avoid untoward personal liability for the driver under *Johnson* would be for this court to extend the collateral source rule immunity from the public entity to the public employee.

The first alternative would patently conflict with this court's approach to the civil liability of public employees in *Johnson*. . . .

The second alternative would mechanically follow the rules established in *Johnson* and *Souza,* but would totally undermine the effect of *Souza* by indirectly imposing the rule upon the public entity by means of the indemnification process. . . .

The third approach would extend the collateral source rule immunity from the public entity to its employees and increase the unjustified discrimination against tort victims who happen to be injured by public entities rather than private individuals. . . .

In view of the several legitimate and important functions of the collateral source rule in our present approach to the law of torts and damages, we find no appropriate justification for labelling the rule "punitive" or for not applying it to public entities and public employees. . . .

Taylor v. Southern Pacific Transportation Co.

Supreme Court of Arizona, 1981.
130 Ariz. 516.

■ CAMERON, JUSTICE. . . . On 2 November 1974, a collision occurred at a railroad crossing between a train and a car driven by plaintiff, Dennis Taylor, in which his wife Kathy was a passenger. The train was owned by defendant, Southern Pacific Transportation Company, and was being operated by co-defendant Wilber Biggerstaff. Kathy Taylor died as a result of the accident, and Taylor filed suit against the defendants for negligently causing the wrongful death of his wife. At the time of the accident, Dennis and Kathy Taylor had been married for approximately two months.

Before trial, Taylor moved for an order in limine to prevent the defendants from mentioning Taylor's remarriage. The motion was granted. Upon violation of this order, Taylor moved for a mistrial and for sanctions. Taylor's motion was taken under advisement.

The trial then proceeded through nine more days of testimony. Evidence was introduced through expert testimony to show the amount of damages Taylor would suffer throughout his lifetime as a result of the loss of homemaking services and income that the deceased would have been expected to contribute to the marriage [both recognized as items of damage recoverable under the governing wrongful death statute]. After six days of deliberation, the jury returned a verdict finding Biggerstaff not liable, but finding in favor of Taylor against defendant Southern Pacific for $7,000 compensatory damages and $200 punitive damages.

Thereafter, the trial court granted Taylor's motion for new trial against both defendants on all issues finding that the verdict was insufficient and the result of passion or prejudice because of misconduct by defense counsel.

Defendant's motion to reconsider the order for new trial was accompanied by affidavits from all but two jurors stating that they "had no information and drew no conclusion as to the plaintiff's marital status," and that it "played no part in . . . deliberations or judgment." The affidavits were stricken and the motion to reconsider was denied.

EVIDENCE OF REMARRIAGE IN WRONGFUL DEATH CASES

. . . We must first consider whether the trial court erred in excluding evidence of plaintiff's subsequent remarriage. Although this court has previously declined to express an opinion on the rule, the Court of Appeals has cited with approval the subsequent marriage exclusionary rule. In affirming a decision of the trial court to exclude evidence of remarriage, the Court of Appeals stated:

> "The great majority of the states hold that the limitation placed upon the City of Phoenix in connection with the trial of the case now under consideration was the correct ruling. So far as we are informed, Wisconsin and Mississippi are the only states holding against the majority. Arizona's statutory measure of damages in a wrongful death action is found in A.R.S. § 12–613. In part, this section provides:
>
>> 'In an action for wrongful death, the jury shall give such damages as it deems fair and just with reference to the injury resulting from the death to the surviving parties who may be entitled to recover, and also having regard to the mitigating or aggravating circumstances attending the wrongful act, neglect or default.' . . ."

. . . Unlike statutes in other states that specifically allow for evidence of marriage to be introduced, see Fla. Stat. Ann. § 768.21(6)(c) (West) (1980 Supp.), our statute is silent on the issue.

Historically, the refusal to consider the surviving spouse's marital status in wrongful death cases has been attributed to three avenues of thought. One view is that damages should be calculated as of the time of death. Another reason to exclude evidence of remarriage has been that the decedent's contributions relative to the contributions of the new spouse would be too speculative to calculate accurately. Lastly, and most often, it is advanced that the collateral source rule, which disallows evidence of payments to the injured party from other sources to be credited against the tortfeasor's liability, should be invoked to exclude evidence of remarriage. . . .

The collateral source rule is most often applied in cases where an injured party recovers from a tortfeasor amounts for which plaintiff has already been compensated by his insurer. . . . There should be no windfall for a tortfeasor because he injured an insured instead of a non-insured. Likewise, we believe a person guilty of wrongful death should not benefit from the spouse's remarriage. Remarriage of the spouse before the lawsuit is over should not result in a windfall for the person who negligently caused the death of the previous spouse. To so hold might well encourage a surviving spouse not to remarry until after the lawsuit for wrongful death is settled, not necessarily a socially desirable result. We see no need to change the law in Arizona that a plaintiff's remarriage is not admissible in a suit for wrongful death.

MISCONDUCT OF DEFENDANTS' ATTORNEYS

Before trial and pursuant to Taylor's motion in limine, the trial court issued an order preventing the defendants from bringing up plaintiff's current marital status. The order read:

"IT IS FURTHER ORDERED granting plaintiff's oral motion in limine and ORDERING that the defendant not bring up the marital status of the plaintiff, until further Order of this Court."

On the first full day of testimony, defendant asked the following question of Dennis Taylor on cross-examination:

"Q . . . Now, are you implying that since Kathy's death you have done without homemaking services?"

Before the witness could answer and out of the hearing of the jury, the objection to the question was sustained. The court found that the question violated the pretrial order despite defendants' contention that the question sought to establish mitigation of damages and not the plaintiff's current marital status. After this bench conference, cross-examination of Mr. Taylor continued with the following question:

"Q . . . How many times have you been married, Mr. Taylor?"

Before he could answer, objection to the question was sustained. At a conference in chambers later that day, Taylor moved for a mistrial on the basis that defendants had again violated the in limine order and that the question posed on cross-examination created an impermissible inference that Taylor was currently married. The trial court ruled that the questions violated the in limine order. . . .

Defendants . . . contend:

"The relevancy of that question is plainly and simply this—that a person who has experienced multiple marriages is likely to have suffered less grief from the loss of one than a person who has experienced and lost but one. The jury is entitled to take that into consideration."

Even if we were to agree that this statement of the law was correct, it does not excuse the fact that the trial court had ruled on the question and ordered the defendants to make no mention of Taylor's remarriage. The defendants are, in effect, trying to justify the violation of the trial court's order by arguing the wisdom of the order itself. This they may not do.

Neither are we persuaded that the purpose of the questions was unrelated to the evidence prohibited by the order of the court in limine. The evidence is sufficient from which the trial court could find that the questions were an attempt to evade the clear directions of the court. Instead of requesting permission out of the presence of the jury to ask the questions, counsel chose to ask them in the presence of the jury. This they did at their peril. We find no error. . . .

G. TORT AND CONTRACT

1. FORESEEABILITY

Hampton v. Federal Express Corp.

United States Court of Appeals, Eighth Circuit, 1990.
917 F.2d 1119.

■ RE, CHIEF JUDGE. . . . In March, 1988, Carl Gerome Hampton, a 13-year old cancer patient at Children's Memorial Hospital in Omaha, Nebraska, was awaiting a bone marrow transplant. A transplant operation was scheduled at the University of Iowa Hospital in Iowa City, Iowa, where five potential bone marrow donors had been found.

On March 21, 1988, in order to match Carl with the most suitable donor, five samples of Carl's blood were sent by the shipper, the Children's Memorial Hospital in Omaha, to Dr. Nancy Goeken, at the Veterans Administration Medical Center in Iowa City. The shipper, the Children's Memorial Hospital, entered into a contract with the carrier, Federal Express, for the transport of the blood samples.

In a paragraph entitled "Damages or Loss," the contract of carriage, set forth in the airbill, stated:

> "We are liable for no more than $100 per package in the event of physical loss or damage, unless you fill in a higher **Declared Value** to the left and document higher actual loss in the event of a claim. We charge 30¢ for each additional $100 of declared value up to the maximum shown in our Service Guide."

. . . It is not disputed that the blood samples were never received by Dr. Goeken, that Carl Hampton, the infant cancer patient, never obtained a bone marrow transplant, and that he died on May 19, 1988.

Alleging causes of action for personal injury, wrongful death, and loss of services, Carl Jerry Hampton, individually and on behalf of his deceased son, Carl Gerome Hampton, filed suit in the United States District Court for the Western District of Missouri, seeking $3,081,000 in damages. On the basis of the released value doctrine, the district court granted Federal Express' motion for partial summary judgment, and entered judgment in favor of Hampton for $100.

[The court first discussed the "released value doctrine," which permits freight carriers to limit their liability for harm to shipped items to a stated value under certain circumstances. The court indicated that Hampton was bound by the limitation of liability in the contract between the shipper, Children's Memorial Hospital, and Federal Express, but it went on to discuss the validity of Hampton's underlying claims to relief.]

[E]ven if it were to be assumed that Hampton may sue as a third party beneficiary of the contract between the shipper and the carrier, on the facts presented he still cannot recover in contract.

It is a fundamental principle of the law of damages that, in contract cases, a plaintiff can only recover for a loss which, in the ordinary course of events, would result from the defendant's breach or for a loss which was in the contemplation of the parties. In the words of the Restatement, "[d]amages are not recoverable for loss that the party in breach did not have reason to foresee as a probable result of the breach when the contract was made." Restatement (Second) of Contracts § 351(1) (1981). This rule of damages may be traced to Hadley *v.* Baxendale, 9 Ex. 341, 156 Eng. Rep. 145 (1854) . . . .

Hampton, in this case, cannot dispute that Federal Express had no knowledge of Hampton or of the contents of the package that it accepted for delivery. Hence, even apart from the limitation of liability provision, since the damages suffered by Hampton were not reasonably foreseeable, they would not be recoverable in a breach of contract action.

The tort law of negligence, however, does not provide as clear a rule as to whether a defendant may be held liable for injuries or damages that are not reasonably foreseeable. . . .

Under [the rule of Palsgraf *v.* Long Island R.R., 248 N.Y. 339 (1928)], it is only when the defendant owes a duty to the plaintiff that the defendant is liable for all damages, whether or not reasonably foreseeable, caused by the defendant's negligent act. Notwithstanding the variety of views that have emerged from *Palsgraf* and related cases, the Restatement has adopted the *Palsgraf* approach. See Restatement (Second) of Torts § 281 comment c, illustration 1 (1965).

Clearly, Federal Express had no knowledge of Hampton, and did not know that the package contained blood samples. It is equally clear that the shipper, Children's Memorial Hospital, did not declare a value higher than $100 for the package. Under these circumstances, Federal Express could not reasonably foresee any injury to Hampton, or the nature and extent of the injury. In accordance with the reasoning in *Palsgraf,* since there was no duty, there could be no recovery for negligence, and therefore the defendant, Federal Express, could not be held liable to the unforeseeable plaintiff, Hampton. Indeed, under any of the general principles and theories of the common law that have been considered and applied, it would seem clear that Hampton has no cause of action.

Under the circumstances of this case, involving a contract of carriage, it would also seem unreasonable and unjust to hold Federal Express liable to Hampton. If Federal Express had known of the contents of the package, it might have charged a higher rate, exercised additional care, have obtained insurance, or might not have accepted the responsibility. Since Federal Express had no knowledge of the contents, and hence could not reasonably foresee the injury and damages that could be suffered, plaintiff Hampton cannot recover on its cause of action founded in tort. . . .

NOTES ON CONSEQUENTIAL DAMAGES IN TORT AND CONTRACT

1. The classic case on consequential damages for breach of contract is Hadley *v.* Baxendale, 9 Ex. 341, 156 Eng. Rep. 145 (Court of Exchequer, 1854). Plaintiffs, owners of a steam mill, delivered to defendant, a carrier, a broken mill shaft essential to the functioning of the mill. The defendant agreed to transport the shaft to a maker of mill shafts, to be used as a model for a replacement shaft. The defendant was late in delivering the mill shaft and the plaintiffs sued for profits lost as a result of the delay. The court stated that:

> "Where two parties have made a contract which one of them has broken, the damages which the other party ought to receive in respect of such breach of contract should be such as may fairly and reasonably be considered either arising naturally, *i.e.*, according to the usual course of things, from such breach of contract itself, or such as may reasonably be supposed to have been in the contemplation of both parties, at the time they made the contract, as the probable result of the breach of it. Now, if the special circumstances under which the contract was actually made were communicated by the plaintiffs to the defendants, and thus known to both parties, the damages resulting from the breach of such a contract, which they would reasonably contemplate, would be the amount of injury which would ordinarily follow from a breach of contract under these special circumstances so known and communicated. But, on the other hand, if these special circumstances were wholly unknown to the party breaking the contract, he, at the most, could only be supposed to have had in his contemplation the amount of injury which would arise generally, and in the great multitude of cases not affected by any special circumstances, from such a breach of contract. For, had the special circumstances been known, the parties might have specially provided for the breach of contract by special terms as to the damages in that case; and of this advantage it would be very unjust to deprive them."

Id. at 354–55, 156 Eng. Rep. at 152.

2. In another action against the same carrier it was stated that "whether any particular class of expenses is reasonable or not [and therefore recoverable] depends upon the usage of trade, and other circumstances. It is not a question for the Judge, but for the jury, to decide what are reasonable expenses." Chief Baron Pollock in Black *v.* Baxendale, 1 Ex. 410, 412, 154 Eng. Rep. 174, 175 (1847).

3. In Victoria Laundry (Windsor), Ltd. *v.* Newman Industries, Ltd., [1949] 2 K.B. 528 (Court of Appeal, 1949), Asquith, L.J., made the following comments about the "two rules" of Hadley *v.* Baxendale:

> "For this purpose, knowledge 'possessed' is one of two kinds; one imputed, the other actual. Everyone, as a reasonable person, is taken to know the 'ordinary course of things' and consequently what loss is liable to result from a breach of contract in that

ordinary course. This is the subject matter of the 'first rule' in Hadley *v.* Baxendale. But to this knowledge, which a contract-breaker is assumed to possess whether he actually possesses it or not, there may have to be added in a particular case knowledge which he actually possesses, of special circumstances outside the 'ordinary course of things,' of such a kind that a breach in those special circumstances would be liable to cause more loss. Such a case attracts the operation of the 'second rule' so as to make additional loss also recoverable.

"In order to make the contract-breaker liable under either rule it is not necessary that he should actually have asked himself what loss is liable to result from a breach. As has often been pointed out, parties at the time of contracting contemplate not the breach of the contract, but its performance. It suffices that, if he had considered the question, he would as a reasonable man have concluded that the loss in question was liable to result.

"Nor, finally, to make a particular loss recoverable, need it be proved that upon a given state of knowledge the defendant could, as a reasonable man, foresee that a breach must necessarily result in that loss. It is enough if he could foresee it was likely so to result."

Id. at 539–40.

4. Pipkin borrowed money at a high interest rate to finance construction of a motel. Thomas Hill, a mortgage lender, agreed to provide a mortgage loan at a lower rate "to provide a payout of the construction loan upon the completion of construction." Thomas Hill later refused to make the promised loan. At the time of the breach, credit was tight and Pipkin was unable to obtain another long-term mortgage loan. Instead, it refinanced the construction loan and sued Thomas Hill for the difference between the agreed interest rate on the mortgage loan and the much higher interest rate it was paying on the refinanced construction loan.

The court held for Pipkin, awarding him the actual cost of the refinanced construction loan through the date of trial (less the interest they plaintiffs would have paid the defendant during that period), plus the difference between the agreed rate and the prevailing rate for a long-term mortgage from the date of trial. The court said:

"[D]efendant argues that the trial court properly denied plaintiffs any recovery of the interest they paid on the demand note which refinanced the temporary construction loan. In our view, this contention by a defaulting lender, fully aware of the purpose for which plaintiffs had secured its commitment, is entirely unrealistic. . . .

"[W]e harbor no doubt that a committed permanent lender on a substantial building project certainly must foresee that a breach of his commitment a relatively short time before the date he has contracted to provide the money to pay off the interim construction loan will result in substantial harm to the borrower."

Pipkin *v.* Thomas Hill, Inc., 298 N.C. 278, 291 (1979).

Were Pipkin's damages within the contemplation of the parties at the time of the contract?

Were Pipkin's damages direct damages, resulting naturally from the breach, or consequential damages?

5. Uttley agreed to deliver and install a ventilated hopper for pignuts to Parson's farm. Over a period of several months after Uttley delivered the hopper, the pignuts became increasingly moldy and the plaintiffs' pigs began to fall ill. Uttley returned and fixed the ventilator, but 254 pigs eventually died. Parsons sued for the value of the lost pigs, as consequential damages resulting from the breach. The judges of the Court of Appeal agreed that Parsons should recover, but differed in their reasoning.

Lord Denning, M.R., stated that:

> "Remoteness of damage is beyond doubt a question of law. In C. Czarnikow Ltd. *v.* Koufos [1969] A.C. 350 the House of Lords said that, in remoteness of damage, there is a difference between contract and tort. In the case of a *breach of contract,* the court has to consider whether the consequences were of such a kind that a reasonable man, at the time of making the contract, would *contemplate* them as being of a very substantial degree of probability. . . .
>
> "In the case of a *tort,* the court has to consider whether the consequences were of such a kind that a reasonable man, at the time of the tort committed, would *foresee* them as being of a much lower degree of probability. . . .
>
> "I find it difficult to apply those principles universally to all cases of contract or to all cases of tort: and to draw a distinction between what a man "contemplates" and what he "foresees." I soon begin to get out of my depth. . . . I go back with relief to the distinction drawn in legal theory by Professors Hart and Honoré in their book CAUSATION IN THE LAW (1959). They distinguish between those cases in contract in which a man has suffered no damage to person or property, but only *economic loss,* such as, loss of profit or loss of opportunities for gain in some future transaction: and those in which he claims damages for an *injury actually done* to his person or damage actually done to his property (including his livestock) or for ensuing expense (damnum emergens) to which he has actually been put. . . .
>
> "I would suggest as a solution that in the former class of case—loss of profit cases—the defaulting party is only liable for the consequences if they are such as, at the time of the contract, he ought reasonably to have *contemplated* as a *serious* possibility or real danger. . . .
>
> "In the second class of case—the physical injury or expense case—the defaulting party is liable for any loss or expense which he ought reasonably to have *foreseen* at the time of the breach as a possible consequence, even if it was only a *slight* possibility."

Parsons (Livestock), Ltd. *v.* Uttley Ingham & Co., Ltd., [1978] Q.B. 791, 801–03 (Court of Appeal 1977).

Scarman, L.J. (with whom Orr, L.J. concurred) stated that:

> "I agree with Lord Denning M.R. in thinking that the law must be such that, in a factual situation where all have the same actual or imputed knowledge and the contract contains no term limiting the damages recoverable for breach, the amount of damages recoverable does not depend upon whether, as a matter of legal classification, the plaintiff's cause of action is breach of contract or tort. It may be that the necessary reconciliation is to be found . . . in holding that the difference between "reasonably foreseeable" (the test in tort) and "reasonably contemplated" (the test in contract) is semantic, not substantial. . . .
>
> "The court's task, therefore, is to decide what loss to the plaintiffs it is reasonable to suppose would have been in the contemplation of the parties as a serious possibility had they had in mind the breach when they made their contract. . . .
>
> "I would agree with MCGREGOR ON DAMAGES, 13th ed. (1972), pp. 131–132 that
>
>> '. . . [I]n contract as in tort, it should suffice that, if physical injury or damage is within the contemplation of the parties, recovery is not to be limited because the degree of physical injury or damage could not have been anticipated.'
>
> "This is so, in my judgment, not because there is, or ought to be, a specific rule of law governing cases of physical injury but because it would be absurd to regulate damages in such cases upon the necessity of supposing the parties had a prophetic foresight as to the exact nature of the injury that does in fact arise. It is enough if upon the hypothesis predicated physical injury must have been a serious possibility. Though in loss of market or loss of profit cases the factual analysis will be very different from cases of physical injury, the same principles, in my judgment, apply. Given the situation of the parties at the time of contract, was the loss of profit, or market, a serious possibility, something that would have been in their minds had they contemplated breach?
>
> "It does not matter, in my judgment, if they thought that the chance of physical injury, loss of profit, loss of market, or other loss as the case may be, was slight, or that the odds were against it, provided they contemplated as a serious possibility the type of consequence, not necessarily the specific consequence, that ensued upon breach. Making the assumption as to breach that the judge did, no more than common sense was needed for [the defendant] to appreciate that food affected by bad storage conditions might well cause illness in the pigs fed upon it."

Id. at 807–13.

Evra Corp. v. Swiss Bank Corp.

United States Court of Appeals, Seventh Circuit, 1982.
673 F.2d 951.

■ POSNER, CIRCUIT JUDGE. The question—one of first impression—in this diversity case is the extent of a bank's liability for failure to make a transfer of funds when requested by wire to do so. The essential facts are undisputed. In 1972 Hyman-Michaels Company, a large Chicago dealer in scrap metal, entered into a two-year contract to supply steel scrap to a Brazilian corporation. Hyman-Michaels chartered a ship, the *Pandora,* to carry the scrap to Brazil. The charter was for one year, with an option to extend the charter for a second year; specified a fixed daily rate of pay for the hire of the ship during both the initial and the option period, payable semi-monthly "in advance"; and provided that if payment was not made on time the *Pandora*'s owner could cancel the charter. Payment was to be made by deposit to the owner's account in the Banque de Paris et des Pays-Bas (Suisse) in Geneva, Switzerland.

The usual method by which Hyman-Michaels, in Chicago, got the payments to the Banque de Paris in Geneva was to request the Continental Illinois National Bank and Trust Company of Chicago, where it had an account, to make a wire transfer of funds. Continental would debit Hyman-Michaels' account by the amount of the payment and then send a telex to its London office for retransmission to its correspondent bank in Geneva—Swiss Bank Corporation—asking Swiss Bank to deposit this amount in the Banque de Paris account of the *Pandora's* owner. The transaction was completed by the crediting of Swiss Bank's account at Continental by the same amount.

When Hyman-Michaels chartered the *Pandora* in June 1972, market charter rates were very low, and it was these rates that were fixed in the charter for its entire term—two years if Hyman-Michaels exercised its option. Shortly after the agreement was signed, however, charter rates began to climb and by October 1972 they were much higher than they had been in June. The *Pandora*'s owners were eager to get out of the charter if they could. At the end of October they thought they had found a way, for the payment that was due in the Banque de Paris on October 26 had not arrived by October 30, and on that day the *Pandora*'s owner notified Hyman-Michaels that it was canceling the charter because of the breach of the payment term. Hyman-Michaels had mailed a check for the October 26 installment to the Banque de Paris rather than use the wire-transfer method of payment. It had done this in order to have the use of its money for the period that it would take the check to clear, about two weeks. But the check had not been mailed in Chicago until October 25 and of course did not reach Geneva on the twenty-sixth.

When Hyman-Michaels received notification that the charter was being canceled it immediately wired payment to the Banque de Paris, but the *Pandora's* owner refused to accept it and insisted that the charter was indeed canceled. The matter was referred to arbitration in accordance with the charter. On December 5, 1972, the arbitration panel ruled in favor of Hyman-Michaels. The panel noted that previous arbitration panels had "shown varying degrees of latitude to Charterers"; "In all cases, a pattern of obligation on Owners' part to protest, complain, or warn of intended withdrawal was expressed as an essential prerequisite to withdrawal, in spite of the clear wording of the operative clause. No such advance notice was given by Owners of M/V Pandora." One of the three members of the panel dissented; he thought the *Pandora*'s owner was entitled to cancel.

Hyman-Michaels went back to making the charter payments by wire transfer. On the morning of April 25, 1973, it telephoned Continental Bank and requested it to transfer $27,000 to the Banque de Paris account of the *Pandora*'s owner in payment for the charter hire period from April 27 to May 11, 1973. Since the charter provided for payment "in advance," this payment arguably was due by the close of business on April 26. The requested telex went out to Continental's London office on the afternoon of April 25, which was nighttime in England. Early the next morning a telex operator in Continental's London office dialed, as Continental's Chicago office had instructed him to do, Swiss Bank's general telex number, which rings in the bank's cable department. But that number was busy, and after trying unsuccessfully for an hour to engage it the Continental telex operator dialed another number, that of a machine in Swiss Bank's foreign exchange department which he had used in the past when the general number was engaged. We know this machine received the telexed message because it signaled the sending machine at both the beginning and end of the transmission that the telex was being received. Yet Swiss Bank failed to comply with the payment order, and no transfer of funds was made to the account of the *Pandora*'s owner in the Banque de Paris.

No one knows exactly what went wrong. One possibility is that the receiving telex machine had simply run out of paper, in which event it would not print the message although it had received it. Another is that whoever took the message out of the machine after it was printed failed to deliver it to the banking department. Unlike the machine in the cable department that the Continental telex operator had originally tried to reach, the machines in the foreign exchange department were operated by junior foreign exchange dealers rather than by professional telex operators, although Swiss Bank knew that messages intended for other departments were sometimes diverted to the telex machines in the foreign exchange department.

At 8:30 a.m. the next day, April 27, Hyman-Michaels in Chicago received a telex from the *Pandora*'s owner stating that the charter was canceled because payment for the April 27–May 11 charter period had not been made. Hyman-Michaels called over to Continental and told them to keep trying to effect payment through Swiss Bank even if the *Pandora's* owner rejected it. This instruction was confirmed in a letter to

Continental dated April 28, in which Hyman-Michaels stated: "please instruct your London branch to advise their correspondents to persist in attempting to make this payment. This should be done even in the face of a rejection on the part of Banque de Paris to receive this payment. It is paramount that in order to strengthen our position in an arbitration that these funds continue to be readily available." Hyman-Michaels did not attempt to wire the money directly to the Banque de Paris as it had done on the occasion of its previous default. Days passed while the missing telex message was hunted unsuccessfully. Finally Swiss Bank suggested to Continental that it retransmit the telex message to the machine in the cable department and this was done on May 1. The next day Swiss Bank attempted to deposit the $27,000 in the account of the *Pandora*'s owner at the Banque de Paris but the payment was refused.

Again the arbitrators were convened and rendered a decision. In it they ruled that Hyman-Michaels had been "blameless" up until the morning of April 27, when it first learned that the Banque de Paris had not received payment on April 26, but that "being faced with this situation," Hyman-Michaels had "failed to do everything in [its] power to remedy it. The action taken was immediate but did not prove to be adequate, in that [Continental] Bank and its correspondent required some 5/6 days to trace and effect the lost instruction to remit. [Hyman-Michaels] could have ordered an immediate duplicate payment—or even sent a Banker's check by hand or special messengers, so that the funds could have reached owner's Bank, not later than April 28th." By failing to do any of these things Hyman-Michaels had "created the opening" that the *Pandora*'s owner was seeking in order to be able to cancel the charter. It had "acted imprudently." The arbitration panel concluded, reluctantly but unanimously, that this time the *Pandora*'s owner was entitled to cancel the agreement. The arbitration decision was confirmed by a federal district court in New York.

Hyman-Michaels then brought this diversity action against Swiss Bank, seeking to recover its expenses in the second arbitration proceeding plus the profits that it lost because of the cancellation of the charter. The contract by which Hyman-Michaels had agreed to ship scrap steel to Brazil had been terminated by the buyer in March 1973 and Hyman-Michaels had promptly subchartered the *Pandora* at market rates, which by April 1973 were double the rates fixed in the charter. Its lost profits are based on the difference between the charter and subcharter rates. . . .

The case was tried to a district judge without a jury. In his decision, he . . . ruled that . . . Swiss Bank had been negligent and under Illinois law was liable to Hyman-Michaels for $2.1 million in damages. This figure was made up of about $16,000 in arbitration expenses and the rest in lost profits on the subcharter of the *Pandora*. . . . The case comes to us on Swiss Bank's appeal from the judgment in favor of Hyman-Michaels. . . .

When a bank fails to make a requested transfer of funds, this can cause two kinds of loss. First, the funds themselves or interest on them may be lost, and of course the fee paid for the transfer, having bought nothing, becomes a loss item. These are "direct" (sometimes called "general") damages. Hyman-Michaels is not seeking any direct damages in this case and apparently sustained none. It did not lose any part of the $27,000; although its account with Continental Bank was debited by this amount prematurely, it was not an interest-bearing account so Hyman-Michaels lost no interest; and Hyman-Michaels paid no fee either to Continental or to Swiss Bank for the aborted transfer. A second type of loss, which either the payor or the payee may suffer, is a dislocation in one's business triggered by the failure to pay. Swiss Bank's failure to transfer funds to the Banque de Paris when requested to do so by Continental Bank set off a chain reaction which resulted in an arbitration proceeding that was costly to Hyman-Michaels and in the cancellation of a highly profitable contract. It is those costs and lost profits—"consequential" or, as they are sometimes called, "special" damages—that Hyman-Michaels seeks in this lawsuit, and recovered below. It is conceded that if Hyman-Michaels was entitled to consequential damages, the district court measured them correctly. The only issue is whether it was entitled to consequential damages. . . .

The rule of Hadley *v.* Baxendale—that consequential damages will not be awarded unless the defendant was put on notice of the special circumstances giving rise to them—has been applied in many Illinois cases, and *Hadley* cited approvingly. See, *e.g.*, Siegel *v.* Western Union Telegraph Co., 312 Ill. App. 86, 92–93 (1941). In *Siegel,* the plaintiff had delivered $200 to Western Union with instructions to transmit it to a friend of the plaintiff's. The money was to be bet (legally) on a horse, but this was not disclosed in the instructions. Western Union misdirected the money order and it did not reach the friend until several hours after the race had taken place. The horse that the plaintiff had intended to bet on won and would have paid $1650 on the plaintiff's $200 bet if the bet had been placed. He sued Western Union for his $1450 lost profit, but the court held that under the rule of Hadley *v.* Baxendale Western Union was not liable, because it "had no notice or knowledge of the purpose for which the money was being transmitted."

The present case is similar, though Swiss Bank knew more than Western Union knew in *Siegel;* it knew or should have known, from Continental Bank's previous telexes, that Hyman-Michaels was paying the Pandora Shipping Company for the hire of a motor vessel named *Pandora.* But it did not know when payment was due, what the terms of the charter were, or that they had turned out to be extremely favorable to Hyman-Michaels. And it did not know that Hyman-Michaels knew the *Pandora*'s owner would try to cancel the charter, and probably would succeed, if Hyman-Michaels was ever again late in making payment, or that despite this peril Hyman-Michaels would not try to pay until the last possible moment and in the event of a delay in transmission would not do everything in its power to minimize the consequences of the delay. Electronic funds transfers are not so unusual as to automatically place a bank on notice of extraordinary consequences if such a transfer goes awry. Swiss Bank did not have enough information to infer that if it lost a $27,000 payment order it would face a liability in excess of $2 million.

It is true that in both *Hadley* and *Siegel* there was a contract between the parties and here there was none. We cannot be certain that the Illinois courts would apply the principles of those cases outside of the contract area. As so often in diversity cases, there is an irreducible amount of speculation involved in attempting to predict the reaction of a state's courts to a new issue. The best we can do is to assume that the Illinois courts would look to the policies underlying cases such as *Hadley* and *Siegel* and, to the extent they found them pertinent, would apply those cases here. We must therefore ask what difference it should make whether the parties are or are not bound to each other by a contract. On the one hand, it seems odd that the absence of a contract would enlarge rather than limit the extent of liability. After all, under Swiss law the absence of a contract would be devastating to Hyman-Michaels' claim. Privity is not a wholly artificial concept. It is one thing to imply a duty to one with whom one has a contract and another to imply it to the entire world.

On the other hand, contract liability is strict. A breach of contract does not connote wrongdoing; it may have been caused by circumstances beyond the promisor's control—a strike, a fire, the failure of a supplier to deliver an essential input. And while such contract doctrines as impossibility, impracticability, and frustration relieve promisors from liability for some failures to perform that are beyond their control, many other such failures are actionable although they could not have been prevented by the exercise of due care. The district judge found that Swiss Bank had been negligent in losing Continental Bank's telex message and it can be argued that Swiss Bank should therefore be liable for a broader set of consequences than if it had only broken a contract. But *Siegel* implicitly rejects this distinction. Western Union had not merely broken its contract to deliver the plaintiff's money order; it had "negligently misdirected" the money order. "The company's negligence is conceded." Yet it was not liable for the consequences.

Siegel, we conclude, is authority for holding that Swiss Bank is not liable for the consequences of negligently failing to transfer Hyman-Michaels' funds to Banque de Paris; reason for such a holding is found in the animating principle of *Hadley v. Baxendale,* which is that the costs of the untoward consequence of a course of dealings should be borne by that party who was able to avert the consequence at least cost and failed to do so. In *Hadley* the untoward consequence was the shutting down of the mill. The carrier could have avoided it by delivering the engine shaft on time. But the mill owners, as the court noted, could have avoided it simply by having a spare shaft. Prudence required that they have a spare shaft anyway, since a replacement could not be obtained at once even if there was no undue delay in carting the broken shaft to and the replacement shaft from the manufacturer. The court refused to imply a duty on the part of the carrier to guarantee the mill owners against the consequences of their own lack of prudence, though of course if the parties had stipulated for such a guarantee the court would have enforced it. The notice requirement of *Hadley v. Baxendale* is designed to assure that such an improbable guarantee really is intended.

This case is much the same, though it arises in a tort rather than a contract setting. Hyman-Michaels showed a lack of prudence throughout. It was imprudent for it to mail in Chicago a letter that unless received the next day in Geneva would put Hyman-Michaels in breach of a contract that was very profitable to it and that the other party to the contract had every interest in canceling. It was imprudent thereafter for Hyman-Michaels, having narrowly avoided cancellation and having (in the words of its appeal brief in this court) been "put . . . on notice that the payment provision of the Charter would be strictly enforced thereafter," to wait till arguably the last day before payment was due to instruct its bank to transfer the necessary funds overseas. And it was imprudent in the last degree for Hyman-Michaels, when it received notice of cancellation on the last possible day payment was due, to fail to pull out all the stops to get payment to the Banque de Paris on that day, and instead to dither while Continental and Swiss Bank wasted five days looking for the lost telex message. Judging from the obvious reluctance with which the arbitration panel finally decided to allow the *Pandora*'s owner to cancel the charter, it might have made all the difference if Hyman-Michaels had gotten payment to the Banque de Paris by April 27 or even by Monday, April 30, rather than allowed things to slide until May 2.

This is not to condone the sloppy handling of incoming telex messages in Swiss Bank's foreign department. But Hyman-Michaels is a sophisticated business enterprise. It knew or should have known that even the Swiss are not infallible; that messages sometimes get lost or delayed in transit among three banks, two of them located 5000 miles apart, even when all the banks are using reasonable care; and that therefore it should take its own precautions against the consequences—best known to itself—of a mishap that might not be due to anyone's negligence.

We are not the first to remark the affinity between the rule of Hadley *v.* Baxendale and the doctrine, which is one of tort as well as contract law and is a settled part of the common law of Illinois, of avoidable consequences. If you are hurt in an automobile accident and unreasonably fail to seek medical treatment, the injurer, even if negligent, will not be held liable for the aggravation of the injury due to your own unreasonable behavior after the accident. If in addition you failed to fasten your seat belt, you may be barred from collecting the tort damages that would have been prevented if you had done so. Hyman-Michaels' behavior in steering close to the wind prior to April 27 was like not fastening one's seat belt; its failure on April 27 to wire a duplicate payment immediately after disaster struck was like refusing to seek medical attention after a serious accident. The seat-belt cases show that the doctrine of avoidable consequences applies whether the tort victim acts imprudently before or after the tort is committed. Hyman-Michaels did both.

The rule of Hadley *v.* Baxendale links up with tort concepts in another way. The rule is sometimes stated in the form that only foreseeable damages are recoverable in a breach of contract action. So expressed, it corresponds to the tort principle that limits liability to the foreseeable consequence of the defendant's carelessness. The amount of care that a person ought to take is a function of the probability and magnitude of the harm that may occur if he does not take care. See, *e.g.*, United States *v.* Carroll Towing Co., 159 F.2d 169 (2d Cir. 1947). If he does not know what that probability and magnitude are, he cannot determine how much care to take. That would be Swiss Bank's dilemma if it were liable for consequential damages from failing to carry out payment orders in timely fashion. To estimate the extent of its probable liability in order to know how many and how elaborate fail-safe features to install in its telex rooms or how much insurance to buy against the inevitable failures, Swiss Bank would have to collect reams of information about firms that are not even its regular customers. It had no banking relationship with Hyman-Michaels. It did not know or have reason to know how at once precious and fragile Hyman-Michaels' contract with the *Pandora*'s owner was. These were circumstances too remote from Swiss Bank's practical range of knowledge to have affected its decisions as to who should man the telex machines in the foreign department or whether it should have more intelligent machines or should install more machines in the cable department, any more than the falling of a platform scale because a conductor jostled a passenger who was carrying fireworks was a prospect that could have influenced the amount of care taken by the Long Island Railroad. See Palsgraf *v.* Long Island R.R., 248 N.Y. 339 (1928).

In short, Swiss Bank was not required in the absence of a contractual undertaking to take precautions or insure against a harm that it could not measure but that was known with precision to Hyman-Michaels, which could by the exercise of common prudence have averted it completely. As Chief Judge Cardozo (the author of *Palsgraf*) remarked in discussing the application of Hadley *v.* Baxendale to the liability of telegraph companies for errors in transmission, "The sender can protect himself by insurance in one form or another if the risk of nondelivery or error appears to be too great. . . . The company, if it takes out insurance for itself, can do no more than guess at the loss to be avoided." . . .

The legal principles that we have said are applicable to this case were not applied below. Although the district judge's opinion is not entirely clear, he apparently thought the rule of Hadley *v.* Baxendale inapplicable and the imprudence of Hyman-Michaels irrelevant. He did state that the damages to Hyman-Michaels were foreseeable because "a major international bank" should know that a failure to act promptly on a telexed request to transfer funds could cause substantial damage; but *Siegel* . . . make clear that that kind of general foreseeability, which is present in virtually every case, does not justify an award of consequential damages.

We could remand for new findings based on the proper legal standard, but it is unnecessary to do so. The undisputed facts, recited in this opinion, show as a matter of law that Hyman-Michaels is not entitled to recover consequential damages from Swiss Bank. . . .

2. ECONOMIC LOSS

General Electric Co. v. Lowe's Home Centers, Inc.

Supreme Court of Georgia, 2005.
279 Ga. 77.

■ FLETCHER, CHIEF JUSTICE. . . . Lowe's Home Centers, Inc. operated a retail store on a 5.8-acre parcel of land in Rome, Georgia until 1998. During the 1990s, Lowe's sought to replace the retail store with a much larger "superstore," which would also require the acquisition of adjacent property. Lowe's therefore entered into an agreement with a developer, Horne Properties, under which Horne would buy adjacent property and lease it to Lowe's. All of the relevant property is located near a General Electric Company plant where polychlorinated biphenyls (PCBs) were used. After PCBs were discovered on the first parcel of adjacent property sought by Horne, Lowe's and Horne canceled their agreements with respect to this property. Lowe's and Horne then entered into a second agreement for a different, eight-acre adjacent parcel that is the subject of this case. After testing revealed PCBs on this property and on Lowe's existing property, Horne and Lowe's canceled their agreements for the second parcel, which was permitted by the contractual terms.

Lowe's then filed suit against GE in the United States District Court for the Northern District of Georgia alleging trespass, nuisance, negligence, and negligence per se in addition to federal environmental claims. The jury awarded Lowe's $18 million in lost profits associated with the planned superstore; $2 million for the reduction of rental value of Lowe's existing property; and $163,581 for Lowe's costs of investigating and responding to the contamination. On appeal, the Eleventh Circuit certified to this Court [the following question: "Can Lowe's recover lost profits when its own property was damaged, but additional property, also damaged but not belonging to Lowe's, was necessary to complete the Relocation Store upon which the lost profit award was premised?"]

The "economic loss rule" generally provides that . . . a plaintiff can recover in tort only those economic losses resulting from injury to his person or damage to his property; a plaintiff cannot recover economic losses associated with injury to the person or damage to the property of another. Lowe's argues that because it planned to use both its property and the unowned property for a single enterprise, lost profits associated with the combined property are recoverable even under the economic loss rule. GE, on the other hand, argues that Georgia law only permits recovery for damage to the property that Lowe's actually owned. For the following reasons, GE is correct. . . .

In Byrd *v.* English, this Court denied recovery to a customer of Georgia Electric Light Company who lost power when the defendants damaged power conduits on third party property. This Court stated that:

> "If the plaintiff can recover of these defendants upon this cause of action, then a customer of his, who was injured by the delay occasioned by the stopping of his work, could also recover from them; and one who had been damaged through his delay could in turn hold them liable; and so on without limit to the number of persons who might recover on account of the injury done to the property of the company owning the conduits. To state such a proposition is to demonstrate its absurdity."

117 Ga. at 193–194. . . .

Lowe's attempts to conflate the damage to both properties by showing that it planned to use both for a single enterprise. In doing so, it seeks to make this a "hybrid" case to which existing case law does not neatly apply. But in fact existing case law does neatly apply—it provides that Lowe's can recover for damage to its own property and that the owner of the other property can recover for damage to its property.

Established Georgia law is clear that an "option to purchase land does not, before acceptance, vest in the holder of the option any interest, legal or equitable, in the land which is the subject of the option." Martin *v.* Schindley, 264 Ga. 142, 143 (1994). Lowe's had even less than an option in the adjacent property—it had a lease agreement with Horne, and Horne had the option. As noted earlier, both Lowe's and Horne were contractually permitted to cancel their agreements in the event of contamination, and both did so. Therefore, it is clear that Lowe's did not have a sufficient property interest in the adjacent land to permit recovery.

Policy considerations also favor GE's position and disfavor Lowe's position. Lowe's position would significantly expand the reach of Georgia tort law by allowing double recovery for the same wrongdoing if, for example, the current owner of the adjacent land in this case also made a claim for recovery. In addition, under Lowe's theory, nothing would prevent Horne, who had an option to purchase the adjacent property, from being the *third* party to recover from GE for its lost profits—again associated with the same damage. This new exception to the economic loss rule would also be murky and could give rise to substantial litigation. In contrast, GE's position provides the certainty of a bright-line rule, affords predictability to courts and parties alike, and avoids the unfairness to defendants that would come with duplicative liability for the same damage.

Because we hold that Lowe's may not recover lost profits relating to its planned superstore under the economic loss rule, we need not address the second certified question as to whether lost profits would be prohibited by the new business rule. . . .

NOTES

1. In East River Steamship Corp. *v.* Transamerica Delaval, Inc., 476 U.S. 858 (1986), the U.S. Supreme Court, exercising admiralty jurisdiction, applied a version of the economic loss rule to hold that the plaintiffs could not bring a products liability claim when the defective product had caused no harm to persons or property. The plaintiffs were ship charterers; the defendants had manufactured and installed turbines that malfunctioned, causing harm to the turbines and consequential loss of profits while the ships were out of service. The Court held that when a defective product injures only itself, and otherwise causes purely economic harm, the safety rationale for strict products liability does not apply and a tort claim is not available. Consequently, plaintiffs are limited to claims based on breach of contract or warranty. Otherwise, the Court said, "contract law would drown in a sea of tort."

> "Permitting recovery for all foreseeable claims for purely economic loss could make a manufacturer liable for vast sums. It would be difficult for a manufacturer to take into account the expectations of persons downstream who may encounter its product. In this case, for example, if the charterers—already one step removed from the transaction—were permitted to recover their economic losses, then the companies that subchartered the ships might claim their economic losses from the delays, and the charterers' customers also might claim their economic losses, and so on."

Id. at 874. The distinction between tort and contract mattered because the contract between the manufacturer and the shipbuilder limited liability for breach of warranty and the plaintiff charterers agreed to take the ships "as is." The Court also reasoned that the rule of Hadley *v.* Baxendale and privity restrictions provide appropriate brakes on a contract claim for purely economic loss.

2. The economic loss rule has been applied to limit recovery for the ripple effects of environmental disasters, although courts have taken a less absolute approach. In Louisiana ex rel. Guste *v.* M/V Testbank, 752 F.2d 1019 (5th Cir. 1985), for example, a carrier transporting toxic chemicals

through the Mississippi Gulf River Outlet Channel collided with another vessel, resulting in a massive spill of toxic chemicals. After a white chemical haze developed around the vessels, residents of the area were evacuated and the outlet was closed for two weeks. A variety of plaintiffs, including commercial fishermen, "shipping interests, marina and boat rental operators, wholesale and retail seafood enterprises not actually engaged in fishing, seafood restaurants, tackle and bait shops, and recreational fishermen" sued the chemical carrier for economic losses. The district court allowed claims by fishermen but granted summary judgment against all other plaintiffs, whether or not their losses were sufficiently foreseeable to satisfy the requirement of proximate cause. The Fifth Circuit affirmed, with four judges dissenting and three filing separate opinions. The majority stated that:

> "Review of the foreseeable consequences of the collision of the *Sea Daniel* and *Testbank* demonstrates the wave upon wave of successive economic consequences and the managerial role plaintiffs would have us assume. The vessel delayed in St. Louis may be unable to fulfill its obligation to haul from Memphis, to the injury of the shipper, to the injury of the buyers, to the injury of their customers. Plaintiffs concede, as do all who attack the requirement of physical damage, that a line would need to be drawn—somewhere on the other side, each plaintiff would say in turn, of its recovery. Plaintiffs advocate not only that the lines be drawn elsewhere but also that they be drawn on an ad hoc and discrete basis. The result would be that no determinable measure of the limit of foreseeability would precede the decision on liability. We are told that when the claim is too remote, or too tenuous, recovery will be denied. Presumably then, as among all plaintiffs suffering foreseeable economic loss, recovery will turn on a judge or jury's decision. There will be no rationale for the differing results save the 'judgment' of the trier of fact. Concededly, it can 'decide' all the claims presented, and with comparative if not absolute ease. The point is not that such a process cannot be administered but rather that its judgments would be much less the products of a determinable rule of law. In this important sense, the resulting decisions would be judicial products only in their draw upon judicial resources.
>
> "The bright line rule of damage to a proprietary interest, as most, has the virtue of predictability with the vice of creating results in cases at its edge that are said to be 'unjust' or 'unfair.' Plaintiffs point to seemingly perverse results, where claims the rule allows and those it disallows are juxtaposed—such as vessels striking a dock, causing minor but recoverable damage, then lurching athwart a channel causing great but unrecoverable economic loss. The answer is that when lines are drawn sufficiently sharp in their definitional edges to be reasonable and predictable, such differing results are the inevitable result—indeed, decisions are the desired product. But there is more. The line drawing sought

by plaintiffs is no less arbitrary because the line drawing appears only in the outcome—as one claimant is found too remote and another is allowed to recover. The true difference is that plaintiffs' approach would mask the results. The present rule would be more candid, and in addition, by making results more predictable, serves a normative function. It operates as a rule of law and allows a court to adjudicate rather than manage.

"That the rule is identifiable and will predict outcomes in advance of the ultimate decision about recovery enables it to play additional roles. Here we agree with plaintiffs that economic analysis, even at the rudimentary level of jurists, is helpful both in the identification of such roles and the essaying of how the roles play. Thus it is suggested that placing all the consequence of its error on the maritime industry will enhance its incentive for safety. While correct, as far as such analysis goes, such *in terrorem* benefits have an optimal level. Presumably, when the cost of an unsafe condition exceeds its utility there is an incentive to change. As the costs of an accident become increasing multiples of its utility, however, there is a point at which greater accident costs lose meaning, and the incentive curve flattens. When the accident costs are added in large but unknowable amounts the value of the exercise is diminished.

"With a disaster inflicting large and reverberating injuries through the economy, as here, we believe the more important economic inquiry is that of relative cost of administration, and in maritime matters administration quickly involves insurance. Those economic losses not recoverable under the present rule for lack of physical damage to a proprietary interest are the subject of first party or loss insurance. The rule change would work a shift to the more costly liability system of third party insurance. For the same reasons that courts have imposed limits on the concept of foreseeability, liability insurance might not be readily obtainable for the types of losses asserted here. . . . By contrast, first party insurance is feasible for many of the economic losses claimed here. Each businessman who might be affected by a disruption of river traffic or by a halt in fishing activities can protect against that eventuality at a relatively low cost since his own potential losses are finite and readily discernible. Thus, to the extent that economic analysis informs our decision here, we think that it favors retention of the present rule."

Id. at 1028–29.

3. Some courts have refused to apply a *per se* rule against recovery of purely economic consequences of negligence. An example is People Express Airlines, Inc. *v.* Consolidated Rail Corporation, 100 N.J. 246 (1985), in which the Supreme Court of New Jersey recognized a claim for economic loss by an airline forced to evacuate its terminal following a chemical spill. The court said:

"The troublesome concern reflected in cases denying recovery for negligently-caused economic loss is the alleged potential for infinite liability, or liability out of all proportion to the defendant's fault. This objection is also not confined to negligently-caused economic injury. The same objection has been asserted and, ultimately, rejected by this Court and others in allowing recovery for other forms of negligent torts and in the creation of the doctrine of strict liability for defective products and ultrahazardous activities. The answer to the allegation of unchecked liability is not the judicial obstruction of a fairly grounded claim for redress. Rather, it must be a more sedulous application of traditional concepts of duty and proximate causation to the facts of each case.

"It is understandable that courts, fearing that if even one deserving plaintiff suffering purely economic loss were allowed to recover, all such plaintiffs could recover, have anchored their rulings to the physical harm requirement. While the rationale is understandable, it supports only a limitation on, not a denial of, liability. The physical harm requirement capriciously showers compensation along the path of physical destruction, regardless of the status or circumstances of individual claimants. Purely economic losses are borne by innocent victims, who may not be able to absorb their losses. In the end, the challenge is to fashion a rule that limits liability but permits adjudication of meritorious claims. The asserted inability to fix crystalline formulae for recovery on the differing facts of future cases simply does not justify the wholesale rejection of recovery in all cases. . . .

"Judicial discomfiture with the rule of nonrecovery for purely economic loss throughout the last several decades has led to numerous exceptions in the general rule. Although the rationalizations for these exceptions differ among courts and cases, two common threads run throughout the exceptions. The first is that the element of foreseeability emerges as a more appropriate analytical standard to determine the question of liability than a *per se* prohibitory rule. The second is that the extent to which the defendant knew or should have known the particular consequences of his negligence, including the economic loss of a particularly foreseeable plaintiff, is dispositive of the issues of duty and fault.

"One group of exceptions is based on the "special relationship" between the tortfeasor and the individual or business deprived of economic expectations. . . ." . . .

"One thematic motif that may be extrapolated from these decisions to differentiate between those cases in which recovery for economic losses was allowed and denied is that of foreseeability as it relates to both the duty owed and proximate cause. The traditional test of negligence is what a reasonably prudent person would foresee and do in the circumstances; duty is clearly defined by knowledge of the risk of harm or the reasonable apprehension of that risk. In the above-cited cases, the defendants knew or reasonably should have foreseen both that particular plaintiffs or an identifiable class of plaintiffs were at risk and that ascertainable economic damages would ensue from the conduct. Thus, knowledge or special reason to know of the consequences of the tortious conduct in terms of the persons likely to be victimized and the nature of the damages likely to be suffered will suffice to impose a duty upon the tortfeasor not to interfere with economic well-being of third parties. . . .

"We hold therefore that a defendant owes a duty of care to take reasonable measures to avoid the risk of causing economic damages, aside from physical injury, to particular plaintiffs or plaintiffs comprising an identifiable class with respect to whom defendant knows or has reason to know are likely to suffer such damages from its conduct. A defendant failing to adhere to this duty of care may be found liable for such economic damages proximately caused by its breach of duty. . . .

"Among the facts that persuade us that a cause of action has been established [in this case] is the close proximity of the North Terminal and People Express Airlines to the Conrail freight yard; the obvious nature of the plaintiff's operations and particular foreseeability of economic losses resulting from an accident and evacuation; the defendants' actual or constructive knowledge of the volatile properties of ethylene oxide; and the existence of an emergency response plan prepared by some of the defendants (alluded to in the course of oral argument), which apparently called for the nearby area to be evacuated to avoid the risk of harm in case of an explosion. We do not mean to suggest by our recitation of these facts that actual knowledge of the eventual economic losses is necessary to the cause of action; rather, particular foreseeability will suffice. The plaintiff still faces a difficult task in proving damages, particularly lost profits, to the degree of certainty required in other negligence cases. The trial court's examination of these proofs must be exacting to ensure that damages recovered are those reasonably to have been anticipated in view of the defendants' capacity to have foreseen that this particular plaintiff was within the risk created by their negligence."

Id. at 253–68. See also J'Aire Corp. *v.* Gregory, 24 Cal.3d 799 (1979) (rejecting a *per se* rule against recovery for negligently inflicted economic loss).

3. EMOTIONAL DISTRESS IN CONTRACT CASES

B & M Homes, Inc. v. Hogan

Supreme Court of Alabama, 1979.
376 So.2d 667.

■ EMBRY, JUSTICE. . . . The Hogans entered into a written agreement to buy both a lot and a house to be constructed on that lot. . . . The agreed purchase price was $37,500. . . .

During the construction of the house, Mrs. Hogan discovered a hairline crack in the concrete slab that extended from the front porch through the den and informed Morrow [an agent of B & M Homes who acted as nominal seller] of this. He informed her that such cracks were common and told her not to worry about it. B & M Homes completed construction of the house and the Hogans received a warranty of completion of construction signed by Morrow on behalf of B & M Homes. The Hogans then moved into the house. After they moved in they reported several defects in the house to Morrow and repairmen were sent to fix those defects. After a couple of months the crack in the slab widened and extended through the house causing severe damage.

Again, Morrow was notified. He sent a man to repair some of the damage caused by the crack in the slab; however, nothing was done to repair the slab itself. There is expert testimony to the effect the slab probably could not be permanently repaired. There is also testimony the defective slab seriously decreased the value of the house; the Hogans' expert witness testified the defective slab made the house worthless. . . .

Appellants contend the trial court erred by failing to grant their motion to strike mental anguish as an element of damages from the Hogans' complaint. We find mental anguish a proper element of damages in this case. . . .

[T]he Hogans' case was submitted to the jury on two theories stated in separate counts: one for breach of an implied covenant, to their written purchase contract, to build their home in a workmanlike manner using first class materials; and one for breach of express warranty. In both counts, appellees alleged damages for mental anguish as follows:

> ". . . the plaintiffs have suffered mental anguish and are still suffering mental anguish with regard to the condition of such home in that they fear for their safety in the house not being structurally sound; . . . ."

At the close of the trial, B & M Homes filed a motion to strike the above allegation from both causes of action. The motion was denied. It can be assumed the jury awarded damages for mental anguish since the verdict was for $75,000 and the highest appraisal of the value of the house had it been built without defects was $42,500.

Evidence was introduced, over appellants' objection, that the Hogans were worried and concerned for their safety due to these facts: (1) the house was structurally defective and they believed its defective condition might cause the gas and water lines to burst; and (2) they were forced to live in the defective house because they could not afford to move.

In Alabama the general rule is that mental anguish is not a recoverable element of damages arising from breach of contract. This court, however, has traditionally recognized exceptions to this rule in certain cases . . . . The exceptions are stated in the following excerpt from F. Becker Asphaltum Roofing Co. *v.* Murphy, 141 So. 630 (1932) . . . :

> "The general rule is that damages cannot be recovered for mental anguish in an action of assumpsit. The ground on which the right to recover such damages is denied, is that they are too remote, were not within the contemplation of the parties, and that the breach of the contract is not such as will naturally cause mental anguish. 'Yet where the contractual duty or obligation is so coupled with matters of mental concern or solicitude, or with the feelings of the party to whom the duty is owed, that a breach of that duty will necessarily or reasonably result in mental anguish or suffering, it is just that damages therefor be taken into consideration and awarded.'
>
> "Another exception is where the breach of the contract is tortious, or attended with personal injury, damages for mental anguish may be awarded."

This case clearly falls within the first exception delineated in *F. Becker Asphaltum*. It was reasonably foreseeable by appellants that faulty construction of appellees' house would cause them severe mental anguish. The largest single investment the average American family will make is the purchase of a home. The purchase of a home by an individual or family places the purchaser in debt for a period ranging from twenty (20) to thirty (30) years. While one might expect to take the risk of acquiring a defective home if that person bought an older home, he or she certainly would not expect severe defects to exist in a home they contracted to have newly built. Consequently, any reasonable builder could easily foresee that an individual would undergo extreme mental anguish if their newly constructed house contained defects as severe as those shown to exist in this case. In any event, this court long ago set down the principle that the person who contracts to do work concerning a person's residence subjects himself to possible liability for mental anguish if that work is improperly performed and causes severe defects in that residence or home. The court clearly indicated this when it referred to the plaintiff's residence in *F. Becker Asphaltum* as ". . . her 'castle,' the habitation which she had provided to protect her against the elements . . . ." While such language might be dramatic, it is a clear indication that contracts dealing with residences are in a special category and are exceptions to the general damages rule applied in contract cases which prohibits recovery for mental anguish. . . .

Appellants contend, that before recovery for mental anguish or suffering can be allowed, the mental anguish has to be corroborated by physical symptoms, *i.e.*, becoming physically sick or ill. We reject this contention. The cases have not required mental anguish to be corroborated by the presence of physical symptoms. This is demonstrated by the fact that the cases have allowed recovery for annoyance and inconvenience. Appellees were only required to present evidence of their mental anguish, which they did; the question of damages for mental anguish then became a question of fact for the jury to decide. . . .

NOTES ON RECOVERY FOR EMOTIONAL DISTRESS

1. Compare Hancock *v.* Northcutt, 808 P.2d 251 (Alaska 1991), in which the Supreme Court of Alaska stated:

> "[B]reach of a house construction contract is not especially likely to result in serious emotional disturbance. Such contracts are not so highly personal and laden with emotion as contracts where emotional damages have typically been allowed to stand on their own. Examples of the latter include contracts to marry, to conduct a funeral, to sell a sealed casket, to conduct a cesarean birth, to surgically rebuild a nose, to provide promised maternity medical coverage, to provide medical services, and to keep a daughter informed of her mother's health. Further, the typical damages for breach of house construction contracts can appropriately be calculated in terms of monetary loss. By contrast, the damages in contracts of a more personal nature in which emotional disturbance damages are allowed are usually intangible. Thus, there would ordinarily be only a nominal recovery unless emotional disturbance damages were allowed."

808 P.2d at 258–59. Other portions of the *Northcutt* case are reprinted in Chapter Four, below.

2. Valentine, an employee of General American Credit, was terminated without cause in violation of a job security provision in her employment contract. Valentine sued for breach of contract, claiming both economic losses and emotional distress. The Michigan Supreme Court denied the claim for emotional distress:

> "Valentine may not recover mental distress damages for breach of the employment contract, although such damages may have been foreseeable and she might not be "made whole" absent an award of mental distress damages. . . .
>
> "Under the rule of Hadley *v.* Baxendale, literally applied, damages for mental distress would be recoverable for virtually every breach of contract. . . .
>
> "In determining what damages are recoverable, the courts of this state have qualified the general rule, pursuant to which mental

distress damages for breach of contract are not recoverable, with a narrow exception. Rather than look to the foreseeability of loss to determine the applicability of the exception, the courts have considered whether the contract 'has elements of personality' and whether the 'damage suffered upon the breach of the agreement is capable of adequate compensation by reference to the terms of the contract.' . . .

"An employment contract will indeed often have a personal element. Employment is an important aspect of most persons' lives, and the breach of an employment contract may result in emotional distress. The primary purpose in forming such contracts, however, is economic and not to secure the protection of personal interests. The psychic satisfaction of the employment is secondary.

"Mental distress damages for breach of contract have not been awarded where there is a market standard by which damages can be adequately determined. Valentine's monetary loss can be estimated with reasonable certainty according to the terms of the contract and the market for, or the market value of, her service. . . .

"We conclude, because an employment contract is not entered into primarily to secure the protection of personal interests and pecuniary damages can be estimated with reasonable certainty, that a person discharged in breach of an employment contract may not recover mental distress damages."

Valentine *v.* General American Credit, Inc., 420 Mich. 256, 259–63 (1984).

H. CONTRACTUAL LIMITATIONS ON DAMAGES

1. LIQUIDATED DAMAGES AND PENALTIES

Space Master International, Inc. v. Worcester

United States Court of Appeals, First Circuit, 1991.
940 F.2d 16.

■ BOWNES, SENIOR CIRCUIT JUDGE. This is an appeal from a summary judgment in favor of plaintiff-appellee Space Master International, Inc. ("Space Master"). The City of Worcester, defendant-appellant, hired Space Master to construct modular classrooms to alleviate overcrowding in the City's public schools. Under the publicly-bid contract, the City agreed to pay Space Master $1,514,559 to install within 120 days twenty-three modular classroom buildings at nine school sites. If performance exceeded 120 days, the City reserved the right to assess Space Master liquidated damages of $250 per day plus $100 per day per site.

Space Master completed its work over 200 days late; the city retained $254,400 in liquidated damages. Space Master then sued the City in the United States District Court of Massachusetts, seeking the ds on the grounds that the liquidated damages provision ..orceable. . . .

Under the Restatement of Contracts:

> "Damages for breach by either party may be liquidated in the agreement but only at an amount that is reasonable in the light of the anticipated or actual loss caused by the breach and the difficulties of proof of loss. A term fixing unreasonably large liquidated damages is unenforceable on grounds of public policy."

Restatement (Second) of Contracts § 356(1) (1979). Two factors combine to determine whether an amount fixed as liquidated damages is not so unreasonably large as to be unenforceable. First, to be reasonable the amount must approximate actual loss or loss anticipated at the time the contract was executed. Second, "[t]he greater the difficulty either of proving that loss has occurred or of establishing its amount with the requisite certainty . . . the easier it is to show that the amount fixed is reasonable." Restatement (Second) of Contracts § 356 comment b.

Considerable deference is given to the parties' reasonable agreement as to the amount of liquidated damages where losses are difficult to quantify. That deference, however, is not unlimited. In Colonial at Lynnfield, Inc. *v.* Sloan, we found that the liquidated damages provision at issue was a reasonable estimate of difficult to ascertain damages. We nonetheless found that the liquidated damages provision was an unenforceable penalty because no loss had been sustained as a result of the breach. 870 F.2d at 765. Liquidated damages must compensate for loss rather than punish for breach: "[A]n exaction of punishment for a breach which could produce no possible damage has long been deemed oppressive and unjust."

There can be no question that the injury sustained by the City is difficult to quantify in monetary terms. Because Space Master breached its promise to provide classrooms for the City within 120 days, children had to attend classes in hallways, gymnasiums, auditoriums, and libraries; educational programs were compromised; and morale among teachers, students and administrators suffered. These conditions continued for over 200 days past the contract deadline. . . .

The basic question is whether the City intended the liquidated damages provision in the contract to compensate it for a loss difficult to quantify in monetary terms or intended it as a penalty to spur timely performance. We turn, therefore, to the evidence before the district court. Dr. John E. Durkin, Superintendent of the Worcester Public Schools, stated in an affidavit:

> "When the contract was executed, it was difficult to ascertain the value of actual damages that would result from a delay in the contract's completion. The City could have incurred costs for the completion of the classroom delivery and

installation by another contractor. The City might have decided to lease additional classroom space from a private party. The City could have paid to refurbish other public properties to be used as classroom space. The City could have incurred damages in the form of interest payments due on the borrowing that was done to pay for the contract at issue. The City could have incurred costs to pay for its own personnel for additional time that was required because of the need to supervise and monitor the completion of the necessary work to alleviate the overcrowding. The City could have been damaged by the continuing overcrowding problems and the impact such problems had on the quality of education that could be offered by the City."

This statement suggests that the liquidated damages clause was meant to compensate for loss that might be incurred rather than to penalize.

Other testimony by Durkin indicated that the liquidated damages clause was intended to penalize for late performance rather than to compensate the City for injury it would incur as a result of late performance. The deposition of Durkin reads in pertinent part:

> "Q: Well, did you give them any instructions to insure that those provisions would be included in the contract?
>
> "A: I didn't originate those figures, other than the fact that I knew that there were penalty clauses in the contract. The specifics came from—
>
> "Q: And by penalty clause, you refer to those three?
>
> "A: That's what I would consider penalty.
>
> "Q: And by penalty what do you mean, doctor, basically what is here?
>
> "A: That's my interpretation of penalty, that if the modular classrooms were not in place on time and accepted by the city, that there would be these assessments made against the provider.
>
> "Q: To penalize the contractor for his late performance?
>
> "A: I think more to encourage the contractor to deliver the modulars on time and to meet the provisions of the contract.
>
> "Q: So to provide a financial incentive to the contractor to finish the units on time?
>
> "A: I believe was the motivating factor, yes." . . .

In light of the contradictory and ambiguous statements, there was a genuine issue of material fact as to whether the City intended the liquidated damages provision to provide reasonable compensation or impose a penalty in the event of Space Master's breach. The grant of Space Master's motion for summary judgment was error. . . .

NOTES ON LIQUIDATED DAMAGES

1. The rule suggested in *dicta* in *Space Master*, that a liquidated damages clause that was reasonable at the time of contracting may nevertheless be unenforceable if the breach causes no actual loss, was subsequently rejected by the Massachusetts Supreme Judicial Court, although the rule has been followed in some other states. In Kelly *v.* Marx, 428 Mass. 877 (1999), the court faced the question "whether enforceability of a liquidated damages clause is to be tested by analyzing the circumstances at contract formation, the prospective or 'single look' approach, or when the breach occurs, the retrospective or 'second look' approach." *Id.* at 879. It chose the single look approach and upheld a liquidated damages clause in a real estate contract although the plaintiffs were able to sell their house to another buyer, for a higher price, with virtually no delay. The court said:

> "The plaintiffs argue that application of a 'second look' approach would allow the court to guard against undue windfalls, such as the one the defendants would receive here if they were to keep the deposit, because the defendants suffered no loss from the breach of the sale. We disagree. In essence, the plaintiffs want to undo the agreement between the parties, who expect to receive stipulated damages, not damages resolved by a court examining postbreach circumstances. The parties agreed to the extent of their damages when they agreed on a liquidated damages clause. '[T]he proper course is to enforce contracts according to their plain meaning and not to undertake to be wiser than the parties, and therefore that in general when parties say that a sum is payable as liquidated damages they will be taken to mean what they say and will be held to their word.' Guerin *v.* Stacy, 175 Mass. 595, 597 (1900) (Holmes, C.J.)."

Id. at 881.

In a footnote, the court commented on Restatement (Second) of Contracts § 356(1) (quoted in *Space Master*). In particular, it took issue with the Restatement's illustration 4, in which a contractor delayed in constructing a race track, but the breach caused no loss because the track was otherwise barred from operating during the period of the delay. According to the Restatement, a clause providing for liquidated damages is unenforceable in these circumstances. The Massachusetts court stated:

> "We disagree with the *Restatement*'s illustration. It contradicts the express language of § 356(1), which permits liquidated damages where the agreement is "reasonable in light of the anticipated *or* actual loss" (emphasis added). In the illustration, the liquidated damages were reasonable in light of the owners' anticipated or potential loss, and, therefore, should have been enforced."

Id. at 880 n.4.

2. Carborundum, the manufacturer of a product used in making steel, entered into a contract with a distributor for bagging and storage of the product. Carborundum undertook to ship a certain minimum amount of the product and to pay the contract rate for handling the guaranteed minimum amount, whether or not it actually shipped that amount. The steel industry experienced a downturn, Carborundum failed to ship the minimum amount, and the distributor sued for the agreed minimum payment, as liquidated damages. Judge Posner, writing for the court, stated that:

> "The hardest issue in the case is whether the formula in the minimum-guarantee clause imposes a penalty for breach of contract or is merely an effort to liquidate damages. Deep as the hostility to penalty clauses runs in the common law . . . , we still might be inclined to question, if we thought ourselves free to do so, whether a modern court should refuse to enforce a penalty clause where the signator is a substantial corporation, well able to avoid improvident commitments. Penalty clauses provide an earnest of performance. The clause here enhanced Carborundum's credibility in promising to ship the minimum amount guaranteed by showing that it was willing to pay the full contract price even if it failed to ship anything. On the other side it can be pointed out that by raising the cost of a breach of contract to the contract breaker, a penalty clause increases the risk to his other creditors; increases (what is the same thing and more, because bankruptcy imposes 'deadweight' social costs) the risk of bankruptcy; and could amplify the business cycle by increasing the number of bankruptcies in bad times, which is when contracts are most likely to be broken. But since little effort is made to prevent businessmen from assuming risks, these reasons are no better than makeweights.
>
> "A better argument is that a penalty clause may discourage efficient as well as inefficient breaches of contract. Suppose a breach would cost the promisee $12,000 in actual damages but would yield the promisor $20,000 in additional profits. Then there would be a net social gain from breach. After being fully compensated for his loss the promisee would be no worse off than if the contract had been performed, while the promisor would be better off by $8,000. But now suppose the contract contains a penalty clause under which the promisor if he breaks his promise must pay the promisee $25,000. The promisor will be discouraged from breaking the contract, since $25,000, the penalty, is greater than $20,000, the profits of the breach; and a transaction that would have increased value will be forgone.
>
> "On this view, since compensatory damages should be sufficient to deter inefficient breaches (that is, breaches that cost the victim more than the gain to the contract breaker), penal damages could have no effect other than to deter some efficient breaches. But this overlooks the earlier point that the willingness to agree to a penalty clause is a way of making the promisor and his promise credible and may therefore be essential to inducing

> some value-maximizing contracts to be made. It also overlooks the more important point that the parties (always assuming they are fully competent) will, in deciding whether to include a penalty clause in their contract, weigh the gains against the costs—costs that include the possibility of discouraging an efficient breach somewhere down the road—and will include the clause only if the benefits exceed those costs as well as all other costs.
>
> "On this view the refusal to enforce penalty clauses is (at best) paternalistic—and it seems odd that courts should display parental solicitude for large corporations. But however this may be, we must be on guard to avoid importing our own ideas of sound public policy into an area where our proper judicial role is more than usually deferential. The responsibility for making innovations in the common law of Illinois rests with the courts of Illinois, and not with the federal courts in Illinois. And like every other state, Illinois, untroubled by academic skepticism of the wisdom of refusing to enforce penalty clauses against sophisticated promisors, continues steadfastly to insist on the distinction between penalties and liquidated damages."

Lake River Corp. *v.* Carborundum Co., 769 F.2d 1284, 1288–89 (7th Cir. 1985).

3. In re Trans World Airlines, Inc. (Interface Group-Nevada, Inc. *v.* Trans World Airlines, Inc.), 145 F.3d 124 (1998), grew out of the 1992 bankruptcy of TWA. In a transaction that may have been tax-motivated, Interface Group purchased two airplanes for $25,200,000 and leased them to TWA for a period of about eight years. In the early 1990s, TWA defaulted on rent, then filed a bankruptcy petition. The lease provided that in case of default, TWA agreed to pay Interface a sum named on a schedule of "termination values," minus the actual rental or resale value of the planes. The court determined that this formula bore no reasonable relation to Interface's expected loss in case of breach and therefore was an unenforceable penalty. It then stated that:

> "Interface does not cite any case in which a court enforced an otherwise invalid liquidated damages provision merely because it was freely negotiated by sophisticated parties. Contracts that are void as against public policy are unenforceable regardless of how freely and willingly they were entered into."

Id. at 135.

Compare Uzan *v.* 845 UN Ltd. Partnership, 10 A.D.3d 230 (N.Y. App. Div. 2004), in which the court allowed Donald Trump to enforce a provision calling for forfeiture of an $8 million down payment as liquidated damages for breach of a condominium purchase agreement. The defendants were "Turkish billionaires" who agreed to buy four luxury condominiums in the Trump World Tower but repudiated the agreement after the twin towers of the World Trade Center were destroyed by terrorists on September 11, 2001. The court relied in part on the customary use of non-refundable 20%–25% down payments in real estate transactions in New York, and in part on the lenient approach New York courts traditionally had taken to enforcement of down payment provisions in real estate contracts. According to the court, "There is no question that this was an arm's length transaction. The parties were sophisticated business people, represented by counsel, who spent two months at the bargaining table before executing the amended purchase agreements."

4. Donna and Manuel Diosdado had been married for five years when Manuel had an affair with another woman. After Donna discovered the affair, the couple remained married but signed a "Marital Settlement Agreement" drafted by Manuel's lawyer. The agreement imposed a "legal obligation of emotional and sexual fidelity" on the parties, defined "any act of kissing on the mouth or touching in any sexual manner of any person outside of said marital relationship" as a breach of the obligation of fidelity, and acknowledged the parties' "mutual understanding that any such breach of fidelity by one party hereto may cause serious emotional, physical and financial injury to the other." A further provision stated that if either party breached the obligation of fidelity, and the parties consequently divorced, the party who committed the breach would pay "liquidated damages for said breach in the sum of $50,000."

Five years later, Manuel had another affair. In Diosdado *v.* Diosdado, 97 Cal. App. 4th 470 (Cal. App. 2002), the court refused to enforce the agreement:

> "[Under California's no-fault divorce law, the] family law court may not look to fault in dissolving the marriage, dividing property, or ordering support. Yet this agreement attempts to penalize the party who is at fault for having breached the obligation of sexual fidelity, and whose breach provided the basis for terminating the marriage. This penalty is in direct contravention of the public policy underlying no-fault divorce."

Id. at 474.

5. Does the existence of a liquidated damages clause affect decisions to breach a contract? That question was explored in experimental work by Professor Tess Wilkinson-Ryan. She analyzed her findings in this way:

> "Psychologists and behavioral economists have observed in many contexts that actors are more likely to defy a social norm when the penalty for their noncooperation is real and explicit, but not so harsh as to deter the behavior on its own terms. I argue here that weak sanctions in economics games serve the same function as liquidated-damages clauses in efficient breach situations. The liquidated-damages clause makes the remedy for breach explicit but not unduly punitive. Under these conditions, I predicted that people would be more willing to breach a contract, an action normally dictated against by social and moral norms. Data reported here suggests that people prefer to breach a contract with a liquidated-damages clause to one with an identical remedy provided by the rule of expectation damages. One interpretation of these results, supported by both descriptive and normative

> scholarship in this field, is that liquidated-damages clauses encourage efficient breach by changing the parties' understanding of the content of the promise."

Tess Wilkinson-Ryan, Do Liquidated Damages Encourage Breach? A Psychological Experiment, 108 Mich. L. Rev. 633, 637 (2010).

2. LIMITS ON REMEDIES

Mandle v. Owens

Court of Appeals of Indiana, 1975.
164 Ind. App. 607.

■ LOWDERMILK, JUDGE. Plaintiffs-appellants (Mandles), by newspaper advertisement, offered their residence in Terre Haute, Indiana, for sale. Defendants-appellees (Owenses) after examining the house, entered into an agreement with Mandles to purchase the house for $30,000. Owenses at the time of the agreement made an earnest money deposit in the amount of $300.00 on the house in the form of a check. . . .

The contract entered into by and between the parties reads, in part, as follows:

> ". . . If offer is accepted and we fail to complete the purchase of the real estate herein mentioned as provided herein, the amount of Three Hundred ($300.00) dollars will be forfeited to you."

. . . On August 8, Owens called Mandles and informed them that he and his wife had decided not to proceed with the purchase of the Mandle house-that they had found something they liked better. . . .

Mandles, having moved from Terre Haute to their new home in Maryland, advertised the Terre Haute property for sale after they were informed by Owenses that they would not take the property. They were unsuccessful and having a deadline to meet on the Maryland property, on August 28, listed the Terre Haute property with a Terre Haute realtor.

The property was sold for $29,500. A brokerage fee of $2,065 was paid the realtor. The Terre Haute property was refinanced and other expenses in the amount of $436.00 were incurred. Mandles also claim additional expenses [for a motel stay, telephone usage, and interest on a loan, totaling $305.17]. . . .

[The Mandles sued for breach of the agreement to sell the property. The trial court found "[t]hat the clause referred to . . . is a liquidated damages clause which was intended by the parties as compensation for a breach of the contract by the buyers and was a good faith attempt on the part of the parties to estimate the damages which would probably flow from a breach thereof and is fair and reasonable and was intended by the parties to be the sole remedy in the event of the buyers' breach under the contract." Nevertheless, the court found that the plaintiffs suffered no injury, and thus entered judgment for the Owenses, the defendants.]

While liquidated damages may be proper in some cases involving real estate sales where damages are uncertain, such is not the case here. The greater part of the damages which resulted from the failure of Owens to complete the contract were clearly and accurately shown by the evidence at trial. Given such reasonable certainty of proof, we must conclude that the $300 figure was at best arbitrary—there is nothing to show that the stipulated sum has any relation to anticipated loss.

Inasmuch as we have found the sum to be a penalty, it necessarily follows that the contract provision above was not intended as the sole remedy for breach. . . .

Judgment reversed and cause remanded to the trial court with instructions to restate its conclusions of law in accordance with this opinion and to hear further evidence on the amount of damages sustained by Mandles . . . as the result of Owenses' breach of the contract and to give Owenses credit for the $300 earnest money payment paid to Mandles and render its judgment accordingly.

NOTES ON UNDERCOMPENSATORY DAMAGES PROVISIONS

1. Was the remedy agreed to in Mandle *v.* Owen a penalty? Was it a reasonable estimate of probable loss? Was it fundamentally unfair?

2. The Denver Burglar Alarm company agreed to install a burglar alarm system in Niccoli's place of business and to dispatch an agent to the site if the alarm went off. The contract between the parties provided that "the Contractor's liability hereunder shall be limited to a fixed sum of fifty dollars or ten percent of the annual service charge whichever is greater, as liquidated damages, and not as a penalty, and this liability shall be exclusive."

Niccoli's business was burglarized and Niccoli sued for damages. The trial court limited damages to $50, as specified in the contract. The appellate court affirmed, stating that damages were difficult to estimate and the facts "leave little doubt that this contractual provision was intended to operate as a liquidated damages clause rather than a penalty." Niccoli *v.* Denver Burglar Alarm, Inc., 490 P.2d 304, 306 (Colo. App. 1971).

Was the agreed remedy a penalty? Was it a reasonable estimate of probable loss? Was it fundamentally unfair?

3. Sonitrol agreed to install a burglar alarm system in Core-Mark's warehouse, to monitor microphones installed at the site, and to notify the police if operators heard a burglary in progress. The contract provided that Sonitrol "is not an insurer and . . . insurance, if any, covering personal injury and property loss or damage on client's premises shall be obtained by client." United States Fire Insurance Co. *v.* Sonitrol Management Corp., 192 P.3d 543, 545 (Colo. App. 2008), In case of "a failure to perform any of its obligations or a failure of the equipment to properly operate," Sonitrol's

liability was limited to $500, and the limited remedy "shall be exclusive and shall apply if loss or damage, irrespective of cause or origin, results directly or indirectly to persons or property from performance or non-performance of any of dealer's obligations or from negligence, active or otherwise, of dealer . . . ." *Id.* at 545–46.

As described by the court:

> "In December 2002, a burglar entered Core-Mark's warehouse while it was closed over the weekend. He returned a little later with two confederates, and the three looted the warehouse for approximately three hours. They made no effort to be quiet, but shouted to each other, threw boxes around, and used a noisy gravity chute lined with steel rollers to move boxes. When they were ready to leave, one of the burglars smashed boxes of flammable liquids, pulled down large jugs of methanol, and set two fires at 8:42 a.m. The fire department arrived on the scene eleven minutes later at 8:53 a.m., alerted by a passerby, but it was too late to save the property.
>
> "During this episode, Sonitrol's off-site monitoring center received audio activations caused by the noise the burglars created. Two different Sonitrol employees received the alarms and reacted as follows: (1) audio activation at 1:35 a.m., no replay of stored audio, alarm reset in 36 seconds, no call to police; (2) audio activation at 6:50 a.m., no replay of stored audio, alarm reset in 4 seconds, no call to police; (3) audio activation at 7:29 a.m., no replay of stored audio, alarm reset in 40 seconds, no call to police; (4) audio activation at 7:56 a.m., no replay of stored audio, alarm reset in 1 minute and 49 seconds, no call to police; (5) audio activation at 8:36 a.m., no replay of stored audio, alarm reset in 2 minutes and 10 seconds, no call to police; (6) audio activation at 8:44 a.m., operator replayed stored audio, no call to police; (7) 8:46 a.m. (four minutes after fire started), the telephone connection between warehouse and monitoring center was severed. At 9:05, the Sonitrol employee called the fire department, which had been at the scene for twelve minutes.
>
> "Despite the fire department's efforts, the fire burned for a week and destroyed the building and all the inventory, resulting in a loss of approximately $20 million."

Id. at 546.

The trial court entered summary judgment, limiting Core-Mark's remedy to the $500 stipulated in the contract. The Colorado Court of Appeals reversed, holding that Core-Mark was entitled to a trial on the question of whether Sonitrol had acted "willfully and wantonly:"

> "Exculpatory clauses insulating a party from its own negligence, though disfavored, are permitted in Colorado if one party is not at a significant disadvantage in bargaining. However, an exculpatory clause is against public policy if it enforces a release from willful and wanton conduct. . . .

> "We need not decide here whether the clause in question is a limitation of liability clause, a liquidated damages clause, or an exculpatory clause, because the general rule applies to all of them. . . .
>
> "Therefore, although the district court properly found that the limitation of liability clause shielded Sonitrol from claims for simple negligence . . . , the district court should not have granted summary judgment before determining the issue of willful and wanton conduct."

Id. at 548–49.

Pierce v. Catalina Yachts, Inc.

Supreme Court of Alaska, 2000.
2 P.3d 618.

■ BRYNER, JUSTICE. . . . In June 1992 Jim and Karen Pierce purchased a forty-two-foot sailboat newly built by Catalina Yachts. Catalina gave the Pierces a limited warranty, promising to repair or pay for repair of any below-waterline blisters that might appear in the gel coat—a smooth outer layer of resin on the boat's hull.[1] The warranty expressly disclaimed Catalina's responsibility for consequential damages.

In June 1994 the Pierces hauled the boat out of the water to perform maintenance and discovered gel-coat blisters on its hull and rudder. They promptly notified Catalina of the problem and submitted a repair estimate of $10,645, which included the cost of removing and replacing the gel coat below the waterline. Catalina refused to accept this estimate, insisting that the hull only needed minor patching. Six months later, after their repeated efforts failed to convince Catalina that the gel coat needed to be replaced, the Pierces sued the company, claiming tort and contract damages. . . .

Before trial, the superior court ruled that the limited warranty's provision barring consequential damages was not unconscionable. Based on this ruling, the court later precluded the Pierces from submitting their consequential damages claim to the jury, restricting the Pierces' recovery on their claim of breach of contract to their cost of repair, as specified in the limited warranty. The jury awarded the Pierces $12,445 as the reasonable cost of repair, specifically finding that the Pierces had given Catalina timely notice of the blister problem, that Catalina breached its gel-coat warranty, that it acted in bad faith in failing to honor its warranty obligations, and that the Pierces could not have avoided any of their losses. . . .

The Pierces' consequential damages argument requires us to consider a question of first impression concerning how a warranty

---

[1] This limited warranty provided, in relevant part: "Catalina will repair or, at its option, pay for 100% of the labor and material costs necessary to repair any below-the-waterline gel coat blisters that occur within the first year after the boat is placed in the water."

provision that creates a limited remedy interacts with another provision that excludes consequential damages: if the limited remedy fails, should the exclusion of consequential damages survive?

Alaska's commercial code addresses these issues in AS 45.02.719.[3] The first paragraph of this provision, subsection .719(a), authorizes . . . parties entering into commercial transactions to "limit or alter the measure of damages recoverable under [chapter 7 of the U.C.C.], as by limiting the buyer's remedies to . . . repair and replacement of nonconforming goods or parts" and to agree that the limited remedy is "exclusive, in which case it is the sole remedy." But when a limited remedy fails, the second paragraph of AS 45.02.719, subsection .719(b), nullifies the warranty's limitation, restoring the buyer's right to rely on any authorized remedy: "If circumstances cause an exclusive or limited remedy to fail of its essential purpose, remedy may be had as provided in the code."

Courts construing U.C.C. subsection .719(b) agree that a limited warranty to repair "fails of its essential purpose," "when the seller is either unwilling or unable to conform the goods to the contract."

The policy behind the failure of essential purpose rule is to insure that the buyer has "at least minimum adequate remedies." [U.C.C. § 2–719 official comment 1.] Typically, a limited repair/replacement remedy fails of its essential purpose where (1) the "[s]eller is unsuccessful in repairing or replacing the defective part, regardless of good or bad faith; or (2)[t]here is unreasonable delay in repairing or replacing defective components."

Here, by specifically finding that the Pierces' boat experienced gel-coat blisters, that the Pierces gave Catalina timely notice of the problem, that Catalina thereafter breached its obligations under the limited gel-coat warranty, and that the Pierces could not have avoided their damages, the jury effectively determined that the gel-coat warranty had failed of its essential purpose. Under subsection .719(b), then, the Pierces

---

[3] AS 45.02.719 mirrors U.C.C. § 2–719, providing:

"(a) Subject to (b) and (c) of this section and AS 45.02.718 on liquidation and limitation of damages,

"(1) the agreement may provide for remedies in addition to or in substitution for those provided in this chapter and may limit or alter the measure of damages recoverable under this chapter, as by limiting the buyer's remedies to return of the goods and repayment of the price or to repair and replacement of nonconforming goods or parts; and

"(2) resort to a remedy as provided is optional unless the remedy is expressly agreed to be exclusive, in which case it is the sole remedy.

"(b) If circumstances cause an exclusive or limited remedy to fail of its essential purpose, remedy may be had as provided in the code.

"(c) Consequential damages may be limited or excluded unless the limitation or exclusion is unconscionable. Limitation of consequential damages for injury to the person in the case of consumer goods is prima facie unconscionable, but limitation of damages where the loss is commercial is not."

seemingly can pursue any remedy available under the commercial code, including consequential damages.

But the Pierces' right to consequential damages under subsection .719(b) is not as certain as it seems. The last paragraph of AS 45.02.719, subsection .719(c), separately provides that consequential damages may be limited or excluded "unless the limitation or exclusion is unconscionable." By validating consequential damages exclusions subject only to unconscionability, subsection .719(c) casts doubt upon subsection .719(b)'s implied promise that, when a limited remedy fails, the buyer may claim consequential damages because they are a "remedy . . . provided in the code." . . .

Courts addressing this dilemma in other jurisdictions have come to differing conclusions. Some have found the two subsections to be dependent, ruling that when a warranty fails, subsection .719(b)'s command to restore all available remedies trumps subsection .719(c)'s approval of a specific clause that bars consequential damages, regardless of whether that clause might itself be unconscionable. Other courts have applied a case-by-case analysis. But the majority of jurisdictions view these subsections to be independent, ruling that when a warranty fails, a separate provision barring consequential damages will survive under subsection .719(c) as long as the bar itself is not unconscionable.

We believe that the majority approach best serves the Uniform Commercial Code's underlying purposes "to simplify, clarify and modernize the law governing commercial transactions; to permit the continued expansion of commercial practices through custom, usage and agreement of the parties; [and] to make uniform the law among the various jurisdictions." [U.C.C. § 1–102(2) (1996).] Moreover, this approach balances the purposes of subsections .719(b) and (c) by allowing parties latitude to contract around consequential damages, while protecting buyers from unconscionable results. We therefore adopt the independent approach as the most sensible rule in light of precedent, reason, and policy. . . .

In determining whether an exclusion is unconscionable, courts examine the circumstances existing when the contract was signed, asking whether "there was . . . reason to conclude that the parties could not competently agree upon the allocation of risk." Chatlos Systems, Inc. *v.* National Cash Register Corp., 635 F.2d 1081, 1087 (3d Cir. 1980). Courts are more likely to find unconscionability when a consumer is involved, when there is a disparity in bargaining power, and when the consequential damages clause is on a pre-printed form; conversely, they are unlikely to find unconscionability when "such a limitation is freely negotiated between sophisticated parties, which will most likely occur in a commercial setting . . . ."

In addition to inquiring into the circumstances at the time of the sale, courts examine the case "[f]rom the perspective of later events," inquiring whether "it appears that the type of damage claimed . . . came within the realm of expectable losses." The reason for the limited warranty's failure affects this analysis . . . . And in examining why a limited remedy failed of its essential purpose, courts consider it significant if the seller acted unreasonably or in bad faith.

In the present case, the nature of the Pierces' warranty and the circumstances surrounding Catalina's breach weigh heavily against enforcing the consequential damages bar. The contract at issue was a consumer sale, not a commercial transaction between sophisticated businesses with equivalent bargaining power. Catalina unilaterally drafted the damages bar and evidently included it in a preprinted standard limited warranty. Moreover, the jury's sizable award for the reasonable cost of repairing the boat's gel coat establishes that Catalina's breach deprived the Pierces of a substantial benefit of their bargain. Though some gel-coat blistering might have been foreseeable, a defect of this magnitude does not fit neatly "within the realm of expectable losses."

But the decisive factor in this case is the nature of Catalina's breach, which caused the limited remedy to fail of its essential purpose. The jury specifically found that Catalina acted in bad faith in failing to honor its warranty. This finding virtually establishes a "circumstance[ ] resulting in failure of performance that makes it unconscionable to enforce the parties' allocation of risk." Because the jury found that Catalina consciously deprived the Pierces of their rights under the warranty, the company cannot conscionably demand to enforce its own warranty rights against the Pierces . . . .

CHAPTER 4

MEASURING DAMAGES

A. LOST VALUE

Portland General Electric Co. v. Taber

Court of Appeals of Oregon, 1997.
146 Or. App. 735.

■ HASELTON, JUDGE. . . . The sole issue presented is whether the proper measure of damages when a motorist negligently destroys a wooden power pole is: (a) the undepreciated cost of the lost pole or (b) the full replacement cost of a new pole. The trial court determined that, as a matter of law, PGE's recovery was limited to the lost pole's undepreciated value. We affirm.

The material facts are undisputed. PGE owns and operates an electrical distribution system, which includes approximately 235,000 wooden power poles. The age of the poles varies, with roughly 40 percent being in service for more than 40 years; the oldest is 84 years old. Among the factors that affect the life of any individual pole may be rot and decay, insect infestation, lightning strikes, other accidental destruction, and systemic relocation or restructuring. Improved treatment processes have extended the useful life of properly treated wooden poles. PGE does not replace poles on a fixed schedule, but, instead, inspects and treats poles on a seven-year cycle and replaces them on an "as necessary" basis.

PGE depreciates its poles, as a capital asset, for tax and accounting purposes. Poles are depreciated as a group, rather than individually, based on the projected useful life of all wooden transmission poles in the system. The projected useful life, for tax and accounting purposes, is 37 years.

There is no market for used power poles, and such poles have no salvage or retirement value. Historically, until 1993, whenever one of its wooden transmission poles was negligently damaged or destroyed, PGE calculated its damages for the loss of the pole as the original cost of the pole less any depreciation previously taken (the "undepreciated cost" method). Thus, if a 17-year-old pole was damaged or destroyed, PGE would invoice damages for 20/37 of the pole's total original cost.[1] On July 1, 1993, PGE altered its methodology and began invoicing allegedly liable third parties for the full replacement cost of a new power pole, rather than the undepreciated cost of the damaged pole. Under the new "full replacement cost" method, if the third party actually pays the full cost of

[1] In addition, PGE would seek damages for the costs of removing and replacing the damaged pole, excluding the pole's cost.

the new pole, PGE does not depreciate the new pole for tax and accounting purposes. If the third party pays for part of the new pole, PGE depreciates the balance of the cost.

On June 20, 1994, defendant Taber's pickup truck struck and damaged a wooden power pole owned by PGE, which had been installed in 1934 and was still fully functional. PGE brought this action, seeking to recover damages of $2,213 for removing and replacing the damaged pole and $407.85 for the cost of the new pole itself. Defendant agreed to pay PGE $2,213 for costs, exclusive of the actual cost of the new pole, but disputed PGE's claim for the full replacement cost of a new pole. In particular, defendant asserted that the "undepreciated value" measure of damages should control and that, under that method, PGE was not entitled to any damages, because the pole's actual age (60 years) exceeded the 37-year average useful life that PGE assumed for depreciation purposes.

On September 12, 1993, a car driven by intervenor Farmers' insured, Johnson, struck and damaged a PGE power pole that had been installed in 1976. As with Taber, PGE sought to recover the full cost of a new pole ($908.22),[2] rather than the pole's undepreciated value ($467.73). Farmers moved to intervene, ORCP 33, in the Taber litigation because the issue presented there, as to the correct measure of damages, was identical to that raised by PGE's claim against Johnson. Farmers sought a declaration that the "undepreciated cost" method was the correct measure of damages. Neither PGE nor Taber objected, and the trial court allowed Farmers' intervention.

PGE then moved for summary judgment, and Taber and Farmers cross-moved, on the dispositive replacement cost issue. The trial court granted Taber's and Farmers' cross-motions for summary judgment. PGE appeals.

The question is one of first impression in Oregon. That question seems simple. Nevertheless, it has engendered a substantial division of opinion in other jurisdictions. That disagreement suggests, quite correctly, that although the question is straight-forward, the answer is not.

Despite that complexity, the overarching principles that guide our inquiry are clear. In assessing compensatory damages for tortious injury to property, the measure of damages is to be determined "not only by what might be right for an injured person to receive in order to afford just compensation, but also by what is just to compel the other party to pay." Mock *v.* Terry, 251 Or. 511, 513 (1968). Generally, where property has been damaged, the measure of damages is the difference in value before and after the injury. Similarly, where property is destroyed, the measure of damages is generally the market value of the property. Where,

---

[2] The record does not explain the difference between the replacement costs of the poles in the Taber and Johnson cases.

however, the property that is damaged or destroyed had no market value, "other means of valuation must necessarily be resorted to in order to appraise the property." Prettyman *v.* Railway etc. Co., 13 Or. 341, 344 (1886).

Here, it is undisputed that there was no market and, hence, no market value for used wooden power poles. Accordingly, our task is to identify the appropriate "other means of valuation," that justly compensates plaintiff while not unfairly assessing defendant.

The parties espouse starkly contrasting methodologies, with PGE invoking the "full replacement cost" rule adopted in 14 states, and Taber and Farmers urging a variation of the "depreciated value" approach adopted in five states. Each contends that the other's approach yields unconscionable windfalls, but that its own achieves, or at least approximates, just compensation. As described below, there is—notwithstanding their Manichean oversimplification—some merit in both positions.

The original, and most frequently quoted, "full cost of replacement" case is N.J. Power & Light Co. *v.* Mabee, 41 N.J. 439 (1964). The premise of that holding, which is reiterated in virtually every "majority rule" decision, is that, because it is impossible to predict the life of any particular power pole, only the full cost replacement ensures that the power company will be fully compensated for its loss:

> "If the life of every pole were 36 years and if it were clear that each pole would be replaced at the end of that period defendants could well urge that a new pole clearly conferred a benefit beyond the amount of the damage done. The difficulty is that there is no discernible life expectancy of an individual pole and that although the period of 36 years is used for accounting purposes, the pole that was destroyed might well have served for a much longer period and the new pole may last for but a few years. Moreover, because of changes in circumstances or in technology, it cannot be known whether the pole would ever have been replaced. In short, at least upon the record before us, we cannot say with reasonable assurance that the installation of a new pole did more than remedy the wrong done. An injured party should not be required to lay out money, as defendants' approach would require, upon a questionable assumption that one day its worth will be recaptured." *Id.*

Conversely, the minority "undepreciated cost" rule turns on the premise that requiring a party to replace a used power pole with a new pole confers an unfair windfall on the utility and that relating damages to the pole's undepreciated cost, representing the loss of the balance of the *average* projected useful life, effects fair compensation. Younger *v.* Appalachian Power Company, 214 Va. 662 (1974), exemplifies that view:

"The record shows that Appalachian periodically inspects its transmission system and replaces poles deteriorated in normal usage. From this experience, Appalachian can determine the average useful life of poles in the system. Since in the normal course of doing business Appalachian must bear the expense of replacement costs at some reasonable ascertainable future time, recovery from a tortfeasor of full replacement costs at an earlier time would overcompensate the injury sustained. Thus, if a pole deteriorated in normal usage was to be replaced and an automobile damaged it an hour before the replacement crew arrived with the new pole, Appalachian would gain a windfall if the tortfeasor is required to pay the full replacement costs Appalachian was about to expend. On the other hand, if an automobile damaged a pole an hour after it had been replaced in the normal course of replacement, Appalachian would be less than whole if the tortfeasor is permitted to pay less than full replacement costs. In each case, the actual injury sustained by Appalachian is related to the useful life of the pole. In the former case, Appalachian would have enjoyed the full anticipated use of its property and incurred no unanticipated expense. In the latter case, Appalachian would have been deprived of the full anticipated use of its property and would have incurred an expense which, but for the tort, would have been deferred for the useful life of the pole."

See also Puget Sound Power and Light Co. *v.* Strong, 59 Wash. App. 430, 434–35 (1990), *rev'd.*, 117 Wash. 2d 400 (1991) (rejecting "total cost replacement" in favor of "undepreciated value" measure where defendant destroyed 14-year-old pole: "Puget would gain an estimated additional fourteen years of service life if it were permitted to recover the cost of a new pole. Such compensation exceeds the loss incurred by Puget and, thus, would result in a windfall to Puget.").

In related fashion, in Ohio Power Co. *v.* Zemelka, 19 Ohio App. 2d 213 (1969), the court held that, just as the utility relied on "sound accounting principles," in projecting poles' useful life for accounting and taxation purposes and in assessing other costs associated with the removal and replacement of damaged poles, the same actuarial assumptions should bind the utility in determining the value of a lost pole:

"We feel that justice is a two-way street. Just as plaintiff is entitled to be compensated for such items as cost of pole storage and administration and engineering expenses, because the application of sound accounting principles establishes that these indirect expenses are properly part of the damages suffered by a utility company when one of its utility poles is damaged, so defendants are entitled to use sound accounting principles to establish the life expectancy of a utility pole so that the depreciation of such a utility pole can be readily determined by the application of sound accounting principles."

"It is true that a utility pole has a variable life expectancy, just as any other item of personal property, such as an automobile, furniture, etc., but sound accounting principles can establish a life expectancy of such items. . . . All variables can be attacked on the basis of uncertainty; however, for business and legal reasons, we need to establish uniform definite standards for variable expenses on the basis of sound accounting principles. We feel that there is no difference in the application of sound accounting principles to determine the accrued depreciation of a damaged utility pole with a variable life expectancy than to determine the indirect costs of repairing the damaged pole by the application of sound accounting principles to the variable costs of such expenses."

As the dispute is framed by the parties, we are, thus, faced with an "either/or" choice between two contending formulations. That choice is, frankly, less than satisfying for at least three reasons.

First, it is beyond dispute that either measure of damages will, at least in some circumstances, produce seemingly unjust results. For example, if the "full replacement cost" method were applied here, PGE would, in effect, be allowed to trade a 60-year-old pole, which has survived 23 years past its projected useful life, for a brand new pole. Conversely, if the "undepreciated cost" method were applied to the same 60-year-old pole, Taber would pay nothing for PGE's loss of a pole that was fully functioning and useful until Taber's pickup damaged it—and that might still be in use but for Taber's negligence. Second, many, if not all, of the decisions that adopt either rule speak in terms of the speculative nature of projecting the life expectancy of *any particular pole*. It is true that "there is no discernible life expectancy to any individual pole." However, with all respect to those courts, and to the present litigants who invoke their reasoning, their apparent preoccupation with that truism seems inapt. This dispute is special, perhaps unique, in that it concerns the appropriate valuation of (1) peculiar property (power poles), (2) that is owned by a very limited class of persons (utilities), and (3) whose valuation is the subject of frequent disputes and litigation. To be blunt: This dispute is not about the fairness or "speculativeness" of valuing the loss of a single 60-year-old power pole in Clackamas County; it is, instead, about the proper method of compensating PGE for the loss of any of the 235,000 poles in its transmission system. Our task, then, is to identify the measure of damages that most closely effects just compensation *systemically*, in power pole loss cases in the aggregate.

Third, our performance of that task is skewed by the fact that the parties present us with only two options and the evidentiary record was tailored to those two options only. There are, at least in the abstract, alternative methodologies that might mitigate the cross-cutting "windfall" concerns and better effectuate just compensation.[7] However, because of the manner in which the record was developed on summary judgment, there is no basis on this record for determining the practicability of such approaches. We cannot prescribe them in an evidentiary void.

Faced with the "either/or" choice, we opt for the "undepreciated cost" approach. That measure, although imperfect, comes closer to promoting just compensation in power pole damage cases as a whole than does the "full replacement cost" method.

Our holding rests on reasoning similar to *Ohio Power*'s observation that "justice is a two-way street." The only evidence in this record as to the average useful life of PGE's wooden power poles in the aggregate is that, for tax and accounting purposes, PGE depreciates the poles on the basis of a 37-year useful life. We fully appreciate that different considerations *may* underlie projections of useful life for tax and accounting purposes, as opposed to property loss valuation purposes. Nevertheless, PGE has not explained why it should reap the benefit of a 37-year useful life for tax depreciation purposes but, concurrently, claim that the 37-year figure is not an accurate benchmark of average projected life in crafting a measure of damages that applies to all power poles. Nor does PGE explain why the "undepreciated cost" approach, which it has applied historically, became somehow unjust or incompletely remedial as of July 1, 1993.

Conversely, adoption and application of the "full cost replacement" measure in every power pole loss case would systematically overcompensate PGE. In every case, PGE would be receiving a new pole for a used and depreciated pole. Regardless of whether that might yield an appreciable windfall in any given case, the inescapable consequence would be that PGE would be unjustly overcompensated in the aggregate.

The trial court did not err in adopting and applying the "undepreciated cost" measure of damages. . . .

NOTES ON VALUE

1. Hughes marketed a product called Replex, buying it in bulk from a manufacturer and repackaging it for retail sale. An employee of Ocean Electric, working above the space where Hughes stored its inventory of Replex in bottled bulk form, caused a flood that damaged the stored bottles. Hughes claimed damages of $4.06 per bottle, the retail price.

---

[7] For example, during oral argument, we explored with counsel a method by which the life expectancy of power poles would be projected, actuarially, in a fashion similar to human life mortality tables. Thus, even if the *average* useful life of a wooden power pole in PGE's system were assumed to be 37 years, a 60-year-old pole might (hypothetically) have a projected remaining life of 12 years, and damages could be based on that period. Similarly, two-year-old power poles might, as a class, have an average projected life of 30 years, and damages to any particular two-year-old pole would be based on that 28 years of "lost life." In response to our inquiries, counsel explained that the record contained no evidence as to whether the actuarial data necessary to implement such an approach existed or could be practicably developed.

> "In order to achieve the objective of restoring the plaintiff to a financially equal position had the damage not occurred, damages for loss of personal property are to be measured based upon the market value of the property on the date of the loss. The market value of property or goods is determined by looking at the price which would be agreed upon at a voluntary sale between a willing seller and a willing purchaser. . . .
>
> "The appropriate economic market to be used in approximating reasonable market value is the usual market where the property or goods had been purchased. The usual market for the owner of goods held for subsequent resale, is the wholesale selling market, because a retailer will replace destroyed or damaged goods at the wholesale price, and thus be restored to the prior financial position.
>
> "Applying these principles to the present case, the fair market value of Hughes' damages must be calculated based upon the usual market where Hughes purchased the Replex, which was the wholesale selling market, where Hughes could purchase Replex for $.635 per bottle. . . . [A]llowing Hughes to recover the retail value of the damaged goods . . . would, in essence, allow Hughes to recover 'lost profits' that were *never lost* in the first place."

Ocean Electric Co. *v.* Hughes Laboratories, Inc., 636 So.2d 112, 113–15 (Fla. Dist. Ct. App. 1994).

2. In United States *v.* Eden Memorial Park Association, 350 F.2d 933 (9th Cir. 1965), the federal government condemned land that was zoned for cemetery purposes, in order to make way for an interstate highway. The court, quoting from a manual on real estate appraisal, said that:

> "Appraisers commonly think of value in three ways: 1. The current cost of reproducing a property less depreciation from all sources, that is, deterioration and functional and economic obsolescence. 2. The value which the property's net earning power will support, based upon a capitalization of net income. 3. The value indicated by recent sales of comparable properties in the market. The three approaches—Cost, income, and market data—are based on these three facets of value."

Id. at 935.

In Foster *v.* United States, 2 Cl. Ct. 426 (1983), another eminent domain case, the government condemned property in which the plaintiffs held a mineral interest in riprap rock (used in construction and landscaping). The plaintiff claimed compensation in the amount of $5,029,532, based on capitalized income. The court said:

> "The capitalization of income approach has become acceptable in recognition of situations where income producing potential is a key element for both buyer and seller in many negotiations in arriving at a fair price. As to mining properties, plaintiffs contend that the calculation of future income from the extraction of the mineral provides a more accurate measure of value than so-called

comparable sales data because mineral deposits inherently must be quite dissimilar. . . .

"Although a computation by the capitalization of income approach involves multiplication of tonnage volumes by net income per ton, the operator's interest in a mineral estate has a different function than as a measure of an operator's profit. The operator's interest is a separate right to produce and sell the mineral. When bought and sold on the open market, it commands a price that represents a present value, measured by an estimate of what can be earned by exercise of the right. The value placed on an operator's interest is not compensation for the consequential damages of lost future business profits; it is compensation for the taking of an interest in real property.

"In a particular case, each approach to valuation appropriately can be useful as a tool to arrive at an amount equivalent to the hypothetical fair market value, when the buyer and seller each is fully informed and acts in the absence of constraints."

Id. at 448–49.

Ultimately, the court concluded that the plaintiff's proof of capitalized income was insufficient. The plaintiff failed to establish, among other things, the quantity of rock it controlled, the quality of the rock, the future demand for riprap, the costs of transporting rock, and the relevant extraction technology. The court also noted that the expected income stream from the property must be discounted to present value, and took issue with plaintiff's discount rate. Accordingly, the plaintiffs were entitled to $28,000.

Averett v. Shircliff

Supreme Court of Virginia, 1977.
218 Va. 202.

■ I'ANSON, CHIEF JUSTICE. Plaintiff, James V. Shircliff, instituted this action against the defendant, Henry T. Averett, to recover damages to his automobile, certain personal property in the trunk of the car, and the loss of use of his vehicle as a result of defendant's negligence in the operation of an automobile which collided with plaintiff's vehicle. The defendant admitted liability, and the case was tried by a jury on the issue of damages only. The jury returned a verdict for the plaintiff and awarded $4,000 as damages to the car and $160 for damages to the personal property in the car.

Plaintiff moved the court to set aside the jury's verdict and award him judgment as a matter of law in the amount of $8,059 on the ground that under the Restatement of the Law of Torts, § 928,[1] he "had a right

---

[1] Section 928 of the Restatement of the Law of Torts reads as follows:

"Where a person is entitled to a judgment for harm to chattels not amounting to a total destruction in value, the damages include compensation for

"(a) the difference between the value of the chattel before the harm and the value after the harm or, at the plaintiff's election, the reasonable cost of repair or

to elect" as his measure of damages the difference in the value of the automobile before and after the accident. . . . [The trial judge accepted this argument, set aside the jury's verdict, and entered judgment in the amount of $8,059, representing $7,899 for lost market value of the car and $160 for damages to personal items in the car.]

The question presented is what is the proper measure of damages in the present case. The precise issue has not heretofore been decided by us.

In Norview Cars *v.* Crews, 208 Va. 148, 149–150 (1967), we quoted the general rule[2] with its exception and the Restatement rule. However, we found it unnecessary to adopt either the general rule and the contended for "special circumstances" exception thereto or the Restatement rule, "if there be, indeed, any real difference between the two rules," because of the stipulation plaintiff had entered into in the trial court.

In an annotation entitled "Damages: Injury to Pleasure Vehicles," at 169 A.L.R. 1100 (1947), numerous cases are collected, and the general rule with its exception is stated and applied to variant circumstances. The author of the annotation, in summarizing the principles on the issue, states:

> "Where the automobile is totally destroyed the measure of damages is the market value of the automobile as at the time of destruction.
>
> "Where the automobile is damaged but not completely destroyed the measure of damages is basically the difference between market value at the time of the injury and market value after the injury, which, where the injury is susceptible of repairs, is ordinarily measured by the cost of reasonable repairs necessary to restore the automobile to its original condition . . . together with . . ."

the diminution in value of the injured property after repairs are made. *Id.* at 1100–01.

Most jurisdictions confronted with situations such as exist in the present case have held that where an automobile has been damaged but not totally destroyed and it is reasonably susceptible of repairs, the

---

> restoration where feasible, with due allowance for any difference between the original value and the value after repairs, and
>
> "(b) the loss of use."

2 The general rule was quoted from Riddle *v.* Baltimore & O.R. Co., 137 W.Va. 733, 751 (1952), as follows:

> "In the valuation of personal property, which has been damaged but not destroyed, the measure of damages is the difference between the market value of the property immediately before and immediately after the property was damaged, plus necessary and reasonable expenses incurred by the owner in connection with the injury. . . . An exception to this rule is that where tangible personal property can be restored by repairs and the repairs would be less than the diminution in value because of the injury, the amount recoverable is the reasonable cost of restoring the property to its former condition. . . ."

measure of damages is the cost of repairs and any diminution of the automobile's market value which results from the car having been injured after the repairs; that is, the cost of repairs plus any amount of depreciation in value of the vehicle as repaired.

Instruction 1a granted by the trial court is in accord with the above principles. It reads, in pertinent part, as follows:

> "The Court instructs the jury that in the valuation of personal property, which has been damaged but not destroyed, the measure of damages is the difference between the market value of the property immediately before and immediately after the property was damaged.
>
> "The Court further instructs the jury that an exception to this rule is that where personal property can be restored by repairs and the repairs would be less than the diminution in value because of the injury, the amount recoverable is the reasonable cost of restoring the property to its former condition.
>
> "Thus, if you believe from the preponderance of the evidence that the car involved could not be restored to its former condition by repairs, the measure of damages is the difference between the market value of the car immediately before and immediately after the accident.
>
> "And if you believe from a preponderance of the evidence that the car involved could be restored to its former condition by repairs, the measure of damage is the reasonable cost of repairs, with reasonable allowance for depreciation."

There is little difference between the rule set out in Instruction 1a and the Restatement rule. Both rules are merely evidentiary methods for determining that amount which will reasonably compensate the owner for his actual pecuniary loss sustained as a result of a negligent or wrongful act. The reasonable cost of repairs is one of the evidentiary factors in determining the market value of an automobile after it has been damaged.

The only significant difference in the two rules is that under the Restatement rule a plaintiff has the option of recovering either the difference in the value of the vehicle immediately before and immediately after the accident or the reasonable cost of repairs plus any depreciation in value after repairs. But we think that the jury, not the plaintiff, should make that determination based on the evidence presented. . . .

For the reasons stated, we reverse the judgment, reinstate the verdict of the jury, and enter judgment thereon for the plaintiff in the amount of $4,160. . . .

Burgess v. Shampooch Pet Industries, Inc.

Court of Appeals of Kansas, 2006.
35 Kan. App. 2d 458.

■ BUSER, P.J. . . . On April 10, 2004, Burgess took Murphy [her dog] to Shampooch in Kansas City, Kansas, for pet grooming services. Two days prior, on April 8, 2004, a veterinarian had examined Murphy and determined the dog was in good health. Moreover, Murphy appeared healthy when Burgess left her at Shampooch. Burgess returned later, retrieved the newly groomed Murphy and paid the $30 bill.

Upon leaving Shampooch, Burgess noticed Murphy was acting strangely and was limping. Burgess immediately returned to the business and a representative of Shampooch denied any responsibility for Murphy's injury. The following day, Burgess sought treatment for Murphy at Veterinary Specialty and Emergency Center in Overland Park, Kansas. On April 13, 2004, 3 days after her ill-fated grooming, Murphy underwent surgery to repair a dislocated hip. Veterinary treatment also included x-rays, blood work-up, anesthesia, intravenous fluids, sutures, and pain medications. As a result, Burgess incurred veterinary bills totaling $1,308.89. According to the district court, Burgess testified at trial that Murphy "was back to her usual self within a short time after her treatment."

Burgess filed a [small claims] petition for damages in Wyandotte County District Court alleging negligence by Shampooch caused Murphy's dislocated hip. Following a trial to the court, judgment was entered for Burgess and against Shampooch in the amount of $1,308.89 plus court costs. Shampooch filed a timely appeal.

In its determination of damages the district court ruled that "a pet is different than a motor vehicle or a piece of machinery or other items of personal property in that a pet has no real market value." The district court relied on Kansas Power & Light Co. *v.* Thatcher, 14 Kan. App. 2d 613 (1990), a case involving the destruction of a 35-year-old wooden utility pole, for the legal proposition: "When measuring damages to personal property where the item damaged has no market value, other relevant factors must be considered such as *cost of repair,* the original value, the loss of use, any special value to the owner, the loss of expected profits, and the cost of replacement." (Emphasis added.) With *Thatcher* as precedent, the trial court awarded Burgess the cost of Murphy's repair—$1,308.89 to reimburse Burgess for payment of Murphy's veterinary bills.

Shampooch appeals the district court's decision that a pet does not have a market value. To the contrary, Shampooch contends:

> "People put dollar values—and therefor[e] market values—on their pets all the time. Sometimes it's just 'a good home'; sometimes it's a specific dollar value in a want ad; sometimes people actually have their pets put to sleep because they don't

want to pay the vet bills for curing or fixing some existing damage or injury to the pet, thus putting a value on their pet at least less than vet bills. There are a number of ways to establish market values for pets."

Shampooch contends the damages awarded should be limited to Murphy's market value. This contention is predicated on the general rule that when repairs can restore personal property to its previous condition, the measure of damages is the fair and reasonable cost of repairs not to exceed the value of the property before damage. . . .

In response, Burgess tacitly acknowledges that Murphy may have value but observes:

> "[W]hat is the value of a wet face licking received first thing in the morning? To a 'cat person' it is probably nothing but to a dog owner who has raised her friend from a puppy it is like the Master Card ad—priceless. What is the value of years of companionship, of training, of shared love? To put a value on a family pet all of this must be considered."

Burgess argues in support of the district court's damage award, however, because by

> "allowing her the veterinary bills, the trial court put Burgess back into the position she was in prior to entering Shampooch Pet Grooming. She had a pet who could walk without pain, again. She did not have to find another pet, housebreak it, treat and care for it, feed it, walk it, love it and travel the many thousands of steps involved in a 13 year journey."

. . . There exists in the United States a prevailing view regarding the proper measure of damages in cases involving the injury to or death of pet dogs. As one legal commentator summarized the legal landscape:

> "Companion animals have played a myriad of important roles in their human caregivers' lives since prehistoric times. More than inanimate objects, they provide companionship, affection, solace, and uncritical acceptance of their human guardians. The law, however, has valued them as commodities by restricting recovery for their destruction or injury to their fair market value. The fair market value of ordinary pets, unless they have special qualities as breeding or working animals, is usually close to zero and, as a result, plaintiffs whose pets are destroyed through another's negligent or intentional act are left with minimal damage recoveries." Livingston, The Calculus of Animal Valuation: Crafting a Viable Remedy, 82 Neb. L. Rev. 783, 847 (2004).

Another approach to evaluating damages in cases involving pet dogs is characterized as the "value to the owner" measure of damages . . . .

Several jurisdictions have found that where recovery is sought for a dog's injury . . . , the owner is entitled to recover the reasonable veterinary expenses incurred in treating those injuries. See Kaiser *v.* United States, 761 F. Supp. 150 (D.D.C. 1991) ($1786.50 in veterinary fees awarded pursuant to the Federal Tort Claims Act for injury to dog shot by United States Capitol Police officer); Kurash *v.* Layton, 251 N.J. Super. 412 (1991) ($851 in veterinary fees awarded to owner whose dog sustained injuries when it was impregnated by defendant's trespassing dog) . . . .

[The traditional rule] that the recovery of damages must not "exceed the value of the animal" makes sense in the economic marketplace but is certainly problematic in the case of a pet dog whose value is typically noneconomic. . . .

Consistent with this long-standing common-sense jurisprudence, we find the district court did not err in its award of damages to Burgess. We hold that when an injured pet dog with no discernable market value is restored to its previous health, the measure of damages may include, but is not limited to, the reasonable and customary cost of necessary veterinary care and treatment. . . .

[T]he award of the amount Burgess spent on veterinary bills is in accord with the very purpose of the law of damages—to make Burgess whole and return her to the position she was in prior to Shampooch's tortious conduct. It can hardly be said that a lesser award—for example, Murphy's original purchase price of $175 depreciated over 13 years—would "make good the injury done," or fairly and adequately compensate Burgess for her out-of-pocket expenses.

Finally, Shampooch hyperbolically claims: "To allow this ruling to stand in its current state would open the proverbial 'floodgates' of high dollar litigation on behalf of animals with market value substantially less than the claims." We disagree. Our holding is premised upon the finding that Murphy's veterinary care and treatment were necessary and that the costs were reasonable and customary. We do not address those special cases wherein a pet dog may receive extraordinary veterinary care and treatment or may incur veterinary costs that are unusual or unreasonable. . . .

NOTES ON INJURY TO PETS

1. Many courts continue to limit damages for injury to pets to the market value of the pet. *E.g.*, Soucek *v.* Banham, 524 N.W.2d 478 (1994). The "value to the owner" measure has gained ground but is often quite restricted. For example, in Mitchell *v.* Heinrichs, 27 P.3d 309 (2001), the court said:

> "We agree with those courts that recognize that the actual value of the pet to the owner, rather than the fair market value, is sometimes the proper measure of the pet's value. . . . Where, as here, there may not be any fair market value for an adult dog, the

'value to the owner may be based on such things as the cost of replacement, original cost, and cost to reproduce.' Thus, an owner may seek reasonable replacement costs—including such items as the cost of purchasing a puppy of the same breed, the cost of immunization, the cost of neutering the pet, and the cost of comparable training. Or an owner may seek to recover the original cost of the dog, including the purchase price and, again, such investments as immunization, neutering, and training. Moreover, as some courts have recognized, it may be appropriate to consider the breeding potential of the animal, and whether the dog was purchased for the purpose of breeding with other purebreds and selling the puppies. But while these damages may more accurately reflect the animal's actual value to the owner, Mitchell may not recover damages for her dog's sentimental value as a component of actual value to her as the dog's owner."

Id. at 313–14.

2. Claims for emotional distress and loss of consortium in connection with injury to a pet have not fared well. For example, in Kondaurov *v.* Kerdasha, 271 Va. 646 (2006), the plaintiff, who suffered from multiple sclerosis, anxiety, and depression, had acquired a dog, Sushi, "to help her maintain emotional stability and prevent or moderate her 'stress attacks.' . . . A witness testified that the plaintiff and Sushi 'were inseparable. . . . Sushi was Eve's very best friend in the world. . . . [T]he most unconditional source of love in Eve's life, period.' " When the defendant negligently hit the plaintiff's car, Sushi's tail was injured, leading to a partial amputation. The court recited that:

> "Several witnesses stated that the dog suffered such a shock as a result of the accident that she would cower under a bed or hide in a closet when she heard a siren outside. They added that the plaintiff had become distraught because of the dog's condition and would have to go under the bed or into the closet and stay there with the dog to comfort her. The plaintiff's psychiatrist testified as an expert witness that the plaintiff was 'devastated by what happened emotionally and by what happened to her dog.' His opinion was that the effects of the accident had made the plaintiff's underlying depression and anxiety disorder more difficult to treat and had created an 'almost catastrophic downhill ride for her,' leaving her subject to 'feelings of fear, feelings of danger, feelings of terror, cinematic tension, tremor, motor tics.' "

Id. at 652–53.

Discussing the plaintiff's claims for emotional distress, the court said:

> "[T]he plaintiff was clearly entitled to be compensated in damages for any emotional distress she suffered as a consequence of the physical impact she sustained in the accident. Such distress might include shock and fright at being struck three times, turned over, left hanging upside down in her seatbelt and experiencing physical pain. It might also include anxiety as to the extent of her

injuries, worry as to her future well-being, her ability to lead a normal life and to earn a living. It might include fear of disability, deformity, or death. . . .

"Injury to, or loss of, a plaintiff's personal property, as a result of a defendant's negligence, stands upon a different footing. Damages for such losses are confined to the diminution in the value of the property resulting from the accident, plus reasonable and necessary expenses incurred.

"It is beyond debate that animals, particularly dogs and cats, when kept as pets and companions, occupy a position in human affections far removed from livestock. Especially in the case of owners who are disabled, aged or lonely, an emotional bond may exist with a pet resembling that between parent and child, and the loss of such an animal may give rise to grief approaching that attending the loss of a family member. The fact remains, however, that the law in Virginia, as in most states that have decided the question, regards animals, however beloved, as personal property . . . . Our decisions have never approved an award of damages for emotional distress resulting from negligently inflicted injury to personal property. . . . We conclude that permitting such an award would amount to a sweeping change in the law of damages, a subject properly left to legislative consideration."

Id. at 656–58.

Matter of Rothko

Court of Appeals of New York, 1977.
43 N.Y.2d 305.

■ COOKE, JUDGE. Mark Rothko, an abstract expressionist painter whose works through the years gained for him an international reputation of greatness, died testate on February 25, 1970. The principal asset of his estate consisted of 798 paintings of tremendous value, and the dispute underlying this appeal involves the conduct of his three executors in their disposition of these works of art. In sum, that conduct as portrayed in the record and sketched in the opinions was manifestly wrongful and indeed shocking.

Rothko's will was admitted to probate on April 27, 1970 and letters testamentary were issued to Bernard J. Reis, Theodoros Stamos and Morton Levine. Hastily and within a period of only about three weeks and by virtue of two contracts each dated May 21, 1970, the executors dealt with all 798 paintings.

By a contract of sale, the estate executors agreed to sell to Marlborough A.G., a Liechtenstein corporation (hereinafter MAG), 100 Rothko paintings as listed for $1,800,000, $200,000 to be paid on execution of the agreement and the balance of $1,600,000 in 12 equal interest-free installments over a 12-year period. Under the second agreement, the executors consigned to Marlborough Gallery, Inc., a domestic corporation (hereinafter MNY), "approximately 700 paintings listed on a Schedule to be prepared," the consignee to be responsible for costs covering items such as insurance, storage, restoration and promotion. By its provisos, MNY could sell up to 35 paintings a year from each of two groups, pre-1947 and post-1947, for 12 years at the best price obtainable but not less than the appraised estate value, and it would receive a 50% commission on each painting sold, except for a commission of 40% on those sold to or through other dealers.

[Two of the three executors had obvious conflicts of interest in entering these contracts. Reis was a director and officer of MNY. Stamos was a "not too successful" artist who, shortly after his appointment as an executor of the Rothko estate, contracted with MNY for sale of his own paintings. Levine had no personal interest in the MNY-MAG contracts but knew of the other executors' conflicting interests. Prior to trial, a number of the paintings were sold.]

Petitioner Kate Rothko, decedent's daughter and a person entitled to share in his estate by virtue of an election under EPTL 5–3.3, instituted this proceeding to remove the executors, to enjoin MNY and MAG from disposing of the paintings, to rescind the aforesaid agreements between the executors and said corporations, for a return of the paintings still in possession of those corporations, and for damages. . . .

[The trial court awarded damages against Levine for the value of the paintings sold by MNY and MAG at the time of sale, $6,464,880, minus proceeds paid by MNY and MAG to the estate, about $1,500,000. The court held Reis and Stamos jointly and severally liable for the same amount plus an additional $2,787,120, representing the increase in the value of the paintings between the date of sale and the date of the decree, as found by the court.]

The measure of damages was the issue that divided the Appellate Division. The contention of Reis, Stamos, MNY and MAG, that the award of appreciation damages was legally erroneous and impermissible, is based on a principle that an executor authorized to sell is not liable for an increase in value if the breach consists only in selling for a figure less than that for which the executor should have sold. For example, Scott states:

> "The beneficiaries are not entitled to the value of the property at the time of the decree if it was not the duty of the trustee to retain the property in the trust and the breach of trust consisted *merely* in selling the property for too low a price" (3 Scott, TRUSTS [3d ed.], § 208.3, p. 1687 [emphasis added]).
>
> "If the trustee is guilty of a breach of trust in selling trust property for an inadequate price, he is liable for the difference between the amount he should have received and the amount which he did receive. He is not liable, however, for any

subsequent rise in value of the property sold." (*Id.*, § 208.6, pp. 1689–1690.)

A recitation of similar import appears in Comment *d* under Restatement, Trusts 2d (§ 205): "*d.* Sale for less than value. If the trustee is authorized to sell trust property, but in breach of trust he sells it for less than he should receive, he is liable for the value of the property at the time of the sale less the amount which he received. If the breach of trust consists *only* in selling it for too little, he is not chargeable with the amount of any subsequent increase in value of the property under the rule stated in Clause (c), as he would be if he were not authorized to sell the property. See § 208." (Emphasis added.) However, employment of "merely" and "only" as limiting words suggests that where the breach consists of some misfeasance, other than solely for selling "for too low a price" or "for too little," appreciation damages may be appropriate. Under Scott and the Restatement, the trustee may be held liable for appreciation damages if it was his or her duty to retain the property, the theory being that the beneficiaries are entitled to be placed in the same position they would have been in had the breach not consisted of a sale of property that should have been retained. The same rule should apply where the breach of trust consists of a serious conflict of interest—which is more than merely selling for too little.

The reason for allowing appreciation damages, where there is a duty to retain, and only date of sale damages, where there is authorization to sell, is policy oriented. If a trustee authorized to sell were subjected to a greater measure of damages he might be reluctant to sell (in which event he might run a risk if depreciation ensued). On the other hand, if there is a duty to retain and the trustee sells there is no policy reason to protect the trustee; he has not simply acted imprudently, he has violated an integral condition of the trust.

"If a trustee in breach of trust transfers trust property to a person who takes with notice of the breach of trust, and the transferee has disposed of the property . . . [i]t seems proper to charge him with the value at the time of the decree, since if it had not been for the breach of trust the property would still have been a part of the trust estate" (4 Scott, TRUSTS [3d ed.], § 291.2). This rule of law which applies to the transferees MNY and MAG also supports the imposition of appreciation damages against Reis and Stamos, since if the Marlborough corporations are liable for such damages either as purchaser or consignees with notice, from one in breach of trust, it is only logical to hold that said executors, as sellers and consignors, are liable also *pro tanto*.

Contrary to assertions of appellants and the dissenters at the Appellate Division, Menzel *v.* List, 24 N.Y.2d 91 (1969), is authority for the allowance of appreciation damages. There, the damages involved a breach of warranty of title to a painting which at one time had been stolen from plaintiff and her husband and ultimately sold to defendant. Here, the executors, though authorized to sell, did not merely err in the amount they accepted but sold to one with whom Reis and Stamos had a self-interest. To make the injured party whole, in both instances the quantum of damages should be the same. In other words, since the paintings cannot be returned, the estate is therefore entitled to their value at the time of the decree, *i.e.*, appreciation damages. These are not punitive damages in a true sense, rather they are damages intended to make the estate whole. Of course, as to Reis, Stamos, MNY and MAG, these damages might be considered by some to be exemplary in a sense, in that they serve as a warning to others, but their true character is ascertained when viewed in the light of overriding policy considerations and in the realization that the sale and consignment were not merely sales below value but inherently wrongful transfers which should allow the owner to be made whole. . . .

NOTE ON PROPERTY THAT FLUCTUATES IN VALUE

In Broadwater *v.* Old Republic Surety, 854 P.2d 527 (Utah 1993) the plaintiff purchased stock in a venture, which was never effectively transferred on the issuer's books. After a series of efforts to rectify the problem, the plaintiff sued the issuer and a transfer agent for conversion of the stock. Between the date when the issuer first refused to complete the transfer and the date of trial, the value of the stock rose significantly, then fell. The court said:

> "As a general rule, the measure of damages for the conversion of property is the value of the property at the time of the conversion, plus interest. That remedy is inadequate, however, when the property converted, such as stock, fluctuates in value. The injury to the owner of converted stocks is not merely in the loss of control over the stock, 'but in the sale of it at an unfavorable time, and for an unfavorable price.'
>
> "Recognizing the unfairness of the general rule as applied to the conversion of stock and other property with fluctuating values, the courts at common law held that the proper measure of damages should be the highest value of the property between the date of conversion and the date of trial. That measure proved unsatisfactory because it allowed a plaintiff to ride the stock market at the defendant's risk and expense until trial, which might not take place until years after the conversion.
>
> "In the late nineteenth century, the New York Court of Appeals adopted what has become known as the New York rule, which sets the measure of damages as the highest intermediate value of the stock between the time of conversion and a reasonable time after the owner receives notice of the conversion. The New York rule indemnifies the owner of the converted stock for his or her loss, while requiring the owner to mitigate damages by replacing the stock within a reasonable time after notice of the conversion. The rule affords the owner of the stock a reasonable opportunity to consult counsel, employ other brokers, watch the

> market to determine when it would be advisable to purchase replacement stock, and raise funds should the owner decide to repurchase.
>
> "In our view, the New York rule continues to provide the fairest measure of damages to all involved. The rule indemnifies a plaintiff for the conversion of stock without affording a windfall at the expense of the defendant, who, more often than not, committed the conversion due to honest mistake or inadvertence.
>
> "What constitutes a reasonable time varies with the particular facts and circumstances of each case. Depending upon the individual circumstances, courts have held that anywhere from a few days to several months, or even years, may be reasonable. . . .
>
> "We believe that under the circumstances of this case, it was not error for the trial court to conclude that plaintiff was reasonable in delaying the mitigation of her damages for more than ninety days."

Id. at 531–32.

Varjabedian v. City of Madera

Supreme Court of California, 1977.
20 Cal.3d 285.

■ MOSK, JUSTICE. Defendant City of Madera appeals from a judgment awarding plaintiffs approximately $73,000 for damages caused by the city's operation of a sewage treatment plant near plaintiffs' property. Recovery was on a nuisance theory. Plaintiffs cross-appeal from a judgment on the pleadings for defendant on plaintiffs' cause of action in inverse condemnation. . . .

Plaintiffs Michael and Judith Ann Varjabedian acquired a vineyard of approximately 80 acres in Madera County, and in 1971 moved onto the property with their three children. In 1972 defendant city began operation of a new waste water treatment plant on land located some 600 feet from plaintiffs' residence. The plant emits odors which are blown onto plaintiffs' property by the prevailing winds.

The Varjabedians noticed septic smells on their property as soon as sewage was delivered to the new plant in June 1972. There followed a lengthy period during which they repeatedly complained of the odors to city officials and were told that corrective efforts were being made and assured that the plant would eventually be odor-free. On advice of counsel, Michael Varjabedian began to keep a log of the occurrence and intensity of the smells, and of his attempts to persuade the city to remedy the situation. Finally, in July 1973 the instant lawsuit was filed against the city by all five family members.

In their complaint, plaintiffs set forth four theories of recovery: negligence in the design, construction and operation of the plant; maintenance of a nuisance; maintenance of a dangerous and defective condition; and inverse condemnation. When the case came to trial in June 1974, plaintiffs voluntarily dismissed the causes of action for negligence and maintenance of a defective condition. The remaining two counts were the object of defendant's motion for judgment on the pleadings. The trial judge granted the motion as to the inverse condemnation theory, stating his belief that recovery on that cause required "physical damage to the property."

As to the nuisance cause of action the motion was denied, and the case went to trial on that theory. Plaintiffs sought recovery for permanent diminution in the value of their property caused by the nuisance, as well as compensation for personal discomfort. They further sought special damages for the anticipated loss of a Cal-Vet loan which financed the purchase of the bulk of the vineyard. In support of this claim, plaintiffs contended they would be compelled to move off the property and would therefore forfeit their loan under Military and Veterans Code section 987.2. Damages were requested to cover the cost of refinancing the land purchase at a higher rate.

The jury returned a verdict for plaintiffs awarding damages as follows: $32,000 to the Varjabedians for the loss in value of their real property; $30,000 special damages for loss of the Cal-Vet loan; and $11,000 other damages distributed among the five named plaintiffs.

Defendant relies upon alleged error in the instructions to the jury regarding the measure of property damage for which the city could be liable in nuisance. The challenged instruction read: "In determining the compensation, if any, to be awarded Plaintiffs for damage to their property proximately caused by a permanent nuisance, in addition to other damage as to which I have instructed you or will instruct you, they are entitled to recover the difference, if any, in the present fair market value of the property as the same would have been without the construction of the sewage treatment plant by the City of Madera, and the present fair market value after said plant was constructed and put into operation." . . .

Defendant argues, however, that the instruction . . . allowed the jury to consider effects of the sewage plant on the market value of the Varjabedians' property caused by aspects of the plant other than its production of odors. It is true that under the instruction, which simply calls for a comparison of the market value of the Varjabedians' land before and after the construction of the plant, the jury could have considered decreases in market value provoked by such considerations as the unappealing aesthetic qualities of the sewer plant or anxiety caused by mere knowledge of its proximity. Undoubtedly, not all of such factors fall within the definition of nuisance; in those respects, therefore, the instruction failed to satisfy the requirements of the law of nuisance . . . .

We decline to speculate, however, on which of the potentially depressive effects of sewer plant construction on property values—other than odors—constitute nuisances, or if nuisances, which are expressly authorized, because of our belief that any error in the instruction in this case was not prejudicial to defendant. There was no evidence of negative impact on plaintiffs' property value, to which the jury was exposed, which did not relate directly to the odors. The only testimony regarding the nonolfactory impact of the sewer plant was that of defendant's expert, one Freeman, who estimated that in the absence of constant foul odors there was no depreciation of the farmland. The testimony of plaintiff's expert, one Salaberry, that the sewage plant had caused a depreciation of $56,000 was based solely on the existence of the smells. Indeed, the court kept Salaberry's written report from the jury because it contained language which might have misled the jury into estimating damages before and after the construction of the plant rather than before and after the emission of odors. And although the challenged instruction gave some sanction to the jury's consideration of precisely the same erroneous comparison, this tendency was minimized by other instructions which tied damages to those proximately caused by a permanent nuisance. In the light of the evidence and the totality of the court's instructions, the potential for prejudice contained in the erroneous instruction on damages was minimal. . . .

Defendant next asserts that plaintiffs' recovery for the anticipated loss of their Cal-Vet loan was speculative and therefore improper (Civ. Code, § 3283). The trial court treated the certainty of the future loss of the loan as a question of fact for the jury, and instructed as follows: "If, under the evidence you should find that there is a permanent nuisance, and if you further find that it is reasonably certain that plaintiffs Michael C. and Judith Ann Varjabedian will by reason thereof move from their property, then you may consider any damages that it is reasonably certain they will suffer from the loss of their Cal-Vet loan." The submission of the issue to the jury as a question of fact was proper, and the instruction requirement of "reasonable certainty" satisfied Civil Code section 3283. . . .

The total amount of damages awarded for loss of the loan was adequately supported by testimony of plaintiff's expert, a banker, that this was the present value of the additional obligations the Varjabedians would incur if forced to refinance their farm. We do not find the amount excessive. . . .

We turn now to plaintiffs' appeal from the judgment on the pleadings entered against their claim in inverse condemnation. Despite plaintiffs' successful nuisance recovery, we cannot say on the basis of the record before us that the challenged ruling, if erroneous, was necessarily harmless. We therefore reach the issue whether the court erred in denying plaintiffs' claim in inverse condemnation. . . .

[T]he California Constitution requires that "just compensation" be paid when "private property" is "taken or damaged for public use." In this case, the trial judge gave as his reason for denying compensation under this provision plaintiffs' failure to allege "physical damage to the property" or a "trespass." Defendant urges no other grounds in support of the judgment, and we consider none.

In assessing whether plaintiffs' allegations may serve as a basis for inverse liability, we note that physical damage to property is not invariably a prerequisite to compensation. Rather, the determination of the scope of the just compensation clause rests on its construction "as a matter of interpretation and policy." The contending policies which guide that construction have often been described as follows: "on the one hand the policy underlying the eminent domain provision in the Constitution is to distribute throughout the community the loss inflicted upon the individual by the making of the public improvements. . . . On the other hand, fears have been expressed that compensation allowed too liberally will seriously impede, if not stop, beneficial public improvements because of the greatly increased cost."

Several factors present militate in favor of a distribution throughout the relevant community of the type of loss involved here. Plaintiffs' claim stems from the recurring violation of their property by a gaseous effluent. As such, the injury is not far removed from those core cases of direct physical invasion which indisputably require compensation. Thus, damage from invasions of water or other liquid effluents often provides the basis for inverse liability. Moreover, plaintiffs' complaint which includes, inter alia, the claim that their land was made "untenantable for residential purposes" is clearly sufficient to depict a permanent and "substantial impairment" in their use of the land.

At the same time, fears that "compensation . . . will seriously impede, if not stop" the beneficial construction of sewage treatment plants might be realized if courts were to award compensation for every objectionable odor, however insubstantial or widely dispersed, produced by such facilities. But the problem of reconciling this consideration with the competing policy of loss-distribution is not presented in its most difficult form by the appeal of the present judgment, since it appears from the Varjabedians' allegations that their property may have been peculiarly burdened by the odors so as to bring the case within the doctrine of Richards *v.* Washington Terminal Co., 233 U.S. 546 (1914). In *Richards* the plaintiff complained of "inconvenience . . . in the occupation of his property" caused by "gases and smoke" emanating from a nearby railroad. The United States Supreme Court ruled that under the "taking" clause of the Fifth Amendment to the federal Constitution, the plaintiff could not recover for "those consequential damages that are necessarily incident to proximity to the railroad . . . ." Yet the landowner was entitled to compensation for "gases and smoke emitted from locomotive engines while in [a] tunnel, and forced out of it by means of [a] fanning system through a portal located so near to plaintiff's property that these gases and smoke materially contribute to injure the furniture and to render the house less habitable than otherwise . . . ." Construing federal statutes immunizing the railroad from nuisance liability "in light of the Fifth

Amendment" the court concluded "they do not authorize the imposition of so direct and peculiar and substantial a burden upon plaintiff's property without compensation to him."

Of course, *Richards* may be distinguished from this case with respect to the nature of the public facility involved, or on the ground that there is no device here which directs the noxious gases onto plaintiffs' property. However, such factual differences do not render the underlying principle of *Richards* inapplicable to the problem at hand, particularly when it is considered together with the California Constitution, which protects a somewhat broader range of property values from government destruction than does the analogous federal provision. If a plaintiff can establish that his property has suffered a "direct and peculiar and substantial" burden as a result of recurring odors produced by a sewage facility—that he has, as in *Richards,* been in effect "singled out" to suffer the detrimental environmental effects of the enterprise—then the policy favoring distribution of the resulting loss of market value is strong and the likelihood that compensation will impede necessary public construction is relatively slight. In these circumstances, the necessity of breathing noxious sewage fumes may be a burden unfairly and unconstitutionally imposed on the individual landowner.

Here plaintiffs allege their farm was directly in the path of the odors as they were blown from defendant's facility by the prevailing winds. Plaintiffs should have been given the opportunity—through amendment of their pleadings if necessary—to demonstrate that the burden on their farm was sufficiently direct, substantial, and peculiar to come within the principle of *Richards,* as applied above. On that showing the Varjabedians can base a claim in inverse condemnation. It follows that the trial court's judgment on that count must be reversed. . . .

NOTE

Homeowners sued an airport authority for nuisance in the form of noise, exhaust, and vibrations. The defendant argued that the nuisance was permanent and the statute of limitations on claims of permanent nuisance had run. The California Supreme Court noted that air traffic conducted in compliance with federal regulations could not be enjoined. However:

> "It does not follow . . . that simply because commercial flights operated in compliance with federal law may not be enjoined, the nuisance at issue is a permanent one. . . .
>
> "Two distinct classifications have emerged in nuisance law which determine the remedies available to injured parties and the applicable statute of limitations. On the one hand, permanent nuisances are of a type where 'by one act a permanent injury is done, [and] damages are assessed once for all.' The cases finding the nuisance complained of to be unquestionably permanent in nature have involved solid structures, such as a building encroaching upon the plaintiff's land, a steam railroad operating

over plaintiff's land, or regrade of a street for a rail system. In such cases, plaintiffs ordinarily are required to bring one action for all past, present and future damage within three years after the permanent nuisance is erected. . . .

"On the other hand, if a nuisance is a use which may be discontinued at any time, it is considered continuing in character and persons harmed by it may bring successive actions for damages until the nuisance is abated. Recovery is limited, however, to actual injury suffered prior to commencement of each action. Prospective damages are unavailable.

"The classic example of a continuing nuisance is an ongoing or repeated disturbance, such as the one before us today, caused by noise, vibration or foul odor. Indeed, even more substantial physical invasions of land have been held to be continuing in character. . . . [T]he distinction to be drawn is between encroachments of a permanent nature erected upon one's lands, and a complaint made, not of the location of the offending structures, but of the continuing use of such structures. The former are permanent, the latter is not.

"In case of doubt as to the permanency of the injury the plaintiff may elect whether to treat a particular nuisance as permanent or continuing. . . . As the United States Supreme Court noted in [United States *v.* Dickinson, 331 U.S. 745, 749 (1946)] '[i]f suit must be brought, lest he jeopardize his rights, as soon as his land is invaded, other contingencies would be running against him—for instance, the uncertainty of the damage and the risk of res judicata against recovering later for damage as yet uncertain. . . .' "

Baker *v.* Burbank-Glendale-Pasadena Airport Authority, 39 Cal.3d 862, 868–870 (1985).

B. LOST BARGAIN

1. MEASURES OF DAMAGES FOR BREACH OF CONTRACT

Sullivan v. O'Connor

Supreme Judicial Court of Massachusetts, 1973.
363 Mass. 579.

■ KAPLAN, JUSTICE. The plaintiff patient secured a jury verdict of $13,500 against the defendant surgeon for breach of contract in respect to an operation upon the plaintiff's nose. . . .

[T]he plaintiff alleged that she, as patient, entered into a contract with the defendant, a surgeon, wherein the defendant promised to perform plastic surgery on her nose and thereby to enhance her beauty and improve her appearance; that he performed the surgery but failed to achieve the promised result; rather the result of the surgery was to disfigure and deform her nose, to cause her pain in body and mind, and to subject her to other damage and expense. . . .

The jury returned a verdict for the plaintiff on the contract count, and for the defendant on the negligence count. . . .

The plaintiff was a professional entertainer, and this was known to the defendant. The agreement was as alleged in the declaration. More particularly, judging from exhibits, the plaintiff's nose had been straight, but long and prominent; the defendant undertook by two operations to reduce its prominence and somewhat to shorten it, thus making it more pleasing in relation to the plaintiff's other features. Actually the plaintiff was obliged to undergo three operations, and her appearance was worsened. Her nose now had a concave line to about the midpoint, at which it became bulbous; viewed frontally, the nose from bridge to midpoint was flattened and broadened, and the two sides of the tip had lost symmetry. This configuration evidently could not be improved by further surgery. The plaintiff did not demonstrate, however, that her change of appearance had resulted in loss of employment. . . .

The judge instructed the jury, first, that the plaintiff was entitled to recover her out-of-pocket expenses incident to the operations. Second, she could recover the damages flowing directly, naturally, proximately, and foreseeably from the defendant's breach of promise. These would comprehend damages for any disfigurement of the plaintiff's nose—that is, any change of appearance for the worse—including the effects of the consciousness of such disfigurement on the plaintiff's mind, and in this connection the jury should consider the nature of the plaintiff's profession. Also consequent upon the defendant's breach, and compensable, were the pain and suffering involved in the third operation, but not in the first two. . . .

The plaintiff . . . excepted to the judge's refusal of a request to charge that the plaintiff could recover the difference in value between the nose as promised and the nose as it appeared after the operations. However, the plaintiff in her brief expressly waives this exception. . . .

It has been suggested on occasion that agreements between patients and physicians by which the physician undertakes to effect a cure or to bring about a given result should be declared unenforceable on grounds of public policy. But there are many decisions recognizing and enforcing such contracts, and the law of Massachusetts has treated them as valid, although we have had no decision meeting head on the contention that they should be denied legal sanction. These causes of action are, however, considered a little suspect, and thus we find courts straining sometimes to read the pleadings as sounding only in tort for negligence, and not in contract for breach of promise, despite sedulous efforts by the pleaders to pursue the latter theory. . . .

If an action on the basis of contract is allowed, we have next the question of the measure of damages to be applied where liability is found.

Some cases have taken the simple view that the promise by the physician is to be treated like an ordinary commercial promise, and accordingly that the successful plaintiff is entitled to a standard measure of recovery for breach of contract—"compensatory" ("expectancy") damages, an amount intended to put the plaintiff in the position he would be in if the contract had been performed, or, presumably, at the plaintiff's election, "restitution" damages, an amount corresponding to any benefit conferred by the plaintiff upon the defendant in the performance of the contract disrupted by the defendant's breach. Thus in Hawkins *v.* McGee, 84 N.H. 114, the defendant doctor was taken to have promised the plaintiff to convert his damaged hand by means of an operation into a good or perfect hand, but the doctor so operated as to damage the hand still further. The court, following the usual expectancy formula, would have asked the jury to estimate and award to the plaintiff the difference between the value of a good or perfect hand, as promised, and the value of the hand after the operation. (The same formula would apply, although the dollar result would be less, if the operation had neither worsened nor improved the condition of the hand.) If the plaintiff had not yet paid the doctor his fee, that amount would be deducted from the recovery. There could be no recovery for the pain and suffering of the operation, since that detriment would have been incurred even if the operation had been successful; one can say that this detriment was not "caused" by the breach. But where the plaintiff by reason of the operation was put to more pain than he would have had to endure, had the doctor performed as promised, he should be compensated for that difference as a proper part of his expectancy recovery. . . .

Other cases, including a number in New York, without distinctly repudiating the *Hawkins* type of analysis, have indicated that a different and generally more lenient measure of damages is to be applied in patient-physician actions based on breach of alleged special agreements to effect a cure, attain a stated result, or employ a given medical method. This measure is expressed in somewhat variant ways, but the substance is that the plaintiff is to recover any expenditures made by him and for other detriment (usually not specifically described in the opinions) following proximately and foreseeably upon the defendant's failure to carry out his promise. This, be it noted, is not a "restitution" measure, for it is not limited to restoration of the benefit conferred on the defendant (the fee paid) but includes other expenditures, for example, amounts paid for medicine and nurses; so also it would seem according to its logic to take in damages for any worsening of the plaintiff's condition due to the breach. Nor is it an "expectancy" measure, for it does not appear to contemplate recovery of the whole difference in value between the condition as promised and the condition actually resulting from the treatment. Rather the tendency of the formulation is to put the plaintiff back in the position he occupied just before the parties entered upon the agreement, to compensate him for the detriments he suffered in reliance upon the agreement. This kind of intermediate pattern of recovery for breach of contract is discussed in the suggestive article by Fuller and Perdue, The Reliance Interest in Contract Damages, 46 Yale L.J. 52, 373, where the authors show that, although not attaining the currency of the standard measures, a "reliance" measure has for special reasons been applied by the courts in a variety of settings, including noncommercial settings.

For breach of the patient-physician agreements under consideration, a recovery limited to restitution seems plainly too meager, if the agreements are to be enforced at all. On the other hand, an expectancy recovery may well be excessive.... Where ... the doctor has been absolved of negligence by the trier, an expectancy measure may be thought harsh. We should recall here that the fee paid by the patient to the doctor for the alleged promise would usually be quite disproportionate to the putative expectation recovery. To attempt, moreover, to put a value on the condition that would or might have resulted, had the treatment succeeded as promised, may sometimes put an exceptional strain on the imagination of the fact finder....

There is much to be said, then, for applying a reliance measure to the present facts, and we have only to add that our cases are not unreceptive to the use of that formula in special situations. We have, however, had no previous occasion to apply it to patient-physician cases.[5]

The question of recovery on a reliance basis for pain and suffering or mental distress requires further attention. We find expressions in the decisions that pain and suffering (or the like) are simply not compensable in actions for breach of contract. The defendant seemingly espouses this proposition in the present case. True, if the buyer under a contract for the purchase of a lot of merchandise, in suing for the seller's breach, should claim damages for mental anguish caused by his disappointment in the transaction, he would not succeed; he would be told, perhaps, that the asserted psychological injury was not fairly foreseeable by the defendant as a probable consequence of the breach of such a business

[5] In Mt. Pleasant Stable Co. *v.* Steinberg, 238 Mass. 567, the plaintiff company agreed to supply teams of horses at agreed rates as required from day to day by the defendant for his business. To prepare itself to fulfill the contract and in reliance on it, the plaintiff bought two "Cliest" horses at a certain price. When the defendant repudiated the contract, the plaintiff sold the horses at a loss and in its action for breach claimed the loss as an element of damages. The court properly held that the plaintiff was not entitled to this item as it was also claiming (and recovering) its lost profits (expectancy) on the contract as a whole. (The loss on sale of the horses is analogous to the pain and suffering for which the patient would be disallowed a recovery in Hawkins *v.* McGee, 84 N.H. 114, because he was claiming and recovering expectancy damages.) The court in the *Mt. Pleasant* case referred, however, to Pond *v.* Harris, 113 Mass. 114, as a contrasting situation where the expectancy could not be fairly determined. There the defendant had wrongfully revoked an agreement to arbitrate a dispute with the plaintiff (this was before such agreements were made specifically enforceable). In an action for the breach, the plaintiff was held entitled to recover for his preparations for the arbitration which had been rendered useless and a waste, including the plaintiff's time and trouble and his expenditures for counsel and witnesses. The context apparently was commercial but reliance elements were held compensable when there was no fair way of estimating an expectancy. A noncommercial example is Smith *v.* Sherman, 4 Cush. 408, 413–414, suggesting that a conventional recovery for breach of promise of marriage included a recompense for various efforts and expenditures by the plaintiff preparatory to the promised wedding.

contract. But there is no general rule barring such items of damage in actions for breach of contract. It is all a question of the subject matter and background of the contract, and when the contract calls for an operation on the person of the plaintiff, psychological as well as physical injury may be expected to figure somewhere in the recovery, depending on the particular circumstances. . . . Again, it is said in a few of the New York cases, concerned with the classification of actions for statute of limitations purposes, that the absence of allegations demanding recovery for pain and suffering is characteristic of a contract claim by a patient against a physician, that such allegations rather belong in a claim for malpractice. These remarks seem unduly sweeping. Suffering or distress resulting from the breach going beyond that which was envisaged by the treatment as agreed, should be compensable on the same ground as the worsening of the patient's condition because of the breach. Indeed it can be argued that the very suffering or distress "contracted for"—that which would have been incurred if the treatment achieved the promised result—should also be compensable on the theory underlying the New York cases. For that suffering is "wasted" if the treatment fails. Otherwise stated, compensation for this waste is arguably required in order to complete the restoration of the status quo ante.[6]

In the light of the foregoing discussion, all the defendant's exceptions fail: the plaintiff was not confined to the recovery of her out-of-pocket expenditures; she was entitled to recover also for the worsening of her condition, and for the pain and suffering and mental distress involved in the third operation. These items were compensable on either an expectancy or a reliance view. We might have been required to elect between the two views if the pain and suffering connected with the first two operations contemplated by the agreement, or the whole difference in value between the present and the promised conditions, were being claimed as elements of damage. But the plaintiff waives her possible claim to the former element, and to so much of the latter as represents the difference in value between the promised condition and the condition before the operations. . . .

Glendale Federal Bank, FSB v. United States

United States Court of Appeals, Federal Circuit, 2001.
239 F.3d 1374.

■ PLAGER, SENIOR CIRCUIT JUDGE. The issue in this case is how to measure the damages sustained by savings and loan institutions as a result of the breach by the United States of contracts it made with these

---

[6] Recovery on a reliance basis for breach of the physician's promise tends to equate with the usual recovery for malpractice, since the latter also looks in general to restoration of the condition before the injury. But this is not paradoxical, especially when it is noted that the origins of contract lie in tort. A few cases have considered possible recovery for breach by a physician of a promise to sterilize a patient, resulting in birth of a child to the patient and spouse. If such an action is held maintainable, the reliance and expectancy measures would, we think, tend to equate, because the promised condition was preservation of the family status quo.

organizations during the savings and loan crisis of the late 1970s and early 1980s. In Winstar Corp. *v.* United States, 64 F.3d 1531 (Fed. Cir. 1995), this court upheld the judgment of the Court of Federal Claims holding the United States liable for breach of contract as a consequence of the enactment of the Financial Institutions Recovery, Reform and Enforcement Act. The judgment of this court was affirmed by the Supreme Court and the matter was remanded to the Court of Federal Claims for a trial on damages.

The trial in this case, the first of more than 120 *Winstar*-related cases, ultimately took more than 150 days conducted over a period of fourteen months, and produced more than 20,000 pages of trial transcript. The trial court made a conscious decision that the trial in this case would serve to air and test many of the models and theories at issue in most of the other cases. We have the benefit of a carefully reasoned and extensive opinion from the trial judge. . . .

On April 12, 1999, the trial court entered a judgment awarding plaintiff Glendale Federal Bank, FSB ("Glendale") $908,948,000 in restitution and non-overlapping reliance damages for the breach of contract . . . .

The Federal Savings and Loan Insurance Corporation ("FSLIC") was established by Congress to insure the deposits of savings and loan institutions (also known as "S & Ls" or "thrifts"), and the Federal Home Loan Bank Board ("FHLBB") was established to safeguard the soundness of those institutions. Pursuant to this regulatory scheme, thrifts that desired to provide depositors with the insurance guaranteed under the program were required to maintain a certain level of capital.

Interest rates soared during the late 1970s and early 1980s, causing the savings and loan industry serious economic problems. At that time, thrifts' liabilities were principally short-term deposits, while their assets were primarily long-term fixed-rate mortgages. When interest rates soared, the value of the long-term fixed-rate assets plummeted, and the thrifts had to pay higher rates on their liabilities. As a result, many thrifts experienced difficulty remaining solvent and many became insolvent.

The Government's insurance fund lacked sufficient funds to liquidate even a small percentage of the thrifts that became insolvent. Consequently, the FSLIC and the FHLBB began to consider proposals for outside investors and thrifts to acquire other thrifts through mergers to prevent an exhaustion of the insurance fund.

[To encourage solvent thrifts to acquire insolvent thrifts, the government permitted the acquirers to engage in an accounting maneuver in which a sum corresponding to the negative net worth of the acquired thrift was entered on the acquirer's books as an intangible asset known as "supervisory goodwill." The entry for supervisory good will reflected an assumption that eventually, mortgage loans owned by the acquired thrift would be paid off and interest rates on deposits would return to normal. In this way, the acquirers could meet federal capital requirements for savings and loans and remain technically solvent.]

In 1981, the Government and Glendale, an S & L institution primarily doing business in California, entered into negotiations concerning Glendale's possible acquisition of First Federal Savings and Loan Association of Broward County, Florida ("Broward"). The FHLBB found that Broward's financial condition was deteriorating and projected that Broward's regulatory capital would fall to zero by June 1982. Although Glendale was also losing money, the federal regulators determined that Glendale was nevertheless a financially strong institution, had no material management problems, and had the strength to absorb Broward and remain viable for some years.

In November 1981, the FHLBB approved Glendale's acquisition of Broward in a voluntary merger, and the Government and Glendale entered into a contract memorializing the arrangement. At the time of the merger, the market value of the liabilities of Broward exceeded the market value of its assets by $734 million. Pursuant to its contract with the Government, Glendale was permitted to book Broward's resulting market value deficit or net excess liabilities (negative net worth) as supervisory goodwill, an asset for purposes of meeting regulatory capital requirements. This supervisory goodwill was to be amortized over forty years, or until 2021.

Not long after the merger, interest rates declined, and the asset squeeze experienced by the industry eased. For a variety of reasons, some in the Government began to doubt the wisdom of the contracts that had been made with the salvaging S & Ls. In August of 1989, Congress enacted the Financial Institutions Recovery, Reform and Enforcement Act ("FIRREA"). . . .

FIRREA and its implementing regulations repudiated the Government's obligation to recognize Glendale's goodwill as an asset for purposes of regulatory capital over the contract's forty-year amortization period by requiring Glendale to deduct goodwill in determining its regulatory capital on a greatly accelerated schedule. In addition to mandating the phase-out of goodwill as an asset includable in calculating a thrift's regulatory capital ratios, FIRREA and its implementing regulations also changed the minimum requirements for capital. . . .

In response to the phase-out of goodwill, Glendale reduced its size from $25.6 billion in total assets to $14.4 billion and, in 1990, ceased most high credit-risk lending. Although shrinking reduced its losses, Glendale nonetheless failed the risk-based capital requirement in March of 1992 and the core capital requirement in December 1992.

To return to compliance, in 1993 Glendale raised $451 million from new investors. Glendale incurred $24.2 million in transaction costs in this recapitalization. In 1994, Glendale sold its Florida Division, including Broward. In 1995, Glendale sold University Savings, its Washington subsidiary. In 1998, Glendale merged with California Federal Bank.

Glendale brought this action claiming the enactment of FIRREA breached an agreement by the Government to give Glendale favorable regulatory treatment in connection with its merger with Broward. As noted, the courts that reviewed the matter held that FIRREA's enactment rendered the Government liable to Glendale for breach of contract; the matter was remanded to the trial court for a trial on damages. . . .

[T]he trial court concluded that on the facts of the case Glendale was not entitled to expectancy damages. This conclusion appears to rest upon problems of proof, coupled with certain evidentiary issues related to inconsistent positions taken at different stages of the litigation by Glendale's key witnesses. In this appeal, Glendale does not challenge that ruling by the trial court.

When proof of expectancy damages fails, the law provides a fall-back position for the injured party—he can sue for restitution. . . .

Restitution is sometimes described in terms of taking from the breaching party any benefits he received from the contract and returning them to the non-breaching party. . . .

In the case before us, the trial court, faced with a situation in which expectancy damages were ruled out but with a legitimate claim by the plaintiff for a remedy for the Government's breach, fashioned a restitutionary remedy based on the assumed risk that Glendale undertook when it acquired Broward. This was done by taking the value of Broward's obligations or debts at the time the contract was made, and subtracting from it Broward's then-assets. The resulting figure, a negative $798,291,000, was deemed to be the amount that the Government benefited from the contract, and to which Glendale was entitled as restitutionary damages.

Glendale supports the trial court's conclusion by arguing that Glendale's assumption of the market value of Broward's net liabilities was a benefit to the Government because Glendale thus relieved the Government of its imminent responsibility for those liabilities. . . .

[T]he action taken by the purchasing S & L in acquiring the failing thrift did not result in the Government, specifically the FSLIC, saving the dollar value of the net obligations of the thrift. For one, it is not at all clear that but for Glendale's purchase of Broward the Government would have been called upon to make up that deficit then and there. Glendale was only one of a number of potential acquirers of Broward. Alternatively, rather than approve a merger, the Government had open to it the option of hiring new and better management to run Broward and make a go of it, just as Glendale itself did. In a very real sense, what the Government received in exchange for its promise was time—time to deal with other failing S & Ls, time to see what the market would do before having to commit substantial resources to the problem. Though the value of time was more than zero, there is no proof of what in fact it was worth.

It is important to remember that, even after Glendale's merger with Broward, the Government was not free of potential liability for the failing thrift. Had interest rates not come down, and Broward, and perhaps Glendale as well, failed, the Government's contingent liability would have matured, and the FSLIC would have had to step in at that time and assume the very losses that Glendale now claims were benefits the Government received.

Fortunately for both the industry and the Government, the facts of the case are that interest rates did come down, market forces allowed the thrift industry to escape impending doom, and neither Glendale nor the Government was called upon to pay the potential losses the fear of which was the motivation for the scenario in the first place.

This case, then, presents an illustration of the problem in granting restitution based on an assumption that the non-breaching party is entitled to the supposed gains received by the breaching party, when those gains are both speculative and indeterminate. We do not see how the restitution award granted by the trial court, measured in terms of a liability that never came to pass, and based on a speculative assessment of what might have been, can be upheld; accordingly we vacate the trial court's damage award on this theory.

This does not mean that Glendale is without a remedy. . . . [T]he trial court recognized [a] third category of damages, known as reliance damages, and added specified reliance damages to the total award it granted plaintiff.

The underlying principle in reliance damages is that a party who relies on another party's promise made binding through contract is entitled to damages for any losses actually sustained as a result of the breach of that promise. See *Restatement (Second) of Contracts* § 344(b) ("[Judicial remedies serve to protect the promisee's] reliance interest, which is his interest in being reimbursed for loss caused by reliance on the contract by being put in as good a position as he would have been in had the contract not been made.") . . . .

In the case at bar, the trial court awarded reliance damages for post-breach events, which the court denominated non-overlapping reliance damages. More specifically, it awarded Glendale damages for the following: lost historic cost of funds advantage over its competitors in the amount of $335,400,000; increased deposit insurance premiums in the amount of $11,480,000; increased Office of Thrift Supervision assessments in the amount of $4,675,000; transaction costs from the sale of University Savings in the amount of $4,472,000; transaction costs from the 1993 recapitalization in the amount of $24,235,000; and custodial fees paid to the Federal Home Loan Bank in the amount of $524,932.

Note that, unlike restitution in which the critical event that fixes the damages is when the contract was entered into, in reliance damages the critical event is the breach itself. Damages consequent to that breach may be the result of actions before or after the breach. Though the trial court limited Glendale's reliance damages to post-breach damages, since otherwise there would be a problem with duplication of the restitution elements, there is nothing inherent in the concept to prevent a court from awarding reliance damages for pre-breach activities from which ascertainable losses as a result of the breach can be shown.

In a case like the one before us, for all the reasons we have explained, we conclude that, for purposes of measuring the losses sustained by Glendale as a result of the Government's breach, reliance damages provide a firmer and more rational basis than the alternative theories argued by the parties. We recognize the appeal in the restitution approach, but we find that keying an award to a liability that was at most a paper calculation, and which ignores the reality of subsequent events as they impacted on the parties, and particularly the plaintiff, is not justifiable. Reliance damages will permit a more finely tuned calculation of the actual losses sustained by plaintiff as a result of the Government's breach. . . .

NOTE

In a second appeal, the court upheld the trial court's award of $381 million for reliance losses, most of them attributable to Glendale's position as a "wounded bank" after it failed to meet capital requirements. The court said that "the focus of a recovery based on the reliance interest is the real costs incurred for capital and services that the thrift would not have incurred but for the contract and its subsequent breach," and that the court's assessment of these costs was "fair and reasonable." Glendale Federal Bank, FSB *v.* United States, 378 F.3d 1308, 1311–1313 (Fed. Cir. 2004).

2. MEASURING LOST EXPECTANCY

Wilson v. Hays

Court of Civil Appeals of Texas, 1976.
544 S.W.2d 833.

■ JAMES, JUSTICE. This is a suit by the buyer against the seller for breach of an oral contract to sell and deliver used bricks. Trial was had to a jury, which rendered a verdict favorable to the Plaintiff buyer, pursuant to which verdict the trial court entered judgment. We affirm in part and reverse and render in part.

Plaintiff-Appellee W.D. Hays was in the business of buying and selling used building materials. Defendant-Appellant Bobby Wilson doing business as Wilson Salvage Co. was in the business of wrecking or demolishing buildings. In March 1972, Defendant Wilson was in the process of wrecking some buildings in Midland, Texas. Plaintiff Hays became interested in buying the used, uncleaned brick from Defendant Wilson's demolition work. Whereupon, Hays and Wilson entered into an oral agreement whereby Wilson agreed to sell and deliver 600,000 used uncleaned bricks to Hays at a price of one cent per brick, and Hays agreed to buy said bricks at said price. Hays paid Wilson $6,000.00 in advance. Wilson delivered the uncleaned brick to a designated area where Hays had people hired to clean and stack the bricks. Wilson delivered a lesser number of bricks than 600,000, thereby precipitating this suit.

Plaintiff-Appellee Hays brought this suit for the return of the proportionate part of the purchase price paid for the bricks he did not get, plus damages. In answer to special issues the jury found:

> (1) That Bobby Wilson orally agreed with Hays that he, Bobby Wilson, would sell and deliver to Hays at least 600,000 bricks at a price of one cent per brick; . . .
>
> (6) That Bobby Wilson did not deliver 600,000 uncleaned bricks to Hays (but)
>
> (6A) delivered only 400,000 bricks to Hays;
>
> (7) The market value of used bricks in Midland, Texas in April 1972, was five cents per brick;
>
> (8) Hays suffered lost profits in the amount of $6250.00 by virtue of the failure of Bobby Wilson to deliver to Hays at least 600,000 bricks;
>
> (9) That Hays saved $2605.00 in expenses in consequence of the failure of Bobby Wilson to deliver to him (Hays) at least 600,000 bricks.

Pursuant to the jury verdict, the trial court entered judgment in favor of Plaintiff Hays against Defendant Bobby Wilson in the amount of $13,645.00, plus accrued interest at 6% per annum from and after May 15, 1972, up to Jan. 27, 1976, same being the date of the trial court's judgment, plus interest at 9% per annum from and after the date of said judgment. From this judgment, Defendant Wilson appeals. . . .

Plaintiff-Appellee Hays' remedies and measures of damages as a buyer of goods in the case at bar are governed by Sections 2.711, 2.712, 2.713, and 2.715 of the Texas Business and Commerce Code. We herewith quote the portions of said sections that bear upon the case at bar:

"Sec. 2.711. Buyer's Remedies in General; . . .

> "(a) Where the seller fails to make delivery or repudiates . . . the buyer may cancel and whether or not he has done so may in addition to recovering so much of the price as has been paid
>
> "(1) 'cover' and have damages under the next section as to all the goods affected whether or not they have been identified to the contract; or

"(2) recover damages for non-delivery as provided in this chapter (Section 2.713)."

"Section 2.712. 'Cover'; Buyer's Procurement of Substitute Goods

"(a) After a breach within the preceding section the buyer may 'cover' by making in good faith and without unreasonable delay any reasonable purchase of or contract to purchase goods in substitution for those due from the seller.

"(b) The buyer may recover from the seller as damages the difference between the cost of cover and the contract price together with any incidental or consequential damages as hereinafter defined (Section 2.715), but less expenses saved in consequence of the seller's breach.

"(c) Failure of the buyer to effect cover within this section does not bar him from any other remedy."

"Section 2.713. Buyer's Damages for Non-Delivery or Repudiation

"(a) . . . the measure of damages for non-delivery or repudiation by the seller is the difference between the market price at the time when the buyer learned of the breach and the contract price together with any incidental and consequential damages provided in this chapter (Sec. 2.715), but less expenses saved in consequence of the seller's breach."

"Section 2.715. Buyer's Incidental and Consequential Damages

"(a) Incidental damages . . . (not applicable).

"(b) Consequential damages resulting from the seller's breach include

"(1) any loss resulting from general or particular requirements and needs of which the seller at the time of contracting had reason to know and which could not reasonably be prevented by cover or otherwise; . . . ."

Let us analyze the verdict and judgment in the light of the foregoing statutory provisions. In the first place, it is established that Plaintiff Hays paid $6000.00 for 600,000 used bricks at the rate of one cent per brick, whereas he received only 400,000 bricks. Therefore he paid $2000 for 200,000 bricks that he never got, and he is thereby entitled to recover $2000.00 under Section 2.711 for "recovering so much of the price as has been paid."

Next, under Section 2.713, he is entitled to damages for "non-delivery or repudiation," and here his measure of damages is the difference between the market price and the contract price. The contract price of the 200,000 bricks not delivered is established at $2000.00. The market price at the appropriate time and place of the undelivered bricks was five cents per brick or $10,000.00. This jury finding of market value (five cents per brick) although challenged by Appellant for legal and factual insufficiency, is amply supported by the evidence and is well within the range of probative testimony. Therefore under Section 2.713 and appropriate jury findings, Plaintiff is entitled to $8000.00 damages (or $10,000.00 market price less $2000.00 contract price) for non-delivery.

Now we come to the problem of "consequential damages . . . less expenses saved in consequence of the seller's breach" as mentioned in Sec. 2.713 and which damages are provided for in Sec. 2.715. As stated, the jury found Hays sustained lost profits of $6250.00 (Special Issue No. 8) and saved $2605.00 expenses (No. 9), thereby suffering a lost profits net of $3645.00, which last-named amount was included in the $13,645.00 judgment total. This $3645.00 lost profits amount has no support in the evidence. Under Sec. 2.715, "consequential damages" includes "any loss . . . which could not reasonably be prevented by cover or otherwise." There is no evidence in the record whatever that Plaintiff Hays at any time made any effort to cover or in any other manner attempt to prevent or mitigate a loss resulting from the Defendant Wilson's non-delivery of the 200,000 bricks in question. In the absence of such a showing these consequential damages are unauthorized under Section 2.715. The burden of proving the extent of loss incurred by way of consequential damage is on the buyer. This being so, we are of the opinion that there is no evidence to support these jury findings concerning consequential damages, and that the trial court's judgment insofar as it awarded Plaintiff Hays $3645.00 lost profits is improper and this amount should be deleted from said judgment. . . .

We therefore affirm in part and reverse and render in part the trial court's judgment as follows: Plaintiff-Appellee Hays is hereby awarded judgment against Defendant-Appellant Wilson in the amount of $10,000.00, plus interest at six percent per annum from and after May 15, 1972 up until January 27, 1976, the date of the entry of the trial court's judgment, together with interest from the date of the trial court's judgment upon the amount then due at the rate of nine percent per annum until paid. . . .

NOTE

Credit Agricole and Chameleon Finance Company entered into an interest rate swap agreement. As explained by the court that decided their ensuing dispute:

> "Interest rate 'swaps' are agreements to exchange fixed-rate and floating-rate interest obligations. Typically, each party agrees to make interest payments to the other calculated by reference to an agreed amount, the 'notional amount' in swap parlance. One party pays interest on the notional amount at a fixed rate; the other

at a floating rate. When the agreement expires, the obligations are netted and the party owing the greater amount, if any, pays the excess. Swap agreements are used to manage interest rate risk or to speculate on interest rate movements. . . .

"Business Week has described swap agreements in this manner: 'In a typical interest-rate swap, one party agrees to pay a variable interest rate to another party in exchange for receiving a fixed rate payment. For example, say a company that has issued $100 million in 10-year, fixed-rate 7% bonds thinks interest rates will fall. It could enter into a swap contract where it agrees to make variable-rate interest payments for 10 years to another party, equal to three percentage points over the two-year Treasury rate of 4%. In exchange, it would get fixed payments of 7%—equal to the interest payments it is paying bondholders. If rates fall, so do the company's payments—even though its bondholders are still receiving 7%. The other party to this deal, say an insurance company, may have issued floating-rate notes and wanted to protect against a rise in rates. The swaps dealers—mostly banks—that create, market, and broker these deals—have made billions.' David Greising, *Chicago's Swaps Sweepstakes,* Business Week, June 14, 1993."

Caisse Nationale de Credit Agricole *v.* CBI Industries, Inc., 90 F.3d 1264, 1267 & n.1 (7th Cir. 1996).

The swap agreement between Credit Agricole and Chameleon called for a swap of floating and fixed interest rates on a "notional amount" of $35 million, with periodic payments of the difference. The agreement also included a "swaption," giving Credit Agricole the option to extend the agreement for an additional two years by notice on or before January 16, 1994. As it happened, January 16 and January 17 were, respectively, a Sunday and a holiday. Credit Agricole gave notice of intent to extend the swap on January 19; Chameleon argued that the option had expired and refused to honor the swap agreement. Based on a provision of New York law, the court determined that this notice was effective and Chameleon was bound for an additional two years. It concluded by stating that "Credit is entitled to 'expectation damages,' which means Credit should be placed in the same economic position it would have been in had both parties performed."

Should Credit Agricole be compensated for loss of its expectancy?

If so, what are its damages?

United Virginia Bank v. Dick Herriman Ford, Inc.

Supreme Court of Virginia, 1974.
215 Va. 373.

■ COCHRAN, JUSTICE. On September 7, 1972, United Virginia Bank of Fairfax (Bank) filed its motion for judgment against Dick Herriman Ford, Inc. (Dealer), alleging damages resulting from breach of a contract to record a first lien in favor of the Bank on the application for title to an automobile purchased from the Dealer by Scott Burdette, to whom the Bank made a loan for a portion of the purchase price.

The case was tried before the court, sitting without a jury. At the conclusion of the Bank's evidence the Dealer moved to strike the evidence on the ground that a prima facie case had not been made out. The trial court granted the motion and on October 12, 1973, entered a final order awarding summary judgment for the Dealer. In the final order, however, the court held that there was a contract between the Bank and the Dealer, that the Dealer had breached the contract and had thereby damaged the Bank and was liable therefor, but that the Bank had "failed to establish the value of the automobile at the time that its right to repossession accrued," so that the court could not assess the measure of damages. . . .

The trial court's action in entering summary judgment for the Dealer would have been permissible . . . had it followed a finding that there was no liability on the part of the Dealer. But the court erred in taking such action after finding that the Dealer was liable to the Bank and that the Bank had been damaged by the Dealer's breach of contract.

The Bank was not required to prove the value of the vehicle at the time of Burdette's default. The Bank is entitled to be put in the same position as it would have been in if the contract had been performed. If the Dealer had fulfilled its contractual obligations the Bank would have been protected by a first lien on the title certificate issued in the name of the borrower covering the amount of his indebtedness to the Bank. Damages within the reasonable contemplation of the parties at the time the contract was made would comprise the amount of the indebtedness to be secured, diminished by payments actually received.

The general rule is that damages are to be determined at the time of breach of a contract. Evidence of fluctuations in value after the breach is irrelevant.

To require the Bank to prove the value of the automobile as of the date its right of repossession accrued would be to reward the Dealer, at the Bank's expense, for the Dealer's breach of contract. We hold, therefore, that the general rule should apply in this case and that damages should be determined as of the date of breach of the contract between the Bank and the Dealer. This requires a determination of the value of the vehicle at that time, because the Bank is not entitled to damages in excess of the value of the collateral of which it was deprived.

A litigant is not required to prove his damages with precision, particularly where the violator of the contract has made it impossible for him to do so, provided the evidence permits an intelligent and reasonable estimate of the damages. Here, the amount of the obligation to be protected by the first lien that was never perfected was $4,525.92. This is rebuttable evidence that the value of the vehicle at the time the contract was breached was not less than that amount. The title application, however, signed by the Dealer, disposes of the question of value, for it shows that the purchase price paid for the vehicle was $4,560.00. We hold that $4,525.92 was the measure of damages caused by the Dealer's breach of contract, less credits for payments received by the Bank after the contract was breached, reducing the damages to $3,771.98.

As value has been established by the evidence, we reverse the final order of October 12, 1973, and enter final judgment for the Bank in the amount of $3,771.98. . . .

In re WorldCom, Inc.

United States Bankruptcy Court, S.D.N.Y, 2007.
361 B.R. 675.

■ ARTHUR J. GONZALEZ, BANKRUPTCY JUDGE. [The background facts of this case appear in Chapter Four, above. The question before the court was whether Michael Jordon's claim against MCI Worldcom for breach of an endorsement contract should be disallowed or reduced because Jordan failed to minimize damages by seeking an alternative endorsement contract.]

Jordan argues that as a "lost volume seller" he was under no obligation to mitigate damages. . . .

"A lost volume seller is one who has the capacity to perform the contract that was breached in addition to other potential contracts due to unlimited resources or production capacity." Precision Pine & Timber, Inc. *v.* United States, 72 Fed. Cl. 460, 490 (Fed. Cl. 2006). A lost volume seller does not minimize its damages by entering into another contract because it would have had the benefit of both contracts even if the first were not breached. The lost volume seller has two expectations, the profit from the breached contract and the profit from one or more other contracts that it could have performed at the same time as the breached contract. . . .

The lost volume seller theory is recognized in the Restatement (2d) of Contracts, §§ 347, 350 (1981). The lost volume seller theory applies to contracts for services as well as goods.

This case offers a twist on the typical lost volume seller situation. In what the Court regards as the typical situation, the non-breaching seller has a near-inexhaustible supply of inventory. In the typical situation, when a buyer breaches an agreement to buy a good or service from the seller, the item is returned to inventory and the lost volume seller continues in its efforts to sell its goods or services. However, the transactions that occur following the breach are not necessarily the result of the breach but fundamentally the result of the seller continuing efforts to market its goods and services. It is this continuous effort coupled with a virtually limitless supply that warrants the lost volume exception to mitigation. As stated above, the transactions that may occur after the breach would in the context of the lost volume seller have occurred independent of the breach. Here, Jordan lacked a nearly limitless supply and had no intention of continuing to market his services as a product endorser. . . .

To claim lost volume seller status, Jordan must establish that he would have had the benefit of both the original and subsequent contracts if MCI had not rejected the Agreement. Although there is no definitive set of elements that the non-breaching party must show, many cases seem to follow the language from the Restatement (2d), Section 347, that the non-breaching party must show that it "could and would have entered into" a subsequent agreement.

In his arguments, Jordan focuses primarily on his *capacity* to enter subsequent agreements, arguing that the loss of MCI's sixteen-hour annual time commitment hardly affected his ability to perform additional endorsement services. On this prong alone, Jordan likely would be considered a lost volume seller of endorsement services because he had sufficient time to do multiple endorsements. Although he does not have the "infinite capacity" that some cases discuss, a services provider does not need unlimited capacity but must have the requisite capacity and intent to perform under multiple contracts at the same time. . . .

Jordan has not shown he could and *would have* entered into a subsequent agreement. Rather, the evidence shows that Jordan did not have the "subjective intent" to take on additional endorsements. The testimony from Jordan's representatives establishes that although Jordan's popularity enabled him to obtain additional product endorsements in 2003, Jordan desired to scale back his level of endorsements. Jordan's financial and business advisor, Curtis Polk . . . , testified that at the time the Agreement was rejected, Jordan's desire was "not to expand his spokesperson or pitchman efforts with new relationships." . . . Jordan's agent, David Falk . . . , testified that "there might have been twenty more companies that in theory might have wanted to sign him" but that Jordan and his representatives wanted to avoid diluting his image. Jordan's Memorandum for Summary Judgment stated that at the time the Agreement was rejected, Jordan had implemented a strategy of not accepting new endorsements because of a belief that new deals would jeopardize his ability to achieve his primary goal of National Basketball Association ("NBA") franchise ownership. . . .

One of the classic examples of the lost volume seller is found in Neri *v.* Retail Marine Corp., 30 N.Y.2d 393, 399–400 (1972):

> "[I]f a private party agrees to sell his automobile to a buyer for $2,000, a breach by the buyer would cause the seller no loss (except incidental damages, *i.e.*, expense of a new sale) if the seller was able to sell the automobile to another buyer for $2,000. But the situation is different with dealers having an unlimited supply or standard-priced goods. Thus, if an

> automobile dealer agrees to sell a car to a buyer at the standard price of $2,000, a breach by the buyer injures the dealer, even though he is able to sell the automobile to another for $2,000. If the dealer has an inexhaustible supply of cars, the resale to replace the breaching buyer costs the dealer a sale, because, had the breaching buyer performed, the dealer would have made two sales instead of one. The buyer's breach, in such a case, depletes the dealer's sales to the extent of one, and the measure of damages should be the dealer's profit on one sale."

This example would surely have a different result if the car dealership was winding down its business and had agreed to sell one of its last cars to a buyer. . . .

Because the evidence establishes, among other things, that Jordan would not have entered into subsequent agreements, Jordan has not established that he is a lost volume seller. This theory thus does not relieve Jordan from the duty to mitigate damages. . . .

The Debtors are to settle an order consistent with this opinion.

NOTE

Most authorities have agreed that Section 2–708 of the Uniform Commercial Code was intended to recognize the lost volume theory in sales of goods:

> "§ 2–708. Seller's Damages for Non-acceptance or Repudiation.
>
> "(1) Subject to subsection (2) and to the provisions of this Article with respect to proof of market price, the measure of damages for non-acceptance or repudiation by the buyer is the difference between the market price at the time and place for tender and the unpaid contract price together with any incidental damages provided in this Article, but less expenses saved in consequence of the buyer's breach.
>
> "(2) If the measure of damages provided in subsection (1) is inadequate to put the seller in as good a position as performance would have done then the measure of damages is the profit (including reasonable overhead) which the seller would have made from full performance by the buyer, together with any incidental damages provided in this Article, due allowance for costs reasonably incurred and due credit for payments or proceeds of resale."

3. LOST USE

Bumann v. Maurer

Supreme Court of North Dakota, 1972.
203 N.W.2d 434.

■ MAXWELL, DISTRICT JUDGE. . . . The facts were ably presented in Justice Paulson's opinion on that appeal, and need no reiteration at length here. In essence the suit was instituted by the plaintiffs (respondents) for two purposes. One was to require the defendants (appellants) to specifically perform an agreement to convey real estate. The other was to recover damages imputable to tardiness in transferring possession of the land.

After issue was joined, and when trial was first imminent, the defendants relented and did convey the property to the plaintiffs. That left open only the issue of damages alleged to have sprouted from laggardly performance.

Trial of that question was had in Kidder County District Court on February 1, 1972. A jury verdict for the plaintiffs was brought in for the sum of $8,292.33. Judgment in that amount was thereafter entered. . . .

The leading issue on this appeal we esteem to be propriety of a portion of the trial court's jury charge. The defendants, (whom we shall for simplicity hereinafter call "sellers") press upon us with skill and zeal the criticism that one of the trial court's instructions obliged the jurors to use an inappropriate guide for measuring damages. With this view we are disposed to agree. The challenged instruction was, we find, inappropriate under the facts.

At the trial, the plaintiffs (hereinafter "buyers") advocated, and the court gave instructions on damages based upon Sec. 32–03–09 NDCC. That section reads:

> "For the breach of an obligation arising from contract, the measure of damages, except when otherwise expressly provided by the laws of this state, is the amount which will compensate the party aggrieved for all the detriment proximately caused thereby or which in the ordinary course of things would be likely to result therefrom. No damages can be recovered for a breach of contract if they are not clearly ascertainable in both their nature and origin."

The sellers resisted use of this statute as the legal basis for damages. Noting that this section, by its own terms, applied only when no other specific law controlled, sellers insisted there was a specifically applicable statute. They claimed Sec. 32–03–13 was singularly designed for this type of case. It states:

> "The detriment caused by the breach of an agreement to convey an estate in real property is the difference between the

> price agreed to be paid and the value of the estate agreed to be conveyed at the time of the breach and the expenses properly incurred in examining the title, and in preparing to enter upon the land, and the amount paid on the purchase price, if any, with interest thereon from the time of the breach."

While we do, as already mentioned, adopt sellers' position that the trial court erred by giving an instruction founded on Sec. 32–03–09, we do not find the alternative suggestion to be appropriate either. On the contrary, we believe the trial court properly resisted sellers' solicitations to give instructions based on Sec. 32–03–13. Use of that statute is warranted only when specific performance is impossible or impracticable. The appellate court in California, recently construed the very statute of that state from which ours was copied; it said: "A simple reading of the statute discloses that by its explicit terms it is adaptable only to a failure to convey, and not to a delay in conveying." Christensen *v.* Slawter, 173 Cal. App. 2d 325 (1959).

The sellers here rely on the case Missouri Slope Auction *v.* Wachter, 107 N.W.2d 349, decided by this court in 1961. We there approved as a measure of damages "the difference between the price to be paid under the contract and the value of the land at the time of the breach." However, in that case, conveyance could not be accomplished under any circumstances. The sellers had agreed to sell property to which they had no title. Here there was no such an impediment. The contract did not fail—it merely suffered long delay.

The damages in this case arose because, in defiance of their contractual obligation to convey and deliver, the sellers wrongfully occupied and used the real estate. There is a specific statute governing damages in such circumstances. Sec. 32–03–21 is titled "Damages for wrongful occupation of realty" and the pertinent part reads as follows:

> "The detriment caused by the wrongful occupation of real property . . . is deemed to be the value of the use of the property for the time of such occupation . . . and the costs, if any, of recovering the possession." . . .

Sec. 32–03–21 speaks of "the value of the use" as the proper gauge of recovery for the period of wrongful occupation. This value may be found by either of two routes. The aggrieved party may require the party at fault to make an accounting and deliver over the fruits of the illegitimate possession. Or he may, at his election, recover the fair rental value of the property. . . .

The authorities seem generally to concur in the view that delay in performance of an agreement to convey can be the root of special as well as general damages. . . .

Care, however, must be taken that double compensation is not given for the same element of injury, first as general damages, and again as an item of special damages. . . .

Evidence of several other items of special damage was admitted by the court. This evidence included (1) the expense of locating a new farm, (2) the cost of moving to it, (3) additional expense for school transportation, and (4) extra school tuition paid. It was not error to submit these matters to the jury—provided, of course, they were accompanied by proper instructions.

Recoverable special damages must meet the orthodox text laid down in the celebrated English case Hadley *v.* Baxendale, 156 Eng. Rep. 145 (1854). They must be "such as may reasonably be supposed to have been in the contemplation of the parties at the time they made the contract, as the probable result of the breach of it." The burden is upon the party claiming special damages to show that the injury was reasonably within the contemplation of the parties. . . .

NOTE

McKee agreed to sell and Smith agreed to buy a parcel of land. The closing was delayed beyond the agreed dates when Smith requested, and McKee denied, permission to test the water level on the property (a prerequisite for government approval of a subdivision). The court determined that testing was authorized under the purchase and sale contract, and, accordingly, that McKee was responsible for the delay.

Can McKee recover interest on the purchase price during the period of delay? See Smith *v.* McKee, 116 N.M. 34 (1993).

4. COST OF REPAIR

Hancock v. Northcutt

Supreme Court of Alaska, 1991.
808 P.2d 251.

■ MATTHEWS, CHIEF JUSTICE. This case involves a dispute between the owner-builders of an earth-sheltered concrete house, Carol and Melvin Northcutt, and the concrete contractors for the house, Herb and Marge Hancock. The house consists of seven joined pods which may be covered with dirt for insulation. The Northcutts made an oral contract with the Hancocks for construction of the pods. The terms of the contract are in dispute. The Northcutts claim that for $65,000 the Hancocks agreed to complete all structural concrete work. The Hancocks dispute the original price, and claim that they performed extra work not contemplated in the original contract, for which they were to be paid on a time and material basis. Construction was delayed. Each side blames the other for the delay. Following delays, all seven pods were poured. The Northcutts believed some of the work to be defective. The Hancocks offered to cure the problems but the Northcutts refused, ordering them off the job. . . .

The Northcutts then sued the Hancocks. The Northcutts' amended complaint states that the Hancocks breached the contract by failing to perform in a timely and professional manner, and by changing the design of the Northcutts' structure. . . . The Hancocks counterclaimed for the amount allegedly due under the contract plus extra work performed.

The contract was made in May of 1982. The Hancocks first poured concrete in September of 1982 and made their last pour on October 30, 1982. The Hancocks were ordered off the job prior to filing a lien in November of 1982. The Northcutts finished the house and closed on their $160,000 mortgage about 90 days later. They have lived in the house since that time. However, they do not occupy pod seven because they believe it may collapse and have installed timber cribbing in certain sections of the house to prevent a sudden collapse. . . .

The jury, guided by a special verdict form, awarded the Northcutts $455,984 as the cost of demolishing and rebuilding the house, $19,600 for moving and storage costs and temporary housing during reconstruction, $7,200 for past lost use of portions of the house, $28,486 for costs incurred by construction delays, and $175,000 for emotional distress. Compensatory damages thus totaled $686,271.[1] . . .

[The trial court's Instruction 40 stated:]

> ". . . The usual way of deciding what damages to award to the plaintiffs is to give them the reasonable cost of putting the house in the same condition it would have been in had the defendants kept their promise.
>
> "However, if you find that it would be impractical and grossly wasteful, in proportion to the benefit to be gained, to repair the house so that it matches its promised condition, then you should not use this first method unless you find it is more likely than not true:
>
> "(1) the house has a special significance to the plaintiffs; or
>
> "(2) the plaintiffs are more likely than not to demolish and rebuild the house; or
>
> "(3) the house as is creates a dangerous condition.
>
> "If you find one or more of the above conditions to be more likely true than not true, you may determine that cost of repair is the approximate measure of damages in this case.
>
> "Otherwise, for all conditions that can be repaired at disproportionate and wasteful expense, you should use the following method of measuring damages. You should award to the plaintiffs a sum which represents the difference between the value of the performance that the defendants promised and the value of the performance that the defendants actually gave.
>
> "If you decide that some defects are repairable, but that others can be repaired only at a disproportionate and wasteful

---

1 The jury also awarded $1 for lost aesthetic value.

> expense, then you should use the cost of repair to measure damages for the repairable defects and the drop in value to measure the damages for the remaining non-repairable defects."

The jury, in answer to the questions posed in the special verdict form, found that it would be impractical and grossly wasteful to put the house in the same condition it would have been in had the Hancocks kept their promise. However, the jury also found that at least one of the three conditions existed. It thus awarded the Northcutts $455,894 as the "reasonable cost to put the house in the condition it would have been in had the defendants kept their promise." The parties agree that this represents the sum of $68,465 for removing the present house and $387,519 for rebuilding the house. . . .

The Hancocks note that the most the house would have been worth if it had been properly built was $190,000 as of the time of its completion in 1982. As of the time of trial, because of a depressed real estate market, the house would have been worth approximately $142,500.

In our view, the instruction was a misstatement of the law. In Advanced, Inc. *v.* Wilks, 711 P.2d 524 (Alaska 1985), a case which involved another earth-sheltered concrete house, we approved a jury instruction which told the jury that damages should be the reasonable cost of remedying construction defects unless such costs were impractical and grossly wasteful, in which case a difference in value approach should be used. . . .

We went on to explain that an owner's recovery should not necessarily be limited to diminution in value "whenever that figure is less than the cost of repair." *Id.* at 527. In support of this we cited Restatement (Second) of Contracts § 348, comment c (1981). this comment makes it clear that while a cost of repair figure somewhat in excess of damages under the comparative value approach may be tolerated because of proof difficulties, a gross excess will not be. The comment states, in relevant part:

> "Sometimes, especially if the performance is defective as distinguished from incomplete, it may not be possible to prove the loss in value to the injured party with reasonable certainty. In that case he can usually recover damages based on the cost to remedy the defects. Even if this gives him a recovery somewhat in excess of the loss in value to him, it is better that he receive a *small windfall* than that he be undercompensated by being limited to the resulting diminution in the market price of his property.
>
> "Sometimes, however, such a large part of the cost to remedy the defects consists of the cost to undo what has been improperly done that the cost to remedy the defects will be clearly disproportionate to the probable loss in value to the injured party. Damages based on the cost to remedy the defects

> would then give the injured party a recovery greatly in excess of the loss in value to him and result in a substantial windfall. Such an award will not be made. It is sometimes said that the award would involve 'economic waste,' but this is a misleading expression since an injured party will not, even if awarded an excessive amount of damages, usually pay to have the defects remedied if to do so will cost him more than the resulting increase in value to him." (Emphasis added) . . .

There is . . . a theoretical basis for awarding cost to cure damages which greatly exceed the value differential measure, although cases where this has actually been done are rare. What is required are assurances that the injured party will effect a cure for legally sufficient reasons. A hornbook on contracts states:

> "It is usually said that this second measure of recovery [value differential damages] is appropriate '[i]f it is made to appear that physical reconstruction and completion in accordance with the contract will involve unreasonable economic waste by destruction of usable property or otherwise.' *It seems apparent however, that the true rationale is that recovery for the cost of remedying the defect would involve unjust enrichment.* In all likelihood, if the owner were to recover this amount in such circumstances he would pocket the recovery. Most likely he would not undertake to remedy the defect . . . . The end result would be that the owner would have a structure substantially in compliance with the contract and a sum of money far in excess of the pecuniary harm done to him. Economic waste, then, is merely a criterion by which one can determine whether or not the owner reasonably would remedy the defect or would utilize the building in its defective state. Another criterion is whether the owner's purpose is to gratify personal taste and fancy. If so, he may be entitled to damages measured by the cost of completion *even if this involves economic waste.*"

J. Calamari and J. Perillo, TREATISE ON CONTRACTS § 14–29, at 560–61 (1977) (emphasis added).

Accordingly, if warranted by the evidence, an instruction like that in question might be proper if it required a finding that the injured party would probably rebuild. Thus, if the instruction were to state that cost of cure damages were appropriate, even if grossly wasteful, if the house has special significance to the plaintiffs *and* the plaintiffs are more likely than not to demolish and rebuild the house, it would not be erroneous. The same is true if the instruction were to say that if the house is dangerous *and* the plaintiffs are more likely than not to demolish and rebuild it, cost of cure damages could be awarded. However, the exceptions in Instruction 40 are stated in the disjunctive. Thus the jury could have found merely that the house creates a dangerous condition, or that the house has special significance to the plaintiffs, without also finding that the plaintiffs are more likely than not to demolish and rebuild it.

The instruction as given therefore allows the possibility of unjust enrichment of the plaintiffs. Assuming their house to have no value, their loss is $190,000, which is what their house would have been worth in 1982 had it been built properly, plus demolition costs of $68,465. The jury awarded them $387,519 plus the costs of demolition. They can now demolish their house, buy another house comparable in size for $190,000 ($142,500 using values as of the time of trial) and profit by $197,519. On the facts of this case, this seems likely. Neither Mrs. nor Mr. Northcutt testified that they would rebuild an earth-sheltered concrete house given another chance.

For this reason, the jury's award of $387,519 as the cost of rebuilding the house must be vacated.[6] The jury's award of storage costs and temporary housing during reconstruction must also be reversed as these items necessarily assume that the house will be rebuilt.

[The court went on to discuss, and reject, the Northcutts' claim to damages for emotional distress.]

The case is remanded for a new trial to determine the value the house would have had if it had been built as promised. Since the jury found that the house as built had no value, this will represent damages under the difference in value approach.

Bellizzi v. Huntley Estates, Inc.

Court of Appeals of New York, 1957.
3 N.Y.2d 112.

■ DYE, J. The defendant-respondent, a real estate developer, on or about August 19, 1950, contracted to sell to the plaintiff-appellant a lot designated as No. 235 in its development and to build a house thereon in accordance with its demonstration model known as "The 1951 Kent" which, among other features, had an attached garage with an access driveway substantially at street level. When the construction work was commenced, the defendant encountered rock close to the surface and, instead of excavating same, as might have been done without too much trouble at the time, it placed the house thereon, with the result that from the entrance of the garage to the street, a distance of 43 feet, there was a difference in elevation of 9 feet and 8 inches. This amounted to a 22½% grade, which is so steep that the driveway cannot be used safely and conveniently. As a matter of fact, the evidence shows that a grade of 12% is considered the permissive maximum. While the plans are silent as to the grade of the driveway, the defendant does not now claim that the

[6] The demolition costs found by the jury, $68,465, may stand as both parties agree that this is the amount found by the jury for demolition and that the jury necessarily found that the house was not structurally sound and "was going to have to be replaced and had no value."

grade of the existing driveway is reasonable or that plaintiff has no cause for complaint. It defends against plaintiff's claim for damages on the sole ground that the trial court erred when it excluded evidence offered by it as to the value of the property and should not have refused to charge that the measure of damages "is the difference between the value of the building as constructed and its value had it been constructed conformably to the contract or the cost of repairs, whichever is the lesser." Instead, the trial court charged in substance that the measure of damage is "the fair and reasonable cost to remedy the defect in this controversy or to get a reasonably usable driveway."

The Appellate Division adopted the defendant's contention largely in reliance on Jacob & Youngs *v.* Kent, 230 N.Y. 239, 244. In that case, we had applied the "difference in value" rule simply because the proof failed to show any substantial damage or loss in value, since the wrought iron galvanized pipe, as furnished, was substantially the same in quality, weight, market price, serviceability and appearance as pipe of "Reading" manufacture called for in the contract specifications and that the cost of replacing same with the "Reading" pipe as specified "would be great, but the difference in value . . . would be either nominal or nothing"; in other words, replacement of the pipe, under the circumstances in that case, would have constituted economic waste.

However, this litigation poses an entirely different kind of breach, the consequence of which is to burden plaintiff with an unusable, unsafe and unsightly driveway. While it is unfortunate that the defendant elected to build the garage at an unsuitable elevation in order to avoid the cost of excavating unforeseen rock and that to correct the defect will now cost much more than initially, nonetheless, that loss should not fall on the innocent owner whose protests made at the time were put off by the president of the defendant corporation with assurances not to worry, that when finished the grade would not exceed 10% and that the plaintiff would be happy when he got into his home.

The "difference in value" rule in defective performance of construction contracts seems to be applied only when it would be unfair to apply the general rule. In a case such as the present when the variance is so substantial as to render the finished building partially unusable and unsafe, the measure of damage is "the market price of completing or correcting the performance" (5 WILLISTON ON CONTRACTS [Rev. ed.], § 1363, p. 3825.) It is only "If the defect is not thus remediable, damages are based on the difference between the value of the defective structure and that of the structure if properly completed." (*Id.* at 3825–3826.) This rule we have long applied.

Here, there is uncontradicted evidence that the dangerous and unsatisfactory driveway can be corrected. When that is done, the plaintiff will have received no more than he was entitled to under his contract and the defendant will have given no more than it obligated itself to furnish. . . .

Appalachian Power Co. v. John Stewart Walker, Inc.

Supreme Court of Virginia, 1974.
214 Va. 524.

■ POFF, JUSTICE. . . . For a number of years prior to 1970, Appalachian conducted a sales promotion program designed to encourage real estate developers to build "all electric" residences. Under that program, Appalachian agreed to install underground rather than overhead electrical service. Against the cost of installation, the developer was allowed a credit based upon anticipated revenues. If the credit exceeded the cost, installation was provided free of charge to the developer. In order to calculate the credit, Appalachian needed a plat of the subdivision.

[In the fall of 1969, Appalachian agreed orally to install underground electric lines in a subdivision to be developed by Walker and to provide a written confirmation of the agreement. In April, 1970, the State Corporation Commission ruled utility promotions of the kind offered by Appalachian unlawful, with an exception for pre-existing written contracts. At trial, the jury found that Appalachian was obligated to provide a written contract, and consequently was liable for Walker's lost expectancy. It returned a verdict for $6,000.]

Walker's evidence tended to show that the lack of underground electrical facilities reduced the sale value of the 20 lots by $8,000.00. Appalachian's evidence tended to show that the cost of installation was $3,546.00. The trial court granted Walker's instruction based on the "value" formula, refused Appalachian's instruction based on the "cost" formula, and overruled Appalachian's motion to set aside the jury verdict based on the "value" formula.

A successful plaintiff is entitled to recover those damages which are "the natural and direct result of the breach of the contract." And "[t]he object of the law in awarding damages is to make amends or reparations by putting the party injured in the same position, as far as money can do it, as he would have been if the contract had been performed."

Whether the "value" formula or the "cost" formula is applicable "will depend upon the facts and [the] circumstances of the particular case." We have recognized application of the "value" formula in an appropriate case. The test is the nature of the motivation which induced the promisee to make the contract. If his primary interest was the value of the result performance would have produced, then the "value" formula is applicable; if performance itself, then the "cost" formula.

The uncontradicted evidence was that Walker was developing Locksview Subdivision to sell lots; that his reason for wanting underground electrical service was to enhance the marketability and market price of the lots; and that the lack of such service impaired both by a measurable degree. The first jury found that such impairment was the natural and direct result of Appalachian's breach of a contractual duty. We find no error in the formula applied by the trial court's instructions. . . .

■ [The opinion of JUSTICE CARRICO, dissenting on other grounds, is omitted.]

5. AVOIDABLE COSTS

F. Enterprises, Inc. v. Kentucky Fried Chicken Corp.

Supreme Court of Ohio, 1976.
47 Ohio St. 2d 154.

■ STEPHENSON, J. . . . On January 20, 1968, appellees entered into an option with the H. Corporation for the purchase of a parcel of real estate fronting 170 feet on Morse Road in Franklin County for the sum of $85,000. Shortly thereafter, negotiations began between appellees and appellant, resulting in a contract between the parties for a 20-year lease at a monthly rental of $1,100 for 85 feet of the frontage on Morse Road, which was about 50 percent of the whole of the tract under option by appellees. It was agreed that as a part of the lease, appellees would construct a building on the leased premises not to exceed a cost of $40,000, appellees having the option to require appellant to erect the building with appellant being reimbursed by appellees in a sum not to exceed $40,000.

On August 12, 1968, appellant notified appellees by letter that it would not enter into the lease. On November 18, 1968, appellees exercised their option for the whole tract. The fair rental value of the 85-foot tract, if improved with a building, was $9,025 per year; without improvement, the fair rental value was $3,825 per year. The judgment of $28,508.89 was determined by the trial court in accordance with the opinion of the Court of Appeals.*

* The method of calculation by the trial court was as follows:

Contract rental per year	$ 13,200
Market rental value per year	(9,025)
Difference	4,175
Interest income on unexpended $40,000 for building, per year	(2,400)
Difference	1,775
Term of lease in years	× 20
Result	$ 35,500
Discounted value of $35,500 to current value	$ 20,809.41
Interest at six percent	7,699.48
Damage Award	$ 28,508.89

In their brief in the Court of Appeals, appellees state an arithmetical error was made in such calculation and that the correct figure should have been $28,842.58. Appellees waived any claim of error in such respect and such is not an issue in this appeal.

Appellant urges this method of calculation is erroneous in that, upon appellant's breach of the contract, appellees were required to minimize their damage, and, since appellees were not required to exercise their option, even though, in fact, they did so, that appellant's liability for damages should be further reduced by a deduction for interest income for 20 years on one-half of the purchase price of the whole tract. Appellant then asserts that since over the twenty-year period such interest income, which is $51,000, when added to the interest income on the sum unexpended for the building, $48,000, would exceed the difference between the fair market rental and the proposed lease rental for the term of lease, appellees suffered no damage and should recover nothing, except, perhaps, nominal damages. In short, appellant's argument is that appellees either suffered no damage or were, in fact, benefited by appellant's breach of the contract. Such conclusion is untenable and unsupportable under the record. We conclude that not only is appellant not entitled to the further reduction asserted, but also, that the courts below erred in allowing the deduction for the interest upon the $40,000 cost of the proposed building.

We agree with the Court of Appeals that the general rule of damages to be applied when there is an anticipatory breach by a proposed lessee of a contract to make a lease, which is a contract that vests no estate in the prospective lessee, is the difference between the fair market rental of the property proposed to be leased and the agreed rental to be paid in the proposed lease, such sum discounted to present value, together with any special damages arising from the breach. Such rule is one of almost universal application, is consistent with general contract law, and represents the weight of authority. The general rule of necessity is formulated upon the basis of, and takes into consideration, any expenditures for improvements the lessor is required to make under the contract, inasmuch as the agreed payments in the proposed lease reflect such improvements. Such rule, therefore, gives to the defaulting prospective lessee the benefit of any expenditures, such as erection of a building, the prospective of such expenditures in rental obtainable for the improved property on the open market.

Where the courts below erred in their computation of the damage award was, after giving appellant the benefit of the investment by appellees of the $40,000 to help produce the rental income of $9,025, to again give appellant credit for the interest income upon the $40,000. Such $40,000, if invested in the building, could not be at the same time retained by appellees and also constitute a source of interest income to them.

When a contract is repudiated at a time when the injured party has not yet performed, ordinarily a savings to the injured party occurs by reason of not having to perform his promise. Such savings is deducted from the compensation under the contract the injured party would have received from the breaching party had the contract been fully performed, since the injured party is only entitled to a damage award which places him in as good a position as he would have been had the contract been fully performed. It is upon this principle that appellant relies; although, in its brief, appellant's argument is framed in the context of the doctrine of avoidable consequences. As will be seen hereafter non-exercise of the purchase of the land by the appellees, under the facts of this case, would not have effected a saving to appellees but actually increased their damages from the breach of the contract by appellant.

The doctrine of avoidable consequences is a rule also arising from the cardinal principle that the damage award should put the injured party in as good a position had the contract not been breached at the least cost to the defaulting party. It is applied, in substance, to prevent an inclusion in the damage award of such damages that could have been avoided by reasonable affirmative action by the injured party without substantial risk to such party.

Whatever should be the rule with respect to the breach of a lease by a lessee, a question not before us, as to the breach by a prospective lessee of a contract to make a lease, we agree with the rule, representing the weight of authority, that recovery of damages by the prospective lessor is limited to only those damages arising from the breach which could not, by reasonable effort on his part without undue risk or expense, have been averted or reduced.

It is to be noted that the general rule of damages gives recognition to a prospective lessor's obligation to minimize damages by renting on the open market to others. Thus, as stated in Branning Manufacturing Co. *v.* Norfolk-Southern R. Co., 138 Va. 43, 60 (1924), "[I]n effect, the measure of damages stated minimizes the damages of the plaintiff in such case, which is a duty which rests upon the plaintiff in all such cases." To the extent that the prospective lessor has made a "good" or "bad" bargain, it will be reflected in a difference between the agreed rental and market rental. Conceivably, the market rental could exceed the agreed rental so that no pecuniary loss is suffered by the prospective lessor by the prospective lessee's breach.

In order to comply with the contract to make a lease, the prospective lessor at the time of execution of the lease, must own or otherwise have an interest in the premises to let to the prospective lessee. In the ordinary case where the prospective lessor owns the premises at the time of contract, the value thereof, whatever the actual cost, is reflected both in the agreed rental and the fair market rental. What should be the rule, however, if, as here, the parcel is not owned by the prospective lessor but is only the subject of an option? If the prospective lessee does not breach the contract but demands compliance, the prospective lessor is legally required, irrespective of the market value, to exercise his option for whatever sum was agreed to in order to perform his obligation under the contract for the lease.

Conceivably, by the expenditure of the option price, coupled with his obligations under the proposed contract of lease, the result would not be a pecuniary gain but, rather, a loss by the prospective lessor. In such a situation the prospective lessor suffers no damage and might monetarily gain by the breach of the contract by the prospective lessee. Since the general rule of damages would not reflect such fact in such a situation, a deduction from the sum arrived at by application of the general rule of damages above set forth would be proper. However, under the facts of this case it is manifest that the non-exercise of the option would have been to appellees' monetary detriment and not benefit.

Appellees assert, and we agree, three alternatives were available to them upon the breach of the contract. First, they could decline exercise of the option and take no further action under the contract. In this event, they would have expended no funds and, as a result, had available to them the $42,500 (unexpended for land) and $40,000 (unexpended for building) to invest for a return of interest for the term of the proposed lease. Secondly, they could expend the $42,500 in buying the land and invest the $40,000 and receive interest for the term of the lease. Under this alternative they would derive the return from the fair market rental of the unimproved parcel ($3,825 per year) in addition to the interest return upon the $40,000 for the 20-year period. Thirdly, they could have exercised the option for $42,500 as to the parcel here considered, erected the building and rented the improved tract upon the open market for $9,025, effecting an eleven percent return upon the investment.

Simple mathematical calculation of the above alternatives discloses that the non-exercise of the option, would have resulted in the greatest damage to appellees. Additionally, the non-exercise of the option would have required appellees to forego any profit that could be realized by a sale of the other half of the parcel not the subject of the proposed lease. The exercise of the option was thus a prerequisite to appellees' minimization of their damage. It follows, therefore, that since the exercise of the option did not increase but, rather, decreased appellees' pecuniary loss, no deduction from the difference between the agreed rental and fair market rental was warranted.

It follows that appellant is not entitled to the further reduction sought in the award of damages entered by the trial court. . . .

6. EXPECTANCY DAMAGES FOR TORTS

Coghlan v. Wellcraft Marine Corp.

United States Court of Appeals, Fifth Circuit, 2001.
240 F.3d 449.

■ EDITH H. JONES, CIRCUIT JUDGE. . . . In May 1998, the Coghlans, residents of Texas, purchased an Aquasport 205, a type of recreational fishing boat manufactured by Wellcraft Marine Corporation. Wellcraft is a Delaware corporation with its principal place of business in Florida. The boat cost about $28,000. The Coghlans' purchase was motivated, at least in part, by Wellcraft's marketing campaign for this line of boats, which emphasized the advantages of all-fiberglass construction. In addition to rot-resistance and durability, it is generally believed among mariners that all-fiberglass boats tend to hold their value better than their wood-fiberglass hybrid counterparts.

The Coghlans assert that they relied on Wellcraft's representations that the Aquasport 205 was made entirely of fiberglass. A few months after the purchase, they discovered that the deck of the Aquasport 205 is actually composed of 1.5 inches of plywood encased entirely within fiberglass. Disappointed by this revelation, the Coghlans filed suit against Wellcraft . . . .

The Coghlans' suit alleged [among other things] fraud, negligent misrepresentation, breach of contract, deceptive trade practices, unjust enrichment and civil conspiracy. . . .

The district court . . . concluded that the Coghlans had failed to allege any real damages, a required element for each of their causes of action. . . .

The district court did not consider whether Texas or Florida law, the only two arguable candidates, governs the Coghlans' various state claims . . . .

The only damage sought by the Coghlans is the benefit of their bargain with Wellcraft, or the difference in value between what they were promised, an all fiberglass boat, and what they received, a hybrid wood-fiberglass boat. Along with the "out of pocket" damages formula, which measures the difference between what the plaintiff paid in consideration and what he actually received, "benefit of the bargain" is a standard method for measuring damages in fraudulent representation and certain contract cases. The benefit of the bargain measure of damages is neither novel nor exotic. A simple example proffered by the Coghlans at oral argument makes the common-sense nature of benefit of the bargain damages clear: if a man buys what is represented to him as an 18k gold ring, but later discovers that the ring is merely 10k gold, he is entitled to the difference in value between the 18k ring that he bargained for and the 10k ring that he received. . . .

Texas and Florida both follow the "flexibility theory" in fraud actions, which permits a trial court to instruct the jury under either the out-of-pocket rule or the benefit of the bargain rule, whichever will more fully compensate the defrauded party. Therefore, regardless whether Texas or Florida law is applied, it was improper to dismiss the Coghlans' fraud claim on the pleadings; a fraud claim seeking benefit of the bargain damages is legally cognizable in both Texas and Florida. . . .

Texas courts have held that benefit of the bargain damages are not recoverable in a claim for negligent misrepresentation. In Texas negligent misrepresentation actions the plaintiff can recover only the amount necessary to compensate for direct pecuniary loss.

Florida has been less explicit in its treatment of this issue. However, it appears that Florida courts do allow the recovery of benefit of the bargain damages in negligent misrepresentation actions. . . .

While we share the district court's implicit concern over the rise of "no-injury" product liability law suits, the district court acted prematurely in dismissing this case *sua sponte* on the pleadings: the determination that there has been no injury in this case must be an evidentiary one, since the relevant state jurisdictions recognize benefit of the bargain damages for the claims that the Coghlans allege. . . .

NOTES

1. Bull induced Reno to buy shares of stock in an oil refining company by misrepresenting the condition and capacity of the company's refining plant and the company's business prospects. Reno paid $5000 for the shares. A jury awarded damages of $6000 for fraud. The court said:

> "The purpose of an action for deceit is to indemnify the party injured. All elements of profit are excluded. The true measure of damage is indemnity for the actual pecuniary loss sustained as the direct result of the wrong. The plaintiff paid $5,000 for the stock purchased by him. If he were entitled to recover at all, it was the difference between that amount and the value of the stock which he received with interest from that time. He was not entitled to anything else."

Reno *v.* Bull, 226 N.Y. 546, 553 (1919).

2. The Hyatt Regency Chicago hotel, owned by Kato Kagaku Company, entered a contract with Roboserve, in which Roboserve agreed to install 1000 minibars in the hotel and the Hyatt agreed "to use 'reasonable endeavors' to place those guests most likely to use minibars in the Robobar rooms and to encourage them to make purchases from the minibars." After Roboserve had installed 900 minibars, Kato proposed a pause in installation and a one year "test period" to compare the performance of Roboserve's minibars with minibars supplied by a competitor, ServiSystems. Kato agents indicated that if Roboserve cooperated with the test scheme, the winner of the test would obtain additional, maybe national, business from Hyatt hotels. Roboserve acquiesced and won the test, then learned that before proposing the test, Kato had already committed to shift all its minibar business to ServiSystems.

A jury found that Kato had defrauded Roboserve and returned a verdict of $1 million as compensatory damages for fraud (as well as $7 million as punitive damages for fraud). The Court of Appeals for the Seventh Circuit rejected the award, saying:

> "Roboserve is entitled to recover for those out-of-pocket losses attributable to Kato's misrepresentations, including the loss of its time and resources in preparing proposals for adding new Robobars

to the HRC. Testimony at trial indicated that Roboserve incurred $12,810 in attorney's fees and costs. We believe the evidence also indicates that officials at Roboserve, independent of its attorney, expended a substantial amount of time and effort preparing for and conducting negotiations with Hyatt, for which Roboserve deserves compensation. We assume the jury took this into account when calculating the damages and, in addition to the $12,810 in attorney's fees, awarded Roboserve $25,000 in out-of-pocket losses for the wasted time and effort of its employees.

"The jury's $1 million verdict, however, went far beyond compensation for Roboserve's out-of-pocket losses. It obviously included benefit-of-the-bargain damages. But what bargain? There was a misleading contest that could have resulted in a contract for the winner. There were hints of Hyatt placing Robobars in a number of other hotels throughout the country. But this alleged fraud did not induce any contract. . . . The most that has been shown is that through a misleading 'contest' and 'negotiations' that were designed to delay, Hyatt wasted Roboserve's time and efforts, induced it not to enforce its existing contractual right to install 100 more minibars, and unjustly raised its expectations of future business and profits. However objectionable, such mistreatment does not entitle Roboserve to damages for what might have been had it actually consummated a broader agreement with Hyatt. . . . Thus there was no basis for an award of benefit-of-the-bargain damages."

Roboserve, Inc. *v.* Kato Kagaku Company, Ltd., 78 F.3d 266, 274–75 (7th Cir. 1996).

C. PERSONAL INJURY

1. NON-ECONOMIC COMPONENTS OF PERSONAL INJURY DAMAGES

Fertile v. St. Michael's Medical Center

Supreme Court of New Jersey, 2001.
169 N.J. 481.

■ LONG, J. The core issues presented on this appeal are rather straightforward: in the face of a concededly excessive damages award, when is the remedy of a new damages trial conditioned on plaintiffs' acceptance of a remittitur order appropriate; when is a new trial on all issues mandated; and by what standard is the amount of a remittitur order to be assessed?

On April 4, 1996, plaintiffs, Danialie Fertile, an infant by her guardian ad litem, Marlene Fertile, and Marlene Fertile, individually, (collectively, plaintiffs) filed a complaint against Dr. Angela Buontempo and St. Michael's Medical Center (collectively, defendants). The complaint alleged that Danialie was severely injured as a result of Dr. Buontempo's malpractice and that Mrs. Fertile suffered severe emotional distress as a result. The gravamen of the complaint, as elucidated in discovery, was that Dr. Buontempo delivered Danialie vaginally when a caesarean (c-section) section was indicated.

A five day trial ensued at which the following evidence was introduced. On June 24, 1994, Mrs. Fertile was admitted to St. Michael's Medical Center in the early morning hours experiencing labor. At approximately 6:45 p.m., Dr. Cecil Holgado, a second-year resident, examined Mrs. Fertile and found her labor progressing satisfactorily. At his 9 p.m. examination, Dr. Holgado observed that Mrs. Fertile's cervix had stopped dilating, probably because of fetal pelvic disproportion, a condition in which the mother's pelvis cannot accommodate the size of the baby. Because the baby showed no signs of distress, Dr. Holgado recommended to Dr. Debra Rosenzweig, the attending physician, that Mrs. Fertile deliver by c-section. At approximately 9:15 p.m., Dr. Holgado asked Dr. Buontempo (another second-year resident) to follow Mrs. Fertile while he performed a c-section on another patient. Dr. Holgado advised Dr. Buontempo of his plans to perform a c-section on Mrs. Fertile. . . .

At 9:40 p.m., because Mrs. Fertile was fully dilated and the baby's head was at the vaginal opening, Dr. Buontempo concluded that a caesarian section was no longer an appropriate option and that the baby had to be delivered vaginally. Accordingly, she sent a nurse to the operating room to inform Dr. Rosenzweig, who along with Dr. Holgado, was engaged in another delivery.

Dr. Buontempo summoned assistance. She recognized the potential that Danialie would be a large baby, given Mrs. Fertile's obesity and her substantial weight gain during pregnancy. Such large babies present a risk of shoulder dystocia, a condition that occurs when the baby's shoulder is stuck against the mother's pubic bone and obstructed in its passage from the vagina.

Danialie was large, and her shoulder was wedged behind Mrs. Fertile's pubic bone. Dr. Buontempo freed the baby by changing Mrs. Fertile's position, pressing on her pubic bone, and enlarging the surgical incision to expand her vagina. In the course of her birth, Danialie was injured, resulting in an atrophied and partially paralyzed arm. . . .

A pediatric neurologist, Dr. Daniel Adler, testified for plaintiffs that as a result of traction on her head during birth Danialie suffered a brachial plexus injury, paralyzing some of her arm muscles and weakening others, resulting in a limited range of right arm motion. She is unable to move her right hand, thumb or fingers but can place a light object in her right hand and hold it there; her condition will not improve. . . .

A jury awarded Danialie damages in the amount of $15 million and Mrs. Fertile damages in the amount of $3 million. Defendants filed a motion for a new trial or, in the alternative, a remittitur. The trial court denied a new trial concluding that no trial error had occurred. However, stating that the verdict "took my breath away," the court concluded that it was excessive and remitted $10 million of the $15 million dollar award to Danialie and all but $250,000 of the award to Mrs. Fertile, on the condition that plaintiffs accept that amount. Otherwise, defendants would be entitled to a new damages trial. Plaintiffs agreed to the remittitur order. . . .

Once the trial court determines that a "manifest denial of justice" has occurred, a new trial is warranted. The scope of the new trial depends on the nature of the injustice. Where trial error affecting liability occurs, the new trial will encompass all issues. Where the quantum of damages is the sole source of the court's determination that a denial of justice has taken place, other remedies are available including remittitur and additur.[2]

Because it is conceded that the damages award in favor of Danialie was excessive, our focus is on remittitur. Remittitur "describes the power of a court upon a motion for a new trial due to excessive damages rendered by a jury to require the plaintiff to consent to a decrease in the award to a specified amount as a condition for denial of the motion." In other words, remittitur denies a defendant a new trial if a plaintiff consents to a specified reduction in the jury award.

Remittitur is designed to bring excessive damages awarded by a jury to the level that the court knows is within the limits of a proper verdict and thereby avoid the necessity of a new trial. Remittitur has long been employed by courts and legislatures to eliminate retrials for excessive verdicts. In fact, the practice of remittitur began to take hold in America in the nineteenth century. By the latter half of the 1800's most state and federal courts accepted the doctrine. Remittitur was formally recognized by the United States Supreme Court in 1886 . . . . Remittitur has been attacked as an unconstitutional infringement on the guarantee of a trial by jury. However, the United States Supreme Court [has] recognized remittitur, although disapproving additur, the difference being that the former is a calculation within the jury's verdict whereas the latter is not. . . .

Because the use of remittitur avoids the unnecessary expense and delay of a new trial, when confronted with excessive verdicts New Jersey courts should, if possible, resort to an order of remittitur. That is the action the trial court took in this case, and that the Appellate Division set aside. . . .

---

[2] Additur refers to "[t]he power of a court, on motion for a new trial due to inadequate damages rendered by jury verdict, to require the defendant to consent to an increase to a stipulated amount of the award as a condition for denial of the motion for a new trial. . . ."

The standard applicable to [review of a trial-level remittitur] is similar to that governing a new trial. . . . Obviously, assessing the amount of a remittitur is a slightly more complicated function than merely determining entitlement to a new damages trial. It not only involves the conclusion that the damages award cannot stand because it constitutes a manifest denial of justice but also a determination that the remitted amount is what a reasonable jury, properly instructed, would have awarded.

Different approaches have developed for determining the proper amount of a remittitur order: one is to award the lowest amount supported by the record; a second is to award the highest amount supported by the record; and a third is to award damages in between the highest and lowest amounts supported by the record. Because the process of remittitur is essentially to "lop-off" excess verdict amounts, and not to substitute the court's weighing and balancing for that of the jury, remitting the award to the highest figure that could be supported by the evidence is the most analytically solid approach. Indeed, commentators have concluded that such an approach "tampers least with the intentions of the jurors, who by implication wanted to fully compensate the plaintiffs . . . ." Irene Deaville Sann, Remittiturs (and Additurs) in the Federal Courts: An Evaluation With Suggested Alternatives, 38 Case W. Res. L. Rev. 157, 191 (1987/88).

We have carefully reviewed this record in light of the aforementioned standards, and find no reason to interfere with the remittitur order. The trial court fully and carefully explained how it determined that the jury verdict was excessive and how it reached the remitted number. In so doing, it properly relied on the evidence it saw and heard. In addition, it based the decision on its own common knowledge, as well as its experience with other injury verdicts, and particularly on Danialie's extended life expectancy. The court stated:

> ". . . What's devastating to one is so so to another. So, it has to be an individual situation. Certainly we know that we have, it's certainly no solace to the parents of this child that we have much more severely injured children with brain damage babies etc. It doesn't give any solace that, oh, well, it's only, you know a brachioplexis injury as opposed to a brain damage. That doesn't do the plaintiff in this case any good. But I have to look at it all around, the quality of life, and what's available there because as I say everybody is a little bit different. . . .
>
> "And I looked at that and I say that in good conscience I can't let the dollar amount stand and it's a hard place to put and I look at it all, yes, there is a young woman who certainly is precocious, is bright, intellectually has the world open to her, but yet there are still some everyday things that are going to cause some problems that you think very simply is how easy it is to do certain things that we take for granted for everyday with

> two arms that you can't do with only one. It is something that goes on and on and on, and I do have to consider the life expectancy overall. Remember we do have as of this time she was just short of five and the life expectancy of a little over 70, so you're talking 75 years and hopefully and god willing she'll have longevity longer than that because we know as we get older that it extends, but the jury looked at it from that point of view. In evaluating I've even watched her again today, a charming young lady but with a very noticeable injury that is not something that's going to take a discerning eye to see. It's something that is going to, you know, jump up and hit anybody who sees it. It is something that is going to if you don't need a psychiatrist or anybody on that basis to say that it's always to be some sort of a problem to someone to adapt with it and all, but in this court's opinion the 15 million dollars just is a bit of an overreach and somewhat interlaced with [emotion]."

The court ultimately concluded that $5,000,000 was an appropriate and just award, underscoring that Danialie's injury "is devastating and visible and with [her] for a lifetime." Having reviewed the trial record and the videotape, we cannot say that the court was wide of the mark or that the remittitur order constituted a manifest denial of justice.

Consorti v. Armstrong World Industries, Inc.

United States Court of Appeal, Second Circuit, 1995.
72 F.3d 1003.

■ LEVAL, CIRCUIT JUDGE. Owens-Corning Fiberglass Corporation ("OCF"), a fabricator of asbestos pipe-covering products, appeals from jury verdicts in favor of John Consorti, a pipe insulation worker who developed mesothelioma as the result of exposure to asbestos dust . . . .

Consorti began to suffer back problems in August 1991. In February 1992, he was diagnosed with pleural mesothelioma, an incurable cancer of the lining of the lung. He died after trial, at the age of 51, in November 1993.

Consorti initiated his asbestos personal injury action in August 1992 against numerous defendants in the Southern District of New York. His suit was one of the many thousands of asbestos cases reassigned by the Multi-District Litigation Panel to the Eastern District of Pennsylvania for discovery and pre-trial proceedings. Because of his rapidly advancing illness, his case was deemed an emergency "hardship" and was remanded to the Southern District of New York for expedited trial. It was consolidated for trial in 1993 with three other cases of mesothelioma due to asbestos exposure. . . .

In summation, plaintiffs' counsel . . . suggested awards of $8 million for John Consorti's past pain and suffering, plus $4 million for his future suffering. The jury returned a verdict that awarded exactly those amounts. The jury found John's remaining life expectancy to be nine months. . . .

OCF claims that the award to John Consorti of $12 million for his pain and suffering was excessive and should be set aside. We agree.

We note at the start, our finding in no way deprecates the enormous suffering that John Consorti endured. He developed a tumor which gradually enveloped his spine. The tumor pressed against his vocal cords, causing him to lose his voice and choke. It interfered with eating, swallowing, even breathing. His circulatory system was impaired, causing painful and disfiguring swelling of his head and neck. And, as his disease progressed, it became increasingly difficult (later impossible) for him to walk or to care for himself. His pain grew worse as time passed, and was, of course, deepened by the certainty of imminent death. We take it as a given that reasonable people of his age, in good mental and physical health, would not have traded one-quarter of his suffering for a hundred million dollars, much less twelve.

It does not follow that courts should permit a verdict of a hundred million dollars, or twelve million, to stand. While the law seeks by reasonable compensation to make a plaintiff whole, we must recognize that compensation for suffering can be accomplished only in a symbolic and arbitrary fashion. There are at least two serious shortcomings to the endeavor. First, money awards do not make one whole; they do not alleviate pain. Second, there is no rational scale that justifies the award of any particular amount, as opposed to some very different amount, in compensation for a particular quantum of pain.

We acknowledge furthermore that a judge's training in law gives the judge no greater ability than a jury to determine the dollar amount that appropriately compensates any particular level of suffering. This recognition can lead judges to abdicate responsibility for review of jury verdicts. As we have no greater knowledge than jurors of the amount of money that suitably compensates for suffering, the question arises why our assessment should take precedence over theirs?

Nonetheless, there are important reasons why courts cannot properly leave it to juries to set the limits of compensation for such injuries. Even where the law is incapable of furnishing a rational answer, it seeks at least to be evenhanded, fair, and predictable. It should be our goal that persons who endure a similar degree of suffering can expect to receive a roughly similar award of compensation, and that similarly situated defendants be burdened by similar judgments. If each jury is given unbridled authority to set the level of damages, awards will vary widely and unpredictably. Great discrepancies in awards destroy the fairness of the judicial system, as well as the predictability of litigation. This vigilance must be directed not only against awards that are too high, but also against those that are too low. See, *e.g.*, In re Brooklyn Navy Yard Asbestos Litigation, 971 F.2d 831, 853–54 (2d Cir. 1992) (ordering new trial on issue of pain and suffering where award of $25,000 was so low, given evidence of lengthy and intense suffering, as to shock the conscience). Such goals cannot be achieved unless courts exercise responsibility to keep jury awards within limits.

The unpredictability of jury awards is pernicious not only because it is unfair. Widely varying jury verdicts make it difficult for risk bearers to structure their behavior to efficiently manage risk. While it is an aim of tort law to deter wrongful conduct, see *Restatement (Second) of Torts* § 901 (1977), at the same time tort law seeks to avoid over-deterrence that would stifle socially valuable enterprise.

> ". . . Where liability costs are relatively predictable, they can be avoided (where it is efficient to do so) or 'built in' to the costs of goods and services. . . . But errors in valuation may cause over-deterrence—the taking of too many costly precautions, or withdrawal from risky activity altogether. For example, during the liability insurance crisis of the 1980s, many obstetricians reportedly stopped delivering babies, and some manufacturers ceased development or production of certain drugs and goods. . . ."

Randall R. Bovbjerg et al., Valuing Life and Limb in Tort: Scheduling "Pain and Suffering," 83 Nw. U. L. Rev. 908, 925 (1989). When courts fail to exercise the responsibility to curb excessive verdicts, the effects are uncertainty and an upward spiral. One excessive verdict, permitted to stand, becomes precedent for another still larger one. Unbridled, spiraling, excessive judgments predictably impose huge costs on society.

A failure by courts to impose limits on jury verdicts would cause serious social dislocation. At the first level, unchecked costs attributable to tort liability, and resultant increases in insurance premiums, would inevitably raise the price of goods and services to the public. More serious exaggeration in unchecked jury awards can cause bankruptcies in productive enterprises, with consequent disappearance of jobs, and even bankruptcies among insurers, leaving segments of society unprotected. Finally, in the circumstance represented by asbestos litigation, where it appears virtually certain that the resources of major defendants will eventually be completely consumed by their liabilities, allowing excessive awards to stand in the early stages of the litigation of the many thousands of cases they face will mean that over-compensation of the early plaintiffs will leave insufficient resources for the equally deserving plaintiffs whose cases are heard later.

For all these reasons, even if courts have no better ability than jurors to measure the dollar value of pain, they must accept the responsibility of controlling the limits of jury awards. . . .

The question we face is how much money John Consorti may be awarded in damages by reason of his pain and suffering. This is an issue of substantive rights under the laws of New York. . . .

We therefore . . . look to the law of New York to determine whether the award was excessive. Like a New York court, we will "look . . . to other jury awards condoned by the courts of" New York, recognizing that "New York appellate courts regard prior awards as not binding but instructive."

The standard for determining excessiveness and the appropriateness of remittitur in New York is somewhat ambiguous. Prior to 1986, New York law employed the same standard as the federal courts, which authorized remittitur only if the jury's verdict was so excessive that it "shocked the conscience of the court." In 1986, New York State legislated a new standard that required the Appellate Division of the Supreme Court to exercise closer control over jury awards. The new CPLR § 5501(c) provides,

> "In reviewing a money judgment in an action in which an itemized verdict is required . . . in which it is contended that the award is excessive or inadequate and that a new trial should have been granted unless a stipulation is entered to a different award, the appellate division shall determine that an award is excessive or inadequate *if it deviates materially from what would be reasonable compensation.*"

N.Y. Civ. Prac. L. & R. § 5501(c) (McKinney Supp. 1995) (emphasis added). This standard requires the reviewing court to determine the range it regards as reasonable, and to determine whether the particular jury award deviates materially from that range, taking corrective action if it does. Material deviation from reasonableness is less than that deviation required to find an award so excessive as to "shock the conscience." . . .

In discussing below the question of excessiveness of the jury's award to [Tabolt, another plaintiff in the consolidated action] of $7.5 million for pain and suffering, Judge Sweet converted the $4.5 million *McPadden* award to a monthly figure of $409,090.91 for McPadden's 11 months of suffering. Multiplication of that figure by Tabolt's 18 months of suffering produced a figure of $7,363,636.36, which was not substantially lower than the jury's award to Tabolt. Although it was not expressly discussed, the district court presumably used the same conversion of the *McPadden* award to a monthly amount to justify the jury's $12 million award to Consorti, whose disease the jury predicted to run 32 months from onset to death. Twelve million expressed as a monthly figure over 32 months is $375,000, which is below the $409,090.91 monthly figure Judge Sweet extrapolated from the *McPadden* judgment.

We disagree with the district court's use of *McPadden* to justify the jury's award to Consorti for two reasons. First, rigid application of a monthly multiplier for diseases of significantly different durations is an oversimplification, as well as inconsistent with New York precedent. Unquestionably, the duration of suffering is a relevant factor. But it cannot be automatically assumed that suffering which lasts 30 months, from onset of illness to death, should command a verdict three times that of a case where ten months pass from onset to death. In many cases, the degree of average daily suffering will be greater in a case where the disease progresses rapidly. The fact that McPadden's disease progressed three times more rapidly than Consorti's does not necessarily justify an award for Consorti nearly three times the size of McPadden's. . . .

Justice Helen Freedman is the trial judge to whom all New York asbestos litigation has been assigned by administrative order. In the period shortly prior to the Consorti trial, Justice Freedman rendered numerous judgments reducing awards in comparable cases of mesothelioma to levels far below what the jury awarded to Consorti. In Didner *v.* Keene Corp., Justice Freedman reduced a $3.25 million award to $2.3 million; the plaintiff had suffered 26–27 months of pain and suffering due to mesothelioma. N.Y.L.J., Jan. 4, 1991, at 22 (N.Y. Sup. Ct. Dec. 17, 1990), *aff'd,* 188 A.D.2d 15 (App. Div.1993). The court concluded that while Didner's pain and suffering was severe, "courts in this jurisdiction have not countenanced awards of this size for two plus years of pain and suffering."

Four months later, in the consolidated Brooklyn Navy Yard litigation, Justice Freedman reduced fourteen pain and suffering awards in mesothelioma death cases. The jury awards for pain and suffering from mesothelioma that Justice Freedman considered ranged from a low of $1 million, for a course of disease that took only three months, to a high of $5 million, in a case of 34 months of suffering. The jury awards thus ranged from 8% to 42% of this jury's award to Consorti. Justice Freedman found all those awards excessive under New York law. Those most comparable in duration to Consorti's were two awards of $5 million in cases where the suffering lasted 34 and 35 months. Justice Freedman reduced these to $3 million. And as to three awards ranging from $3.2 to $4.25 million, for suffering periods of 26 to 29 months, they were reduced to $2.2 to $2.4 million.

While it is difficult, especially without a study of the complete record, to evaluate the pertinence of one judgment for pain and suffering for another, the strong pattern of Justice Freedman's rulings is helpful in evaluating the Consorti awards. In the face of so substantial a pattern of New York judgments communicating that New York courts find excessiveness in such cases at far lower levels, we believe it was error for the district court to conclude that the jury's $12 million award was within the range accepted by New York law.

Although we recognize that John Consorti's suffering was very great, Justice Freedman's cases also all involved deaths from mesothelioma. It is not suggested to us that the suffering of the plaintiffs she considered was any less horrendous. . . .

Given the consistent pattern, over a considerable number of cases of death by mesothelioma, of reduction of jury verdicts for pain and suffering by New York courts to figures ranging from approximately $1 million to a maximum of $3 million, we conclude an award exceeding $3.5 million would deviate materially from what is deemed reasonable under New York law. Accordingly, we direct entry of a conditional order of a new trial on the issue of damages for pain and suffering, unless plaintiffs accept remittitur to that amount. . . .

OCF [also] claims that error occurred during summation, when plaintiffs' counsel made specific dollar recommendations to the jury as to appropriate awards for pain and suffering. He suggested $8 million for John Consorti's pain and suffering to date and $4 million for future pain and suffering. . . .

OCF's protest is undermined by the fact that its own counsel was the first to suggest a value for Consorti's pain and suffering. Earlier in the summations, counsel for OCF told the jury:

> "And I feel that to make a suggestion to you that he's not entitled to any compensation would not be fair . . . [if you decide] that he was entitled to maybe $750,000 to maybe even a million dollars, I don't think that that would be an unfair figure."

While this court has not adopted a per se rule about the propriety of suggested damage amounts, we wish to emphasize that specifying target amounts for the jury to award is disfavored. Such suggestions anchor the jurors' expectations of a fair award at a place set by counsel, rather than by the evidence. A jury is likely to infer that counsel's choice of a particular number is backed by some authority or legal precedent. Specific proposals have a real potential to sway the jury unduly. While under the circumstances present here we do not yet reach the point of holding that it is error to permit such recommendations, it is not a desirable practice. We encourage trial judges to bar such recommendations. . . .

Epping v. Commonwealth Edison Co.

Appellate Court of Illinois, 2000.
315 Ill. App. 3d 1069.

■ JUSTICE WOLFSON delivered the opinion of the court.

One sunny Thursday—April 18, 1996—Nancy Epping (Epping) was driving south on Route 31 toward Algonquin when, in seconds, her life changed forever.

Mark Schleehauf, a Commonwealth Edison (Edison) employee, was driving his Edison "stake truck" north on Route 31. He just finished eating a pear and leaned over to throw away the core. In that split second he failed to see the car in front of him slow to a stop to make a left-hand turn into the YMCA. When Schleehauf looked up it was too late. He tried to swerve to the right, but hit the car, which was driven by Reverend James Bensing. Bensing's car was forced over the centerline and into oncoming southbound traffic. Bensing's car plowed into Epping's car.

Epping sustained serious injuries, including: multiple open fractures of the right proximal tibial plateau (in the area of the knee); an open fracture of the right foot; a large wound over the top of the right foot; a closed fracture of the left ankle; a fractured left wrist; and a fractured and dislocated left hip with cracked pelvis. Epping had to be extricated from her car and air-lifted by helicopter to Lutheran General Hospital.

Edison admitted liability for the accident. Epping's suit against Edison proceeded to trial on the issue of damages.

The jury learned that when the accident occurred Epping was 49 years old, had been married for 28 years, was the mother of one daughter and a grandmother of one. Epping was a part-time teacher of anthropology at McHenry County Community College and the executive director of the Elgin Public Museum. She traveled extensively as the president of the Midwest Museum Conference. She had been named the Business Woman of the Year and the YWCA Woman of the Year. She enjoyed sailing and reading.

After the accident, Epping's injuries caused her to undergo 32 operations and procedures between 1996 and 1999. The jury viewed photographs of Epping's severely deformed leg and foot. It saw a video depicting a day in Epping's life.

The jury learned that Epping is unable to walk and needs assistance getting out of bed, getting into a chair, or getting onto the toilet. It learned she requires assistance attending to matters of personal hygiene. She can no longer drive a car and, because her left wrist joint has been "fixed" in place, she has difficulty maneuvering her own wheelchair. Epping's right leg is called "flail leg" and cannot support her weight. Doctors are optimistic that with further reconstructive surgery Epping might have the future ability to independently "ambulate" around the interior of her home with the aid of a walker or by holding on to furniture. But there is still the potential that Epping's right leg will have to be amputated.

Despite a number of surgeries, Epping continues to experience difficulty with her left hip. Epping will never be able to return to work, independently ambulate outside her home, or be able to perform the normal tasks of living—cleaning, cooking, or taking care of household chores. Her life expectancy is 32 years.

After receiving all the evidence and the instructions, the jury awarded Epping $4.5 million for past and future economic damages, along with $9 million for non-economic damages, which consisted of $2,250,000 each for disability, disfigurement, and past and future pain and suffering. . . .

Edison challenges the propriety of awarding Epping $9 million in non-economic damages. It asks for a remittitur of $5 million or, in the alternative, a new trial on damages.

Edison contends $9 million falls outside the realm of fair and reasonable compensation. It reaches this conclusion mainly on its belief that the award is disproportionately high when viewed in light of awards given in other cases where, it says, the injuries were as severe as or more severe than the injuries sustained by Epping in this case. . . .

Edison misstates the standard by which we review a damages verdict. The power to order a remittitur of damages—a long recognized and accepted part of Illinois law—should be employed only when an award falls outside the range of fair and reasonable compensation, appears to be the result of passion or prejudice, or is so large that it shocks the judicial conscience. Remittitur should not be applied when the award "falls within the flexible range of conclusions which can be reasonably supported by the facts."

There is no mathematical formula for deciding whether an award is fair and reasonable. Factors which may be considered are: the extent of the injuries suffered and permanency of the plaintiff's condition, the plaintiff's age, the possibility of future deterioration, the extent of the plaintiff's medical expenses, and the restrictions imposed on the plaintiff by the injuries.

Courts in this State have "traditionally declined to make ... comparisons [among verdicts] in determining whether a particular award is excessive . . . ." . . . As we said in Barry *v.* Owens-Corning Fiberglas Corp., 282 Ill. App. 3d 199, 207 (1996):

> "Establishing predictability of outcome for people similarly situated has surface attraction, but the courts of this State never have imposed on juries a requirement of conformity in damage awards."

This case is not about an injury to an arm or a leg. It is about the nature and extent of injuries to a particular woman. It is about the life she is required to lead because of the defendant's negligence. We will not compare. . . .

[A] damages award for a personal injury "must be examined in the light of the particular injury involved, with humble deference to the discretion of the jury and the judgment of the trial court." Kopczick *v.* Hobart Corp., 308 Ill. App. 3d 967, 979 (1999).

As we have said, jurors, when considering damages, "use their combined wisdom and experience to reach fair and reasonable judgments. We are neither trained nor equipped to second-guess those judgments about pain and suffering and familial losses incurred by other human beings. To pretend otherwise would be sheer hubris." Barry *v.* Owens-Corning Fiberglas Corp., 282 Ill. App. 3d at 207.

Admittedly, there is no litmus test for determining when the outer limits of a reasonable jury award are reached. That is why we examine the record for indications that the award was a product of passion or prejudice. That is why we do what judges often are called upon to do—determine whether fairness and rationality have been maltreated.

Reviewing the facts and circumstances of this case, there is no question Epping has suffered and will continue to suffer severe debilitating injuries. We cannot agree with Edison's characterization of Epping's injuries as "orthopedic injuries—but that is it."

Although Epping has not, as yet, suffered the loss of a limb, the top inch or more of the tibia bone near the right knee has been removed, resulting in "flail leg." The leg can turn in any direction and can bear no weight. Epping may not be a paraplegic, but her mobility is severely impaired. Any hope of walking independently depends on undergoing more painful surgery.

Epping's left hip also suffered severe trauma. Even after major reconstructive surgeries, the hip joint repeatedly becomes dislocated. The joint is held together with artificial replacement parts and numerous screws. Both the hip and the leg, doctors testified, were competent producers of pain. Epping has been on pain medication, as well as anti-depressants, since the accident.

Edison cannot deny Epping's injuries and surgeries have resulted in severe deformities to her right leg and foot. But it would have us reduce the jury's award because Epping's disfigurements are not readily visible and, consequently, are less repulsive to public eyes. We find no persuasive force in the fact that the disfigurements are capable of being hidden by clothes. Epping must suffer the indignities of these deformities each day—a constant reminder of the pain and suffering she has already suffered and will continue to suffer in the future.

Edison suggests "the enormity of the award" can be readily recognized if we consider the return Epping might expect if she invested her award of damages at the prevailing interest rate. Juries are not asked to reduce future noneconomic damages to present cash value—we see no reason for us to engage in investment analysis or advice.

Finally, we reject Edison's suggestion that a reduction of the damages award in this case might assist businessmen or individuals in determining what constitutes adequate insurance coverage. Our duty is to decide cases, not to assist in coverage planning. This argument, like the "reduction in systemic costs of tort liability" rationale . . . , does not inspire principled analysis. As our supreme court said, "The difficulty in quantifying compensatory damages for noneconomic injuries is not alleviated by imposing an arbitrary limitation or cap on all cases, without regard to the facts or circumstances."

The record is replete with evidence that supports the jury's award. It cannot be said the award is the product of passion or prejudice. Nor does it shock our judicial conscience. The $9 million award, therefore, does not exceed a fair and reasonable amount. . . .

McDougald v. Garber

Court of Appeals of New York, 1989.
73 N.Y.2d 246.

■ CHIEF JUDGE WACHTLER. This appeal raises fundamental questions about the nature and role of nonpecuniary damages in personal injury litigation. By nonpecuniary damages, we mean those damages awarded to compensate an injured person for the physical and emotional consequences of the injury, such as pain and suffering and the loss of the ability to engage in certain activities. Pecuniary damages, on the other hand, compensate the victim for the economic consequences of the injury, such as medical expenses, lost earnings and the cost of custodial care.

The specific questions raised here deal with assessment of nonpecuniary damages and are (1) whether some degree of cognitive awareness is a prerequisite to recovery for loss of enjoyment of life and (2) whether a jury should be instructed to consider and award damages for loss of enjoyment of life separately from damages for pain and suffering. We answer the first question in the affirmative and the second question in the negative.

On September 7, 1978, plaintiff Emma McDougald, then 31 years old, underwent a Caesarean section and tubal ligation at New York Infirmary. Defendant Garber performed the surgery; defendants Armengol and Kulkarni provided anesthesia. During the surgery, Mrs. McDougald suffered oxygen deprivation which resulted in severe brain damage and left her in a permanent comatose condition. This action was brought by Mrs. McDougald and her husband, suing derivatively, alleging that the injuries were caused by the defendants' acts of malpractice.

A jury found all defendants liable and awarded Emma McDougald a total of $9,650,102 in damages, including $1,000,000 for conscious pain and suffering and a separate award of $3,500,000 for loss of the pleasures and pursuits of life. The balance of the damages awarded to her were for pecuniary damages—lost earnings and the cost of custodial and nursing care. Her husband was awarded $1,500,000 on his derivative claim for the loss of his wife's services. On defendants' posttrial motions, the Trial Judge reduced the total award to Emma McDougald to $4,796,728 by striking the entire award for future nursing care ($2,353,374) and by reducing the separate awards for conscious pain and suffering and loss of the pleasures and pursuits of life to a single award of $2,000,000. Her husband's award was left intact. On cross appeals, the Appellate Division affirmed and later granted defendants leave to appeal to this court.

We note at the outset that the defendants' liability for Emma McDougald's injuries is unchallenged here . . . .

Also unchallenged are the awards in the amount of $770,978 for loss of earnings and $2,025,750 for future custodial care—that is, the pecuniary damage awards that survived defendants' posttrial motions.

What remains in dispute, primarily, is the award to Emma McDougald for nonpecuniary damages. At trial, defendants sought to show that Mrs. McDougald's injuries were so severe that she was incapable of either experiencing pain or appreciating her condition. Plaintiffs, on the other hand, introduced proof that Mrs. McDougald responded to certain stimuli to a sufficient extent to indicate that she was aware of her circumstances. Thus, the extent of Mrs. McDougald's cognitive abilities, if any, was sharply disputed.

The parties and the trial court agreed that Mrs. McDougald could not recover for pain and suffering unless she were conscious of the pain. Defendants maintained that such consciousness was also required to support an award for loss of enjoyment of life. The court, however, accepted plaintiffs' view that loss of enjoyment of life was compensable without regard to whether the plaintiff was aware of the loss. Accordingly, because the level of Mrs. McDougald's cognitive abilities was in dispute, the court instructed the jury to consider loss of enjoyment of life as an element of nonpecuniary damages separate from pain and suffering. . . .

We conclude that the court erred, both in instructing the jury that Mrs. McDougald's awareness was irrelevant to their consideration of damages for loss of enjoyment of life and in directing the jury to consider that aspect of damages separately from pain and suffering.

We begin with the familiar proposition that an award of damages to a person injured by the negligence of another is to compensate the victim, not to punish the wrongdoer. The goal is to restore the injured party, to the extent possible, to the position that would have been occupied had the wrong not occurred. To be sure, placing the burden of compensation on the negligent party also serves as a deterrent, but purely punitive damages—that is, those which have no compensatory purpose—are prohibited unless the harmful conduct is intentional, malicious, outrageous, or otherwise aggravated beyond mere negligence.

Damages for nonpecuniary losses are, of course, among those that can be awarded as compensation to the victim. This aspect of damages, however, stands on less certain ground than does an award for pecuniary damages. An economic loss can be compensated in kind by an economic gain; but recovery for noneconomic losses such as pain and suffering and loss of enjoyment of life rests on "the legal fiction that money damages can compensate for a victim's injury." We accept this fiction, knowing that although money will neither ease the pain nor restore the victim's abilities, this device is as close as the law can come in its effort to right the wrong. We have no hope of evaluating what has been lost, but a monetary award may provide a measure of solace for the condition created.

Our willingness to indulge this fiction comes to an end, however, when it ceases to serve the compensatory goals of tort recovery. When that limit is met, further indulgence can only result in assessing damages that are punitive. The question posed by this case, then, is whether an award of damages for loss of enjoyment of life to a person whose injuries preclude any awareness of the loss serves a compensatory purpose. We conclude that it does not.

Simply put, an award of money damages in such circumstances has no meaning or utility to the injured person. An award for the loss of enjoyment of life "cannot provide [such a victim] with any consolation or ease any burden resting on him. . . . He cannot spend it upon necessities or pleasures. He cannot experience the pleasure of giving it away."

We recognize that, as the trial court noted, requiring some cognitive awareness as a prerequisite to recovery for loss of enjoyment of life will result in some cases "in the paradoxical situation that the greater the degree of brain injury inflicted by a negligent defendant, the smaller the award the plaintiff can recover in general damages." The force of this argument, however—the temptation to achieve a balance between injury and damages—has nothing to do with meaningful compensation for the victim. Instead, the temptation is rooted in a desire to punish the defendant in proportion to the harm inflicted. However relevant such retributive symmetry may be in the criminal law, it has no place in the law of civil damages, at least in the absence of culpability beyond mere negligence.

Accordingly, we conclude that cognitive awareness is a prerequisite to recovery for loss of enjoyment of life. We do not go so far, however, as to require the fact finder to sort out varying degrees of cognition and determine at what level a particular deprivation can be fully appreciated. With respect to pain and suffering, the trial court charged simply that there must be "some level of awareness" in order for plaintiff to recover. We think that this is an appropriate standard for all aspects of nonpecuniary loss. No doubt the standard ignores analytically relevant levels of cognition, but we resist the desire for analytical purity in favor of simplicity. A more complex instruction might give the appearance of greater precision but, given the limits of our understanding of the human mind, it would in reality lead only to greater speculation.

We turn next to the question whether loss of enjoyment of life should be considered a category of damages separate from pain and suffering.

There is no dispute here that the fact finder may, in assessing nonpecuniary damages, consider the effect of the injuries on the plaintiff's capacity to lead a normal life. Traditionally, in this State and elsewhere, this aspect of suffering has not been treated as a separate category of damages; instead, the plaintiff's inability to enjoy life to its fullest has been considered one type of suffering to be factored into a general award for nonpecuniary damages, commonly known as pain and suffering.

Recently, however, there has been an attempt to segregate the suffering associated with physical pain from the mental anguish that stems from the inability to engage in certain activities, and to have juries provide a separate award for each.

Some courts have resisted the effort, primarily on the ground that duplicative and therefore excessive awards would result. Other courts have allowed separate awards, noting that the types of suffering involved are analytically distinguishable. Still other courts have questioned the propriety of the practice but held that, in the particular case, separate awards did not constitute reversible error.

In this State, the only appellate [courts] to address the question . . . were persuaded that the distinctions between the two types of mental anguish justified separate awards and that the potential for duplicative awards could be mitigated by carefully drafted jury instructions. In addition, the courts opined that separate awards would facilitate appellate review concerning the excessiveness of the total damage award.

We do not dispute that distinctions can be found or created between the concepts of pain and suffering and loss of enjoyment of life. If the term "suffering" is limited to the emotional response to the sensation of pain, then the emotional response caused by the limitation of life's activities may be considered qualitatively different. But suffering need not be so limited—it can easily encompass the frustration and anguish caused by the inability to participate in activities that once brought pleasure. Traditionally, by treating loss of enjoyment of life as a permissible factor in assessing pain and suffering, courts have given the term this broad meaning.

If we are to depart from this traditional approach and approve a separate award for loss of enjoyment of life, it must be on the basis that such an approach will yield a more accurate evaluation of the compensation due to the plaintiff. We have no doubt that, in general, the total award for nonpecuniary damages would increase if we adopted the rule. That separate awards are advocated by plaintiffs and resisted by defendants is sufficient evidence that larger awards are at stake here. But a larger award does not by itself indicate that the goal of compensation has been better served.

The advocates of separate awards contend that because pain and suffering and loss of enjoyment of life can be distinguished, they must be treated separately if the plaintiff is to be compensated fully for each distinct injury suffered. We disagree. Such an analytical approach may have its place when the subject is pecuniary damages, which can be calculated with some precision. But the estimation of nonpecuniary damages is not amenable to such analytical precision and may, in fact, suffer from its application. Translating human suffering into dollars and cents involves no mathematical formula; it rests, as we have said, on a legal fiction. The figure that emerges is unavoidably distorted by the translation. Application of this murky process to the component parts of nonpecuniary injuries (however analytically distinguishable they may be) cannot make it more accurate. If anything, the distortion will be amplified by repetition.

Thus, we are not persuaded that any salutary purpose would be served by having the jury make separate awards for pain and suffering and loss of enjoyment of life. We are confident, furthermore, that the trial advocate's art is a sufficient guarantee that none of the plaintiff's losses will be ignored by the jury.

The errors in the instructions given to the jury require a new trial on the issue of nonpecuniary damages to be awarded to plaintiff Emma McDougald. . . .

■ TITONE, J. (dissenting.) The majority's holding represents a compromise position that neither comports with the fundamental principles of tort compensation nor furnishes a satisfactory, logically consistent framework for compensating nonpecuniary loss. Because I conclude that loss of enjoyment of life is an objective damage item, conceptually distinct from conscious pain and suffering, I can find no fault with the trial court's instruction authorizing separate awards and permitting an award for "loss of enjoyment of life" even in the absence of any awareness of that loss on the part of the injured plaintiff. Accordingly, I dissent. . . .

Unquestionably, recovery of a damage item such as "pain and suffering" requires a showing of some degree of cognitive capacity. Such a requirement exists for the simple reason that pain and suffering are wholly subjective concepts and cannot exist separate and apart from the human consciousness that experiences them. In contrast, the destruction of an individual's capacity to enjoy life as a result of a crippling injury is an objective fact that does not differ in principle from the permanent loss of an eye or limb. As in the case of a lost limb, an essential characteristic of a healthy human life has been wrongfully taken, and, consequently, the injured party is entitled to a monetary award as a substitute, if, as the majority asserts, the goal of tort compensation is "to restore the injured party, to the extent possible, to the position that would have been occupied had the wrong not occurred."

Significantly, this equation does not suggest a need to establish the injured's awareness of the loss. The victim's ability to comprehend the degree to which his or her life has been impaired is irrelevant, since, unlike "conscious pain and suffering," the impairment exists independent of the victim's ability to apprehend it. Indeed, the majority reaches the conclusion that a degree of awareness must be shown only after injecting a new element into the equation. Under the majority's formulation, the victim must be aware of the loss because, in addition to being compensatory, the award must have "meaning or utility to the injured person." This additional requirement, however, has no real foundation in law or logic. "Meaning" and "utility" are subjective value judgments that have no place in the law of tort recovery, where the primary goal is to find ways of quantifying, to the extent possible, the worth of various forms of human tragedy.

Moreover, the compensatory nature of a monetary award for loss of enjoyment of life is not altered or rendered punitive by the fact that the unaware injured plaintiff cannot experience the pleasure of having it. The fundamental distinction between punitive and compensatory damages is that the former exceed the amount necessary to replace what the plaintiff lost. As the Court of Appeals for the Second Circuit has observed, "[t]he fact that the compensation [for loss of enjoyment of life] may inure as a practical matter to third parties in a given case does not transform the nature of the damages."

Ironically, the majority's expressed goal of limiting recovery for nonpecuniary loss to compensation that the injured plaintiff has the capacity to appreciate is directly undercut by the majority's ultimate holding, adopted in the interest of "simplicity," that recovery for loss of enjoyment of life may be had as long as the injured plaintiff has "some level of awareness," however slight. Manifestly, there are many different forms and levels of awareness, particularly in cases involving brain injury. Further, the type and degree of cognitive functioning necessary to experience "pain and suffering" is certainly of a lower order than that needed to apprehend the loss of the ability to enjoy life in all of its subtleties. Accordingly, the existence of "some level of awareness" on the part of the injured plaintiff says nothing about that plaintiff's ability to derive some comfort from the award or even to appreciate its significance. Hence, that standard does not assure that loss of enjoyment of life damages will be awarded only when they serve "a compensatory purpose," as that term is defined by the majority. . . .

Having concluded that the injured plaintiff's awareness should not be a necessary precondition to recovery for loss of enjoyment of life, I also have no difficulty going on to conclude that loss of enjoyment of life is a distinct damage item which is recoverable separate and apart from the award for conscious pain and suffering. The majority has rejected separate recovery, in part because it apparently perceives some overlap between the two damage categories and in part because it believes that the goal of enhancing the precision of jury awards for nonpecuniary loss would not be advanced. However, the overlap the majority perceives exists only if one assumes, as the majority evidently has, that the "loss of enjoyment" category of damages is designed to compensate only for "*the emotional response* caused by the limitation of life's activities" and "*the frustration and anguish caused by* the inability to participate in activities that once brought pleasure" (emphasis added), both of which are highly *subjective* concepts.

In fact, while "pain and suffering compensates the victim for the physical and mental discomfort caused by the injury; . . . loss of enjoyment of life compensates the victim for the limitations on the person's life created by the injury," a distinctly *objective* loss. In other words, while the victim's "emotional response" and "frustration and anguish" are elements of the award for pain and suffering, the "limitation of life's activities" and the "inability to participate in activities" that the majority identifies are recoverable under the "loss of enjoyment of life" rubric. Thus, there is no real overlap, and no real basis for concern about potentially duplicative awards where, as here, there is a properly instructed jury.

Finally, given the clear distinction between the two categories of nonpecuniary damages, I cannot help but assume that permitting separate awards for conscious pain and suffering and loss of enjoyment of life would contribute to accuracy and precision in thought in the jury's deliberations on the issue of damages. . . .

NOTE

On the question of damages for loss of enjoyment of one's life, the Ohio Supreme Court stated:

> "Courts throughout the United States have differed on whether damages may be awarded for loss of enjoyment of life in addition to, and separate from, an award for other elements of damages such as pain and suffering, or an award for general damages. . . .
>
> "The damage with which we deal here is the claimed impairment of one's physical capacity to enjoy the amenities of life. This concept entails providing compensation for the deprivation of one's ability to engage in those activities, and perform those functions, which were part of, and provided pleasure to, one's life prior to the injury. This type of claimed damage is distinguishable from those types of damages that are based upon recognized categories of bodily pain and mental suffering. The claim of damages for deprivation or impairment of life's usual activities has, in other jurisdictions, been applied to a wide variety of pleasurable activities shown to have been curtailed by the injuries received by the plaintiff. Such damages include loss of ability to play golf, dance, bowl, play musical instruments, engage in specific outdoor sports, along with other activities. These types of experiences are all positive sensations of pleasure, the loss of which could provide a basis for an award of damages to the plaintiff in varying degrees depending upon his involvement, as shown by the evidence. Such proof differs from the elements of mental suffering occasioned by the plaintiff's injury such as nervousness, grief, shock, anxiety, and so forth. Although the loss of the ability to engage in a usual pleasant activity of life is an emotional experience, it is a loss of a positive experience rather than the infliction of a negative experience.
>
> "In a review and weighing of all factors involved in this discussion, we find it reasonable to treat the claimed inability to

perform usual functions (both basic and hedonic) as a separate and distinct element of damage. . . .

"[T]he many jurisdictions which have not permitted 'loss of enjoyment of life' as a separate element of damages made their determination on the basis that this would lead to a duplication of damages, in that the jury would have included that loss within the element of pain and suffering or the permanency of the disability. We recognize the validity of such fears, and with the aim of avoiding the feared duplication, shall herewith set forth new provisions to Section 23.01 of OJI. Our intent is that the trial court shall henceforth instruct the jury that if it awards damages for loss of ability to perform usual activities (which will also encompass the permanency of the disability suffered), the jury must not award additional damages for that same loss when considering any other element of damages, such as physical and mental pain and suffering, as such additional award would be duplicative.

"In the appropriate case, where there have been allegations of and evidence adduced on the plaintiff's inability to perform usual activities, occasioned by the injuries received, the trial court shall give these additional instructions to the jury:

> 'If you find from the greater weight of the evidence that, as a proximate cause of the injuries sustained, the plaintiff has suffered a permanent disability which is evidenced by way of the inability to perform the usual activities of life such as the basic mechanical body movements of walking, climbing stairs, feeding oneself, driving a car, etc., or by way of the inability to perform the plaintiff's usual specific activities which had given pleasure to this particular plaintiff, you may consider, and make a separate award for, such damages.
>
> 'Any amounts that you have determined will be awarded to the plaintiff for any element of damages shall not be considered again or added to any other element of damages. You shall be cautious in your consideration of the damages not to overlap or duplicate the amounts of your award which would result in double damages. For example, any amount of damages awarded to the plaintiff for pain and suffering must not be awarded again as an element of damages for the plaintiff's inability to perform usual activities. In like manner, any amount of damages awarded to the plaintiff for the inability to perform usual activities must not be considered again as an element of damages awarded for the plaintiff's pain and suffering, or any other element of damages.' "

Fantozzi *v.* Sandusky Cement Products Co., 64 Ohio St. 3d 601, 612–618 (1992).

Hagerty v. L & L Marine Services, Inc.

United States Court of Appeals, Fifth Circuit, 1986.
788 F.2d 315.

■ REAVLEY, CIRCUIT JUDGE. William L. Hagerty was accidently soaked with toxic chemicals while doing duty as a Jones Act seaman. He sues for his damages which include pain and suffering, mental anguish due to the fear of developing cancer, and the medical expense of regular checkups to monitor against that disease. The district court granted summary judgment for the defendants on the ground that no cause of action had accrued. We reverse and remand.

The traditional tort rules may be restated. A tortious cause of action accrues when the victim suffers harm caused by the defendant's wrong. The injury or harm may occur simultaneously with the tortious conduct in the case of a traumatic event or the injury may be latent and not manifested and discovered until some later date. When the fact of the injury does occur, if discovered by the victim, the cause of action accrues. The victim is then entitled to sue for his damages, past and present, as well as his probable future damages, and limitation also begins to run on the time within which suit may be instituted. The victim is entitled to only one cause of action and, if his injuries subsequently worsen, he has no further opportunity for recompense.

The present appeal raises, primarily, the question of whether a cause of action has accrued. We hold that Hagerty suffered physical injuries and was entitled to pursue this action. The element of fear of cancer and attendant medical costs will be urged upon remand, and we therefore address that issue. Finally, we volunteer our dissatisfaction with the single cause of action rule in face of the recurring problem of injured people facing the possibility of cancer. Those victims should be entitled to recover for present injuries and, also, for the cancer when and if it later develops; they should neither be entitled nor compelled to recover for cancer damages until those damages can be realistically assessed. . . .

The cause of action has accrued if Hagerty's injury was discernible on the occasion when he was drenched with the toxic chemical. Albertson *v.* T.J. Stevenson & Co., 749 F.2d 223 (5th Cir. 1984). Dizziness, leg cramps, and a persistent stinging sensation in feet and fingers suggest some harm or injury. The prospects of cancer are of some significance only because that affected Hagerty's appraisal of the significance of what had occurred. Whether a person has suffered harm and whether it is nominal or significant may depend upon that person's own feelings and response. One person might ignore headaches and temporary lassitude, while another—possibly because of a lower pain threshold or because of a greater awareness of the potential consequences—might be so disturbed as to suffer injury and be charged by law with the accrual of a cause of action. In *Albertson* we held that limitations barred the Jones Act and general maritime law claims because the plaintiff's headaches and nausea and a subsequent loss of consciousness gave the plaintiff knowledge of the critical facts that he had suffered more than a minor injury. While the early effects of Hagerty's exposure may not have been as severe as those of Albertson, we hold that they suffice to present an issue of physical injury and to render summary judgment improper.

Upon trial the plaintiff is entitled to recover damages for all of his past, present and probable future harm attributable to the defendant's tortious conduct. Those damages include pain and suffering and mental anguish. The present fear or anxiety due to the possibility of contracting cancer constitutes a present fact of mental anguish and may be included in recoverable damages. The increase in the risk of his contracting cancer may not be included, however.

Defendants contend that a plaintiff's cancerphobia should not be considered a present injury unless accompanied by "physical manifestations." Only a physical injury requirement, they argue, will ensure against the proliferation of "unworthy claims." It would also deny worthy claims, perhaps that of Hagerty. We believe the courts have better devices with which to choose between the worthy and the unworthy.

Cancerphobia is merely a specific type of mental anguish or emotional distress. Courts have long allowed plaintiffs to recover for psychic and emotional harm in Federal Employers' Liability Act or Jones Act/maritime cases. Indeed, these statutes are intended to provide broad coverage for all work-related "injuries," whether characterized as mental or physical. Furthermore, while neither the parties' nor our own research has uncovered any claims for cancerphobia under the Jones Act or FELA, courts have often recognized such claims in other contexts.

The physical injury requirement, like its counterpart, the physical impact requirement, was developed to provide courts with an objective means of ensuring that the alleged mental injury is not feigned. We believe that notion to be unrealistic. It is doubtful that the trier of fact is any less able to decide the fact or extent of mental suffering in the event of physical injury or impact. With or without physical injury or impact, a plaintiff is entitled to recover damages for serious mental distress arising from fear of developing cancer where his fear is reasonable and causally related to the defendant's negligence. The circumstances surrounding the fear-inducing occurrence may themselves supply sufficient indicia of genuineness. It is for the jury to decide questions such as the existence, severity and reasonableness of the fear.

Here, Hagerty has testified that he studied the characteristics of the chemicals he dealt with and thus knew before his exposure that dripolene was a carcinogen. In addition, he felt physical effects after the first dousing; having previously watched benzene absorb into his finger, these effects triggered anxiety because he realized that his entire body had absorbed the chemical. He further testified that he saw a doctor after the exposure and advised his co-worker to do the same. His doctor advised him to undergo periodic medical testing for cancer. In addition to doing so, he subsequently left his job as a tankerman out of concern for future accidents. From this evidence, we conclude that Hagerty has presented sufficient indicia of genuineness so as to make summary judgment of his cancerphobia claim improper.

In addition to any damages for mental distress, Hagerty correctly asserts that he is entitled to recover for the continuing expense of his periodic medical checkups. A plaintiff ordinarily may recover reasonable medical expenses, past and future, which he incurs as a result of a demonstrated injury. Moreover, under the "avoidable consequences rule," he is required to submit to treatment that is medically advisable; failure to do so may bar future recovery for a condition he could thereby have alleviated or avoided. Hagerty testified that he undergoes the checkups at the advice of his physician to ensure early detection and treatment of a possible cancerous condition. We agree that the reasonable cost of those checkups may be included in a damage award to the extent that, in the past, they were medically advisable and, in the future, will probably remain so.

Hagerty also urges that he be allowed to recover damages for his increased risk of contracting cancer in the future. In his brief, he does not specify exactly what he believes that "increased risk" to be; we assume, however, that it is not greater than fifty percent.

Recent commentators have argued for recognition of a claim for "increased risk," whether greater or less than fifty percent. . . . [W]e conclude that a plaintiff can recover only where he can show that the toxic exposure more probably than not *will* lead to cancer. Because he does not allege that he has cancer or will probably develop it in the future, Hagerty does not state a claim for this possible effect of his dousing.

In *Albertson*, this court decided that the single cause of action rule barred the plaintiff's suit for complications to his initial injury from trichloroethylene exposure. That result is consistent with the vast majority of latent diseases cases under state tort law, particularly those involving asbestos exposure. The victim of exposure to toxic substances which cause present harm and which may at some future time cause cancer or other serious disease is further victimized by the single cause of action rule. If Hagerty, for example, cannot prove a future probability of his contracting cancer when his trial is conducted but thereafter does contract the disease because of the 1982 exposure at Guyanilla, he will have no remedy for his damages suffered from cancer. He could not, however, have postponed this suit to protect himself from the catastrophic damages because, having suffered some injury, he was forced to sue or suffer the same fate as Albertson.

Even when there is evidence that the increased risk of cancer exceeds fifty percent, the rule does not work well. A plaintiff, if suffering any injury, is forced to seek cancer damages although the extent of those damages is yet highly speculative. They may be nothing at all because what was probable may not occur. The extent of the disease may be limited or the suffering and expenses may be enormous.

The rule has its disadvantages for all parties. Consider the case of Jackson *v.* Johns-Manville Sales Corp., 781 F.2d 394 (5th Cir. 1986) (*en banc*). The prognosis of Jackson's future cancer was not predicated on the detection of any personal physiology, not from results of a cytogenetic test or a showing of immunodysfunction in Jackson himself. It was based entirely on the experience of all persons who have developed asbestosis from heavy exposure to asbestos dust; over fifty percent of those people have in the past died from bronchogenic carcinoma. Should all plaintiffs who make that showing recover for cancer damages, and if they match the experience upon which the testimony is based, over forty percent of them will not contract cancer even though they will have been awarded the damages. The onset of cancer, its extent and the amount of damages are too speculative to be decided in this manner.

At least in the toxic chemical or asbestos cases, the disease of cancer should be treated as a separate cause of action for all purposes. There should be no cause of action or beginning of the running of limitations until the diagnosis of the disease. Nor should damages for that disease be recoverable unless and until that time. A prior but distinct disease, though the tortfeasor may have paid reparations, should not affect the cause of action and damages for the subsequent disease.

A few courts have been willing to construe the "single injury" rule so as not to preclude a later suit for latent disease. . . .

When the proper case is presented, this panel hopes that the en banc court will consider this problem, if Congress has not acted upon it by that time. . . .

2. TORT REFORM

Beginning in the mid-1980s, legislatures in many states enacted a wide variety of statutes designed to rein in tort liability. These statutes were motivated in part by a crisis in the insurance industry, which tort reform proponents attributed to increasingly high damage awards. Common statutory limitations include caps on non-economic damages, caps on damages in particular types of actions, restrictions on punitive damages, abolition or limitation of the collateral source rule, and limits on contingent fee arrangements.

Federal constitutional challenges to tort reform have not been successful. Challenges based on due process, equal protection, jury trial, and open-access-to-court provisions of state constitutions have brought mixed results. See, *e.g.*, Fein *v.* Permanente Medical Group, 38 Cal.3d 137 (1985) (upholding a cap on non-economic damages and other restrictions); Carson *v.* Maurer, 120 N.H. 925 (1980) (invalidating a cap on non-economic damages and other restrictions on equal protection grounds); Smith *v.* Department of Insurance, 507 So.2d 1080 (Fla. 1987) (invalidating a cap on non-economic damages based on a state constitutional provision guaranteeing that "courts shall be open to every person for redress of any injury)." For a wider survey, see 3 STEIN ON PERSONAL INJURY DAMAGES, ch. 19 (1997).

Tort reform statutes are premised on perceptions about damages award patterns that often do not reflect reality. Interest groups may portray damages as ever-increasing and out of control. The following discussion, based on Theodore Eisenberg, Empirical Effect of Tort Reform, in RESEARCH HANDBOOK ON THE ECONOMICS OF TORTS (Jennifer Arlen ed., 2014), focuses on information about the pattern of damages awards in tried cases and on the effect of tort reform in medical malpractice cases.

A. Compensatory Awards in State Court Trials over Time

The best available data on damages awarded at trial in state courts are from the Civil Justice Survey of State Courts, a National Center for State Courts (NCSC)–Bureau of Justice Statistics (BJS) project. The Civil Justice Survey gathers data directly from state court clerks' offices on tort, contract, and property cases disposed of by trial in fiscal year 1991–1992 (referred to hereafter as 1991) and in calendar years 1996, 2001, and 2005. Each of these time periods corresponds to a separate data set. The first three datasets covered state courts of general jurisdiction in a random sample of 45 or 46 of the 75 most populous counties in the United States. The 2001 Civil Justice Survey data included 46 counties; the 1991–92 and 1996 data included 45. The 2005 Civil Justice Survey included 46 of the 75 most populous counties selected to maintain backwards compatibility with the earlier Civil Justice Surveys and expanded coverage by adding 110 counties to represent the 3,066 smaller counties not included in the country's 75 largest counties.[i]

Table 1 shows the mean and median compensatory award for each year, subdivided by jury trials and judge trials. Data on judge trials was not gathered in the 1991 study.

---

[i] For summaries of the data and methodology in the Civil Justice Surveys, see Bureau of Justice Statistics Bulletin: Civil Justice Survey of State Courts, 2001: Civil Trial Cases and Verdicts in Large Counties, 2001 (Apr. 2004); Bureau of Justice Statistics Bulletin: Civil Justice Survey of State Courts, 1996: Civil Trial Cases and Verdicts in Large Counties (1996); Bureau of Justice Statistics Special Report: Civil Justice Survey of State Courts, 1992: Civil Jury Cases and Verdicts in Large Counties (July 1995); Bureau of Justice Statistics Special Report: Civil Justice Survey of State Courts, 2005: Civil Bench and Jury Trials in State Courts, 2005 (Oct. 2008); Codebook, Inter-university Consortium for Political and Social Research, Civil Justice Survey of State Courts, 2005 [United States], Study No. 2386. The initial Civil Justice Survey dataset (1991–92) included only jury trials. The three subsequent datasets include jury and bench trials. The three datasets include all completed trials in most of the counties.

Table 1. Mean and Median Compensatory Award 1991 to 2005, State Court Trials

Year	Mean	Median	N	Mean	Median	N
	Compensatory award, juries			Compensatory award, judges		
1991	510,197	60,730	3,053	data on judges not gathered		
1996	1,351,195	58,335	3,005	197,116	32,328	1,377
2001	736,728	42,311	3,086	204,840	26,361	1,204
2005	722,950	40,000	2,954	218,074	29,035	1,470
Total	828,824	50,062	12,098	207,017	28,900	4,051

Note. Amounts are in 2005 dollars. Unweighted results reported.

Additional information on award trends over time is available in Seth A. Seabury, Nicholas M. Pace, and Robert T. Reville, Forty Years of Civil Jury Verdicts, 1 J. Empirical Legal Stud. 1 (2004). That study covers a longer time period but has smaller geographical coverage than the NCSC-BJS data. The authors summarize their results as follows:

> "This article examines the long-term trends in jury verdicts reached in tort trials using 40 years of data from San Francisco County, CA and Cook County, IL. Our data come from the RAND Institute for Civil Justice (ICJ), which has been collecting and analyzing data on jury verdicts for the past 20 years. However, while the ICJ data include verdicts rendered in some jurisdictions from as far back as 1959, previous reports have focused their analysis on smaller time periods of just 20, 10, or 5 years. This report uses verdicts reached in the years 1960–1999 in San Francisco County and Cook County and, as such, this is the first time all the collections of ICJ data have ever been combined into a single, unified sample for multidecade analysis, albeit for two counties only. The 40 years of data that we analyze here comprise, to our knowledge, the longest time series on jury decisions ever collected in a uniform manner, offering an unprecedented opportunity to study the long-term behavior of jury verdicts. . . .
>
> "Our results are striking. Not only do we show that real average awards have grown by less than real income over the 40 years in our sample, we also find that essentially all of this growth can be explained by changes in observable case characteristics and claimed economic losses (particularly claimed medical costs). However, focusing on the average award masks considerable heterogeneity in the growth rates for different kinds of cases. In particular, we find that the average award in automobile cases declined after controlling for claimed medical costs, offsetting persistent and unexplained growth in the average awards for other tort cases. In general, though, the

growth (or decline) does not appear substantial enough to support claims of radically changing jury behavior over the past 40 years. Rising claimed medical costs appear to be one of the most important factors driving increases in jury verdicts."

Id. at 2–3.

B. Compensatory Awards by Type of Case

The 1991 to 2005 NCSC-BJS the studies referred to above also allow a breakdown of awards by type of cases. Table 2 shows, for each case type, the mean and median compensatory award for the four time periods aggregated together.

Table 2. Mean and Median Compensatory Award 1991 to 2005, State Court Trials

Case type	Mean	Median	N	Mean	Median	N
	Compensatory award, juries			Compensatory award, judges		
Motor vehicle tort	284,206	22,321	5,533	340,469	16,884	490
Premises liability	586,069	91,740	1,493	383,584	47,301	137
Products liability, asbestos	1,601,555	492,123	170	163,539	163,539	1
Products liability, other	3,401,697	500,000	110	196,470	72,807	17
Intentional tort	595,789	50,187	403	166,042	38,109	112
Medical malpractice	1,953,097	455,079	769	283,941	227,723	26
Professional malpractice, other	1,137,275	172,974	125	453,526	54,982	39
Slander/libel	935,421	34,624	68	561,010	18,655	21
Animal attack	477,036	95,667	160	78,490	38,278	10
Conversion	477,468	114,752	22	198,644	20,000	31
False arrest, impris., prosec.	364,069	187,470	14	40,017	31,054	3
Other or unknown tort	5,667,438	108,885	528	178,577	38,306	68
Fraud	1,106,499	78,914	453	450,943	44,147	350
Seller plaintiff	375,319	64,374	604	141,030	33,523	1,487
Buyer plaintiff	399,929	58,038	656	144,632	17,497	493
Employment dispute, discrimination	456,153	175,000	257	95,981	59,929	21
Employment dispute, other	1,758,913	85,815	222	78,479	28,312	114
Rental/lease agreement	217,821	47,250	101	96,434	24,358	319
Tortious interference	2,192,856	142,996	98	118,301	32,001	62
Partnership dispute	1,503,790	127,494	24	196,731	86,844	20

Other or unknown contract	737,784	83,260	138	210,936	38,147	85
Subrogation	45,235	8,862	22	28,825	7,517	23
Other or unknown real property	114,427	4,166	84	263,377	24,341	114
Unknown	399,810	48,866	22			0
Total	829,605	50,000	12,076	207,271	28,834	4,043

Note. Amounts are in 2005 dollars. Unweighted results reported.

C. Federal and State Damages Comparison

In General Civil Jury Trial Litigation in State and Federal Courts: A Statistical Portrait, 5 J. Empirical Legal Stud. 593 (2008), Thomas H. Cohen compared federal jury trial data available from the Administrative Office of the United States Courts with the NCSC-BJS state jury trial court data for 1991 to 2001. The article limited the federal data to the same geographic locales or counties as the state data. Some of the results are summarized as follows:

> "Table 3 examines the median damage awards garnered by plaintiffs who prevailed in civil jury trials concluded in state and federal district courts in 1992, 1996, and 2001. Overall, the median damage awards were consistently and substantially higher in the federal as opposed to the state courts.[14] These findings mirror the Eisenberg et al. study which also observed larger federal damage awards (Eisenberg et al., 1995–1996).
>
> "In the federal courts, half of plaintiffs who won at trial received damages of $228,000 or more; in comparison, the median damage awards in the state courts were $48,000. In tort jury trials, the median damage awards were approximately five times higher in the federal ($199,000) than in the state ($41,000) courts. When automobile accident cases are excluded from the tort award calculation, the median damage amounts for tort cases in state courts becomes higher ($105,000), but is still substantially lower compared to tort cases tried in the federal courts ($221,000). Contract cases tried in the federal courts also manifested higher median awards compared to their state counterparts ($311,000 federal vs. $77,000 state).

[14] Median, as opposed to mean, damage awards are presented because of the limitations inherent in the federal damage award data field. The reliability of the AOUSC damage award field has been questioned because of the way in which damage award data are recorded. . . .

Table 3. Mean and Median Compensatory Award 1991 to 2005, State Court Trials

Case Types	State Civil Jury Trials			
	Number	Median Damage Awards	Confidence lower	Interval upper
Total	15,814	$48,000	$42,000	$56,000
All torts	12,448	41,000	35,000	49,000
All contracts	3,300	77,000	68,000	88,000
All real property	66	80,000	35,000	185,000
Non-motor-vehicle torts total	5,243	$105,000	$94,000	$119,000
All other torts	3,744	73,000	63,000	85,000
Medical malpractice	948	349,000	309,000	379,000
Asbestos	303	189,000	134,000	233,000
Product liability	247	347,000	151,000	433,000
Motor vehicle torts	7,205	$23,000	$19,000	$26,000

	Federal Civil Jury Trials	
	Number	Median Damage Awards
Total	1,496	$228,000
All torts	944	199,000
All contracts	528	311,000
All real property	24	156,000
Non-motor-vehicle torts total	616	$221,000
All other torts	434	163,000
Product liability	138	702,000
Medical malpractice	37	508,000
Asbestos	7	164,000
Motor vehicle torts	328	$151,000

Note: Table includes only those state and federal general civil jury trials with award payouts to plaintiffs. Eighty-seven percent of plaintiff winners in federal jury trials were awarded damages and 97.4% of plaintiff winners in state jury trials were awarded damages. Award data were rounded to the nearest thousand. Damage awards adjusted for inflation in 2001 dollars. Confidence intervals were calculated using WesVar Software for state jury trials. No confidence intervals were calculated for federal jury trials because the federal data are not from a sample.

"Although the data seem to show that federal juries are inclined to award damages that are significantly higher compared to state juries, these differences are driven mostly by federal diversity jurisdictional mandates. In addition to the requirement that the litigants are from different states or countries, a diversity case cannot be brought into the federal courts unless the amount in controversy being litigated is over $75,000.[15] The $75,000 figure is almost two times higher than the $48,000 median award imposed by juries in state courts. The amount in controversy requirements leads to higher damage awards in the federal courts and makes comparisons of state and federal jury awards problematic.

"Even though the monetary amounts being litigated in the federal courts are generally higher than the state courts, the amount of damages being awarded tend to follow similar patterns. Overall, the medical malpractice and product liability case categories manifested some of the highest damages awards in both court systems. The median damage award for medical malpractice trials in state courts ($349,000) was approximately nine times greater than the $41,000 median award figure for all tort trials. In the federal courts, medical malpractice trials produced median awards that were approximately three times greater compared to the overall tort case category ($508,000 medical malpractice award vs. $199,000 total tort award). Similar patterns manifested themselves in the product liability case category where the median awards in the state ($349,000) and federal ($702,000) courts were substantially higher compared to the average tort case in both venues. In automobile accident trials, the median awards in both the state ($23,000) and federal ($151,000) courts were significantly lower compared to the overall tort case category.

"The award patterns noted in these data are similar to those described by Eisenberg et al. who observed that "product liability and medical malpractice cases in both court systems generate mean and median awards well above other areas of the law . . . motor vehicle cases are at the low end of the . . . award-level spectrum [and] contact cases group between the high and low end tort areas" (Eisenberg et al., 1995–1996: 438).

"A major difference between Eisenberg's and the extant study concerns the award amounts for asbestos trials. In federal courts, Eisenberg noted that asbestos cases were "literally in a world of their own" with median and mean damage awards in the millions of dollars. Current data shows a decline in the damages being awarded to litigants in federal asbestos jury

[15] The minimum value required was $10,000 until 1989 and $50,000 until 1996, when it was raised to $75,000 in P.L. 104–317, Federal Courts Improvement Act.

> trials. In 1992, 1996, and 2001, seven asbestos trials were concluded in the federal district courts in which the plaintiffs prevailed and received damages. The median damage awards for these cases were $164,000. The decline in asbestos damage awards can be attributed to numerous factors including the multi-district transfer of these cases and an overall reduction in the number of asbestos cases decided by trial."

Id. at 603–06.

D. Non-Economic Damages

Tort reform legislation often places special limits on non-economic damages such as damages for pain and suffering. The worry is that unless these damages are restricted, fact-finders will have too much discretion and awards will be excessive or uneven. One empirical study, however, suggests that non-economic damages are not as unruly as they often are assumed to be.

In Yun-chien Chang, Theodore Eisenberg, Tsung Hsien Li, and Martin T. Wells, Pain and Suffering Damages in Person Injury Cases: An Empirical Study, 14 J. Empirical Legal Stud. 199 (2017), the authors looked at patterns of pain and suffering awards in Taiwan and the United States. They began with the premise that pain and suffering cannot be sufficiently quantified to serves the aim of optimal deterrence of wrongs. The next-best aim is predictability, which allows for settlement.

Taiwanese courts do not use civil juries and tort awards are generally much lower in Taiwan than in the United States. Nevertheless, the authors found that in both countries, pain and suffering awards were closely correlated with elements of economic damages and other factors that were relatively easy to quantify and also logically connected to pain. In particular, pain and suffering awards tracked awards for medical expenses and were consistent with the level of injury suffered. These findings suggest that, despite significant differences in procedure, fact-finding, and background social and economic conditions, pain and suffering awards are reasonably predictable across jurisdictions.

On a less positive note, the authors also found that pain and suffering awards correlated with the amount of pain and suffering damages requested by the plaintiff. This suggests that factfinders' assessment of non-economic damages is subject to a cognitive bias known as the anchoring effect, in which exposure to a salient numerical figure may affect outcomes whether or not the figure is logically related to the question to be decided. Anchoring may not undermine predictability, but it introduces a normatively irrelevant element into legal decisionmaking.

E. Medical Malpractice Tort Reform in Particular

McDougald was a medical malpractice case and medical malpractice perhaps has been the most active area of tort reform. Medical malpractice liability has an important characteristic as an object of study. Relevant information about patients' condition and medical treatment often is preserved in accessible form. The preserved information enables ex post assessment of defendant behavior through expert review of medical records. No area of law has been as scrutinized with respect to whether legal system outcomes correlate with a standard of care. Both the need for reform and its effects can be assessed through studies exploiting information available to assess evidence of the standard of care. In addition, society's strong interest in law's effect on physician behavior has generated many studies.

The least disputable crisis in the medical malpractice field is underclaiming by victim patients. A medical malpractice liability system persists because the scope and impact of medical malpractice is massive. A 1999 Institute of Medicine report found that medical error caused between 44,000 and 98,000 deaths and over one million injuries each year, with an associated cost of $17 to $29 billion. Linda T. Kohn et al., eds., TO ERR IS HUMAN: BUILDING A SAFER HEALTH SYSTEM (1999). A 1993 report on New York hospitals stated that medical injury accounts for more deaths than all other accidents combined. Paul C. Weiler et al., A MEASURE OF MALPRACTICE: MEDICAL INJURY, MALPRACTICE LITIGATION, AND PATIENT COMPENSATION (1993). Evidence indicates that this problem has not materially diminished over time, though important initiatives exist. Most victims of tortious behavior never claim at all and the vast majority of people who are injured as result of poor medical care do not file a claim. *E.g.*, Weiler et al.

But this crisis has not been the object of emphasis by groups such as the American Medical Association (AMA). Their focus with respect to reform has been on whether the legal system's functioning in the medical malpractice cases that are brought should be changed to limit recoveries of the relatively small fraction of victims who do bring claims. The efforts at tort reform to protect physicians and reduce insurance and litigation costs are too numerous to systematically review here. The topics addressed here are how the legal system performs in medical malpractice cases, the effects of liability and liability reform on physician behavior, the effects of liability reform on physician availability, the effects of damages caps on insurance premiums and victim recoveries, and the effects of selected miscellaneous reforms.

(1) The Performance of the Legal System

One approach to medical malpractice reform is to focus on frivolous lawsuits. Nevertheless, there is evidence from medical malpractice studies suggesting that frivolous suits are rare. For example, a study of 1,452 closed malpractice claims from five liability insurers concluded that, "The vast majority of resources go toward resolving and paying claims that involve [medical] errors." David M. Studdert et al., Claims, Errors, and Compensation Payments in Medical Malpractice Litigation, 354 New England J. Medicine 2024 (2006). A different view has been taken by the AMA. Under a headline of "Meritless lawsuits cost everyone," the AMA stated in 2006 that there were 125,000 lawsuits currently in the system. American Medical Association, AMERICA'S MEDICAL LIABILITY CRISIS (2006). It failed to note that studies suggest the vast majority of the lawsuits involved verifiable medical injuries.

To the extent tort reforms based on socially constructed beliefs about frivolous suits curtail medical malpractice actions, the reforms, by promoting hospitals' ability to externalize costs of poor care, likely undermine improving the medical malpractice system.

(2) Studies of Filed and Litigated Claim Outcomes

Despite claims of a lawsuit lottery, and inexpert judges and juries second-guessing medical professionals, the overwhelming evidence is that the legal system's disposition of medical malpractice claims is strongly associated with the quality of medical care that was delivered.

Table 4 summarizes the results of 12 empirical studies of claims of medical malpractice. Seven of the studies, those above the horizontal line in the middle of the table (and with a "Yes" in the table's last column), focus solely on claims that reached the lawsuit stage or had information enabling one to separate claims that terminated before the filing of a lawsuit from those that did not. The other five studies, those below the line, cover claims for medical error, but do not report separate results for lawsuits.

Table 4. Medical Malpractice Claim Outcomes and Quality of Care

Study	Sample	Good care outcome	Uncertain care outcome	Poor care outcome	Lawsuit results discernable
Cheney et al. (1989)	1,004 anesthesia-related lawsuits, 1985 to 1988, from 17 insurance companies; anesthesiologists assessed appropriateness of care	47% payment rate; median payments much lower in good care cases ($10,000 for nondisabling injury; $93,000 for disabling injury; $115,000 for death)		89% payment rate	Yes
Cranberg et al. (2007)	42 closed malpractice claims (38 lawsuits), 1986 to 2006, against Harvard-affiliated	4% payment rate		32% payment rate	Yes

	medical institutions; assessment by neurologists				
Farber & White (1991)	252 lawsuits filed and concluded, 1977 to 1989, against one hospital; experts evaluated quality of care	24% payment rate; mean $14,109	69% payment rate; mean $146,160	89% payment rate; mean $203,209	Yes
Peeples et al. (2002)	81 malpractice lawsuits filed in NC between 1991 and 1995 that progressed to pretrial mediation; care based on reports that ins. co. obtained from experts in specialty	11.1% payment rate	36.8% payment rate	86.2% payment rate	Yes
Sloan et al. (1993)	187 FL closed claims, with interviews, involving permanent injury at birth or in emergency departments, 10/1985 through 3/1988	43% payment rate[a]	75% payment rate[a]	79% payment rate[a]	Yes
Spurr & Howze (2001)	165 lawsuits closed between 1987 and 1995 against one hospital; continuous measure of care quality	for 90 settled cases and 55 dropped cases, the only significant variable was the strength of the evidence of negligence			Yes
Taragin et al. (1992)	8,231 closed cases involving NJ physicians insured by one company, 1977 to 1992; physician care prospectively	low rate (24% est.)b of payment in cases with defensible care	middle rate of payment in unclear cases	high payment rate in cases with poor care	Yes

	determined by ins. co.			
Brennan et al. (1996)[c]	46 malpractice claims arising from hospitalizations in NY in 1984, closed as of 12/31/1995; physician reviewers assessed degree of liability	43% payment rate (16 of 37); 24.3% (9 of 37) non-nuisance payments (>$25,000)	56% payment rate (5/9)	No
Ogburn et al. (1988)	87 cases involving perinatal death or injury from closed claims of St. Paul Co. filed 1980 to 1982; care assessed by five obstetricians	55% payment rate	90% payment rate	No
Rosenblatt & Hurst (1989)	33 obstetric cases in which suit was filed and/or payment made in lawsuits against a single insurer, closed 1982 to 1988; author reviewed clinical abstract to assess negligence	0% payment rate	95% payment rate	No
Sloan & Hsieh (1990)	6,612 FL closed claims from 10/1985 through 3/1988; avoidable injury classified by physicians based on ins. co. summary	Cases with avoidable injury significantly associated with probability of payment		No
Studdert et al. (2006)	1,452 closed malpractice claims from five liability insurers, 1984–2004; reviews by board-certified	28% payment rate	73% payment rate	No

	physicians, fellows, or final-year residents in specialty			

Notes. a=author's calculation based on Tables 8.1 to 8.3 in Sloan et al. (1993); b=estimate derived from Figure 1 in Taragin et al. (1992); c= Brennan et al. (1996) is a follow-up of Weiler et al. (1993).

Table 4 provides evidence relating to two major issues. First, the results provide little evidence of a random or out-of-control system of medical malpractice litigation. In those studies in which one can separate results for cases that reach the legal system, only two studies suggest a recovery rate in good care cases much in excess of 20 percent. Two of the four studies with high payment rates in good care cases do not distinguish between cases that reached the lawsuit stage and those that did not. And only one large study (N>1,000) shows a payment rate above 30 percent in good care cases.

Second, a great concern about medical care is the high rate of negligent events and the low rate at which such events to lead recovery. Claims that reach the legal system do not suffer from this gap. Conditional on a lawsuit being filed, every study but one shows a high rate of payment in poor care cases. Thus, potentially misleading impressions about the medical malpractice system, such as the AMA's statement as of 2006 that "75 percent of medical liability claims are closed without a payment to the plaintiff" depend wholly on failing to distinguish between weak cases, which tend not receive payment, and strong cases, which every study shows to receive payment at a higher rate than that suggested by the AMA.

The most invoked study about the relation been care and claim outcomes has been the Harvard Medical Malpractice Study (HMPS) (Weiler et al. 1993). It is also the most questioned study, and it is not clear that one can separate lawsuit outcomes from more general claims outcomes that do not result in lawsuits. Critics note an important feature of its design. When two expert reviewers assigned to a file split on the propriety of the physician's conduct, the case was classified as one that should not have led to liability. Divided opinion cases comprised about one-third of the sample, which rendered the summary results highly sensitive to how these ambiguous cases were classified. Over two-thirds of the claims reviewed for negligence were determined by at least one of two reviewers to involve negligent care. This may explain why the HMPS, as shown in Table 4 (Brennan, et al. 1996), has by far the smallest difference of any study between recovery rates in good care and poor care cases.

The studies summarized in Table 4 likely understate the performance of the medical malpractice claims system (including lawsuits) in cases in which victims file claims. Physicians systematically overstate the effect of the malpractice system on their practice. Michelle

M. Mello et al., Changes In Physician Supply And Scope Of Practice During A Malpractice Crisis: Evidence from Pennsylvania, 26 Health Affairs 425 (2007). Physicians also overestimate the likelihood a malpractice claim by as much as an order of magnitude, and substantially underestimate the risk to patients of iatrogenic injuries.

If physicians substantially overstate the risk of being sued, and underestimate injury rates, they likely tend to regard questionable practices as satisfying the relevant standard of care. This understandable within-profession tendency is complemented by the absence of any patient advocate in the ex post evaluations of physician performance. The combination of misperceived risk, within-profession natural protectiveness, and the absence of the patient's side of the story, likely exaggerates the extent to which the Table 4 studies find good care situations in which payments were made.

(3) Claim Patterns, Verdicts, and Awards Over Time

Claims of wild fluctuations or dramatic increases in medical malpractice litigation have not been verified. Bernard Black et al., Stability, Not Crisis: Medical Malpractice Claim Outcomes in Texas, 1988–2002, 2 J. Empirical Legal Stud. 207 (2005). One study considered 31,521 closed claims in Florida from 1990 through 2003. Neil Vidmar et al., Uncovering the "Invisible" Profile of Medical Malpractice Litigation: Insights from Florida, 54 DePaul Law Review 315 (2005). After 1997 only paid claims were required to be reported by statute, a change withdrawn in 2003. Claim frequency was stable over 1990 to 1997, averaging about 2,600 per year, with the number of zero-payment claims dropping during this period. The number of paid claims increased over 1990–2003, with a growth rate by one measure of 26 percent. The increase disappears once one adjusts for population growth and paid claims per physician did not increase. The number of paid claims per 100,000 Florida residents declined slightly from 9.96 in 1990 to 9.74 in 2003, and the number of paid claims per 100 physicians fell from 3.98 in 1990 to 3.33 in 2002. Mean payments for paid claims increased substantially. In real 2003 dollars, the mean payment increased from $177,000 in 1990 to $300,000 in 2003. Median payments increased from $49,000 in 1990 to $150,000 in 2003. The authors attribute these changes to (1) a significant increase in the severity of the injuries claimants sustained, and (2) larger awards within injury-severity categories, possibly driven by the growing cost of health care.

But studies of trial verdict outcomes establish increases in medical malpractice verdict amounts over time. Seabury et al., *supra*, report data on from jury verdict reporters covering Cook County, Illinois and San Francisco, California for the period 1960 to 1999. Claimed medical losses were flat over time until the late 1980s and early 1990s, when they increased sharply. Regression results suggest that claimed non-medical economic losses and claimed medical losses account for essentially all the observed growth in average tort awards in the two counties. This trend was especially apparent in products liability trials where the median award amounts were three times higher in 2005 ($748,000) than they were in 1996 ($241,000).

(4) Effect of Caps on Awards, Insurance Premiums, Recoveries, and Patient Safety

There is persistent evidence that caps on noneconomic damages, such as those at issue in *McDougald*, reduce payouts. A 2004 Congressional Budget Office (CBO) review concludes that caps on damages are fairly consistently found to reduce the number of lawsuits, awards, and the loss ratio.

Reform-generated reduction of awards leads to reduced malpractice insurance premiums. A review of studies concluded that the more rigorous studies consistently showed that damages caps reduced medical malpractice premiums. Leonard J. Nelson et al., Damages Caps in Medical Malpractice Cases, 85 Milbank Quarterly 259 (2007). But insurance reductions caused by caps may not have had the intended effects. One study found that no reform measure was associated with improved financial solvency of hospitals. Charles R. Ellington et al., State Tort Reforms and Hospital Malpractice Costs, 38 J. Law, Medicine & Ethics 127 (2007). Another study concluded that caps on damages have reduced insurer payments and insurance premiums but that caps have not improved safety. Frank A. Sloan and Lindsey M. Chepke, MEDICAL MALPRACTICE (2008).

Evidence suggests that greater savings to hospitals and insurers can be achieved not at the expense of patient victims. Grunebaum et al. (2011) found that an enhanced safety program in obstetrics at New York's Cornell Weill Medical Center reduced claims paid, even in the highly visible and risky ob/gyn specialty. Average yearly compensation payments decreased from $27.6 million between 2003–2006 to $2.6 million between 2007–2009, sentinel events (defined as an unexpected occurrence involving death or serious physical or psychological injury, or the risk thereof) decreased from 5 in 2000 to none in 2008 and 2009. Caps that reduce premiums by brute force likely discourage more painstaking but socially desirable efforts to improve safety.

(5) Effects on Physician Behavior

Research on whether state tort reform legislation affects medical decisionmaking generates mixed results. Some more credible studies find that health care savings from eliminating defensive medicine would be in the one to two percent range. CBO (2009). Studies that assess whether tort liability is associated with physician behavior are mixed. Two of the most studied areas are behavior by obstetrician/gynecologists (ob/gyns) and behavior with respect to heart attacks.

a. Behavior by Ob/gyns

Fully reconciling all the ob/gyn results relating to liability pressure is difficult. On balance, the available evidence does not support a consistent association between liability pressure and increased cesarean rates. Increased cesarean rates can be attributable to factors other than liability pressure and studies with reasonable control groups of physicians without liability pressure tend not to find an association. Studies that use actual physician experience, rather than insurance premiums, to measure malpractice pressure, tend not to find increased cesarean rates. Studies that find an association between liability pressure and increased rates tend to use aggregated premium pressure or tort reform statutes, and no control group of physicians removed from liability pressure. They are less persuasive than studies using individualized pressure and control groups. And even studies of this kind provide mixed results.

b. Acute Myocardial Infarction (AMI) Patients

Praveen Dhankhar et al., Effect of Medical Malpractice on Resource Use and Mortality of AMI Patients, 4 J. Empirical Legal Stud. 163 (2007) suggest that an increase in medical malpractice risk leads to a reduction in resource use and improvement in health outcome for patients with less severe medical conditions. For patients with more severe medical conditions, medical malpractice is associated with an improvement in mortality. They find no evidence that the costs of defensive medicine for most AMI patients are escalating. The threat of a malpractice lawsuit lowers the mortality rate of AMI patients, which they interpret as contradicting the widely view that defensive medicine has no positive effect on health status of patients.

This work casts doubt on the generalizability of the widely cited Kessler and McClellan findings with respect to tort reform and AMI treatment. Daniel P. Kessler and Mark B. McClellan, Do Doctors Practice Defensive Medicine? 111 Quarterly J. Econ. 353 (1996). Using data on all elderly Medicare beneficiaries, they found that the costs of treating patients for AMI or ischemic heart disease was lower, without a denigration in outcomes, in states with "direct" tort reforms such as limitations on damages. In their later study on the same patients, they found that indirect tort reforms, such as period payments or limits on joint and several liability, had little impact. How Liability Law Affects Medical Productivity, 21 J. Health Econ. 931 (2002). Sloan and Shadle reassessed the Kessler-McClellan papers using a data set with more years of data and a broader measure of costs. They found no significant effect of tort reform on cost or outcomes. The absence of effect is consistent with the balance of evidence for behavior by ob/gyns. Frank Sloan and John H. Shadle, Is There Empirical Evidence for "Defensive Medicine"? A Reassessment, 28 J. Health Econ. 481 (2009).

(6) Liability Effects on Doctor Availability

Many studies assess the effect of malpractice, insurance, and tort reform on the supply of doctors. Y. Tony Yang et al. note that conventional wisdom within the medical community is that dramatic increases in insurance premiums cause physicians to relocate or discontinue their practices. A Longitudinal Analysis of the Impact of Liability Pressure on the Supply of Obstetrician-Gynecologists, 5 J. Empirical Legal Stud. 21 (2008). After assessing the relevant literature, they conclude, "Overall, clear evidence of a widespread diminution in overall physician supply has not been established" (p. 22). Analysis of the relevant studies suggests that this is a reasonable summary of the state of knowledge. Table 5 expands on a table in Mello et al., *supra*, to summarize the results of studies of physician supply. The studies are about evenly split between finding effects and not finding effects.

An important preliminary issue is whether a study examines actual practice or surveys physicians. Studies of actual practice report more modest effects than studies based on physician surveys. While 43 percent of high-risk Pennsylvania specialist survey respondents said they restricted their practice, only three percent were found to have done so in Mello et al.'s study of actual practices.

Table 5. Studies of the Effect of the Malpractice Environment on Physician Supply

Study	Malpractice risk measure	Data years	Analysis	Findings
Baicker & Chandra (2005)	Premiums/claims payments	1993–2001	State-level regression models comparing number of physicians in 2001 and 1993	Not significant. Neither premiums nor payments were associated with the overall physician supply
Donohue & Ho (2007)	Damage caps	1991–2004	Randomization inference	Not significant.
Encinosa & Hellinger (2005)	Damage caps	1985–2000	D-in-D comparing counties that did and did not get damage caps	Significant. Damage caps >= $250,000 associated with 2% more physicians per capita
Erus (2004)	Premiums/AMA deems state in crisis/number of claims/claims payments	1997–2002	State-level random coefficients models	Not significant. Total number of physicians not significantly affected by the crisis; effect on new physicians
Gius (2000)	Premiums	1994–1996	State-level model using instrumental variables to control for endogeneity	Significant. Malpractice premiums have a negative impact on the physician supply

			between salaries and physician supply	
Grumbach (1997)	Premiums	1980–1989	Physician-level model of discontinuance of obstetrics practice in NY	Not significant. No association between level of increase in premiums and discontinuation of obstetric practice
Hellinger & Encinosa (2003)	Damage caps	1985–2000	State-level OLS regression	Significant. States with caps average 12% more physicians per capita
Kessler et al. (2005)	Damage caps and less direct tort reform	1985–2001	D-in-D comparing states that did and did not change tort laws	Significant. Damage caps associated with 3% higher growth in physician supply after 3 years
Klick & Stratmann (2007)	Damage caps	1980–2001	D-in-D comparing doctors in high-risk specialties with those in low-risk specialties in states with and without tort reform	Significant. Damages caps associated with 6.1% more physicians per 100,000 population in the 5 highest-risk specialties and 4.1% more in the 10 highest-risk specialties
Matsa (2005)	Damage caps	1970–2000	County-level regression model of all states	Not significant. No overall association; increase of specialists in rural areas
Mello et al. (2007a)	Effect of insurance crisis	1993–2002	Supply of physicians during insurance crisis in PA	Overall supply of high-risk specialists did not drop; ob/gyn supply decreased by 8% but supply of physicians delivering babies increased slightly
Polsky et al. (2010)	Premiums	1998–2004	FL, NY, PA hospital discharge data and county premiums	Significant. Increasing malpractice premiums are negatively associated with

				supply of obstetricians
Xu (2009)	Premiums, malpractice claims	2006	Logistic regression of discontinuing obstetric care and malpractice burden in Michigan	Not significant. Malpractice payments were not associated with family physicians' discontinuation of obstetric services. No evidence of prior malpractice claims or payments affecting ob/gyns' decision to cease obstetric care
Yang et al. (2008)	Premiums/tort reform	1992–2002	50 state mixed-effects model assessing relation between malpractice risk and number of ob/gyns	Not significant. No significant association between supply of ob/gyns and premiums or tort reforms

Notes. D-in-D=difference-in-difference; OLS=ordinary least squares regression. Mello et al. (2007) include an early version of Helland and Showalter (2009), which is excluded from this table because it did not examine the number of physicians.

The inconsistency of the results across physician supply studies is striking. Effects on both the overall supply of physicians and on the high-risk area of ob/gyns do not yield a consistent picture. Studies that measure malpractice risk using premiums tend not to find robust physician supply effects. Studies that measure malpractice risk using damages caps are more likely to find physician supply effects.

3. ECONOMIC COMPONENTS OF PERSONAL INJURY DAMAGES

Richmond v. Zimbrick Logging, Inc.

Court of Appeals of Oregon, 1993.
124 Or. App. 631.

■ DURHAM, JUDGE. . . . Plaintiff was injured when a logging truck, owned by defendant Zimbrick Logging, Inc. and driven by defendant Pyle, struck the car in which she was a passenger. Plaintiff is a homemaker and a minister's wife. She has been married since 1971. Since then, she has not been employed outside the home, except for odd jobs. At the time of the accident, four of plaintiff's five children were still at home, and she was "home schooling" the three youngest. Before the accident, plaintiff helped her husband in his work as a minister by volunteering at his church, assisting him with janitorial work and performing other church duties. She did not testify that she had plans to begin a career outside the home. Her husband testified that they did not have any such plans at the time of the accident. The parties stipulated that plaintiff incurred medical expenses of $5,971.60 for her injuries, and that her family spent $1,428.35 for household help while plaintiff was recovering. The jury awarded plaintiff non-economic damages of $30,000 and $37,399.95 in economic damages. Because the amount of special economic damages was $7,399.95, the award necessarily included $30,000 for impaired earning capacity. . . .

ORS 18.560(2)(a) [governing damages for personal injuries] provides, in part:

> " 'Economic damages' means objectively verifiable monetary losses including . . . loss of income and past and future impairment of earning capacity . . . ."

Defendants argue that, in the absence of past earnings or an intention to work outside the home in the future, plaintiff has no "objectively verifiable" loss. Consequently, they claim that there is no foundation of relevance for expert testimony on earning capacity, and no evidence from which the jury could find that plaintiff suffered an impairment of earning capacity.

However, plaintiff is not required to prove that she has worked in the past or intended to do so in the future. Oregon, like most jurisdictions, recognizes that the impairment of a person's earning capacity is an injury distinct from a loss of earnings.

> "In determining past and future loss of earning capacity the question is not whether plaintiff would have worked, by choice. A person is entitled to compensation for the lost *capacity* to earn, whether he would have chosen to exercise it or not."

Harper, James and Gray, THE LAW OF TORTS 549, § 25.8 (2d ed 1986). . . .

Thus, a plaintiff who is not employed at the time of injury and does not submit proof of wage loss may prove a diminished earning capacity through other evidence.

Plaintiff presented the testimony of Andy Huckfeldt, a vocational rehabilitation counselor. Huckfeldt first calculated plaintiff's loss of earning capacity by estimating the value of her services as a minister's wife. He also calculated her earning potential by examining career alternatives based on her education and abilities. Using the 1987 census survey, he looked at the average earnings in the United States for a 38-year-old woman with a high school diploma. He multiplied the number of years until her retirement at 65 by the average earnings of such a person and arrived at a figure in excess of $459,540. Finally, Huckfeldt calculated plaintiff's potential lifetime earnings, if she were employed at $5.00 per hour, at approximately $280,000. He testified that plaintiff had lost half of that earning capacity, because her injuries limited her ability to work to 20 hours per week. The court instructed the jury that this final computation was the maximum that it could award for impaired earning capacity. The jury awarded less than 25 percent of that figure. Defendants argue that Huckfeldt's testimony is irrelevant and should not have been admitted, because plaintiff has not worked and has "no ambition to work outside the home." . . .

[The Oregon Supreme Court, in Wilson *v.* B.F. Goodrich, 292 Or. 626, 633 (1982)] held that, despite the inherent speculation in the task, the jury "necessarily must draw some inferences from the available evidence as to the individual's likely level of earnings and continuity of employment over many years. . . ."

The jury could draw the necessary inferences about plaintiff's diminished earning capacity from the evidence about the extent and permanence of her injury, her educational attainment, vocational and avocational skills, earning history, age and other facts that bear on the question whether the "economic horizon of the [plaintiff] has been shortened because of the injuries." Courts regularly permit juries to base their judgment on such evidence, especially in the case of an injured housewife . . . .

We conclude that the trial court correctly determined that Huckfeldt's testimony was admissible because plaintiff was not required to provide a foundation that she intended to seek employment outside her home. That testimony and other evidence in the record adequately support the verdict for future impairment of earning capacity. . . .

O'Shea v. Riverway Towing Co.

United States Court of Appeals, Seventh Circuit, 1982.
677 F.2d 1194.

■ POSNER, CIRCUIT JUDGE. This is a tort case under the federal admiralty jurisdiction. We are called upon to decide questions of contributory negligence and damage assessment . . . .

On the day of the accident, Margaret O'Shea was coming off duty as a cook on a towboat plying the Mississippi River. A harbor boat operated by the defendant, Riverway Towing Company, carried Mrs. O'Shea to shore and while getting off the boat she fell and sustained the injury complained of. The district judge found Riverway negligent and Mrs. O'Shea free from contributory negligence, and assessed damages in excess of $150,000. Riverway appeals only from the finding that there was no contributory negligence and from the part of the damage award that was intended to compensate Mrs. O'Shea for her lost future wages. . . .

The more substantial issues in this appeal relate to the computation of lost wages. Mrs. O'Shea's job as a cook paid her $40 a day, and since the custom was to work 30 days consecutively and then have the next 30 days off, this comes to $7200 a year although, as we shall see, she never had earned that much in a single year. She testified that when the accident occurred she had been about to get another cook's job on a Mississippi towboat that would have paid her $60 a day ($10,800 a year). She also testified that she had been intending to work as a boat's cook until she was 70—longer if she was able. An economist who testified on Mrs. O'Shea's behalf used the foregoing testimony as the basis for estimating the wages that she lost because of the accident. He first subtracted federal income tax from yearly wage estimates based on alternative assumptions about her wage rate (that it would be either $40 or $60 a day); assumed that this wage would have grown by between six and eight percent a year; assumed that she would have worked either to age 65 or to age 70; and then discounted the resulting lost-wage estimates to present value, using a discount rate of 8.5 percent a year. These calculations, being based on alternative assumptions concerning starting wage rate, annual wage increases, and length of employment, yielded a range of values rather than a single value. The bottom of the range was $50,000. This is the present value, computed at an 8.5 percent discount rate, of Mrs. O'Shea's lost future wages on the assumption that her starting wage was $40 a day and that it would have grown by six percent a year until she retired at the age of 65. The top of the range was $114,000, which is the present value (again discounted at 8.5 percent) of her lost future wages assuming she would have worked till she was 70 at a wage that would have started at $60 a day and increased by eight percent a year. The judge awarded a figure—$86,033—near the mid-point of this range. He did not explain in his written opinion how he had arrived at this figure, but in a preceding oral opinion he stated that he was "not certain that she would work until age 70 at this type of work," although "she certainly was entitled to" do so and "could have earned something"; and that he had not "felt bound by [the economist's] figure of eight per cent increase in wages" and had "not found the wages based on necessarily a 60 dollar a day job." If this can be taken to mean that he thought Mrs. O'Shea would probably have worked till she was 70, starting at $40 a day but moving up from there at six rather than eight percent a year, the economist's estimate of the present value of her lost future wages would be $75,000.

There is no doubt that the accident disabled Mrs. O'Shea from working as a cook on a boat. The break in her leg was very serious: it reduced the stability of the leg and caused her to fall frequently. It is impossible to see how she could have continued working as a cook, a job performed mostly while standing up, and especially on a boat, with its unsteady motion. But Riverway argues that Mrs. O'Shea (who has not worked at all since the accident, which occurred two years before the trial) could have gotten some sort of job and that the wages in that job should be deducted from the admittedly higher wages that she could have earned as a cook on a boat.

The question is not whether Mrs. O'Shea is totally disabled in the sense, relevant to social security disability cases but not tort cases, that there is no job in the American economy for which she is medically fit. It is whether she can by reasonable diligence find gainful employment, given the physical condition in which the accident left her. Here is a middle-aged woman, very overweight, badly scarred on one arm and one leg, unsteady on her feet, in constant and serious pain from the accident, with no education beyond high school and no work skills other than cooking, a job that happens to require standing for long periods which she is incapable of doing. It seems unlikely that someone in this condition could find gainful work at the minimum wage. True, the probability is not zero; and a better procedure, therefore, might have been to subtract from Mrs. O'Shea's lost future wages as a boat's cook the wages in some other job, discounted (*i.e.*, multiplied) by the probability—very low—that she would in fact be able to get another job. But the district judge cannot be criticized for having failed to use a procedure not suggested by either party. The question put to him was the dichotomous one, would she or would she not get another job if she made reasonable efforts to do so? This required him to decide whether there was a more than 50 percent probability that she would. We cannot say that the negative answer he gave to that question was clearly erroneous.

Riverway argues next that it was wrong for the judge to award damages on the basis of a wage not validated, as it were, by at least a year's employment at that wage. Mrs. O'Shea had never worked full time, had never in fact earned more than $3600 in a full year, and in the year preceding the accident had earned only $900. But previous wages do not put a cap on an award of lost future wages. If a man who had never worked in his life graduated from law school, began working at a law firm at an annual salary of $35,000, and was killed the second day on the job, his lack of a past wage history would be irrelevant to computing his lost future wages. The present case is similar if less dramatic. Mrs. O'Shea did not work at all until 1974, when her husband died. She then lived on her inheritance and worked at a variety of part-time jobs till January 1979, when she started working as a cook on the towboat. According to her testimony, which the trial judge believed, she was then working full time. It is immaterial that this was her first full-time job and that the accident occurred before she had held it for a full year. Her job history was typical of women who return to the labor force after their children are grown or, as in Mrs. O'Shea's case, after their husband dies, and these women are, like any tort victims, entitled to damages based on what they would have earned in the future rather than on what they may or may not have earned in the past.

If we are correct so far, Mrs. O'Shea was entitled to have her lost wages determined on the assumption that she would have earned at least $7200 in the first year after the accident and that the accident caused her to lose that entire amount by disabling her from any gainful employment. And since Riverway neither challenges the district judge's (apparent) finding that Mrs. O'Shea would have worked till she was 70 nor contends that the lost wages for each year until then should be discounted by the probability that she would in fact have been alive and working as a boat's cook throughout the damage period, we may also assume that her wages would have been at least $7200 a year for the 12 years between the date of the accident and her seventieth birthday. But Riverway does argue that we cannot assume she might have earned $10,800 a year rather than $7200, despite her testimony that at the time of the accident she was about to take another job as a boat's cook where she would have been paid at the rate of $60 rather than $40 a day. The point is not terribly important since the trial judge gave little weight to this testimony, but we shall discuss it briefly. Mrs. O'Shea was asked on direct examination what "pay you would have worked" for in the new job. Riverway's counsel objected on the ground of hearsay, the judge overruled his objection, and she answered $60 a day. The objection was not well taken. Riverway argues that only her prospective employer knew what her wage was, and hence when she said it was $60 she was testifying to what he had told her. But an employee's wage is as much in the personal knowledge of the employee as of the employer. If Mrs. O'Shea's prospective employer had testified that he would have paid her $60, Riverway's counsel could have made the converse hearsay objection that the employer was really testifying to what Mrs. O'Shea had told him she was willing to work for. Riverway's counsel could on cross-examination have probed the basis for Mrs. O'Shea's belief that she was going to get $60 a day in a new job, but he did not do so and cannot complain now that the judge may have given her testimony some (though little) weight. . . .

D. LOSS OF CONSORTIUM

Whittlesey v. Miller

Supreme Court of Texas, 1978.
572 S.W.2d 665.

■ MCGEE, JUSTICE. The question presented by this appeal is whether one spouse has an independent action for loss of consortium as a result of physical injuries caused to the other spouse by the negligence of a third party. The vehicle Stewart Miller was driving was involved in a collision with a vehicle driven by David Whittlesey in June 1974. In March 1976, Miller and Whittlesey entered into a settlement agreement whereby Miller released Whittlesey from liability in connection with the accident for consideration of $9,650. In June 1976, Ann Miller, Stewart's wife, sued Whittlesey for damages, alleging that Whittlesey's negligence had caused personal injury to her husband, thereby depriving her of her husband's consortium. Whittlesey was granted a summary judgment on the basis that a Texas wife could not recover for loss of consortium for the alleged negligent injury to her husband. The court of civil appeals reversed and remanded. We affirm the judgment of the court of civil appeals.

The marital relationship is the primary familial interest recognized by the courts. The remedy for the negligent or intentional impairment of this relationship is a tort action for loss of consortium.[1] Consortium has been the subject of many different definitions by the courts, but it can generally be defined to include the mutual right of the husband and wife to that affection, solace, comfort, companionship, society, assistance, and sexual relations necessary to a successful marriage. This definition primarily consists of the emotional or intangible elements of the marital relationship. In Texas, it does not include the "services" rendered by a spouse to the marriage.[2] These elements have been referred to as a conceptualistic unity, and the action accrues upon the substantial impairment of them.

The loss of consortium can arise from either the intentional or negligent conduct of a third party toward the marital relationship. The intentional impairment of consortium can result in actions for either alienation of affections or criminal conversation. Both actions have been recognized by prior Texas decisions.

The husband's right to recover for the negligent impairment of consortium has existed at common law, although there are no decisions by this court expressly holding this. It has only been within the past 25 years, however, that the wife's cause of action in the United States has been recognized. . . .

Comment *a* to [the Restatement (Second) of Torts § 693 (1977)] characterizes the spouse who suffered the bodily harm as a result of the tortious conduct as the "impaired spouse"; the spouse who brings the independent consortium action is characterized as the "deprived spouse." We find these designations to be pertinent and will use them in the balance of this opinion to assist in simplifying the discussion.

The present action for negligent impairment of consortium contemplates a single tortious act which injures both spouses by virtue of their relationship to each other. While the impaired spouse sustains direct physical injuries, the deprived spouse sustains damage to emotional interests stemming from their relationship. In the respective causes of action, the impaired spouse would have the exclusive right to recover for the normal damages associated with such an injury—bodily

---

[1] The phrase "loss of consortium" is more accurately described as an element of damage rather than a cause of action. But courts have so frequently used the phrase to denote those actions in which loss of consortium is the major element of damage that "loss of consortium" has come to be referred to as a cause of action.

[2] The term "services" is generally taken to include the performance by a spouse of household and domestic duties. In Texas, it is a concept that is entirely separate and distinct from that of consortium. In our community property system the husband and wife are equal; as such, a spouse's services counterbalance the other spouse's duty to support the community with earnings. Furthermore, the services of the spouse performing such are thus recoverable as a damage to the community.

injuries, medical expenses, pain and suffering, loss of earnings, et cetera. The deprived spouse would have the right to bring an action for the loss of consortium and seek recovery on the basis of harm to the intangible or sentimental elements. Finally, while the deprived spouse's suit for loss of consortium is considered to be derivative of the impaired spouse's negligence action to the extent that the tortfeasor's liability to the impaired spouse must be established, the consortium action is, nevertheless, independent and apart from that of the impaired spouse's negligence action.

It has been argued that the deprived spouse's loss of consortium is an injury that is too indirect to be compensated because the elements involved are too intangible or conjectural to be measured in pecuniary terms by a jury. We do not agree, for to do so would mean that a jury would also be incompetent to award damages for pain and suffering. The character of harm to the intangible or sentimental elements is not illusory. The loss of companionship, emotional support, love, felicity, and sexual relations are real, direct, and personal losses. It is recognized that these terms concern subjective states which present some difficulty in translating the loss into a dollar amount. The loss, however, is a real one requiring compensation, and "the issue generally must be resolved by the 'impartial conscience and judgment of jurors who may be expected to act reasonably, intelligently and in harmony with the evidence.' " . . .

Providing either spouse with a cause of action for loss of consortium would allow us to keep pace with modern society by recognizing that the emotional interests of the marriage relationship are as worthy of protection from negligent invasion as are other legally protected interests.

Therefore, we hold that either spouse has a cause of action for loss of consortium that might arise as a result of an injury caused to the other spouse by a third party tortfeasor's negligence. This holding not only aligns Texas with the majority of jurisdictions recognizing the action for either spouse, but it also corrects a paradox in the law of this state in that heretofore the marital relationship has been protected from only intentional invasions. . . .

Reagan v. Vaughn

Supreme Court of Texas, 1990.
804 S.W.2d 463.

■ GONZALEZ, JUSTICE. In this case, we are presented with the issue of whether a child has a right to recover damages for loss of consortium and mental anguish when a parent is injured but not killed by the tortious conduct of a third party. . . .

David Reagan was involved in a fight with another patron in the parking lot of K-Jacs Saloon in Pasadena, Texas. During the course of the fight, the manager of the bar, Vaughn, struck Reagan on the head with a baseball bat. Reagan suffered a severe brain injury and now functions at the level of a six- or seven-year-old child. Reagan and his minor daughter, Julia, sued Vaughn as well as the owners of K-Jacs, Keith Nichols and Ernest Rosenovac. The jury found that Vaughn, Nichols, and Rosenovac were each 20% negligent and that Reagan was 40% negligent. The jury awarded damages in the amount of $2,432,000 to Reagan and $405,000 to Julia. ($200,000 for loss of "parental care, nurture and guidance:" $25,000 for mental anguish in the past and $180,000 for mental anguish in the future). The trial court rendered judgment in conformity with the verdict.

This court has never addressed the issue of whether a child may recover damages for the loss of parental companionship, love, and society when a parent is injured. . . .

In the present case, Reagan was not killed; thus our analysis does not include interpretation of the wrongful death statute. Rather, we must decide whether, given our previous recognition of the significance of injuries to the familial relationship, this court should recognize a common law cause of action for loss of consortium damages that result from injury to a parent. . . .

In Sanchez *v.* Schindler, 651 S.W.2d 249 (Tex. 1983) [reprinted below], we recognized that the death of a child inflicts upon his parents a loss of love, advice, comfort, companionship and society. Likewise, in Cavnar *v.* Quality Control Parking, Inc., 696 S.W.2d 549 (Tex. 1985), we held that a child suffers equivalent losses from the death of a parent. And in Whittlesey *v.* Miller, 572 S.W.2d 665 (Tex. 1978) [reprinted above], we acknowledged that nonfatal injury to a spouse can result in a real, direct, and personal loss to the other spouse. We would be hard pressed to say that a serious, permanent and disabling injury to a parent does not potentially visit upon the child an equally serious deprivation. In the present case, Julia Reagan has been deprived of essentially any opportunity for further parent-child exchange with her father. A child faced with Julia's circumstances can no longer experience the joy of shared experiences with her parent, and she is denied the care, guidance, love, and protection ordinarily provided by her parent. There is no principled reason to accord the parent-child relationship second class status . . . . The obvious and unquestionable significance of the parent-child relationship compels our recognition of a cause of action for loss of parental consortium.

Respondents have suggested that recognition of this cause of action will somehow have the snowball effect of leading to recognition of actions in favor of siblings, grandparents, close friends, and so on. We have little difficulty limiting recovery to the parent-child relationship. We recognize, as did the Wisconsin Supreme Court, that the two relationships likely to be most severely affected by a negligent injury to a person are the husband and wife relationship and that of the parent and child:

> "The distinction between the interests of children and those of other relatives is rational and easily applied. Most children are dependent on their parents for emotional sustenance. This is rarely the case with more remote relatives. Thus, by limiting the plaintiffs in the consortium action to the victim's children, the courts would ensure that the losses compensated would be both real and severe."

Theama *v.* City of Kenosha, 117 Wis.2d 508, 521 (1984). Consistent with our prior recognition that adult children may recover for the wrongful death of a parent, we decline to limit the right of recovery under this cause of action to minor children. . . .

Respondents assert that the jury's award of mental anguish damages to Julia violates Freeman *v.* City of Pasadena, 744 S.W.2d 923 (Tex. 1988), in which we held that a stepfather who was not located at or near the scene of an accident involving injury to his stepsons could not recover for negligent infliction of mental anguish.

A claim for negligent infliction of mental anguish is separate and distinct from a child's claim for loss of parental consortium and loss of consortium does not include an element of mental anguish. A cause of action for loss of consortium is derivative of the parent's claim for personal injuries. In order to recover, the child must prove that the defendant is liable for the personal injuries suffered by her parent, and any defense that tends to constrict or exclude the defendant's liability to the injured parent will have the same effect on the child's consortium action.

On the other hand, a claim for negligent infliction of mental anguish that is not based upon the wrongful death statute requires that the plaintiff prove that he or she was, among other things, located at or near the scene of the accident, and that the mental anguish resulted from a direct emotional impact upon the plaintiff from the sensory and contemporaneous observance of the incident, as contrasted with learning of the accident from others after the occurrence. Julia has not met either of these requirements and therefore may not recover for mental anguish.

We hold that children may recover for loss of consortium when a third party causes serious, permanent, and disabling injuries to their parent. In order to successfully maintain a claim for loss of parental consortium resulting from injury to the parent-child relationship, the plaintiff must show that the defendant physically injured the child's parent in a manner that would subject the defendant to liability. The child may recover for such non-pecuniary damages as loss of the parent's love, affection, protection, emotional support, services, companionship, care, and society. Factors that the jury may consider in determining the amount of damages include, but are not limited to, the severity of the injury to the parent and its actual effect upon the parent-child relationship, the child's age, the nature of the child's relationship with the parent, the child's emotional and physical characteristics, and whether other consortium giving relationships are available to the child. . . .

OPINION ON MOTION FOR REHEARING

■ GONZALEZ, JUSTICE. . . . [W]hen the facts are disputed, there must be a threshold finding by the finder of fact that the injury to the parent was a serious, permanent, and disabling injury before the finder of fact determines the consortium damage issue.

■ HECHT, JUSTICE, concurring and dissenting. . . . Today the Court creates a new personal injury cause of action, holding for the first time that a person is entitled to money damages for a diminution in parental love, advice, comfort, companionship and society occasioned by tortious injury to the parent. The Court extends this newly allowed recovery to adult as well as minor children, although the only child in this case is a minor. It equivocates on the rather important matter of how seriously a parent must be injured before the child can recover . . . . Henceforth every person whose parent is, or within any applicable limitations period has been, personally injured—either intentionally, or in a motor vehicle accident, or by a fall, or from using an unreasonably dangerous product, or while receiving medical or health care, or as a result of any other tortious misconduct—has a separate damage claim against the person causing the injuries. In the future, simple personal injury claims cannot be absolutely resolved without the concurrence of the injured person's children. Today's decision is breathtaking in its scope. . . .

If ever there were a case that cried out for recovery for loss of parental consortium, this is not it. The circumstances of David Reagan's injury and any consequent loss to his daughter, Julia, vivify the *in*appropriateness of awarding a person money because his or her parent has been hurt. Brushing facts aside, the Court simply idealizes that "[a] child faced with Julia's circumstances can no longer experience the joy of shared experiences with the parent and is denied the care, guidance, love, and protection ordinarily provided by a parent." The Court is conspicuously vague about what Julia's circumstances are exactly, and about whether the evidence shows that she would have had the sort of relationship with her father, but for his injury, that other children "ordinarily" have. The concurring opinion picks up the Court's refrain, adding that children in Julia's circumstances—not Julia herself, but children *like* Julia—face "sorrow and grief . . . on a daily basis." There is absolutely no evidence in the record before us that Julia faces, or has ever faced, sorrow and grief on account of her father's injury. There is some evidence to the contrary.

These panegyrics, while moving as they are no doubt intended to be, have little to do with the reality of this case. The Court's preference for generalities calls for a recapitulation of the facts here in some detail.

When his wife of some four years filed for divorce, David Reagan left her and their four-year-old daughter, Julia, in Indiana and moved to

Houston. Unemployed, the 22-year-old Reagan became a "regular" at K-Jacs Saloon, a beer joint in a "rough" part of town. K-Jacs was owned by Keith Jack Nichols and Ernest Rosenovac, and managed by Lester Gene "Lucky" Vaughn. Vaughn's duties included protecting the barmaids and waitresses from harassment and breaking up fights among the patrons, routine occurrences at K-Jacs and other bars in its neighborhood. Reagan spent two or three nights a week at K-Jacs during the three months he stayed with his sister. Vaughn testified that he had seen Reagan in the bar on several prior occasions and that Reagan seemed like a nice kid.

On Friday, the thirteenth of June, Reagan arrived at K-Jacs early, about 3:30 or 4:00 p.m. One of the waitresses, Elizabeth "Tina" Lamb, testified that Reagan said he was very upset because he was about to return to Indiana to finish up his divorce. He began drinking immediately, Lamb stated, and continued to drink heavily throughout the evening, roaming around in the bar, increasingly intoxicated and increasingly violent. Reagan stayed until K-Jacs closed at 2:00 a.m. Nearly three hours later his blood alcohol level was .226 gm/dl, more than twice the level for legal intoxication.

Richard Lepper testified that he noticed while talking with Reagan during the evening that Reagan was unstable. Concerned that Reagan was in no condition to be driving, Lepper said he offered to take Reagan to get something to eat and then home. Lepper stated that as he and Reagan were walking out across the parking lot, Reagan stopped to talk to two girls in a car. When they drove off, Lepper said, Reagan got into an argument with three cowboys who were standing nearby. Lepper, who had been stabbed on the K-Jacs parking lot on a separate occasion, testified that he begged Reagan to leave, but the argument turned into a scuffle, and when he tried to pull Reagan away from the others, Reagan turned, enraged, and began to fight like a wild man.

About that time Ronnie Di Simone and his wife, Donna, were also leaving K-Jacs. They had been to a movie earlier in the evening and had stopped by on the way home. Di Simone testified that as he walked out of the bar he saw Reagan, whom he had seen at K-Jacs on prior occasions, grabbing through the open window of a car at a man inside and shouting, "I'm going to whip your ass." Di Simone said that he walked over to Reagan and tried to persuade him to leave, but Reagan whirled around and said, "If I can't whip him, I'm going to whip you." Di Simone said that Reagan hit him, and the two began to fight. After a few minutes, Di Simone stated, Vaughn came out of the bar and separated them, telling them that he had called the police and that they had better go home. Vaughn testified that he was cleaning up in the bar after it closed when he was told that there was fighting outside. He stated that he told one of the bartenders to call the police, went outside and stopped the fight, and then returned inside. Several spectators verified that Vaughn warned everyone to leave and told them that the police were on their way.

Reagan, however, was wild-eyed and uncontrollable, according to Di Simone, and came at him again. Vaughn testified that when he heard that Reagan and Di Simone were still fighting, he again instructed an employee to call the police and went outside to break them up. This time, Vaughn stated, he grabbed Reagan, threw him on the ground, and sat on him until Reagan promised he would go home if Vaughn would let him up. Di Simone stated that he tried to walk away while Vaughn pinned Reagan on the ground, but that as soon as Reagan got up he came at Di Simone again. Di Simone testified that Reagan shouted that "he was in a fighting mood and he was going to whip some son-of-a-bitch."

Vaughn testified that having failed in his efforts to separate Reagan and Di Simone, he went inside K-Jacs, instructed one of the waitresses again to call the police, retrieved a baseball bat he kept under the bar, and went back outside. By this time Reagan and Di Simone had been fighting off and on for nearly half an hour. Several witnesses testified that as Vaughn tried again to break up the pair, Di Simone hit Reagan so that he fell, striking his head against a concrete curb on the parking lot. Reagan got up and lunged, screaming, at Vaughn who was using the baseball bat to push Di Simone away. Lamb and another K-Jacs waitress, Diane Jackson, who were watching the fight, testified that Vaughn was only trying to settle the two down. But Reagan, Lamb stated, would not stop cursing and fighting. Another onlooker, Ronnie McFadden, testified that Reagan was fighting as if he were not afraid of anything.

As to some of the details of the events of the evening the recollections of the witnesses vary. But every witness present testified that when Reagan came up behind Vaughn, someone yelled that there was a knife. Waitresses Lamb and Jackson heard it, although they did not see anyone with a knife. McFadden heard someone shout, "Look out, Lucky, he's got a knife!" Don Morgan, a K-Jacs patron who was still inside the bar, heard the same thing. Neither McFadden nor Morgan actually saw a knife. However, Vaughn, Di Simone and Di Simone's wife all testified that they not only heard the shout but saw a knife in Reagan's hand. Henry Willis, a passerby who drove into the parking lot to see what was happening, also heard the same outcry and saw Reagan with a knife.

As soon as someone yelled that there was a knife, Di Simone kicked at Reagan, and as he did, Vaughn turned and swung the bat, hitting Reagan in the side of the head. Reagan fell to the ground motionless. Vaughn and several others immediately loaded Reagan into a vehicle to take him to the hospital. When the police arrived at 2:44 a.m., the parking lot was clear. The knife, if there was one, was never found.

As a result of his injury, Reagan suffered serious, permanent, debilitating brain damage. Although he is able to care for himself in many respects, he cannot function as an adult. A physician testified at trial that Reagan behaves much like a six-year-old child and will never significantly improve.

The only evidence of the nature of the relationship between Reagan and his daughter, Julia, is the testimony of Reagan's two sisters, Geneva Dale Showalter and Donita Cooper. Neither Julia, who was eleven years old at the time of trial, nor her mother, Tressa, appeared at trial or offered testimony. Reagan appeared but did not testify. . . .

With a few sentences in a footnote, the Court dismisses the fact that its decision today is the view of only a very small minority of American jurisdictions, adding lamely that it need not follow a rule just because the great majority of other states do. . . .

The Court attempts to premise its analysis upon the proposition that the common law is ever developing and subject to reexamination in light of changing conditions. . . .

There . . . does not appear to have been much if any change in the nature of family relationships in what the Court calls "our modern society" to warrant recognizing recovery for loss of parental consortium for the first time. The significance of the parent-child relationship is, as the Court states, "obvious and unquestionable." But this fact is hardly a recent discovery. Surely we cannot claim to have attained a more enlightened appreciation of the parental relationship in an age when divorce and child abuse are at least as commonplace as ever, and the Court does not say that we can. . . .

The right to recover damages for loss of consortium resulting from injury to a personal relationship cannot depend upon whether the relationship is "worthy of protection." The test proves everything and nothing. . . .

To characterize certain close, personal relationships as "worthy of protection" and the loss of such relationships a "serious deprivation" is unavoidably demeaning to others. . . . If recovery for loss of consortium really depended upon whether the injured relationship was "worthy of protection"—and it certainly should not—that determination ought to be left to the finder of fact to be made from the evidence adduced in each case. Not even the Court is willing to go so far, preferring categorization over individual determination.

Whether to allow recovery for loss of consortium must not depend upon the worth of the relationship injured or the seriousness of the loss. The emotional, spiritual attributes of all kinds of personal relationships are immeasurable. The Court's "worthy of protection" standard is alluring rhetoric but very flawed and unfortunately offensive reasoning. Allowing damages for loss of consortium must instead depend on the ability of our legal system to determine appropriate monetary compensation for such intangible, emotional injuries . . . .

If David Reagan had simply decided to abandon Julia, she would have suffered as serious a deprivation of his care and affection as she has in this case, but she would not have a cause of action against him, no matter how reprehensible his actions. Although parents in this state are obliged to support their children financially, they have no legal duty to provide them affection. A daughter cannot sue her father for failing to love her. . . .

Julia cannot recover for the loss of her father's consortium caused by her parents' decision to divorce and her mother's decision to remarry. She cannot sue her stepfather for damages for ordering Reagan not to telephone Julia. The injury to Julia's relationship with her father caused by her parents' divorce, her father's move to Texas, and her mother's remarriage is no less real than the injury caused by Lucky Vaughn; only the latter, however, is compensable under the Court's rule. . . .

The rule the Court adopts is unmanageable. It extends the right to recover monetary damages for an intangible loss which cannot be measured. It does nothing to prevent overlapping recovery when there are multiple claimants as a result of a single occurrence. It is not limited to claims by minor children, and is not clearly limited to instances involving serious injury to the parent. And it is likely that the recovery the Court allows will result in additional friction in relationships already marred by physical injury. . . .

The Court takes no notice of the immense difficulties inherent in the task [of assessing damages for loss of parental consortium]. The Court holds that jurors awarding damages for loss of parental consortium may take into account "the severity of the injury to the parent and its actual effect upon the parent-child relationship, the child's age, the nature of the child's relationship with the parent, the child's emotional and physical characteristics, and whether other consortium giving relationships are available to the child." I doubt whether jurors will find these factors to be of much help. Regarding the child's age, for example, I cannot tell whether the Court thinks injury is greater when the child has become close to the parent but is less in need of parental guidance, or when the child is an infant and does not know the parent but is very much in need of some parental care. Considering the child's personality, I do not know if the Court thinks that injury involving a well-adjusted, stable child is worth more or less than injury involving an emotionally insecure child. Regarding the availability of "other consortium giving relationships," I cannot tell whether the Court actually thinks that a child in a larger family suffers less from parental injury than an only child. I simply do not see how the Court can imagine that anyone, even a juror, can use these factors to arrive at a monetary value for loss of parental consortium. The factors are as imponderable as the loss itself, and applying them is mostly guesswork. . . .

There is nothing in the evidence in this case to indicate that Julia should get $405,000 for her loss. The jury appears simply to have accepted some of the figures suggested by Reagan's counsel in argument. The jury might just as well have assessed damages at $1,000 or $1,000,000; I doubt seriously whether either award would have been set aside as either inadequate or excessive. In future cases, some children will "hit the jackpot" while others will be awarded little or nothing, depending mostly on factors like which attorney is more persuasive, which party is more sympathetic, and the geographical location of the trial—none of which have anything whatever to do with any loss that may have been suffered. In no case will any real loss be restored. I can see very little justification for a rule which allows such lottery-like awards and serves as much or more to benefit lawyers than the children the rule professes to protect. . . .

Further complicating assessment of damages for a child's loss of parental consortium is the difficulty in preventing such recovery from overlapping or conflicting with damages awarded to the injured parent or to any sibling. Apart from any claim by the child, the injured parent may ask the fact finder to consider as an element of any damages assessed the impairment in performing parental responsibilities that the parent claims to have suffered. If damages are assessed for this element of recovery, the injury to the parent-child relationship has been compensated at least in part. Under the rule the Court adopts today, each of the injured parent's children may also sue for damages to the parent-child relationship. To prevent multiple recovery for the same injury, the damages awarded the parent and each child should not overlap each other. Also, the damage awards should not be conflicting: that is, a child should not be awarded damages for loss of consortium when the injured parent has not recovered damages for any loss of ability to love and care for the child; and recovery by similarly situated children should not be greatly disparate. . . .

The far-reaching effects of the Court's legislation today seem to have escaped its notice. Before today, the only persons who could claim damages resulting from the tortious infliction of nonfatal bodily injury were the injured person and his or her spouse. Now the children of the injured person may assert their own claims. The potential liability for a single incident of bodily injury has thus been multiplied. The liability for injury to a person with children may be greater than for a person who is childless, resulting in an unpredictable range of exposure. Someone who injures a single person may get off relatively lightly compared with someone else who inflicts no greater injury on a married person with children. . . .

I was not aware that there was a public clamor for more personal injury lawsuits. Many of the damage claims allowed by the Court in today's decision will be paid ultimately by the public in the form of increased costs of goods and services, and increased insurance premiums. . . .

The Court does not even pause to acknowledge these current conditions in light of which it is to reexamine the established common law rule. It does not take evidence on the benefits and costs of the rule it adopts, as it might if it were a legislature. . . .

E. WRONGFUL DEATH

Liff v. Schildkrout

Court of Appeals of New York, 1980.
49 N.Y.2d 622.

■ JASEN, JUDGE. . . . The first issue for our resolution is whether a surviving spouse, in his or her individual capacity, may maintain a common-law cause of action in this State for loss of consortium due to death which is independent and distinct from a statutory action for wrongful death. While we recognize the attractive nature of plaintiffs' arguments, we decline the invitation to change the law of this State and adhere to our [prior] pronouncement . . . that all causes of action arising from the death of an individual must be maintained in accordance with statutory authority.

Although the origin of the common-law notion that "[i]n a civil court, the death of a human being could not be complained of as an injury" has been the subject of much speculation and the cited theoretical underpinnings of the rule itself have drawn serious questions as to their continued vitality, there is simply no room left for debate that the common law of this State, despite numerous opportunities and forceful requests to change, does not recognize suits to recover damages for the wrongful death of an individual. This is not to say that a decedent's distributees are without a remedy, for a cause of action for wrongful death has been expressly authorized by statute in this State since 1847 and is now embodied in EPTL [Estates, Powers and Trusts Law] 5–4.1. (See N.Y. Const., art. I, § 16 [right of action to recover for injuries resulting in death may not be abrogated].) Thus, the cause of action for wrongful death has been dubbed "a child of statute."

Perhaps the most forthright justification for the refusal by the courts of this State to establish a common-law cause of action for wrongful death is the very existence of the statutory right. . . . The courts have deferred to the wisdom of the Legislature in striking the sensitive balance as to the causes of action which should be permitted to be maintained due to the wrongful death of another and also the measure of damages recoverable. In short, legislative enactments have preempted this area; the rights accorded by statute being in derogation of the common law, the right to sue for injury sustained due to the death of another must be founded in statutory authority.

Nor can it be said that a spouse's cause of action for loss of consortium exists in the common law independent of the injured spouse's right to maintain an action for injuries sustained. In this regard, we adopt the reasoning set forth in Osborn *v.* Kelley, 61 A.D.2d 367, 370, "that insofar as plaintiff is attempting to recover for loss of consortium for the period prior to decedent's death, a cause of action is stated. Such a cause of action, however, is a derivative one. The wrongful death statute created a new cause of action based not upon damage to the estate of the deceased because of death, but rather for the pecuniary injury to the surviving spouse and next of kin of the decedent. Since a decedent has no cause of action to recover damages for his death, plaintiff has no derivative cause of action to recover for loss of consortium due to decedent's death."

In sum, we decline the invitation to recognize a common-law cause of action on behalf of the surviving spouse for permanent loss of consortium due to the wrongful death of his or her marital partner. Any cause of action or, indeed, remedy predicated upon the loss of one's spouse must be founded in statutory authority.

Having so concluded, it becomes necessary to determine the issue whether loss of consortium can be claimed as an element of damages within a wrongful death action. Resolution of this issue centers upon an examination of the statutory language embodied in EPTL 5–4.3.

That section—which delineates the measure of damages in wrongful death actions—provides in pertinent part: "The damages awarded to the plaintiff may be such sum as the jury or, where issues of fact are tried without a jury, the court or referee deems to be fair and just compensation for the pecuniary injuries resulting from the decedent's death to the persons for whose benefit the action is brought. In every such action, in addition to any other lawful element of recoverable damages, the reasonable expenses of medical aid, nursing and attention incident to the injury causing death and the reasonable funeral expenses of the decedent paid by the distributees, or for the payment of which any distributee is responsible, shall also be proper elements of damage."

The qualifying phrase "pecuniary injuries" has been retained since the enactment of the first wrongful death statute in this State and has been consistently construed by the courts as excluding recovery for grief, and loss of society, affection and conjugal fellowship—all elements of the generic phrase "loss of consortium." While it is true that one factor often cited by courts in refusing recovery for loss of consortium—that loss of consortium is incapable of measurement in monetary terms—has been repudiated by this court, there still exists a fundamental reason why we should not change the present rule of law.

The Legislature, by including the pecuniary injury limitation in its statutory scheme, clearly intended that damages for loss of consortium should not be recoverable in wrongful death actions. The courts, under such circumstances, are not free to consider the relative merits of the arguments in favor of, or in opposition to, this limitation for the Legislature has "struck the balance for us." As shown, the courts of this State have consistently honored this legislative policy of limitation on damages and, given the failure of the Legislature to amend the statute, we conclude that the Legislature has approved this finding and implementation of legislative intent.

In short, we now reaffirm the principle that a claim for loss of consortium will not be recognized within a wrongful death action in this State. If a change should be made, it is for the Legislature, and not the courts, to make. . . .

NOTE

Compare with *Liff* the following passages from Krouse *v.* Graham, 19 Cal.3d 59 (1977):

> "The statutory cause of action for wrongful death, created in California in 1862, provided that 'pecuniary or exemplary' damages were to be awarded by the jury in the amount found 'just' under all the circumstances. Ten years after its enactment, the statute was amended to remove the words 'pecuniary or exemplary,' retaining the language that 'damages may be given as under all the circumstances of the case, may be just, . . .' Nonetheless, in subsequent decisional law a theory developed that damages for wrongful death were recoverable only for the 'pecuniary' losses suffered by the decedent's heirs.
>
> "California case law, however, has not restricted wrongful death recovery only to those elements with an ascertainable economic value, such as loss of household services or earning capacity. On the contrary, as early as 1911, we held that damages could be recovered for the loss of a decedent's 'society, comfort and protection,' though only the 'pecuniary value' of these losses was held to be a proper element of recovery. Other cases have held admissible such evidence as the closeness of the family unit, the warmth of feeling between family members, and the character of the deceased as 'kind and attentive' or 'kind and loving.' Not only was wrongful death compensation awarded historically to heirs who had been financially dependent upon their deceased relatives, but adult children received substantial awards for the wrongful death of retired, elderly parents and parents received compensatory damages for the death of young children. These cases suggest a realization that if damages truly were limited to 'pecuniary' loss, recovery frequently would be barred by the heirs' inability to prove such loss. The services of children, elderly parents, or nonworking spouses often do not result in measurable net income to the family unit, yet unquestionably the death of such a person represents a substantial 'injury' to the family for which just compensation should be paid."

Id. at 67–68.

Yowell v. Piper Aircraft Corporation

Supreme Court of Texas, 1986.
703 S.W.2d 630.

■ SPEARS, JUSTICE. This is a wrongful death and survival case. On February 22, 1977, Howard Reed Yowell, James Luther Ward, Jr., Jimmy Kenneth Fulkerson, and Fabe Ingram, Jr. were killed in a crash of a Piper PA–31–310 aircraft near Springdale, Arkansas. The airplane sustained a mid-air breakup at about 10,000 feet and crashed to the ground. There were no survivors. . . .

This court has not specifically addressed loss of inheritance damages in prior wrongful death cases. . . .

Clearly, heirs or devisees may suffer pecuniary loss to the extent the decedent would have accumulated property and passed it on to the heirs at his later, natural death. In Texas, the plaintiffs do not receive a double recovery when they receive loss of inheritance damages because the decedent's estate has no cause of action for lost future earnings.

The Texas wrongful death statute gives a specified group of survivors a cause of action for losses they sustain as a result of their decedent's wrongful death. Some states' statutes give the decedent's estate, rather than certain classes of survivors, a cause of action for loss of future accumulated property occasioned by wrongful death. Loss of inheritance under the Texas statute is very similar to "loss of the estate." Under a loss of inheritance claim, however, the claimant must prove not only the probability that the deceased would have accumulated money or assets, but also the probability that the decedent would have left this accumulation by will or inheritance to the statutory beneficiaries. . . .

The relatively few courts which have denied this type of recovery have done so not by excluding the loss from pecuniary damages but by holding the amount of the loss too speculative. Though probably nothing is more certain than the uncertainty of human life, presuming that thrifty persons will accumulate an estate and leave it to their heirs at death is no more speculative than finding any of the other recognized elements of pecuniary loss in a wrongful death action, such as lost support, guidance, and training. "Statutes giving damages for injuries resulting in death necessarily deal with probabilities," and necessarily indeterminate damages are properly left to the sound sense of the jury.

Recovery for loss of inheritance is proper. Had the injured person survived, his recovery would include lost future earnings which presumably would increase the personal estate and, at death, pass to heirs or beneficiaries. Preventing the heir's recovery would protect the wrongdoer from the consequences of the wrong.

We define loss of inheritance damages in Texas as the present value that the deceased, in reasonable probability, would have added to the estate and left at natural death to the statutory wrongful death beneficiaries but for the wrongful act causing the premature death. True, not every wrongful death beneficiary sustains loss of inheritance damages. If the decedent would have earned no more than he and his family would have used for support, or if the decedent would have outlived the wrongful death beneficiary, loss of inheritance damages would properly be denied. This is for the jury to decide. . . .

Mitchell v. Buchheit

Supreme Court of Missouri, 1977.
559 S.W.2d 528.

■ MORGAN, CHIEF JUSTICE. . . . [T]he Court of Appeals . . . transferred the case to this court "for the purpose of [our] reexamining the existing law," relative to whether or not the surviving parents of a minor child, in an action for wrongful death, may recover for pecuniary benefits which they reasonably could have expected after majority of the deceased child.

Decedent was 19 years and 10 months of age, unmarried, and living with his parents when killed in an accident involving two motor vehicles. The parents instituted a wrongful death action; and, judgment was entered on a jury verdict in their favor for $12,500. . . .

[P]laintiffs contend that the award of $12,500 was inadequate, and that such an unacceptable result was caused by the trial court erroneously refusing to admit evidence or permit argument that circumstances were such that plaintiffs reasonably could have expected pecuniary benefits from their son after he reached majority. . . .

The Court of Appeals agreed with plaintiffs and would have remanded the cause for a new trial as to damages; but, being bound by the latest pronouncements of the substantive law by this court, ordered transfer. We agree that a reassessment of the issue is proper and necessary.

In this state, the Wrongful Death Act was enacted originally in 1855. It has been revised several times since, including 1879, 1905, 1955, 1967 and 1973 Amendments. Throughout, and to this date, the interpretation placed upon the statute by the courts of this state was delineated best in Oliver *v.* Morgan, 73 S.W.2d 993 (Mo. 1934), wherein this court stated that:

> "It is . . . clearly the law that the basis of the recovery [for the death of a minor child] is the value of the child's services to the parents during the child's minority, and that from this must be deducted the expenses of the support and maintenance of the child during that period. . . . So long as the statute permits a recovery in such a case of only the *pecuniary* loss to the plaintiffs, the plaintiffs must prove and the jury find an actual pecuniary loss in order to recover." . . .

The case of Parsons *v.* Missouri Pacific Railway Co., 6 S.W. 464 (Mo. 1888), relied on in the *Oliver* case, provided the predicate upon which the rule has continued to rest. . . .

The statute was amended as seen in Laws 1905, page 135, (§ 5425, R. S. Mo. 1909) and survived as § 537.080(3). It provides, in part, that:

> ". . . if there be no husband, wife, minor child or minor children, natural born or adopted as hereinbefore indicated, or if the deceased be an unmarried minor and there be no father or mother, then in such case suit may be instituted and recovery had by the administrator or executor of the deceased and the amount recovered shall be distributed according to the laws of descent . . . ."

Recovery, therefore, was no longer limited to the parents in a wrongful death case involving a minor. An administrator or executor could recover as a trustee. Logically, no framework remained for the idea a deceased had to be legally obligated to furnish support to the beneficiary. It was sufficient if there existed "a reasonable probability of pecuniary benefit to one from the continuing life of another . . . ."

Later cases, oddly enough, did not undertake to reassess the limitations created in the *Parsons* case, although doubts as to the validity thereof did appear. For instance, in McCrary *v.* Ogden, 267 S.W.2d 670 (Mo. 1954), this court stated: "Whether our past interpretations of the section, to the effect that recovery is limited to pecuniary loss and in the case of an infant, to the value of services during minority only, are basically correct, may be debatable but we have consistently so construed the section." . . .

We have concluded that the holding in the *Parsons* case is not tenable under the present statutory provisions, nor can it stand on its own logic. Parents, seeking to recover for the death of a minor child, should not be prohibited from trying to establish a reasonable probability of pecuniary benefit from the continued life of said child beyond the age of minority. . . .

The judgment heretofore entered is affirmed except as to damages and the cause is remanded to the trial court for a new trial on that issue only.

Sanchez v. Schindler

Supreme Court of Texas, 1983.
651 S.W.2d 249.

■ SPEARS, JUSTICE. Eugene and Angelica Sanchez brought this wrongful death action against Charles Schindler and his parents for the death of their minor son, Johnny Sanchez, arising from a collision between Johnny's motorcycle and Schindler's pick-up truck. The jury found for plaintiffs on the liability issues. On the damages issues, however, they found that Mr. and Mrs. Sanchez sustained no pecuniary loss, but awarded $102,500.00 in damages for the mental anguish suffered by Mrs. Sanchez. The trial court disregarded the jury's answers to the special issues on mental anguish. The court of appeals affirmed the trial court's denial of recovery for mental anguish. . . .

In the past a surviving parent's damages in an action for the death of a child under the Texas Wrongful Death Act have been limited to the pecuniary value of the child's services and financial contributions, minus the cost of his care, support and education. The Texas statute does not expressly limit recovery to pecuniary loss. Tex. Rev. Civ. Stat. Ann. article 4671 creates a cause of action for "actual damages on account of the injuries causing the death. . . ." Article 4677 provides that "[t]he jury may give such damages as they may think proportionate to the injury resulting from such death." Like most states, Texas patterned its wrongful death statutes after Lord Campbell's Act. The Fatal Accident Act, 9 & 10 Vict., ch. 93 § 1 (1846). The English court ruled that Lord Campbell's Act limited recovery to pecuniary loss. In March *v.* Walker, 48 Tex. 372, 375 (1877), this court held that since the language of the Texas Wrongful Death Act was based on Lord Campbell's Act, the measure of damages under the Texas statute would also be restricted to pecuniary loss.

Sanchez argues the pecuniary loss rule is based on an antiquated concept of the child as an economic asset, and should be rejected. We agree. It is time for this court to revise its interpretation of the Texas Wrongful Death statutes in light of present social realities and expand recovery beyond the antiquated and inequitable pecuniary loss rule. If the rule is literally followed, the average child would have a negative worth. Strict adherence to the pecuniary loss rule could lead to the negligent tortfeasor being rewarded for having saved the parents the cost and expense of rearing a child. The real loss sustained by a parent is not the loss of any financial benefit to be gained from the child, but is the loss of love, advice, comfort, companionship and society. We, therefore, reject the pecuniary loss limitation and allow a plaintiff to recover damages for loss of companionship and society and damages for mental anguish for the death of his or her child. In this case, Mrs. Sanchez pleaded for the recovery of damages for mental anguish, and the jury awarded her $102,500 pursuant to the special issues on mental anguish. She has preserved her argument on appeal to this court. . . .

This court has recognized previously that injuries to the familial relationship are significant injuries and are worthy of compensation. In Whittlesey *v.* Miller, 572 S.W.2d 665, 668 (Tex. 1978), we held that either spouse has a cause of action for loss of consortium suffered as a result of an injury to the other spouse by a tortfeasor's negligence. . . . A parent's claim for damages for the loss of companionship of a child is closely analogous. . . .

The jurisdictions that do not limit recovery to pecuniary loss realize that damages for loss of companionship and society of a child are not too uncertain to be measured in pecuniary terms in an attempt to redress the actual loss which a parent suffers. These elements of damage are not too speculative to be given a monetary value. Recovery is allowed in other tort areas for injuries which are equally intangible; *e.g.*, pain and suffering. The fear of excessive verdicts is not a sufficient justification for denying recovery for loss of companionship. The judicial system has adequate safeguards to prevent recovery of damages based on sympathy or prejudice rather than fair and just compensation for the plaintiff's injuries.

A parent's recovery under the wrongful death statute includes the mental anguish suffered as a result of the child's wrongful death. The destruction of the parent-child relationship results in mental anguish, and it would be unrealistic to separate injury to the familial relationship from emotional injury. Injuries resulting from mental anguish may actually be less nebulous than pain and suffering, or injuries resulting from loss of companionship and consortium. A plaintiff should be permitted to prove the damages resulting from a tortfeasor's negligent infliction of emotional trauma. This includes recovery for mental anguish.

In this case Mrs. Sanchez proved she is suffering from traumatic depressive neurosis. She presented testimony that she is despondent and disoriented, has been forced to seek medical attention for her neurosis and has frequent neck and shoulder pains and headaches. Mrs. Sanchez has proved that she suffered mental anguish, and therefore, is entitled to recover the $102,500 awarded to her by the jury for her mental anguish. . . .

■ POPE, CHIEF JUSTICE, dissenting. I respectfully dissent because I believe the court should not overturn its long-standing decisions and reinterpret the Texas Wrongful Death Statute to authorize recovery for mental anguish. In 1877, this court ruled that since the Texas Wrongful Death Statute was borrowed from Lord Campbell's Act, the measure of damages under the Texas statute was the same as the English act—pecuniary loss only. March *v.* Walker, 48 Tex. 372, 375 (1877). Texas courts have consistently followed the pecuniary loss rule.

The majority reverses this well-established rule. If we were dealing with the common law rather than the statute, I might be persuaded by the majority's reasoning. There is strong evidence, however, that the Texas Legislature intended to limit recovery to pecuniary losses when it enacted the Texas Wrongful Death Statute. The Texas statute was patterned after the English statute. Both statutes provided that "the jury may give such damages as they may think proportioned to the injury resulting from such death . . . ." When the Texas Legislature adopted the statute in 1860, the English statute and every American statute patterned after it had already been interpreted to limit recovery to pecuniary losses. See G. Field, THE LAW OF DAMAGES § 630 (1878). The majority does not dispute that the Texas Legislature at the inception of the statute intended to apply the pecuniary loss rule to the Texas statute. The continued use of the same language for more than a century while the courts have time and again consistently held that mental anguish may not be recovered shows that the courts' construction is in accord with the legislature's intent. E. Crawford, CONSTRUCTION OF STATUTES, § 224 (1940).

There are times when we have properly stuffed new meaning into old words of some statute. We should proceed modestly, however, when the Texas Legislature has addressed the provisions of this specific statute many times since we handed down March *v.* Walker, 48 Tex. 372 (1877). The Texas Wrongful Death Statute has been codified and recodified on four occasions since our decision in March. Article 4671 of the act, which authorizes the cause of action, has been amended five times. The Sixty-Third Legislature addressed the specific matter of damages under the statute and enacted article 4675a to permit proof of remarriage of the surviving spouse as evidence of reduced damages. Four bills introduced in the Sixty-Sixth Legislature and three bills introduced in the Sixty-Seventh Legislature would have expanded recovery to include mental anguish. None of these bills passed. This summary of legislative consideration of damages under the Texas Wrongful Death Statute shows that the legislature has accepted some and rejected other proposals to change decisions about damages under the statute.

The Texas Legislature now has under consideration Senate Bill 30 and House Bills 255 and 800. Those bills, if enacted, would permit parents to recover damages for mental anguish, loss of society, and loss of companionship resulting from the death of a child. House Bill 800 has been reported favorably from a House committee. While the majority may be impatient with what they consider a less desirable statutory policy, I would adhere to settled principles of statutory construction. There is, for example, a presumption that the legislature acts "with full knowledge of all decisions on the subject matter of the legislation rendered before its enactment." Craft *v.* Craft, 579 S.W.2d 506, 508 (Tex. Civ. App.—Dallas), *writ ref'd per curiam*, 580 S.W.2d 814 (Tex. 1979).

The Texas Wrongful Death Statute created a right that did not exist at common law. We are now dealing with that statute—not the common law. The force of prior judicial construction of statutes has been expressed by this court in a number of thoughtful opinions. In Cunningham *v.* Cunningham, 120 Tex. 491 (1931), we announced a principle of statutory construction that we have respected:

> "Nothing is better settled than that the Legislature must be regarded as intending statutes, when repeatedly re-enacted, as is the case here, to be given that interpretation which has been settled by the courts."

Upon these principles this court refused to overturn a long-standing interpretation that the Texas Wrongful Death Statute did not have extra-territorial force. Marmon *v.* Mustang Aviation, Inc., 430 S.W.2d 182 (Tex. 1968). In *Marmon*, the petitioner argued that the doctrine that the state had no power to give extra-territorial effect had become outmoded by force of the most significant contacts doctrine. This court, while accepting the doctrine in other contexts, rejected that approach, saying:

> "If this proposition be accepted as sound, it does not necessarily follow that we should now hold that Article 4671 has extra-territorial thrust. It would be far-reaching, to say the least, for us to say that an enactment of the Legislature adopted over a hundred years ago now has a different meaning and a more far-reaching thrust than it did when construed by this court in 1884."

The legislature subsequently amended the statute to give it extra-territorial force.

The majority announces a novel rule of statutory construction. It first appeared in the jurisprudence of Texas in a concurring opinion three years ago. Bedgood *v.* Madalin, 600 S.W.2d 773 (Tex. 1980) (Spears, J., concurring). That new rule is that a legislature's inaction is a signal that courts are free to move into legislative policy matters. The majority opinion states that legislative inaction should no longer thwart what they consider a better policy. It then imposes that policy judicially.

This rule assumes that repeated unfruitful efforts to amend the Texas Wrongful Death Statute concerning damages are proof of inaction. The legislature has in fact often acted. An effective way of defeating a weak or bad bill is to avoid voting on it. The legislature's refusal to vote on the many proposals to change the measure of damages is an opinion of that branch of government that there is no pressing need to change the present law. Legislatures act affirmatively and negatively; but in either instance, the legislative will is expressed. For us to ignore defeated legislation is as misleading as it would be for a court to reject from our common law decisions those cases which hold for the defendant. See 2 A. Sutherland, STATUTORY CONSTRUCTION, § 45.10 (4th ed. 1973). When we refuse the claims of plaintiffs and hold for defendants, we are still handing down legal opinions and guidelines, just as the legislature makes a statement of its intent by defeating legislation.

The judiciary should exercise caution before substituting its subjective notions for legislative materials. The new rule authorizes judicial resolution of policy matters of great public import without benefit of or compliance with ordinary checks and balances, open meetings limitations, public hearings, democratic legislative debate, a bicameral consideration, an executive veto, or other legislative safeguards. It is one thing for a court to decide that an interpretation of a statute is erroneous; it is quite another and more serious matter for a court to decide that a statute is unwise. I would respect the separation of powers and exercise judicial restraint before entering a policy field where our judgment is at best a minority subjective decision.

A second reading of the majority opinion shows that the many cases cited in support of its proposed new rule relate to loss of society, which is not here involved. It is not until we reach the penultimate paragraph of the majority opinion that we are told that the majority's new rule is actually supported only by "several states." According to the majority, three states allow recovery for mental anguish under statutes similar to Texas' statute: Arizona, South Carolina, and Washington.

The Washington Supreme Court quite properly applied the Washington Legislature's 1967 amended statute that provided for a parent's recovery. Wilson *v.* Lund, 80 Wash.2d 91 (1971). We do not have a statute, as Washington does, that says:

> "damages may be recovered for the loss of love and companionship of the child and for injury to or destruction of the parent-child relationship . . . ."

Wash. Rev. Code § 4.24.010. The Arizona Supreme Court abandoned the pecuniary loss rule as a result of a 1956 amendment which authorized

> "such damages as it [the jury] deems fair and just with reference to the injury resulting from the death to the surviving parties who may be entitled to recover . . . ."

Ariz. Rev. Stat. Ann. § 12–613. See Boise *v.* Cole, 99 Ariz. 198 (1965). The South Carolina Supreme Court has always construed its statute to permit mental anguish damages. See Norhden *v.* Northeastern Railroad Co., 59 S.C. 87 (1900). The important distinction is that none of these courts had to overturn an established statutory construction. The majority does not cite a single case in which a court has authorized damages for mental anguish by overruling a longstanding statutory construction that has been ratified by legislative re-enactment of the existing statute and ratified by legislative rejection of amendments authorizing mental anguish damages. Yet that is what the majority does today.

Other states that have achieved the result sought by the majority have waited until the statutory policy was changed by the legislature's amendment of the statute. A minority of eleven jurisdictions permit recovery for mental anguish, and ten of those jurisdictions declared their policy by amending their statutes. The majority can muster no substantial precedent for its in-house change of legislative policy.

The majority opinion does not clearly delineate the proof required to recover its newly created damages for mental anguish. Some of the language in the opinion suggests that any mental anguish, however slight, is compensable. The established threshold for recovering mental anguish damages requires proof of willful tort, gross negligence, willful and wanton disregard, or physical injury resulting from the mental anguish. This threshold is universally applied in the common law and statutory law of this state. *E.g.*, Farmers & Merchants State Bank of Krum *v.* Ferguson, 617 S.W.2d 918, 921 (Tex. 1981) (Uniform Commercial Code); Duncan *v.* Luke Johnson Ford, Inc., 603 S.W.2d 777, 779 (Tex. 1980) (deceptive trade practices); Billings *v.* Atkinson, 489 S.W.2d 858, 861 (Tex. 1973) (invasion of privacy); Fisher *v.* Carrousel Motor Hotel, Inc., 424 S.W.2d 627, 630 (Tex. 1967) (assault and battery).

The Texas Deceptive Trade Practices Act, like the Texas Wrongful Death Statute, authorizes the recovery of "actual damages." We have repeatedly held that "actual damages" under the Deceptive Trade Practices Act means those damages recoverable at common law and that damages for mental anguish require proof of physical injury or conduct worse than negligence. In this case, Mrs. Sanchez has satisfied the threshold for recovering mental anguish damages by proving a resulting physical injury. In future cases, we should continue to adhere to the universally established standard for mental anguish damages.

The decisions of this court have made the Wrongful Death Statute certain, and to that extent our decisions are a part of the statute. To change our decisions is to change the statute when the evidence is that the legislature has not seen any need to make the change. For this court to do so is to intrude upon the legislative policy arena. Horack, Jr., Congressional Silence: A Tool of Judicial Supremacy, 25 Tex. L. Rev. 247, 261 (1947).

I would affirm the judgments of the courts below.

MCGEE and BARROW, JJ., join in this dissenting opinion.

■ [The concurring opinion of JUSTICE RAY, upon motion for rehearing, is omitted.]

F. WRONGFUL LIFE

Anderson v. St. Francis-St. George Hospital, Inc.

Supreme Court of Ohio, 1996.
77 Ohio St. 3d 82.

On May 25, 1988, Edward H. Winter was admitted to appellant St. Francis-St. George Hospital, Inc. ("the hospital"), complaining of chest pains and fainting. Shortly after admission, Winter discussed his treatment with his personal physician, Dr. George E. Russo, who supplemented the orders on Winter's chart to provide for "No Code Blue," indicating Winter's desire not to be resuscitated. Winter's reason for not wanting to be resuscitated stemmed from his fear of suffering the same fate as his wife, who had seriously deteriorated following an emergency resuscitation. However, Dr. Russo did not order the discontinuation of the cardiac monitoring equipment.

In the early morning hours of May 28, Winter suffered ventricular tachycardia. Despite the "No Code Blue" order, and due in part to the fact that Winter was attached to a heart monitor, a nurse defibrillated Winter once and succeeded in reviving him. Upon regaining consciousness, Winter expressed his gratitude to the nurse for saving his life. . . .

On May 30, Winter suffered a stroke that paralyzed his right side. In June, he was transferred to another hospital, from which he was released in July. Winter lived with his daughter and son-in-law for several months following his discharge from the hospital. In April 1989, Winter moved to a nursing home. Although Winter remained partially paralyzed until his death in April 1990, he enjoyed numerous visits and outings with his family.

Before his death, Winter initiated this action against the hospital for damages resulting from the hospital's failure to obey the "No Code Blue" order. . . .

■ MOYER, CHIEF JUSTICE. We are presented with the following question: Where a medical provider administers a life-prolonging treatment or procedure to a patient against the patient's instructions, is the medical provider liable for all foreseeable consequential damages resulting from the treatment or procedure? . . .

American jurisprudence has developed at least three civil actions relating to the beginning and the extension of life: "wrongful life," "wrongful birth" and "wrongful living." Generally, a claim for "wrongful life" is brought by a child seeking damages against a physician or hospital for negligently failing to properly sterilize the parent.

A "wrongful birth" action is a claim brought by the parents of an impaired child seeking to recover damages for the birth of the child. The parents claim that due to the negligence of the physician, they were prevented from exercising their right to terminate the pregnancy or avoid conception altogether.

In a claim for "wrongful living," which is the basis for recovery in this case, the plaintiff . . . asserts a right to enforce an informed, competent decision to reject live-saving treatment. . . . [T]he plaintiff is asserting a liberty interest in refusing unwanted medical treatment. It is the denial of this liberty interest, when the medical professional either negligently or intentionally disregards the express wishes of a patient, that gives rise to the wrongful living cause of action.

Some form of valuation of life pervades the legal issue in all three of the causes of action. In reality, a claim of wrongful living is a *damages* concept, just as a claim for "wrongful whiplash" or "wrongful broken arm". . . .

Because a person has a right to die, a medical professional . . . is required by a legal duty to accede to a patient's express refusal of medical treatment. . . .

[O]nce it is established that but for the conduct of the medical professional, death would have resulted, the causation element of a "wrongful living" claim is satisfied.

Assuming that the plaintiff can show a duty, breach of the duty, and proximate cause between the breach and the prolongation of life, the difficult issue is what damages flow from the "harm" caused the plaintiff. There is perhaps no issue that better demonstrates the outer bounds of liability in the American civil justice system than this issue.

This court has recognized "the impossibility of a jury placing a price tag" on the benefit of life. We have also disapproved of awarding damages on the relative merits of "being versus nonbeing." . . .

There are some mistakes, indeed even breaches of duty or technical assaults, that people make in this life that affect the lives of others for which there simply should be no monetary compensation. See Heiner *v.* Moretuzzo, 73 Ohio St. 3d 80, 88 (1995) (affirming that "not every wrong is deserving of a legal remedy"). . . .

Anderson never presented any evidence that the defibrillation itself caused or contributed to Winter's suffering a stroke in any way *other than by simply prolonging his life*. . . .

The only damages that appellee may recover are those damages suffered by Winter due directly to the battery [entailed in unwanted treatment]. Where the battery was physically harmless, however, the plaintiff is entitled to nominal damages only.

We also observe that unwanted life-saving treatment does not go undeterred. Where a patient clearly delimits the medical measures he or she is willing to undergo, and a health care provider disregards such instructions, the consequences for that breach would include the damages arising from any battery inflicted on the patient, as well as appropriate licensing sanctions against the medical professionals.

In the present case, Winter suffered no damages as a result of the defibrillation of his heart, *i.e.*, no tissue burns or broken bones. Anderson concedes that he is not seeking nominal damages. There is no issue to be decided by the trial court upon remand. Therefore, we reverse the judgment of the court of appeals and enter judgment for appellant. . . .

■ [The concurring opinion of JUSTICE DOUGLAS and dissenting opinion of JUSTICE PFIEFFER are omitted.]

G. LOSS WITHOUT DAMAGE

1. NOMINAL DAMAGES

Freund v. Washington Square Press, Inc.

Court of Appeals of New York, 1974.
34 N.Y.2d 379.

▪ RABIN, JUDGE. In this action for breach of a publishing contract, we must decide what damages are recoverable for defendant's failure to publish plaintiff's manuscript. In 1965, plaintiff, an author and a college teacher, and defendant, Washington Square Press, Inc., entered into a written agreement which, in relevant part, provided as follows. Plaintiff ("author") granted defendant ("publisher") exclusive rights to publish and sell in book form plaintiff's work on modern drama. Upon plaintiff's delivery of the manuscript, defendant agreed to complete payment of a nonreturnable $2,000 "advance." Thereafter, if defendant deemed the manuscript not "suitable for publication," it had the right to terminate the agreement by written notice within 60 days of delivery. Unless so terminated, defendant agreed to publish the work in hardbound edition within 18 months and afterwards in paperbound edition. The contract further provided that defendant would pay royalties to plaintiff, based upon specified percentages of sales. (For example, plaintiff was to receive 10% of the retail price of the first 10,000 copies sold in the continental United States.) If defendant failed to publish within 18 months, the contract provided that "this agreement shall terminate and the rights herein granted to the Publisher shall revert to the Author. In such event all payments theretofore made to the Author shall belong to the Author without prejudice to any other remedies which the Author may have." . . .

Plaintiff performed by delivering his manuscript to defendant and was paid his $2,000 advance. Defendant thereafter merged with another publisher and ceased publishing in hardbound. Although defendant did not execute its 60-day right to terminate, it has refused to publish the manuscript in any form.

[The trial court found that the cost of hardcover publication to the plaintiff was the natural and probable consequence of the breach and awarded $10,000.00 to cover this cost.]

The Appellate Division . . . affirmed, finding that the cost of publication was the proper measure of damages. In support of its conclusion, the majority analogized to the construction contract situation where the cost of completion may be the proper measure of damages for a builder's failure to complete a house or for use of wrong materials. The dissent concluded that the cost of publication is not an appropriate measure of damages and consequently, that plaintiff may recover nominal damages only. We agree with the dissent. In so concluding, we look to the basic purpose of damage recovery and the nature and effect of the parties' contract. . . .

[T]he law awards damages for breach of contract to compensate for injury caused by the breach—injury which was foreseeable, *i.e.*, reasonably within the contemplation of the parties, at the time the contract was entered into. . . . But it is equally fundamental that the injured party should not recover more from the breach than he would have gained had the contract been fully performed.

Measurement of damages in this case according to the cost of publication to the plaintiff would confer greater advantage than performance of the contract would have entailed to plaintiff and would place him in a far better position than he would have occupied had the defendant fully performed. Such measurement bears no relation to compensation for plaintiff's actual loss or anticipated profit. Far beyond compensating plaintiff for the interests he had in the defendant's performance of the contract—whether restitution, reliance or expectation—an award of the cost of publication would enrich plaintiff at defendant's expense.

Pursuant to the contract, plaintiff delivered his manuscript to the defendant. In doing so, he conferred a value on the defendant which, upon defendant's breach, was required to be restored to him. Special Term, in addition to ordering a trial on the issue of damages, ordered defendant to return the manuscript to plaintiff and plaintiff's restitution interest in the contract was thereby protected.

At the trial on the issue of damages, plaintiff alleged no reliance losses suffered in performing the contract or in making necessary preparations to perform. Had such losses, if foreseeable and ascertainable, been incurred, plaintiff would have been entitled to compensation for them.

As for plaintiff's expectation interest in the contract, it was basically two-fold—the "advance" and the royalties. (To be sure, plaintiff may have expected to enjoy whatever notoriety, prestige or other benefits that might have attended publication, but even if these expectations were compensable, plaintiff did not attempt at trial to place a monetary value on them.) There is no dispute that plaintiff's expectancy in the "advance" was fulfilled—he has received his $2,000. His expectancy interest in the royalties—the profit he stood to gain from sale of the published book—while theoretically compensable, was speculative. Although this work is not plaintiff's first, at trial he provided no stable foundation for a reasonable estimate of royalties he would have earned had defendant not breached its promise to publish. In these circumstances, his claim for royalties falls for uncertainty.

Since the damages which would have compensated plaintiff for anticipated royalties were not proved with the required certainty, we agree with the dissent in the Appellate Division that nominal damages alone are recoverable. Though these are damages in name only and not at all compensatory, they are nevertheless awarded as a formal vindication of plaintiff's legal right to compensation which has not been given a sufficiently certain monetary valuation.

In our view, the analogy by the majority in the Appellate Division to the construction contract situation was inapposite. In the typical construction contract, the owner agrees to pay money or other consideration to a builder and expects, under the contract, to receive a completed building in return. The value of the promised performance to the owner is the properly constructed building. In this case, unlike the typical construction contract, the value to plaintiff of the promised performance—publication—was a percentage of sales of the books published and not the books themselves. Had the plaintiff contracted for the printing, binding and delivery of a number of hardbound copies of his manuscript, to be sold or disposed of as he wished, then perhaps the construction analogy, and measurement of damages by the cost of replacement or completion, would have some application.

Here, however, the specific value to plaintiff of the promised publication was the royalties he stood to receive from defendant's sales of the published book. Essentially, publication represented what it would have cost the defendant to confer that value upon the plaintiff, and, by its breach, defendant saved that cost. The error by the courts below was in measuring damages not by the value to plaintiff of the promised performance but by the cost of that performance to defendant. Damages are not measured, however, by what the defaulting party saved by the breach, but by the natural and probable consequences of the breach *to the plaintiff*. In this case, the consequence to plaintiff of defendant's failure to publish is that he is prevented from realizing the gains promised by the contract—the royalties. But, as we have stated, the amount of royalties plaintiff would have realized was not ascertained with adequate certainty and, as a consequence, plaintiff may recover nominal damages only.

Accordingly, the order of the Appellate Division should be modified to the extent of reducing the damage award of $10,000 for the cost of publication to six cents, but with costs and disbursements to the plaintiff. . . .

2. LOSS OF RIGHTS

Carey v. Piphus

Supreme Court of the United States, 1978.
435 U.S. 247.

■ MR. JUSTICE POWELL delivered the opinion of the Court. . . .

Respondent Jarius Piphus was a freshman at Chicago Vocational High School during the 1973–1974 school year. On January 23, 1974, during school hours, the school principal saw Piphus and another student standing outdoors on school property passing back and forth what the principal described as an irregularly shaped cigarette. The principal approached the students unnoticed and smelled what he believed was the strong odor of burning marihuana. He also saw Piphus try to pass a packet of cigarette papers to the other student. When the students became aware of the principal's presence, they threw the cigarette into a nearby hedge.

The principal took the students to the school's disciplinary office and directed the assistant principal to impose the "usual" 20-day suspension for violation of the school rule against the use of drugs. The students protested that they had not been smoking marihuana, but to no avail. Piphus was allowed to remain at school, although not in class, for the remainder of the school day while the assistant principal tried, without success, to reach his mother. . . .

Piphus and his mother . . . filed suit against petitioners . . . under 42 U.S.C. § 1983 . . . charging that Piphus had been suspended without due process of law in violation of the Fourteenth Amendment. The complaint sought declaratory and injunctive relief, together with actual and punitive damages in the amount of $3,000. Piphus was readmitted to school under a temporary restraining order after eight days of his suspension. . . .

[T]he District Court declined to award damages because "the record is completely devoid of any evidence which could even form the basis of a speculative inference measuring the extent of [Piphus's] injuries." . . .

[T]he Court of Appeals held that even if the District Court found on remand that [Piphus's suspension was] justified, [he] would be entitled to recover substantial "nonpunitive" damages simply because [he] had been denied procedural due process. . . .

The legislative history of § 1983 . . . demonstrates that it was intended to "[create] a species of tort liability" in favor of persons who are deprived of "rights, privileges, or immunities secured" to them by the Constitution. . . .

[Piphus seems] to make two different arguments in support of the holding below. First, [he contends] that substantial damages should be awarded under § 1983 for the deprivation of a constitutional right *whether or not* any injury was caused by the deprivation. This, [he says,] is appropriate both because constitutional rights are valuable in and of themselves, and because of the need to deter violations of constitutional rights. . . . Second, [Piphus argues] that even if the purpose of a § 1983 damages award is, as petitioners contend, primarily to compensate persons for injuries that are caused by the deprivation of constitutional rights, every deprivation of procedural due process may be *presumed* to cause some injury. This presumption, [Piphus says], should relieve them from the necessity of proving that injury actually was caused. . . .

Rights, constitutional and otherwise, do not exist in a vacuum. Their purpose is to protect persons from injuries to particular interests, and their contours are shaped by the interests they protect.

Our legal system's concept of damages reflects this view of legal rights. "The cardinal principle of damages in Anglo-American law is that of *compensation* for the injury caused to plaintiff by defendant's breach of duty." 2 F. Harper & F. James, LAW OF TORTS § 25.1, p. 1299 (1956). The Court implicitly has recognized the applicability of this principle to actions under § 1983 by stating that damages are available under that section for actions "found . . . to have been violative of . . . constitutional rights *and to have caused compensable injury*. . . ." . . . .[11]

The parties . . . disagree as to the . . . holding of the Court of Appeals that [Piphus is] entitled to recover substantial—although unspecified—damages to compensate them for "the injury which is inherent in the nature of the wrong," even if their suspensions were justified and even if they fail to prove that the denial of procedural due process actually caused them some real, if intangible, injury. [Piphus submits] that the holding is correct because injury fairly may be "presumed" to flow from every denial of procedural due process. [His] argument is that in addition to protecting against unjustified deprivations, the Due Process Clause also guarantees the "feeling of just treatment" by the government. [He contends] that the deprivation of protected interests without procedural due process, even where the premise for the deprivation is not erroneous, inevitably arouses strong feelings of mental and emotional distress in the individual who is denied this "feeling of just treatment." [He analogizes his] case to that of defamation *per se,* in which "the plaintiff is relieved from the necessity of producing any proof whatsoever that he has been injured" in order to recover substantial compensatory damages. . . .

As we have observed in another context, the doctrine of presumed damages in the common law of defamation *per se* "is an oddity of tort law, for it allows recovery of purportedly compensatory damages without evidence of actual loss." The doctrine has been defended on the grounds that those forms of defamation that are actionable *per se* are virtually certain to cause serious injury to reputation, and that this kind of injury is extremely difficult to prove. Moreover, statements that are defamatory *per se* by their very nature are likely to cause mental and emotional distress, as well as injury to reputation, so there arguably is little reason to require proof of this kind of injury either. But these considerations do

---

[11] This is not to say that exemplary or punitive damages might not be awarded in a proper case under § 1983 with the specific purpose of deterring or punishing violations of constitutional rights. Although we imply no approval or disapproval of any of these cases, we note that there is no basis for such an award in this case. The District Court specifically found that petitioners did not act with malicious intention to deprive respondents of their rights or to do them other injury . . . . We also note that the potential liability of § 1983 defendants for attorney's fees, provides additional—and by no means inconsequential—assurance that agents of the State will not deliberately ignore due process rights.

not support [Piphus's] contention that damages should be presumed to flow from every deprivation of procedural due process.

First, it is not reasonable to assume that every departure from procedural due process, no matter what the circumstances or how minor, inherently is as likely to cause distress as the publication of defamation *per se* is to cause injury to reputation and distress. Where the deprivation of a protected interest is substantively justified but procedures are deficient in some respect, there may well be those who suffer no distress over the procedural irregularities. Indeed, in contrast to the immediately distressing effect of defamation *per se,* a person may not even know that procedures *were* deficient until he enlists the aid of counsel to challenge a perceived substantive deprivation.

Moreover, where a deprivation is justified but procedures are deficient, whatever distress a person feels may be attributable to the justified deprivation rather than to deficiencies in procedure. But as the Court of Appeals held, the injury caused by a justified deprivation, including distress, is not properly compensable under § 1983. This ambiguity in causation, which is absent in the case of defamation *per se,* provides additional need for requiring the plaintiff to convince the trier of fact that he actually suffered distress because of the denial of procedural due process itself.

Finally, we foresee no particular difficulty in producing evidence that mental and emotional distress actually was caused by the denial of procedural due process itself. Distress is a personal injury familiar to the law, customarily proved by showing the nature and circumstances of the wrong and its effect on the plaintiff. In sum, then, although mental and emotional distress caused by the denial of procedural due process itself is compensable under § 1983, we hold that neither the likelihood of such injury nor the difficulty of proving it is so great as to justify awarding compensatory damages without proof that such injury actually was caused. . . .

Even if [Piphus's suspension was] justified, and even if [he] did not suffer any other actual injury, the fact remains that [he was] deprived of their right to procedural due process. . . .

Common-law courts traditionally have vindicated deprivations of certain "absolute" rights that are not shown to have caused actual injury through the award of a nominal sum of money. By making the deprivation of such rights actionable for nominal damages without proof of actual injury, the law recognizes the importance to organized society that those rights be scrupulously observed; but at the same time, it remains true to the principle that substantial damages should be awarded only to compensate actual injury or, in the case of exemplary or punitive damages, to deter or punish malicious deprivations of rights.

Because the right to procedural due process is "absolute" in the sense that it does not depend upon the merits of a claimant's substantive assertions, and because of the importance to organized society that procedural due process be observed, we believe that the denial of procedural due process should be actionable for nominal damages without proof of actual injury. We therefore hold that if, upon remand, the District Court determines that [Piphus's suspension was] justified, [Piphus] nevertheless will be entitled to recover nominal damages not to exceed one dollar from petitioners. . . .

■ MR. JUSTICE MARSHALL concurs in the result.

■ MR. JUSTICE BLACKMUN took no part in the consideration or decision of this case.

Memphis Community School District v. Stachura

Supreme Court of the United States, 1986.
477 U.S. 299.

■ JUSTICE POWELL delivered the opinion of the Court. . . .

Respondent Edward Stachura is a tenured teacher in the Memphis, Michigan, public schools. When the events that led to this case occurred, respondent taught seventh-grade life science, using a textbook that had been approved by the School Board. The textbook included a chapter on human reproduction. During the 1978–1979 school year, respondent spent six weeks on this chapter. As part of their instruction, students were shown pictures of respondent's wife during her pregnancy. Respondent also showed the students two films concerning human growth and sexuality. These films were provided by the County Health Department, and the Principal of respondent's school had approved their use. Both films had been shown in past school years without incident.

After the showing of the pictures and the films, a number of parents complained to school officials about respondent's teaching methods. These complaints, which appear to have been based largely on inaccurate rumors about the allegedly sexually explicit nature of the pictures and films, were discussed at an open School Board meeting held on April 23, 1979. Following the advice of the School Superintendent, respondent did not attend the meeting, during which a number of parents expressed the view that respondent should not be allowed to teach in the Memphis school system. The day after the meeting, respondent was suspended with pay. The School Board later confirmed the suspension, and notified respondent that an "administration evaluation" of his teaching methods was underway. No such evaluation was ever made. Respondent was reinstated the next fall, after filing this lawsuit.

Respondent sued the School District, the Board of Education, various Board members and school administrators, and two parents who had participated in the April 23 School Board meeting. The complaint alleged that respondent's suspension deprived him of both liberty and property without due process of law and violated his First Amendment right to academic freedom. Respondent sought compensatory and punitive damages under 42 U.S.C. § 1983 for these constitutional violations.

At the close of trial on these claims, the District Court instructed the jury as to the law governing . . . liability. . . . In addition to [an] instruction on the standard elements of compensatory damages, the court explained that punitive damages could be awarded, and described the standards governing punitive awards. Finally, . . . the court charged that damages also could be awarded based on the value or importance of the constitutional rights that were violated:

> "If you find that the Plaintiff has been deprived of a Constitutional right, you may award damages to compensate him for the deprivation. . . . In one sense, no monetary value we place upon Constitutional rights can measure their importance in our society or compensate a citizen adequately for their deprivation. However, just because these rights are not capable of precise evaluation does not mean that an appropriate monetary amount should not be awarded.
>
> "The precise value you place upon any Constitutional right which you find was denied to Plaintiff is within your discretion. You may wish to consider the importance of the right in our system of government, the role which this right has played in the history of our republic, [and] the significance of the right in the context of the activities which the Plaintiff was engaged in at the time of the violation of the right."

The jury found petitioners liable, and awarded a total of $275,000 in compensatory damages and $46,000 in punitive damages. The District Court entered judgment notwithstanding the verdict as to one of the defendants, reducing the total award to $266,750 in compensatory damages and $36,000 in punitive damages. . . .

The instructions at issue here cannot be squared with Carey *v.* Piphus, 435 U.S. 247 (1978) . . . . The jurors in this case were told that, in determining how much was necessary to "compensate [respondent] for the deprivation" of his constitutional rights, they should place a money value on the "rights" themselves by considering such factors as the particular right's "importance . . . in our system of government," its role in American history, and its "significance . . . in the context of the activities" in which respondent was engaged. These factors focus, not on compensation for provable injury, but on the jury's subjective perception of the importance of constitutional rights as an abstract matter. *Carey* establishes that such an approach is impermissible. The constitutional right transgressed in *Carey*—the right to due process of law—is central to our system of ordered liberty. We nevertheless held that *no* compensatory damages could be awarded for violation of that right absent proof of actual injury. *Carey* thus makes clear that the abstract value of a constitutional right may not form the basis for § 1983 damages.

Respondent nevertheless argues that *Carey* does not control here, because in this case a *substantive* constitutional right—respondent's First Amendment right to academic freedom—was infringed. The argument misperceives our analysis in *Carey*. That case does not establish a two-tiered system of constitutional rights, with substantive rights afforded greater protection than "mere" procedural safeguards. We did acknowledge in *Carey* that "the elements and prerequisites for recovery of damages" might vary depending on the interests protected by the constitutional right at issue. But we emphasized that, whatever the constitutional basis for § 1983 liability, such damages must always be designed "to *compensate injuries* caused by the [constitutional] deprivation." That conclusion simply leaves no room for non-compensatory damages measured by the jury's perception of the abstract "importance" of a constitutional right.

Nor do we find such damages necessary to vindicate the constitutional rights that § 1983 protects. Section 1983 presupposes that damages that compensate for actual harm ordinarily suffice to deter constitutional violations. Moreover, damages based on the "value" of constitutional rights are an unwieldy tool for ensuring compliance with the Constitution. History and tradition do not afford any sound guidance concerning the precise value that juries should place on constitutional protections. Accordingly, were such damages available, juries would be free to award arbitrary amounts without any evidentiary basis, or to use their unbounded discretion to punish unpopular defendants. Such damages would be too uncertain to be of any great value to plaintiffs, and would inject caprice into determinations of damages in § 1983 cases. We therefore hold that damages based on the abstract "value" or "importance" of constitutional rights are not a permissible element of compensatory damages in such cases.

Respondent further argues that the challenged instructions authorized a form of "presumed" damages—a remedy that is both compensatory in nature and traditionally part of the range of tort law remedies. . . .

Presumed damages are a *substitute* for ordinary compensatory damages, not a *supplement* for an award that fully compensates the alleged injury. When a plaintiff seeks compensation for an injury that is likely to have occurred but difficult to establish, some form of presumed damages may possibly be appropriate. In those circumstances, presumed damages may roughly approximate the harm that the plaintiff suffered and thereby compensate for harms that may be impossible to measure. . . . [T]he instructions at issue in this case did not serve this purpose, but instead called on the jury to measure damages based on a subjective evaluation of the importance of particular constitutional values. Since such damages are wholly divorced from any compensatory purpose, they cannot be justified as presumed damages.[14] Moreover, no rough substitute for compensatory damages was required in this case, since the jury was fully authorized to compensate respondent for both monetary and nonmonetary harms caused by petitioners' conduct. . . .

■ JUSTICE BRENNAN and JUSTICE STEVENS join the opinion of the Court and also join JUSTICE MARSHALL'S opinion concurring in the judgment.

■ JUSTICE MARSHALL, with whom JUSTICE BRENNAN, JUSTICE BLACKMUN, and JUSTICE STEVENS join, concurring in the judgment. . . . Following *Carey,* the Courts of Appeals have recognized that invasions of constitutional rights sometimes cause injuries that cannot be redressed by a wooden application of common-law damages rules. In Hobson *v.* Wilson, 737 F.2d 1, 57–63 (D.C. Cir. 1984), *cert. denied,* 470 U.S. 1084 (1985), which the Court cites, plaintiffs claimed that defendant Federal Bureau of Investigation agents had invaded their First Amendment rights to assemble for peaceable political protest, to associate with others to engage in political expression, and to speak on public issues free of unreasonable government interference. The District Court found that the defendants had succeeded in diverting plaintiffs from, and impeding them in, their protest activities. The Court of Appeals for the District of Columbia Circuit held that that injury to a First Amendment-protected interest could itself constitute compensable injury wholly apart from any "emotional distress, humiliation and personal indignity, emotional pain, embarrassment, fear, anxiety and anguish" suffered by plaintiffs. The court warned, however, that that injury could be compensated with substantial damages only to the extent that it was "reasonably quantifiable"; damages should not be based on "the so-called inherent value of the rights violated."

I believe that the *Hobson* court correctly stated the law. When a plaintiff is deprived, for example, of the opportunity to engage in a demonstration to express his political views, "[i]t is facile to suggest that no damage is done." Loss of such an opportunity constitutes loss of First Amendment rights "in their most pristine and classic form." There is no

---

[14] For the same reason, Nixon *v.* Herndon, 273 U.S. 536 (1927) and similar cases do not support the challenged instructions. In *Nixon,* the Court held that a plaintiff who was illegally prevented from voting in a state primary election suffered compensable injury. This holding did not rest on the "value" of the right to vote as an abstract matter; rather, the Court recognized that the plaintiff had suffered a particular injury—his inability to vote in a particular election—that might be compensated through substantial money damages.

Nixon followed a long line of cases, going back to Lord Holt's decision in Ashby *v.* White, 2 Ld. Raym. 938, 92 Eng. Rep. 126 (1703), authorizing substantial money damages as compensation for persons deprived of their right to vote in particular elections. Although these decisions sometimes speak of damages for the value of the right to vote, their analysis shows that they involve nothing more than an award of presumed damages for a nonmonetary harm that cannot easily be quantified . . . .

The "value of the right" in the context of these decisions is the money value of the particular loss that the plaintiff suffered—a loss of which "each member of the jury has personal knowledge." It is *not* the value of the right to vote as a general, abstract matter, based on its role in our history or system of government. Thus, whatever the wisdom of these decisions in the context of the changing scope of compensatory damages over the course of this century, they do not support awards of noncompensatory damages such as those authorized in this case.

reason why such an injury should not be compensable in damages. At the same time, however, the award must be proportional to the actual loss sustained.

The instructions given the jury in this case were improper because they did not require the jury to focus on the loss actually sustained by respondent. Rather, they invited the jury to base its award on speculation about "the importance of the right in our system of government" and "the role which this right has played in the history of our republic," guided only by the admonition that "[i]n one sense, no monetary value we place on Constitutional rights can measure their importance in our society or compensate a citizen adequately for their deprivation." These instructions invited the jury to speculate on matters wholly detached from the real injury occasioned respondent by the deprivation of the right. Further, the instructions might have led the jury to grant respondent damages based on the "abstract value" of the right to procedural due process—a course directly barred by our decision in *Carey*.

The Court therefore properly remands for a new trial on damages. I do not understand the Court, however, to hold that deprivations of constitutional rights can never themselves constitute compensable injuries. Such a rule would be inconsistent with the logic of *Carey,* and would defeat the purpose of § 1983 by denying compensation for genuine injuries caused by the deprivation of constitutional rights.

H. TIME, TAXES, AND RELATED MATTERS

1. ACCOUNTING FOR TAXES

Norfolk and Western Railway v. Liepelt

Supreme Court of the United States, 1980.
444 U.S. 490.

▪ MR. JUSTICE STEVENS delivered the opinion of the Court.

In cases arising under the Federal Employers' Liability Act [FELA], most trial judges refuse to allow the jury to receive evidence or instruction concerning the impact of federal income taxes on the amount of damages to be awarded. . . . [T]he two questions presented by the certiorari petition in this wrongful death action [are]: (1) whether it was error to exclude evidence of the income taxes payable on the decedent's past and estimated future earnings; and (2) whether it was error for the trial judge to refuse to instruct the jury that the award of damages would not be subject to income taxation.

In 1973 a fireman employed by petitioner suffered fatal injuries in a collision caused by petitioner's negligence. Respondent, as administratrix of the fireman's estate, brought suit under the FELA to recover the damages that his survivors suffered as a result of his death. In 1976, after a full trial in the Circuit Court of Cook County, the jury awarded respondent $775,000. . . .

The evidence supporting the damages award included biographical data about the decedent and his family and the expert testimony of an economist. The decedent, a 37-year-old man, was living with his second wife and two young children and was contributing to the support of two older children by his first marriage. His gross earnings in the 11 months prior to his death on November 22, 1973 amounted to $11,988. Assuming continued employment, those earnings would have amounted to $16,828.26 in 1977.

The expert estimated that the decedent's earnings would have increased at a rate of approximately five percent per year, which would have amounted to $51,600 in the year 2000, the year of his expected retirement. The gross amount of those earnings, plus the value of the services he would have performed for his family, less the amounts the decedent would have spent upon himself, produced a total which, when discounted to present value at the time of trial, amounted to $302,000.

Petitioner objected to the use of gross earnings, without any deduction for income taxes, in respondent's expert's testimony and offered to prove through the testimony of its own expert, an actuary, that decedent's federal income taxes during the years 1973 through 2000 would have amounted to about $57,000. Taking that figure into account, and making different assumptions about the rate of future increases in salary and the calculation of the present value of future earnings, petitioner's expert computed the net pecuniary loss at $138,327. As already noted, the jury returned a verdict of $775,000.

Petitioner argues that the jury must have assumed that its award was subject to federal income taxation; otherwise, it is argued, the verdict would not have exceeded respondent's expert's opinion by such a large amount. For that reason, petitioner contends that it was prejudiced by the trial judge's refusal to instruct the jury that "your award will not be subject to any income taxes, and you should not consider such taxes in fixing the amount of your award."

Whether it was error to refuse that instruction, as well as the question whether evidence concerning the federal taxes on the decedent's earnings was properly excluded, is a matter governed by federal law. . . .

In a wrongful-death action under the FELA, the measure of recovery is "the damages . . . [that] flow from the deprivation of the pecuniary benefits which the beneficiaries might have reasonably received . . . ." The amount of money that a wage earner is able to contribute to the support of his family is unquestionably affected by the amount of the tax he must pay to the Federal Government. It is his after-tax income, rather than his gross income before taxes, that provides the only realistic measure of his ability to support his family. It follows inexorably that the wage earner's income tax is a relevant factor in calculating the monetary loss suffered by his dependents when he dies.

Although federal courts have consistently received evidence of the amount of the decedent's personal expenditures and have required that the estimate of future earnings be reduced by "taking account of the earning power of the money that is presently to be awarded," they have generally not considered the payment of income taxes as tantamount to a personal expenditure and have regarded the future prediction of tax consequences as too speculative and complex for a jury's deliberations.

Admittedly there are many variables that may affect the amount of a wage earner's future income-tax liability. The law may change, his family may increase or decrease in size, his spouse's earnings may affect his tax bracket, and extra income or unforeseen deductions may become available. But future employment itself, future health, future personal expenditures, future interest rates, and future inflation are also matters of estimate and prediction. Any one of these issues might provide the basis for protracted expert testimony and debate. But the practical wisdom of the trial bar and the trial bench has developed effective methods of presenting the essential elements of an expert calculation in a form that is understandable by juries that are increasingly familiar with the complexities of modern life. We therefore reject the notion that the introduction of evidence describing a decedent's estimated after-tax earnings is too speculative or complex for a jury.

Respondent argues that if this door is opened, other equally relevant evidence must also be received. For example, she points out that in discounting the estimate of future earnings to its present value, the tax on the income to be earned by the damages award is now omitted. Logically, it would certainly seem correct that this amount, like future wages, should be estimated on an after-tax basis. But the fact that such an after-tax estimate, if offered in proper form, would also be admissible does not persuade us that it is wrong to use after-tax figures instead of gross earnings in projecting what the decedent's financial contributions to his survivors would have been had this tragic accident not occurred.

Respondent also argues that evidence concerning costs of litigation, including her attorneys' fees, is equally pertinent to a determination of what amount will actually compensate the survivors for their monetary loss. In a sense this is, of course, true. But the argument that attorney's fees must be added to a plaintiff's recovery if the award is truly to make him whole is contrary to the generally applicable "American Rule." . . . In any event, it surely is not proper for the Judiciary to ignore the demonstrably relevant factor of income tax in measuring damages in order to offset what may be perceived as an undesirable or unfair rule regarding attorney's fees.

Section 104(a)(2) of the Internal Revenue Code provides that the amount of any damages received on account of personal injuries is not taxable income. The section is construed to apply to wrongful-death awards; they are not taxable income to the recipient.

Although the law is perfectly clear, it is entirely possible that the members of the jury may assume that a plaintiff's recovery in a case of this kind will be subject to federal taxation, and that the award should be increased substantially in order to be sure that the injured party is fully compensated. . . . Judge Aldisert, writing for the Third Circuit, [said]:

> "We take judicial notice of the 'tax consciousness' of the American public. Yet, we also recognize . . . that few members of the general public are aware of the special statutory exception for personal injury awards contained in the Internal Revenue Code." . . .

. . . In this case the respondent's expert witness computed the amount of pecuniary loss at $302,000, plus the value of the care and training that decedent would have provided to his young children; the jury awarded damages of $775,000. It is surely not fanciful to suppose that the jury erroneously believed that a large portion of the award would be payable to the Federal Government in taxes, and that therefore it improperly inflated the recovery. . . .

We hold that it was error to refuse the requested instruction in this case. That instruction was brief and could easily be understood. It would not complicate the trial by making additional qualifying or supplemental instructions necessary. It would not be prejudicial to either party, but would merely eliminate an area of doubt or speculation that might have an improper impact on the computation of the amount of damages. . . .

■ MR. JUSTICE BLACKMUN, with whom MR. JUSTICE MARSHALL joins, dissenting. . . .

In my view, by mandating adjustment of the award by way of reduction for federal income taxes that would have been paid by the decedent on his earnings, the Court appropriates for the tortfeasor a benefit intended to be conferred on the victim or his survivors. And in requiring that the jury be instructed that a wrongful-death award is not subject to federal income tax, the Court opens the door for a variety of admonitions to the jury not to "misbehave," and unnecessarily interjects what is now to be federal law into the administration of a trial in a state court. . . .

By not taxing the award, Congress has bestowed a benefit. Although the parties disagree over the origin of the tax-free status of the wrongful-death award, it is surely clear that the lost earnings could be taxed as income. . . .

While Congress has not articulated its reasons for not taxing a wrongful-death award, it is highly unlikely that it intended to confer this benefit on the tortfeasor. Two more probable purposes for the exclusion are apparent. First, taxing the award could involve the same uncertainties and complexities noted by respondent and the majority of the courts of this country as a reason for not taking income taxes into account in computing the award. Congress may have decided that it is simply not worthwhile to enact a complex and administratively burdensome system in order to approximate the tax treatment of the income if, in fact, it had been earned over a period of time by the decedent. Second, Congress may have intended to confer a humanitarian benefit on the victim or victims of the tort. . . .

Whichever of these concerns it was that motivated Congress, transfer of the tax benefit to the FELA tortfeasor-defendant is inconsistent with that purpose. If Congress felt that it was not worth the effort to estimate the decedent's prospective tax liability on behalf of the public fisc, it is unlikely that it would want to require this effort on behalf of the tortfeasor. And Congress would not confer a humanitarian benefit on tort victims or their survivors in the Internal Revenue Code, only to take it away from victims or their survivors covered by the FELA. I conclude, therefore, that any income tax effect on lost earnings should not be considered in the computation of a damages award under the FELA. . . .

The required instruction is purely cautionary in nature. It does not affect the determination of liability or the measure of damages. It does nothing more than call a basically irrelevant factor to the jury's attention, and then directs the jury to forget that matter. . . . [T]he instruction required by the Court seems to me to be both unwise and unjustified, and almost an affront to the practical wisdom of the jury.

It also is "entirely possible" that the jury "may" increase its damages award in the belief that the defendant is insured, or that the plaintiff will be obligated for substantial attorney's fees, or that the award is subject to state (as well as federal) income tax, or on the basis of any number of other extraneous factors. Charging the jury about every conceivable matter as to which it should not misbehave or miscalculate would be burdensome and could be confusing. . . .

NOTES ON TAX TREATMENT OF DAMAGES

1. As a general matter, damage awards (or settlements) are taxable in the year in which they are paid. Thus, if a court awards damages for lost profits resulting from a breach of contract, the plaintiff must pay income tax on the award. (Damages based on harm to capital assets are subject to capital gains tax under the involuntary conversion provisions of the Internal Revenue Code, I.R.C. § 1033.) The plaintiff's tax liability extends to funds earmarked for payment of attorney's fees, although this is not income the plaintiff will enjoy.

Personal injury awards, however, are singled out for special treatment. I.R.C. § 104(a)(2) provides an exclusion for compensatory damages for physical personal injuries. Punitive damages and damages for emotional distress, on the other hand, are taxable.

In a brief but interesting insurrection, a panel of the United States Court of Appeals for the District of Columbia held in 2006 that taxation of damages for emotional distress violated the Sixteenth Amendment. Murphy *v.* I.R.S., 460 F.3d 79 (D.C. Cir. 2006). The same panel later reheard the case and reversed its decision. Murphy *v.* I.R.S., 493 F.3d 170 (D.C. Cir. 2007).

2. Norfolk & Western Railway *v.* Liepelt is a decision under the Federal Employers' Liability Act and therefore is not binding in state court actions based on state law. In Otis Elevator Co. *v.* Reid, 101 Nev. 515 (1985), the court made the following observations with respect to the propriety of tax exemption instructions under state law:

> "Jurisdictions which have considered the propriety of these instructions are divided into three groups. The majority prohibit tax instructions under any circumstances. The minority view, exemplified by the United States Supreme Court decision in [*Liepelt*], requires trial courts to give the instruction upon request of counsel. In a few jurisdictions, the instruction may be given at the discretion of trial court.
>
> "In determining whether a tax exemption instruction is appropriate under the latter rule, other jurisdictions have focused on whether the jury has been exposed to the issue of taxes during trial, either by the evidence or by comments by counsel. We conclude that tax exemption instructions are appropriate only as curative devices designed to eliminate any prejudice resulting from the jury's exposure to tax-related issues at trial."

Id. at 522.

2. COMPUTING FUTURE LOSSES

Jones & Laughlin Steel Corp. v. Pfeifer

Supreme Court of the United States, 1983.
462 U.S. 523.

■ STEVENS, JUSTICE. Respondent was injured in the course of his employment as a loading helper on a coal barge. As his employer, petitioner was required to compensate him for his injury under § 4 of the Longshoremen's and Harbor Workers' Compensation Act (the Act). 44 Stat. 1426, 33 U.S.C. § 904. . . .

The District Court arrived at its final award by taking 12½ years of earnings at respondent's wage at the time of injury ($325,312.50), subtracting his projected hypothetical earnings at the minimum wage ($66,352) and the compensation payments he had received under § 4 ($33,079.14), and adding $50,000 for pain and suffering. The court did not increase the award to take inflation into account, and it did not discount the award to reflect the present value of the future stream of income. The Court instead decided to follow a decision of the Supreme Court of Pennsylvania, which had held "as a matter of law that future inflation shall be presumed equal to future interest rates with these factors offsetting." Kaczkowski *v.* Bolubasz, 491 Pa. 561, 583 (1980). . . .

The District Court found that respondent was permanently disabled as a result of petitioner's negligence. He therefore was entitled to an award of damages to compensate him for his probable pecuniary loss over the duration of his career, reduced to its present value. It is useful at the outset to review the way in which damages should be measured in a hypothetical inflation-free economy. We shall then consider how price inflation alters the analysis. . . .

In calculating damages, it is assumed that if the injured party had not been disabled, he would have continued to work, and to receive wages at periodic intervals until retirement, disability, or death. An award for impaired earning capacity is intended to compensate the worker for the diminution in that stream of income. The award could in theory take the form of periodic payments, but in this country it has traditionally taken the form of a lump sum, paid at the conclusion of the litigation. The appropriate lump sum cannot be computed without first examining the stream of income it purports to replace.

The lost stream's length cannot be known with certainty; the worker could have been disabled or even killed in a different, non-work-related accident at any time. The probability that he would still be working at a given date is constantly diminishing. Given the complexity of trying to make an exact calculation, litigants frequently follow the relatively simple course of assuming that the worker would have continued to work up until a specific date certain. In this case, for example, both parties agreed that the petitioner would have continued to work until age 65 (12½ more years) if he had not been injured.

Each annual installment[11] in the lost stream comprises several elements. The most significant is, of course, the actual wage. In addition, the worker may have enjoyed certain fringe benefits, which should be included in an ideal evaluation of the worker's loss but are frequently excluded for simplicity's sake. On the other hand, the injured worker's lost wages would have been diminished by state and federal income taxes. Since the damages award is tax-free, the relevant stream is ideally of *after-tax* wages and benefits. Moreover, workers often incur unreimbursed costs, such as transportation to work and uniforms, that the injured worker will not incur. These costs should also be deducted in estimating the lost stream.

In this case the parties appear to have agreed to simplify the litigation, and to presume that in each installment all the elements in the stream would offset each other, except for gross wages. However, in attempting to estimate even such a stylized stream of annual

[11] Obviously, another distorting simplification is being made here. Although workers generally receive their wages in weekly or biweekly installments, virtually all calculations of lost earnings, including the one made in this case, pretend that the stream would have flowed in large spurts, taking the form of annual installments.

installments of gross wages, a trier of fact faces a complex task. . . . Even in an inflation-free economy—that is to say one in which the prices of consumer goods remain stable—a worker's wages tend to "inflate." This "real" wage inflation reflects a number of factors, some linked to the specific individual and some linked to broader societal forces.

With the passage of time, an individual worker often becomes more valuable to his employer. His personal work experiences increase his hourly contributions to firm profits. To reflect that heightened value, he will often receive "seniority" or "experience" raises, "merit" raises, or even promotions. Although it may be difficult to prove when, and whether, a particular injured worker might have received such wage increases, they may be reliably demonstrated for some workers.

Furthermore, the wages of workers as a class may increase over time. Through more efficient interaction among labor, capital, and technology, industrial productivity may increase, and workers' wages may enjoy a share of that growth. Such productivity increases—reflected in real increases in the gross national product per worker-hour—have been a permanent feature of the national economy since the conclusion of World War II. Moreover, through collective bargaining, workers may be able to negotiate increases in their "share" of revenues, at the cost of reducing shareholders' rate of return on their investments. . . .

To summarize, the first stage in calculating an appropriate award for lost earnings involves an estimate of what the lost stream of income would have been. The stream may be approximated as a series of after-tax payments, one in each year of the worker's expected remaining career. In estimating what those payments would have been in an inflation-free economy, the trier of fact may begin with the worker's annual wage at the time of injury. If sufficient proof is offered, the trier of fact may increase that figure to reflect the appropriate influence of individualized factors (such as foreseeable promotions) and societal factors (such as foreseeable productivity growth within the worker's industry).

Of course, even in an inflation-free economy the award of damages to replace the lost stream of income cannot be computed simply by totaling up the sum of the periodic payments. For the damages award is paid in a lump sum at the conclusion of the litigation, and when it—or even a part of it—is invested, it will earn additional money. . . .

The discount rate should be based on the rate of interest that would be earned on "the best and safest investments." Once it is assumed that the injured worker would definitely have worked for a specific term of years, he is entitled to a risk-free stream of future income to replace his lost wages; therefore, the discount rate should not reflect the market's premium for investors who are willing to accept some risk of default. Moreover, since under Norfolk & Western R. Co. *v.* Liepelt, 444 U.S. 490 (1980), the lost stream of income should be estimated in after-tax terms, the discount rate should also represent the after-tax rate of return to the injured worker.[21]

Thus, although the notion of a damage award representing the present value of a lost stream of earnings in an inflation-free economy rests on some fairly sophisticated economic concepts, the two elements that determine its calculation can be stated fairly easily. They are: (1) the amount that the employee would have earned during each year that he could have been expected to work after the injury; and (2) the appropriate discount rate, reflecting the safest available investment. The trier of fact should apply the discount rate to each of the estimated installments in the lost stream of income, and then add up the discounted installments to determine the total award.[22]

Unfortunately for triers of fact, ours is not an inflation-free economy. Inflation has been a permanent fixture in our economy for many decades, and there can be no doubt that it ideally should affect both stages of the calculation described in the previous section. . . .

The first stage of the calculation required an estimate of the shape of the lost stream of future income. For many workers, including respondent, a contractual "cost-of-living adjustment" automatically increases wages each year by the percentage change during the previous year in the consumer price index calculated by the Bureau of Labor Statistics. Such a contract provides a basis for taking into account an additional societal factor—price inflation—in estimating the worker's lost future earnings.

The second stage of the calculation requires the selection of an appropriate discount rate. Price inflation—or more precisely, anticipated price inflation—certainly affects market rates of return. If a lender knows that his loan is to be repaid a year later with dollars that are less valuable than those he has advanced, he will charge an interest rate that is high enough both to compensate him for the temporary use of the loan proceeds and also to make up for their shrinkage in value.[23]

---

[21] The arithmetic necessary for discounting can be simplified through the use of a so-called "present value table," such as those found in R. Wixon, ACCOUNTANTS' HANDBOOK, at 29.58–29.59 (1956 ed.), or S. Speiser, RECOVERY FOR WRONGFUL DEATH 2d § 8:4, at 713–718 (1975). These tables are based on the proposition that if *i* is the discount rate, then "the present value of $1 due in *n* periods must be $1/(1 + i)^n$." Wixon, *supra*, at 29.57. In this context, the relevant "periods" are years; accordingly, if "*i*" is a market interest rate, it should be the effective *annual* yield.

[22] At one time it was thought appropriate to distinguish between compensating a plaintiff "for the loss of time from his work which has actually occurred up to the time of trial" and compensating him "for the time which he will lose in the future." C. McCormick, DAMAGES § 86 (1935). This suggested that estimated future earning capacity should be discounted to the date of trial, and a separate calculation should be performed for the estimated loss of earnings between injury and trial. It is both easier and more precise to discount the entire lost stream of earnings back to the date of injury—the moment from which earning capacity was impaired. The plaintiff may then be awarded interest on that discounted sum for the period between injury and judgment, in order to ensure that the award when invested will still be able to replicate the lost stream.

[23] The effect of price inflation on the discount rate may be less speculative than its effect on the lost stream of future income. The latter effect always requires a prediction of the future,

At one time many courts incorporated inflation into only one stage of the calculation of the award for lost earnings. In estimating the lost stream of future earnings, they accepted evidence of both individual and societal factors that would tend to lead to wage increases even in an inflation-free economy, but required the plaintiff to prove that those factors were not influenced by predictions of future price inflation. No increase was allowed for price inflation, on the theory that such predictions were unreliably speculative. In discounting the estimated lost stream of future income to present value, however, they applied the market interest rate.

The effect of these holdings was to deny the plaintiff the benefit of the impact of inflation on his future earnings, while giving the defendant the benefit of inflation's impact on the interest rate that is used to discount those earnings to present value. Although the plaintiff in such a situation could invest the proceeds of the litigation at an "inflated" rate of interest, the stream of income that he received provided him with only enough dollars to maintain his existing *nominal* income; it did not provide him with a stream comparable to what his lost wages would have been in an inflationary economy. This inequity was assumed to have been minimal because of the relatively low rates of inflation.

In recent years, of course, inflation rates have not remained low. There is now a consensus among courts that the prior inequity can no longer be tolerated. There is no consensus at all, however, regarding what form an appropriate response should take.

Our sister common law nations generally continue to adhere to the position that inflation is too speculative to be considered in estimating the lost stream of future earnings; they have sought to counteract the danger of systematically undercompensating plaintiffs by applying a discount rate that is below the current market rate. . . . [I]n Australia, the High Court has adopted a 2% rate, on the theory that it represents a good approximation of the long-term "real interest rate."

In this country, some courts have taken the same "real interest rate" approach as Australia. They have endorsed the economic theory

---

for the existence of a contractual cost-of-living adjustment gives no guidance about how big that adjustment will be in some future year. However, whether the discount rate also turns on predictions of the future depends on how it is assumed that the worker will invest his award.

On the one hand, it might be assumed that at the time of the award the worker will invest in a mixture of safe short-term, medium-term, and long-term bonds, with one scheduled to mature each year of his expected worklife. In that event, by purchasing bonds immediately after judgment, the worker can be ensured whatever future stream of nominal income is predicted. Since all relevant effects of inflation on the market interest rate will have occurred at that time, future changes in the rate of price inflation will have no effect on the stream of income he receives. . . . On the other hand, it might be assumed that the worker will invest exclusively in safe short-term notes, reinvesting them at the new market rate whenever they mature. Future market rates would be quite important to such a worker. Predictions of what they will be would therefore also be relevant to the choice of an appropriate discount rate, in much the same way that they are always relevant to the first stage of the calculation. . . . We perceive no intrinsic reason to prefer one assumption over the other, but most "offset" analyses seem to adopt the latter.

suggesting that market interest rates include two components—an estimate of anticipated inflation, and a desired "real" rate of return on investment—and that the latter component is essentially constant over time.[25] They have concluded that the inflationary increase in the estimated lost stream of future earnings will therefore be perfectly "offset" by all but the "real" component of the market interest rate.[26]

Still other courts have preferred to continue relying on market interest rates. To avoid undercompensation, they have shown at least tentative willingness to permit evidence of what future price inflation will be in estimating the lost stream of future income. . . .

Finally, some courts have applied a number of techniques that have loosely been termed "total offset" methods. What these methods have in common is that they presume that the ideal discount rate—the after-tax market interest rate on a safe investment—is (to a legally tolerable degree of precision) completely offset by certain elements in the ideal computation of the estimated lost stream of future income. They all assume that the effects of future price inflation on wages are part of what offsets the market interest rate. The methods differ, however, in their assumptions regarding which if any other elements in the first stage of the damages calculation contribute to the offset. . . .

The litigants and the *amici* in this case urge us to select one of the many rules that have been proposed and establish it for all time as the exclusive method in all federal trials for calculating an award for lost earnings in an inflationary economy. We are not persuaded, however, that such an approach is warranted. For our review of the foregoing cases leads us to draw three conclusions. First, by its very nature the calculation of an award for lost earnings must be a rough approximation. Because the lost stream can never be predicted with complete confidence, any lump sum represents only a "rough and ready" effort to put the

---

[25] In his dissenting opinion in Pennant Hills Restaurant Pty. Ltd. *v.* Barrell Insurances Pty. Ltd., 55 A.L.J.R. 258, 266–267 (1981), Justice Stephen explained the real interest rate approach to discounting future earnings, in part, as follows:

> "It rests upon the assumption that interest rates have two principal components: the market's own estimation of likely rates of inflation during the term of a particular fixed interest investment, and a 'real interest' component, being the rate of return which, in the absence of all inflation, a lender will demand and a borrower will be prepared to pay for the use of borrowed funds. It also relies upon the alleged economic fact that this 'real interest' rate, of about two per cent, will always be much the same and that fluctuations in nominal rates of interest are due to the other main component of interest rates, the inflationary expectation."

[26] What is meant by the "real interest rate" depends on how one expects the plaintiff to invest the award. If one assumes that the injured worker will immediately invest in bonds having a variety of maturity dates, in order to ensure a particular stream of future payments, then the relevant "real interest rate" must be the difference between (1) an average of short-term, medium-term, and long-term market interest rates in a given year and (2) the average rate of price inflation in *subsequent* years (*i.e.*, during the terms of the investments). . . .

It appears more common for "real interest rate" approaches to rest on the assumption that the worker will invest in low-risk short-term securities and will reinvest frequently. Under that assumption, the relevant real interest rate is the difference between the short-term market interest rate in a given year and the average rate of price inflation during that same year. Several studies appear to have been done to measure this difference. . . .

plaintiff in the position he would have been in had he not been injured. Second, sustained price inflation can make the award substantially less precise. Inflation's current magnitude and unpredictability create a substantial risk that the damage award will prove to have little relation to the lost wages it purports to replace. Third, the question of lost earnings can arise in many different contexts. In some sectors of the economy, it is far easier to assemble evidence of an individual's most likely career path than in others. . . .

In calculating an award for a longshoreman's lost earnings caused by the negligence of a vessel, the discount rate should be chosen on the basis of the factors that are used to estimate the lost stream of future earnings. If the trier of fact relies on a specific forecast of the future rate of price inflation, and if the estimated lost stream of future earnings is calculated to include price inflation along with individual factors and other societal factors, then the proper discount rate would be the after-tax market interest rate. But since specific forecasts of future price inflation remain too unreliable to be useful in many cases, it will normally be a costly and ultimately unproductive waste of longshoremen's resources to make such forecasts the centerpiece of litigation under § 5(b). As Judge Newman has warned, "The average accident trial should not be converted into a graduate seminar on economic forecasting." For that reason, both plaintiffs and trial courts should be discouraged from pursuing that approach.

On the other hand, if forecasts of future price inflation are not used, it is necessary to choose an appropriate below-market discount rate. As long as inflation continues, one must ask how much should be "offset" against the market rate. Once again, that amount should be chosen on the basis of the same factors that are used to estimate the lost stream of future earnings. If full account is taken of the individual and societal factors (excepting price inflation) that can be expected to have resulted in wage increases, then all that should be set off against the market interest rate is an estimate of future price inflation. This would result in one of the "real interest rate" approaches described above. Although we find the economic evidence distinctly inconclusive regarding an essential premise of those approaches,[30] we do not believe a trial court adopting such an approach in a suit under § 5(b) should be reversed if it adopts a rate between one and three percent and explains its choice.

There may be a sound economic argument for even further setoffs. In 1976, Professor Carlson of the Purdue University Economics Department wrote an article in the American Bar Association Journal contending that in the long run the societal factors excepting price inflation—largely productivity gains—match (or even slightly exceed) the "real interest rate." Carlson, Economic Analysis v. Courtroom Controversy, 62 ABA J. 628 (1976). He thus recommended that the

[30] The key premise is that the real interest rate is stable over time. It is obviously not perfectly stable, but whether it is even relatively stable is hotly disputed among economists. . . .

estimated lost stream of future wages be calculated without considering either price inflation or societal productivity gains. All that would be considered would be individual seniority and promotion gains. If this were done, he concluded that the entire market interest rate, including both inflation and the real interest rate, would be more than adequately offset.

Although such an approach has the virtue of simplicity and may even be economically precise, we cannot at this time agree with the Court of Appeals for the Third Circuit that its use is mandatory in the federal courts. Naturally, Congress could require it if it chose to do so. And nothing prevents parties interested in keeping litigation costs under control from stipulating to its use before trial. But we are not prepared to impose it on unwilling litigants . . . .

On remand, the decision on whether to reopen the record should be left to the sound discretion of the trial court. . . .

3. PREJUDGMENT INTEREST

Woodline Motor Freight, Inc. v. Troutman Oil Co.

Supreme Court of Arkansas, 1997.
327 Ark. 448.

■ ARNOLD, CHIEF JUSTICE. . . . On March 11, 1992, Lattermore Belcher was driving his automobile near the intersection of Seventh and Cypress Streets in North Little Rock when he collided with a tractor-trailer driven by William Moore, an employee of appellant Woodline Motor Freight, Inc. Due to the impact of the collision, Moore lost control of his rig and crashed into a convenience store and gas station owned by Troutman Oil and leased by Crosland. The building and its contents were destroyed. Troutman and Crosland sued Belcher and Woodline for negligence. Troutman claimed $202,000.00 in property damage and $175,500.00 in lost profits, while Crosland claimed $31,426.05 in property damage and $150,000.00 in lost profits. . . . The jury returned a special verdict awarding Troutman $100,000.00 for property damage and $15,000.00 for lost profits, and Crosland $31,426.05 for property damage and $24,000.00 for lost profits.

Following a hearing on the issue of prejudgment interest, the trial court entered judgment February 20, 1996, awarding prejudgment interest on the property damage at the rate of six percent per annum. As a result, Troutman was awarded an additional $23,000.00, and Crosland an additional $7,232.30. . . .

[L]ike other courts, we have struggled with this subject over the years. In our very early cases, we followed the rule that, if the damaged or destroyed property had a market value, or other definite standards of determining the value, at the time of loss, damage or destruction, prejudgment interest was allowable.

In 1961, we announced the rule that prejudgment interest was not allowable in tort actions. . . . However, in 1979, we returned to the former rule, allowing prejudgment interest for damage to "knee-high" soybeans totally destroyed by heavy rains within a 48-hour period. . . .

After thorough consideration of our caselaw in this area, we . . . embrace the general rule that prejudgment interest is not recoverable on claims that are neither liquidated as a dollar sum nor ascertainable by fixed standards. Prejudgment interest is allowable where the amount of damages is definitely ascertainable by mathematical computation, or if the evidence furnishes data that make it possible to compute the amount without reliance on opinion or discretion.

Applying this test, the remaining question is whether prejudgment interest was properly allowed under the circumstances presented in this case. In answering this question, a review of the testimony at trial is instructive. Gerald Hodges, Sr. of Radford Equipment Company in Little Rock prepared a bid proposal for appellee Troutman to replace the service station and convenience store. The bid, totaling $203,128.00, included separate estimates to replace the building, the canopy over the gasoline pumps, the building mansard or fascia, the fuel equipment, and fuel work. It was Hodges's opinion that it would not have been cost effective to repair the old building, which measured 2,500 square feet. His bid was to replace the building with a very similar building, which would measure 2,400 square feet. During cross-examination, Hodges admitted that competitive bids could vary.

Jim Davenport, Chief Building Inspector for the city of North Little Rock, inspected the damage to the service station and convenience store. On direct examination, Davenport testified that he told Troutman that the building could not be repaired and that it would have to be torn down. However, on cross examination, he stated that he never told Troutman that he had to tear down the car wash. According to Davenport, he left it up to Troutman whether to repair the car wash and fuel island canopy. However, Troutman testified that it was his understanding that the entire building would have to be torn down.

Woodline presented the testimony of Denver Fletcher of Crockett Adjustments, who retained the services of an engineer to determine what part of the building structure could be reutilized. Fletcher then met with a builder who prepared an estimate of the cost of the repairs, which amounted to $62,939.87.

In light of this testimony, it was impossible to compute the amount of Troutman's damages without reliance on opinion or discretion. There was conflicting testimony as to whether the building needed to be completely torn down, or whether part of the structure could have been repaired. Accordingly, the estimates to repair or replace Troutman's building varied substantially, indicating that, at the time of the loss, the amount due Troutman was neither liquidated as a dollar sum nor ascertainable by fixed standards. . . .

Turning to Crosland's damages, Crosland testified that he and another employee made an inventory list of the items destroyed, among which included equipment, furniture, cigarettes, beer and other merchandise. According to Crosland, he "placed a true market value, *to the best of his knowledge,* on every item listed." He testified that he consulted the State Health Department to determine whether the intact beer inside the beer cooler had to be destroyed. Crosland personally assigned a figure representing the cost to each item. In light of Crosland's reliance on subjective opinion as to value, we cannot agree that, at the time of the loss, the amount due him was liquidated as a dollar sum or ascertainable by fixed standards.

Based upon the foregoing, we hold that the trial court erred in awarding prejudgment interest on the property damages awarded to Troutman and Crosland. Accordingly, the judgment of the trial court is reversed and remanded.

NOTES

1. Is there any cogent reason for the rule the court applied?

2. In General Motors Corp. *v.* Devex Corp., 461 U.S. 648 (1983), the U.S. Supreme Court held that prejudgment interest "should ordinarily be awarded" in patent infringement cases. Amendments to the patent laws provided for "damages adequate to compensate for the infringement, but in no event less than a reasonable royalty." 35 U.S.C. § 284. The Court concluded that full compensation was the primary purpose of the statute as amended, and that the traditional rule limiting prejudgment interest to liquidated amounts of damages was inconsistent with that purpose.

> "In the typical case an award of prejudgment interest is necessary to ensure that the patent owner is placed in as good a position as he would have been in had the infringer entered into a reasonable royalty agreement.[10] An award of interest from the time that the royalty payments would have been received merely serves to make the patent owner whole, since his damages consist not only of the value of the royalty payments but also of the foregone use of the money between the time of infringement and the date of the judgment."

Id. at 655–56.

3. Courts may be more favorable to prejudgment interest in particular contexts, such as breach of fiduciary duty or violation of a special duty of care. See, *e.g.*, Bullis *v.* Security Pacific National Bank, 21 Cal.3d 801 (1978)

[10] The traditional view, which treated prejudgment interest as a penalty awarded on the basis of the defendant's conduct, has long been criticized on the ground that prejudgment interest represents "delay damages" and should be awarded as a component of full compensation. A rule denying prejudgment interest not only undercompensates the patent owner but may also grant a windfall to the infringer and create an incentive to prolong litigation. There is no reason why an infringer should stand in a better position than a party who agrees to pay a royalty and then fails to pay because of financial difficulties.

(bank negligence). See also Tripp *v.* Swoap, 17 Cal.3d 671 (1976) (erroneous denial of welfare benefits).

4. In the following case, the Seventh Circuit expressed a strongly favorable view of prejudgment interest.

Matter of Oil Spill by Amoco Cadiz Off Coast of France on March 16, 1978

United States Court of Appeals, Seventh Circuit, 1992.
954 F.2d 1279.

■ PER CURIAM. On the morning of March 16, 1978, the supertanker AMOCO CADIZ broke apart in a severe storm, spewing most of its load of 220,000 tons of Iranian crude into the seas off Brittany. The wreck resulted in one of the largest oil spills in history, damaging approximately 180 miles of coastline in one of the most important tourist and fishing regions in France. The clean up took more than six months and involved equipment and resources from all over the country. The disaster has had lasting effects on the environment, the economy, and the people of Brittany . . . .

[The supertanker was commissioned by Amoco International Oil Co. and constructed by Astilleros Espanoles, a Spanish shipbuilding company. The immediate cause of the accident that destroyed it was a failed steering system. In the wake of the accident, the Republic of France, and numerous French municipalities, businesses, and individuals, sued Amoco and Astilleros for damage caused by the spill. Petroleum Insurance Limited (PIL) also sued, claiming reimbursement for the value of the spilled oil cargo.

[In 1990, following four years of consolidated trials on liability and damages, the district court awarded principle amounts of approximately $61 million to the French parties and $20 million to PIL. It also awarded prejudgment interest at a rate of 7.22%. As a guide to the rate of prejudgment interest, the district court referred to a federal statute providing that post-judgment interest should be calculated according to the auction price of 52-week U.S. Treasury bills immediately prior to the date of judgment. One of the many issues raised on appeal was the award of prejudgment interest.]

We start with a discussion of principles. . . .

Money today is not a full substitute for the same sum that should have been paid years ago. Prejudgment interest therefore is an ordinary part of any award under federal law.

By committing a tort, the wrongdoer creates an involuntary creditor. It may take time for the victim to obtain an enforceable judgment, but once there is a judgment the obligation is dated as of the time of the injury. In voluntary credit transactions, the borrower must pay the market rate for money. (The market rate is the minimum appropriate rate for prejudgment interest, because the involuntary creditor might have charged more to make a loan.) Prejudgment interest at the market rate puts *both* parties in the position they would have occupied had compensation been paid promptly.

To see this, consider what would have happened if the French parties had borrowed $60 million to finance the cleanup in April 1978, and Amoco had put that sum in trust to fund an award of damages (just as Amoco actually put 77 million francs in trust in France). The victims would have had to pay the market rate of interest, which at times during this case has exceeded 20% per annum. If they arranged to repay the debt in a single balloon payment at the end (when they recouped from Amoco), and if the rate of interest averaged 12%, then by April 1991 the victims would owe their creditors $262 million. Meanwhile the trust fund, lending out its assets at the market rate of 12%, would have grown to $262 million. Scores would be fully settled if Amoco tendered its interest in the fund: it would thus "pay" $60 million as of 1978, and the victims would receive $60 million as of 1978; the lenders who financed the cleanup would receive full payment for the use of their money. . . .

Victims who finance their own cleanup lend to themselves; forced to devote money to a project not of their own choosing (money they otherwise could have lent out at the market rate of interest), they are entitled to compensation for the "hire" of this capital. Tortfeasors who choose to reinvest their money in their business (as Amoco has done) rather than create a trust fund must believe that the returns in their enterprise exceed the market rate. Having earned this higher rate of return for the duration of the litigation, they are in no position to complain when called on to pay prejudgment interest. An injurer allowed to keep the return on this money has profited by the wrong. So we reiterate . . . that compound prejudgment interest is the norm in federal litigation.

Interest at what rate? Surely the market rate. That is what the victim must pay—either explicitly if it borrows money or implicitly if it finances things out of cash on hand—and the rate the wrongdoer has available to it. To return to the trust fund example, if the market rate were 12% it would be unthinkable to set a prejudgment rate of interest at 7.5%, order Amoco to turn over $154 million to the victims (the value of $60 million invested at 7.5% compound interest for 13 years), and authorize Amoco to retain the other $108 million. The victims would owe their creditors $108 million, and the tortfeasor would be the wealthier. Yet that would be the upshot of computing prejudgment interest at less than the market rate—an effect that does not depend on the existence of an express trust but is as powerful if the victims and the tortfeasor both use internal financing. All of this is just the flip side of discounting to present value in a tort case for future loss. As *prepaid* damages must be reduced at a market rate that takes account of inflation, so *postpaid* damages must be increased.

What, then, is the market rate? Some of the district judge's discussion, coupled with his use of the rate on Treasury securities as of the date of his opinion, implies that the court thought that the market rate is the rate for *safe* securities at the *end* of the case. Yet . . . , an involuntary tort creditor is not safe. The defendant may go out of business (or encounter less serious reverses), or hide assets, during the litigation. Any market interest rate reflects three things: the social return on investment (that is, the amount necessary to bid money away from other productive uses), the expected change in the value of money during the term of the loan (*i.e.*, anticipated inflation), and the risk of nonpayment. The best estimate of these three variables is the amount *the defendant* must pay for money, which reflects variables specific to that entity. Amoco has publicly traded notes and debentures; a court could draw an interest rate directly from them. . . . [U]nless it engages in such refined rate-setting, a court should use the "prime rate"—that is, the rate banks charge for short-term unsecured loans to creditworthy customers. This rate may miss the mark for any particular party, but it is a market-based estimate. . . .

[I]t should be plain that the market rate in question is the one *during* the litigation—when the defendant had the use of money that the court has decided belongs to the plaintiff—not the going rate at the end of the case. It is 13 1/2 years since the AMOCO CADIZ ran aground. Market rates have been above 20% and below 10% for different portions of the period. As it would be inappropriate to award prejudgment interest at a 20% rate if that happened to prevail in the last week of a case (and the rate had been 5% for the preceding decade), so it is inappropriate to use a low rate such as 7% for which money may be rented at the conclusion, when higher rates persisted during the bulk of the case. . . . The market rate includes a prediction of inflation—which is why it is necessary to use the rates in force during the case and not whatever rate prevails at the end. . . .

According to Amoco, three equitable considerations support a denial of all interest [to the French plaintiffs.] First, this has been a lengthy case, so that interest has mounted dramatically. Much of that delay is attributable to the French plaintiffs, Amoco submits. Second, the French plaintiffs (especially the Côtes du Nord parties) submitted inflated, even fraudulent, claims. Third, French courts do not award compound prejudgment interest. . . .

Many cases say that district courts have discretion to adjust the rate of interest or deny interest altogether. . . . What reasons would justify an exercise of discretion against the prevailing plaintiff? We remarked in [a prior opinion] that "[s]ubstantial, unexplained delay in filing suit might be such a reason, because delay shifts the investment risk to the defendant, allowing the plaintiff to recover interest without bearing the corresponding risk.". . . A court also may deny interest when it is too difficult to determine which parts of an award are eligible. Beyond these hints, courts have done little to sketch the limits of acceptable discretion. Limits there must be—for what is the point of computing the principal amount of damages in intricate detail if the judge may turn around and increase (or reduce) the value of that award by a factor of three on the basis of vague equitable concerns? . . .

None of the three considerations Amoco offers could support a denial of interest even had the district court been inclined to exercise its discretion in Amoco's favor. Start with the passage of time: this is a reason to award interest, not to deny it. Amoco does not contend that the plaintiffs delayed in filing suit, and although 13 years is a regrettably long time to reach final decision, it is not uncommon for a case of this magnitude. As for exaggerated and fraudulent claims: these may be a basis of sanctions under Fed. R. Civ. P. 11 and 37, but sanctions must be proportioned to the wrong. No one would suppose that the appropriate sanction for filing even a bushel basket full of bogus claims is a $100 million fine. Yet that is Amoco's position. Return to the trust fund example: Amoco ponies up $60 million in April 1978, and by April 1991 the fund contains $262 million. The district court must apportion this fund between the parties. Could a court even *think* of saying: "Complete redress of the plaintiffs' injuries calls for an award of the entire $262 million, but because many of the claims during the course of the litigation were inflated, I shall award the plaintiffs $149 million and return the other $113 million to the defendant."? Not a chance. This is, however, the consequence of interest at the rate of 7.22% rather than 12%—and Amoco's preferred position (no interest) implies a penalty of $202 million for exaggeration. . . .

The right way to deal with exaggerated claims is to cut down on those claims, not to deny interest on proven entitlements. . . . The right way to deal with French law on prejudgment interest is to decide whether it governs. If it does, apply it; if it does not, then apply American law (as the district judge did) rather than attempt some compromise between the bodies of law. . . .

We hold that the French plaintiffs are entitled to prejudgment interest at the market rates that prevailed during the 1980s. . . . Because Amoco has not challenged the proposed rate of 11.9%, we adopt it. . . .

Amoco has little reason to shed crocodile tears. Exxon reportedly spent $2 billion to clean up the oil the EXXON VALDEZ spilled off Alaska; it has agreed to pay another $1 billion as damages and to pay a criminal fine of $125 million. Amoco will be called on to pay only $61 million plus interest to redress a spill that not only was larger but also occurred in a more densely populated area. Calling the $61 million the result of inflated or fraudulent claims taxes credulity.

The district court awarded PIL the same 7.22% rate of interest as it had the French plaintiffs but without compounding. . . .

For reasons we have already given, 7.22% is not the market rate and is not justifiable on any other ground. Even the "equitable" arguments Amoco asserts against the French plaintiffs are unavailable against PIL. We therefore hold that PIL is entitled to prejudgment interest at the prime rate. PIL contends that the average rate between the catastrophe and judgment is 12.31% per annum. (This exceeds the rate the French plaintiffs have calculated, because it includes the high-interest period between March 1978 and the end of 1979, which was excluded from the French plaintiffs' claim.) Again, Amoco does not contest this calculation. . . .

The parties agree that courts of the United Kingdom award simple rather than compound prejudgment interest. . . .

Parties may provide for compound interest by contract; by incorporating the law of the United Kingdom without a separate provision on this question, the parties assented to simple interest. . . .

To sum up: all decisions on jurisdiction and liability are affirmed. The computation of damages is affirmed with the following exceptions: . . .

> 4. The French plaintiffs are entitled to compound prejudgment interest at a rate of 11.9% per annum from January 1, 1980, implying a multiplier of 3.3162.
>
> 5. PIL is entitled to simple prejudgment interest at the rate of 12.31% per annum from March 16, 1978. . . .

4. FOREIGN CURRENCY CONVERSION

Competex, S.A. v. LaBow

United States Court of Appeals, Second Circuit, 1986.
783 F.2d 333.

■ JON O. NEWMAN, CIRCUIT JUDGE. This appeal presents issues concerning currency conversion in the context of enforcing a foreign judgment. Specifically, the question is whether a judgment debtor may satisfy an American judgment that was based on an English judgment by paying the amount of the English judgment in pounds. . . .

LaBow, a New Yorker, lost a substantial sum of money through speculation in copper on the London Metal Exchange. His broker, Competex, a Swiss corporation, satisfied these debts. Competex sued LaBow for breach of contract in the English High Court of Justice, Queen's Bench Division, and obtained a default judgment for £187,929.82, which included principal, interest, and costs.

Competex then brought this diversity action to enforce the English judgment. Following a bench trial, Judge Werker held that the English judgment was entitled to recognition and enforcement. Because determination of the date on which to convert a foreign currency debt into dollars is a substantive question, Judge Werker was compelled to apply New York law. New York uses the breach-day conversion rule.

In applying the breach-day rule, Judge Werker reasoned that Competex's American claim was based on the English judgment rather than on the underlying contract. Competex's American claim had therefore accrued upon the date of entry of the English judgment, and Judge Werker applied the conversion rate prevailing on that date: £1 = $2.20. He entered judgment for $583,201.78, which included interest and a fee award pursuant to Fed. R. Civ. P. 56(g). . . .

The pound depreciated substantially relative to the dollar between the dates of the English and American judgments. On the date of the American judgment, the conversion rate was: £1 = $1.50. The pound continued to depreciate. As a result, LaBow moved, pursuant to Fed. R. Civ. P. 60(b), for a clarification of the American judgment and a declaration that he could satisfy the American judgment by paying the underlying English judgment in pounds. While this motion was pending, LaBow borrowed the necessary funds and paid the English judgment, with interest, in pounds. Judge Sprizzo denied LaBow's Rule 60(b) motion and held that the American judgment could be satisfied only by paying the dollar amount specified in that judgment. He credited LaBow's payment against the American judgment at the conversion rate prevailing on the date of payment: £1 = $1.20. This calculation left a balance owing on the American judgment of approximately $236,000. LaBow appeals the denial of his Rule 60(b) motion.

Because of the procedural posture of this case, we are faced with a narrow issue: whether Judge Sprizzo's denial of LaBow's Rule 60(b) motion was proper. Rule 60(b) is not a substitute for appeal. LaBow may not relitigate the bases for the enforcing judgment entered by Judge Werker. Specifically, LaBow may not challenge Judge Werker's application of the breach-day conversion rule. However, review of the Rule 60(b) denial requires some exploration of the currency conversion problem because determination of a state's rule for deeming enforcing judgments satisfied turns on the rationale for the state's currency conversion rule.

For illustrative purposes, the following example will be helpful. Defendant defaults on a contractual obligation to pay plaintiff £1. Plaintiff brings suit in an English court and receives judgment for that amount, at which time the prevailing conversion rate is: £1 = $1. For simplicity and to keep the discussion focused on the pertinent points, we assume that the value of the dollar remains constant (*i.e.*, constant against gold and all currencies except the pound) but that fluctuation in the value of the pound causes a change in the exchange rate for the dollar. Initially, we consider what would happen if the pound depreciates relative to the dollar, so that £1 = $.60. Plaintiff then brings an action on the English judgment in an American state court. We will further assume that defendant has sufficient property in both jurisdictions to satisfy any judgments against it.

If the English judgment is entitled to enforcement, a state court applying New York's breach-day rule would enter judgment for $1, in accordance with the conversion rate prevailing on the date the English judgment debt became due. The asserted purpose of this rule is to assure that plaintiff will be made whole by protecting him against fluctuation in relative currency values. Thus, had defendant paid plaintiff £1 on the date of the English judgment and had plaintiff converted this amount into dollars on that date, plaintiff would be in possession of $1 on the date of the American judgment. On the surface, the breach-day rule appears to do no more than regard as done that which ought to have been done.

However, the breach-day rule does more than make plaintiff whole. It generously allows him to reap the benefit of appreciation in the value of the pound without risking loss as a result of the pound's depreciation. In our example, plaintiff was insulated from any loss as a result of the pound's depreciation. His right to receive $1 was completely unaffected by the pound's depreciation. However, had the pound appreciated relative to the dollar, so that £1 = $1.30, plaintiff would simply have executed on the English judgment. He would receive £1, the equivalent of $1.30. Since the original obligation was worth only $1, plaintiff would make $.30 as a result of the pound's appreciation.

Of course, this game of creditor's choice is possible only if the judgment debtor has property in both jurisdictions sufficient to satisfy either judgment. The proposed *Restatement of Foreign Relations Law* suggests a more extreme rule of creditor's preference that can enable the creditor to benefit from currency fluctuations even if the debtor does not have property in both jurisdictions. See *Restatement of Foreign Relations Law of the United States* § 823 comment c (Tent. Draft No. 6, 1985). According to the Restatement, if the foreign currency has depreciated since the foreign obligation accrued, an American court should follow the breach-day rule and apply the conversion rate prevailing at the time of accrual. In our example, if the value of £1 goes from $1 to $.60, the American court enters judgment for $1, and plaintiff loses nothing as a result of the pound's depreciation. However, if the foreign currency appreciates, an American court, according to the Restatement, should follow the judgment-day rule and apply the conversion rate prevailing on the date of the American judgment. In our example, if the value of £1 goes from $1 to $1.30, the American court enters judgment for $1.30, and plaintiff makes $.30. Thus, under the Restatement's approach, the judgment debtor need not have property in England for the judgment creditor to be allowed to engage in currency speculation without risk.

It might be argued that the judgment debtor can avoid these unfavorable consequences by immediately satisfying the first judgment. Indeed, it could be argued that these consequences are fitting punishment for failure to pay debts justly due. However, these arguments assume that the original judgment is valid and enforceable. It might be that the original judgment is arguably not entitled to foreign recognition. There is no justification for forcing defendant to choose between waiving all defenses to the enforcement action by satisfying the original judgment and assuming the risk of currency fluctuation.[8] Moreover, post-judgment interest, which compensates the judgment creditor for the time value of money, is ordinarily the only "punishment" for delay in paying judgment debts.

The gamesmanship of the breach-day rule can be avoided by selecting a conversion rule of general application that is neutral between the parties with respect to currency fluctuation. There are three methods by which neutrality can be achieved, depending on whether the original or the enforcing judgment is viewed as primary. If the original judgment is viewed as primary, which seems theoretically superior, neutrality can be achieved, first, by entering the enforcing judgment in the currency of the original jurisdiction (foreign-currency-judgment rule) or, second, by entering the enforcing judgment for an amount of dollars to be determined by converting the original judgment into dollars as of the date of payment (payment-day rule). If the enforcing judgment is viewed as primary, the third method for achieving neutrality is by converting the original judgment into dollars as of the date of the enforcing judgment (judgment-day rule).

Entry of judgment in a foreign currency is allowed in England, France, and Germany. Despite the obvious appeal of this approach, which preserves the original judgment inviolate and places on both parties the risk of fluctuation in the value of the currency of the original judgment, it has received little support in the United States for a procedural reason. Most American courts have assumed that American judgments must be entered in dollars. This assumption has rested on either common law notions of sovereignty or, at least in part, on the now repealed section 20 of the Coinage Act of 1792. This assumption probably deserves reexamination in light of the repeal of section 20.[9]

The payment-day rule is economically equivalent to the foreign-currency-judgment rule. . . . [I]n the United States, there has been some concern that a judgment must be entered in dollars for a sum certain. Although the Federal Rules contain no explicit obstacle to the entry of a judgment for an amount of dollars to be determined in the future (by reference to ascertainable figures), the payment-day rule has found little favor in this country.

---

8 This point would seem even stronger in the breach-of-contract context than in the judgment-on-a-judgment context. There is no reason to require a defendant to pay a plaintiff merely because the plaintiff has a colorable contract claim.

9 Section 20, now repealed, was formerly codified at 31 U.S.C. § 371, and stated:

> "The money of account of the United States shall be expressed in dollars or units, dimes or tenths, cents or hundredths, . . . and all accounts in the public offices and all proceedings in the courts shall be kept and had in conformity to this regulation."

American courts wishing to avoid the procedural objections to the foreign-currency-judgment or payment-day rules while choosing a neutral conversion rule may apply the judgment-day rule. The neutrality of the judgment-day rule may be illustrated by a return to our example. If plaintiff holds an English judgment for £1 and the value of £1 depreciates from $1 to $.60 as of the date of the American judgment, the American court enters judgment for $.60, and plaintiff loses $.40. But that is merely the consequence of holding an obligation in pounds. Had plaintiff executed on his English judgment, he would have lost the equivalent of $.40 as a result of the pound's depreciation. Conversely, if the value of £1 appreciates from $1 to $1.30, the American court enters judgment for $1.30, and plaintiff makes $.30, the equivalent of what he would have made had he executed on the English judgment. Thus, the judgment-day rule allows the plaintiff to speculate in pounds for as long as he wishes, but he now engages in true speculation. His gains and losses are registered with equal force in England and in the United States, and any incentive for forum shopping disappears. After entry of the American judgment, the judgment creditor is insulated from fluctuation in the value of the pound but takes the risk of fluctuation in the value of the dollar. But that is merely the consequence of holding a judgment in dollars.

If we were free to choose a conversion rule, we would select either the judgment-day or the payment-day rule. However, as noted, we are not free to do so because the conversion question is one of New York law and because we are reviewing only the denial of LaBow's Rule 60(b) motion. Our task is to predict what satisfaction of judgment rule New York would apply.

Bearing in mind the consequences previously discussed of the various possible conversion rules, we believe that New York's choice of the breach-day conversion rule clearly implies that New York would require satisfaction of a New York enforcing judgment by payment of the dollar amount specified in that judgment and would not consider an enforcing judgment satisfied by payment of the amount of the underlying judgment in foreign currency. The breach-day rule protects the judgment creditor against fluctuation in currency values to the point of allowing him to speculate without risk. It would be anomalous to suggest that New York would allow its creditor's preference rule to be undercut by giving the judgment debtor the opportunity to satisfy his New York judgment by paying the underlying judgment in depreciated pounds. Therefore, Judge Sprizzo was correct in holding that Competex's American judgment could be satisfied only in dollars. . . .

NOTE ON FOREIGN CURRENCY JUDGMENTS

In Matter of Oil Spill by Amoco Cadiz Off Coast of France on March 16, 1978, reprinted in part above, the Seventh Circuit approved a judgment entered in pounds. The court said:

"PIL opens with the argument that a court of the United States *must* enter judgment in dollars. What's wrong with sterling? PIL is an English corporation; sterling is its native currency. PIL expresses concern that Amoco will refuse to pay; how do you execute a pound-denominated judgment against assets in the United States? Or what would happen, PIL wonders, if Amoco timed its satisfaction of the judgment to take account of movements in the currency markets? Courts all over the world enter judgment in currencies other than their own. . . . Collection is simple once you recognize that dollars may be turned into any other currency, so that a judgment nominally in marks or yen may be satisfied in dollars. 'A judgment denominated in a foreign currency may be satisfied either in that currency or by payment of an equivalent amount in dollars measured by the rate of exchange in effect on the date of payment.' *Restatement (3d) of the Foreign Relations Law of the United States* § 823 comment b (1986). Delay in payment also creates no special problem. As soon as the court announces the award, the parties may eliminate exchange risk by using the currency futures markets. For example, if PIL wants to hedge against the risk that the pound will fall against the dollar, it can buy a dollar futures contract, promising to pay in sterling. When Amoco satisfies the judgment with sterling, PIL can close its futures position and receive the dollar value of the award. . . .

"Judgment in a foreign currency is especially attractive when the commercial activity took place in that currency. Parties that conduct their dealings in francs, rubles, pesos, yuan, bolivars, or australs either accept the risk of changes in the value of that currency or have made provisions to hedge against that risk. Computing an award in cruzeiros and then converting to dollars creates a risk that the parties did not accept—the risk that the judge will select an inapt date or use a currency no one had included in hedging plans. Fights over conversion dates are inevitable whenever judges enter dollar awards to redress injuries denominated in other currencies. Thus the English rule should be used in the United States too—not because the choice-of-law provision in this contract requires it, but because it is the right rule for commerce. The court should enter the judgment in the currency the parties themselves selected for their dealings, the currency in which the loss is felt. All problems about conversion dates vanish, and the parties' hedging strategies (or lack thereof) proceed unimpeded."

Matter of Oil Spill by Amoco Cadiz Off Coast of France on March 16, 1978, 954 F.2d 1279, 1327–28 (7th Cir. 1992).

PART III

EQUITY

CHAPTER 5

THE HISTORY OF EQUITY

A. INTRODUCING EQUITY

Equity is a complex word with multiple senses. Sometimes it refers to interpreting a law according to its spirit rather than its letter. Sometimes *equity* refers to a moral reading of the law's requirements, often accompanied by an intervention to prevent someone from exploiting the law's rigidity. For example, a court might prevent someone who has a legal right or power from using it to opportunistically take advantage of another person, as in cases telling landowners they cannot build spite fences. At other times *equity* is used as a rough synonym for *justice* or *fairness*. Another sense is the most important one for a course on remedies: *equity* is a technical term for the doctrines and remedies developed by courts of equity, especially by the English Court of Chancery.

In this chapter, the word is usually used in this last, technical sense. Nevertheless, it is good to remember the other senses the word can have. They have profoundly shaped the development of equity as a body of law. Even when *equity* is used as a technical term, its other senses may not be far behind.

1. A SKETCH OF EQUITY'S HISTORY

The Origin of Equity

Frederic William Maitland, EQUITY 1–11
(A. H. Chayton & W. J. Whittaker eds. 1910).[i]

. . . [S]uppose that we ask the question—What is Equity? We can only answer it by giving some short account of certain courts of justice which were abolished over thirty years ago. In the year 1875 we might have said "equity is that body of rules which is administered only by those Courts which are known as Courts of Equity." The definition of course would not have been very satisfactory, but now-a-days we are cut off even from this unsatisfactory definition. We have no longer any courts which are merely courts of equity. Thus we are driven to say that Equity now is that body of rules administered by our English courts of justice which, were it not for the operation of the Judicature Acts, would be administered only by those courts which would be known as Courts of Equity.

[i] On Maitland and his achievements—he is considered the greatest English legal historian—see the centennial tribute by T.F.T. Plucknett, 26 N.Y.U. L. Rev. 1 (1951).

This, you may well say, is but a poor thing to call a definition. Equity is a certain portion of our existing substantive law, and yet in order that we may describe this portion and mark it off from other portions we have to make reference to courts that are no longer in existence. Still I fear that nothing better than this is possible. The only alternative would be to make a list of the equitable rules and say that Equity consists of those rules. This, I say, would be the only alternative, for if we were to inquire what it is that all these rules have in common and what it is that marks them off from all other rules administered by our courts, we should by way of answer find nothing but this, that these rules were until lately administered, and administered only, by our courts of equity.

Therefore for the mere purpose of understanding the present state of our law, some history becomes necessary. . . .

In Edward I's day [r. 1272–1307], at the end of the thirteenth century, three great courts have come into existence, the King's Bench, the Common Bench or Court of Common Pleas and the Exchequer. Each of these has its own proper sphere, but as time goes on each of them attempts to extend its sphere and before the middle ages are over a plaintiff has often a choice between these three courts and each of them will deal with his case in the same way and by the same rules. The law which these courts administer is in part traditional law, in part statute law. Already in Edward I's day the phrase "common law" is current. It is a phrase that has been borrowed from the canonists—who used "*jus commune*" to denote the general law of the Catholic Church; it describes that part of the law that is unenacted, nonstatutory, that is common to the whole land and to all Englishmen. It is contrasted with statute, with local custom, with royal prerogative. It is not as yet contrasted with equity, for as yet there is no body of rules which bears this name.

One of the three courts, namely, the Exchequer, is more than a court of law. From our modern point of view it is not only a court of law but a "government office," an administrative or executive bureau; our modern Treasury is an offshoot from the old Exchequer. What we should call the "civil service" of the country is transacted by two great offices or "departments"; there is the Exchequer which is the fiscal department, there is the Chancery which is the secretarial department, while above these there rises the king's permanent Council. At the head of the Chancery stands the Chancellor, usually a bishop; he is we may say the king's secretary of state for all departments, he keeps the king's great seal and all the already great mass of writing that has to be done in the king's name has to be done under his supervision.

He is not as yet a judge, but already he by himself or his subordinates has a great deal of work to do which brings him into a close connection with the administration of justice. One of the duties of that great staff of clerks over which he presides is to draw up and issue those writs whereby actions are begun in the courts of law—such writs are sealed with the king's seal. A man who wishes to begin an action must go to the Chancery and obtain a writ. Many writs there are which have been formulated long ago; such writs are writs of course (*brevia de cursu*), one obtains them by asking for them of the clerks—called Cursitors—and paying the proper fees. But the Chancery has a certain limited power of inventing new writs to meet new cases as they arise. That power is consecrated by a famous clause of the Second Statute of Westminster authorizing writs *in consimili casu*. Thus the Chancellor may often have to consider whether the case is one in which some new and some specially worded writ should be framed. This however is not judicial business. The Chancellor does not hear both sides of the story, he only hears the plaintiff's application, and if he grants a writ the courts of law may afterwards quash that writ as being contrary to the law of the land.

But by another route the Chancellor is brought into still closer contact with the administration of justice. Though these great courts of law have been established there is still a reserve of justice in the king. Those who can not get relief elsewhere present their petitions to the king and his council praying for some remedy. Already by the end of the thirteenth century the number of such petitions presented in every year is very large, and the work of reading them and considering them is very laborious. In practice a great share of this labour falls on the Chancellor. He is the king's prime minister, he is a member of the council, and the specially learned member of the council. It is in dealing with these petitions that the Chancellor begins to develop his judicial powers.

In course of time his judicial powers are classified as being of two kinds. It begins to be said that the Court of Chancery, "Curia Cancellariae"—for the phrase is used in the fourteenth century—has two sides, a common law side and an equity side, or a Latin side and an English side. Let us look for a moment at the origin of these two kinds of powers, and first at that which concerns us least.

(1) Many of these petitions of which I have spoken seek for justice not merely from the king but against the king. If anybody is to be called the wrongdoer, it is the king himself. For example, he is in possession of land which has been seized by his officers as an escheat while really the late tenant has left an heir. Now the king can not be sued by action—no writ will go against him; the heir if he wants justice must petition for it humbly. Such matters as these are referred to the Chancellor. Proceedings are taken before him; the heir, it may be, proves his case and gets his land. The number of such cases, cases in which the king is concerned, is very large—kings are always seizing land on very slight pretexts—and forcing other people to prove their titles. Gradually a quite regular and ordinary procedure is established for such cases—a procedure very like that of the three courts of law. The proceedings are enrolled in Latin—just as the proceedings of the three courts of law are enrolled in Latin (hence the name "Latin side" of the Court of Chancery)—and if a question of fact be raised, it is tried by jury. The Chancellor himself does not summon the jury or preside at the trial, he

sends the question for trial to the King's Bench. All this is by no means unimportant, but it does not concern us very much at the present time.

(2) Very often the petitioner requires some relief at the expense of some other person. He complains that for some reason or another he can not get a remedy in the ordinary course of justice and yet he is entitled to a remedy. He is poor, he is old, he is sick, his adversary is rich and powerful, will bribe or will intimidate jurors, or has by some trick or some accident acquired an advantage of which the ordinary courts with their formal procedure will not deprive him. The petition is often couched in piteous terms, the king is asked to find a remedy for the love of God and in the way of charity. Such petitions are referred by the king to the Chancellor. Gradually in the course of the fourteenth century petitioners, instead of going to the king, will go straight to the Chancellor, will address their complaints to him and adjure him to do what is right for the love of God and in the way of charity. Now one thing that the Chancellor may do in such a case is to invent a new writ and so provide the complainant with a means of bringing an action in a court of law. But in the fourteenth century the courts of law have become very conservative and are given to quashing writs which differ in material points from those already in use. But another thing that the Chancellor can do is to send for the complainant's adversary and examine him concerning the charge that has been made against him. Gradually a procedure is established. The Chancellor having considered the petition, or "bill" as it is called, orders the adversary to come before him and answer the complaint. The writ whereby he does this is called a subpoena—because it orders the man to appear upon pain of forfeiting a sum of money, *e.g. subpoena centum librarum*. It is very different from the old writs whereby actions are begun in the courts of law. They tell the defendant what is the cause of action against him—he is to answer why he assaulted and beat the plaintiff, why he trespassed on the plaintiff's land, why he detains a chattel which belongs to the plaintiff. The subpoena, on the other hand, will tell him merely that he has got to come before the Chancellor and answer complaints made against him by A.B. Then when he comes before the Chancellor he will have to answer on oath, and sentence by sentence, the bill of the plaintiff. This procedure is rather like that of the ecclesiastical courts and the canon law than like that of our old English courts of law. It was in fact borrowed from the ecclesiastical courts, not from their ordinary procedure but from the summary procedure of those courts introduced for the suppression of heresy. The defendant will be examined upon oath and the Chancellor will decide questions of fact as well as questions of law.

I do not think that in the fourteenth century the Chancellors considered that they had to administer any body of substantive rules that differed from the ordinary law of the land. They were administering the law but they were administering it in cases which escaped the meshes of the ordinary courts. The complaints that come before them are in general complaints of indubitable legal wrongs, assaults, batteries, imprisonments, disseisins and so forth—wrongs of which the ordinary courts take cognizance, wrongs which they ought to redress. But then owing to one thing and another such wrongs are not always redressed by courts of law. In this period one of the commonest of all the reasons that complainants will give for coming to the Chancery is that they are poor while their adversaries are rich and influential—too rich, too influential to be left to the clumsy processes of the old courts and the verdicts of juries. However this sort of thing can not well be permitted. The law courts will not have it and parliament will not have it. Complaints against this extraordinary justice grow loud in the fourteenth century. In history and in principle it is closely connected with another kind of extraordinary justice which is yet more objectionable, the extraordinary justice that is done in criminal cases by the king's council. Parliament at one time would gladly be rid of both—of both the Council's interference in criminal matters, and the Chancellor's interference with civil matters. And so the Chancellor is warned off the field of common law—he is not to hear cases which might go to the ordinary courts, he is not to make himself a judge of torts and contracts, of property in lands and goods.

But then just at this time it is becoming plain that the Chancellor is doing some convenient and useful works that could not be done, or could not easily be done by the courts of common law. He has taken to enforcing uses or trusts. Of the origin of uses or trusts you will have read and I shall have something to say about it on another occasion. I don't myself believe that the use came to us as a foreign thing. I don't believe that there is anything Roman about it. I believe that it was a natural outcome of ancient English elements. But at any rate I must ask you not to believe that either the mass of the nation or the common lawyers of the fourteenth and fifteenth centuries looked with disfavour upon uses. No doubt they were troublesome things, things that might be used for fraudulent purposes, and statutes were passed against those who employed them for the purpose of cheating their creditors or evading the law of mortmain. But I have not a doubt that they were very popular, and I think we may say that had there been no Chancery, the old courts would have discovered some method of enforcing these fiduciary obligations. That method however must have been a clumsy one. A system of law which will never compel, which will never even allow, the defendant to give evidence, a system which sends every question of fact to a jury, is not competent to deal adequately with fiduciary relationships. On the other hand the Chancellor had a procedure which was very well adapted to this end. To this we may add that very possibly the ecclesiastical courts (and the Chancellor you will remember was almost always an ecclesiastic) had for a long time past been punishing breaches of trust by spiritual censures, by penance and excommunication. And so by general consent, we may say, the Chancellor was allowed to enforce uses, trusts or confidences.

Thus one great field of substantive law fell into his hand—a fruitful field, for in the course of the fifteenth century uses became extremely popular. Then, as we all know, Henry VIII [r. 1509–1547]—for it was rather the king than his subservient parliament—struck a heavy blow at uses. The king was the one man in the kingdom who had everything to gain and nothing to lose by abolishing uses, and as we all know he merely succeeded in complicating the law, for under the name of "trusts" the Chancellors still reigned over their old province. And then there were some other matters that were considered to be fairly within his jurisdiction. An old rhyme[ii] allows him "fraud, accident, and breach of confidence"—there were many frauds which the stiff old procedure of the courts of law could not adequately meet, and "accident," in particular the accidental loss of a document, was a proper occasion for the Chancellor's interference. No one could set any very strict limits to his power, but the best hint as to its extent that could be given in the sixteenth century was given by the words "fraud, accident and breach of confidence." On the other hand he was not to interfere where a court of common law offered an adequate remedy. A bill was "demurrable for want of equity" on that ground.

In the course of the sixteenth century we begin to learn a little about the rules that the Chancellors are administering in the field that is thus assigned to them. They are known as "the rules of equity and good conscience." As to what they have done in remoter times we have to draw inferences from very sparse evidence. One thing seems pretty plain. They had not considered themselves strictly bound by precedent.[iii] Remember this, our reports of cases in courts of law go back to Edward I's day—the middle ages are represented to us by the long series of Year Books. On the other hand our reports of cases in the Court of Chancery go back no further than 1557; and the mass of reports which come to us from between that date and the Restoration in 1660 is a light matter. This by

---

[ii] ["These three give place in court of conscience, Fraud, accident, and breach of confidence."]

[iii] [John Selden, a lawyer and scholar and the most learned man in seventeenth century England, said:

> "Equity in Law is the same that the spirit is in Religion, what ever one pleases to make it. Sometimes they Goe according to conscience sometime according to Law some time according to the Rule of the Court. Equity is A Roguish thing, for Law wee have a measure know what to trust too. Equity is according to the conscience of him that is Chancellor, and as that is larger or narrower soe is equity. Tis all one as if they should make the Standard for the measure wee call A foot, to be the Chancellors Foot; what an uncertain measure would this be; One Chancellor has a long foot another A short foot a third an indifferent foot; this the same thing in the Chancellors Conscience."

John Selden, TABLE TALK 43 (Pollock ed. 1927).

Compare Lord Chancellor Eldon's response to this concern in Gee *v.* Pritchard, 2 Swanst. 402, 414 (1818):

> "The doctrines of this Court ought to be as well settled, and made as uniform almost as those of the common law, laying down fixed principles, but taking care that they are applied according to the circumstances of each case. I cannot agree that the doctrines of this Court are to be changed with every succeeding judge. Nothing would inflict on me greater pain, in quitting this place, than the recollection that I had done any thing to justify the reproach that the equity of this Court varies like the Chancellor's foot."]

itself is enough to show us that the Chancellors have not held themselves very strictly bound by case law, for men have not cared to collect cases. Nor do I believe that to any very large extent the Chancellors had borrowed from the Roman Law—this is a disputed matter, Mr. Spence has argued for their Romanism, Mr. Justice Holmes against it. No doubt through the medium of the canon law these great ecclesiastics were familiar with some of the great maxims which occur in the *Institutes* or the *Digest.* One of the parts of the *Corpus Juris Canonici,* the Liber Sextus, ends with a bouquet of these high-sounding maxims—*Qui prior est tempore potior est jure,* and so forth, maxims familiar to all readers of equity reports. No doubt the early Chancellors knew these and valued them—but I do not believe that we ought to attribute to them much knowledge of Roman law or any intention to Romanise the law of England. For example, to my mind the comparison sometimes drawn between the so-called double ownership of England, and the so-called double ownership of Roman law can not be carried below the surface. In their treatment of uses or trusts the Chancellors stick close, marvelously close, to the rules of the common law—they often consulted the judges, and the lawyers who pleaded before them were common lawyers, for there was as yet no "Chancery Bar." On the whole my notion is that with the idea of a law of nature in their minds they decided cases without much reference to any written authority, now making use of some analogy drawn from the common law, and now of some great maxim of jurisprudence which they have borrowed from the canonists or the civilians.

In the second half of the sixteenth century the jurisprudence of the court is becoming settled. The day for ecclesiastical Chancellors is passing away. Wolsey is the last of the great ecclesiastical Chancellors, though in Charles I's day [r. 1625–49] we have one more divine in the person of Dr. Williams. Ellesmere, Bacon, Coventry, begin to administer an established set of rules which is becoming known to the public in the shape of reports and they begin to publish rules of procedure. In James I's day [r. 1603–25] occurred the great quarrel between Lord Chancellor Ellesmere and Chief Justice Coke which finally decided that the Court of Chancery was to have the upper hand over the courts of law. If the Chancery was to carry out its maxims about trust and fraud it was essential that it should have a power to prevent men from going into the courts of law and to prevent men from putting in execution the judgments that they had obtained in courts of law. In fraud or in breach of trust you obtain a judgment against me in a court of law; I complain to the Chancellor, and he after hearing what you have to say enjoins you not to put in force your judgment, says in effect that if you do put your judgment in force you will be sent to prison. Understand well that the Court of Chancery never asserted that it was superior to the courts of law; it never presumed to send to them such mandates as the Court of King's Bench habitually sent to the inferior courts, telling them that they must do this or must not do that or quashing their proceedings—the Chancellor's injunction was in theory a very different thing from a mandamus, a prohibition, a certiorari, or the like. It was addressed not to the judges, but to the party. You in breach of trust have obtained a judgment—the Chancellor does not say that this judgment was wrongly granted, he does not annul it, he tells you that for reasons personal to yourself it will be inequitable for you to enforce that judgment, and that you are not to enforce it. For all this, however, it was natural that the judges should take umbrage at this treatment of their judgments. Coke declared that the man who obtained such an injunction was guilty of the offence denounced by the Statutes of Praemunire, that of calling in question the judgments of the king's courts in other courts (these statutes had been aimed at the Papal curia). King James had now a wished-for opportunity of appearing as supreme over all his judges, and all his courts, and acting on the advice of Bacon and other great lawyers he issued a decree in favour of the Chancery. From this time forward the Chancery had the upper hand. It did not claim to be superior to the courts of law, but it could prevent men from going to those courts, whereas those courts could not prevent men from going to it.

Its independence being thus secured, the court became an extremely busy court. Bacon said that he had made 2,000 orders in a year, and we are told that as many as 16,000 causes were pending before it at one time: indeed it was hopelessly in arrear of its work. Under the Commonwealth [1649–60] some vigorous attempts were made to reform its procedure. Some were for abolishing it altogether. It was not easily forgotten that the Court of Chancery was the twin sister of the Court of Star Chamber. The projects for reform came to an end with the Restoration. Still it is from the Restoration or thereabouts—of course a precise date can not be fixed—that we may regard the equity administered in the Chancery as a recognised part of the law of the land. Usually, though not always, the great seal is in the keeping of a great lawyer—in 1667 Sir Orlando Bridgman, the great conveyancer, has it; in 1673 Sir Heneage Finch, afterwards Lord Nottingham, who has been called the father of equity; in 1682 Sir Francis North, afterwards Lord Guilford; in 1693 Sir John Somers, afterwards Lord Somers, a great common lawyer. I think that Anthony Ashley, Earl of Shaftesbury, the famous Ashley of the Cabal, was the last non-lawyer who held it, and he held it for but one year, from 1672 to 1673. Then during the eighteenth century there comes a series of great Chancellors. In 1705 Cowper, in 1713 Harcourt, in 1725 King, in 1733 Talbot, in 1737 Hardwicke, in 1757 Northington, in 1766 Camden, in 1778 Thurlow, in 1793 Loughborough, in 1801 Eldon. In the course of the century the Chancery reports improve; the same care is spent upon reporting the decrees of the Chancellors that has long been spent on reporting the judgments of the judges in the courts of common law. Gradually, too, a Chancery bar forms itself, that is to say, some barristers begin to devote themselves altogether to practising before the Chancellor, and do not seek for work elsewhere. Lastly, equity makes its way into the textbooks as a part, and an important part, of the law of the land. . . .

Equity Comes to America

Austin Wakeman Scott & Sydney Post Simpson, CASES AND OTHER MATERIALS ON CIVIL PROCEDURE 161–163 (1950).

The American colonies were settled before English equity had been reduced to a system under Lord Eldon. Under the pioneer conditions in America, there was little need for the elaborate machinery of the English Court of Chancery, which was in large part concerned with family settlements and the transactions of wealthy landowners. Whether there was any substantial hostility in the colonies to equity as such has been disputed. Pound takes the position that the very notion of equity and of discretion in the application of law went counter to Puritan ideas, and that this was an important reason for the hostility to equity in England during the Commonwealth and in the New England colonies. Chafee has suggested that there was no real hostility to equity as such in the colony of Massachusetts Bay, and explains the failure of some of the colonies to set up separate courts of chancery on the ground that this would have been unnecessary and expensive. Whether this was the primary reason for the reluctance of the New England colonies to set up separate equity courts, or whether the reason lay rather in Puritan hostility to equity and to a feeling that the Court of Chancery in England was sister to the hated Courts of Star Chamber and High Commission, are questions which cannot be answered with confidence in the present state of the colonial records. It seems clear that the fact that in some colonies chancery powers were vested in the royal governors or persons appointed by them did not increase the popularity of equity, and it is also clear that the colonists generally became much attached to the institution of trial by jury in civil cases. . . . There were, however, regularly constituted courts of chancery in some of the colonies.

After the Revolution, most of the newly constituted states established courts of chancery, but at first these for the most part administered only a rough layman's equity. There was no American equity jurisprudence; the English precedents were inaccessible and not well settled, and there was in any event a hostility to all things English; many of the judges were laymen. The history of equity in the United States as a system of law as distinguished from a system of lay magisterial discretion in hard cases dates from the second decade of the [nineteenth] century. Joseph Story became a Justice of the Supreme Court of the United States and began to sit in equity cases in the Circuit Court for Massachusetts in 1811; James Kent became Chancellor of New York in 1814. At that time the equity of the English Court of Chancery was becoming settled under Lord Eldon, and the time was ripe for the building of an American equity jurisprudence. The judicial labors of Kent and Story did much to domesticate equity in the United States; their writings, perhaps, did even more. Most of the original states developed courts with full equity powers comparatively early in the [nineteenth] last century, and the newer states created such courts.

But history has left its mark. The New England states were slow in developing full equity jurisdiction—indeed, Massachusetts did not have it until 1877—so that early New England equity cases are apt to turn upon the meaning of particular statutes granting partial jurisdiction. Pennsylvania equity, also, has had a checkered history; prior to 1836 there were no equity courts at all, with the result that the common-law courts absorbed a considerable amount of equity into the law, sometimes in a rather awkward fashion, and that there was a considerable amount of equitable relief by special acts of the legislature. In Georgia, there were jury trials in all equity cases as late as 1830; and in North Carolina, there is jury trial of right in some equity cases today. Moreover, the civil law origin of the law of Louisiana and the Spanish influences on the law of Texas have had their effect on equity in those states.

By Article III, Section 2 of the Constitution of the United States "The judicial Power shall extend to all Cases, in Law and Equity" of certain classes. By the second clause of the same section the Supreme Court is given original jurisdiction of certain cases, chiefly "those in which a State shall be a Party." Since this clause makes no distinction between law and equity, it is apparent that the original jurisdiction of the Supreme Court extends to both. When the first Congress created the inferior federal courts by the Judiciary Act of 1789, it followed the same plan. No separate equity courts were created; the same courts, circuit and district, were to administer law and equity, but on different sides of the court and by a different procedure. Some of the states followed this lead; others retained the system of separate courts. Then, beginning with 1848, when the Code of Procedure proposed and drafted by David Dudley Field was adopted in New York, there came a vigorous movement to merge or fuse law and equity. This movement spent its original force by about 1887, when some twenty-two states and territories had adopted codes of procedure purporting to abolish the distinction between actions at law and suits in equity, but was revived, as evidenced by the Illinois Civil Practice Act of 1933 and the Federal Rules of Civil Procedure of 1938. . . .

2. THE MAXIMS OF EQUITY

Some equitable principles have come to be expressed in the form of maxims. The maxims of equity are not rules that determine the outcome in cases. They are better seen as concerns, as statements of principle that focus the attention of judges. As justices of the High Court of Australia have put it, a maxim of equity "is not a specific rule or principle of law. It is a summary statement of a broad theme which underlines equitable concepts and principles."[iv]

[iv] Corin *v.* Patton (1990) 169 CLR 540, 557 (Mason, C.J. and McHugh, J.), quoted in R. P. Meagher, W. M. C. Gummow & J. R. F. Lehane, EQUITY: DOCTRINES AND REMEDIES 71 (3d ed. 1992).

There is no agreement on the exact number and source of these maxims. Nevertheless, they are frequently referred to and sometimes relied upon by the courts. Here are twelve:

1. Equity acts *in personam.*
2. Equity regards substance rather than form.
3. Equity follows the law.
4. Equity will not suffer a wrong to be without a remedy.
5. He who seeks equity must do equity.
6. He who comes into equity must come with clean hands.
7. Equity aids the vigilant, not those who slumber on their rights.
8. Equity regards as done that which ought to be done.
9. Equity imputes an intention to fulfill an obligation.
10. Equity is equality.
11. Equity delights to do justice and not by halves.
12. When the equities are equal, the law prevails.

These traditional maxims of equity have inspired light-hearted additions, such as the following:

13. He who seeks equity must do so with full pockets.
14. Equity is not for the squeamish.
15. Equity can be grumpy before its first cup of coffee.
16. Equity is crunchy on the outside, soft and chewy on the inside.[v]

3. EQUITY ACTS *IN PERSONAM*

J.R. v. M.P.

Court of Common Pleas, 1459.
Yearbook, 37 Henry 6, 13, pl. 3.[vi]

Debt upon an obligation [*i.e.*, a sealed bond] by J.R. of London against M.P. and J.B., citizens and aldermen of London.

Choke, for the defendants. The action lies not; for formerly, on such a day in the feast of the Holy Trinity, in the year last past, the said defendants made a bill to the Chancellor of England containing the matter following: that the defendants had purchased of J.R. certain debts due to him, giving their obligation therefor; that these debts being only choses in action could not vest in the defendants so as to give them any

---

[v] Eugene Volokh, Lost Maxims of Equity, 52 J. Leg. Ed. 619 (2002).

[vi] The case was translated and condensed by James Barr Ames, second dean of Harvard Law School (1895–1910) and a former editor of this book.

action for the recovery of the debts, but the duty remained all the time in J.R., so that the defendants had no *quid pro quo*; that their obligation was, on this account, void and worthless, but that the common law gave them no relief against their obligation; wherefore they prayed for a writ against J.R. to appear, under a certain penalty, before the king in Chancery to answer to this matter. A *subpoena* issued. The parties appeared, and because the matter was doubtful in law, the Chancellor [Waynflete] adjourned them to the Exchequer Chamber. There the matter was rehearsed and well debated before him and the justices of both benches [*i.e.*, King's Bench and Common Pleas]. And it was the opinion of all the justices that, as no duty was vested in the defendants by the bargain, the obligation ought in conscience to be surrendered to them, or the plaintiff ought to release the defendants. The Chancellor ordered him to give up the obligation [*i.e.*, deliver the sealed bond] to be cancelled in the Chancery or to make an acquittance or release. The plaintiff refusing to do either, was committed for contempt to the Fleet prison until he should obey, and still remains there. And we do not think an action lies upon the obligation.

Demurrer. And now a *supersedeas* is issued out of Chancery, relating all these matters and commanding that they shall not proceed.[vii]

Billing, for the plaintiff. The decree [*i.e.*, the Chancery decision] is not that the obligation is null and void in the law, but that the plaintiff shall bring it in to be cancelled. This proves clearly that the obligation is in force until cancelled. The decree [*i.e.*, the equitable decision] is not a bar here.

Littleton, for the defendants. I think otherwise, that it is a bar. What was done in Chancery was by the advice of all the justices, and by the order to bring in the obligation to be cancelled, the obligation loses its force. For as soon as he brings it in, the court will cancel it or redeliver it to the defendants, and so in effect it is null and void in law.

Laicon, contra. Sir, the decree is merely that he bring in the obligation to be cancelled, so it is clear that it is still in force. For if the obligation by this decree had lost its force, the plaintiff would not be ordered to prison.

Boef. It is proved that the obligation is not yet surrendered, but remains with the plaintiff. Therefore it is still in force, and that is why he is still in prison.

NEEDHAM, J. The matter is [not] a bar, because the obligation is still in force . . . .

[vii] [A *supersedeas* commands a lower court to stay proceedings before it. This *supersedeas* aimed to stay the proceedings at law. Counsel for the plaintiff argued successfully that it should not be obeyed by the Common Bench in this instance. However, he recognized that the situation would be different if the *supersedeas* concerned a matter of privilege. "If an officer of the Chancery be impleaded here, in that case if he wishes to buy a *supersedeas* because he is minister of that court, you would stop proceedings because of their privilege, for otherwise all the clerks and ministers of Chancery might be impleaded here."]

DANBY, J., contra. By the decree the obligation loses its force as fully as if it had been cancelled.

MOYLE, J., to the same effect.

DANVERS, J. This is not like an obligation made by an infant, or under duress. In those cases the obligation is void; not so here. The plea is bad.

ASHTON, J., contra. The decree is the same in effect as if it had ordered that the obligation should be null and void.

PRISOT, C.J. In the use of writs of *subpoena* the Chancery is not a court of record,[viii] for it is only to examine the conscience. We here are bound to the law, and cannot go beyond. It belongs to them to examine the conscience. For when the deed is good and always has been so, their examination will not make it bad, nor will their examination make it good and legal in our law. And since the defendants cannot have any remedy by our law, they shall sue there to be restored to their obligation; and the effect of their power and decree is to restore the party to his obligation, or to compel the plaintiff to make an acquittance or release. But to execute this, the Chancery can do nothing but order him to prison, there to remain until he will obey. And this is all that court can do. And if the party will lie in prison rather than give up the obligation, the other is without remedy, and so the Chancellor has no power to nullify the obligation.

NOTES ON THE NATURE OF EQUITABLE DECREES

1. "If judgment be given in an action at common law, the Chancellor cannot alter or meddle with the judgment, but he may proceed against the person for corrupt conscience, because he will take advantage of the law against conscience." Anonymous, Litt. 37, 124 Eng. Rep. 124 (Common Pleas 1626).

2. Injunctions against domestic judgments have lost most of their former importance as a result of the merger of law and equity courts, the recognition of traditionally equitable defenses in merged courts, and the procedural rules that enable merged courts to correct procedural injustices by vacating their own judgments or granting new trials.

3. C, a judgment creditor of D, sued D and got a temporary injunction in July against any transfer of D's land pending a hearing. On August 11, before any hearing was held, D paid C, and with his consent sold the land to X. The injunction remained in place until November when C obtained an order dissolving it and dismissing the bill. Meanwhile, on August 17, P, another judgment creditor of D, filed a bill against D and X to set aside the sale as in violation of the injunction. The sale was held valid. Herman *v.* Sartor, 107 Tenn. 235 (1901).

[viii] [At the time of this decision, this meant that the Chancery did not follow the common law.]

4. B has a right with respect to A's land which is enforceable only in equity. A conveys the land to X with a covenant against incumbrances. X is subject to B's equitable right. X can recover damages from A in an action at law for breach of the covenant. Roberts *v.* Levy, 3 Abb. Pr. (n.s.) 311 (N.Y. Common Pleas 1867); New York *v.* New York & South Brooklyn Ferry & Steam Transp. Co., 231 N.Y. 18 (1921).

5. Christopher Columbus Langdell, first dean of Harvard Law School (1870–1895), wrote:

> "Indeed, as a rule, the chancellor, like the ecclesiastical courts, had no jurisdiction *in rem,* and hence could only enforce his orders and decrees by process *in personam*; though whether this was a cause or a consequence of his adopting the ecclesiastical procedure may be doubtful. To some extent, however, the chancellor has asserted and maintained the right to proceed *in rem*. Thus, when all process against the person has been exhausted without effect, he will issue a writ of sequestration against the property of the delinquent. So when a defendant has been decreed to deliver possession of land to the plaintiff, as a last resort a writ of assistance will be issued to the sheriff to put the plaintiff in possession. But, with these exceptions, chancery exercises all its powers by process of contempt against the person.

C.C. Langdell, SUMMARY OF EQUITY PLEADING 35 (2d ed. 1883).

Langdell also noted:

> "After all, these are scarcely exceptions to the rule that the chancellor has no jurisdiction *in rem*. When he issues and enforces a writ of sequestration, or a writ of assistance, he merely exerts physical power over the possession of property, and this he can do, though he have no jurisdiction whatever *in rem*. A court which possesses that jurisdiction can by its judgment or decree take the title to property out of one person and put it in another. . . . So when the property of a judgment debtor is seized and sold to satisfy the judgment, the title of the judgment debtor is as effectively transferred to the purchaser as if the sale had been made by the judgment debtor himself. . . . This power of creating and extinguishing titles the chancellor never had nor claimed to have, except when it was given him by statute. It is true that he frequently directed the sale of property, but it was by his control over the person of the owner that he made the sale effective, *i.e.*, when the sale had been made he compelled the owner to execute a deed pursuant to the sale; and hence, when the owner was out of the jurisdiction, or labored under any incapacity, *e.g.*, that of infancy, the chancellor was powerless. He could not even make the appointment of a new trustee effective, except by compelling the old trustee or his heir, or whoever held the legal title, to convey to the new trustee. When it became the practice to resort to chancery for the partition of land, what the chancellor really did was, first, to inquire and ascertain *how* the property should be divided, and then

to compel the parties to divide accordingly by the execution of mutual conveyances. So when the chancellor undertook the settlement of a disputed boundary, he first ascertained what the true boundary line was, and then compelled the parties by mutual conveyances to establish that as the boundary line. . . . Indeed, it may be stated broadly that a decree in chancery has not in itself (*i.e.*, independently of what may be done under it) any legal operation whatever. If a debt, whether by simple contract or by specialty, be sued for in a court of law, and judgment recovered, the original debt is merged in the judgment, and extinguished by it, and the judgment creates a new debt of a higher nature, and of which the judgment itself is conclusive evidence. But if the same debt be sued for in the court of chancery (as it frequently may be) and a decree obtained for its payment, not one of the effects before stated is produced by the decree. . . . Again, if a claim be made the subject of an action at law, and judgment be rendered for the defendant upon the merits, the judgment is conclusive evidence that the claim was not well founded, and it will therefore furnish a perfect defence to any future action upon the same claim; but a decree in equity against the validity of a claim is never a defence to an action at law upon the same claim. Here again, however, the chancellor will make his decrees equal to judgments so far as it is in his power to do so; and therefore a decree in chancery against a claim upon its merits will always be a defence to any future suit in chancery upon the same claim, not as destroying the claim or as proving conclusively its invalidity, but as furnishing a sufficient reason why chancery should not again take cognizance of it. Such a decree will also be (what is sometimes called) an equitable defence to any action at law upon the same claim, *i.e.*, the chancellor will enjoin the prosecution of any such action, upon the ground that the plaintiff having elected to make his claim the subject of a suit in equity, and that suit having been defended successfully upon the merits, it is not right that the defendant should be vexed again by the same claim. Accordingly, when A and B demand the same thing of C, and for that reason C, the demand being a legal one, files a bill of interpleader against A and B, and the chancellor decides that the thing demanded belongs to A, and awards it to him, he also directs a perpetual injunction to issue against B to restrain him from suing C at law for the same thing, and that is C's only protection.

"Upon the whole, therefore, the weakness of the chancellor's jurisdiction is as conspicuous as its strength; its strength being that it can always command the obedience of suitors; its weakness being that it has substantially no resource beyond commanding such obedience. It should be observed, however, that, while its element of strength is necessary to the existence of the jurisdiction, its element of weakness is not. The chancellor might in the beginning, like the court of admiralty, have been clothed with the same jurisdiction *in rem* as *in personam;* but if he had been, equity would

> now be a very different thing from what it is, and its machinery would be very different from what it is. . . . However that may be, any one who wishes to understand the English system of equity as it is, and as it has been from the beginning, must study its weakness as well as its strength."

Id. at 35–38 n. 4.

Federal Trade Commission v. Affordable Media, LLC

United States Court of Appeals, Ninth Circuit, 1999.
179 F.3d 1228.

■ WIGGINS, J. [A company called Sterling marketed gadgets on late night television, 11:00 p.m. to 4:00 a.m. Its products included a water-filled dumbbell called the "Aquabell," a talking pet tag, and a plastic-wrap dispenser called the "KenKut." Denyse and Michael Anderson formed another company, Financial, which used telemarketing techniques to sell investments in Sterling's enterprise, known as "media units."]

The media units sold for $5,000. Each media unit entitled the investor to participate in the sale of Sterling's products from 201 of the late-night commercials. Each product sold for $20.00. The investor would receive $7.50 for each product sold during his 201 commercials, up to a maximum of five products per commercial. According to Financial's telemarketers, the investors would likely receive $37.50 per commercial (from five products sold during each commercial) for a total of $7,537.50—an astronomical fifty percent return in sixty to ninety days. Financial, for its part, would receive forty-five percent of the investor's $5,000.00 investment, an amount that the Andersons assert is the industry standard. [Financial raised an estimated $13,000,000 from media unit investors, resulting in $6,300,000 in commissions for itself.]

Perhaps unsurprisingly to those not involved in the media-unit project, it turned out that Sterling could not sell enough Talking Pet Tags and Aquabells to return the promised yields to the media-unit investors. Instead, it appears that Sterling used later investors' investments to pay the promised yields to earlier investors—a classic Ponzi scheme.

[Shortly before the Andersons began selling media units, they established an asset protection trust under the law of the Cook Islands, a fifteen-island nation in the South Pacific. At the time of the case, most or all of the commissions the Andersons had earned from sales of media units were held in this trust.

[Asset protection trusts are devices to avoid payment of creditors by placing assets outside the reach of courts of the United States. In a majority of United States jurisdictions, a party who creates a trust and also retains a beneficial interest in the trust cannot prevent creditors from reaching his or her own interest. A typical asset protection trust is established in a friendly jurisdiction, such as the Cook Islands, that does not allow creditors to reach any interest held in trust. Settlors such as the Andersons transfer their assets to co-trustees consisting of themselves and a local bank or financial institution. The primary power of the institutional trustee is a power to remove the settlors as co-trustees if certain adverse events occur ("events of duress"), such as an action by or on behalf of the settlor's creditors. If the settlors are removed as co-trustees, then at least nominally, they have no further access to trust assets and no further control over the decisions of the institutional trustee. Local courts enforce the trust as written, treating the institutional trustee as the sole trustee after an event of duress and refusing to give access to the settlor's assets. Some asset protection trusts, including the trust established by the Andersons, add a further level of complexity by designating the settlors as "protectors" of the trust with power to override decisions of the institutional trustee.

[In April, 1998, the Federal Trade Commission filed a complaint against the Andersons and Financial for fraudulent telemarketing of media units in violation of a variety of federal laws. The FTC requested, and the district court granted, a preliminary injunction requiring the Andersons to repatriate any assets held outside the United States for their benefit, including the assets in their Cook Islands trust.]

In response to the preliminary injunction, the Andersons faxed a letter to [the institutional trustee, AsiaCiti Trust Limited], instructing AsiaCiti . . . to repatriate the assets to the United States to be held under the control of the district court. AsiaCiti thereupon notified the Andersons that the temporary restraining order was an event of duress under the trust, removed the Andersons as co-trustees under the trust because of the event of duress, and refused to provide an accounting or repatriation of the assets. . . .

At a hearing on June 4, 1998, the district court found the Andersons in civil contempt of court for failing to repatriate the trust assets to the United States and failing to provide an accounting of the trust's assets. The district court, however, continued the hearing until June 9, then until June 11, and finally until June 17, in an effort to allow the Andersons to purge themselves of their contempt. . . . At the close of the June 17 hearing, the district judge ordered the Andersons taken into custody because they had not purged themselves of their contempt. We affirm the district court.[3]

The standard for finding a party in civil contempt is well settled:

> "The moving party has the burden of showing by clear and convincing evidence that the contemnors violated a specific and definite order of the court. The burden then shifts to the contemnors to demonstrate why they were unable to comply."

---

[3] [On] December 22, 1998, the district court ordered the Andersons released but found that they remain in contempt of court. Because they remain in contempt, their appeal of the court's order finding them in contempt has not been rendered moot. . . .

. . . . The Andersons do not dispute that the trust assets have not been repatriated to the United States. Instead, the Andersons claim that compliance with the temporary restraining order is impossible because the trustee, in accordance with the terms of the trust, will not repatriate the trust assets to the United States.

A party's inability to comply with a judicial order [normally] constitutes a defense to a charge of civil contempt. . . .

[W]e are not certain that the Andersons' inability to comply in this case would be a defense to a finding of contempt. It is readily apparent that the Andersons' inability to comply with the district court's repatriation order is the intended result of their own conduct—their inability to comply and the foreign trustee's refusal to comply appears to be the precise goal of the Andersons' trust. . . .

We leave for another day the resolution of this more difficult question because we find that the Andersons have not satisfied their burden of proving that compliance with the district court's repatriation order was impossible. It is well established that a party petitioning for an adjudication that another party is in civil contempt does not have the burden of showing that the other party has the capacity to comply with the court's order. Instead, the party asserting the impossibility defense must show "categorically and in detail" why he is unable to comply.

In the asset protection trust context, moreover, the burden on the party asserting an impossibility defense will be particularly high because of the likelihood that any attempted compliance with the court's orders will be merely a charade rather than a good faith effort to comply. . . .

> ". . . . [T]he settlor should be aware that, although his trust will probably prove unassailable by domestic creditors, he may face minor hassles while defending his trust in court. In particular, if a creditor attacks an offshore trust in United States court, the settlor may face contempt of court orders during the proceedings. . . . [T]here is a possibility that the court will . . . order the settlor to collect his assets from the trust and turn them over to the court. If the settlor does not comply with these orders, a court may hold him in contempt. However, there are ways around such a conflict. . . . [T]he settlor could comply with the court order and 'order' his trustee to turn over the funds, knowing full well that the trustee will not comply with his request. Thereby, the settlor would technically comply with the court's orders, escape contempt of court charges, and still rest assured that his assets will remain protected."

James T. Lorenzetti, The Offshore Trust: A Contemporary Asset Protection Scheme, 102 Commercial L.J. 138, 158 (1997). . . .

Given these considerations, we cannot find that the district court clearly erred in finding that the Andersons' compliance with the repatriation order was not impossible because the Andersons remain in control of their Cook Islands trust. . . .

The Andersons had previously been able to obtain in excess of $1 million from the trust in order to pay their taxes. Given their ability to obtain, with ease, such large sums from the trust, we share the district court's skepticism regarding the Andersons' claim that they cannot make the trust assets subject to the court's jurisdiction.

[The court also pointed to the Andersons' position as "protectors" under the trust, a position they had attempted to abandon after the district court entered its repatriation order.]

We, therefore, affirm the district court's finding the Andersons in contempt. Given the nature of the Andersons' so-called "asset protection" trust, which was designed to frustrate the power of United States' courts to enforce judgments, there may be little else that a district court judge can do besides exercise its contempt powers to coerce people like the Andersons into removing the obstacles they placed in the way of a court. Given that the Andersons' trust is operating precisely as they intended, we are not overly sympathetic to their claims and would be hesitant to overly-restrict the district court's discretion, and thus legitimize what the Andersons have done.

Affirmed.

Lewis v. North Kingstown

Supreme Court of Rhode Island, 1887.
16 R.I. 15.

■ DURFEE, C.J. This bill sets out that the complainants are owners in possession of a lot of land situate on Washington Street, in the village of Wickford, in the town of North Kingstown, in highway district No. 37 of said town, on which lot there is a building belonging to them; that the defendant John H. Weeden, the surveyor of highways of said district, acting under orders of the town council of said town, the members whereof are likewise made defendants, has entered on said lot, and is engaged in [razing] said building and taking away the foundations . . . and grading said lot, thereby throwing the estate open to the public, and obliterating its boundaries, to the irreparable injury of the complainants. The bill prays that the defendants may be enjoined from carrying out their purposes, and from further interfering in any way with the estate, and for general relief. The bill was filed February 28, 1885. The defendants, by their answer, filed May 27, 1885, admit that they are or were doing as charged, but deny that the lot is part and parcel of the estate of the complainants, and allege that it is and ever has been, from a time when the memory of man runneth not to the contrary, part and parcel of a public highway, and that the building had stood thereon by sufferance of the town. The defendants also by supplemental answer, filed September 28, 1886, allege that their purposes have been fully carried out by removing the building and foundations and grading the lot, and set up that the complainants ought not to maintain their bill, because their remedy is complete at law. To both answers the complainants have filed general replications. In this state of the pleadings, the defendants move that the bill be dismissed, because the complainants have an adequate remedy at law, and, in support of their motion, contend: *first,* that the bill does not state a case for equitable relief; and, *second,* if it does, that the case stated has ceased to exist by reason of the removal of the building and foundations, and the grading of the lot. . . .

We do not think the motion should be granted because of the statements of the supplemental answer, since those statements are controverted by the replication. Moreover, if they were admitted, we do not think they would make a case for dismissal. It ought not to be in the power of a defendant in an injunction bill to oust the court of its jurisdiction by committing, *pendente lite,* the very acts to prevent which the suit was begun, and such, we think, is the law. "It is well settled," says the Supreme Judicial Court of Massachusetts, "with little or no conflict of authority, that when a defendant in a bill in equity disenables himself, pending the suit, to comply with an order for specific relief, the court will proceed to afford relief by way of compelling compensation to be made, and for this purpose will retain the bill and determine the amount of such compensation, although its nature and measure are precisely the same as the party would otherwise recover as damages in an action at law." It may be that an amendment of the bill, setting forth the acts committed by the defendants *pendente lite,* will be necessary, notwithstanding the supplemental answer, if the complainants desire not only an injunction from further interference but also an award of damages, but if so the complainants should have an opportunity to make it. . . .

B. THE PARTIAL FUSION OF LAW AND EQUITY

1. EARLY REFORMS

Steps Toward Merger

Austin Wakeman Scott & Sydney Post Simpson, CASES AND OTHER MATERIALS ON CIVIL PROCEDURE 232–236 (1950).

The movement for the procedural merger of law and equity had its chronological beginning in the United States with the activities of the New York Commissioners on Practice and Pleading [led by David Dudley Field]. Their report of 1848 proposed that the distinction between law and equity be abolished, and this proposal was embodied in the Code of Procedure adopted by the legislature of New York in that year and widely copied in many other states within a relatively brief period. A little later, as a result of the investigations of two Royal Commissions, substantial legislative changes were made in the English practice which brought about some degree of fusion but of a less complete character. The English legislation, unlike that of New York and the states which copied the New York code, did not purport to combine law and equity, but did permit equitable defenses and some degree of equitable relief in actions at law and extended the jurisdiction of the Court of Chancery to decide questions of law. Later English legislation (1858) gave the courts of law a limited jurisdiction to grant equitable relief in some cases. . . . In 1875, England made effective a completely unified procedure. In 1915, Congress for the first time permitted equitable defenses in actions at law in the federal courts, and allowed the transfer of causes from law to equity or from equity to law. In the provision as to transfer of causes, Congress followed the lead of a number of non-code states. In recent years the movement for more complete unification of civil procedure has made considerable headway, the most noteworthy events being the adoption of a new system of practice by the state of Illinois in 1933 and the promulgation by the Supreme Court of the United States in 1938 of unified rules of civil procedure for the federal district courts, pursuant to the statutory authorization of 1934, and the thoroughgoing merger in New Jersey in 1948.

In studying the procedural merger of law and equity, four main types of legislation come into consideration.

1. *Equitable Defenses and Counterclaims at Law.* The English legislation of 1854, the federal legislation of 1915, and the statutes of most non-code states permit the defendant in an action at law to set up what are commonly denominated "equitable defenses." The main purpose of the earlier legislation of this character seems to have been to deal with cases where the defendant in an action at law could secure in equity a perpetual and unconditional injunction against the prosecution of the action . . . .

Under the code system of unified procedure it would appear that no special statutory authorization of equitable defenses or counterclaims was necessary, but doubts which arose under the pioneer New York Code of Procedure led to its amendment to include the following provision: "The defendant may set forth by answer, as many defences and counterclaims as he may have, whether they be such as have been heretofore denominated legal or equitable, or both." Similar sections are contained in most of the codes of civil procedure in the states which have adopted code practice.

2. *Expansion of the Power of Equity.* Under the classical English practice, the powers of the Court of Chancery were limited by three self-imposed restrictions: (1) The Court was reluctant to decide questions of legal right or title in suits to enjoin torts; (2) it was sometimes reluctant to decide questions of law and was in the habit of stating cases for the opinion of one of the courts of common law on such questions; (3) it would not give damages in lieu of specific performance or damages in cases

where equitable relief turned out to be impracticable or was refused for some other reason not affecting the merits. The first two of these limitations were removed by statute in 1852, the third by statute in 1858. . . .

The difficulties met by this English legislation have not been so serious in the United States, and there is little legislation of similar character in this country.

3. *Transfer of Causes From Law to Equity or From Equity to Law.* Under the old practice a plaintiff who failed in a suit in equity because he was found to have an adequate remedy at law or for some other reason not affecting the merits such as impracticability of the remedy in equity, had to begin a new action at law. Similarly, a plaintiff who sought relief at law which could be given only in equity had to bring a new suit in equity. . . . This resulted in substantial and unnecessary expense in every such case, and in some cases the Statute of Limitations had run on the plaintiff's cause of action before he found out that he had sued in the wrong court. Where law and equity are administered in the same court but by different procedures, as in a considerable number of the United States, these difficulties could readily be met by providing that an action or suit brought on the wrong side of the court might be transferred to the other side of the court, with appropriate amendment of the pleadings. . . .

4. *Unification of Legal and Equitable Procedure.* None of the methods heretofore discussed eliminates all the difficulties resulting from separate law and equity procedure. In consequence, the most usual form of legislative change to meet these difficulties has been some kind of unification of legal and equitable procedure.

2. RULES ESTABLISHING UNIFIED PROCEDURE

The Field Code adopted in New York and a number of other states formally abolished the distinction between actions at law and suits in equity.[ix] Specifically, the New York Code of Procedure of 1848 provided in Section 62 that: "The distinctions between actions at law and suits in equity, and the forms of all such actions and suits, heretofore existing, are abolished; and, there shall be in this state, hereafter, but one form of action, for the enforcement or protection of private rights and the redress of private wrongs, which shall be denominated a civil action."

Rule 1 of the Federal Rules of Civil Procedure, first promulgated in 1938, provides that "[t]here shall be one form of action to be known as 'civil action.' " Comments state that the purpose of the Federal Rules is "to secure the just, speedy, and inexpensive determination of every action." The Federal Rules also incorporate procedural devices formerly available only on the equity side of the federal courts. Under these modern procedural rules a court may grant a successful litigant the relief

[ix] For further discussion, see Kellen Funk, Equity Without Chancery: The Fusion of Law and Equity in the Field Code of Civil Procedure, New York 1846–76, 36 J. Leg. Hist. 152 (2015).

or remedy to which that litigant is entitled, whether the relief was formerly denominated legal or equitable. The defendant may also raise any defense whether formerly denominated legal or equitable.

Although the Federal Rules of Civil Procedure merged the procedures of law and equity, and almost all states now have merged procedures as well, the unified procedures do not affect the right to a jury trial in civil cases. The jury trial right is "preserved" (not made universal) in state and federal constitutional provisions and rules of procedure. One implication is that distinctions must still be made between legal and equitable decisionmaking.

3. RECOGNITION OF EQUITABLE DECREES AT LAW (AND JUDGMENTS IN EQUITY)

Mutual Life Insurance Co. v. Newton

Supreme Court of New Jersey, 1888.
50 N.J. Law 571.

To an action upon a bond a plea was filed, setting forth that, before the bringing of the action, a decree for deficiency had been made in a suit of foreclosure of a mortgage given for the same debt. Held, a good plea.

On motion to strike out plea.

The declaration is upon a bond for $8,000, made by the defendant to the plaintiffs. It states that this bond was accompanied by a mortgage made by the defendant, upon certain lands of his, to the plaintiffs, to secure the sum mentioned in said bond. That upon the foreclosure of this mortgage a sum was realized, which was applied to the payment of the said $8,000, leaving a balance of $3,877.53 still due. The defendant filed a plea setting up that the sum of $3,877.53 is the amount of a deficiency declared and decreed by the Court of Chancery as still due and owing upon the proceeding in foreclosure set forth in the declaration; that the bond sued on is the bond which accompanied the mortgage, and was set forth in the bill of complaint to foreclose the said mortgage; that after such decree of foreclosure was made and entered in the Court of Chancery, and after the sale of the lands, there remained the said deficiency of $3,877.53, which was decreed by the Court of Chancery to be still due; that on the 15th day of August, 1881, a statement or abstract of such decree was filed in the office of the clerk of the supreme court, whereby the said sum became a judgment of this court, and is still a judgment.

■ REED, J. The motion to strike out the plea raises the question, whether a party who has taken a personal decree in equity for a deficiency in the amount raised on the foreclosure of a mortgage can afterwards bring an action at law upon the accompanying bond. The view of the pleader was that the recovery by way of a decree under the statute was a bar against any other action upon the original cause of action. The notion of the plaintiffs' counsel is that a decree is not a judgment in a sense that implies a merger of the original cause of action, and that, therefore, the bond is still suable. The point made is that no action will lie on a decree as it will upon a judgment and therefore a decree, has not the qualities of a judgment in respect to its effect in extinguishing the original ground of the suit. . . .

The law in England may be regarded as settled, that upon foreign decrees an action at law will lie. . . . The right to bring actions upon domestic decrees the English courts had denied; but this denial was put upon the ground that such actions were unnecessary, because the court which made the decree could, within its own jurisdiction, enforce it, and so an action was unnecessary.

[A prior New Jersey case] relied upon the case of Hugh *v.* Higgs, [21 U.S. 697 (1823)], as establishing the law in the federal courts against an action at law on a decree. Whatever force this case may have had once is now entirely dissipated by the case of Pennington *v.* Gibson, [57 U.S. 65 (1853)], in his opinion in which case Mr. Justice Daniel remarked: "We lay it down as the general rule that, in every instance in which an action of debt can be maintained upon a judgment at law for a sum of money awarded by such judgment, the like action can be maintained upon a decree in equity for an ascertained and specific amount, and nothing more." . . .

In treating the question as an open one, I have no doubt that an action will lie upon a domestic decree for the payment of money only in the same degree as it will lie upon a judgment . . . . I think it might be admitted that the right of an action at law upon a domestic decree could be denied upon the ground that such an action is unnecessary and vexatious because of the fact that the court which made the decree can enforce it in all respects. It was upon this ground that the English courts and one or two of the American courts early denied the right of bringing such an action at law.

The denial of a right of action upon such ground would not, in my judgment, render such a decree less conclusive in bar of another suit for the same cause of action; for the question is whether the decree amounts to a determination of the rights of the parties in respect to the identical matter involved in the present action. If so, it is a bar. The doctrine of *res adjudicata* is plain and intelligible, and amounts simply to this, that a cause of action once finally determined, without appeal, between the parties, on the merits, by a competent tribunal, cannot afterwards be litigated by a new proceeding, either by the same or any other tribunal. . . .

And this is true, whether the first adjudication is in a court of law or equity. A decree in chancery may be given in evidence between the same parties, or those claiming under them, for their judgments must be of authority in those cases where the law gives them jurisdiction; for it were very absurd that the law should give them jurisdiction, and yet not suffer what is done by force of that jurisdiction to be full proof.

Hence it is settled that a verdict and judgment of a court of record or a decree in chancery puts an end to all further controversy concerning the points thus decided between the parties to the suit. . . . If the decree is final, then its result is to merge the original cause of action. As was remarked in the case of Barnes *v.* Gibbs, 31 N. J. Law, 319, in regard to a judgment: "The doctrine of merger arises out of the quality which renders the judgment conclusive upon the parties as to the question which is involved. If the plaintiff be permitted to sue on the original cause of action, it is treating it, although judicially settled, as open to controversy."

I am of the opinion that when the plaintiff invoked the Court of Chancery to give him the statutory decree for deficiency, and he obtained it, his right to bring a new suit on the bond was gone. Nor is it easy to perceive the occasion for such an action.

The power to file the decree of the court in the supreme [court] clerk's office, the power to have execution in any county in the state, the right to sue upon the decree in foreign jurisdictions, all tend to make the decree an efficient instrument for the collection of the debt. The motion to strike is refused, with costs.

NOTES ON THE PRECLUSIVE EFFECT OF EQUITABLE DECREES

1. The town of Solon, after issuing bonds, sued bondholders (including the Williamsburgh Savings Bank), claiming that the bonds had not been validly issued and requesting that they be cancelled (an equitable remedy). The court held that the bonds were valid and dismissed the town's complaint. Subsequently, the bank brought an action against the town to recover interest due on the bonds (an action at law). In defense, the town claimed that the bonds were invalid. The court held in favor of the bank. The court's explanation for this ruling was as follows:

> "[In the first suit, by the town against the bank, the bank] might have defended upon other grounds, those peculiar to equity, and independent of the main and central issue, but it did not. One such ground might have been that there was an adequate remedy at law, but that was waived because not raised by demurrer on the one hand, or by pleading the defense on the other. . . . Another such defense might possibly have been laches, but that was not interposed, and was explicitly shut out from the decision. . . . On the trial, no merely equitable question was raised, save and except that if the bonds were invalid on their face, the remedy was at law, which the court correctly overruled. . . . The plaintiff municipality deliberately chose the forum of equity, saying that it was afraid of the courts of law and of the multitude of suits which might follow and especially of some in the Federal courts; and before the tribunal which it voluntarily selected was bound to show, and could only

succeed by showing, that the identical bonds here in controversy were void. . . .

"The town has had its day in court, a full opportunity to assail and test the bonds, a patient hearing and direct decision upon all the questions now raised. It would be hard to find a case to which the doctrine of *res adjudicata* could more justly and clearly apply than this."

Williamsburgh Savings Bank *v.* Solon, 136 N.Y. 465, 473–4 (1893).

2. The Restatement (Second) of Judgments makes these observations about how the merger of law and equity affected "merger" and "bar" (older names for doctrines of claim preclusion):

" *'Legal' and 'equitable' phases of a claim.* When 'law' and 'equity' with their distinctive remedies were separately administered, a plaintiff had to choose between the two "sides" when he brought his action, and the choice could be difficult, as the dividing line was not exact. Also, it was sometimes impossible to dispose completely in a single action of an entire transaction or controversy, since it might require a combination of legal and equitable remedies. The difficult remedial situation created by the law-equity division naturally had important restrictive effects on the operation of the doctrines of merger and bar. These are overcome when law and equity are "merged" or unified into the "one form of action" so that a pleader may and is expected to demand in a single action any and all remedies suited to the case. The point is emphasized by the customary provision in modern rules or codes of procedure that, except where judgment is by default, "every final judgment shall grant the relief to which the party in whose favor it is rendered is entitled, even if the party has not demanded such relief in his pleadings." *See* Rule 54(c) of the Federal Rules of Civil Procedure.

"*(1) Remission from 'law' to 'equity' or 'equity' to 'law' unnecessary and improper.* Formerly, if the plaintiff brought an action at law in which judgment was given for the defendant because the plaintiff's remedy was solely by a suit in equity, the plaintiff was not precluded from maintaining a suit in equity. Conversely, if the plaintiff brought a suit in equity which was dismissed because his remedy was solely by an action at law, the plaintiff was not precluded from maintaining an action at law; this was true, for example, where the suit in equity was dismissed because the plaintiff had an adequate remedy at law, or on the ground of such delay or hardship or impropriety of the plaintiff's conduct as barred a suit in equity but not an action at law.

"In a unified system of procedure, the plaintiff in the situations mentioned would ordinarily be entitled to be awarded in the first action any remedy called for by the facts, whether the remedy would formerly have been denominated legal or equitable; hence one action should suffice.

"(2) *'Legal' and 'equitable' relief possible in single action.* Formerly, a plaintiff who brought a suit in equity to enjoin the continuance of wrongful conduct might not be permitted to demand in the same suit the prior damages resulting from the wrong, or, where the system was somewhat less strict, might be permitted, but would not be obligated to make the demand in the same suit (a demand for 'cleanup' damages). Accordingly, judgment in the equity suit either would not preclude an action by the plaintiff at law to recover the damages, or in the laxer systems, would preclude the action only if the plaintiff had in fact sought the damage remedy in the equity suit. Today, after unification, the damage remedy would be considered part of the unitary claim for purposes of merger and bar. So also a judgment granting or denying specific performance of a contract should preclude an action for money damages for breach.

"(3) *Alternative relief in a single action on a contract as written or as reformed.* Formerly, when the plaintiff brought an action at law for breach of a written contract and failed to prove a breach, and judgment was accordingly given for the defendant, the plaintiff was not precluded from a suit in equity to reform the contract on the ground of mistake or fraud or some other ground, and to enforce the contract as reformed. Today, in a unified system, he would ordinarily be precluded from a second action, assuming, as would very likely be the case, that the facts basing the proposed second action were part of the same transaction as those grounding the first."

Restatement (Second) of Judgments § 25, comment *i* (1982).

4. EQUITY IN THE UNITED STATES TODAY

It is often said that law and equity have merged in the United States, but that is only partly true. Since the adoption of the Federal Rules of Civil Procedure in 1938, the procedures of the federal courts are merged and they no longer have separate "sides" for law and equity. The state systems are administered as follows:

(1) Equity may be administered in the same court and by the same procedure as law. This is now the rule in Alabama, Alaska, Arizona, Arkansas, California, Colorado, Connecticut, Florida, Georgia, Hawaii, Idaho, Illinois (except Cook County), Indiana, Kansas, Kentucky, Louisiana, Maine, Maryland, Massachusetts, Michigan, Minnesota, Missouri, Montana, Nebraska, Nevada, New Hampshire, New Mexico, New York, North Carolina, North Dakota, Ohio, Oklahoma, Oregon, Pennsylvania, Rhode Island, South Carolina, South Dakota, Texas, Utah, Vermont, Virginia, Washington, West Virginia, Wisconsin, and Wyoming, as well as the District of Columbia. In some of these jurisdictions, caveats could be added. For example, Georgia distinguishes law and equity for purposes of trial and appellate jurisdiction.

(2) Equity may be administered in the same court as law, but on a different side or in a different division of the court. This was the federal rule prior to September 16, 1938, and is the rule in New Jersey and Cook County, Illinois. Where there are different sides or divisions, statutes usually provide for the easy transfer of cases from law to equity and the reverse. Compare Iowa, where there are unified courts that administer law and equity as "distinct and separate jurisdictions" (in the words of the state constitution).

(3) Equity may be administered in a separate court from law and by a different procedure. This was the English rule prior to 1875, and is still the rule followed in Delaware, Mississippi, and Tennessee.

Outside of institutions and procedure, there remains a significant distinction between law and equity. Some bodies of substantive law were equitable in their origins (*e.g.*, fiduciary law), and these substantive areas have inherited many equitable doctrines and attitudes. In other areas of substantive law, legal rules may expressly incorporate equitable principles (*e.g.*, the Uniform Commercial Code, § 1–103(b)). In all of these areas, lawyers who understand equitable principles have a strategic advantage in litigation over lawyers who do not. In addition, the maxims of equity continue to be relied on by courts to focus their decisionmaking. See, *e.g.*, Roger Young & Stephen Spitz, SUEM—Spitz's Ultimate Equitable Maxim: In Equity, Good Guys Should Win and Bad Guys Should Lose, 55 S.C. L. Rev. 175 (2003). And judicial decisions continue to be shaped by equity precedents.

Most important of all, the distinction between law and equity is still pervasive in remedies. Courts routinely ask whether the remedy the plaintiff seeks is legal or equitable. And a lot can turn on the answer—including who decides the case (judge or jury), what defenses the defendant can raise, and how the plaintiff can enforce the remedy. See Samuel L. Bray, The System of Equitable Remedies, 63 UCLA L. Rev. 530 (2016). Equitable relief historically was, and continues to be, viewed by courts as more discretionary and tailored to the facts than legal relief, although discretion enters into the measurement of damages as well.

In short, despite legislative measures to unify legal and equitable procedure, equity has not disappeared from either the vocabulary of adjudication or the law of remedies. The following two cases are illustrative. The first is an example of a state supreme court invoking equity to prevent one person from opportunistically taking advantage of another. The second is an example of the Supreme Court of the United States defining its equitable powers—specifically its power to give the equitable remedy of a preliminary injunction—in terms of the traditional practice of the English Chancery. Both cases show the continuing significance of equity in American law. Indeed, one could go further. Not only does equity continue to be significant, but the Supreme Court of the

United States and courts in England, Australia, and Canada have shown a resurgent interest in the distinction between law and equity.[x]

Strank v. Mercy Hospital of Johnstown

Supreme Court of Pennsylvania, 1955.
383 Pa. 54.

■ HORACE STERN, CHIEF JUSTICE. . . . The facts are set forth in the opinion of this court on a former appeal. Briefly stated, they are that the defendant institution conducts a school of nursing in conjunction with its hospital, that plaintiff, then a minor, enrolled in the school as a student nurse and paid the expenses incidental thereto, that she successfully completed the work prescribed for the first two years of the course but was dismissed in her third and final year of training because she had broken a rule of the school in remaining away overnight without permission; (she explained the circumstances of this infraction). She does not seek reinstatement as a student in the school but only that defendant give her transfer credits for the work she has completed in order that she may secure advanced standing in some other nursing school; this the defendant has refused to do. Plaintiff brought an action in mandamus to compel defendant to give her the credits; to her complaint defendant filed a preliminary objection raising the question of jurisdiction. We held that a writ of mandamus could not issue to enforce a right or duty which was not imposed by law but rested solely on contract, and therefore that the complaint in mandamus must be dismissed.

Following this decision plaintiff instituted the present proceedings in equity. She filed a complaint, and, after defendant filed preliminary objections thereto, an amended complaint, in which she set forth her oral arrangements with the school at the time she entered, later confirmed in part by writing and carried out by both parties for a period of two years. She alleged that these arrangements and understandings imposed upon defendant the legal duty to give her proper credits for work completed, and that, because of defendant's refusal to do so, she has suffered great damage by loss of time for which she has no adequate remedy at law. Defendant again filed preliminary objections, among them that the court did not have jurisdiction to entertain such an action in equity. . . .

There is not the slightest merit in defendant's contention that the court in equity was without jurisdiction to enter upon these proceedings; indeed the case is one peculiarly for determination by such a court. Under the Acts of June 16, 1836, and February 14, 1857, the courts of common pleas have the jurisdiction and powers of a court of chancery in all cases

[x] On this phenomenon, see J. D. Heydon, M. J. Leeming, & P. G. Turner, MEAGHER, GUMMOW AND LEHANE'S EQUITY: DOCTRINES AND REMEDIES xxi-xxiii (5th ed. 2015); Samuel L. Bray, The Supreme Court and the New Equity, 68 Vand. L. Rev. 997 (2015); Joshua S. Getzler, Patterns of Fusion, in THE CLASSIFICATION OF OBLIGATIONS 157 (Peter Birks ed., 1997). To read more about equity, a good starting point is Henry Smith, Fusing the Equitable Function in Private Law, in PRIVATE LAW IN THE 21ST CENTURY 173 (Kit Barker, Karen Fairweather, & Ross Grantham eds., 2017).

such as those in which they had theretofore possessed jurisdiction and powers under the Constitution and laws of the Commonwealth, and also so far as relates to the affording of specific relief when a recovery in damages would be an inadequate remedy. They have jurisdiction not only for the prevention of acts contrary to law and prejudicial to the rights of individuals, but also for the enforcement of obligations whether arising under express contracts, written or oral, or implied contracts, including those in which a duty may have resulted from long recognized and established customs and usages, as in this case, perhaps, between an educational institution and its students. Moreover, it is the peculiar province of equity to afford relief where the measurement of damages in such cases cannot be formulated and applied in a suit at law because of their being necessarily speculative and indeterminate, and therefore the legal remedy is not adequate and complete. Indeed it might be said that it would be a reproach to our system of jurisprudence if plaintiff should be found entitled to the transfer credits which she seeks, but nevertheless neither law nor equity can furnish her any adequate means of redress. . . .

Grupo Mexicano de Desarrollo, S.A. v. Alliance Bond Fund, Inc.

Supreme Court of the United States, 1999.
527 U.S. 308.

■ JUSTICE SCALIA delivered the opinion of the Court.

This case presents the question whether, in an action for money damages, a United States District Court has the power to issue a preliminary injunction preventing the defendant from transferring assets in which no lien or equitable interest is claimed.

I

Petitioner Grupo Mexicano de Desarrollo, S.A. (GMD), is a Mexican holding company. In February 1994, GMD issued $250 million of 8.25% unsecured, guaranteed notes due in 2001 (Notes), which ranked *pari passu* in priority of payment with all of GMD's other unsecured and unsubordinated debt. Interest payments were due in February and August of every year. Four subsidiaries of GMD (which are the remaining petitioners) guaranteed the Notes. Respondents are investment funds which purchased approximately $75 million of the Notes.

Between 1990 and 1994, GMD was involved in a toll road construction program sponsored by the Government of Mexico. In order to elicit private financing, the Mexican Government granted concessions to companies that would build and operate the system of toll roads. GMD was both an investor in the concessionaries and among the construction companies hired by the concessionaries to build the toll roads. Problems in the Mexican economy resulted in severe losses for the concessionaries, who were therefore unable to pay contractors like GMD. In response to these problems, in 1997, the Mexican Government announced the Toll Road Rescue Program, under which it would issue guaranteed notes (Toll Road Notes) to the concessionaries, in exchange for their ceding to the Government ownership of the toll roads. . . . In the fall of 1997, GMD announced that it expected to receive approximately $309 million of Toll Road Notes under the program.

Because of the downturn in the Mexican economy and the related difficulties in the toll road program, by mid-1997 GMD was in serious financial trouble. . . . As a result of these financial problems, neither GMD nor its subsidiaries (who had guaranteed payment) made the August 1997 interest payment on the Notes.

Between August and December 1997, GMD attempted to negotiate a restructuring of its debt with its creditors. On August 26, Reuters reported that GMD was negotiating with the Mexican banks to reduce its $256 million bank debt, and that it planned to deal with this liability before negotiating with the investors owning the Notes. On October 28, GMD publicly announced that it would place in trust its right to receive $17 million of Toll Road Notes, to cover employee compensation payments, and that it had transferred its right to receive $100 million of Toll Road Notes to the Mexican Government (apparently to pay back taxes). GMD also negotiated with the holders of the Notes (including respondents) to restructure that debt, but by December these negotiations had failed.

On December 11, respondents accelerated the principal amount of their Notes, and, on December 12, filed suit for the amount due in the United States District Court for the Southern District of New York . . . . The complaint alleged that "GMD is at risk of insolvency, if not insolvent already"; that GMD was dissipating its most significant asset, the Toll Road Notes, and was preferring its Mexican creditors by its planned allocation of Toll Road Notes to the payment of their claims . . .; and that these actions would "frustrate any judgement" respondents could obtain. Respondents sought breach-of-contract damages of $80.9 million, and requested a preliminary injunction restraining petitioners from transferring the Toll Road Notes or Receivables. . . .

On December 23, the District Court entered an order in which it found that . . . respondents had demonstrated irreparable injury; and that it was "almost certain" that respondents would succeed on the merits of their claim. It preliminarily enjoined petitioners "from dissipating, disbursing, transferring, conveying, encumbering or otherwise distributing or affecting any [petitioner's] right to, interest in, title to or right to receive or retain, any of the [Toll Road Notes]." . . .

III

We turn, then, to the merits question whether the District Court had authority to issue the preliminary injunction in this case pursuant to Federal Rule of Civil Procedure 65. The Judiciary Act of 1789 conferred on the federal courts jurisdiction over "all suits . . . in equity." We have long held that "[t]he 'jurisdiction' thus conferred . . . is an authority to administer in equity suits the principles of the system of judicial remedies which had been devised and was being administered by the English Court of Chancery at the time of the separation of the two countries." Atlas Life Ins. Co. *v.* W.I. Southern, Inc., 306 U.S. 563, 568 (1939). See also, *e.g.*, Stainback *v.* Mo Hock Ke Lok Po, 336 U.S. 368, 382, n. 26 (1949); Guaranty Trust Co. *v.* York, 326 U.S. 99, 105 (1945); Gordon *v.* Washington, 295 U.S. 30, 36 (1935). "Substantially, then, the equity jurisdiction of the federal courts is the jurisdiction in equity exercised by the High Court of Chancery in England at the time of the adoption of the Constitution and the enactment of the original Judiciary Act, 1789 (1 Stat. 73)." A. Dobie, HANDBOOK OF FEDERAL JURISDICTION AND PROCEDURE 660 (1928). "[T]he substantive prerequisites for obtaining an equitable remedy as well as the general availability of injunctive relief are not altered by [Rule 65] and depend on traditional principles of equity jurisdiction." 11A Charles Alan Wright, Arthur R. Miller, & Mary Kay Kane, FEDERAL PRACTICE AND PROCEDURE § 2941, p. 31 (2d ed. 1995). We must ask, therefore, whether the relief respondents requested here was traditionally accorded by courts of equity. . . .

The United States as *amicus curiae*, however, contends that the preliminary injunction issued in this case is analogous to the relief obtained in the equitable action known as a "creditor's bill." This remedy was used (among other purposes) to permit a judgment creditor to discover the debtor's assets, to reach equitable interests not subject to execution at law, and to set aside fraudulent conveyances. It was well established, however, that, as a general rule, a creditor's bill could be brought only by a creditor who had already obtained a judgment establishing the debt. The rule requiring a judgment was a product, not just of the procedural requirement that remedies at law had to be exhausted before equitable remedies could be pursued, but also of the substantive rule that a general creditor (one without a judgment) had no cognizable interest, either at law or in equity, in the property of his debtor, and therefore could not interfere with the debtor's use of that property. . . .

The United States asserts that there were exceptions to the general rule requiring a judgment. The existence and scope of these exceptions is by no means clear. . . .

Justice Ginsburg concedes that federal equity courts have traditionally rejected the type of provisional relief granted in this case. She invokes, however, "the grand aims of equity," and asserts a general power to grant relief whenever legal remedies are not "practical and efficient," unless there is a statute to the contrary. . . . We do not question the proposition that equity is flexible; but in the federal system, at least, that flexibility is confined within the broad boundaries of traditional equitable relief. To accord a type of relief that has never been available before—and especially (as here) a type of relief that has been specifically disclaimed by longstanding judicial precedent—is to invoke a "default rule," not of flexibility but of omnipotence. When there are indeed new conditions that might call for a wrenching departure from past practice, Congress is in a much better position than we both to perceive them and to design the appropriate remedy. Despite Justice Ginsburg's allusion to the "increasing complexities of modern business relations," and to the bygone "age of slow-moving capital and comparatively immobile wealth," we suspect there is absolutely nothing new about debtors' trying to avoid paying their debts, or seeking to favor some creditors over others—or even about their seeking to achieve these ends through "sophisticated . . . strategies." The law of fraudulent conveyances and bankruptcy was developed to prevent such conduct; an equitable power to restrict a debtor's use of his unencumbered property before judgment was not.

Respondents argue (supported by the United States) that the merger of law and equity changed the rule that a general creditor could not interfere with the debtor's use of his property. But the merger did not alter substantive rights. "Notwithstanding the fusion of law and equity by the Rules of Civil Procedure, the substantive principles of Courts of Chancery remain unaffected." Stainback, *supra*, at 382, n. 26. Even in the absence of historical support, we would not be inclined to believe that it is merely a question of procedure whether a person's unencumbered assets can be frozen by general-creditor claimants before their claims have been vindicated by judgment. It seems to us that question goes to the substantive rights of all property owners. In any event it appears, as we have observed, that the rule requiring a judgment was historically regarded as serving, not merely the procedural end of assuring exhaustion of legal remedies (which the merger of law and equity could render irrelevant), but also the substantive end of giving the creditor an interest in the property which equity could then act upon.

[The Court distinguished two prior cases involving injunctions against asset transfers on the ground that the injunctions in question were either in aid of independent equity jurisdiction or authorized by statute.]

IV

. . . The requirement that the creditor obtain a prior judgment is a fundamental protection in debtor-creditor law—rendered all the more important in our federal system by the debtor's right to a jury trial on the legal claim. . . . [B]y adding, through judicial fiat, a new and powerful weapon to the creditor's arsenal, the new rule could radically alter the balance between debtor's and creditor's rights which has been developed over centuries through many laws—including those relating to bankruptcy, fraudulent conveyances, and preferences. Because any rational creditor would want to protect his investment, such a remedy might induce creditors to engage in a "race to the courthouse" in cases involving insolvent or near-insolvent debtors, which might prove financially fatal to the struggling debtor. (In this case, we might observe, the respondents did not represent all of the holders of the Notes; they were an active few who sought to benefit at the expense of the other noteholders as well as GMD's other creditors.) . . .

We do not decide which side has the better of these arguments. We set them forth only to demonstrate that resolving them in this forum is incompatible with the democratic and self-deprecating judgment we have long since made: that the equitable powers conferred by the Judiciary Act of 1789 did not include the power to create remedies previously unknown to equity jurisprudence. Even when sitting as a court in equity, we have no authority to craft a "nuclear weapon" of the law like the one advocated here. Joseph Story made the point many years ago:

> "If, indeed, a Court of Equity in England did possess the unbounded jurisdiction, which has been thus generally ascribed to it, of correcting, controlling, moderating, and even superceding the law, and of enforcing all the rights, as well as charities, arising from natural law and justice, and of freeing itself from all regard to former rules and precedents, it would be the most gigantic in its sway, and the most formidable instrument of arbitrary power, that could well be devised. It would literally place the whole rights and property of the community under the arbitrary will of the Judge, acting, if you please, *arbitrio boni judicis*, and it may be, *ex aequo et bono*, according to his own notions and conscience; but still acting with a despotic and sovereign authority. A Court of Chancery might then well deserve the spirited rebuke of Seld[e]n; 'For law we have a measure, and know what to trust to—Equity is according to the conscience of him, that is Chancellor; and as that is larger, or narrower, so is Equity. 'T is all one, as if they should make the standard for the measure the Chancellor's foot. What an uncertain measure would this be? One Chancellor has a long foot; another a short foot; a third an indifferent foot. It is the same thing with the Chancellor's conscience.' " 1 COMMENTARIES ON EQUITY JURISPRUDENCE § 19, at 21.

The debate concerning this formidable power over debtors should be conducted and resolved where such issues belong in our democracy: in the Congress.

* * *

Because such a remedy was historically unavailable from a court of equity, we hold that the District Court had no authority to issue a preliminary injunction preventing petitioners from disposing of their assets pending adjudication of respondents' contract claim for money damages. We reverse the judgment of the Second Circuit and remand the case for further proceedings consistent with this opinion. . . .

■ JUSTICE GINSBURG, with whom JUSTICE STEVENS, JUSTICE SOUTER, and JUSTICE BREYER join, concurring in part and dissenting in part.

. . . The Judiciary Act of 1789 gave the lower federal courts jurisdiction over "all suits . . . in equity." We have consistently interpreted this jurisdictional grant to confer on the district courts "authority to administer . . . the principles of the system of judicial remedies which had been devised and was being administered" by the English High Court of Chancery at the time of the founding. Atlas Life Ins. Co. *v.* W.I. Southern, Inc., 306 U.S. 563, 568 (1939).

As I see it, the preliminary injunction ordered by the District Court was consistent with these principles. We long ago recognized that district courts properly exercise their equitable jurisdiction where "the remedy in equity could alone furnish relief, and . . . the ends of justice requir[e] the injunction to be issued." Watson *v.* Sutherland, 5 Wall. 74, 79 (1867). Particularly, district courts enjoy the "historic federal judicial discretion to preserve the situation [through provisional relief] pending the outcome of a case lodged in court." 11A Charles Alan Wright, Arthur R. Miller, & Mary Kay Kane, FEDERAL PRACTICE AND PROCEDURE § 2943, p. 79 (2d ed. 1995). The District Court acted in this case in careful accord with these prescriptions, issuing the preliminary injunction only upon well-supported findings that Alliance had "[no] adequate remedy at law," would be "frustrated" in its ability to recover a judgment absent interim injunctive relief, and was "almost certain" to prevail on the merits.

The Court holds the District Court's preliminary freeze order impermissible principally because injunctions of this kind were not "traditionally accorded by courts of equity" at the time the Constitution was adopted. In my view, the Court relies on an unjustifiably static conception of equity jurisdiction. From the beginning, we have defined the scope of federal equity in relation to the *principles* of equity existing at the separation of this country from England, we have never limited federal equity jurisdiction to the specific practices and remedies of the pre-Revolutionary Chancellor.

Since our earliest cases, we have valued the adaptable character of federal equitable power. We have also recognized that equity must evolve over time, "in order to meet the requirements of every case, and to satisfy the needs of a progressive social condition in which new primary rights and duties are constantly arising and new kinds of wrongs are constantly committed." Union Pacific R. Co. *v.* Chicago, R.I. & P.R. Co., 163 U.S. 564, 601 (1896). A dynamic equity jurisprudence is of special importance in the commercial law context. As we observed more than a century ago: "It must not be forgotten that in the increasing complexities of modern business relations equitable remedies have necessarily and steadily been expanded, and no inflexible rule has been permitted to circumscribe them." *Id.* at 600–601. On this understanding of equity's character, we have upheld diverse injunctions that would have been beyond the contemplation of the 18th-century Chancellor. . . .

I do not question that equity courts traditionally have not issued preliminary injunctions stopping a party sued for an unsecured debt from disposing of assets pending adjudication. . . . But it is one thing to recognize that equity courts typically did not provide this relief, quite another to conclude that, therefore, the remedy was beyond equity's capacity. I would not draw such a conclusion.

Chancery may have refused to issue injunctions of this sort simply because they were not needed to secure a just result in an age of slow-moving capital and comparatively immobile wealth. By turning away cases that the law courts could deal with adequately, the Chancellor acted to reduce the tension inevitable when justice was divided between two discrete systems. But as the facts of this case so plainly show, for creditors situated as Alliance is, the remedy at law is worthless absent the provisional relief in equity's arsenal. Moreover, increasingly sophisticated foreign-haven judgment proofing strategies, coupled with technology that permits the nearly instantaneous transfer of assets abroad, suggests that defendants may succeed in avoiding meritorious claims in ways unimaginable before the merger of law and equity. . . .

Contrary to the Court's suggestion, this case involves no judicial usurpation of Congress' authority. Congress, of course, can instruct the federal courts to issue preliminary injunctions freezing assets pending final judgment, or instruct them not to, and the courts must heed Congress' command. Indeed, Congress has restricted the equity jurisdiction of federal courts in a variety of contexts. See Yakus *v.* United States, 321 U.S. 414, 442, n. 8 (1944) (cataloging statutes regulating federal equity power).

The Legislature, however, has said nothing about preliminary freeze orders. . . . I would find the default rule in the grand aims of equity. Where, as here, legal remedies are not "practical and efficient," Payne *v.* Hook, 7 Wall. 425, 431 (1869), the federal courts must rely on their "flexible jurisdiction in equity . . . to protect all rights and do justice to all concerned," Rubber Co. *v.* Goodyear, 9 Wall. 805, 807 (1870). No countervailing precedent or principle holds the federal courts powerless to prevent a defendant from dissipating assets, to the destruction of a plaintiff's claim, during the course of judicial proceedings. Accordingly, I would affirm the judgment of the Court of Appeals and uphold the District Court's preliminary injunction.

C. THE RIGHT TO TRIAL BY JURY

As indicated in the two cases reprinted in the last section, the state and federal courts continue to distinguish between their legal and equitable powers. For those who want a more complete merger of law and equity, perhaps the greatest obstacle has been the right to jury trial. Professor Zechariah Chafee, Jr., is reported to have said that the guarantee of jury trial "is the sword in the bed that prevents the complete union of law and equity."[xi] These materials consider the right to a jury trial and its entrenchment of the line between law and equity.

Colclasure v. Kansas City Life Ins. Co.

Supreme Court of Arkansas, 1986.
290 Ark. 585.

■ DUDLEY, JUSTICE. The appellee, Kansas City Life Insurance Company, loaned $450,000.00 to appellants. The installment promissory note evidencing the debt was secured by a mortgage on appellants' farm. When appellants defaulted on an annual installment payment, appellee accelerated the maturity date, made demand, and filed suit for foreclosure in chancery court. The appellants answered, and, in addition, filed a complaint in circuit court alleging that the appellee had indicated that a prospective buyer of the farm would be allowed to assume the debt, but then would not permit the assumption. Appellants filed motions to transfer the foreclosure suit to circuit court, to consolidate the cases, and to demand a jury trial. Appellee moved to dismiss the suit in circuit court, or, alternatively, to transfer and consolidate in chancery court. The trial court consolidated the cases in chancery court, with the circuit court complaint being treated as a counterclaim, and denied the demand for a jury trial. . . .

Appellants . . . contend that Article 2, Section 7 of the Constitution of Arkansas and the Arkansas Rules of Civil Procedure guarantee them the right to a trial by jury. The argument is without merit. The constitutional right to a jury trial is limited to those cases which were so triable at common law. A defendant in a mortgage foreclosure proceeding did not have a right to a jury trial at common law. . . .

Foreclosure proceedings are equitable proceedings even though the chancellor may render an in personam judgment in addition to granting foreclosure. This is in line with our continued application of the clean-up doctrine, which allows the equity court, once it has properly acquired jurisdiction, to decide law issues incidental to or essential to the determination of the equitable issues. Appellants do not question that the law issue was incidental to the equitable issue in this case. . . .

Our current constitution was ratified in 1874, and, by that time, our common law was replete with decisions upholding the clean-up doctrine. The constitution was obviously drafted with full knowledge of the clean-up doctrine, and the two are fully compatible.

The appellants next contend that the Seventh Amendment to the Constitution of the United States and Beacon Theatres, Inc. *v.* Westover, 359 U.S. 500 (1959), prevent the application of the clean-up doctrine. . . . Even if [the Seventh Amendment] were held to apply to equity cases where the clean-up doctrine is invoked, [it] would not afford appellants

[xi] Chafee, a former editor of this book, made the remark in an unpublished lecture.

the relief they seek since the Supreme Court of the United States has long recognized that the Seventh Amendment has not been, and should not be, extended to the states through the Fourteenth Amendment. . . .

NOTES

1. At the time of the decision in Colclasure *v.* Kansas City Life Insurance Co., Arkansas still had separate courts of law and equity. The courts were merged procedurally by an amendment to the state constitution, effective in 2001. The merger, however, is unlikely to affect the right to jury trial in a mortgage foreclosure; state courts have often reached the same result, based on the clean-up doctrine, despite a full procedural merger. See, *e.g.*, Anderson *v.* Wooten, 549 So.2d 40, 44 (Ala. 1989).

2. The Seventh Amendment to the United States Constitution provides:

> "In suits at common law, where the value in controversy shall exceed twenty dollars, the right of trial by jury shall be preserved, and no fact tried by jury, shall be otherwise re-examined in any Court of the United States, than according to the rules of the Common Law."

State constitutions typically contain similar provisions; however, state courts are free to read their own constitutions differently than the Supreme Court has read the Seventh Amendment, and they have often done so. State and federal courts have generally agreed that the right to jury trial exists in actions at law but not in actions in equity; the interpretive differences concern what should count as legal and equitable actions in a procedurally merged judicial system. The complications of merger are exacerbated by the assertion of new causes of action, joinder of causes of action, and counterclaims.

3. The analysis applied in *Colclasure*, namely asking how the case before the court would have been tried at the time a given constitutional provision was adopted, is sometimes referred to as the "historical" test of the right to jury trial. Federal courts, applying the Seventh Amendment to United States Constitution, have taken a different approach. The Supreme Court formulated its "dynamic" version of the right to jury trial in a series of decisions beginning in the 1950s. It is called "dynamic" because instead of protecting the jury trial right only in what would have been actions at law in 1791, it is meant to adjust the scope of the right over time, typically expanding its scope as new procedures enlarge the domain of "law." Despite the difference in nomenclature, history plays a significant role in both the "historical" and "dynamic" tests.

In the dynamic approach, the focus is not on "cases" viewed as a whole but rather on individual claims. When a case combines legal and equitable claims, the parties are entitled to a jury trial on any factual question raised by the legal components of the case, and these questions must be tried first to avoid preclusion. See Beacon Theatres, Inc. *v.* Westover, 359 U.S. 500 (1959) (request for declaratory judgment did not eliminate the right to jury trial on underlying antitrust claims); Dairy Queen, Inc. *v.* Wood, 369 U.S.

469 (1962) (request for equitable accounting for trademark infringement did not eliminate the right to jury trial on underlying contract claims); Ross *v.* Bernhard, 396 U.S. 531 (1970) (right to jury trial extends to legal claims asserted in shareholder derivative actions, although the derivative procedure was historically equitable). A prominent example of the dynamic analysis is the next case.

Chauffeurs, Teamsters and Helpers, Local No. 391 v. Terry

Supreme Court of the United States, 1990.
494 U.S. 558.

[The plaintiffs, unionized truck drivers, were transferred to a new location where other drivers, also members of the union, had been laid off. More layoffs led to disputes between the two groups of drivers, which led in turn to proceedings before the union's grievance committee. The grievance committee, interpreting seniority provisions of the governing collective bargaining agreement, ultimately decided against the plaintiffs.

[The plaintiffs then brought an action against the employer for breach of the collective bargaining agreement and against the union for breach of the duty of fair representation. Initially, the plaintiffs sought an injunction requiring the employer to comply with the plaintiffs' interpretation of the seniority rules, reinstatement with seniority, back pay, and damages against the union for lost wages and benefits. After the employer filed a bankruptcy petition, the plaintiffs voluntarily dismissed the action against the employer but continued to pursue their damage claim against the union. They also requested a jury trial.]

■ JUSTICE MARSHALL delivered the opinion of the Court, except as to Part III–A.

This case presents the question whether an employee who seeks relief in the form of backpay for a union's alleged breach of its duty of fair representation has a right to trial by jury. We hold that the Seventh Amendment entitles such a plaintiff to a jury trial. . . .

II

The duty of fair representation is inferred from unions' exclusive authority under the National Labor Relations Act (NLRA) to represent all employees in a bargaining unit. The duty requires a union "to serve the interests of all members without hostility or discrimination toward any, to exercise its discretion with complete good faith and honesty, and to avoid arbitrary conduct." A union must discharge its duty both in bargaining with the employer and in its enforcement of the resulting collective-bargaining agreement. Thus, the Union here was required to pursue respondents' grievances in a manner consistent with the principles of fair representation.

Because most collective-bargaining agreements accord finality to grievance or arbitration procedures established by the collective-bargaining agreement, an employee normally cannot bring a § 301 action against an employer unless he can show that the union breached its duty of fair representation in its handling of his grievance. Whether the employee sues both the labor union and the employer or only one of those entities, he must prove the same two facts to recover money damages: that the employer's action violated the terms of the collective-bargaining agreement and that the union breached its duty of fair representation.

III

We turn now to the constitutional issue presented in this case—whether respondents are entitled to a jury trial. The Seventh Amendment provides that "[i]n Suits at common law, where the value in controversy shall exceed twenty dollars, the right of trial by jury shall be preserved." The right to a jury trial includes more than the common-law forms of action recognized in 1791; the phrase "Suits at common law" refers to "suits in which *legal* rights [are] to be ascertained and determined, in contradistinction to those where equitable rights alone [are] recognized, and equitable remedies [are] administered." Parsons *v.* Bedford, 3 Pet. 433, 447 (1830); see also *ibid.* ("[T]he amendment then may well be construed to embrace all suits which are not of equity and admiralty jurisdiction, whatever may be the peculiar form which they may assume to settle legal rights"). The right extends to causes of action created by Congress. Since the merger of the systems of law and equity, this Court has carefully preserved the right to trial by jury where legal rights are at stake. As the Court noted in Beacon Theatres, Inc. *v.* Westover, 359 U.S. 500, 501 (1959), "Maintenance of the jury as a fact-finding body is of such importance and occupies so firm a place in our history and jurisprudence that any seeming curtailment of the right to a jury trial should be scrutinized with the utmost care."

To determine whether a particular action will resolve legal rights, we examine both the nature of the issues involved and the remedy sought. "First, we compare the statutory action to 18th-century actions brought in the courts of England prior to the merger of the courts of law and equity. Second, we examine the remedy sought and determine whether it is legal or equitable in nature." Tull *v.* United States, 481 U.S. 412, 417–418 (1987). The second inquiry is the more important in our analysis.

A

An action for breach of a union's duty of fair representation was unknown in 18th-century England; in fact, collective bargaining was unlawful. We must therefore look for an analogous cause of action that existed in the 18th century to determine whether the nature of this duty of fair representation suit is legal or equitable.

The Union contends that this duty of fair representation action resembles a suit brought to vacate an arbitration award because respondents seek to set aside the result of the grievance process. In the 18th century, an action to set aside an arbitration award was considered equitable. 2 J. Story, COMMENTARIES ON EQUITY JURISPRUDENCE § 1452, pp. 789–790 (13th ed. 1886) (equity courts had jurisdiction over claims that an award should be set aside on the ground of "mistake of the arbitrators"); see, *e.g.*, Burchell *v.* Marsh, 17 How. 344 (1855) (reviewing bill in equity to vacate an arbitration award). . . .

The arbitration analogy is inapposite, however, to the Seventh Amendment question posed in this case. No grievance committee has considered respondents' claim that the Union violated its duty of fair representation; the grievance process was concerned only with the employer's alleged breach of the collective-bargaining agreement. Thus, respondents' claim against the Union cannot be characterized as an action to vacate an arbitration award . . . .

The Union next argues that respondents' duty of fair representation action is comparable to an action by a trust beneficiary against a trustee for breach of fiduciary duty. Such actions were within the exclusive jurisdiction of courts of equity. 2 Story, *supra*, § 960, p. 266. This analogy is far more persuasive than the arbitration analogy. Just as a trustee must act in the best interests of the beneficiaries, a union, as the exclusive representative of the workers, must exercise its power to act on behalf of the employees in good faith. Moreover, just as a beneficiary does not directly control the actions of a trustee, an individual employee lacks direct control over a union's actions taken on his behalf.

The trust analogy extends to a union's handling of grievances. In most cases, a trustee has the exclusive authority to sue third parties who injure the beneficiaries' interest in the trust, including any legal claim the trustee holds in trust for the beneficiaries. The trustee then has the sole responsibility for determining whether to settle, arbitrate, or otherwise dispose of the claim. Similarly, the union typically has broad discretion in its decision whether and how to pursue an employee's grievance against an employer. Just as a trust beneficiary can sue to enforce a contract entered into on his behalf by the trustee only if the trustee "improperly refuses or neglects to bring an action against the third person," Restatement (Second) of Trusts, § 282(2) (1959), so an employee can sue his employer for a breach of the collective-bargaining agreement only if he shows that the union breached its duty of fair representation in its handling of the grievance.

Respondents contend that their duty of fair representation suit is less like a trust action than an attorney malpractice action, which was historically an action at law. . . .

The attorney malpractice analogy is inadequate in several respects. Although an attorney malpractice suit is in some ways similar to a suit alleging a union's breach of its fiduciary duty, the two actions are fundamentally different. The nature of an action is in large part controlled by the nature of the underlying relationship between the parties. Unlike employees represented by a union, a client controls the significant decisions concerning his representation. Moreover, a client can fire his attorney if he is dissatisfied with his attorney's performance. This option is not available to an individual employee who is unhappy with a union's representation, unless a majority of the members of the bargaining unit share his dissatisfaction. Thus, we find the malpractice analogy less convincing than the trust analogy.

Nevertheless, the trust analogy does not persuade us to characterize respondents' claim as wholly equitable. The Union's argument mischaracterizes the nature of our comparison of the action before us to 18th-century forms of action. As we observed in Ross *v.* Bernhard, 396 U.S. 531 (1970), "The Seventh Amendment question depends on the nature of the *issue* to be tried rather than the character of the overall action." As discussed above, to recover from the Union here, respondents must prove both that McLean [breached] the collective-bargaining agreement and that the Union breached its duty of fair representation.[6] When viewed in isolation, the duty of fair representation issue is analogous to a claim against a trustee for breach of fiduciary duty. The § 301 issue, however, is comparable to a breach of contract claim—a legal issue.

Respondents' action against the Union thus encompasses both equitable and legal issues. The first part of our Seventh Amendment inquiry, then, leaves us in equipoise as to whether respondents are entitled to a jury trial.

B

Our determination under the first part of the Seventh Amendment analysis is only preliminary. In this case, the only remedy sought is a request for compensatory damages representing backpay and benefits. Generally, an action for money damages was "the traditional form of relief offered in the courts of law." Curtis *v.* Loether, 415 U.S. 189, 196 (1974). . . . [T]he remedy respondents seek has none of the attributes that must be present before we will find an exception to the general rule and characterize damages as equitable, we find that the remedy sought by respondents is legal.

---

[6] The dissent characterizes this opinion as "pars[ing] legal elements out of equitable claims." The question whether the Seventh Amendment analysis requires an examination of the nature of each element of a typical claim is not presented by this case. The claim we confront here is not typical; instead, it is a claim consisting of discrete issues that would normally be brought as two claims, one against the employer and one against the union. Had the employer remained a defendant in this action, the dissent would surely agree that the . . . claim against the employer was a separate claim. The Seventh Amendment analysis should not turn on the ability of the plaintiff to maintain his suit against both defendants, when the issues in the suit remain the same even when he can sue only the union. Consideration of the nature of the two issues in this hybrid action is therefore warranted.

First, we have characterized damages as equitable where they are restitutionary, such as in "action[s] for disgorgement of improper profits." Tull, *supra*, at 424. The backpay sought by respondents is not money wrongfully held by the Union, but wages and benefits they would have received from McLean had the Union processed the employees' grievances properly. Such relief is not restitutionary.

Second, a monetary award "incidental to or intertwined with injunctive relief" may be equitable. *Ibid.* Because respondents seek only money damages, this characteristic is clearly absent from the case.[8]

The Union argues that the backpay relief sought here must nonetheless be considered equitable because this Court has labeled backpay awarded under Title VII of the Civil Rights Act as equitable. . . .

Assuming, without deciding, that such a Title VII plaintiff has no right to a jury trial, the Union's argument does not persuade us that respondents are not entitled to a jury trial here. Congress specifically characterized backpay under Title VII as a form of "equitable relief." Congress made no similar pronouncement regarding the duty of fair representation. Furthermore, the Court has noted that backpay sought from an employer under Title VII would generally be restitutionary in nature, in contrast to the damages sought here from the Union. Thus, the remedy sought in this duty of fair representation case is clearly different from backpay sought for violations of Title VII. . . .

We hold, then, that the remedy of backpay sought in this duty of fair representation action is legal in nature. Considering both parts of the Seventh Amendment inquiry, we find that respondents are entitled to a jury trial on all issues presented in their suit.

IV

On balance, our analysis of the nature of respondents' duty of fair representation action and the remedy they seek convinces us that this action is a legal one. Although the search for an adequate 18th-century analog revealed that the claim includes both legal and equitable issues, the money damages respondents seek are the type of relief traditionally awarded by courts of law. Thus, the Seventh Amendment entitles

---

[8] Both the Union and the dissent argue that the backpay award sought here is equitable because it is closely analogous to damages awarded to beneficiaries for a trustee's breach of trust. Such damages were available only in courts of equity because those courts had exclusive jurisdiction over actions involving a trustee's breach of his fiduciary duties.

The Union's argument, however, conflates the two parts of our Seventh Amendment inquiry. Under the dissent's approach, if the action at issue were analogous to an 18th-century action within the exclusive jurisdiction of the courts of equity, we would necessarily conclude that the remedy sought was also equitable because it would have been unavailable in a court of law. This view would, in effect, make the first part of our inquiry dispositive. We have clearly held, however, that the second part of the inquiry—the nature of the relief—is more important to the Seventh Amendment determination. The second part of the analysis, therefore, should not replicate the "abstruse historical" inquiry of the first part, Ross, *supra*, at 538, n. 10, but requires consideration of the general types of relief provided by courts of law and equity.

respondents to a jury trial, and we therefore affirm the judgment of the Court of Appeals. . . .

■ JUSTICE BRENNAN, concurring in part and concurring in the judgment.

I agree with the Court that respondents seek a remedy that is legal in nature and that the Seventh Amendment entitles respondents to a jury trial on their duty of fair representation claims. . . . I do not join that part of the opinion which reprises the particular historical analysis this Court has employed to determine whether a claim is a "Sui[t] at common law" under the Seventh Amendment, because I believe the historical test can and should be simplified.

The current test, first expounded in Curtis *v.* Loether, requires a court to compare the right at issue to 18th-century English forms of action to determine whether the historically analogous right was vindicated in an action at law or in equity, and to examine whether the remedy sought is legal or equitable in nature. However, this Court, in expounding the test, has repeatedly discounted the significance of the analogous form of action for deciding where the Seventh Amendment applies. I think it is time we dispense with it altogether. I would decide Seventh Amendment questions on the basis of the relief sought. If the relief is legal in nature, *i.e.*, if it is the kind of relief that historically was available from courts of law, I would hold that the parties have a constitutional right to a trial by jury—unless Congress has permissibly delegated the particular dispute to a non-Article III decisionmaker and jury trials would frustrate Congress' purposes in enacting a particular statutory scheme.

I believe that our insistence that the jury trial right hinges in part on a comparison of the substantive right at issue to forms of action used in English courts 200 years ago needlessly convolutes our Seventh Amendment jurisprudence. For the past decade and a half, this Court has explained that the two parts of the historical test are not equal in weight, that the nature of the remedy is more important than the nature of the right. . . . The time has come to borrow William of Occam's razor and sever this portion of our analysis. . . .

Requiring judges, with neither the training nor time necessary for reputable historical scholarship, to root through the tangle of primary and secondary sources to determine which of a hundred or so writs is analogous to the right at issue has embroiled courts in recondite controversies better left to legal historians. . . .

In addition, modern statutory rights did not exist in the 18th century, and even the most exacting historical research may not elicit a clear historical analog. The right at issue here, for example, is a creature of modern labor law quite foreign to Georgian England. . . .

To rest the historical test required by the Seventh Amendment solely on the nature of the relief sought would not, of course, offer the federal courts a rule that is in all cases self-executing. Courts will still be required to ask which remedies were traditionally available at law and which only in equity. But this inquiry involves fewer variables and simpler choices, on the whole, and is far more manageable than the scholasticist debates in which we have been engaged. Moreover, the rule I propose would remain true to the Seventh Amendment, as it is undisputed that, historically, "[j]urisdictional lines [between law and equity] were primarily a matter of remedy." McCoid, Procedural Reform and the Right to Jury Trial: A Study of Beacon Theaters, Inc. *v.* Westover, 116 U. Pa. L. Rev. 1 (1967). See also Redish, Seventh Amendment Right to Jury Trial: A Study in the Irrationality of Rational Decision Making, 70 Nw. U. L. Rev. 486, 490 (1975) ("In the majority of cases at common law, the equitable or legal nature of a suit was determined not by the substantive nature of the cause of action but by the remedy sought").[7] . . .

We can guard this right and save our courts from needless and intractable excursions into increasingly unfamiliar territory simply by retiring that prong of our Seventh Amendment test which we have already cast into a certain doubt. . . .

■ [The opinion of JUSTICE STEVENS, concurring in part and concurring in the judgment, is omitted.]

■ JUSTICE KENNEDY, with whom JUSTICE O'CONNOR and JUSTICE SCALIA join, dissenting.

This case asks whether the Seventh Amendment guarantees the respondent union members a jury trial in a duty of fair representation action against their labor union. The Court is quite correct, in my view, in its formulation of the initial premises that must govern the case. Under Curtis *v.* Loether, 415 U.S. 189, 194 (1974), the right to a jury trial in a statutory action depends on the presence of "legal rights and remedies." To determine whether rights and remedies in a duty of fair representation action are legal in character, we must compare the action

---

[7] There are, to be sure, some who advocate abolishing the historical test altogether. Contrary to the intimations in JUSTICE KENNEDY'S dissent, I am not among them. I believe that it is imperative to retain a historical test for determining when parties have a right to jury trial for precisely the same reasons JUSTICE KENNEDY does. It is mandated by the language of the Seventh Amendment and it is a bulwark against those who would restrict a right our forefathers held indispensable. Like JUSTICE KENNEDY, I have no doubt that courts can and do look to legal history for the answers to constitutional questions, and therefore the Seventh Amendment test I propose today obliges courts to do exactly that.

Where JUSTICE KENNEDY and I differ is in our evaluations of which historical test provides the more reliable results. That three learned Justices of the Supreme Court cannot arrive at the same conclusion in this very case, on what is essentially a question of fact, does not speak well for the judicial solvency of the current test. My concern is not merely the competence of courts to delve into this peculiarly recalcitrant aspect of legal history and certainly not, as JUSTICE KENNEDY summarizes it, the "competence of the Court to understand legal history" in general. My concern is that all too often the first prong of the current test requires courts to measure modern statutory actions against 18th-century English actions so remote in form and concept that there is no firm basis for comparison. In such cases, the result is less the discovery of a historical analog than the manufacture of a historical fiction. By contrast, the nature of relief available today corresponds more directly to the nature of relief available in Georgian England. Thus the historical test I propose, focusing on the nature of the relief sought, is not only more manageable than the current test, it is more reliably grounded in history. JUSTICE KENNEDY JUSTICE KENNEDY

to the 18th-century cases permitted in the law courts of England, and we must examine the nature of the relief sought. I agree also with those Members of the Court who find that the duty of fair representation action resembles an equitable trust action more than a suit for malpractice.

I disagree with the analytic innovation of the Court that identification of the trust action as a model for modern duty of fair representation actions is insufficient to decide the case. The Seventh Amendment requires us to determine whether the duty of fair representation action "is more similar to cases that were tried in courts of law than to suits tried in courts of equity." Tull *v.* United States, 481 U.S. 412, 417 (1987). Having made this decision in favor of an equitable action, our inquiry should end. . . .

I

. . . JUSTICE MARSHALL, speaking for four Members of the Court, states an important and correct reason for finding the trust model better than the malpractice analogy. He observes that the client of an attorney, unlike a union member or beneficiary, controls the significant decisions concerning his litigation and can fire the attorney if not satisfied. Put another way, although a lawyer acts as an agent of his client, unions and trustees do not serve as agents of their members and beneficiaries in the conventional sense of being subject to their direction and control in pursuing claims. An individual union member cannot require his union to pursue a claim and cannot choose a different representative. A trustee, likewise, may exercise proper discretion in deciding whether to press claims held in trust, and in general does not act as an agent of his beneficiaries, see Taylor *v.* Davis, 110 U.S. 330, 334–335 (1884) ("A trustee is not an agent. An agent represents and acts for his principal. . . . [A trustee] has no principal"); 1 A. Scott, LAW OF TRUSTS § 8, pp. 74–79 (3d ed. 1967) (distinguishing trustees from agents). . . .

The relief available in a duty of fair representation action also makes the trust action the better model. . . . The court may order an injunction compelling the union, if it is still able, to pursue the employee's claim, and may require monetary compensation, but it cannot award exemplary or punitive damages. This relief parallels the remedies prevailing in the courts of equity in actions against trustees for failing to pursue claims. . . .

These remedies differ somewhat from those available in attorney malpractice actions. Because legal malpractice was a common-law claim, clients sued their attorneys for breach of professional obligations in the law courts. No one maintains that clients could obtain from these courts the injunctive relief offered in duty of fair representation actions. . . . Although the parties have not cited any punitive damages award in an attorney malpractice action prior to 1791, courts have awarded such damages since the 19th century. . . .

II

The Court relies on two lines of precedents to overcome the conclusion that the trust action should serve as the controlling model. The first consists of cases in which the Court has considered simplifications in litigation resulting from modern procedural reforms in the federal courts. JUSTICE MARSHALL asserts that these cases show that the Court must look at the character of individual issues rather than claims as a whole. The second line addresses the significance of the remedy in determining the equitable or legal nature of an action for the purpose of choosing the most appropriate analogy. . . . Under these cases, the Court decides that the respondents have a right to a jury because they seek money damages. These authorities do not support the Court's holding.

A

In three cases we have found a right to trial by jury where there are legal claims that, for procedural reasons, a plaintiff could have or must have raised in the courts of equity before the systems merged. In Beacon Theatres, Inc. *v.* Westover, 359 U.S. 500 (1959), Fox, a potential defendant threatened with legal antitrust claims, brought an action for declaratory and injunctive relief against Beacon, the likely plaintiff. Because only the courts of equity had offered such relief prior to the merger of the two court systems, Fox had thought that it could deprive Beacon of a jury trial. Beacon, however, raised the antitrust issues as counterclaims and sought a jury. We ruled that, because Beacon would have had a right to a jury trial on its antitrust claims, Fox could not deprive it of a jury merely by taking advantage of modern declaratory procedures to sue first. . . .

In Dairy Queen, Inc. *v.* Wood, 369 U.S. 469 (1962), we held, in a similar manner, that a plaintiff, by asking in his complaint for an equitable accounting for trademark infringement, could not deprive the defendant of a jury trial on contract claims subsumed within the accounting. Although a court of equity would have heard the contract claims as part of the accounting suit, we found them severable under modern procedure.

In Ross *v.* Bernhard, 396 U.S. 531 (1970), a shareholder-plaintiff demanded a jury trial in a derivative action asserting a legal claim on behalf of his corporation. The defendant opposed a jury trial. In deciding the case, we recognized that only the courts of equity had procedural devices allowing shareholders to raise a corporation's claims. We nonetheless again ruled that modern procedure allowed trial of the legal claim to a jury.

These three cases responded to the difficulties created by a merged court system. They stand for the proposition that, because distinct courts of equity no longer exist, the possibility or necessity of using former equitable procedures to press a legal claim no longer will determine the right to a jury. JUSTICE MARSHALL reads these cases to require a jury trial whenever a cause of action contains legal issues and would require a jury trial in this case because the respondents must prove a breach of the collective-bargaining agreement as one element of their claim.

I disagree. The respondents, as shown above, are asserting an equitable claim. Having reached this conclusion, the *Beacon*, *Dairy Queen*, and *Ross* cases are inapplicable. Although we have divided self-standing legal claims from equitable declaratory, accounting, and derivative procedures, we have never parsed legal elements out of equitable claims absent specific procedural justifications. Actions which, beyond all question, are equitable in nature may involve some predicate inquiry that would be submitted to a jury in other contexts. For example, just as the plaintiff in a duty of fair representation action against his union must show breach of the collective-bargaining agreement as an initial matter, in an action against a trustee for failing to pursue a claim the beneficiary must show that the claim had some merit. But the question of the claim's validity, even if the claim raises contract issues, would not bring the jury right into play in a suit against a trustee. . . .

B

The Court also rules that, despite the appropriateness of the trust analogy as a whole, the respondents have a right to a jury trial because they seek money damages. The nature of the remedy remains a factor of considerable importance in determining whether a statutory action had a legal or equitable analog in 1791, but we have not adopted a rule that a statutory action permitting damages is by definition more analogous to a legal action than to any equitable suit. In each case, we look to the remedy to determine whether, taken with other factors, it places an action within the definition of "Suits at common law." . . .

III

The Court must adhere to the historical test in determining the right to a jury because the language of the Constitution requires it. The Seventh Amendment "preserves" the right to jury trial in civil cases. We cannot preserve a right existing in 1791 unless we look to history to identify it. Our precedents are in full agreement with this reasoning and insist on adherence to the historical test. No alternatives short of rewriting the Constitution exist. See F. James, CIVIL PROCEDURE § 8.5, p. 352 (1965) ("For good or evil, both the constitutio[n] and the charters of the merged procedure embody the policy judgment, quite deliberately made, to leave the extent of jury trial about where history had come to place it"); Shapiro & Coquillette, The Fetish of Jury Trial in Civil Cases: A Comment on Rachal *v.* Hill, 85 Harv. L. Rev. 442, 449 (1971) ("Even the most ardent critic of any historical test would concede that matters that would have fallen entirely within the jurisdiction of a court of equity or admiralty in 1791 do not come within the definition of a suit at 'common law' under the seventh amendment"). If we abandon the plain language of the Constitution to expand the jury right, we may expect Courts with opposing views to curtail it in the future.

It is true that a historical inquiry into the distinction between law and equity may require us to enter into a domain becoming less familiar with time. Two centuries have passed since the Seventh Amendment's ratification, and the incompleteness of our historical records makes it difficult to know the nature of certain actions in 1791. The historical test, nonetheless, has received more criticism than it deserves. Although our application of the analysis in some cases may seem biased in favor of jury trials, the test has not become a nullity. We do not require juries in all statutory actions. The historical test, in fact, resolves most cases without difficulty.

I would hesitate to abandon or curtail the historical test out of concern for the competence of the Court to understand legal history. We do look to history for the answers to constitutional questions. Although opinions will differ on what this history shows, the approach has no less validity in the Seventh Amendment context than elsewhere.

If Congress has not provided for a jury trial, we are confined to the Seventh Amendment to determine whether one is required. Our own views respecting the wisdom of using a jury should be put aside. Like JUSTICE BRENNAN, I admire the jury process. Other judges have taken the opposite view. But the judgment of our own times is not always preferable to the lessons of history. Our whole constitutional experience teaches that history must inform the judicial inquiry. Our obligation to the Constitution and its Bill of Rights, no less than the compact we have with the generation that wrote them for us, do not permit us to disregard provisions that some may think to be mere matters of historical form. . . .

Marseilles Hydro Power, LLC v. Marseilles Land and Water Co.

United States Court of Appeals, Seventh Circuit, 2002.
299 F.3d 643.

■ POSNER, CIRCUIT JUDGE. The plaintiff ("the power company") owns a disused hydroelectric plant built in 1912. When functional the plant was powered by water from a canal, owned by the defendant ("the canal company"), that connects the plant to the Illinois River. A contract between the parties' predecessors required the owner of the plant to pay rent to the owner of the canal and required the latter to keep the canal in good repair. The requirement had no practical significance when the plant was not being used. But the current owner of the plant, that is, the power company, decided to put the plant back into service and so it became concerned about the state of the canal and in particular feared that the canal's wall was about to collapse. The canal company refused to repair it, and so the power company brought this suit to enforce the canal company's duty under the contract and moved for a preliminary injunction; but before the motion could be heard, the canal wall collapsed. The canal company counterclaimed for the rent due under the contract, rent that the power company refused to pay until the canal was repaired. After a bench trial, the judge awarded judgment for the power company both on its complaint and on the canal company's counterclaim. The judgment seems (the reason for this hedge will appear momentarily) to include an order injunctive in character that entitles the power company to enter upon the canal company's property for the purpose of repairing the canal wall and to obtain a lien on the property for the cost of the repair. . . .

[T]he canal company's principal argument, and the only one we strictly need to consider, is that it was entitled to a jury trial. Rule 38(b) of the civil rules gives a party only ten days "after the service of the last pleading directed to the issue" (that is, "any issue triable of right by a jury," *id.*) to demand a jury trial on that issue. The canal company filed its demand within ten days after serving on the power company its counterclaim demanding payment of the rent specified in the contract for the use of the canal, which the power company had decided to withhold until the canal was repaired. The district judge thought the demand had come too late, because the rent issue was clearly flagged in the power company's complaint; part of the declaratory judgment sought was a declaration that the power company owed no rent until the canal was back in working order.

The power company and the judge were confused by the word "issue" in Rule 38(b). They think it means that if an issue *could* give rise to a claim for damages, either party can demand that it be tried to a jury. That is not correct. If the only relief sought is equitable, such as an injunction or specific performance (a type of affirmative injunction), neither the party seeking that relief nor the party opposing it is entitled to a jury trial. Rule 38(a), so far as applicable to this case, creates a right to a jury trial merely coextensive with the Seventh Amendment, which in turn confines that right to "Suits at common law." A suit seeking only equitable relief is not a suit at common law, regardless of the nature of the issues likely or even certain to arise in the case, most of which indeed might be legal, such as whether the canal company broke its contract with the power company, an issue normally determined by the common law of contracts rather than by some principle of equity jurisprudence.

We state this proposition (that a suit for equitable relief is not a suit at common law regardless of the nature of the issues in the case) with confidence though mindful of the statement in Chauffeurs, Teamsters & Helpers Local No. 391 *v.* Terry, 494 U.S. 558, 565 (1990) (a plurality opinion, but the statement in question was agreed to by a majority of the Justices), that "to determine whether a particular action will resolve legal rights, and therefore give rise to a jury trial right, we examine both the nature of the issues involved and the remedy sought. First, we compare the statutory action to 18th-century actions brought in the courts of England prior to the merger of the courts of law and equity. Second, we examine the remedy sought and determine whether it is legal or equitable in nature. The second inquiry is the more important in our analysis." This formula for guiding the Seventh Amendment inquiry has been repeated frequently by lower courts . . . . But the historical inquiry, and the criticism of it, are not about unsettling the principle that there is no right to a jury trial when the plaintiff is seeking only equitable relief; that principle is firm; the inquiry is to determine whether a modern *legal* right has a sufficient analogy to a right enforced by common law courts in the eighteenth century to be enforceable by "a suit at common law" within the meaning of the Seventh Amendment.

The complaint in this case sought an injunction against the canal company's preventing the power company from going on the canal company's land to repair the canal at the latter's expense, as well as specific performance (the granting of a lien), also a form of equitable relief. If that were all, then, as if we have just seen, it would be clear that there was no right to a jury trial. But declaratory relief was also sought. Despite the equitable origins of such relief, the Supreme Court has said that actions for declaratory judgments are "neither legal nor equitable." (So much for the historical test for Seventh Amendment rights.) Rule 57 of the civil rules provides that "the procedure for obtaining a declaratory judgment pursuant to [the Declaratory Judgment Act, 28 U.S.C. § 2201] shall be in accordance with these rules, and the right to trial by jury may be demanded under the circumstances and in the manner provided in Rules 38 and 39." In other words, casting one's suit in the form of a suit for a declaratory judgment, or adding a claim for a declaratory judgment to one's other claim or claims for relief, does not create a right to a jury trial. Rather, as the Third Circuit put it nicely in Owens-Illinois, Inc. *v.* Lake Shore Land Co., 610 F.2d 1185, 1189 (3d Cir. 1979), "If the declaratory judgment action does not fit into one of the existing equitable patterns but is essentially an inverted law suit—an action brought by one who would have been a defendant at common law—then the parties have a right to a jury. But if the action is the counterpart of a suit in equity, there is no such right." We prefer the formulation that we just quoted from *Owens-Illinois* to that in Petition of Rosenman & Colin, 850 F.2d 57, 60 (2d Cir. 1988): "the nature of the underlying dispute determines whether a jury trial is available." The "nature of the underlying dispute" here is breach of contract, but a plaintiff who is seeking equitable relief and not damages cannot wrest an entitlement to a jury trial by the facile expedient of attaching a claim for declaratory judgment. Otherwise anyone seeking an injunction could obtain a jury trial.

So neither the power company nor the canal company had a right to demand a jury trial on the basis of the complaint. Any such right would have had to arise later. It did arise later; it arose when the canal company counterclaimed for the withheld rent. Founded on an alleged breach of contract by the power company, the counterclaim was a claim for damages and hence—despite its being a counterclaim rather than a free-standing lawsuit, since a counterclaim *is* a suit, only joined for economy with an existing suit—it was a suit at common law within the meaning of the Seventh Amendment. The canal company's demand for a jury, filed within ten days after the counterclaim, was the earliest either party could have demanded a jury trial. At that point the fact that there was a common issue underlying both the equitable and the legal claims, namely the duty if any of the power company to pay rent, and under that issue perhaps the deeper issue of which party had actually broken the contract, became significant. Common issues, if triable at all in the sense that their resolution requires resolving a material dispute of fact, as was the case here, must be tried to a jury in order to prevent a judge's determination from foreclosing a party's right to have the issues in a common law suit tried by a jury. Dairy Queen, Inc. *v.* Wood, 369 U.S. 469, 472–73, 479 (1962). So the demand for a jury trial was timely and its rejection error; and until the jury trial to which the canal company is entitled is completed issuance of an injunction is premature. . . .

FURTHER NOTES ON THE SEVENTH AMENDMENT RIGHT TO A JURY TRIAL

1. The Supreme Court has held that the Seventh Amendment is inapplicable in administrative proceedings, as long as the rights at stake are "public" rights rather than traditional tort or contract rights of private parties. See Curtis *v.* Loether, 415 U.S. 189 (1974); Atlas Roofing Co. *v.* Occupational Safety and Health Review Commission, 430 U.S. 442 (1977).

2. Parties that are within the equitable jurisdiction of a bankruptcy court generally do not have a right to a jury trial. Langenkamp *v.* Culp, 498 U.S. 42 (1990). But cf. Granfinanciera, S.A. *v.* Nordberg, 492 U.S. 33 (1989) (holding that a non-party to a bankruptcy proceeding, in receipt of a fraudulent or preferential transfer from the debtor, is entitled to a jury trial).

3. Section 504(c) of the Copyright Act permits a copyright owner "to recover, instead of actual damages and profits, an award of statutory damages, in a sum of not less than $500 or more than $20,000 as the court considers just." The Supreme Court deemed the statute to be silent on the question of jury trial, and held that the Seventh Amendment provides a right to a jury determination of the amount of statutory damages:

> "The Seventh Amendment provides that '[i]n Suits at common law, where the value in controversy shall exceed twenty dollars, the right of trial by jury shall be preserved. . . .' . . . The Seventh Amendment . . . applies not only to common-law causes of action, but also to 'actions brought to enforce statutory rights that are analogous to common-law causes of action ordinarily decided in English law courts in the late 18th century, as opposed to those customarily heard by courts of equity or admiralty.' To determine whether a statutory action is more analogous to cases tried in courts of law than to suits tried in courts of equity or admiralty, we

examine both the nature of the statutory action and the remedy sought."

Feltner *v.* Columbia Pictures Television, Inc., 523 U.S. 340, 347–48 (1998).

4. Takings claims seeking relief in the form of money damages under the Fifth and Fourteenth Amendments carry a right to a jury trial. City of Monterey *v.* Del Monte Dunes, Ltd., 526 U.S. 687 (1999) (plurality opinion). Damages are not, however, the only remedies available for suits under the Takings Clause. See generally Thomas W. Merrill, Anticipatory Remedies for Takings, 128 Harv. L. Rev. 1630 (2015).

5. Restitutionary remedies allow a recovery measured by the defendant's gain, not the plaintiff's loss. Whether there is a right to a jury trial depends on whether the plaintiff has a legal claim (*e.g.*, quasi-contract) or seeks an equitable remedy (*e.g.*, accounting for profits, constructive trust, equitable lien). See, *e.g.*, Fischer Imaging Corp. v. General Electric Co., 187 F.3d 1165, 1172–73 (10th Cir. 1999) (reversing and remanding for a new trial because the district court struck the plaintiff's demand for a jury trial in a statutory action analogous to quasi-contract). For discussion of how to distinguish legal and equitable restitution, see Chapter Thirteen, Section A (Restitution: Legal and Equitable).

CHAPTER 6

EQUITABLE POWERS AND LIMITING PRINCIPLES

A. ENFORCEMENT OF EQUITABLE DECREES

1. THE DUTY TO OBEY

The Cape May and Schellinger's Landing Railroad Co. v. Johnson

Court of Chancery of New Jersey, 1882.
35 N.J. Eq. 422.

■ VAN FLEET, V.C. The defendants are before the court on a charge of contempt. On the 20th day of June, 1881, an order was made directing the city council of the city of Cape May to desist and refrain from passing a certain ordinance, and also to show cause, at a subsequent day, why an injunction should not issue restraining the same act. The order was granted at Newark about midday on the day of its date. The council, it was understood, were to meet on the evening of the same day for the purpose of doing the act which the order was intended to restrain. The distance between the point where the order was made and the point where the defendants were to meet, rendered an actual service of the order impossible before the next day. Notice of the fact that an order had been made prohibiting the passage of the ordinance was sent to the president of the council by telegraph, which he received before the council convened on the evening of the 20th, and afterwards read to the council in open meeting. A special messenger, sent by the complainants, gave the council the same notice while they were in session on the evening of the 20th. The council the next day (June 21st) passed the ordinance.

The facts just stated are undisputed. They show that the defendants are guilty. The regularity, validity or correctness of the order contemned cannot be examined on this proceeding. While an order of a court remains in force it must be obeyed. Even if it was improvidently granted or irregularly obtained, it must nevertheless be respected until it is annulled by the proper authority. The rule upon this subject has been laid down with great clearness and force by Lord Truro. He says: "It is an established rule of this court that it is not open to any party to question the orders of this court, or any process issued under the authority of this court, by disobedience. I know of no act which this court may do which may not be questioned in a proper form and on a proper application; but I am of opinion that it is not competent for any one . . . to disobey an injunction, or any other order of the court, on the ground that such orders were made improvidently. Parties must take a proper course to question their validity, but while they exist they must be obeyed. I consider the rule to be of such importance to the interests and safety of the public, and to the due administration of justice, that it ought on all occasions to be inflexibly maintained." . . .

The notice that the defendants had of the order, at the time they violated the command, was, according to the authorities, entirely sufficient. Where the charge is that the defendant has willfully contemned the authority of the court, all that need be shown is that he knew of the existence of the order at the time he violated it. Lord Eldon held that if a defendant is in court when an injunction is granted, he has sufficient notice of it to make it his duty to respect it. He also held that if the defendant is not in court when an order for an injunction is made, but is informed that such an order has been made, by a person who was in court when the order was made, he has sufficient notice of the injunction to render him liable to punishment for its breach. . . .

Notice, to be sufficient, need possess but two requisites—first, it must proceed from a source entitled to credit; and second, it must inform the defendant clearly and plainly from what act he must abstain. The notice in the case under consideration possessed both requisites. It was sent by the counsel who obtained the order, and it not only informed the defendants what act the order prohibited, but warned them, if they disregarded the order, their disobedience would be a contempt of the authority of the court. There is nothing in the conduct of the defendants indicating that they had the least doubt concerning the authenticity of the notice or the truth of its contents. They made no inquiry respecting its authenticity or its truth, but say that they consulted counsel whether or not they could safely disregard it, and were advised that they could. This advice, to say the least of it, was both injudicious and dangerous. It affords the defendants neither justification nor palliation. They must be adjudged guilty of contempt.

The complainants, since the proceeding for contempt was instituted, have voluntarily brought the order to show cause why an injunction should not issue to hearing, and it has been decided against them. While the fact that the order contemned was improvidently or erroneously made, neither justifies nor excuses the defendants, it is a matter which it is proper the court should consider in awarding punishment.

Each of the six defendants must pay to the clerk, for the use of the state, a fine of $10, and they must also jointly pay the taxed costs of this proceeding.

United States v. United Mine Workers of America

Supreme Court of the United States, 1947.
330 U.S. 258.

■ MR. CHIEF JUSTICE VINSON delivered the opinion of the Court.

In October, 1946, the United States was in possession of, and operating, the major portion of the country's bituminous coal mines.[1] [The United Mine Workers and the Secretary of the Interior had negotiated a labor agreement. The UMW claimed, and attempted to exercise, authority to terminate the agreement unilaterally. The Secretary argued that the union had no such authority, and obtained a temporary restraining order from a federal district court, prohibiting the union from organizing a strike. The mine workers nevertheless commenced a general strike, and the U.S. moved for an order to show cause why the union should not be punished for contempt. The defendants responded that the Norris-La Guardia Act, which limited the power of federal courts to enjoin strikes, prohibited the court from entering the restraining order. The district court determined that the Norris-LaGuardia Act did not apply, extended the restraining order, and fined the union and its president $3.5 million and $10,000, respectively, for criminal and civil contempt.]

Defendants' first and principal contention is that the restraining order and preliminary injunction were issued in violation of the Clayton and Norris-LaGuardia Acts. We have come to a contrary decision. . . .

Although we have held that the Norris-LaGuardia Act did not render injunctive relief beyond the jurisdiction of the District Court, there are alternative grounds which support the power of the District Court to punish violations of its orders as criminal contempt. . . .

In the case before us, the District Court had the power to preserve existing conditions [by a temporary restraining order] while it was determining its own authority to grant injunctive relief. The defendants, in making their private determination of the law, acted at their peril. Their disobedience is punishable as criminal contempt.

Although a different result would follow were the question of jurisdiction frivolous and not substantial, such contention would be idle here. The applicability of the Norris-LaGuardia Act to the United States in a case such as this had not previously received judicial consideration . . . .

Proceeding further, we find impressive authority for the proposition that an order issued by a court with jurisdiction over the subject matter

[1] The United States had taken possession of the mines pursuant to Executive Order 9728 of May 21, 1946, in which the President, after determining that labor disturbances were interrupting the production of bituminous coal necessary for the operation of the national economy during the transition from war to peace, directed the Secretary of Interior to take possession of and operate the mines and to negotiate with representatives of the miners concerning the terms and conditions of employment. . . .

and person must be obeyed by the parties until it is reversed by orderly and proper proceedings. This is true without regard even for the constitutionality of the Act under which the order is issued. This is true without regard even for the constitutionality of the Act under which the order is issued. In Howat *v.* Kansas, 258 U.S. 181, 189 (1922), this Court said:

> "An injunction duly issuing out of a court of general jurisdiction with equity powers, upon pleadings properly invoking its action, and served upon persons made parties therein and within the jurisdiction, must be obeyed by them, however erroneous the action of the court may be, even if the error be in the assumption of the validity of a seeming, but void law going to the merits of the case. It is for the court of first instance to determine the question of the validity of the law, and until its decision is reversed for error by orderly review, either by itself or by a higher court, its orders based on its decision are to be respected, and disobedience of them is contempt of its lawful authority, to be punished."

Violations of an order are punishable as criminal contempt even though the order is set aside on appeal or though the basic action has become moot.

We insist upon the same duty of obedience where, as here, the subject matter of the suit, as well as the parties, was properly before the court; where the elements of federal jurisdiction were clearly shown; and where the authority of the court of first instance to issue an order ancillary to the main suit depended upon a statute, the scope and applicability of which were subject to substantial doubt. The District Court on November 29 affirmatively decided that the Norris-LaGuardia Act was of no force in this case and that injunctive relief was therefore authorized. Orders outstanding or issued after that date were to be obeyed until they expired or were set aside by appropriate proceedings, appellate or otherwise. Convictions for criminal contempt intervening before that time may stand.

It does not follow, of course, that simply because a defendant may be punished for criminal contempt for disobedience of an order later set aside on appeal, that the plaintiff in the action may profit by way of a fine imposed in a simultaneous proceeding for civil contempt based upon a violation of the same order. The right to remedial relief falls with an injunction which events prove was erroneously issued, and a fortiori when the injunction or restraining order was beyond the jurisdiction of the court. . . . If the Norris-LaGuardia Act were applicable in this case, the conviction for civil contempt would be reversed in its entirety.

Assuming, then, that the Norris-LaGuardia Act applied to this case and prohibited injunctive relief at the request of the United States, we would set aside the preliminary injunction of December 4 and the judgment for civil contempt; but we would, subject to any infirmities in the contempt proceedings or in the fines imposed, affirm the judgments for criminal contempt as validly punishing violations of an order then outstanding and unreversed. . . .

■ MR. JUSTICE FRANKFURTER, concurring in the judgment. . . .

A majority of my brethren find that neither the Norris-LaGuardia Act nor the War Labor Disputes Act limited the power of the district court to issue the orders under review. I have come to the contrary view. But to suggest that the right to determine so complicated and novel an issue could not be brought within the cognizance of the district court, and eventually of this Court, is to deny the place of the judiciary in our scheme of government. And if the district court had power to decide whether this case was properly before it, it could make appropriate orders so as to afford the necessary time for fair consideration and decision while existing conditions were preserved. To say that the authority of the court may be flouted during the time necessary to decide is to reject the requirements of the judicial process.

It does not mitigate such defiance of law to urge that hard-won liberties of collective action by workers were at stake. The most prized liberties themselves pre-suppose an independent judiciary through which these liberties may be, as they often have been, vindicated. When in a real controversy, such as is now here, an appeal is made to law, the issue must be left to the judgment of courts and not the personal judgment of one of the parties. This principle is a postulate of our democracy.

And so I join the opinion of the Court insofar as it sustains the judgment for criminal contempt upon the broad ground of vindicating the process of law. . . .

■ MR. JUSTICE RUTLEDGE, dissenting. . . .

Since in my opinion the order was jurisdictionally invalid when issued, by virtue of the War Labor Disputes Act and its adoption of the Norris-LaGuardia Act's policy, it follows that the violation gave no sufficient cause for sustaining the conviction for contempt. Lewis and the United Mine Workers necessarily took the risk that the order would be found valid on review and, in that event, that punishment for contempt would apply. They did not take the risk that it would apply in any event, even if the order should be found void as beyond the jurisdiction of the Court to enter. . . .

The power of the federal courts to issue stay orders to maintain the status quo pending appeal, like other matters affecting their jurisdiction except in the case of this Court's original jurisdiction, is subject to Congress' control. That control has been exercised, in my view, to exclude such jurisdiction in cases of this character. And, this being true, I do not think either we or any other court subject to that mandate has power to punish as for contempt the violation of such an order issued in contravention of Congress' command.

Walker v. City of Birmingham

Supreme Court of the United States, 1967.
388 U.S. 307.

■ MR. JUSTICE STEWART delivered the opinion of the Court.

On Wednesday, April 10, 1963, officials of Birmingham, Alabama, filed a bill of complaint in a state circuit court asking for injunctive relief against 139 individuals and two organizations. The bill and accompanying affidavits stated that during the preceding seven days:

> "[R]espondents [had] sponsored and/or participated in and/or conspired to commit and/or to encourage and/or to participate in certain movements, plans or projects commonly called 'sit-in' demonstrations, 'kneel-in' demonstrations, mass street parades . . . ."

It was alleged that this conduct was "calculated to provoke breaches of the peace," "threaten[ed] the safety, peace and tranquility of the City," and placed "an undue burden and strain upon the manpower of the Police Department." . . .

The circuit judge granted a temporary injunction as prayed in the bill, enjoining the petitioners from, among other things, participating in or encouraging mass street parades or mass processions without a permit as required by a Birmingham ordinance.

Five of the eight petitioners were served with copies of the writ early the next morning. Several hours later four of them held a press conference. There a statement was distributed, declaring their intention to disobey the injunction because it was "raw tyranny under the guise of maintaining law and order." At this press conference one of the petitioners stated: "That they had respect for the Federal Courts, or Federal Injunctions, but in the past the State Courts had favored local law enforcement, and if the police couldn't handle it, the mob would."

That night a meeting took place at which one of the petitioners announced that "[i]njunction or no injunction we are going to march tomorrow." The next afternoon, Good Friday, a large crowd gathered in the vicinity of Sixteenth Street and Sixth Avenue North in Birmingham. A group of about 50 or 60 proceeded to parade along the sidewalk while a crowd of 1,000 to 1,500 onlookers stood by, "clapping, and hollering, and [w]hooping." Some of the crowd followed the marchers and spilled out into the street. At least three of the petitioners participated in this march.

Meetings sponsored by some of the petitioners were held that night and the following night, where calls for volunteers to "walk" and go to jail were made. On Easter Sunday, April 14, a crowd of between 1,500 and 2,000 people congregated in the midafternoon in the vicinity of Seventh Avenue and Eleventh Street North in Birmingham. One of the petitioners was seen organizing members of the crowd in formation. A group of about 50, headed by three other petitioners, started down the sidewalk two abreast. At least one other petitioner was among the marchers. Some 300 or 400 people from among the onlookers followed in a crowd that occupied the entire width of the street and overflowed onto the sidewalks. Violence occurred. Members of the crowd threw rocks that injured a newspaperman and damaged a police motorcycle.

The next day the city officials who had requested the injunction applied to the state circuit court for an order to show cause why the petitioners should not be held in contempt for violating it. At the ensuing hearing the petitioners sought to attack the constitutionality of the injunction on the ground that it was vague and overbroad, and restrained free speech. They also sought to attack the Birmingham parade ordinance upon similar grounds, and upon the further ground that the ordinance had previously been administered in an arbitrary and discriminatory manner.

The circuit judge refused to consider any of these contentions, pointing out that there had been neither a motion to dissolve the injunction, nor an effort to comply with it by applying for a permit from the city commission before engaging in the Good Friday and Easter Sunday parades. Consequently, the court held that the only issues before it were whether it had jurisdiction to issue the temporary injunction, and whether thereafter the petitioners had knowingly violated it. Upon these issues the court found against the petitioners, and imposed upon each of them a sentence of five days in jail and a $50 fine, in accord with an Alabama statute.

The Supreme Court of Alabama affirmed. That court, too, declined to consider the petitioners' constitutional attacks upon the injunction and the underlying Birmingham parade ordinance:

> "It is to be remembered that petitioners are charged with violating a temporary injunction. We are not reviewing a denial of a motion to dissolve or discharge a temporary injunction. Petitioners did not file any motion to vacate the temporary injunction until after the Friday and Sunday parades. Instead, petitioners deliberately defied the order of the court and did engage in and incite others to engage in mass street parades without a permit.
>
> "We hold that the circuit court had the duty and authority, in the first instance, to determine the validity of the ordinance, and, until the decision of the circuit court is reversed for error by orderly review, either by the circuit court or a higher court, the orders of the circuit court based on its decision are to be respected and disobedience of them is contempt of its lawful authority, to be punished. Howat *v.* State of Kansas, 258 U.S. 181 (1922)."

Howat *v.* State of Kansas was decided by this Court almost 50 years ago. That was a case in which people had been punished by a Kansas trial court for refusing to obey an antistrike injunction issued under the state industrial relations act. They had claimed a right to disobey the court's order upon the ground that the state statute and the injunction based upon it were invalid under the Federal Constitution. The Supreme Court of Kansas had affirmed the judgment, holding that the trial court "had general power to issue injunctions in equity, and that even if its exercise of the power was erroneous, the injunction was not void, and the defendants were precluded from attacking it in this collateral proceeding . . . that, if the injunction was erroneous, jurisdiction was not thereby forfeited, that the error was subject to correction only by the ordinary method of appeal, and disobedience to the order constituted contempt."

This Court, in dismissing the writ of error, not only unanimously accepted but fully approved the validity of the rule of state law upon which the judgment of the Kansas court was grounded:

> "An injunction duly issuing out of a court of general jurisdiction with equity powers, upon pleadings properly invoking its action, and served upon persons made parties therein and within the jurisdiction, must be obeyed by them, however erroneous the action of the court may be, even if the error be in the assumption of the validity of a seeming, but void law going to the merits of the case. It is for the court of first instance to determine the question of the validity of the law, and until its decision is reversed for error by orderly review, either by itself or by a higher court, its orders based on its decision are to be respected, and disobedience of them is contempt of its lawful authority, to be punished."

The rule of state law accepted and approved in Howat *v.* State of Kansas is consistent with the rule of law followed by the federal courts.

In the present case, however, we are asked to hold that this rule of law, upon which the Alabama courts relied, was constitutionally impermissible. We are asked to say that the Constitution compelled Alabama to allow the petitioners to violate this injunction, to organize and engage in these mass street parades and demonstrations, without any previous effort on their part to have the injunction dissolved or modified, or any attempt to secure a parade permit in accordance with its terms. Whatever the limits of Howat *v.* State of Kansas, we cannot accept the petitioners' contentions in the circumstances of this case.

Without question the state court that issued the injunction had, as a court of equity, jurisdiction over the petitioners and over the subject matter of the controversy. And this is not a case where the injunction was transparently invalid or had only a frivolous pretense to validity. We have consistently recognized the strong interest of state and local governments in regulating the use of their streets and other public places. . . .

The generality of the language contained in the Birmingham parade ordinance upon which the injunction was based would unquestionably raise substantial constitutional issues concerning some of its provisions. The petitioners, however, did not even attempt to apply to the Alabama courts for an authoritative construction of the ordinance. Had they done so, those courts might have given the licensing authority granted in the ordinance a narrow and precise scope. . . . [I]t could not be assumed that this ordinance was void on its face.

The breadth and vagueness of the injunction itself would also unquestionably be subject to substantial constitutional question. But the way to raise that question was to apply to the Alabama courts to have the injunction modified or dissolved. The injunction in all events clearly prohibited mass parading without a permit, and the evidence shows that the petitioners fully understood that prohibition when they violated it.

The petitioners also claim that they were free to disobey the injunction because the parade ordinance on which it was based had been administered in the past in an arbitrary and discriminatory fashion. In support of this claim they sought to introduce evidence that, a few days before the injunction issued, requests for permits to picket had been made to a member of the city commission. One request had been rudely rebuffed, and this same official had later made clear that he was without power to grant the permit alone, since the issuance of such permits was the responsibility of the entire city commission. Assuming the truth of this proffered evidence, it does not follow that the parade ordinance was void on its face. The petitioners, moreover, did not apply for a permit either to the commission itself or to any commissioner after the injunction issued. Had they done so, and had the permit been refused, it is clear that their claim of arbitrary or discriminatory administration of the ordinance would have been considered by the state circuit court upon a motion to dissolve the injunction.

This case would arise in quite a different constitutional posture if the petitioners before disobeying the injunction, had challenged it in the Alabama courts, and had been met with delay or frustration of their constitutional claims. But there is no showing that such would have been the fate of a timely motion to modify or dissolve the injunction. There was an interim of two days between the issuance of the injunction and the Good Friday march. The petitioners give absolutely no explanation of why they did not make some application to the state court during that period. The injunction had issued *ex parte*; if the court had been presented with the petitioners' contentions, it might well have dissolved or at least modified its order in some respects. If it had not done so, Alabama procedure would have provided for an expedited process of appellate review. It cannot be presumed that the Alabama courts would have ignored the petitioners' constitutional claims. Indeed, these contentions were accepted in another case by an Alabama appellate court that struck down on direct review the conviction under this very ordinance of one of these same petitioners.

The rule of law upon which the Alabama courts relied in this case was one firmly established by previous precedents. We do not deal here, therefore, with a situation where a state court has followed a regular past practice of entertaining claims in a given procedural mode, and without notice has abandoned that practice to the detriment of a litigant who finds his claim foreclosed by a novel procedural bar. This is not a case where a procedural requirement has been sprung upon an unwary litigant when prior practice did not give him fair notice of its existence.

The Alabama Supreme Court has apparently never in any criminal contempt case entertained a claim of nonjurisdictional error. . . .

These precedents clearly put the petitioners on notice that they could not by-pass orderly judicial review of the injunction before disobeying it. Any claim that they were entrapped or misled is wholly unfounded, a conclusion confirmed by evidence in the record showing that when the petitioners deliberately violated the injunction they expected to go to jail.

The rule of law that Alabama followed in this case reflects a belief that in the fair administration of justice no man can be judge in his own case, however exalted his station, however righteous his motives, and irrespective of his race, color, politics, or religion. This Court cannot hold that the petitioners were constitutionally free to ignore all the procedures of the law and carry their battle to the streets. One may sympathize with the petitioners' impatient commitment to their cause. But respect for judicial process is a small price to pay for the civilizing hand of law, which alone can give abiding meaning to constitutional freedom. . . .

■ MR. CHIEF JUSTICE WARREN, whom MR. JUSTICE BRENNAN and MR. JUSTICE FORTAS join, dissenting.

. . . Petitioners were served with copies of the injunction at various times on Thursday and on Good Friday. Unable to believe that such a blatant and broadly drawn prior restraint on their First Amendment rights could be valid, they announced their intention to defy it and went ahead with the planned peaceful demonstrations on Easter weekend. On the following Monday, when they promptly filed a motion to dissolve the injunction, the court found them in contempt, holding that they had waived all their First Amendment rights by disobeying the court order.

These facts lend no support to the court's charges that petitioners were presuming to act as judges in their own case, or that they had a disregard for the judicial process. They did not flee the jurisdiction or refuse to appear in the Alabama courts. Having violated the injunction, they promptly submitted themselves to the courts to test the constitutionality of the injunction and the ordinance it parroted. They were in essentially the same position as persons who challenge the constitutionality of a statute by violating it, and then defend the ensuing criminal prosecution on constitutional grounds. It has never been thought that violation of a statute indicated such a disrespect for the legislature that the violator always must be punished even if the statute was unconstitutional. On the contrary, some cases have required that persons seeking to challenge the constitutionality of a statute first violate it to establish their standing to sue. Indeed, it shows no disrespect for law to violate a statute on the ground that it is unconstitutional and then to submit one's case to the courts with the willingness to accept the penalty if the statute is held to be valid. . . .

The only circumstance that the court can find to justify anything other than a *per curiam* reversal is that Commissioner Connor had the foresight to have the unconstitutional ordinance included in an *ex parte* injunction . . . .

I do not believe that giving this Court's seal of approval to such a gross misuse of the judicial process is likely to lead to greater respect for the law any more than it is likely to lead to greater protection for First Amendment freedoms. The *ex parte* temporary injunction has a long and odious history in this country, and its susceptibility to misuse is all too apparent from the facts of the case. As a weapon against strikes, it proved so effective in the hands of judges friendly to employers that Congress was forced to take the drastic step of removing from federal district courts the jurisdiction to issue injunctions in labor disputes. The labor injunction fell into disrepute largely because it was abused in precisely the same way that the injunctive power was abused in this case. Judges who were not sympathetic to the union cause commonly issued, without notice or hearing, broad restraining orders addressed to large numbers of persons and forbidding them to engage in acts that were either legally permissible or, if illegal, that could better have been left to the regular course of criminal prosecution. The injunctions might later be dissolved, but in the meantime strikes would be crippled because the occasion on which concerted activity might have been effective had passed. Such injunctions so long discredited as weapons against concerted labor activities, have now been given new life by this Court as weapons against the exercise of First Amendment freedoms. Respect for the courts and for judicial process was not increased by the history of the labor injunction. . . .

The Alabama Circuit Court did not issue this temporary injunction to preserve existing conditions while it proceeded to decide some underlying dispute. There was no underlying dispute before it, and the court in practical effect merely added a judicial signature to a preexisting criminal ordinance. Just as the court had no need to issue the injunction to preserve its ability to decide some underlying dispute, the city had no need of an injunction to impose a criminal penalty for demonstrating on the streets without a permit. The ordinance already accomplished that. In point of fact, there is only one apparent reason why the city sought this injunction and why the court issued it: to make it possible to punish petitioners for contempt rather than for violating the ordinance, and thus to immunize the unconstitutional statute and its unconstitutional application from any attack. I regret that this strategy has been so successful. . . .

■ MR. JUSTICE DOUGLAS, with whom THE CHIEF JUSTICE, MR. JUSTICE BRENNAN, and MR. JUSTICE FORTAS concur, dissenting.

. . . Howat *v.* State of Kansas states the general rule that court injunctions are to be obeyed until error is found by normal and orderly review procedures. But there is an exception where "the question of jurisdiction" is "frivolous and not substantial." United States *v.* United Mine Workers, 330 U.S. 258, 293 (1947). . . . In the present case the collision between this state court decree and the First Amendment is so obvious that no hearing is needed to determine the issue. . . .

A court does not have jurisdiction to do what a city or other agency of a State lacks jurisdiction to do. The command of the Fourteenth Amendment, through which the First Amendment is made applicable to the States, is that no "State" shall deprive any person of "liberty" without due process of law. The decree of a state court is "state" action in the constitutional sense, as much as the action of the state police, the state prosecutor, the state legislature, or the Governor himself. An ordinance—unconstitutional on its face or patently unconstitutional as applied—is not made sacred by an unconstitutional injunction that enforces it. It can and should be flouted in the manner of the ordinance itself. . . .

■ MR. JUSTICE BRENNAN, with whom THE CHIEF JUSTICE, MR. JUSTICE DOUGLAS, and MR. JUSTICE FORTAS join, dissenting.

. . . In the present case we are confronted with a collision between Alabama's interest in requiring adherence to orders of its courts and the constitutional prohibition against abridgment of freedom of speech, more particularly "the right of the people peaceably to assemble," and the right "to petition the Government for a redress of grievances." . . .

The vitality of First Amendment protections has . . . been deemed to rest in large measure upon the ability of the individual to take his chances and express himself in the face of such restraints, armed with the ability to challenge those restraints if the State seeks to penalize that expression. The most striking examples of the right to speak first and challenge later, and of peculiar moment for the present case, are the cases concerning the ability of an individual to challenge a permit or licensing statute giving broad discretion to an individual or group, such as the Birmingham permit ordinance, despite the fact that he did not attempt to obtain a permit or license. . . .

Yet by some inscrutable legerdemain these constitutionally secured rights to challenge prior restraints invalid on their face are lost if the State takes the precaution to have some judge append his signature to an *ex parte* order which recites the words of the invalid statute. . . .

The Court today lets loose a devastatingly destructive weapon for infringement of freedoms jealously safeguarded not so much for the benefit of any given group of any given persuasion as for the benefit of all of us. . . . Convictions for contempt of court orders which invalidly abridge First Amendment freedoms must be condemned equally with convictions for violation of statutes which do the same thing. I respectfully dissent.

NOTES

1. One of the petitioners in *Walker* was Dr. Martin Luther King. A number of the participants in the Easter Sunday march were prosecuted for violation of the Birmingham parade ordinance on which the order in *Walker* was based. Included among their number was the Rev. Fred L. Shuttlesworth, a Baptist minister who had also been one of the petitioners in *Walker*.

Rev. Shuttlesworth was convicted and sentenced to 90 days' imprisonment at hard labor, and the sentence was lengthened when he defaulted on the payment of about $100 in fines and costs. The Alabama Court of Appeals reversed Rev. Shuttlesworth's conviction, finding among other things that there was a pattern of discrimination in how the ordinance was enforced. When the Alabama Supreme Court reinstated the conviction, it was reversed by the U.S. Supreme Court on the ground that the ordinance was unconstitutional. Shuttlesworth *v.* Birmingham, 394 U.S. 147 (1969). Writing for the Court, Justice Stewart remarked:

> "This ordinance as it was written . . . fell squarely within the ambit of the many decisions of this Court over the last 30 years, holding that a law subjecting the exercise of First Amendment freedoms to the prior restraint of a license, without narrow, objective, and definite standards to guide the licensing authority, is unconstitutional. . . . And our decisions have made clear that a person faced with such an unconstitutional licensing law may ignore it and engage with impunity in the exercise of the right of free expression for which the law purports to require a license."

Id. at 150–51.

2. Willy commenced a wrongful discharge action against his employer in state court and the employer removed the action to federal court. Willy challenged the jurisdiction of the district court, arguing that the claim did not arise under federal law. The district court concluded that it had subject matter jurisdiction, granted the employer's motion to dismiss, and imposed sanctions on Willy's lawyer for filing papers that "created a blur of absolute confusion" (including a 1,200 page, unindexed, unnumbered pile of materials), and for relying on a nonexistent Federal Rule of Evidence. On appeal, the Fifth Circuit Court of Appeals reversed and remanded the case to the state court, holding that the district court had no subject matter jurisdiction. The court, however, upheld the Rule 11 sanctions. The Supreme Court affirmed, stating that "the maintenance of orderly procedure, even in the wake of a jurisdiction ruling later found to be mistaken—justifies the conclusion that the sanction ordered here need not be upset." Willy *v.* Coastal Corporation, 503 U.S. 131, 137 (1992).

3. Goodson, an Arkansas trial judge, ordered Wood, a newspaper editor, to refrain for a day from publishing the results of a jury trial in a rape case, pending the resolution of a related case against defendants charged with participating in the rape. Wood published, and Goodson held him in contempt. The Arkansas Supreme Court vacated the contempt conviction, saying:

> "Every court that has had an occasion to rule upon the freedom of the press to publish court proceedings, has held that whatever transpires in the court room is public property and those who see and hear it may report it without judicial censorship. . . .
>
> "No court, as we have indicated, has the power to prohibit the news media from publishing that which transpires in open court. Consequently it follows that the order not to publish was void and also subject to collateral attack."

Wood *v.* Goodson, 485 S.W.2d 213, 216–17 (Ark. 1972).

2. PERSONS BOUND BY THE DECREE

Lord Wellesley v. Earl of Mornington

Chancery, 1848.
11 Beavan 181, 50 Eng. Rep. 786.

. . . The plaintiff, having failed in his motion to commit [*i.e.*, imprison] Mr. Batley for a breach of the injunction, which applied to the Earl only, and not to his agents, now moved to commit him for the contempt, in being party and privy to, and in aiding and assisting the breach of the injunction, which restrained the Defendant, the earl of Mornington, from cutting timber, &c., Batley at the time knowing that these acts were forbidden.

It was proved that Batley, who was the agent and manager of the Earl, from the time of granting the injunction in 1846, had cut trees and underwood, and appropriated the produce to the purposes of the earl, and that he had interfered in letting the property and taking fines [*i.e.*, payments from tenants to lords]. All these acts were in breach of the injunction, and some of them had been done after Batley had been served with clear and distinct notice of the terms of the injunction.

Mr. Roupell and *Mr. Heathfield,* in support of the motion. The former motion failed in consequence of this technical objection—that it was to commit for a breach of an injunction which accidentally omitted the words "servants and agents." The present motion is in a different form, and seeks to commit *for the contempt*, in knowingly assisting in a breach of the injunction.

The court will interfere, where a person, though not enjoined, willfully assists in the act forbidden by the court, as in Lewes *v.* Morgan, 5 Price, 42, where after an injunction granted against Morgan from receiving rents, Lewes, the solicitor of Morgan, with knowledge of the order, received them, an order was made for his committal for the contempt.

So, where a party assaults an officer of the court in the discharge of his duty; or displaces a receiver; or interferes with the execution of its process; or obstructs or interferes with the due course of justice; the court interferes and punishes for the contempt. . . .

The Master of the Rolls [Langdale]. Does the plaintiff press for a committal?

Mr. Roupell stated that it was not his desire to press for the committal.

The Master of the Rolls. By the forbearance of the plaintiff, I am spared the painful necessity of making an order. If the matter had been pressed, I should have found it my duty to commit Mr. Batley for his contempt in intermeddling with these matters; some of his acts in contravention of the injunction are distinctly proved, though with respect to others there may be some shadow of doubt.

Batley, in the position in which he was, and knowing the duty of the Earl of Mornington, ought to have taken care not to do any acts, in violation of the order of the court. I am glad to be relieved from the necessity of ordering a committal, but Batley must pay the costs of the motion. . . .

NOTE

Lord Wellesley *v.* Earl of Mornington marked a change from Iveson *v.* Harris, 7 Ves. Jun. 251, 32 Eng. Rep. 102 (1802), in which Lord Chancellor Eldon made the following remark:

> "I have no conception, that it is competent to this court to hold a man bound by an injunction, who is not a party in the cause for the purpose of the cause. . . .
>
> "The court has no right to grant an injunction against a person whom they have not brought, or attempted to bring, before the court by *subpoena*."

Rigas v. Livingston

Court of Appeals of New York, 1904.
178 N.Y. 20.

■ CULLEN, J. The plaintiff was the occupant of a fruit stand on the sidewalk in front of No. 89 Park Row in the city of New York. The appellant Levy was the tenant and occupant of the store in front of which the plaintiff's stand was located. Levy was anxious that the stand should be removed, and applied to the city authorities to have such removal effected. Thereupon the plaintiff brought an action in the Supreme Court against the commissioner of public works of the borough of Manhattan and the superintendent of the bureau of incumbrances to enjoin them from interfering with his stand. A temporary injunction was granted . . . . This order purported in terms not only to restrain the defendants, but also "all persons having knowledge of this injunction order." Thereafter one Rosenblum, the son-in-law of Levy, landlord of the building, brought proceedings in the Municipal Court to dispossess Levy from his store. In these proceedings Levy made default and a warrant for his removal was issued. Acting under this warrant, Loewenthal, a city marshal, and Dickman, the attorney for the landlord, removed and destroyed the plaintiff's stand. Thereafter application was made to punish Levy, Dickman, and Loewenthal for contempt. The proof tended to show that all of them were notified of the existence of the injunction. The Special Term adjudged the parties guilty of a civil contempt in impairing and prejudicing the plaintiff's rights, and fined them the sum of $150. . . .

The Special Term found that [Levy] "did, by trick and scheme, violate said injunction order and caused said stand to be removed." . . . [The] facts and the relationship between Levy and Rosenblum create a very strong suspicion that Levy was a prime mover in all the transactions, but it is doubtful whether, in the face of Levy's sworn denial, they were sufficient, in these proceedings, which are *quasi* criminal, to establish his guilt.

However this may be, we are of opinion that the removal of the stand, though illegal, was not a violation of the injunction. The parties might have been sued for their trespass civilly and, it is possible, criminally; however great their fault it was not a contempt of court. . . . In terms the Code authorizes an injunction against the defendants only, not the whole world. . . .

It is true that persons not parties to the action may be bound by an injunction if they have knowledge of it, provided they are servants or agents of the defendants or act in collusion or combination with them. Such was the case of Daly *v.* Amberg (126 N.Y. 490), where the agents and employees of the manager of a theater disobeyed an injunction granted against their employer to restrain the representation of a play at his theater. . . . [T]he underlying principle in all cases of this class, on which is founded the power of the court to punish for the violation of its mandate persons not parties to the action, is that the parties so punished were acting either as the agents or servants of the defendants or in combination or collusion with them or in assertion of their rights or claims. Persons, however, who are not connected in any way with the parties to the action are not restrained by the order of the court. . . . [T]he injunction order determined that *prima facie* the plaintiff was authorized to maintain his stand as against the city of New York and its authorities. This was the only right passed upon on the application for the injunction and the only right which could have been passed upon. The injunction order, therefore, properly restrained the city authorities from interfering with the plaintiff's stand. Had any of the city officials or their employees or agents or any third parties acting in aid of or in connivance with them interfered with the stand, they would have committed a contempt of court. But it is not pretended that the city officials against whom the action was brought, or either of them, in any way, directly or indirectly, by act or solicitation, took part in the subsequent trespass on the plaintiff's property. The parties who removed the stand neither acted nor assumed to act under any right or authority of the city officials, but in execution of the process of another court issued on a judgment not based on any claim of the city that the stand was a nuisance, but on a right asserted by a landlord to dispossess a defaulting tenant. It is true that this process offered no justification for the trespass on the plaintiff's property. That fact did not make them guilty of contempt, but liable as trespassers. A thief might have come along in the night and stolen the plaintiff's stand. He would have been guilty of larceny, but not of contempt of court. . . .

■ PARKER, CH. J., GRAY, O'BRIEN, HAIGHT, and MARTIN, JJ., concur. VANN, J., dissents.

Paramount Pictures Corp. v. Carol Publishing Group, Inc.

United States District Court, S.D.N.Y., 1998.
25 F. Supp. 2d 372.

■ SCHEINDLIN, DISTRICT JUDGE. [Sam Ramer, a self-described "Trekker," wrote a book called *The Joy of Trek: How to Enhance Your Relations with a STAR TREK Fan*. The book, which provided a detailed guide to the various Star Trek movie and television series, was published by Carol Publishing. Paramount Pictures Corporation, the owner of copyrights covering the Star Trek productions, sued for infringement and requested a preliminary injunction. The court found that Paramount had established a likelihood of success on the merits of its infringement claim, and, on June 1, 1998, enjoined Ramer, Carol Publishing, "and their agents, servants, employees, and attorneys, and all persons, firms, or corporations acting in active concert with them" from publishing or distributing the book.]

In December 1997, Carol Publishing shipped nearly 6,000 copies of *The Joy of Trek* to various retailers and distributors. The books were sold on a return basis, whereby unsold inventory would be returned to Carol Publishing by early 1999. By June 24, 1998, an estimated 1,200 to 1,500 copies of *The Joy of Trek* had been purchased from retailers and distributors and 1,000 copies had been returned to Carol Publishing. After Judge Conti issued the June 1, 1998 preliminary injunction, Steven Schragis [a Carol Publishing manager] instructed his staff to stop shipping or selling any copies of *The Joy of Trek*. [In the phase of the case reprinted here, Paramount requested a supplemental order clarifying whether the distributors and retailers currently in possession of copies of the book were subject to the preliminary injunction and therefore open to punishment for contempt.] . . .

[Fed. R. Civ. P.] 65(d) provides that "[e]very order granting an injunction . . . is binding only upon the parties to the action, their officers, agents, servants, employees, and attorneys, and upon those persons in active concert or participation with them who receive actual notice of the order by personal service or otherwise." While a court "cannot lawfully enjoin the world at large," an injunction binds a nonparty who has actual notice of an order and acts in concert with the enjoined party. In order for a nonparty to be bound, that entity must either aid and abet the defendant or be legally identified with it.

Because a court's power to enjoin is limited to the conduct of a party, it is the relationship between the party enjoined and the nonparty that determines the permissible scope of an injunction. See Alemite Mfg. Corp. *v.* Staff, 42 F.2d 832, 833 (2d Cir. 1930) ("[T]he only occasion when a person not a party may be punished is when he has helped to bring about, not merely what the decree has forbidden, . . . but what it has the power to forbid, an act of a party."). A nonparty in active concert cannot violate an injunction unless the enjoined party is also in contempt. See United Pharmacal Corp. *v.* United States, 306 F.2d 515, 516–17 (1st Cir. 1962) ("[I]f the person enjoined is not involved in the contempt, an employee, and by the same token one in active concert or participation, cannot be either, because the decree has not been violated."); see also Heyman *v.* Kline, 444 F.2d 65, 65–66 (2d Cir. 1971) (Rule 65(d) does not authorize jurisdiction over persons who act independently and whose rights have not been adjudicated).

Nor does an injunction reach backwards in time to action taken prior to the time it was issued. See United Pharmacal, 306 F.2d at 517 ("past contractual relationship is not controlling" on question of whether nonparty violated injunction); cf. Waffenschmidt *v.* MacKay, 763 F.2d 711, 724 (5th Cir. 1985) (nonparties aided and abetted enjoined party where they accepted note after receiving notice of court's order prohibiting transfer of funds); Forschner Group, Inc. *v.* New Trends, Vrolixs J.–C., Civ. A. No. B–89–531, 1994 WL 708129, at *7–8 (D. Conn. Aug.10, 1994) (nonparty acted in concert with defendant by negotiating agreement with defendant's successor in interest after entry of injunction and distributing enjoined goods pursuant to that agreement). Each case is fact specific. For example, in O & L Associates *v.* Del Conte, 601 F. Supp. 1463, 1464–65 (S.D.N.Y. 1985), a nonparty movie studio had acquired from defendants the "universal right, in perpetuity" to use the name "The Flirts" in connection with the movie, "The Karate Kid," before defendants were enjoined from using the name in any manner. Judge Edward Weinfeld, of this court, found that "an arm's length transaction involving totally distinct entities" and occurring eight months prior to the entry of the court's order failed to demonstrate that the nonparty acted in concert with defendants. . . .

The injunction at issue extends neither to a "past contractual relationship" between Carol Publishing and nonparty retailers and distributors nor to independent action taken by nonparties on their own behalf. Thus, the threshold question is whether the sales transactions between Carol Publishing and the nonparties now selling *The Joy of Trek* were complete before the injunction issued. . . . Under New York's Uniform Commercial Code, "[u]nless otherwise agreed, if delivered goods may be returned by the buyer even though they conform to the contract, the transaction is . . . a 'sale or return' if the goods are delivered primarily for resale." And, "[a]lthough a buyer retains the right to return goods, a completed sale is generally deemed to have taken place and title passes to the buyer." Thus, the retailers and distributors' purchases of *The Joy of Trek* became final before the entry of the injunction. . . .

Because the nonparty retailers and distributors have not been shown to be in "active concert or participation" with Carol Publishing, Defendant has no obligation to notify them of this Order. Paramount, however, may decide to notify the booksellers that it will consider any further sales of *The Joy of Trek* to be an act of copyright infringement that it intends to pursue in court. . . .

United States v. Hall

United States Court of Appeals, Fifth Circuit, 1972.
472 F.2d 261.

■ WISDOM, CIRCUIT JUDGE. This case presents the question whether a district court has power to punish for criminal contempt a person who, though neither a party nor bearing any legal relationship to a party, violates a court order designed to protect the court's judgment in a school desegregation case. We uphold the district court's conclusion that in the circumstances of this case it had this power, and affirm the defendant's conviction for contempt.

On June 23, 1971, the district court entered a "Memorandum Opinion and Final Judgment" in the case of Mims *v.* Duval County School Board. The court required the Duval County [Jacksonville], Florida school board to complete its desegregation of Duval County schools . . . by pairing and clustering a number of schools which had theretofore been predominantly one-race schools. This order culminated litigation begun eleven years before. This Court affirmed the district court's order in Mims *v.* Duval County School Board. The district court retained jurisdiction to enter such orders as might be necessary in the future to effectuate its judgment.

Among the schools marked for desegregation under the plan approved by the district court was Ribault Senior High School, a predominantly white school. The plan directed pairing of Ribault with William E. Raines Senior High School, a predominantly black school, so that the black enrollment would be 59 percent at Raines and 57 percent at Ribault. After the desegregation order was put into effect racial unrest and violence developed at Ribault, necessitating on one occasion the temporary closing of the school. On March 5, 1972, the superintendent of schools and the sheriff of Jacksonville filed a petition for injunctive relief in the *Mims* case with the district court. This petition alleged that certain black adult "outsiders" had caused or abetted the unrest and violence by their activities both on and off the Ribault campus. The petition identified the appellant Eric Hall, allegedly a member of a militant organization known as the "Black Front," as one of several such outsiders who, in combination with black students and parents, were attempting to prevent the normal operation of Ribault through student boycotts and other activities. As relief the petitioners requested an order "restraining all Ribault Senior High School students and any person acting independently or in concert with them from interfering with the orderly operation of the school and the Duval County School system, and for such other relief as the court may deem just and proper."

At an ex parte session on March 5, 1972, the district court entered an order providing in part:

> "1. All students of Ribault Senior High School, whether in good standing or under suspension, and other persons acting independently or in concert with them and having notice of this order are hereby enjoined and restrained from
>
> > "(a) Obstructing or preventing the attendance in classes of students and faculty members;
> >
> > "(b) Harassing, threatening or intimidating any faculty, staff member or employee of Ribault Senior High School or the Duval County School Board;
> >
> > "(c) Harassing, threatening or intimidating any student en route to and from school;
> >
> > "(d) Destroying or attempting to destroy, defacing or attempting to deface any structure, buildings, materials or equipment of Ribault Senior High School or the Duval County School Board;
> >
> > "(e) Committing any other act to disrupt the orderly operation of Ribault Senior High School or any other school of the Duval County School System;
>
> "2. Until further order of this Court, no person shall enter any building of the Ribault Senior High School or go upon the school's grounds except the following:
>
> > "(a) Students of Ribault Senior High School while attending classes or official school functions;
> >
> > "(b) The faculty, staff, and administration of Ribault Senior High School and other employees of the Duval County School Board having assigned duties at the school;

> "(c) Persons having business obligations which require their presence on the school's premises;
>
> "(d) Parents of Ribault Senior High School students or any other person who has the prior permission of the principal or his designee to be present on the school's premises;
>
> "(e) Law enforcement officials of the City of Jacksonville, the State of Florida or the United States Government."

The order went on to provide that "[a]nyone having notice of this order who violates any of the terms thereof shall be subject to arrest, prosecution and punishment by imprisonment or fine, or both, for criminal contempt under the laws of the United States of America. . . ." The court ordered the sheriff to serve copies of the order on seven named persons, *including Eric Hall.* Hall was neither a party plaintiff nor a party defendant in the *Mims* litigation, and in issuing this order the court did not join Hall or any of the other persons named in the order as parties.

On March 9, 1972, four days after the court issued its order, Hall violated that portion of the order restricting access to Ribault High School by appearing on the Ribault campus. When questioned by a deputy United States marshal as to the reasons for his presence, Hall replied that he was on the grounds of Ribault for the purpose of violating the March 5, order. The marshal then arrested Hall and took him into custody. After a nonjury trial, the district court found Hall guilty of the charge of criminal contempt and sentenced him to sixty days' imprisonment.

On this appeal Hall raises two related contentions. Both contentions depend on the fact that Hall was not a party to the *Mims* litigation and the fact that, in violating the court's order, he was apparently acting independently of the *Mims* parties. He first points to the common law rule that a nonparty who violates an injunction solely in pursuit of his own interests cannot be held in contempt. Not having been before the court as a party or as the surrogate of a party, he argues that in accordance with this common law rule he was not bound by the court's order. Second, he contends that Rule 65(d) of the Federal Rules of Civil Procedure prevents the court's order from binding him, since Rule 65(d) limits the binding effect of injunctive orders to "parties to the action, their officers, agents, servants, employees, and attorneys, and . . . those persons in active concert or participation with them who receive actual notice of the order by personal service or otherwise." We reject both contentions. . . .

In [prior cases holding that nonparties acting in pursuit of their own interests cannot be punished for violating an injunction], the activities of third parties, however harmful they might have been to the plaintiffs' interests, would not have disturbed in any way the adjudication of rights and obligations as between the original plaintiffs and defendants. . . . The activities of Hall, however, threatened both the plaintiffs' right and the defendant's duty as adjudicated in the *Mims* litigation. In *Mims* the plaintiffs were found to have a constitutional right to attend an integrated school. The defendant school board had a corresponding constitutional obligation to provide them with integrated schools and a right to be free from interference with the performance of that duty. Disruption of the orderly operation of the school system, in the form of a racial dispute, would thus negate the plaintiffs' constitutional right and the defendant's constitutional duty. In short, the activities of persons contributing to racial disorder at Ribault imperiled the court's fundamental power to make a binding adjudication between the parties properly before it.

Courts of equity have inherent jurisdiction to preserve their ability to render judgment in a case such as this. This was the import of the holding in United States *v.* United Mine Workers of America, 330 U.S. 258 (1947). . . .

The integrity of a court's power to render a binding judgment in a case over which it has jurisdiction is at stake in the present case. In *Mine Workers* disruptive conduct prior to the court's decision could have destroyed the court's power to settle a controversy at least potentially within its jurisdiction. Here the conduct of Hall and others, if unrestrained, could have upset the court's ability to bind the parties in *Mims,* a case in which it unquestionably had jurisdiction. Moreover, the court retained jurisdiction in *Mims* to enter such further orders as might be necessary to effectuate its judgment. Thus disruptive conduct would not only jeopardize the effect of the court's judgment already entered but would also undercut its power to enter binding desegregation orders in the future.

The principle that courts have jurisdiction to punish for contempt in order to protect their ability to render judgment is also found in the use of in rem injunctions. Federal courts have issued injunctions binding on all persons, regardless of notice, who come into contact with property which is the subject of a judicial decree. A court entering a decree binding on a particular piece of property is necessarily faced with the danger that its judgment may be disrupted in the future by members of an undefinable class—those who may come into contact with the property. The in rem injunction protects the court's judgment. The district court here faced an analogous problem. The judgment in a school case, as in other civil rights actions, inures to the benefit of a large class of persons, regardless of whether the original action is cast in the form of a class action. At the same time court orders in school cases, affecting as they do large numbers of people, necessarily depend on the cooperation of the entire community for their implementation.

As this Court is well aware, school desegregation orders often strongly excite community passions. School orders are, like in rem orders, particularly vulnerable to disruption by an undefinable class of persons who are neither parties nor acting at the instigation of parties. In such cases, as in voting rights cases, courts must have the power to issue orders similar to that issued in this case, tailored to the exigencies of the situation and directed to protecting the court's judgment. The peculiar problems posed by school cases have required courts to exercise broad and flexible remedial powers. Similarly broad applications of the power to punish for contempt may be necessary, as here, if courts are to protect their ability to design appropriate remedies and make their remedial orders effective. . . .

Similarly, we conclude that Rule 65(d), as a codification rather than a limitation of courts' common-law powers, cannot be read to restrict the inherent power of a court to protect its ability to render a binding judgment. . . . By deciding *Mims* and retaining jurisdiction the district court had, in effect, adjudicated the rights of the entire community with respect to the racial controversy surrounding the school system. Moreover, as we have noted, in the circumstances of this case third parties such as Hall were in a position to upset the court's adjudication. This was not a situation which could have been anticipated by the draftsmen of procedural rules. In meeting the situation as it did, the district court did not overstep its powers.

We do not hold that courts are free to issue permanent injunctions against all the world in school cases. Hall had notice of the court's order. Rather than challenge it by the orderly processes of law, he resorted to conscious, willful defiance. . . .

We hold, then, that the district court had the inherent power to protect its ability to render a binding judgment between the original parties to the *Mims* litigation by issuing an interim ex parte order against an undefinable class of persons. We further hold that willful violation of that order by one having notice of it constitutes criminal contempt. The judgment of the district court is affirmed.

NOTE

In Spallone *v.* United States, 493 U.S. 265 (1990), the Supreme Court held that a district court order against four Yonkers city councilmembers for refusing to vote in favor of legislation implementing a consent decree earlier approved by the city was an abuse of discretion. The aim of the consent decree was to end residential racial segregation within the city of Yonkers. The City of Yonkers was a party to the action, but the individual councilmembers were not. The Court stated:

> "We hold that the District Court, in view of the 'extraordinary' nature of the imposition of sanctions against the individual councilmembers, should have proceeded with such contempt sanctions first against the city alone in order to secure compliance with the remedial orders. Only if that approach failed to produce compliance within a reasonable time should the question of imposing contempt sanctions against petitioners even have been considered. This limitation accords with the doctrine that a court

must exercise [t]he least possible power adequate to the end proposed."

3. CONTEMPT

Anonymous

Court of King's Bench, 1631.
Dyer 188b, 73 Eng. Rep. 416n.

■ RICHARDSON CH. JUST. de C. Banc al Assises at Salisbury in Summer 1631, fuit assault per prisoner la condemne pur felony que puis son condemnation ject un Bickbat a le dit Justice que narrowly mist & pur ceo immediately fuit Indictment drawn per Noy envers le prisoner, & don dexter manus ampute & fix al Gibbet sur que luy mesme immediatement hange in presence de Court.

International Union, United Mine Workers of America v. Bagwell

Supreme Court of the United States, 1994.
512 U.S. 821.

■ JUSTICE BLACKMUN delivered the opinion of the Court.

We are called upon once again to consider the distinction between civil and criminal contempt. Specifically, we address whether contempt fines levied against a union for violations of a labor injunction are coercive civil fines, or are criminal fines that constitutionally could be imposed only through a jury trial. We conclude that the fines are criminal and, accordingly, we reverse the judgment of the Supreme Court of Virginia.

Petitioners, the International Union, United Mine Workers of America, and United Mine Workers of America, District 28 (collectively, the union), engaged in a protracted labor dispute with the Clinchfield Coal Company and Sea "B" Mining Company (collectively, the companies) over alleged unfair labor practices. In April 1989, the companies filed suit in the Circuit Court of Russell County, Virginia, to enjoin the union from conducting unlawful strike-related activities. The trial court entered an injunction which, as later amended, prohibited the union and its members from, among other things, obstructing ingress and egress to company facilities, throwing objects at and physically threatening company employees, placing tire-damaging "jackrocks" on roads used by company vehicles, and picketing with more than a specified number of people at designated sites. The court additionally ordered the union to take all steps necessary to ensure compliance with the injunction, to place supervisors at picket sites, and to report all violations to the court. . . .

As a result of . . . contempt proceedings, the court levied over $64 million in fines against the union, approximately $12 million of which was ordered payable to the companies. Because the union objected to payment of any fines to the companies and in light of the law enforcement burdens posed by the strike, the court ordered that the remaining roughly $52 million in fines be paid to the Commonwealth of Virginia and Russell and Dickenson Counties, "the two counties most heavily affected by the unlawful activity."

While appeals from the contempt orders were pending, the union and the companies settled the underlying labor dispute, agreed to vacate the contempt fines, and jointly moved to dismiss the case. A special mediator representing the Secretary of Labor, and the governments of Russell and Dickenson Counties, supported the parties' motion to vacate the outstanding fines. The trial court granted the motion to dismiss, dissolved the injunction, and vacated the $12 million in fines payable to the companies. After reiterating its belief that the remaining $52 million owed to the counties and the Commonwealth were coercive, civil fines, the trial court refused to vacate these fines, concluding they were "payable in effect to the public." . . .

The Court of Appeals of Virginia reversed and ordered that the contempt fines be vacated pursuant to the settlement agreement. . . .

On consolidated appeals, the Supreme Court of Virginia reversed. The court held that whether coercive, civil contempt sanctions could be settled by private parties was a question of state law, and that Virginia public policy disfavored such a rule, "if the dignity of the law and public respect for the judiciary are to be maintained." The court also rejected petitioners' contention that the outstanding fines were criminal and could not be imposed absent a criminal trial. Because the trial court's prospective fine schedule was intended to coerce compliance with the injunction and the union could avoid the fines through obedience, the court reasoned, the fines were civil and coercive and properly imposed in civil proceedings. . . .

"Criminal contempt is a crime in the ordinary sense," Bloom *v.* Illinois, 391 U.S. 194, 201 (1968), and "criminal penalties may not be imposed on someone who has not been afforded the protections that the Constitution requires of such criminal proceedings," Hicks *v.* Feiock, 485 U.S. 624, 632 (1988). For "serious" criminal contempts involving imprisonment of more than six months, these protections include the right to jury trial. In contrast, civil contempt sanctions, or those penalties designed to compel future compliance with a court order, are considered to be coercive and avoidable through obedience, and thus may be imposed in an ordinary civil proceeding upon notice and an opportunity to be heard. Neither a jury trial nor proof beyond a reasonable doubt is required.

Although the procedural contours of the two forms of contempt are well established, the distinguishing characteristics of civil versus criminal contempts are somewhat less clear. In the leading early case addressing this issue in the context of imprisonment, Gompers *v.* Bucks Stove & Range Co., 221 U.S. 418, 441 (1911), the Court emphasized that whether a contempt is civil or criminal turns on the "character and purpose" of the sanction involved. Thus, a contempt sanction is considered civil if it "is remedial, and for the benefit of the complainant. But if it is for criminal contempt the sentence is punitive, to vindicate the authority of the court." *Ibid.*

As *Gompers* recognized, however, the stated purposes of a contempt sanction alone cannot be determinative. "[W]hen a court imposes fines and punishments on a contemnor, it is not only vindicating its legal authority to enter the initial court order, but it also is seeking to give effect to the law's purpose of modifying the contemnor's behavior to conform to the terms required in the order." Hicks, 485 U.S. at 635. Most contempt sanctions, like most criminal punishments, to some extent punish a prior offense as well as coerce an offender's future obedience. The *Hicks* Court accordingly held that conclusions about the civil or criminal nature of a contempt sanction are properly drawn, not from "the subjective intent of a State's laws and its courts," but "from an examination of the character of the relief itself."

The paradigmatic coercive, civil contempt sanction, as set forth in *Gompers*, involves confining a contemnor indefinitely until he complies with an affirmative command such as an order "to pay alimony, or to surrender property ordered to be turned over to a receiver, or to make a conveyance." 221 U.S. at 442. Imprisonment for a fixed term similarly is coercive when the contemnor is given the option of earlier release if he complies. In these circumstances, the contemnor is able to purge the contempt and obtain his release by committing an affirmative act, and thus " 'carries the keys of his prison in his own pocket.' " Gompers, 221 U.S. at 442 (quoting In re Nevitt, 117 F. 448, 451 (8th Cir. 1902)).

By contrast, a fixed sentence of imprisonment is punitive and criminal if it is imposed retrospectively for a "completed act of disobedience," Gompers, 221 U.S. at 443, such that the contemnor cannot avoid or abbreviate the confinement through later compliance. Thus, the *Gompers* Court concluded that a 12-month sentence imposed on Samuel Gompers for violating an anti-boycott injunction was criminal. When a contempt involves the prior conduct of an isolated, prohibited act, the resulting sanction has no coercive effect. "[T]he defendant is furnished no key, and he cannot shorten the term by promising not to repeat the offense." Id. at 442.

This dichotomy between coercive and punitive imprisonment has been extended to the fine context. A contempt fine accordingly is considered civil and remedial if it either "coerce[s] the defendant into compliance with the court's order, [or] . . . compensate[s] the complainant for losses sustained." United States *v.* Mine Workers, 330 U.S. 258, 303–304 (1947). Where a fine is not compensatory, it is civil only if the contemnor is afforded an opportunity to purge. Thus, a "flat, unconditional fine" totaling even as little as $50 announced after a finding of contempt is criminal if the contemnor has no subsequent opportunity to reduce or avoid the fine through compliance.

A close analogy to coercive imprisonment is a per diem fine imposed for each day a contemnor fails to comply with an affirmative court order. Like civil imprisonment, such fines exert a constant coercive pressure, and once the jural command is obeyed, the future, indefinite, daily fines are purged. Less comfortable is the analogy between coercive imprisonment and suspended, determinate fines. In this Court's sole prior decision squarely addressing the judicial power to impose coercive civil contempt fines, *Mine Workers*, it held that fixed fines also may be considered purgable and civil when imposed and suspended pending future compliance. *Mine Workers* involved a $3,500,000 fine imposed against the union for nationwide post-World War II strike activities. Finding that the determinate fine was both criminal and excessive, the Court reduced the sanction to a flat criminal fine of $700,000. The Court then imposed and suspended the remaining $2,800,000 as a coercive civil fine, conditioned on the union's ability to purge the fine through full, timely compliance with the trial court's order. The Court concluded, in light of this purge clause, that the civil fine operated as "a coercive imposition upon the defendant union to compel obedience with the court's outstanding order."

This Court has not revisited the issue of coercive civil contempt fines addressed in *Mine Workers*. Since that decision, the Court has erected substantial procedural protections in other areas of contempt law, such as criminal contempts and summary contempts. Lower federal courts and state courts such as the trial court here nevertheless have relied on *Mine Workers* to authorize a relatively unlimited judicial power to impose noncompensatory civil contempt fines.

Underlying the somewhat elusive distinction between civil and criminal contempt fines, and the ultimate question posed in this case, is what procedural protections are due before any particular contempt penalty may be imposed. Because civil contempt sanctions are viewed as nonpunitive and avoidable, fewer procedural protections for such sanctions have been required. To the extent that such contempts take on a punitive character, however, and are not justified by other considerations central to the contempt power, criminal procedural protections may be in order.

The traditional justification for the relative breadth of the contempt power has been necessity: Courts independently must be vested with "power to impose silence, respect, and decorum, in their presence, and submission to their lawful mandates, and . . . to preserve themselves and their officers from the approach and insults of pollution." Anderson *v.* Dunn, 6 Wheat. 204, 227 (1821). Courts thus have embraced an inherent contempt authority, as a power "necessary to the exercise of all others." United States *v.* Hudson, 7 Cranch 32, 34 (1812).

But the contempt power also uniquely is "liable to abuse." Bloom, 391 U.S. at 202. Unlike most areas of law, where a legislature defines both the sanctionable conduct and the penalty to be imposed, civil contempt proceedings leave the offended judge solely responsible for identifying, prosecuting, adjudicating, and sanctioning the contumacious conduct. Contumacy "often strikes at the most vulnerable and human qualities of a judge's temperament," *id.* at 202, and its fusion of legislative, executive, and judicial powers "summons forth . . . the prospect of 'the most tyrannical licentiousness.'" Young *v.* United States ex rel. Vuitton et Fils S.A., 481 U.S. 787, 822 (1987) (Scalia, J., concurring in judgment), quoting Anderson, 6 Wheat., at 228. Accordingly, "in [criminal] contempt cases an even more compelling argument can be made [than in ordinary criminal cases] for providing a right to jury trial as a protection against the arbitrary exercise of official power." Bloom, 391 U.S. at 202.

Our jurisprudence in the contempt area has attempted to balance the competing concerns of necessity and potential arbitrariness by allowing a relatively unencumbered contempt power when its exercise is most essential, and requiring progressively greater procedural protections when other considerations come into play. The necessity justification for the contempt authority is at its pinnacle, of course, where contumacious conduct threatens a court's immediate ability to conduct its proceedings, such as where a witness refuses to testify, or a party disrupts the court. Thus, petty, direct contempts in the presence of the court traditionally have been subject to summary adjudication, "to maintain order in the courtroom and the integrity of the trial process in the face of an actual obstruction of justice." Codispoti *v.* Pennsylvania, 418 U.S. 506, 513 (1974). In light of the court's substantial interest in rapidly coercing compliance and restoring order, and because the contempt's occurrence before the court reduces the need for extensive factfinding and the likelihood of an erroneous deprivation, summary proceedings have been tolerated.

Summary adjudication becomes less justifiable once a court leaves the realm of immediately sanctioned, petty direct contempts. If a court delays punishing a direct contempt until the completion of trial, for example, due process requires that the contemnor's rights to notice and a hearing be respected. There "it is much more difficult to argue that action without notice or hearing of any kind is necessary to preserve order and enable [the court] to proceed with its business," particularly "in view of the heightened potential for abuse posed by the contempt power." Taylor *v.* Hayes, 418 U.S. 488, 498, 500 (1974). Direct contempts also cannot be punished with serious criminal penalties absent the full protections of a criminal jury trial. Bloom, 391 U.S. at 210.

Still further procedural protections are afforded for contempts occurring out of court, where the considerations justifying expedited procedures do not pertain. Summary adjudication of indirect contempts is prohibited, and criminal contempt sanctions are entitled to full criminal process. Certain indirect contempts nevertheless are appropriate for imposition through civil proceedings. Contempts such as failure to comply with document discovery, for example, while occurring outside the court's presence, impede the court's ability to adjudicate the proceedings before it and thus touch upon the core justification for the contempt power. Courts traditionally have broad authority through means other than contempt—such as by striking pleadings, assessing costs, excluding evidence, and entering default judgment—to penalize a party's failure to comply with the rules of conduct governing the litigation process. Such judicial sanctions never have been considered criminal, and the imposition of civil, coercive fines to police the litigation process appears consistent with this authority. Similarly, indirect contempts involving discrete, readily ascertainable acts, such as turning over a key or payment of a judgment, properly may be adjudicated through civil proceedings since the need for extensive, impartial factfinding is less pressing.

For a discrete category of indirect contempts, however, civil procedural protections may be insufficient. Contempts involving out-of-court disobedience to complex injunctions often require elaborate and reliable factfinding. Such contempts do not obstruct the court's ability to adjudicate the proceedings before it, and the risk of erroneous deprivation from the lack of a neutral factfinder may be substantial. Under these circumstances, criminal procedural protections such as the rights to counsel and proof beyond a reasonable doubt are both necessary and appropriate to protect the due process rights of parties and prevent the arbitrary exercise of judicial power.

In the instant case, neither any party nor any court of the Commonwealth has suggested that the challenged fines are compensatory. At no point did the trial court attempt to calibrate the fines to damages caused by the union's contumacious activities or indicate that the fines were "to compensate the complainant for losses sustained." Mine Workers, 330 U.S. at 303–304. The nonparty governments, in turn, never requested any compensation or presented any evidence regarding their injuries, never moved to intervene in the suit, and never actively defended the fines imposed. The issue before us accordingly is limited to whether these fines, despite their noncompensatory character, are coercive civil or criminal sanctions.

The parties propose two independent tests for determining whether the fines are civil or criminal. Petitioners argue that because the injunction primarily prohibited certain conduct rather than mandated affirmative acts, the sanctions are criminal. Respondents in turn urge that because the trial court established a prospective fine schedule that the union could avoid through compliance, the fines are civil in character.

Neither theory satisfactorily identifies those contempt fines that are criminal and thus must be imposed through the criminal process. . . . The distinction between mandatory and prohibitory orders is easily applied in the classic contempt scenario, where contempt sanctions are used to enforce orders compelling or forbidding a single, discrete act. In such cases, orders commanding an affirmative act simply designate those actions that are capable of being coerced.

But the distinction between coercion of affirmative acts and punishment of prohibited conduct is difficult to apply when conduct that can recur is involved, or when an injunction contains both mandatory and prohibitory provisions. Moreover, in borderline cases injunctive provisions containing essentially the same command can be phrased either in mandatory or prohibitory terms. Under a literal application of petitioners' theory, an injunction ordering the union: "Do not strike," would appear to be prohibitory and criminal, while an injunction ordering the union: "Continue working," would be mandatory and civil. In enforcing the present injunction, the trial court imposed fines without regard to the mandatory or prohibitory nature of the clause violated. Accordingly, even though a parsing of the injunction's various provisions might support the classification of contempts such as rock throwing and placing tire-damaging "jackrocks" on roads as criminal and the refusal to place supervisors at picket sites as civil, the parties have not asked us to review the order in that manner. In a case like this involving an injunction that prescribes a detailed code of conduct, it is more appropriate to identify the character of the entire decree.

Despite respondents' urging, we also are not persuaded that dispositive significance should be accorded to the fact that the trial court prospectively announced the sanctions it would impose. Had the trial court simply levied the fines after finding the union guilty of contempt, the resulting "determinate and unconditional" fines would be considered "solely and exclusively punitive." . . .

[T]he fact that the trial court announced the fines before the contumacy, rather than after the fact, does not in itself justify respondents' conclusion that the fines are civil or meaningfully distinguish these penalties from the ordinary criminal law. Due process traditionally requires that criminal laws provide prior notice both of the conduct to be prohibited and of the sanction to be imposed. The trial court here simply announced the penalty—determinate fines of $20,000 or $100,000 per violation—that would be imposed for future contempts. The union's ability to avoid the contempt fines was indistinguishable from the ability of any ordinary citizen to avoid a criminal sanction by conforming his behavior to the law. The fines are not coercive day fines, or even suspended fines, but are more closely analogous to fixed, determinate, retrospective criminal fines which petitioners had no opportunity to purge once imposed. We therefore decline to conclude that the mere fact that the sanctions were announced in advance rendered them coercive and civil as a matter of constitutional law.

Other considerations convince us that the fines challenged here are criminal. The union's sanctionable conduct did not occur in the court's presence or otherwise implicate the court's ability to maintain order and adjudicate the proceedings before it. Nor did the union's contumacy involve simple, affirmative acts, such as the paradigmatic civil contempts examined in *Gompers*. Instead, the Virginia trial court levied contempt fines for widespread, ongoing, out-of-court violations of a complex injunction. In so doing, the court effectively policed petitioners' compliance with an entire code of conduct that the court itself had imposed. The union's contumacy lasted many months and spanned a substantial portion of the State. The fines assessed were serious, totaling over $52 million. Under such circumstances, disinterested factfinding and evenhanded adjudication were essential, and petitioners were entitled to a criminal jury trial.

In reaching this conclusion, we recognize that this Court generally has deferred to a legislature's determination whether a sanction is civil or criminal, and that "[w]hen a State's proceedings are involved, state law provides strong guidance about whether or not the State is exercising its authority in a nonpunitive, noncriminal manner." Hicks, 485 U.S. at 631. We do not deviate from either tradition today. Where a single judge, rather than a legislature, declares a particular sanction to be civil or criminal, such deference is less appropriate. Moreover, this Court has recognized that even for state proceedings, the label affixed to a contempt ultimately "will not be allowed to defeat the applicable protections of federal constitutional law." *Ibid.* We conclude that the serious contempt fines imposed here were criminal and constitutionally could not be imposed absent a jury trial.

Our decision concededly imposes some procedural burdens on courts' ability to sanction widespread, indirect contempts of complex injunctions through noncompensatory fines. Our holding, however, leaves unaltered the longstanding authority of judges to adjudicate direct contempts summarily, and to enter broad compensatory awards for all contempts through civil proceedings. Because the right to trial by jury applies only to serious criminal sanctions, courts still may impose noncompensatory, petty fines for contempts such as the present ones without conducting a jury trial. We also do not disturb a court's ability to levy, albeit through the criminal contempt process, serious fines like those in this case.

Ultimately, whatever slight burden our holding may impose on the judicial contempt power cannot be controlling. The Court recognized more than a quarter century ago:

> "We cannot say that the need to further respect for judges and courts is entitled to more consideration than the interest of the individual not be subjected to serious criminal punishment

without the benefit of all the procedural protections worked out carefully over the years and deemed fundamental to our system of justice. Genuine respect, which alone can lend true dignity to our judicial establishment, will be engendered, not by the fear of unlimited authority, but by the firm administration of the law through those institutionalized procedures which have been worked out over the centuries." Bloom, 391 U.S. at 208. . . .

The judgment of the Supreme Court of Virginia is reversed. . . .

■ JUSTICE SCALIA, concurring. . . . The use of a civil process for contempt sanctions "makes no sense except as a consequence of historical practice." Weiss *v.* United States, 510 U.S. 163, 198 (1994) (Scalia, J., concurring in part and concurring in judgment). As the scope of injunctions has expanded, they have lost some of the distinctive features that made enforcement through civil process acceptable. It is not that the times, or our perceptions of fairness, have changed (that is in my view no basis for either tightening or relaxing the traditional demands of due process); but rather that the modern judicial order is in its relevant essentials not the same device that in former times could always be enforced by civil contempt. So adjustments will have to be made. We will have to decide at some point which modern injunctions sufficiently resemble their historical namesakes to warrant the same extraordinary means of enforcement. We need not draw that line in the present case, and so I am content to join the opinion of the Court.

■ [The concurring opinion of JUSTICE GINSBURG is omitted.]

NOTES

1. Criminal contempt is administered in a criminal proceeding separate from the underlying case. Civil contempt, in contrast, is administered in a civil proceeding adjunct to the underlying case. The difference between civil and criminal contempt affects such matters as the effect of the plaintiff's voluntary dismissal of the equity suit, the application of the Statute of Limitations for crimes, the availability of the privilege against self-incrimination, the burden of proof, the procedure and scope of appellate review, and the power of the executive to pardon a person adjudged to be in contempt.

2. Vuitton informed a federal district court that Klayminc was violating an injunction barring Klayminc from infringing Vuitton's trademark. The judge appointed Vuitton's lawyers to investigate and prosecute the alleged contempt on behalf of the United States. Based on over one hundred audio and video tapes documenting a scheme to produce and sell counterfeit handbags, Klayminc was convicted of criminal contempt. On appeal, the Supreme Court invoked its supervisory power over the federal courts to reverse the conviction. A majority of the justices agreed "that courts possess inherent authority to initiate contempt proceedings for disobedience to their orders, which authority necessarily encompasses the ability to appoint a private attorney to prosecute the contempt." Yet, because of the

potential for conflict of interest, a federal court should not appoint "counsel for a party that is the beneficiary of a court order . . . as prosecutor in a [criminal] contempt action alleging a violation of that order." Young *v.* United States ex rel. Vuitton et Fils S.A., 481 U.S. 787 (1987).

3. In another case, Vuitton obtained a consent decree ordering Carousel, a handbag store, to stop selling counterfeit Vuitton bags. Shortly afterward, a Vuitton lawyer discovered counterfeit bags for sale at Mirage, a handbag store owned jointly by the sole proprietor of Carousel and two of his brothers. Vuitton asked the district judge who approved the consent decree to hold the three brothers in contempt for violation of the decree, but the judge refused. On appeal, the Second Circuit Court of Appeals held that if the district court determined on remand that the three brothers were acting in concert with Carousel in selling the counterfeit bags, Vuitton was entitled to compensatory damages for losses caused by the violation:

> "Generally, the sanctions imposed after a finding of civil contempt serve two functions: to coerce future compliance and to remedy past noncompliance. So far as the first of these functions is concerned, the district judge, sitting in equity, is vested with wide discretion in fashioning a remedy. By contrast, once the plaintiff has proved that he has suffered harm because of a violation of the terms of an injunction, compensatory damages are appropriate.
>
> "[A] compensatory fine in civil contempt . . . is employed not to vindicate the court's authority but to make reparation to the injured party and restore the parties to the position they would have held had the injunction been obeyed. The district court is not free to exercise its discretion and withhold an order in civil contempt awarding damages, to the extent they are established.
>
> "Since the plaintiff should be made whole for the harm he has suffered, it is appropriate for the court also to award the reasonable costs of prosecuting the contempt, including attorney's fees, if the violation of the decree is found to have been willful."

Vuitton et Fils S. A. *v.* Carousel Handbags, 592 F.2d 126 (2d Cir. 1979).

Chadwick v. Janecka

United States Court of Appeals, Third Circuit, 2002.
312 F.3d 597.

■ ALITO, CIRCUIT JUDGE. . . . In November 1992, Mrs. Barbara Chadwick filed for divorce in the Delaware County (Pennsylvania) Court of Common Pleas. During an equitable distribution conference in February 1993, Mr. Chadwick informed the state court and Mrs. Chadwick that he had unilaterally transferred $2,502,000.00 of the marital estate to satisfy an alleged debt to Maison Blanche, Ltd., a Gibraltar partnership.

It was later discovered that (1) one of the principals of Maison Blanche had returned $869,106.00 from Gibraltar to an American bank account in Mr. Chadwick's name and that these funds had then been used to purchase three insurance annuity contracts; (2) $995,726.41 had been transferred to a Union Bank account in Switzerland in Mr. Chadwick's name; and (3) $550,000.00 in stock certificates that the petitioner claimed he had transferred to an unknown barrister in England to forward to Maison Blanche had never been received. The state court then entered a freeze order on the marital assets on April 29, 1994.

In May 1994, Mr. Chadwick redeemed the annuity contracts and deposited the funds in a Panamanian bank. After a hearing on July 22, 1994, the court determined that Mr. Chadwick's transfer of the money was an attempt to defraud Mrs. Chadwick and the court. At that time, the court ordered petitioner to return the $2,502,000.00 to an account under the jurisdiction of the court, to pay $75,000.00 for Mrs. Chadwick's attorney's fees and costs, to surrender his passport, and to remain within the jurisdiction. Mr. Chadwick refused to comply, and Mrs. Chadwick thereafter filed a petition to have him held in civil contempt. Mr. Chadwick failed to appear at any of the three contempt hearings, but his attorney was present. The court found Mr. Chadwick in contempt of the July 22, 1994, order and issued a bench warrant for his arrest.

After learning of the bench warrant, Mr. Chadwick fled the jurisdiction but was arrested and detained on April 5, 1995. The state court determined that Mr. Chadwick had the present ability to comply with the terms of the July 22, 1994, order and set bail at $3,000,000. Mr. Chadwick could have been released from custody either by posting bail or by complying with the July 22, 1994, order. To date, he has done neither.

Since his confinement, Mr. Chadwick has applied eight times to the state courts and six times to the federal court to gain release from incarceration. [The present appeal arose from a federal habeas corpus petition, which the district court granted on the ground that the order committing Chadwick to jail had "lost its coercive effect" and should now be treated as a criminal sanction, imposed without sufficient procedural protections.] . . .

To determine whether a contempt order is civil or criminal, Supreme Court jurisprudence requires an examination of the "character and purpose" of the sanction imposed. See International Union *v.* Bagwell, 512 U.S. 821, 827 (1994); Gompers *v.* Buck's Stove & Range Co., 221 U.S. 418, 441 (1911). Civil confinement "is remedial, and for the benefit of the complainant," whereas criminal confinement "is punitive, to vindicate the authority of the court. . . ." Gompers, 221 U.S. at 441. . . .

The Supreme Court has never endorsed the proposition that confinement for civil contempt must cease when there is "no substantial likelihood of compliance." On the contrary, in words that might as well have been written to describe the case now before us, the *Bagwell* Court stated that "[t]he paradigmatic coercive, civil contempt sanction . . . involves confining a contemnor *indefinitely* until he complies with an affirmative command such as an order to pay alimony, or to surrender property ordered to be turned over to a receiver. . . ." . . .

[T]he state courts have repeatedly found that Mr. Chadwick has the present ability to comply with the July 1994 state court order . . . .

Our decision does not preclude Mr. Chadwick from filing a new federal habeas petition if he claims that he is *unable* for some reason to comply with the state court's order. And, needless to say, our decision imposes no restrictions on the state courts' ability to grant relief.

Pounders v. Watson

Supreme Court of the United States, 1997.
521 U.S. 982.

■ PER CURIAM. . . . Respondent Penelope Watson is an attorney who represented William Mora in a multidefendant murder trial in the Superior Court of the State of California in and for the County of Los Angeles. The Honorable William Pounders presided over the case, and he is the petitioner here. On April 7, 1994, counsel for one of Mora's codefendants repeatedly raised in open court the issue of the punishment defendants might receive if they were convicted. Judge Pounders stated that possible punishment "is not a subject that's open to discussion. It should not be explored." Though it is not clear whether this was said at a bench conference only or reiterated in open court, it seems respondent remained at the defense table during the bench conference. Her co-counsel, Joseph Gutierrez, was at the bench on behalf of their client Mora. In later proceedings, Judge Pounders noted that "Miss Watson is no more than six feet away from us when we're at the side bar conference. She's at the end of the center table closest to the bench and only a matter of feet away."

On April 20, counsel for a different codefendant again raised the issue of punishment. Judge Pounders stated in open court: "[T]he subject of sentencing of Mr. Fernandez is not part of the conversation. But more than that, it is prejudicial under Cal. Evid. Code Ann. § 352 (West 1966). It's not a subject the jury is entitled to discuss. This is not a death penalty case, so penalties are not something to discuss. . . ."

The next day, respondent's co-counsel Gutierrez asked a series of questions in which he stated that defendants were "looking at life in prison." At a bench conference, while respondent remained at the defense table, Judge Pounders told Gutierrez:

> "You had an ulterior motive in bringing out the amount of time [the witness] spent [in prison], and I think it's to show the contrast between what he got and what your clients may be facing. . . . I'm saying that's the last time I want to hear anything about a sentence. . . . You've covered it. Do not cover it again."

After the side bar, Gutierrez apologized in open court:

> "Judge, I would just like the record to reflect that I apologize to this court for asking the question as to or informing this witness through my question that he served six months in jail and three years probation. . . . I obviously defied the Court Order, and I misunderstood the Court and I apologize."

In response, Judge Pounders said in open court:

> "It's simply that punishment is not an issue for this jury to decide, and the more that counsel want to harp on this issue of punishment, the more inappropriate it becomes."

On June 21, while respondent was questioning Mora, the following examination and colloquy occurred:

> By Ms. Watson: "[T]hroughout this trial sometimes you've had to get up at 4:00 in the morning and not go to sleep until 10:00 at night?
>
> "Ms. Walker [for the People of California]: Objection, your honor, relevance.
>
> "The Court: Sustained.
>
> "By Ms. Watson: And during that four years [that you have been in prison], you were facing the death penalty until just the day before we started.
>
> "Ms. Walker: Your honor, People are going to object.
>
> "The Court: Sustained.
>
> "Ms. Walker: Ask Miss Watson to be admonished and the Court—
>
> "The Court: Sustained. We've already talked about this at side bar. Follow the Court's admonitions.
>
> "By Ms. Watson: You're facing life without possibility of parole?"

At that point, Judge Pounders called counsel to the bench. The judge asked respondent why he should not hold her in contempt for discussing punishment after he had "at least twice ordered counsel not to cover" the issue. Respondent replied, "I think it goes to [Mora's] state of mind as to why he would take this risk at this point in revealing that he was the person who called 911." When the judge asked why respondent did not raise the point at sidebar, particularly when her co-counsel Gutierrez had been admonished for raising the issue, Watson responded: "I wasn't at side bar with any of that involving Mr. Gutierrez. . . ." The judge said, "You're in violation of a court order. You do not think that's relevant to anything?" Watson responded, "I didn't think it was."

Judge Pounders then found respondent in contempt for violating Cal. Civ. Proc. Code Ann. § 1209(a)(5) (West 1997), which provides that "[d]isobedience of any lawful judgment, order, or process of the court" is grounds for contempt. The next day, on June 22, the judge issued a written order of contempt finding that "the questions asked by contemnor of Defendant Mora in the presence of the jury had as its [sic] sole purpose improperly advising the jury of the potential penalty for the defendants in violation of the court order." He found "contemnor was aware of the Order," since she was

> "at all times . . . present (a) at or immediately adjacent to all side bar conferences and (b) present in open court on April 7, 1994, when the initial warning was given, and (c) on April 20, 1994, when the warning was repeated in open court, and (d) on April 21, 1994, when co-counsel Mr. Gutierrez apologized in open court for defying that same order."

The court imposed a 2-day jail sentence to be served after trial.

On July 8, two days after the murder case was submitted to the jury, Judge Pounders gave respondent another opportunity to justify her actions. She again explained and argued through her counsel that she thought her questions were relevant and "not covered by the court's previous rulings or admonitions." Judge Pounders was not convinced. Respondent, he noted, did not ask for a side bar for clarification. He found:

> "I think she has permanently prejudiced this jury in favor of her client. . . . They know the penalty he's facing . . . and they know that the person that was killed [a gang member] isn't worth that penalty, and so they are not going to find him guilty of the major charge. . . .
>
> "And when the penalty is as extreme as this one is presented to the jury, I think that's a prejudice that cannot be overcome. . . .
>
> "And I believe that the result is going to be that [the jury] will not find Mr. Mora guilty of the main offense, which is murder, that they may not find him guilty of much at all."

Respondent's habeas petitions to the District Court of Appeals and the California Supreme Court were denied. . . .

Respondent appealed to the United States Court of Appeals for the Ninth Circuit, arguing that her due process rights were violated because she did not have notice of the prohibited conduct and because the trial judge could not have known without a hearing whether her conduct was willful. The Court of Appeals did not dispute the state trial court's findings on these points. Instead, it held that "her conduct was not so disruptive as to justify use of summary contempt procedure."

Longstanding precedent confirms the power of courts to find summary contempt and impose punishment. . . . As we have recognized, however, the contempt power may be abused. We have held the summary contempt exception to the normal due process requirements, such as a hearing, counsel, and the opportunity to call witnesses, "includes only charges of misconduct, in open court, in the presence of the judge, which disturbs the court's business, where all of the essential elements of the misconduct are under the eye of the court, are actually observed by the court, and where immediate punishment is essential to prevent 'demoralization of the court's authority' before the public." . . .

Where misconduct occurs in open court, the affront to the court's dignity is more widely observed, justifying summary vindication. . . .

In this case the state trial court made an express finding that respondent willfully refused to comply with the court's order. Again and again the trial court admonished counsel, both in open court and at bench conferences when respondent was sitting a few feet away, not to discuss punishment. After respondent asked her client whether he had been facing the death penalty, the court sustained an objection and said "We've already talked about this at side bar. Follow the Court's admonitions." Undaunted, respondent's next question was, "You're facing life without possibility of parole?" . . .

All that is before us is [a ruling by the Court of Appeals] that respondent's conduct was not disruptive enough to justify contempt, and on this issue we are in disagreement with the Court of Appeals. Nothing in our cases supports a requirement that a contemnor "engage in a pattern of repeated violations that pervaded the courtroom" before she may be held in summary contempt. To the contrary, in United States *v.* Wilson, 421 U.S. 309 (1975), summary contempt convictions were upheld after a single refusal to give immunized testimony, "not delivered disrespectfully." . . . And we have not required that a court determine a contemnor would have repeated the misconduct but for summary punishment. While we have approved, in the context of reviewing a federal contempt order, the equitable principle that only " 'the least possible power adequate to the end proposed' should be used in contempt cases," we found that principle satisfied in the circumstances in *Wilson* because, during an ongoing trial, the court is justified in acting swiftly "to prevent a breakdown of the proceedings." Likewise, in Sacher *v.* United States, 343 U.S. 1, 5 (1952), the Court upheld summary contempt convictions of counsel where the misconduct had the following characteristics: "It took place in the immediate presence of the trial judge; it consisted of breaches of decorum and disobedience in the presence of the jury of his orders and rulings upon the trial; the misconduct was professional in that it was that of lawyers" and conviction was based "upon a course of conduct long-continued in the face of warnings that it was regarded by the court as contemptuous." . . .

The trial court's finding that respondent's comments had prejudiced the jury—together with its assessment of the flagrance of respondent's defiance—support the finding of the need for summary contempt to vindicate the court's authority.

While the Due Process Clause no doubt imposes limits on the authority to issue a summary contempt order, the states must have latitude in determining what conduct so infects orderly judicial proceedings that contempt is permitted. . . .

The ruling of the Court of Appeals, not reviewed en banc, introduced uncertainty into routine proceedings of the many state courts within the Court of Appeals' large geographical jurisdiction. The judgment is reversed. . . .

■ JUSTICE STEVENS, with whom JUSTICE BREYER joins, dissenting. . . .

Given that the respondent in this case asked two inappropriate questions over the course of a three and a half month long trial and that the trial continued without incident for two weeks after her contemptuous conduct, a substantial question exists as to whether fair procedure required a hearing before another judge. Neither the Court nor the petitioner contends that this summary contempt power was exercised to prevent the "actual obstruction of justice," such that a hearing before an entirely disinterested judge would have been impractical. . . .

NOTE

Yengo, a lawyer, was representing one defendant in a complex, multi-defendant conspiracy trial. At the outset of the case, the judge ordered all lawyers to be present and punctual throughout the trial and to make no conflicting plans. In the middle of the trial, Yengo was absent for two days, sending an unprepared colleague to take his place. On Yengo's return, the judge cleared the courtroom and asked him to explain. When Yengo responded that he had gone to Bermuda on business, the judge held him in contempt and fined him $500.

Was this a direct contempt, in the presence of the court?

Compare In re Yengo, 84 N.J. 111 (1980) with In re Lynch, 369 N.J. Super. 93 (2004).

NOTES ON SUMMARY CRIMINAL CONTEMPT

1. Although traditionally there was no right to jury trial in criminal contempt proceedings, the Supreme Court ruled in Bloom *v.* Illinois, 391 U.S. 194 (1968), that the Sixth Amendment right to trial by jury applies in cases of criminal contempt. The Sixth Amendment guarantees a right to trial by jury in prosecutions for serious, as opposed to petty, crimes. The distinction between serious and petty crimes turns on the penalty that the courts are legislatively authorized to impose on convicted offenders. In the event that no such maximum penalty exists, as is typically true of contempt, the actual punishment imposed upon the contemnor is determinative. If the punishment is a jail term in excess of six months, the crime is serious. If the punishment is a jail term of six months or less, the crime is presumed to be petty. In Blanton *v.* City of North Las Vegas, Nevada, 489 U.S. 538 (1989), the Court found that a possible fine of $1,000 did not make a drunk driving offense with a maximum six month prison term a serious crime. In Muniz *v.* Hoffman, 422 U.S. 454 (1975), the Court held that there was no right to jury trial in a criminal contempt proceeding where a fine of $10,000 was imposed

on a union with 13,000 dues-paying members. But the Court has not ruled out the possibility that a fine alone could bring the jury trial right into play in a case of criminal contempt.

2. Mayberry was proceeding *pro se* in a criminal case. In the course of the trial, he spoke abusively to the judge, calling him, for example, a "stumbling dog." Mayberry also attempted to disrupt the proceedings when the judge charged the jury. The attempt was unsuccessful, and Mayberry was found guilty as charged. When he appeared for sentencing in the underlying criminal case, the judge pronounced him guilty of contempt and sentenced him to 11–22 years in prison for his contemptuous behavior. On appeal, the Supreme Court held that, given the personal nature of Mayberry's attacks on the trial judge and the judge's decision to delay the contempt proceedings until the end of the trial, due process required that a different judge preside over the adjudication of Mayberry's contempt. Mayberry *v.* Pennsylvania, 400 U.S. 455 (1971).

3. Little was on trial in a North Carolina trial court for carrying a concealed weapon. After the judge denied Little's request for a continuance on the ground that his lawyer was tied up in another trial, Little attempted a *pro se* defense. In his summation, he characterized himself as a political prisoner and asserted that the judge was biased and had prejudged the case. The judge summarily held him in contempt, stating that his remarks were disrespectful and tended to subvert justice. (The judge also stated in his written order that, following the contempt conviction, Little "called the undersigned presiding judge a 'M____ F____.' "[i]) The Supreme Court reversed the conviction:

> "We hold that in the context of this case petitioner's statements in summation did not constitute criminal contempt. The court's denial of the continuance forced petitioner to argue his own cause. He was therefore clearly entitled to as much latitude in conducting his defense as we have held is enjoyed by counsel vigorously espousing a client's cause. There is no indication, and the State does not argue, that petitioner's statements were uttered in a boisterous tone or in any wise actually disrupted the court proceeding. Therefore, [t]he vehemence of the language used is not alone the measure of the power to punish for contempt. The fires which it kindles must constitute an imminent, not merely a likely, threat to the administration of justice. The danger must not be remote or even probable; it must immediately imperil . . . . [T]he law of contempt is not made for the protection of judges who may be sensitive to the winds of public opinion. Judges are supposed to be men of fortitude, able to thrive in a hardy climate. Trial courts . . . must be on guard against confusing offenses to their sensibilities with obstruction to the administration of justice."

In re Little, 404 U.S. 553 (1972).

[i] Cf. Dogberry's insistence that it be written down that he was called "an ass," in *Much Ado About Nothing*, Act IV, Scene 2.

4. Eaton was on trial in the Municipal Court of Tulsa, Oklahoma, for violating a municipal ordinance. Responding to cross-examination, he referred to an alleged assailant as "chicken shit." In consequence, he was prosecuted and convicted under an information that charged him with "direct contempt," in violation of another Tulsa ordinance, "by his insolent behavior during open court and in the presence of [the judge], to wit: by using the language 'chicken-shit.'" The Supreme Court held that this incident could not constitutionally support a conviction for criminal contempt. Eaton *v.* City of Tulsa, 415 U.S. 697 (1974).

5. Malone and Kennedy were spectators in a courtroom. Because they felt that courts do not always serve the cause of justice, they refused to rise, as requested by the bailiff, when the judge entered and left the courtroom. The judge held them in contempt of court and sentenced Malone to be confined ten days and Kennedy thirty days. The appellate court reversed the sentences, finding that it was a sufficient punishment that Malone and Kennedy had been excluded from the courtroom and held in custody for several hours. United States ex rel. Robson *v.* Malone, 412 F.2d 848 (7th Cir. 1969).

NOTES ON CONTEMPT BY ATTORNEYS

1. Martina, an attorney, was called before a trial judge to explain his failure to appear on behalf of a client charged with issuing a bad check. Martina explained that he had an agreement with the prosecutor that the client could attend court on her own, then added that "[m]y reasons for not showing up were personal reasons. I am trying to make a living. This was a pro bono matter and I felt that my client was not unintelligent. She was fully informed. I simply entered an appearance to expedite it." Rather than hold Martina in contempt the judge informed Martina that the matter would be referred to the Professional Conduct Committee. Martina replied, "Thank you, and I should advise the court I intend to bring you to the Judicial Conduct Committee. I think your actions . . . were quite frankly ignominious." The judge then punished Martina summarily for direct criminal contempt, imposing a fine of five hundred dollars and a jail sentence of fifteen days. The Supreme Court of New Hampshire upheld the trial court's use of the summary contempt procedure, but ultimately remanded the case for further proceedings on the ground that the defendant was not notified of the precise conduct punished. State *v.* Martina, 135 N.H. 111 (1991).

2. Wendy, an attorney, was held in contempt when he refused to proceed with a scheduled criminal trial. Substituting for a law partner who was busy in another court at the time, Wendy had represented the client at an arraignment and during some pretrial matters. When the case was called for trial, however, Wendy explained that he was a tax lawyer, had never tried a case in court, and had merely substituted for his partner during the earlier stages of the proceedings. On appeal, the court held that he could not be held in contempt for refusing to proceed with the trial of the criminal case. United States *v.* Wendy, 575 F.2d 1025 (2d Cir. 1978).

3. Snyder, a lawyer whose application for a fee for representing an indigent defendant had been returned to him for additional documentation, wrote the district judge a letter which stated in part:

> "In the first place, I am appalled by the amount of money which the federal court pays for indigent criminal defense work. The reason that so few attorneys in Bismarck accept this work is for that exact reason. We have, up to this point, still accepted the indigent appointments, because of a duty to our profession, and the fact that nobody else will do it.
>
> "Now, however, not only are we paid an amount of money which does not even cover our overhead, but we have to go through extreme gymnastics even to receive the puny amounts which the federal courts authorize for this work. We have sent you everything we have concerning our representation, and I am not sending you anything else. You can take it or leave it.
>
> "Further, I am extremely disgusted by the treatment of us by the Eighth Circuit in this case, and you are instructed to remove my name from the list of attorneys who will accept criminal indigent defense work. I have simply had it.
>
> "Thank you for your time and attention."

The district judge forwarded the letter to the chief judge of the circuit, who was responsible under the Act for approving expenditures in excess of $1,000.00. The chief judge found the letter disrespectful and ultimately suspended Snyder from practice in the federal courts in the circuit when he refused to apologize for his remarks. In re Snyder, 472 U.S. 634 (1985) (holding that Snyder's conduct did not warrant his suspension from practice).

4. EXECUTION OF DECREES FOR PAYMENT OF MONEY

Brown v. Brown

Court of Appeals of Maryland, 1980.
287 Md. 273.

■ DIGGES, JUDGE. . . . The parties to this dispute, Ronald K. Brown, appellant, and Joyce A. Brown, appellee, were divorced on October 22, 1976, by decree of the Circuit Court for Prince George's County. The decree incorporated a previously executed separation agreement which differs in a material way from most such contracts in only one respect. Its unusual aspect is contained in Paragraph 7, which states:

> "The husband and wife acknowledge that a child, Lisa Graninger, age 6, was born to wife prior to the marriage of the parties. That despite the fact that the husband is not the natural father of Lisa, in consideration of his love for the child and other good and valuable consideration, the husband agrees to pay support to the wife for Lisa Graninger the sum of $30.00 per week . . . commencing on the 5th day of July, 1976, and to

> continue until [the] child becomes eighteen years of age, is emancipated or dies, whichever first occurs."

. . . [T]he appellant soon fell into arrears in the agreed support payments for Lisa. Following a hearing as to whether he was in contempt of court for failing to make these payments, Judge Robert J. Woods, on October 17, 1978, found Mr. Brown to be in default in the amount of $1729.95, adjudged him to be in contempt of court, and subsequently sentenced the stepfather to serve a term of 179 days in jail. . . .

The gravamen of the stepfather's claim . . . [is] Article III, section 38 of the Maryland Constitution . . . :

> ". . . No person shall be imprisoned for debt, but a valid decree of a court of competent jurisdiction or agreement approved by decree of said court for the support of a wife or dependent children, or for the support of an illegitimate child or children, or for alimony, shall not constitute a debt within the meaning of this section.[2]"

. . . [T]he stepfather reasons in this Court that there exists no legal duty, independent of agreement, to support his stepchild, and that his contractual assumption of the obligation to make the weekly payments for Lisa, being voluntary, cannot subject him to incarceration for his failure to pay. . . .

The evident purpose of the framers was to abolish the useless, and sometimes cruel, imprisonment of persons who, having honestly become indebted to another, were unable to pay as promised. However, early in the development of the case law under this section, a distinction was drawn by this Court between a "debt" within the meaning of section 38, and a legal "duty" arising from or imposed by law. . . . This dichotomy between duty and debt was first applied in this State in a domestic relation context in Dickey *v.* Dickey, 154 Md. 675 (1928) . . . :

> "[T]he obligation to pay alimony in a divorce proceeding is not regarded as a debt but a duty growing out of the marital relation and resting upon a sound public policy, and so this obligation may be enforced by attachment of the person for contempt, and the defendant be imprisoned . . . ."

The [1950 and 1962] amendments abolished . . . technical distinctions between alimony on the one hand, and wife support and the support of dependent children, on the other, so that all three obligations now purport to be enforceable by attachment and imprisonment of the defendant. Furthermore, an agreement for support or alimony which is approved by a court of competent jurisdiction, is equated to a decree of

---

[2] . . . For the first one hundred years of its existence, the provision simply read "No person shall be imprisoned for debt." In 1950 the section was amended by adding "but a valid decree of a court of competent jurisdiction or agreement approved by decree of said court for the support of a wife or dependent children, or for alimony, shall not constitute a debt within the meaning of this section." The section was further amended in 1962 by the addition of the language ", or for the support of an illegitimate child or children."

such court, so that neither is a debt within the contemplation of the constitutional prohibition against imprisonment for nonpayment. . . .

[S]ince the primary purpose of the original enactment of section 38's imprisonment prohibition was to safeguard personal liberty, we believe that, in the absence of a clear indication of an intent to abridge the broad scope of this protection, any doubts concerning the class of children whose support the framers intended could be enforced by imprisonment, should be resolved in favor of the liberty of the citizen. . . . [T]he obligation of the appellant here to support his stepchild is contractual, and consequently quite different from a father's noncontractual duty to support his natural or adopted child. The 1950 and 1962 amendments to section 38 do not address obligations such as the one entered into by the appellant, with the consequence that his agreement to aid in the support of his stepdaughter created nothing more than a debt for which the constitution affords him immunity from incarceration when he failed to discharge his contractual obligation. . . .

The chancellor reasoned that, whether Mr. Brown's agreement to contribute to Lisa's support is technically a debt within the scope of section 38, imprisonment as a contempt is available by virtue of the appellant's disregard of a direct order by the court to pay. . . . While we recognize that there is, in some of our sister states, authority to the contrary, the decisions of this Court make clear that although there are

> "various [other] remedies at the command of chancery for the purpose of executing or compelling the performance and fulfillment of a decree[,] . . . when the decree only directs the payment of money, a party defendant, who has been brought into court under process of contempt to compel the performance of such a decree, may not be imprisoned." . . .

NOTES

1. For a decision permitting imprisonment as a method for coercing payment of a money judgment, see Reeves *v.* Crownshield, 274 N.Y. 74 (1937).

2. Originally, when contempt sanctions and sequestration failed to persuade a defendant to comply with an order commanding the payment of money, equity courts had no further means of enforcing the decree. However, beginning in 1785, American legislatures began to enact statutes authorizing the execution of money decrees in the same manner as legal judgments. Such laws now exist throughout the country. This change in attitude toward the enforcement of money decrees has been so complete that Fed. R. Civ. P. 69(a), for example, now states, "Process to enforce a judgment for the payment of money shall be a writ of execution, unless the court directs otherwise."

3. In Bearden *v.* Georgia, 461 U.S. 660 (1983), the Supreme Court held that the imprisonment of an indigent probationer for failing to pay a fine and restitution was unconstitutional if he had "made all reasonable efforts to pay," but was unable to do so "through no fault of his own."

5. MASTERS AND RECEIVERS

Courts of equity (and merged courts exercising equitable powers) traditionally have exercised the power to enlist masters or receivers to assist in preparing and implementing decrees. Masters and receivers are appointed by the court at the parties' expense.

Masters are appointed to handle some aspect of a pending litigation. They have been used, for example, to conduct hearings and investigations, find facts on particular issues, recommend appropriate sanctions, verify accounts, determine the value of property, and compute damages. The use of masters in the federal courts is governed by Fed. R. Civ. P. 53.

Receivers are appointed to manage property. Because a receiver acts on behalf of the appointing court, the law considers the court to have possession of property in the receiver's custody. It follows that interference with the receiver's possession is punishable as contempt. Appointment of receivers in federal courts is authorized by Fed. R. Civ. P.66.

Madden v. Rosseter

Supreme Court of New York, New York County, 1921.
114 Misc. 416.

■ FORD, J. Plaintiff is a resident of New York and the defendant of California. Each owns a half interest in the thoroughbred stallion Friar Rock, which the plaintiff now values at $250,000. In fact the defendant paid the plaintiff $30,000 for a half interest in the horse more than two and half years ago.

Under the written agreement of sale dated June 29, 1918, the defendant was to have possession and use of Friar Rock in California during the seasons of 1919 and 1920, the plaintiff to have him for use in Kentucky during the seasons of 1921 and 1922; "thereafter on new arrangements mutually satisfactory."

The season of 1921 is now open or opening and plaintiff by the agreement is entitled in his turn to possess and use the stallion, but defendant flatly refuses to abide by his agreement unless the plaintiff enters into a new agreement which is unsatisfactory to him.

The defendant has utterly no right to insist upon any conditions of any kind for returning the horse to plaintiff except those expressed in the agreement of sale and those require his shipment forthwith to the plaintiff's stock farm in Kentucky. Indeed he has already been kept by the defendant so far beyond the reasonable time of shipment as to substantially prejudice the plaintiff's rights. The horse should have been sent in August or September of 1920 in order to get the stallion acclimated and fit for the season of 1921, during which the plaintiff is entitled to his possession.

Personal service of the summons upon the defendant has been made in this state and he has duly appeared by his attorneys. Upon the verified complaint and affidavits the plaintiff now asks for a mandatory injunction requiring the defendant to ship Friar Rock to Kentucky as provided in the agreement and enjoining other disposition of him; also for a receiver of the stallion with power to proceed to California and to take appropriate steps there or elsewhere, including the invoking of the aid of the courts of that or any other state, or of the Federal courts, to gain possession of the animal and ship him to the plaintiff's stock farm in Kentucky.

Plaintiff's application for relief is quite novel but so is the situation in which he finds himself. Already his rights have been prejudiced and further irreparable damage is threatening him. There must be a remedy and I do not believe this court is powerless to give it to him. The relief prayed for seems to be the most practicable and appropriate which is available to him. The courts of sister states may be relied upon to aid in serving the ends of justice whenever our own process falls short of effectiveness.

The motion will be granted and the amount of the receiver's bond will be fixed upon settlement of the order. . . .

NOTES

1. Madden *v.* Rosseter was affirmed without opinion, 196 App. Div. 891 (1921). The receiver carried out the order of the court "with tact and diplomacy," and was allowed a fee of $5,000 for his services. 117 Misc. 244, 245 (1921).

2. Receivers are not only used to manage private property. In recent years, they have also been appointed to manage institutions such as schools, prisons, and public housing agencies. The case that follows is an example.

Perez v. Boston Housing Authority

Supreme Judicial Court of Massachusetts, 1980.
379 Mass. 703.

■ KAPLAN, JUSTICE. Nine persons, tenants in various developments of the Boston Housing Authority (BHA), brought this action for themselves and on behalf of the whole class of tenants of BHA similarly situated, seeking to vindicate their statutory rights to decent, safe, and sanitary housing. The judge below found at successive stages of the action that many of the units and common facilities of BHA housing were in substandard conditions in violation of the State sanitary code. In order to right the wrong and provide a remedy, the judge attempted a number of expedients, based essentially on exercise of his injunctive powers, to guide and compel performance by BHA. These failed. After much effort, a comprehensive consent decree was formulated. This also failed. The judge found upon lengthy trial that a major cause of the failures was lack of willing and competent leadership on the part of the five-member Board of BHA. Finally, as an ultimate recourse, after nearly five years of litigation, the judge took the step of ordering appointment of a "receiver"[2] . . . who would assume temporarily the functions of the Board, subject to court order, this again with a view to securing, to the extent that competent management contending with financial stringency could do so, the minimal statutory rights upon which the action was grounded. We have to decide whether this remedial step—certainly an exceptional one—exceeded the bounds of legality or discretion. We hold that it did not, and affirm the judgment appealed from. . . .

1. Appointment of "master." [A] conference was held in April, 1975. . . . The "consensus" of those attending was that BHA would need expert assistance to accomplish any improvements . . . . [The judge] rejected at that time the more intrusive course of appointing a receiver, as suggested by the plaintiffs. Instead, he appointed Robert B. Whittlesey to serve as master.[6] The master was to gather information through investigation and through consultation with the personnel of BHA and any others, official or private, who could be of help. He might prepare draft orders responding to "especially intolerable individual situations." He was also charged with preparing certain plans. . . . BHA was charged with a duty of assisting the master, including the furnishing of all data that he might require. . . .

We skip here to November, 1978. In that eighteenth month of [a consent decree that went into effect in 1977], the master forwarded to BHA some twenty-six notices of substantial noncompliance. . . . [P]laintiffs applied . . . for vacation of the decree, and as further relief, for the appointment of a receiver . . . .

[T]he court on consent of the parties consolidated the applications for hearing. . . . A massive record was generated. The judge filed findings, rulings, opinion, and judgment on July 25, 1979. From this judgment the present appeal is taken. . . .

BHA's liability being established, the problem posed by this important litigation has been to find remedies appropriate and efficient to restore the properties as far as possible to the levels prescribed for human habitation. . . .

BHA could not fairly deny the legitimacy of the use of . . . affirmative injunctions against it in the attempt to achieve the ultimate goal of conformance with the sanitary code. A narrower and more plausible

---

2 We place quotation marks around the words "receiver" and "master," when they first appear in this opinion, to signify that they are not the exact equivalents of the officers of court who usually go by those names.

6 The master's prior experience as a civil engineer and city planner appears of record. He is not a lawyer. Just before this appointment he served as executive director of Greater Boston Community Development, Inc., which gave technical assistance to sponsors of low and moderate income housing.

contention is that the equitable remedy of a receivership goes too far and exceeds the power or jurisdiction of the court. . . .

The power to compel affirmative action by injunction draws with it a power in the court to call to its assistance any agents or officers—we may call them parajudicial officers—whose services appear to be reasonably necessary to attain a legitimate objective. (Indeed the power may be said to inhere in a court whether sitting on the "law" or "equity" side according to the historical division.) . . .

BHA evidently would put receivers in a separate class, and their appointment beyond the powers of an equity court, when the effect of the receivership would be virtually to take over the main functions of public officials (who, by hypothesis, have been in violation of law). We think no such prohibitory rule attaches, although, as we shall emphasize, a receivership must be thoroughly justified on the facts, is always to be considered a remedy of "last resort," and therefore is not often applied in practice. . . .

The circle we are urged to draw around the figure of the receiver would be a highly artificial one. As noted, remedial injunctions have gone against officials directing them what to do, and to that extent we can say that the officials have been supplanted as a practical matter. The injunctions, moreover—which have become familiar in institutional reform litigation prisons, mental health facilities, schools, legislative reapportionment, and so forth—have often been very detailed, tightly controlling the officials initially found delinquent and leaving them with minimal discretion in correcting those delinquencies. . . . [A]s injunctions meet with indifference or violation on the part of the defendant officials, there is justification for the more detailed directions further confining or eliminating discretion. . . .

Still further, it is characteristic of decrees in the fields of institutional reform that they appoint sundry parajudicial officers to assist the court not only in delineating remedies, but often in conducting or overseeing the actual implementation of the remedies. These agents or officers of the court are given functions accommodated to the particular needs. They are called by different names: masters, special masters, examiners, experts, monitors, referees, commissioners, administrators, observers, visitors, ombudsmen, committees, panels, etc. . . .

Finally, we have examples, where exigent facts exist, of the appointment of receivers, eo nomine, to take over temporarily the essential functions of the delinquent officials and in substance to replace them. . . .

A combination of conditions existed here, however, that looked finally to a receivership remedy. There had been massive trouble with eliciting performance of injunctive orders and finally of a comprehensive decree. There could be little doubt that to persist in that course—

retention of the consent decree or reversion to a regime of injunction without consent—could end only in frustration. True leadership of BHA had in fact lapsed. Be it noted that the question was not whether members of the Board were or were not trying hard. The statutory rights of tenants were not to be equated merely with the Board's best efforts. The tenants were entitled to a leadership that had the potential for reaching out to achieve the objectives set by the law. Receivership had not been decided upon precipitately; although earlier sought by the plaintiffs, it had been refused until experience with the consent decree under the existing BHA management established to the satisfaction of the judge that a change of command was indispensable. The Board cannot justly complain of being superseded when it failed, over a long period and after fair opportunity, to secure performance to the level of the injunctive orders and then the consent decree, a decree not thrust upon it but voluntarily adopted.

In holding that the judge did not commit error in finally approving a receivership, we observe that that remedy appears much less drastic in the present situation than it would be in the more typical situations of institutional reform. There is no question here of Federal power entering upon relationships created by the State. Indeed receivership here, installed by a State court in a State setting, does not invade any "line" department or unit of city or State: although, as indicated, BHA is a public body, it functions in many respects as a business corporation to which receivership is readily adapted. The work of a receiver, although beset by collateral problems of no mean difficulty, will focus, after all, on property conservation and rehabilitation. Moreover the problems, both central and collateral, have been canvassed and put in some order by the consent decree whose due performance was beyond the capacities of the old team but may be within the competence of the new. That, at any rate, is a hope not too distant from expectation. . . .

BHA argues that the judgment herein would offend against the principle of separation of powers which finds expression in art. 30 of the Declaration of Rights of our Constitution. But if it is a function of the judicial branch to provide remedies for violations of law, including violations committed by the executive branch, then an injunction with that intent does not derogate from the separation principle, nor, by extension, does a receivership otherwise properly instituted. To the contrary, when the executive persists in indifference to, or neglect or disobedience of court orders, necessitating a receivership, it is the executive that could more properly be charged with contemning the separation principle. . . .

Tied to the "separation" argument, and not too slyly, is an intimation that the courts would do well to stay out of this housing problem, for if the receivership meets with little more success than the current administration of BHA, then the courts will be substituted for BHA as the target of criticism; and the question is left—not squarely stated but immanent—whether that would be good for the courts. Amid these tears shed by anticipation for the courts, we acknowledge the possibility that a receivership will not succeed, but the facts of record suggest to us the certainty that the present administration has failed and would very probably continue to do so. It becomes a conscientious duty, within the law, even at the risk implied, to allow the receivership experiment to go forward as a last resort. . . .

It is right and proper that BHA should be operated as the Legislature declared it should be. But there has been a breakdown, resulting in widespread violations of law by BHA, which necessitates and therefore must evoke extraordinary action. To say that this court has been most reluctant to approve the temporary receivership is to understate the matter. No judge or court could enjoy the prospect of interfering with local authority and assuming a measure of supervision over a large outside enterprise, least of all one sliding downhill. Nevertheless the violations of law are there, and on the facts remedial efforts cannot stop short of receivership. . . .

6. WRITS OF ASSISTANCE AND WRITS OF SEQUESTRATION

Hamilton v. Nakai

United States Court of Appeals, Ninth Circuit, 1971.
453 F.2d 152.

■ DUNIWAY, CIRCUIT JUDGE. [The Hopi Indian Tribe brought an action in federal district court to determine the rights of the Hopi and Navajo Indian Tribes in a reservation in Arizona and to quiet title to the Hopis' interest in the land. In 1962, the district court held that the Hopi and Navajo tribes had undivided and equal interests in a specified portion of the reservation.]

On March 13, 1970, the Hopi Indian Tribe petitioned the District Court for an order of compliance or writ of assistance to enforce its rights as a co-tenant. More specifically, in paragraphs 3 and 4 of their prayer for relief, the Hopi requested an order:

> "3. Directing the defendants to forthwith grant and permit the joint use and possession of the surface, including all resources . . . and to remove such Navajo livestock from said lands as is necessary to accomplish such joint use without further damage to said lands."
>
> "4. Directing the Clerk of this court to issue a writ of assistance to compel performance of the judgment of [the] court entered herein on September 28, 1962, and to allow the plaintiff, the Hopi Tribe, to enter upon said joint use area, and with the Navajo Tribe to jointly and equally use and benefit from the grazing forage and all other surface resources of said area. . . ."

The District Court denied the Hopi's petition on August 3, 1970. . . .

The equitable jurisdiction of a federal court extends to supplemental or ancillary bills brought for the purpose of effectuating a decree of the same court. In *Root* the Court emphasized that "[t]he jurisdiction of courts of equity to interfere and effectuate their own decrees by injunctions or writs of assistance, in order to avoid the relitigation of questions once settled between the same parties, is well settled." Root *v.* Woolworth, 150 U.S. 401, 411–412 (1893). . . .

[T]he power of the court to issue the order requiring compliance or to enforce the judgment by a writ of assistance follows from the principle that a court's power to afford a remedy must be coextensive with its jurisdiction over the subject matter. The [district court] adjudged joint and equal title in the Hopi and Navajo Tribes to a portion of the . . . reservation, and the right to joint possession follows that title even though . . . the original decree did not make explicit provisions concerning possession.

These principles have found expression not only in judicial decisions, but also in a specific statutory enactment, the "All Writs" Act, 28 U.S.C. § 1651(a):

> "The Supreme Courts and all courts established by Act of Congress may issue all writs necessary or appropriate in aid of their respective jurisdictions and agreeable to the usages and principles of law."

The present case meets all the requirements of § 1651(a). First, if the allegations of the Hopi's petition are true, "necessity" rests on the side of the Hopi. They allege that the Navajo have denied to the Hopi the joint use and benefit of the property in question, and that the United States, as trustee and guardian of the property, has neglected its duty to see that the original decree was effectively implemented. . . .

[O]nce jurisdiction has attached, powers under § 1651(a) should be broadly construed. . . .

Finally, a writ of assistance in a suit to quiet title is also "agreeable to the usages and principles of law." [The district] court did not direct that joint possession of the joint use area be delivered to the Hopi, but the court did quiet their title, as co-tenants, and determined that both tribes, for the common use and benefit of their respective members, have joint undivided and equal rights. In these circumstances a writ of assistance is "agreeable to the usages and principles of law." . . .

Nor does it matter that the request for a writ of assistance or possession follows by a number of years the rendering of the decree quieting title. . . .

We are told that it would not be possible to grant the relief sought because many Navajo are permanently settled on the lands in question. In support of the argument we are then confronted with a parade of horribles. Are the Navajo to be ordered to share their hogans with the Hopi? Must they share such gardens as they have, or stock corrals, etc.?

Obviously, where the tract of land is large and the population is sparse, these are straw men. A District Judge is not a creature without judgment or imagination. He can hear testimony from the parties and from representatives of the United States as to what the actual situation is, and can tailor the relief to be afforded to the facts that confront him, always bearing in mind that the objective is to achieve what the court has decreed, the exercise by the Hopi and the Navajo of their "joint, undivided and equal interests as to the surface and subsurface and all resources appertaining thereto [in the lands in question], subject to the trust title of the United States." . . .

NOTES

1. In United States *v.* New York Telephone Co., 434 U.S. 159 (1977), the Court considered whether the All Writs Act allowed a federal court to order a non-party to assist the government in executing a search warrant. Writing in dissent, Justice Stevens offered a succinct overview of the All Writs Act:

> "The All Writs Act was originally enacted, in part, as § 14 of the Judiciary Act of 1789. The Act was, and is, necessary because federal courts are courts of limited jurisdiction having only those powers expressly granted by Congress, and the statute provides these courts with the procedural tools—the various historic common-law writs—necessary for them to exercise their limited jurisdiction. The statute does not contain, and has never before been interpreted as containing [an] open-ended grant of authority to federal courts . . . . Instead, in the language of the statute itself, there are two fundamental limitations on its scope. The *purpose* of any order authorized by the Act must be to aid the court in the exercise of its jurisdiction; and the *means* selected must be analogous to a common-law writ."

Id. at 186–87. The majority in *New York Telephone Co.* decided that the statute did authorize the order, invoking a hodgepodge of considerations, including the lack of burden, the non-party's status as a highly regulated public utility, and congressional intent that could be inferred from other statutes.

2. A federal prosecutor trying to execute a search warrant argued that the All Writs Act allowed the court to order Apple to bypass passcode security on drug trafficker's phone. A federal magistrate judge rejected the argument, in large part because Congress's deliberate failure to give the executive such deencryption authority meant the order would not be "agreeable to the usages and principles of law." In re Apple, Inc., 149 F. Supp. 3d 341 (E.D.N.Y. 2016). For a contrasting opinion, see Matter of Search of an Apple iPhone Seized During Execution of a Search Warrant on a Black Lexus IS300, California License Plate 35KGD203, No. ED 15–0451M, 2016 WL 618401 (C.D. Cal. Feb. 16, 2016) (ordering Apple to modify its software to allow the Federal Bureau of Investigation to access a locked iPhone, and invoking as authority the All Writs Act).

3. When a court enters a legal judgment for possession—for example, in an action of ejectment—and the defendant does not comply voluntarily, the judgment is enforced by a sheriff or federal marshal, acting as an officer of the court. When the court enters an equitable decree that requires surrender of possession, a writ of assistance enables the court to enlist the services of the sheriff or marshal in a roughly equivalent way, as a supplement to the court's contempt powers.

Sequestration was an additional means of enforcing equity decrees against recalcitrant defendants. If jailing the defendant for contempt was impractical or undesirable, the court could instead seize the defendant's assets and hold them to coerce compliance with the decree. Yet, as described in the materials below, the court traditionally could not sell the assets.

Sequestration

Roger North, THE LIFE OF THE RIGHT HONOURABLE FRANCIS NORTH, BARON OF GUILFORD, LORD KEEPER OF THE GREAT SEAL, UNDER KING CHARLES II AND KING JAMES II 197 (1742).

But Sequestrations were not heard of till the Lord Coventry's Time [1625–40], when Sir John Read lay in the Fleet (with 10,000 *l.* in an Iron Cash-Chest in his Chamber) for Disobedience to a Decree, and would not submit and pay the Duty. This being represented to the Lord Keeper as a great Contempt and Affront put upon the Court, he authorised Men to go and break up his Iron Chest, and pay the Duty and Costs, and leave the rest to him, and discharged his Commitment: From thence came Sequestrations; which now are so established as to run of course after all other Process fails, and is but in Nature of a grand Distress, the best Process at Common Law after a Summons, such as a *Subpoena* is; what need all that Grievance and Delay of the intervening Process?

Shaw v. Wright

Chancery, 1795.
3 Ves. 22, 20 Eng. Rep. 872.

Bill against a trustee to have the trusts of a will carried into execution. A sequestration issued for want of answer, under which some leasehold houses were taken. The plaintiffs petitioned that the sequestrators be ordered to sell the houses and account for the proceeds. This relief was denied.

Loughborough, L.C.: "The order would do you no good. I should not have much difficulty in selling, not only perishable commodities, but if the sequestrators were in possession of rents paid in kind, or the natural produce of a farm; but how shall I make a title? By whom? I cannot well order the sequestrators to sell without at the same time warranting the title: then I do not know how I can do that. It does not transfer the term to the sequestrators. It is only a process to compel an appearance, the performance of a duty. All profits I will direct them to apply. The difficulty is this: if the sequestrators sell, and the purchasers should be brought before this Court to complete their contracts, I could not compel them to pay the money. I cannot make a man take a title, which he is to support a bill for an injunction. You will not find any instance of an order to sell under a sequestration a subject, which passes by title and not by delivery."

7. FORECLOSURE AND PARTITION

Eaton v. McCall

Supreme Judicial Court of Maine, 1894.
86 Me. 346.

■ WISHWELL, J. Bill in equity between parties resident in this state to foreclose a mortgage upon real estate situated in Nova Scotia.

The defendant failing to appear, the bill was taken *pro confesso*. . . .

[T]his court has the power to make a decree compelling a mortgagor, over whom it has jurisdiction, to make a conveyance of the mortgaged premises, after failure to pay the amount ascertained to be due, within the time fixed by a decree of the court which time should not be less than the statutory period allowed for redemption in the place where the land is situated.

But as to when and under what circumstances this power should be exercised by the court, is, we think, another and quite different question. It must be remembered that no decree of the court would be operative except one against the mortgagor, or person having the right to redeem, commanding a conveyance. The court could not proceed in the usual and customary method, by decreeing either a strict foreclosure, or a foreclosure by a judicial sale. Neither the decree itself, nor any conveyance under it, except by the person in whom the title is vested, can operate beyond the jurisdiction of the court. A court cannot send its process into another state, nor can it deliver possession of land in another jurisdiction. It can only accomplish foreclosure of such a mortgage by its decree *in personam*, compelling a conveyance.

We do not think that a chancery court should exercise this power except under unusual or extraordinary circumstances. Wherever it is necessary in order to prevent loss or to protect the rights of a mortgagee, it may be done; for instance, in the case of a mortgage upon property situated both within and without the state, where, unless a sale of the entire property could be made at one time, great loss might ensue, or in other cases where an equally good reason existed. But ordinarily we think that the holder of a mortgage should be required to resort to the remedies of the courts of the jurisdiction in which the land is situated. This is in accordance with the principle, than which none is better established, that the disposition of real estate, whether by deed, descent, or by any other mode, must be governed by the law of the state where the same is situated.

In this case there are no reasons, either alleged or apparent, why the holder of this mortgage cannot foreclose the same according to the law of the place where the land is situated, without loss or great inconvenience.

We think, therefore, that the entry should be,

Bill dismissed without prejudice.

Wimer v. Wimer

Supreme Court of Appeals of Virginia, 1888.
82 Va. 890.

Appeal from decree of circuit court of Highland county . . . . The purpose of this suit was to have partition of the lands whereof George Wimer, of Philip, died seized in fee, among the several parties then owning it as tenants in common. These lands consisted of several adjoining tracts . . . situated on Dry Run, partly in said county and partly in Pendleton county, in West Virginia. Defendants demurred to the bill and answered it, . . . denying the jurisdiction of the said circuit court to make partition of land situated in West Virginia, &c. The court appointed commissioners to make the partition, if practicable, as prayed for, and accordingly they did make and report such partition as well of the lands lying in West Virginia as of those lying in Virginia. . . .

■ HINTON, J., delivered the opinion of the court.

The question in this case is one of importance, but of little intrinsic difficulty. It is this: Has a court in Virginia, when the defendants have appeared and answered, jurisdiction to partition lands, the major part of which lies within another State?

Now, it is a fundamental maxim of international jurisprudence that every State or nation possesses an exclusive sovereignty and jurisdiction within its own territory, and the "direct consequence of this rule is," says a learned author, "that the laws of every State affect and bind directly all property, whether real or personal, within its territory." STORY'S CONFLICT OF LAWS, 5, 18. Another consequence of this maxim is, that no State can, by its laws, and no court, which is but a creature of the State, can, by its judgments or decrees, directly bind or affect property beyond the limits of that State; and hence it is axiomatic that no writ of sequestration, or execution, or any order, judgment or decree of a foreign court, can be directly enforced against real estate situate without the limits of the foreign State. . . .

But . . . it is undoubtedly well settled that in cases of fraud, trust or contract, courts of equity will, whenever jurisdiction over the parties has been acquired, administer full relief without regard to the nature or situation of the property in which the controversy had its origin, and even where the relief sought consists in a decree for the conveyance of property which lies beyond the control of the court, provided it can be reached by the exercise of its powers over the person, and the relief asked is of such a nature as the court is capable of administering. Penn *v.* Lord Baltimore, 2 Lead. Cas. Eq. 1806, *et seq.*, and notes; Farley *v.* Shippen, Wythe, 254; 2 Story, Eq. Jur. § 1290 *et seq.*

But even as to these cases it must be borne in mind that the decrees of the foreign court do not directly affect the land, but operate upon the person of the defendant, and compel him to execute the conveyance, and it is the conveyance which has the effect, and not the decree. If, however, the relief asked cannot be administered by a decree *in personam,* without going further and acting upon the land, the court will refuse to entertain the bill. . . .

Now, tested by these principles, it is perfectly manifest that a court of chancery in Virginia has no jurisdiction to decree a partition of lands in another State, and this, for the plain reason before given that the right to transfer, partition and change real estate, belongs exclusively to the State within whose territory it is situate. In order to make a partition the court must invade by its officers the soil of another State, and divide up and allot its lands to suit the views of a foreign jurisdiction. This cannot be done.

For these reasons the decree of the circuit court of Highland County must be reversed, and the bill will be dismissed. . . .

NOTES

1. Tenants in common hold an undivided interest in the land: each has a right of possession with respect to the whole tract. The parties in *Wimer* became tenants in common when George Wimer died without bequeathing the land to anyone in his will.

2. Dean Langdell explained the partition procedure this way:

> "[W]hen common-law courts were in the habit of entertaining suits for the partition of land, the partition was made by the court itself without any act of the owners of the property whatever. The court first rendered judgment that partition be made . . .; whereupon a writ was issued to the sheriff, directing him to make a partition of the land pursuant to the judgment, and report the same to the court. When this had been done, the court rendered another and final judgment that the partition so made remain firm and stable forever . . .; and by force of this latter judgment each party acquired the exclusive title to the share allotted to himself, and ceased to have any title to the shares allotted to the others."

C. C. Langdell, SUMMARY OF EQUITY PLEADING 35 (2d ed. 1883).

B. TERRITORIAL LIMITS AND EQUITABLE POWERS

Alpern v. Coe

Supreme Court of Pennsylvania, 1945.
352 Pa. 208.

■ JONES, JUSTICE. This appeal grows out of a suit in equity instituted by the plaintiff in the Court of Common Pleas of Allegheny County for the purpose of having a constructive trust impressed upon certain real estate situate in that county. Marie Moody, one of the defendants, is the record owner of the property. The other defendants are her husband, Duard Moody, and her brother, Charles Coe. Coe, a resident of Allegheny County, was served personally with the bill of complaint. The Moodys are residents of West Virginia and were served at their residence in that State. . . .

It is the contention of the Moodys that the relief sought by the plaintiff would necessarily be *in personam* as to them and that the court lacks the power to summon persons from beyond its territorial jurisdiction and make them answerable for relief of such nature. . . .

In substance, the bill avers that Coe purchased the property in question under circumstances which constituted a fraud on the rights of the plaintiff who was . . . then carrying on negotiations for the purchase of the property; that Coe stood in a relation of trust and confidence to the plaintiff by whom he was employed; and that, in aid of the fraud alleged, Coe had taken title to the property in the name of his sister, Marie Moody . . . . The relief prayed for is that Marie Moody and her husband be declared trustees of the property for the benefit of the plaintiff [and] that they be directed to convey it to the plaintiff . . . .

[A Pennsylvania statute enacted in 1859 authorized service of process on non-resident defendants in actions relating to land within the state. A statute enacted in 1901 provided that:

> "in any proceedings at law or *in equity*, in any of the courts of this Commonwealth having jurisdiction, if the said court shall order a conveyance to be executed by either of the parties to the said proceeding of his or her interest in any lands or tenements to any other party or person, and the party so ordered shall neglect or refuse to comply with the said order and make the said conveyance, . . . *it shall be lawful for the said court to order . . . that such conveyance be made* by the sheriff, prothonotary or clerk, or by a trustee specially appointed for that purpose; *and the said conveyance* having been duly executed . . . , *shall be good and effective* to convey the interest of the recusant, neglecting, . . . party, to the extent ordered by the court, *the same as if it had been duly executed and delivered* by such party personally."]

The effect of statutes, such as the Pennsylvania acts to which we have referred, has been the virtual abolition of "the ancient doctrine that the decree in equity can only act upon the person of a party." See Pomeroy's EQUITY JURISPRUDENCE, §§ 134, 135, 428, 1317, 1318. A Pennsylvania court of equity, having jurisdiction of the subject matter, can act in rem with respect to lands lying within its territorial jurisdiction. The Act of 1859 operates to make the court's decrees in rem effective as to nonresident defendants who have been served in accordance with the provisions of that act, while the Act of 1901 makes available the efficient means for effectuating the court's orders or decrees in such regard without the defendant's personal compliance. . . .

NOTE

Alpern *v.* Coe was decided shortly before the jurisdictional rules of Pennoyer *v.* Neff, 95 U.S. 714 (1877), were modified by the "minimum contacts" rule of International Shoe Co. *v.* Washington, 326 U.S. 310 (1945). Later, limits on *in rem* jurisdiction were imposed by Shaffer *v.* Heitner, 433 U.S. 186 (1977). Nevertheless, modern jurisdictional rules do not solve the problem of enforcing *in personam* decrees against non-residents. Even when the defendant has sufficient contacts with the forum state, if the defendant is physically absent and sequestration of local property is ineffective, the court does not have an airtight way to coerce the defendant to obey.

To resolve this difficulty, states enacted statutes such as Pennsylvania's Act of 1901. The statutes are of two types. One type is a "vesting" statute, providing that the court's decree has the effect of a conveyance of title and can be recorded as such in the local registry of deeds. The second type is an "appointive" statute similar to the Pennsylvania act, authorizing the court to order a sheriff or clerk to execute a deed on behalf of the defendant. The deed can then be recorded in the registry of deeds. See Fed. R. Civ. P. 70 (providing for both vesting and appointive procedures).

Assume the governing statute is of the appointive type. When the court uses the statutory procedure to enforce a decree for conveyance of title, does it act *in personam* or *in rem*?

Penn v. Lord Baltimore

Chancery, 1750.
1 Vesey Senior 444, 27 Eng. Rep. 1132.

[In settlement of a dispute over the boundaries of the territories of Pennsylvania and Maryland, William Penn and Lord Baltimore entered into an agreement providing that a survey line should be drawn between their lands. Penn brought suit for specific performance of the agreement; Lord Baltimore entered a number of objections, including the claim that the court could not decree specific performance of an agreement regarding foreign lands.]

■ LORD CHANCELLOR [HARDWICKE]. I directed this cause to stand over for judgment, not so much from any doubt of what was the justice of the case, as by reason of the nature of it, the great consequence and importance, and the great labour and ability of the argument on both sides; it being for the determination of the right and boundaries of two great provincial governments and three counties; of a nature worthy of the judicature of a Roman senate rather than of a single judge: and my consolation is, that if I should err in my judgment, there is a judicature equal in dignity to a Roman senate that will correct it [*i.e.*, the House of Lords].

It is unnecessary to state the case on all the particular circumstances of evidence; which will fall in more naturally, and very intelligibly, under the particular points arising in the cause.

The relief prayed must be admitted to be the common and ordinary equity dispensed by this court; the specific performance of agreements being one of the great heads of this court, and the most useful one, and better than damages at law, so far as relates to the thing *in specie*; and more useful in a case of this nature than in most others; because no damages in an action of covenant could be at all adequate to what is intended by the parties, and to the utility to arise from this agreement, *viz.* the settling and fixing these boundaries in peace, to prevent the disorder and mischief, which in remote countries, distant from the seat of government, are most likely to happen, and most mischievous. Therefore the remedy prayed by a specific performance is more necessary here than in other cases: provided it is proper in all respect: and the relief sought must prevail, unless sufficient objections are shewn by defendant; who has made many and various for that purpose.

First, the point of jurisdiction ought in order to be considered: and though it comes late, I am not unwilling to consider it. . . . It is certain, that the original jurisdiction in cases of this kind relating to boundaries between provinces, the dominion, and proprietary government, is in the King and council . . . . This court therefore has no original jurisdiction on the direct question of the original right of the boundaries; and this bill does not stand in need of that. It is founded on articles executed in *England* under seal for mutual consideration; which gives jurisdiction to the King's courts both of law and equity, whatever be the subject matter. . . . The conscience of the party was bound by this agreement; and being within the jurisdiction of this court, which acts *in personam,* the court may properly decree it as an agreement, if a foundation for it. . . .

As to the court's not inforcing the execution of their judgment; if they could not at all, I agree, it would be in vain to make a decree; and that the court cannot inforce their own decree *in rem,* in the present case: but that is not an objection against making a decree in the cause; for the strict primary decree in this court as a court of equity is *in personam,* long before it was settled, whether this court could issue to put into possession in a suit of lands in England; which was first begun and settled in the time of James I. [r. 1603–25] but ever since done by injunction or writ of assistance to the sheriff: but the court cannot to this day as to lands in Ireland or the plantations. In Lord King's time [Ch. 1725–33] in the case of Richardson *v.* Hamilton, Attorney-General of Pennsylvania, which was a suit of land and a house in the town of Philadelphia, the court made a decree, though it could not be inforced *in rem.* In the case of Lord Anglesey of land lying in Ireland, I decreed for distinguishing and settling the parts of the estate, though impossible to inforce that decree *in rem,* but the party being in England, I could inforce it by process of contempt *in personam* and sequestration, which is the proper jurisdiction of this court. . . .

I am of opinion therefore to decree a specific performance of this agreement.

NOTES

1. The order entered by Lord Chancellor Hardwicke, which appears at 3 Vesey Senior *194, 28 Eng. Rep. 498 (1750), decreed:

> "that the said articles, and the several matters and things therein contained, should be performed and carried into execution by and between the said parties, and every of them; and to that end, that the Plaintiffs T.P. and R.P. the father, in their own right, and as standing in the place of J.P. deceased; and the Defendant, the Lord B. should respectively, before the end of three calendar months from that day, execute, under their hands and seals, two several proper instruments, appointing and authorizing proper persons, not more than seven on each side, with full powers to the said seven persons respectively, or any three or more of them, for the actual running, marking, and laying out the part of a circle, and the several lines in the said articles mentioned: and such commissioners were to give due notice to each other, and to fix and agree upon a time or times to begin and proceed in the running, marking, and laying out the same.
>
> "that the same should be begun, at the furthest, some time in the month of November then next, and be proceeded in according to the said article; and that the said lines should be marked out by visible stones, posts, trees, pillars, buildings, land marks, or other certain boundaries, which might remain and continue; and that such boundaries should be marked on one side with the arms of the Defendant the Lord B.; and on the other side, with the arms of the Plaintiffs the Penns; and that such lines should be completely so run, marked, and laid out, on or before the last day of April 1752; and when so done, that a true and exact plan and survey thereof, with the best, and most exact, and certain description that could be given of the same, should be made up, signed, and sealed by the commissioners on both sides, and by their principals, and be entered in all the public offices in the provinces of Maryland and Pennsylvania, and the three lower counties of Newcastle, Kent, and Sussex; and that a true copy of such respective instruments for appointing commissioners, when prepared, should be delivered by the solicitor of the one party, to the solicitor of the other party; and

> in case the parties should differ about such instruments, or either of them, the Master was to settle the same. . . . [A]nd that after the said limits and boundaries should be so set out and ascertained by the commissioners, the Plaintiffs . . . and the Defendant . . . should respectively release and convey to each other, and their heirs, their respective rights, titles, interests, powers, prerogatives, claims, demands, and pretensions, in or to the respective territories, districts, and lands severally allotted to them, according to the tenth article contained in the said articles of agreement."

In 1763, the responsibility for completing the survey was put in the hands of Jeremiah Mason and Charles Dixon. Part of the boundary drawn by these two men is still known as the Mason-Dixon line.

2. Arglasse filed a bill in England to be relieved against a grant of annuity or rent-charge upon his lands in Ireland. He claimed that this grant was obtained by fraud. The defendant's jurisdictional argument, that the matter was examinable only in the Irish Court of Chancery, was overruled. Arglasse *v.* Muschamp, 1 Vern. 75, 135, 23 Eng. Rep. 322, 369 (Ch. 1682). Lord Chancellor Nottingham said:

> "This is surely only a jest put upon the jurisdiction of this court by the common lawyers; for when you go about to bind the lands, and grant a sequestration to execute a decree, then they readily tell you, that the authority of this court is only to regulate a man's conscience, and ought not to affect the estate, but that this court must *agere in personam* only; and when, as in this case, you prosecute the person for a fraud, they tell you, you must not intermeddle here, because the fraud, though committed here, concerns lands that lie in Ireland, which makes the jurisdiction local; and so would wholly elude the jurisdiction of this court. But certainly they forget the case of Archer and Preston, in which case, if in any, the jurisdiction was local, the matter there being not only for land that lay in Ireland, but of a title under the act of settlement there; yet the defendant coming into England, a bill was exhibited against him here, and a *ne exeat regno* [writ to restrain a person from leaving the kingdom] granted, and he put to answer a contract made for those lands; and when he departed into Ireland without answering, he was sent for over by a special order from the King, and made to answer the contempt, and to abide the justice of this court; for the King will maintain the authority of his courts, when they act according to law and reason. . . .
>
> "[A]nd as to the objection, that this court was deficient in power in this case to compel a performance of its decree, because it could not sequester the lands in question, he looked upon that as an objection of no weight; and it did not appear to him, but the defendant might have other lands in England."

3. Watts, the holder of a prior equity in Ohio land, brought an equity action against Massie, a resident of Kentucky, in the federal court in Kentucky. Watts sought a decree ordering Massie to convey to him legal title

to the Ohio land. Watts prevailed, and Massie appealed on the ground that the federal court in Kentucky lacked jurisdiction over the case. The Supreme Court rejected this argument and affirmed the decree in Massie *v.* Watts, 6 Cranch 148 (1810). Chief Justice Marshall explained:

> "Where the defendant in the original action is liable to the plaintiff, either in consequence of contract, or as trustee, or as the holder of a legal title acquired by any species of *mala fides* practised on the plaintiff, the principles of equity give a court jurisdiction wherever the person may be found, and the circumstance, that a question of title may be involved in the inquiry, and may even constitute the essential point on which the case depends, does not seem sufficient to arrest that jurisdiction."

4. The California Development Company diverted water from the Colorado River in Mexico and transported the water by canal to California. The Mexican diversion caused flooding that harmed property of the New Liverpool Salt Company, located in California. The Salt Company sued the Development Company in a federal district court in California for wrongful diversion. The court entered a decree requiring the Development Company to cease diverting water in a harmful manner. It explained its decision as follows:

> "It is . . . objected that the court had no jurisdiction to decree an injunction in effect abating a nuisance caused by the construction of intakes in the republic of Mexico, and it is claimed that there is a rule supporting this objection to the effect that a court of equity can never compel a defendant to do anything which is not capable of being physically done within the territorial jurisdiction of the court. This rule undoubtedly obtains where the property injured is itself outside the jurisdiction of the court . . . .
>
> "The injury charged in the present case was an injury to property within the jurisdiction of the court, and the party charged with the commission of the injury was also within the jurisdiction of the court. . . . Why may not a court restrain a party over whom it has jurisdiction from injuring property within its jurisdiction? How does it affect the question of jurisdiction or venue to say that the party on whom the court must act may find it necessary to do things outside the jurisdiction of the court in order to comply with the order of the court? May this not often happen, and would it not happen oftener, if it were determined that such an excuse was sufficient to defeat the jurisdiction of the court? In criminal law he who on one side of a boundary shoots a person on the other side is amenable where the blow is received. . . .
>
> "In civil actions the jurisdiction of the court depends upon the question whether the action is local or transitory. . . .
>
> "In Miller & Lux *v.* Rickey, 127 F. 573, the action was brought in the Circuit Court for the District of Nevada to restrain the defendants from the wrongful diversion of the waters naturally flowing down the stream of both forks of the Walker river having

their source in California, and flowing down into and through the state of Nevada, where the lands of the complainant were situated.

"The alleged diversion was in the state of California, and the injury caused by such diversion was in the state of Nevada. It was contended on behalf of the defendant that the Circuit Court in Nevada was without jurisdiction, first, because the suit was of a local nature, and could not be brought outside of the state of California; second, because the water right in controversy was in California; third, because the wrongs and injury alleged to have been committed by the defendant were committed wholly in the state of California; fourth, that complete relief could not be decreed by the Nevada court in favor of the complainant without reaching the property rights of the defendant which were situated wholly in California. . . . The court says on page 580:

> 'That this court has jurisdiction over the person of the defendant is unquestioned. It can reach him by injunction, and punish him for contempt if he violates it. This doctrine had its foundation in the equity courts of England at an early day. . . .'

". . . We are of the opinion . . . that the court had jurisdiction in the present case to protect property within its jurisdiction, and to restrain the defendant from diverting the waters of the Colorado river to the damage of such property, notwithstanding the defendant may find it necessary in complying with the decree of the court to perform acts beyond the jurisdiction of the court."

The Salton Sea Cases, California Development Co. *v.* New Liverpool Salt Co., 172 F. 792 (9th Cir. 1909).

5. Thus equity was willing to control the defendant's extraterritorial acts, but it did so in order to protect the plaintiff. Even at their broadest, these extraterritorial injunctions would not control the actions of the defendant against non-parties. In a more recent development, federal district courts have granted "national injunctions." These injunctions restrain a federal defendant from enforcing a statute, regulation, or order against *anyone*, not just the plaintiffs. These decrees remain controversial. See generally Samuel L. Bray, Multiple Chancellors: Reforming the National Injunction, 131 Harv. L. Rev. (forthcoming 2017); Michael T. Morley, De Facto Class Actions? Plaintiff- and Defendant-Oriented Injunctions in Voting Rights, Election Law, and Other Constitutional Cases, 39 Harv. J.L. & Pub. Pol'y 487 (2016).

Deschenes v. Tallman

Court of Appeals of New York, 1928.
248 N.Y. 33.

■ CARDOZO, C.J. The complaint is for the foreclosure of a purchase-money mortgage. The answer is a counterclaim for breach of a covenant of seizin [an assurance that the seller had title to the estate conveyed]. Whether seizin was lacking is the question to be answered.

Plaintiffs sold the land to the defendant Francis Tallman in April, 1925. A predecessor in title was Miller & Lockwell, Limited, a Canadian corporation. By a decree of the courts of the Province of Quebec, made in 1911, the corporation was adjudged insolvent, and its property, real and personal, was ordered to be sold by two liquidators duly appointed according to the laws of the Province. The liquidators conveyed the land to the plaintiffs, who thereafter sold to Tallman with covenant of seizin. The land is located in the city of New York. The defendants insist that the title does not pass under a deed by foreign liquidators.

A second and confirmatory deed, made in December, 1926, is also the subject of attack. After the sale to Tallman, the plaintiffs procured the execution of a quitclaim deed by the Canadian corporation. This deed, made by the corporation to the defendant Francis Tallman, contains a recital that it is given "in confirmation of a deed" made by the liquidators, "it being the opinion of the liquidators that this deed is necessary for the beneficial winding up of the party of the first part and they having requested the execution of the same." The statutes of Canada are to the effect that the corporate life survives the appointment of a liquidator until the winding up is finished, but that the powers of the directors cease "except in so far as the court or liquidator sanctions the continuance of the same." The defendants insist that the later deed, being made under compulsion, adds nothing to the first one, and leaves the title where it was.

The answer demands judgment for the cancellation of the purchase-money mortgage, the return of the cash payment, and reimbursement for the value of subsequent improvements.

We think the counterclaim must fail.

There is no need to determine what effect would be given to the liquidators' deed considered by itself. . . .

If the deed by the liquidators be assumed to be inoperative, there was none the less a conveyance of title upon delivery by the corporation of a confirmatory deed of grant. A judgment of a foreign court will not avail of its own force to transfer the title to land located in this State. It will not avail though a conveyance be executed by the sheriff or a master or other agent of the court in fulfillment of its mandate. "The court, not having jurisdiction of the *res,* cannot affect it by its decree, nor by a deed made by a master in accordance with the decree." But the rule is different where the conveyance is executed by the owner, though he act under compulsion. The conveyance, and not the judgment, is then the source of title. As to this the law has been undoubted since Penn *v.* Lord Baltimore. The distinction is between a judgment directed against the *res* itself, and one directed against the person of the owner, who acts upon the *res*. His deed transmits the title irrespective of the pressure exerted on his will. . . .

Burnley v. Stevenson

Supreme Court of Ohio, 1873.
24 Ohio St. 474.

[General Scott agreed to convey certain lands, originally part of the Virginia military district and now part of Ohio, to Evans in return for his services as a surveyor. After the services were performed, but before the lands were conveyed, Scott died. In a suit by Evans for specific performance of the contract with Scott, a Circuit Court in Kentucky, having jurisdiction of the heirs and legal representatives of Scott, ordered the lands to be conveyed to Evans. A commissioner appointed by the court executed and delivered to Evans a deed in fee simple for the lands. Plaintiffs, claiming through Scott's heirs and legal representatives, now sue in Ohio to recover possession of the lands from the defendant, a successor of Evans.]

■ MCILVAINE, J. . . .

1. The jurisdiction of the Circuit Court to pronounce the decree, is the first inquiry involved in this proposition.

It appears from the record before us, that the Circuit Court of Kentucky which pronounced the decree, was a court of general equity jurisdiction; that some of the defendants in the cause were properly served with the process of the court, and that all others voluntarily appeared and submitted themselves to its jurisdiction, and that the subject-matter of the bill on which the decree was rendered, was the enforcement of a trust and the specific performance of a contract to convey lands situate in the State of Ohio.

That courts exercising chancery powers in one state have jurisdiction to enforce a trust, and to compel the specific performance of a contract in relation to lands situate in another state, after having obtained jurisdiction of the persons of those upon whom the obligation rests, is a doctrine fully settled by numerous decisions.

2. It does not follow, however, that a court having power to compel the parties before it to convey lands situated in another state, may make its own decree to operate as such conveyance. Indeed, it is well settled that the decree of such court can not operate to transfer title to lands situate in a foreign jurisdiction. And this, for the reason that a judgment or decree *in rem* can not operate beyond the limits of the jurisdiction or state wherein it is rendered. And if a decree in such case can not effect the transfer of the title to such lands, it is clear that a deed executed by a master, under the direction of the court, can have no greater effect. The master's deed to Evans must therefore be regarded as a nullity.

The next inquiry then is as to the force and effect of the decree rendered by the Circuit Court directing the heirs of Gen. Scott to convey the land in Ohio to Evans. This decree was *in personam,* and bound the consciences of those against whom it was rendered. In it, the contract of their ancestor to make the conveyance was merged. The fact that the title which had descended to them was held by them in trust for Evans, was thus established by the decree of a court of competent jurisdiction. Such decree is record evidence of that fact, and also of the fact that it [had] become and was their duty to convey the legal title to him. The performance of that duty might have been enforced against them in that court by attachment as for contempt; and the fact that the conveyance was not made in pursuance of the order, does not affect the validity of the decree in so far as it determined the equitable rights of the parties in the land in controversy. In our judgment, the parties, and those holding under them with notice, are still bound thereby.

3. Under our code of practice, equitable as well as legal defenses may be set up in an action for the recovery of land. The defendant in the court below set up this decree of the Circuit Court of Kentucky as a defense to the plaintiffs' action. That it did not constitute a good defense at law may be admitted, but we think, in equity, it was a sufficient defense.

The constitution of the United States declares that full faith and credit shall be given in each state to the records and judicial proceedings of every other state, and provides that Congress may prescribe the mode of proving such records and proceedings, and the effect thereof. By an act of May 26, 1790, Congress declared that the "records and judicial proceedings of the state courts," when properly authenticated, "shall have the same faith and credit given to them in every court within the United States, as they have, by law or usage, in the courts of the state from whence they are or shall be taken." When, therefore, a decree rendered by a court in a sister state, having jurisdiction of the parties and of the subject-matter, is offered as evidence, or pleaded as the foundation of a right, in any action in the courts of this state, it is entitled to the same force and effect which it had in the state where it was pronounced. That this decree had the effect in Kentucky of determining the equities of the parties to the land in this state, we have already shown; hence the courts of this state must accord to it the same effect. True, the courts of this state can not enforce the performance of that decree, by compelling the conveyance through its process of attachment; but when pleaded in our courts as a cause of action, or as a ground of defense, it must be regarded as conclusive of all the rights and equities which were adjudicated and settled therein, unless it be impeached for fraud. . . .

NOTES

1. In addition to the Full Faith and Credit Clause of the Constitution (Article 4, Section 1) Congress has by statute required state and federal courts to give full faith and credit to each others' "judicial proceedings." 28 U.S.C. § 1738.

2. The U.S. Supreme Court held early on that the Full Faith and Credit Clause and accompanying legislation require that when one state has

entered a money judgment, other states' courts must accept the judgment as *res judicata* on matters decided and allow a local action to enforce the judgment according to local enforcement procedures. Thus, in Fauntleroy *v.* Lum, 210 U.S. 230 (1908), a Mississippi court was compelled to grant recovery on a Missouri money judgment, although the original cause of action was a contract made in Mississippi and illegal under Mississippi law.

For many years, however, there was speculation that equity decrees pertaining to land in another state might not have the same preclusive effect as money judgments. Either because the subject matter was local land or because the decree was equitable, it was thought that situs courts might be free to refuse to recognize decrees that conflicted with important local policies, such as policies about division of marital property. See, *e.g.*, McElreath *v.* McElreath, 345 S.W.2d 722 (Tex. 1961); cf. Fall *v.* Eastin, 215 U.S. 1, 7–8 (1909) (holding that situs was not required to recognize a deed resulting from *in rem* enforcement of another state's decree). In Baker *v.* General Motors Corp., 522 U.S. 222, 234 (1998), the Court appeared to lay the matter to rest, stating that "[w]e see no reason why the preclusive effect of an adjudication on parties . . . should differ depending solely up on the type of relief sought in a civil action." At the same time, the court reiterated that full faith and credit does not require the courts of the situs state to provide the same enforcement mechanisms available in the forum state.

3. Various difficult problems of conflict of laws and domestic relations are raised by a suit in one state based on an alimony decree entered in another state or a foreign country. Much depends on (a) whether the second suit is for accrued installments only, or also seeks to obtain an order for the payment of future installments; and (b) whether the original decree is capable of modification by the court which rendered it, either as to future installments or as to past installments still unpaid.

C. INJUNCTIONS AGAINST FOREIGN SUITS

1. GROUNDS FOR ISSUANCE

Lord Portarlington v. Soulby

Chancery, 1834.
3 Myl. & K. 104, 40 Eng. Rep. 40.

■ THE LORD CHANCELLOR [LORD BROUGHAM]. This was a motion to dissolve an injunction, granted to restrain the Defendants from suing in Ireland upon a bill of exchange for £1000,[ii] accepted by the Plaintiff, payable to a person of the name of Aldridge, by whom it was indorsed and passed away to Mr. Brook, a retail dealer in wines, and by him to the Defendants.

[ii] [A bill of exchange is an instrument in which A orders B to pay C a sum certain at a definite future time. A check is a demand bill of exchange. The person who promises to pay a bill is called the acceptor. In the example, B is the acceptor.]

The ground of the injunction is, that the bill was given by Lord Portarlington for money lost at play. . . .

The case . . . is reduced to this. An illegal consideration distinctly stated, and not denied, with several circumstances leading to the belief, that the Defendants now know such to have been the origin of the bill; and several circumstances also shewing that it was taken by their late partner under suspicion, and yet without inquiry.

It is, then, impossible to doubt that the injunction was well granted, and the whole question would be free from difficulty but for one peculiarity in the case; the action is brought in Ireland, and the interposition of this Court is sought to stop proceedings there. That this is an unusual proceeding must be admitted, but I do not see any ground for questioning the competency of it.

Soon after the restoration [1660], and when this, like every other branch of the Court's jurisdiction was, if not in its infancy, at least far from that maturity which it attained under the illustrious series of chancellors, the Nottinghams and Macclesfields, the parents of equity, the point received a good deal of consideration in . . . Love *v.* Baker, 1 Ch. Cas. 67 [1665]. In Love *v.* Baker it appears that one only of several parties who had begun proceedings in the Court of Leghorn [in Livorno, Italy] was resident within the jurisdiction here, and the Court allowed the *subpoena* to be served on him, and that this should be good service on the rest. So far there seems to have been very little scruple in extending the jurisdiction. Lord Clarendon refused the injunction to restrain those proceedings at Leghorn, after advising with the other judges; but the report adds, "[but examine this further], for all the bar was of another opinion;" and it is said that, when the argument against issuing it was used, that this Court had no authority to bind a foreign Court, the answer was given, that the injunction was not directed to the foreign Court, but to the party within the jurisdiction here. A very sound answer, as it appears to me; for the same argument might apply to a Court within this country, which no order of this Court ever affects to bind, our orders being only pointed at the parties to restrain them from proceeding.

Accordingly this case of Love *v.* Baker has not been recognized or followed in later times. . . .

In truth, nothing can be more unfounded than the doubts of the jurisdiction. That is grounded, like all other jurisdiction of the Court, not upon any pretension to the exercise of judicial and administrative rights abroad, but on the circumstance of the person of the party on whom this order is made being within the power of the Court. If the Court can command him to bring home goods from abroad, or to assign chattel interests, or to convey real property locally situate abroad . . .; in precisely the like manner it can restrain the party being within the limits of its jurisdiction from doing anything abroad, whether the thing forbidden be a conveyance or other act *in pais* [done outside of court], or the instituting or prosecution of an action in a foreign Court. . . .

As to the argument that the Courts of Equity in Ireland can, if applied to, restrain the action, the same consideration would prevent an injunction from ever issuing to stay proceedings in this country; for it might be said that the Court of Exchequer [which, at the time, had equity jurisdiction] has the power of restraining, and therefore there needs no interposition of the Court of Chancery. It suffices to say that the Court in which the action [that is, the action the plaintiff sought to enjoin] is brought is a court of common law, and has no jurisdiction as such to stop the proceeding upon the ground now set forth.

I am, therefore, of opinion that this injunction was well issued, and that it must be continued, and that this motion must be refused, with costs.

Castanho v. Brown & Root (U.K.), Ltd.

House of Lords, 1980.
[1981] A.C. 557.

[Castanho, a Portuguese citizen, worked aboard a ship harbored in England. His employer and the owner of the ship was Brown & Root, an English subsidiary of a Texas corporation. Like the parent corporation, the subsidiary had offices in Texas. While working aboard ship, Castanho was paralyzed in an accident. When he was in a hospital in England, English solicitors sued on his behalf for damages and received interim payments of £27,250. Meanwhile, Castanho was moved back to Portugal. Then, as the House of Lords puts it, "a firm of Texan attorneys contacted the plaintiff in order to persuade him to bring proceedings in Texas where higher damages could be obtained." Castanho made an agreement with the Texas firm to allow it to sue on his behalf in Texas, providing that the English action was not to be concluded until after there was a decision in the Texas case. The English solicitors who represented Castanho filed for a discontinuance of the English action.]

■ LORD SCARMAN. My Lords, this is an appeal by defendants from an order of the Court of Appeal . . . , whereby, allowing the plaintiff's appeal from the judge, the court restored the plaintiff's notice of discontinuance of his action in England and discharged an injunction which the [trial] judge had granted restraining the plaintiff from proceeding with his claim in America. Put shortly, the trial judge required the plaintiff to proceed in England; the Court of Appeal allowed him to proceed in America. . . .

The question in the appeal is, therefore, whether the plaintiff should be restrained by the English court from pursuing his claim for damages in the American courts. It is a question of great importance to the parties. In the American courts the plaintiff claims punitive as well as compensatory damages ($5m. compensation, and "at least" $10m. punitive or exemplary). In England he has no claim for punitive damages: and the scale of compensatory damages is much less. . . .

Injunction, being an equitable remedy, operates in personam. It has been used to order parties amenable to the court's jurisdiction "to take, or to omit to take, any steps and proceedings in any other court of justice, whether in this country or in a foreign country." Bushby *v.* Munday [1821] 5 Madd. 297, 307. The English court . . . "does not pretend to any interference with the other court; it acts upon the defendant by punishment for his contempt in his disobedience to the order of the court." . . .

I turn to consider what criteria should govern the exercise of the court's discretion to impose a stay or grant an injunction. It is unnecessary now to examine the earlier case law. The principle is the same whether the remedy sought is a stay of English proceedings or a restraint upon foreign proceedings. The modern statement of the law is to be found in *The Atlantic Star* [1974] A.C. 436. It had been thought that the criteria for staying (or restraining) proceedings were two-fold: (1) that to allow the proceedings to continue would be oppressive or vexatious, and (2) that to stay (or restrain) them would not cause injustice to the plaintiff. In *The Atlantic Star* this House . . . extended and re-formulated[ ] the criteria, treating the epithets "vexatious" and "oppressive" as illustrating but not confining the jurisdiction. . . . The "critical equation," [Scott L.J. said,] was between "any advantage to the plaintiff" and "any disadvantage to the defendant." . . .

In MacShannon *v.* Rockware Glass Ltd. [1978] A.C. 795, 812[,] my noble and learned friend, Lord Diplock, interpreted the majority speeches in *The Atlantic Star* as an invitation to drop the use of the words "vexatious" and "oppressive" . . . and formulated his distillation of principle in words which are now very familiar:

> "In order to justify a stay two conditions must be satisfied, one positive and the other negative: (a) the defendant must satisfy the court that there is another forum to whose jurisdiction he is amenable in which justice can be done between the parties at substantially less inconvenience or expense, and (b) the stay must not deprive the plaintiff of a legitimate personal or juridical advantage which would be available to him if he invoked the jurisdiction of the English court."

Transposed into the context of the present case, this formulation means that to justify the grant of an injunction the defendants must show: (a) that the English court is a forum to whose jurisdiction they are amenable in which justice can be done at substantially less inconvenience and expense, and (b) the injunction must not deprive the plaintiff of a legitimate personal or juridical advantage which would be available to him if he invoked the American jurisdiction. . . .

The fact that the plaintiff can sue in Texas defendants who have an office and substantial assets in Texas and that under the law there he has the legitimate personal and juridical advantage of the prospect of a much greater recovery than if he were to sue in England cannot be discarded as of little weight merely because an English award would not be regarded as unjustly low in Portugal. The discretion is not to be exercised upon such a comparison, even if there were (which there was not) any evidence to guide the judge's speculation as to the Portuguese possibilities. The balance is between the English and the American proceedings; the relative elements of plaintiff's advantage and defendant's disadvantage in each have to be weighed. The balance is not to be confused by uncertain legal, social and economic elements arising outside the two sets of litigation. . . .

The only additional expense incurred by the defendants as a result of the plaintiff suing first in England has been that of legal costs, which are recoverable by the defendants. Texas is as natural and proper a forum for suing a group of Texan-based companies as England—even though England, as the scene of the accident, is also a natural and proper forum. . . .

My conclusion is, therefore, that the Court of Appeal was right to discharge the injunction. . . .

■ [LORD WILBERFORCE, LORD DIPLOCK, LORD KEITH OF KINKEL, and LORD BRIDGE OF HARWICH concurred.]

Kaepa, Inc. v. Achilles Corp.

United States Court of Appeals, Fifth Circuit, 1996.
76 F.3d 624.

■ WIENER, CIRCUIT JUDGE. . . . This case arises out of a contractual dispute between two sophisticated, private corporations: Kaepa, an American company which manufactures athletic shoes; and Achilles, a Japanese business enterprise with annual sales that approximate one billion dollars. In April 1993, the two companies entered into a distributorship agreement whereby Achilles obtained exclusive rights to market Kaepa's footwear in Japan. The distributorship agreement expressly provided that Texas law and the English language would govern its interpretation, that it would be enforceable in San Antonio, Texas, and that Achilles consented to the jurisdiction of the Texas courts.

Kaepa grew increasingly dissatisfied with Achilles's performance under the contract. Accordingly, in July of 1994, Kaepa filed suit in Texas state court, alleging (1) fraud and negligent misrepresentation by Achilles to induce Kaepa to enter into the distributorship agreement, and (2) breach of contract by Achilles. Thereafter, Achilles removed the action to federal district court, and the parties began a laborious discovery process which to date has resulted in the production of tens of thousands of documents. In February 1995, after appearing in the Texas action, removing the case to federal court, and engaging in comprehensive discovery, Achilles brought its own action in Japan, alleging mirror-image claims: (1) fraud by Kaepa to induce Achilles to enter into the distributorship agreement, and (2) breach of contract by Kaepa.

Back in Texas, Kaepa promptly filed a motion asking the district court to enjoin Achilles from prosecuting its suit in Japan (motion for an antisuit injunction). . . . The district court . . . granted Kaepa's motion to enjoin, ordering Achilles to refrain from litigating the Japanese action and to file all of its counterclaims with the district court. . . .

Achilles's primary argument is that the district court failed to give proper deference to principles of international comity when it granted Kaepa's motion for an antisuit injunction. . . .

[F]ederal courts have the power to enjoin persons subject to their jurisdiction from prosecuting foreign suits. The circuits differ, however, on the proper legal standard to employ when determining whether that injunctive power should be exercised. We have addressed the propriety of an antisuit injunction on two prior occasions . . . . Emphasizing . . . the need to prevent vexatious or oppressive litigation, we concluded that a district court does not abuse its discretion by issuing an antisuit injunction when it has determined "that allowing simultaneous prosecution of the same action in a foreign forum thousands of miles away would result in inequitable hardship and tend to frustrate and delay the speedy and efficient determination of the cause." . . .

Achilles urges us to give greater deference to comity and apply the latter, more restrictive standard. We note preliminarily that, even though the standard [we have] espoused . . . focuses on the potentially vexatious nature of foreign litigation, it by no means excludes the consideration of principles of comity. We decline, however, to require a district court to genuflect before a vague and omnipotent notion of comity every time that it must decide whether to enjoin a foreign action.

In the instant case, for example, it simply cannot be said that the grant of the antisuit injunction actually threatens relations between the United States and Japan. First, no public international issue is implicated by the case: Achilles is a private party engaged in a contractual dispute with another private party. Second, the dispute has been long and firmly ensconced within the confines of the United States judicial system: Achilles consented to jurisdiction in Texas; stipulated that Texas law and the English language would govern any dispute; appeared in an action brought in Texas; removed that action to a federal court in Texas; engaged in extensive discovery pursuant to the directives of the federal court; and only then, with the federal action moving steadily toward trial, brought identical claims in Japan. Under these circumstances, we cannot conclude that the district court's grant of an antisuit injunction in any way trampled on notions of comity.

On the contrary, the facts detailed above strongly support the conclusion that the prosecution of the Japanese action would entail "an absurd duplication of effort" and would result in unwarranted inconvenience, expense, and vexation. Achilles's belated ploy of filing as putative plaintiff in Japan the very same claims against Kaepa that Kaepa had filed as plaintiff against Achilles smacks of cynicism, harassment, and delay. Accordingly, we hold that the district court did not abuse its discretion by granting Kaepa's motion for an antisuit injunction. . . .

For the foregoing reasons, the district court's grant of Kaepa's motion to enjoin the litigation of Achilles's action in Japan is

AFFIRMED.

■ GARZA, CIRCUIT JUDGE, dissenting. International comity represents a principle of paramount importance in our world of ever increasing economic interdependence. Admitting that "comity" may be a somewhat elusive concept does not mean that we can blithely ignore its cautionary dictate. Unless we proceed in each instance with respect for the independent jurisdiction of a sovereign nation's courts, we risk provoking retaliation in turn, with detrimental consequences that may reverberate far beyond the particular dispute and its private litigants. Amicable relations among sovereign nations and their judicial systems depend on our recognition, as federal courts, that we share the international arena with co-equal judicial bodies, and that we therefore act to deprive a foreign court of jurisdiction only in the most extreme circumstances. . . .

The filing of a second parallel action in another jurisdiction does not necessarily conflict with or prevent the first court from exercising its legitimate concurrent jurisdiction. In the ordinary case, both forums should be free to proceed to a judgment, unhindered by the concurrent exercise of jurisdiction in another court. . . .

By focusing on the potential hardship to Kaepa of having to litigate in two forums, the majority applies an analysis that is more appropriately brought to bear in the context of a motion to dismiss for *forum non conveniens.* Considerations that are appropriate in deciding whether to decline jurisdiction are not as persuasive when deciding whether to deprive another court of jurisdiction. . . . A dismissal on grounds of *forum non conveniens* by either court in this case would satisfy the majority's concern with avoiding hardship to the parties, without harming the interests of international comity. The district court is not in a position, however, to make the *forum non conveniens* determination on behalf of the Japanese court. In light of the important interests of international comity, the decision by a United States court to deprive a foreign court of jurisdiction must be supported by far weightier factors than would otherwise justify that court's decision to decline its own jurisdiction on *forum non conveniens* grounds. . . .

[A] district court should look to only two factors in determining whether to issue an antisuit injunction: (1) whether the foreign action threatens the jurisdiction of the district court; and (2) whether the foreign action was an attempt to evade important public policies of the district court. . . .

2. EFFECT OF INJUNCTIONS AGAINST SUIT

Dobson v. Pearce

Court of Appeals of New York, 1854.
12 N.Y. 156.

The action was commenced in the New York superior court, on the 26th of September, 1850. The complaint was upon a judgment for $612.93, recovered in that court in April, 1846, in favor of one Olney against Pearce, the defendant in this suit, alleging an assignment thereof from Olney to Dobson, the plaintiff, just previous to the commencement of the action.

The defendant by his answer alleged that the judgment was entered in a suit commenced against him, in favor of Olney, by the service of a *capias* [a writ formerly used to start actions at law] upon him in February, 1846, when he was casually in New York, he then and ever after being a resident of Connecticut; that Olney had no just or legal demand against him, when the *capias* was served, and that he was induced by fraudulent representations and assurances of Olney, made to him after the *capias* was served, and upon which he relied, to the effect that no further proceedings would be taken in the suit, not to appear therein; and that afterwards Olney fraudulently and without the knowledge of the defendant procured the judgment mentioned in the complaint to be entered in the suit upon a false and unfounded claim, and known so to be by Olney at the time; that in 1848 Olney commenced an action of debt on the judgment, against the defendant, in the superior court of the State of Connecticut. Thereupon the defendant commenced a suit in chancery against Olney, before the same court in Connecticut alleging that the judgment was procured to be entered by fraud on the part of Olney, and praying the court to perpetually enjoin him from further prosecuting it. Olney appeared in and defended the chancery suit by attorney; and on the 10th of September, 1850, a decree was made therein, declaring the judgment fraudulent and perpetually enjoining Olney from further prosecuting the action upon it; that in submission to this decree the action upon the judgment in the superior court of Connecticut was discontinued; and that the pretended assignment to the plaintiff was made after the decree and with full knowledge of it and of the fraud in procuring the judgment. . . .

The . . . trial was had before Justice Duer and a jury, in 1853. On this trial the plaintiff proved the judgment described in the complaint, and the assignment thereof by Olney to the plaintiff, on the 11th of September, 1850, and rested.

The defendant offered in evidence a duly authenticated copy of the record of the proceedings in the suit in chancery in the superior court of Connecticut, mentioned in the answer. The counsel for the plaintiff objected to it as evidence; the objection was overruled and the same received and read in evidence, and plaintiff's counsel excepted. . . .

The justice before whom the cause was tried instructed the jury that the record of the proceedings, finding and decree of the superior court of Connecticut in the chancery suit, was conclusive evidence against the plaintiff to sustain the allegations in the defendant's answer, if the jury found that Olney appeared in that suit by an attorney who was authorized by him to do so; that if the jury did not so find, then this record did not affect the plaintiff. The counsel for the plaintiff excepted to such instructions. The jury rendered a verdict in favor of the defendant [and the court entered judgment accordingly].

■ W.F. ALLEN, J. . . . A judgment rendered by a court of competent jurisdiction cannot be impeached collaterally for error or irregularity, but is conclusive until set aside or reversed by the same court or some other court having appellate jurisdiction. The jurisdiction of the court in which a judgment has been recovered is, however, always open to inquiry; and if it has exceeded its jurisdiction, . . . the judgment void. The want of jurisdiction has always been held to be a valid defence to an action upon the judgment, and a good answer to it when set up for any purpose. . . .

[I]t is unquestionable that a court of chancery has power to grant relief against judgments when obtained by fraud. Any fact which clearly proves it to be against conscience to execute a judgment, and of which the injured party could not avail himself at law, but was prevented by fraud or accident, unmixed with any fault or negligence in himself or his agents, will justify an interference by a court of equity.

Under our present judiciary system, the functions of the courts of common law and of chancery are united in the same court, and the distinctions between actions at law and suits in equity, and the forms of all such actions and suits, are abolished, and the defendant may set forth by answer as many defences as he may have, whether they be such as have been heretofore denominated legal or equitable, or both. . . . The intent of the legislature is very clear, that all controversies respecting the subject matter of the litigation should be determined in one action, and the provisions are adapted to give effect to that intent. Whether, therefore, fraud or imposition in the recovery of a judgment could heretofore have been alleged against it collaterally at law or not, it may now be set up as an equitable defence to defeat a recovery upon it. Under the head of equitable defences are included all matters which would before have authorized an application to the court of chancery for relief against a legal liability, but which, at law, could not have been pleaded in bar. The facts alleged by way of defence in this action would have been good cause for relief against the judgment in a court of chancery, and under our present system are, therefore, proper matters of defence; and there was no necessity or propriety for a resort to a separate action to vacate the judgment. In Connecticut, although law and equity are administered by the same judges, still the distinction between these systems is preserved. . . .

The right of the plaintiff in the judgment was a personal right and followed his person; and, aside from the fact that he had resorted to the courts of Connecticut to enforce his claim under the judgment, the courts of that state, having obtained jurisdiction of his person by due service of process within the state, had full power to pronounce upon the rights of the parties in respect to the judgment and to decree concerning it. It necessarily follows that the decree of the superior court of Connecticut, sitting as a court of chancery, directly upon the question of fraud, is conclusive upon the parties to that litigation and all persons claiming under them with notice of the adjudication. The judgment of a court of competent jurisdiction upon a point litigated between the parties is conclusive in all subsequent controversies where the same point comes again in question between the same parties. In the State of Connecticut, it is quite clear the question of fraud would not be an open question between the parties, but would be considered entirely settled by the decree of the court of that state; and as full faith and credit are to be given by each state to the judicial proceedings of every other state, that is, the same credit, validity and effect as they would have in the state in which they were had, the parties are concluded in the courts of this state by the judgment of the court in Connecticut directly upon the question in issue. The decree of the court of chancery of the State of Connecticut as an operative decree, so far as it enjoined and restrained the parties, had and has no extraterritorial efficacy, as an injunction does not affect the courts of this state; but the judgment of the court upon the matters litigated is conclusive upon the parties everywhere and in every forum where the same matters are drawn in question. It is not the particular relief which was granted which affects the parties litigating in the courts of this state; but it is the adjudication and the determination of the facts by that court, the final decision that the judgment was procured by fraud, which is operative here and necessarily prevents the plaintiff from asserting any claim under it. The court acquired jurisdiction of the parties by the commencement of the action, and the service of process upon the defendant therein, and his appearance by an authorized attorney; and the withdrawal of the action of debt upon the judgment did not deprive it of jurisdiction thus acquired. . . .

James v. Grand Trunk Western Railroad Co.

Supreme Court of Illinois, 1958.
14 Ill.2d 356.

[The plaintiff, a resident of Michigan and the administratrix of a Michigan estate, brought an action in Illinois against the defendant, an Illinois railroad corporation, seeking to recover under the Michigan wrongful death statute for a death caused by an accident in Michigan. The railroad then sued the administratrix in Michigan and obtained an injunction enjoining her from proceeding with her action in Illinois, based on a Michigan venue statute restricting venue in suits against railroads to the county in which plaintiff resides, if the railroad lines traverse that county. The administratrix then asked the Illinois court to restrain the defendant railroad from enforcing its Michigan injunction. The Illinois trial court refused to grant the requested order.]

■ BRISTOW, JUSTICE. . . . The issues are essentially whether the Illinois court, having prior jurisdiction of a wrongful death action instituted by a nonresident plaintiff, must recognize an out-of-State injunction restraining the plaintiff from proceeding with that action; and whether the Illinois court, to protect its jurisdiction of the wrongful death action, may issue a counter injunction restraining defendant from enforcing its injunction against plaintiff in the State of her residence. . . .

On this appeal plaintiff argues that she had an unquestionable right to file the action in the Illinois court; that where a court has obtained prior jurisdiction of an action, injunctive relief is proper to prevent defendant from transferring the action elsewhere through an action in another forum; and that neither the full-faith-and-credit clause nor comity require the Illinois court to respect the Michigan venue statute and the decision of the Michigan court in this case.

The defendant argues, however, that this court will not, by counterinjunction, aid a citizen of another State to violate an injunction against prosecuting an action in Illinois; that the counterinjunction cannot be justified to protect the prior injunction of the Illinois court, since the Michigan injunction was *in personam* only; and that such counterinjunction would compel a party to give up vested rights and would violate the full-faith-and-credit and due-process clauses of the Federal constitution. . . .

With reference to the Michigan injunction, while we quite agree with defendant's repeated assertion that a court of equity has power to restrain persons within its jurisdiction from instituting or proceeding with foreign actions, we note that the exercise of such power by equity courts has been deemed a matter of great delicacy, invoked with great restraint to avoid distressing conflicts and reciprocal interference with jurisdiction.

Illinois has consistently followed the course of refusing to restrain the prosecution of a prior instituted action pending in a sister State unless a clear equity is presented requiring the interposition of the court to prevent a manifest wrong and injustice; and neither a difference of remedy afforded by the domicile and the forum nor mere inconvenience and expense of defending will constitute grounds for such an injunction. . . .

Conversely, where other States have enjoined litigants from proceeding with a previously instituted Illinois action, this jurisdiction has followed the overwhelming judicial opinion that neither the full-faith-and-credit clause nor rules of comity require compulsory recognition of such injunctions so as to abate or preclude the disposition of the pending case. . . .

While it is not the province of this court to adjudge the constitutionality of the Michigan venue statute, it may be noted that similar statutes confining transitory actions to the State of plaintiff's residence have been held unconstitutional. In Tennessee Coal, Iron, & Railroad Co. *v.* George, 233 U.S. 354, 360 (1914), the court stated . . . : "But venue is no part of the right; and a state cannot create a transitory cause of action and at the same time destroy the right to sue on that transitory cause of action in any court having jurisdiction. That jurisdiction is to be determined by the law of the court's creation, and cannot be defeated by the extraterritorial operation of a statute of another state, even though it created the right of action."

In the light of this reasoning, we cannot escape the observation that if statutes prohibiting or circumscribing the export of causes of action may not be given extraterritorial effect, it is hard to see why an equity decree should be entitled to any greater recognition. A court should be subject to the same limitations.

Therefore, it is evident that legal consistency, as well as the weight of authority, do not require us to recognize the Michigan injunction, and we may retain jurisdiction and proceed with plaintiff's wrongful death action. Such a course, however, is not practicable in the instant case, unless plaintiff, who is subject to imprisonment and other coercive tactics if she fails to dismiss her Illinois action, is protected by enjoining defendant from enforcing the Michigan injunction by contempt proceedings. A plaintiff cannot be expected or required to risk imprisonment so that the court may retain jurisdiction of a cause.

This brings us to the ultimate issue in this case: whether the court which first acquires jurisdiction of the parties and of the merits of the cause can issue a counterinjunction restraining a party before it from enforcing an out-of-State injunction which requires the dismissal of the local cause and ousts the forum of jurisdiction.

There is no quarrel with the basic principle that a court has a duty, as well as power, to protect its jurisdiction over a controversy in order to decree complete and final justice between the parties and may issue an injunction for that purpose, restraining proceedings in other courts.

Defendant, however, claims that there is no reason to invoke this principle in the instant case since the Michigan injunction in no way interferes with the jurisdiction of this court, but merely affects the litigants. In support thereof defendant cites the equitable maxim, "equity acts *in personam*," invoked since the days of Coke and Bacon to obviate open conflicts between law and equity courts, and the general principle that courts of equity have the power to prevent those amenable to their own process from instituting or carrying on suits in other States which will result in injury or fraud.

In applying these principles to the instant case, we cannot close our eyes to the fact that the intended effect of the Michigan injunction, though directed at the parties and not at this court, is to prevent the Illinois court from adjudicating a cause of action of which it had proper jurisdiction. For it is patent that if the litigants are coerced to dismiss the Illinois action, it is our rightfully acquired jurisdiction that is thereby destroyed. Therefore, the Michigan injunction was in everything but form an order restraining the Illinois court and determining the cases it may properly try. . . .

Under our analysis of the authorities, if Illinois were not the appropriate forum to try this, or any other transitory action, the defense of *forum non conveniens* could be interposed, and, if meritorious, the Illinois court would dismiss the case. However, this court need not, and will not, countenance having its right to try cases, of which it has proper jurisdiction, determined by the courts of other States, through their injunctive process. We are not only free to disregard such out-of-State injunctions, and to adjudicate the merits of the pending action, but we can protect our jurisdiction from such usurpation by the issuance of a counterinjunction restraining the enforcement of the out-of-State injunction.

It was therefore error for the trial court to dismiss plaintiff's supplemental complaint and her motion for a counterinjunction . . . .

Reversed and remanded, with directions.

■ SCHAEFER, JUSTICE (dissenting). . . . I agree with the majority that the Michigan injunction is not entitled to full faith and credit.

But the question in this case goes a step beyond the issue as to full faith and credit. What is here sought is a counter-injunction to restrain the railroad from enforcing the injunction entered by the Michigan court. The difficulties that attend the kind of injunction that the Michigan court entered were stated long ago by Chancellor Walworth: "If this court should sustain an injunction bill to restrain proceedings previously commenced in a sister state, the court of that state might retaliate upon the complainant, who was defendant in the suit there; and, by process of attachment, might compel him to relinquish the suit subsequently commenced here. By this course of proceeding, the courts of different states would indirectly be brought into collision with each other in regard to jurisdiction; and the rights of suitors might be lost sight of in a useless struggle for what might be considered the legitimate powers and rights of courts." What was there said with respect to an initial injunction applies with added force to a counterinjunction. Just as the first injunction sired the second, so the second might sire a third. The ultimate end is not foreseeable.

The place to stop this unseemly kind of judicial disorder is where it begins. . . .

D. INJUNCTIONS AND FEDERALISM

1. STATE INJUNCTIONS AGAINST FEDERAL PROCEEDINGS

Donovan v. City of Dallas

Supreme Court of the United States, 1964.
377 U.S. 408.

■ MR. JUSTICE BLACK delivered the opinion of the Court.

The question presented here is whether a state court can validly enjoin a person from prosecuting an action *in personam* in a district or appellate court of the United States which has jurisdiction both of the parties and of the subject matter.

The City of Dallas, Texas, owns Love Field, a municipal airport. In 1961, 46 Dallas citizens who owned or had interests in property near the airport filed a class suit in a Texas court to restrain the city from building an additional runway and from issuing and selling municipal bonds for that purpose. The complaint alleged many damages that would occur to the plaintiffs if the runway should be built and charged that issuance of the bonds would be illegal for many reasons. The case was tried, summary judgment was given for the city, the Texas Court of Civil Appeals affirmed, the Supreme Court of Texas denied review, and we denied certiorari. Later 120 Dallas citizens, including 27 of the plaintiffs in the earlier action, filed another action in the United States District Court for the Northern District of Texas seeking similar relief. . . . None of the bonds would be approved, and therefore under Texas law none could be issued, so long as there was pending litigation challenging their validity. The city filed a motion to dismiss and an answer to the complaint in the federal court. But at the same time the city applied to the Texas Court of Civil Appeals for a writ of prohibition to bar all the plaintiffs in the case in the United States District Court from prosecuting their case there. The Texas Court of Civil Appeals denied relief, holding that it was without power to enjoin litigants from prosecuting an action in a federal court and that the defense of *res judicata* on which the city relied could be raised and adjudicated in the United States District Court. On petition for mandamus the Supreme Court of Texas took a different view, however, held it the duty of the Court of Civil Appeals to prohibit the litigants from further prosecuting the United States District Court case . . . . The United States District Court in an unreported opinion dismissed the case pending there. Counsel Donovan, who is one of the petitioners here, excepted to the dismissal and then filed an appeal from that dismissal in the United States Court of Appeals for the Fifth

Circuit. The Texas Court of Civil Appeals thereupon cited Donovan and the other United States District Court claimants for contempt . . . .

Early in the history of our country a general rule was established that state and federal courts would not interfere with or try to restrain each other's proceedings. That rule has continued substantially unchanged to this time. An exception has been made in cases where a court has custody of property, that is, proceedings *in rem* or *quasi in rem*. In such cases this Court has said that the state or federal court having custody of such property has exclusive jurisdiction to proceed. In Princess Lida *v.* Thompson, 305 U.S. 456 (1939), this Court said "where the judgment sought is strictly in personam, both the state court and the federal court, having concurrent jurisdiction, may proceed with the litigation at least until judgment is obtained in one of them which may be set up as res judicata in the other." It may be that a full hearing in an appropriate court would justify a finding that the state-court judgment in favor of Dallas in the first suit barred the issues raised in the second suit, a question as to which we express no opinion. But plaintiffs in the second suit chose to file that case in the federal court. They had a right to do this, a right which is theirs by reason of congressional enactments passed pursuant to congressional policy. And whether or not a plea of *res judicata* in the second suit would be good is a question for the federal court to decide. While Congress has seen fit to authorize courts of the United States to restrain state-court proceedings in some special circumstances, it has in no way relaxed the old and well-established judicially declared rule that state courts are completely without power to restrain federal-court proceedings in *in personam* actions like the one here. And it does not matter that the prohibition here was addressed to the parties rather than to the federal court itself. . . .

Petitioners being properly in the federal court had a right granted by Congress to have the court decide the issues they presented, and to appeal to the Court of Appeals from the District Court's dismissal. . . . That right was granted by Congress and cannot be taken away by the State. The Texas courts were without power to take away this federal right by contempt proceedings or otherwise. . . .

The Court of Civil Appeals . . . acted on the assumption that petitioners were guilty of "willful disobedience of a *valid* order." Since we hold the order restraining petitioners from prosecuting their case in the federal courts was not valid, but was invalid, petitioners have been punished for disobeying an invalid order. Whether the Texas court would have punished petitioners for contempt had it known that the restraining order petitioners violated was invalid, we do not know. However, since that question was neither considered nor decided by the Texas court, we leave it for consideration by that court on remand. We express no opinion on that question at this time. . . .

Judgment of Texas Supreme Court reversed, judgment of Texas Court of Civil Appeals vacated, and case remanded with directions.

■ MR. JUSTICE HARLAN, whom MR. JUSTICE CLARK and MR. JUSTICE STEWART join, dissenting. . . .

Given the Texas Supreme Court's finding, amply supported by the record and in no way challenged by this Court, that this controversy "has reached the point of vexatious and harassing litigation," I consider both the state injunction and the ensuing contempt adjudication to have been perfectly proper.

The power of a court in equity to enjoin persons subject to its jurisdiction from conducting vexatious and harassing litigation in another forum has not been doubted until now. . . .

NOTES

1. On remand, the Texas Court of Civil Appeals declined to hold the *Donovan* petitioners in contempt for having violated the invalid writ of prohibition and remitted the fines and costs that they had paid. City of Dallas *v.* Brown, 384 S.W.2d 724 (Tex. Civ. App. 1964).

2. *Donovan* involved a state court's attempt to enjoin further prosecution of a pending federal suit. In General Atomic Co. *v.* Felter, 434 U.S. 12 (1977) (*per curiam*), the Court held that *Donovan* also bars injunctions aimed at prospective litigation in the federal courts.

2. FEDERAL INJUNCTIONS AGAINST STATE PROCEEDINGS OR INSTITUTIONS

Younger v. Harris

Supreme Court of the United States, 1971.
401 U.S. 37.

■ MR. JUSTICE BLACK delivered the opinion of the Court.

Appellee, John Harris, Jr., was indicted in a California state court, charged with violation of the California Penal Code §§ 11400 and 11401, known as the California Criminal Syndicalism Act, set out below.[1] He

[1] "§ 11400. *Definition*

" 'Criminal syndicalism' as used in this article means any doctrine or precept advocating, teaching or aiding and abetting the commission of crime, sabotage (which word is hereby defined as meaning wilful and malicious physical damage or injury to physical property), or unlawful acts of force and violence or unlawful methods of terrorism as a means of accomplishing a change in industrial ownership or control, or effecting any political change."

"§ 11401. *Offense; punishment*

"Any person who:

"1. By spoken or written words or personal conduct advocates, teaches or aids and abets criminal syndicalism or the duty, necessity or propriety of committing crime, sabotage, violence or any unlawful method of terrorism as a means of accomplishing a change in industrial ownership or control, or effecting any political change; or

"2. Wilfully and deliberately by spoken or written words justifies or attempts to justify criminal syndicalism or the commission or attempt to commit crime, sabotage, violence or unlawful methods of terrorism with intent to approve, advocate or further the doctrine of criminal syndicalism; or

then filed a complaint in the Federal District Court, asking that court to enjoin the appellant, Younger, the District Attorney of Los Angeles County, from prosecuting him, and alleging that the prosecution and even the presence of the Act inhibited him in the exercise of his rights of free speech and press, rights guaranteed him by the First and Fourteenth Amendments. Appellees Jim Dan and Diane Hirsch intervened as plaintiffs in the suit, claiming that the prosecution of Harris would inhibit them as members of the Progressive Labor Party from peacefully advocating the program of their party, which was to replace capitalism with socialism and to abolish the profit system of production in this country. Appellee Farrell Broslawsky, an instructor in history at Los Angeles Valley College, also intervened claiming that the prosecution of Harris made him uncertain as to whether he could teach about the doctrines of Karl Marx or read from the Communist Manifesto as part of his classwork. . . . A three-judge Federal District Court, convened pursuant to 28 U.S.C. § 2284, held that it had jurisdiction and power to restrain the District Attorney from prosecuting, held that the State's Criminal Syndicalism Act was void for vagueness and overbreadth in violation of the First and Fourteenth Amendments, and accordingly restrained the District Attorney from "further prosecution of the currently pending action against plaintiff Harris for alleged violation of the Act." . . .

In this Court the brief for the State of California, filed at our request, . . . argues that . . . issuance of the injunction was a violation of a longstanding judicial policy and of 28 U.S.C. § 2283, which provides:

> "A court of the United States may not grant an injunction to stay proceedings in a State court except as expressly authorized by Act of Congress, or where necessary in aid of its jurisdiction, or to protect or effectuate its judgments."

. . . [W]e have concluded that the judgment of the District Court, enjoining appellant Younger from prosecuting under these California statutes, must be reversed as a violation of the national policy forbidding federal courts to stay or enjoin pending state court proceedings except under special circumstances. We express no view about the circumstances under which federal courts may act when there is no

---

"3. Prints, publishes, edits, issues or circulates or publicly displays any book, paper, pamphlet, document, poster or written or printed matter in any other form, containing or carrying written or printed advocacy, teaching, or aid and abetment of, or advising, criminal syndicalism; or

"4. Organizes or assists in organizing, or is or knowingly becomes a member of, any organization, society, group or assemblage of persons organized or assembled to advocate, teach or aid and abet criminal syndicalism; or

"5. Wilfully by personal act or conduct, practices or commits any act advised, advocated, taught or aided and abetted by the doctrine or precept of criminal syndicalism, with intent to accomplish a change in industrial ownership or control, or effecting any political change;

"Is guilty of a felony and punishable by imprisonment in the state prison not less than one nor more than 14 years."

prosecution pending in state courts at the time the federal proceeding is begun. . . .

Since the beginning of this country's history Congress has, subject to few exceptions, manifested a desire to permit state courts to try state cases free from interference by federal courts. . . . [A] judicial exception to the longstanding policy evidenced by the statute has been made where a person about to be prosecuted in a state court can show that he will, if the proceeding in the state court is not enjoined, suffer irreparable damages. See Ex parte Young, 209 U.S. 123 (1908).

The precise reasons for this longstanding public policy against federal court interference with state court proceedings have never been specifically identified but the primary sources of the policy are plain. One is the basic doctrine of equity jurisprudence that courts of equity should not act, and particularly should not act to restrain a criminal prosecution, when the moving party has an adequate remedy at law and will not suffer irreparable injury if denied equitable relief. The doctrine may originally have grown out of circumstances peculiar to the English judicial system and not applicable in this country, but its fundamental purpose of restraining equity jurisdiction within narrow limits is equally important under our Constitution, in order to prevent erosion of the role of the jury and avoid a duplication of legal proceedings and legal sanctions where a single suit would be adequate to protect the rights asserted. This underlying reason for restraining courts of equity from interfering with criminal prosecutions is reinforced by an even more vital consideration, the notion of "comity," that is, a proper respect for state functions, a recognition of the fact that the entire country is made up of a Union of separate state governments, and a continuance of the belief that the National Government will fare best if the States and their institutions are left free to perform their separate functions in their separate ways. This, perhaps for lack of a better and clearer way to describe it, is referred to by many as "Our Federalism," and one familiar with the profound debates that ushered our Federal Constitution into existence is bound to respect those who remain loyal to the ideals and dreams of "Our Federalism." The concept does not mean blind deference to "States' Rights" any more than it means centralization of control over every important issue in our National Government and its courts. The Framers rejected both these courses. What the concept does represent is a system in which there is sensitivity to the legitimate interests of both State and National Governments, and in which the National Government, anxious though it may be to vindicate and protect federal rights and federal interests, always endeavors to do so in ways that will not unduly interfere with the legitimate activities of the States. It should never be forgotten that this slogan, "Our Federalism," born in the early struggling days of our Union of States, occupies a highly important place in our Nation's history and its future.

This brief discussion should be enough to suggest some of the reasons why it has been perfectly natural for our cases to repeat time and time again that the normal thing to do when federal courts are asked to enjoin pending proceedings in state courts is not to issue such injunctions. . . .

In [cases following *Ex parte Young*], the Court stressed the importance of showing irreparable injury, the traditional prerequisite to obtaining an injunction. In addition, however, the Court also made clear that in view of the fundamental policy against federal interference with state criminal prosecutions, even irreparable injury is insufficient unless it is "both great and immediate." Certain types of injury, in particular, the cost, anxiety, and inconvenience of having to defend against a single criminal prosecution, could not by themselves be considered "irreparable" in the special legal sense of that term. Instead, the threat to the plaintiff's federally protected rights must be one that cannot be eliminated by his defense against a single criminal prosecution. . . .

This is where the law stood when the Court decided Dombrowski *v.* Pfister, 380 U.S. 479 (1965), and held that an injunction against the enforcement of certain state criminal statutes could properly issue under the circumstances presented in that case. In *Dombrowski,* unlike many of the earlier cases denying injunctions, the complaint made substantial allegations that:

> "the threats to enforce the statutes against appellants are not made with any expectation of securing valid convictions, but rather are part of a plan to employ arrests, seizures, and threats of prosecution under color of the statutes to harass appellants and discourage them and their supporters from asserting and attempting to vindicate the constitutional rights of Negro citizens of Louisiana."

. . . These circumstances . . . sufficiently establish the kind of irreparable injury, above and beyond that associated with the defense of a single prosecution brought in good faith, that had always been considered sufficient to justify federal intervention. . . .

It is against the background of these principles that we must judge the propriety of an injunction under the circumstances of the present case. Here a proceeding was already pending in the state court, affording Harris an opportunity to raise his constitutional claims. There is no suggestion that this single prosecution against Harris is brought in bad faith or is only one of a series of repeated prosecutions to which he will be subjected. In other words, the injury that Harris faces is solely "that incidental to every criminal proceeding brought lawfully and in good faith," and therefore under the settled doctrine we have already described he is not entitled to equitable relief "even if such statutes are unconstitutional." . . .

It is undoubtedly true, as the Court stated in *Dombrowski,* that "[a] criminal prosecution under a statute regulating expression usually involves imponderables and contingencies that themselves may inhibit the full exercise of First Amendment freedoms." But this sort of "chilling effect," as the Court called it, should not by itself justify federal intervention. In the first place, the chilling effect cannot be satisfactorily eliminated by federal injunctive relief. In *Dombrowski* itself the Court stated that the injunction to be issued there could be lifted if the State obtained an "acceptable limiting construction" from the state courts. The Court then made clear that once this was done, prosecutions could then be brought for conduct occurring before the narrowing construction was made, and proper convictions could stand so long as the defendants were not deprived of fair warning. The kind of relief granted in *Dombrowski* thus does not effectively eliminate uncertainty as to the coverage of the state statute and leaves most citizens with virtually the same doubts as before regarding the danger that their conduct might eventually be subjected to criminal sanctions. The chilling effect can, of course, be eliminated by an injunction that would prohibit any prosecution whatever for conduct occurring prior to a satisfactory rewriting of the statute. But the States would then be stripped of all power to prosecute even the socially dangerous and constitutionally unprotected conduct that had been covered by the statute, until a new statute could be passed by the state legislature and approved by the federal courts in potentially lengthy trial and appellate proceedings. . . .

Moreover, the existence of a "chilling effect," even in the area of First Amendment rights, has never been considered a sufficient basis, in and of itself, for prohibiting state action. Where a statute does not directly abridge free speech, but—while regulating a subject within the State's power—tends to have the incidental effect of inhibiting First Amendment rights, it is well settled that the statute can be upheld if the effect on speech is minor in relation to the need for control of the conduct and the lack of alternative means for doing so. Just as the incidental "chilling effect" of such statutes does not automatically render them unconstitutional, so the chilling effect that admittedly can result from the very existence of certain laws on the statute books does not in itself justify prohibiting the State from carrying out the important and necessary task of enforcing these laws against socially harmful conduct that the State believes in good faith to be punishable under its laws and the Constitution.

Beyond all this is another, more basic consideration. Procedures for testing the constitutionality of a statute "on its face" in the manner apparently contemplated by *Dombrowski,* and for then enjoining all action to enforce the statute until the State can obtain court approval for a modified version, are fundamentally at odds with the function of the federal courts in our constitutional plan. The power and duty of the judiciary to declare laws unconstitutional is in the final analysis derived from its responsibility for resolving concrete disputes brought before the courts for decision; a statute apparently governing a dispute cannot be applied by judges, consistently with their obligations under the Supremacy Clause, when such an application of the statute would conflict with the Constitution. But this vital responsibility, broad as it is, does not amount to an unlimited power to survey the statute books and pass judgment on laws before the courts are called upon to enforce them. . . . [A]nalyzing a proposed statute, pinpointing its deficiencies, and requiring correction of these deficiencies before the statute is put into effect, is rarely if ever an appropriate task for the judiciary. . . . In light of this fundamental conception of the Framers as to the proper place of the federal courts in the governmental processes of passing and enforcing laws, it can seldom be appropriate for these courts to exercise any such power of prior approval or veto over the legislative process.

For these reasons, fundamental not only to our federal system but also to the basic functions of the Judicial Branch of the National Government under our Constitution, we hold that the *Dombrowski* decision should not be regarded as having upset the settled doctrines that have always confined very narrowly the availability of injunctive relief against state criminal prosecutions. We do not think that opinion stands for the proposition that a federal court can properly enjoin enforcement of a statute solely on the basis of a showing that the statute "on its face" abridges First Amendment rights. There may, of course, be extraordinary circumstances in which the necessary irreparable injury can be shown even in the absence of the usual prerequisites of bad faith and harassment. For example, as long ago as Watson *v.* Buck, 313 U.S. 387, 402 (1941), we indicated:

> "It is of course conceivable that a statute might be flagrantly and patently violative of express constitutional prohibitions in every clause, sentence and paragraph, and in whatever manner and against whomever an effort might be made to apply it."

Other unusual situations calling for federal intervention might also arise, but there is no point in our attempting now to specify what they might be. It is sufficient for purposes of the present case to hold, as we do, that the possible unconstitutionality of a statute "on its face" does not in itself justify an injunction against good-faith attempts to enforce it, and that appellee Harris has failed to make any showing of bad faith, harassment, or any other unusual circumstance that would call for equitable relief. Because our holding rests on the absence of the factors necessary under equitable principles to justify federal intervention, we have no occasion to consider whether 28 U.S.C. § 2283, which prohibits an injunction against state court proceedings "except as expressly authorized by Act of Congress" would in and of itself be controlling under the circumstances of this case. . . .

■ MR. JUSTICE STEWART, with whom MR. JUSTICE HARLAN joins, concurring. . . .

In basing its decisions on policy grounds, the Court does not reach any questions concerning the independent force of the federal anti-injunction statute . . . .

The Court confines itself to deciding the policy considerations that in our federal system must prevail when federal courts are asked to interfere with pending state prosecutions. Within this area, we hold that a federal court must not, save in exceptional and extremely limited circumstances, intervene by way of either injunction or declaration in an existing state criminal prosecution.[3] Such circumstances exist only when there is a threat of irreparable injury "both great and immediate." A threat of this nature might be shown if the state criminal statute in question were patently and flagrantly unconstitutional on its face, or if there has been bad faith and harassment—official lawlessness—in a statute's enforcement. In such circumstances the reasons of policy for deferring to state adjudication are outweighed by the injury flowing from the very bringing of the state proceedings, by the perversion of the very process that is supposed to provide vindication, and by the need for speedy and effective action to protect federal rights.

■ [The concurring opinion of MR. JUSTICE BRENNAN is omitted.]

■ MR. JUSTICE DOUGLAS, dissenting.

The fact that we are in a period of history when enormous extrajudicial sanctions are imposed on those who assert their First Amendment rights in unpopular causes emphasizes the wisdom of Dombrowski *v.* Pfister. There we recognized that in times of repression, when interests with powerful spokesmen generate symbolic pograms against nonconformists, the federal judiciary, charged by Congress with special vigilance for protection of civil rights, has special responsibilities to prevent an erosion of the individual's constitutional rights. . . .

The special circumstances when federal intervention in a state criminal proceeding is permissible are not restricted to bad faith on the part of state officials or the threat of multiple prosecutions. They also exist where for any reason the state statute being enforced is unconstitutional on its face. . . .

If the "advocacy" which Harris used was an attempt at persuasion through the use of bullets, bombs, and arson, we would have a different case. But Harris is charged only with distributing leaflets advocating political action toward his objective. He tried unsuccessfully to have the state court dismiss the indictment on constitutional grounds. He resorted to the state appellate court for writs of prohibition to prevent the trial,

---

[3] The negative pregnant in this sentence—that a federal court may, as a matter of policy, intervene when such "exceptional and extremely limited circumstances" are found—is subject to any further limitations that may be placed on such intervention by 28 U.S.C. § 2283.

but to no avail. He went to the federal court as a matter of last resort in an effort to keep this unconstitutional trial from being saddled on him.

The "anti-injunction" statute, 28 U.S.C. § 2283, is not a bar to a federal injunction under these circumstances. That statute was adopted in 1793, and reflected the early view of the proper role of the federal courts within American federalism.

Whatever the balance of the pressures of localism and nationalism prior to the Civil War, they were fundamentally altered by the war. The Civil War Amendments made civil rights a national concern. Those Amendments, especially § 5 of the Fourteenth Amendment, cemented the change in American federalism brought on by the war. Congress immediately commenced to use its new powers to pass legislation. Just as the first Judiciary Act and the "anti-injunction" statute represented the early views of American federalism, the Reconstruction statutes, including the enlargement of federal jurisdiction, represent a later view of American federalism.

One of the jurisdiction-enlarging statutes passed during Reconstruction was the Act of April 20, 1871. Beyond its jurisdictional provision that statute, now codified as 42 U.S.C. § 1983 provides:

> "Every person who, under color of any statute, ordinance, regulation, custom, or usage, of any State or Territory, subjects, or causes to be subjected, any citizen of the United States or other person within the jurisdiction thereof *to the deprivation of any rights, privileges, or immunities secured by the Constitution* and laws, shall be liable to the party injured in an action at law, *suit in equity,* or other proper proceeding for redress." (Emphasis added.)

A state law enforcement officer is someone acting under "color of law" even though he may be misusing his authority. And prosecution under a patently unconstitutional statute is a "deprivation of . . . rights, privileges, or immunities secured by the Constitution." "Suit[s] in equity" obviously includes injunctions.

I hold to the view that § 1983 is included in the "expressly authorized" exception to § 2283. . . . There is no more good reason for allowing a general statute dealing with federalism passed at the end of the 18th century to control another statute also dealing with federalism, passed almost 80 years later, than to conclude that the early concepts of federalism were not changed by the Civil War. . . .

NOTES

1. If no state proceeding was pending at the time the federal suit was filed, the *Younger* rule does not bar federal courts from granting either injunctive or declaratory relief. See Wooley *v.* Maynard, 430 U.S. 705 (1977); Steffel *v.* Thompson, 415 U.S. 452 (1974). However, abstention is required if a state proceeding is begun "before any proceedings of substance on the

merits have taken place in the federal court." See Hicks *v.* Miranda, 422 U.S. 332 (1975).

2. *Younger* suggests that abstention is required only when the constitutional claim can be raised in the pending state court proceeding. In Moore *v.* Sims, 442 U.S. 415, 425–26 (1979), the Court stated that *Younger* abstention is "appropriate unless state law clearly bars the interposition of the constitutional claims," and upheld an abstention when some of those claims could only be raised in the state court by counterclaim. In Middlesex County Ethics Committee *v.* Garden State Bar Association, 457 U.S. 423 (1982), the Court deemed it sufficient that a state forum became available while the question of abstention was being litigated in the federal appellate courts.

3. Gibson *v.* Berryhill, 411 U.S. 564 (1973), involved a controversy over whether Alabama optometrists could lawfully work for business corporations, which came before the Alabama Board of Optometry. Thirteen optometrists employed by Lee Optical filed a § 1983 suit in federal court, challenging the Board's ability to give them the fair and impartial hearing to which they felt entitled under the Due Process Clause. The trial court found the Board members biased, and granted the plaintiffs' request for an injunction against the pending license revocation proceedings.

On appeal, the Supreme Court rejected the Board's contention that *Younger* required the federal trial court to abstain and dismiss the injunction action. The Court explained that

> "[*Younger* abstention] naturally presupposes the opportunity to raise and have timely decided by a competent state tribunal the federal issues involved. Here the predicate for a Younger *v.* Harris dismissal was lacking, for the appellees alleged, and the District Court concluded, that the State Board of Optometry was incompetent by reason of bias to adjudicate the issues pending before it. . . . Nor, in these circumstances, would a different result be required simply because judicial review, *de novo* or otherwise, would be forthcoming at the conclusion of the administrative proceedings."

Id. at 577.

4. A year after *Younger*, the Court held that § 1983 actions fall within the "expressly authorized" exception to the anti-injunction act. Mitchum *v.* Foster, 407 U.S. 225 (1972). However, as *Younger* itself demonstrates, § 1983 actions are not exempt from the abstention principles set out in *Younger*.

5. In Samuels *v.* Mackell, 401 U.S. 66 (1971), decided the same day as *Younger,* the Court held that federal courts may not grant declaratory relief when *Younger* forbids them from granting injunctive relief. Two justices have expressed the opinion that the *Younger* principles prevent federal district courts from awarding damages under § 1983 to the defendant in a pending state prosecution, but the Court has not decided the question. See Deakins *v.* Monaghan, 484 U.S. 193, 205–210 (1988) (White, J., joined by O'Connor, J., concurring).

6. In Huffman *v.* Pursue, 420 U.S. 592 (1975), the Court applied *Younger* in the context of a state public nuisance action against a movie theater specializing in pornographic films. The state proceeding was a civil proceeding, brought under a state statute providing for closure of any theater found to show obscene films and also for a preliminary injunction pending a finding of obscenity. The theater sued in federal district court, arguing that the state statute imposed an unconstitutional prior restraint. The Court held that, at least in the circumstances of the case, the district court should not interfere with the state proceeding, and also that the theater must exhaust state appellate remedies before seeking relief in federal court:

> "The component of *Younger* which rests upon the threat to our federal system is . . . applicable to a civil proceeding such as this quite as much as it is to a criminal proceeding. . . .
>
> "Appellee's argument, that because there may be no civil counterpart to federal habeas it should have contemporaneous access to a federal forum for its federal claim, apparently depends on the unarticulated major premise that every litigant who asserts a federal claim is entitled to have it decided on the merits by a federal, rather than a state, court. We need not consider the validity of this premise in order to reject the result which appellee seeks. Even assuming, *arguendo,* that litigants are entitled to a federal forum for the resolution of all federal issues, that entitlement is most appropriately asserted by a state litigant when he seeks to *relitigate* a federal issue adversely determined in *completed* state court proceedings. . . .
>
> "Appellee apparently relies on the facts that the Allen County Court of Common Pleas had already issued its judgment and permanent injunction when this action was filed, and that no appeal from that judgment has ever been taken to Ohio's appellate courts. . . .
>
> "Virtually all of the evils at which *Younger* is directed would inhere in federal intervention prior to completion of state appellate proceedings, just as surely as they would if such intervention occurred at or before trial. . . .
>
> "Federal post-trial intervention . . . deprives the States of a function which quite legitimately is left to them, that of overseeing trial court dispositions of constitutional issues which arise in civil litigation over which they have jurisdiction. We think this consideration to be of some importance because it is typically a judicial system's appellate courts which are by their nature a litigant's most appropriate forum for the resolution of constitutional contentions. Especially is this true when, as here, the constitutional issue involves a statute which is capable of judicial narrowing. In short, we do not believe that a State's judicial system would be fairly accorded the opportunity to resolve federal issues arising in its courts if a federal district court were permitted to substitute itself for the State's appellate courts. We therefore

> hold that *Younger* standards must be met to justify federal intervention in a state judicial proceeding as to which a losing litigant has not exhausted his state appellate remedies."

Id. at 604–09.

The Supreme Court later clarified that ordinary rules of issue preclusion apply when plaintiffs in § 1983 actions attempt to relitigate matters previously decided in state proceedings. The Court said:

> "There is, in short, no reason to believe that Congress intended to provide a person claiming a federal right an unrestricted opportunity to relitigate an issue already decided in state court simply because the issue arose in a state proceeding in which he would rather not have been engaged at all."

Allen *v.* McCurry, 449 U.S. 90, 104 (1980).

7. Since *Huffman,* the Court has held *Younger* principles applicable in other civil enforcement proceedings. See Moore *v.* Sims, 442 U.S. 415 (1979) (child custody proceedings); Trainor *v.* Hernandez, 431 U.S. 434 (1977) (action to recover welfare payments wrongly received). In another group of cases, abstention was required to preclude federal interference with "orders . . . in furtherance of the state courts' ability to perform their judicial functions." Pennzoil Co. *v.* Texaco, Inc., 481 U.S. 1 (1987) (judgment lien and supersedeas bond); see Juidice *v.* Vail, 430 U.S. 327 (1977) (civil contempt order). Beyond these lines of cases, however, the Court has indicated that *Younger* abstention should not be applied. Sprint Communications, Inc. *v.* Jacobs, 134 S. Ct. 584 (2013).

O'Shea v. Littleton

Supreme Court of the United States, 1974.
414 U.S. 488.

■ MR. JUSTICE WHITE delivered the opinion of the Court.

[Nineteen individuals—seventeen black and two white—brought a class action in federal district court against the prosecuting attorney and police commissioner of Cairo, Illinois and two judges of the Alexander County Circuit Court. The plaintiffs alleged a pattern of race discrimination in administration of justice in Alexander County, including discrimination by the judicial defendants in bail and sentencing decisions and jury fee requirements. The plaintiffs sought injunctive relief, which likely would involve continued monitoring of the practices of the Circuit Court. The district court dismissed the case; the court of appeals reversed.]

We reverse the judgment of the Court of Appeals. The complaint failed to satisfy the threshold requirement imposed by Art. III of the Constitution that those who seek to invoke the power of federal courts must allege an actual case or controversy. Plaintiffs in the federal courts "must allege some threatened or actual injury resulting from the putatively illegal action before a federal court may assume jurisdiction." . . .

None of the named plaintiffs is identified as having himself suffered any injury in the manner specified. . . . At oral argument, respondents' counsel stated that some of the named plaintiffs-respondents, who could be identified by name if necessary, had actually been defendants in proceedings before petitioners and had suffered from the alleged unconstitutional practices. Past exposure to illegal conduct does not in itself show a present case or controversy regarding injunctive relief, however, if unaccompanied by any continuing, present adverse effects. . . .

Of course, past wrongs are evidence bearing on whether there is a real and immediate threat of repeated injury. . . . Apparently, the proposition is that *if* respondents proceed to violate an unchallenged law and *if* they are charged, held to answer, and tried in any proceedings before petitioners, they will be subjected to the discriminatory practices that petitioners are alleged to have followed. But it seems to us that attempting to anticipate whether and when these respondents will be charged with crime and will be made to appear before either petitioner takes us into the area of speculation and conjecture. . . .

The foregoing considerations obviously shade into those determining whether the complaint states a sound basis for equitable relief; and even if we were inclined to consider the complaint as presenting an existing case or controversy, we would firmly disagree with the Court of Appeals that an adequate basis for equitable relief against petitioners had been stated. The Court has recently reaffirmed the "basic doctrine of equity jurisprudence that courts of equity should not act, and particularly should not act to restrain a criminal prosecution, when the moving party has an adequate remedy at law and will not suffer irreparable injury if denied equitable relief." Younger *v.* Harris, 401 U.S. 37, 43–44 (1971). Additionally, recognition of the need for a proper balance in the concurrent operation of federal and state courts counsels restraint against the issuance of injunctions against state officers engaged in the administration of the State's criminal laws in the absence of a showing of irreparable injury which is "both great and immediate." *Id.* at 46. . . .

What [respondents] seek is an injunction aimed at controlling or preventing the occurrence of specific events that might take place in the course of future state criminal trials. . . . Apparently the order would contemplate interruption of state proceedings to adjudicate assertions of non-compliance by petitioners. This seems to us nothing less than an ongoing federal audit of state criminal proceedings which would indirectly accomplish the kind of interference that Younger *v.* Harris and related cases sought to prevent.

A federal court should not intervene to establish the basis for future intervention that would be so intrusive and unworkable. . . . An injunction of the type contemplated by respondents and the Court of

Appeals would disrupt the normal course of proceedings in the state courts via resort to the federal suit for determination of the claim *ab initio,* just as would the request for injunctive relief from an ongoing state prosecution against the federal plaintiff which was found to be unwarranted in *Younger*. Moreover, it would require for its enforcement the continuous supervision by the federal court over the conduct of the petitioners in the course of future criminal trial proceedings involving any of the members of the respondents' broadly-defined class. . . . [S]uch a major continuing intrusion of the equitable power of the federal courts into the daily conduct of state criminal proceedings is in sharp conflict with the principles of equitable restraint which this Court has recognized . . . .

Respondents have failed, moreover, to establish the basic requisites of the issuance of equitable relief in these circumstances—the likelihood of substantial and immediate irreparable injury, and the inadequacy of remedies at law. We have already canvassed the necessarily conjectural nature of the threatened injury to which respondents are allegedly subjected. And if any of the respondents are ever prosecuted and face trial, or if they are illegally sentenced, there are available state and federal procedures which could provide relief from the wrongful conduct alleged. Open to a victim of the discriminatory practices asserted under state law are the right to a substitution of judge or a change of venue, review on direct appeal or on postconviction collateral review, and the opportunity to demonstrate that the conduct of these judicial officers is so prejudicial to the administration of justice that available disciplinary proceedings, including the possibility of suspension or removal, are warranted. In appropriate circumstances, moreover, federal habeas relief would undoubtedly be available. . . .

Whatever may be the case with respect to civil liability generally, or civil liability for willful corruption, we have never held that the performance of the duties of judicial, legislative, or executive officers, requires or contemplates the immunization of otherwise criminal deprivations of constitutional rights. . . .

■ [The concurring opinion of MR. JUSTICE BLACKMUN is omitted.]

■ MR. JUSTICE DOUGLAS, with whom MR. JUSTICE BRENNAN and MR. JUSTICE MARSHALL concur, dissenting.

The respondents in this case are black and indigent citizens of Cairo, Illinois. Suing in federal court, they alleged that since the early 1960's black citizens of Cairo have been actively seeking equal opportunity and treatment in employment, housing, education, and ordinary day-to-day relations with the white citizens and officials of Cairo. In this quest, blacks have engaged in a boycott of local merchants deemed to have engaged in racial discrimination.

Alleging that this quest for equality has generated substantial antagonism from white governmental officials, respondents brought a class action under 42 U.S.C. §§ 1981, 1982, 1983, and 1985, seeking to represent citizens of Cairo who have been subjected in the past, and continue to be subjected, to the allegedly discriminatory and unconstitutional administration of criminal justice in Alexander County, Illinois, which includes Cairo. Among their other claims, respondents alleged that petitioners Michael O'Shea and Dorothy Spomer, both now judges in Alexander County, engage in acts which deprive them and members of their class of their constitutional rights. These judges allegedly set bond in criminal cases without regard to the facts of individual cases and as punishment, and not merely to assure the appearance of defendants at trial; impose higher sentences and harsher conditions of sentencing on blacks than on white citizens; and require respondents and members of their class, when charged with violations of city ordinances which carry fines and possible jail penalties, to pay for a trial by jury if the fine cannot be paid. . . .

This is a more pervasive scheme for suppression of Blacks and their civil rights than I have ever seen. It may not survive a trial. But if this case does not present a "case or controversy" involving the named plaintiffs, then that concept has been so watered down as to be no longer recognizable. This will please the white superstructure, but it does violence to the conception of even-handed justice envisioned by the Constitution. . . .

It will be much more appropriate to pass on the nature of any equitable relief to be granted after the case has been tried. It may be that when the case is ended, no injunction against any state proceeding will be asked for or will seem appropriate. Or the injunctive relief in final analysis may come down to very narrow and discrete orders prohibiting precise practices. The Court labels this an "ongoing federal audit of state criminal proceedings." . . . I would cross the bridge of remedies only when the precise contours of the problem have been established after a trial. . . .

Furthermore, the respondents do not primarily allege individual instances of excessively harsh treatment . . . but rather a pattern of discriminatory treatment, especially in favor of prosperous white defendants. . . . A single instance of sentencing by itself might not strike the conscience of a reviewing court, but when coupled with a pattern of discriminatory treatment could well justify the equitable intervention of a federal court. A class suit where evidence could be developed showing a pattern of discriminatory bail and sentencing decisions by the petitioners would be the one appropriate vehicle in which these claims could be developed. . . .

NOTES

1. The Court has held that judges are absolutely immune from damages suits under § 1983 for judicial acts performed by them within their jurisdiction. Pierson *v.* Ray, 386 U.S. 547 (1967).

2. In Rizzo *v.* Goode, 423 U.S. 362 (1976), residents of Philadelphia brought a § 1983 class action in federal district court against the mayor, city manager, and police commissioner, alleging that the defendants had failed to address a pattern of police misconduct. The district court entered an injunction requiring the defendants to take measures to respond to complaints and to control the misconduct. The Supreme Court reversed, primarily on the ground that, in the absence of a policy condoning misconduct, there was no present case or controversy between the plaintiffs and the defendants. The Court also invoked federalism:

> "[T]he principles of federalism which play such an important part in governing the relationship between federal courts and state governments, though initially expounded and perhaps entitled to their greatest weight in cases where it was sought to enjoin a criminal prosecution in progress, have not been limited either to that situation or indeed to a criminal proceeding itself. We think those principles likewise have applicability where injunctive relief is sought, not against the judicial branch of the state government, but against those in charge of an executive branch of an agency of state or local governments . . . ."

Id. at 380.

New Orleans Public Service, Inc. v. Council of City of New Orleans

Supreme Court of the United States, 1989.
491 U.S. 350.

■ JUSTICE SCALIA delivered the opinion of the Court.

[New Orleans Public Service, Inc. (NOPSI), a subsidiary of Middle South Utilities, Inc., was a producer, wholesaler, and retailer of electricity. In 1974, NOPSI and other Middle South subsidiaries agreed to jointly finance construction of Grand Gulf 1, a nuclear reactor. Costs were much higher than anticipated, exceeding $3 billion. Consequently, electricity from Grand Gulf 1 proved to be more expensive than electricity from conventional sources.

[The Federal Energy Regulatory Commission (FERC), which has exclusive authority over interstate power transmission, conducted proceedings to allocate the costs and output of Grand Gulf 1 among the Middle South subsidiaries. FERC implicitly accepted Middle South's argument that construction of the reactor was prudent. It allocated 17 percent of the costs to NOPSI.

[After FERC announced its allocation of costs, NOPSI sought a rate increase from the New Orleans City Council, which had final authority over NOPSI's retail rates. The Council conducted an investigation and concluded that NOPSI had acted imprudently in reviewing the investment and in failing to sell its share following the 1979 nuclear accident at Three Mile Island. It then entered an order disallowing rate increases for $135 million of the Grand Gulf 1 costs (about 1/3 of NOPSI's share).

[NOPSI filed a petition for review of the Council's order in state court. It then filed a suit in federal district court, seeking declaratory and injunctive relief on the ground that the Council's rate order was preempted by federal law. The district court indicated agreement with NOPSI's preemption claim, but determined that it should abstain from deciding the case. After the district court dismissed the preemption claim, NOPSI amended its state court complaint to include the preemption claim.]

Before proceeding to the merits of the abstention issues, it bears emphasis that the Council does not dispute the District Court's *jurisdiction* to decide NOPSI's pre-emption claim. Our cases have long supported the proposition that federal courts lack the authority to abstain from the exercise of jurisdiction that has been conferred. . . . Underlying these assertions is the undisputed constitutional principle that Congress, and not the judiciary, defines the scope of federal jurisdiction within the constitutionally permissible bounds.

That principle does not eliminate, however, and the categorical assertions based upon it do not call into question, the federal courts' discretion in determining whether to grant certain types of relief—a discretion that was part of the common-law background against which the statutes conferring jurisdiction were enacted. Thus, there are some classes of cases in which the withholding of authorized equitable relief because of undue interference with state proceedings is "the normal thing to do." Younger *v.* Harris, 401 U.S. 37, 45 (1971). We have carefully defined, however, the areas in which such "abstention" is permissible, and it remains "the exception, not the rule." As recently as last Term we described the federal courts' obligation to adjudicate claims within their jurisdiction as "virtually unflagging." . . .

[The Court first considered the *Burford* abstention doctrine, which holds that federal courts must not enjoin parties from proceeding in state court when "(1) . . . there are difficult questions of state law bearing on policy problems of substantial public import whose importance transcends the result in the case then at bar; or (2) . . . the exercise of federal review of the question in a case and in similar cases would be disruptive of state efforts to establish a coherent policy with respect to a matter of substantial public concern." In the Court's view, the *Burford* doctrine was not implicated in NOPSI's case because NOPSI was not pressing state law claims in federal court and interstate regulation of rates for electricity "does *not* demand significant familiarity with, and will not disrupt state resolution of, distinctively local regulatory facts or policies."]

[O]ne of the issues in the present case is whether the principle of *Younger* can properly be extended to this type of suit. . . . First, NOPSI argues that *Younger* does not require abstention in the face of a substantial claim that the challenged state action is completely pre-empted by federal law. Such a claim, NOPSI contends, calls into question the prerequisite of *Younger* abstention that the State have a legitimate, substantial interest in its pending proceedings. . . .

[W]hen we inquire into the substantiality of the State's interest in its proceedings we do not look narrowly to its interest in the *outcome* of the particular case—which could arguably be offset by a substantial federal interest in the opposite outcome. Rather, what we look to is the importance of the generic proceedings to the state. . . . Because pre-emption-based challenges merit a similar focus, the appropriate question here is not whether Louisiana has a substantial, legitimate interest in reducing NOPSI's retail rate below that necessary to recover its wholesale costs, but whether it has a substantial, legitimate interest in regulating intrastate retail rates. It clearly does. . . .

NOPSI's second argument [is] that *Younger*'s posited exception for state statutes "flagrantly and patently violative of express constitutional prohibitions" ought to apply equally to state proceedings and orders flagrantly and patently violative of federal pre-emption . . . . [W]e do not have to decide the matter here, since the proceeding and order at issue do not meet that description. The Council has not sought directly to regulate interstate wholesale rates; nor has it questioned the validity of the FERC-prescribed allocation of power within the Grand Gulf system, or the FERC-prescribed wholesale rates; nor has it reexamined the prudence of NOPSI's agreement to participate in Grand Gulf 1 in the first place. . . .

[T]herefore, . . . NOPSI's challenge must stand or fall upon the answer to the question whether the Louisiana court action is the type of proceeding to which *Younger* applies. Viewed in isolation, it plainly is not. Although our concern for comity and federalism has led us to expand the protection of *Younger* beyond state criminal prosecutions, to civil enforcement proceedings, and even to civil proceedings involving certain orders that are uniquely in furtherance of the state courts' ability to perform their judicial functions, it has never been suggested that *Younger* requires abstention in deference to a state judicial proceeding reviewing legislative or executive action. Such a broad abstention requirement would make a mockery of the rule that only exceptional circumstances justify a federal court's refusal to decide a case in deference to the States.

In asserting that *Younger* is applicable, however, respondents focus not upon the Louisiana court action in isolation, but upon that action as a mere continuation of the Council proceeding. . . .

Respondents' case for abstention still requires, however, that the *Council proceeding* be the sort of proceeding entitled to *Younger* treatment. We think it is not. While we have expanded *Younger* beyond criminal proceedings, and even beyond proceedings in courts, we have never extended it to proceedings that are not "judicial in nature." The Council's proceedings in the present case were not judicial in nature. . . .

As a challenge to completed legislative action, NOPSI's suit [was] no different in substance from a facial challenge to an allegedly unconstitutional statute or zoning ordinance—which we would assuredly not require to be brought in state courts. It is true, of course, that the federal court's disposition of such a case may well affect, or for practical purposes pre-empt, a future—or, as in the present circumstances, even a pending—state-court action. But there is no doctrine that the availability or even the pendency of state judicial proceedings excludes the federal courts. Viewed, as it should be, as no more than a state-court challenge to completed legislative action, the Louisiana suit comes within none of the exceptions that *Younger* and later cases have established. . . .

■ [The concurring opinion of JUSTICE BRENNAN is omitted.]

■ CHIEF JUSTICE REHNQUIST, concurring in Parts I and I–B and concurring in the judgment. . . .

Nothing in the Court's opinion curtails our prior application of *Younger* to certain administrative proceedings which *are* "judicial in nature"; nor does it alter our prior case law indicating that such proceedings should be regarded as "ongoing" for the purposes of *Younger* abstention until state appellate review is completed. With this understanding, I join the portion of the Court's opinion holding that *Younger* abstention is inappropriate here. . . .

■ [The concurring opinion of JUSTICE BLACKMUN is omitted.]

NOTES

1. The Supreme Court has explained a third federal abstention doctrine, the *Pullman* doctrine, in the following terms:

> "In Railroad Commission *v.* Pullman Co., 312 U.S. 496 (1941), this Court held that federal courts should abstain from decision when difficult and unsettled questions of state law must be resolved before a substantial federal constitutional question can be decided. By abstaining in such cases, federal courts will avoid both unnecessary adjudication of federal questions and needless friction with state policies. . . ."

Hawaii Housing Authority *v.* Midkiff, 467 U.S. 229, 236 (1984). Unlike abstention under *Younger* and *Burford*, *Pullman* abstention generally results in the stay, rather than the dismissal, of the federal action pending the outcome of state court proceedings. As in *Younger* and *Burford*, in *Pullman* the Court grounded its abstention analysis in equity precedents, concluding that abstention was required by "important considerations of policy in the administration of federal equity jurisdiction." 312 U.S. at 501.

2. The Court has also held that federal courts should sometimes abstain from decision in cases that duplicate state proceedings. This form of abstention, however, is appropriate only in "exceptional" cases, when a

parallel federal suit is highly inconvenient or impractical: otherwise, federal courts must honor their "virtually unflagging" duty to exercise jurisdiction. Colorado River Water Conservation District *v.* United States, 424 U.S. 800 (1976). When the relief sought is a declaratory judgment, federal courts may have greater discretion to abstain. See Wilton *v.* Seven Falls Co., 515 U.S. 277 (1995).

Missouri v. Jenkins

Supreme Court of the United States, 1995.
515 U.S. 70.

■ CHIEF JUSTICE REHNQUIST delivered the opinion of the Court.

As this school desegregation litigation enters its 18th year, we are called upon again to review the decisions of the lower courts. In this case, the State of Missouri has challenged the District Court's order of salary increases for virtually all instructional and noninstructional staff within the Kansas City, Missouri, School District (KCMSD) and the District Court's order requiring the State to continue to fund remedial "quality education" programs because student achievement levels were still "at or below national norms at many grade levels."

A general overview of this litigation is necessary for proper resolution of the issues upon which we granted certiorari. This case has been before the same United States District Judge since 1977. In that year, the KCMSD, the school board, and the children of two school board members brought suit against the State and other defendants. Plaintiffs alleged that the State, the surrounding suburban school districts (SSD's), and various federal agencies had caused and perpetuated a system of racial segregation in the schools of the Kansas City metropolitan area. . . .

After a trial that lasted 7 1/2 months, the District Court . . . determined that the State and the KCMSD were liable for an intradistrict violation, *i.e.*, they had operated a segregated school system within the KCMSD. . . .

In June 1985, the District Court issued its first remedial order and established as its goal the "elimination of all vestiges of state imposed segregation." The District Court determined that "[s]egregation ha[d] caused a system wide *reduction* in student achievement in the schools of the KCMSD." . . .

The District Court, pursuant to plans submitted by the KCMSD and the State, ordered a wide range of quality education programs for all students attending the KCMSD. . . .

The KCMSD was awarded an AAA rating in the 1987–1988 school year, and there is no dispute that since that time it has "maintained and greatly exceeded AAA requirements." The total cost for these quality education programs has exceeded $220 million.

The District Court also set out to desegregate the KCMSD . . . . Because it had found no interdistrict violation, the District Court could not order mandatory interdistrict redistribution of students between the KCMSD and the surrounding SSD's. . . . [T]he District Court determined that "[a]chievement of AAA status, improvement of the quality of education being offered at the KCMSD schools, magnet schools, as well as other components of this desegregation plan can serve to maintain and hopefully attract non-minority student enrollment."

In November 1986, the District Court approved a comprehensive magnet school and capital improvements plan and held the State and the KCMSD jointly and severally liable for its funding. . . . The District Court adopted the magnet-school program . . . because it believed "that the proposed magnet plan [was] so attractive that it would draw non-minority students from the private schools who have abandoned or avoided the KCMSD, and draw in additional non-minority students from the suburbs." . . . Since its inception, the magnet-school program has operated at a cost, including magnet transportation, in excess of $448 million. . . .

In June 1985, the District Court ordered substantial capital improvements to combat the deterioration of the KCMSD's facilities. . . .

[T]he total cost of capital improvements ordered has soared to over $540 million. . . .

As part of its desegregation plan, the District Court has ordered salary assistance to the KCMSD. . . . The total cost of this component of the desegregation remedy since 1987 is over $200 million.

The District Court's desegregation plan has been described as the most ambitious and expensive remedial program in the history of school desegregation. . . . [T]he KCMSD, which has pursued a "friendly adversary" relationship with the plaintiffs, has continued to propose ever more expensive programs. As a result, the desegregation costs have escalated and now are approaching an annual cost of $200 million. These massive expenditures have financed

> "high schools in which every classroom will have air conditioning, an alarm system, and 15 microcomputers; a 2,000-square-foot planetarium; green houses and vivariums; a 25-acre farm with an air-conditioned meeting room for 104 people; a Model United Nations wired for language translation; broadcast capable radio and television studios with an editing and animation lab; a temperature controlled art gallery; movie editing and screening rooms; a 3,500-square-foot dust-free diesel mechanics room; 1,875-square-foot elementary school animal rooms for use in a zoo project; swimming pools; and numerous other facilities."

Not surprisingly, the cost of this remedial plan has "far exceeded KCMSD's budget, or for that matter, its authority to tax." . . .

Almost 25 years ago, in Swann *v.* Charlotte-Mecklenburg Board of Education, 402 U.S. 1 (1971), we dealt with the authority of a district court to fashion remedies for a school district that had been segregated in law in violation of the Equal Protection Clause of the Fourteenth Amendment. Although recognizing the discretion that must necessarily adhere in a district court in fashioning a remedy, we also recognized the limits on such remedial power:

> "[E]limination of racial discrimination in public schools is a large task and one that should not be retarded by efforts to achieve broader purposes lying beyond the jurisdiction of the school authorities. One vehicle can carry only a limited amount of baggage. It would not serve the important objective of Brown [v. Board of Education, 347 U.S. 483 (1954),] to seek to use school desegregation cases for purposes beyond their scope, although desegregation of schools ultimately will have impact on other forms of discrimination." *Id.* at 22–23.

. . . [I]n Milliken *v.* Bradley, 433 U.S. 267 (1977), we articulated a three-part framework derived from our prior cases to guide district courts in the exercise of their remedial authority.

> "In the first place, like other equitable remedies, the nature of the desegregation remedy is to be determined by the nature and scope of the constitutional violation. . . . Second, the decree must indeed be *remedial* in nature, that is, it must be designed as nearly as possible 'to restore the victims of discriminatory conduct to the position they would have occupied in the absence of such conduct.' Third, the federal courts in devising a remedy must take into account the interests of state and local authorities in managing their own affairs, consistent with the Constitution."

. . . Because "federal supervision of local school systems was intended as a temporary measure to remedy past discrimination," Board of Education of Oklahoma City Public Schools *v.* Dowell, 498 U.S. 237, 247 (1991), we also have considered the showing that must be made by a school district operating under a desegregation order for complete or partial relief from that order. In Freeman *v.* Pitts, 503 U.S. 467 (1992), we stated that

> "[a]mong the factors which must inform the sound discretion of the court in ordering partial withdrawal are the following: [1] whether there has been full and satisfactory compliance with the decree in those aspects of the system where supervision is to be withdrawn; [2] whether retention of judicial control is necessary or practicable to achieve compliance with the decree in other facets of the school system; and [3] whether the school district has demonstrated, to the public and to the parents and students of the once disfavored race, its good-faith commitment to the whole of the courts' decree and to those

> provisions of the law and the Constitution that were the predicate for judicial intervention in the first instance." *Id.* at 491.

The ultimate inquiry is "whether the [constitutional violator] ha[s] complied in good faith with the desegregation decree since it was entered, and whether the vestiges of past discrimination ha[ve] been eliminated to the extent practicable." *Id.* at 492.

Proper analysis of the District Court's orders challenged here, then, must rest upon their serving as proper means to the end of restoring the victims of discriminatory conduct to the position they would have occupied in the absence of that conduct and their eventual restoration of "state and local authorities to the control of a school system that is operating in compliance with the Constitution." *Id.* at 489. . . .

The proper response to an intradistrict violation is an intradistrict remedy, that serves to eliminate the racial identity of the schools within the affected school district by eliminating, as far as practicable, the vestiges of *de jure* segregation in all facets of their operations. . . .

Instead of seeking to remove the racial identity of the various schools within the KCMSD, the District Court has set out on a program to create a school district that was equal to or superior to the surrounding SSD's. Its remedy has focused on "desegregative attractiveness," coupled with "suburban comparability." . . .

We previously have approved of intradistrict desegregation remedies involving magnet schools. Magnet schools have the advantage of encouraging voluntary movement of students within a school district in a pattern that aids desegregation on a voluntary basis, without requiring extensive busing and redrawing of district boundary lines. As a component in an intradistrict remedy, magnet schools also are attractive because they promote desegregation while limiting the withdrawal of white student enrollment that may result from mandatory student reassignment.

The District Court's remedial plan in this case, however, is not designed solely to redistribute the students within the KCMSD in order to eliminate racially identifiable schools within the KCMSD. Instead, its purpose is to attract nonminority students from outside the KCMSD schools. But this *inter* district goal is beyond the scope of the *intra*district violation identified by the District Court. In effect, the District Court has devised a remedy to accomplish indirectly what it admittedly lacks the remedial authority to mandate directly: the inter district transfer of students. . . .

Respondents argue that the District Court's reliance upon desegregative attractiveness is justified in light of the District Court's statement that segregation has "led to white flight from the KCMSD to suburban districts." The lower courts' "findings" as to "white flight" are . . . inconsistent with the typical supposition, bolstered here by the record evidence, that "white flight" may result from desegregation, not *de jure* segregation. . . .

It is certainly theoretically possible that the greater the expenditure per pupil within the KCMSD, the more likely it is that some unknowable number of nonminority students not presently attending schools in the KCMSD will choose to enroll in those schools. Under this reasoning, however, every increased expenditure, whether it be for teachers, noninstructional employees, books, or buildings, will make the KCMSD in some way more attractive, and thereby perhaps induce nonminority students to enroll in its schools. But this rationale is not susceptible to any objective limitation. . . .

Nor are there limits to the duration of the District Court's involvement. . . . [O]ur cases recognize that local autonomy of school districts is a vital national tradition, and that a district court must strive to restore state and local authorities to the control of a school system operating in compliance with the Constitution.

The District Court's pursuit of the goal of "desegregative attractiveness" results in so many imponderables and is so far removed from the task of eliminating the racial identifiability of the schools within the KCMSD that we believe it is beyond the admittedly broad discretion of the District Court. In this posture, we conclude that the District Court's order of salary increases, which was "grounded in remedying the vestiges of segregation by improving the desegregative attractiveness of the KCMSD," is simply too far removed from an acceptable implementation of a permissible means to remedy previous legally mandated segregation.

Similar considerations lead us to conclude that the District Court's order requiring the State to continue to fund the quality education programs because student achievement levels were still "at or below national norms at many grade levels" cannot be sustained. . . .

In one . . . order relied upon by the Court of Appeals, the District Court stated that the KCMSD had not reached anywhere close to its "maximum potential because the District is still at or below national norms at many grade levels."

But this clearly is not the appropriate test . . . . The basic task of the District Court is to decide whether the reduction in achievement by minority students attributable to prior *de jure* segregation has been remedied to the extent practicable. . . .

In reconsidering this order, the District Court should apply our three-part test from Freeman *v.* Pitts. . . . [I]mproved achievement on test scores is not necessarily required for the State to achieve partial unitary status as to the quality education programs, the District Court should sharply limit, if not dispense with, its reliance on this factor. Just as demographic changes independent of *de jure* segregation will affect the racial composition of student assignments, so too will numerous external factors beyond the control of the KCMSD and the State affect minority student achievement. So long as these external factors are not the result of segregation, they do not figure in the remedial calculus. . . .

The District Court also should consider that many goals of its quality education plan already have been attained . . . .

■ JUSTICE O'CONNOR, concurring. . . . When the District Court found that KCMSD was racially segregated, the constitutional violation from which all remedies flow in this case, it also found that there was neither an interdistrict violation nor significant interdistrict segregative effects. Whether the white exodus that has resulted in a school district that is 68% black was caused by the District Court's remedial orders or by natural, if unfortunate, demographic forces, we have it directly from the District Court that the segregative effects of KCMSD's constitutional violation did not transcend its geographical boundaries. In light of that finding, the District Court cannot order remedies seeking to rectify regional demographic trends that go beyond the nature and scope of the constitutional violation. . . .

■ JUSTICE THOMAS, concurring. It never ceases to amaze me that the courts are so willing to assume that anything that is predominantly black must be inferior. Instead of focusing on remedying the harm done to those black schoolchildren injured by segregation, the District Court here sought to convert the Kansas City, Missouri, School District (KCMSD) into a "magnet district" that would reverse the "white flight" caused by *de*segregation. . . .

The mere fact that a school is black does not mean that it is the product of a constitutional violation. . . .

According to the District Court, the schools whose student bodies were more than 90% black constituted "vestiges" of the prior *de jure* segregation, which the State and the KCMSD had an obligation to eliminate. Later, in the course of issuing its first "remedial" order, the District Court added that a "system wide reduction in student achievement in the schools of . . . KCMSD" was also a vestige of the prior *de jure* segregation. In a subsequent order, the District Court indicated that post-1954 "white flight" was another vestige of the pre-1954 segregated system.

In order for a "vestige" to supply the ground for an exercise of remedial authority, it must be clearly traceable to the dual school system. . . . District courts must not confuse the consequences of *de jure* segregation with the results of larger social forces or of private decisions. . . .

Given that desegregation has not produced the predicted leaps forward in black educational achievement, there is no reason to think that black students cannot learn as well when surrounded by members of their own race as when they are in an integrated environment. Indeed, it may very well be that what has been true for historically black colleges is true for black middle and high schools. . . .

"Racial isolation" itself is not a harm; only state-enforced segregation is. After all, if separation itself is a harm, and if integration therefore is the only way that blacks can receive a proper education, then there must be something inferior about blacks. Under this theory, segregation injures blacks because blacks, when left on their own, cannot achieve. To my way of thinking, that conclusion is the result of a jurisprudence based upon a theory of black inferiority. . . .

Not only did the court subscribe to a theory of injury that was predicated on black inferiority, it also married this concept of liability to our expansive approach to remedial powers. We have given the federal courts the freedom to use any measure necessary to reverse problems—such as racial isolation or low educational achievement—that have proven stubbornly resistant to government policies. We have not permitted constitutional principles such as federalism or the separation of powers to stand in the way of our drive to reform the schools. Thus, the District Court here ordered massive expenditures by local and state authorities, without congressional or executive authorization and without any indication that such measures would attract whites back to KCMSD or raise KCMSD test scores. The time has come for us to put the genie back in the bottle.

The Constitution extends "[t]he judicial Power of the United States" to "all Cases, in Law and Equity, arising under this Constitution, the Laws of the United States, and Treaties made . . . under their Authority." Art. III, §§ 1, 2. I assume for purposes of this case that the remedial authority of the federal courts is inherent in the "judicial Power," as there is no general equitable remedial power expressly granted by the Constitution or by statute. As with any inherent judicial power, however, we ought to be reluctant to approve its aggressive or extravagant use, and instead we should exercise it in a manner consistent with our history and traditions.

Motivated by our worthy desire to eradicate segregation, however, we have disregarded this principle and given the courts unprecedented authority to shape a remedy in equity. Although at times we have invalidated a decree as beyond the bounds of an equitable remedy, see Milliken *v.* Bradley, 418 U.S. 717 (1974) (*Milliken I*), these instances have been far outnumbered by the expansions in the equity power. . . .

In upholding these court-ordered measures, we indicated that trial judges had virtually boundless discretion in crafting remedies once they had identified a constitutional violation. As *Swann* put it, "[o]nce a right and a violation have been shown, the scope of a district court's equitable powers to remedy past wrongs is broad, for breadth and flexibility are inherent in equitable remedies." 402 U.S., at 15. We did say that "the nature of the violation determines the scope of the remedy," *id.*, at 16, but our very next sentence signaled how weak that limitation was: "In default by the school authorities of their obligation to proffer acceptable remedies, a district court has broad power to fashion a remedy that will assure a unitary school system," *ibid.*

It is perhaps understandable that we permitted the lower courts to exercise such sweeping powers. Although we had authorized the federal courts to work toward "a system of determining admission to the public schools on a nonracial basis" in Brown *v.* Board of Education, 349 U.S. 294, 300–301 (1955) (*Brown II*), resistance to *Brown I* produced little desegregation by the time we decided Green *v.* School Board of New Kent County, 391 U.S. 430 (1968). Our impatience with the pace of desegregation and with the lack of a good-faith effort on the part of school boards led us to approve such extraordinary remedial measures. But such powers should have been temporary and used only to overcome the widespread resistance to the dictates of the Constitution. The judicial overreaching we see before us today perhaps is the price we now pay for our approval of such extraordinary remedies in the past. . . .

Such extravagant uses of judicial power are at odds with the history and tradition of the equity power and the Framers' design. The available historical records suggest that the Framers did not intend federal equitable remedies to reach as broadly as we have permitted. Anticipating the growth of our modern doctrine, the Anti-Federalists criticized the Constitution because it might be read to grant broad equitable powers to the federal courts. In response, the defenders of the Constitution "sold" the new framework of government to the public by espousing a narrower interpretation of the equity power. . . .

Two clear restraints on the use of the equity power—federalism and the separation of powers—derive from the very form of our Government. Federal courts should pause before using their inherent equitable powers to intrude into the proper sphere of the States. . . . A structural reform decree eviscerates a State's discretionary authority over its own program and budgets and forces state officials to reallocate state resources and funds to the desegregation plan at the expense of other citizens, other government programs, and other institutions not represented in court. When district courts seize complete control over the schools, they strip state and local governments of one of their most important governmental responsibilities, and thus deny their existence as independent governmental entities. . . .

■ JUSTICE SOUTER, with whom JUSTICE STEVENS, JUSTICE GINSBURG, and JUSTICE BREYER join, dissenting. . . .

After *Brown*, neither the State nor the KCMSD moved to dismantle this system of separate education "root and branch," despite their affirmative obligation to do that under the Constitution. . . . Ten years later, in the 1983–1984 school year, 24 schools remained racially isolated with more than 90 percent black enrollment. . . .

Since the District Court found that segregation had caused, among other things, "a system wide *reduction* in student achievement in the schools of the KCMSD," it ordered the adoption, starting in 1985, of a series of remedial programs to raise educational performance. . . .

[I]t would be error to require that the students in a school district attain the national average test score as a prerequisite to a finding of partial unitary status, if only because all sorts of causes independent of the vestiges of past school segregation might stand in the way of the goal. That said, test scores will clearly be relevant in determining whether the improvement programs have cured a deficiency in student achievement to the practicable extent. . . .

[T]he District Court did not ground its orders of salary increases solely on the goal of attracting students back to the KCMSD. From the start, the District Court has consistently treated salary increases as an important element in remedying the systemwide reduction in student achievement resulting from segregation in the KCMSD. . . .

[T]he Court has nothing to justify its rejection of the District Court's finding that segregation caused white flight but its supposition that flight results from integration, not segregation. The supposition, and the distinction on which it rests, are untenable. At the more obvious level, there is in fact no break in the chain of causation linking the effects of desegregation with those of segregation. There would be no desegregation orders and no remedial plans without prior unconstitutional segregation as the occasion for issuing and adopting them, and an adverse reaction to a desegregation order is traceable in fact to the segregation that is subject to the remedy. . . .

■ JUSTICE GINSBURG, dissenting. . . . The Court stresses that the present remedial programs have been in place for seven years. But compared to more than two centuries of firmly entrenched official discrimination, the experience with the desegregation remedies ordered by the District Court has been evanescent.

In 1724, Louis XV of France issued the Code Noir, the first slave code for the Colony of Louisiana, an area that included Missouri. When Missouri entered the Union in 1821, it entered as a slave State.

Before the Civil War, Missouri law prohibited the creation or maintenance of schools for educating blacks: "No person shall keep or teach any school for the instruction of negroes or mulattoes, in reading or writing, in this State." Act of Feb. 16, 1847, § 1, 1847 Mo. Laws 103.

Beginning in 1865, Missouri passed a series of laws requiring separate public schools for blacks. The Missouri Constitution first permitted, then required, separate schools. See Mo. Const. Art. IX, § 2 (1865); Mo. Const. Art. XI, § 3 (1875).

After this Court announced its decision in Brown *v.* Board of Education, 347 U.S. 483 (1954), Missouri's Attorney General declared these provisions mandating segregated schools unenforceable. The statutes were repealed in 1957 and the constitutional provision was rescinded in 1976. Nonetheless, 30 years after *Brown*, the District Court found that "the inferior education indigenous of the state-compelled dual school system has lingering effects in the Kansas City, Missouri School District." The District Court concluded that "the State . . . cannot defend its failure to affirmatively act to eliminate the structure and effects of its past dual system on the basis of restrictive state law." Just ten years ago, in June 1985, the District Court issued its first remedial order.

Today, the Court declares illegitimate the goal of attracting nonminority students to the Kansas City, Missouri, School District, and thus stops the District Court's efforts to integrate a school district that was, in the 1984/1985 school year, sorely in need and 68.3% black. Given the deep, inglorious history of segregation in Missouri, to curtail desegregation at this time and in this manner is an action at once too swift and too soon.

CHAPTER 7

INJUNCTIONS

The classic equitable remedy is the injunction, an *in personam* order by the court to a defendant, requiring the defendant to do or to refrain from doing some act. Professor Zechariah Chafee, Jr., one of the twentieth century's great equity scholars and the editor of some previous editions of this book, described injunctions as "a kit of tools which can be employed effectively in all sorts of ways after one has been thoroughly accustomed to handling them." Zechariah Chafee, Jr., Foreword, in Edward D. Re, SELECTED ESSAYS ON EQUITY i, iii (1955).

Injunctive relief may be sought to preserve a state of affairs pending the outcome of litigation, to prevent a threatened injury from happening, or to limit the adverse consequences of an injurious act. It may be denied if it is premature, oppressive, impractical, or impossible to enforce.

The first sections of this chapter address the standards for granting an injunction as final relief in a case. The somewhat different standards courts apply to interlocutory injunctions are taken up in Section F.

A. PREVENTATIVE AND REPARATIVE INJUNCTIONS

Vane v. Lord Barnard

Court of Chancery, 1716.
2 Vern. 738, 23 Eng. Rep. 1082.

The defendant, on the marriage of the plaintiff, his eldest son, with the daughter of Morgan Randyll and 10,000*l.* portion, settled (*inter alia*) Raby Castle on himself for life, without impeachment of waste,[i] remainder to his son for life, and to his first and other sons in tail male.

The defendant, the Lord Barnard, having taken some displeasure against his son, got two hundred workmen together, and of a sudden in a few days, stript the castle of the lead, iron, glass doors, and boards, &c., to the value of 3000*l.*

The court [LORD COWPER, L.C.], upon filing the bill (and plea and answer put in by Lord Barnard), granted an injunction to stay committing of waste, in pulling down the castle; and now, upon the hearing of the cause, decreed, not only the injunction to continue, but that the castle should be repaired, and put into the same condition it was in, in August, 1714, and for that purpose a commission was to issue to ascertain what ought to be repaired, and a master to see it done at the

[i] [This means that the tenant, Lord Barnard, could not be called to account in the law courts for waste committed during his tenure.]

expense and charge of the defendant, the Lord Barnard; and decreed the plaintiff his costs.

NOTES

1. In 1908, Dean Christopher Langdell wrote,

> "When . . . justice requires that a tort should be specifically repaired, it would seem to be much more feasible for a court of equity itself to undertake the repair of it, at the expense of the tortfeasor, than to attempt to compel the latter to repair it. . . . [Yet the only instance seems to be Vane *v.* Lord Barnard.] The decree directed the master to see the castle repaired at the defendant's expense. Whether the decree was ever performed or not does not appear. It is said not to have been performed during the defendant's life."

C. C. Langdell, BRIEF SURVEY OF EQUITABLE JURISDICTION 37 (2d ed. 1908). Today, courts often rely on masters and receivers in complex cases. See Chapter Six, Section A(5) (Masters and Receivers).

2. The classic injunction is an order designed to stop a wrong from occurring, or from continuing to occur in the future. The injunction typically is negative in form: do not do an act, or cease doing an act. If the wrong has not yet occurred, the injunction protects the plaintiff's rights very effectively, by preventing a violation. If the wrong is already in progress, a complete remedy includes both an injunction and compensation for harm done.

Professor Owen Fiss distinguished three types of injunctions: preventative injunctions, reparative injunctions, and structural injunctions. A preventative injunction prevents future wrongs, as just described: Lord Barnard is commanded to cease wrecking the castle. A reparative injunction, in Fiss's words, "seeks to eliminate the effects of a past wrong." Owen M. Fiss, THE CIVIL RIGHTS INJUNCTION 10 (1978). Lord Barnard must not only stop wasting the castle, but repair the harm he has done. In a sense, repairing the castle is preventative: it prevents the future harm the plaintiff would suffer in a damaged castle; but Fiss believed the notion of repair was necessary to capture an important feature of injunctive relief.

Less common are injunctions in Fiss's third category, structural injunctions. These combine preventative and reparative orders with a commitment to long-run judicial management in order to bring about institutional reform. Examples include judicial management of a racially segregated school district or an overcrowded prison.

3. Reparative injunctions are mandatory: they require the defendant to perform some affirmative act. Courts traditionally resisted mandatory injunctions, which place a different sort of burden on the defendant and may require additional supervision by the court. Courts have become somewhat more comfortable with mandatory injunctive relief, at least at the stage of final relief. Even so, it is still easier to obtain a prohibitory injunction than a mandatory one. On occasion, courts revert to the habit of phrasing essentially mandatory injunctions in the negative.

Foulkes v. Hays

Supreme Court of Washington, 1975.
85 Wash.2d 629.

■ UTTER, ASSOCIATE JUSTICE. This is an appeal from an order of the Adams County Superior Court granting respondent Kenny Foulkes' "motion to correct election fraud or error" and setting aside the results of a recount in an election for County Commissioner. Appellant Gordon Hays, the winning candidate in the recount, appeals its nullification; respondent Foulkes, the winner in the original tally, cross-appeals the court's refusal to reinstate it and order of a new election. We affirm both aspects of the trial court's judgment.

Appellant Hays was the incumbent and respondent Foulkes the challenger in the November 1974 Adams County Commissioner race. The first tally of votes in that contest established respondent as winner by 37 votes out of 3,025. Appellant requested a recount. The recount was held 14 days after the results of the initial count were known and resulted in appellant being declared elected by 71 votes. Almost all of the change in the results came from 12 of the 30 county precincts.

Respondent filed in superior court a timely challenge to the election results . . . , alleging some votes counted for appellant in the recount were marked by someone other than the voter after the original count was completed. . . . In the trial, testimony was taken as to the procedures by which the original tally was made and the way the ballots were kept between the time of the initial balloting and that of the recount. It showed that in that interim the ballots were placed in envelopes sealed with wax. The envelopes, in turn, were locked in canvas bags with the key to each bag tied to the outside, and the bags were stored in a vault at the County Auditor's office, accessible to several persons during working hours. Further testimony was heard from a document examiner called by respondent, who said that, in his opinion, 46 of 53 ballots he had selected as suspect (from all of the ballots from the 12 swing precincts) contained votes for the appellant made by someone other than the voter who marked the rest of the ballot. . . .

Additional testimony was then taken from two more experts with contradicting views on the conclusions of the first. Another document examiner, called by respondent, agreed that some ballots had been marked by two persons, though he differed with the first expert as to the legitimacy of certain ones. A graphoanalyst, one trained to determine personality traits from handwriting, called by appellant, disagreed and said that every one of the ballots from the 12 challenged precincts were marked by a single person.

On the basis of all this testimony, the court found enough ballots had been altered between the time of the original tally and the recount to change the outcome of the election. From this finding, and the fact that the keys to the padlocked sacks of ballots were accessible, it concluded the election officers had been guilty of "neglect of duty" . . . in failing to properly safeguard the ballots from tampering. . . . Since the exact number of ballots which had been altered could not be ascertained, the court determined that the proper remedy for this neglect was the holding of a new election. . . .

Appellant's most basic challenge is to the power of courts to inquire into the conduct of elections and order new elections to correct improprieties therein under RCW 29.04.030.[2] The broad language and murky legislative history of this statute show it to be a statutory recognition of the power of superior courts, acting within their general equity jurisdiction, to intervene in cases of election fraud or wrongdoing. Such jurisdiction would exist even without such recognition by virtue of Const. art. 4, § 6, unless it were "by law vested exclusively in some other court." We have upheld its exercise in quo warranto proceedings to contest election results brought completely independent of statutory remedies. This authority, whether based on a specific statute or the general equity jurisdiction, carries with it "all the means to carry it into effect." RCW 2.28.150. Where appropriate, these necessary and proper powers would include the power to order a new election where no other remedy would adequately correct distortions in election results caused by fraud or neglect. . . .

Respondent's cross-appeal urges us to reinstate the results of the original tally of votes and overturn the trial court's order of a new election. He provides neither authority nor sound argument for his position. The expert testimony heard below indicated it was impossible to tell exactly how many ballots had been fraudulently altered, though the number specifically identified as tainted fell short of making up appellant's margin of victory. In light of this, the trial court was correct in holding that the irregularity was such that the actual result of the voting could not be ascertained and a new election should be held. It did not, therefore, abuse its equitable discretion in ordering such an election. . . .

NOTES ON REMEDIES INVOLVING ELECTIONS

1. In 1996, Montana voters adopted (by initiative) a state law that limited corporate spending on political campaigns. In 1998, another initiative, imposing restrictions on mining, was certified for the November ballot. Business-oriented associations challenged the spending law, and also sought an injunction to delay or set aside the mining initiative, on the ground that mining companies had been wrongly excluded from mounting a

---

[2] RCW 29.04.030 provides:

"Any justice of the supreme court, judge of the court of appeals, or judge of the superior court in the proper county shall, by order, require any person charged with error, wrongful act or neglect [in connection with ballots] to forthwith correct the error, desist from the wrongful act, or perform the duty and to do as the court orders or to show cause forthwith why the error should not be corrected, the wrongful act desisted from, or the duty or order not performed . . . ."

campaign against it. On October 22, 1998, the district court concluded that the 1996 spending limit was unconstitutional, but refused to delay voting on the mining initiative. On November 3, voters adopted the mining initiative. The district court again refused injunctive relief. The Court of Appeals for the Ninth Circuit agreed that the spending limit was invalid, yet also affirmed the district court's decision to deny injunctive relief:

> "A state election violates due process 'if it is conducted in a manner that is fundamentally unfair.' Of course, 'the voiding of a state election is a drastic if not staggering remedy.' In determining whether to void an election, we balance the constitutional violation against the 'countervailing equitable factors' such as 'the extremely disruptive effect of election invalidation and the havoc it wreaks upon local political continuity.'
>
> "Here, even though there was evidence that [the spending limit] had affected [the mining companies'] ability to campaign, there was also evidence that it had no substantial impact. Eleven days remained before the election after the district court lifted the [spending] restrictions. And the state has a significant interest in avoiding the costs of a special election. In these circumstances, we cannot say that the district court abused its discretion in failing to void the results of the election."

Montana Chamber of Commerce *v.* Argenbright, 226 F.3d 1049, 1058 (9th Cir. 2000).

2. In August 2016, a federal district court held that the North Carolina legislature had drawn state legislative districts in a way that violated the Voting Rights Act. The court ordered the drawing of new districts, but allowed the existing ones to be used in the impending November 2016 election. Then, shortly after the election, the court ordered additional relief: a March 2017 deadline for new districts to be drawn, and a special election for the affected districts in November 2017. In effect, the district court was changing the term in office for a number of state legislators from two years to one year; in the affected districts, the newly elected legislators would also have a term of one year. In North Carolina *v.* Covington, 137 S.Ct. 1624, 1625–26 (2017) (*per curiam*), the Supreme Court reversed, stating that:

> "Relief in redistricting cases is 'fashioned in the light of well-known principles of equity.' Reynolds *v.* Sims, 377 U.S. 533, 585 (1964). A district court therefore must undertake an 'equitable weighing process' to select a fitting remedy for the legal violations it has identified, taking account of 'what is necessary, what is fair, and what is workable.' And in the context of deciding whether to truncate existing legislators' terms and order a special election, there is much for a court to weigh. Although this Court has never addressed whether or when a special election may be a proper remedy for a racial gerrymander, obvious considerations include the severity and nature of the particular constitutional violation, the extent of the likely disruption to the ordinary processes of

governance if early elections are imposed, and the need to act with proper judicial restraint when intruding on state sovereignty. We do not suggest anything about the relative weight of these factors (or others), but they are among the matters a court would generally be expected to consider in its 'balancing of the individual and collective interests' at stake. Swann *v.* Charlotte-Mecklenburg Board of Education, 402 U.S. 1, 16 (1971).

"Rather than undertaking such an analysis in this case, the District Court addressed the balance of equities in only the most cursory fashion. As noted above, the court simply announced that '[w]hile special elections have costs,' those unspecified costs 'pale in comparison' to the prospect that citizens will be 'represented by legislators elected pursuant to a racial gerrymander.' That minimal reasoning would appear to justify a special election in every racial-gerrymandering case—a result clearly at odds with our demand for careful case-specific analysis. For that reason, we cannot have confidence that the court adequately grappled with the interests on both sides of the remedial question before us. And because the District Court's discretion 'was barely exercised here,' its order provides no meaningful basis for even deferential review. Winter *v.* Natural Resources Defense Council, Inc., 555 U.S. 7, 27 (2008)."

B. EQUITABLE RIPENESS

Gustafson v. Cotco Enterprises, Inc.

Court of Appeals of Ohio, 1974.
42 Ohio App. 2d 45.

■ LYNCH, PRESIDING JUDGE. Defendant is appealing [an order] of the trial court which enjoined it from constructing and operating a "drag strip" on its property in Berlin Township because such operation constituted a nuisance and was an unreasonable interference with plaintiffs' use and enjoyment of their property. . .

On June 28, 1973, defendant acquired title to approximately 150 acres of land situated in Berlin Township with considerable frontage on the north side of U. S. Route 224, just to the east of Berlin Township Center. The deed was recorded on July 2, 1973. The purchase price was $85,000. Shortly after the purchase of the property, defendant made known its intention to construct and operate a drag strip.

Plaintiffs are the owners or occupiers of land situated in Berlin Township. Several of the plaintiffs live on property immediately adjacent to defendant's land and others live at various distances from defendant's land. The entire area adjacent to defendant's property is residential-agricultural. There are homes and farms, and a few small commercial establishments. Some of the farms are devoted to the raising of livestock as well as crops.

Approximately July 10, 1973, some of the plaintiffs met with officers of the defendant corporation and discussed the proposed drag strip operation. By letter dated July 12, 1973, plaintiffs notified defendant of their opposition to the construction of the proposed drag strip because they felt it would result in irreparable damage to their lives, to their property values and to their village, and that legal action would be taken if defendant would not reconsider its proposed use of its newly acquired property.

Defendant commenced clearing its land and a few days later on July 17, 1973, plaintiffs filed their complaint for injunctive relief. Berlin Township has not enacted any zoning laws or regulations.

Plaintiffs agree that drag strip racing is not a nuisance per se. . . . Plaintiffs further agree that the proposed drag strip is not unlawful because it does not violate any zoning ordinance in Berlin Township.

We agree with the holdings of several courts that the operation of a drag strip racing track in the vicinity of residential and agricultural properties may constitute. . . a nuisance in fact because of extraordinary noise during races that owners and occupants of residential property in the vicinity of such track are entitled to have such operation enjoined. . . .

Ohio Jurisprudence 2d 143, 144, Nuisances, Section 55 states as follows:

> "A court of equity may enjoin a threatened or anticipated nuisance, public or private, where it clearly appears that a nuisance will necessarily result from the contemplated act or thing which it is sought to enjoin. If the conceded facts show that the defendant contemplates the doing of things that will constitute a continuing public nuisance, injunction is the proper remedy. But the court must see plainly that the acts will constitute a nuisance before it will issue an injunction. The degree of proof required before a court will enjoin an anticipated nuisance must be convincing, and if the act or thing sought to be enjoined may or may not become a nuisance, depending on the use or manner of its operation, or other circumstances, equity will not interfere. . . ."

. . . Defendant planned to build a quarter mile asphalt track running north from U.S. Route 224 roughly in the center of this property. The track would be approximately 1100 feet from their west property line at the entrance side of their property and 600 feet from their property lines on the top section. The track would be one of the biggest and most modern in this area. The track would operate on Sundays from April to October with time trials scheduled from 8 a.m. to 11 a.m. and races from noon to 6 p.m. An estimated 3,000 spectators would attend each racing day, but their spectator stands capacity would be for 5,000 people with parking space available for 10,000 automobiles. Plans were for a 12 foot high security fence constructed of three-quarter inch plywood to be erected all around the property, and for 50 poles for floodlights containing 3 to 5 lightbulbs with 500 to 1500 wattage pointed downwards.

Defendant estimated that it would have about 280 time trials and races per Sunday. If the business was profitable, defendant would consider running races twice a week. Defendant's officers were hoping eventually to be able to handle a major event which would be a two day affair with 750 race cars and 50,000 people. The three officers and shareholders of defendant testified that they had considerable experience with drag racing. Two have worked for the National Hot Rod Association.

Defendant wrote a letter of intent dated March 23, 1973, to the National Hot Rod Association in which it stated that it planned to build a new and modern Drag Strip according to the requirements and specifications of the National Hot Rod association in order to obtain the approval of said association. The National Hot Rod Association does not allow jet engines on their sanctioned tracks because they are unsafe.

Defendant planned to curtail dust by use of blacktop or grass, to turn the lights downward at the race track to curtail reflection light beyond their property, to erect barrier fences for sound reduction, to control traffic by cooperating with the Mahoning County sheriff's office to set up a traffic pattern, and to prohibit the use of alcoholic beverages on the premises. The evidence was in conflict as to the effectiveness of barrier fences to reduce sound.

Defendant estimated that the following kinds of cars would be raced at their track: Stock or factory cars—70%; modified cars, dragster or rails—1 to 5%; funny cars—less than 1%. About 50% of the stock cars would be without mufflers and about 70% of all the cars that would race would be without mufflers.

Funny cars are specially designed and built for drag racing and cost a minimum of $25,000. Some of them use a mixture of nitro and other fuel. They develop between 1,500 and 1,800 horsepower.

Plaintiff's testimony was that part of the thrill of any drag race track was the noise and speed of the cars that would participate in the races. The racers start at a dead stop with their motors running at full speed and reach speeds of from 50 to 220 miles per hour by the time they travel the one-quarter mile length of the track. While two cars are racing each other, other cars are warming up their motors in preparation for racing. When the cars start racing, they peel rubber. Mufflers slow the exhaust and reduce the horsepower of a car so that they are removed to obtain the highest speed. Anything that tends to slow down a car is eliminated.

Funny cars and most of the rail cars do a burnout. The tires are coated with resin. Smoke is created that extends two to four hundred feet. There is nothing on the highway comparable to the noise of a funny car while in operation. A semi-truck or tractor trailer on the highway produces one-fourth to one-third of the noise of a funny car. The rail cars are also extremely loud.

Plaintiffs' expert sound engineer recorded sounds at Dragway 42, which is west of Salem, Ohio. The readings for stock cars racing averaged from 86 to 99 decibels at two separate points 500 feet from the starting line with the average background readings being 81 decibels and 88 decibels. The readings for funny cars at a distance of 1,000 feet from the starting line ranged from 100 to 104 decibels even though there were several trees and dense shrubbery between the recording device and the race track.

Defendant's sound expert also recorded sounds at Drag Strip 42 in West Salem, Ohio, and testified that at a distance of 3,500 feet from the starting line of the race tract, he had average readings of 82 decibels with a maximum of 84 decibels. By comparison, at 36 feet from the south side of U. S. 224 in Berlin Center, immediately across the street from defendant's property, the average passing automobile was 75 decibels and the average passing truck was 90 decibels.

Several of plaintiffs' witnesses had either attended drag strip races or resided near drag strips. They testified that at the drag strips the racing of engines, the big blast, and rumbling noise and squealing of tires at the start of the race had no comparison either to the traffic noise on U. S. Route 224 or to the noise in a mill. The sound is comparable to a nearby rocket and artillery fire in the Korean War.

Witnesses residing from four-tenths to six-tenths of a mile from drag strip race tracks testified that the noise and vibrations emanating from such tracks is so loud and aggravating that normal conversations are not possible, television sets have to be turned up and windows facing the drag strip have to be closed. It shakes the windows of the house and interferes with social activities outside the house. Sleep is impeded or interrupted.

Plaintiff, John Hawkins, who is an experienced realtor living in Berlin Center, testified that approximately 100 people live in Berlin Center; that Berlin Center has developed into a quiet residential community, and that the proposed drag strip would "kill the market" for residential and agricultural properties immediately adjacent to defendant's property . . . because of the noise and the character of some of the people who attend drag strip races. Two of the plaintiffs unsuccessfully tried to sell their properties when they learned of defendant's proposed drag strip.

The Methodist Church is located on the south side of U. S. 224 about 300 feet west of defendant's property and holds services from 9:45 a.m. until noon on Sundays and sometimes in the evenings; 300 members attended services the Sunday before the trial. One of the reasons for the opposition of plaintiff, John Hawkins, to this proposed drag strip was its proximity to the Methodist Church and defendant's proposed running of time trials during church services on Sunday. . . .

Defendant introduced evidence indicating that it had incurred considerable expense in preparation for its proposed drag strip; however, we find that plaintiffs were diligent in notifying defendant of their opposition to this drag strip and in filing this lawsuit. We are not impressed with plaintiffs' contentions that this proposed drag strip will increase traffic and will disturb them because of fumes, dust, dirt and lighting.

However, we find that there is clear and convincing evidence to support the trial court's finding that the proposed drag strip race track would create such an unreasonable amount of noise that serious interference to plaintiffs, who are the owners and occupants of surrounding property, in their use and enjoyment of their property would be caused, so as to constitute a nuisance. Therefore, we affirm this part of the trial court's decision.

Judgment affirmed as to enjoining defendant from constructing and operating its proposed "drag strip" on its property in Berlin Center.

NOTES ON EQUITABLE RIPENESS

1. Ripeness in the sense required for an injunction is sometimes termed "equitable ripeness" or "remedial ripeness." It overlaps with but is distinct from constitutional ripeness, which implements the jurisdictional requirement of a present "case or controversy." See, *e.g.*, City of Los Angeles *v.* Lyons, 461 U.S. 95, 103, 105, 109, 111–13 (1983) (treating equitable requirements as more strict than the constitutional requirement); see also Samuel L. Bray, The System of Equitable Remedies, 63 UCLA L. Rev. 530, 549 & n.85, 578–579 (2016).

Courts vary in their statements of the standard of equitable or remedial ripeness. A number of courts have referred to a "reasonable likelihood" of harm or a "substantial probability" that harm will occur. Some use stricter formulations, such as "reasonable certainty" or "imminent" harm.

2. Equitable ripeness has several components. One is the likelihood the defendant will take an action (sometimes phrased in terms of the defendant's "propensity"). Another is the likelihood that the act will cause harm. Another is the likelihood that the act will be unlawful.

3. In Nicholson *v.* Connecticut Half-Way House, Inc., the defendant purchased a home in a residential neighborhood intending to open a halfway house for prisoners released on parole. Neighbors sought an injunction against the proposed use of the property. The court denied injunctive relief, saying that the plaintiffs' "present fear of what may happen in the future, although genuinely felt, rests completely on speculation." 153 Conn. 507, 511 (1966).

State of Tennessee v. Feezell

Supreme Court of Tennessee, 1966.
22 McCanless 17.

■ WHITE, JUSTICE. The Honorable Glenn W. Woodlee, Chancellor . . . heard this case which was brought in the name of the State of Tennessee, under T.C.A. § 23–301 et seq., on behalf of twenty-six citizens of Blount County, all similarly situated, to enjoin the establishment of a crematory by Defendant Feezell in a "rural or rural residential" area in said county. . . .

Petitioners aver in their bill that the proposed establishment and operation of the crematory is a public or private nuisance and said establishment and operation should be enjoined immediately. . . .

A demurrer was filed to the petition stating essentially that it sought an injunction for an anticipated injury which constitutes no basis for injunctive relief. Excellent trial briefs were prepared by both parties, and in a memorandum opinion and decree, the chancellor sustained the demurrer and dismissed the petition on the ground that the suit was premature. Motion for a new trial having been overruled, appeal was perfected to this Court.

The question presented for determination by the Court is essentially this: Does a cause of action exist to enjoin, as a nuisance, a proposed cremation establishment in a rural or rural residential area under averments of the residents of the area that it will cause mental anguish, depressed feelings, physical discomfort and lower property values? We do not think so.

We believe that for an injunction suit to be sustained prior to the alleged nuisance coming into being, it must be sufficiently shown in the original bill or petition that the proposed establishment is a nuisance per se; that is within itself.

> "A nuisance at law or a nuisance per se is an act, occupation, or structure which is a nuisance at all times and under any circumstances, *regardless of location or surroundings*. Nuisances in fact or per accidens are those which become nuisances by reason of circumstances and surroundings and an act may be found to be a nuisance as a matter of fact where the natural tendency of the act is to create danger or inflict injury on person or property." 66 C.J.S. Nuisances § 3 (1950). (Emphasis supplied.)

> "Other definitions are: any act or omission or use of property or thing which is of itself hurtful to the health, tranquility, or morals, or which outrages the decency of the community; that which *cannot* be so *conducted* or *maintained* as to be *lawfully carried on* or *permitted* to *exist;* and, as related to private persons, an act or use of property of a continuing nature, offensive to and legally injurious to health and property, or both." 39 Am. Jur., Nuisances, § 11 (1942). (Emphasis supplied.)

It is perhaps misleading to define a nuisance per se as one which exists "at all times and under any circumstances, regardless of location or surroundings." Actually, a nuisance cannot exist without surrounding circumstances, because it is the surrounding circumstances that determine whether an injury is occasioned; and it is axiomatic that some injury must be occasioned or be at least imminent because of the alleged "nuisance."

There is, in at least one case in this State, an indication that the difference between a nuisance per se, and a nuisance per accidens is that in the former, injury in some form is certain to be inflicted, while in the latter, the injury is uncertain or contingent until it actually occurs. This case held that where injury from a nuisance is not real and immediate and certain to occur, but only uncertain or contingent, the nuisance will not be enjoined anticipatory to its going into operation. . . .

We do not say that an anticipatory nuisance is not enjoinable under any circumstances. If the injury anticipated is imminent and certain to occur, there may, in fact, be a proper case for immediate abatement, provided, of course, the injury is recognized as otherwise actionable at law and equity. We do not say that mental disturbances or "psychic" injuries caused by a nuisance, public or private, are not such as may be actionable at law or equity. They can, in fact, be very real to the complainants. We do say, however, that allegations in the petition must be sufficient, in defining the circumstances and mode of operation surrounding the undertaking, to persuade the court, if they are proved, that injury is imminent and certain. We are convinced that proof of the alleged location of defendant's crematory and the alleged mode of operation and physical appearance of the same will be insufficient to foretell certain injury.

Our research has uncovered no case involving the attempted abatement of a human cremation establishment. Possibly the closest analogy would be the operation of a funeral parlor—at least as regards "psychic" injuries and lowered property values. . . .

As regards funeral parlors or undertaking establishments, the majority rule in this country, according to an annotation in 39 A.L.R. 2d 1000 (1955), is

> "that if an undertaking establishment in a purely residential section causes from its normal operations, depressing feelings to families in the immediate neighborhood, and, as a constant reminder of death, appreciably impairs their happiness or weakens their powers of resistance and depreciates the values of their properties, such an establishment constitutes a nuisance."

. . . Our holding in the instant cases does not, perhaps, coincide precisely with some of the cases following the majority rule. . . . Nevertheless, we are limited in the instant case to an examination of those factors alleged in the petition, proof of which would not indicate certain injury, either emotional or physical, to petitioners. Residences in a rural area are sparsely situated and there is no allegation in the bill that any residence is in close proximity to the proposed crematory, but that it is to be located in "an entirely rural area."

There is, of course, a minority rule, the gist of which is that mental suffering or depressed feelings are not actionable injuries where funeral parlors are proposed for residential areas. . . .

Because we find the allegations in the petition insufficient, even if proved, to persuade us that a nuisance is sure to be created by the operation of a crematory in this particular location, we, therefore, affirm the ruling of the trial court as set forth in a splendid memorandum opinion. . . .

Town of Monroe v. Renz

Appellate Court of Connecticut, 1997.
46 Conn. App. 5.

■ LANGENBACH, JUDGE. The defendants appeal from the judgment of the trial court permanently enjoining them from using a rock crusher and from blasting rock to supply the rock crusher in their sand and gravel operation at 201 Turkey Roost Road in the town of Monroe. . . .

The parties have shared a long journey through many proceedings before administrative agencies and state and federal trial courts. In 1973, the named defendant, Ronald Renz, purchased a 133 acre parcel of land located in a residential zone in Monroe. The property has been used continuously for sand and gravel excavation since the 1940s and its use as such constitutes a valid prior nonconforming use with respect to the subsequently enacted zoning regulations that established the area as a two acre residential zone.

From 1973 through 1987, the on-site excavation of naturally occurring deposits of sand and gravel remained essentially the same. By 1987, those deposits began to be depleted, and commercial demand for bank run gravel declined. The demand for crushed stone, however, increased. To compete for contracts to provide crushed stone, the defendants installed a rock crusher in 1988. The rock crushing operation consisted of two rock crushers that worked in tandem sending crushed materials down conveyor belts to two screens that sized the stones. Bucket loaders continuously fed blasted rock into the crushing plant. Blasting was conducted once a month to feed the crushing plant. Between blasts, drilling machines constantly drilled into rock formations in preparation for the next blast. Each blast required up to 200 holes fifty feet deep that were packed with up to 28,000 pounds of explosives. The blasting created sheer rock cliffs between sixty and 100 feet in height.

In response to that activity, the town issued a cease and desist order . . . . [A series of legal proceedings followed, first before zoning authorities and then in superior court. Up to the time of final judgment, the defendant continued to operate its rock crusher on a limited basis, according to an interim plan agreed to by the parties. Ultimately, the superior court found in favor of the plaintiffs and entered a permanent injunction ordering the defendant to cease the rock crushing operation. The defendant appealed, and the plaintiffs cross-appealed for additional relief. The appellate court affirmed the judgment for the plaintiffs on substantive zoning issues and approved the injunction against further rock-crushing.]

The plaintiffs next claim that the trial court improperly failed to order the rock crusher removed.

"A party seeking injunctive relief has the burden of alleging and proving irreparable harm and lack of an adequate remedy at law. . . . A prayer for injunctive relief is addressed to the sound discretion of the court and the court's ruling can be reviewed only for the purpose of determining whether the decision was based on an erroneous statement of law or an abuse of discretion." As noted by the trial court, *Levin, J.*, in its July 21, 1995 memorandum of decision, and not amended by its September 14, 1995 decision, "Even in an action brought by a zoning enforcement officer to require conformity with the zoning regulations, the granting of injunctive relief, which must be compatible with the equities of the case, rests within the trial court's sound discretion. Those equities should take into account the gravity and wilfulness of the violation, as well as the potential harm to the defendants. The proof of violations does not . . . obligate the court mechanically to grant the requested injunction for every violation."

In their motion to reargue on the issue of a mandatory injunction requiring removal of the rock crusher from the defendants' premises, the plaintiffs' argument was solely: "The defendants' disdain of five court orders is reasonable concern to the plaintiffs that the defendants *may* continue to utilize the machinery which is prohibited under the zoning regulations. There is no legal justification for its presence." The plaintiffs did not allege any other harm requiring an order of removal. The trial court properly took note of the equities, including the "gravity and wilfulness of the violations" and the "potential harm to the defendants" before refusing to order the rock crusher removed. In ruling on this issue, the trial court stated: "While the defendants have . . . not been reluctant to relitigate issues previously settled, they have not previously violated an order of this court, nor may the court presume that they will do so. Injunctive relief may not lie where it is predicated on the fears and apprehensions of the party applying for it or where it would be incompatible with the equities of the case . . . and likewise the power of equity to grant such relief may be exercised only under demanding circumstances. . . . The extraordinary nature of injunctive relief requires that the harm complained of is occurring or will occur if the injunction is not granted." The court concluded that such harm was not demonstrated and refused to order the removal of the rock crusher.

Our review of the record and the trial court's opinion in this case leads us to conclude that the trial court neither incorrectly stated the law nor abused its discretion. The trial court properly declined to order the requested injunction. . . .

C. EQUITABLE MOOTNESS

Federal Trade Commission v. Accusearch Inc.

United States Court of Appeals, Tenth Circuit, 2009.
570 F.3d 1187.

■ HARTZ, CIRCUIT JUDGE. Abika.com is a website that has sold various personal data, including telephone records. The Federal Trade Commission (FTC) brought suit against the operator of the website, Accusearch Inc., and its president and owner, Jay Patel (collectively, Accusearch), to curtail Accusearch's sale of confidential information and to require it to disgorge its profits from the sale of information in telephone records. The FTC alleged that Accusearch's trade in telephone records (which are protected from disclosure under § 702 of the Telecommunications Act of 1996, 47 U.S.C. § 222 (2006)) constituted an unfair practice in violation of § 5(a) of the Federal Trade Commission Act (FTCA), 15 U.S.C. § 45(a) (2006). The district court granted the FTC summary judgment, and after further briefing entered an injunction restricting Accusearch's future trade in telephone records and other personal information. . . .

Although the parties characterize the Abika.com website differently, they do not dispute the essential aspects of its operation. Any person interested in Abika.com's services could access the website through a search engine or by typing its address into an Internet browser. A visitor to the website would first see its homepage, which displayed various categories of information that could be searched. The record contains one printout of the website from December 20, 2006, and one from November 27, 2007. The printouts show that some searches advertised on the homepage targeted information generally contained in government records, such as "court dockets," "sex offender records," and "Tax . . . Liens." Other search categories related to intimate personal information, such as "Romantic Preferences," "Personality traits," and "Rumors."

Accusearch stresses on appeal that the search services offered on Abika.com were primarily services provided by third-party researchers, who were required by Accusearch to provide assurances that they would perform their work in accordance with applicable law. The researchers had no direct contact with Abika.com's customers. As Accusearch explains, "all information passed between [customer] and researcher went through Abika.com, as an intermediary." In placing a search order, a customer paid Accusearch an "administrative search fee," and selected the type of search desired, not a specific researcher or a search identified with a specific researcher. Accusearch would forward the search request to a researcher who could fulfill it. After completing a search, the researcher would send the results to Accusearch and bill Accusearch directly. Accusearch would then email the results to the customer and post them on the customer's Abika.com account. A customer could know that a third-party researcher was involved in a transaction only by reading boilerplate contained on the website and in Accusearch's email correspondence. And even then, the customer was not provided contact information for any researcher.

From February 2003 to January 2006 the Abika.com website advertised access to personal telephone records. The website stated that its customers could acquire "details of incoming or outgoing calls from any phone number, prepaid calling card or Internet Phone," and that "Phone searchers are available for every country of the world." Abika.com's customers could purchase both cellphone and landline records. The website specified that cellphone records would detail the numbers dialed from a particular cellphone and generally include the "date, time and duration of the calls" made. Landline records would include the same information, save for the specific time at which calls were made.

Acquisition of this information would almost inevitably require someone to violate the Telecommunications Act or to circumvent it by fraud or theft. The Act forbids telecommunications carriers from disclosing telephone records absent customer consent or the applicability of one of several exceptions. . . .

Although Accusearch (remarkably, in our view) maintained that it relied in good faith on its researchers' commitment to obey the law in acquiring information, it represented that it ceased offering telephone records in January 2006 after learning that a subsidiary of one of its researchers possibly obtained telephone data fraudulently.

The FTC filed suit against Accusearch on May 1, 2006, roughly four months after Accusearch ceased to offer telephone records. . . .

[On appeal from the district court's grant of summary judgment in favor of the FTC, Accusearch argued that it had broken no laws and was not subject to FTC action. Accusearch also claimed that the district court had erred in granting an injunction because Accusearch had voluntarily ceased dealing in telephone records.

[The court rejected Accusearch's substantive arguments, concluding that Accusearch had engaged in an unfair trade practice by encouraging third parties to violate the Telecommunications Act. It also concluded that Accusearch was not entitled to immunity under the Communications Decency Act, which protects certain types of Internet service providers, such as message boards, from liability for content provided by others.]

The FTCA provides that "in proper cases the Commission may seek, and after proper proof, the court may issue, a permanent injunction." 15 U.S.C. § 53(b). Although Accusearch ceased dealing in telephone records before the FTC filed its complaint, the district court determined that prospective injunctive relief was appropriate to prevent Accusearch from engaging in similar unfair practices with respect to telephone records or the other information it provided. . . .

A "court's power to grant injunctive relief survives the discontinuance of the illegal conduct." United States *v.* W.T. Grant Co., 345 U.S. 629 (1953). When, as in this case, a defendant has ceased offending conduct, the party seeking injunctive relief must demonstrate to the court "that there exists some cognizable danger of recurrent violation, something more than the mere possibility which serves to keep the case alive." *Id.* In assessing the likelihood of recurrence, a court may consider "all the circumstances," including the "bona fides of the expressed intent to comply, the effectiveness of the discontinuance and, in some cases, the character of the past violations." *Id.* We review the decision to grant a permanent injunction for abuse of discretion. The district court's discretion in this context is "necessarily broad and a strong showing of abuse must be made to reverse it." *Id.* at 633.

Accusearch has not persuaded us that the district court abused its discretion. True, Accusearch ceased offering telephone records before litigation commenced. But, as the district court noted, because Accusearch remained in the "information brokerage business" it had the capacity to "engag[e] in similar unfair acts or practices" in the future. See also *ibid.* ("effectiveness of the discontinuance" is a factor in assessing likelihood of recurrence). In Accusearch's view it has proved the absence of any need for prospective relief by expressing a willingness to disgorge nearly $200,000 in ill-gotten profits. But a district court is best situated to judge the sincerity of a litigant's contrition, and Accusearch has given us no ground to second-guess the district court's judgment. See United States *v.* Oregon State Medical Society, 343 U.S. 326, 333 (1952) (courts must "beware of efforts to defeat injunctive relief by protestations of repentance and reform").

Accusearch also argues that the injunction was improper because 18 U.S.C. § 1039, enacted by Congress after this suit was filed, criminalizes the sale and receipt of confidential telephone records absent customer consent. *Id.* § 1039(a)–(c) (Supp. 2008). Stressing that the government could prosecute under § 1039 if it resumed its trade in telephone records, Accusearch asserts that prospective injunctive relief would be redundant, and, as such, improper, because a proper injunction must "enhance the already existing power of the Government to act."

To be sure, injunctions against criminalized conduct have historically been disfavored. But in keeping with the characteristic flexibility of equitable remedies, they have never been absolutely prohibited. An injunction can have several advantages over the threat posed by a criminal statute. To begin with, it can encompass conduct not barred by the statute. Here, the injunction covers all "individually identifiable" consumer information, whereas the criminal statute covers only telephone records, see 18 U.S.C. § 1039(a)–(c), (h)(1). Also, because an injunction can be drawn more precisely than a criminal statute, it can have a greater deterrent effect by removing any doubt in the mind of the enjoined party that particular conduct is forbidden. Furthermore, proving a violation of an injunction is generally less burdensome than proving a criminal violation. For example, to violate § 1039 one must act "knowingly and intentionally." The injunction, on the other hand, imposes no scienter requirement and the law does not necessarily imply one. And a violation need not be proved to a jury beyond a reasonable doubt. The district court did not impose an inconsequential injunction. Thus, Accusearch's argument fails on its own terms. . . .

■ [The concurring opinion of CIRCUIT JUDGE TYMKOVICH is omitted.]

D. EQUITABLE DISCRETION IN GRANTING INJUNCTIVE RELIEF

Injunctions and other equitable remedies have traditionally been viewed as extraordinary. The Chancellors would intervene only when legal remedies failed. Today the rhetoric of equity continues: courts often say that equitable remedies are available only when legal remedies are inadequate, or, in a phrase that is usually synonymous, when equitable relief is necessary to prevent irreparable harm. Professor Douglas Laycock has argued that in practice courts do not follow this rule. Instead, they grant equitable remedies whenever equitable relief is likely to be more effective, all things considered. See Douglas Laycock, THE DEATH OF THE IRREPARABLE INJURY RULE (1991). Yet it remains the case that courts treat the decision to grant an equitable remedy as discretionary, at least to some degree. They weigh the plaintiff's need for an injunction against the hardship an injunction would impose on the defendant; they inquire with particular care into the conduct of both parties leading up to the dispute; they consider the burden an injunction would place on the court and the effects it may have on third parties or the public. The sum of these considerations, compared to the shortcomings of a damage remedy, is probably the best way to understand the modern meaning of the phrases "irreparable injury" and "adequacy of legal remedies."

The cases that follow illustrate the courts' attitudes toward using injunctions to prevent wrongs. Similar considerations come into play for another equitable remedy, specific performance, which is discussed in Chapter Eight, below.

1. IN GENERAL

A.W. Chesterton Co. v. Chesterton

United States Court of Appeals, First Circuit, 1997.
128 F.3d 1.

■ LYNCH, CIRCUIT JUDGE. This appeal involves the duties imposed by Massachusetts law on a minority shareholder in a closely held corporation. Arthur W. Chesterton ("Chesterton"), a minority shareholder in the A.W. Chesterton Company, frustrated in his efforts to dispose of his shares, proposed to transfer a portion of his stock in the Company to two shell corporations. Because such a transfer would terminate the Company's advantageous Subchapter S status under the Internal Revenue Code, the district court found that the proposed transfer violated Chesterton's fiduciary duty to the Company and enjoined him from proceeding with the transfer. . . . We affirm. . . .

The Company has been a closely held Massachusetts corporation since its inception in 1885, and is currently owned and operated by the descendants of the Company's founder, Arthur W. Chesterton. Chesterton, the defendant in this case and the grandson of the original Arthur Chesterton, is currently the Company's largest shareholder, with 27.06% of the Company's stock. The Company and its affiliates manufacture mechanical seals, packaging, pumps and related products, which are distributed throughout the world.

Two corporate events set the stage. The first occurred in 1975, when the shareholders of the Company approved the Company's Restated Articles of Organization ("the Articles"). The Articles provide the Company with a right of first refusal in the event that a shareholder seeks to transfer her shares to an individual or entity outside the immediate Chesterton family. The shareholder must give the Company 30 days notice; the Company may avoid the sale by opting to purchase the stock within the 30 days. If the Company declines the option, the shareholder may proceed with the sale as planned. Part of Chesterton's argument focuses on the fact that he had complied with these provisions of the Articles when he proposed his stock transfer.

The second occurred in 1985, when the Company's Board of Directors voted to change the Company's status under the Internal Revenue Code from a Subchapter C corporation to a Subchapter S corporation. The Board perceived Subchapter S status as advantageous to the Company because it allows shareholders in a small business corporation to avoid the double taxation of income to which shareholders in a Subchapter C corporation are subject. The income of a Subchapter C corporation is taxed first at the corporate level when the company earns income, and a second time at the shareholder level when the shareholders receive the income in the form of dividends. A Subchapter S corporation, in contrast, is not taxed at the corporate level; rather, each shareholder pays income tax individually in proportion to her share of ownership in the corporation.

In order to qualify for Subchapter S treatment, a corporation must be a domestic corporation which does not: (1) have more than seventy-five shareholders, (2) have a corporation or other non-individual as a shareholder, (3) have a non-resident alien as a shareholder, and (4) have more than one class of stock. Failure to abide by any of these limitations results in automatic termination of Subchapter S status.

After the Company Board voted to adopt Subchapter S status, the officers and directors sought to inform the shareholders about the benefits and limitations of the S election, and recommended that the shareholders give their consent. Under the Internal Revenue Code, the unanimous consent of the shareholders of a corporation is required in order to finalize a Subchapter S election. 26 U.S.C. 1362(a)(2). As an officer and director of the Company at the time, Chesterton was heavily involved in this process. He led and participated in shareholder meetings regarding the Subchapter S election. At those meetings the shareholders were provided with information regarding the benefits of Subchapter S election, as well as the limitations it imposed. The shareholders unanimously consented to the Subchapter S election. Implicit in this consent was a general understanding among the shareholders that they would take no action that would adversely affect the Company's Subchapter S status.

In the early 1990's, Chesterton became discontented with the Company's performance, including its declining profits, heavy debt, and credit problems. Chesterton also objects to a financial arrangement that the Company has with Chesterton International, B.V. ("BV"), a Company affiliate. Under the arrangement, the affiliate BV pays the Company a large management fee, which has allowed the Company to continue to pay dividends to its shareholders, despite its poor financial performance. Chesterton believes that this arrangement masks the Company's dire financial straits. He also objects to the arrangement because much of the management fee is funnelled into Company pension plans, from which Chesterton does not benefit because he is not a current Company employee.

Because of his dissatisfaction with the Company, Chesterton sought to sell his Company stock. He found little interest because all he could offer was a minority of shares. After some failed efforts to locate an investor willing to purchase his stock outright, Chesterton devised the scheme at issue in this case. Chesterton proposed to transfer a portion of his shares to two shell corporations which are wholly-owned by him. Chesterton complied with the Articles of Organization by providing the Company with the proper notice of his proposed transfer so that it could purchase his shares. The Company, however, declined because it lacks the ability to purchase the shares.

When the Company would not purchase his shares, Chesterton sought to proceed with the transfer. But that transfer would have a deleterious effect on the Company's tax status. The Company and its shareholders derive significant tax benefits from the Company's status as a Subchapter S corporation. . . . Once a corporation loses its Subchapter S status, it cannot reattain that status for a minimum of five years. In fact, loss of Subchapter S status would have a more severe effect on the Company because it is currently grandfathered under an old provision which exempted Subchapter S corporations from taxes on the sale of corporate assets. Even if the Company eventually regained its Subchapter S status, it would permanently lose its grandfathered status.

Fearing the loss of its Subchapter S status, the Company and its shareholders instituted suit, seeking to enjoin Chesterton from effectuating his plan. . . . After a bench trial, the district court ruled that the proposed transfers would violate Chesterton's fiduciary duty under Massachusetts law and that they would result in irreparable harm to the Company. The court enjoined the transfers . . . .

We review the district court's grant of a permanent injunction for abuse of discretion. The standard for issuing a permanent injunction requires the district court to find that (1) plaintiffs prevail on the merits; (2) plaintiffs would suffer irreparable injury in the absence of injunctive relief; (3) the harm to plaintiffs would outweigh the harm the defendant would suffer from the imposition of an injunction; and (4) the public interest would not be adversely affected by an injunction. The district court found, and we agree, that the public interest was not at issue in this case. We turn to the remaining three factors.

[The court first determined that, as a minority shareholder in a closely held corporation, Chesterton owed fiduciary obligations to the majority, which he breached by pursuing a strategy that advanced his personal interests but harmed the interests of the corporation. Thus, the plaintiffs prevailed on the merits. The court then turned to the second factor, irreparable harm.]

The district court found that the Company would suffer irreparable harm from the loss of its Subchapter S status, in part because that harm is not measurable. Chesterton argues that because the harm to the Company from the loss of its Subchapter S status is entirely financial, equitable relief is inappropriate. Where the harm is not measurable, it is not an abuse of discretion to award equitable relief. The loss of advantageous tax status can form the basis for a finding of irreparable harm. The district court found that the actual degree of the injury was not measurable, "because the amount of the increased tax liability would be contingent on the Company's future earnings and distributions." This finding is supported by the record and common sense, and is not an abuse of discretion. . . .

The final consideration regarding the propriety of injunctive relief is whether, on balance, the harm plaintiffs will suffer from the proposed transfers outweighs the harm that Chesterton will suffer if his transfers are enjoined. The district court found that an injunction would not harm Chesterton because the proposed sales would do little to advance his efforts to sell the stock. The court stated that, "if [Chesterton] was unable to find a buyer for his shares in the Company, it strains logic to believe that he would be able to find a buyer for shares in [the shell corporations] when their primary assets are the very same shares he was previously unable to sell." Chesterton claims that by transferring the shares to his shell corporations, he will somehow increase the liquidity of those shares. The claim is counter-intuitive and no evidence was presented to support it. On this record, the district court's finding that the potential harm to plaintiffs outweighs the harm to defendant was proper. . . .

2. TRESPASS

Wheelock v. Noonan

Court of Appeals of New York, 1888.
108 N.Y. 179.

■ FINCH, J. The findings of the trial court establish that the defendant, who was a total stranger to the plaintiff, obtained from the latter a license to place upon his unoccupied lots in the upper part of the city of New York a few rocks for a short time, the indefiniteness of the period having been rendered definite by the defendant's assurance that he would remove them in the spring. Nothing was paid or asked for this permission, and it was not a contract in any just sense of the term but merely a license which by its terms expired in the next spring. During the winter, and in the absence and without the knowledge of plaintiff, the defendant covered six of the lots of plaintiff with "huge quantities of rock," some of them ten or fifteen feet long, and piled to the height of fourteen to eighteen feet. This conduct was a clear abuse of the license and in excess of its terms, and so much so that if permission had been sought upon a truthful statement of the intention it would undoubtedly have been refused. In the spring the plaintiff, discovering the abuse of his permission, complained bitterly of defendant's conduct and ordered him to remove the rocks to some other locality. The defendant promised to do so but did not, and in the face of repeated demands has neglected and omitted to remove the rocks from the land.

The court found as matter of law from these facts that the original permission given did not justify what was done either as it respected the quantity of rock or the time allowed; that after the withdrawal of the permission in the spring and the demand for the removal of the rock the defendant was a trespasser, and the trespass was a continuing one which entitled plaintiff to equitable relief; and awarded judgment requiring defendant to remove the rocks before March 15, 1886, unless for good cause shown the time for such removal should be extended by the court. . . .

It is now said that the remedy was at law; that the owner could have removed the stone and then recovered of the defendant for the expense incurred. But to what locality could the owner remove them? He could not put them in the street; the defendant presumably had no vacant lands of his own on which to throw the burden; and it would follow that the owner would be obliged to hire some vacant lot or place of deposit, become responsible for the rent, and advance the cost of men and machinery to effect the removal. If any adjudication can be found throwing such burden upon the owner, compelling him to do in advance for the trespasser what the latter is bound to do, I should very much doubt its authority. On the contrary the law is the other way. And all the cases which give to the injured party successive actions for the continuance of the wrong are inconsistent with the idea that the injured party must once for all remove it. Such is neither an adequate remedy nor one which the plaintiff was bound to adopt.

But it is further said that he could sue at law for the trespass. That is undoubtedly true. The case of Uline *v.* New York Central and Hudson River Railroad Company (101 N.Y. 98) demonstrates upon abundant authority that in such action only damages to its date could be recovered, and for the subsequent continuance of the trespass, new actions following on in succession would have to be maintained. But in a case like the present would that be an adequate remedy? In each action the damages could not easily be anything more than the fair rental of the lot. It is difficult to see what other damages could be allowed, not because they would not exist, but because they would be quite uncertain in amount and possibly somewhat speculative in their character. The defendant, therefore, might pay those damages and continue his occupation, and if there were no other adequate remedy, defiantly continue such occupation, and, in spite of his wrong, make of himself, in effect, a tenant who could not be dispossessed. The wrong in every such case is a continued unlawful occupation and any remedy which does not or may not end it, is not adequate to redress the injury, or restore the injured party to his rights. On the other hand such remedy in a case like the present might result to the wrong-doer in something nearly akin to persecution. He is liable to be sued every day, *die de diem,* for the renewed damages following from the continuance of the trespass, and while ordinarily there is no sympathy to be wasted on a trespasser, yet such multiplicity of suits should be avoided and especially under circumstances like those before us. The rocks could not be immediately removed. The courts have observed that peculiarity of the case and shaped their judgment to give time. It may take a long time and during the whole of it the defendant would be liable to daily actions.

For reasons of this character it has very often been held that while ordinarily courts of equity will not wield their power merely to redress a trespass, yet they will interfere under peculiar circumstances, and have often done so where the trespass was a continuing one, and a multiplicity of suits at law was involved in the legal remedy. . . .

In Avery *v.* New York Central and Hudson River Railroad Company (106 N.Y. 142), to which we have been referred since the argument, we were disposed to sustain a mandatory injunction requiring defendant to remove so much of a fence as obstructed plaintiff's right of way, although the obstruction was not a nuisance but an invasion of a private right. In that case, the equitable remedy was not challenged by either counsel or the court, and evidently stood upon the grounds here invoked; those of a continuing trespass the remedy for which at law would be inadequate, and involve repeated actions by the injured party for damages daily occurring.

These views of the case enable us to support the judgment rendered. It should be affirmed, with costs. . . .

NOTES ON ENJOINING TRESPASS

1. The reluctance of early courts to enjoin trespass stemmed in part from the Chancellors' belief that disputes about title ought to be resolved in the law courts. In America, this attitude was reinforced by the popularity of jury trials and many lawyers' ignorance of equity.

2. From an early date, courts routinely granted injunctions to protect easements. An example is Brooks *v.* Wheeler, 243 N.Y. 28 (1926), a case involving a right of way claimed by the plaintiffs:

> "The complaint alleges that defendant has erected encroachments on the right of way and asks that he be required to remove them . . . .
>
> "When the case came on for trial it was tried by jury as an action in ejectment. . . .
>
> "The rule is elementary that an incorporeal hereditament may not be recovered in ejectment. . . . The proper remedy against one who bars another from possessing and exercising his incorporeal rights is in equity. . . .
>
> "The complaint is sufficiently broad to sustain an action in equity."

Id. at 30–32.

Lucy Webb Hayes National Training School v. Geoghegan

United States District Court, District of Columbia, 1967.
281 F. Supp. 116.

■ HOLTZOFF, DISTRICT JUDGE. The plaintiff's prima facie case tends to show the following facts: that defendant Ellen S. Geoghegan has been a patient for a considerable length of time at Sibley Memorial Hospital, which is maintained and operated by the plaintiff corporation. The hospital is a private hospital. Evidence has been further introduced tending to show that the hospital came to the conclusion that the patient no longer needs hospital care but can be adequately provided for at a nursing home.

After a series of negotiations on June 2nd, 1967 the president of the hospital corporation made a formal demand on the defendant Thomas Geoghegan, the husband of the other defendant, that Ellen Geoghegan, his wife, be transferred from Sibley Memorial Hospital. This demand is worded as follows: "I again request you to make arrangements for the transfer of your wife, Ellen Geoghegan, from Sibley Memorial Hospital." The mere fact that the polite word "request" is used does not detract from the tenor of the letter as a demand.

What, then, is the status of the defendant Ellen Geoghegan when her departure from the hospital has been demanded by the hospital? Manifestly she becomes a trespasser. This action is brought for an injunction to require her removal from the hospital as a trespasser. Obviously an action for damages would be an inadequate remedy.

A private hospital has a right to accept or decline any patient. It has a moral duty to reserve its accommodations for persons who actually need medical and hospital care and it would be a deviation from its purposes to act as a nursing home for aged persons who do not need constant medical care but who need nursing care. There are homes for the aged, there are nursing homes and similar institutions. Hospitals have a duty not to permit their facilities to be diverted to the uses for which hospitals are not intended.

The correspondence introduced in evidence shows that the male defendant takes the position that his wife should remain in the hospital for the remainder of her life. For the hospital to permit that would be to allow a diversion of its facilities to purposes for which they are not intended and would not be in the public interest. An action for damages, of course, would present no solution so far as the plaintiff is concerned because the husband is able and willing to pay whatever the hospital would charge.

It has been established for a great many years that equity will enjoin a continuing trespass or a series of repeated trespasses where an action for damages would not be an adequate remedy. . . . The Court of Appeals of New York State in Wheelock *v.* Noonan, 108 N.Y. 179, stated, "It has very often been held that while, ordinarily, courts of equity will not wield their power merely to redress a trespass, yet they will interfere under peculiar circumstances, and have often done so where the trespass was a continuing one, and a multiplicity of suits at law was involved in the legal remedy."

This Court had occasion to consider this matter in Potomac Electric Power Co. *v.* Washington Chapter of the Congress of Racial Equality, 210 F. Supp. 418, 419, and stated, "It is well established that equity may enjoin continuing trespasses, repeated or irreparable injuries to property, or a course of illegitimate interference with business activities, if a remedy by an action for damages is not adequate. This is one of the traditional functions of equity."

It is argued by counsel for the defendants that the plaintiff has a remedy by way of an action of ejectment in this court. Such an action is a very cumbersome one and resort is had to it very rarely. It is also argued by counsel for the defendants that an action may be brought for forcible entry and detainer in the Court of General Sessions under the local statute, D.C. Code, Title 11, Section 735. These considerations do not detract from the power of equity to exercise its power to grant redress by way of injunction.

It is clear that in this case the damages in an action at law would obviously be inadequate, as has already been stated. . . .

Peters v. Archambault

Supreme Judicial Court of Massachusetts, 1972.
361 Mass. 91.

■ CUTTER, JUSTICE. The plaintiffs by this bill seek to compel the defendants (the Archambaults) to remove a portion of the Archambault house which encroaches on the plaintiffs' land in Marshfield. The plaintiffs and the Archambaults owned adjoining ocean-front lots. Both lots are registered (G.L. c. 185). Neither certificate of title shows the Archambault lot to have any rights in the plaintiffs' lot.

The Archambaults' predecessor in title obtained a building permit in 1946 and built a house partly on their own lot and partly on the plaintiffs' lot, of which the total area is about 4,900 square feet. Each lot had a frontage of only fifty feet on the adjacent way. The encroachment contains 465 square feet, and the building extends fifteen feet, three inches, onto the plaintiffs' lot, to a depth of thirty-one feet, four inches. The trial judge found that it will be expensive to remove the encroaching portion of the Archambaults' building. He ruled . . . that there had been established no estoppel of, or laches on the part of, the plaintiffs in seeking to have the encroachment removed. It appears from the evidence that the Archambaults bought their lot from one vendor and the plaintiffs on June 14, 1966, bought their lot from another vendor. The judge found no evidence of any permission by the owners of the plaintiffs' lot for the encroachment. The encroachment was discovered on July 14, 1966, when the plaintiffs had a survey of their land made.

A final decree ordered the removal of the encroachment. The Archambaults appealed. . . .

In Massachusetts a landowner is ordinarily entitled to mandatory equitable relief to compel removal of a structure significantly encroaching on his land, even though the encroachment was unintentional or negligent and the cost of removal is substantial in comparison to any injury suffered by the owner of the lot upon which the encroachment has taken place. In rare cases, referred to in our decisions as "exceptional," courts of equity have refused to grant a mandatory injunction and have left the plaintiff to his remedy of damages, "where the unlawful encroachment has been made innocently, and the cost of removal by the defendant would be greatly disproportionate to the injury to the plaintiff from its continuation, or where the substantial rights of the owner may be protected without recourse to an injunction, or where an injunction would be oppressive and inequitable. . . . But these are the exceptions. What is just and equitable in cases of this sort depends very much upon the particular facts and circumstances disclosed." . . .

The present record discloses no circumstances which would justify denial of a mandatory injunction for removal of an encroachment taking away over nine per cent ($^{465}/_{4900}$) of the plaintiffs' lot. The exceptions . . . to the general Massachusetts rule, hitherto recognized as sufficient to justify denial of mandatory relief, have related to much less significant invasions of a plaintiff's land, or have involved circumstances not here present. The invasion of the plaintiffs' lot is substantial and not de minimis. Photographs and maps in evidence, portraying the encroachment, show that the intrusion of the Archambaults' building on the plaintiffs' small lot greatly increases the congestion of that lot. The plaintiffs were entitled to receive whatever was shown by the land registration certificate as belonging to their grantor, unencumbered by any unregistered prescriptive easement or encroachment. . . .

■ TAURO, CHIEF JUSTICE (dissenting). The plaintiffs and defendants are owners of adjoining lots, with dwellings, both registered under G.L. c. 185. The defendants acquired title to their lot on June 18, 1954, and the plaintiffs acquired their title on June 14, 1966. The plaintiffs seek removal of a portion of the defendants' dwelling which encroaches on their land. This encroachment existed in full view from June, 1946, when the defendants' predecessor in title erected the dwelling, until July 14, 1966, when the plaintiffs had their property surveyed for the purpose of erecting a retaining wall. During this period, neither the plaintiffs' predecessor in title nor the plaintiffs raised any objection to the location of the defendants' dwelling. It is reasonable to infer that prior to taking title the plaintiffs viewed the property. Thus they had actual notice of the location of the defendants' dwelling and its relative position to their own dwelling.

The plaintiffs do not seek money damages but rather a decree for the removal of the encroachment on their land which, in effect, would result in the destruction of the defendants' dwelling. . . . I believe that the record before us sets forth unusual circumstances which would justify this court in denying a mandatory injunction and leaving the plaintiffs to seek their remedy at law for damages. Moreover, the granting of injunctive relief in the circumstances of this case would be "oppressive and inequitable."

To conclude, as does the majority opinion, that this court must grant a mandatory injunction because the facts in the instant case do not precisely fit the factual pattern adjudged to be "exceptional" in prior Massachusetts cases is illogical and untenable. Courts, especially courts of equity, should not be restricted to so fossilized a concept of what the law is or should be. The cause of justice deserves a better fate. The overwhelming weight of authority in other jurisdictions recognizes and applies the doctrine I urge be adopted here. . . .

In the totality of circumstances, I conclude that equity does not, in the exercise of our sound discretion, require us to grant injunctive relief. Removal imposes upon the defendants substantial cost and inconvenience which are entirely disproportionate to the injury to the plaintiffs. Where, as here, it appears that the plaintiffs were content with the status quo until fortuitous discovery of the encroachment, it would be oppressive and inequitable for this court to grant a mandatory injunction against the defendants who have acted in good faith, albeit their predecessor in title made a mistake which remained undiscovered for some twenty years. Hardship alone is of course not a ground for denial of injunctive relief, but this court should take relative hardship into account, if, as in the instant case, the owner of the encroaching structure is not guilty of an intentional trespass. The view I express is not only in accordance with our own case law but also in accordance with decisions in other jurisdictions. Here, it appears not only that the defendants have always acted in good faith but that the initial trespass was committed many years before they acquired title to their lot. . . .

If we were to refuse injunctive relief, common sense suggests that, in all probability, this dispute would be settled eventually without the need for the destruction of the defendants' dwelling. This could be accomplished through an agreement by the plaintiffs to voluntarily relocate their boundary line in return for payment by the defendants of an amount negotiated between them. The parties would then have their certificates of title reformed to reflect the agreement. In the alternative, the plaintiffs could bring an action at law and the court would make an impartial assessment of damages. The placing of the potent weapon of injunctive relief in the hands of the plaintiffs is hardly conducive to a fair and just settlement. In circumstances such as those in the instant case, the court in Christensen *v.* Tucker, 114 Cal. App. 2d 554, 563, said: "[T]he injunction should be denied, otherwise, the court would lend itself to what practically amounts to extortion." I would dismiss the bill and relegate the plaintiffs to their remedy at law.

Kratze v. Independent Order of Oddfellows, Garden City Lodge No. 11

Supreme Court of Michigan, 1993.
442 Mich. 136.

■ BOYLE, JUSTICE. . . . The full backdrop of the case is aptly summarized by the Court of Appeals:

> "[Oddfellows] Lodge No. 11 purchased Lots 2911 and 2912 of Folker's Garden City Acres No. 18 in December 1948. Already existing on the lots at the time of their purchase was a building foundation upon which the previous owners had intended to erect a church. Lodge No. 11 instead erected its meeting hall on this foundation.
>
> "In September 1985, plaintiff entered into an option agreement to purchase Lots 2901 to 2910 of Folker's Garden City Acres No. 18. This property is adjacent to and abuts the property owned by Lodge No. 11. Plaintiff gave a deposit of $1,000 and agreed to purchase the property for $18,000. He intended to erect multiple-unit dwellings on the property.
>
> "Plaintiff caused two surveys of the property to be done. As a result of the first survey, plaintiff received in early 1986 a 'schematic' of his property that showed the northeast corner of the building owned by Lodge No. 11 touching plaintiff's property line. A site plan for a sixty-two-unit apartment building was prepared using this schematic and submitted to Garden City for approval on March 27, 1986. A short time later, plaintiff learned, as a result of the second survey, that the northeast corner of the building owned by Lodge No. 11 encroached 1.2 feet onto his property.[1] Nevertheless, in May 1986 plaintiff purchased the property for $18,000 as agreed.
>
> "The Garden City Planning Commission approved plaintiff's site plan on August 28, 1986, as submitted, without knowledge of the encroachment. However, as a result of the encroachment, plaintiff was unable to secure title insurance and, without title insurance, to secure financing for his project.
>
> "In July, 1987 plaintiff filed the instant action in the Wayne Circuit Court, seeking damages resulting from the encroachment. Following a one-day bench trial, the court ordered the encroachment removed and found Lodge No. 11 . . . liable for damages totalling $797,215.46, exclusive of costs and interest."

. . . Fashioning an appropriate remedy where a structure encroaches on the land of another poses special problems and has resulted in special

---

1 This second survey was done because plaintiff had "determined that there could possibly be an encroachment."

solutions. "In such cases the approach is to balance several factors—the relative hardship to the parties and the equities between them—and to grant or deny the injunction as the balance may seem to indicate." Dan B. Dobbs, REMEDIES § 5.6 at 355 (1973).[6] . . .

In balancing the hardships and equities regarding encroachment, courts are guided by two central considerations: An interest in avoiding judicial approval of private eminent domain by the encroacher, and an interest in preventing extortion by the encroachee, who may use the injunction to "compromise" the claim. . . .

While a court is not bound to engage in a balancing of the relative hardships and equities if the encroachment resulted from an intentional or wilful act, we agree with the defendant's assertion that there is no evidentiary support that the encroachment was wilful or intentional, and that the trial court erred in issuing a mandatory injunction without balancing the relative hardships to the parties.

The injury to the plaintiff as a result of the encroachment is slight. The building encroaches only 1.2 feet and was not noted in the initial survey. Furthermore, enough property remains to satisfy the city set-back requirements, even without the encroached-upon strip of land.

Although the plaintiff argues that the encroachment prevents the construction of an apartment building on the property, trial testimony showed that there would be no impediments to site plan approval, title insurance, or construction financing, if the encroached-upon property were excluded from the plaintiff's holdings. On the other hand, testimony at trial, to which no objection was raised, indicates that, because of the age of the [defendant's encroaching] structure, neither the building, nor the wall, could be moved without causing the building to collapse.

Examining the character, conduct, and motives of the parties, it is apparent that the plaintiff knew before purchasing the property that a portion of the Oddfellows' building stood on the property he intended to purchase. As an attorney with thirty years experience in the building and construction industry, he also knew that he would not be able to obtain clear title to the 1.2-foot encroachment. Without clear title, neither title

---

[6] The relative hardships to the parties is but one of the many factors a court may consider when determining the propriety of issuing an injunction against a tort. See, *e.g.*, *Restatement (Second) of Torts* § 936 (1979), which provides:

> "(1) The appropriateness of the remedy of injunction against a tort depends upon a comparative appraisal of all of the factors in the case, including the following primary factors:
>
> "(a) the nature of the interest to be protected,
>
> "(b) the relative adequacy to the plaintiff of injunction and of other remedies,
>
> "(c) any unreasonable delay by the plaintiff in bringing suit,
>
> "(d) any related misconduct on the part of the plaintiff,
>
> "(e) the relative hardship likely to result to defendant if an injunction is granted and to plaintiff if it is denied,
>
> "(f) the interests of third persons and of the public, and
>
> "(g) the practicability of framing and enforcing the order or judgment."

insurance nor construction financing was available, and without construction financing, construction could not begin. Despite knowing of the problems associated with such a purchase, the plaintiff purchased the property.

Furthermore, the original site plan submitted to the Garden City Planning Commission called for sixty-two units to be built on the property and was submitted to the commission on the basis of the initial property survey, which showed only that the defendant's building was abutting the plaintiff's property line. Within days of this submission, plaintiff's second survey discovered the encroachment. At that point, according to trial testimony, plaintiff should have submitted a revised site plan that showed the encroachment. He did not, and, almost six months later, the commission approved the sixty-two unit development even though density requirements in effect at the time would have allowed only fifty-six units to be built on the property. . . .

Against the plaintiff's conduct, we weigh the defendant's conduct. It is not contested that the foundation for the Oddfellows' meeting hall stood where it now stands when the Oddfellows purchased the property in 1948. The meeting hall was built on the existing foundation. The defendant was unaware of the encroachment until the plaintiff brought it to its attention, and, being made aware, inquired about purchasing the strip from the plaintiff. . . . Although it is unclear which party bears responsibility for the breakdown of negotiations, defendant contends with record support that plaintiff's only solution to the problem was for the Oddfellows to move the structure.[7]

On balance, the hardship to the defendant as a result of removing the encroachment outweighs the hardship to the plaintiff as a result of allowing the encroaching structure to remain. Under the totality of the circumstances, the balance of hardships weighs heavily in the defendant's favor. Thus, the order to remove the encroachment was not consistent with justice and equity and should be vacated. . . .

Where the wrong consists of a trespass to property resulting in an injury to the land, the general measure of damages is the diminution in value of the property if the injury is permanent or irreparable. If the injury is reparable, or temporary, the proper measure of damages is the cost of restoration of the property to its original condition, if less than the value of the property before the injury. The rule is, however, flexible in its application. The ultimate goal is compensation for the harm or damage done. Thus, whatever method is most appropriate to compensate a plaintiff for the loss may be used. . . .

In the instant case, the structure is physically permanent because it is "likely to continue without any clear stopping point." Dobbs, *supra*, § 5.4 at 339. It is legally permanent because, as we today hold, the order

[7] At trial, plaintiff testified that he would prefer to have the building torn down because, in his opinion, the building was an eyesore and presented a safety hazard.

to remove it should not have been issued. We recognize, however, that it is the defendant trespasser who seeks to pay permanent damages and thus acquire a right of private eminent domain. We do not sanction private takings of private lands for private purposes. However, we also cannot ignore an award of damages in an amount that creates the possibility of a "compromise" equity should not sanction.[15]

Thus, we hold that the Court of Appeals erred in stating the measure of damages as the diminution in value or cost of repairs to the property. Because the trespass is permanent, the correct measure of damages is the diminution in value of the property itself as represented by the value of the property without the encroachment, minus the value of the property with the encroachment or, alternatively, the value of the strip of land on which the building sits.

In the instant case, the plaintiff had agreed to pay $18,000 for the property before learning of the encroachment. Even after the encroachment was discovered, he paid the asking price for the property. Thus, the encroachment did not devalue the property. On remand, the plaintiff is entitled to recover only the alternative value of the 1.2-foot strip of land on which the structure is located, rather than the value of the rest of the property that he still has the benefit of using.

The Court of Appeals allowed two items of special damage to stand: the cost of the plaintiff's employees' time spent in attempting to remedy the situation, and the cost of a second survey done on the property after the initial survey disclosed that the Oddfellows' building came dangerously close to encroaching on the property that the plaintiff intended to purchase. We do not agree that the plaintiff is entitled to recover for the time his employees spent in attempting to remedy the encroachment. Had he avoided rushing through the project in the first instance, his employees' time would not have been spent in pursuit of a solution to the problem. Given the fact that we cannot conclude from the record that plaintiff attempted to negotiate removal of the encroachment, damages for his employees' activities are too speculative.

The plaintiff is also not entitled to recover for the costs of the second survey because this expense was not caused by the defendant's tort. The survey occurred before the plaintiff exercised his option to purchase and was necessary to enable him to make the decision to purchase. . . .

---

[15] . . . It is not difficult to imagine a scenario where the plaintiff would "settle" for the property itself in satisfaction of the judgment. The plaintiff would then own the final two lots, which abut the property he already owns on both sides of the Oddfellows' property.

Lindsey v. Clark

Supreme Court of Appeals of Virginia, 1952.
193 Va. 522.

■ BUCHANAN, J., delivered the opinion of the court. . . .

In 1937 the Clarks were the owners of four adjoining lots, Nos. 31, 32, 33 and 34, each fronting 25 feet on the east side of Magnolia avenue in West Waynesboro, and running back 150 feet to a 20-foot alley. The Clark residence was on Nos. 31 and 32.

By deed dated July 24, 1937, the Clarks conveyed to C. W. Six and Mabel G. Six, his wife, the latter being a daughter of the Clarks, the front two-thirds of Lots 33 and 34, being a frontage of 50 feet and extending back 100 feet. On the rear one-third of these two lots Clark erected a dwelling and garage for rental purposes. After this conveyance the Sixes built a house on their property, approximately 15 feet from the Clark line on the north and about 8 feet from their own line on the south. The Clark deed to the Sixes contained this reservation:

> "There is reserved, however, a right-of-way ten (10) feet in width, along the South side of the two lots herein conveyed, for the benefit of the property in the rear."

By deed of January 16, 1939, the Sixes conveyed their property to William H. McGhee and wife, with the same reservation; and by deed of March 16, 1944, the McGhees conveyed the property to the Lindseys, without any reservation.

These three deeds were all made with general warranty and both the deed to the Sixes and the deed to the McGhees were duly recorded prior to the date of the deed to the Lindseys.

Notwithstanding that the 10-foot right of way was reserved by Clark along the south side of the property conveyed to the Sixes, now owned by the Lindseys, Clark proceeded to use it along the north side of the Six property, and has so used it ever since, without objection by the Sixes, or by the McGhees, or by the Lindseys until a few months before this suit was brought. There is no explanation of this change of location. . . .

The Lindseys contend that the Clarks now have no right of way across their property because none was reserved along the north side and the one reserved on the south side has been abandoned and thereby extinguished. . . .

Abandonment is a question of intention. . . .

[M]ere non-use of an easement created by deed, for a period however long, will not amount to abandonment. . . .

Very clearly [Clark] had no intention of abandoning that right of way. He was evidently mistaken as to where it was located . . . .

The residence built by the Sixes, and now occupied by the Lindseys, encroaches by about two feet on the 10-foot alley when located on the south side, and the Lindsey property on that side within the 10-foot space is terraced and planted with shrubbery and a tree. The Lindseys argue that the Clarks are estopped from claiming a right of way on that side because Clark knew where the Sixes were building the house. The only testimony about that is from Six, who said that Clark was away at work when the house was being built but came and went every day to and from his home on the adjoining property, saw where the house was located and made no objection; but Six also said that Clark had nothing to do with locating the house. There is no evidence that Clark knew, any more than Six knew, that the house was encroaching on the right of way. Clark did not think the right of way was on that side. . . .

The Lindseys had both actual and constructive knowledge of the situation. The driveway was there on the north side when they bought the property and Lindsey testified he could see where cars had been using it. They negligently failed to have their title examined but they are, of course, chargeable with the information contained in the recorded deeds.

The suit therefore developed this situation: The Clarks were entitled to a 10-foot right of way along the south side of the Lindsey property. That right of way was partially blocked by the Lindsey house with its terraces and shrubbery. To require their removal would be very expensive to the Lindseys and damaging to their property. The Clarks were willing to let their right of way continue to be located on the north side.

The court was well warranted in resolving the matter by applying the maxim "He who seeks equity must do equity." That means that "he who seeks the aid of an equity court subjects himself to the imposition of such terms as the settled principles of equity require, and that whatever be the nature of the controversy between the parties, and whatever be the nature of the remedy demanded, the court will not confer its equitable relief on the party seeking its interposition and aid, unless he has acknowledged and conceded, or will admit and provide for, all the equitable rights, claims, and demands justly belonging to the adversary party, and growing out of, or necessarily involved in, the subject matter of the controversy." 30 C.J.S., Equity, § 91, p. 461. 2 POMEROY'S EQUITY JURISPRUDENCE, 5th ed., § 385, pp. 51–2.

A court of equity may in a case in which the principles and rules of equity demand it, condition its granting of the relief sought by the complainant upon the enforcement of a claim or equity held by the defendant which the latter could not enforce in any other way.

The decree of the trial court provided: "The Court will not require the expensive removal of the obstruction, so long as the right-of-way along the north side of the property is made available. . . ." . . .

3. NUISANCE

Campbell v. Seaman

Court of Appeals of New York, 1876.
63 N.Y. 568.

■ EARL, J. The plaintiffs owned about forty acres of land, situate in the village of Castleton, on the east bank of the Hudson river, and had owned it since about 1849. During the years 1857, 1858 and 1859 they built upon it an expensive dwelling-house, and during those years, and before and since, they improved the land by grading and terracing, building roads and walks through the same, and planting trees and shrubs, both ornamental and useful.

The defendant had for some years owned adjoining lands, which he had used as a brick-yard. The brick-yard is southerly of plaintiff's dwelling-house about 1,320 feet, and southerly of their woods about 567 feet. In burning bricks defendant had made use of anthracite coal. During the burning of a kiln sulphuric acid gas is generated, which is destructive to some kinds of trees and vines. The evidence shows, and the referee found, that gas coming from defendant's kilns had, during the years 1869 and 1870, killed the foliage on plaintiff's white and yellow pines and Norway spruce, and had, after repeated attacks, killed and destroyed from 100 to 150 valuable pine and spruce trees, and had injured their grape vines and plum trees, and he estimated plaintiff's damages from the gas during those years at $500.

This gas did not continually escape during the burning of a kiln, but only during the last two days, and was carried into and over plaintiff's land only when the wind was from the south.

It is a general rule that every person may exercise exclusive dominion over his own property, and subject it to such uses as will best subserve his private interests. Generally, no other person can say how he shall use or what he shall do with his property. But this general right of property has its exceptions and qualifications. *Sic utere tuo ut alienum non laedas* [use your property as not to injure your neighbor's] is an old maxim which has a broad application. It does not mean that one must never use his own so as to do any injury to his neighbor or his property. Such a rule could not be enforced in civilized society. Persons living in organized communities must suffer some damage, annoyance and inconvenience from each other. For these they are compensated by all the advantages of civilized society. . . .

But every person is bound to make a reasonable use of his property so as to occasion no unnecessary damage or annoyance to his neighbor. If he make an unreasonable, unwarrantable or unlawful use of it, so as to produce material annoyance, inconvenience, discomfort or hurt to his neighbor, he will be guilty of a nuisance to his neighbor. And the law will hold him responsible for the consequent damage. As to what is a reasonable use of one's own property cannot be defined by any certain general rules, but must depend upon the circumstances of each case. A use of property in one locality and under some circumstances may be lawful and reasonable, which, under other circumstances, would be unlawful, unreasonable and a nuisance. To constitute a nuisance, the use must be such as to produce a tangible and appreciable injury to neighboring property, or such as to render its enjoyment specially uncomfortable or inconvenient.

Within the rules thus referred to, that defendant's brick burning was a nuisance to plaintiffs cannot be doubted. . . .

But the claim is made that although the brick burning in this case is a nuisance, a court of equity will not and ought not to restrain it, and the plaintiffs should be left to their remedy at law to recover damages, and this claim must now be examined. . . .

The plaintiffs had built a costly mansion and had laid out their grounds and planted them with ornamental and useful trees and vines, for their comfort and enjoyment. How can one be compensated in damages for the destruction of his ornamental trees, and the flowers and vines which surrounded his home? How can a jury estimate their value in dollars and cents? The fact that trees and vines are for ornament or luxury entitles them no less to the protection of the law. Every one has the right to surround himself with articles of luxury, and he will be no less protected than one who provides himself only with articles of necessity. The law will protect a flower or a vine as well as an oak. These damages are irreparable too, because the trees and vines cannot be replaced, and the law will not compel a person to take money rather than the objects of beauty and utility which he places around his dwelling to gratify his taste or to promote his comfort and his health.

Here the injunction also prevents a multiplicity of suits. The injury is a recurring one, and every time the poisonous breath from defendant's brick-kiln sweeps over plaintiffs' land they have a cause of action. Unless the nuisance be restrained the litigation would be interminable. The policy of the law favors, and the peace and good order of society are best promoted by the termination of such litigations by a single suit.

The fact that this nuisance is not continual, and that the injury is only occasional, furnishes no answer to the claim for an injunction. The nuisance has occurred often enough within two years to do the plaintiffs large damage. Every time a kiln is burned some injury may be expected, unless the wind should blow the poisonous gas away from plaintiffs' lands. Nuisances causing damage less frequently have been restrained.

It matters not that the brick-yard was used before plaintiffs bought their lands or built their houses. One cannot erect a nuisance upon his land adjoining vacant lands owned by another and thus measurably control the uses to which his neighbor's land may in the future be subjected. He may make a reasonable and lawful use of his land and thus cause his neighbor some inconvenience, and probably some damage which the law would regard as *damnum absque injuria* [loss or harm without injury in the legal sense]. But he cannot place upon his land anything which the law would pronounce a nuisance, and thus compel his neighbor to leave his land vacant, or to use it in such way only as the neighboring nuisance will allow.

It is claimed that the plaintiffs so far acquiesced in this nuisance as to bar them from any equitable relief. I do not perceive how any acquiescence short of twenty years can bar one from complaining of a nuisance, unless his conduct has been such as to estop him. There is no proof that plaintiffs, when they bought their lands, knew that any one intended to burn any bricks upon the land now owned by defendant. From about 1840 to 1853 no bricks were burned there. Then from 1853 to 1857 bricks were burned there, and then not again until 1867. From 1857 to 1867 the brick yard was plowed and used for agricultural purposes. Before suit brought, plaintiffs objected to the brick burning. No act or omission of theirs induced the defendant to incur large expenses or to take any action which could be the basis of an estoppel against them, and therefore there was no acquiescence or laches which should bar the plaintiffs, within any rule laid down in any reported case. . . .

The defendant claims a prescriptive right to burn bricks upon his land and to cause the poisonous vapors to flow over plaintiffs' lands. Assuming that defendant could acquire by lapse of time and continuous user the prescriptive right which he claims, there has not here been a continuous use and exercise of the right for twenty consecutive years. . . .

We cannot apprehend that our decision in this case can improperly embarrass those engaged in the useful trade of brick making. Similar decisions in England, where population and human habitations are more dense, do not appear to have produced any embarrassment. In this country there can be no trouble to find places where brick can be made without damage to persons living in the vicinity. It certainly cannot be necessary to make them in the heart of a village or in the midst of a thickly settled community. . . .

NOTES ON ENJOINING NUISANCES

1. As indicated in Campbell *v.* Seaman, injunctions are standard remedies for nuisance. Damages are assumed to be a sufficiently imperfect remedy to justify injunctive relief, unless injunctive relief will impose on the defendant an "undue hardship." This inquiry is also called the "balance of equities" or "balance of hardships." The balancing of equities is not merely a cost-benefit analysis, for it includes other considerations, such as the fault of the parties. See Douglas Laycock, The Neglected Defense of Undue Hardship (and the Doctrinal Train Wreck in *Boomer v. Atlantic Cement*), 4 J. Tort L. 1 (2012). Although this doctrine is often raised as a defense in property tort cases, it can be invoked whenever the plaintiff has sought equitable relief. *E.g.*, North Carolina *v.* Covington, 137 S.Ct. 1624 (2017) (*per curiam*). For

further discussion, see Chapter Sixteen, Section B(4) (Undue Hardship). Note that comparing hardships is not only a remedial consideration but an element of the substantive law of nuisance, as the next case illustrates.

2. Public nuisances are those that interfere with public use of property or affect entire communities. The proper plaintiff is a public officer, such as a state attorney general. However, a private landowner who is specially affected by the nuisance, differently from the general public, may seek an injunction against the same activity. Compare Exxon Valdez Alaska Native Class *v.* Exxon Corp., 104 F.3d 1196 (9th Cir. 1997) (refusing to allow a private suit by "Alaska Natives" based on the Exxon Valdez oil spill) with Tushbant *v.* Greenfields, Inc., 308 Mich. 626 (1944) (allowing a neighboring store to enjoin a disorderly restaurant line on a public sidewalk).

Boomer v. Atlantic Cement Co.

Court of Appeals of New York, 1970.
26 N.Y.2d 219.

■ BERGAN, JUDGE. Defendant operates a large cement plant near Albany. These are actions for injunction and damages by neighboring land owners alleging injury to property from dirt, smoke and vibration emanating from the plant. A nuisance has been found after trial, temporary damages have been allowed; but an injunction has been denied.

[There were seven homeowner-plaintiffs in the case. Permanent damages to the plaintiffs, meaning damages for loss of market value if the nuisance were not enjoined, totaled about $185,000. Construction costs for the plant were more than $45 million, and the plant employed about 300 workers from the neighboring town. The factory appears to have been built after the plaintiffs built their homes.]

The public concern with air pollution arising from many sources in industry and in transportation is currently accorded ever wider recognition accompanied by a growing sense of responsibility in State and Federal Governments to control it. Cement plants are obvious sources of air pollution in the neighborhoods where they operate.

But there is now before the court private litigation in which individual property owners have sought specific relief from a single plant operation. The threshold question raised by the division of view on this appeal is whether the court should resolve the litigation between the parties now before it as equitably as seems possible; or whether, seeking promotion of the general public welfare, it should channel private litigation into broad public objectives.

A court performs its essential function when it decides the rights of parties before it. Its decision of private controversies may sometimes greatly affect public issues. Large questions of law are often resolved by the manner in which private litigation is decided. But this is normally an incident to the court's main function to settle controversy. It is a rare exercise of judicial power to use a decision in private litigation as a purposeful mechanism to achieve direct public objectives greatly beyond the rights and interests before the court.

Effective control of air pollution is a problem presently far from solution even with the full public and financial powers of government. In large measure adequate technical procedures are yet to be developed and some that appear possible may be economically impracticable.

It seems apparent that the amelioration of air pollution will depend on technical research in great depth; on a carefully balanced consideration of the economic impact of close regulation; and of the actual effect on public health. It is likely to require massive public expenditure and to demand more than any local community can accomplish and to depend on regional and interstate controls.

A court should not try to do this on its own as a by-product of private litigation and it seems manifest that the judicial establishment is neither equipped in the limited nature of any judgment it can pronounce nor prepared to lay down and implement an effective policy for the elimination of air pollution. This is an area beyond the circumference of one private lawsuit. It is a direct responsibility for government and should not thus be undertaken as an incident to solving a dispute between property owners and a single cement plant—one of many—in the Hudson River valley.

The cement making operations of defendant have been found by the court at Special Term to have damaged the nearby properties of plaintiffs in these two actions. That court, as it has been noted, accordingly found defendant maintained a nuisance and this has been affirmed at the Appellate Division. The total damage to plaintiffs' properties is, however, relatively small in comparison with the value of defendant's operation and with the consequences of the injunction which plaintiffs seek.

The ground for the denial of injunction, notwithstanding the finding both that there is a nuisance and that plaintiffs have been damaged substantially, is the large disparity in economic consequences of the nuisance and of the injunction. This theory cannot, however, be sustained without overruling a doctrine which has been consistently reaffirmed in several leading cases in this court and which has never been disavowed here, namely that where a nuisance has been found and where there has been any substantial damage shown by the party complaining an injunction will be granted.

The rule in New York has been that such a nuisance will be enjoined although marked disparity be shown in economic consequence between the effect of the injunction and the effect of the nuisance.

The problem of disparity in economic consequence was sharply in focus in Whalen *v.* Union Bag & Paper Co. (208 N.Y. 1). A pulp mill entailing an investment of more than a million dollars polluted a stream in which plaintiff, who owned a farm, was "a lower riparian owner." The economic loss to plaintiff from this pollution was small. This court, reversing the Appellate Division, reinstated the injunction granted by the Special Term against the argument of the mill owner that in view of "the slight advantage to plaintiff and the great loss that will be inflicted on defendant" an injunction should not be granted. "Such a balancing of injuries cannot be justified by the circumstances of this case," Judge Werner noted. He continued: "Although the damage to the plaintiff may be slight as compared with the defendant's expense of abating the condition, that is not a good reason for refusing an injunction."

Thus the unconditional injunction granted at Special Term was reinstated. The rule laid down in that case, then, is that whenever the damage resulting from a nuisance is found not "unsubstantial," viz., $100 a year, injunction would follow. This states a rule that had been followed in this court with marked consistency.

There are cases where injunction has been denied. McCann *v.* Chasm Power Co. (211 N.Y. 301) is one of them. There, however, the damage shown by plaintiffs was not only unsubstantial, it was non-existent. Plaintiffs owned a rocky bank of the stream in which defendant had raised the level of the water. This had no economic or other adverse consequence to plaintiffs, and thus injunctive relief was denied. Similar is the basis for denial of injunction in Forstmann *v.* Joray Holding Co. (244 N.Y. 22) where no benefit to plaintiffs could be seen from the injunction sought. Thus if . . . the damage to plaintiffs in these present cases from defendant's cement plant is "not unsubstantial," an injunction should follow.

Although the court at Special Term and the Appellate Division held that injunction should be denied, it was found that plaintiffs had been damaged in various specific amounts up to the time of the trial and damages to the respective plaintiffs were awarded for those amounts. The effect of this was, injunction having been denied, plaintiffs could maintain successive actions at law for damages thereafter as further damage was incurred.

The court at Special Term also found the amount of permanent damage attributable to each plaintiff, for the guidance of the parties in the event both sides stipulated to the payment and acceptance of such permanent damage as a settlement of all the controversies among the parties. The total of permanent damages to all plaintiffs thus found was $185,000. This basis of adjustment has not resulted in any stipulation by the parties.

This result at Special Term and at the Appellate Division is a departure from a rule that has become settled; but to follow the rule literally in these cases would be to close down the plant at once. This court is fully agreed to avoid that immediately drastic remedy; the difference in view is how best to avoid it.

One alternative is to grant the injunction but postpone its effect to a specified future date to give opportunity for technical advances to permit defendant to eliminate the nuisance; another is to grant the injunction conditioned on the payment of permanent damages to plaintiffs which would compensate them for the total economic loss to their property present and future caused by defendant's operations. For reasons which will be developed the court chooses the latter alternative.

If the injunction were to be granted unless within a short period—*e.g.*, 18 months—the nuisance be abated by improved methods, there would be no assurance that any significant technical improvement would occur.

The parties could settle this private litigation at any time if defendant paid enough money and the imminent threat of closing the plant would build up the pressure on defendant. If there were no improved techniques found, there would inevitably be applications to the court at Special Term for extensions of time to perform on showing of good faith efforts to find such techniques.

Moreover, techniques to eliminate dust and other annoying by-products of cement making are unlikely to be developed by any research the defendant can undertake within any short period, but will depend on the total resources of the cement industry nationwide and throughout the world. The problem is universal wherever cement is made.

For obvious reasons the rate of the research is beyond control of defendant. If at the end of 18 months the whole industry has not found a technical solution a court would be hard put to close down this one cement plant if due regard be given to equitable principles.

On the other hand, to grant the injunction unless defendant pays plaintiffs such permanent damages as may be fixed by the court seems to do justice between the contending parties. All of the attributions of economic loss to the properties on which plaintiffs' complaints are based will have been redressed.

The nuisance complained of by these plaintiffs may have other public or private consequences, but these particular parties are the only ones who have sought remedies and the judgment proposed will fully redress them. The limitation of relief granted is a limitation only within the four corners of these actions and does not foreclose public health or other public agencies from seeking proper relief in a proper court.

It seems reasonable to think that the risk of being required to pay permanent damages to injured property owners by cement plant owners would itself be a reasonable effective spur to research for improved techniques to minimize nuisance.

The power of the court to condition on equitable grounds the continuance of an injunction on the payment of permanent damages seems undoubted. . . .

Thus it seems fair to both sides to grant permanent damages to plaintiffs which will terminate this private litigation. The theory of damage is the "servitude on land" of plaintiffs imposed by defendant's nuisance. . . .

The judgment, by allowance of permanent damages imposing a servitude on land, which is the basis of the actions, would preclude future recovery by plaintiffs or their grantees.

This should be placed beyond debate by a provision of the judgment that the payment by defendant and the acceptance by plaintiffs of permanent damages found by the court shall be in compensation for a servitude on the land.

Although the Trial Term has found permanent damages as a possible basis of settlement of the litigation, on remission the court should be entirely free to re-examine this subject. It may again find the permanent damage already found; or make new findings.

The orders should be reversed, without costs, and the cases remitted to Supreme Court, Albany County to grant an injunction which shall be vacated upon payment by defendant of such amounts of permanent damage to the respective plaintiffs as shall for this purpose be determined by the court.

■ JASEN, JUDGE (dissenting). I agree with the majority that a reversal is required here, but I do not subscribe to the newly enunciated doctrine of assessment of permanent damages, in lieu of an injunction, where substantial property rights have been impaired by the creation of a nuisance.

It has long been the rule in this State, as the majority acknowledges, that a nuisance which results in substantial continuing damage to neighbors must be enjoined. To now change the rule to permit the cement company to continue polluting the air indefinitely upon the payment of permanent damages is, in my opinion, compounding the magnitude of a very serious problem in our State and Nation today.

In recognition of this problem, the Legislature of this State has enacted the Air Pollution Control Act (Public Health Law, §§ 1264 to 1299–m) declaring that it is the State policy to require the use of all available and reasonable methods to prevent and control air pollution.

The harmful nature and widespread occurrence of air pollution have been extensively documented. Congressional hearings have revealed that air pollution causes substantial property damage, as well as being a contributing factor to a rising incidence of lung cancer, emphysema, bronchitis and asthma.

The specific problem faced here is known as particulate contamination because of the fine dust particles emanating from defendant's cement plant. The particular type of nuisance is not new, having appeared in many cases for at least the past 60 years. It is interesting to note that cement production has recently been identified as a significant source of particulate contamination in the Hudson Valley.

This type of pollution, wherein very small particles escape and stay in the atmosphere, has been denominated as the type of air pollution which produces the greatest hazard to human health. We have thus a nuisance which not only is damaging to the plaintiffs, but also is decidedly harmful to the general public.

I see grave dangers in overruling our long-established rule of granting an injunction where a nuisance results in substantial continuing damage. In permitting the injunction to become inoperative upon the payment of permanent damages, the majority is, in effect, licensing a continuing wrong. It is the same as saying to the cement company, you may continue to do harm to your neighbors so long as you pay a fee for it. Furthermore, once such permanent damages are assessed and paid, the incentive to alleviate the wrong would be eliminated, thereby continuing air pollution of an area without abatement.

It is true that some courts have sanctioned the remedy here proposed by the majority in a number of cases, but none of the authorities relied upon by the majority are analogous to the situation before us. In those cases, the courts, in denying an injunction and awarding money damages, grounded their decision on a showing that the use to which the property was intended to be put was primarily for the public benefit. Here, on the other hand, it is clearly established that the cement company is creating a continuing air pollution nuisance primarily for its own private interest with no public benefit.

This kind of inverse condemnation may not be invoked by a private person or corporation for private gain or advantage. Inverse condemnation should only be permitted when the public is primarily served in the taking or impairment of property. The promotion of the interests of the polluting cement company has, in my opinion, no public use or benefit.

Nor is it constitutionally permissible to impose servitude on land, without consent of the owner, by payment of permanent damages where the continuing impairment of the land is for a private use. . . .

In sum, then, by constitutional mandate as well as by judicial pronouncement, the permanent impairment of private property for private purposes is not authorized in the absence of clearly demonstrated public benefit and use.

I would enjoin the defendant cement company from continuing the discharge of dust particles upon its neighbors' properties unless, within 18 months, the cement company abated this nuisance. . . .

I believe it is incumbent upon the defendant to develop such devices, since the cement company, at the time the plant commenced production (1962), was well aware of the plaintiffs' presence in the area, as well as the probable consequences of its contemplated operation. Yet, it still chose to build and operate the plant at this site.

In a day when there is a growing concern for clean air, highly developed industry should not expect acquiescence by the courts, but should, instead, plan its operations to eliminate contamination of our air and damage to its neighbors. . . .

Spur Industries, Inc. v. Del E. Webb Development Co.

Supreme Court of Arizona, 1972.
108 Ariz. 178.

■ CAMERON, VICE CHIEF JUSTICE. . . . Although numerous issues are raised, we feel that it is necessary to answer only two questions. They are:

> 1. Where the operation of a business, such as a cattle feedlot is lawful in the first instance, but becomes a nuisance by reason of a nearby residential area, may the feedlot operation be enjoined in an action brought by the developer of the residential area?
>
> 2. Assuming that the nuisance may be enjoined, may the developer of a completely new town or urban area in a previously agricultural area be required to indemnify the operator of the feedlot who must move or cease operation because of the presence of the residential area created by the developer?"

The area in question is located in Maricopa County, Arizona, some 14 to 15 miles west of the urban area of Phoenix, on the Phoenix-Wickenburg Highway, also known as Grand Avenue. About two miles south of Grand Avenue is Olive Avenue which runs east and west. . . .

Farming started in this area about 1911. . . . By 1950, the only urban areas in the vicinity were the agriculturally related communities of Peoria, El Mirage, and Surprise . . . . [T]he community of Youngtown was commenced in 1954. Youngtown is a retirement community appealing primarily to senior citizens.

In 1956, Spur's predecessors in interest . . . developed feedlots, about 1/2 mile south of Olive Avenue . . . . The area is well suited for cattle feeding and in 1959, there were 25 cattle feeding pens or dairy operations within a 7 mile radius of the location developed by Spur's predecessors. . . .

In May of 1959, Del Webb began to plan the development of an urban area to be known as Sun City. For this purpose, the Marinette and the Santa Fe Ranches, some 20,000 acres of farmland, were purchased for $15,000,000 or $750.00 per acre. This price was considerably less than the price of land located near the urban area of Phoenix . . . .

By September 1959, Del Webb had started construction of a golf course south of Grand Avenue and Spur's predecessors had started to level ground for more feedlot area. In 1960, Spur purchased the property in question and began a rebuilding and expansion program extending both to the north and south of the original facilities. By 1962, Spur's expansion program was completed and had expanded from approximately 35 acres to 114 acres.

Accompanied by an extensive advertising campaign, homes were first offered by Del Webb in January 1960 and the first unit to be completed was south of Grand Avenue and approximately 2 1/2 miles north of Spur. By 2 May 1960, there were 450 to 500 houses completed or under construction. At this time, Del Webb did not consider odors from the Spur feed pens a problem and Del Webb continued to develop in a southerly direction . . . .

By December 1967, Del Webb's property had extended south to Olive Avenue and Spur was within 500 feet of Olive Avenue . . . . Del Webb filed its original complaint alleging that in excess of 1,300 lots in the southwest portion were unfit for development for sale as residential lots because of the operation of the Spur feedlot.

Del Webb's suit complained that the Spur feeding operation was a public nuisance because of the flies and the odor which were drifting or being blown by the prevailing south to north wind over the southern portion of Sun City. At the time of the suit, Spur was feeding between 20,000 and 30,000 head of cattle, and the facts amply support the finding of the trial court that the feed pens had become a nuisance to the people who resided in the southern part of Del Webb's development. The testimony indicated that cattle in a commercial feedlot will produce 35 to 40 pounds of wet manure per day, per head, or over a million pounds of wet manure per day for 30,000 head of cattle, and that despite the admittedly good feedlot management and good housekeeping practices by Spur, the resulting odor and flies produced an annoying if not unhealthy situation as far as the senior citizens of southern Sun City were concerned. There is no doubt that some of the citizens of Sun City were unable to enjoy the outdoor living which Del Webb had advertised and that Del Webb was faced with sales resistance from prospective purchasers as well as strong and persistent complaints from the people who had purchased homes in that area. . . .

It is noted . . . that neither the citizens of Sun City nor Youngtown are represented in this lawsuit and the suit is solely between Del E. Webb Development Company and Spur Industries, Inc.

It is clear that as to the citizens of Sun City, the operation of Spur's feedlot was both a public and a private nuisance. They could have successfully maintained an action to abate the nuisance. Del Webb, having shown a special injury in the loss of sales, had a standing to bring suit to enjoin the nuisance. The judgment of the trial court permanently enjoining the operation of the feedlot is affirmed. . . .

A suit to enjoin a nuisance sounds in equity and the courts have long recognized a special responsibility to the public when acting as a court of equity. . . .

In addition to protecting the public interest, however, courts of equity are concerned with protecting the operator of a lawfully, albeit noxious, business from the result of a knowing and willful encroachment by others near his business.

In the so-called "coming to the nuisance" cases, the courts have held that the residential landowner may not have relief if he knowingly came into a neighborhood reserved for industrial or agricultural endeavors and has been damaged thereby . . . .

Were Webb the only party injured, we would feel justified in holding that the doctrine of "coming to the nuisance" would have been a bar to the relief asked by Webb, and, on the other hand, had Spur located the feedlot near the outskirts of a city and had the city grown toward the feedlot, Spur would have to suffer the cost of abating the nuisance as to those people locating within the growth pattern of the expanding city. . . .

We agree, however, with the Massachusetts court that:

> "The law of nuisance affords no rigid rule to be applied in all instances. It is elastic. It undertakes to require only that which is fair and reasonable under all the circumstances. In a commonwealth like this, which depends for its material prosperity so largely on the continued growth and enlargement of manufacturing of diverse varieties, 'extreme rights' cannot be enforced. . . ." Stevens *v.* Rockport Granite Co., 216 Mass. 486, 488 (1914).

There was no indication in the instant case at the time Spur and its predecessors located in western Maricopa County that a new city would spring up, full-blown, alongside the feeding operation and that the developer of that city would ask the court to order Spur to move because of the new city. Spur is required to move not because of any wrongdoing on the part of Spur, but because of a proper and legitimate regard of the courts for the rights and interests of the public.

Del Webb, on the other hand, is entitled to the relief prayed for (a permanent injunction), not because Webb is blameless, but because of the damage to the people who have been encouraged to purchase homes in Sun City. It does not equitably or legally follow, however, that Webb, being entitled to the injunction, is then free of any liability to Spur if Webb has in fact been the cause of the damage Spur has sustained. It does not seem harsh to require a developer, who has taken advantage of the lesser land values in a rural area as well as the availability of large tracts of land on which to build and develop a new town or city in the area, to indemnify those who are forced to leave as a result.

Having brought people to the nuisance to the foreseeable detriment of Spur, Webb must indemnify Spur for a reasonable amount of the cost of moving or shutting down. It should be noted that this relief to Spur is limited to a case wherein a developer has, with foreseeability, brought into a previously agricultural or industrial area the population which makes necessary the granting of an injunction against a lawful business and for which the business has no adequate relief.

It is therefore the decision of this court that the matter be remanded to the trial court for a hearing upon the damages sustained by the defendant Spur as a reasonable and direct result of the granting of the permanent injunction. Since the result of the appeal may appear novel and both sides have obtained a measure of relief, it is ordered that each side will bear its own costs. . . .

4. CONVERSION (EQUITABLE REPLEVIN)

Burr v. Bloomsburg

Court of Chancery of New Jersey, 1927.
101 N.J. Eq. 615.

■ BERRY, VICE CHANCELLOR. This bill seeks the recovery from the defendant of a diamond ring which came into defendant's possession on the death of her husband, and to which she claims title by virtue of her husband's will. The complainant claims the ring as her own property by virtue of a gift from her mother, now deceased, and seeks the aid of this court on the ground that the ring has a peculiar sentimental value by reason of its associations and because damages at law would be an inadequate remedy. This suit is in the nature of an equitable replevin. The evidence submitted at the final hearing showed that the complainant's father, Robert Bloomsburg, died at Bordentown, N.J., in 1899; that many years before his death he purchased an unset diamond for his wife, the mother of the complainant, and with the intention of having it set in a ring for her; and that at the time of the purchase the complainant accompanied her father. On their return home the complainant's father took the unset stone from his pocketbook and handed it to his wife, telling her it was for her, and that she could have it set any way that she liked. Because she thought the stone was too large for her, however, she declined to have it set in a ring for herself, and after some months it was set in a ring for complainant's father, and he wore it until his death in 1899. While on his deathbed, and in the presence of the complainant, he handed the ring to his wife and said:

> "This is the last gift, Jennie, I will ever give you. If you are hungry, you can sell it for food; if not, it goes to Mary, then to Pud, and then to the baby."

"Mary" was a daughter of Robert Bloomsburg, and "Pud" was the complainant; "Pud" being the father's pet name for her. The "baby" was the daughter of the complainant. These, together with a brother, George Bloomsburg, the husband of the defendant, comprised the family of

Robert Bloomsburg. All of Robert Bloomsburg's family, with the exception of complainant, are now dead.

After the father's death, complainant's mother wore the ring until after the death of her daughter Mary, about three years later. She then gave the ring to complainant in George's presence. Complainant retained the ring until June 10, 1909, when, at his request, she loaned it to her brother and took from him a receipt in his own handwriting, in the following form:

> "In case of my death I promise to return my father's ring to his family. [Signed] George A. Bloomsburg, June 10, 1909."

Some time later in a letter written by George Bloomsburg to complainant, he said:

> "About the paper regarding the ring, won't you kindly send it to me, and I will make it all right with you in some other way. It would make things a great deal more pleasant for me if you will do this."

It seems that the defendant had started some family controversy about this ring and importuned her husband to get it from the complainant, which he finally did in an effort to appease the defendant. Complainant, however, refused to surrender the receipt.

When complainant's father died, he left a will of which he appointed his wife and his daughter Mary, executrices, and his son George, executor. The ring was inventoried as a part of the assets of the estate and appraised at $250. The estate was not formally settled through the courts, but apparently was adjusted out of court by agreement between complainant and her brother long after the death of their mother and the complainant's sister.

Some time before June 10, 1909, when the ring was delivered by complainant to her brother, the controversy then having arisen over its possession and ownership, he insisted that if she desired to retain the ring she would have to pay him $400, which she finally consented to do, and gave him her note for that amount. The note was finally paid on June 16, 1910, by complainant's check drawn to the order of George A. Bloomsburg for $416. It is significant that this payment was made over a year after the ring was delivered by complainant to her brother. If she did not own the ring at that time, I cannot understand why she would have paid the note, as it is reasonable to suppose that upon a surrender of her claim to the ring the note would have been canceled.

George Bloomsburg retained possession of the ring until his death in 1925. He left a will dated December 16, 1905, in which he devised all of his property to his wife, who is the defendant in this suit. A codicil to that will, dated October 9, 1914, contains the following paragraph:

> "Whereas, since the making of my last will and testament to which this codicil is attached, I have executed a certain

> writing which might be considered a bequest of my diamond ring left me by my father, Robert Bloomsburg. I do hereby give and bequeath to my beloved wife, Mary A. Bloomsburg, the said diamond ring above referred to, absolutely for her benefit, behoof and use forever."

It is by virtue of this provision of the codicil that defendant claims title to the ring in question. The truth is, however, that the diamond ring had not been left to him by his father, and the statement in the codicil that it had been was a plain attempt to evade his obligation to return it to his sister.

Undoubtedly "this court has jurisdiction to enforce the restitution or delivery of a specific chattel which has a peculiar artificial value, and for which therefore adequate compensation cannot be obtained at law; and that, too, whether possession has been got by the wrongdoer through a trust or not." . . . This jurisdiction has been exercised by the Court of Chancery since very early times.

The earliest leading case on the subject, and perhaps the one most frequently cited, is Pusey *v.* Pusey, 1 Vernon, 273 (1684). That case involved the possession of a horn anciently given to the Pusey family by the Danish King Canute and which time out of mind had gone along with the plaintiff's estate. The horn bore this inscription:

> "Kyng Knowd geve Wyllyam Pewse This horne to hold, by they lond."

It was held the bill was maintainable for the recovery of the specific chattel. The next reported case pertinent to this inquiry, and to which my attention has been directed, is Duke of Somerset *v.* Cookson, 3 P. Wms. 389 (1735). It involved the possession of an old silver patera [sacrificial plate or saucer] bearing a Greek inscription and dedication to Hercules, which had been dug up on the plaintiff's estate. It had come into defendant's possession, and the Duke brought a bill in equity to compel its delivery in specie undefaced. Defendant demurred on the ground that the remedy was at law, but the demurrer was overruled. In Fells *v.* Read, 3 Vesey, 70 (1796), a suit was brought to recover a tobacco box of a remarkable kind which had belonged to a club, and the Lord Chancellor stated the reason of the equitable remedy as follows:

> "The Pusey horn, the patera of the Duke of Somerset, were things of that sort of value, that a jury might not give two-pence beyond the weight. It was not to be cast to the estimation of people, who had not those feelings. In all cases, where the object of the suit is not liable to a compensation by damages, it would be strange, if the law of this country did not afford any remedy. It would be great injustice, if an individual cannot have his property without being liable to the estimate of people, who have not his feelings upon it."

. . . [W]hile the equitable principles here involved are usually treated under the head of "Specific Performance" in works on equity jurisprudence, the jurisdiction of this court is not confined to that head; "it is freely exercised to enforce the surrender of chattels *in specie* which have been *tortiously obtained or are wrongfully detained.*" POMEROY'S SPECIFIC PERFORMANCE OF CONTRACTS (3d ed.), § 12 [emphasis added in case]. . . .

[H]ere suit is not brought to enforce a written agreement. It is rather to enforce the right of the complainant to the return of the ring by reason of her ownership, amply proved . . . .

It is also insisted that mere sentiment or personal desire for a particular object affords no basis for an equitable action such as this. That may be true as an abstract proposition; but when that sentiment or desire is based upon or born of facts and circumstances which endow the chattel with a special, aside from its intrinsic, value, to the extent of a pretium affectionis, it is not true. In such cases there is and can be no measure of damages in money. While this ring itself, as a piece of jewelry, may have a definite value in dollars and cents, how can the sentiment, the imaginary value put upon it by complainant's fancy, because of her affection for the one from whom she obtained it, be valued in terms of money any more than could a value be placed upon the "touch of a vanished hand" or "the sound of a voice that is still?" The real question here is whether or not this ring has a "pretium affectionis." If it has, whether because of sentiment, desire, or what not, provided it be real, "not . . . founded in weakness and folly," and not assumed for the occasion, then this court has jurisdiction, and relief should not be denied. . . .

There is here an abundance of proof to establish a "pretium affectionis" in this ring. The stone had been bought by complainant's father for her mother; it was later set in a ring which he wore during the balance of his lifetime, and which, on his deathbed, and in complainant's presence, he gave to her mother with the injunction not to part with it except that she be hungry and it was needed for bread, and that after her death it was to go first to the daughter Mary, then to complainant, and eventually to complainant's daughter.

That it does have a real and not a pretended sentimental value is evidenced by the fact that the complainant cherished it from then until now; that she refused to sell it even to her own brother; that rather than be deprived of it she acquiesced in her brother's demands for the payment of a considerable sum of money to him on the pretense that it was property of the father's estate, when, in fact, it was her very own; that after the loan of the ring to her brother, ostensibly to prevent domestic discord, she refused to surrender the receipt which he had given for it and finally instituted this suit to recover the ring itself rather than its money value.

These facts show conclusively to my mind that the ring has had the pretium affectionis impressed upon it. To the defendant, it is merely a piece of jewelry, necessary to the gratification of envy or avarice, but to the complainant it recalls the daydreams of youth and the childhood memories of maturer years. It is endowed with a sentimental fancy, which, even though imaginary, can no more be estimated in dollars and cents than can mother love or the guileless and trusting affection of the child. "There is no standard by which the price of affection can be adjusted, and no scale to graduate the feelings of the heart." To agree with defendant's argument would be to admit that sentiment should be commercialized; but when sentiment and the finer feelings of the heart are measured in terms of money, then will this world cease to be a fit habitation for man. "It would be a reproach to the country not to indulge" the complainant in her desire. . . .

As to the payment of some $400 to the brother, the surviving executor of her father's will, she did not fix this value. It was not a price set upon the article by her; it was a demand of the defendant's husband, reluctantly complied with by the complainant under duress. It was, in effect, the price of peace, and I do not consider that by paying this price the complainant has in any way set a value on the chattel in controversy which could bind her or prejudice her in this action. The fact is, she was under no obligation in law or otherwise to pay a dollar. The property was already hers. The payment was no more than a gratuity or a peace offering.

For the reasons above expressed I will advise a decree for the complainant.

NOTES ON REPLEVIN

1. When a defendant wrongfully withholds a chattel belonging to the plaintiff, the plaintiff may bring an action of replevin. In replevin, the recovery is specific rather than substitutionary—that is, it gives the plaintiff possession of the chattel itself rather than damages for its value. It is historically a legal action, and so does not rely on the court's equitable powers. In a traditional replevin action, the plaintiff would file an action of replevin and post a bond, whereupon the sheriff seized the chattel from the defendant and delivered it to the plaintiff pending trial. Modern statutes are likely to require an adversary hearing prior to seizure, and also to permit the defendant to retain the property by posting a counter-bond.

2. In contrast, the plaintiff in Burr *v.* Bloomsburg sought an equitable decree requiring the defendant to return her ring. Some courts will call this an injunction; other courts refer to the remedy of equitable replevin. Whichever term is used, equitable replevin permits the plaintiff to avoid statutory replevin procedures and to enforce the court's order by contempt.

E. MODIFICATION OF INJUNCTIONS

Ladner v. Siegel

Supreme Court of Pennsylvania, 1930.
298 Pa. 487.

[Siegel proposed to build a public garage and gas station on a block he owned in Philadelphia. Neighbors sued and obtained an injunction, on the ground that the proposed use would constitute a nuisance. Siegel later adopted a limited plan to rent parking space to tenants of neighboring apartment buildings. He applied to the trial court for modification of the injunction, which the court granted. The modified decree read:]

> "And now, to wit, May 14, 1929, the decree heretofore entered in the above-entitled case on the 2d day of March, 1928, which reads as follows,
>
> > 'And now, to wit, March 2, 1928, in consideration of the foregoing case, it is ordered, adjudged and decreed as follows:
> >
> > '1. That the defendants, Clarence R. Siegel and William M. Anderson be and are hereby enjoined as follows:
> >
> > '(a) From maintaining and operating garage building built in the center of the block of ground surrounded by Forty-Seventh, Forty-Eighth, Pine and Spruce Streets, Philadelphia, as a public garage.
> >
> > 'Defendants to bear the cost.'
>
> "Be and the same is hereby amended so as to read as follows:
>
> > '1. That the defendants, Clarence R. Siegel and William M. Anderson be and are hereby enjoined.
> >
> > '(a) From maintaining and operating garage buildings built in the center of the block of ground surrounded by Forty-Seventh, Forty-Eighth, Pine and Spruce Streets, Philadelphia, as a public garage.
> >
> > '(b) Nothing in this injunction, however, shall prevent the defendants, Clarence R. Siegel and William M. Anderson, from using the said garage building for the storage of automobiles by the tenants of Garden Court Apartments, situate at the northeast corner Forty-Seventh and Pine Streets in the City of Philadelphia or by the tenants of the apartment houses now being erected at the northwest corner Forty-Seventh and Pine Streets or by any other apartment house erected in the block bounded by Forty-Seventh, Forty-Eighth, Pine and Spruce Streets. Leave is hereby given to the plaintiffs and any of them to

> apply to this court at any time for specific orders in connection with the operation of the building as actual operation shall show to be necessary or proper . . . .' "

■ KEPHART, J. . . . An injunction is the form of equitable proceeding which protects civil rights from irreparable injury, either by commanding acts to be done, or preventing their commission, there being no adequate remedy at law. Granting an injunction rests in the sound discretion of the court, that discretion to be exercised under well-established principles, and there are no statutory limitations on the power of the court in relation thereto. While the decree in such action is an adjudication of the facts and the law applicable thereto, it is none the less executory and continuing as to the purpose or object to be attained; in this it differs from other equitable actions. It operates until vacated, modified, or dissolved. An injunction contemplates either a series of continuous acts or a refraining from action. A preventive injunction constantly prevents one party from doing that which would cause irreparable damage to his neighbor's property rights. The final decree continues the life of such proceeding, not only for the purpose of execution, but for such other relief as a chancellor may in good conscience grant under the law. . . .

The injunction in this case prevented an anticipated injury to a property right. The chancellor in granting it placed the protecting arm of the court about this right, and prevented Siegel from using his property in such a way as would injure his neighbors. It was to remain as long as the court felt that protection necessary to complainant's rights, or until conditions demanded a modification of that protection or its entire removal. The power of the chancellor to modify in such cases cannot be controlled by term rules, otherwise equity would cease to be equity and become a hard and fast taskmaster. . . .

The modification of a decree in a preventive injunction is inherent in the court which granted it, and may be made, (a) if, in its discretion judicially exercised, it believes the ends of justice would be served by a modification, and (b) where the law, common or statutory, has changed, been modified or extended, and (c) where there is a change in the controlling facts on which the injunction rested. . . .

An injunction decree does not create a right; it protects the right of the owner to the enjoyment of his property from injurious interference by the uses of other land. The right protected is an attribute of property existing through the application of common-law principles. A decree preventing its injury does not give to the complaining party a perpetual or vested right either in the remedy, the law governing the order, or the effect of it. He is not entitled to the same measure of protection at all times and under all circumstances. A decree protecting a property right is given subject to the rules governing modification, suspension, or dissolution of an injunction. The decree is an ambulatory one, and marches along with time affected by the nature of the proceeding. . . .

Sawyer v. Davis

Supreme Judicial Court of Massachusetts, 1884.
136 Mass. 239.

The plaintiffs, who were manufacturers in Plymouth, were restrained by a decree of this court, made on October 1, 1881, upon a bill in equity brought by the present defendants, from ringing a bell on their mill before the hour of six and one half o'clock in the morning; which decree was affirmed by the full court on September 7, 1882. On March 28, 1883, the Legislature passed an act, which took effect upon its passage, as follows: "Manufacturers and others employing workmen are authorized, for the purpose of giving notice to such employees, to ring bells and use whistles and gongs of such size and weight, in such manner and at such hours as the board of aldermen of cities and the selectmen of towns may in writing designate." (St. 1883, c. 84.) On April 18, 1883, the selectmen of Plymouth granted to the plaintiffs a written license to ring the bell on their mill in such manner, and at such hours, beginning at five o'clock in the morning, as they were accustomed to do prior to the injunction of this court.

The prayer of the bill was that the injunction might be dissolved, or that the decree might be so modified as to enable the plaintiffs to act under their license without violating the decree of this court; and for other and further relief. . . .

■ C. ALLEN, J. Nothing is better established than the power of the Legislature to make what are called police regulations, declaring in what manner property shall be used and enjoyed, and business carried on, with a view to the good order and benefit of the community, even although they may to some extent interfere with the full enjoyment of private property, and although no compensation is given to a person so inconvenienced. . . . In this conflict of rights, police regulations by the Legislature find a proper office in determining how far and under what circumstances the individual must yield with a view to the general good. For example, if, in a neighborhood thickly occupied by dwelling-houses, any one, for his own entertainment or the gratification of a whim, were to cause bells to be rung and steam-whistles to be blown to the extent that is usual with the bells and steam-whistles of locomotive engines near railroad stations in large cities, there can be no doubt that it would be an infringement of the rights of the residents, for which they could find ample remedy and vindication in the courts. But if the Legislature, with a view to the safety of life, provides that bells shall be rung and whistles sounded, under those circumstances, persons living nearby must necessarily submit to some annoyance from this source, which otherwise they would have a right to be relieved from. . . .

But the argument is urged upon us with great force, that in the present case there had been a judicial determination that the ringing of the bell, at the hours now authorized by the terms of the statute and the designation of the selectmen, was a private nuisance to the defendants, not growing out of any public right, and that the statute ought not, as a matter of construction, to be held applicable to this case; or, if such is its necessary construction, that it is unconstitutional, as interfering with their vested rights. . . .

The injunction which was awarded by the court, upon the facts which appeared at the hearing, did not imply a vested right in the present defendants to have it continued permanently. Though a final determination of the case before the court, and though binding and imperative upon the present plaintiffs, and enforceable against them by all the powers vested in a court of equity, yet they were at liberty at any time, under new circumstances making it inequitable for it to be longer continued, to apply to the court for a review of the case and a dissolution of the injunction. In respect to such a state of facts, an injunction can never be said to be final, in the sense that it is absolute for all time. . . . [A] declaration by the Legislature that, in its judgment, it is reasonable and necessary for certain branches of business to be carried on in particular ways, notwithstanding the incidental disturbance and annoyance to citizens, is certainly a change of circumstances which is entitled to the highest consideration of the court; and in the present case we cannot doubt that it is sufficient to entitle the plaintiffs to relief from the operation of the injunction.

The method of procedure to which the plaintiffs have resorted is the usual and proper one in such circumstances. . . .

Jefferson v. Big Horn County

Supreme Court of Montana, 2000.
300 Mont. 284.

■ JUSTICE JIM REGNIER delivered the Opinion of the Court.

[In 1989, members of the Crow Indian tribe filed an action against the state of Montana and Big Horn County claiming that land they owned within the Crow reservation was exempt from property taxes. Based on a decision of the Court of Appeals for the Ninth Circuit holding that property taxes apply only to land allotted to individual owners under the Indian General Allotment Act of 1887 (GAA), the district court granted summary judgment for the plaintiffs.] . . .

On August 28, 1990, the District Court issued an order implementing its Judgment. The District Court required Big Horn County to refund taxes paid under protest and remove the Crow Tribe Members from the tax rolls. The court stated that "[t]his declaratory ruling establishes a future tax exempt status for land that is located within the Crow Reservation, has never been subject to the General Allotment Act and is owned by an enrolled Crow Tribe member." The District Court also stated that its order granting summary judgment in favor of the Crow Tribe Members "established as a matter of law that Defendants may not collect property tax on a Crow Tribe member's land within the Crow Reservation that is not and never has been subject to the General Allotment Act."

On June 20, 1997, Big Horn County filed a Motion for Partial Vacation of Judgment and Supporting Memorandum requesting the District Court vacate that portion of its order establishing a future tax exempt status for the Crow Tribe Members pursuant to Rule 60(b), Montana R. Civ. P. [governing relief from judgment]. Big Horn County claimed that subsequent federal decisions had established that alienable land owned by enrolled members of tribes was subject to state ad valorem taxes even if it had not been patented in fee pursuant to the GAA. The court did not rule on the motion within 60 days and it was deemed denied under Rule 60(c), Montana R. Civ. P.

On December 12, 1997, Big Horn County filed a Motion to Dissolve Injunction . . . , asserting that due to a change in the applicable law, there were insufficient grounds to continue the initial order. On October 2, 1998, Big Horn County supplemented its motion to dissolve the injunction with a copy of [a decision of the Supreme Court of the United States that resolved a conflict among circuits and held that all alienable Indian lands are subject to taxation.] . . .

On December 18, 1998, the District Court granted Big Horn's motion and dissolved that portion of its Judgment dated August 28, 1990, which had granted a future tax exempt status to the Crow Tribe Members. The Crow Tribe Members appeal. . . .

The Crow Tribe Members assert that the District Court was barred by the doctrine of res judicata from dissolving a portion of its judgment. The State contends that the portion of the judgment which had established a future tax exempt status for the Plaintiffs was a form of injunctive relief that the District Court could modify or dissolve . . . .

"Any order which requires a person to refrain from a particular act for any period of time, no matter what its purpose is an 'injunction.' " Sheridan County Elec. Co-op. *v.* Ferguson, 124 Mont. 543, 554 (1951). . . .

[Montana statutes governing relief against illegally imposed taxes] did not preclude the District Court from ordering injunctive relief, nor could the court's declaratory judgment exempt the Plaintiffs' property from future taxation without a further order of injunctive relief. Because that portion of the District Court's Judgment which ordered a "future tax exempt status" was an order granting prospective relief by restraining the Defendants from imposing an ad valorem property tax on Plaintiffs' property in the future, it was injunctive relief. Accordingly, the only remaining issue is whether the court was authorized to modify or dissolve its injunction. . . .

A court may modify or dissolve perpetual injunctive relief based on a subsequent change in the judicial interpretation of a law. In Santa Rita Oil Co. *v.* State Board of Equalization, 112 Mont. 359, 368 (1941), we stated that "[t]he latter point hardly requires citation to authority, for obviously it is not equitable to continue to restrain a party from actions no longer unlawful [when] the change in law has come about . . . through an authoritative change in judicial construction by courts." . . .

> "An injunction is merely the process by which the court enforces equity and it has not only the power but the duty to modify or annul its injunction as equity demands. A final or permanent injunction is a continuing process over which the equity court necessarily retains jurisdiction in order to do equity. And if the court of equity later finds that the law has changed or that equity no longer justifies the continuance of the injunction, it may and should free the defendant's hands from the fetters by which until then its activities have been prevented, thus leaving it free to perform its lawful duties."

112 Mont. at 370. . . .

[A] court has the inherent power to modify or vacate an injunction when the law upon which that injunction was based has been changed by subsequent judicial interpretation. . . . The Crow Tribe Members concede that the judicial interpretation of the law upon which that relief was based has subsequently changed . . . . Accordingly, we conclude that the District Court did not err when it vacated the injunctive portion of its judgment. . . .

■ JUSTICE TERRY N. TRIEWEILER dissenting.

The majority opinion is predicated on the majority's conclusion that the judgment . . . was in the nature of injunctive, rather than declaratory relief, and that, therefore, principles of *res judicata* did not bar reconsideration of the issues resolved by that judgment. I disagree.

As noted in the Court's original judgment:

. . . Plaintiffs' action was brought pursuant to Title 15, Chapter 1, Part 4 [of the Montana Code], which provides the method for protesting property taxes and recovering those amounts which have been unlawfully imposed. Section 15–1–404 . . . specifically provides as follows:

> "The remedies hereby provided shall supersede the remedy of injunction and all other remedies which might be invoked to prevent the collection of taxes or licenses alleged to be irregularly levied or demanded, except in unusual cases where the remedies hereby provided are deemed by the court to be inadequate."

34 Section 15–1–406 . . . provides . . . :

> (1) An aggrieved taxpayer may bring a declaratory judgment action in the district court seeking a declaration that:
>
> . . .
>
> (b) a tax . . . was illegally or unlawfully imposed . . . .

Relief was granted pursuant to § 15–1–408 . . . which provides that:

> If the district court determines that the tax was illegally or unlawfully imposed or exceeded the taxing authority of the entity imposing the tax, the judgment may direct:
>
> > (1) that the revenue collected under the illegal tax be directly refunded to the taxpayers who have paid the illegal tax and who have not been excluded from the action; [or] . . .
> >
> > (4) any other remedy as the court considers appropriate.

In this case, the court . . . ordered that illegally collected taxes be refunded to the taxpayers who brought the action and that they not be collected in the future. [B]oth forms of relief were pursuant to the declaratory judgment action provided for in § 15–1–406, MCA. They were not in the form of injunctive relief . . . .

The declaratory relief was sufficient to exempt the taxpayer's property from taxation on a stand-alone basis. It was not necessary to additionally enjoin Big Horn County or the State of Montana from prospective conduct. Any incidental language to that effect was gratuitous, unnecessary, and, in fact, contrary to the specific prohibition of injunctive relief found at § 15–1–404. . . .

For these reasons, when federal decisional law changed . . . the only procedure available to the State or to the county for relief from that judgment was . . . . Rule 60(b). . . . Big Horn County filed a motion for Rule 60(b) . . . relief. . . . [N]either the county nor the State appealed from the District Court's denial of their Rule 60(b) motion. Therefore, the District Court's denial is final.

NOTES

1. The majority and dissent in Jefferson *v.* Big Horn County differed over the nature of the remedy granted by the district court, a debatable point. Assuming the remedy was an injunction, however, the majority's discussion of modification is uncontroversial.

2. In 1963, a federal district court found that Oklahoma City was operating a "dual" school system, in which school children were intentionally segregated by race. In 1972, the court found that the city had failed to eliminate the effects of segregation by voluntary efforts, and entered a decree establishing the "Finger Plan," which provided for busing among schools.

In 1977, the district court found that the Finger Plan had been successful, resulting in a "unitary" school system in substantial compliance with constitutional requirements, and that the school board had manifested its "desire and intent to follow the law." Accordingly, it terminated its jurisdiction over the case, without formally dissolving the injunction.

By 1984, changes in housing patterns had resulted in increasingly longer bus routes for children. In response, the school board adopted a new plan, assigning students in grades kindergarten through four to neighborhood schools. As a result of this plan, thirty-three of sixty-four elementary schools were substantially single-race schools. In 1985, parties representing black children and their parents moved to re-open the case.

The district court found that school district remained unitary, that continuing segregation resulted from housing patterns that had developed independently of the former segregation of schools, that the Finger Plan was no longer viable, and that the school board had complied in good faith with the court's orders. It concluded that the 1977 desegregation decree should be vacated. The Court of Appeals for the Tenth Circuit reversed, citing a prior Supreme Court decision, United States *v.* Swift & Co., 286 U.S. 106 (1932), for the proposition that a decree should remain in effect unless the defendant shows a "grievous wrong evoked by new and unforeseen conditions" that imposes "extreme and unexpectedly oppressive hardships" on the defendant.

The Supreme Court reversed the Court of Appeals, stating that:

> "Considerations based on the allocation of powers within our federal system, we think, support our view that quoted language from *Swift* does not provide the proper standard to apply to injunctions entered in school desegregation cases. Such decrees, unlike the one in *Swift,* are not intended to operate in perpetuity. Local control over the education of children allows citizens to participate in decisionmaking, and allows innovation so that school programs can fit local needs. The legal justification for displacement of local authority by an injunctive decree in a school desegregation case is a violation of the Constitution by the local authorities. Dissolving a desegregation decree after the local authorities have operated in compliance with it for a reasonable period of time properly recognizes that 'necessary concern for the important values of local control of public school systems dictates that a federal court's regulatory control of such systems not extend beyond the time required to remedy the effects of past intentional discrimination.' "

Board of Education of Oklahoma City Public Schools *v.* Dowell, 498 U.S. 237, 248 (1991). Justices Marshall, Blackmun, and Stevens dissented. See also Freeman *v.* Pitts, 503 U.S. 467 (1992) (holding that "federal courts have the authority to relinquish supervision and control of school districts in incremental stages, before compliance has been achieved in every area of school operations").

3. Courts have applied the standards articulated in *Dowell* when called upon to modify or dissolve consent decrees or injunctive orders designed to curb other constitutional violations. For example, in King *v.* Greenblatt, 53 F. Supp. 2d 117 (D. Mass. 1999), the Commonwealth of Massachusetts moved to vacate or terminate consent decrees put in place twenty-five years earlier that governed operations at treatment facilities for

civilly committed sexually dangerous persons. The court granted the motion, but elected to *terminate*, rather than *vacate*, the consent decrees:

> "The Commonwealth has phrased its motion alternatively, to vacate or terminate the consent decrees. In Inmates of Suffolk Co. Jail *v.* Sheriff of Suffolk Co., 952 F. Supp. 869, 883–84 (D. Mass. 1997), the defendants asked the district court to enter an order that vacated the consent decree. In that case, the district court decided to terminate, but not vacate, the decrees. As the district judge stated in that case, a consent decree is 'an adjudication of an ongoing obligation based on a claim of "violation of a Federal right" that was at least one part of the subject matter of the civil action in which the Consent Decree was entered. That adjudication may still have pragmatic consequences even after the prospective relief that had earlier been included in the Consent Decree has been terminated.' . . . . I believe a record of the past should be preserved and, accordingly, I grant the motion to terminate the consent decrees."

Id. at 139.

4. Emergency Hospital excluded Dr. James Stephens from performing surgery in the hospital. Dr. Stephens sued the hospital, claiming that, as a physician in good standing, he was entitled under the hospital's constitution and by-laws to perform surgery there. The court entered an order stating that the hospital and its employees "are hereby enjoined and perpetually restrained from interfering with or failing to aid or assist Dr. James A. Stephens . . . in the surgical treatment of his patients in the said hospital . . . ."

After the court entered its order, the hospital amended its by-laws to require that surgeons seeking to operate in the hospital must obtain approval from the hospital's directors. Dr. Stephens did not apply for approval. Relying on the new by-law, the hospital excluded him from performing surgery. Dr. Stephens requested that the hospital be punished for contempt. The hospital replied that the new by-law had altered the factual and legal basis for the injunction. The court said:

> "[The hospital] contends that, if its interpretation of the facts relied upon and the legal consequences flowing therefrom as nullifying the continuing authority of the injunction, is correct, it should be exonerated from the charge of contempt and that only in the event that such interpretation is erroneous can it be deemed guilty of the contempt charged.
>
> "That contention assumes that the court granting the injunction had no power to rescind or modify its final decree after it had become enrolled, no matter what changes had occurred in the conditions or the relations of the parties after the decree. There is obviously no force in these contentions."

Emergency Hospital of Easton *v.* Stevens, 146 Md. 159, 165–66 (1924).

F. INTERLOCUTORY INJUNCTIONS

Interlocutory injunctions are injunctions granted before a full trial has been held, to preserve the court's ability to decide the case as well as the parties' rights pending adjudication. There are two important types of interlocutory injunctions: temporary restraining orders and preliminary injunctions. A temporary restraining order may be granted *ex parte* based on affidavits submitted by the plaintiff; the order is followed by notice and a hearing and expires after ten days unless extended by the court. A preliminary injunction is granted after notice and a hearing, and normally extends until final judgment.

Abbott Laboratories v. Mead Johnson & Co.

United States Court of Appeals, Seventh Circuit, 1992.
971 F.2d 6.

■ FLAUM, CIRCUIT JUDGE. Abbott Laboratories (Abbott) filed this interlocutory appeal, 28 U.S.C. § 1292(a)(1), after the district court denied its motion for a preliminary injunction against Mead Johnson & Company (Mead). Abbott seeks relief under § 43(a) of the Lanham Act (the Act), 15 U.S.C. § 1125(a), to halt Mead's alleged false advertising and trade dress infringement practices in the oral electrolyte maintenance solution (OES) market. . . .

Oral electrolyte maintenance solutions are over-the-counter medical products used to prevent dehydration in infants suffering from acute diarrhea or vomiting. They are clear liquids, comprised almost exclusively of water, electrolytes and dissolved carbohydrates, and are ingested orally. While OES products do not actually cure diarrhea or nausea, they maintain the fluid balance of infants inflicted with these maladies by facilitating the body's absorption of fluids and electrolytes. The OES market is a small (approximately $45 million in annual sales) but important one . . . .

Abbott and Mead are, for all practical purposes, the only two competitors in the United States OES market. Abbott's product is called "Pedialyte," while Mead's is called "Ricelyte." Competition in this market is of surprisingly recent vintage, as Pedialyte enjoyed a virtual monopoly until Mead introduced Ricelyte in 1990. The two products are virtually identical; only their carbohydrate components differ. This difference is crucial to understanding the dispute in this case, so we briefly provide some background.

Pedialyte is known as a "glucose-based solution" because its carbohydrate component is glucose. Glucose is a monomer. Monomers are the simplest carbohydrate molecules, and serve as the building blocks for larger carbohydrates, known as oligimers or polymers. . . .

Ricelyte, unlike Pedialyte, is not a glucose-based solution, for it is manufactured with carbohydrates known as "rice syrup solids." When producing Ricelyte, Mead takes whole rice kernels and separates out the two carbohydrates, amylose and amylopectin, found naturally in rice. Amylose and amylopectin, like starch, are complex carbohydrates comprised of thousands of monomers bonded together. Mead then hydrolyzes the rice carbohydrates—biochemists have long known how to replicate natural hydrolysis in the laboratory—into rice syrup solids, which are much shorter polymer chains, but still more complex than the monomer glucose. It is important for our purposes to emphasize that rice syrup solids, while hydrolytically *derived* from rice carbohydrates, are not actually "rice carbohydrates" as the term is used in the scientific and medical communities. . . .

The OES market, unlike typical consumer product markets, is "professionally driven," meaning that Abbott and Mead do not promote their product directly to consumers, but rather to physicians and nurses, who in turn recommend them to consumers. . . .

Since Pedialyte is the incumbent and Ricelyte the challenger, Mead launched a promotional campaign designed to convince physicians and nurses to recommend Ricelyte over Pedialyte. The campaign does so by emphasizing that Ricelyte's carbohydrate components (*i.e.,* rice syrup solids) come from rice, while Pedialyte's carbohydrate component is glucose. Mead focuses on rice for a fairly simple reason. Over the past decade, medical researchers worldwide, many sponsored by the World Health Organization (WHO), have studied the effectiveness of OES products made with powdered whole grains of rice, which are known as "rice-based," or whole grain, solutions. These studies have found that rice-based solutions have significant advantages over glucose-based solutions, like Pedialyte, when it comes to combatting the dehydrative effects of diarrhea. Despite their medical superiority, however, rice-based solutions face two obstacles to commercial viability. First, rice grain powder, unlike glucose and rice syrup solids, cannot be completely dissolved in water, making rice-based solutions cloudy and susceptible to separation, and less palatable to consumers as a result. Second, rice-based solutions are subject to early spoilage, and hence have too brief a shelf life for commercial distribution.

Ricelyte, according to Mead, fashions a compromise between the marketability and appearance of glucose-based solutions and the medical effectiveness of whole grain solutions. Its rice syrup solids are derived from rice, but are soluble and do not spoil, making Ricelyte more marketable than whole grain solutions. There remain, however, significant differences between Ricelyte and rice-based solutions. As noted, the carbohydrate components of rice-based solutions are actual rice carbohydrates . . . , *not* the less complex rice syrup solids used in Ricelyte. Moreover, rice-based solutions, unlike Ricelyte, also contain the non-carbohydrate components of rice, including proteins, fats, fiber and other organic materials.

Nonetheless, Mead's promotional campaign plays up Ricelyte's association with rice. First, it forges a direct link between Ricelyte and rice. To take an obvious example, the name "Ricelyte" conveys the message that the product contains or is made from rice. Further, some of Mead's advertisements describe Ricelyte as a "rice-based oral electrolyte solution," while others claim that Ricelyte contains "rice carbohydrate molecules." The visual background of many advertisements consists of an illustration of rice grains cascading into a clear liquid pool. Second, Mead's campaign implies, and at times directly states, that Ricelyte's link to rice makes it superior to Pedialyte. Some advertisements proclaim that "worldwide results confirm the benefits of rice" and that rice "has been used for centuries to help manage diarrhea." The statement "Rice Makes A Difference" appears in nearly all Ricelyte advertisements, in most instances as a subtitle to "New Ricelyte." In addition, a number of ads tout certain (alleged) specific benefits of Ricelyte vis-a-vis Pedialyte, including lower osmolality, better fluid absorption, and reduced stool output—all the consequence of Ricelyte's link to rice. . . .

The court's analysis followed the venerable four-part preliminary injunction standard, about which we speak at greater length in the following section. With regard to the false advertising claim under § 43(a)(2), the court ruled that Abbott had established a likelihood of success on the merits. It found certain of Mead's advertisements, including those claiming that Ricelyte is "rice-based," to be literally false, and others, including those maintaining that Ricelyte has a lower osmolality than Pedialyte, to be literally true but misleading. Nonetheless, the court declined to enjoin Mead's promotional campaign pending a full trial because the other three preliminary injunction factors tipped the equities in Mead's favor: (1) if Abbott were to prevail on the merits, any harm it would suffer prior to final judgment could be adequately compensated with money damages and would not be irreparable; (2) the balance of hardships favored Mead; and (3) the public interest would be disserved by a preliminary injunction. . . .

Despite our recent efforts to clarify the law of preliminary injunctions, confusion persists, as demonstrated by the contrasting spins both parties place upon the four-part preliminary injunction standard. . . .

As a threshold matter, a party seeking a preliminary injunction must demonstrate (1) some likelihood of succeeding on the merits, and (2) that it has "no adequate remedy at law" and will suffer "irreparable harm" if preliminary relief is denied. If the moving party cannot establish either of these prerequisites, a court's inquiry is over and the injunction must be denied. If, however, the moving party clears both thresholds, the court must then consider: (3) the irreparable harm the non-moving party will suffer if preliminary relief is granted, balancing that harm against the irreparable harm to the moving party if relief is denied; and (4) the public interest, meaning the consequences of granting or denying the injunction to non-parties.

The court, sitting as would a chancellor in equity, then "weighs" all four factors in deciding whether to grant the injunction, seeking at all times to "minimize the costs of being mistaken." We call this process the "sliding scale" approach: the more likely it is the plaintiff will succeed on the merits, the less the balance of irreparable harms need weigh towards its side; the less likely it is the plaintiff will succeed, the more the balance need weigh towards its side.[2]

This weighing process, as noted, also takes into consideration the consequences to the public interest of granting or denying preliminary relief.[3] While we have at times framed the sliding scale approach in mathematical terms, it is more properly characterized as subjective and intuitive, one which permits district courts to "weigh the competing considerations and mold appropriate relief." . . .

Section 43(a)(2) of the Act prohibits the use of false or misleading statements or representations of fact in commercial advertising, and establishes a private remedy for any violation thereof. The provision applies with equal force to (1) statements which are literally false and (2) statements which, while literally true or ambiguous, convey a false impression or are misleading in context, as demonstrated by actual consumer confusion. . . .

The "Rice Claims." . . . [W]e agree with the district court that Mead's rice claims falsely represent that Ricelyte has certain qualities that it in fact does not actually have, and hence are literally false in violation of § 43(a)(2).

---

[2] Mead, pointing to an isolated dictum . . . states that if the balance of irreparable harms (factor number 3 in the text) tips toward the defendant, the preliminary injunction must be denied regardless of the strength of plaintiff's case on the merits. This statement is erroneous. It is the balance of harms *discounted* by the parties' relative chances of succeeding on the merits (and taking account of the public interest), not the *undiscounted* balance of harms, that must weigh in plaintiff's favor for a preliminary injunction to issue. . . .

To illustrate our point, consider the following. Plaintiff X seeks a preliminary injunction against defendant Y. Suppose that the (undiscounted) balance of irreparable harms tips slightly toward Y—in other words, that X will be irreparably harmed $9x$ if the court denies preliminary relief, while Y will be harmed $10x$ if the court grants it. Suppose further that X has a 99 percent chance of succeeding on the merits, Y a one percent chance, and that the public interest is not implicated by the case. The proper course in this instance—recognizing, of course, that quantifying the factors to this degree of precision is likely impossible—would be to grant preliminary relief, for that is the course that would minimize the cost of error. Weighing the equities *as a whole* favors X, making preliminary relief appropriate, even though the undiscounted balance of harms favors Y.

[3] Both parties state that a plaintiff, to obtain a preliminary injunction, must show that the injunction would not harm the public interest. This, in effect, adds a third threshold to our preliminary injunction standard by making the public interest factor dispositive. Although the statement finds support from a dictum . . . , we question whether it accurately characterizes the law of the circuit. The public interest is one factor courts must consider in weighing the equities; it is not dispositive. Suppose, to take a simple example, that the balance of harms tips significantly in plaintiff's favor, that plaintiff has an overwhelming chance of succeeding on the merits, but that granting the injunction would ever so slightly impair the public interest (*e.g.*, by removing one of ten products from a given product market). In this instance, preliminary relief would be proper even though it might harm the public interest.

The "Ricelyte" Name. . . . In [the context of Mead's promotional campaign], the name "Ricelyte" implies more than the permissible message that Ricelyte is produced from rice or contains rice syrup solids derived from rice carbohydrates. It also implies that Ricelyte actually contains rice and rice carbohydrates—or at least we can say that Abbott has established a strong likelihood of so proving at trial. . . .

The Comparison Claims. The district court made two other significant findings: (1) Mead's statement that Ricelyte has a lower osmolality than Pedialyte, while literally true, is misleading because the difference in osmolality has no therapeutic significance; and (2) Mead's claim that Ricelyte is superior to Pedialyte in terms of fluid absorption and stool output does not have a firm scientific grounding, and hence is false. . . . While remaining neutral as to the merits, we believe that Abbott has established the requisite likelihood of proving its case at trial, particularly in light of the deference we owe the meticulous and carefully reasoned findings entered by the district court. At argument the parties informed us that they soon anticipate the release of another study bearing upon the fluid absorption and water output issue; this study should help resolve whether Mead's claims are false or misleading. . . .

[W]e agree with the district court's determination that Abbott has established a likelihood of success on the merits . . . .

The second preliminary injunction threshold requires Abbott to establish that it will be irreparably harmed if it does not receive preliminary relief, and that money damages and/or an injunction ordered at final judgment would not rectify that harm. The district court determined that Abbott did not clear this threshold. In so holding, the court acknowledged the well-established presumption that injuries arising from Lanham Act violations are irreparable, even absent a showing of business loss. This presumption, it appears, is based upon the judgment that it is virtually impossible to ascertain the precise economic consequences of intangible harms, such as damage to reputation and loss of goodwill, caused by such violations.

There can be no doubt that Mead's Ricelyte campaign, which attempts to convince consumers that Pedialyte is an inferior OES product, has dented Abbott's reputation. The district court nonetheless found the presumption of irreparable harm rebutted owing to the unusual structure of the OES market. It reasoned as follows: Pedialyte enjoyed a virtual monopoly prior to Ricelyte's entry into the market. Any injunction, entered after a full trial, would remove Ricelyte from the market, thereby restoring Pedialyte's monopoly and lost market share. Under these circumstances, one could easily measure the sales Abbott lost while waiting for final judgment. As far as the future is concerned, Abbott's reputational damage will have no tangible economic impact because Pedialyte will have regained its monopoly, leaving those who need OES products with no other choice. It appears, then, that we are faced with a rare situation—any harm to Abbott's reputation and goodwill wreaked by Mead's promotional campaign between now and final judgment will be fully compensable in money damages, and therefore cannot be considered irreparable. Put another way, the fact that injunctive relief in Abbott's favor at final judgment would boot Ricelyte from the market renders compensable any injuries Abbott will have suffered in the interim. . . .

The district court's conclusion rests upon two assumptions. First, the court assumed that if final judgment forced Mead to withdraw Ricelyte, Abbott's losses would be limited to past lost sales in the OES market. In our view, this assumption overlooks the fact that Mead's promotional campaign will probably have lingering, incalculable economic consequences even if final relief on the merits drives Ricelyte from the market. Any monopoly Abbott regains is unlikely to last very long. (We of course do not mean to imply that Abbott deserves a monopoly, or that a monopoly would benefit the OES market, but only that Abbott's damages would be difficult to calculate in the event it could not sustain a monopoly.) It is almost certain that Mead will re-enter, or some other company will enter, the OES market shortly after Ricelyte departs; the market has a proven potential for growth, and the dominant player has proven potentially vulnerable. Pedialyte's loss of goodwill will have tangible economic consequences once competition reemerges, because doubts planted by the Ricelyte campaign will linger in the minds of consumers and physicians, who may avail themselves of an alternative to Pedialyte if given the choice. Moreover, any shifts in the OES market between now and final judgment will affect the closely related competition between Abbott and Mead in the immense infant formula market, which accounts for more than $1.5 billion in annual sales. . . .

[T]he district court [also] erred by assuming in the first instance that granting final injunctive relief to Abbott would necessarily mean the end of Ricelyte. Granted, some of the relief sought by Abbott—*e.g.,* an order requiring Mead to recall Ricelyte, change its label, and immediately cease use of the "Ricelyte" name—would eliminate Ricelyte from the market at least temporarily, and perhaps permanently. But other relief—*e.g.,* an order prohibiting Mead from purveying the false "rice claims" and directing it to issue corrective advertisements and brochures—would not have such drastic consequences. These less severe remedies would leave Ricelyte a viable, albeit somewhat discredited, competitor with at least part of its current market share.

The district court did not address the possibility of ordering these intermediate forms of relief after a full trial on the merits. This, we believe, constitutes an error of law. It is axiomatic that injunctions, preliminary as well as permanent, have their basis in equity. When faced with a motion for a preliminary injunction, a district court must remain flexible, and weigh the equities as to each element of preliminary relief sought by the plaintiff. The same applies to final relief if, as here, the potential parameters of a permanent injunction will influence the equities that govern the propriety of issuing a preliminary injunction. The importance of flexibility is enhanced where those equities depend in great measure upon which preliminary and permanent remedies are ordered. We therefore find that the district court abused its discretion by restricting its focus to those final remedies, to the exclusion of all others, that would eliminate Ricelyte from the market. . . .

Less severe relief, as we just observed, would leave Ricelyte a viable competitor in the OES market, making it extremely difficult to measure Abbott's damages. Some consumers, particularly new parents, would choose Ricelyte for reasons unrelated to Mead's promotional campaign. Other consumers would inevitably choose Ricelyte on the basis of impressions formed during that campaign; this group includes, for example, consumers who accepted their physicians' initial recommendation to purchase Ricelyte but who were not subsequently informed that the recommendation rested upon false premises. . . .

We next consider the public interest. The district court concluded that granting Abbott's request for a preliminary injunction would disserve the public interest. Ricelyte, the court reasoned, is a safe and effective product whose presence in the market has promoted the public welfare by focusing attention upon OES products and increasing their use. The court also believed that forcing Ricelyte from the market would restore Abbott's former virtual monopoly, dousing competitive incentives to invest in additional research and develop more effective OES products.

We agree with the district court that forcing Ricelyte from the market would harm the public interest. It is a rare case where purging a safe and effective product serves broad societal interests. This is particularly so when the purged product is one of only two in a given market; monopolies, as a general rule, carry substantial social costs, including higher prices, lower output, and a reduced incentive to engage in product innovation beneficial to consumers. The costs are even higher when, as here, important health concerns are involved.

But we decline to accept the court's implicit assumption that granting Abbott preliminary relief would necessarily mean the demise of Ricelyte, for the same reasons we just rejected that assumption with regard to final injunctive relief. As noted, some forms of intermediate relief, such as ordering Mead to purge the false aspects of its promotional campaign and issue corrective advertising, would leave Ricelyte a viable competitor. In fact, such relief would serve, rather than disserve, the public interest in truthful advertising, an interest that lies at the heart of the Lanham Act. . . .

The district court also determined that the balance of hardships tilted in Mead's favor—in other words, that the irreparable harm to Mead of granting preliminary relief would outweigh the irreparable harm to Abbott of denying such relief. . . .

Having found that the district court (1) overstated the irreparable harm to Mead and the public interest of granting a preliminary injunction, and (2) possibly overlooked the irreparable harm to Abbott of denying an injunction, we cannot accept its conclusion that the equities weigh in Mead's favor as to Abbott's false advertising claim under § 43(a)(2). . . .

One final note. As we have emphasized throughout, the district court's analysis suffered from its near exclusive focus upon the most drastic remedies requested by Abbott (*e.g.*, product recall) to the exclusion of less severe remedies (*e.g.*, corrective advertising). This focus, we learned at argument, resulted from the district court's decision to adopt, nearly verbatim, the proposed findings of fact and conclusions of law submitted by the parties; obviously, the court selected some of Abbott's proposals and some of Mead's. Each party, it appears, tried to hit a home run, Abbott by submitting conclusions of law granting it all the relief it sought, and Mead by submitting conclusions of law granting Abbott nothing. Neither offered alternative conclusions that steered a reasonable middle ground. So, when it came time for the court to assess the impact upon the parties and the public of granting or denying preliminary relief, the court considered only the impact of either granting the most severe relief or shutting Abbott out altogether.

Of course there is nothing wrong and everything right with zealous advocacy. But counsel, when drafting proposed conclusions of law for the district court, should bear in mind a crucial observation to which we alluded above: courts retain a great deal of flexibility when fashioning preliminary relief, and the equities weighed under the four-part preliminary injunction standard can shift as the nature of that relief varies. Nor do we cast aspersions upon the widespread practice in the busy district courts of adopting many or most of the parties' proposed findings of fact and conclusions of law, particularly if skillfully and wisely drafted. Nonetheless, district judges also should bear in mind our observations regarding the nature of preliminary relief, and, when presented with proposed findings and conclusions that hug the extremes, consider developing alternatives of their own. . . .

NOTES ON PRELIMINARY INJUNCTIONS

1. In addition to the four-part test outlined in *Abbott Laboratories*, courts often state that the proper function of a preliminary injunction is to preserve the *status quo* pending trial. *E.g.*, Univ. of Texas *v.* Camenisch, 451 U.S. 390, 395 (1981). This is fair enough, if preserving the *status quo* is understood loosely as protecting the court's ability to reach a decision in the case, and protecting the parties' rights from irreparable harm that might occur before the court can make that decision. "*Status quo*," however, is a slippery term that can cause difficulties when applied literally.

Another traditional limitation on preliminary injunctive relief is that courts will not grant mandatory injunctions prior to trial. Although that restriction is no longer absolute, courts still favor preliminary injunctions that are prohibitory.

Both principles are illustrated by Cooling *v.* Security Trust Co., 29 Del. Ch. 286 (1946). Security Trust served as both the trustee of a testamentary trust and an executor of the settlor's will. The statute of limitations governing objections to the accounts filed by Security Trust as executor was about to run. The plaintiff, representing minor beneficiaries of the trust, requested a preliminary injunction requiring Security Trust, as trustee, to file objections to the accounts it had submitted as executor. The court granted the injunction, stating that:

> "[I]t has been said in some American decisions that a mandatory *interlocutory* injunction would never be granted. This doctrine is not only opposed to the overwhelming weight of authority, but is contrary to the principle which regulates the administration of preventive relief, and is manifestly absurd. . . .
>
> "However, it is equally important to emphasize that a mandatory preliminary injunction should only issue to preserve the status quo in the true sense of that term. In my opinion, the issuance of the injunction here served that purpose. This court recognizes that the power exists, but it also realizes that there are stringent prerequisites to the exercise of the power.
>
> "Only by the issuance of the mandatory preliminary injunction could it be assured that a possible trust asset would not be lost here. When such a showing is made, I feel that this court has the power and the duty to issue an appropriate injunction."

Id. at 291–92.

Similarly, in Trautwein *v.* Moreno Mutual Irrigation Co., 22 F.2d 374 (9th Cir. 1927), the court granted a preliminary injunction permitting the plaintiff to transport water through the defendant's irrigation system. That court said:

> "While it is generally true that the office of a preliminary injunction is to preserve the status quo until upon final hearing the court may grant full relief, and that this can be accomplished by an injunction prohibitory in form, it sometimes happens that the status quo is a condition, not of rest, but of action. . . . Inasmuch as the defendants were not transporting or carrying water for the plaintiffs immediately prior to the demand in question, it is doubtful whether the status quo in this case was a condition of action; but, after all, the question rests very largely in the discretion of the court, and the principal consideration is the relative inconvenience to the parties that will result from granting or refusing the relief."

Id. at 376.

2. "Irreparable injury" has a distinctive meaning for a preliminary injunction. For a permanent injunction, it is often used synonymously with "no adequate remedy at law." For further discussion, see Section D of this

chapter (Equitable Discretion in Granting Injunctive Relief). But for a preliminary injunction, an injury is "irreparable" if it would not be remedied by the plaintiff's winning on the merits at trial.

3. The four-part test for preliminary relief in *Abbott Laboratories* is standard in most courts. Yet courts differ in the methods and priorities they use in applying the test. For example, the Court of Appeals for the Third Circuit has said the first two parts of the test—likelihood of success on the merits and irreparable injury—are threshold requirements that must be met before a district court goes on to weigh the other considerations. Reilly *v.* City of Harrisburg, 858 F.3d 173, 176 (3d Cir. 2017), as amended (June 26, 2017). By contrast, the Court of Appeals for the Ninth Circuit considers the parts of the test "on a sliding scale, such that a stronger showing of one element may offset a weaker showing of another." Recycle for Change *v.* City of Oakland, 856 F.3d 666, 669 (9th Cir. 2017). And some courts that apply a sliding scale also emphasize the fact-specific decisions that a court has to make when deciding to give a preliminary injunction: "Once all the equitable factors are before the judge, however, a classic discretionary decision must be made involving how much weight to give individual components of the calculus and to what direction the balance of equity tips." Jones *v.* Markiewicz-Qualkinbush, 842 F.3d 1053 (7th Cir. 2016).

Nevertheless, there are questions about whether the sliding-scale approach is consistent with the U.S. Supreme Court's decision in Winter *v.* Natural Resources Defense Council, Inc., 555 U.S. 7 (2008). For contrasting views on that question, see the opinions in Diné Citizens Against Ruining Our Environment *v.* Jewell, 839 F.3d 1276 (10th Cir. 2016).

4. The black-letter rule, sometimes honored in the breach, is "that a preliminary injunction is an extraordinary and drastic remedy, one that should not be granted unless the movant, *by a clear showing,* carries the burden of persuasion." Mazurek *v.* Armstrong, 520 U.S. 968, 972 (1997) (quoting 11A C. Wright, A. Miller, & M. Kane, FEDERAL PRACTICE AND PROCEDURE § 2948, pp. 129–130 (2d ed. 1995) (emphasis in original)).

5. The "confusion" the court referred to in *Abbott Laboratories* stemmed primarily from American Hospital Supply Corp. *v.* Hospital Products, Ltd., 780 F.2d 589 (7th Cir. 1986), in which Judge Posner made the following statements about preliminary injunctions:

> "A district judge asked to decide whether to grant or deny a preliminary injunction must choose the course of action that will minimize the costs of being mistaken. Because he is forced to act on an incomplete record, the danger of a mistake is substantial. And a mistake can be costly. If the judge grants the preliminary injunction to a plaintiff who it later turns out is not entitled to any judicial relief—whose legal rights have not been violated—the judge commits a mistake whose gravity is measured by the irreparable harm, if any, that the injunction causes to the defendant while it is in effect. If the judge denies the preliminary injunction to a plaintiff who it later turns out is entitled to judicial relief, the judge commits a mistake whose gravity is measured by

the irreparable harm, if any, that the denial of the preliminary injunction does to the plaintiff.

"These mistakes can be compared, and the one likely to be less costly can be selected, with the help of a simple formula: grant the preliminary injunction if but only if P x Hp > (1–P) x Hd, or, in words, only if the harm to the plaintiff if the injunction is denied, multiplied by the probability that the denial would be an error (that the plaintiff, in other words, will win at trial), exceeds the harm to the defendant if the injunction is granted, multiplied by the probability that granting the injunction would be an error. That probability is simply one minus the probability that the plaintiff will win at trial; for if the plaintiff has, say, a 40 percent chance of winning, the defendant must have a 60 percent chance of winning (1.00−.40 = .60). The left-hand side of the formula is simply the probability of an erroneous denial weighted by the cost of denial to the plaintiff, and the right-hand side simply the probability of an erroneous grant weighted by the cost of grant to the defendant.

"This formula, a procedural counterpart to Judge Learned Hand's famous negligence formula, see United States *v.* Carroll Towing Co., 159 F.2d 169, 173 (2d Cir. 1947), is not offered as a new legal standard; it is intended not to force analysis into a quantitative straitjacket but to assist analysis by presenting succinctly the factors that the court must consider in making its decision and by articulating the relationship among the factors. It is actually just a distillation of the familiar four (sometimes five) factor test that courts use in deciding whether to grant a preliminary injunction. The court asks whether the plaintiff will be irreparably harmed if the preliminary injunction is denied (sometimes also whether the plaintiff has an adequate remedy at law), whether the harm to the plaintiff if the preliminary injunction is denied will exceed the harm to the defendant if it is granted, whether the plaintiff is reasonably likely to prevail at trial, and whether the public interest will be affected by granting or denying the injunction (*i.e.*, whether third parties will be harmed—and these harms can then be added to Hp or Hd as the case may be). The court undertakes these inquiries to help it figure out whether granting the injunction would be the error-minimizing course of action, which depends on the probability that the plaintiff is in the right and on the costs to the plaintiff, the defendant, or others of granting or denying the injunction. See also Leubsdorf, The Standard for Preliminary Injunctions, 91 Harv. L. Rev. 525 (1978). The formula is new; the analysis it capsulizes is standard."

Id. at 593–94.

The Posner/Leubsdorf formula provoked much criticism, some of it from judges who feared increased appellate scrutiny of trial courts' decisions to grant or deny preliminary injunctions. In a subsequent decision, the Seventh Circuit clarified its position as follows:

"These cases [*i.e.*, *American Hospital Supply* and a prior case in which the court questioned the notion of trial court "discretion," Roland Machinery Co. *v.* Dresser Industries, 749 F.2d 380 (7th Cir. 1984)] would be troublesome if the verbal and mathematical formulae and the discussion of discretion are misinterpreted to establish a rigid approach to the preliminary injunction question. *Roland* and *American Hospital,* in accord with the assurances of the panel in each case that no change in the substantive law was intended, maintain the traditional equitable character of the remedy . . . .

"[A]s those opinions also emphasize, a formula is not a substitute for, but an aid to, judgment. A mathematical formula can create a false impression that the elements of the formula, the magnitudes and probabilities, can be accurately quantified and that through a specified type of mental calculus the singularly "correct" result can be arrived at with some exactitude. The obvious problem with this is that the impression is false: a figure representing the probability of success can be arrived at only through a subjective estimate by the court and the magnitudes of harm are rarely susceptible to quantification because of the subjective values, externalities, and effects on the public interest that may be involved in an injunction case. In fact, it is the inability to measure damage that often is the reason the plaintiff is seeking the injunction. Thus the equation relies on the same type of subjective, impressionistic weighing that has been part of the traditional preliminary injunction determination. . . .

"While the use of an equation has no impact upon the nature of the district court's inquiry, the implication that a 'correct' answer can be achieved would represent a change in the law and is thus of greater concern. It must be remembered that preliminary injunctions have the dual characteristic of being equitable, such that there is no 'right' to obtain one, and being 'by [their] very nature, interlocutory, tentative, provisional, ad interim, impermanent, mutable, not fixed or final or conclusive, characterized by its for-the-time-beingness.' The temporary nature of the remedy mitigates, without eliminating, the concern with the possibility of mistake and need for the 'correct' answer. More significantly, the equitable personality of injunctive relief requires the result to be a 'just' or 'fair' result rather than a 'correct' result. The district judge, sitting as a chancellor in equity considering a preliminary injunction, endeavors to achieve a rough justice between the parties that will maintain the status quo pending trial. . . . Thus it is impossible to think in terms of a single correct result. In each case there exist a number of fair accommodations. If a rigid formulaic approach is used, where the motion is granted only if X > Y or so many stated criteria are met, one of the central questions, what kind or degree of relief is appropriate, is not answered. As the type of relief varies the parameters of the injunction equation will also change, making it very difficult to achieve the accurate, cost-minimizing result. Implicit in equity's connection to the vague concept of fairness is a need for flexibility. *Roland* and *American Hospital* do not limit in any way the ability of the district courts to flexibly weigh the competing considerations and mold appropriate relief in preliminary injunction cases."

Lawson Products, Inc. *v.* Avnet, Inc., 782 F.2d 1429, 1434–36 (7th Cir. 1986).

6. Consider the following dispute:

"Plaintiff Caterpillar, Inc. ('Caterpillar') is . . . engaged in the design, manufacturing and marketing of earth-moving, construction and materials handling machinery and engines for world-wide sales. . . . In 2002, Caterpillar reported $20.15 billion in multi-national sales and revenues, primarily from the sale of the goods and services listed above bearing its marks. Caterpillar also licenses its marks for use on various products such as clothing, footwear, clothing accessories, and a children's product line from which it reported a total of $850 million in sales and revenues in 2002.

[Caterpillar sued Walt Disney Company and Buena Vista Home Entertainment, Inc., claiming that the Disney film "George of the Jungle 2" ("George 2"), violated Caterpillar's trademark rights. George 2, which was produced in video format only, was scheduled for release on October 21, 2003. Prior to the suit, the defendants engaged in "a national marketing campaign to raise awareness for the release of George 2 in various media outlets throughout the country. These advertisements . . . highlighted the expected release date." Caterpillar requested a temporary restraining order enjoining release of the film in its current form.]

"George 2 is an 87 minute comedy primarily targeted at children. It chronicles the exploits of its eponymous hero following the first movie. George is a noble man of nature described as the 'klutzy king of the jungle' on the website who possesses an unusually thick and durable cranium. He is blessed with a lovely wife Ursula and a five-year-old son. George is also a friendly fellow, beloved by most of the creatures living on Ape Mountain. Indeed, he is a linguist of the highest order by virtue of being able to converse with apparently every animal species in their native tongue. His speeches are admirable for their laconic directness and economy of words. He is a hardy fellow in that he is blessed with an incredible constitution that allows him to survive his rather routine bone-crushing collisions with various inanimate objects throughout the movie that would cripple or kill an ordinary man. There is one area where George is deficient, however, in that he is naive and not particularly skilled in navigating the civilized dissembling world of modern society; thereby confirming Maharbal's observation to Hannibal following the Battle of Cannae in 216 BC that the gods do not give all their gifts to one man.

"The plot of the movie revolves around the Machievellian machinations of Ursula's worldly mother, Beatrice, and Ursula's sophisticated fumbling former fiancee, Lyle, to separate George from his beloved wife and son. In his misguided quest for Ursula's love and hand in marriage, Lyle conceives a plot to steal George's deed to Ape Mountain, which would allow him to send his 'dastardly disciples' on dozers to destroy Ape Mountain. Presumably, the destruction of George and Ursula's home would somehow drive Ursula back into Lyle's waiting arms. To make a long story short, Lyle succeeds in obtaining the deed to Ape Island by theft. With this deed in hand, Lyle's minions move into action which is where Caterpillar enters the picture, *in media res*.

"The problem with George 2 from Caterpillar's perspective is that Lyle's minions are shown in the movie driving Caterpillar bulldozers. These are genuine Caterpillar products bearing the Caterpillar and Cat trademarks on them with no apparent alterations. There are four separate scenes featuring the Caterpillar bulldozers. Three of these scenes show brief glimpses of the bulldozers moving toward Ape Mountain at various angles in which a viewer could make out the Caterpillar trademarks. However, these scenes are brief, averaging approximately ten seconds apiece. The final scene is a seven minute battle scene between George and his animal allies against these bulldozers driven by Lyle's minions. Caterpillar's marks are clearly visible in several instances during this battle. While the action is occurring onscreen, the narrator will occasionally chime in with descriptions of the machines as 'deleterious dozers,' 'maniacal machines' and other similar comments. The bulldozers, however, are not computer animated and look and perform as expected of their type; and it is clear that the bulldozers are operated by Lyle's henchmen. George and his allies manage to decommission these bulldozers in several different ways, generally involving instances of combustible ape flatulence and projectile coconuts and animal feces.

[Caterpillar's principal claims were trademark infringement and trademark dilution under the federal Lanham Act. The cause of action for trademark infringement is designed to protect against product confusion, which occurs when consumers associate the infringer's product (George 2) with the trademark holder's business (Caterpillar). The cause of action for trademark dilution protects against harm to a trademark, including harm by "tarnishment" of the reputation of the trademark and products associated with it.]"

Should the court grant preliminary relief? See Caterpillar, Inc. *v.* Walt Disney Co., 287 F. Supp. 2d 913, 915–17 (C.D. Ill. 2003).

Coyne-Delany Co. v. Capital Development Board

United States Court of Appeals, Seventh Circuit, 1983.
717 F.2d 385.

■ POSNER, CIRCUIT JUDGE. The principal questions for decision are the extent of the district court's power to deny damages to a defendant injured by the issuance of a preliminary injunction that is later reversed on appeal, and the proper standard for exercising that power.

The genesis of this case is an otherwise unrelated civil rights suit brought by inmates of the Illinois state prison at Stateville complaining about living conditions. A decree was entered requiring the prison to replace all of the plumbing fixtures in one of the prison's cellhouses. The state's Capital Development Board let a contract for the first of two projected phases of the work to Naal Plumbing & Heating Co., which subcontracted with Coyne-Delany Company for the flush valves required in the project. . . . The valves were installed, and malfunctioned. After Coyne-Delany shipped redesigned valves which also malfunctioned, the prison authorities asked the Capital Development Board to designate another valve subcontractor in the bidding specifications for the second phase of the contract. The Board complied, designating Sloan [Company].

Bids were received, but on May 7, 1979, two days before they were to be opened, Coyne-Delany sued the Board under section 1 of the Civil Rights Act of 1871, 42 U.S.C. § 1983, and on May 8 it obtained a temporary restraining order against the Board's opening the bids. The state asked that Coyne-Delany be ordered to post a $50,000 bond, pointing out that the temporary restraining order was preventing it from proceeding with the entire project and that indefinite delay could be extremely costly. But Judge Perry . . . required a bond of only $5,000, in the belief that the temporary restraining order would be in effect for only a week until Judge Bua could hear the motion for a preliminary injunction. However, at the preliminary-injunction hearing Judge Bua issued the injunction but refused to increase the bond. . . .

The premise of Coyne-Delany's civil rights suit against the Capital Development Board was that under Illinois law as expounded by the Illinois Appellate Court in Polyvend, Inc. *v.* Puckorius, 61 Ill. App. 3d 163 (1978), Coyne-Delany, as an indirect bidder on the plumbing contract for the Stateville cellhouse, had a property right of which it was deprived without due process of law by the Board's requiring Naal to use Sloan valves merely because the prison authorities had determined—unreasonably in Coyne-Delany's opinion—that Coyne-Delany's valves were defective. When he issued the preliminary injunction Judge Bua said that Coyne-Delany was likely to prevail on the merits, especially given the Board's refusal to submit the dispute over the quality of Coyne-Delany's valves to an impartial expert for binding determination, as Coyne-Delany had proposed. This court reversed the grant of the preliminary injunction, however. Noting that *Polyvend* had been reversed by the Illinois Supreme Court, after Judge Bua had granted the preliminary injunction to Coyne-Delany, we held that under Illinois law a bidder, and *a fortiori* an indirect bidder, has no property right in being allowed to bid on a public contract and that Coyne-Delany therefore had no claim against the Board under the Fourteenth Amendment.

Our decision came down on February 22, 1980, and a few days later the Board at last opened the bids that had been submitted back in May 1979. Naal was the low bidder, with a bid of $214,000, but its bid had lapsed because of the passage of time, and the Board had to solicit new bids. The new bids were opened on May 9, 1980. Although Naal's new bid, $270,000, was higher than its old bid had been, Naal was again the low bidder and was awarded the contract.

The Board then joined Hanover Insurance Company, the surety on the injunction bond, as an additional defendant in Coyne-Delany's civil rights suit, pursuant to Rule 65.1 of the Federal Rules of Civil Procedure, and moved the district court to award the Board damages of $56,000 for the wrongfully issued preliminary injunction and statutory costs (filing fees and the like, see 28 U.S.C. § 1920) of $523 which the Board had incurred in the district court. Judge Bua refused to award either costs or damages. His opinion states, "the Court must weigh the equitable factors of the case, including whether the case was filed in good faith or is frivolous. . . . [T]he parties have stipulated that the case was filed in good faith and without malice. Further, it is apparent that the case was not frivolous. The law as it existed at the time the case was filed clearly favored the plaintiffs. It would be unreasonable to require a party to anticipate a change in the law and would be unconscionable to label a suit filed in good faith as frivolous where there is such a subsequent change."

There is no dispute over the amount of costs claimed by the Board; and while Coyne-Delany has not conceded that the Board incurred damages of $56,000 as a result of the delay of the project and the district court made no finding with respect to those damages, they undoubtedly exceeded $5,000, the amount of the injunction bond . . . . The specifications for the second round of bids were apparently the same as those for the first round. The Board must therefore have lost much more than $5,000 on the difference in the bids alone. And it may well have incurred other costs from the delay of the project by a year. . . .

The language of Rule 65(c), governing damages on an injunction bond, is . . . : "No restraining order or preliminary injunction shall issue except upon the giving of security by the applicant, in such sum as the court deems proper, for the payment of such costs and damages as may be incurred or suffered by any party who is found to have been wrongfully enjoined or restrained." The court is not told in so many words to order the applicant to pay the wrongfully enjoined party's damages. But it is told to require a bond or equivalent security in order to ensure that the plaintiff will be able to pay all or at least some of the damages that the defendant incurs from the preliminary injunction if it turns out to have been wrongfully issued. The draftsmen must have intended that when such damages were incurred the plaintiff . . . would normally be required to pay the damages, at least up to the limit of the bond.

Yet some courts treat the district court's discretion to award or deny damages under an injunction bond as completely open-ended unless the plaintiff acted in bad faith in seeking the preliminary injunction. The principal cases, Page Communications Engineers, Inc. *v.* Froehlke, 475 F.2d 994 (D.C. Cir. 1973) (*per curiam*), and H & R Block, Inc. *v.* McCaslin, 541 F.2d 1098 (5th Cir. 1976) (*per curiam*), rely on Russell *v.* Farley, 105 U.S. 433 (1882), where the Supreme Court stated that "in the absence of an imperative statute to the contrary, the court should have the power to mitigate the terms imposed [in granting the injunction], or to relieve from them altogether, whenever in the course of the proceedings it appears that it would be inequitable or oppressive to continue them." Although the statement partakes of dictum because the injunction had not been dissolved completely, a more important point is the absence, at the time the case was decided, of any statute or rule of court dealing with security for federal court injunctions. The Court discussed state statutes and rules, precursors of Rule 65(c), requiring injunction bonds, and only then stated that because of the absence of a federal statute or rule the federal courts "must *still* be governed in the matter by the general principles and usages of equity." The implication is that a rule requiring an injunction bond would have changed the Court's result—would have been the "imperative statute" to which it referred.

Page and *H & R Block* do not consider this reading of *Russell* or cite Houghton *v.* Cortelyou, 208 U.S. 149 (1908), where the Court narrowed the discretion that *Russell* had given district courts to relieve from liability under an injunction bond. And they dismiss Rule 65(c)'s requirement of a bond or other security by pointing out that the district court can require a bond of nominal amount in appropriate cases, for example if the plaintiff is indigent. But it is one thing to say that the requirement of a bond can in effect be waived when there is a good reason for doing so . . . and another to say that where a substantial bond is clearly required by the equities of the case the district court nevertheless has carte blanche to excuse the plaintiff from paying any damages on the bond.

Most cases hold, contrary to *Page* and *H & R Block,* that a prevailing defendant is entitled to damages on the injunction bond unless there is a good reason for not requiring the plaintiff to pay in the particular case. We agree with the majority approach. Not only is it implied by the text of Rule 65(c) but it makes the law more predictable and discourages the seeking of preliminary injunctions on flimsy (though not necessarily frivolous) grounds.

When rules prescribe a course of action as the norm but allow the district court to deviate from it, the court's discretion is more limited than it would be if the rules were nondirective. . . . The judge must have a good reason for departing from such a principle in a particular case. It is not a sufficient reason for denying costs or damages on an injunction bond that the suit had as in this case been brought in good faith. That would be sufficient only if the presumption were against rather than in favor of awarding costs and damages on the bond to the prevailing party . . . . The award of damages on the bond is not punitive but compensatory.

A good reason for not awarding such damages would be that the defendant had failed to mitigate damages. The district court made no reference to any such failure in this case and we can find no evidence that there was any; the Board's requesting and obtaining a 30-day extension of time for filing its appeal brief, the factor stressed by Coyne-Delany, did not create material or unreasonable delay. A good reason not for denying but for awarding damages in this case, unmentioned by the district court, was that the bond covered only a small fraction of the defendant's damages. The Board asked for and should have been granted a much larger bond; and when the heavy damages that the Board had predicted in asking for the larger bond materialized, it had a strong equitable claim to recover its damages up to the limit of the bond. . . .

Although the district court's decision cannot stand, both because it applies an incorrect standard and because it fails to consider and evaluate the full range of factors (which might in an appropriate case include, but is not exhausted by, the plaintiff's good faith) that would be relevant under the proper standard, we are not prepared to hold that the Board is entitled as a matter of law to its costs and to its injunction damages up to the limit of the bond. The district court did allude to one factor, besides mere absence of bad faith, that supported its ruling—the change in the applicable law after the preliminary injunction was issued. The law on which the court had relied in issuing the injunction was contained in an intermediate state appellate court decision and of course such decisions are reversed with some frequency. We do not believe that a change in the law is always a good ground for denying costs and injunction damages to a prevailing party, but it is a legitimate consideration, perhaps especially where the prevailing party is a state agency that benefited from a change in the law of its state. In a sense, this is a case where one state agency (the Board) is seeking to benefit from the confusing signals sent out by another state agency (the court system)—though we do not mean to suggest that the Illinois Supreme Court was rushing fraternally to the aid of another state agency when it reversed *Polyvend.* In any event, a remand is necessary to allow Judge Bua to consider and weigh all the relevant factors identified in this opinion—bearing in mind the principle of preference that we have indicated should guide his equitable determination.

It remains to consider whether on remand the Board should be allowed to seek injunction damages above the limit of the bond. The surety cannot be required to pay more than the face amount of the bond, but it is a separate question whether the plaintiff can be. However, the

Ninth Circuit has held in a scholarly opinion that the bond is the limit of the damages the defendant can obtain for a wrongful injunction, even from the plaintiff, provided the plaintiff was acting in good faith, which is not questioned here. Buddy Systems, Inc. *v.* Exer-Genie, Inc., 545 F.2d 1164, 1167–68 (9th Cir. 1976). (Another exception might be where the plaintiff was seeking restitution rather than damages.) The Supreme Court has cited *Buddy Systems* in dictum for the proposition that "a party injured by the issuance of an injunction later determined to be erroneous has no action for damages in the absence of a bond." Although there was a bond in the present case, it states unequivocally: "The obligation of this bond is limited to $5,000.00." In asking for more, the Board is necessarily relying not on the bond but on some principle of equity that [the Court] says does not exist.

Rightly or wrongly, American common law, state and federal, does not attempt to make the winner of a lawsuit whole by making the loser reimburse the winner's full legal expenses, even when the winner is the defendant, who unlike a prevailing plaintiff does not have the consolation of a damage recovery. In noninjunctive suits, except those brought (or defended) in bad faith, the winner can recover only his statutory costs, invariably but a small fraction of his expenses of suit. It would be incongruous if a prevailing defendant could obtain the full, and potentially the staggering, consequential damages caused by a preliminary injunction. The preliminary injunction in this case halted work on a major construction project for a year; it could easily have been two or three years, and the expenses imposed on the defendant not $56,000 but $560,000. . . .

A defendant's inability to obtain damages in excess of the bond unless the plaintiff was acting in bad faith can have unfortunate results, which are well illustrated by this case where the district court required too small a bond. But a defendant dissatisfied with the amount of bond set by the district court can, on appeal from the preliminary injunction, ask the court of appeals to increase the bond, which the defendant here did not do. . . .

Since Coyne-Delany is conceded to have brought this suit in good faith, the Board is not entitled to any damages above the $5,000 fixed in the bond. . . .

Friends for All Children, Inc. v. Lockheed Aircraft Corporation

United States Court of Appeals, District of Columbia Circuit, 1984.
746 F.2d 816.

■ STARR, CIRCUIT JUDGE. This is a tort action on behalf of Vietnamese orphans for injuries suffered in a tragic aviation accident in South Vietnam in 1975. The suit is over eight years old, and this appeal is the fourth before this court. Seven years after the action was filed, the

District Court granted partial summary judgment on a motion on behalf of the Vietnamese children adopted by non-U.S. parents, holding that Lockheed was liable for the cost of diagnostic examinations of the children. Finding that approximately forty adopted Vietnamese children living in France faced irreparable injury unless they promptly obtained diagnostic examinations, the court entered a mandatory injunction *pendente lite.* The injunction ordered Lockheed to create a $450,000 fund from which reasonable expenses of diagnostic examinations would be paid. . . .

Lockheed claims that even if partial summary judgment was appropriate, the entry of a preliminary mandatory injunction, ordering it to pay $450,000 into the Registry of the District Court, was improper. Lockheed argues that it is always impermissible for a court to provide interim equitable relief in a suit the ultimate objective of which is the recovery of money damages—the classic remedy at law. Lockheed invokes no less an authority than Learned Hand as the *fons et origo* of this doctrine. In Sims *v.* Stuart, 291 F. 707 (S.D.N.Y. 1922), Judge Hand displayed no hesitation in rejecting the plaintiff's motion for a mandatory injunction ordering a collector of customs in advance of trial to return money that the plaintiff contended had illegally been seized. Judge Hand stated:

> "The acts charged constitute, on the plaintiff's theory, a conversion, nothing more. Under the guise of a mandatory injunction I do not see how I can give final relief in advance of answer and trial in such a case. It is, of course, true that equity will at times affirmatively restore the status quo ante pending the suit. But never, so far as I know, will it take jurisdiction over a legal claim merely to hurry it along by granting final relief at the outset of a cause. . . . I cannot suppose that it would anywhere be seriously contended that upon a conversion of money the victim might file a bill in equity and get final relief by mandatory injunction."

Judge Hand's remarks have enjoyed wide and lasting currency. In Enercons Virginia, Inc. *v.* American Security Bank, N.A., 720 F.2d 28 (D.C. Cir. 1983), this court recently had occasion to quote *Sims* in reversing a temporary restraining order enjoining a bank from refusing to honor a cashier's check payable to the plaintiff. The *Enercons* court emphasized that since the plaintiff's action was a "straightforward action on a negotiable instrument," the plaintiff possessed an adequate remedy at law and the injunction was impermissible.

We have no quarrel whatever with *Sims'* result. But, critically, the *Sims* line of cases differs from the instant case in one vital respect: in those cases liability had not yet been determined, whereas here the defendant has already been adjudicated as *liable* for the costs of reasonable diagnostic testing. Only the computation of the *amount* of damages remains for the trier of fact. In our view, the *Sims* rule should not rigidly be erected as an absolute bar to a limited intervention by equity designed to prevent irreparable harm in those circumstances where, as here, the defendant's liability has already been determined through stipulation or partial summary judgment prior to trial. The invocation of equity in such a case reflects a common-sense notion of fairness that undergirds equity jurisprudence: it is more just that a defendant already adjudged liable bear the risk that an interim computation of damages will be fixed too high by the court than to have the plaintiff bear the risk of receiving damages too late to be of any use.

To be sure, the language of *Sims* and other cases cited by Lockheed seems to announce flatly that courts should not entertain interim equitable relief when a remedy at law—money damages—is deemed adequate to provide final relief in the plaintiff's action. In short, equity is perceived in these cases as an interloper threatening to trample law's well-cultivated garden. We cannot agree, however, that equity should never, under any circumstances, be permitted to provide interim relief in an action at law. While our legal system quite properly views damages ultimately as an adequate compensation for a particular kind of loss, it simply does not follow that equity may never be properly called upon, in order to prevent irreparable injury, to accelerate recovery of a portion of damages likely to be awarded when liability has already been determined. Lockheed's counsel commendably admitted at oral argument that once summary judgment was granted, the only circumstance preventing the award of damages for diagnostic examinations was the need to conduct individual trials for the approximately forty French plaintiffs on the issue of the reasonable cost for such examinations. The inability of normal legal channels to provide plaintiffs the necessary relief to prevent their suffering irreparable harm provides under these circumstances the classic case warranting the chancellor's intervention.

Moreover, in the circumstances of this case, we believe that a slavish adherence to *Sims'* dictum would be inconsistent with the deep-rooted power of equity to do what is necessary and appropriate to achieve justice in the individual case. Other courts have refused to forbid rigidly the entry of preliminary injunctions that create monetary funds, the proceeds of which are to be used to prevent injury. . . . [F]unds for diagnostic examinations do not simply represent compensation for past injury, but are required to prevent future injury. To allow this injunction to stand therefore creates no new equitable principle. . . .

Finally, appropriate to the novelty of the case before us, we emphasize the narrowness of today's holding. We hold only that a preliminary injunction requiring the defendant to create a fund to pay for diagnostic exams is proper when the defendant has been held liable for the cost of such examinations and when the delay inherent in trying the case to compute the amount of the defendant's liability will result in irreparable injury. Moreover, under our holding, plaintiffs must show that they meet the traditional standards governing the award of equitable relief, and the District Court must seek to minimize the prospect that a plaintiff will receive any funds that a trier of fact will subsequently fail to award. . . .

In re O'Connell

District Court of Appeal of California, First District, 1925.
75 Cal. App. 292.

■ KNIGHT, J. The petitioner, Daniel O'Connell, by virtue of a writ of injunction issued in a divorce proceeding to which he was a party, was ordered excluded, during the pendency of said action, from the dwelling-house theretofore occupied by him with his wife under the marital relation, and, for violating said injunction, was adjudged guilty of contempt of court and sentenced to pay a fine and to be imprisoned. He now seeks release on *habeas corpus*.

The circumstances leading up to the contempt proceedings are as follows: On June 2, 1923, petitioner, upon his cross-complaint, obtained an interlocutory judgment of divorce from Mrs. O'Connell, whereby the property in question was assigned to him as his sole and separate property. Later, by a decree in equity, rendered in a suit commenced by Mrs. O'Connell in June, 1925, said interlocutory judgment was annulled, upon the ground that said interlocutory judgment had been obtained through . . . fraud. Thereupon Mrs. O'Connell, upon notice to petitioner, applied for and was granted, in the divorce proceeding, said writ of injunction, enjoining petitioner, during the pendency of said action, "from entering the dwelling-house now occupied by the said plaintiff and known and designated as No. 900 Balboa Street in the City and County of San Francisco, State of California, and from living in said dwelling-house during the pendency of said action and from annoying or harassing the said plaintiff in any way during the pendency of said action. . . ." [Mr. O'Conner appealed the order, and continued to occupy the house pending the outcome of the appeal. The trial court held him in contempt.] . . .

The question is whether said writ of injunction is mandatory or prohibitory in its nature and effect. If it be mandatory, its operation was stayed by appeal, and it was beyond the power of the court to punish as a contempt failure to comply with its mandatory terms pending appeal; but if it be prohibitory its operation could not be stayed by appeal and the enforcement thereof was at all times within the jurisdiction of the court. . . .

In the instant case, upon the rendition of said decree in equity, the parties to said divorce proceeding, by operation of law as well as by the express declaration of said decree itself, were restored to the same position as if said interlocutory judgment had never been entered. . . . It follows that the effect of said decree was merely to again place said divorce action at issue, Mrs. O'Connell claiming . . . absolute ownership in said property by virtue of a deed to her from petitioner, and petitioner alleging . . . that said property constituted a homestead and that Mrs. O'Connell's title was merely that of a trustee; and both parties were in actual possession of said property. In that state of the record the plain effect of said injunction *pendente lite,* in relation to the occupancy of said premises, was to oust petitioner from the possession which he theretofore held and to compel him to turn over to the other party to the litigation, prior to final determination of their respective rights in said property, the sole and exclusive possession thereof. Manifestly, said injunction, in the respect noted, did not operate merely to preserve *in statu quo* the subject of the litigation, but went further to the extent of attempting to change the *status* of the parties in relation to the possession of the property in dispute. Therefore . . . it must be held that in so far as said injunction sought to exclude petitioner from said premises, it was mandatory in its effect and consequently its operation was stayed by the appeal therefrom. . . .

The remaining features of said injunction, wherein petitioner was enjoined from harassing and annoying or otherwise interfering with the person of Mrs. O'Connell, and from making any alterations in said premises, are, we believe, purely prohibitive in their nature, and therefore self-executing and not stayed by appeal. Those features become immaterial here, however, owing to the fact that the act for which petitioner was adjudged guilty of contempt was his refusal to discontinue in the occupation of the premises . . . .

The writ is granted and the petitioner is discharged from custody.

NOTE

Appeals of preliminary injunctions are governed by procedural rules that vary from court to court. In the federal courts, most preliminary injunctions (other than trial-related orders) are appealable. State courts may or may not allow interlocutory appeal. Where interlocutory appeals are allowed, procedural rules typically authorize either the trial court, the appellate court, or both, to stay the effect of the injunction pending resolution of the appeal.

What reasons would support the rule in In re O'Connell that mandatory orders are automatically stayed during appeal?

CHAPTER 8

MEASURING INJUNCTIVE RELIEF

A. SCOPE AND SPECIFICITY

Collins v. Wayne Iron Works

Supreme Court of Pennsylvania, 1910.
227 Pa. 326.

■ Opinion by MOSCHZISKER, J. The plaintiff below, appellee here, filed a bill against the defendant below, appellant here, alleging a nuisance from the noise created by the operation of defendant's works. . . .

The learned court below found: "The noises of which complaint is made are not reasonably endurable or bearable, and render the dwelling of complainant during the operation of said iron works uncomfortable and unfit for use as the residence of a reasonable and ordinary person." The following decree was entered: "It is ordered, adjudged, and decreed that you, Wayne Iron Works, your servants, agents, and employees, do abate the nuisance complained of in said bill, and you are hereby enjoined and restrained from the operation of your works by at any time making noises with air drills, power hammers, power chippers, riveting machines, or other tools or apparatus so as to render the premises of the plaintiff described in the said bill unfit for use and enjoyment as a residence by a reasonable and normal person."

The defendant contends: first, that the decree does not specifically point out the things that it is required to do or to refrain from doing in order to abate the nuisance which the court found to exist; and, second, that the evidence in the case does not justify such a sweeping decree as the one entered.

The entry of an injunction is, in some respects, analogous to the publication of a penal statute. It is a notice that certain things must be done or not done, under a penalty to be fixed by the court. Such a decree should be as definite, clear, and precise in its terms as possible, so that there may be no reason or excuse for misunderstanding or disobeying it; and, when practicable, it should plainly indicate to the defendant all of the acts which he is restrained from doing, without calling upon him for inferences or conclusions about which persons may well differ. In the present instance the only definite thing that the defendant is ordered to do is "to abate the nuisance complained of in said bill." As the evidence does not show any improper or negligent operation of the machinery, and as the defendant's conclusion as to what constitutes "a reasonable and normal person" may well differ from that of the plaintiff, it would seem that the only safe way to comply with the decree would be to entirely stop the running of its machinery. Where the facts and equities call for it, a chancellor is required to give relief by injunction; but such injunction should never go beyond the requirements of the particular case, and under no circumstances should a decree be entered the apparent practical effect of which will be to close an industrial plant, if it is possible to frame another form of decree which will give such relief as the plaintiff is entitled to. . . . [A]n important question is: Can the noise by any reasonable means be so moderated so as to accord with the degree of quietness the plaintiff has a right to enjoy; and, if it can, by what means? . . .

We find no manifest error in any of the findings of fact made by the court below; but in addition thereto, the testimony suggests, and is sufficient to sustain, the further finding that the disturbance of the standard of comfort normally prevailing in the neighborhood of the plaintiff's residence, and the consequent annoyance to the plaintiff, are caused by the defendant's permitting the use of tools and apparatus of a noisy character on its premises outside of its buildings, by their use inside of certain of its buildings with the windows and doors open, and at times by the use of such tools and apparatus until late in the evenings. On this finding, a definite decree can be entered enjoining the defendant from operating tools, machines, or apparatus of a noisy character between certain hours, and requiring it to carry on all such operations on the inside of buildings with windows securely closed and with doors shut. This decree will probably afford the relief required. At least such a measure of relief should be first tried before the entry of a decree that may mean the closing of the defendant's works, the ruin of a prosperous business, and the loss of employment to many men. . . .

The twenty-second assignment of error, which goes to the form of the decree, is sustained, and the decree entered by the court below is modified; and it is now adjudged, ordered, and decreed that the Wayne Iron Works, its servants, agents, and employees, are restrained from working its plant in such a manner as to create the nuisance complained of, and to that end they are enjoined from operating drills, power hammers, power chippers, riveting machines, or other tools, machines, or apparatus of a noisy character between the hours of 7 p.m. and 7 a.m.; and from operating such tools, machines, and apparatus of a noisy character at any time unless on the inside of buildings with all windows securely closed with double sash, and with the doors shut . . . .

NOTE

The requirement of specificity is incorporated in Fed. R. Civ. P. 65 and similar state procedural rules. Fed. R. Civ. P. 65(d) provides that:

> "Every order granting an injunction and every restraining order must:
>
> "(A) state the reasons why it issued;

"(B) state its terms specifically; and

"(C) describe in reasonable detail—and not by referring to the complaint or other document—the act or acts restrained or required."

205 Corp. v. Brandow

Supreme Court of Iowa, 1994.
517 N.W.2d 548.

■ HARRIS, JUSTICE. . . . Plaintiff 205 Corporation hired Ron Brandow to manage The Tavern, a restaurant it owns and operates in West Des Moines, Iowa. At the time 205 Corporation provided Brandow with recipes for The Tavern's pizza sauce, pizza crust, and grinder sandwiches. The secret recipes for pizza sauce and grinders were known only to 205 Corporation's president, Charles Celsi, and by the former owner of The Tavern. Several current and former employees knew the pizza crust recipe.

205 Corporation later terminated Brandow's employment. Brandow subsequently provided pizza and grinder recipes to his new employer, Mustards Restaurant, in Windsor Heights, Iowa. 205 Corporation then sued Mustards and Ron Brandow personally. 205 Corporation claimed misappropriation of trade secrets by Mustards and Brandow under Iowa Code chapter 550 (1991). 205 Corporation also alleged Brandow breached his duties of loyalty and to conceal The Tavern's recipes and alleged that Mustards induced Brandow's breaches. . . .

Under Iowa's trade secret Act . . . a trade secret means:

"[I]nformation, including but not limited to a formula, pattern, compilation, program, device, method, technique, or process that is both of the following:

"a. Derives independent economic value, actual or potential, from not being generally known to, and not being readily ascertainable by proper means by a person able to obtain economic value from its disclosure or use.

"b. Is the subject of efforts that are reasonable under the circumstances to maintain its secrecy."

Iowa Code § 550.2(4). . . .

205 Corporation . . . offered the following evidence . . . :

1. The value of the recipes was attested to by The Tavern's owner, Charles Celsi. He purchased the restaurant for $455,000 and testified that the most valuable assets purchased were the recipes.

2. There was testimony by 205 Corporation's expert, a department chairman of the Culinary Institute of America, and defendants' expert that they could not determine the exact

amount of specific ingredients found in the recipes without access to prohibitively expensive chemical analysis machinery. Even if such a machine was used, both experts testified it could not determine the underlying process by which the pizza and grinders were assembled.

3. There was independent evidence of The Tavern's popularity as shown by several highly-prized local food awards.

Other evidence bolstered a finding that the recipes were not generally known or ascertainable. While the core ingredients were determinable with resort to a rare and expensive machine, the exact assembly and baking processes used could not be determined.

Beyond independent economic value, 205 Corporation was required to show that it expended reasonable efforts under the circumstances to maintain secrecy of their recipes. . . .

205 Corporation showed that, when it purchased The Tavern, the former owner testified that none of the recipes were used by or given to the public. Brandow was told the recipes were confidential and were not to be left anywhere readily accessible to others, and all recipes, including the crust recipe, were in a safe deposit box at all times.

But realities of crust preparation differed from those involved with sauce preparation to an extent requiring a different confidentiality procedure. In order to maintain freshness the crust had to be prepared daily. The kitchen employees who prepared the dough were thus necessarily made aware of the recipe. Accordingly, in contrast to other recipes, the crust recipe became known to all employees. Evidence was in conflict on the issue whether these employees considered the crust recipe confidential.

The key to this second element of the trade secret test is found in the words "reasonable under the circumstances." Given the evidence of the special needs inherent in crust preparation, we think substantial evidence supported the conclusion that plaintiff's secrecy procedures were reasonable under the circumstances. . . .

[T]he trial court granted 205 Corporation's request for a permanent injunction, as follows:

> "The defendants and their officers, agents, and employees, are hereby permanently enjoined and restrained from using, divulging, and communicating to anyone else any of the trade secrets or confidential information which includes all or any part of the plaintiff's recipes for pizza sauce, pizza dough or grinders or any substantially similar recipes thereto."

Defendants challenge the dimensions of the injunction, not the court's authority to order one. The injunction is assailed as improperly vague and overly broad, both in scope and duration. Defendants point to the "substantially similar" language and the permanent nature of the injunction. It is clear that an injunction should be limited to the requirements of the case. "The acts or things enjoined should be definitely specified, and they should be set forth with certainty and clearness so that persons bound by the decree may readily know what they must refrain from doing without speculation or conjecture." 42 Am. Jur. 2d *Injunction* § 296, at 1095.

In defendants' "substantially similar" challenge they contend all pizza recipes use similar ingredients. Defendants argue the injunction thus effectively prohibits them from selling any pizza, or at best requires them to speculate on the meaning of the prohibition.

Similar language was disallowed by other courts. American Can Co. *v.* Mansukhani, 742 F.2d 314, 333 (7th Cir. 1984) (disallowing injunction forbidding sale of inks "compositionally similar" to plaintiff's inks and "attributed principally" to use of plaintiff's trade secrets as impermissibly vague); Peggy Lawton Kitchens, Inc. *v.* Hogan, 403 Mass. 732 (1989) (vacating injunction that restricted the sale of cookies, "substantially derived" from plaintiff's formula). There is however substantial contra authority. See, *e.g.*, Mead Corp. *v.* Lane, 54 Ohio App. 3d 59 (1988) (allowing injunction that prohibited use of formula for jet print ink, purge fluid, and "compositionally similar" formulas); Televation Telecommunications Systems, Inc. *v.* Saindon, 169 Ill. App. 3d 8 (1988) (permitting injunction forbidding manufacture or sale of any product similar to, or based on, or incorporating plaintiff's product that could add features to an existing in-house phone system).

We think defendants exaggerate the scope of the prohibition. They are on solid ground in challenging a prohibition that would ban the use or sale of readily available ingredients common to all pizza. But we do not think this prohibition reaches that far. We understand the words "substantially similar," used in the context of the challenged order, to extend only to any unique ingredients or qualities in 205 Corporation's recipes. So understood, we reject defendants' challenge.

The same is true with respect to defendants' protest concerning the injunction's duration. It is a permanent injunction in the sense that it will not expire at a given time. But it can extend only to the time required for independent development of the recipe. Anything more would be punitive, and beyond the proper function of injunctive relief.

Upon defendants' future application, the injunction should be dissolved, if defendants show an independent determination of the recipe's ingredients. . . .

NOTE

Was the injunction, as interpreted by the appellate court, specific enough to give guidance? Could the court have made the order more specific?

Calvin Klein Cosmetics Corp. v. Parfums de Coeur, Ltd.

United States Court of Appeals, Eighth Circuit, 1987.
824 F.2d 665.

■ LAY, CHIEF JUDGE. . . . [Calvin Klein Cosmetics Corporation (Calvin Klein)] distributes high-priced fragrance products under the registered trademark OBSESSION through prestigious department stores and has spent substantial sums to advertise these products. [Parfums de Coeur, Ltd. (Parfums)] manufactures an imitation of the OBSESSION scent, which it calls CONFESS and which it markets as part of its "Designer Imposters" [sic] line of designer perfume imitations. Parfums distributes the CONFESS fragrance in the form of a body spray and spray cologne through discount retailers and drugstore chains at prices far below those of OBSESSION products.[3]

Parfums' body spray container displays the slogan, "If you like OBSESSION you'll love CONFESS." Body spray containers are sold both with and without an accompanying store display that bears the slogan "If you like OBSESSION by CALVIN KLEIN, you'll *love* CONFESS." In both slogans, the word CONFESS is printed in bolder type than the other words, and the terms OBSESSION and CALVIN KLEIN are both denoted as registered marks through the use of the ® registered trademark symbol. Near the bottom of the store display appear the words "Fragrance Body Spray" and "Designer Imposters by Parfums de Coeur."

Calvin Klein filed a motion for a preliminary injunction, seeking to enjoin all of Parfums' packaging and promotional materials and all use by Parfums of the "like/love" slogan. . . . In an order filed June 30, 1986, the district court found that the information on the body spray container viewed as a whole was ambiguous and did not provide sufficient information for the consumer to adequately compare the two products, thus creating a likelihood of consumer confusion as to the source or origin of CONFESS and its relationship to OBSESSION. Finding that Calvin Klein would probably succeed on the merits at trial, the district court preliminarily enjoined distribution or sale of the body spray container. It did not, however, enjoin the use of the "like/love" slogan itself but stated that the "like/love" phrase could be used in conjunction with appropriate disclaimers or other source-identifying information. The district court also refused to preliminarily enjoin the store display, finding that the display's combination of the "like/love" slogan with the phrase "Designer Imposters by Parfums de Coeur" adequately informed consumers as to the source of CONFESS and invited consumers to compare the two products in a manner that lessened the likelihood of confusion. Finally, the district court included in its order as Paragraph 1(b) language prohibiting Parfums from "[u]sing any packaging, labeling, display

---

[3] The 2.5 ounce CONFESS body spray container costs approximately three dollars; OBSESSION products retail for up to 160 dollars for one ounce of perfume.

materials, or other advertising or promotional materials in connection with CONFESS products which are likely to confuse, deceive, or mislead the public into believing that CONFESS products are associated with, sponsored by, or otherwise affiliated with OBSESSION products or plaintiff Calvin Klein Cosmetics Corporation." . . .

[W]e believe that the district court did not abuse its discretion in expressly refusing to preliminarily enjoin all uses by Parfums of the "like/love" slogan. "Like/love" slogans have been found by courts both to contribute to likely consumer confusion and to *not* create likely consumer confusion. In reaching either conclusion, courts do not focus solely on the "like/love" slogan but on the overall context in which that phrase appears.

The district court correctly recognized that numerous factors may be weighed in determining whether there is a likelihood of confusion and that no one factor is dispositive in reaching that conclusion. Factors that the district court weighed here include the OBSESSION mark's strength as a widely recognized trademark, the close relationship between CONFESS and OBSESSION products, and the manner in which the OBSESSION mark is used by Parfums. In enjoining the body spray container but not the store display, the district court found that while the slogan does invite consumers to compare CONFESS with OBSESSION, the spray container as a whole was insufficient to denote the source of CONFESS as a Parfums, not a Calvin Klein, product. It specifically contrasted the container design with Parfums' prominent uses of the phrase "Designer Imposters by Parfums de Coeur" on the store display, which it found adequately cured any likely confusion as to source. A manufacturer does not commit unfair competition merely because it refers to another's product by name in order to win over customers interested in a lower cost copy of that product if the reference is truthful and does not likely confuse consumers into believing that the copy is from the same source as the original. . . .

Parfums [in its cross-appeal] requests that this court vacate Paragraph 1(b) of the June 30 order on the grounds that it is prejudicially overbroad and does not conform to the requirements of Fed. R. Civ. P. 65(d). . . . Broad language in an injunction that essentially requires a party to obey the law in the future is not encouraged and may be struck from an order for injunctive relief, for it is basic to the intent of Rule 65(d) that those against whom an injunction is issued should receive fair and precisely drawn notice of what the injunction actually prohibits. Rule 65(d)'s specificity requirement is designed to prevent uncertainty and confusion on the part of those to whom the injunction is directed, to avoid the possible founding of contempt citations on an order that is too vague to be understood, and to ascertain that the appellate court knows precisely what it is reviewing.

Although the degree of particularity required of an injunction depends on the subject matter involved, we agree with Parfums that Paragraph 1(b) too broadly requires Parfums to guess at what kind of conduct would be deemed trademark infringement. Moreover, the proceedings to date reveal that the very harm that the specificity requirement is designed to protect against has occurred here in the form of repeated contempt motions brought by Calvin Klein against Parfums, all of which, as far as this court can determine, have been denied by the district court. In view of these circumstances, we vacate Paragraph 1(b) of the district court's June 30, 1986, order.

[The court then approved a subsequent order of the district court permitting Parfums to market its body spray in the current packaging, with a disclaimer firmly affixed to the package.]

NOTES

1. Injunctions that require the defendant to comply with applicable law run afoul of both the specificity requirement and the principle that injunctive relief should be tailored to the rights violation under dispute.

2. Express Publishing Co., the publisher of a San Antonio newspaper, refused to bargain with the San Antonio Newspaper Guild, the union representative elected by its employees. The National Labor Relations Board, exercising injunctive power conferred on it by the National Labor Relations Act, ordered Express Publishing "upon request to bargain collectively with the . . . Guild" and "if understandings are reached to embody such understandings in a signed agreement if requested to do so by the Guild." It further enjoined Express Publishing from:

> "In any manner interfering with, restraining, or coercing its employees in the exercise of their rights to self-organization, to form, join, or assist labor organizations, to bargain collectively through representatives of their own choosing, and to engage in concerted activities for the purposes of collective bargaining or other mutual aid and protection, as guaranteed in Section 7 of the [NLRA]."

On appeal, the Court of Appeals for the Fifth Circuit, struck the language just quoted, and the Supreme Court affirmed. The Court said:

> "[T]he authority conferred on the Board to restrain the practice which it has found the employer to have committed is not an authority to restrain generally all other unlawful practices which it has neither found to have been pursued not persuasively to be related to the proven unlawful conduct. . . .
>
> "A federal court [and likewise the NLRB] has broad power to restrain acts which are of the same type or class as unlawful acts which the court has found to have been committed or whose commission in the future unless enjoined, may fairly be anticipated from the defendant's conduct in the past. But the mere fact that a court has found that a defendant has committed an act in violation of a statute does not justify an injunction broadly to obey the statute and thus subject the defendant to contempt proceedings if he shall at any time in the future commit some new violation unlike

and unrelated to that with which he was originally charged. This Court will strike from an injunction decree restraints upon the commission of unlawful acts which are thus dissociated from those which a defendant has committed.

"It is a salutary principle that when one has been found to have committed acts in violation of a law he may be restrained from committing other related unlawful acts. But we think that without sacrifice of that principle, the National Labor Relations Act does not contemplate that an employer who has unlawfully refused to bargain with his employees shall for the indefinite future, conduct his labor relations at the peril of a summons for contempt on the Board's allegation, for example, that he has discriminated against a labor union in the discharge of an employee, or because his supervisory employees have advised other employees not to join a union. . . .

"The breadth of the order, like the injunction of a court, must depend upon the circumstances of each case, the purpose being to prevent violations, the threat of which in the future is indicated because of their similarity or relation to those unlawful acts which the Board has found to have been committed by the employer in the past. . . . That justification is lacking here."

National Labor Relations Board *v.* Express Publishing Co., 312 U.S. 426, 434–37 (1941).

B. DOING JUSTICE

Merrill Lynch, Pierce, Fenner & Smith, Inc. v. Stidham

United States Court of Appeals, Fifth Circuit, 1981.
658 F.2d 1098.

■ JAMES C. HILL, CIRCUIT JUDGE. Merrill Lynch, Pierce, Fenner & Smith, Incorporated (hereinafter Merrill Lynch) brought this action in United States District Court, Middle District of Georgia, to enjoin Reese M. Stidham, III, H. Paige Scarborough, and John A. Bruner (hereinafter defendants) from violating noncompetition and nondisclosure terms in their respective employment contracts. The district court granted the injunction which we vacate in part and affirm in part.

Defendants Stidham, Scarborough, and Bruner were employed by Merrill Lynch on December 30, 1974, March 14, 1977, and June 19, 1978, respectively. Contemporaneous with his hiring, each was placed in an "account executive training program," which involved intensive as well as expensive training at Merrill Lynch's New York headquarters. To these defendants, this program was an absolute necessity: neither Stidham, Scarborough nor Bruner had any prior securities experience, and obviously none of the three defendants met the strict license and registration requirements applicable to dealers in securities. The training period, during which defendants were compensated as salaried employees but generated no income for Merrill Lynch, lasted approximately one-half year. Following licensing, defendants became "account executives" stockbrokers with the Athens, Georgia office of Merrill Lynch.

In connection with his employment, each defendant executed a contract with Merrill Lynch containing two restrictive covenants, which are the essence of this litigation. These promises constitute the first two paragraphs of the agreements between the parties and provide:

> "1. All records of Merrill Lynch, including the names and addresses of its clients, are and shall remain the property of Merrill Lynch at all times during my employment with Merrill Lynch and after termination for any reason of my employment with Merrill Lynch, and that none of such records nor any part of them is to be removed from the premises of Merrill Lynch either in original form or in duplicated or copied form, and that the names, addresses, and other facts in such records are not to be transmitted verbally except in the ordinary course of conducting business for Merrill Lynch.
>
> "2. In the event of termination of my services with Merrill Lynch for any reason, I will not solicit any of the clients of Merrill Lynch whom I served or whose names became known to me while in the employ of Merrill Lynch in any community or city served by the office of Merrill Lynch, or any subsidiary thereof, at which I was employed at any time for a period of one year from the date of termination of my employment. . . ."

Defendants, it is fair to say, were successful with Merrill Lynch. Their salaries prior to their respective resignations from Merrill Lynch ranged from approximately $54,000 to $84,000 per year [high salaries at the time]. Nonetheless, they were receptive when in mid-1980 they were courted by a major southeastern securities firm, Atlanta-based Robinson-Humphrey Company, Incorporated. By August 1980, each had accepted a position with that firm to open and operate its new Athens office. The district court found that prior to informing Merrill Lynch of their plans, defendants duplicated various records containing vital sales information[2] and provided Robinson-Humphrey with client names and addresses so that the latter might dispatch announcements of its new office opening to investors likely to take advantage of it.[3]

On September 12, 1980 defendants resigned. Five days later Merrill Lynch brought suit. . . .

---

[2] These records are known in the securities business as "holding pages." They contain a given customer's name and an inventory of his holdings.

[3] The district court further found that some of Merrill Lynch's clients were "personally contacted, told of the planned opening of a Robinson-Humphrey office and asked to authorize a transfer of securities held by Merrill Lynch to Robinson-Humphrey. Defendant Bruner even went so far as to sign the name (sic) of some of the customers serviced by him to a required transfer form which only the customer can sign."

A. Noncompetition Clause

. . . Through the noncompetition covenant here at issue, then, Merrill Lynch sought no more than to prevent employees it trained at considerable expense from filling the coffers of a competitor by virtue of Merrill Lynch's efforts. . . . The covenant here at issue is reasonable. Nonetheless it fails. The Supreme Court of Georgia has injected a bright-line test into this area by requiring an express geographical description of the territory covered, without reference to the overall reasonableness of the limitation in light of the nature of the profession or trade involved. No such express territorial limitation is found in this covenant. . . .[7]

B. Nondisclosure Clause

In its January 15, 1981 order, the district court permanently enjoined defendants "[f]rom directly or indirectly violating paragraph 1 of the subject contracts by in any way using all or any portion of Merrill Lynch's records copied, extracted, or verbally transmitted by either defendant to Robinson-Humphrey from Merrill Lynch's records. . . ."

Paragraph 1 of the employment agreement contains three clauses, only the first of which ("[a]ll records . . . are and shall remain the property of Merrill Lynch . . . during employment . . . and after termination. . . .) reaches beyond the temporal existence of an employment relationship. The other two clauses, which prohibit removal of records or duplicates as well as verbal transmission of their contents, apply during the employment relationship. The entire paragraph, then, is no more than an agreement between parties (1) fixing title to physical documents and (2) requiring confidentiality during employment. The perpetuality of the title agreement is not offensive nor is the confidentiality agreement unreasonable. The injunction does, however, have a twist to it, which we approve. As a result of the district court's finding blatant breach of paragraph 1 by defendants during the employment relationship, the court enjoined defendants from reaping the benefits of the ill-gotten information into the post-employment period. Thus, while the confidentiality covenant itself was not of perpetual duration, the district court's injunction with regard to nondisclosure is. We decline to disturb the nondisclosure aspect of the injunction. It is not an abuse of discretion and its terms are "peculiarly for the discretion of the district judge sitting as a chancellor." . . .

NOTES

1. Valco Cincinnati, Inc. *v.* N & D Machining Service, Inc., reprinted in Chapter One, above, is similar in effect. Courts typically limit trade secrets injunctions to the defendant's illegal headstart: the period of time it would have taken the defendant to reverse engineer or independently

[7] . . . In [a recent case], the Georgia court reviewed its authorities and concluded that the question . . . was "not an open one." Like the King of Siam, we express some "puzzlement." . . . [W]e would, with deference, suggest a fresh look [at the rule].

develop the plaintiff's secrets process or machine. See 205 Corp. *v.* Brandow, reprinted above. In *Valco*, however, the court held that, when the defendant's theft of secrets was "egregious," a perpetual injunction was within the equitable discretion of the trial court. Thus, the plaintiff ended up with a remedy greater than its legal right.

2. A somewhat different example is Bailey *v.* Proctor, 160 F.2d 78 (1st Cir. 1947). Prior to the Investment Company Act of 1940, there were no limitations on the capital structure of investment trusts. The Aldred Trust, a trust organized before 1940, issued nearly $6 million worth of debentures, which are debt securities, to provide capital for its investments. Debenture holders were entitled to a return of their investments on a set date, plus a fixed rate of interest. They had no voting control over management of the trust. Control was vested in the holders of common stock, who had made a much smaller capital investment in the trust (the owners of common stock at the time of the suit paid about $150,000 for their shares).

This capital structure, which was forbidden (prospectively) by the Investment Company Act of 1940, gave controlling common stock holders a powerful incentive to make risky investments at the expense of debenture holders. If a high-risk investment failed, the owners of common stock would lose at most their small investment in the trust, while debenture holders would lose their much larger investment. If a high-risk investment prospered, the common stock holders would reap the benefit as the equity value of the trust increased, while debenture holders would receive only the agreed return of their initial investment, plus interest.

The Aldred trust became insolvent in the 1930s. In 1944, with the trust still deep in insolvency, the then-controlling stock holder caused the trust to make a large investment in the stock of a race track venture (Eastern Racing Association, which managed Boston's Suffolk Downs). Debenture holders, backed by the Securities and Exchange Commission, sued, alleging gross breach of trust by the controlling stock holder. The district court placed the trust in receivership.

Following the end of World War II, interest in horseracing suddenly revived, the value of the trust's race track shares increased dramatically, and the trust returned to solvency. Meanwhile, Bailey and others purchased the controlling shares in the trust.

In 1946, acting on petitions by the receiver and the SEC, the district court ordered a sale of the race track stock and a liquidation of the trust. Bailey appealed, arguing that because the trust was now solvent and the current management was not corrupt, there was no legal basis for liquidating the trust. The Court of Appeals for the First Circuit affirmed the district court's order:

> "The 'free stock,' representing only a small investment and often no equity, controlled the operations, policies and management of the almost $6,000,000 investment of the debenture holders. The inability to earn interest requirements induces the controlling shareholders to engage in capital appreciation investments or in speculative ventures to insure them a profit in one way or another,

e. g., [the prior holder of the free stock's] activities in the Eastern Racing Association stock. The present holders of the free stock, the appellants here, purchased control of Aldred, which has $5,900,000 principal amount of debentures, for $150,000. Their equity at present shows an appreciation of some $2,500,000 as a result of general market increases and the favorable sale of Eastern Racing Association stock. . . .

"[T]he court could not feel assured that a recurrence of the events leading up to the present receivership was impossible. Insolvency was likely; insufficient earnings to cover interest requirements was possible. In such event, nothing would prevent the controlling shareholders, either appellants or their successors, from embarking on new speculation to the detriment of the debenture holders. The court properly felt that the debenture holders were entitled now to cash salvaged from what had happened to be a doomed enterprise. . . .

"The Act itself does not require the liquidation or reorganization of existing investment companies which do not conform to the new statutory standards. But when a court of equity has exercised its jurisdiction to appoint receivers of an investment company pursuant to a complaint charging gross abuse of trust on the part of the trustees or officers, we deem it proper for the court, in determining what would be the appropriate remedy in order to afford complete relief, to take account of the fact that the capital structure is not in conformity with the standards and safeguards which Congress has now written into law. That fact, in conjunction with the other facts in the case, may well render it fair and equitable to require the liquidation of the company . . . ."

Id. at 83.

Did the court's order match the debenture holders' legal rights?

C. PROPHYLACTIC INJUNCTIONS

Equal Employment Opportunity Commission v. Wilson Metal Casket Co.

United States Court of Appeals, Sixth Circuit, 1994.
24 F.3d 836.

■ KEITH, CIRCUIT JUDGE. . . . Wilson Metal, a Tennessee corporation owned and operated by Elmer Wilson ("Wilson"), hired William Ellis on January 11, 1974 and Barbara Ellis on August 6, 1979. William and Barbara are married. Wilson Metal employed Dawn Bryan McMullan ("McMullan") on April 20, 1987.

In 1982, while Barbara Ellis' husband was on temporary medical leave, Wilson relocated Barbara's work station to a building separate from the main plant. Wilson repeatedly followed Barbara Ellis as she walked through the building and whenever she reached an isolated spot he grabbed her, held her, kissed her, and fondled her, touching her breasts and buttocks. He also made sexual comments, requested she meet him after working hours, and forced her to accompany him to isolated areas of the plant and to perform oral sex on him. When William Ellis returned to work, Wilson moved Barbara Ellis' work station back to the main plant and stopped demanding oral sex. The sexual harassment, however, continued.

On September 18, 1984, William Ellis phoned Wilson at home and said he knew Wilson was having an affair with his wife and demanded that it stop. Wilson's wife overheard her husband's side of the conversation and became upset. Wilson announced the incident at a meeting of his employees, including the Ellises. The Ellises denied any allegations of a sexual relationship between Wilson and Barbara Ellis. Wilson, however, fired the Ellises and gave them separation slips which stated they were terminated because of the telephone call and its effect upon Mrs. Wilson.

In 1987, Dawn McMullan worked for Wilson Metal for approximately three months. During McMullan's employment, anytime she was in isolated parts of the plant, Wilson fondled her breasts and buttocks, and sexually propositioned her. In July 1987, McMullan telephoned Wilson and told him she was not coming to work that day because of his continued sexual advances. Wilson told her she was terminated.

On October 31, 1984, William and Barbara Ellis filed separate charges with the EEOC alleging Wilson Metal discriminated against them and other female employees by either subjecting them to sexual harassment or retaliating against their protests of sexual harassment in violation of Title VII. After an investigation, the EEOC found reason to believe: (1) Wilson Metal had sexually harassed Barbara Ellis; (2) Wilson Metal discharged William and Barbara Ellis because they objected to Wilson's sexual harassment; (3) Wilson engaged in a common practice of making sexual advances toward female employees; and (4) at least two other female employees were forced to quit because of Wilson's advances.

[Following a trial in federal district court, the court awarded backpay to the discharged employees and entered an injunction against Elmer Wilson.]

Wilson Metal argues the injunction . . . is overly broad and enjoins lawful conduct. Specifically, the injunction enjoins Wilson from "asking any female employee to accompany him off the premises of the Company unless accompanied by at least one other employee, and kissing or placing his hands on any female employee in the work place." None of this conduct, according to Appellant is, in and of itself, unlawful.

A district court has broad discretionary powers to craft an injunction to the specific violations found to ensure that the employer complies with the law. The proper scope of an injunction is to enjoin conduct which has been found to have been pursued or is related to the proven unlawful conduct. "In fashioning relief against a party who has transgressed the governing legal standard, a court of equity is free to proscribe activities that, standing alone, would have been unassailable."

In the instant case, a distinct pattern of sexual harassment emerged. Wilson either waited until female employees were alone with him in isolated portions of the facilities or transferred them to isolated areas. Once they were isolated, he grabbed them and fondled their breasts and buttocks. With Barbara Ellis, in addition to unwanted fondling, Wilson forced her to engage in oral sex and sexual intercourse. Wilson also sexually propositioned female employees and asked them to accompany him off the company's premises. Based on this pattern of behavior, the injunction appropriately enjoins conduct which allowed sexual harassment to occur. Thus, the district court did not abuse its discretion. . . .

Zappaunbulso v. Zappaunbulso

Superior Court of New Jersey, Appellate Division, 2004.
367 N.J. Super. 216.

■ REISNER, J.A.D. This case presents the novel issue whether a trial court may order a defendant, already subject to a restraining order under the Prevention of Domestic Violence Act, to move out of a house in the victim's neighborhood. In this case defendant had rented the house and moved in, despite a pending motion by his ex-wife to preclude him from doing so. The trial judge ordered him to move out of the house within thirty days because defendant had a history of stalking and harassing his ex-wife and the trial judge found that his purpose in moving into her neighborhood was to continue his course of harassment. We affirm. . . .

Plaintiff Alisa Zappaunbulso (n/k/a Trombetta) (plaintiff) and Defendant Anthony Zappaunbulso (defendant) were married in 1993. In April 2001, plaintiff filed for divorce on grounds of extreme cruelty.

On June 29, 2001, plaintiff sought a temporary restraining order (TRO) against defendant, claiming that he was harassing her. She alleged that he came home intoxicated after midnight, yelled and screamed at her when she refused his sexual advances, and threatened to "get even" with her. As part of her TRO application, plaintiff also certified to a past history of domestic violence. She alleged that several months before this incident, defendant kicked down the door while she was inside the bathroom. Defendant also threw chairs and other furniture at her in front of their two young children and would kick, punch or throw objects in her presence when he was angry. He constantly criticized and verbally abused her and would scream at her for no reason. Plaintiff also stated that, at times, the defendant would try to control her by following her throughout the house, restricting her ability to leave or take the children with her outside of the house.

As a result of the June 29, 2001 application, plaintiff was granted temporary custody of the children and exclusive possession of the marital residence. Defendant was barred from the residence and prohibited from harassing or stalking plaintiff. However, on July 19, 2001, after a final hearing, the trial court dismissed the domestic violence complaint and vacated the restraining order.

On July 24, 2001, plaintiff filed another domestic violence complaint and received a temporary restraining order on the basis of harassment by the defendant. She alleged that after the hearing on July 19, 2001, defendant called her cell phone multiple times throughout the day without leaving a message and then called the house telephone at 12:30 a.m. . . . Four days later, defendant appeared at the house without notice and demanded access. Later that day, he called plaintiff numerous times on her cell phone from 10:25 p.m. to 1:24 a.m. without leaving a message. When he called the house telephone at 1:28 a.m., she answered because she did not want the phone to wake up the children. At that time defendant stated that he wished to see the children on Wednesday. When plaintiff informed him that he was not to call the house at unreasonable times and that he had to give notice before visiting the house, he screamed at her and told her that he could call and visit whenever he wanted. Plaintiff, shaken and fearful, had a friend stay with her through the night.

As a result of the July 24, 2001 complaint, an order was entered again granting plaintiff temporary custody of the children and exclusive possession of the marital residence. Defendant was prohibited from any further acts of domestic violence; he was barred from the residence and plaintiff's parents' residence and prohibited from contacting, harassing or stalking the plaintiff. In addition, defendant could not visit the children but could telephone them from 6:00 p.m. to 7:00 p.m. daily. Defendant was restricted to calling the plaintiff's cell phone only to alert her that he would be calling the children so that she would have them answer the telephone.

On August 1, 2001, the domestic violence complaint was dismissed incident to the settlement of the divorce case, and the restraints were incorporated into a consent order entered in the divorce action. Under the terms of the consent order, plaintiff was awarded sole possession of the house. Defendant was permitted visitation with the children from Tuesday, 4:30 p.m. to Wednesday, 8:30 a.m. and Friday, 4:30 p.m. to Sunday, 6:00 p.m. He was required to pick-up and drop-off the children at the curbside of the marital residence; plaintiff was to stay inside the house during drop-off and pick-up. Defendant could only call plaintiff on her cell phone to discuss the children or to speak to the children from 9:00 a.m. to 8:00 p.m., although the children were able to call the defendant at any time. These restrictions on visitation and communication with the children were incorporated into the final judgment of divorce, which was entered on April 25, 2002.

On March 3, 2003, plaintiff filed another domestic violence complaint and another temporary restraining order was issued against defendant. Plaintiff alleged that defendant appeared outside her house "screaming, cursing and calling [her] crazy," and that he called her house and cell phone repeatedly. Defendant also made derogatory comments about her in the children's presence and threatened, in front of the children, that he would call the police and have her arrested. Plaintiff recited a history of additional abuse, alleging that defendant drove by her house often, banged on her garage door and looked through her front door window. He called plaintiff and screamed at her, threatening that he was going to take the children away from her. He would also appear and confront plaintiff at the children's school and at their dental appointments.

As a result of the March 3, 2003 complaint, defendant was again prohibited from further acts of domestic violence. He was barred from plaintiff's place of employment and from going to her residence, except for the curbside pick-up and drop-off of the children. He was prohibited from leaving the car during pick-up or drop-off. Defendant was also prohibited from communicating with, harassing or stalking plaintiff.

On March 12, 2003, Judge Allen-Jackson entered a Final Restraining Order continuing all of the previously imposed restraints. Defendant was also specifically prohibited from parking in plaintiff's neighbor's driveway and watching her home. The Children's Bill of Rights was incorporated in the order, specifying that the children would not be asked to "choose sides" between the parties, not be told about the divorce proceedings, and not be told "bad things" about the other parent.

In April 2003, plaintiff became aware that defendant might be planning to move into a house in her neighborhood. . . . On April 10, 2003, plaintiff's attorney filed a motion to enforce litigant's rights to "prohibit the defendant from moving into a house approximately two blocks and four homes away from the plaintiff." Plaintiff . . . alleged that her house and 20 Daytona Drive are located within the same housing development in Sewell, Gloucester County, and that the defendant's proposed residence had a direct sight line to plaintiff's house. In her certification in support of the motion, she attested that defendant made the following threats to her:

a. "I'm moving on your street whenever a house goes up for sale;"

b. "I'm gonna be your neighbor. You'll see I'll get you;"

c. "Once I get a house near you, I'm going back to court to fight for custody, that way the kids won't have to change schools."

. . . On April 17, 2003, the defendant, pro se, filed an order to show cause seeking permission to move into 20 Daytona Drive. His papers acknowledged that plaintiff's motion to bar him from moving in was scheduled for May 2, 2003. Judge Allen-Jackson refused to entertain the order to show cause. Instead of waiting for a decision on the May 2, 2003 motion, defendant signed a lease on 20 Daytona Drive on April 23, 2003.

At the May 2, 2003 hearing . . . defendant appeared pro se. He contended he had searched for housing elsewhere, but could not find anything else as affordable and convenient. He denied that plaintiff's house was visible from his house or that they would need to pass each other's houses in order to enter or leave the housing development. He contended that his purpose in moving to Daytona Drive was not to harass his ex-wife, but to be closer to his children. He stated:

> "My children can walk to this home, they have friends here, . . . and here they know the children. So, all they have to do is leave their mother's home, stay on this sidewalk, ride their bikes or walk, come up to here, turn and go right to [defendant's house]."

. . . Judge Allen-Jackson noted that the parties were last before her as a result of the defendant stalking and harassing the plaintiff, and on that occasion defendant had been parked in a neighbor's driveway and watching plaintiff's house. Judge Allen-Jackson concluded that "[n]ow it appears that every time she wants to leave in order to go some place she's got to pass by [his house] in order to get back to the main street." She found forcing plaintiff to drive past defendant's house would violate the intent of the restraining order and would be intimidating, in violation of the Prevention of Domestic Violence Act. The court found that plaintiff would feel harassed or stalked every time she had to pass defendant's house. She also did not believe defendant's purported reasons for moving into the neighborhood. . . .

Based on these findings, Judge Allen-Jackson executed an order restraining the defendant from residing at 20 Daytona Drive, Sewell, New Jersey and ordered him to vacate the residence in thirty days.

Domestic violence is a serious problem in our society. Described as a "pattern of abusive and controlling behavior injurious to its victims," domestic violence "persists as a grave threat to the family, particularly to women and children.

Pursuant to the Prevention of Domestic Violence Act (the Act), harassment is an act of domestic violence. The statute on harassment states a person commits a petty disorderly persons offense if, with purpose to harass another, he . . . (c) [e]ngages in any other course of alarming conduct or of repeatedly committed acts with purpose to alarm or seriously annoy such other person. . . .

Remedies under the Act are liberally construed for the protection and safety of the victims and the public at large. Accordingly, upon finding a violation of the Act, the court shall grant any relief necessary to prevent further abuse.

Specific remedies listed in the Act, include an order restraining the defendant from further acts of domestic violence, granting plaintiff possession of the marital residence, and restricting the defendant from communicating, stalking or harassing the victim. The Act further authorizes

> (6) An order restraining the defendant from entering the residence, property, school, or place of employment of the victim or of other family or household members of the victim *and requiring the defendant to stay away from any specified place that is named in the order and is frequented regularly by the victim or other family or household members.*

... Given defendant's documented history of stalking and harassing his ex-wife, and the restraining order limiting his access to the children, we conclude that Judge Allen-Jackson properly enjoined him from residing in plaintiff's immediate neighborhood. . . .

CPC International, Inc. v. Skippy Inc.

United States Court of Appeals, Fourth Circuit, 2000.
214 F.3d 456.

■ WILKINSON, CHIEF JUDGE. This case involves a protracted dispute over the use of the trademark SKIPPY. . . .

In 1923, Percy L. Crosby created a cartoon featuring a school-aged child named Skippy. The cartoon was syndicated and the Skippy character was marketed in cartoon books, magazine articles, and novels. Crosby obtained a federal trademark SKIPPY for cartoons depicting the humorous juvenile character. This mark was transferred to appellant Skippy, Incorporated, sometime after 1932. Appellant Joan Crosby Tibbetts is Percy Crosby's daughter and the current president of Skippy. Skippy currently owns a trademark SKIPPY for the cartoon comic strip.

CPC International and its predecessors have sold peanut butter in the United States under the trademark SKIPPY since 1933. CPC owns a federal trademark SKIPPY for peanut butter.

In 1986, CPC brought suit alleging that Skippy had engaged in trademark infringement and unfair competition. Skippy had licensed the right to use "the word mark SKIPPY, the comic strip SKIPPY, [and] the fanciful character SKIPPY" on the packaging of caramel corn, popcorn, and nuts. The district court found that the use of the mark SKIPPY on caramel corn or any other food product constituted trademark infringement because it would create a likelihood of confusion with CPC's trademark in SKIPPY Peanut Butter.

Accordingly, the district court issued an order (the 1986 order) that enjoined Skippy and Joan Tibbetts (1) "from continuing to offer to license, offer to sell, distribute, advertise or promote a caramel corn and peanut product or any other food product under the trademark SKIPPY or any mark confusingly similar thereto"; and (2) "from communicating in any manner with anyone that [Skippy's] rights in the trademark SKIPPY include the right to use SKIPPY on peanut butter and food products and, conversely, that CPC has no rights in the SKIPPY trademark in connection with these products."

In 1997, Skippy registered the domain name Skippy.com. The web site recounted the "Life and Times" of Percy Crosby, including his childhood, military career, and the popular success enjoyed by the Skippy cartoon character. It also included stories of an FBI investigation, "CPC's Malicious Prosecution," and "CPC's Fraud on the Courts." A "legal notice" on the web site stated "SKIPPY and the image of the character SKIPPY are trademarks and copyrights of SKIPPY, INC. Neither these marks nor the copyrighted works of Percy Crosby may be used without the permission of SKIPPY, INC."

[In 1999, CPC asked the district court to hold Skippy and Tibbetts in contempt for violation of the 1986 order. In response, the district court issued a second order (the 1999 order) requiring Skippy and Tibbetts to remove about ten pages of material from the Skippy.com web site. The 1999 order also provided that in case of future violations the court would impose a $500 per day damage award against Skippy and Tibbetts.]

We find that the district court's injunctive decree suffers from two related deficiencies. First, the injunction fails to comply with the terms of Fed. R. Civ. P. 65(d). Second, the injunction's substantial overbreadth raises serious First Amendment concerns. We shall address each of these problems in turn. . . .

The district court's 1999 order . . . silences a substantial quantity of speech from Skippy's web site, including commentary on the ongoing litigation and the alleged mistreatment of Skippy cartoon creator Percy Crosby. Yet the district court does not explain how these statements violate the 1986 order. There are no findings that relate the redacted statements to the 1986 order. Nor are there any reasons given for issuance of the injunction. What is to be removed is clear from the order; however, the reason for redacting these materials is not. Such a terse and sweeping injunction does not comply with the requirements of Rule 65(d).

It is not clear to us how Skippy's web site violated either part of the 1986 order. The 1986 order first enjoined Skippy from offering to license or promote "a caramel corn and peanut product or any other food product under the trademark SKIPPY or any mark confusingly similar thereto." There is no allegation here that Skippy has licensed or sold its trademark for the promotion or packaging of any food product.

The 1986 order also enjoined Skippy from "communicating in any manner" that its rights in the SKIPPY trademark "include the right to use SKIPPY on peanut butter and food products and, conversely, that CPC has no rights in the SKIPPY trademark in connection with these products." CPC makes much of the fact that some of the redacted statements are false and allege that CPC "pirated" and "stole" the SKIPPY trademark. The web site at various points claims that CPC's ownership of the trademark SKIPPY was procured by wrongful actions. Yet rather than denying CPC's ownership of the mark, these comments presuppose that CPC now owns the trademark SKIPPY for peanut butter and food products. The statements largely reflect Ms. Tibbetts' opinion that CPC's ownership is unjust and that it was made possible only through decades of "predatory conduct." . . . [For example, the] redacted portions include the following statements:

> "During this time, Crosby's famous Skippy trademark and its valuable good will was pirated by a bankrupt peanut butter company, which later merged with a Fortune 500 company, making a fortune in illicit sales under the Skippy brand name."
>
> "Percy Crosby referred to the NRA as Roosevelt's 'New Russian Administration,' unaware that it was by means of the NRA peanut butter code that a bankrupt California food packer (Rosefield) would steal Skippy and make a fortune. . . ."

The district court also ordered Skippy to remove statements discussing the pending lawsuit:

> "Immediately after the release of this web site, CPC filed a motion in court to silence Joan Crosby Tibbetts from publishing the true story of Skippy. Ms. Tibbetts is in need of your support to help protect the property rights of Skippy that her father lived and died to preserve. For more information on how you can help, please email Joan Crosby Tibbetts. Your support of Skippy is very much appreciated!"

. . . Further, the district court ordered removal of a Skippy cartoon reprinted from Life magazine with the added caption "Why is [CPC] bullying the little Skippy once again?" It is unclear how these comments and cartoons concerning the litigation between Skippy and CPC relate to the proscribed conduct, because they seem mainly to solicit assistance with pending litigation and to criticize CPC for its legal actions. . . .

The absence of proper findings serves to illuminate a further defect in the district court's order. The injunction against Skippy is not narrowly tailored to remedy specific violations of the 1986 order. As such it implicates serious First Amendment concerns. . . .

The Supreme Court has recognized the risks of overbroad injunctions, especially when First Amendment considerations are at stake. An injunction must "burden no more speech than necessary to serve a significant government interest." Injunctions must be narrowly tailored and should prohibit only unlawful conduct. An "order must be tailored as precisely as possible to the exact needs of the case."

The district court failed to articulate any correlation between the redactions and the government's interest in enforcing trademark law. The basic objectives of trademark law are to encourage product differentiation, promote the production of quality goods, and provide consumers with information about the quality of goods. It is hard to see what "significant government interest" is served here. CPC's trademark has not been used for any commercial gain, nor has the trademark been used in a way that confuses the public. In the 1986 case, the district court found that when Skippy licensed the SKIPPY trademark for use on food products this constituted unfair competition because of the possibility of confusion between the caramel corn products and CPC's Skippy Peanut Butter. The web site, however, does not create any such confusion between the Skippy cartoon character and Skippy Peanut Butter. While there certainly is a strong state interest in preventing trademark infringement and unfair competition, there has been no finding that suppressing significant portions of Skippy's web site serves such an interest.

First Amendment interests are at stake here because Ms. Tibbetts tells her side of the story on the Skippy web site—how a big corporation worked to steal her father's cartoon trademark and then used the trademark to make a fortune. This is an admittedly partisan account and one that vexes CPC. Yet just because speech is critical of a corporation and its business practices is not a sufficient reason to enjoin the speech. As the First Circuit stated, if a trademark owner could "enjoin the use of his mark in a noncommercial context found to be negative or offensive, then a corporation could shield itself from criticism by forbidding the use of its name in commentaries critical of its conduct." . . .

D. DAMAGES IN COMBINATION WITH INJUNCTIVE RELIEF

Hutton v. Gliksberg

California Court of Appeal, 1982.
128 Cal. App. 3d 240.

■ ASHBY, ASSOCIATE JUSTICE. Plaintiffs Brian G. Hutton and Albert S. Ruddy (hereinafter Buyers) brought this action against defendants Mike and Sheina Gliksberg (hereinafter Sellers) to compel specific performance of a contract for the purchase and sale of real property. The trial court granted a judgment in favor of Buyers, compelling Sellers to convey the property and awarding incidental compensation. Sellers appeal.

On March 3, 1977, the parties executed a written contract for the purchase and sale of an apartment building at 426–428 Spaulding Drive in Beverly Hills, California, for $750,000. [Buyers agreed to pay $250,000 in cash and obtain a $400,000 loan, secured by a first mortgage. Sellers agreed to provide an additional loan of $100,000, secured by a second mortgage. The parties] executed escrow instructions dated March 7 which called for escrow to close on or before April 21, 1977, time being of the essence. As of April 21, Buyers had performed their obligations but

Sellers had not provided escrow with the necessary documents. On April 22, Sellers, in writing, canceled the escrow. . . .

In addition to ordering Sellers to convey the property, the trial court made a monetary award to buyers, totaling $122,219, to compensate Buyers for the fact that at the time specified for performance in the contract, Buyers had a loan commitment for $400,000 at 9 1/4 percent interest, whereas at the time of the judgment, prevailing mortgage rates were 14 percent. . . .[6]

In California the compensation which may be awarded incident to a decree of specific performance is not for breach of contract and is not legal damages. The complainant affirms the contract and asks that it be performed. Since the time for performance has passed, the court relates that performance back to that date, by treating the parties as if the change in ownership had taken place at that time. Thus the buyer is entitled to the rents and profits from the time the contract should have been performed, and the seller is entitled to an offset for the interest on the purchase money which he would have received had the contract been performed. The process is more like an accounting between the parties than an assessment of damages. . . . We have found no California case which upholds an award, incident to specific performance, in the nature of the award granted here

However, we conclude that in the circumstances of this case Buyers should receive compensation for the difference in interest rates. Specific performance is an action in equity. In a world of change, equitable remedies have been expanded to meet increasing complexities. Equity is not bound by rigid precedent, but has the flexibility to adjust the remedy in order to do right and justice. Recent decisions in other states have approved this sort of award, and we conclude such an award is justified in this case. . . .

Sellers obviously knew that the purchase was being financed because the contract provided for Buyers to procure a new first trust deed loan for $400,000 at current rates and charges, and for Sellers to provide a $100,000 second trust deed loan with an interest rate 1/4 percent more than the interest on the first trust deed loan. The first trust deed lender, Santa Fe Federal Savings, notified escrow on April 4, 1977, that the loan had been approved. We reject Sellers' contention that it was not reasonably within the contemplation of the parties that if Sellers delayed or refused to convey the property, Buyers could be subjected to a higher interest rate. We do not agree with Sellers that this increased cost is remote and collateral to the contract, as was found with respect to the buyers' increased cost of renting other premises in [a prior case]. . . .

---

[6] This was calculated as follows: Monthly payments on a $400,000 loan for 30 years at 14 percent would be $4,739.49; monthly payments on a $400,000 loan for 30 years at 9 1/4 percent would be $3,290.70. The difference, $1,448.79 per month over a period of 30 years would be $521,564.40. The present value of $521,564.40 payable over 30 years discounted at 14 percent, is $122,219.

Moreover, in this case, Sellers were to make a $100,000 loan at an interest rate 1/4 percent higher than Buyers' rate on the first trust deed loan. By refusing to perform until a later time when interest rates are much higher, Sellers obtain a higher rate of return on their loan. In effect, Sellers would profit by their own wrong. Equity cannot permit this.

Thus we conclude that the trial court was empowered to grant compensation to Buyers, incidental to specific performance, for the differential in interest rates. Sellers contend, however, that . . . Buyers will not actually suffer the amount of damages calculated by the court unless Buyers hold the property for the entire 30-year term of the loan, and that Buyers can reap a windfall profit at the expense of Sellers by reselling the property any time sooner than 30 years. We disagree. . . .

[I]f in the future Buyers resell the property subject to a 14 percent or higher loan, they will get a lower purchase price than if they could resell the property subject to a 9 1/4 percent loan. . . .

Furthermore, we foresee tremendous practical difficulties in attempting to fashion a remedy which would involve Sellers in providing partial financing to Buyers over an indefinite period of time or which could require the parties to come back to court if Buyers resold or refinanced the property. We conclude the trial court acted properly in calculating the amount of compensation.

NOTE

In negotiations for a sale of lakefront property by the Forsters to the Bosses, the Forsters represented that the Bosses would be able to obtain a boat dock permit. This representation was false because the Forsters possessed a conflicting permit, which they intended to retain. The Forsters also promised to remove a swim dock, which they failed to remove. The trial court ordered the Forsters to yield up their boat dock permit and remove the swim dock. A jury also awarded $12,250 as consequential damages, based on the difference in the values of the property with and without a boat dock permit and the cost of removing the swim dock. Is this a sensible combination of remedies? See Forster *v.* Boss, 97 F.3d 1127 (8th Cir. 1996).

I. H. P. Corp. v. 210 Central Park South Corp.

Court of Appeals of New York, 1963.
12 N.Y.2d 329.

■ BURKE, JUDGE. . . . The facts alleged were that plaintiff was the lessee in possession of the street level floor in the building of one of the defendants; that all of the defendants caused the premises to be broken into at night on two occasions during which certain damage was done to the leasehold; that each time barriers were placed on the means of access to bar plaintiff from the premises, all with the purpose of harassing plaintiff into surrendering its valuable lease; that similar acts will occur in the future unless restrained by the court. The relief requested was an injunction and . . . "$5,000 plus exemplary damages besides injunction."

Defendants challenge the propriety of the award, not as a matter of the law of damages but rather on the procedural ground that "the function of a court of equity goes no further than to award compensatory damages as incidental to injunctive relief: it may not assess exemplary damages." Defendants' position, aside from the right to a jury trial, which we think is waived here, is based on an erroneous concept of the court system of this State. We have one court of general jurisdiction which administers *all* of New York law, be that law of legal or equitable origin. Therefore, defendants are mistaken when they suggest that a Justice of the Supreme Court of the State of New York cannot apply a particular principle of New York law to a case before him for decision where that principle is properly applicable to the facts as determined. The court in Dunkel *v.* McDonald (272 App. Div. 267, affd. on other issues, 298 N.Y. 586), which the Appellate Division overruled in reaching its conclusion in this case, mistook the issue in stating that "The court has no power in an action in equity to award exemplary or punitive damages. . . . The function of a court of equity goes no further than to award as incidental to other relief, or in lieu thereof, compensatory damages; it may not assess exemplary damages." This, as we have said, presupposes a court intrinsically limited to granting remedies solely equitable in historical origin. There is no such court in this State.

No amount of authority in other States should persuade us that Judge Cardozo was wrong when he said "The whole body of principles, whether of law or of equity, bearing on the case, becomes the reservoir to be drawn upon by the court in enlightening its judgment." Maitland expressed the same view when he predicted that "The day will come when lawyers will cease to inquire whether a given rule be a rule of equity or a rule of common law; suffice it that it is a well-established rule administered by the High Court of Justice." (Maitland, EQUITY [1909], p. 20.) Needless to say, we have accepted Maitland's and Judge Cardozo's understanding of the consequences of the merger. . . .

Assuming that defendants had a constitutional right to a jury trial of the issues of fact supporting the award of exemplary damages (an assumption which is not free from uncertainty), it is clear that the failure to move to separately state and number the causes of action or to demand a jury trial constituted a waiver of any such right. . . .

The judgment should, therefore, be affirmed, without costs.

NOTE

Traditionally, punitive damages are not available in equity. In Superior Construction Co. *v.* Elmo, 204 Md. 1 (1954), the court reversed an award of punitive damages made in conjunction with a decree enjoining a continuing trespass. According to the appellate court, the Elmos had waived any claim to punitive damages by bringing their case in equity. Moreover, the court continued, it would be inappropriate for equity courts to award "clean-up" damages without statutory authorization because "equity will permit only what is just and right with no element of vengeance." *Id.* at 20. For further discussion of punitive damages in equity, see note 6 on p. 895.

CHAPTER 9

SPECIFIC PERFORMANCE OF CONTRACTS

In the days of separate law and equity courts, the legal remedy in an action for breach of contract was damages. When damages were deemed to be inadequate, an equity court could order the defendant to perform the contract according to its terms. Because specific performance was historically an equitable remedy, courts continue to invoke equitable doctrines in determining whether to grant or deny this remedy, as illustrated by the materials in this chapter.

A. STANDARDS FOR GRANTING SPECIFIC PERFORMANCE

1. ADEQUACY OF LEGAL REMEDIES

Tower City Grain Co. v. Richman

Supreme Court of North Dakota, 1975.
232 N.W.2d 61.

■ PEDERSON, JUDGE. . . . The Richmans entered into an oral contract to sell 10,000 bushels of 58-pound test weight wheat to Tower City Grain. The terms of the contract are in dispute. The Richmans contend that . . . the contract was entered into on or about December 15, 1972. Tower City Grain contends that . . . the date of the contract was January 2, 1973. . . . It is undisputed that there was no date set for the delivery of the grain. Delivery was to be made upon availability of storage or rail transportation [as determined by Tower City Grain]. . . .

The Richmans testified that they made repeated inquiries throughout the spring and summer of 1973 concerning the delivery of the grain. On each of these occasions, the Richmans were told either that they were next on the list or that the elevator was full and no boxcars were available for shipment.

The Richmans contend that Tower City Grain was accepting grain deliveries from other farmers during this time period. Tower City Grain argues that the grain accepted was for resale as seed or to fill contracts that had been entered into prior to the contract with the Richmans.

Tower City Grain pointed out that this method of buying grain had been its custom for almost forty years. It did agree, however, that the time lag between the date of the contract and the date it called for delivery was unusual, but noted that in times of boxcar shortages such delays did occur. The Richmans admitted that they had been doing business with Tower City Grain for over thirty years and that this was the customary transaction between the parties, but also stated that they had never waited for such a long time to deliver their grain. Tower City Grain alleges that the Richmans were asked to deliver the grain on July 17, 1973. The Richmans contend that the actual date was much later than July 17, possibly not until September of 1973.

The Richmans refused to deliver the 10,000 bushels of wheat to Tower City Grain because the delay in calling for delivery of the grain constituted a breach of the contract. Tower City Grain then brought this action for specific performance of the oral contract. . . .

On September 27, 1974, the court rendered a memorandum decision. . . . [T]he trial court found that on or about January 2, 1973, the parties entered into an oral agreement to sell 10,000 bushels of 58-pound test weight wheat for $2.25 per bushel, that delivery was to be made upon availability of storage and/or rail transportation, and that this course of dealing and usage of trade was customary in the business of both parties. The court further found that in reliance upon the oral contract Tower City Grain entered into an agreement to sell the wheat to a third party and that the Richmans still retained the 10,000 bushels of wheat.

The trial court then ordered judgment in favor of Tower City Grain granting specific performance of the contract. . . .

[Section] 41–02–95, N.D.C.C. (§ 2–716 of the Uniform Commercial Code), is controlling in the instant case and states, in part:

> "1. Specific performance may be decreed where the goods are unique or in other proper circumstances.
>
> "2. The decree for specific performance may include such terms and conditions as to payment of the price, damages, or other relief as the court may deem just."

While the Richman's contention that fungible goods were not a proper subject for the remedy of specific relief under prior laws is correct, the adoption of the Uniform Commercial Code in 1966 liberalized the discretion of the trial court to grant specific performance in a greater number of situations. The Official Comment to § 2–716, provides in pertinent part:

> "1. The present section continues in general prior policy as to specific performance and injunction against breach. However, without intending to impair in any way the exercise of the court's sound discretion in the matter, this Article seeks to further a more liberal attitude than some courts have shown in connection with the specific performance of contracts of sale.
>
> "2. In view of this Article's emphasis on the commercial feasibility of replacement, a new concept of what are 'unique' goods is introduced under this section. Specific performance is no longer limited to goods which are already specific or ascertained at the time of contracting. The test of uniqueness

under this section must be made in terms of the total situation which characterizes the contract."

In addition, § 41–01–06 (1–106), N.D.C.C., states that "the remedies provided by this title shall be liberally administered to the end that the aggrieved party may be put in as good a position as if the other party had fully performed . . . ." We cannot presume that an award of damages fails to put an aggrieved party in as good a position as if the other party had fully performed. . . . There was no finding or conclusion to that effect by the trial court in this case.

A complaint which prays for the equitable remedy of specific performance must clearly show that the legal remedy of damages is inadequate. A defendant should not be deprived of a jury trial, to which he would be entitled in an action at law, unless the plaintiff is clearly entitled to the equitable remedy he seeks.

Historically, specific performance, which is an equitable remedy, was applied primarily to contracts relating to goods which were 'unique.' All real estate was deemed to be unique, and so were goods which had sentimental value as distinguished from market value. Another basis for invoking specific performance was the inadequacy of the remedy at law. . . .

Our examination of the record discloses no evidence upon which such finding could be based. The fact that the complaint prayed for specific performance and that the Richmans have in their possession the type and quantity of wheat called for in the contract are not adequate to support such finding. . . .

Without holding that specific performance can never be invoked to enforce a contract for grain or other fungible goods, we conclude that it was a manifest abuse of discretion and an error as a matter of law for the trial court to grant such remedy under the circumstances of this case. . . .

NOTES

1. If Tower City Grain wants specific performance, why not grant the remedy?

2. Bromage sued Genning in equity for specific performance of a covenant to lease land. In response, Genning obtained a writ of prohibition (an order directing another court not to exceed its authority) from the Court of King's Bench. As Chief Justice Coke saw it, a decree ordering specific performance would "subvert the intent of the covenantor, for he intends to be at his election either to lose the damages or to make the lease . . . ." Bromage *v.* Genning, 1 Rolle 368, 81 Eng. Rep. 540 (K.B. 1616).

Kitchen v. Herring

Supreme Court of North Carolina, 1851.
42 N.C. 190.

■ PEARSON, J. In December 1846, the defendant, Herring, executed a contract in writing in these words, "Rec'd. of John L. Kitchen payment in full for a certain tract of land lying on the South west side of Black River, adjoining the lands of William Haffland and Martial, for which I am to give him a good deed etc." The defendant Pridgen wrote the contract and is a subscribing witness. The plaintiff was put into possession in March 1847. Pridgen united with him; and the other defendant, Musgrove, under a contract with Pridgen, with a large number of hands, commenced cutting down the timber, which constitutes the chief value of the land. Pridgen was the surety of the plaintiff, to a note of $325, given payable at three months for the price of the land. In January, Herring executed a deed for the land to Pridgen, and under this title the plaintiff was turned out of possession.

The prayer of the Bill is for a specific performance, for an account of the profits and for an injunction. After the Bill was filed, an arrangement was made, by which Musgrove continued his operations in getting timber, and agreed to account with the successful party. . . .

It was further insisted, that, as it appears by the plaintiff's own showing, that "the land is chiefly valuable on account of the timber," this case does not come within the principle, on which a specific performance is decreed.

The position is new, and the Counsel admitted, that there was no authority to sustain it, but he contended with earnestness, that it was so fully sustained by "the reason of the thing," as to justify a departure from a well settled rule of this Court under the maxim, *cessante ratione cessat lex* [the reason for the law ceasing, the law ceases].

The argument failed wholly to prove, that "the reason of the thing" called for an exception. The principle in regard to land was adopted, not because it was fertile or rich in minerals, or *valuable for timber,* but simply because it was *land*—a favorite and favored subject in England, and every country of Anglo Saxon origin. Our constitution gives to land preeminence over every other species of property; and our law, whether administered in Courts of law or of equity, gives to it the same preference. Land, whether rich or poor, cannot be taken to pay debts until the personal property is exhausted. Contracts concerning land must be in writing. Land must be sold at the Court House, must be conveyed by deeds duly registered, and other instances "too tedious to mention." The principle is, that land is *assumed* to have a peculiar value, so as to give an equity for a specific performance, without reference to its quality or quantity. The same is assumed as to slaves, while in regard to other property, less favored, a specific performance will not be decreed, unless there be peculiar circumstances; for, if with the money, an article of the same description can be bought in market—corn, cotton, etc., the remedy at law is adequate. . . .

NOTE

1. For a rare contrary decision, see Suchan *v.* Rutherford, 90 Idaho 288 (1966) (denying specific performance of a contract to buy farm land of a type that was "common to the general area," frequently traded, and comparatively easy to value).

2. Most courts hold that specific performance is available to both parties to a land sale contract. Initially, the reason given was "mutuality of remedy," a supposed requirement of remedial symmetry. Modern courts are likely to cite the difficulties entailed in marketing real property and in proving market value as reasons to grant specific performance to sellers.

Laclede Gas Co. v. Amoco Oil Co.

United States Court of Appeals, Eighth Circuit, 1975.
522 F.2d 33.

■ ROSS, CIRCUIT JUDGE. . . . On September 21, 1970, Midwest Missouri Gas Company (now Laclede), and American Oil Company (now Amoco), the predecessors of the parties to this litigation, entered into a written agreement which was designed to provide central propane gas distribution systems to various residential developments in Jefferson County, Missouri, until such time as natural gas mains were extended into these areas. The agreement contemplated that as individual developments were planned the owners or developers would apply to Laclede for central propane gas systems. If Laclede determined that such a system was appropriate in any given development, it could request Amoco to supply the propane to that specific development. This request was [to be] made in the form of a supplemental form letter; and if Amoco decided to supply the propane, it bound itself to do so by signing this supplemental form. . . .

For its part Laclede agreed to "[i]nstall, own, maintain and operate all distribution facilities." . . . Laclede also promised to pay Amoco "the Wood River Area Posted Price for propane plus four cents per gallon for all amounts of commercial propane gas delivered" to it under the agreement.

Since it was contemplated that the individual propane systems would eventually be converted to natural gas, one paragraph of the agreement provided that Laclede should give Amoco 30 days written notice of this event, after which the agreement would no longer be binding for the converted development.

Another paragraph gave Laclede the right to cancel the agreement [after the first year, by giving notice 30 days prior to the end of that year or any subsequent year].

There was no provision under which Amoco could cancel the agreement.

For a time the parties operated satisfactorily under this agreement, and some 17 residential subdivisions were brought within it by supplemental letters. However, for various reasons, including conversion to natural gas, the number of developments under the agreement had shrunk to eight by the time of trial. These were all mobile home parks.

During the winter of 1972–73 Amoco experienced a shortage of propane and voluntarily placed all of its customers, including Laclede, on an 80% Allocation basis, meaning that Laclede would receive only up to 80% of its previous requirements. . . .

[The following spring, Amoco repudiated the contract. Laclede sued for breach and requested specific performance. The trial court found the contract to be unenforceable for lack of mutual obligation. The Court of Appeals disagreed, finding that Laclede had assumed a bargained-for obligation to purchase its requirements of propane for designated subdivisions from Amoco.]

Since he found that there was no binding contract, the district judge did not have to deal with the question of whether or not to grant the injunction prayed for by Laclede. . . .

[W]e have carefully reviewed the very complete record on appeal and conclude that the trial court should grant the injunctive relief prayed. We are satisfied that this case falls within that category in which specific performance should be ordered as a matter of right.

There is simply no requirement in the law that both parties be mutually entitled to the remedy of specific performance in order that one of them be given that remedy by the court.

While a court may refuse to grant specific performance where such a decree would require constant and long-continued court supervision, this is merely a discretionary rule of decision which is frequently ignored when the public interest is involved.

Here the public interest in providing propane to the retail customers is manifest, while any supervision required will be far from onerous.

Section 370 of the Restatement of Contracts (1932) provides:

> "Specific enforcement will not be decreed unless the terms of the contract are so expressed that the court can determine with reasonable certainty what is the duty of each party and the conditions under which performance is due."

We believe these criteria have been satisfied here. As discussed in part I of this opinion, as to all developments for which a supplemental agreement has been signed, Amoco is to supply all the propane which is reasonably foreseeably required, while Laclede is to purchase the required propane from Amoco and pay the contract price therefor. The parties have disagreed over what is meant by "Wood River Area Posted

Price" in the agreement, but the district court can and should determine with reasonable certainty what the parties intended by this term and should mold its decree, if necessary accordingly. Likewise, the fact that the agreement does not have a definite time of duration is not fatal since the evidence established that the last subdivision should be converted to natural gas in 10 to 15 years. This sets a reasonable time limit on performance and the district court can and should mold the final decree to reflect this testimony.

It is axiomatic that specific performance will not be ordered when the party claiming breach of contract has an adequate remedy at law. This is especially true when the contract involves personal property as distinguished from real estate.

However, in Missouri, as elsewhere, specific performance may be ordered even though personalty is involved in the "proper circumstances." And a remedy at law adequate to defeat the grant of specific performance "must be as certain, prompt, complete, and efficient to attain the ends of justice as a decree of specific performance." . . .

We are satisfied that Laclede has brought itself within this practical approach taken by the Missouri courts. As Amoco points out, Laclede has propane immediately available to it under other contracts with other suppliers. And the evidence indicates that at the present time propane is readily available on the open market. However, this analysis ignores the fact that the contract involved in this lawsuit is for a long-term supply of propane to these subdivisions. The other two contracts under which Laclede obtains the gas will remain in force only until March 31, 1977, and April 1, 1981, respectively; and there is no assurance that Laclede will be able to receive any propane under them after that time. . . . Also it is unclear as to whether or not Laclede can use the propane obtained under these contracts to supply the Jefferson County subdivisions, since they were originally entered into to provide Laclede with propane with which to "shave" its natural gas supply during peak demand periods. Additionally, there was uncontradicted expert testimony that Laclede probably could not find another supplier of propane willing to enter into a long-term contract such as the Amoco agreement, given the uncertain future of worldwide energy supplies. And, even if Laclede could obtain supplies of propane for the affected developments through its present contracts or newly negotiated ones, it would still face considerable expense and trouble which cannot be estimated in advance in making arrangements for its distribution to the subdivisions.

Specific performance is the proper remedy in this situation . . . .

NOTES

1. Eastern Rolling Mill, a steel company, agreed to deliver its accumulation of steel scrap to Michlovitz over a period of five years, at prices calculated on the basis of trade journal quotes. The Maryland Supreme Court

upheld a decree of specific performance, finding that uncertainties about the quantity and price of the scrap to be delivered over the remaining term of the contract made a damage remedy impractical:

> "The scrap is not to be delivered according to specified tonnage, but as it accumulates, which in the past has been at the rate of one and two, and occasionally three, carloads of scrap a day, so the quantities vary from quarter to quarter. If the plant should cease to operate or suffer an interruption, there would be no scrap accumulating for delivery under the contracts, and its deliveries would end or be lessened. Neither are the prices for the scrap constant during the period of the contracts, but change from quarter to quarter according to the quotations of two specified materials on the Philadelphia market . . . . By what method would a jury determine the future quarterly tonnage, the quarterly contract price, and quarterly market price during these coming years? How could it possibly arrive at any fair ascertainment of damages? Any estimate would be speculative and conjectural, and not, therefore, compensatory."

Eastern Rolling Mill Co. *v.* Michlovitz, 157 Md. 51, 66–67 (1929).

2. Northeastern Baseball, Inc. (NBI) desired to locate a Triple A minor league baseball team in Scranton, Pennsylvania. Jordan Kobritz, general partner of Triple-A Baseball Club Associates, agreed to transfer a team then playing in Maine to NBI. Kobritz breached the agreement and NBI sued for specific performance. The court granted specific relief, saying:

> "We think the facts of this case bring it well within the ambit of the rules requiring specific performance. The contract's terms are unambiguous; there is no problem in drafting a clear order. NBI showed its ability and willingness to perform on the closing day and presented convincing evidence of its inability to purchase another Triple-A team. . . . [T]he Triple-A franchise has no readily ascertainable market value, it cannot be easily obtained from other sources, and it is of special interest to NBI.
>
> "There can be no doubt that what NBI sought, a Triple-A franchise, was unique. Nor can it be gainsaid that money damages, even if ascertained, could not 'obtain the duplicate or the substantial equivalent of the promised performance . . . .' . . .
>
> "As to damages, [Kobritz] only offer[s] an amount for the year 1987, based on the difference in profits between a Triple-A team and a Double-A team for that year. This formulation does not take into account the difference in location or facilities. Nor [does Kobritz] discuss how to measure future lost profits or how to compensate NBI for any added expenses it will incur in obtaining a Triple-A team in the future-assuming one becomes available for purchase."

Triple-A Baseball Club Associates *v.* Northeastern Baseball, Inc., 832 F.2d 214, 224–25 (1st Cir. 1987).

3. Between 2001 and 2004, Exelon Generation Co., an electric utility engaged in nuclear power production, entered into a series of contracts with General Atomic Technologies Corp. (GATC), a nuclear technology company that owned significant North American uranium deposits. In these contracts, GATC agreed to supply Exelon with stated amounts of uranium, at stated prices, in the years 2007–2009. The contracts included an ambiguous damage limitation that certainly excluded consequential damages and may also have limited Exelon's damage remedy to the agreed price for the amounts of uranium to be delivered (as opposed to the actual cost of covering by buying uranium from another source).

Before delivering any uranium, GATC repudiated the contracts, and Exelon sued for breach. The court granted summary judgment in favor of Exelon on its claim of breach, but refused to grant specific performance.

> "GATC contends that Exelon is not entitled to specific performance because money damages are an adequate remedy in this case. Under New York's version of the UCC, '[s]pecific performance may be decreed where the goods are unique or in other proper circumstances.' N.Y. U.C.C. Law § 2–716(1) (McKinney 2008). Though a comment to this provision indicates that it 'seeks to further a more liberal attitude than some courts have shown in connection with the specific performance of contracts of sale,' *id.*, cmt. 1, Exelon has offered no evidence from which a finding reasonably could be made that the goods in question were unique or that 'other proper circumstances' exist. . . .
>
> "The Court . . . rejects Exelon's argument that damages are inadequate because it requires a reliable stream of uranium and if it had to purchase uranium on the spot market, doing so would raise the market price, causing its subsequent purchases to be more expensive. The Court has a hard time seeing how that would make damages inadequate; it would seem that it would simply increase the amount recoverable as damages. *Cf.* 12 Corbin on Contracts § 1146 (2007) ("Specific performance of a contract for the sale of [goods] will not, apart from statute, be decreed if such [goods] are readily procurable in the market. The cost of obtaining them can be ascertained; and money damages are adequate."). In any event, however, Exelon has failed to offer admissible evidence that reasonably would permit a finding that this hypothetical effect would occur. Exelon points to a report by its expert witness Gene Clark, which includes a statement that a purchase of 525,000 pounds of uranium on the open market would have the effect of raising the market price. As GATC argues, however, neither Clark nor Exelon has offered any foundation supporting the admissibility of this particular opinion. . . .
>
> "For these reasons, the Court grants summary judgment in favor of GATC on [Exelon's request for specific performance]."

Exelon Generation Co., LLC *v.* General Atomics Technologies Corp., 559 F. Supp. 2d 892, 900 (N.D. Ill. 2008). Was the legal remedy adequate? Was adequacy of the legal remedy the problem?

4. At the end of World War II, new cars were in short supply. Vandover Motors agreed to sell Albert Boeving the thirteenth Buick to come into Vandover's possession after the date of the agreement. Later Vandover refused to deliver the car and Boeving sought specific performance. The trial court refused to grant specific relief but the appellate court reversed: "[P]laintiff desired this car to be used in his business and for social duties. It certainly could not be obtained elsewhere except at considerable expense, trouble or loss, which cannot be estimated in advance, and under such circumstances he did not have an adequate remedy at law." Boeving *v.* Vandover, 240 Mo. App. 117, 128 (1949). Cf. Fortner *v.* Wilson, 202 Okl. 563 (1950) (denying specific performance on similar facts).

5. Welton claimed that General Securities Corporation had agreed to sell him 60 shares of stock in the St. Louis Aviation Corporation, but had refused to give him the stock certificate when he tendered payment. Welton alleged further that St. Louis Aviation Corporation stock was not listed on any stock exchange and that its market value was thus not readily ascertainable. He requested specific performance of the contract. The trial court overruled GSC's demurrer to Welton's bill and its decision was affirmed on appeal. General Securities Corp. *v.* Welton, 223 Ala. 299 (1931).

6. In Heilman *v.* Union Canal Co., 37 Pa. 100 (1860), the court made these remarks:

> "The fact, if it be so, that this remedy may not be successful in realizing the fruits of a recovery at law, on account of the insolvency of the defendants, is not of itself a ground of equitable interference. The remedy is what is to be looked at. If it exist, and is ordinarily adequate, its possible want of success is not a consideration."

This is the traditional, although not universal, rule in contract cases. Yet a damage remedy against an insolvent defendant is certainly inadequate in a practical sense. The reason for the traditional rule may be to maintain equality among creditors. See Douglas Laycock, THE DEATH OF THE IRREPARABLE INJURY RULE 76–77 (1991). Note that the Bankruptcy Code, 11 U.S.C. § 365, permits a trustee in bankruptcy to "reject" executory contracts, leaving the promisee with a damage claim for breach.

In tort cases, courts are more likely to take insolvency into account in assessing the adequacy of damages.

Rubinstein v. Rubinstein

Court of Appeals of New York, 1968.
23 N.Y.2d 293.

■ KEATING, JUDGE. Henry and Leo Rubinstein are distant relatives. For some years they had successfully operated a number of joint enterprises. In July, 1965 they owned an equal number of shares in two corporations, one of which operated a grocery business on Third Avenue in New York

City ("Premium") and the other a delicatessen business on First Avenue ("Kips Bay"). In addition, the cousins had equal interests in two other corporations. One held title to real property on which the Kips Bay delicatessen was conducted and the other to the adjoining parcel.

Prior to July, 1965 differences arose. The cousins decided on a parting of the ways. On July 20, 1965, with each party represented by his own counsel, an agreement was signed. Its basic outline was this. Each business was valued at $70,000. Henry was to choose immediately between the two businesses. Leo would get the other. The agreement also provided that whoever took the Kips Bay delicatessen would also take the realty located there. Although the agreement established a procedure by which the realty was to be valued, it appears that the realty played an insignificant part in the negotiations.

At the time the agreement was executed, Henry and Leo deposited $5,000 with their respective lawyers. The agreement stated this sum would "be held in escrow by each respective attorney, to be applied towards the payment that each of the parties may have to make to the other party upon the closing of the above transaction." Any surplus, after the necessary adjustments, was to be returned to Henry and Leo at the time of the closing. These two provisions, which appear in paragraph numbered "8," are then followed by this clause: "In the event that either of the parties hereto shall default or refuse to consummate this transaction, then the aforesaid $5,000.00 deposited by such defaulting party shall be forfeited as liquidated damages and such sum shall be paid by the escrowee thereof to the other party."

The day after the execution of the agreement Henry sent a letter to Leo's lawyer in which he elected to take the Kips Bay property. The agreement provided that the closing would take place within one week. Apparently, disputes arose as to how various details of the transaction should be worked out, and in October of 1965 the deal still had not been consummated. At this point, Henry instituted this suit in Supreme Court, New York County, for specific performance. An answer was interposed by the defendant in which he counterclaimed for specific performance, also alleging the lack of an adequate remedy at law.

Leo thereafter had a complete change of mind. He changed lawyers and in September, 1966 moved to strike the complaint from the equity calendar on the ground that the quoted provision of the agreement relegated Henry to an action at law for $5,000. Henry cross-moved for summary judgment for specific performance. Leo then moved for leave to serve a proposed amended answer to remove the counterclaim for equitable relief.

Special Term found that it "is clear that the defendant does not desire to go through with the contract," and ruled that plaintiff was entitled to summary judgment, but held that the clause quoted above constituted not only a liquidated damages provision but, as a matter of law, it constituted the sole relief to which plaintiff was entitled. The correctness of this holding is the principal legal issue presented by this appeal. . . .

We conclude that the pertinent clause does not preclude the relief of specific performance, that plaintiff does not have an adequate remedy at law and that the agreement is enforceable by a court of equity. Therefore, plaintiff's motion for summary judgment for specific performance should have been granted.

We may immediately dispose of a preliminary argument, namely, that plaintiff has an adequate remedy at law. On its face the principal aim of this agreement was to sever the parties' relationship and to enable each party to own completely, separately and without interference by the other one half the joint business. It is evident that this result cannot be achieved by a damage award, and respondent does not seriously argue that plaintiff has an adequate remedy at law.

We turn then to the main question presented by this appeal, whether the agreement by its terms or in light of surrounding circumstances precludes specific performance. Nothing in the language of the contract explicitly states that the liquidated damages provision was to be plaintiff's sole and exclusive remedy, but both Special Term and the Appellate Division majority found the liquidated damages provision itself precluded specific performance. This is made clear by the following language in the prevailing opinion: "Properly considered, clause Eight in the contract relating to the $5,000 was nothing more than an option, affording the plaintiff a choice not to go forward, if he was willing to forfeit $5,000."

In relying on the liquidated damages clause alone the majority was clearly in error. The law is now well settled that a liquidated damages provision will not in and of itself be construed as barring the remedy of specific performance. For there to be a complete bar to equitable relief there must be something more, such as explicit language in the contract that the liquidated damages provision was to be the sole remedy. . . .

It is interesting to note that nowhere in this contract can be found the word "option" although this is the term used by the Appellate Division majority to describe the instant contract. Absent, therefore, an unambiguous provision, the majority below was in error in finding that the language itself precluded specific performance and for a very sound reason. Generally, the law presumes that the primary purpose of a contract, not expressly stated to be an option, is performance of the act promised and not nonperformance. Penalty clauses and even liquidated damages clauses are generally inserted to help secure performance and to avoid litigation as to quantum of damages. In this way, it is hoped to induce performance by making delay or breaches unprofitable.

Moreover, the first reference to the $5,000 is that it was to be used in connection with the "closing." This clause signifies that the escrow deposit was not even intended to assure performance, which was presumed, but it was contemplated that it would be used in connection with the performance of the contract in question. Also to be considered is the fact that the closing—originally scheduled to take place within 48 hours—was set for a week later. This surely evinces an intent that the contract be specifically performed.

The agreement grew out of a deterioration in the personal relations of the two cousins. Its first goal was the severance of their partnership. Defendant's interpretation would only provide Henry with the "right" to continue as Leo's partner if Leo did not like the division. It would be preposterous for the parties to enter into an agreement providing that, at the risk of $5,000, the parties shall see if they can agree to a division. We may not presume persons act so irrationally. If the defendant desired the Kips Bay property as well as a severance, he could have demanded the right of first choice. Or some alternative method for dividing the business would have been devised. The fact that defendant was willing to give plaintiff the right to select the property indicates that his major desire was to terminate a relationship, which was no longer bearable, rather than to obtain a right to pay $5,000 for the privilege of being restored to the *status quo ante*.

Nor is there anything in the surrounding circumstances which discloses a design that the liquidated damages clause is intended to bar specific performance. On this point it is of significance that the same lawyer who represented the defendant at the time the agreement was made counterclaimed for specific performance. Defendant thus indicated that it was his understanding that the agreement could be specifically enforced.

The conclusion is clear. The agreement here does not bar plaintiff from seeking the remedy of specific performance. There being no question that defendant defaulted, plaintiff has his choice of remedies and he has elected specific performance.

A final point raised by the respondent is that equitable relief should not be granted since the agreement is allegedly ambiguous, vague, preliminary in nature and incomplete. This contention is distinctly without merit. . . .

If any serious difficulties as to the meaning of various terms of the agreement do ultimately arise, and at present defendant has shown none, oral testimony as to the meaning of the term in the agreement would appear proper. In any event, the propriety of equitable relief is one which should be resolved by the trial court since it is clear that the agreement does not, as a matter of law, bar equitable relief. . . .

■ [The dissenting opinion of CHIEF JUSTICE FULD and JUSTICE BERGAN is omitted.]

2. HARDSHIP, SUPERVISION, AND RELATED CONCERNS

Van Wagner Advertising Corp. v. S & M Enterprises

Court of Appeals of New York, 1986.
67 N.Y.2d 186.

■ KAYE, JUDGE. . . . By agreement dated December 16, 1981, Barbara Michaels leased to plaintiff, Van Wagner Advertising, for an initial period of three years plus option periods totaling seven additional years space on the eastern exterior wall of a building on East 36th Street in Manhattan. Van Wagner was in the business of erecting and leasing billboards, and the parties anticipated that Van Wagner would erect a sign on the leased space, which faced an exit ramp of the Midtown Tunnel and was therefore visible to vehicles entering Manhattan from that tunnel.

In early 1982 Van Wagner erected an illuminated sign and leased it to Asch Advertising, Inc. for a three-year period commencing March 1, 1982. However, by agreement dated January 22, 1982, Michaels sold the building to defendant S & M Enterprises. Michaels informed Van Wagner of the sale in early August 1982, and on August 19, 1982 S & M sent Van Wagner a letter purporting to cancel the lease as of October 18 pursuant to section 1.05, which provided:

> "Notwithstanding anything contained in the foregoing provisions to the contrary, Lessor (or its successor) may terminate and cancel this lease on not less than 60 days prior written notice in the event and only in the event of:
>
> "a) a bona fide sale of the building to a third party unrelated to Lessor."

Van Wagner abandoned the space under protest and in November 1982 commenced this action for declarations that the purported cancellation was ineffective and the lease still in existence, and for specific performance and damages.

[The trial court concluded that the parties to the lease intended that only an owner making a sale, and not the purchaser, could terminate the lease. Therefore, S & M had no right to cancel Van Wagner's lease. Nevertheless, the trial court declined to order specific performance.]

Given defendant's unexcused failure to perform its contract, we next turn to a consideration of remedy for the breach: Van Wagner seeks specific performance of the contract, S & M urges that money damages are adequate but that the amount of the award was improper.[2]

---

[2] We note that the parties' contentions regarding the remedy of specific performance in general, mirror a scholarly debate that has persisted throughout our judicial history, reflecting fundamentally divergent views about the quality of a bargained-for promise. While the usual remedy in Anglo-American law has been damages, rather than compensation "in kind," the current trend among commentators appears to favor the remedy of specific performance but the view is not unanimous.

Whether or not to award specific performance is a decision that rests in the sound discretion of the trial court, and here that discretion was not abused. Considering first the nature of the transaction, specific performance has been imposed as the remedy for breach of contracts for the sale of real property, but the contract here is to lease rather than sell an interest in real property. While specific performance is available, in appropriate circumstances, for breach of a commercial or residential lease, specific performance of real property leases is not in this State awarded as a matter of course (see Gardens Nursery School *v.* Columbia University, 94 Misc.2d 376, 378).[3]

Van Wagner argues that specific performance must be granted in light of the trial court's finding that the "demised space is unique as to location for the particular advertising purpose intended." The word "uniqueness" is not, however, a magic door to specific performance. A distinction must be drawn between physical difference and economic interchangeability. The trial court found that the leased property is physically unique, but so is every parcel of real property and so are many consumer goods. Putting aside contracts for the sale of real property, where specific performance has traditionally been the remedy for breach, uniqueness in the sense of physical difference does not itself dictate the propriety of equitable relief.

By the same token, at some level all property may be interchangeable with money. Economic theory is concerned with the degree to which consumers are willing to substitute the use of one good for another (see Kronman, Specific Performance, 45 U. Chi. L. Rev. 351, 359), the underlying assumption being that "every good has substitutes, even if only very poor ones," and that "all goods are ultimately commensurable" (*id.*). Such a view, however, could strip all meaning from uniqueness, for if all goods are ultimately exchangeable for a price, then all goods may be valued. Even a rare manuscript has an economic substitute in that there is a price for which any purchaser would likely agree to give up a right to buy it, but a court would in all probability order specific performance of such a contract on the ground that the subject matter of the contract is unique.

The point at which breach of a contract will be redressable by specific performance thus must lie not in any inherent physical uniqueness of the property but instead in the uncertainty of valuing it: "What matters, in measuring money damages, is the volume, refinement, and reliability of the available information about substitutes for the subject matter of the breached contract. When the relevant information is thin and unreliable, there is a substantial risk that an award of money damages will either exceed or fall short of the promisee's actual loss. Of course this risk can

---

[3] But see 5A Corbin, CONTRACTS § 1143, at 131; at 7, n. 62; 11 Williston, CONTRACTS § 1418A [3d ed.]; Pomeroy and Mann, SPECIFIC PERFORMANCE OF CONTRACTS § 9, at 18–19 [3d ed. 1926]; Restatement [Second] of Contracts § 360 comment a, illustration 2; Restatement [Second] of Contracts § 360 comment e.

always be reduced—but only at great cost when reliable information is difficult to obtain. Conversely, when there is a great deal of consumer behavior generating abundant and highly dependable information about substitutes, the risk of error in measuring the promisee's loss may be reduced at much smaller cost. In asserting that the subject matter of a particular contract is unique and has no established market value, a court is really saying that it cannot obtain, at reasonable cost, enough information about substitutes to permit it to calculate an award of money damages without imposing an unacceptably high risk of undercompensation on the injured promisee. Conceived in this way, the uniqueness test seems economically sound." (45 U. Chi. L. Rev. at 362.) This principle is reflected in the case law, and is essentially the position of the Restatement (Second) of Contracts, which lists "the difficulty of proving damages with reasonable certainty" as the first factor affecting adequacy of damages (Restatement [Second] of Contracts § 360[a]).

Thus, the fact that the subject of the contract may be "unique as to location for the particular advertising purpose intended" by the parties does not entitle a plaintiff to the remedy of specific performance.

Here, the trial court correctly concluded that the value of the "unique qualities" of the demised space could be fixed with reasonable certainty and without imposing an unacceptably high risk of undercompensating the injured tenant. Both parties complain: Van Wagner asserts that while lost revenues on the Asch contract may be adequate compensation, that contract expired February 28, 1985, its lease with S & M continues until 1992, and the value of the demised space cannot reasonably be fixed for the balance of the term. S & M urges that future rents and continuing damages are necessarily conjectural, both during and after the Asch contract, and that Van Wagner's damages must be limited to 60 days—the period during which Van Wagner could cancel Asch's contract without consequence in the event Van Wagner lost the demised space. S & M points out that Van Wagner's lease could remain in effect for the full 10-year term, or it could legitimately be extinguished immediately, either in conjunction with a bona fide sale of the property by S & M, or by a reletting of the building if the new tenant required use of the billboard space for its own purposes. Both parties' contentions were properly rejected.

First, it is hardly novel in the law for damages to be projected into the future. Particularly where the value of commercial billboard space can be readily determined by comparisons with similar uses—Van Wagner itself has more than 400 leases—the value of this property between 1985 and 1992 cannot be regarded as speculative. Second, S & M having successfully resisted specific performance on the ground that there is an adequate remedy at law, cannot at the same time be heard to contend that damages beyond 60 days must be denied because they are conjectural. If damages for breach of this lease are indeed conjectural, and cannot be calculated with reasonable certainty, then S & M should be compelled to perform its contractual obligation by restoring Van Wagner to the premises. Moreover, the contingencies to which S & M points do not, as a practical matter, render the calculation of damages speculative. While S & M could terminate the Van Wagner lease in the event of a sale of the building, this building has been sold only once in 40 years; S & M paid several million dollars, and purchased the building in connection with its plan for major development of the block. The theoretical termination right of a future tenant of the existing building also must be viewed in light of these circumstances. If any uncertainty is generated by the two contingencies, then the benefit of that doubt must go to Van Wagner and not the contract violator. Neither contingency allegedly affecting Van Wagner's continued contractual right to the space for the balance of the lease term is within its own control; on the contrary, both are in the interest of S & M. Thus, neither the need to project into the future nor the contingencies allegedly affecting the length of Van Wagner's term render inadequate the remedy of damages for S & M's breach of its lease with Van Wagner.

The trial court, additionally, correctly concluded that specific performance must be denied on the ground that such relief "would be inequitable in that its effect would be disproportionate in its harm to defendant and its assistance to plaintiff." It is well settled that the imposition of an equitable remedy must not itself work an inequity, and that specific performance would not be an undue hardship. This conclusion is "not within the absolute discretion of the Supreme Court." Here, however, there was no abuse of discretion; the finding that specific performance would disproportionately harm S & M and benefit Van Wagner has . . . support in the proof regarding S & M's projected development of the property. . . .

NOTE

Was the legal remedy adequate? Should the court have granted specific performance? No, Yes

Link v. State

Supreme Court of Montana, 1979.
180 Mont. 469.

■ JACK D. SHANSTROM, DISTRICT JUDGE. . . . The facts are as follows: On June 15, 1946, after extensive negotiations, the Montana State Park Commission entered into an agreement with Henry A. Link, John G. Link, Jr., Elmer F. Link and Louis W. Link, a copartnership doing business as Link Bros. (. . . referred to as "concessionaires"). This agreement gave concessionaires the right to operate concessions at Lewis and Clark Caverns State Park in return for payment to the State of 10 percent of the gross receipts from the concessions. The concessionaires also agreed to construct certain permanent improvements on the premises, including buildings, booths and storerooms, a water system, and possibly a mountain railroad. All such improvements were to become the property of the Park Commission upon construction and were to be leased to concessionaires. The agreement had a life of 25 years, and concessionaires had an option to renew.

Concessionaires did construct a system to transport visitors between the concession area and the cavern entrances. This system, which came to be called a "mountain railroad," consisted of two components. Visitors were carried back and forth between the concession area and the lower cavern entrance in a sight-seeing car pulled on railroad tracks by a Jeep. A hoist and tram lifted the visitors approximately 300 feet at a 30 degree incline from the lower to the upper cave entrance. Visitors walked through the cave from the upper to the lower entrance. Concessionaires operated this railroad from 1947 to 1950.

[In 1950, the State of Montana decided to assume control of the mountain railroad. Accordingly, the Park Commission and the concessionaires signed a supplemental agreement in which the Commission agreed to "take over the operation and maintenance of the said mountain railroad" and to "operate said mountain railroad, tram and hoist, and handle the visiting public thereon in such a way as to encourage said public to use the other facilities of the Concessionaires at said Lewis and Clark Caverns State Park, and to operate said railroad in a manner that is beneficial to the business of the Concessionaires . . . ." The Commission also agreed to pay the concessionaires an agreed percentage of the railroad fare charged to visitors. In exchange, the concessionaires relinquished their right to operate the railroad and waived any right to reimbursement for their expenses in constructing the railroad.]

In 1970, the concessionaires exercised their option to renew the amended agreement for an additional 25 years.

In 1973 a large gear broke in the cable car hoist and was not replaced by the Commission. This caused the tramway portion of the system to be closed. The Commission made repairs to the other portions of the railroad from 1973 to 1975, but in 1976 the Commission refused to spend more money on the mountain railroad and discontinued its use. The track was removed, and a gravel pathway was constructed from the concession area to the cavern entrance. Park visitors have used the pathway since that time.

[The court first found that the contract was valid and obligated the Park Commission to repair, maintain, and operate the railroad over the term of the contract (as extended). It rejected the State's argument that the railroad was obsolete, reasoning that "repairs, maintenance, or replacement could have been done by defendants. They refused to do so because of costs and not because of reasons beyond their control."]

The last question to be determined by this Court is whether the District Court erred in ordering specific performance of the contract rather than awarding damages. Defendants contend that by ordering specific performance the court is put in the position of supervising a complex construction project and that such a decree cannot be precise enough to be enforceable. Furthermore, they contend that damages could be awarded by using attendance figures for the last several years and thereby estimating the damages to the concessionaires. Finally, they assert that specific performance would cost the State a minimum of $250,000 and therefore would operate more harshly on defendants than its refusal would operate on plaintiffs.

Plaintiffs have been put in the position that, even if they could determine their past losses by the attendance figure, the loss of their future business because of the inconvenience to the patrons of Lewis and Clark Caverns by not having transportation to take them back and forth would be impossible to determine and denial of specific performance would operate more harshly on plaintiffs than granting it would on defendants. . . .

The District Court in this case found that the Commission breached the contract in the past, was now breaching the contract, and intended in the future to breach its contractual obligations with the Links. It could only speculate as to the money damages that such breaches had caused in the past and would cause in the future. Loss of the mountain railroad has so completely changed the nature of plaintiffs' operation that it would be impossible to establish a reasonable damage figure. The only just, reasonable and feasible solution was to compel specific performance and return the Links to the position they were in at the time the March 1950 contract was entered into, where the Links could run the railroad and the visiting public would again be served with transportation facilities to the mouth of the cave. All the court is ordering is that the Commission return to the Links what it had received: a working and operable railroad and tram system.

Defendants argue that the District Court was powerless to grant specific performance because the District Court would then be engaged in continuous protracted supervision and direction with the requirement of special knowledge, skill and judgment. This is not so. A court sitting in equity has all of the power requisite to render justice between the parties, particularly where "the intent and disposition of the department is not to perform its contractual obligations. . . ."

The order of the District Court compelling specific performance of the contract is affirmed. The date by which performance is to be completed, however, is hereby changed to grant the State two years from the date of the issuance of this opinion in which to perform.

NOTE

The mountain railroad was never restored.

Lane v. Newdigate

Chancery, 1804.
10 Ves. Jun. 192, 32 Eng. Rep. 818.

The plaintiff was assignee of a lease, granted by the defendant, for the purpose of erecting mills and other buildings; with covenants for the supply of water from canals and reservoirs on the defendant's estates, reserving to the defendant the right of working and using his then or future collieries, either with regard to the supply of water, or other uses of the collieries, or any locks for the passage of his boats or otherwise: the liberties and privileges granted being, as expressed in the lease, intended to be subordinate to the use and enjoyment of the collieries: the defendant to have due regard to the mills, &c. and doing as little mischief as the nature of the case would admit.

The bill prayed, that the defendant may be decreed so to use and manage the waters of the canals as not to injure the plaintiff in the occupation of his manufactory; and, in particular, that he may be restrained from using the locks, and thereby drawing off the waters which would otherwise run to and supply the manufactory; and that he may be decreed to restore the cut for carrying the waste waters from the Arbury Canal to Kenilworth Pool, and to restore Kenilworth Stopgate and the banks of the canal to their former height; and also to repair such stop-gates, bridges, canals, and towing-paths, as were made previously to granting the lease; and that he may be decreed to make compensation for the injury sustained by their having been suffered to go out of repair; and that he may be decreed to remove the locks, which have been made since the lease, and to make compensation for the injury sustained by the said locks having been made so near the manufactory; thereby injuring the machinery; and, that he may be decreed to pay the plaintiff the expense he has been put to by working the steam engine, to supply the want of water.

The *Lord Chancellor*, upon the motion for the injunction, expressed a difficulty, whether it is according to the practice of the court to decree or order repairs to be done.

Mr. Romilly, in support of the injunction, said the repairs to be done in this case are in effect nothing more than was done in Robinson *v.* Lord Byron, 1 Bro. C.C. 588, *viz.* raising the damheads, so that the water shall not escape; as it will otherwise.

■ THE LORD CHANCELLOR [ELDON]. So, as to restoring the stop-gate, the same difficulty occurs. The question is, whether the court can specifically order that to be restored. I think I can direct it in terms that will have that effect. The injunction, I shall order, will create the necessity of restoring the stop-gate; and attention will be had to the manner in which he is to use these locks; and he will find it difficult, I apprehend, to avoid completely repairing these works.

The order pronounced was, that the defendant, his agents, &c., be restrained until farther order, from farther impeding, obstructing, or hindering, the plaintiff from navigating the canal for the necessary purposes of the mill, or from using and enjoying the demised premises, and the mills and buildings erected thereon, or the liberties and privileges, granted by the indenture of lease, &c., contrary to the covenant, by continuing to keep the said canals, or the banks, gates, locks, or works of the same respectively, out of good repair, order, or condition; and also from farther troubling, molesting, and preventing, the plaintiff, contrary to the covenant, in the use and enjoyment of the said mills and buildings, or the liberty, privilege, and power of drawing for the use of the said mill from the canals, &c., a sufficient quantity of water for the use and working of the said mill, by diverting, draining, or drawing off water; or preventing the same by the use of any lock or locks, erected by the defendant, from remaining and continuing in the said canals, or by continuing the removal of the stop-gate, mentioned in the pleadings in the action brought by the plaintiff, to have been erected; and by means of which the water could and would have been kept and retained in the said pool for the use of the mill; but nothing in this order is to extend, to diminish, lessen, hinder, or prejudice the working, using, or enjoying, by the defendant of his present and future collieries, either with regard to the supply of water for his fire engine, or other uses of the collieries, or of any locks to be erected for the passage of his boats, or otherwise: the defendant having due regard to the said mills, and doing as little damage thereto, as the nature of the case will admit.

Jones v. Parker

Supreme Judicial Court of Massachusetts, 1895.
163 Mass. 564.

■ HOLMES, J. The case of Jones *v.* Parker is a bill in equity brought by a lessee upon a lease purporting to begin on September 1, 1893, and to demise part of a basement in a building not yet erected. The lessor "covenants to deliver possession of the same to the lessee upon completion of said building, and thereafter, during the term of this lease, reasonably to heat and light the demised premises." It is alleged that the building has been completed, but that the defendants refuse to complete the premises with apparatus sufficient to heat and light the same, and to deliver the same to the plaintiff. It also is alleged that the occupancy of the premises for the purpose contemplated in the lease was impossible without the construction in the premises of proper apparatus for heating and lighting them before delivery to the plaintiff. The prayer is for specific performance of the covenant quoted, and for damages. The defendant demurs.

It does not need argument to show that the covenant is valid. Whether it should be enforced specifically admits of more doubt, the questions being whether it is certain enough for that purpose and whether a decree for specific performance would not call on the court to do more than it is in the habit of undertaking. We are of opinion that specific performance should be decreed. With regard to the want of certainty of the covenant, if the plaintiff were left to an action at law, a jury would have to determine whether what was done amounted to a reasonable heating and lighting. A judge sitting without a jury would find no difficulty in deciding the same question. We do not doubt that an expert would find it as easy to frame a scheme for doing the work. The other question is practical rather than a matter of precedent. It fairly is to be supposed, in the present case, that the difference between the plaintiff and the defendants is only with regard to the necessity of some more or less elaborate apparatus for light and heat, a difference which lies within a narrow compass and which can be adjusted by the court. There is no universal rule that courts of equity never will enforce a contract which requires some building to be done. They have enforced such contracts from the earliest days to the present time. . . .

City Stores Co. v. Ammerman

United States District Court, District of Columbia, 1967.
266 F. Supp. 766.

[A group of developers, planning to build a shopping center, solicited City Stores' help in obtaining a zoning change. In exchange, the developers promised to "give [City Stores] the opportunity to become one of . . . [the] center's major tenants with rental and terms at least equal to that of any other major department store in the center." City Stores provided the sought-after assistance and the land was rezoned. However, the developers did not offer to lease space in the shopping center to City Stores. City Stores brought an action for specific performance.]

■ GASCH, DISTRICT JUDGE. [In the first part of the opinion, the court held that the parties had made a valid contract.]

Whether the option contract secured by plaintiff in this case is sufficiently definite to be the subject of a decree for specific performance is quite another question, which does not concern the validity or existence of the contract but only the nature of the remedy available to plaintiff.

It is not contested by the plaintiff that if it were to accept a lease tendered by defendants in accordance with the contract, there would be numerous complex details left to be worked out. The crucial elements of rate of rental and the amount of space can readily be determined from the Hecht and Woodward & Lothrop leases. But some details of design, construction and price of the building to be occupied by plaintiff at Tyson's Corner would have to be agreed to by the parties, subject to further negotiation and tempered only by the promise of equal terms with other tenants. The question is whether a court of equity will grant specific performance of a contract which has left such substantial terms open for future negotiation. . . .

[T]he 1926 case of Morris *v.* Ballard, 16 F.2d 175, held that an option to purchase property which contained a provision as to price "on terms to be agreed upon" was specifically enforceable by a court of equity. The court in that case held that "it became the duty of defendant, upon proper demand, either to accept the agreed purchase price in cash or to specify such terms as were acceptable to him. He had no right to refuse arbitrarily and unconditionally to accept payment solely for the purpose of defeating the option. Such a refusal would operate as a fraud upon the plaintiff." The court further held that the clause "on terms to be agreed upon"

> *"was in good conscience a stipulation that he would in fact agree with plaintiff upon reasonable terms of payment, and would not arbitrarily refuse to proceed with the sale. . . ."* (Emphasis added.) *Id.* at 383, 384.

. . . I therefore hold as a matter of law that the mere fact that a contract, definite in material respects, contains some terms which are subject to further negotiation between plaintiff and defendant will not bar a decree for specific performance, if in the court's discretion specific performance should be granted. . . .

The question whether a contract which also calls for construction of a building can or should be specifically enforced apparently never has been decided before in this jurisdiction. The parties have cited no cases on this point. . . .

It is apparent from the nature of the contract involved in this case that even were it possible to arrive at a precise measure of damages for breach of a contract to lease a store in a shopping center for a long period of years—which it is not—money damages would in no way compensate the plaintiff for loss of the right to participate in the shopping center enterprise and for the almost incalculable future advantages that might accrue to it as a result of extending its operations into the suburbs. Therefore, I hold that the appropriate remedy in this case is specific performance.

Some jurisdictions in the United States have opposed granting specific performance of contracts for construction of buildings and other contracts requiring extensive supervision of the court, but the better view, and the one which increasingly is being followed in this country, is that such contracts should be specifically enforced unless the difficulties of supervision outweigh the importance of specific performance to the plaintiff. This is particularly true where the construction is to be done on land controlled by the defendant, because in that circumstance the plaintiff cannot employ another contractor to do the construction for him at defendant's expense. In the case at bar, the fact that more than mere construction of a building is involved reinforces the need for specific enforcement of the defendants' duty to perform their entire contractual obligation to the plaintiff. . . .

The defendants contend that the granting of specific performance in this case will confront the court with insuperable difficulties of supervision, but after reviewing the evidence, I am satisfied that the standards to be observed in construction of the plaintiff's store are set out in the Hecht and Woodward & Lothrop leases with sufficient particularity as to make design and approval of plaintiff's store a fairly simple matter, if the parties deal with each other in good faith and expeditiously, as I shall hereafter order.

For example, Article VIII, Sec. 8.1, Paragraph (G) of the Hecht lease (the Woodward & Lothrop lease contains a similar provision) says:

> "The quality of (i) the construction, (ii) the construction components, (iii) the decorative elements (including landscaping irrigation systems for the landscaping) and (iv) the furnishings; and the general architectural character and general design, the materials selection, the decor and the treatment values, approach and standards of the Enclosed Mall shall be comparable, at minimum, to the qualities, values, approaches and standards as of the date hereof of the enclosed mall at Topanga Plaza Shopping Center, Los Angeles, California. . . ."

The existing leases contain further detailed specifications which will be identical to those in the lease granted to plaintiff. The site for plaintiff's store has already been settled by the design of the center. Although the exact design of plaintiff's store will not be identical to the design of any other store, it must be remembered that all of the stores are to be part of the same center and subject to its overall design requirements. If the parties are not in good faith able to reach an agreement on certain details, the court will appoint a special master to help settle their differences, unless they prefer voluntarily to submit their disagreements to arbitration. . . .

During the course of this proceeding, the plaintiff has examined the leases executed between defendants and Hecht and Woodward & Lothrop and has indicated its willingness to accept a lease with terms equal to the Hecht lease. I therefore find that the plaintiff has exercised its option, and is entitled to specific performance of a lease on terms equal to those contained in the Hecht lease. . . .

NOTE

In Kearns-Gorsuch Bottle Co. *v.* Hartford-Fairmont Co., 1 F.2d 318, 319 (S.D.N.Y. 1921), the court made these observations:

> "[P]rotracted supervisions of a business should not be assumed, but it is not true that it cannot be assumed. Everything depends on how insistently the justice of the case demands the

court's assumptions of difficult, unfamiliar, and contentious business problems. The tendency of the times is to take on harder and longer jobs. As a judge of first instance I would not nowadays hesitate to undertake any business enterprise for which, with the support of competent receivers, I thought a reasonably intelligent judge reasonably fit. Yet it might easily be that most appellate courts would still reverse that discretionary order. But the reversal could only logically or lawfully rest on an ascertained abuse of discretion; the error would be in degree, not kind."

De Rivafinoli v. Corsetti

Court of Chancery of New York, 1833.
4 Paige 264.

This case came before the chancellor on an order for the complainant to show cause why a ne exeat [a writ forbidding a person from leaving the territorial jurisdiction of the court] granted against the defendant should not be discharged, or the amount for which the defendant was held to bail reduced. The bill, which was filed in September, 1833, stated that the defendant, in the March preceding, had agreed with the complainant, as manager of the Italian theatre in the City of New-York, to sing, gesticulate and recite, in the capacity of *primo basso,* in all the operas, serious, semi-serious and comic, farces, oratorios, concerts, cantatas and benefits, which should be ordered by the complainant, or his authorized agents, in any city of the United States, where the complainant should think proper; and that he should be present at the times which should be appointed for rehearsals, and contribute to the interest and good conduct of the enterprise, submitting himself to the regulations made by the complainant, and to the fines in such regulations established, for the term of eight months, commencing on the first of November, 1833. For which singing, gesticulating, reciting, etc. the complainant agreed to pay him $1192, in sixteen half monthly payments; each payment to be made in advance, at the commencement of the half month for which the same was to be paid; and to allow the defendant one benefit, he bearing half the expense thereof. And that the defendant also agreed not to make use of his talents in any other theatre, or public hall, without the permission of the complainant, or his agents. For the performance of which agreement each party bound himself to the other, under the penalty of a fine of one third of the salary of the defendant; which fine was to be paid by the party in default, without objection, or exception. The bill further alleged that the complainant had entered into a contract with the trustees of the Italian opera house, in New-York, under heavy penalties, to commence the performance of Italian operas, with a first rate company, on the first of November, 1833; and that he had engaged the defendant as one of such company, and had gone to Europe to procure others to make up a troupe, complete in all its departments. That the defendant was a skilful musician, and was well qualified to sing, perform and exhibit Italian operas, in the capacity in which he had been engaged by the complainant; who had made all his arrangements, and his selections of other performers, in this country and in Europe, on the faith of the defendant's performing his engagement. That the services of the defendant were necessary, in the capacity in which he was engaged, to make up the troupe, or company, and his place could not be supplied without great expense and delay. And also that the complainant would be exposed to great damage, loss and inconvenience, and be liable to fail in his contract to obtain a first rate company by the first of November, if the defendant did not perform his engagement. The bill further charged that the defendant, since the making of the agreement, and in violation thereof, had entered into a contract with another person to go to the Havana as an opera singer, and to be there on the same day on which, by his agreement with the complainant, his services were to commence at New-York; and that he was about to leave this state for Cuba, in fraud and violation of the rights of the complainant. The bill therefore prayed for a specific performance of the contract with the complainant; that the defendant might be decreed to sing, gesticulate and recite, in the capacity of *primo basso,* according to his said agreement; that he might be restrained from leaving the state; and for general relief. The bill also prayed for a ne exeat; which was granted by an injunction master. And the defendant being unable to find bail, was committed to prison . . . .

■ The CHANCELLOR [WALWORTH]. The material facts alleged in the complainant's bill are not denied; and for the purpose of this application, they must be taken to be true. There is an affidavit, annexed to the bill, that the defendant has declared his intention of going to the Havana; and the defendant has not denied such intention, although he swears he has not made any engagement to go there. Upon the merits of the case, I suppose it must be conceded that the complainant is entitled to a specific performance of this contract; as the law appears to have been long since settled that a bird that can sing and will not sing must be made to sing. (*Old adage.*) In this case it is charged in the bill, not only that the defendant can sing, but also that he has expressly agreed to sing, and to accompany that singing with such appropriate gestures as may be necessary and proper to give an interest to his performance. And from the facts disclosed, I think it is very evident also that he does not intend to gratify the citizens of New-York, who may resort to the Italian opera either by his singing, or by his gesticulations. Although the authority before cited shows the law to be in favor of the complainant, so far at least as to entitle him to a decree for the singing, I am not aware that any officer of this court has that perfect knowledge of the Italian language, or possesses that exquisite sensibility in the auricular nerve which is necessary to understand, and to enjoy with a proper zest, the peculiar beauties of the Italian opera, so fascinating to the fashionable world. There might be some difficulty, therefore, even if the defendant was compelled to sing under the direction and in the presence of a master in chancery, in ascertaining whether he performed his engagement according to its spirit and intent. It would also be very difficult for the master to determine what effect coercion might produce upon the defendant's singing, especially in the livelier airs; although the fear of imprisonment would unquestionably deepen his seriousness in the graver parts of the drama. But one thing at least is certain; his songs will be neither comic, or even semi-serious, while he remains confined in that dismal cage, the debtor's prison of New-York. I will therefore proceed to inquire whether the complainant had any legal right thus to change the character of his native warblings, by such a confinement, before the appointed season for the dramatic singing had arrived.

From the terms of the agreement, as stated in the bill it is evident that there can be no breach thereof until the 1st of November next, when the engagement of the defendant was to commence. Even when that time arrives, the complainant will not be entitled to the defendant's services until he shall have paid, or tendered to him, a half month's salary in advance. A specific performance cannot be decreed, upon the present bill, because at the time it was filed, the complainant had no right of action against the defendant, either at law or in equity. And I believe this court has never yet gone so far as to sustain a bill quia timet, because the complainant apprehended that the defendant might not be willing to perform an engagement for personal services; and where, from the peculiar nature of those services, they could not be performed until a future day. The writ of ne exeat is in the nature of equitable bail; and to entitle the complainant to such bail, there must be a present debt or duty, or some existing right to relief against the defendant or his property, either at law, or in equity. The writ in this case therefore was prematurely granted; and the rule to discharge it must be made absolute.

NOTES

1. On De Rivafinoli *v.* Corsetti, see 3 G. Odell, ANNALS OF THE NEW YORK STAGE (1927).

2. Traditionally, courts have refused specific relief to either party to an employment contract. Title VII of the Civil Rights Act of 1964, which bars employment discrimination on the basis of race, color, religion, sex, or national origin, creates a significant exception. Remedies for violations of Title VII are set forth in 42 U.S.C. § 2000e–5(g)(1):

> "If the court finds that the respondent has intentionally engaged in or is intentionally engaging in an unlawful employment practice charged in the complaint, the court may enjoin the respondent from engaging in such unlawful employment practice, and order such affirmative action as may be appropriate, which may include, but is not limited to, reinstatement or hiring of employees, with or without back pay (payable by the employer, employment agency, or labor organization, as the case may be, responsible for the unlawful employment practice), or any other equitable relief as the court deems appropriate. . . ."

Lumley v. Wagner

Chancery, 1852.
1 De G.M. & G. 604, 42 Eng. Rep. 687.

The bill in this suit was filed on the 22d April 1852, by Benjamin Lumley, the lessee of Her Majesty's Theatre, against Johanna Wagner, Albert Wagner, her father, and Frederick Gye, the lessee of Covent Garden Theatre: it stated that in November 1851 Joseph Bacher, as the agent of the Defendants Albert Wagner and Johanna Wagner, came to and concluded at Berlin an agreement in writing in the French language, bearing date the 9th November 1851, and which agreement, being translated into English, was as follows:—

[Mademoiselle Wagner agreed to sing at Drury Lane for three months, beginning April 1, 1852. She also agreed "not to use her talents at any other theatre . . . without the written authorization of Mr. Lumley."]

The bill then stated that J. and A. Wagner subsequently made another engagement with the Defendant F. Gye, by which it was agreed that the Defendant J. Wagner should, for a larger sum than that stipulated by the agreement with the Plaintiff, sing at the Royal Italian Opera, Covent Garden, and abandon the agreement with the Plaintiff. The bill then stated that the Defendant F. Gye had full knowledge of the previous agreement with the Plaintiff, and that the Plaintiff had received a protest from the Defendants J. and A. Wagner, repudiating the agreement on the allegation that the Plaintiff had failed to fulfil the pecuniary portion of the agreement.

The bill prayed that the defendants Johanna Wagner and Albert Wagner might be restrained from violating or committing any breach of the [quoted] article of the agreement; that the defendant Johanna Wagner might be restrained from singing and performing or singing at the Royal Italian Opera, Covent Garden, or at any other theatre or place without the sanction or permission in writing of the plaintiff during the existence of the agreement with the plaintiff; and that the defendant Albert Wagner might be restrained from permitting or sanctioning the defendant Johanna Wagner singing and performing or singing as aforesaid; that the defendant Frederick Gye might be restrained from accepting the professional services of the defendant Johanna Wagner as a singer and performer or singer at the said Royal Italian Opera, Covent Garden, or at any other theatre or place, and from permitting her to sing and perform or to sing at the Royal Italian Opera, Covent Garden, during the existence of the agreement with the plaintiff, without the permission or sanction of the plaintiff. . . .

The plaintiff having obtained an injunction from the Vice-Chancellor, Sir James Parker, on the 9th May, 1852, the defendants now moved by way of appeal before the Lord Chancellor, to discharge . . . [this] order. . . .

■ THE LORD CHANCELLOR [ST. LEONARDS]. The question which I have to decide in the present case arises out of a very simple contract the effect of which is that the defendant Johanna Wagner should sing at Her Majesty's Theatre for a certain number of nights, and that she should not sing elsewhere (for that is the true construction) during that period. As I understand the points taken by the defendants' counsel in support of this appeal, they in effect come to this, namely, that a court of equity ought not to grant an injunction except in cases connected with specific performance, or where the injunction being to compel a party to forbear from committing an act (and not to perform an act), that injunction will complete the whole of the agreement remaining unexecuted.

I have then to consider how the question stands on principle and on authority, and in so doing I shall observe upon some of the cases which have been referred to and commented upon by the defendants in support of their contention. The first was that of Martin *v.* Nutkin, 2 P.W. 266 [1725], in which the court issued an injunction restraining an act from being done where it clearly could not have granted any specific performance: but then it was said that that case fell within one of the exceptions which the defendants admit are proper cases for the interference of the court, because there the ringing of the bells, sought to be restrained, had been agreed to be suspended by the defendant in consideration of the erection by the plaintiffs of a cupola and clock, the agreement being in effect the price stipulated for the defendant's relinquishing bell-ringing at stated periods; the defendant having accepted the benefit, but rejected the corresponding obligation, Lord Macclesfield first granted the injunction which the Lords Commissioners, at the hearing of the cause, continued for the lives of the plaintiffs. That case, therefore, however it may be explained as one of the exceptional cases, is nevertheless a clear authority showing that this court has granted an injunction prohibiting the commission of an act in respect of which the court could never have interfered by way of specific performance. . . .

The present is a mixed case, consisting not of two correlative acts to be done, one by the plaintiff and the other by the defendants, which state of facts may have and in some cases has introduced a very important difference—but of an act to be done by J. Wagner alone, to which is superadded a negative stipulation on her part to abstain from the commission of any act which will break in upon her affirmative covenant—the one being ancillary to, concurrent, and operating together with the other. The agreement to sing for the plaintiff during three months at his theatre, and during that time not to sing for anybody else, is not a correlative contract, it is in effect one contract; and though beyond all doubt this court could not interfere to enforce the specific performance of the whole of this contract, yet in all sound construction, and according to the true spirit of the agreement, the engagement to perform for three months at one theatre must necessarily exclude the right to perform at the same time at another theatre. It was clearly intended that J. Wagner was to exert her vocal abilities to the utmost to aid the theatre to which she agreed to attach herself. I am of opinion, that if she had attempted, even in the absence of any negative stipulation, to perform at another theatre, she would have broken the spirit and true meaning of the contract as much as she would now do with reference to the contract into which she has actually entered.

Wherever this court has not proper jurisdiction to enforce specific performance, it operates to bind men's consciences, as far as they can be bound, to a true and literal performance of their agreements; and it will not suffer them to depart from their contracts at their pleasure, leaving the party with whom they have contracted to the mere chance of any damages which a jury may give. The exercise of this jurisdiction has, I believe, had a wholesome tendency towards the maintenance of that good faith which exists in this country to a much greater degree perhaps than in any other; and although the jurisdiction is not to be extended, yet a judge would desert his duty who did not act up to what his predecessors have handed down as the rule for his guidance in the administration of such an equity.

It was objected that the operation of the injunction in the present case was mischievous, excluding the defendant J. Wagner from performing at any other theatre while this court had no power to compel her to perform at Her Majesty's Theatre. It is true, that I have not the means of compelling her to sing, but she has no cause of complaint, if I compel her to abstain from the commission of an act which she has bound herself not to do, and thus possibly cause her to fulfil her engagement. The jurisdiction which I now exercise is wholly within the power of the court, and being of opinion that it is a proper case for interfering, I shall leave nothing unsatisfied by the judgment I pronounce. The effect too of the injunction, in restraining J. Wagner from singing elsewhere may, in the event of an action being brought against her by the plaintiff, prevent any such amount of vindictive damages being given against her as a jury might probably be inclined to give if she had carried her talents and exercised them at the rival theatre: the injunction may also, as I have said, tend to the fulfillment of her engagement; though, in continuing the injunction, I disclaim doing indirectly what I cannot do directly. . . .

NOTES

1. The parties in this case were distinguished figures in the world of music. See Zechariah Chafee, Jr., Sidney Post Simpson & John Phillip Maloney, CASES ON EQUITY 288–90 (3d ed. 1951). Gye was also well-known in the field of law, for he was involved in what became leading cases in equity, torts, contracts, and partnership. Besides the principal case, see Lumley *v.* Gye, 2 E. & B. 216, 118 Eng. Rep. 749 (1853); Bettini *v.* Gye, L.R. 1 Q.B.D. 183 (1876); Knox *v.* Gye, L.R. 5 H.L.C. 656 (1871–72); James Barr Ames, CASES ON PARTNERSHIP 163 (1894).

2. In spite of the injunction restraining her from singing for Gye, Mademoiselle Wagner did not perform her contract to sing for Lumley. After the decision in the principal case, Lumley sued Gye at law for damages for inducing Mademoiselle Wagner to break her contract with Lumley, alleging that Gye had "maliciously enticed and procured her" to leave Lumley's employment. A demurrer to Lumley's declaration was overruled in the leading case of Lumley *v.* Gye, 2 E. & B. 216, 118 Eng. Rep. 749 (1853). Thereafter, at the trial of the action Lumley was awarded nominal damages. See Benjamin. Lumley, REMINISCENCES OF THE OPERA 328–33 (1864); Zechariah Chafee, Jr., Equitable Servitudes on Chattels, 41 Harv. L. Rev. 945, 975 & n. 89 (1928).

3. The leading American case involved an attempt by Napoleon Lajoie, the Philadelphia Phillies' Hall of Fame second baseman, to repudiate his contract with the Phillies and play for their crosstown rivals, the Athletics. The trial court refused to enjoin him from breaching the exclusivity clause of his contract, but the state supreme court reversed, saying:

> "The court below finds from the testimony that 'the defendant is an expert baseball player in any position; that he has a great reputation as a second baseman; that his place would be hard to fill with as good a player; that his withdrawal from the team would weaken it, as would the withdrawal of any good player, and would probably make a difference in the size of the audiences attending the game.' We think that, in thus stating it, he puts it very mildly, and that the evidence would warrant a stronger finding as to the ability of the defendant as an expert ball player. He has been for several years in the service of the plaintiff club, and has been re-engaged from season to season at a constantly increasing salary. He has become thoroughly familiar with the action and methods of the other players in the club, and his own work is peculiarly meritorious as an integral part of the team work which is so essential. In addition to these features which render his services of peculiar and special value to the plaintiff, and not easily replaced, Lajoie is well known, and has great reputation among the patrons of the sport, for ability in the position which he filled, and was thus a most attractive drawing card for the public. He may not be the sun in the baseball firmament, but he is certainly a bright particular star. We feel, therefore, that the evidence in this case justifies the conclusion that the services of the defendant are of such a unique character, and display such a special knowledge, skill, and ability, as renders them of peculiar value to the plaintiff, and so difficult of substitution that their loss will produce 'irreparable injury,' in the legal significance of that term, to the plaintiff. The action of the defendant in violating his contract is a breach of good faith, for which there would be no adequate redress at law, and the case, therefore, properly calls for the aid of equity in negatively enforcing the performance of the contract by enjoining against its breach."

Philadelphia Ball Club *v.* Lajoie, 202 Pa. 210, 217 (1902). Despite this decision, Lajoie did not return to the Phillies.

4. Cohen worked for the Ticor Title Insurance Company as a title insurance salesman. His job involved forming and maintaining relationships with law firms that might be interested in title insurance. Cohen was quite successful; his compensation (salary and bonuses) for 1997 was more than $1.1 million and his expense reimbursements for the year, covering club memberships, sports tickets, Broadways shows, and the like, were over $150,000.

In 1995, Cohen signed a heavily negotiated employment contract with Ticor, which allowed Cohen, but not Ticor, to terminate his employment with Ticor on 30 days' notice. Cohen, however, agreed not to engage in the title insurance business in the state of New York for six months following termination of employment.

In 1998, Cohen gave notice to Ticor and immediately went to work for a competitor, TitleServ. Ticor sued, seeking injunctive relief. The district court enjoined Cohen from engaging in the title insurance business for six months. The Court of Appeals for the Second Circuit affirmed. It noted that under New York law, anti-competition covenants in employment agreements are enforceable if the they are reasonable in their temporal and geographic scope, and if an injunction is necessary either to prevent disclosure of trade secrets or confidential customer lists, or because "the employee's services to the employer are deemed special or unique." In the court's view, Cohen's services were unique; therefore the anti-competition covenant was enforceable whether or not Cohen had appropriated, or was likely to appropriate, confidential information:

> "Unique services have been found in various categories of employment where the services are dependent on an employee's special talents; such categories include musicians, professional athletes, actors and the like. In those kinds of cases injunctive relief has been available to prevent the breach of an employment contract where the individual performer has such ability and reputation that his or her place may not easily be filled. We recognized this category of uniqueness in the case of the services of an acrobat who, in his performance, with one hand lifted his co-performer, a grown man, from a full length position on the floor, an act described as 'the most marvelous thing that has ever been [done] before.' Shubert Theatrical Co. *v.* Rath, 271 F. 827, 829–30 (2d Cir. 1921). We later said that where services are unique the issuance of an injunction 'is not an open question in this court,' and commented that this 'principle is equally well settled in the courts of New York.' Associated Newspapers *v.* Phillips, 294 F. 845, 850 (2d Cir. 1923) (employee writer of feature articles for the daily press provided unique services). . . .
>
> "[T]o fall within this category of employees against whom equity will enforce a negative covenant, it is not necessary that the employee should be the only 'star' of his employer, or that the

> business will grind to a halt if the employee leaves. Hence, as noted earlier, in determining uniqueness the inquiry now focuses more on the employee's relationship to the employer's business than on the individual person of the employee.
>
> "The trial court found Cohen's relationships with clients were 'special' and qualified as unique services. It deemed these relationships unique for several reasons. First, since the costs and terms of title insurance in New York are fixed by law, competition for business relies more heavily on personal relationships. Second, since potential clients—New York law firms with real estate practices—are limited and well known throughout the industry, maintaining current clients from this established group is crucial. Third, the trial court noted that . . . Cohen had negotiated his employment contract and the non-compete clause with the assistance of counsel and not from an inferior bargaining position."

Ticor Title Insurance Co. *v.* Cohen, 173 F.3d 63, 70–71 (2d Cir. 1999).

5. Montague hired Flockton to act in his theater for a season. They later renewed their agreement for another season. Flockton received a few better offers during the second season and refused to complete the season with Montague, who hired Palmer to perform in Flockton's place in his next play. When Montague learned that Flockton was going to act in other theaters before the end of the season, he obtained an injunction barring Flockton from doing so. Montague *v.* Flockton, L.R. 16 Eq. 189 (1873). Although there was no explicit exclusivity provision in Flockton's contract with Montague, the judge thought it plain that "a man agreeing to act in one particular theatre during the season" is agreeing to "act there and not anywhere else." Given the retention of Palmer, an injunction would leave Flockton unemployed, but the court viewed this as a problem of his own making.

Rogers v. Runfola & Associates, Inc.

Supreme Court of Ohio, 1991.
57 Ohio St. 3d 5.

. . . In 1971, Thomas Runfola, acting as a sole proprietor, began operating a court reporting service under the name of "Runfola and Associates." In February 1977, Runfola incorporated the business . . . .

In 1972, while attending school, Rogers began working for Runfola. Rogers continued to work for Runfola after completing school, and on June 1, 1975, she signed an employment contract. On September 19, 1977, Marrone, at the age of nineteen, began working for Runfola and he also signed a contract. Marrone testified that Runfola indicated to him that if Marrone should ever become unhappy with the firm, he would not be held to the contract. At the time appellees filed their complaint, both contracts were for a term of one year and subject to automatic renewal.

Rogers' and Marrone's employment contracts contained a covenant not to compete. The covenants in each contract are virtually identical and both preclude appellees from engaging in court reporting or public stenography as an employee or otherwise in Franklin County, for a period of two years. The covenant also bans appellees from ever diverting or soliciting any of Runfola's clients and bars appellees from ever using any client list, notes, transcripts, exhibits, files, records or any documents received by or on behalf of Runfola.

On April 28, 1988, appellees each submitted a letter of resignation to Dennis Mowery, the general manager of Runfola. Appellees met with Mowery and, among other things, expressed to him that they both had decided to terminate their employment. At this meeting, Rogers and Marrone also agreed that in order to effect the transition, they would continue to work until their contract anniversary dates, and stated they were reasonably certain they would open their own firm locally. In response, counsel for Runfola sent letters to appellees reminding them of their agreements not to compete. . . .

■ DOUGLAS, JUSTICE. The primary issue we are asked to decide is whether the covenants not to compete contained within appellees' employment contracts are reasonable in light of the guidelines pronounced by this court in Raimonde *v.* Van Vlerah, 42 Ohio St. 2d 21 (1975).

[The court first determined that the employment contracts were valid.]

In *Raimonde*, . . . we stated:

> "1. A covenant not to compete which imposes unreasonable restrictions upon an employee will be enforced to the extent necessary to protect an employer's legitimate interests.
>
> "2. A covenant restraining an employee from competing with his former employer upon termination of employment is reasonable *if the restraint is no greater than is required for the protection of the employer, does not impose undue hardship on the employee, and is not injurious to the public*." (Emphasis added.)

Further, in *Raimonde*, we acknowledged that courts are empowered to fashion a reasonable covenant between the parties and, in so doing, they should consider the following factors:

> ". . . [T]he absence or presence of limitations as to time and space, . . . whether the employee represents the sole contact with the customer; whether the employee is possessed with confidential information or trade secrets; whether the covenant seeks to eliminate competition which would be unfair to the employer or merely seeks to eliminate ordinary competition; whether the covenant seeks to stifle the inherent skill and experience of the employee; whether the benefit to the employer is disproportional to the detriment to the employee; whether the

> covenant operates as a bar to the employee's sole means of support; whether the employee's talent which the employer seeks to suppress was actually developed during the period of employment; and whether the forbidden employment is merely incidental to the main employment. . . ."

Keeping the foregoing factors in mind, we conclude that the restraints and resultant hardships on appellees do exceed that which is reasonable to protect Runfola's legitimate business interests. Geographically, appellees are prohibited from engaging in court reporting or public stenography in Franklin County for two years. Appellees are also restricted, for a lifetime, from soliciting or diverting any of Runfola's clients. Court reporting is a unique profession. Appellees attended school to become court reporters and have worked as reporters for most of their adult lives. Rogers' and Marrone's testimony indicated that court reporting is the only profession in which they have become proficient. Imposing such space and time restrictions is unreasonable and will create an undue hardship on appellees.

Although we conclude that the covenants not to compete create an excessive hardship on appellees, our inquiry, nevertheless, cannot end here. We must also determine whether some restrictions prohibiting appellees from competing are necessary to protect Runfola's business interests. The record reflects that Runfola played a large role in appellees' development as successful court reporters. While employed by Runfola, Rogers and Marrone gained valuable experience in the business which included the use of computerized technology. Runfola invested time and money in equipment, facilities, support staff and training. Much of this training and support, undoubtedly, inured to the benefit of the appellees. Runfola also developed a clientele with which appellees had direct contact. Appellees' assignments were taken under the Runfola name. Indeed, Runfola has a legitimate commercial interest to protect.

Thus, balancing the restraints and projected hardships on appellees with Runfola's interests, and upon the authority of *Raimonde*, we modify the restrictions as to space and time . . . .

[W]e hold that appellees shall, sixty days from the date of this order, be prohibited for a period of one year from engaging in court reporting or public stenography as a business, as employees, or otherwise, within the city limits of Columbus, Ohio, and be prohibited for a period of one year from engaging in court reporting or the stenography business with any person, firm or other business entity with an office located within the city limits of Columbus, Ohio. Further, appellees shall, from the date of this order, be prohibited for a period of one year from soliciting or diverting any of Runfola's clients that have employed Runfola seeking advice, assistance or services. Finally, we remand this case to the trial court on the sole issue of damages. Upon remand, the trial court should determine what damages, if any, appellees have caused Runfola by disregarding the covenant not to compete, as modified, by this court. . . .

■ [The separate opinion of JUSTICE BROWN, concurring in part and dissenting in part, is omitted.]

NOTES

1. Hirshberg worked as a managing accountant (one step below partnership) for BDO Seidman, a national accounting firm. In his employment contract with BDO Seidman, Hirshberg agreed to pay liquidated damages to the firm if, within 18 months after termination of his employment, he performed accounting services for any client of the firm's Buffalo office. Hirshberg resigned in 1993 and proceeded to perform services for former clients of the Buffalo office, including both clients developed by the firm and clients Hirschberg had brought to the firm.

The New York Court of Appeals first concluded that Hirshberg, despite his professional status, was not a "unique" employee. Then, treating enforcement by liquidated damages as equivalent to enforcement by specific performance, the court applied a three part test of reasonableness for enforcement of employee agreements not to compete: the restraint on competition must be "no greater than is required for the protection of the legitimate interest of the employer," it must not impose undue hardship on the employee, and it must not injure the public. The court found that Hirshberg's contract violated the first element of the test, because it applied not only to client relationships initiated and supported by the firm, but also to client relationships developed independently.

Based on this finding, the court remanded for partial enforcement of the contract. It said:

> "The issue of whether a court should cure the unreasonable aspect of an overbroad employee restrictive covenant through the means of partial enforcement or severance has been the subject of some debate among courts and commentators. A legitimate consideration against the exercise of this power is the fear that employers will use their superior bargaining position to impose unreasonable anti-competitive restrictions, uninhibited by the risk that a court will void the entire agreement, leaving the employee free of any restraint. The prevailing, modern view rejects a per se rule that invalidates entirely any overbroad employee agreement not to compete. Instead, when, as here, the unenforceable portion is not an essential part of the agreed exchange, a court should conduct a case specific analysis, focusing on the conduct of the employer in imposing the terms of the agreement Under this approach, if the employer demonstrates an absence of overreaching, coercive use of dominant bargaining power, or other anti-competitive misconduct, but has in good faith sought to protect a legitimate business interest, consistent with reasonable standards of fair dealing, partial enforcement may be justified. . . .
>
> "Here, the undisputed facts and circumstances militate in favor of partial enforcement. The covenant was not imposed as a condition of defendant's initial employment, or even his continued

employment, but in connection with promotion to a position of responsibility and trust just one step below admittance to the partnership. There is no evidence of coercion or that the Manager's Agreement was part of some general plan to forestall competition. Moreover, no proof was submitted that BDO imposed the covenant in bad faith, knowing full well that it was overbroad. Indeed, as already discussed, the existence of our 'learned profession' precedents, and decisions in other States upholding the full terms of this type of agreement, support the contrary conclusion.

"The Appellate Division's fear that partial enforcement will require rewriting the parties' agreement is unfounded. No additional substantive terms are required. The time and geographical limitations on the covenant remain intact. The only change is to narrow the class of BDO clients to which the covenant applies. Moreover, to reject partial enforcement based solely on the extent of necessary revision of the contract resembles the now-discredited doctrine that invalidation of an entire restrictive covenant is required unless the invalid portion was so divisible that it could be mechanically severed, as with a 'judicial blue pencil.' Thus, we conclude that severance is appropriate, rendering the restrictive covenant partially enforceable."

BDO Seidman *v.* Hirshberg, 93 N.Y.2d 382, 394–95 (1999). But cf. Peat Marwick Main & Co. *v.* Haass, 818 S.W.2d 381 (Texas 1991) (refusing partial enforcement of an overbroad covenant not to compete).

2. A provision of Merrill Lynch's company-funded pension plan stated that if a former employee entered into competition with the firm after termination of employment, the employee would forfeit his or her pension and profit-sharing benefits. On August 30, 1974, Merrill Lynch fired Post and Maney without cause; on September 4 they began work for another brokerage. The New York Court of Appeals held that forfeiture in the event of an involuntary discharge without cause is *per se* unreasonable. Post *v.* Merrill Lynch, Pierce, Fenner & Smith, Inc., 48 N.Y.2d 84 (1979). The court did not say whether the same reasoning would preclude specific enforcement of a covenant not to compete following an involuntary discharge without cause.

B. SCOPE AND CONSEQUENCES OF THE SPECIFIC PERFORMANCE REMEDY

1. TAILORING THE REMEDY

Dalton v. Educational Testing Service

Court of Appeals of New York, 1995.
87 N.Y.2d 384.

[Educational Testing Service (ETS) refused to release Dalton's SAT scores based on its suspicion that an imposter had taken the test. Dalton brought a suit for specific performance and money damages. The lower court held that ETS breached its contract with Dalton and ordered ETS to release SAT score. The Appellate Division affirmed.]

■ KAYE, CHIEF JUDGE. The primary question before us is whether [ETS], a standardized testing firm, complied with procedures specified in its contract with high school senior Brian Dalton in refusing to release Dalton's [SAT] score. Because the factual findings underlying the trial court's determination that ETS failed to act in good faith in following those procedures were affirmed by the Appellate Division, have support in the record and are consequently beyond the scope of our review, we conclude—as did the trial court and Appellate Division—that ETS breached its contract with Dalton. Though we agree, moreover, with the courts below that specific performance is the appropriate remedy, we nevertheless conclude that the promised performance was good-faith compliance with the stated procedures, not release of the questioned scores as ordered by those courts.

In May 1991, Brian Dalton took the SAT, which was administered by ETS, at Holy Cross High School in Queens where Dalton was a junior. Six months later, in November, he took the examination a second time, as a senior, this time at John Bowne High School in Queens, and his combined score increased 410 points.

Because Dalton's score increased by more than 350 points, his test results fell within the ETS category of "Large Score Differences" or "discrepant scores." In accordance with ETS policy, members of the ETS Test Security Office therefore reviewed his May and November answer sheets. Upon a finding of disparate handwriting, the answer sheets were submitted to a document examiner, who opined that they were completed by separate individuals. Dalton's case was then forwarded to the Board of Review, which preliminarily decided that substantial evidence supported cancelling Dalton's November score.

Upon registering for the November SAT, Dalton had signed a statement agreeing to the conditions in the New York State edition of the Registration Bulletin, which reserved to ETS "the right to cancel any test score . . . if ETS believes that there is reason to question the score's validity." The Registration Bulletin further provided that, if "the validity of a test score is questioned because it may have been obtained unfairly, ETS [will] notif[y] the test taker of the reasons for questioning the score" and offer the test-taker the following five options: (1) the opportunity to provide additional information, (2) confirmation of the score by taking a free retest, (3) authorization for ETS to cancel the score and refund all fees, (4) third-party review by any institution receiving the test score or (5) arbitration.

As specified in the Registration Bulletin, ETS apprised Dalton of its preliminary decision to cancel his November SAT score in a letter from Test Security Specialist Celeste M. Eppinger. Noting the handwriting disparity and the substantial difference between his May and November test results, Eppinger informed Dalton that "[t]he evidence suggests that someone else may have completed your answer sheet and that the questioned scores may be invalid." She advised him that he could supply "any additional information that will help explain" this or, alternatively, elect one of the other options.

Eppinger enclosed the Procedures for Questioned Scores pamphlet with her letter, which reiterated the test-taker's right to "submit additional relevant information" to the Board of Review supporting the validity of questioned scores. In cautioning test-takers to provide only information "relevant to the questions being raised," the Procedures for Questioned Scores explained, "[f]or example, character references or testimonial letters do not explain handwriting differences." As to the four additional options, the guide further explained, "ETS also offers other options . . . if additional information doesn't resolve the questions about the validity of the scores. The option to provide additional information to resolve these questions may be used in combination with one or more of the[se] options."

Dalton opted to present additional information to the Board of Review, including the following: verification that he was suffering from mononucleosis during the May examination; diagnostic test results from a preparatory course he took prior to the November examination (he had taken no similar course prior to the May SAT) that were consistent with his performance on that test; a statement from an ETS proctor who remembered Dalton's presence during the November examination; and statements from two students—one previously unacquainted with Dalton—that he had been in the classroom during that test. Dalton further provided ETS with a report from a document examiner obtained by his family who concluded that Dalton was the author of both sets of answer sheets.

ETS, after several Board of Review meetings, submitted the various handwriting exemplars to a second document examiner who, like its first, opined that the May and November tests were not completed by the same individual. As a result, ETS continued to question the validity of Dalton's November score.

At this point plaintiff Peter Dalton, father and natural guardian of Brian Dalton, filed a [suit] to prohibit ETS from cancelling Dalton's November SAT score and to compel immediate release of the score. Following a 12-day nonjury trial, the trial court found that ETS failed "to make even rudimentary efforts to evaluate or investigate the information" furnished by Dalton and thus concluded that ETS failed to act in good faith in determining the legitimacy of Dalton's score, thereby breaching its contract. The trial court premised this conclusion on its determination that the ETS Board of Review members failed to evaluate the information submitted because they believed Dalton's presence at the November SAT to be wholly irrelevant to the handwriting issue and that he could controvert the Board's preliminary finding that the score was invalid solely by taking a retest. As a remedy for the contractual breach, the trial court ordered ETS to release the November SAT score.

The Appellate Division affirmed. It too found that ETS ignored the documentation provided by Dalton and considered only the reports of its own document examiners. Like the trial court, the Appellate Division concluded that this failure to evaluate as well as to investigate Dalton's information constituted a breach of contract. In light of these factual determinations, we agree that ETS breached its contract with Dalton but differ as to the scope of the relief.

By accepting ETS' standardized form agreement when he registered for the November SAT, Dalton entered into a contract with ETS. Implicit in all contracts is a covenant of good faith and fair dealing in the course of contract performance.

Encompassed within the implied obligation of each promisor to exercise good faith are "any promises which a reasonable person in the position of the promisee would be justified in understanding were included." This embraces a pledge that "neither party shall do anything which will have the effect of destroying or injuring the right of the other party to receive the fruits of the contract." Where the contract contemplates the exercise of discretion, this pledge includes a promise not to act arbitrarily or irrationally in exercising that discretion. The duty of good faith and fair dealing, however, is not without limits, and no obligation can be implied that "would be inconsistent with other terms of the contractual relationship."

The parties here agreed to the provisions in the Registration Bulletin, which expressly permit cancellation of a test score so long as ETS found "reason to question" its validity after offering the test-taker the five specified options. Nothing in the contract compelled ETS to prove that the test-taker cheated. Nor did the invitation to the test-taker to furnish ETS with relevant information reasonably and realistically translate into any requirement that ETS conduct a field investigation or gather evidence to verify or counter the test-taker's documentation. Indeed, such an obligation would be inconsistent with the contractual language placing the burden squarely on the test-taker to overcome the ETS finding of score invalidity. ETS, therefore, was under no duty, express or implied, to initiate an external investigation into a questioned score.

The contract, however, did require that ETS consider any relevant material that Dalton supplied to the Board of Review. The Registration Bulletin explicitly afforded Dalton the option to provide ETS with relevant information upon notification that ETS questioned the legitimacy of his test score. Having elected to offer this option, it was certainly reasonable to expect that ETS would, at the very least, consider any relevant material submitted in reaching its final decision.

Dalton triggered this implied-in-law obligation on the part of ETS by exercising his contractual option to provide ETS with information. Significantly, Dalton heeded the advice in the Procedures for Questioned Scores and tendered numerous documents that did more than simply deny allegations of wrongdoing or attest to his good character, such as medical evidence regarding his physical condition, statements by fellow test-takers, the statement of a classroom proctor and consistent diagnostic test results.

Nevertheless, with the exception of the document examiner's report, ETS disputes the relevancy of this information. Specifically, ETS maintains that the sole issue before the Board of Review was the disparate handwriting and that evidence regarding Dalton's health (apart from a damaged arm) or presence during both examinations is irrelevant to resolving that issue.

To be sure, the Procedures for Questioned Scores warned Dalton "to provide only additional information that is relevant to the questions being raised." The Eppinger letter to Dalton, however, informed him that his November score was possibly invalid precisely because ETS believed "that someone else may have completed [his] answer sheet." Thus, ETS expressly framed the dispositive question as one of suspected impersonation. Because the statements from the classroom proctor and November test-takers corroborated Dalton's contention that he was present at and in fact took the November examination, they were relevant to this issue.

Likewise, inasmuch as the medical documentation concerning Dalton's health at the time of the May SAT provided an explanation for his poor performance on that examination, and the consistent diagnostic test results demonstrated his ability to achieve such a dramatic score increase, these items were also germane to the question whether it was Dalton or an imposter who completed the November examination. Indeed, in its manual, Policies and Procedures Concerning Scores of Questionable Validity—which details internal ETS procedure regarding questioned scores—ETS offers several examples of "relevant information" that a test-taker might provide, including "a doctor's report that the candidate was under the influence of medication at the time the low score was earned." Regarding "a case of possible impersonation" in particular, the manual suggests that "other test results might demonstrate that the questioned score is not inconsistent with other measures of the candidate's abilities." Thus, Dalton's material fell within ETS' own definition of relevancy, as expressed in its manual and letter to Dalton.

The critical question then is whether the Board of Review made any effort to consider this relevant information submitted by Dalton. That is a factual inquiry. . . .

Several Board of Review members—each member alone had the power to order release of Dalton's November score—testified that they believed information establishing Dalton's presence during the November examination to be irrelevant to their determination and, moreover, that only a successful retest would validate Dalton's score. Thus, there is support in the record for the factual determinations of the trial court and Appellate Division and they are binding on us. This is so notwithstanding inconsistent testimony by Board members that the Board did review Dalton's information but found it unpersuasive. In light of the affirmed findings, the Court of Appeals simply does not have authority to weigh conflicting evidence and make its own factual determinations . . . .

Consequently, this case is factually distinct from those relied upon by ETS, where the testing service considered but then rejected information provided by the test-taker. When ETS fulfills its contractual obligation to consider relevant material provided by the test-taker and otherwise acts in good faith, the testing service—not the courts—must be the final arbiter of both the appropriate weight to accord that material and the validity of the test score. This Court will not interfere with that discretionary determination unless it is performed arbitrarily or irrationally.

Where, however, ETS refuses to exercise its discretion in the first instance by declining even to consider relevant material submitted by the test-taker, the legal question is whether this refusal breached an express or implied term of the contract, not whether it was arbitrary or irrational. Here, the courts below agreed that ETS did not consider the relevant information furnished by Dalton. By doing so, ETS failed to comply in good faith with its own test security procedures, thereby breaching its contract with Dalton. . . .

In an analogous context, we have refused to compel a university to issue a degree to a student who had not fulfilled the academic requirements (see Matter of Olsson *v.* Board of Higher Education, 49 NY2d 408). This reluctance to interfere with the exercise of academic discretion is motivated by sound considerations of public policy. "When an educational institution issues a diploma to one of its students, it is, in effect, certifying to society that the student possesses all of the knowledge and skills that are required by his [or her] chosen discipline" (*id.* at 413). Likewise, we have held that a college did not act arbitrarily in declining to "round off" a student's failing grade so that she could graduate.

The comparison between ETS and academic institutions is surely not exact, inasmuch as judicial restraint in matters of academic achievement is based, in part, on the inherently subjective nature of the evaluation to be made by professional educators. Still, similar policy concerns militate against directing ETS to release a questioned score. When a standardized testing service reports a score, it certifies to the world that the test-taker possesses the requisite knowledge and skills to achieve the particular score. Like academic credentials, if courts were to require testing services to release questioned scores, "the value of these credentials from the point of view of society would be seriously undermined." Given the reliance that students, educational institutions, prospective employers and others place on the legitimacy of scores released by ETS, requiring challenged scores to be reported would be contrary to the public interest and exceed the scope of ETS' promised performance.

While courts as a matter of policy are reluctant to intrude upon academic discretion in educational matters, they stand ready as a matter of law and equity to enforce contract rights. Where a contract is breached, moreover, and the injured party is entitled to specific performance, the remedy must be a real one, not an exercise in futility.

Dalton is entitled to relief that comports with ETS' contractual promise—good-faith consideration of the material he submitted to ETS. We cannot agree with Dalton's assumption that ETS will merely rubber-stamp its prior determination without good-faith attention to his documentation and that reconsideration by ETS will be an empty exercise. Our conclusion that the contract affords Dalton a meaningful remedy rests also on the provision in the Procedures for Questioned Scores allowing Dalton to utilize one or more of the remaining four options in combination with renewed consideration by the Board of Review. Those options—including third-party review by any institution receiving the test score as well as arbitration—remain available should ETS determine that the information submitted fails to resolve its concerns about the validity of the November score. . . .

■ [The dissenting opinion of JUDGE LEVINE is omitted.]

2. ENFORCEMENT AGAINST ASSIGNEES AND SUCCESSORS

Kunzman v. Thorsen

Supreme Court of Oregon, 1987.
303 Or. 600.

■ CAMPBELL, JUSTICE. [In 1977, the Kunzmans, as vendors, entered into an installment sale contract with McNabb, as vendee, for conveyance of a farm. The same year, McNabb assigned the contract to the Thorsens. The Thorsens took possession of the farm, made payments due under the installment contract, built a barn, gave a mortgage to secure a loan, and rented out pasture. There was no further contact between the Kunzmans and McNabb. In 1984, the Thorsens defaulted and the Kunzmans sued them for specific performance of the contract. Under Oregon law, both parties to a land sale contract are routinely entitled to specific performance.]

A vendor's rights against the assignee of a land sale contract derive from the vendor's status as third party beneficiary to the contract of assignment between the vendee and the vendee's assignee. No independent obligation arises between the vendor and the assignee as a result of the acceptance of contract benefits. The scope of the assignment defines the scope of relief available to the vendor. In essence, the vendor's action is one for specific performance of the assignee's agreement to assume the vendee's duties.

The dispute in this case is over construction of the instrument of assignment. That instrument conveys to the assignees "all of the vendee's right, title and interest in and to" the land sale contract "and to the real estate described therein." The issue is whether this broad and inclusive language was intended by the parties to impose upon the assignees duties of performance under the original contract. . . .

In contracts for the sale of goods that ambiguity has been resolved in favor of a presumption that the assignee has assumed the contract duties. ORS 72.2100(4) reads:

> "An assignment of 'the contract' or of 'all my rights under the contract' or an assignment in similar general terms is an assignment of rights and unless the language or the circumstances (as in an assignment for security) indicate the contrary, it is a delegation of performance of the duties of the assignor and its acceptance by the assignee constitutes a promise by the assignee to perform those duties. This promise is enforceable by either the assignor or the other party to the original contract."

The Restatement (Second) of Contracts . . . adopted the same presumption as a general rule of contract construction. Restatement (Second) Contracts § 328 (1981).[2] The justification advanced for this rule is that it most probably conforms to the parties' intent and to their understanding of the meaning of such broad language of assignment. However, the Restatement (Second) includes a caveat in which the American Law Institute reserves its opinion as to whether that presumption "applies to an assignment by a purchaser of his rights under a contract for the sale of land." Restatement (Second) Contracts § 328 (1981). The Institute explains this reticence in a comment:

> "When the purchaser under a land contract assigns his rights, the assignment has commonly been treated like a sale of land 'subject to' a mortgage. In this view acceptance of the assignment does not amount to an assumption of the assignor's duties unless the contract of assignment so provides either expressly or by implication. . . . Decisions refusing to infer an

---

[2] . . . Restatement (Second) Contracts § 328 (1981) reads:

"(1) Unless the language or the circumstances indicate the contrary, as in an assignment for security, an assignment of 'the contract' or of 'all my rights under the contract' or an assignment in similar general terms is an assignment of the assignor's rights and a delegation of his unperformed duties under the contract.

"(2) Unless the language or the circumstances indicate the contrary, the acceptance by an assignee of such an assignment operates as a promise to the assignor to perform the assignor's unperformed duties, and the obligor of the assigned rights is an intended beneficiary of the promise. . . ."

> assumption of duties by the assignee have been influenced by doctrinal difficulties in the recognition of rights of assignees and beneficiaries. Those difficulties have now been overcome, and it is doubtful whether adherence to such decisions carries out the probable intent of the parties in the usual case. But since the shift in doctrine has not yet produced any definite changes in the body of decisions, the Institute expresses no opinion on the application of Subsection (2) to an assignment by a purchaser under a land contract."

Restatement (Second) Contracts § 328, *comment c* at 46 (1981).

In Hodges *v.* Servine, 211 Or. 428 (1957), this court stated the rule of interpretation for use in such cases . . . :

> ". . . [T]he assignee of a contract for the purchase of land or other property assumes no liability to the vendor by reason of the assignment alone. But [w]here the assignee claims the benefits of the contract he becomes subject to its burdens as fully and to the same extent as though he were the original party to the contract." . . .

211 Or. at 437–38. . . .

In Langel *v.* Betz, 250 N.Y. 159 (1928), . . . the court recognized that "[t]he assignee may . . . expressly or impliedly, bind himself to perform the assignor's duties," and noted that under its previous decisions "where the assignee of the vendee invokes the aid of a court of equity in an action for specific performance, he impliedly binds himself to perform on his part," but that the converse of this rule, "that the assignee of the vendee would be bound when the vendor began the action," did not follow from those decisions.

The *Langel* court next discussed and rejected the rule of the first Restatement presuming assumption by the assignee . . . :

> "The [rule of the first Restatement] is a complete reversal of our present rule of interpretation as to the probable intention of the parties. It is, perhaps, more in harmony with modern ideas of contractual relations than is 'the archaic view of a contract as creating a strictly personal obligation between the creditor and debtor,' which prohibited the assignee from suing at law in his own name and which denied a remedy to third party beneficiaries. . . . [B]ut the law remains that no promise of the assignee to assume the assignor's duties is to be inferred from the acceptance of an assignment of a bilateral contract, in the absence of circumstances surrounding the assignment itself which indicate a contrary intention."

. . . . [In Hodges *v.* Servine,] [t]his court joined the New York court in rejecting the Restatement rule and requiring some objective manifestation of intent to be bound where the words of assignment are ambiguous. However, this court held in *Hodges* that a claim of the contract benefits creates a presumption that the assignee assumed the contract obligations.

As we read the opinion in *Hodges,* the court was impressed less with the fact that the assignees sought restitution for their expenditures than with the fact that the assignees took possession of the land and made payments directly to the vendors, behaving generally as if they were party to the original contract. This interpretation of *Hodges* is supported by the only other cases in which this court has determined that acceptance of contract benefits imposed liability upon a contract assignee. . . .

From this mash of precedent we distill the following principle: An assignee "claims the benefits" of a land sale contract when he or she exercises the rights in the contract's subject matter conferred upon the vendee by the contract. Where a party accepts a broadly worded assignment of a land sale contract, "steps into the shoes" of the assignor and asserts the interests the contract conveys, the presumption arises that the assignee intended also to assume the duties the contract imposes.

Defendants aver that "every assignee, even assignees for security purposes, 'claim the benefits' of contracts assigned to them," and they express concern that the Court of Appeals' decision consequently renders every contract assignee liable for performance of the contract assigned. This concern is unfounded.

Accepting the benefits of a contract does not *impose* liability on an assignee. The *Hodges* rule is a rule of construction only. It considers the probable intent of the parties at the time the assignment was made for the purpose of determining whether expansive words of the assignment imply an assumption of duties by the assignee. Where the parties clearly intend otherwise (as evinced either by the terms of the assignment or by the surrounding circumstances, *e.g.*, an assignment for security), the implication that the assignee assumed the vendor's contractual duties is dispelled.

Defendants further contend that vendees under land sale contracts will be unable to assign their interests in land as freely as mortgagors or grantors of trust deeds, pointing out that holders of those interests can assign their interests in the land "subject to" the mortgage or trust deed. Of course, nothing prevents the parties to an assignment of a vendee's interest in a land sale contract from including such a provision or otherwise limiting the assignee's exposure in the instrument of assignment.

The rule developed in *Hodges* [and other Oregon cases] is closer to that of the Restatement and the UCC than it is to the probable majority rule on this issue. However, we are not persuaded that a more rigorous test than that adopted in this court's previous decisions is needed to safeguard the interests of the parties to a land sale contract or to its subsequent assignment. . . .

NOTES

1. Langel *v.* Betz (the New York decision discussed in *Kunzman*) has been much criticized, but it continues to exert some influence.

2. In Epstein *v.* Gluckin, 233 N.Y. 490 (1922), the court held that, by bringing an action for specific performance, the assignee of the vendee was impliedly bound to perform the duties of the assignor. The court stated: "What equity exacts today as a condition of relief is the assurance that the decree [of specific performance], if rendered, will operate without injustice or oppression either to plaintiff or to defendant." *Id.* at 494.

Walgren v. Dolan

California Court of Appeal, Fourth District, 1990.
226 Cal. App. 3d 572.

■ FROELICH, ASSOCIATE JUSTICE. . . . On August 28, 1986, Walgren entered into a contract with Dolan, Sr., for the purchase of property offered for sale by Dolan, Sr., through a real estate agent. The contract provided that $1,000 would be placed immediately in escrow, and another $14,000 would be deposited by Walgren shortly thereafter as down payment. The contract further provided that should the seller be unable to furnish a marketable title, seller would agree to "perfect said title at his expense."

The property subject to this contract was allegedly represented by both Dolan, Sr., and the real estate agent to be property owned by Dolan, Sr. However, formal legal and record title was held by a trust. According to testimony presented by Walgren, at the time the contract was signed neither Walgren nor the real estate agent had actual knowledge of how the property title was vested. No separate inquiry was made by Walgren or the real estate agent as to the true nature of title. Walgren deposited $1,000 in escrow; however, when Walgren tendered an additional $14,000 cashier's check for the balance of the down payment, the escrow company refused to accept it. Two months later, Dolan, Sr., died.

Defendant Dolan [Jr.] is now and was at the time the contract was signed the trustee of the trust under which the property was held. At the time the trust was created, Dolan, Sr., and his wife were the settlors and sole beneficiaries of the trust. According to the terms of the trust, all duties of the trustee were exercisable only pursuant to the written instructions of Dolan, Sr., and his wife, or the survivor of them. When Dolan, Sr.'s wife died, the trust was to be divided in two equal shares, the wife's share to become "irrevocably vested" in her appointees. Such vesting was subject, however, to a life estate for the benefit of the surviving husband, as well as discretionary authority in the trustee to invade principal for the husband's benefit. Respondents contend this vesting, which occurred when she in fact predeceased Dolan, Sr., altered the power of Dolan, Sr., over the disposition of property in the trust. The trust provisions, however, seem clear: Until the time of his death Dolan, Sr., had complete control over disposition of property in the trust, even though his beneficial interest therein, arguably, was reduced to a moiety. . . .

Our focus . . . is entirely upon the question of the alleged flaw in the contract based upon the status of record title in the trustee, rather than in the name of the individual who executed the agreement of sale—Dolan, Sr.

Analysis of this question is assisted by approaching it in two segments: first, would the contract have been specifically enforceable against Dolan, Sr., and his trustee absent the factor of his death; and second, if it would have been enforceable, does Dolan, Sr.'s death in any way impair that right?

The beneficiary of an ordinary trust is empowered to convey only his beneficial interest in the trust property. Since the beneficiary holds only equitable title, the legal title residing in the trustee, the beneficiary has no power to convey absolute ownership of trust property. The Dolan trust was not, however, an ordinary trust. The beneficiary had retained absolute control over trust property, having (even after the death of the cobeneficiary) the complete power to direct the trustee to purchase or sell realty. It would seem inequitable, indeed, to permit one with absolute power over title to realty to decline to perform an agreement for sale of the realty because bare legal title was held in the name of a trustee. . . .

Where . . . a party holds the equitable title to realty and has the power to "call for" legal title, it is established that specific performance is available. . . .

[E]nforcement of a sale by a vendee to a subpurchaser is usually described as based upon the doctrine of equitable conversion. The vendee having a right to acquire title from the titleholder of the realty becomes an equitable owner; having the power to "call" for legal title, he should be required to respond in specific performance to the subpurchaser. The rationale would seem applicable to any situation in which the vendor has equitable title and the power to control conveyance of legal title. Hence, when the beneficiary of a trust agrees to convey trust realty, and has the power by the terms of the trust to require a deed execution by the trustee, specific performance should be available. . . .

We . . . conclude that specific performance (assuming all other requisites of the remedy are established) is available in California to a vendee who has an agreement to purchase realty executed by the holder of beneficial interest in a trust which is legal titleholder, where the beneficiary has the power under the terms of the trust to require a conveyance by the trustee. . . .

Concluding, then, that the Dolan-Walgren contract of sale was enforceable during the lives of the parties, is there any defense provided by the death of Dolan, Sr.? We conclude there is not. The enforceability of contracts in general (other than those for personal services) survives the death of a contracting party. When a vendor dies before conveyance, an action for specific performance may be maintained against his heirs and devisees. Although Walgren's action for damages presumably should have been brought against Dolan, Sr.'s estate, the action for specific performance necessarily had to be brought against the successors-in-interest to the title to the realty, which would be either the trustees or the successor beneficiaries of the trust. . . .

The record here does not disclose whether title to the property remained in the hands of Dolan as trustee, or had been distributed to the beneficiaries of the trust. All these parties were named as defendants, however, and hence it appears all necessary parties were before the court. . . .

NOTES

1. Dolan, Sr. was no longer in a position to perform the contract. Dolan, Jr. (as trustee) was not a party to the contract, nor was he an assignee who assumed the vendor's duties, yet he was required to perform. Although the court did not refer to the doctrine of equitable conversion (discussed in the next section), equitable conversion may help to explain the result.

2. Mr. Colby agreed, in consideration of marriage, to leave his residence to Mrs. Colby. Mr. Colby later secretly changed his will. The court allowed Mrs. Colby to enforce the agreement against her husband's devisee:

> "There was a legal binding contract alleged in the complaint, made upon a good and sufficient consideration, which the plaintiff fully and faithfully performed upon her part; the deceased failed to perform on his part; he failed to vest her with the title to the property in question, and in consequence of such failure on the part of the deceased, the title to the house and lot descended to the defendants who are his heirs at law; the relief to which the plaintiff is entitled is a conveyance from these heirs of the title to the premises in fulfillment of the contract of their ancestor. . . . While an agreement to make a certain disposition of property by a last will is one which, strictly speaking, is not capable of a specific execution, yet it has been held to be within the jurisdiction of a court of equity to do what is equivalent to a specific performance of such an agreement, by requiring those upon whom the legal title has descended to convey the property in accordance with its terms. And the court will not allow this *post mortem* remedy to be defeated by any devise inconsistent with the agreement."

Colby *v.* Colby, 30 N.Y.S. 677, 678 (1894).

3. EQUITABLE CONVERSION

Shay v. Penrose

Supreme Court of Illinois, 1962.
25 Ill.2d 447.

■ HOUSE, JUSTICE. . . . Carol M. Shay individually acquired six parcels of real estate in her lifetime. Between 1955 and 1960 she executed contracts for deed to separate purchasers of four of the properties. None of the contracts is set out in full but it appears from the pleadings that they are the type of contract for deed in common usage by the profession. Each provided for a down payment with the balances payable in varying amounts per month together with interest on the balances from time to time unpaid. Each buyer went into possession under his contract. Provisions were made for delivery of abstracts of title showing merchantable title in seller, title examination by the buyers, methods of perfecting any title defects, and delivery of warranty deeds upon receipt of final payment. The seller retained an option of forfeiture in the event the buyer failed to perform his covenants, including that of making the specified payments.

On July 31, 1960, Carol M. Shay died intestate and was survived by her husband Arthur R. Shay, the plaintiff, who is also made a party as administrator, and her sister Grace Penrose. [Under the governing rules of intestate succession, title to the decedent's personal property vested in her administrator at her death, pending distribution to the statutory heirs, while real property vested in directly in her heirs. Grace Penrose, as an heir of Carol Shay, claimed a one-half interest in the four parcels of land subject to contract, and sought to have the land partitioned.].

The trial court held that equitable conversion had occurred at the time of execution of the contracts so that the four tracts were not subject to partition by heirs of the seller. Defendant's basic contention is that equitable conversion does not apply to a long term contract for the sale of real estate prior to the time that both parties have performed all acts necessary to complete the contract except tender of final payment and delivery of the deed.

Equitable conversion is the treating of land as personalty and personalty as land under certain circumstances. Hence, as between the parties and those claiming through them, when the owner of land enters into a valid and enforceable contract for its sale he continues to hold the legal title, but in trust for the buyer; and the buyer becomes the equitable owner and holds the purchase money in trust for the seller. The conversion takes place at the time of entering into contract. It stems from the basic equitable principle that equity regards as done that which ought to be done. The doctrine of equitable conversion has been recognized in Illinois, as it has in practically every other jurisdiction, since earliest times.

We would be less than candid if we said that this court has been consistent in applying the doctrine. . . . We believe the correct view to be that expressed in the majority of the cases which hold equitable conversion takes place at the instant a valid and enforceable contract is entered into and that the buyer at that time acquires an equitable title. . . .

The defendant seeks, in effect, a definitive rule of application of the doctrine in the several fields where it may be invoked, such as dower, insurance, joint tenancy and the like. The issue here presented is devolution of title at the death of the seller and we concern ourselves in this opinion only with that issue. . . .

The defendant seems to read special significance into the long term nature of these contracts and suggests that a seller needs the protection of the courts. The simple answer is that a seller voluntarily enters into such a contract and is deemed to know the legal implication of his acts. To base application of the doctrine of equitable conversion upon the length of time the contracts have to run would leave titles in an utter state of confusion. It is a matter of common knowledge, admitted by defendant, that contracts for deed are useful to and increasingly used in our society. As a matter of policy, entirely aside from the legal desirability of a doctrine almost universally accepted, certainty and stability of titles dictate that application of the doctrine cannot depend upon the flexible element suggested by defendant.

[At the time of Mrs. Shay's death, one buyer was behind in payments and another had requested permission to assign the purchase contract. The doctrine of equitable conversion determined who had legal authority to deal with these problems.]

Equitable conversion took place at the time of execution of the contracts, so that upon the death of the seller the plaintiff [Arthur Shay] became entitled to the entire unpaid balance of the purchase prices as personal representative of the decedent, since it was personal property under the doctrine of equitable conversion. The option to declare the contract in default and the right to consent to the assignment were therefore vested in the plaintiff as administrator. . . .

NOTES

1. Edward and Bess Panushka owned a motel as tenants by entireties. In 1952, they entered into an installment contract for sale of the motel to the Lessmans, which provided for a conveyance of title upon full payment of the price. The Lessmans took possession and made regular payments according to the contract. In 1955, with several years remaining on the installment contract, Mr. Panushka died. Mrs. Panushka argued that as the surviving tenant by entireties, she was entitled to the full balance due from the Lessmans. Her stepson argued that the Panushkas' interest in the motel was converted to personal property when they signed the installment contract, and that Oregon law recognizes the estate of tenancy by entireties for real

property only. Therefore, at the time of Mr. Panushka's death, the Panushkas owned the balance due from the Lessmans as tenants in common and one half of the balance became an asset of Mr. Panushka's estate.

A majority of the court agreed with the stepson, saying:

> "In equity a binding and enforceable contract for the sale and purchase of real estate is recognized for most purposes in this court, as well as in other jurisdictions, as if specifically executed and performed. This concept is derived from the maxim that equity considers as done that which was agreed to be done.
>
> "An equitable conversion, therefore, takes place when a contract for the sale of real property becomes binding upon the parties. Thenceforth, the purchaser of the land is deemed the equitable owner thereof, and the seller is considered the owner of the purchase price. Upon the execution of the contract, the two contracting parties change positions. The purchaser's interest is 'land,' and the right and interest conferred by the contract upon the vendor is 'personal property,' i. e., ownership of the right to receive the purchase money. The naked legal title, which the vendor holds in trust as security for the payment of the purchase money, descends to his heirs to be held by them for the benefit of the purchaser, but the vendor has no *interest* in the *land* which is subject to descent. Upon the vendor's death, his interest in the purchase money passes to his personal representative as personalty, and is distributable among the deceased vendor's next of kin. In short, as a result of the equitable conversion, the vendor holds an encumbered legal title, charged with the equitable interest of the purchaser, which is subject to be defeated by the purchaser's performance of the contract but so long as the contract remains executory, no title to the land is conveyed in law to the purchaser. Subsequent holders of the legal title with notice are likewise treated as trustees for the purchaser, as are heirs and devisees. This trust cannot be terminated either by the vendor or by anyone, with notice of the trust, claiming under, by or through the vendor, except for a breach by the purchaser of the conditions of the contract. The purchaser is called, by some courts, the trustee of the purchase money for the vendor. Other courts, adhering in strict theory, do not say 'trustee,' but designate the purchaser a contracting party bound by an obligation to pay the vendor or his personal representative money for the land purchased."

Panushka *v.* Panushka, 221 Or. 145, 149–51 (1960).

A dissenting justice argued that the doctrine of equitable conversion should not apply in the circumstances of the case:

> "The fiction [of equitable conversion] is indulged in so that an equitable result may be reached; it is not appropriately used if it defeats the intention of the parties. . . .
>
> "The majority applies the doctrine without inquiry as to whether its application will defeat or carry out the intention of the

> parties; the conversion of real into personal property is regarded as an inevitable conclusion once it is determined that a contract for the sale of land was entered into. We should not misapply an equitable principle to produce an inequitable result.
>
> "There were no circumstances in the instant case suggesting the need for indulging in the fiction that the real property interest of Edward and Bess Panushka was personal property. As a matter of fact, the circumstances point to the probability that the use of the fiction operates to defeat the intention of the vendors. It is reasonable to assume that the vendors intended the survivorship feature which characterized their interest in the land to continue as to the unpaid purchase money falling due after the death of one of the spouses."

Id. at 167–70. The outcome of the *Panushka* case has been altered by statute. O.R.S. § 93.240, and Oregon courts have retreated from some of the technical implications of equitable conversion.

2. As the courts indicated in Shay *v.* Penrose and Panushka *v.* Panushka, equitable conversion arises from the routine availability of specific performance to enforce certain categories of contracts. It can have a variety of consequences, some of which are sensible and some of which are not.

3. Stevens and Cureton, vendors, agreed to sell land to Kee. Kee gave Stevens and Cureton promissory notes for the purchase price and Stevens and Cureton undertook to deliver a deed when the notes were paid. Stevens and Cureton then assigned the notes to Walker and Treholm, the plaintiffs. Later, they assigned all their assets, including the land in question, for the benefit of creditors, "subject to a contract of sale to A.M. Kee."

Kee became insolvent. Walker and Trenholm sued for specific performance of the purchase and sale contract (in other words, for payment of the notes), and requested that the land be sold and the proceeds applied to pay the amount due on the notes. Stevens's and Cureton's creditors objected, claiming title to the land. The court found that the assignment from Stevens and Cureton to Walker and Trenholm was "not merely an endorsement of the paper as promissory notes, but a sale and transfer of the land trade and all rights incident thereto." Accordingly, by virtue of the doctrine of equitable conversion, Walker and Trenholm were entitled to the proceeds of the land:

> "It is true that Kee executed no mortgage to secure the purchase-money of the land. It is also true that, according to our decided cases, we have not, in this State, what is known technically as 'the vendor's lien,' as declared and enforced in the English Chancery—that is, a lien upon land sold to secure the purchase-money, whether the vendor has, or has not, executed titles to the vendee. But as to all executory contracts for the sale of land in which the title-deed is not executed, but the vendor gives a bond for titles, we have what is equivalent to the vendor's lien in the well-

recognized equity doctrine of specific performance of contracts for the sale of land. . . .

"The contract in this case was executory, and the vendors, Stevens & Cureton, had the right to require specific performance, and the only question is whether the assignees of the notes have the same right. . . .

"Judge Story says: '. . . The general principle is, that from the time of the contract for the sale of the land, the vendor as to the land becomes a trustee for the vendee, and the vendee as to the purchase-money a trustee for the vendor, who has a lien upon the land therefor. And every subsequent purchaser from either, with notice, becomes subject to the same equities as the party would from whom he purchased.' "

Walker & Trenholm *v.* Kee, 16 S.C. 76, 88–89 (1881).

4. Timko, as vendee, entered into a contract with Useful Homes Corporation for purchase and sale of a lot in a planned subdivision for $1000. Timko agreed to pay the price in installments and Useful Homes agreed to convey the land upon payment of the final installment. Timko made payments as required, then asked for a deed. Meanwhile, Useful Homes had run into financial difficulty and sold the tract to Sunshine Home Builders, which sold Timko's lot to another buyer, Madacsi, for $1100. When the problem came to light, Sunshine repurchased Timko's lot and offered Timko a deed. Timko refused and demanded instead the $1100 that Madacsi had paid for the lot.

The court held for Timko, based on equitable conversion:

"The Useful Homes Corporation, upon making its contract with the Timkos, held the lots in trust for them and the Sunshine Home Builders, Inc., assumed the trust when it acquired the legal title; and when it sold the lots to Madacsi, it became charged with the price upon the same trust. The repurchase of the lots and its offer to convey them cannot relieve the Sunshine Home Builders, Inc., from paying to the complainant the price received from Madacsi. It is optional with the complainant to demand the price or a conveyance, but the option is absolute in her. She has made her choice, and the defendant is bound by it. . . .

"The principle is of course applied only in instances of wrongful conduct by the trustee. In the instant case it does not appear that the sale of the complainant's lots to Madacsi was accidental. . . . The officials of the Sunshine Builders, Inc., when they sold the complainant's lots, were none too careful of her rights, and, it would appear, were under a cloud when the new, the present officials were forced to take over the management. After the complainant made demand for her deed, they sought to make amends, by recapturing the title to the lots, but we cannot distinguish between managements; the corporation is the responsible trustee. . . ."

Timko *v.* Useful Homes Corp., 114 N.J. Eq. 433 (1933). See also Gassner *v.* Lockett, 101 So.2d 33 (Fla. 1958) (allowing the first buyer of a lot to recover profits the seller obtained from a second sale of the land, although the seller, who was "old, senile, and extremely forgetful," had made a good faith mistake).

5. In the case of In re Boyle's Estate, 154 Iowa 249 (1912), a vendee under an executory purchase and sale contract claimed rent collected by the vendor. The court held that although the vendee became the "equitable owner" of the land when the contract was signed, he was not entitled to rent unless he was presently entitled to possession.

6. Moses Bros. entered into an installment land sale contract with Johnson. The contract provided that Johnson would get title if he paid the accruing taxes and the unpaid purchase money (plus interest) as due. It also provided that, should Johnson default on any installment payment, Moses Bros. could cancel the contract, retake possession, keep some of the money paid by Johnson as rent (at a rate of $60 per year), and return the rest to Johnson.

Johnson took possession of the land when the contract was signed. Before his first payment was due, Moses Bros. sought an injunction barring him from cutting timber on the land, "except for repairs, fences, and other necessary purposes." The appellate court held that the injunction should be granted:

> "When a vendor of real estate enters into an executory agreement to convey title on the payment of the purchase-money, he sustains, in substance, the same relation to the vendee, as a mortgagee does to a mortgagor. Each has a legal title, which, in the absence of stipulations for possession, will maintain an action of ejectment. Each can retain his legal title against the other party, until the purchase-money, or mortgage debt is paid unless he permits the other to remain in undisturbed possession for twenty years. And yet each is at last but a trustee of the legal title for the mortgagee or vendee, if the purchase-money, or mortgage debt, as the case may be, is paid, or seasonably tendered. The same mutual rights and remedies, legal and equitable, and the same limitation to the right of recovery, obtain in the one relation and in the other. . . .
>
> "In King *v.* Smith, 2 Har. 239, 24 Eng. Ch. Rep. 239, it was said to be an established rule, 'that if the security of the mortgagee is insufficient, and the court is satisfied of that fact, the mortgagor will not be allowed to do that which would directly impair the security—cut timber upon the mortgaged premises. . . . The cases decide, that a mortgagee out of possession is not, of course, entitled to an injunction to restrain the mortgagor from cutting timber on the mortgaged property. If the security is sufficient, the court will not grant an injunction merely because the mortgagor cuts, or threatens to cut timber. There must be a special case made out before the court will interfere. The difficulty is in determining what is meant by a 'sufficient security.' Suppose the mortgage debt, with all the expenses, to be £1,000, and the property to be worth £1,000,

> that is, in one sense, a sufficient security; but no mortgagee, who is well advised, would lend his money, unless the mortgaged property was worth one-third more than the amount lent at the time of the mortgage.' This was considered the rule, and the only safe rule, under English values. In that country, land values were, in a measure, stationary. In this, they are fluctuating. To be a 'sufficient security,' with us, there should be a much broader margin between the amount of the debt and the estimated value of the property mortgaged for its security, than is considered sufficient in that older country. . . .
>
> "The bill charges, and the answer admits, that the land, which is the subject of this suit, is in value not exceeding the sum of the purchase-money that remains unpaid. The bill also charges that the defendant is insolvent. . . ."

Moses *v.* Johnson, 88 Ala. 517, 517 (1890).

7. If a land contract fails of performance without the purchaser's default (for example, because of defects of title, delay by the vendor, or non-compliance with the Statute of Frauds), the general rule is that the purchaser has an action against the vendor to recover any payments made on account of the purchase price. The purchaser also has an equitable lien on the land to the extent of his payments, which is enforceable in equity against the vendor's grantee unless for value without notice. This lien is implied by law without mention in the contract, like the grantor's lien of which it has been called the counterpart. However, the destruction of the grantor's lien, by statute or otherwise, does not usually destroy the purchaser's lien.

8. Equitable conversion may also play a role, for better or worse, in assigning the risk of loss if the property is damaged before the conditions have been met for formal conveyance. This problem is illustrated in the following cases.

4. RISK OF LOSS

Skelly Oil Co. v. Ashmore

Supreme Court of Missouri, 1963.
365 S.W.2d 582.

[Skelly Oil Co. contracted to buy land from the Ashmores. A building on the land, which Skelly intended to demolish, was destroyed by fire before the closing date. The day after the fire, Skelly notified the Ashmores that the fire would have no effect on the deal; Skelly, in turn, learned that the Ashmores had insurance on the building. The Ashmores received $10,000 on the insurance policy. Skelly sought specific performance of the contract with a $10,000 abatement in the price. The trial court gave this relief and the Ashmores appealed.]

■ HYDE, JUDGE. . . . The contract of sale here involved contained no provision as to who assumed the risk of loss occasioned by a destruction of the building, or for protecting the building by insurance or for allocating any insurance proceeds received therefor. When the parties met to close the sale on April 16, the purchaser's counsel informed vendors and their attorney he was relying on Standard Oil Co. *v.* Dye, 223 Mo. App. 926, for purchaser's claim to the $10,000 insurance proceeds on the building. Purchaser made no claim to the $4,000 paid vendors for the loss of the furniture and fixtures. It is stated in 3 AMERICAN LAW OF PROPERTY, § 11.30, p. 90, that in the circumstances here presented at least five different views have been advanced for allocating the burden of fortuitous loss between vendor and purchaser of real estate. We summarize those mentioned: (1) The view first enunciated in Paine *v.* Meller (Ch. 1801, 6 Ves. Jr. 349, 31 Eng. Reprint 1088) is said to be the most widely accepted; holding that from the time of the contract of sale of real estate the burden of fortuitous loss was on the purchaser even though the vendor retained possession. (2) The loss is on the vendor until legal title is conveyed, although the purchaser is in possession, stated to be a strong minority. (3) The burden of loss should be on the vendor until the time agreed upon for conveying the legal title, and thereafter on the purchaser unless the vendor be in such default as to preclude specific performance, not recognized in the decisions. (4) The burden of the loss should be on the party in possession, whether vendor or purchaser, so considered by some courts. (5) The burden of loss should be on the vendor unless there is something in the contract or in the relation of the parties from which the court can infer a different intention; . . . "this rather vague test" has not received any avowed judicial acceptance, although it is not inconsistent with jurisdictions holding the loss is on the vendor until conveyance or jurisdictions adopting the possession test. . . .

We do not agree that we should adopt the arbitrary rule of Paine *v.* Meller and Standard Oil Co. *v.* Dye, that there is equitable conversion from the time of making a contract for sale and purchase of land and that the risk of loss from destruction of buildings or other substantial part of the property is from that moment on the purchaser. . . .

We take the view stated in an article on Equitable Conversion by Contract, 13 Columbia Law Review 369, 386, Dean Harlan F. Stone, later Chief Justice Stone, in which he points out that the only reason why a contract for the sale of land by the owner to another operates to effect conversion is that a court of equity will compel him specifically to perform his contract. He further states: "A preliminary to the determination of the question whether there is equitable ownership of land must therefore necessarily be the determination of the question whether there is a contract which can be and ought to be specifically performed *at the very time when the court is called upon to perform it. . . .*" . . .

[W]e believe the Massachusetts rule is the proper rule. It is thus stated in Libman *v.* Levenson, 236 Mass. 221: When "the conveyance is to be made of the whole estate, including both land and buildings, for an entire price, and the value of the buildings constitutes a large part of the total value of the estate, and the terms of the agreement show that they constituted an important part of the subject matter of the contract . . . the contract is to be construed as subject to the implied condition that it no longer shall be binding if, before the time for the conveyance to be made, the buildings are destroyed by fire. The loss by the fire falls upon the vendor, the owner; and if he has not protected himself by insurance, he can have no reimbursement of this loss; but the contract is no longer binding upon either party. If the purchaser has advanced any part of the price, he can recover it back. If the change in the value of the estate is not so great, or if it appears that the buildings did not constitute so material a part of the estate to be conveyed as to result in an annulling of the contract, specific performance may be decreed, *with compensation for any breach of agreement,* or relief may be given in damages." . . . The reason for the Massachusetts rule is that specific performance is based on what is equitable; and it is not equitable to make a vendee pay the vendor for something the vendor cannot give him.

However, the issue in this case is not whether the vendee can be compelled to take the property without the building but whether the vendee is entitled to enforce the contract of sale, with the insurance proceeds substituted for the destroyed building. We see no inequity to defendants in such enforcement since they will receive the full amount ($20,000.00) for which they contracted to sell the property. Their contract not only described the land but also specifically stated they sold it "together with the buildings, driveways and all construction thereon." While the words "Service Station Site" appeared in the caption of the option contract and that no doubt was the ultimate use plaintiff intended to make of the land, the final agreement made by the parties was that plaintiff would take it subject to a lease of the building which would have brought plaintiff about $6,150.00 in rent during the term of the lease. Moreover, defendants' own evidence showed the building was valued in the insurance adjustment at $16,716.00 from which $4,179.00 was deducted for depreciation, making the loss $12,537.00. Therefore, defendants are not in a very good position to say the building was of no value to plaintiff. Furthermore, plaintiff having contracted for the land with the building on it, the decision concerning use or removal of the building, or even for resale of the entire property, was for the plaintiff to make. Statements were in evidence about the use of the building and its value to plaintiff made by its employee who negotiated the purchase but he was not one of plaintiff's chief executive officers nor possessed of authority to bind its board of directors. The short of the matter is that defendants will get all they bargained for; but without the building or its value plaintiff will not.

We therefore affirm the judgment and decree of the trial court.

■ STORCKMAN, JUDGE (dissenting). . . . The evidence is convincing that Skelly Oil Company was buying the lot as a site for a service station and that in so using it they not only wanted the Jones's lease terminated but intended to tear down and remove the building in question. . . .

In short, as to both Skelly and the Ashmores, the destruction of the insured building was a fortuitous circumstance supplying the opportunity to rid the property of a vexatious lease, to dispose of the building, and at the same time resulting in a windfall of $10,000. And the problem, in fact the only seriously contested issue between the parties, is which of them is to have the advantage of this piece of good fortune. Skelly contracted to pay $20,000 for the property. If it is awarded the $10,000 windfall, it will receive a $20,000 lot for $10,000. If the Ashmores retain the $10,000, they will in fact have realized $30,000 for a piece of property they have agreed to sell for $20,000.

Nevertheless, . . . the rule . . . has evolved: "Where the purchaser as equitable owner will bear the loss occasioned by a destruction of the property pending completion of the sale, and the contract is silent as to insurance, the rule quite generally followed is that the proceeds of the vendor's insurance policies, even though the purchaser did not contribute to their maintenance, constitute a trust fund for the benefit of the purchaser to be credited on the purchase price of the destroyed property, the theory being that the vendor is a trustee of the property for the purchaser." Annotation 64 A.L.R.2d 1402, 1406. . . . The rule is not as general as the annotator indicated, and as with the rule upon which it is founded, all the experts agree that it is unsound, their only point of disagreement is as to what the rule should be. . . .

Professor Williston was of the view that the risk of loss should follow possession . . . .

Vance is of the opinion that a rule of "business usage" should be adopted . . . .

Professor Vanneman has pointed out that the basic problem in all these cases is, "should there be a decree for specific performance at all?" He is of the view that the important and controlling factor should be the intention of the parties. If the building was a material part of the transaction, the vendor intending to sell and the vendee intending to buy "land with a building upon it," the vendee should have the benefit of the insurance. . . . This view has the merit of avoiding resort to the legal fictions of equitable ownership and trusteeship. . . .

Automatic application of the doctrine that "equity regards that as done which ought to be done," in the circumstances of this case, begs the question of *what ought to be done.* Because the insurance proceeds may be a windfall to those legally entitled does not necessarily mean that justice will be accomplished by transferring them elsewhere. . . .

A valid legal excuse is a sufficient reason for refusal of specific performance. . . . Destruction of a particular thing upon which the contract depends is generally regarded as a legal excuse for nonperformance . . . .

[T]he majority opinion . . . employs conflicting rules or theories. It purports to adopt one but applies another. It professes to repudiate the equitable conversion theory and to adopt unequivocally the Massachusetts rule, stating: "Instead we believe the Massachusetts rule is the proper rule." This rule as shown by the opinion's quotation from Libman *v.* Levenson, 236 Mass. 221, is that the sales contract will no longer be binding if the buildings are destroyed by fire and "the value of the buildings constitutes a large part of the total value of the estate, and the terms of the agreement show that they constituted an important part of the subject matter of the contract." In the same quotation from the Libman case, the circumstances and terms under which specific performance is granted are stated as follows: "If the change in the value of the estate is not so great, or if it appears that the buildings did not constitute so material a part of the estate to be conveyed as to result in an annulling of the contract, specific performance may be decreed, *with compensation for any breach of agreement, or relief may be given in damages.*"

Obviously the majority opinion did not find that the value of the building constituted "a large part of the total value of the estate" or "an important part of the subject matter of the contract," else it would have declared the sales contract no longer binding under the Massachusetts rule. What it had to find was that the value of the building was not so great or such a material part of the estate to be conveyed as to interfere with the decree of specific performance.

But at this point the majority opinion abandons any pretense of following the Massachusetts rule and switches back to the equitable conversion theory and awards the insurance proceeds as such to the vendee without a determination of compensation for breach or relief to be given in damages. The value of the building for insurance purposes or as a structure to house a retail store is not necessarily the proper measure of the compensation or damages to which the plaintiff is entitled. It might be considerably less than such a figure if Skelly intended to remove the building as soon as it had the legal right to do so. Obviously the Massachusetts rule is not tied in with insurance at all and that is as it should be. Logically the majority opinion should have remanded the case for a determination of the amount of actual damages suffered by Skelly or the compensation to which it is entitled if it still wants specific performance. This is undoubtedly what the Massachusetts rule contemplates. I would find no fault with such a procedure. . . .

On the present record the plaintiff has failed to show a superior equity in the insurance proceeds under the Massachusetts rule or otherwise, and on well-established equitable principles I would leave the legal title to that fund where it is. I would . . . award [Skelly] specific performance . . . on the condition that it pay to the defendants the agreed purchase price of $20,000 less the amount of compensation or damages, if any, that it could establish against the defendants (not the insurance funds) at a plenary hearing of that issue in the trial court.

Dixon v. Salvation Army

California Court of Appeal, Fourth District, 1983.
142 Cal. App. 3d 463.

■ COLOGNE, ACTING PRESIDING JUSTICE. . . . Dixon and the Salvation Army entered a real estate purchase and sale agreement. The Salvation Army agreed to sell to Dixon two parcels, described herein as "8th & K property" and "8th & J property." Both parcels were improved with commercial structures. The 8th & K property included a two-story office building and warehouse building and the 8th and J property included a three-story brick warehouse.

The parties opened an escrow, and the escrow instructions were later amended to reduce the sales price from $1,100,000 to $900,000 because the parties discovered the 8th & J property had certain structural deficiencies.

Before the escrow closed and before either title or possession passed from the Salvation Army to Dixon, one of the two buildings on the 8th & K property was destroyed by fire. The Salvation Army received $240,000 as fire insurance proceeds, but it became apparent during the negotiations following the fire that the destroyed building was significantly underinsured. The Salvation Army could not, of course, deliver the property in the "same general condition minus normal wear and tear as when inspected prior to opening of escrow" as the contract provided and the parties could not agree to a new price of the property as is. This litigation resulted.

Dixon sought and obtained a court declaration that "as a result of the destruction by fire of the improvements on the . . . '8th & K property,' the total purchase price to be paid . . . should be abated to reflect the loss—if any—of the proportionate value of the improvements on the 8th and K property to the total value of all of the property sold" under the agreement. The effect of this order was to authorize Dixon to seek specific enforcement of the contract at an abated price. This price was to be determined by the parties' negotiation or future litigation. The Salvation Army had requested a declaration that the contract should be rescinded or, alternatively, the contract could be enforced without an abatement of the sales price.

The Uniform Vendor and Purchaser Risk Act (Uniform Act) was adopted in California and codified as Civil Code section 1662. This statute provides:

> "Any contract hereafter made in this State for the purchase and sale of real property shall be interpreted as including an agreement that the parties shall have the following rights and duties, unless the contract expressly provides otherwise:

"(a) If, when neither the legal title nor the possession of the subject matter of the contract has been transferred, all or a material part thereof is destroyed without fault of the purchaser or is taken by eminent domain, the vendor cannot enforce the contract, and the purchaser is entitled to recover any portion of the price that he has paid;

"(b) If, when either the legal title or the possession of the subject matter of the contract has been transferred, all or any part thereof is destroyed without fault of the vendor or is taken by eminent domain, the purchaser is not thereby relieved from a duty to pay the price, nor is he entitled to recover any portion thereof that he has paid.

"This section shall be so interpreted and construed as to effectuate its general purpose to make uniform the law of those states which enact it. . . ."

Since neither title nor possession had passed to Dixon, the provisions of subdivision (a) apply and the Salvation Army had the risk of loss. This rule prohibits the Salvation Army from enforcing the contract and permits Dixon to rescind and recover any consideration. The statute is silent, however, on whether Dixon can specifically enforce the contract with or without an abatement in price.

Of the other jurisdictions which have enacted the Uniform Act, New York appears to be the only one which has previously resolved whether the vendee may obtain specific enforcement of the contract at an abated purchase price.

In Rizzo *v.* Landmark Realty Corp., 277 App. Div. 1094 (1950), the court held the Uniform Act precludes a vendor from specifically enforcing a real estate sales contract when a material part of the subject property has been destroyed, but it does not destroy any common law rights of the purchaser to specific performance with abatement. . . .

In Lucenti *v.* Cayuga Apartments, Inc., 59 App. Div. 2d 438 (1977), the court discussed the New York modified version of the Uniform Act. Section 5–1311 of New York's General Obligations Law is in essence the Uniform Act but with the added provision that "if an immaterial part thereof is destroyed without fault of the purchaser or is taken by eminent domain, neither the vendor nor the purchaser is thereby deprived of the right to enforce the contract, but there shall be, to the extent of the destruction or taking, an abatement of the purchase price."

Thus, the New York Legislature has expressly provided for the situation where the vendor has the risk of loss and an immaterial part of the property is destroyed. In *Lucenti,* the court considered a similar situation except found the destruction to the subject property was material. Finding "no logical basis for distinguishing between a loss to a 'material' and an 'immaterial' portion of the premises," the court allowed the vendee to specifically enforce the contract at an abated price. It is clear the court was also applying the common law rule of New York (which permitted the vendee to enforce a contract at an abated purchase price), thus providing no assistance in interpreting the California statute. In applying the common law rule, the New York court recognized, but chose not to follow, the recommendation of the New York Law Revision Commission report of 1936 (the same year New York enacted the Uniform Act), which suggested rescission of the contract was the best remedy when a material part of the subject property was destroyed.

The long established rule in California, stemming from cases occurring after the San Francisco fire of 1906, differs from the common law of New York. In Potts Drug Co. *v.* Benedict, 156 Cal. 322, 334 (1909), the court stated in dictum:

> "Where there is a mere agreement to sell, and title therefore has not passed, the loss falls on the vendor for the same reason. In such a case the vendor is excused from the performance of his contract under *the rule we have discussed* by reason of the destruction of the thing, but he cannot retain money already paid on account of the proposed purchase, or recover moneys remaining unpaid."

Thus, we hold where a material part of the subject property is destroyed without the fault of either party and neither title nor possession has passed to the purchaser, the vendor's performance is excused and the purchaser is entitled to the return of any consideration paid.

We believe the more equitable approach and one more compatible with the Uniform Act is to place the parties in their original position, free to make a new bargain. A rule that denies a vendor the ability to specifically enforce the sales agreement where the material part of the consideration is lost or destroyed calls out for the converse also to be applied. It would be grossly unfair to require either party to accept consideration less than the whole of what was bargained for under these circumstances. If it is unfair to force the purchaser to receive materially damaged property, it is equally unfair to compel the vendor to accept a price substantially below what he bargained for. Although a court in equity has broad powers, it should not use its jurisdiction to remake the contract for the parties, particularly on the critical term of the purchase price. This task is better left to the further negotiations of the parties, with neither compelled to strike an agreement. Specific performance with abatement of the purchase price is not an appropriate remedy for the purchaser. . . .

■ WORK, J., dissenting. . . . Because I find the trial court's disposition properly places the risk of loss, especially on the facts of this case, I would affirm.

The majority opinion omits several significant portions of the dealings between these parties. As a result, it overlooks the equities of this specific transaction and ignores commercial reality.

First, an unusually lengthy escrow period (one year) was given at Salvation Army's request to accommodate its moving out. Seller retained title and possession until close of escrow.

The escrow agreement stated buyer was to evaluate the properties and allocate the purchase price between the buildings and property.

The fire occurred eight months after opening of escrow.

The property consisted of two contiguous parcels of real property in a desirable downtown San Diego location, one (8th and J) improved by a single structure (three-story warehouse) and the other (8th and K) containing two buildings (a warehouse and a two-story office building). Only the two-story office building was destroyed in the fire, leaving two parcels of real property and two buildings.

The allocation was made and the value was generally assessed at $700,000 for the 8th and K property and structures, and $200,000 for the 8th and J parcel and building.[1] . . .

Clearly, a seller bears the risk of loss under the *Potts* analysis until title or possession passes. Civil Code section 1662, adopted after *Potts,* does not change this rule. Consistent with *Potts,* subparagraph (b) imposes the risk of loss upon a buyer when either legal title or possession of the subject property is transferred before destruction. Also, under subparagraph (a) where neither legal title nor possession has passed when all "or a material part" of the premises are destroyed through no fault of the buyer, the seller cannot force performance of the contract and the buyer may recover any prepaid portion of the purchase price.

Potts does refer, in passing, to the elementary rule of the law of sales, *i.e.*, where the loss falls upon the seller because title has not passed, the seller is excused from performing the contract. However, *Potts* only discusses the complete destruction of property, talking in terms of impossibility of performance from the perishing of the person or thing.

The majority assume the loss of one of the three buildings on the two parcels of scarce downtown San Diego real estate materially destroyed the essence of the bargain. This ignores the commercial reality readily visible through our chambers windows. However, it is necessary to engage in this fiction to set aside the ruling of the trial court for, where

---

[1] Before the purchase price was reduced from $1,100,000 to $900,000, the allocation for 8th and J was $400,000. It was reduced after determining structural changes to bring the J Street warehouse up to seismic code would be $550,000 and it was probably more economical to tear the building down and rebuild.

there is an immaterial destruction and the vendor may enforce the contract against the vendee, the vendee is entitled to abatement.[2] . . .

Although the majority opinion states, a rule denying seller the right to specifically enforce a sales agreement where a material (but not immaterial) part of the consideration is lost or destroyed calls out for the converse to be true, this statement lacks foundation. Nor is it relevant, in the context of our fact situation, whether the abatement requested is related to a material or immaterial part of the consideration. The reason a buyer is entitled to abatement for immaterial diminutions of the value of the consideration is because the seller, both statutorily and by common law, may enforce the contract over the buyer's objections. Certainly, if the seller could force the buyer to perform where there is a material part, but less than all, of the consideration destroyed, then an abatement for the reduction of the total value of the contract based upon the destruction of that material part would be equally required. Where the risk of loss remains with the seller, neither an immaterial *or* material loss should bar the buyer from purchasing the remainder at an abated price.

If the risk is foreseeable, a commercial practice by which a party might be expected to insure himself against a risk militates against shifting it to the other party.

Here, the risk of fire was foreseen by seller and specifically insured against. It is only the probability the coverage was inadequate which smarts. It is equitable to place this consciously self-assumed risk upon the seller who was allowed to remain in possession for one year at its own request to obtain benefits it desired.

The majority also make much ado of the fact the destroyed building was underinsured. Whether the building was fully insured, underinsured or completely uninsured is not relevant to the issues involved. It relates only to whether there is in fact an economic loss to seller.

Under the majority analysis, buyer is denied his right to specifically enforce even those land contracts where adequate insurance coverage would give seller its entire contract price, or even more.

If we adhere to the concept that real property is unique and such sales may be specifically enforced, the destruction of one or all structures placed upon a piece of land should not prevent a buyer from electing to specifically enforce a sale even though the sale originally contemplated the land in its improved state. The policy reasons for denying a seller the right to force a materially different package upon an unwilling buyer are far different than those permitting an originally willing seller to refuse to specifically perform a contract to convey real property to the extent the property still exists when enforcement is requested. The majority does not quarrel with the harshness of the rule which forces a buyer in the

---

[2] In total context, the buyer claims the loss of one building does not materially destroy the essence of this bargain. The trial court found in his favor, and buyer's position is commercially realistic.

Potts case to pay full value for a leasehold interest which has been totally destroyed before possession was even turned over to him on a rule the risk of loss passed when paper title was transferred. Why it is so solicitous of concern for hardships which are only imaginary and which the statute, and common law, properly impose upon sellers retaining both title and legal possession when the risk is realized, is beyond me. If the agreement was to sell two parcels of unimproved property for a total of $1,000,000, and one parcel was condemned by the State before title or possession passed, what unfairness is there in permitting the buyer to specifically enforce that portion of the contract regarding the other parcel and, if the parties cannot agree on the proper abatement of the price, to have it determined judicially? (See Skelly Oil Co. *v.* Ashmore (Mo.) 365 S.W.2d 582, 589.) I find no substantive difference here.

NOTES

1. Section 2–406(b) of the Uniform Land Transactions Act provides as follows:

> "(b) . . . In case of a casualty loss or taking by eminent domain while the risk is on the seller:
>
> > "(1) if the loss or taking results in a substantial failure of the real estate to conform to the contract, the buyer may cancel the contract and recover any portion of the price he has paid, or accept the real estate with his choice of (i) a reduction of the contract price equal to the decrease in fair market value caused by the loss or taking, or (ii) the benefit of the seller's insurance coverage or the eminent domain payment for the loss or taking, but without further right against the seller; or
> >
> > "(2) if the real estate substantially conforms to the contract after the loss or taking, the buyer must accept the real estate, but is entitled to his choice of (i) a reduction of the contract price equal to the decrease in fair market value caused by the loss or taking or (ii) the benefit of the seller's insurance coverage or the eminent domain payment with respect to the loss or taking but without further right against the seller."

2. The remedy sought by Dixon and authorized in the Uniform Land Transactions Act—specific performance with an abatement in the price—may apply in other circumstances as well. The following case is an example.

5. ABATEMENT

Billy Williams Builders & Developers, Inc. v. Hillerich

Court of Appeals of Kentucky, 1969.
446 S.W.2d 280.

■ EDMUND P. HILL, JUDGE. Appellees (hereinafter Hillerich) sued appellant (hereinafter Williams) for specific performance of a contract to convey a house and a lot, for damages growing out of the defective construction of the house, and for damages due to delay in performance. Equity directed specific performance and transferred the case to the common law docket, where a jury later returned a verdict for appellees for $3318 in damages resulting from defective construction and for $910.38 in damages occasioned by delay in performance. Williams appeals. . . .

The main thrust of Williams' argument concerns the right of the buyer to have two remedies (1) specific performance of a contract to purchase real estate (a house and a lot) and (2) damages for defective construction and for delay in performance. Williams argues that by complying with the judgment for specific performance and by accepting the deed to the property, Hillerich elected to have one of two inconsistent remedies; and by so doing, he cannot back up to the "forks of the road" and take a road different from the one on which he "first embarked."

In a proper case there can be little doubt that one may be entitled to the specific performance of a contract to purchase real estate and damages for delay in performance. But damages for deficiency of quantity or quality present a more complex question, on which there is some conflict among the authorities. . . .

In [the Restatement (Second) of Contracts § 365] it is said:

> "Specific Enforcement in Part, With Compensation for the Remainder.
>
> "The fact that a part of the promised performance cannot be rendered, or is otherwise such that its specific enforcement would violate some of the rules stated in §§ 360–380, does not prevent the specific enforcement of the remainder, if in all other respects the requisites for specific enforcement of that remainder exist. Compensation for the partial breach that still remains may be awarded in the same proceeding, either as damages, restitution, or an abatement in price. . . ."

. . . It is recognized that specific performance is an equitable remedy devised to apply in cases where common law actions for damages were found inadequate to afford a full remedy. The doctrine, first adopted in England, met with formidable opposition, but it has survived. In fact, its scope has been enlarged down through the years.

We need to keep in mind that in the contract in question vendor (appellant) agreed to sell lot 102 and to construct a house according to "submitted plans and specifications." Not only did appellant agree to convey the lot and residence to be built, but he undertook to build the house according to the "plans and specifications."

Appellees argue that their purpose in entering into the contract was to obtain this particular property in this particular neighborhood due to aged relatives nearby; that they are entitled to specific performance notwithstanding appellant's breach of the contract to construct the house according to plans and specifications. . . .

NOTES

1. Stringer agreed to sell Barnes a fee simple estate in land, but he had no such estate. As Barnes later learned, Stringer's wife had a remainder interest in the land, which she refused to release. Barnes sought specific performance of the contract. The court ruled as follows:

> "The purchaser entered into his contract with the husband in total ignorance of the state of the title, and without any knowledge that the husband could only sell with the concurrence of his wife. The husband, therefore, is bound to convey all the interest that he has according to the principle of the authorities that have been cited, and the Court must endeavor to find out, in the best way it can, what compensation is to be made in respect of the interest which he is unable to convey."

Barnes *v.* Wood, L.R. 8 Eq. 424, 429 (Ch. 1869).

2. Rudd agreed to buy Lascelles' land for £3500. As Rudd knew, Lascelles had inherited the property from her husband and knew virtually nothing about her legal rights. Hence, "[t]here was no representation as to the title the defendant could make as to the property nor as to the nature of her interest, nor any provision for compensation for defects." When he learned of restrictive covenants that significantly reduced the value of the land, Rudd sought specific performance of the contract at a price of £2500. The bill was dismissed:

> "In my opinion the jurisdiction to enforce specific performance with compensation on a vendor, where the contract is silent as to compensation, rests on the equitable estoppel referred to in Mortlock *v.* Buller, 10 Ves. 292, 315, namely, that a vendor representing and contracting to sell an estate as his own cannot afterwards be heard to say he has not the entirety. It probably first arose in cases of small deficiency in the quantity of the land sold, *e.g.*, if a vendor contracted to sell 100 acres and only had 90 acres, he could not resist specific performance on the ground that the contract was to sell 100 acres. This cy-près execution was a purely equitable remedy. . . . In the present case there is obviously no direct representation of that kind, and though a mere offer to sell real property prima facie implies that the vendor has the unincumbered fee simple therein, still, if the purchaser, as in this case, knows that the vendor is ignorant as to the title, he cannot set up any such implication as a representation inducing the contract. The present case, therefore, does not come within the above category. . . .
>
> "Further, the compensation could not be fairly ascertained. If I am to make a new contract for the parties, I must see that it is at a fair price; but I do not ascertain this if I merely find out what would be the value of the property if it were subject to no

> restrictions, and how much less it is worth because of the restrictions. It would be necessary to find out further what the purchaser would have given and what the vendor would have taken for it under the altered conditions. Now, according to the plaintiff's own shewing, he has lost a resale at an advance of 1000*l.*, and, as he put the compensation at 1000*l.*, it looks as if he had contracted to give the right price for the property as it stands. How then can I assume that the purchaser would not still give 3500*l.?* I must not make any bargain that might be unjust to either party. The proposed new bargain would be extremely hard on the vendor. She sells on the basis of income, and she has contracted to sell property producing 125*l.* a year for 3500*l.*, and if the purchaser is right, she is to lose about one-third of the purchase-money. It would be a great hardship to enforce the contract against her with so large an abatement in respect of covenants which do not affect her enjoyment, and I cannot assume that she would have sold for such a reduced sum."

Rudd *v.* Lascelles, 1 Ch. 815, 818–20 (1900).

C. CONTRACTS FOR ARBITRATION

Matter of Grayson-Robinson Stores (Iris Construction Corp.)

Court of Appeals of New York, 1960.
8 N.Y.2d 133.

■ DESMOND, CHIEF JUDGE. Again . . . the courts are called upon to confirm an arbitration award which, conformably to the express powers given by the parties to the arbitrators, directed specific performance of a contract. Appellant, defaulting in performance and losing its case before the arbitrators, now argues to the courts that enforcement of this award would be contrary to public policy. Specific performance of a contract to construct a building, argues appellant, is never ordered by courts of equity because of the necessity of continuous judicial supervision and control of performance. Therefore, so the argument runs, the same courts will not confirm and enforce an arbitration award which decrees specific performance of the same kind of agreement. We disagree. There is no hard and fast rule against applying the remedy of specific performance to such contracts, especially when the parties have by agreement provided for just that remedy.

In 1955 appellant Iris, owner of vacant land in Levittown, Nassau County, entered into a written agreement with respondent Grayson (later assigned by Grayson to its subsidiary respondent Klein) whereby Iris undertook to erect on the Iris tract a building (part of a "shopping center") to be rented by Iris to Grayson for use as a retail department store for a term of 25 years after completion with certain optional provisions for renewals of the term. Possession was to be turned over to

Grayson "on or before September 1, 1957, time being of the essence." The agreement called for arbitration of all disputes and incorporated the rules of the American Arbitration Association which in terms empower the arbitrator in his award to grant any just or equitable remedy or relief "including . . . specific performance."

There were several amendments and extensions of the original contract, but none of these are relevant to our discussion. The plans and specifications for the building were completed or practically completed, a public ground-breaking ceremony was held and excavation commenced, then Iris notified Grayson-Klein that, because of difficulties in getting mortgage money, Iris could not go further unless Grayson-Klein agreed to increase the agreed rent. The tenant declined to pay more. The building has never been completed.

It was, apparently, always the intention of Iris to obtain by mortgage loan the money it needed for construction but there is nothing in the agreement relieving Iris of its obligation, in the event it should find such borrowing to be difficult or impossible. At the arbitration and in the courts Iris has argued "impossibility" but the arbitrators disposed of that issue by ordering Iris to "proceed forthwith with the improvements of the leased premises in accordance with the terms of the said lease, as amended." There was no proof before the arbitrators of any physical or actual impossibility as distinguished from difficulty of financing or additional expense of construction.

It would be quite remarkable if, after these parties had agreed that arbitrators might award specific performance and after the arbitrators had so ordered, frustrate the whole arbitration process by refusing to confirm the award. The only ground suggested for such a refusal is that confirmation would involve the court in supervision of a complex and extended construction contract. We hold that this apprehension or speculation is no deterrent to confirmation by the courts.

There is of course, an old tradition or approach according to which courts have been reluctant to enforce "Contracts which require the performance of varied and continuous acts, or the exercise of special skill, taste, and judgment" because "the execution of the decree would require such constant superintendence as to make judicial control a matter of extreme difficulty." In some instances courts of equity in other States have for some such reasons refused to order specific performance of building contracts. Other courts of equity have gone the other way. . . . Modern writers think that the "difficulty of enforcement" idea is exaggerated and that the trend is toward specific performance. Clearly there is no binding rule that deprives equity of jurisdiction to order specific performance of a building contract. At most there is discretion in the court to refuse such a decree. And here we do not even have an equity suit but a motion made as of right to confirm a completely valid arbitration award conforming in all respects to the express conferral of authority on the arbitrators and meeting all statutory requirements for confirmation.

Assuming that the equity court in an original suit would have discretion to refuse specific performance, and even making the very large assumption that the court would have similar discretionary power to refuse to confirm this award, it remains that such discretion, if any, was exercised the other way in this case, and unanimously affirmed by the Appellate Division. That exercise of discretion was justified on the facts. There is nothing extraordinary about this ordinary building contract. Appellant is simply being required to fulfill its promise. . . .

Arbitration is by consent and those who agree to arbitrate should be made to keep their solemn, written promises. Such is New York State's public policy, plainly written in article 84 of the Civil Practice Act. The courts should follow a "liberal policy of promoting arbitration both to accord with the original intention of the parties and to ease the current congestion of court calendars" (Lawrence Co. *v.* Devonshire Fabrics, 271 F. 2d 402, 410). . . .

■ VAN VOORHIS, JUDGE. (dissenting). If "Arbitration is not merely a step in judicial enforcement of a claim nor auxiliary to a main proceeding, but the full relief sought" (Goodall-Sanford *v.* Textile Workers, 353 U.S. 550, 551), it would relieve the courts if the arbitrators enforced their own awards in specific performance instead of delegating that essential function to the courts after they have been discharged from further duty. Only recently was it settled that an arbitration award will be enforced by the courts which grants, under an appropriate arbitration clause, equitable relief by injunction. More recently it was held that our courts would enforce specific performance of an employment contract on an arbitration award even though a court of equity would not compel a man to work for another or to continue another in his employment. The decision in the present case lends the enforcement machinery of the courts to implement specific performance directed by arbitration that extends beyond any equitable relief which the courts have heretofore granted either on arbitrations or after trial. . . .

Sprinzen v. Nomberg

Court of Appeals of New York, 1979.
46 N.Y.2d 623.

■ JASEN, JUDGE. This appeal requires us to determine whether an arbitrator's award which enforces the terms of a restrictive covenant of employment is unenforceable as being contrary to public policy.

Respondent Murray Nomberg was employed by the petitioner Local 1115 Joint Board in April, 1973 as a business agent in its health-care division. Nomberg's responsibilities included, among other tasks, the negotiation of collective bargaining agreements, the processing of members' grievances, and the general organization of employees at various facilities. Practically all of Nomberg's service occurred in New Jersey, although he did, on occasion, work in Connecticut and Pennsylvania.

Upon commencement of his employment with Local 1115 in April 1973, Nomberg signed an agreement which contained a restrictive covenant. The terms of such covenant provided for a perpetual prohibition against the divulgence of the identity and addresses of union members or the terms and conditions embodied in the union agreements or the revelation of any information obtained by Nomberg during the course of his employment. Further, Nomberg agreed that "[u]pon the termination of his employment . . . he shall not directly or indirectly, within the States of New York, Pennsylvania, New Jersey and Connecticut . . . enter into or engage in organizing workers, either as an individual or as a part of a labor organization, for a period of five (5) years after the date of termination of his employment hereunder." The agreement also contained a sweeping arbitration clause which prescribed that "[a]ll complaints, disputes whatsoever of whatever kind or nature . . . concerning any provision of this contract . . . or otherwise . . . shall be submitted for arbitration" pursuant to a clearly delineated process.

In February, 1976, Nomberg left Local 1115 and began employment as a business representative for Local 144 of the Hotel, Hospital, Nursing Home and Allied Services Union, a union also involved in organizing and representing employees in the healthcare field. With Local 144, Nomberg's geographical responsibilities included only Manhattan and Staten Island, areas with which he had no previous dealings.

Petitioner Local 1115 demanded arbitration to compel compliance with the terms of the restrictive covenant and to enjoin Nomberg from employment as a business representative for Local 144. The parties proceeded to arbitration, where Nomberg, after unsuccessfully contesting the partiality of the arbitrator named in the April, 1973 agreement, walked out of the hearing, refusing to participate further. After petitioner presented its case, the arbitrator ruled that Local 1115 was entitled to the relief sought and issued an award enjoining Nomberg from working for Local 144 until February 6, 1981, five years after his employment ceased with Local 1115, and further restrained Nomberg from engaging in any of the other practices and acts specifically prohibited by the restrictive covenant. . . .

Over the years, courts have had not infrequent occasion to test restrictive covenants against the fabric of prevailing public policy. While it has been consistently asserted that the policy considerations against depriving the public of a person's industry and precluding an individual from pursuing his occupation, thereby preventing him from supporting himself and his family, must be weighed against the enforcement of such covenants, no hard-and-fast rules have yet been formulated and courts have been continuously engaged in the ongoing task of determining what restrictions are reasonable given the peculiar circumstances and context of each individual case. Thus, it can be said with apparent certainty that cases involving restrictive covenants cannot be decided in a vacuum free from external influences. Courts must respond to each case as it presents itself, and often times, as in the present case, must resolve seemingly divergent considerations of public policy.

The issue presented in this case comes to us in an increasingly recurrent posture—to wit: the review of a judgment confirming an arbitrator's award. An agreement to submit to arbitration disputes arising out of a contract, once condemned by the judiciary of this State as tending to oust the courts of their jurisdiction and, thus, declared void as contrary to settled policy, is now favorably recognized as an efficacious procedure whereby parties can select their own nonjudicial forum for the "private and practical" resolution of their disputes "with maximum dispatch and at minimum expense." (Matter of Siegel [Lewis], 40 NY2d 687, 689.)

In furtherance of the laudable purposes served by permitting consenting parties to submit controversies to arbitration, the law has adopted a policy of noninterference, with few exceptions, in this mode of dispute resolution. Quite simply, it can be said that the arbitrator is not bound to abide by, absent a contrary provision in the arbitration agreement, those principles of substantive law or rules of procedure which govern the traditional litigation process. An arbitrator's paramount responsibility is to reach an equitable result, and the courts will not assume the role of overseers to mold the award to conform to their sense of justice. Thus, an arbitrator's award will not be vacated for errors of law and fact committed by the arbitrator and "[e]ven where the arbitrator states an intention to apply a law, and then misapplies it, the award will not be set aside." (Matter of Schine Enterprises [Real Estate Portfolio of N. Y.], 26 NY2d 799, 801).

Despite this policy of according an arbitrator seemingly unfettered discretion in matters submitted to him by the consent of the parties, it is the established law in this State that an award which is violative of public policy will not be permitted to stand. The courts, however, must exercise due restraint in this regard, for the preservation of the arbitration process and the policy of allowing parties to choose a nonjudicial forum, embedded in freedom to contract principles, must not be disturbed by courts, acting under the guise of public policy, wishing to decide the dispute on its merits, for arguably every controversy has at its core some issue requiring the application, or weighing, of policy considerations. Thus, there are now but a few matters of concern which have been recognized as so intertwined with overriding public policy considerations as to either place them beyond the bounds of the arbitration process itself or mandate the vacatur of awards which do violence to the principles upon which such matters rest.

Some examples would be instructive. It has been held that an arbitrator is without power to award punitive damages, a sanction reserved solely to the State and that an agreement to arbitrate, when sought to be enforced by a lender, cannot divest the courts of their responsibility to determine whether a purported sales agreement is in fact a usurious loan, and thus illegal. Matters involving the enforcement of our State's antitrust laws, recognized as representing "public policy of the first magnitude," cannot be left to commercial arbitration, and claims concerning the liquidation of insolvent insurance companies have been held to be beyond the reach of an arbitrator's discretion where a State statute bestows upon the Supreme Court exclusive jurisdiction over these proceedings.

In public school matters, it has been held that agreements which purportedly reflect a bargain by a board of education not to inspect teacher personnel files cannot be enforced through arbitration insofar as such right is supported by statute and public policy. Nor can a board of education surrender its authority to discharge a nontenured teacher at the end of his probationary period to the arbitration process pursuant to a collective bargaining agreement, and an award the terms of which would bestow upon a probationary teacher tenure, as distinguished from procedural guarantees, will be struck down as violative of public policy.

These illustrations of instances where courts will intervene in the arbitration process are, without apparent exception, cases in which public policy considerations, embodied in statute or decisional law, prohibit, in an absolute sense, particular matters being decided or certain relief being granted by an arbitrator. Stated another way, the courts must be able to examine an arbitration agreement or an award on its face, without engaging in extended factfinding or legal analysis, and conclude that public policy precludes its enforcement. This is so because, as has been previously noted, an arbitrator is free to apply his own sense of law and equity to the facts as he has found them to be in resolving a controversy.

Applying these principles to this case, we now hold that disputes involving restrictive covenants of employment can be, by mutual consent of the parties, submitted to arbitration, and an arbitrator's award which specifically enforces such covenants, even to the extent of enjoining an individual from engaging in like employment for a reasonable period of years in the future, will not be vacated on public policy grounds.

While it is true that considerations of public policy militate against the enforcement of restrictive covenants of future employment, these covenants are not per se unenforceable as being null and void. Each case turns upon its own distinct facts. If the restrictive covenant is found, under all the circumstances, to be "reasonable in time and area, necessary to protect the employer's legitimate interests, not harmful to the general public and not unreasonably burdensome to the employee," it will be subject to specific enforcement.

Here, the parties, by reason of a broad arbitration clause contained in their signed agreement, submitted the issue of the enforceability of the restrictive covenant to arbitration, clearly a proper forum for the resolution of their dispute in this private matter. By so doing, the parties placed upon the arbitrator, not the courts, the responsibility of passing upon the merits of their controversy with the expectation that a just, yet practical, result would be reached. While there may be some doubt whether we would have enforced the restrictive covenant now before us had this dispute been adjudicated in the courts, such consideration is irrelevant to the disposition of this case, for courts will not second-guess the factual findings or the legal conclusions of the arbitrator. The utility of the arbitration process itself is derived from its autonomy, and courts must honor the choice of the parties to have their controversy decided within this framework. Insofar as public policy considerations do not absolutely preclude the enforcement of restrictive covenants of future employment for a reasonable period of time or related business concerns, we conclude that the arbitrator had the power to pass upon the issue of both the reasonableness and the necessity of the restrictions imposed upon the employee. Having thus concluded, and acknowledging the wide latitude afforded arbitrators in formulating just relief, the award rendered should not now be disturbed. . . .

NOTES ON ENFORCEABILITY OF ARBITRATION AGREEMENTS

1. Arbitration and arbitration agreements have not always been honored by the courts. But the increasing receptiveness of law to arbitration is now reflected in state and federal statutes. Most states have adopted some variant of the Uniform Arbitration Act, which declares arbitration agreements to be specifically enforceable. Under the Act, specific performance of an agreement to arbitrate existing or future controversies may be ordered directly (by ordering the breaching party to arbitrate) or indirectly (by staying litigation brought in violation of the agreement or appointing persons with the power to act as arbitrators). Other states have adopted statutory reforms of a less comprehensive nature.

On the federal level, the Federal Arbitration Act, 9 U.S.C.A. §§ 1–14, which applies to contracts relating to "maritime transactions" and "transactions involving interstate commerce" other than contracts of employment, is similar to the Uniform Act. Agreements to arbitrate disputes arising out of labor-management contracts to which federal labor law applies are governed by, and specifically enforceable under, section 301 of the Labor Management Relations Act, 29 U.S.C.A. § 185. The Supreme Court has interpreted both these acts as establishing a presumption of arbitrability. See Mitsubishi Motors Corp. *v.* Soler Chrysler-Plymouth, Inc., 473 U.S. 614 (1985); Steelworkers *v.* Enterprise Wheel & Car Corp., 363 U.S. 593 (1960).

Sprinzen's statement that, at least under New York law, "It has been held that an arbitrator is without power to award punitive damages, a sanction reserved solely to the State," has been eroded by interpretation of the FAA. In Garrity *v.* Lyle Stuart, Inc., 40 N.Y.2d 354, 356 (1976), the New York Court of Appeals held that, at a matter of public policy, judges may award punitive damages but arbitrators may not. But in Mastrobuono *v.*

Shearson Lehman Hutton, Inc., 514 U.S. 52 (1995), the Supreme Court applied the FAA to allow securities arbitrators to award punitive damages notwithstanding New York law. Securities arbitrators have been found to award punitive damages at rates that exceed the rates of punitive damages awards by judges and juries. Stephen J. Choi & Theodore Eisenberg, Punitive Damages in Securities Arbitration: An Empirical Study, J. Legal Stud. 497 (2010).

2. Yet, there have been some signs of ambivalence. In Wright *v.* Universal Maritime Service, 525 U.S. 70 (1998), the Supreme Court addressed the question whether a general arbitration clause in a collective bargaining agreement requires an employee to use an arbitration procedure for a federal statutory discrimination claim arising from an alleged violation of the Americans with Disabilities Act. The Court held that the petitioner's statutory claim was not subject to a presumption of arbitrability and a collectively bargained agreement to arbitrate such a claim must be clear.

3. Employees of Giant Foods brought a class action against their employer in federal district court, claiming discrimination based on race, age, and disability. Giant moved for summary judgment, arguing that the governing collective bargaining agreement contained an arbitration clause, and further that the scope of the arbitration clause should be determined by the arbitration.

The Court of Appeals for the Fourth Circuit disagreed:

> "Generally, 'any doubts concerning the scope of arbitrable issues should be resolved in favor of arbitration.' . . . This presumption, however, does not apply to the issue of which claims are arbitrable.
>
> "The Supreme Court has explained the reasons for this reverse presumption. It has stated that the 'willingness of parties to enter into agreements that provide for arbitration of specified disputes would be drastically reduced . . . if a labor arbitrator had the power to determine his own jurisdiction.' And, it has noted that a 'party often might not focus upon that question or upon the significance of having arbitrators decide the scope of their own powers.'
>
> "Nevertheless, the parties can agree to let an arbitrator determine the scope of his own jurisdiction. Their agreement must, however, 'clearly and unmistakably' provide that the arbitrator shall determine what disputes the parties agreed to arbitrate. . . .
>
> "The 'clear and unmistakable' test set forth by the Supreme Court requires more than simply saying that the arbitrator determines the meaning of any disputed contractual terms. The courts have repeatedly rejected the assertion that general arbitration clauses, like the ones at issue here, commit to arbitration disputes over an arbitrator's jurisdiction. . . .
>
> "We stress, however, that arbitration of arbitrability disputes—like other contractual matters—remains a question of the parties' intent. Those who wish to let an arbitrator decide which issues are arbitrable need only state that 'all disputes concerning

> the arbitrability of particular disputes under this contract are hereby committed to arbitration,' or words to that clear effect."

Carson *v.* Giant Food, Inc., 175 F.3d 325, 329–331 (4th Cir. 1999).

4. Another subject of controversy is when the arbitration clause itself is valid. In 2005, the California Supreme Court held that an arbitration clause in a consumer credit agreement, in which the consumer waived both the right to litigate in court and the right to participate in classwide arbitration, was unconscionable. The court explained that:

> "[W]hen the waiver is found in a consumer contract of adhesion in a setting in which disputes between the contracting parties predictably involve small amounts of damages, and when it is alleged that the party with the superior bargaining power has carried out a scheme to deliberately cheat large numbers of consumers out of individually small sums of money, then, at least to the extent the obligation at issue is governed by California law, the waiver becomes in practice the exemption of the party 'from responsibility for[its] own fraud, or willful injury to the person or property of another.' (Civil Code, § 1668.) Under these circumstances, such waivers are unconscionable under California law and should not be enforced."

Discover Bank *v.* Superior Court of Los Angeles, 36 Cal.4th 148, 162–63 (2005). Other state courts followed suit.

In 2011, the U.S. Supreme Court put an end to this line of decisions by holding that the rule of *Discover Bank* was preempted by the Federal Arbitration Act. A majority of five justices concluded that an application of unconscionability doctrine that effectively required companies to submit to classwide arbitration at the election of consumers was contrary to "[t]he overarching purpose of the FAA, [which is] to ensure the enforceability of arbitration agreements according to their terms so as to facilitate streamlined proceedings." AT&T Mobility LLC *v.* Concepcion, 563 U.S. 333, 344 (2011). Four justices dissented.

5. Editors of this text, in collaboration with Professor Geoffrey Miller, conducted a study of the use of arbitration clauses by firms marketing products such as cell phones and credit cards to consumers. Using a sample of 26 consumer contracts and 164 nonconsumer contracts, we compared the firms' use of arbitration clauses in their agreements with consumers with the same firms' use of arbitration clauses in their agreements with other businesses. We found that, despite their public stances in favor of arbitration as a fair and efficient method of dispute resolution, the companies included in our study "overwhelmingly selected arbitration as the method for resolving consumer disputes and permitted litigation as the method for resolving business disputes." Theodore Eisenberg, Geoffrey P. Miller, & Emily Sherwin, Arbitration's Summer Soldiers: An Empirical Study of Arbitration Clauses in Consumer and Nonconsumer Contracts, 41 U. Mich. J. L. Reform 871 (2008). Table 1 summarizes our findings.

Table 1. Rate of Arbitration Clauses by Contract Type

Contract type	Arbitration clause No	Yes	Total
Consumer (N)	6	20	26
Percent	23.1	76.9	100.0
Employment (N)	1	13	14
Percent	7.1	92.9	100.0
Other material contract (N)	138	9	147
Percent	93.9	6.1	100.0
Total (N)	145	42	187
Percent	76.3	23.7	100.0

Sources. Authors' collection of consumer contracts: EDGAR database Form 8–K and Form 10–K, Jan. 1, 2006 to Aug. 13, 2007.

CHAPTER 10

RESCISSION, REFORMATION, AND OTHER REMEDIES

A. RESCISSION

1. NATURE AND EFFECT OF RESCISSION

Estate of McKenney

District of Columbia Court of Appeals, 2008.
953 A.2d 336.

■ STEADMAN, SENIOR JUDGE. In the fall of 2004, Joseph McKenney, Jr., sold his property rights in his deceased mother's estate to Khalid B.M. Eltayeb for $1,200. The principal asset was the mother's home, on which this appeal focuses. Subsequently, after a hearing, the probate court voided the sale and removed Eltayeb as the personal representative of the mother's estate. . . . We affirm.

Geraldine B. McKenney died intestate on November 14, 1990, leaving as her only significant asset her home at 1525 E Street, S.E. Her son, Joseph W. McKenney, Jr., was her sole heir. No probate proceedings were instituted at that time. For more than a decade, the property taxes on the home went unpaid and the amount of unpaid taxes accrued to over $100,000.

In November 2004, Eltayeb approached McKenney at his place of employment. McKenney was a banquet steward who had no experience at all in real estate matters and who lived in a shelter on the grounds of St. Elizabeths Hospital. Eltayeb asked McKenney if he was aware of the $100,000 in outstanding taxes owed and asked whether McKenney "was in any position to do anything with the property." McKenney understood Eltayeb's implication to be that McKenney would need to pay that amount himself and "to pay it at one time." Eltayeb offered to purchase McKenney's interest in the property. McKenney said that he did not know the exact amount of unpaid taxes, but that he thought that he had already lost the home for failing to pay the property taxes. Eltayeb offered McKenney $1,200 for his interest in the property, but he did not disclose the property's value or that there was a right of redemption. He pressed McKenney to make a decision "right away," asserting that the house was facing imminent demolition. Eltayeb introduced McKenney to a man accompanying Eltayeb as a nephew of a prominent local political figure. Eltayeb said that the nephew had the contract for the demolition of the property.

The next day, Eltayeb again met with McKenney at work. Pressed for a decision, McKenney accepted the offer and was paid the first installment of $300. He testified that he felt "pressured into making a quick decision" because Eltayeb claimed that he needed an answer to his offer immediately in order to stop the pending demolition of the property. Over the next three weeks, McKenney received the three remaining $300 installment payments. On at least one occasion, he was again accompanied by the man who supposedly had the contract to demolish the property.

At one point during that period, Eltayeb picked up McKenney at work and they went to meet with Eltayeb's then attorney for "some paperwork." McKenney was presented with an "Irrevocable Assignment of Right" assigning his property interest to Eltayeb. He signed the document although no dollar value was listed in the agreement. Eltayeb's attorney then presented McKenney with pages one, two, and four of a Petition for Probate of his mother's estate. Omitted was page three of the petition as actually filed, which listed the home's value at $150,000 and erroneously stated that McKenney had paid nearly $4,000 in funeral expenses when he had in fact paid none. Moreover, McKenney overheard Eltayeb telling his attorney that the purchase price of property was $1,200. Without being shown the third page, McKenney signed the Petition, which was filed several days later, seeking appointment of Eltayeb as the personal representative.

On December 15, 2004, the trial court held a hearing on the Petition for Probate so that it could "further probe into the circumstances of the transaction." Prior to the hearing, Eltayeb told McKenney not to volunteer too much information and only to answer the questions asked. McKenney testified, but the purchase price of the assignment was never disclosed to the court and the trial judge never inquired, perhaps because the nature of the concerns prompting the hearing was focused elsewhere. At the hearing, Eltayeb's attorney informed the court that he represented the estate—not Eltayeb—and that they were there to "save the house" from a pending tax sale, although he was retained by Eltayeb and served as his personal attorney. The trial judge accepted the Petition for Probate. Eltayeb was appointed the estate's personal representative and conveyed the property to himself by quitclaim deed the next month, which was recorded on January 15, 2005.

In March 2005, McKenney was approached by a third party, who informed him of the property's real value and offered to purchase the property. McKenney filed a petition to remove Eltayeb as personal representative and to rescind the assignment. He then executed an agreement to sell the property for $205,000 minus the outstanding tax debt.

The trial court conducted several days of evidentiary hearings. McKenney testified to the facts of the transaction and the petition for probate as set forth above. To the contrary, Eltayeb testified that he paid

McKenney $48,375 in currency in a similar manner to what McKenney testified, but that he had no receipts, withdrawal records, bank statements, or any other documents confirming the transaction or the source of the funds. Instead, he produced a torn scrap of paper that he purported to contain his notes regarding the payments. When Eltayeb added the amounts of the five alleged installment payments before the court, the sum was $46,400, which was less than the total amount he claimed that he paid McKenney. Eltayeb denied telling McKenney that the man accompanying him had a contract to demolish the home.

Another issue at the hearing was the location of Eltayeb's residence. The address he listed in the Petition for Probate was that of his attorney. Before the trial court, Eltayeb testified that he was a resident of the District of Columbia, even though his vehicle had Virginia "drive-away" license plates, which he claimed were issued for his car detailing business that was located at a friend's home in Alexandria, Virginia, and his cellular telephone number's area code was 703, which is designated for Northern Virginia. He claimed that his residence was 333 I Street, Southwest; however, the electric utility bill for this home, which is air-conditioned, showed zero kilowatt hours billed from December 2003 until October 2004. Furthermore, Eltayeb was unable to produce his driver's license and stated that he is not a registered voter. At the conclusion of the hearings, the trial court found by clear and convincing evidence that Eltayeb made "substantial fraudulent untrue misrepresentations or representations to Mr. McKenney for the purpose of inducing him to execute the irrevocable assignment of his rights in this case, and Mr. McKenney relied upon these misrepresentations. . . ." The court completely discredited Eltayeb's testimony. . . . [I]t then removed Eltayeb as personal representative, and voided both the assignment and quitclaim deed. . . .

Traditionally, a person who was induced to enter into a contract by a misrepresentation has several common law causes of action, including fraud in the inducement sounding in tort and rescission sounding in contract. The distinction between these two may be important because each action requires a different level of proof and allows for different remedies. . . .

The D.C. Circuit has explained that a party can sue for rescission of a contract without establishing all of the elements of fraud:

> "It is well established that misrepresentation of material facts may be the basis for the rescission of a contract, even where the misrepresentations are made innocently, without knowledge of their falsity and without fraudulent intent. The rationale supporting this rule, which has its origins in equity, is that, as between two innocent parties, the party making the representation should bear the loss. Stated another way, the rule is based on the view that 'one who has made a false statement ought not to benefit at the expense of another who

has been prejudiced by relying on the statement.' This rule may be employed 'actively,' as in a suit at equity or law for rescission and restitution, or 'passively,' as a defense to a suit for breach of contract."

Barrer *v.* Women's National Bank, 761 F.2d 752, 757–58 (D.C. Cir. 1985) . . . .

Here, the trial court found that Eltayeb knowingly made fraudulent misrepresentations, which induced McKenney to agree to assign his property rights. The court concluded that Eltayeb falsely represented that the property was subject to imminent demolition and presented a man whom he claimed had the contract to demolish it. From testimony given at the hearing, the court found that Eltayeb knew that these representations were false, material, and made with an intent to deceive, and that McKenney reasonably relied upon them. Even if we assume that the proof was not sufficiently "clear and convincing" to constitute fraud in the strict sense, it was nonetheless sufficient to justify the rescission of the assignment under the principles for rescission set forth above. . . .

In its oral findings of fact, the trial court also found that Eltayeb misrepresented to McKenney that the property had no value and concealed the property's redemption value. There were, in addition, striking irregularities in preparation and presentation of the Petition for Probate, reflecting a possible overall plan of cover-up. And, most notably, Eltayeb's massive untruths in his testimony about the proceedings, as found by the trial judge, cast grave doubt on every aspect of the transaction. . . .

Eltayeb also suggests that McKenney's reliance upon any misstatements was unjustified. . . . [I]t was not facially preposterous for the home to be subject to imminent demolition. McKenney thought that he had already lost the property after failing to pay property taxes for over ten years. Moreover, Eltayeb is hardly in a position to fault McKenney's acceptance of his assertions when he pressed McKenney vigorously for an immediate decision in the face of the impending demolition. On this record, we cannot say as a matter of law that McKenney's reliance was unreasonable.

In sum, there is sufficient evidence that Eltayeb made material misrepresentations that induced McKenney to enter into the agreement to support the trial court's action in voiding the assignment and the quitclaim deed. . . .

NOTE ON LEGAL AND EQUITABLE RESCISSION

Rescission initially was an equitable remedy, available only through a suit by the party seeking to rescind. Over time, however, the law courts developed their own procedure that was similar in practical effect: a promisor entitled to equitable rescission of a contract could treat the contract as rescinded and sue at law for restitution of any value conferred on the other party. Before claiming restitution, however, the promisor was required to return anything of value received from the promisee. There are thus two kinds of rescission, equitable and legal, both historically and today in many jurisdictions in the United States.

The Alaska Supreme Court noted the distinction between the two kinds of rescission in a case about fiduciary duties. Chipp, Heiner, and Knaebel formed a close corporation to conduct mining explorations. Nine years later, the three principals executed a reorganization agreement providing, in effect, that Chipp and Heiner would buy out Knaebel. When disputes arose about the legality and tax consequences of the buy-out agreement, Knaebel sued to rescind based on breach of fiduciary duty. The trial court denied the claim. The Alaska Supreme Court remanded the case for further consideration. Addressing the claim that Knaebel could not obtain rescission without first returning the cash and benefits he had received under the buy-out agreement, the court said:

> "Rescission *at law* is a suit based upon rescission already accomplished. At law the court has nothing to do with the rescission itself; it is only involved if a subsequent suit is brought by plaintiff to recover what he gave to defendant pursuant to the rescinded transaction.
>
> "Restoration or tender [of the benefits received under the transaction being rescinded] before suit is a necessary element in legal rescission, but is wholly superfluous as a prerequisite to the commencement of a suit in equity for rescission or cancellation.
>
> "Equitable rescission differs from rescission at law in that it is not conditioned upon restoration of benefits, nor does it require an offer of restoration.
>
>> 'Since rescission is not accomplished "in equity" until the court so decrees, *the plaintiff has no obligation before suit to make restitution* of goods or money he received from the defendant. . . . [The court has the] capacity to protect the defendant by its decree and to condition rescission upon full restoration.
>>
>> 'This does not mean that the plaintiff is entitled to get back what he gave and keep what he got, too. It means only that *he need not make formal tender before suit.*' "
>
> "Dan B. Dobbs, HANDBOOK ON THE LAW OF REMEDIES § 4.8, at 294 (1973)."

Knaebel *v.* Heiner, 663 P.2d 551, 554 (Alaska 1983).

Is the distinction between legal and equitable rescission merely vestigial? Or are there reasons to retain two forms of rescission, with one form having equity's powers and constraints and the other form being for simpler cases in which judicial unwinding of the transaction is unnecessary?

For an argument that rescission (or one form of rescission?) should be widely available but not especially generous, see Richard R.W. Brooks &

Alexander Stremitzer, Beyond Ex Post Expediency—an Ex Ante View of Rescission and Restitution, 68 Wash. & Lee L. Rev. 1171 (2011).

New York Life Insurance Co. v. Johnson

United States Court of Appeals, Third Circuit, 1991.
923 F.2d 279.

■ DEBEVOISE, DISTRICT JUDGE. This is an appeal from the district court's dismissal of the complaint of plaintiff/appellant New York Life Insurance Company ("New York Life"). . . . New York Life had sought a judgment declaring that a $50,000 insurance policy it had issued on the life of Kirk Johnson, the deceased son of defendant/appellant Lawrence T. Johnson, Sr. ("Mr. Johnson"), was void *ab initio* because it had been induced by fraud. . . .

Pennsylvania substantive law is applicable. The decided Pennsylvania cases have held that an insurance policy obtained by means of a material misrepresentation will, if challenged within the period of contestability, be declared void *ab initio.* No Pennsylvania court has applied this rule in the context of a misrepresentation of smoking habits.

The district court predicted that in a smoking misrepresentation case where the insurance carrier would have issued a life insurance policy at an ascertainable higher premium if supplied with the correct smoking information, the Pennsylvania courts would not apply the "Draconian" remedy of voiding the policy *ab initio.* Rather, the district court concluded, in the present case either the Pennsylvania courts would reduce the proceeds of the policy by the amount by which the premium would have been enlarged had New York Life known of Kirk Johnson's smoking history or else the Pennsylvania courts would reduce the face amount of the policy to that amount of insurance that would have been purchased by the amount of premiums that were in fact paid. The district court recognized "that [this] rule that seems to me a proper and equitable one has no support in any of the decided jurisprudence" and that "[t]he smoking cases, albeit not Pennsylvania cases, are exactly to the contrary of my view." . . .

An examination of the pertinent Pennsylvania cases and cases from other jurisdictions leads us to conclude that the district court did not predict correctly what the Pennsylvania courts would do in the circumstance of this case. We conclude that Pennsylvania law requires that the policy in question be declared void *ab initio.*

The facts are undisputed. They were established by a comprehensive stipulation by the parties, documentary evidence and the testimony of the only witness, Mr. Johnson's expert David T. Warner, a retired insurance company executive.

Kirk Johnson applied for life insurance with New York Life on October 7, 1986. Question 12 of the application required him to provide information as to his past and present smoking habits. In answer to the question he represented that he had not smoked in the past twelve months and that he had never smoked cigarettes. Just above Kirk Johnson's signature at the end of the application is the statement that "[a]ll of the statements which are part of the application . . . are complete and true to the best of the knowledge and belief of those persons who made them."

The true facts were that Kirk Johnson had smoked for thirteen years and that during the month that he applied for the policy he was smoking approximately 10 cigarettes per day. Both Kirk Johnson and his father, Mr. Johnson, were aware of the facts. Had New York Life known these facts it would have offered a life insurance policy to Kirk Johnson, but the premium it would have demanded would have been substantially higher.

Kirk Johnson died on July 17, 1988, within two years of the application for insurance, for reasons unrelated to smoking. Mr. Johnson, the beneficiary, filed a claim for the proceeds of the policy. New York Life investigated and learned of the misrepresentations. It denied the claim and sought to effect rescission by tendering to Mr. Johnson a check for the premiums paid under the policy. The tender was refused and New York Life commenced this declaratory judgment action.

Under Pennsylvania law an insurance policy is void for misrepresentation when the insurer establishes three elements: (1) that the representation was false; (2) that the insured knew that the representation was false when made or made it in bad faith; and (3) that the representation was material to the risk being insured. . . .

In the present case disclosure of the true facts about Kirk Johnson's smoking practices would have caused New York Life to have demanded higher premiums and thus the misrepresentations were material. . . .

The district court distinguished between medical condition or health background misrepresentations (where voiding the policy would be required) and smoking practices misrepresentations. In the former case, according to the district court, the consequences of the misrepresentations are conjectural because one could not know with any assurance at what rate (if any) insurance would have issued had the proper information been supplied. In the smoking misrepresentation situation, on the other hand, one can simply refer to the insurance carrier's underwriting book to determine with precision the premium which would be charged had the proper information been supplied.

Based upon perceived equitable considerations and upon the distinction between health and smoking misrepresentations, the district court reached its determination that Pennsylvania courts would not apply the void *ab initio* rule in the smoking context.

We do not believe that these reasons support the district court's prediction of Pennsylvania law. . . .

It is true that certain medical conditions would preclude obtaining a life insurance policy at any rate. However, it is also true that in many circumstances medical or health background misrepresentations have exactly the same characteristics as smoking practices misrepresentations. In each case it is possible to refer to the underwriters manual and ascertain what premium rate would have been charged if the true facts had been disclosed.

The logic of the district court's opinion would require abrogating the void *ab initio* rule not just in smoking misrepresentation cases but in all misrepresentation cases where, if the true facts were known, the insurance company would have issued a policy at a higher precisely ascertainable rate.

There is no suggestion in Pennsylvania law that there is either a smoking misrepresentation exception or a broader precisely ascertainable rate exception to the void *ab initio* rule. The relevant inquiry is whether the misrepresentation is material. Although not decided in the smoking context, Pennsylvania cases uniformly hold that a policy will be void *ab initio* if issued as a result of a misrepresentation whether the truth would have resulted in no policy being issued or whether the truth would have resulted in the policy being issued with a higher premium. . . .

The Pennsylvania legislature has created one exception to the common law rule. With respect to misrepresentations about age, the statute requires that policies provide that, upon discovery of the misrepresentation, the amount payable "shall be such as the premium would have purchased at the correct age or ages." There are special circumstances applicable to age representations. For example, some persons, particularly among recent immigrants, may not have accurate information about their dates of birth. There are no similar circumstances which would justify removing smoking representations from the general class of representations. It is significant that the Pennsylvania legislature has spoken when it wished to accord special treatment to a particular category of representations.

Although Pennsylvania courts have not had occasion to apply the void *ab initio* rule in the smoking misrepresentation context, other courts have addressed the very issue presented in this case. Applying rescission standards similar to Pennsylvania's, these courts have uniformly voided policies for misrepresentations of smoking habits. . . .

While a court might sympathize with a beneficiary who does not receive the proceeds of a policy obtained by the insured's fraud, there are strong reasons of public policy supporting the rule which we believe prevails in Pennsylvania. If the only consequence of a fraudulent misrepresentation in a life insurance application is to reduce the amount paid under the policy, there is every incentive for applicants to lie. If the lie is undetected during the two year contestability period, the insured will have obtained excessive coverage for which he has not paid. If the lie is detected during the two year period, the insured will still obtain what he could have had if he had told the truth. In essence, the applicant has everything to gain and nothing to lose by lying. The victims will be the honest applicants who tell the truth and whose premiums will rise over the long run to pay for the excessive insurance proceeds paid out as a result of undetected misrepresentations in fraudulent applications. . . .

Therefore, we conclude that the district court erred in predicting what a Pennsylvania court would do when presented with the circumstances of this case. The judgment of the district court will be reversed and the case remanded for entry of a judgment declaring that the policy in question was void *ab initio.*

Hart v. Steel Products, Inc.

Indiana Court of Appeals, 1996.
666 N.E.2d 1270.

■ CHEZEM, JUDGE. . . . This action arose out of the sale of the assets of a steel manufacturing business located in Windfall, Indiana.

In 1990, Paul Hart decided to change careers. Paul was a veterinarian by trade who had maintained a solo practice for seventeen years. In May of 1990, Paul sold his practice and moved with his family to Indiana. Paul then began to look for a business to purchase. During a six-month period, Paul reviewed information he received from various business brokers, relating to businesses for sale such as a lumber yard, jewelry store, metal recycling plant, an unfinished furniture store, and a leather manufacturing plant.

In January of 1991, Paul received information regarding Steel Products, Inc. . . .

Sometime before April 11, 1991, Paul and [Alvah Rochon, Steel Products' general manager] went to the office of Dell Henderson, Steel Products' accountant. Rochon authorized Henderson to release the 1990 financial information to Paul. Steel Products' 1990 financial statements and income tax return showed ordinary income for 1990 of $176,301.94. Paul was not given a copy of the 1990 federal tax return. On April 11, 1991, Paul made [an] offer to purchase the assets of Steel Products. This offer was accepted and the deal was closed on May 1, 1991. Paul formed Hart Steel, Inc. to hold the assets purchased. . . .

In April of 1993, Paul contacted Henderson to retrieve some information from the 1990 federal income tax return. Henderson asked if he wanted information from the original return or the amended return. Upon learning of the amended return, Paul went to [the home of Katherine Scales, Steel Products' sole shareholder] and obtained a copy of it. The amended return showed that for 1990, Steel Products had a loss of $4,344.76.

On April 21, 1993, Harts filed suit against Scales, Rochon, and Steel Products. Harts alleged that the Defendants committed fraud by representing that Steel Products had 1990 ordinary income of $176,301.94 when they knew Steel Products had actually sustained a loss in 1990 of $4,344.76. . . . Defendants counterclaimed, alleging that Harts had failed to pay on the notes they had made in purchasing the assets of Steel Products.

A bench trial was conducted on February 17 and 18, 1995. On April 20, 1995, the trial court entered findings of fact and conclusions of law. A judgment of $215,114.56 was entered in favor of Harts and against Scales; the contract for the sale of Steel Products' assets was ordered rescinded. . . .

Defendants contend the trial court erred in ordering the contract rescinded. Fraud in the inducement of a contract is a basis for rescission. A party bringing an action for fraud has an election between two remedies. He may affirm the contract, retain the benefits, and seek damages; or he may rescind the contract, return any benefits received, and be returned to the *status quo*. If he elects to rescind the contract, he may not recover general damages, but is only entitled to be returned to the *status quo*, which usually necessitates a return of money or other things received or paid under the contract, plus reimbursement as special damages, for any reasonable expenditures incurred as a proximate result of the fraudulent conduct. The rescinding party must also restore all benefits received under the contract.

A plaintiff seeking to rescind a contract bears the burden of proving his right to rescission, and that he is able to return *in specie* any property received under the contract, or its reasonable value if a return *in specie* is impossible. Applications for rescission are addressed to the sound discretion of the trial court. . . .

Defendants argue that rescission was inappropriate in this case because the parties could not be returned to the *status quo*. The parties contracted for the sale of the assets of Steel Products for $292,500.00. The price was composed as follows:

$ 20,000.00	Cash paid to broker
100,000.00	Assumption of existing accounts payable
22,500.00	Assumption of existing obligations on equipment
150,000.00	Note payable to Scales
$292,500.00	Total

As the contract was ordered rescinded, Harts were entitled to a return of their consideration actually paid. The trial court awarded Harts

$215,114.56.[1] This sum was made up of the $100,000.00 in accounts payables that Harts had assumed, and $115,114.56 in additional capital contributions ($80,114.56 made by Harts and $35,000.00 made by another investor) paid into the business after Harts had purchased it.

Defendants argue the $115,114.56 in additional capital contributions cannot properly be characterized as consideration paid for the business because they are actually equity investments in the business. However, the fact that additional equity was invested in the business does not make those contributions not recoverable. Harts purchased the assets of Steel Products. Those assets included land, buildings and equipment, accounts receivable, inventory, goodwill, etc. Out of the revenues generated by these assets, Hart Steel had to pay its operating expenses. As Harts soon discovered after closing the deal, however, there was an insufficient revenue stream to cover the operating expenses. This necessitated that Harts pay Hart Steel's creditors out of their own pockets.

The additional capital contributions had the effect of keeping the value of Hart Steels' assets at a level that they would not have been, but for the payments by Harts. As the contract was rescinded, this increased value of the assets (because Harts paid company bills personally and not out of company revenues) is being transferred back to Steel Products. As such, Defendants should pay Harts for the amount of their payments, because it is those payments which caused the assets to have a greater value than they otherwise would have had.

In a related argument, Defendants also contend there is no way of knowing whether the additional capital contributions are being held by Hart Steel as retained earnings, which would not be transferred to Steel Products upon rescission of the contract. However, even if the funds were held by Hart Steel as retained earnings, there necessarily would be a corresponding increase in Hart Steel's assets (assets = liabilities + stockholders' equity). Thus, contrary to Defendants' contention, the judgment ordering Defendants to pay Harts for their $115,114.56 equity investment does not result in a windfall to plaintiffs; it merely restores the *status quo*. In fact, if the trial court did not order reimbursement of the equity investment, it would be Defendants who actually would be receiving a windfall because the assets returned to Steel Products would be inflated by the $115.114.56 that Harts personally paid to the company's creditors.

Defendants additionally argue the judgment is erroneous because it includes a return of the $100,000.00 in accounts payable assumed by

---

1 At trial, Harts introduced an exhibit listing the monies they sought returned. The exhibit included $47,115.28 paid to Scales on the $150,000 note. Linda Hart testified that all payments to Scales on the note were made out of the assets of the business.

However, the debt to Scales was not a debt of the business, but a debt of Harts. In reality, the payments to Scales out of the business assets were in substance either a dividend or a capital distribution by the company to Harts, who then in turn paid Scales. As such, the trial court correctly excluded this amount as a part of the consideration paid by Harts to Scales.

Harts, and that Harts had not in fact paid this entire amount. Defendants are correct. Upon rescission of the contract, a party is entitled only to the return of the consideration actually paid. The evidence adduced at trial was that Harts actually paid only $87,000 of the $100,000 they assumed in accounts payable. We therefore must remand to the trial court to decrease the judgment by $13,000.00.

Defendants also argue rescission of the contract was inappropriate because they presented evidence that some of the equipment which made up the sale was no longer in existence. However, return of the actual property is not necessary.

At trial, Defendants introduced evidence that a trailer with a 500 gallon gas tank on it was stolen, and that Hart Steel maintained no insurance on the trailer. The result of Harts' failure to maintain insurance on the equipment is that the total assets of the company have been reduced by the fair market value of the trailer. Thus, Defendants are entitled to a credit against the judgment for the fair market value of the trailer.

Defendants also argue they are entitled to a credit for a 2½ ton truck no longer owned by Hart Steel. Paul testified that the truck's engine seized up and it was then sold. However, the difference between this instance and the foregoing is that assets have not been reduced by the fair market value of the truck; it is the truck itself which has a lesser fair market value. Hart Steel received the fair market value of the 2½ ton truck upon its sale. Defendants presented no evidence that the proceeds received from the sale were not deposited into the corporation's accounts. Defendants are not entitled to a credit for the value of the 2½ ton truck.

Lastly, Defendants argue the trial court erred by not entering judgment against Harts on the promissory note payable to Scales, and which was in default. However, as the contract was properly rescinded, the parties are not entitled to any benefits received under the contract, but are only entitled to a return of their consideration actually paid. There was no error. . . .

2. GROUNDS FOR RESCISSION; MISTAKE

Rescission is available for a variety of reasons that undermine the voluntariness of a contract or transfer, including misrepresentation, mistake, duress, undue influence, or fiduciary misconduct. As the court noted in *Estate of McKenney* (above), the standard for rescission based on misrepresentation typically is lower than the standard for granting damages. Thus, most courts require a plaintiff seeking damages for fraud to prove intentional misrepresentation, but will grant rescission on the basis of a material but unknowing misrepresentation. As is usual with equitable remedies, much depends on the particular facts of each case.

In cases of mistake, damages are not an option; rescission is the only avenue available to the party disadvantaged by the mistake. Without delving too far into substantive law, the cases that follow indicate some of the lines of demarcation courts may recognize in response to claims of mistake.

Nelson v. Rice

Arizona Court of Appeals, 2000.
198 Ariz. 563.

■ ESPINOZA, CHIEF JUDGE. . . . After Martha Nelson died in February 1996, Newman and Franz, the co-personal representatives of her estate, employed Judith McKenzie-Larson to appraise the Estate's personal property in preparation for an estate sale. McKenzie-Larson told them that she did not appraise fine art and that, if she saw any, they would need to hire an additional appraiser. McKenzie-Larson did not report finding any fine art, and relying on her silence and her appraisal, Newman and Franz priced and sold the Estate's personal property.

Responding to a newspaper advertisement, Carl Rice attended the public estate sale and paid the asking price of $60 for two oil paintings. Although Carl had bought and sold some art, he was not an educated purchaser, had never made more than $55 on any single piece, and had bought many pieces that had "turned out to be frauds, forgeries or . . . to have been [created] by less popular artists." He assumed the paintings were not originals given their price and the fact that the Estate was managed by professionals, but was attracted to the subject matter of one of the paintings and the frame of the other. At home, he compared the signatures on the paintings to those in a book of artists' signatures, noticing they "appeared to be similar" to that of Martin Johnson Heade. As they had done in the past, the Rices sent pictures of the paintings to Christie's in New York, hoping they might be Heade's work. Christie's authenticated the paintings, *Magnolia Blossoms on Blue Velvet and Cherokee Roses*, as paintings by Heade and offered to sell them on consignment. Christie's subsequently sold the paintings at auction for $1,072,000. After subtracting the buyer's premium and the commission, the Rices realized $911,780 from the sale.

Newman and Franz learned about the sale in February 1997 and thereafter sued McKenzie-Larson on behalf of the Estate, believing she was entirely responsible for the Estate's loss. The following November, they settled the lawsuit because McKenzie-Larson had no assets with which to pay damages. During 1997, the Rices paid income taxes of $337,000 on the profit from the sale of the paintings, purchased a home, created a family trust, and spent some of the funds on living expenses.

The Estate sued the Rices in late January 1998, alleging the sale contract should be rescinded or reformed on grounds of mutual mistake and unconscionability. In its subsequent motion for summary judgment, the Estate argued the parties were not aware the transaction had involved fine art, believing instead that the items exchanged were "relatively valueless, wall decorations." . . . [T]he Rices argued the Estate bore the risk of mistake. . . . The trial court concluded that, although the parties had been mistaken about the value of the paintings, the Estate bore the risk of that mistake . . . .

The Estate first argues that it established a mutual mistake sufficient to permit the reformation or rescission of the sale of the paintings to the Rices.[1] . . . A contract may be rescinded on the ground of a mutual mistake as to a "basic assumption on which both parties made the contract." Restatement (Second) of Contracts § 152, cmt. b (1979). Furthermore, the parties' mutual mistake must have had "such a material effect on the agreed exchange of performances as to upset the very bases of the contract." Restatement (Second) of Contracts, *supra*, § 152, cmt. a. However, the mistake must not be one on which the party seeking relief bears the risk under the rules stated in § 154(b) of the Restatement.

In concluding that the Estate was not entitled to rescind the sale, the trial court found that, although a mistake had existed as to the value of the paintings, the Estate bore the risk of that mistake under § 154(b) of the Restatement . . . . Section 154(b) states that a party bears the risk of mistake when "he is aware, at the time the contract is made, that he has only limited knowledge with respect to the facts to which the mistake relates but treats his limited knowledge as sufficient." . . .

[C]omment c clearly applies here and states:

> "*Conscious ignorance.* Even though the mistaken party did not agree to bear the risk, he may have been aware when he made the contract that his knowledge with respect to the facts to which the mistake relates was limited. If he was not only so aware that his knowledge was limited but undertook to perform in the face of that awareness, he bears the risk of the mistake. It is sometimes said in such a situation that, in a sense, there was not mistake but 'conscious ignorance.' "

Through its personal representatives, the Estate hired two appraisers, McKenzie-Larson and an Indian art expert, to evaluate the Estate's collection of Indian art and artifacts. McKenzie-Larson specifically told Newman that she did not appraise fine art. In his deposition, Newman testified that he had not been concerned that McKenzie-Larson had no expertise in fine art, believing the Estate contained nothing of "significant value" except the house and the Indian art collection. Despite the knowledge that the Estate contained framed art other than the Indian art, and that McKenzie-Larson was not qualified to appraise fine art, the personal representatives relied on her to notify them of any fine art or whether a fine arts appraiser was needed.

---

[1] Reformation is not an available remedy under these facts. It is a remedy to correct a written instrument that fails to express the terms agreed upon by the parties and "is not intended to enforce the terms of an agreement the parties never made."

Because McKenzie-Larson did not say they needed an additional appraiser, Newman and Franz did not hire anyone qualified to appraise fine art. By relying on the opinion of someone who was admittedly unqualified to appraise fine art to determine its existence, the personal representatives consciously ignored the possibility that the Estate's assets might include fine art, thus assuming that risk. . . .

[T]he Estate bore the risk of mistake based on its own conscious ignorance.

Furthermore, under Restatement § 154(c), the court may allocate the risk of mistake to one party "on the ground that it is reasonable in the circumstances to do so." In making this determination, "the court will consider the purposes of the parties and will have recourse to its own general knowledge of human behavior in bargain transactions." Restatement § 154 cmt. d. Here, the Estate had had ample opportunity to discover what it was selling and failed to do so; instead, it ignored the possibility that the paintings were valuable and attempted to take action only after learning of their worth as a result of the efforts of the Rices. Under these circumstances, the Estate was a victim of its own folly and it was reasonable for the court to allocate to it the burden of its mistake.

The Estate also argues that enforcement of the "contract" to sell the paintings is unconscionable. . . .

[T]he Estate contends this is a case of substantive unconscionability, which concerns the actual terms of the contract and the relative fairness of the parties' obligations. Indicia of substantive unconscionability include one-sided terms that oppress or unfairly surprise an innocent party, an overall imbalance in the obligations and rights imposed by the bargain, and significant cost-price disparity. Unconscionability is determined as of the time the parties entered into the contract.

In refusing to rescind the sale on the basis of unconscionability, the trial court stated that, "[w]hile the results of the transaction may seem unconscionable to the [Estate] in hindsight, the terms of the contract certainly were not." We agree. The transaction involved no negotiation, the Estate dictated the terms of the contract by naming a price for each painting, and Carl paid the asking prices. "Courts should not assume an overly paternalistic attitude toward the parties to a contract by relieving one or another of them of the consequences of what is at worst a bad bargain . . . and in declaring the [contract] at issue here unconscionable, we would be doing exactly that." Pacific Am. Leasing, 152 Ariz. 96, 103 (Ariz. App. 1986). . . .

Krezinski v. Hay

Supreme Court of Wisconsin, 1977.
77 Wis.2d 569.

■ DAY, JUSTICE. . . . The plaintiff brought action against Ms. Izetta Hay and her insurer for damages resulting from Ms. Hay's negligent operation of her automobile on State Trunk Highway 31 in Racine county on September 28, 1963. According to the complaint, the plaintiff was driving north on the highway when the defendant negligently drove her car onto the highway from a driveway causing the two automobiles to collide. The plaintiff alleged that she sustained injuries, "among others, traumatic epilepsy, contusions to scalp—occipito parietal area, cervical sprain and right dorsal myositis; numerous other abrasions, contusions and lacerations; severe pain and suffering, shock and mental anguish."

The defendants' answer denied negligent conduct and set forth various affirmative defenses, among which was that on September 5, 1969, the plaintiff, while represented by counsel, executed a release of all claims against the defendants, "in any way growing out of, any and all known and unknown personal injuries, developed or undeveloped, including death and property damage resulting or to result from an accident that occurred on or about the 28th day of September, 1968." The agreement acknowledged receipt by plaintiff of $2,300 as consideration for the release.

The plaintiff filed a reply admitting execution of the release but alleging she and the defendants relied and acted upon a mutual mistake of fact. That mistake was their ignorance the plaintiff was suffering from a latent but present condition as a result of the accident which later manifested itself by grand mal epileptic seizures. This epileptic condition was not observed by plaintiff's physician prior to execution of the release.

The defendant moved for summary judgment . . . .

Releases will be set aside on the ground of mistake only where the mistake is mutual and not unilateral. The mistake of fact must be past or present "for it is obvious that the coming into existence of any future fact must at the time of contracting have been understood to rest in conjecture, and the contingency thereof to have been assumed by both parties." Kowalke *v.* Milwaukee Electric Railway & Light Co., 103 Wis. 472 (1899).

The seemingly all-inclusive language of the release before us is not dispositive of whether there was a mutual mistake of fact.

"[E]ven though a release expressly covers unknown injuries, it is not a bar to an action for such unknown injuries if it can be shown that such unknown injuries were not within the contemplation of the parties when the settlement was agreed upon; however, if the parties did in fact intentionally agree upon a settlement for unknown injuries, such release will be binding. Whether the parties intended the release to cover unknown injuries is usually a question of fact." Doyle *v.* Teasdale, 263 Wis. 328, 336, 346 (1953). . . .

The nature and extent of a party's reliance on a mutually accepted medical diagnosis is a question of fact. If the diagnosis failed to ascertain a then-existing but unknown condition caused by the incident which led to the suit, and the parties relied on the diagnosis as the basis for settlement, the release may be set aside. . . .

Volpe v. Schlobohm

Court of Civil Appeals of Texas, 1981.
614 S.W.2d 615.

■ CORNELIUS, CHIEF JUSTICE. Appellees, Charles H. and Joneen Lou Schlobohm, brought this suit against appellant, Robert M. Volpe, seeking rescission of a partnership agreement. The partnership was originally composed of the Schlobohms, Volpe and Edward R. Wright. Wright withdrew from the partnership before the suit was filed and was not a party. Volpe answered and counterclaimed seeking dissolution, accounting, damages and other relief.

In a trial to the court without the aid of a jury, judgment was rendered for the Schlobohms rescinding the partnership and vesting in them the title to all partnership assets. The judgment decreed that Volpe take nothing on his counterclaim but awarded him . . . the . . . value of his 30% interest in the partnership . . . .

The Schlobohms have been engaged in the food distributing business in Dallas since 1966. Prior to February 1, 1978, they operated a proprietorship which consisted of various distributorships with companies in the prepared food business. Volpe became associated with the Schlobohms as a jobber on June 10 of 1972. On January 28, 1978, the Schlobohms, Volpe and Wright met to discuss the formation of a partnership. Mrs. Schlobohm made notes of the discussions which later formed the basis of a written partnership agreement. The agreement was accepted and agreed to by all parties on February 1, 1978, although it was never signed.

At the commencement of the partnership, Charles Schlobohm was a franchisee of Pepperidge Farms, Volpe was a franchisee of Stella D'Oro, and Wright was a franchisee of Pepperidge Farms. The Schlobohms testified that their Pepperidge Farms franchise was to be excluded from the partnership. Wright also testified that neither of the Pepperidge Farms franchises was to be contributed as a partnership asset. However, the revenues from these franchises were deposited in the partnership account and were divided among the partners according to their percentage interests in the firm. Mr. Volpe testified that he understood that the Pepperidge Farms franchises were to be contributed as partnership assets and that he also understood that he was contributing his Stella D'Oro franchise.

In June of 1978, some four months after the creation of the partnership, Wright withdrew taking his Pepperidge Farms franchise with him. His interest in the partnership was purchased by the Schlobohms with their own funds. Volpe testified that he was not given the opportunity to purchase his pro rata share of Wright's interest; the

Schlobohms asserted that he was given the opportunity but declined to do so because they would not agree to his use of partnership funds to purchase his proportionate interest. Volpe did, however, insist that he was entitled to his proportionate share of Wright's profits and partnership assets; and ultimately this disagreement and the misunderstanding concerning the contribution of the Pepperidge Farms franchises as partnership assets resulted in a deterioration of the relationships between the Schlobohms and Volpe and gave rise to this suit. . . .

The Schlobohms pleaded that the partnership should be rescinded because of ". . . a mutual mistake of material substance . . . , namely, that the parties are unable and/or unwilling to work together to fulfill the purposes and intent of the intended partnership. . . ." At the trial, however, the Schlobohms asserted that the mistake related to the question of whether the Pepperidge Farms franchises were partnership assets, and it was that mistake which formed the basis for the court's grant of rescission. . . .

A partnership agreement, like any other agreement or relationship, may be rescinded when proper grounds exist. Rescission may be authorized either because of a mutual mistake of the parties, or because of a unilateral mistake if the elements of remediable mistake are present.

Although the trial court here based its judgment on remediable mistake, characterizing the misunderstanding about the franchises as a unilateral mistake, the facts found by the trial court actually reveal a mutual mistake of a type which will warrant rescission.

Ordinarily a mutual mistake sufficient to justify rescission exists when both of the parties are laboring under the same misconception as to a common fact, as when the parties know what they have agreed to, but through their common mistake the expression of their contract fails to correctly state that agreement, or when the parties contract on the assumption of a matter material to the contract but not expressed in it, and their common assumption is incorrect. But the mutual mistakes need not be identical. If they relate to the same matter, equitable relief is available even though the mistakes of the parties as to that fact are not the same. Rescission may be granted when there is a mistake of this kind which results in the parties' never having reached a meeting of the minds and thus prevents, ab initio, the formulation of a valid contract. Examples of this type of mistake are found in cases in which the parties, when attempting to formulate their agreement, were laboring under different conceptions as to the subject matter of the agreement, or as to the identity, character or quantity of a matter or thing with reference to which they were attempting to contract. . . . [W]hen one party understands that he is contracting on one set of terms and the other understands that he is contracting on another set of terms, there is no contract unless the circumstances are such as preclude one of the parties from denying that he agreed to the terms set by the other. Of course, this type of mistake will justify relief only if the expression or writing evidencing the purported agreement is uncertain and ambiguous, for if there is no ambiguity with respect to the written or oral expression of the terms neither party will be heard to say that, by his subjective intent, he meant something different from what was actually expressed.

The written partnership agreement involved in this case makes no specific provision concerning whether or not the parties' franchises would be contributed to the firm as partnership assets, and the agreement as a whole is unclear as to whether the franchises were or were not to be included. On the basis of the testimony the trial judge concluded that the franchises were not to be contributed as partnership assets, but he also found that the parties were laboring under opposite understandings with reference to that issue—the Schlobohms thinking that they were not to become partnership assets and Volpe thinking that they were—and that there was no meeting of the minds of the parties on that material issue. Rescission is a proper remedy in such a situation, provided it is possible to restore the contracting parties to their original positions, and provided the rights of innocent third parties have not otherwise intervened. . . .

NOTE

Assuming the court was correct in its analysis of the parties' intent, was rescission an appropriate remedy?

B. REFORMATION

Nash v. Kornblum

Court of Appeals of New York, 1962.
12 N.Y.2d 42.

■ FOSTER, JUDGE. The question before us is whether reformation should be granted where the written executed contract contains an essential term which does not represent the term as originally agreed upon in the oral negotiations. The remaining essential terms were not fixed until the execution of the formal contract.

The development of the negotiations and agreement are set forth as follows. Plaintiff, a fence building company, through its sales estimator, Mr. Harkness, and defendant, who conducted a Summer camp, entered into negotiations on March 17, 1958 concerning new fencing around three tennis courts. Harkness offered to prepare estimates, and by telephone told defendant that he had made an estimate "on 484 feet, of ten-foot high chain-link fence . . . in one width" at $2,040. Because of the amount of money, defendant asked if there was anything else that could be done, to which Harkness replied for less money "we could figure that in hex netting, otherwise the specifications the same as in the chain-link." Although defendant testified Harkness personally came to the camp and viewed the area at this time, which Harkness denied, the realm of discussion was over the cost of fence material. Even with a possible idea of enclosing an additional handball court because of the savings in the use of hex netting, the 484-foot figure, defendant testified, "was a fair estimate of the whole area." In any event, defendant requested both estimates.

Harkness prepared the two estimates, one for chain-link, the other for hex netting, gave them to a stenographer, who typed them on two separate contract forms. Harkness looked them over quickly, and mailed them to defendant. Except as to the differences about to be noted, they are identical.

The first proposal dated March 21, 1958 specifies "Length *484* linear feet," "Height 10—," "Fabric 2—mesh #9 gauge galv. chain link," "Price TWO THOUSAND FORTY DOLLARS ($2,040.00)." This proposal was not accepted by defendant. The second proposed contract dated the same day specifies "Length *968* linear feet," "Height 10," "Fabric 1½—mesh #16 ga. Hex Netting *in two widths of 5 each.*" "Price ONE THOUSAND EIGHT HUNDRED TWENTY NINE DOLLARS ($1,829.00)" (emphasis supplied). Each proposal provides "If more or less fence is erected, an adjustment in price will be made." It should be noted that the second proposal did not state 968 linear feet of fence but simply 968 linear feet; to erect a 10-foot-high fence 484 feet long requires 968 linear feet of 5-foot-wide hex netting. During the first week in April, defendant signed and returned the second proposal, the hex netting offer, together with the requested $600 deposit.

When construction around the tennis courts was almost completed, defendant inquired about enclosing the handball court. Harkness quoted a price based on the tennis court price and, although a letter from plaintiff was sent on May 22, 1958 confirming the estimate and requesting a duplicate letter be signed and returned, the work went on without this additional approval.

At the completion of the fencing work, the job superintendent measured the area fenced. The perimeter of the tennis courts turned out to be 534 feet, and in addition there were 50 feet on each side of the handball court, a total of 634 feet. The total amount of hex netting used was thus 1,268 feet, since the fence was put up in 2 widths of 5 feet each. Plaintiff sent defendant a bill dated May 31, 1958, stating a balance due of $1,794.50. This sum was arrived at by adding $1,829 "as per Contract dated 4/2/58" plus "150—additional fence furnished and installed @ $3.77 per ft. as per estimate dated 5/22/58," a total of $2,394.50 less $600 deposit. On July 5, more than a month later, and without any protest meanwhile, defendant mailed plaintiff a check for only $597.92 together with a letter stating:

> "Enclosed find $597.92 which pays up for 634 feet installed, and which was based on the original contract price. I find you made an error in your calculations. 968 linear feet priced at $1829.00 makes 634 feet equal to $1197.92. Six Hundred dollars has been paid, leaving a balance of $597.92.

"I would like to enclose another area which I estimate about 300 feet. Kindly get in touch with me to make arrangements as we then can use up the remaining 334 feet of our contract."

Thereafter, plaintiff instituted this action to reform the executed contract to read 484 linear feet.

There is no contention in the record that the two original proposals, identical in the most part except for the type of fence material, were not intended for exactly the same ground area. As noted previously, the problem here is that the *ground* linear feet involved in the original estimate (disregarding the actual measurement) was 484 feet. This would mean 484 feet of 10-foot-high chain-link fence; but 968 feet of 5-foot hex-netting fence since a double width was necessary to make the hex-netting fence 10 feet high. Plaintiff contends this contract, as signed, containing the reference to 968 linear feet, was merely a typographical or inadvertent error on the part of the plaintiff's secretary in exactly doubling the ground linear feet, perhaps to reflect the length of 5-foot width fencing, not coming to his attention until the fence was nearly finished, and did not represent the agreement previous to its reduction to writing. Defendant asserts that he signed the contract as written, he tendered payment on the basis of that contract and is even willing to "use up" the remaining ground linear feet of fencing.

The sole issue before us is whether reformation should have been granted. In Ross *v.* Food Specialties (6 N.Y.2d 336, 341) this court stated: "We have consistently and repeatedly held that before a reformation can be granted the plaintiff '*must establish his right to such relief by clear, positive and convincing evidence.* Reformation may not be granted upon a probability nor even upon a mere preponderance of evidence, but only upon a certainty of error' nor may the plaintiff 'secure reformation merely upon a showing that he or his attorney made a mistake. In the absence of fraud, the mistake shown "must be one made by both parties to the agreement so that the intentions of neither are expressed in it." . . . Reformation is not designed for the purpose of remaking the contract agreed upon but, rather, solely for the purpose of stating correctly a mutual mistake shared by both parties to the contract; in other words, it provides an equitable remedy for use when it clearly and convincingly appears that the contract, as written does not embody the true agreement as mutually intended." However, in Hart *v.* Blabey (287 N.Y. 257, 262), this court invoked the equitable doctrine of reformation on the following basis: "Where there is no mistake about the agreement, and the only mistake alleged is in the reduction of that agreement to writing, such mistake of the scrivener, or of either party, no matter how it occurred, may be corrected. In such a case equity will conform the written instrument to the parol agreement which it was intended to embody."

It clearly and convincingly appears from the record here that this is a case of a mistake on the part of the plaintiff's agent in typing the erroneous linear ground measurement, which plaintiff did not discover before submission to the defendant, and the latter, with knowledge of the mistake, trying to take advantage of the error. The writing itself did not represent the understanding of either party as to the area to be fenced which had been agreed upon previous to the writing, and thus did not embody the true agreement, as mutually intended, relating to the area.

This is not a case where the plaintiff unilaterally and mistakenly estimated the linear feet and defendant, without a duty to speak and absent fraud, agreed to the proposal. Should these circumstances have been present in the contract's reduction to writing, there would be no scrivener's mistake or mutual mistake of fact, the agreement would be the intended one by the parties, and equity would not "reform" the executed contract. This set of circumstances is not presented here by the record.

There is clear and convincing evidence that there was an agreement between the parties as to the area to be fenced before the formal written contract was executed, and *then* an error was made, albeit by plaintiff, in the reduction of the antecedent expression of the parties into the complete contract. The only question between the parties on the execution of the written contract was the type of fencing to be constructed and cost thereof, and admittedly these essential terms were not fixed until the formal contract was signed. These latter terms are not sought to be reformed.

The situation presented clearly calls for relief, and the only practicable method of achieving such a result is by the equitable remedy of reformation. The Trial Judge dismissed the complaint with the finding that the proof failed to show fraud on the part of the defendant. In our view of the case it was unnecessary for the plaintiff to establish fraud on the part of the defendant. Perhaps reformation could have been predicated upon a unilateral mistake on one side and deceptive conduct on the other side which tended to obscure the true agreement. However, the situation presented as a result of the scrivener's error was closely akin, if not precisely, to a mutual mistake of fact, and as such was sufficient to call for the application of the equitable doctrine of reformation. Therefore, the judgment should be reversed and the case remitted to Special Term for proceedings not inconsistent with this opinion. . . .

NOTES

1. Suppose Nash discovers the mistake before doing the work. Rather than perform the work at the price initially agreed to, Nash would prefer to avoid the contract and have no further dealings with Kornblum. Assuming, as the court found, that both parties intended a price of $1,829.00 for 484 feet of fence (with adjustments), is rescission an appropriate remedy?

2. Suppose Nash and Kornblum agreed on a fixed price of $2,394.50 for the job of fencing the tennis and handball courts. They arrived at this figure based on a mistaken measurement (provided by a third party), which

both believed to be correct. In fact, the area to be fenced is twice as large as they thought. Nash seeks to reform the contract by doubling the price. Is reformation an available remedy?

Mutual of Omaha Insurance Co. v. Russell

United States Court of Appeals, Tenth Circuit, 1968.
402 F.2d 339.

■ JOHN R. BROWN, CIRCUIT JUDGE. Does the speed of the modern jet age and the restless, irrepressible, increased tempo of all who are in its vortex impose on a flight insurer the obligation toward prospective policy buyers of explaining the distinctive differences of the several available coverages? Does the insurer's attractive sales booth, neon signs heralding the need for and availability of "flight insurance," and the other catchy advertising come-ons carry the inevitable message to scurrying people on the move the notion that the coverage is for the traveler's intended round trip rather than for a definitive period of time? And to avoid this misreading by people in a hurry of printed contracts plain enough that even those who run may read, must the insurer affirmatively take steps by extra-contract informational statements to overcome such misapprehension?

The District Judge, in effect, answered these broad inquiries in the affirmative. The failure to give such informational advice became, in his analysis, a constructive fraud upon which to base reformation of a flight insurance policy which, all now agree, did not by its terms cover the death of the Assured. In more austere terms the main issue presented for decision is whether the Assured is entitled to reformation of a general accident flight insurance policy purchased at Insurer's sales booth in the lobby of an airport. The District Court reformed the contract and awarded plaintiff $20,000. We hold that under the unusual fact situation of this case the insurance policy should not have been reformed and the decision of the District Court must be reversed.

To understand fully the Assured's theory a full recitation of the facts is helpful. Rev. and Mrs. Russell were residents of Kansas City, Kansas. On Thursday, January 24, 1963, upon receiving word that one of her brothers had died in Lubbock, Texas, Mrs. Russell decided to fly to Lubbock for the funeral. Reservations were made for a flight the next day, Friday, but the return flight was left open because the funeral date had not been set. On Friday Rev. and Mrs. Russell and their son went to the airport in Kansas City, Missouri, picked up their tickets at the Continental Airlines counter, and proceeded toward the awaiting plane.

As the three Russells passed one of Insurer's vending machines for dispensing flight insurance, Rev. Russell decided that Mrs. Russell should have insurance to cover her during the trip. This machine dispensed Insurer's policy T–20. In many ways the T–20 affords severely limited coverage in that it provides protection only for accidents while aboard an airplane or in established limousines going to or coming from the airport. On the other hand, the T–20's coverage expressly remains in effect for the duration of the round trip or for twelve months, whichever occurs first. Similarly, since events and covered occurrences were more restrictive, the face amount of insurance per premium dollar was larger than other policies. Had a T–20 been machine-issued the Assured's death would have been covered. But no one had the proper change to operate the machine, so the Russells stepped just south of the machine to one of Insurer's staffed insurance booths. The booth had signs overhead reading "Flight Insurance" and was attended by a Miss Fletcher.

Rev. Russell asked either for flight insurance or insurance to cover his wife on her round trip to Lubbock. Miss Fletcher then asked "How much?", meaning what amount of insurance coverage. Mrs. Russell asked for the least amount and $20,000 was the amount agreed upon. Without then explaining various policies available, Miss Fletcher took out an application form and began to fill it out. She then asked either how long would Mrs. Russell be gone or when would she be returning. Mrs. Russell turned to her husband and asked "Three days?" Rev. Russell said she should allow herself more than that—at least four days. Miss Fletcher completed the form and turned it around for Mrs. Russell's signature. Mrs. Russell signed and paid the $2.25 premium. Miss Fletcher stapled the policy together and handed it to Rev. Russell.

The policy purchased was not, however, the T–20; rather it was the T–18, a significantly different policy. The T–18 is a general accident policy that covers almost all risks—whether air related or not—during the life of the policy. The policy term is stated in terms of twenty-four hour periods on a daily basis up to thirty-one days. The premium is higher on the T–18 for the same dollar amount of insurance, and the T–18 is not sold in vending machines. As the Schedule signed by Mrs. Russell shows, the T–18 was issued for only four days, and expired at 11:00 a.m., Tuesday, January 29, 1963, about twelve hours prior to the Assured's death.

The District Court credited Rev. Russell's testimony that Miss Fletcher never mentioned any other available policies, did not explain the T–18, and did not warn plaintiff that the policy would expire at 11:00 a.m. on Tuesday, January 29, 1963. The Judge also found that the Assured intended to buy insurance that would cover Mrs. Russell's round trip, which both she and her husband thought would occur within four days.

After buying the insurance, Mrs. Russell boarded her plane and arrived safely in Lubbock, Texas. There the funeral was delayed because a son of the deceased had not arrived from England. The funeral was finally held on Tuesday, January 29, and Mrs. Russell was fatally injured when her airplane crashed that night at 10:45 p.m. while attempting to land at the Kansas City, Missouri, airport. The insurance policy had expired by its own terms about twelve hours earlier. The Insurer denied liability.

The Assured then pursued Insurer in this diversity of citizenship suit in Kansas on the theories that either (1) the insurance contract should be construed to cover the death of Mrs. Russell, or (2) the policy should be reformed to provide coverage for the return flight from Lubbock to Kansas City. The District Judge held that the contract was clear and unambiguous and as written did not cover the accident. But now of direct importance he held that as a matter of equity the policy should be reformed to cover the accident. Judgment for $20,000 was entered for the Assured. Insurer appealed contending that it is not liable since the policy had expired and the company was not guilty of any inequitable conduct that would give rise to the remedy of reformation. The Assured cross-appealed contending that the judgment should have been for $90,000, the amount of straight flight insurance (T–20) that $2.25 would have bought, but the Assured did not appeal the decision that the policy could not be construed to cover the accident. Thus the only substantive problem before us is whether the contract should, as a matter of equity, be reformed. . . .

Neither party disagrees about the general principles of equity applicable here. The rub comes in the proper application of those principles to the facts of this case. Reformation is an ancient remedy used to reframe written contracts to reflect accurately the real agreement between contracting parties when, either through mutual mistake or unilateral mistake coupled with actual or equitable fraud by the other party, the writing does not embody the contract as actually made.

But reformation is an extraordinary remedy, and courts exercise it with great caution. Even in situations where obvious mistakes have been made, courts will not rewrite the contract between the parties, but will only enforce the legal obligations of the parties according to their original agreement. Here, of course, the Assured does not contend that mutual mistake occurred and it is well that he does not do so for obviously the Insurer intended to sell the exact policy with the exact coverage that it did. Rather, the Assured's theory rests on another accepted reformation doctrine—mistake by one party coupled with constructive or equitable fraud by the other.

Thus the whole case boils down in reality to one question: Did Insurer have a duty to tell the Assured that several insurance policies were available and to explain fully the provisions and limitations of those policies? Without this supposed duty (and its breach) the District Judge would have had no basis for judge-reformation of the contract to conform to a regular straight flight insurance policy which Insurer was offering for sale. Rules of construction, either generally or with particular reference to the liberalizing impact of traveler haste in acquiring air-flight insurance, are of little help since on construction the Assured fails altogether. The problem is one of the proper scope of the doctrine of equitable fraud and the manner in which that doctrine relates to the duty of an insurer to warn the customer about what he is buying.

As in nearly all cases, an inquiry of this type involves consideration of the competing interests. On the one hand we have the right of the public to be free of fraud and oppression wrought by those in a superior bargaining position. But on the other hand we are confronted with the realities of doing business, the enforcement of contracts, and instability which flows from opening up written contracts to oral accretions.

The Assured urges, and the District Court declared, that an explanation was owing. By whom was it to be given? In what form was it to be offered? Orally or in writing? If orally, how would an insurer conscious of its duty of fair dealing toward a peripatetic public in a hurry assure that an adequate, reliable statement was made? The "explanation" would vary as work shifts changed and sales personnel rotated. They would be expansive or restrictive as the loquacious or taciturn quality of the employee predominated. If the insurer turned to a written statement, how or in what manner would it assure itself that the impatient prospect would pay any more heed to it than the terms of the policy contract? And what happens when, out of an abundance of good faith, an effort is made to explain (in nonlegalese) what a legal document prescribes? And as to either method or a mixture of both, what are the significant distinctions to be pointed out? Which ones to emphasize? To minimize? To omit? How many policies need to be explained? Just the two most common—T–20 and T–18? Or all eleven? In the meantime what is happening to time—that precious irreplaceable which accounts for the traveler's pressure at the airport facing either dispensing machine or an attractive sales person who may well try harder but without benefit of a legal education? The flight would either be missed or the "offer" of flight insurance withdrawn for want of adequate time for equity's mandated "explanation." Hardship, or what seems to be hardship, may sometimes occur if the law adheres to its long-held notions of the non-variability of written contracts. But a too-quick relaxation in the contrails of the jet age might well be worse, not better.

We think that imposing a duty to offer such explanations under circumstances of this kind—requiring as it does an effort by lay persons to interpret the legal meaning of the proposed contract as well as others available—would be fraught with great danger to the stability of contracts. We do not think Kansas would embrace such a view and for Kansas we decline to skywrite such an *Erie* judgment.

The printed contract controls. There it ends. . . .

NOTES

1. Did the parties agree on round-trip insurance?

2. Could Russell have opted for rescission? Would rescission be a sufficient remedy?

NOTES ON RESCISSION, REFORMATION, AND EXTRINSIC EVIDENCE

1. Sabo was employed by Delman, a shoe manufacturer. Sabo alleged that Delman had persuaded Sabo to assign a patent application to Delman, based on an oral promise to manufacture and promote Sabo's design, which Delman never intended to perform. Accordingly, Sabo sought to rescind the assignment on the basis of fraud. Delman pointed to a merger clause in the written assignment, providing that "No verbal understanding or conditions, not herein specified, shall be binding on either party." The New York Court of Appeals reversed a judgment dismissing Sabo's complaint:

> "The parol evidence rule forbids proof of extrinsic evidence to contradict or vary the terms of a written instrument and, accordingly, one who seeks, in a breach of contract action, to *enforce* an oral representation or promise relating to the subject matter of the contract cannot succeed. However, the parol evidence rule has no application in a suit brought to *rescind* a contract on the ground of fraud. In such a case, it is clear [that] evidence of the assertedly fraudulent oral misrepresentation may be introduced to avoid the agreement.
>
> "The provision to which we above referred—that no verbal undertakings or conditions not contained in the writing were to be binding on either party—sometimes termed a merger clause, merely furnishes another reason for applying the parol evidence rule, and, just as that rule is ineffectual to exclude evidence of fraudulent misrepresentations, so this provision may not be invoked to keep out such proof. Indeed, if it were otherwise, a defendant would have it in his power to perpetrate a fraud with immunity, depriving the victim of all redress, if he simply has the foresight to include a merger clause in the agreement. Such, of course, is not the law. . . .
>
> "In the *Ernst Iron Works* case, 270 N.Y. 165, the court wrote, 'A rogue cannot protect himself from liability for his fraud by inserting a printed clause in his contract. This principle disposes of the blanket clause providing that no representation shall be binding unless incorporated in the agreement.' "

Sabo *v.* Delman, 3 N.Y.2d 155, 161–62 (1957).

2. Brandwein, a former insurance agent for Prudential, sued for reformation of his agency contract with Prudential, which omitted to provide for payment of commissions on premiums paid after termination of his employment. Brandwein claimed that, at the time he signed the contract, Prudential had promised to pay such commissions and represented that it would record its promise in a side agreement. The Court of Appeals reversed a judgment dismissing the claim:

> "Plaintiff would not have stated a cause of action had he limited himself to alleging that besides the payments set out in the formal written agreement he had a separate oral promise from defendant for the payment of other commissions. Attempted proof of such a 'side agreement' would probably be inadmissible under

the parol evidence rule. The oral agreement itself would be unenforceable under the Statute of Frauds since on its face and as pleaded it would be such an agreement as could not be performed within a year or before the end of a lifetime. But this complaint contains much more than that. It says that plaintiff's signature on the written agreement was procured from him by a fraudulent representation that defendant intended to write onto its records the collateral agreement. Plaintiff asserts that he does not know whether such record was ever made but that he was at one time assured by defendant that it had been made and later told that it had not. If it is not to be found on defendant's books, says plaintiff, its absence is due to a mutual mistake of the parties or to a mistake on plaintiff's part and a fraud by defendant. Those are the classic grounds for reformation of an instrument in equity.

"As to the alleged defenses, it is settled that neither the Statute of Frauds nor the parol evidence prohibition forbids reformation of a written contract to include material orally agreed upon but, because of mutual mistake or unilateral mistake plus fraud, not inserted in the writing. The authorities so holding are numerous and consistent. The latest application of that rule in this court is Sabo *v.* Delman, the difference between the two cases being that Sabo sued for rescission while the present plaintiff prays for reformation."

Brandwein *v.* Provident Mutual Life Ins. Co., 3 N.Y.2d 491, 495–96 (1957).

C. DECLARATORY JUDGMENT AND EQUITABLE REMEDIES ANALOGOUS TO THE DECLARATORY JUDGMENT

Modern declaratory judgment acts have largely, but not entirely, superseded a variety of equitable remedies that were once quite important in solving procedural difficulties and providing effective protection for rights. Among these were *quia timet* relief, bills of peace, cancellation of documents, and decrees quieting title to property, each of which is briefly described below. In their original forms, these remedies all relied on the power of equity courts to issue *in personam* orders.

There are similarities between these equitable remedies and the modern declaratory judgment, but there are even more differences. The declaratory judgment was created by statute, rather than being developed from equity. A plaintiff seeking a declaratory judgment does not have to meet basic equitable requirements, such as showing there is no adequate remedy at law. And a declaratory judgment is not an *in personam* order, and it is not directly enforceable by contempt. Moreover, in some jurisdictions, a declaratory judgment action can be decided by a jury.

All of these remedies are part of the toolkit of the litigator. They are not sought as frequently as damages and injunctions, but you need to be aware of them, especially when your client needs protection from a suit that someone else might bring.

1. QUIA TIMET

Escrow Agents' Fidelity Corp. v. Abelman

California Court of Appeal, 1992.
4 Cal. App. 4th 491.

■ BOREN, ASSOCIATE JUSTICE. Petitioners challenge an order of the respondent court sustaining, without leave to amend, the demurrer of real party Linda Abelman ("Abelman") to the first cause of action of petitioners' complaint. In that cause of action, petitioners sought relief based on the theory of quia timet, an equitable remedy which allows an aggrieved party to obtain pre-judgment relief to prevent an anticipated injury. Abelman persuaded the respondent court that quia timet was a remedy which no longer exists in the State of California, having been "taken over by, consumed in and now part of a whole statutory scheme of rights."

Although quia timet has by and large been abandoned in favor of other legal and equitable pre-judgment remedies, it is by no means obsolete. Although rarely utilized in general practice, it is widely and effectively used in fidelity and surety bond cases. The respondent court erred, therefore, in sustaining Abelman's demurrer to petitioners' quia timet cause of action.

Petitioner Escrow Agents' Fidelity Corporation (EAFC) is a nonprofit corporation established by the Legislature pursuant to the Escrow Law, Cal. Fin. Code § 17000 et seq., to act as the fidelity surety for the trust obligations of licensed escrow agents in California. The purpose of EAFC is to indemnify its member agents against loss of trust obligations as a result of embezzlement, theft, or mysterious disappearance. The surety coverage is underwritten by petitioner National Union Fire Insurance Company, which issued a "Blanket Crime Policy" for the benefit of EAFC and each of its member agents.

One such agent, Abelman, is alleged to have embezzled over $4 million from Citi Escrow ("Citi") and a related company, 1031 Exchange ("Exchange"). On June 11, 1990, both of those entities filed voluntary Chapter 11 petitions in bankruptcy court. On Citi's behalf, Citi's trustee in bankruptcy made a claim with petitioners in excess of four million dollars, a claim which petitioners are statutorily obligated to pay.

On November 21, 1990, petitioners filed the underlying superior court action against Abelman, to which Abelman demurred. On May 8, 1991, the respondent court sustained, without leave to amend, the demurrer to the first cause of action for equitable relief quia timet and imposition of a constructive trust.

On August 5, 1991, while this petition was pending, Abelman filed a voluntary Chapter 7 bankruptcy petition in the U.S. Bankruptcy Court in Hawaii. Oral argument in this case was continued several times so that petitioners could obtain a transfer of Abelman's bankruptcy case to California, then obtain relief from the automatic stay imposed by [the Bankruptcy Code]. On February 5, 1992, the United States Bankruptcy Court for the Central District of California entered its order granting petitioners' motion for relief from the automatic stay, for the limited purpose of allowing this court to rule on the petition for writ of mandate.

Quia timet (literal translation, "because he fears"), is an action for equitable relief against an anticipated injury. "Bills *quia timet* are in the nature of writs known at the common law as *brevia anticipantia*, or writs of prevention, to accomplish the ends of precautionary justice. They are ordinarily applied to prevent wrongs or anticipated mischief, and not merely to redress them when done. The party asks the aid of the court because he fears some future probable injury to his rights or interests, and not because an injury has already occurred which requires compensation or other relief."

Traditionally, the equitable remedy of quia timet was used in California in real property cases (and, to a lesser extent in personal property cases), "to prevent a mischief, rather than redress it." (Martin *v.* Holm, 197 Cal. 733, 746 (1925) [threatened violation of building restriction]; see also Newport *v.* Hatton, 195 Cal. 132 (1924) ["writ of prevention" to protect remainderman's interest in real property]; German Savings etc. Society *v.* Collins, 145 Cal. 192 (1904) [quia timet action to determine claims and liabilities of parties to $2,500 drawn on forged checks]; Benson *v.* Shotwell, 87 Cal. 49 (1890) [specific performance of a contract to purchase waterfront property in San Francisco]; McGrath *v.* Wallace, 85 Cal. 622 (1890) [action to enjoin a foreclosure sale]; United Land Association *v.* Knight, 85 Cal. 448 (1890) [suit over title to real property]; Archbishop of S.F. *v.* Shipman, 69 Cal. 586 (1886) [action to enjoin a foreclosure sale].)

Even at the time the above cases were decided, quia timet relief was used sparingly. Today, it has for the most part been forsaken in favor of statutory remedies. For example, a party who wants to enjoin a foreclosure sale, prevent a nuisance, or otherwise assert a right to real property (the traditional uses for quia timet), would seek injunctive relief and make effective use of the lis pendens statutes. An aggrieved creditor might avail himself of the attachment law, provided he is fortunate enough to have a debtor with assets to attach. An individual with a claim to personal property has at his disposal the claim and delivery statutes.

Had these statutory remedies completely replaced quia timet, however, it would have been news to the fidelity and surety bond industry, and to those judges of the Los Angeles Superior court who have granted relief in cases similar to this one. "No principle in equity is more familiar, or more firmly established, than that a surety, *after the debt for which he is liable has become due*, without paying or being called on to pay it, may file a bill in equity in the nature of a bill quia timet to compel the principal to exonerate him from liability by its payment, provided no rights of the creditor are prejudiced thereby. . . . The doctrine is not premised on mere fear of loss or liability prior to an obligation's maturity. Rather, only after the obligation becomes payable, the surety, before he pays it, may maintain a suit in equity against the debtor in the nature of a bill quia timet to compel the latter to pay the debt or perform the obligation, provided the creditor could enforce payment or performance but neglects or refuses to do it." (Fireman's Fund Insurance Co. *v.* S.E.K. Construction Co., 436 F.2d 1345, 1349 (10th Cir. 1971), italics in original.)

Quia timet is in fact especially suited to surety cases. "A surety or guarantor is one who promises to answer for the debt, default, or miscarriage of another . . . ." Cal. Civ. Code, § 2787. A surety is obligated by law to pay the creditor of its defaulting principal immediately upon the principal's default or defalcation. Although a surety may file an action at law to compel its principal to perform the obligation on a bond when due, the fact that it may eventually obtain a judgment against the principal is of little comfort to the surety if, in the interim, the principal has absconded with the very funds which could have been used to satisfy the bond. Quia timet allows the surety to prevent the principal from dissipating those funds if the surety knows it will be called upon to "pay the debt or perform the obligation" on the bond, suspects that the principal has some or all of the necessary funds to do so, and fears that the principal may abscond with those funds.

Abelman, without citing any specific authority to support her argument, persuaded the respondent court that quia timet was "a concept that pre-dates movable type, and has virtually no application in modern society." Petitioners have persuaded us otherwise. . . .

NOTE ON QUIA TIMET RELIEF

In a bill *quia timet*, the claimant invokes equity jurisdiction because of fear that the defendant's wrongdoing or neglect will cause injury to the claimant's property rights or other interests. In a loose sense, any preventative injunction issued before an injury has occurred can be considered *quia timet* relief. Preventative injunctions are discussed in Chapter Seven, Section A (Preventative and Reparative Injunctions). See also Fletcher *v.* Bealey, 28 Ch.D. 688 (1885), in which the English Chancery Court considered an injunction against an anticipated nuisance to be *quia timet* relief. The remedies discussed below can also be viewed as forms of *quia timet* relief. To use an analogy from information systems, think of *quia timet* not as the name of a particular remedy, but rather as a "tag" that can be applied to a variety of remedies.

2. BILLS OF PEACE

Yuba Consolidated Gold Fields v. Kilkeary

United States Court of Appeals, Ninth Circuit, 1953.
206 F.2d 884.

■ BYRNE, DISTRICT JUDGE. The appellant, as plaintiff below, filed a complaint in the nature of a "bill of peace" seeking to avoid a multiplicity of legal actions by determining in one equity suit the liability asserted in hundreds of claims for damages resulting from floods of the Yuba River in the winter of 1950. The complaint was dismissed for failure to state a claim upon which relief can be granted and this appeal followed.

The material allegations of the complaint may be summarized as follows: Plaintiff is a citizen of the State of Maine; defendants are all citizens of the State of California; the amount in controversy exceeds $3,000; since March 18, 1905, the plaintiff has been engaged in mining gold by the dredging process in Yuba County; during the month of November, 1950, a series of storms brought heavy precipitation to the section of the Sierra Nevada from the Feather River on the north to the Kern River on the south; the rainfall caused the Yuba River to carry a greater volume of water than had ever before passed down the stream during its recorded history; the flood waters overflowed the south natural banks of the river and broke the south training wall—a cobble embankment that the plaintiff had constructed about the year 1925 as a part of approved projects of flood and debris control; the river's overflow spread over an area of approximately 100 square miles in Yuba County which included large acreages of farm lands, about 2669 separate ownerships of real property, and more than seven residential and business communities; the flood caused an unascertainable amount of heavy damage; claimed items include damage to agricultural lands, orchards, crops, highways, farm produce, machinery, walls and foundations of buildings, furnishings and personal effects in dwellings, automobiles, business, residential and industrial property and lost profits due to interruption of business; a state of emergency was declared in Yuba County, lasting from November 20, 1950, to December 11, 1950, during which about 8,000 persons were forced from their homes for varying lengths of time and received flood and disaster relief from the American Red Cross and others in Marysville; during and after the flood the charge was publicly made that the plaintiff's dredging in the Yuba River had caused the flood and that the plaintiff was responsible for the damage; during November and December, 1950, meetings were held at which various defendants discussed ways and means of prosecuting their claims against the plaintiff, and agreements were circulated providing for payment by claimants of 1% of their respective claims into a fund to be expended for the prosecution of actions against the plaintiff; six actions involving more than one hundred claimants and $853,964.98[1] in claims have been filed against the plaintiff in the Superior Court of Yuba County, California, in which the claimants assert that the plaintiff's operations in the Yuba River were responsible for the flood and the resulting damages, which assertions are unfounded; plaintiff's operations had no causal connection with the flood, were at all times conducted with due care in accordance with good engineering practice and in conformity with the requirements of Federal permits duly issued by statutory authority, and were part of projects approved by statute for debris and flood control that have been in progress on the Yuba River for more than 50 years; the potential claims of the unnamed defendants may run into sums aggregating millions of dollars and if the claims should be asserted and established in amounts comparable with the damage prayers of the suits on file, the resulting liability would exceed the value of the plaintiff's assets and would be beyond its ability to pay.

It is further alleged that the plaintiff has no adequate remedy at law; unless relief in equity is granted plaintiff will be subjected to a multiplicity of actions by the defendants; such actions will involve identical questions of law and fact with respect to the alleged liability of plaintiff; such actions involve damage claims beyond plaintiff's ability to pay and the defendants, therefore, have a common interest in pending and proposed litigation to enforce such claim; and the trial of such actions, potentially numbering hundreds or thousands, cannot be practically or fairly conducted at law.

The prayer of the complaint asks that the court permanently enjoin the defendants from the prosecution, "except in this court and cause," of any suit against the plaintiff for the recovery of any damage alleged to have been caused by the flood; that the court hear and determine all claims of the defendants against the plaintiff and decree such claims to be without right; that declaratory relief be granted "with respect to plaintiff's rights under the statutes pursuant to which said federal permits were issued to plaintiff." . . .

The suits in equity of which federal courts may exercise jurisdiction constitute that body of remedies, procedures, and practices which had been evolved in the English Court of Chancery prior to the adoption of the First Judiciary Act, except as modified by Congress. The granting of relief against multiplicity of legal actions in appropriate situations is part of that historic jurisdiction.

The general doctrine that equity will take cognizance of a matter to prevent a multiplicity of suits is asserted in innumerable decisions, but

---

[1] At the time of the oral argument before this court, the appellant filed a memorandum with respect to the then pending actions at law which disclosed 22 actions pending by 1022 plaintiffs with a total prayer of $2,834,595.08. Subsequently counsel informed the court, by letter, that about 100 of the pending claims have been concluded by compromise and approximately 25 new claims asserted and that there are still pending against appellant actions involving more than 900 claimants for alleged damages exceeding $2,000,000.

when one seeks an answer to the question of the extent of the doctrine he finds uncertainty and a direct conflict of decisions.

Much of the confusion and uncertainty surrounding the doctrine flows from the failure to recognize that its extent and limitations are not identical in every class of cases which furnishes an occasion for its exercise. The class of cases with which we are here concerned is that class wherein a number of persons have separate and individual claims and rights of action against the same party arising from a common cause of transaction and the law defendant seeks to have all of the claims settled in a single suit in equity.

Equity jurisdiction in this class of cases will not be recognized unless there is a common bond or interest held by the number of persons against the single person. The character and essential elements of this common bond or interest constitute the fundamental question upon which the recognition of the equity jurisdiction rests, and it is in the solution of this question that most of the conflict of opinion among the courts has arisen.

Is it necessary that the common bond or interest be a community of interest in the subject matter of the controversy to such an extent as to create *a privity between the individual members of the group,* as well as between each of them and the single adversary party? Or is it sufficient that the common bond or interests consists solely in the fact that the claims of the members of the group have arisen from the same source and all involve and depend upon similar questions of law and fact, so that while the same positive relation exists between the single party on the one side and *each* individual member of the group on the other, *no such legal relation exists between the individual members themselves?* . . .

The majority view is succinctly stated by Pomeroy:[5]

> "... [N]otwithstanding the positive denials by some American courts, the weight of authority is simply overwhelming that the jurisdiction may and should be exercised, either on behalf of a numerous body of separate claimants against a single party, or on behalf of a single party against such a numerous body, although there is no 'common title,' no 'community of right' or of 'interest in the subject-matter,' among these individuals, but where there is and because there is merely a community of interest among them in the questions of law and fact involved in the general controversy, or in the kind and form of relief demanded and obtained by or against each individual member of the numerous body."

The appellees rely upon Hale *v.* Allinson, 188 U.S. 56 (1903). The case does not support their position. It is true that that court denied a bill of peace, but the denial was on the ground that each of the defenses of the multiple parties depended upon different facts. There is no dispute

---

[5] Pomeroy, EQUITY JURISPRUDENCE, 5th ed. 1941, Vol. I sect. 269.

that common questions of law and fact must exist before a court of equity will interfere. The question is whether in addition to common questions of law and fact there must exist a *common title or community right or interest in the subject matter among the defendants.* The Hale *v.* Allinson court said such a community interest was not necessary .... In Bitterman *v.* Louisville & Nashville R.R., 207 U.S. 205 (1907), the Supreme Court sustained a bill of peace and cited Hale *v.* Allinson for the principle that equity jurisdiction would be recognized where "the relief sought against each defendant was the same, and the defenses which might be interposed were common to each defendant and involved like legal questions." . . .

Equity jurisdiction being recognized, the question whether it will be exercised rests in the sound discretion of the chancellor. It must be a legal discretion based on principles of law and not on the arbitrary will of the chancellor. The discretion of the chancellor is directed primarily to the question of whether there is a plain, adequate and complete remedy at law. . . .

Some of the factors to be considered by the chancellor are referred to in Hale *v.* Allinson, where the Supreme Court said each case "must, as we think, be decided upon its own merits and upon a survey of the real and substantial convenience of all parties, the adequacy of the legal remedy, the situations of the different parties, the points to be contested and the result which would follow if jurisdiction should be assumed or denied; these various matters being factors to be taken into consideration upon the question of equitable jurisdiction on this ground, and whether within reasonable and fair grounds the suit is calculated to be in truth one which will practically prevent a multiplicity of litigation, and will be an actual convenience to all parties, and will not unreasonably overlook or obstruct the material interests of any. The single fact that a multiplicity of suits may be prevented by this assumption of jurisdiction is not in all cases enough to sustain it. It might be that the exercise of equitable jurisdiction on this ground, while preventing a formal multiplicity of suits, would nevertheless be attended with more and deeper inconvenience to the defendants than would be compensated for by the convenience of a single plaintiff; and where the case is not covered by any controlling precedent the inconvenience might constitute good ground for denying jurisdiction."

Although the jury trial policy should be considered where the issues are basically legal in their nature, it must be borne in mind "that to sustain a suit in equity in the federal courts it must appear there is no plain, adequate, and complete remedy at law, and, if the remedy at law is not adequate, the right to a jury trial does not exist." The possibility of consolidating the actions at law has a direct bearing on the question of the adequacy of the legal remedy, and the question of removal of all of the actions at law to the federal court, in turn, affects the matter of consolidation. . . .

There is considerable discussion in the briefs of the parties and in the memorandum opinion of the trial court with respect to whether the damages resulted from the negligence of Yuba or were incidental or consequential damages flowing from work performed for the government in accordance with its requirements, by a government contractor. This is a question of fact to be determined by the court in a trial on the merits regardless of whether the trial is at law or in equity. We do not reach that question in the present posture of the case. . . .

The complaint, accepting the facts properly pleaded as established, does state a claim authorizing the exercise of the trial court's discretion. Whether equity jurisdiction should be assumed to prevent a multiplicity of suits, is a question for the trial court. The determination must rest on sound principles of law and the court may require such proof as shall be deemed necessary for the proper exercise of its discretion. We therefore must reverse and remand the case for further proceedings in the trial court not inconsistent with the views expressed here.

NOTES ON BILLS OF PEACE

1. Consider the bearing of the following Federal Rules of Civil Procedure on the need for a bill of peace in a case like *Yuba Consolidated Gold Fields*:

"Rule 19. Required Joinder of Parties

"(a) Persons Required to Be Joined if Feasible.

"(1) *Required Party.* A person who is subject to service of process and whose joinder will not deprive the court of subject-matter jurisdiction must be joined as a party in the action if:

"(A) in that person's absence, the court cannot accord complete relief among existing parties; or

"(B) that person claims an interest relating to the subject of the action and is so situated that the disposing of the action in the person's absence may:

"(i) as a practical matter impair or impede the person's ability to protect the interest; or

"(ii) leave an existing party subject to a substantial risk of incurring double, multiple, or otherwise inconsistent obligations because of the interest.

"(2) *Joinder by Court Order.* If a person has not been joined, as required, the court must order that the person be made a party. A person who refuses to join as a plaintiff may be made either a defendant, or, in a proper case, an involuntary plaintiff.

"(3) *Venue.* If a joined party objects to venue and the joinder would make venue improper, the court must dismiss that party.

"**(b) When Joinder Is Not Feasible.** If a person who is required to be joined if feasible cannot be joined, the court must determine whether, in equity and good conscience, the action should proceed among the existing parties or should be dismissed. The factors for the court to consider include:

"(1) the extent to which a judgment rendered in the person's absence might prejudice that person or the existing parties;

"(2) the extent to which any prejudice could be lessened or avoided by:

"(A) protective provisions in the judgment;

"(B) shaping the relief; or

"(C) other measures;

"(3) whether a judgment rendered in the person's absence would be adequate; and

"(4) whether the plaintiff would have an adequate remedy if the action were dismissed for nonjoinder. . . ."

"Rule 23. Class Actions

"**(a) Prerequisites.** One or more members of a class may sue or be sued as representative parties on behalf of all members only if:

"(1) the class is so numerous that joinder of all members is impracticable;

"(2) there are questions of law or fact common to the class;

"(3) the claims or defenses of the representative parties are typical of the claims or defenses of the class; and

"(4) the representative parties will fairly and adequately protect the interests of the class. . . ."

"Rule 42. Consolidation; Separate Trials

"**(a) Consolidation.** If actions before the court involve a common question of law or fact, the court may:

"(1) join for hearing or trial any or all matters at issue in the actions;

"(2) consolidate the actions; or

"(3) issue any other orders to avoid unnecessary cost or delay. . . ."

2. Bills of peace are sometimes used to prevent the vexatious recurrence of litigation. Cf. Wrenn *v.* Benson, 490 U.S. 89 (1989) (*per curiam*) (directing Supreme Court Clerk "not to accept any further filings from petitioner in which he seeks leave to proceed in forma pauperis . . . unless the affidavit submitted with the filing indicates that petitioner's financial condition has substantially changed"); Mitchell *v.* Wells Fargo Bank, N.A., 295 Ga. 620, 620 (2014).

3. INTERPLEADER

State Farm Fire & Casualty Co. v. Tashire

Supreme Court of the United States, 1967.
386 U.S. 523.

■ MR. JUSTICE FORTAS delivered the opinion of the Court.

Early one September morning in 1964, a Greyhound bus proceeding northward through Shasta County, California, collided with a southbound pickup truck. Two of the passengers aboard the bus were killed. Thirty-three others were injured, as were the bus driver, the driver of the truck and its lone passenger. One of the dead and 10 of the injured passengers were Canadians; the rest of the individuals involved were citizens of five American States. The ensuing litigation led to the present case, which raises important questions concerning administration of the interpleader remedy in the federal courts.

The litigation began when four of the injured passengers filed suit in California state courts, seeking damages in excess of $1,000,000. Named as defendants were Greyhound Lines, Inc., a California corporation; Theron Nauta, the bus driver; Ellis Clark, who drove the truck; and Kenneth Glasgow, the passenger in the truck who was apparently its owner as well. Each of the individual defendants was a citizen and resident of Oregon. Before these cases could come to trial and before other suits were filed in California or elsewhere, petitioner State Farm Fire & Casualty Company, an Illinois corporation, brought this action in the nature of interpleader in the United States District Court for the District of Oregon.

In its complaint State Farm asserted that at the time of the Shasta County collision it had in force an insurance policy with respect to Ellis Clark, driver of the truck, providing for bodily injury liability up to $10,000 per person and $20,000 per occurrence and for legal representation of Clark in actions covered by the policy. It asserted that actions already filed in California and others which it anticipated would be filed far exceeded in aggregate damages sought the amount of its maximum liability under the policy. Accordingly, it paid into court the sum of $20,000 and asked the court (1) to require all claimants to establish their claims against Clark and his insurer in this single proceeding and in no other, and (2) to discharge State Farm from all further obligations under its policy—including its duty to defend Clark in lawsuits arising from the accident. Alternatively, State Farm expressed its conviction that the policy issued to Clark excluded from coverage accidents resulting from his operation of a truck which belonged to another and was being used in the business of another. The complaint, therefore, requested that the court decree that the insurer owed no duty to Clark and was not liable on the policy, and it asked the court to refund the $20,000 deposit.

Joined as defendants were Clark, Glasgow, Nauta, Greyhound Lines, and each of the prospective claimants. Jurisdiction was predicated upon 28 U.S.C. § 1335, the federal interpleader statute,[1] and upon general diversity of citizenship, there being diversity between two or more of the claimants to the fund and between State Farm and all of the named defendants.

An order issued, requiring the defendants to show cause why they should not be restrained from filing or prosecuting "any proceeding in any state or United States Court affecting the property or obligation involved in this interpleader action, and specifically against the plaintiff and the defendant Ellis D. Clark." Personal service was effected on each of the American defendants, and registered mail was employed to reach the 11 Canadian claimants. Defendants Nauta, Greyhound, and several of the injured passengers responded, contending that the policy did cover this accident and advancing various arguments for the position that interpleader was either impermissible or inappropriate in the present circumstances. Greyhound, however, soon switched sides and moved that the court broaden any injunction to include Nauta and Greyhound among those who could not be sued except within the confines of the interpleader proceeding.

When a temporary injunction along the lines sought by State Farm was issued by the United States District Court for the District of Oregon, the present respondents moved to dismiss the action and, in the alternative, for a change of venue—to the Northern District of California, in which district the collision had occurred. After a hearing, the court declined to dissolve the temporary injunction, but continued the motion for a change of venue. The injunction was later broadened to include the protection sought by Greyhound, but modified to permit the filing—although not the prosecution—of suits. The injunction, therefore,

---

1 28 U.S.C. § 1335 provides:

[(a) "The district courts shall have original jurisdiction of any civil action of interpleader or in the nature of interpleader filed by any person, firm, or corporation, association, or society having in his or its custody or possession money or property of the value of $500 or more, or having issued a note, bond, certificate, policy of insurance, or other instrument of value or amount of $500 or more, or providing for the delivery or payment or the loan of money or property of such amount or value, or being under any obligation written or unwritten to the amount of $500 or more, if

"(1) Two or more adverse claimants, of diverse citizenship as defined in section 1332 of this title, are claiming or may claim to be entitled to such money or property, or to any one or more of the benefits arising by virtue of any note, bond, certificate, policy or other instrument, or arising by virtue of any such obligation; and if (2) the plaintiff has deposited such money or property or has paid the amount of or the loan or other value of such instrument or the amount due under such obligation into the registry of the court, there to abide the judgment of the court or has given bond payable to the clerk of the court in such amount and with such surety as the court or judge may deem proper, conditioned upon the compliance by the plaintiff with the future order or judgment of the court with respect to the subject matter of the controversy.

"(b) Such an action may be entertained although the titles or claims of the conflicting claimants do not have a common origin, or are not identical, but are adverse to and independent of one another."]

provided that all suits against Clark, State Farm, Greyhound, and Nauta be prosecuted in the interpleader proceeding.

On interlocutory appeal, the Court of Appeals for the Ninth Circuit reversed. The court found it unnecessary to reach respondents' contentions relating to service of process and the scope of the injunction, for it concluded that interpleader was not available in the circumstances of this case. It held that in States like Oregon which do not permit "direct action" suits against insurance companies until judgments are obtained against the insured, the insurance companies may not invoke federal interpleader until the claims against the insured, the alleged tortfeasor, have been reduced to judgment. Until that is done, said the court, claimants with unliquidated tort claims are not "claimants" within the meaning of § 1335, nor are they "[p]ersons having claims against the plaintiff" within the meaning of Rule 22 of the Federal Rules of Civil Procedure.[3] In accord with that view, it directed dissolution of the temporary injunction and dismissal of the action. . . . Although we reverse the decision of the Court of Appeals upon the jurisdictional question, we direct a substantial modification of the District Court's injunction for reasons which will appear.

Before considering the issues presented by the petition for certiorari, we find it necessary to dispose of a question neither raised by the parties nor passed upon by the courts below. Since the matter concerns our jurisdiction, we raise it on our own motion. The interpleader statute, 28 U.S.C. § 1335, applies where there are "Two or more adverse claimants, of diverse citizenship. . . ." This provision has been uniformly construed to require only "minimal diversity," that is, diversity of citizenship between two or more claimants, without regard to the circumstance that other rival claimants may be co-citizens. The language of the statute, the legislative purpose broadly to remedy the problems posed by multiple claimants to a single fund, and the consistent judicial interpretation tacitly accepted by Congress, persuade us that the statute requires no more. . . . And in a variety of contexts this Court and the lower courts have concluded that Article III poses no obstacle to the legislative extension of federal jurisdiction, founded on diversity, so long as any two adverse parties are not co-citizens. Accordingly, we conclude that the present case is properly in the federal courts.

We do not agree with the Court of Appeals that, in the absence of a state law or contractual provision for "direct action" suits against the insurance company, the company must wait until persons asserting claims against its insured have reduced those claims to judgment before seeking to invoke the benefits of federal interpleader. That may have

[3] We need not pass upon the Court of Appeals' conclusions with respect to the interpretation of interpleader under Rule 22, which provides that "(1) Persons having claims against the plaintiff may be joined as defendants and required to interplead when their claims are such that the plaintiff is or may be exposed to double or multiple liability. . . ." The provisions of this rule supplement and do not in any way limit the joinder of parties permitted in Rule 20. . . .

been a tenable position under the 1926 and 1936 interpleader statutes. These statutes did not carry forward the language in the 1917 Act authorizing interpleader where adverse claimants "may claim" benefits as well as where they "are claiming" them. In 1948, however, in the revision of the Judicial Code, the "may claim" language was restored. Until the decision below, every court confronted by the question has concluded that the 1948 revision removed whatever requirement there might previously have been that the insurance company wait until at least two claimants reduced their claims to judgments. The commentators are in accord.

Considerations of judicial administration demonstrate the soundness of this view which, in any event, seems compelled by the language of the present statute, which is remedial and to be liberally construed. Were an insurance company required to await reduction of claims to judgment, the first claimant to obtain such a judgment or to negotiate a settlement might appropriate all or a disproportionate slice of the fund before his fellow claimants were able to establish their claims. The difficulties such a race to judgment pose for the insurer, and the unfairness which may result to some claimants, were among the principal evils the interpleader device was intended to remedy.

The fact that State Farm had properly invoked the interpleader jurisdiction under § 1335 did not, however, entitle it to an order both enjoining prosecution of suits against it outside the confines of the interpleader proceeding and also extending such protection to its insured, the alleged tortfeasor. Still less was Greyhound Lines entitled to have that order expanded so as to protect itself and its driver, also alleged to be tortfeasors, from suits brought by its passengers in various state or federal courts. Here, the scope of the litigation, in terms of parties and claims, was vastly more extensive than the confines of the "fund," the deposited proceeds of the insurance policy. In these circumstances, the mere existence of such a fund cannot, by use of interpleader, be employed to accomplish purposes that exceed the needs of orderly contest with respect to the fund.

There are situations, of a type not present here, where the effect of interpleader is to confine the total litigation to a single forum and proceeding. One such case is where a stakeholder, faced with rival claims to the fund itself, acknowledges—or denies—his liability to one or the other of the claimants. In this situation, the fund itself is the target of the claimants. It marks the outer limits of the controversy. It is, therefore, reasonable and sensible that interpleader, in discharge of its office to protect the fund, should also protect the stakeholder from vexatious and multiple litigation. In this context, the suits sought to be enjoined are squarely within the language of 28 U.S.C. § 2361, which provides in part:

> "In any civil action of interpleader or in the nature of interpleader under section 1335 of this title, a district court may

> issue its process for all claimants and enter its order restraining them from instituting or prosecuting *any proceeding* in any State or United States court *affecting the property, instrument or obligation involved in the interpleader action . . . .*"

But the present case is another matter. Here, an accident has happened. Thirty-five passengers or their representatives have claims which they wish to press against a variety of defendants: the bus company, its driver, the owner of the truck, and the truck driver. The circumstance that one of the prospective defendants happens to have an insurance policy is a fortuitous event which should not of itself shape the nature of the ensuing litigation. For example, a resident of California, injured in California aboard a bus owned by a California corporation should not be forced to sue that corporation anywhere but in California simply because another prospective defendant carried an insurance policy. And an insurance company whose maximum interest in the case cannot exceed $20,000 and who in fact asserts that it has no interest at all, should not be allowed to determine that dozens of tort plaintiffs must be compelled to press their claims—even those claims which are not against the insured and which in no event could be satisfied out of the meager insurance fund—in a single forum of the insurance company's choosing. There is nothing in the statutory scheme, and very little in the judicial and academic commentary upon that scheme, which requires that the tail be allowed to wag the dog in this fashion.

State Farm's interest in this case, which is the fulcrum of the interpleader procedure, is confined to its $20,000 fund. That interest receives full vindication when the court restrains claimants from seeking to enforce against the insurance company any judgment obtained against its insured, except in the interpleader proceeding itself. To the extent that the District Court sought to control claimants' lawsuits against the insured and other alleged tortfeasors, it exceeded the powers granted to it by the statutory scheme.

We recognize, of course, that our view of interpleader means that it cannot be used to solve all the vexing problems of multiparty litigation arising out of a mass tort. But interpleader was never intended to perform such a function, to be an all-purpose "bill of peace." Had it been so intended, careful provision would necessarily have been made to insure that a party with little or no interest in the outcome of a complex controversy should not strip truly interested parties of substantial rights—such as the right to choose the forum in which to establish their claims, subject to generally applicable rules of jurisdiction, venue, service of process, removal, and change of venue. None of the legislative and academic sponsors of a modern federal interpleader device viewed their accomplishment as a "bill of peace," capable of sweeping dozens of lawsuits out of the various state and federal courts in which they were brought and into a single interpleader proceeding. And only in two reported instances has a federal interpleader court sought to control the underlying litigation against alleged tortfeasors as opposed to the allocation of a fund among successful tort plaintiffs. Another district court, on the other hand, has recently held that it lacked statutory authority to enjoin suits against the alleged tortfeasor as opposed to proceedings against the fund itself.

In light of the evidence that federal interpleader was not intended to serve the function of a "bill of peace" in the context of multiparty litigation arising out of a mass tort, of the anomalous power which such a construction of the statute would give the stakeholder, and of the thrust of the statute and the purpose it was intended to serve, we hold that the interpleader statute did not authorize the injunction entered in the present case. Upon remand, the injunction is to be modified consistently with this opinion. . . .

■ MR. JUSTICE DOUGLAS, dissenting.

While I agree with the Court's view as to "minimal diversity" and that the injunction, if granted, should run only against prosecution of suits against the insurer, I feel that the use which we today allow to be made of the federal interpleader statute is, with all deference, unwarranted. How these litigants are "claimants" to this fund in the statutory sense is indeed a mystery. . . .

This insurance company's policy provides that it will "pay on behalf of the insured all sums which the insured shall become legally obligated to pay." To date the insured has not become "legally obligated" to pay any sum to any litigant. Since nothing is owed under the policy, I fail to see how any litigant can be a "claimant" as against the insurance company. . . .

This construction of the word "claimant" against the fund is borne out, as the Court of Appeals noted, by Rule 22(1) of the Federal Rules of Civil Procedure. That Rule, also based on diversity of citizenship, differs only in the district where the suit may be brought and in the reach of service of process, as the Court points out. But it illuminates the nature of federal interpleader for it provides that only "[p]ersons having claims against the plaintiff [insurer] may be joined as defendants and required to interplead."

Can it be that we have two kinds of interpleader statutes as between which an insurance company can choose: one that permits "claimants" against the insurer ("persons having claims against the plaintiff") to be joined and the other that permits "claimants" against the insured to be joined for the benefit of the insurer even though they may never be "claimants" against the insurer? I cannot believe that Congress launched such an irrational scheme. . . .

NOTES ON INTERPLEADER

1. Interpleader, which originated in the equity courts, allows a person who is ready to perform a duty to determine whom the duty is owed to. The

applicant, who has money or goods claimed by two or more persons, requests that the claimants litigate the title between themselves.[i]

The applicant in an interpleader proceeding seeks relief in the nature of *quia timet*: the applicant fears being subjected to double litigation and, possibly, having to pay twice for the one liability. Relief takes the form of *in personam* orders against the defendants, as described in State Farm Fire & Casualty Co. *v.* Tashire.

Interpleader is available if the applicant can establish that adverse claims that have a reasonable foundation are being asserted against the applicant. If there are two adverse claims, and one is obviously valid and the other obviously void, interpleader is unnecessary. The question is to be determined as of the moment the proceedings are commenced. If, as of that moment, there are two or more adverse claims, and the applicant's liability is limited to only one of them, interpleader should be available.

Liberal provisions for the joinder of parties, found in all modern codes, have greatly diminished the need for the equitable remedy of interpleader. Today, in the states, the right to interpleader is regulated by modern codes and rules of court.

2. On the subject of interpleader, a leading treatise says:

> "The contemporary importance of interpleader is in large measure due to the efforts of Professor Zechariah Chafee, Jr., who, in a notable group of articles, paved the way for the series of reforms by which federal interpleader was modernized and made available in situations where no state court could provide an adequate remedy. There are two kinds of interpleader available in federal court. A statute, 28 U.S.C. § 1335, authorizes interpleader and makes very liberal provisions as to jurisdiction, venue, and service of process. Nonstatutory interpleader is available under Rule 22, but the jurisdictional and procedural requirements there are the same as in an ordinary civil action."
>
> "Before enactment of the federal interpleader statute, there was no effective procedure by which rival claimants of diverse citizenship and residence could be sued in any district in federal court, and territorial limitations on service of process barred state courts from giving relief. This situation is cured by the statute, and the rule supplements the statute."

Charles Alan Wright et al., FEDERAL PRACTICE AND PROCEDURE: FEDERAL PRACTICE DESKBOOK § 79 (Apr. 2017 update).

---

[i] *Interpleader* is not to be confused with *impleader*. Impleader or "third party practice," refers to the procedure whereby a person sought to be held liable on a claim, usually a defendant, in turn and in the same action, makes a claim against a third person for all or part of plaintiff's claim against him. See Fed. R. Civ. Pro. 14. It implies a primary claim against one person, and a subsidiary claim against a third party. *Interpleader* implies adverse claims against the same party.

4. CANCELLATION

Wiard v. Brown

Supreme Court of California, 1881.
59 Cal. 194.

■ MCKEE, J. This is an appeal from a judgment, directing a paper, which constituted the subject-matter in controversy between the parties, to be delivered up and canceled, and from the order denying a motion for a new trial. . . .

[T]he object of the action was to obtain a decree for the cancellation of the following paper, which was signed by the plaintiff, viz.:

> "OAKLAND, July 18th, 1877.
>
> "In consideration of one dollar to me in hand paid, the receipt of which is hereby acknowledged, I hereby contract and agree to sell H. S. Brown, his heirs or assigns, about fifty-six acres of my land, including race-track and improvements, for one hundred and twenty-five thousand dollars, U. S. gold coin, twenty-five thousand dollars to be paid on or before October 1st, and the balance to be secured by mortgage on said land."

The complaint alleges, and it is not denied by the answer, that the paper was executed without consideration, and was never delivered to the defendant Brown; and the Court below found, in substance, that it was only a proposal or offer in writing, made by the plaintiff, and given to the defendant Kennedy, who, as the plaintiff believed, was acting as his agent to communicate it to Brown. Kennedy, having received it for that purpose, sent it to Brown, who read it and approved of the form of it, but immediately sent it back to Kennedy without assenting to its terms, or accepting or agreeing to accept it, and Brown never did, by word or act communicated directly or indirectly by him to the plaintiff, accept the same or agree to accept it.

After the paper had been returned to Kennedy, he denied that he was acting as the agent of the plaintiff, and kept possession of the paper, had it acknowledged by an attesting witness, and recorded, and gave out that it was a subsisting contract between the plaintiff and Brown, in which he and one Putnam were interested with Brown. But neither Brown, nor Kennedy, nor Putnam ever, by word or act, communicated to the plaintiff, accepted, or agreed to accept the proposal. There was, therefore, no mutuality between them, or any of them, and the plaintiff.

Under these circumstances, when the plaintiff discovered that Kennedy had had the paper recorded, he immediately withdrew it as a proposal, and commenced the action for its cancellation. Kennedy, by a verified answer, alone answered the complaint in the action, for himself and Brown. But, before answering, he caused the paper to be transferred by Brown to one Gaskill, who, before the 1st of October, 1877, went through the form of offering to pay the plaintiff the money mentioned in the proposal, and to comply with its terms, and afterwards, being admitted as a party defendant to the action, filed a cross-complaint for a specific performance of the paper as a contract. But the Court, finding that Gaskill took nothing by the assignment from Brown, and that his offer to pay was not made in good faith, and was one which he had not the ability to perform, refused specific performance, and decreed that the paper be delivered up and canceled as a cloud upon the title of the plaintiff.

In this there was no error. . . .

Wherever an instrument of writing exists, which has been obtained without consideration, or has become a nullity, or which, if left outstanding, may cause injury to a plaintiff, or may be vexatiously used against him, after the evidence to impeach or invalidate it is lost or may throw a cloud or suspicion over his title, a court of equity will afford relief by ordering it to be delivered up and cancelled. . . .

NOTE ON CANCELLATION

One may "fear" that a negotiable instrument may be negotiated to a holder in due course (cutting off personal defenses that might otherwise be asserted by the maker). An injunction against the negotiation of a negotiable note does not solve the problem because the injunction acts *in personam*, and thus does not destroy the negotiability of the note. Nor does the doctrine of *lis pendens* apply to the negotiable instrument. Hence, the most effective remedy is a *quia timet* action to cancel the note.

The California Civil Code provides as follows:

> "§ 3412. WHEN CANCELLATION MAY BE ORDERED. A written instrument, in respect to which there is a reasonable apprehension that if left outstanding it may cause serious injury to a person against whom it is void or voidable, may, upon his application, be so adjudged, and ordered to be delivered up or canceled.
>
> "§ 3413. INSTRUMENT OBVIOUSLY VOID. An instrument, the invalidity of which is apparent upon its face, or upon the face of another instrument which is necessary to the use of the former in evidence, is not to be deemed capable of causing injury, within the provisions of the last section."

5. BILLS TO QUIET OR REMOVE A CLOUD ON TITLE

Wathen v. Brown

Court of Special Appeals of Maryland, 1981.
48 Md. App. 655.

■ LOWE, JUDGE. Appellee is the record title holder to a parcel of land and right of way in St. Mary's County. Alleging that appellant claimed ownership by adverse possession, appellee filed a Bill of Complaint to

Quiet Title in the Circuit Court for St. Mary's County. Appellant answered, admitting her claim of ownership by adverse possession . . . . [The trial court entered a decree in favor of the appellee.]

Section 14–108 is one of the "Miscellaneous Rules" set forth in Title 14 of the recent recodification of the Real Property Laws. It was originally enacted in 1955 as a statutory section for the equitable remedy of quieting title to real estate, by authorizing courts of equity to do substantially what they had been doing prior to its enactment.

"§ 14–108. Quieting title.

> "(a) *Conditions.* Any person in actual peaceable possession of property, or, if the property is vacant and unoccupied, in constructive and peaceable possession of it, either under color of title or claim by right by reason of his or his predecessor's adverse possession for the statutory period, when his title to the property is denied or disputed, or when any other person claims, of record or otherwise to own the property, or any part of it, or to hold any lien encumbrance on it, regardless of whether or not the hostile outstanding claim is being actively asserted, and if an action at law or proceeding in equity is not pending to enforce or test the validity of the title, lien, encumbrance, or other adverse claim, the person may maintain a suit in equity in the county where the property lies to quiet or remove any cloud from the title, or determine any adverse claim.
>
> "(b) *Proceeding.* The proceeding shall be deemed in rem or quasi in rem so long as the only relief sought is a decree that the plaintiff has absolute ownership and the right of disposition of the property, and an injunction against the assertion by the person named as the party defendant, of his claim by any action at law or otherwise. Any person who appears of record, or claims to have a hostile outstanding right, shall be made a defendant in the proceedings."

Appellant argues that this statute established a burden of proving actual or constructive possession and that mere evidence of record title (which she concedes in appellee) is insufficient to constitute constructive possession.

The object of a bill to quiet title is to protect the owner of legal title "from being disturbed in his possession and from being harassed by suits in regard to his title by persons setting up unjust and illegal pretensions . . . ." Textor *v.* Shipley, 77 Md. 473 (1893). The statutory requirement of "possession" is that which originally provided equity with jurisdiction; otherwise the complainant would have had to resort to law, having an adequate legal remedy there.

> "In such cases, one being in possession, he cannot have a remedy at law and is obliged therefore to seek the aid of a Court of Equity. If, however, the possession is in another person, his

> remedy is by action of ejectment, and there is no ground for the interposition of a Court of Equity, and for the reason that he has an adequate remedy at law." *Id.*

The alternative to "actual" possession (*i.e.*, title plus vacancy) was early recognized in the case of Baumgardner *v.* Fowler, 82 Md. 631, 640 (1896), which noted that:

> ". . . Courts have held that where a plaintiff has the legal title to lands that are wild, uncultivated and unoccupied, he may invoke the aid of a Court of Equity to remove a cloud upon his title, although he has no other than constructive possession resulting from legal ownership."

In *Baumgardner* this conclusion was coupled with, and apparently predicated upon, the fact that there was no proof that the adverse claimants under a tax sale had taken possession of the lands in dispute under the tax sale deed. Consequently, the plaintiffs could *not* have sued in ejectment to recover the property and thus decide ownership.

Although these cases arose prior to the statute, the statute was seemingly based upon them, and when enacted, it did not dispense with the necessity of showing possession, actual or constructive. Presumably then, if actual possession is not alleged in the Bill of Complaint although title is claimed, the bill is demurrable unless it is alleged that the lands are vacant and unoccupied.

The bill of complaint in this case was clearly demurrable if a demurrer had been filed. In five succinct paragraphs it alleged: (1) that appellee had record title to "Lot Number 5" (a copy of the deed was appended thereto); (2) that appellee had a twenty-foot right of way (evidenced by an appended deed); (3) that appellant's husband had acknowledged the land and right of way in a survey (which was also appended); (4) that appellant claimed both land and right of way by adverse possession; and (5) that the survey was acknowledged on August 29, 1960 and that therefore adverse possession could not have ripened until August 29, 1980. The suit was filed on September 27, 1979, obviously with the intention of tolling the twenty-year adverse possession period. There being no assertion of facts indicative either of actual possession or that the land was vacant and unoccupied (which coupled with the record title would have satisfied constructive possession), had appellant demurred she would have been successful since the bill failed to state on its face a case within the jurisdiction of the court of equity. A bill to quiet title in equity would not have been appropriate because it did not appear that the complainant was in possession of the property in dispute.

Through oversight or cunning, appellant chose not to educate appellee during the crucial twentieth year and elected to answer rather than demur. By admitting that *she claimed* the land and right of way by adverse *possession* as contended by appellee, she underscored the questionable jurisdiction of the equity court, but did naught to raise the issue at that time. On July 14, 1980, just over a month before the crucial date noted in the complaint, a hearing was held. Appellee as noted, rested upon her record title, and appellant, apparently hesitant to chance supplying any defects in appellee's case moved for dismissal and rested upon her motion urging that appellee had failed to supply by proof what she had failed to assert by pleading. Had that proof of right to equity jurisdiction been supplied, even in the absence of a question of the sufficiency of a bill to confer jurisdiction, the court could have based its decree on the evidence without regard to the allegations of the bill. But the evidence was not supplied and the bill was not amended even then, and if a bill fails to state on its face a case within the jurisdiction of equity, that error is fatal at every stage of the case.

The judge sought to avoid this dilemma when faced with the *fait accompli* presented him by the motion to dismiss at the end of appellee's case, by asserting that a fact-finder might draw an inference (which he subsequently seems to have done) of possession from the evidence, which consisted only of the deed and a plat. . . .

No such inference, however, can be drawn from mere paper and the appellee's express contention, admitted by appellant, claimed that appellant was an adverse possessor, which claim necessitates "actual" possession by the possessor. The statutory requirement for constructive possession furthermore, is that the property be "vacant and unoccupied." An inference of vacancy is not available from the proof of bare paper title any more than actual possession by appellee would be inferable in the face of her claim that appellant was claiming possession adversely.

Thus, it did not appear and was not alleged in the present case that appellee was in possession actually or constructively. The object of the suit was to try the question not of possession, but only of right to possession, and such a proceeding is not within the province and jurisdiction of a court of chancery. . . . [T]he Court of Appeals has noted:

> "There is no head of equity jurisprudence under which a party in possession of land can be brought into Court, and made to show his title, in order that that title may be defeated and the possession delivered to the complainants, for this would be substantially to give a chancery suit the effect of an action in ejectment." Polk *v.* Pendleton, 31 Md. 118, 124–125 (1869).

Therefore absent actual or constructive possession, appellee could not bring appellant, who claimed possession adversely, into court to defeat appellant's claim to title. . . .

We will vacate the decree entered below and remand the case for further proceedings which may include the granting of leave to amend the bill of complaint, the introduction of evidence, if any, solely relating to the jurisdictional question of the equity court, or, if necessary, the transfer of the suit to the law side of the court under Md. Rule 515. By doing so, neither party will be improperly prejudiced by a denial of the right to assert fully a claim of ownership in the proper form. Any other remedy appropriately applied would do no more than honor form over substance because a court of conscience erred. . . .

NOTES ON BILLS TO QUIET OR REMOVE A CLOUD ON TITLE

1. The original equitable bill to quiet title was in the nature of a bill of peace, requiring proof that the defendant had sued the plaintiff repeatedly and unsuccessfully at law to obtain possession of the land. See Wehrman *v.* Conklin, 155 U.S. 314 (1894). The equity courts later developed a more flexible remedy, the bill to remove a cloud on title. This remedy, however, had shortcomings of its own. It was available only if the plaintiff was in possession of the property, and only if the competing claim was based on a document that was not invalid on its face and thus would deter an average person from buying the property from the plaintiff. Moreover, the court's decree only determined the validity of any claims based on the document; it did not resolve the broader issue of title to the property.

2. Many jurisdictions have created statutory actions to quiet title that eliminate most of the limitations on the earlier equitable remedies. These actions are commonly designed to settle all of the parties' conflicting claims to the property. Although they may allow non-possessory plaintiffs to sue, they typically preserve the right to jury trial in actions that historically would have been brought at law.

6. DECLARATORY JUDGMENT

Equity decrees are typically coercive: the court orders the defendant to do or not to do some act. This is one application of the maxim that equity acts *in personam*. Yet the ultimate goal of many equity proceedings is a declaration of the plaintiff's rights vis-à-vis the defendant. Actions to rescind or reform a contract are examples. A request for an injunction may also have as its primary motive a declaration of rights between the parties. For example, in Huntworth *v.* Tanner, 87 Wash. 670 (1915), the plaintiff sued to restrain a threatened arrest and prosecution for violation of a penal statute, but the real relief at stake was a declaration that the plaintiff's activities did not violate the law. Such injunctions are often called "anti-suit injunctions," because they are meant to protect against a suit the defendant might have brought.

Modern procedural rules permit plaintiffs to sue directly for declaratory relief without seeking any further remedy against the defendant, provided there is an actual controversy between the parties. In other words, like an "anti-suit injunction," the declaratory judgment can be seen as an "anti-suit" remedy. The effect of the judgment is to settle the rights of the parties. The judgment constitutes a determination on the merits, and, by issue preclusion, precludes relitigation of the issues actually decided by the court. It also lays the foundation for further actions for damages or injunctive relief, if these remedies become necessary.

The principal difficulty in application of declaratory judgment statutes has been determining whether a live case or controversy exists, as illustrated by the following case.

Nashville, Chattanooga & St. Louis Railway v. Wallace

Supreme Court of the United States, 1933.
288 U.S. 249.

■ MR. JUSTICE STONE delivered the opinion of the Court.

Appellant brought suit in the Chancery Court of Davidson county, Tenn., under the Uniform Declaratory Judgments Act of that state, to secure a judicial declaration that a state excise tax levied on the storage of gasoline, is, as applied to appellant, invalid under the commerce clause and the Fourteenth Amendment of the Federal Constitution. A decree for appellees was affirmed by the Supreme Court of the state, and the case comes here on appeal under section 237(a) of the Judicial Code.

After the jurisdictional statement required by Rule 12 was submitted, this Court, in ordering the cause set down for argument, invited the attention of counsel to the question "whether a case or controversy is presented, in view of the nature of the proceedings in the state courts." This preliminary question, which has been elaborately briefed and argued, must first be considered, for the judicial power with which this Court is invested by article 3, § 1, of the Constitution, extends by article 3, § 2, only to "cases" and "controversies"; if no "case" or "controversy" is presented for decision, we are without power to review the decree of the court below.

In determining whether this litigation presents a case within the appellate jurisdiction of this Court, we are concerned, not with form, but with substance. Hence, we look not to the label which the Legislature has attached to the procedure followed in the state courts, or to the description of the judgment which is brought here for review, in popular parlance, as "declaratory," but to the nature of the proceeding which the statute authorizes, and the effect of the judgment rendered upon the rights which the appellant asserts.

Section 1 of the Tennessee Declaratory Judgments Act confers jurisdiction on courts of record "to declare rights . . . whether or not further relief is or could be claimed" and provides that "no action or proceeding shall be open to objection on the ground that a declaratory judgment or decree is prayed for. The declaration may be either affirmative or negative in form and effect; and such declaration shall have the force and effect of a final judgment or decree." By section 2 it is provided that "any person . . . whose rights, status or other legal relations are affected by a statute . . . may have determined any question of construction or validity arising under the . . . statute . . . and obtain a declaration of rights . . . thereunder."

Under section 6, the court may refuse to render a declaratory judgment where, if rendered, it "would not terminate the uncertainty or controversy giving rise to the proceeding." Declaratory judgments may, in accordance with section 7, be reviewed as are other orders, judgments, or decrees, and under section 8 "further relief based on a declaratory judgment or decree may be granted whenever necessary or proper." Section 11 requires that, "when declaratory relief is sought, all persons shall be made parties who have or claim any interest which would be affected by the declaration, and no declaration shall prejudice the rights of persons not parties to the proceeding."

This statute has often been considered by the highest court of Tennessee, which has consistently held that its provisions may only be invoked when the complainant asserts rights which are challenged by the defendant, and presents for decision an actual controversy to which he is a party, capable of final adjudication by the judgment or decree to be rendered. It has also held that no judgment or decree will be rendered when all the parties who will be adversely affected by it are not before the court.

Proceeding in accordance with this statute, appellant filed its bill of complaint in the state chancery court, joining as defendants the appellees, the Attorney General and the state officials charged with the duty of collecting the gasoline privilege tax imposed by the Tennessee statute. The complaint alleged that appellant is engaged in purchasing gasoline outside the state, which it stores within the state pending its use within and without the state in the conduct of appellant's business as an interstate rail carrier; that appellees assert that the statute taxes the privilege of storing gasoline within the state and is applicable to appellant; that they have demanded payment of the tax in a specified amount and have determined to enforce their demand; and that, under the circumstances alleged, the statute as applied to appellant is invalid under the commerce clause and the Fourteenth Amendment. The relief prayed was that the Taxing Act be declared unconstitutional as applied to appellant. The chancery court sustained the appellees' demurrer to the sufficiency in law of the allegations relied on to establish the unconstitutionality of the tax. Its final decree dismissing the bill on the merits has been affirmed by the highest court of the state.

That the issues thus raised and judicially determined would constitute a case or controversy if raised and decided in a suit brought by the taxpayer to enjoin collection of the tax cannot be questioned. The proceeding terminating in the decree below . . . was between adverse parties, seeking a determination of their legal rights upon the facts alleged in the bill and admitted by the demurrer. . . . [V]aluable legal rights asserted by the complainant and threatened with imminent invasion by appellees, will be directly affected to a specific and substantial degree by the decision of the question of law; and . . . the question lends itself to judicial determination and is of the kind which this court traditionally decides. The relief sought is a definitive adjudication of the disputed constitutional right of the appellant, in the circumstances alleged, to be free from the tax; and that adjudication is not . . . subject to revision by some other and more authoritative agency. Obviously the appellant, whose duty to pay the tax will be determined by the decision of this case, is not attempting to secure an abstract determination by the Court of the validity of a statute or a decision advising what the law would be on an uncertain or hypothetical state of facts . . . . Thus the narrow question presented for determination is whether the controversy before us, which would be justiciable in this Court if presented in a suit for injunction, is any the less so because through a modified procedure appellant has been permitted to present it in the state courts, without praying for an injunction or alleging that irreparable injury will result from the collection of the tax.

While the ordinary course of judicial procedure results in a judgment requiring an award of process or execution to carry it into effect, such relief is not an indispensable adjunct to the exercise of the judicial function. This court has often exerted its judicial power to adjudicate boundaries between states, although it gave no injunction or other relief beyond the determination of the legal rights which were the subject of controversy between the parties, and to review judgments of the Court of Claims, although no process issues against the government. As we said in Fidelity National Bank & Trust Co. *v.* Swope, 274 U.S. 132, "Naturalization proceedings; suits to determine a matrimonial or other status; suits for instructions to a trustee or for the construction of a will; bills of interpleader, so far as the stakeholder is concerned; bills to quiet title where the plaintiff rests his claim on adverse possession—are familiar examples of judicial proceedings which result in an adjudication of the rights of litigants, although execution is not necessary to carry the judgment into effect, in the sense that no damages are required to be paid or acts to be performed by the parties."

The issues raised here are the same as those which under old forms of procedure could be raised only in a suit for an injunction or one to recover the tax after its payment. But the Constitution does not require that the case or controversy should be presented by traditional forms of procedure, invoking only traditional remedies. The judiciary clause of the Constitution defined and limited judicial power, not the particular method by which that power might be invoked. It did not crystallize into changeless form the procedure of 1789 as the only possible means for presenting a case or controversy otherwise cognizable by the federal courts. Whenever the judicial power is invoked to review a judgment of a state court, the ultimate constitutional purpose is the protection, by the exercise of the judicial function, of rights arising under the Constitution and laws of the United States. The states are left free to regulate their own judicial procedure. Hence changes merely in the form or method of procedure by which federal rights are brought to final adjudication in the state courts are not enough to preclude review of the adjudication by this Court, so long as the case retains the essentials of an adversary proceeding, involving a real, not a hypothetical, controversy, which is finally determined by the judgment below. As the prayer for relief by injunction is not a necessary prerequisite to the exercise of judicial power, allegations of threatened irreparable injury which are material only if an injunction is asked, may likewise be dispensed with if, in other respects, the controversy presented is, as in this case, real and substantial. . . . Accordingly, we must consider the constitutional questions raised by the appeal. . . .

NOTES

1. Actions for declaratory relief can be initiated in federal as well as state court, provided that federal jurisdictional requirements are met. The federal Declaratory Judgment Act, 28 U.S.C. §§ 2201, 2202, reads as follows:

"§ 2201. CREATION OF REMEDY.

"(a) In a case of actual controversy within its jurisdiction, except with respect to Federal taxes other than actions brought under section 7428 of the Internal Revenue Code of 1986, a proceeding under section 505 or 1146 of title 11, or in any civil action involving an antidumping or countervailing duty proceeding regarding a class or kind of Canadian merchandise, as determined by the administering authority, any court of the United States, upon the filing of an appropriate pleading, may declare the rights and other legal relations of any interested party seeking such declaration, whether or not further relief is or could be sought. Any such declaration shall have the force and effect of a final judgment or decree and shall be reviewable as such. . . .

"§ 2202. FURTHER RELIEF.

"Further necessary or proper relief based on a declaratory judgment or decree may be granted, after reasonable notice and hearing, against any adverse party whose rights have been determined by such judgment."

2. The federal Declaratory Judgment Act was upheld against constitutional challenge in Aetna Life Insurance Co. of Hartford, Connecticut *v.* Haworth, 300 U.S. 227 (1937). The Court found that it had before it "a dispute between parties who face each other in an adversary proceeding," and that the judiciary was being asked "not for an advisory opinion upon a hypothetical basis, but for an adjudication of present right upon established facts." *Id.* at 242.

In subsequent cases the Court has said that a declaratory judgment action can present a constitutional "case" only if it completely resolves the parties' legal dispute, and not if it "would simply carve out one issue in the dispute for separate adjudication." Calderon *v.* Ashmus, 523 U.S. 740, 749 (1998).

D. ACCOUNTING FOR PROFITS

Hurst v. Papierz

Appellate Court of Illinois, First District, 1973.
16 Ill. App. 3d 574.

■ GEORGE J. MORAN, JUSTICE. Counterdefendants appeal from the following decree entered by the Circuit Court of Cook County:

"DECREE

"This cause coming on to be heard on all of the pleadings herein and the Court having considered the Appellate Court Opinion, Judgment and Mandate rendered in this cause, reversing the May 22, 1968, Decree of this Court, and the Court having considered the arguments of counsel and being fully advised in the premises, FINDS:

"(A) That this Court has jurisdiction of the parties hereto and the subject matter hereof.

"(B) That the Appellate Court found that the equities in this cause are with the counterclaimant, ROBERT RAUTH, and against the counterdefendants, STANLEY PAPIERZ, THERESE PAPIERZ, and STANLEY PAPIERZ BUILDERS, INC. . . .

"(C) That the counterdefendants, STANLEY PAPIERZ, THERESE PAPIERZ, and STANLEY PAPIERZ BUILDERS, INC. were found by the Appellate Court to have wrongfully and fraudulently denied ROBERT RAUTH's 30% interest as a joint venturer in the Villa Venice apartment building complex; it was further found that since 1963 said defendants excluded ROBERT RAUTH from the operation and profits of said apartment building complex and that said counterdefendants possessed and operated said apartment buildings and refused to account to ROBERT RAUTH.

"(D) That the Appellate Court found that the counterdefendants, STANLEY PAPIERZ AND THERESE PAPIERZ and the counterplaintiff ROBERT RAUTH, were joint venturers in the real estate development known as "Villa Venice West" and that ROBERT RAUTH owned a 30% interest therein. . . .

"IT IS THEREFORE ORDERED, ADJUDGED, AND DECREED: . . .

"2. That ROBERT RAUTH is hereby decreed to be the owner of a 30% interest in the real estate development known as 'Villa

Venice West' as represented by his ownership of 30% of the outstanding common stock of S.P. Construction, Inc.

"3. That defendants, STANLEY PAPIERZ, THERESE PAPIERZ, and STANLEY PAPIERZ BUILDERS, INC., and any other person, firm or corporation asserting any interest in the following described property shall forthwith convey to S.P. Construction, Inc., a corporation, said premises located in the Village of La Grange, Illinois . . . .

"4. From and after the entry of this Decree, all income, receipts, revenues and proceeds thereafter derived from the operation of 'Villa Venice West,' in whatsoever form, and all assets, including cash on hand, shall become the property of S.P. Construction, Inc.

"5. Michael P. Giambrone is hereby appointed Receiver to manage 'Villa Venice West' until further order of this Court. Said Receiver shall be paid for his services the usual and customary charges paid therefor in the metropolitan Chicago area from the gross collections made by him from 'Villa Venice West.' Said Receiver shall be responsible for the collection of all rentals and payment of all expenses. No extraordinary payments for capital improvements, or otherwise, shall be made by the Receiver without the consent of the parties hereto, and failing such consent, by order of Court. Said Receiver shall submit to the parties a monthly statement with respect to his operation and conduct of 'Villa Venice West.'

"6. From and after the entry of this Decree, all parties hereto shall be and they are hereby enjoined and restrained, until further order of this Court, from paying or disbursing any proceeds derived from the operation of 'Villa Venice West' to any person, firm, or corporation other than S.P. Construction, Inc., excepting the Receiver for the purposes hereinabove described in paragraph 5.

"7. That from and after the entry of this Decree and until further order of this Court, S.P. Construction, Inc. is enjoined and restrained from paying any salaries, dividends, fees, allowances, or emoluments of any kind or description to any of the parties hereto, their transferees or assigns.

"8. That S.P. Construction, Inc. is, from and after the date of this Decree, enjoined and restrained from expending or employing any of its income, assets, or funds in connection with the litigation herein involved, or any other subsequent related cause, whether by way of attorneys' fees, court costs, or otherwise. . . ."

Counterdefendants . . . contend that even though we determine that the trial court properly ordered an accounting, the method by which it is to be taken is contrary to Illinois law. After ordering an accounting, the trial court appointed an accounting firm to determine the net sums due and payable to Robert Rauth from the counterdefendants. We find no authority in law for a method of accounting which does not set forth a procedure by which evidentiary questions may be adjudicated. Whether the suit is referred to a master or is heard by the court itself, each party has a right to be heard in support of his rights. On the hearing they have a right to introduce evidence, cross-examine witnesses and take the various steps authorized by law to protect their rights.

Appellants suggest that the trial court should follow the rules of the Circuit Court of Cook County in taking the accounting, and refer the accounting to a master-in-chancery. Counterdefendants would then submit their accounts before the master and Rauth could then review the accounting and have complete access to the books and records. Rauth could then file objections to the accounting and counterdefendants could then respond to his objections which would establish the issues. An evidentiary hearing could then be held to adjudicate the disputed items and objections to the master's report could then be filed before the circuit court. They state that this is the only procedure deemed proper by the Illinois Supreme Court in complicated accounting suits.

Prior to the passage of the new Illinois Constitution, there was a long line of cases in Illinois which held that in the case of a complicated accounting, the taking of such should be referred to a master in chancery. However, Section 8 of Article VI of the Illinois Constitution now provides that "there shall be no masters in chancery or other fee officers in the judicial system."

In view of the foregoing, the trial court itself must conduct the accounting, try all the issues, administer full relief to the parties and grant a judgment for the balance found due. In so doing, it is suggested that the trial court should follow established accounting procedures, except that it should not refer the case to a master or other fee officer as prohibited by the Illinois Constitution. In addition, it is suggested that the parties use the broad discovery tools available to them in the Supreme Court Rules. . . .

Appointment of a receiver is considered generally to be a harsh remedy. Nevertheless, it resides in the arsenal of equitable remedies to be used when in the sound discretion of the chancellor it is needed to insure complete justice is done between the parties. In equity, the particular circumstances surrounding the case are the criteria by which to judge whether or not the appointment of a receiver was reasonable, *i.e.*, not arbitrary, capricious and an abuse of discretion. Considering that counterdefendants were found to be joint venturers with Rauth and defrauded him and have contumaciously and consistently resisted this conclusion in various ways, including behavior which appears to be continuing bad faith and at the very least a badge of fraud, we hold the appointment of a receiver and the imposition of the complained of temporary injunctions were proper in this case. It is reasonable to fear that there is a danger in this case that the property which belongs to the joint venture may be placed beyond the jurisdiction of the court or in some way involved in transfers, conveyances or subjected to other claims, so as to render it more difficult for the court to give and enforce final relief to which counterclaimant may be found entitled at the conclusion of the accounting.

For the foregoing reasons the judgment of the trial court is affirmed except for that portion which provided for the appointment of the accounting firm to take the accounting. . . .

NOTE ON ACCOUNTING FOR PROFITS

An accounting for profits, also called simply an accounting, is an audit conducted to ascertain the amount of money that one party owes to another. Historically, an accounting culminated in a decree for payment of money. Rauth was entitled to an accounting remedy because his partners in the joint venture were deemed to be fiduciaries, subject to an equitable duty to account for misappropriated funds. Outside the fiduciary context, equity courts have sometimes also required an accounting on the ground that the parties' financial transactions were too complex for a jury to understand. For further discussion of accounting, as well as other equitable restitutionary remedies, see Chapter Thirteen, Section A(2) (Equitable Restitution).

PART IV

UNJUST ENRICHMENT AND RESTITUTIONARY REMEDIES

CHAPTER 11

THE HISTORY OF RESTITUTION

Restitution is an area of law in which the plaintiff's right to recovery is ordinarily based on an unjust enrichment of the defendant at the plaintiff's expense. Although this notion of unjust enrichment has roots in Roman law and in English legal history, it was not recognized as a distinct field of law until the early twentieth century. In 1937, Professors Warren Seavey and Austin Scott compiled the American Law Institute's first Restatement of Restitution. The Restatement brought together a variety of doctrinal rules that seemed to share the feature of relief based on unjust enrichment and, in effect, created a new category of legal doctrine. In part because the sources of restitution are disparate, the field has remained unruly and poorly understood. In trying to grasp this difficult field, history is a good place to start.

A. RESTITUTION AT LAW AND IN EQUITY

Moses v. Macferlan

Court of King's Bench, 1760.
1 W.Bl. 219, 96 Eng. Rep. 120; 2 Burr. 1005, 97 Eng. Rep. 676.

■ LORD MANSFIELD delivered the resolution of the Court . . . .

[This] was an action upon the case, brought in this Court by the now plaintiff, Moses, against the now defendant, Macferlan, (heretofore plaintiff in the Court of Conscience, against the same Moses now plaintiff here,) for money had and received to the use of Moses the now plaintiff in this Court. . . .

It was clearly proved, that the now plaintiff, Moses, had indorsed to the now defendant Macferlan, four several promissory notes, made to Moses himself by one Chapman Jacob, for 30s. each, for value received, bearing date 7th November 1758; and that this was done, in order to enable the now defendant Macferlan to recover the money in his own name, against Chapman Jacob. But previous to the now plaintiff's indorsing these notes, Macferlan assured him "that such his indorsement should be of no prejudice to him:" and there was an agreement signed by Macferlan, whereby he (amongst other things) expressly agreed "that Moses should not be liable to the payment of the money or any part of it; and that he should not be prejudiced, or be put to any costs, or any way suffer, by reason of such his indorsement." Notwithstanding which express condition and agreement, and contrary thereto, the present defendant Macferlan summoned the present plaintiff Moses into the

Court of Conscience,[i] upon each of these four notes, as the indorser thereof respectively, by four separate summonses. Whereupon Moses, (by one Smith who attended the Court of Conscience at their second Court, as solicitor for him and on his behalf,) tendered the said indemnity to the Court of Conscience, upon the first of the said four causes; and offered to give evidence of it, and of the said agreement, by way of defence for Moses in that Court. But the Court of Conscience rejected this defence, and refused to receive any evidence in proof of this agreement of indemnity, thinking that they had no power to judge of it; and gave judgment against Moses, upon the mere foot of his indorsement . . . , (which he himself did not at all dispute,) without hearing his witnesses about the agreement . . . .

The 1st objection is, "that an action of debt would not lie here; and no assumpsit will lie, where an action of debt may not be brought:" some sayings at Nisi Prius, reported by note takers who did not understand the force of what was said, are quoted in support of that proposition. But there is no foundation for it. . . .

[T]he rule . . . settled in [*Slade's Case*] and followed ever since is, "that an action of assumpsit will lie in many cases where debt lies, and in many where it does not lie."

A main inducement, originally, for encouraging actions of assumpsit was, "to take away the wager of law:" and that might give rise to loose expressions, as if the action was confined to cases only where that reason held.

2d objection.—"That no assumpsit lies, except upon an express or implied contract: but here it is impossible to presume any contract to refund money, which the defendant recovered by an adverse suit."

Answer. If the defendant be under an obligation, from the ties of natural justice, to refund; the law implies a debt, and gives this action, founded in the equity of the plaintiff's case, as it were upon a contract ("quasi ex contractu," as the Roman law expresses it).

This species of assumpsit, ("for money had and received to the plaintiff's use,") lies in numberless instances, for money the defendant has received from a third person; which he claims title to, in opposition to the plaintiff's right; and which he had, by law, authority to receive from such third person.

3d objection. Where money has been recovered by the judgment of a Court having competent jurisdiction, the matter can never be brought over again by a new action.

Answer. It is most clear, "that the merits of a judgment can never be over-haled by an original suit, either at law or in equity." Till the

[i] [The Court of Conscience, also known as the Court of Requests, was an inferior law court with limited powers. Its decisions were unappealable.]

judgment is set aside, or reversed, it is conclusive, as to the subject matter of it, to all intents and purposes.

But the ground of this action is consistent with the judgment of the Court of Conscience: it admits the commissioners did right. They decreed upon the indorsement of the notes by the plaintiff: which indorsement is not now disputed. The ground upon which this action proceeds, was no defence against that sentence. . . .

The ground of this action is not, "that the judgment was wrong:" but, "that, (for a reason which the now plaintiff could not avail himself of against that judgment,) the defendant ought not in justice to keep the money." . . .

Money may be recovered by a right and legal judgment; and yet the iniquity of keeping that money may be manifest, upon grounds which could not be used by way of defence against the judgment.

Suppose an indorsee of a promissory note, having received payment from the drawer (or maker) of it, sues and recovers the same money from the indorser who knew nothing of such payment.

Suppose a man recovers upon a policy for a ship presumed to be lost, which afterwards comes home;—or upon the life of a man presumed to be dead, who afterwards appears;—or upon a representation of a risque deemed to be fair, which comes out afterwards to be grossly fraudulent. . . .

One great benefit, which arises to suitors from the nature of this action, is, that the plaintiff needs not state the special circumstances from which he concludes "that, ex æquo & bono, the money received by the defendant, ought to be deemed as belonging to him:" he may declare generally, "that the money was received to his use;" and make out his case, at the trial.

This is equally beneficial to the defendant. It is the most favourable way in which he can be sued: he can be liable no further than the money he has received; and against that, may go into every equitable defence, upon the general issue; he may claim every equitable allowance . . . ; in short, he may defend himself by every thing which shews that the plaintiff, ex æquo & bono, is not intitled to the whole of his demand, or to any part of it. . . .

This kind of equitable action, to recover back money, which ought not in justice to be kept, is very beneficial, and therefore much encouraged. It lies only for money which, ex æquo et bono, the defendant ought to refund: it does not lie for money paid by the plaintiff, which is claimed of him as payable in point of honor and honesty, although it could not have been recovered from him by any course of law; as in payment of a debt barred by the Statute of Limitations, or contracted during his infancy, or to the extent of principal and legal interest upon an usurious contract, or, for money fairly lost at play: because in all these cases, the defendant may retain it with a safe conscience, though by positive law he was barred from recovering. But it lies for money paid by mistake; or upon a consideration which happens to fail; or for money got through imposition, (express, or implied;) or extortion; or oppression; or an undue advantage taken of the plaintiff's situation, contrary to laws made for the protection of persons under those circumstances.

In one word, the gist of this kind of action is, that the defendant, upon the circumstances of the case, is obliged by the ties of natural justice and equity to refund the money.

Therefore we are all of us of opinion that the plaintiff might elect to wave any demand upon the foot of the indemnity, for the costs he had been put to; and bring this action, to recover the 6l. which the defendant got and kept from him iniquitously. . . .

NOTES ON QUASI-CONTRACT

1. Although Lord Mansfield speaks of "equity," it is easy to misunderstand him. Remember that *equity* can be used in multiple senses, including justice and fair dealing and also the more technical sense of remedies and procedures developed by the courts of equity. See Chapter Five, Section A (Introducing Equity). Lord Mansfield is using the term in a more general sense, not in its technical sense. After all, Moses *v.* Macferlan (the latter name is variously spelled) was decided by the Court of King's Bench, not by the Chancellor.

In this case, Lord Mansfield allowed Moses to recover from Macferlan under the common law form of action *indebitatus assumpsit*. This form of action was invented to avoid onerous procedures associated with the ancient action of debt. To accomplish that goal, the action of *indebitatus assumpsit* relied on a fictitious second promise to pay the debt, which allowed the plaintiff to proceed under the new writ, using the more favorable procedures associated with trespass. But Moses *v.* Macferlan and the line of cases it refers to go much further than this. Macferlan's objective was to obtain money from Moses through a fraudulent scheme; he certainly never intended to pay the money back. Thus, the fictitious promise the court enforced was not simply a reiteration of a promise the defendant had actually made, but a promise imputed to him by the court to reach a just result.

Restitution claims of the type recognized in Moses *v.* Macferlan are sometimes referred to as "quasi-contract" claims. Behind the term lies the idea that these claims are not, strictly speaking, in tort or contract, and so some other classification is needed. See A. W. B. Simpson, A HISTORY OF THE COMMON LAW OF CONTRACT: THE RISE OF THE ACTION OF ASSUMPSIT 489–91 (1987). Hence the use of "quasi" before "contract." For further discussion of the terminology of restitution and unjust enrichment, see Chapter Thirteen, Section A (Restitution: Legal and Equitable).

2. The action of *indebitatus assumpsit* spawned what were known as the "common counts." Among these were the count for money had and received, the count for goods sold and delivered, and the count for services rendered (known as *quantum meruit*). As Lord Mansfield noted, these

actions were convenient for plaintiffs because they required no particular factual allegations beyond the fictitious claim that the defendant had made a promise to pay. The common counts are still pleaded in some state courts. Although not expressly mentioned in the Federal Rules of Civil Procedure, the common counts remain available to a plaintiff in federal court. Charles Alan Wright et al., 5 FEDERAL PRACTICE & PROCEDURE: FEDERAL RULES OF CIVIL PROCEDURE § 1222 (3d ed., 2017 update).

Newton v. Porter

Court of Appeals of New York, 1877.
69 N.Y. 133.

■ ANDREWS, J. This is an equitable action brought to establish the right of the plaintiff to certain securities, the proceeds of stolen bonds, and to compel the defendants to account therefor.

In March, 1869, the plaintiff was the owner of $13,000 of government bonds, and of a railroad bond for $1,000, negotiable by delivery, which, on the 12th of March, 1869, were stolen from her, and soon afterwards $11,500 of the bonds were sold by the thief and his confederates, and the proceeds divided between them. William Warner loaned a part of his share in separate loans and took the promissory notes of the borrower therefor. George Warner invested $2,000 of his share in the purchase of a bond and mortgage, which was assigned to his wife Cordelia without consideration.

In January, 1870, William Warner, George Warner, Cornelia Warner and one Lusk were arrested upon the charge of stealing the bonds, or as accessories to the larceny, and were severally indicted in the county of Cortland. The Warners employed the defendants, who are attorneys, to defend them in the criminal proceedings, and in any civil suits which might be instituted against them in respect to the bonds, and to secure them for their services and expenses, and for any liabilities they might incur in their behalf, William Warner transferred to the defendants Miner and Warren promissory notes taken on loans made by him out of the proceeds of the stolen bonds, amounting to $2,250 or thereabouts, and Cordelia Warner, for the same purpose, assigned to the defendant Porter the bond and mortgage above mentioned.

The learned judge at Special Term found that the defendants had notice at the time they received the transfer of the securities, that they were the avails and proceeds of the stolen bonds, and directed judgment against them for the value of the securities, it appearing on the trial that they had collected or disposed of them and received the proceeds.

The doctrine upon which the judgment in this case proceeded, viz.: that the owner of negotiable securities stolen and afterwards sold by the thief may pursue the proceeds of the sale in the hands of the felonious taker or his assignee with notice, through whatever changes the proceeds may have gone, so long as the proceeds or the substitute therefor can be distinguished and identified, and have the proceeds or the property in which they were invested subjected, by the aid of a court of equity, to a lien and trust in his favor for the purposes of recompense and restitution, is founded upon the plainest principles of justice and morality, and is consistent with the rule in analogous cases acted upon in courts of law and equity. It is a general principle of the law of personal property that the title of the owner cannot be divested without his consent. The purchaser from a thief, however honest and *bona fide* the purchase may have been, cannot hold the stolen chattel against the true proprietor, but the latter may follow and reclaim it wherever or in whosoever hands it may be found. . . . The rule that a thief cannot convey a good title to stolen property has an exception in case of money or negotiable securities transferable by delivery, which have been put into circulation and have come to the hands of *bona fide* holders. The right of the owner to pursue and reclaim the money and securities there ends, and the holder is protected in his title. The plaintiff was in this position. The bonds, with the exception stated, had, as the evidence tends to show, been sold to *bona fide* purchasers, and she was precluded from following and reclaiming them.

The right of the plaintiff in equity to have the notes and mortgage while they remained in the possession of the felons or of their assignees with notice, subjected to a lien and trust in her favor, and to compel their transfer to her as the equitable owner, does not, we think, admit of serious doubt. The plaintiff, by the sale of the bonds to *bona fide* purchasers, lost her title to the securities. She could not further follow them. She could maintain an action as for a conversion of the property against the felons. But this remedy in this case would be fruitless, as they are wholly insolvent. Unless she can elect to regard the securities in which the bonds were invested as a substitute, *pro tanto,* for the bonds, she has no effectual remedy. The thieves certainly have no claim to the securities in which the proceeds of the bonds were invested as against the plaintiff. They, without her consent, have disposed of her property, and put it beyond her reach. If the avails remained in their hands, in money, the direct proceeds of the sale, can it be doubted that she could reach it? It is not necessary to decide that, in the case supposed, she would have the legal title to the money, but if that question was involved in the case I should have great hesitation in denying the proposition. That she could assert an equitable claim to the money, I have no doubt. And this equitable right to follow the proceeds would continue and attach to any securities or property in which the proceeds were invested, so long as they could be traced and identified, and the rights of *bona fide* purchasers had not intervened. . . .

In courts of equity the doctrine is well settled and is uniformly applied that when a person, standing in a fiduciary relation, misapplies or converts a trust fund into another species of property, the beneficiary will be entitled to the property thus acquired. The jurisdiction exercised for the protection of a party defrauded by the misappropriation of property, in violation of a duty, owing by the party making the misappropriation, is exceedingly broad and comprehensive. The doctrine is illustrated and applied most frequently in cases of trusts, where trust moneys have been, by the fraud or violation of duty of the trustee, diverted from the purposes of the trust and converted into other property. In such case a court of equity will follow the trust fund into the property into which it has been converted, and appropriate it for the indemnity of the beneficiary. It is immaterial in what way the change has been made, whether money has been laid out in land, or land has been turned into money, or how the legal title to the converted property may be placed. Equity only stops the pursuit when the means of ascertainment fails, or the rights of *bona fide* purchasers for value, without notice of the trust, have intervened. . . .

It is insisted by the counsel for the defendants that the doctrine which subjects property acquired by the fraudulent misuse of trust moneys by a trustee to the influence of the trust . . . has no application to a case where money or property acquired by felony has been converted into other property. There is, it is said, in such cases, no trust relation between the owner of the stolen property and the thief, and the law will not imply one for the purpose of subjecting the avails of the stolen property to the claim of the owner. It would seem to be an anomaly in the law, if the owner who has been deprived of his property by a larceny should be less favorably situated in a court of equity, in respect to his remedy to recover it, or the property into which it had been converted, than one who, by an abuse of trust, has been injured by the wrongful act of a trustee to whom the possession of trust property has been confided. The law in such a case will raise a trust *in invitum* out of the transaction, for the very purpose of subjecting the substituted property to the purposes of indemnity and recompense. . . .

We are of opinion that the absence of the conventional relation of trustee and *cestui que trust* between the plaintiff and the Warners, is no obstacle to giving the plaintiff the benefit of the notes and mortgage, or the proceeds in part of the stolen bonds. . . .

NOTES ON CONSTRUCTIVE TRUST

1. The trust imposed in Newton *v.* Porter was "constructive"—that is, fictitious. Like the promise to pay in Moses *v.* Macferlan, the constructive trust is a device courts use to accomplish restitution of unjust gains. The outcome of the case is not that the defendant will hold the proceeds of the stolen bonds in a continuing trust for the plaintiff; instead, as part of its decree, the court will bring the matter to an end by ordering the defendant to turn over the proceeds to the plaintiff.

2. Dean Ames described the constructive trust this way:

> "An express trust of a chattel is, of course, enforceable in equity. Indeed, since the trustee has the legal title, and there is no common law contract, the jurisdiction of equity is exclusive.
>
> "As to the constructive trusts a distinction must be made.
>
> "If one acquires from the plaintiff by a tort the title to a chattel, or unconscionably retains a title, honestly acquired from the plaintiff, equity might, with propriety, compel him, as a constructive trustee, to reconvey the chattel, just as in early times decrees were made for the payment of money got by fraud, or though properly acquired, unjustly withheld, as in the case of failure of consideration. But at the present day the defrauded person must seek his relief at law, unless damages for the deceit would be an inadequate remedy, either because of the peculiar nature of the chattel, or because of the insolvency of the defendant.
>
> "If, on the other hand, a wrongdoer acquires the title to a chattel from a third person by the misuse of the plaintiff's property; if, for example, a fiduciary, a fraudulent purchaser, or a converter, by a breach of trust or a wrongful transfer of the fraudulently acquired or converted property, acquires in exchange the legal title to a chattel, equity will compel him to hold the newly acquired chattel in trust for the plaintiff. The cases in support of the doctrine that a fiduciary holds the product of the trust fund for the beneficiary are legion. . . . The authorities in favor of the rule that a fraudulent purchaser or a converter come within the same rule, though less numerous, are decisive."

1 James Barr Ames, A SELECTION OF CASES IN EQUITY JURISDICTION 43–44 n.2 (1923).

3. Justice Cardozo, discussing remedies available against an agent charged with misappropriating his employer's opportunity, wrote that:

> "A constructive trust is the formula through which the conscience of equity finds expression. When property has been acquired in such circumstances that the holder of the legal title may not in good conscience retain the beneficial interest, equity converts him into a trustee. We think it would be against good conscience for the plaintiff to retain these profits unless his employer has consented. The tie was close between the employer's business and the forbidden venture. The profits which the agent claims have come from the employer's coffers. If the agent must account as a trustee, the price which the employer pays is to that extent diminished. If the agent retains the profit, the price is to that extent increased. Of course it is true that if Perry had made the purchase alone, without the aid of plaintiff, the employer might be no better off. That is true whenever an agent goes into some competing venture. His associates might have succeeded in diverting equal profits without him. The disability is personal to

> him. Others may divert profits from the business of the principal. He may not. If he does, he must account for them.
>
> "We conclude, therefore, that the plaintiff was chargeable as a trustee if the employer so elected. . . .
>
> "A court of equity in decreeing a constructive trust is bound by no unyielding formula. The equity of the transaction must shape the measure of relief."

Beatty *v.* Guggenheim Exploration Co., 225 N.Y. 380, 386–87 (1919).

The operation of constructive trusts and related equitable restitution remedies is considered in more detail in Chapter Thirteen, below.

B. RESTITUTION AND UNJUST ENRICHMENT

A straightforward principle is at the heart of this area of law. The first Restatement of Restitution began by stating that "[a] person who has been unjustly enriched at the expense of another is required to make restitution to the other." Restatement of Restitution § 1 (1937). The latest Restatement begins with a nearly identical statement of principle: "A person who is unjustly enriched at the expense of another is liable in restitution to the other." Restatement (Third) of Restitution and Unjust Enrichment, § 1 (2011).[ii]

This general principle of unjust enrichment can be seen at work in a number of more specific restitutionary claims and remedies that are available to a plaintiff. As the Illinois Supreme Court put it, "The doctrine of unjust enrichment underlies a number of legal and equitable actions and remedies, including the equitable remedy of constructive trust and the legal actions of *assumpsit* and restitution or quasi-contract." HPI Health Care Services, Inc. *v.* Mt. Vernon Hospital, Inc., 131 Ill. 2d 145, 160 (1989).

The principle that one person should not be enriched at the expense of another has a strong intuitive appeal. Professor Fuller wrote in 1936 that, of the various interests protected by contract remedies, the strongest was the restitution interest:

> "If, following Aristotle, we regard the purpose of justice as the maintenance of an equilibrium of goods among members of society, the restitution interest presents twice as strong a claim to judicial intervention as the reliance interest, since if A not only causes B to lose one unit but appropriates that unity to himself, the resulting discrepancy between A and B is not one unit but two."

Lon L. Fuller & William R. Perdue, Jr., The Reliance Interest in Contract Damages, 46 Yale L.J. 52, 56 (1936).

[ii] There is a first Restatement and a third Restatement; the second Restatement of Restitution was begun but never completed.

Professor Dawson, perhaps the greatest restitution scholar of his time, generalized the point, observing that "rudimentary psychology" tells us that "loss alone is a grievance. But if this loss can be located and identified in the gain received by another, the anguish caused by the loss will be felt as more than doubled." John P. Dawson, UNJUST ENRICHMENT: A COMPARATIVE ANALYSIS 5 (1951).

Not all commentators have agreed that prevention of unjust enrichment is always a laudable objective. Dawson himself said that Karl Marx exploited a similar idea when he "tapped an inexhaustible supply of resentment with the aid of his labor theory of value." *Id.* See also Christopher T. Wonnell, Replacing the Unitary Principle of Unjust Enrichment, 45 Emory L.J. 153, 175–90 (1996) (arguing that the principle of unjust enrichment relies on sentiments akin to envy).

Professor Dawson was particularly skeptical about judicial use of unjust enrichment as a decisional principle rather than as a shorthand way of referring to a body of more concrete rules.

> "[A] general principle prohibiting enrichment though another's loss appears first as a convenient explanation of specific results; it is an instrument for quite practical and intelligible purposes. Yet once the idea has been formulated as a generalization, it has the peculiar faculty of inducing quite sober citizens to jump right off the dock."

Dawson, *supra*, at 8. Comments to Section 1 of the Restatement (Third) of Restitution and Unjust Enrichment reflect a similarly cautious approach to application of the seductive principle of unjust enrichment.

CHAPTER 12

GROUNDS FOR RESTITUTION

In the law of restitution, "unjust enrichment" is an important term. Like tort or contract, unjust enrichment may be the basis for a plaintiff's claim in court. When a plaintiff succeeds on a claim based on unjust enrichment, the relief the court gives is ordinarily measured by the defendant's gain rather than by the plaintiff's loss. That is, a claim based on unjust enrichment is paired with a restitutionary remedy. For an overview of the restitutionary remedies, see Chapter Thirteen, Section A (Restitution: Legal and Equitable).

But courts do not typically appeal to unjust enrichment as an abstract idea. Instead, the law on this subject has developed through a series of recurring scenarios, such as mistaken payments or bad behavior by fiduciaries. In other words, "unjust enrichment" is an umbrella term for a set of more specific scenarios in which courts typically award a restitutionary remedy. As one court noted about the doctrine of unjust enrichment, "While it is said that a defendant is liable if 'equity and good conscience' requires, this does not mean that a moral duty" is sufficient, for "[t]here must be some specific legal principle or situation which [the courts have] established or recognized, to bring a case within the scope of the doctrine." Cohen *v.* Frank Developers, Inc., 118 N.H. 512, 518 (1978).

This chapter discusses the substantive grounds for restitution. Grasping these is necessary for understanding when courts will give a restitutionary remedy. Because the substantive grounds for restitution are neglected at present in the law school curriculum, the lawyer who knows them well is sure to have an advantage over other lawyers in litigation.

A. MISTAKEN PAYMENTS AND OTHER INVOLUNTARY TRANSFERS

Pilot Life Insurance Co. v. Cudd

Supreme Court of South Carolina, 1945.
208 S.C. 6.

■ TAYLOR, JUSTICE. The respondent, Pilot Life Insurance Company, issued its policy, dated April 12, 1936, for $1000 on the life of Lewis Edward Cudd, naming [the appellant, Cudd, who was] the insured's aunt and adoptive mother, as beneficiary; on or about November 18, 1942, the insured sailed from Ceylon as a member of the Merchant Marine aboard the American Export Lines vessel, Swaokla; on January 16, 1943, Elizabeth Blackwell Cudd, who was married to the insured in April,

1942, received the following letter from the War Shipping Administration:

"Re: SA-Lewis E. Cudd

"Dear Madam:

"This letter will advise you that the above-named member of the crew of the indicated vessel has been reported missing as a result of enemy action.

"There was war risk insurance effective upon his life. This office is in possession of documentary evidence that you were designated as the beneficiary of this insurance. . . .

"Yours very truly,

"(s) E. A. Bloomquist

"Chief Adjuster

"Division of Wartime Insurance"

On January 21, 1943, [Elizabeth] received the following telegram from the Navy Department:

"The Navy Department deeply regrets to inform you that your husband, Lewis Edward Cudd, is missing and presumed lost following action in the performance of his duty and in the service of his country. The Coast Guard appreciates your great anxiety and will furnish you further information promptly when received. To prevent possible aid to our enemies please do not divulge the name of his ship—

"Vice-Admiral R. R. Waesche, Commandant,

"U. S. Coast Guard."

On February 9, 1943, the Maritime War Emergency Board issued a Certificate of Presumptive Death [as follows:]

"I hereby certify that the Maritime War Emergency Board has found that Lewis Edward Cudd with the rating of 2nd Cook and Baker is presumed to have died on or about November 28, 1942, as a result of a cause specified in the applicable Decisions of the Maritime War Emergency Board . . . ."

. . . Sometime during the Spring of 1943, appellant communicated this information to the local agent of the respondent . . . .

The local agent inquired of the beneficiary whether or not she had received a Certificate of Presumptive Death and learned it was in the possession of the wife; thereupon respondent communicated with the Maritime War Emergency Board stating that it had been advised of the death of the insured and requested "a copy of the original Certificate of Presumptive Death" and received same under date of May 8, 1943, which was based on the original order of the Board dated February 9, 1943, together with their letter advising: "We believe this will be sufficient for you to pay the beneficiary the amount of the policy carried by you on the deceased." As a result of this death, claims were signed and filed by the appellant. Respondent then issued its check for $1,013.36 covering the face amount of the policy plus a premium payment of $13.36 which had been paid after the date of presumptive death. . . .

On August 20, 1943, the U. S. Coast Guard wrote the wife, Mrs. Elizabeth Cudd . . . as follows:

> "You are advised that this office is in receipt of an official report from the Prisoner of War Information Bureau, through the International Red Cross, that your husband, Lewis Edward Cudd, is a prisoner of War of Japan. He is interned in the Hakodate Prisoner of War Camp located on Hokkaido Island, Japan. . . ."

On October 8, 1945, respondent received from the Maritime War Emergency Board a certificate correcting the Certificate of Presumptive Death. Thereupon respondent's agent called upon the appellant and informed her of same and asked that she refund the money and reinstate the policy, no definite answer being given, respondent wrote and asked that this be done. . . .

That the insured is alive and back in the United States at this time is undisputed. . . .

It is a firmly established general rule that money paid to another under the influence of a mistake of fact, that is, on the mistaken supposition of the existence of a specific fact which would entitle the other to the money, which would not have been paid if it had been known to the payor that the fact was otherwise, may be recovered, provided the payment has not caused such a change in the position of the payee that it would be unjust to require a refund. The ground on which the rule rests is that money paid through misapprehension of facts belongs, in equity and good conscience to the person who paid it. . . .

It is obvious that both parties accepted as a fact that the insured had died shortly after sailing from Ceylon. . . . Appellant contends that there was no mutual mistake but rather a mistake or error of judgment on the part of the insurer, [that the] settlement was made under the realization of an uncertainty, and that the settlement was a compromise of a doubtful liability. . . .

A compromise . . . involves the essential element of a dispute or a controversy. . . . Here there was no dispute, nor claim for double indemnity nor controversy between the parties. Both parties had substantially the same information and proceeded upon the same mistake of fact. . . .

NOTE

In Great American Insurance Co. *v.* Yellen, 58 N.J. Super. 240 (1959), an insurer investigated and rejected a claim for fire damage. When the claim was resubmitted by an agent hired by the insured to pursue the claim, a clerk failed to realize that the claim had already been rejected, and issued a check. The court allowed the insurer to recover:

> "It is the general rule that one who has paid money under a mistake of fact but for which payment would not have been made may have restitution from the payee notwithstanding that the mistake was unilateral and a consequence of the payor's negligence, providing, however, that such restitution will not prejudice the payee. Restatement of Restitution § 59 (1936)."

Id. at 244.

Banque Worms v. BankAmerica International

Court of Appeals of New York, 1991.
77 N.Y.2d 362.

■ ALEXANDER, JUDGE. On April 10, 1989, Security Pacific International Bank (Security Pacific), a Federally chartered banking corporation with offices in New York City, mistakenly wired $1,974,267.97 on behalf of Spedley Securities (Spedley), an Australian corporation, into the account of Banque Worms, a French Bank, maintained with BankAmerica International (BankAmerica), another Federally chartered bank with New York offices. Initially intending to make payment on its debt to Banque Worms under a revolving credit agreement, Spedley instructed Security Pacific, which routinely effected wire transfers for Spedley, to electronically transfer funds from Security Pacific to Banque Worms' account at BankAmerica.

A few hours after directing this wire transfer, Spedley, by a second telex, directed Security Pacific to stop payment to Banque Worms and to make payment instead to National Westminster Bank USA (Natwest USA) for the same amount. At the time Security Pacific received the telexes, Spedley had a credit balance of only $84,500 in its account at Security Pacific, but later that morning, Security Pacific received additional funds sufficient to cover the transaction and then began to execute the transaction. However, in mistaken disregard of Spedley's second telex canceling the wire transfer to Banque Worms, Security Pacific transferred the funds into Banque Worms' account at BankAmerica. The funds were credited to the account after Banque Worms was notified through the Clearing House Interbank Payment System (CHIPS) that the funds had been received. That afternoon, Security Pacific executed Spedley's second payment order and transferred $1,974,267.97 to Natwest USA. Spedley's account at Security Pacific was debited twice to record both wire transfers thus producing an overdraft.

Meanwhile, at Security Pacific's request made prior to the transfer to Natwest USA, BankAmerica agreed to return the funds mistakenly transferred, provided Security Pacific furnished a United States Council on International Banking, Inc. (CIB) indemnity. The indemnity was furnished and the funds returned to Security Pacific on the following day. Banque Worms, however, refused BankAmerica's request that it consent to its account being debited to reflect the return of the funds. Consequently BankAmerica called upon Security Pacific to perform pursuant to the CIB indemnity and return the funds. Security Pacific's attempt to obtain funds from Spedley to cover this indemnity was unavailing because by that time, Spedley had entered into involuntary liquidation.

Banque Worms brought suit against BankAmerica in the United States District Court for the Southern District of New York seeking to compel BankAmerica to recredit $1,974,267.97 to Banque Worms' account. BankAmerica instituted a third-party action against Security Pacific for return of the funds, and Security Pacific counterclaimed against Banque Worms seeking a declaration that neither Banque Worms nor BankAmerica were entitled to the $1,974,267.97. Eventually, for reasons not here pertinent, Security Pacific returned the funds to BankAmerica, BankAmerica recredited Banque Worms' account and was voluntarily dismissed from the case leaving only Banque Worms and Security Pacific as the sole contestants seeking entitlement to the $1,974,267.97. . . .

[T]he District Court, applying the "discharge for value" rule, granted judgment for Banque Worms. Security Pacific appealed to the United States Court of Appeals for the Second Circuit, arguing that New York neither recognized nor applied the "discharge for value" rule in situations such as this; that the controlling rule under New York law was the "mistake of fact" rule pursuant to which, in order to be entitled to retain the mistakenly transferred funds, Banque Worms was required to demonstrate detrimental reliance. The case is before us upon a certified question from the Second Circuit . . . inquiring "[w]hether in this case, where a concededly mistaken wire transfer by [Security Pacific] was made to [Banque Worms], a creditor of Spedley, New York would apply the 'Discharge for Value' rule . . . or, in the alternative, whether in this case New York would apply the rule that holds that money paid under a mistake may be recovered, unless the payment has caused such a change in the position of the receiving party that it would be unjust to require the party to refund."

For the reasons that follow, we conclude that, under the circumstances of this case, the "discharge for value" rule should be applied, thus entitling Banque Worms to retain the funds mistakenly transferred without the necessity of demonstrating detrimental reliance.

In the area of restitution, New York has long recognized the rule that "if A pays money to B upon the erroneous assumption of the former that he is indebted to the latter, an action may be maintained for its recovery. The reason for the rule is obvious. Since A was mistaken in the assumption that he was indebted to B, the latter is not entitled to retain the money acquired by the mistake of the former, even though the mistake is the result of negligence." . . . Where, however, the receiving party has changed its position to its detriment in reliance upon the mistake so that requiring that it refund the money paid would be "unfair," recovery has been denied. . . .

The Restatement of Restitution, on the other hand, has established the "discharge for value" rule which provides that "[a] creditor of another or one having a lien on another's property who has received from a third person any benefit in discharge of the debt or lien, is under no duty to make restitution therefor, although the discharge was given by mistake of the transferor as to his interests or duties, if the transferee made no misrepresentation and did not have notice of the transferor's mistake" (Restatement of Restitution § 14[1]). . . .

Banque Worms . . . invokes the "discharge for value" rule, arguing that because it is a creditor of Spedley and had no knowledge that the wire transfer was erroneous, it is entitled to keep the funds. It points out, as indicated by the official comment to section 14(1) of the Restatement of Restitution, that the "discharge for value" rule is simply a "specific application of the underlying principle of bona fide purchase" set forth in section 13 of the Restatement (Restatement of Restitution § 14, comment a). . . .

[Existing New York precedents,] for the most part, . . . present issues involving more traditional aspects of mistake and restitution, and do not satisfactorily address the unique problems presented by electronic funds transfer technology. . . .

Electronic funds transfers have become the preferred method utilized by businesses and financial institutions to effect payments and transfers of a substantial volume of funds. These transfers, commonly referred to as wholesale wire transfers, differ from other payment methods in a number of significant respects, a fact which accounts in large measure for their popularity. Funds are moved faster and more efficiently than by traditional payment instruments, such as checks. The transfers are completed at a relatively low cost, which does not vary widely depending on the amount of the transfer, because the price charged reflects primarily the cost of the mechanical aspects of the funds transfer. Most transfers are completed within one day and can cost as little as $10 to carry out a multimillion dollar transaction. The popularity of wholesale wire transfers is evidenced by the fact that nearly $1 trillion in transactions occur each day, averaging $5 million per transfer and on peak days, this figure often approaches $2 trillion.

Wholesale wire transfers are generally made over the two principal wire payment systems: the Federal Reserve Wire Transfer Network (Fedwire) and the CHIPS.[2] The CHIPS network handles 95% of the

[2] CHIPS is owned and operated by the New York Clearing House Association and the Federal Reserve Bank owns and operates Fedwire, the largest American wire transfer network.

international transfers made in dollars, transferring an average of $750 billion per day. These funds are transferred through participating banks located in New York because all of the banks belonging to the CHIPS network must maintain a regulated presence in New York. As a result, this State is considered the national and international center for wholesale wire transfers.

The low cost of electronic funds transfers is an important factor in the system's popularity and this is so even though banks executing wire transfers often risk significant liability as a result of losses occasioned by mistakes and errors, the most common of which involve the payment of funds to the wrong beneficiary or in an incorrect amount. Thus, a major policy issue facing the drafters of UCC article 4A was determining how the risk of loss might best be allocated, while preserving a unique price structure. In order to prevent or minimize losses, the industry had adopted and employed various security procedures designed to prevent losses such as the use of codes, identifying words or numbers, call-back procedures and limits on payment amounts or beneficiaries that may be paid. . . .

[I]t was the consensus among various commentators that existing rules of law did not adequately address the problems presented by these wholesale electronic funds transfers. Thus, the National Conference of Commissioners on Uniform State Laws (NCCUSL) and the American Law Institute (ALI) undertook to develop a body of unique principles of law that would address every aspect of the electronic funds transfer process and define the rights and liabilities of all parties involved in such transfers. After extensive investigation and debate and through a number of drafts, in 1989, both the NCCUSL and the ALI approved a new article 4A of the Uniform Commercial Code. In 1990, the New York State Legislature adopted the new article 4A and incorporated it into the New York Uniform Commercial Code (N.Y. UCC art. 4–A). Although the new statute, which became effective January 1, 1991, may not be applied retroactively to resolve the issues presented by this litigation, the statute's legislative history and the history of article 4A of the Uniform Commercial Code from which it is derived and the policy considerations addressed by this legislation, can appropriately inform our decision . . . .

Both the NCCUSL and ALI drafters of article 4A and the New York Legislature sought to achieve a number of important policy goals through enactment of this article. National uniformity in the treatment of electronic funds transfers is an important goal, as are speed, efficiency, certainty (*i.e.*, to enable participants in fund transfers to have better understanding of their rights and liabilities), and finality. Establishing finality in electronic fund wire transactions was considered a singularly important policy goal. Payments made by electronic funds transfers in compliance with the provisions of article 4A are to be the equivalent of cash payments, irrevocable except to the extent provided for in article 4A.

This concern for finality in business transactions has long been a significant policy consideration in this State. . . .

A consequence of this concern has been the adoption of a rule which precludes recovery from a third person, who as the result of the mistake of one or both of the parties to an original transaction receives payment by one of them in good faith in the ordinary course of business and for a valuable consideration. This rule is grounded in "considerations of public policy and convenience for the protection and encouragement of trade and commerce by guarding the security and certainty of business transactions, since to hold otherwise would obviously introduce confusion and danger into all commercial dealings" (44 NY Jur., Payment, § 107).

The "discharge for value" rule is consistent with and furthers the policy goal of finality in business transactions and may appropriately be applied in respect to electronic funds transfers. When a beneficiary receives money to which it is entitled and has no knowledge that the money was erroneously wired, the beneficiary should not have to wonder whether it may retain the funds; rather, such a beneficiary should be able to consider the transfer of funds as a final and complete transaction, not subject to revocation.

We believe such an application accords with the legislative intent and furthers the policy considerations underlying article 4A of the New York Uniform Commercial Code. Although no provision of article 4A calls, in express terms, for the application of the "discharge for value" rule, the statutory scheme and the language of various pertinent sections, as amplified by the Official Comments to the UCC, support our conclusion that the "discharge for value" rule should be applied in the circumstances here presented.

Subject to certain exceptions not here relevant, N.Y. UCC 4–A–209(2) provides that a beneficiary's bank accepts a payment order when the bank pays the beneficiary by crediting the beneficiary's account and notifying the beneficiary of the right to withdraw the credit. When a payment order has been accepted by the beneficiary's bank, cancellation or amendment of that payment order is not effective unless, for example, the order was issued because of a mistake of the sender resulting in a duplicate payment order or an order that directs payment to a beneficiary not entitled to receive the funds. Where a duplicate payment order is erroneously executed or the payment order is issued to a beneficiary different from the beneficiary intended by the sender, the receiving bank in either case is entitled to recover the erroneously paid amount from the beneficiary "to the extent allowed by the law governing mistake and restitution."

More specifically, UCC 4–A–303(3) instructs that "[i]f a receiving bank executes the payment order of the sender by issuing a payment order to a beneficiary different from the beneficiary of the sender's order and the funds transfer is completed on the basis of that error, the sender . . . [is] not obliged to pay the payment order[.] The issuer of the erroneous order is entitled to recover from the beneficiary . . . to the extent allowed by the law governing mistake and restitution." The Official Comment to UCC 4A–303 from which the identical New York statute is derived, explains that although section 4A–402(c) obligates the sender to pay the transfer order to the beneficiary's bank if that bank has accepted the payment order, section 4A–303 takes precedence and "states the liability of the sender and the rights of the receiving bank in various cases of erroneous execution."

Thus, as in the example discussed in comment 2, where the originator's bank mistakenly directs payment of $2,000,000 to the beneficiary's bank but payment of only $1,000,000 was directed by the originator, the originator's bank is obligated to pay the $2,000,000 if the beneficiary's bank has accepted the payment, although the originator need only pay its bank the $1,000,000 ordered. The originator's bank ordinarily would be entitled to recover the excess payment from the beneficiary. The comment points out, however, that "if Originator owed $2,000,000 to Beneficiary and Beneficiary received the extra $1,000,000 in good faith in discharge of the debt, Beneficiary may be allowed to keep it. In this case Originator's Bank has paid an obligation of Originator and under the law of restitution . . . Originator's Bank would be subrogated to Beneficiary's rights against Originator on the obligation paid by Originator's Bank." . . .

Although it seems clear from these provisions of article 4A and the Official Comments that the drafters of UCC article 4A contemplated that the "discharge for value" rule could appropriately be applied in respect to electronic fund transfers, Security Pacific argues that to do so would undermine the low cost structure of wholesale electronic fund transfers and impose extraordinary risks upon banks implementing these enormously large transactions. This argument is unpersuasive. Article 4A contemplates, in the first instance, that a mistake such as occurred here can be effectively held to a minimum through the utilization of "commercially reasonable" security procedures in effecting wire transfers. These security procedures are for the purpose of verifying the authenticity of the order or detecting error in the transmission or content of the payment order or other communication. . . .

Application of the "discharge for value" rule to the circumstances presented here is particularly appropriate. The undisputed facts demonstrate that Security Pacific executed Spedley's initial order directing payment to Banque Worms notwithstanding having already received a cancellation of that order. The District Court also found that the second transfer to Natwest USA was executed despite the fact that Spedley's account did not have sufficient funds to cover this second transfer. Moreover, it appears that, as a creditor of Spedley, Banque Worms was a beneficiary entitled to the funds who made no "misrepresentation and did not have notice of the transferor's mistake."

Accordingly, we conclude, in answer to the certified question, that the "discharge for value" rule as set forth at section 14 of the Restatement of Restitution, should be applied in the circumstances in this case. . . .

Paramount Film Distributing Corp. v. State

Court of Appeals of New York, 1972.
30 N.Y.2d 415.

■ BREITEL, JUDGE. Claimant, a motion picture distributor, seeks recovery of $128,322.50 in motion picture license fees paid to the State from June 10, 1959 to June 10, 1965 when the applicable statutes were nullified. [The New York Court of Appeals declared the statutes void after the United States Supreme Court invalidated a similar Maryland statute on the ground that the statute did not provide for prompt judicial review of licensing decisions.] The fee for original films was $3.50 for each 1,000 feet of film while the fee for copies was $3 plus an additional dollar for each 1,000 feet. Although over a six-year period the fees aggregate an impressive sum, the fee per motion picture distributed in New York was only an inconsiderable expense compared to the cost of production, most often less than $10. Claimant had paid all but a trivial portion of the fees without protest and had not otherwise ever resisted the statutory procedure for licensing or the payment of fees. . . .

A majority at the Appellate Division sustained claimant's right to recover all fees paid since 1959. While $128,322.50 plus interest is now involved, other cases pending bring the claims to just under $2,000,000.

As posed by the parties, the issue is whether the payments of the license fees were voluntary, or involuntary under duress entitling the payor to recover, albeit the payments were made without protest or other action to resist the payments or to recover them.

Two leading New York cases mark clearly when there is a right to recover unprotested taxes or fees.

In Mercury Machine Importing Corp. *v.* City of New York, 3 N.Y.2d 418, this court, over vigorous dissent it is true, held that corporate taxpayers who voluntarily paid an illegally levied tax without protest were not entitled to refunds although the statute under which the taxes were paid was subsequently held unconstitutional. The fulcrum of the determination was the relatively new section of the Civil Practice Act which provided that a mistake being one of law for that reason alone did not forbid recovery for mistake. The taxpayers had made a mistake of law, namely, as to the validity of the taxing statute, but it was held that the mistake did not render the payment involuntary. It was pointed out that in a sense no tax is paid willingly, free from the coercion of law. The precedents were collated and classified and it is unnecessary to repeat what was done there.

In Five Boro Electrical Contractors Association *v.* City of New York, 12 N.Y.2d 146, this court again in an opinion by Judge Van Voorhis, who had written for the court in the *Mercury* case, but this time with unanimous concurrence of the court, permitted the recovery of license fees paid under a city local law without protest by licensed electricians. The distinction was made that the payments then in question were involuntary and under duress, because the electricians would otherwise have been barred from engaging in their occupations. The court held that protest was not required "under the circumstances of this case . . . in view of the compulsory nature of the payment of these exorbitant license fees." Most important, the fees themselves had been the subject of a previous successful attack and the exaction declared unconstitutional because the amounts bore no reasonable relation to the licensing and regulation of electricians under a nonrevenue statute. Again the same authorities cited in the *Mercury* case were reviewed and the distinctions there made repeated to explain the difference in result between the two cases.

The *Mercury* and *Five Boro* cases are not aberrational. They conform generally with distinctions made throughout the country between voluntary and involuntary payments of taxes or fees later declared void, and the necessity for protest in the case of voluntary payments.

Applying the distinctions to this case, the payments by claimant were voluntary, and in the absence of protest at the time, claimant is not entitled to recover the fees it paid just because in a collateral matter on grounds not applicable to it or ever raised by it, the statute has been declared null.

The test of voluntariness in cases involving taxes and fees is sometimes elusive and difficult of application. As noted earlier by Judge Van Voorhis, all taxes and fees in a sense are paid "involuntarily." The difference is often, if not always, one of degree and turns on many factors, including the right of taxing authorities to rely on objection if there be resistance to payment, the likelihood that authentic resistance will be asserted, the unavoidable drastic impact of the taxes or fees on the claimant, and the impact on the public fisc, if revenues raised long ago and expended are subject to reimbursement. Surely one would expect motion picture distributors, and especially a corporation as large as claimant with its staff of lawyers, to protest if the fees were thought illegal. Indeed, the failure to protest indicates that there was no authentic resistance to making the minimal payments for the extensive procedures in licensing motion pictures whose gross yield would be massive compared to the trivial fees imposed.

Moreover, the fees as such have never been held illegal or excessive but on the contrary sustained, and the regulatory services which the fees financed have long ago been rendered and the cost undoubtedly passed on to the patrons of the films. . . . [The license] requirements were overturned because of the invalid procedure under the statute. . . . Notably, in the *Freedman* case [invalidating the Maryland statute] the Supreme Court reiterated its prior holdings that motion pictures were properly subject to licensing and the payment of license fees. . . .

What has been said so far assumes, as the parties have assumed, that restitution is appropriate unless it can be shown that claimant paid its license fees voluntarily. But, if general principles of restitution were to be reached, even if one assumes involuntary or coerced payment, those general principles do not support restitution.

The essential inquiry in any action for unjust enrichment or restitution is whether it is against equity and good conscience to permit the defendant to retain what is sought to be recovered. Such a claim is undoubtedly equitable and depends upon broad considerations of equity and justice. Generally, courts will look to see if a benefit has been conferred on the defendant under mistake of fact or law, if the benefit still remains with the defendant, if there has been otherwise a change of position by the defendant, and whether the defendant's conduct was tortious or fraudulent.

It is difficult to say that the State has received any benefit, let alone unjust enrichment. The fees defrayed the cost of the licensing program, a program which, at least, was intended to further the interests of both the industry and the public. The statute was not a revenue measure, and, *inter alia,* it exacted a regulatory fee to support the program. The difference between regulatory fees and revenue imposts, the latter including unauthorized excessive regulatory fees paid involuntarily, also distinguishes this case from the *Five Boro* case.

Moreover, the funds have been disbursed long ago. Nor has the State acted tortiously or fraudulently in exacting the fees. . . . That the exactions were themselves proper and not tortious, fraudulent, or illegal, and that they have been consumed is significant. Generally, if a plaintiff's recovery will lead to an undue net loss to a defendant by reason of a changed position, as will often be the case when the funds have been disbursed, then the parties being equally innocent, recovery may be denied.

In summary, the payment of license fees without protest was voluntary for purposes of recovery of moneys paid as fees or taxes; hence, no recovery for the fees collected without protest or other resistance may be allowed. Since a small percentage of fees were paid under protest between March and June, 1965, the matter should be remanded so that such fees may be computed, and recovery allowed. . . .

■ BERGAN, JUDGE (dissenting). . . . This court's [prior decision] was a determination that the entire statute "is null and void," a decision embracing the fee provisions. This much must be said about the belief of the majority that the fees as such have never been held illegal. . . .

What seems decisive in the majority's summation of the grounds for decision here is that claimant's "payment of license fees without protest was voluntary for purposes of recovery of moneys paid as fees or taxes." On this aspect of the case, at least, *Five Boro* appears to be indistinguishable and it should be overruled or followed. The need for protest, and not the uses to which the fees were put, was decisive in *Five Boro*. The rule for licensed electricians and licensed motion picture exhibitors should be pretty much the same.

Thus the difference between regulatory fees and revenue imposts played no part in the announced reasons for decision in *Five Boro* and is not a ground to distinguish the present case. . . .

That the State used the proceeds of the license fees collected under the statute in the licensing operation itself does not for the purposes of this case distinguish it from one where the fee or tax is used for general State purposes. Here the program of inspection and licensing expressed in the statute was responsive to the State's belief in the value of censorship to protect public morals and elevate public taste, and so in furtherance of a general public policy. No benefit to the business of motion picture exhibitors was intended or demonstrated in the experience with censorship. . . .

It is true, as the majority has observed, that an action for recovery for unjust enrichment or restitution should appeal to equity and good conscience and this principle ought to apply to an action such as the present one.

Here the good conscience in issue is that of the sovereign which collected the fees under the compulsion of a statute which the sovereign State itself, by its highest court, advisedly held to be "null and void." It seems the part of fair dealing to turn the money back.

The sum is large for the taxpayers as well as the State. As Judge Fuld noted in dissent in *Mercury*: "Modern and enlightened tax administration frowns upon the imposition of technical obstacles to the refunding of illegally collected taxes." . . .

NOTE

Most courts have reached similar results, reasoning either that the taxpayer paid the tax voluntarily or that the taxpayer has no claim because the taxpayer's mistake was a mistake of law. Why?

The Restatement (Third) of Restitution and Unjust Enrichment proposes to reverse the standard outcome:

> "(1) . . . [T]he payment of tax by mistake, or the payment of a tax that is erroneously or illegally assessed or collected, gives the taxpayer a claim in restitution against the taxing authority as necessary to prevent unjust enrichment. . . .
>
> "(2) If restitution pursuant to subsection (1) would disrupt orderly fiscal administration or result in severe public hardship, the court may on that account limit the relief to which the taxpayer would otherwise be entitled."

Restatement (Third) of Restitution and Unjust Enrichment § 19 (2011).

B. UNSOLICITED BENEFITS

Trott v. Dean Witter & Co.

United States District Court, New York, 1977.
438 F.Supp. 842.

■ LASKER, DISTRICT JUDGE. [Trott, attempting to recover money misappropriated from his employer, became acquainted with Franzese, a Dean Witter employee engaged in a misappropriation scheme involving diversion of funds to fictitious accounts. Franzese invited Trott to participate in the scheme. Trott agreed, fearing reprisals if he refused and planning to reveal the scheme after amassing sufficient evidence of the fraud. In the meantime, Trott said nothing to Dean Witter.

[In pursuance of the plan, Franzese issued checks payable by Dean Witter in the amount of $275,000. Trott then notified the Federal Bureau of Investigation, which asked him to continue to cooperate with Franzese while the FBI gathered evidence. Ultimately, the FBI intervened, Franzese was convicted based in part on Trott's testimony, and the money was returned to Dean Witter. Trott sued Dean Witter on a theory of restitution to recover the value of his services in uncovering the fraud. The court denied relief.]

[Dean Witter] argues that Trott was merely a volunteer and cannot be awarded relief in quasi-contract. Certainly no consensual agreement was present here, and Trott's situation does not meet the standards set out in the Restatement relating to quantum meruit recovery when consent is not present. He cannot claim that it was "reasonably necessary" for him to render his services "before it was possible to communicate" with Dean Witter since a period of over two months elapsed from the time Trott joined the plan until the company was alerted. The cases he cites indicate that a greater practical obstacle to communication is intended by this provision than Trott's subjective fear that his story was not credible or that he would be endangered. Nor can we accept Trott's claim that he had "no reason to believe that the owner did not desire him so to act," since Dean Witter points out, with good reason, that the prolongation of the scheme, which represented to plaintiff a chance for federal protection and a reward, placed the company in great danger. While we sympathize with the anxiety felt by Trott upon being confronted with the Franzeses' scheme, we find, as a matter of law, that the course of action which he chose to follow is not one which permits recovery in quantum meruit.

In reaching this conclusion, we reject plaintiff's claim that he cannot be considered an officious intermeddler because he acted during an emergency. Whether an emergency exists cannot be measured from the subjective standpoint of one of the parties, as Trott suggests, and we do not agree that his only alternative upon learning of the scheme was to cooperate with it. It is inconceivable that Dean Witter would have turned a deaf ear to information involving a potential loss of vast amounts of money. And, even if Trott were justified in thinking that the threat of violence from the Franzeses was enough, by itself, to create an emergency, this situation was of plaintiff's own creation in pursuing his acquaintance with the two men independently of any action by Dean Witter. At the least, he could have gone to the F.B.I. as he later did. . . .

Defendant's motion for summary judgment is granted.

Owen v. Tate

Court of Appeal, 1974.
[1976] Q.B. 402.

■ SCARMAN, L.J. . . . I can take the facts from the very succinct statement to be found in the county court judge's judgment. He said:

> "On February 26, 1965, the defendants obtained a loan from Lloyds Bank, Sunderland. This loan was secured by a charge by way of legal mortgage upon the property of a Miss Lightfoot. The plaintiff was in no way concerned with this transaction, and received no money from the defendants. In 1969 Miss Lightfoot became concerned that her deeds were being held by the bank to secure the defendants' loan. She consulted the plaintiff, who offered to help her to get her deeds back. Miss Lightfoot was a former employee of the plaintiff. The plaintiff knew that Miss Lightfoot had cohabited with a Mr. Russell, who had had a dispute with the defendants concerning money. Mr. Russell is now deceased. In order to oblige Miss Lightfoot, and in order to obtain her deeds and keep them in a safe place, the plaintiff deposited £350 with Lloyds Bank and signed a form of guarantee by which he guaranteed payment of all money, limited to £350, due, owing or incurred to Lloyds Bank by the defendants. He did not consult the defendants before doing this. He was not asked to do this by the defendants. His motive was only to help Miss Lightfoot. He did not speak to the defendants at all about the matter. On December 17, 1970, Lloyds Bank applied £350, held by them in support of the plaintiff's said guarantee, in repayment of the defendants' debt. On January 15, 1971, the plaintiff's solicitor demanded from the defendants reimbursement of this sum. The defendants refused and the battle was joined. . . ."

I turn to consider the law. As I understand the law, there are two general rules, both of them well known. The first is conveniently set out in CHITTY ON CONTRACTS . . . : "[i]f the payment is regarded by the law as voluntary, it cannot be recovered." . . .

The second general rule [holds that] . . . :

> ". . . one man, who is compelled to pay money which another is bound by law to pay, is entitled to be reimbursed by the latter."

This appeal requires us to consider the interaction of the two rules in the particular circumstances of this case. . . . I would add that neither rule can be treated as one to which there can conceivably be no exception. The first rule, that a volunteer who makes a payment on behalf of another cannot obtain repayment, does appear to me to have been one to which over the centuries the common law recognised exceptions. The exceptions have been constructed by the judges through a readiness to imply from the circumstances of the case a request or an authority to make the payment. . . .

When one turns to the second general rule, namely, the rule that where a person is compelled by law to make a payment for which another is primarily liable he is entitled to be indemnified, notwithstanding the lack of any request or consent, one again finds that the law recognises exceptions. This rule has been subjected to very careful treatment in Goff and Jones, THE LAW OF RESTITUTION (1966), p. 207. The authors say, after stating the rule in general terms:

> "To succeed in his claim, however, the plaintiff must satisfy certain conditions. He must show (1) that he has been compelled by law to make the payment; (2) that he did not officiously expose himself to the liability to make the payment; (3) that his payment discharged a *liability* of the defendant; and (4) that both he and the defendant were subject to a common demand by a third party, for which, as between the plaintiff and the defendant, the latter was primarily responsible."

In the present case we are very much concerned with the first two of those conditions: whether the plaintiff had been compelled by law to make the payment, and whether he did or did not officiously expose himself to the liability to make the payment. . . .

[A] broad approach is needed to the question whether in circumstances such as these a right of indemnity arises, and that broad approach requires the court to look at all the circumstances of the case. It follows that the way in which the obligation came to be assumed is a relevant circumstance. If, for instance, the plaintiff has conferred a benefit upon the defendant behind his back in circumstances in which the beneficiary has no option but to accept the benefit, it is highly likely that the courts will say that there is no right of indemnity or reimbursement. But (to take the other extreme) if the plaintiff has made a payment in a situation not of his own choosing, but where the law imposes an obligation upon him to make the payment on behalf of the principal debtor, then clearly the right of indemnity does arise. Not every case will be so clear-cut: the fundamental question is whether in the circumstances it was reasonably necessary in the interests of the volunteer or the person for whom the payment was made, or both, that the payment should be made—whether in the circumstances it was "just and reasonable" that a right of reimbursement should arise. . . .

Looking, therefore, at the circumstances as a whole, and giving weight to both phases of the transaction, I come to the conclusion that the plaintiff has failed to make out a case that it would be just and reasonable in the circumstances to grant him a right to reimbursement. Initially he was a volunteer; he has, as I understand the findings of fact of the judge and as I read the documents in the case, established no facts, either initially when he assumed the obligation, or later when he was called upon to make the payment, such as to show that it was just and reasonable that he should have a right of indemnity. I think, therefore, that on the facts as found this appeal fails.

In my judgment, the true principle of the matter can be stated very shortly, without reference to volunteers or to the compulsions of the law, and I state it as follows. If without an antecedent request a person assumes an obligation or makes a payment for the benefit of another, the law will, as a general rule, refuse him a right of indemnity. But if he can show that in the particular circumstances of the case there was some necessity for the obligation to be assumed, then the law will grant him a right of reimbursement if in all the circumstances it is just and reasonable to do so. In the present case the evidence is that the plaintiff acted not only behind the backs of the defendants initially, but in the interests of another, and despite their protest. When the moment came for him to honour the obligation thus assumed, the defendants are not to be criticised, in my judgment, for having accepted the benefit of a transaction which they neither wanted nor sought. . . .

NOTES ON BENEFITS CONFERRED WITHOUT REQUEST

1. Savage's building material accidentally fell into a river. Savage being absent, Glenn recovered it at his own expense. When Savage refused to compensate Glenn for this good deed, Glenn sued for the value of his and his employees' services. Glenn prevailed in the trial court, but its judgment was reversed on appeal. Glenn *v.* Savage, 14 Or. 567 (1887). The Oregon Supreme Court explained:

> "The facts enumerated . . . could not create a legal liability on the part of Savage. They may have been meritorious, and probably beneficial, to Savage, but this was not enough. To make him liable, he must either have requested the performance of the service, or, after he knew of the service, he must have promised to pay for it. The great and leading rule of law is to deem an act done for the benefit of another, without his request, as a voluntary act of courtesy, for which no action can be sustained. The world abounds with acts of this kind, done upon no request; but would more abound with ruinous litigation, and the overthrow of personal

> rights and civil freedom, if the law was otherwise. The law will never permit a friendly act, or such as was intended to be an act of kindness or benevolence, to be afterwards converted into a pecuniary demand. It would be doing violence to some of the kindest and best effusions of the heart to suffer them afterwards to be perverted by sordid avarice. Whatever differences may arise afterwards among men, let those meritorious and generous acts remain lasting monuments of the good offices, intended in the days of good neighborhood and friendship; and let no after-circumstances ever tarnish or obliterate them from the recollection of the parties. So, in Bartholomew *v.* Jackson, 20 Johns. 28, it is said: 'The plaintiff performed the service without the privity or request of the defendant, and there was, in fact, no promise express or implied. If a man humanely bestows his labor, and even risks his life, in voluntarily aiding to preserve his neighbor's house from destruction by fire, the law considers the service rendered as gratuitous, and it therefore forms no ground of action.' "

Id. at 577–78.

2. Harrison was unconscious as a result of a street car accident. Doctors contacted by a spectator tried, unsuccessfully, to save his life. They then sued Cotnam, Harrison's administrator, for the value of their services. The Arkansas Supreme Court determined that restitution was proper: doctors and nurses who provide services for patients who are unable to contract for service have a claim in quasi-contract. Cotnam *v.* Wisdom, 83 Ark. 601 (1907).

Seegers v. Sprague

Supreme Court of Wisconsin, 1975.
70 Wis.2d 997.

■ HANLEY, JUSTICE. The sole issue on this appeal is whether the contractor here may recover the value of goods and services rendered to a general contractor property owner.

The key paragraph in Seegers' complaint was:

> "That on or about the 13th day of October, 1970 at the special instance and the request of the defendant, plaintiffs agreed to furnish certain materials and labor to wit: . . ."

With a further allegation that the agreed labor and materials necessary for septic systems were furnished, demand was made for their value.

The trial court adopted the allegations of the complaint as its findings of fact. Implicit in Sprague's argument on appeal, however, is the contention that the Seegers were always subcontractors of Keller and were without privity to Sprague, contrary to the conclusion accepted by the court.

Defendant Sprague places heavy reliance on Utschig *v.* McClone, 16 Wis.2d 506 (1962), for the proposition that a subcontractor cannot obtain direct relief against a property owner without an express contract. *Utschig* acknowledged that the subcontractor may avail himself of a construction lien, but his primary remedy was to proceed against the main contractor who employed him. No attempt was made to prove an express contract between Sprague and the Seegers. The lien remedy has been terminated. Further, contractor Keller is "among the missing." This was brought out through the testimony of Sprague. Apparently some dispute over Keller's workmanship had arisen and he had commenced suit. Sprague counterclaimed, seemingly for the costs of defective work. The absence of Keller has suspended that action. Sprague claimed, however, to have paid Keller for the septic systems.

The latter testimony is argued as defeating the Seegers' claim which is denominated by Sprague as "unjust enrichment." *Utschig* had contained language that an owner is not liable on an implied contract simply because he received subcontractors services, but did not state that such theory would be unsuccessful under all circumstances. . . .

Respondents claim to avoid [precedents] restricting unjust enrichment by denying that this theory was involved. They reiterate that the action is on quantum meruit. They also deny that the evidence establishes that they were subcontractors. . . .

In an oral decision after the trial, the court stated:

> "Well, there is conflicting testimony in the matter concerning Mr. Sprague's contact with one or both of the Seegers Brothers prior to commencement . . . . Eugene Seegers testified that he saw Mr. Sprague on the job and discussed with him the change in the size of the tanks. . . . It would lead the court to believe that Mr. Sprague was aware that some person other than Mr. Keller, the plumber, was installing the septic system. . . ."

Awareness of the subcontractor and his work does not establish unjust enrichment, but is an essential element of recovery. The above quoted language, read in connection with the findings, indicates that the court found some privity contact but did not find that [the] Seegers were "in the position of contractors with Donald Sprague" as the respondents would hope. . . .

In reviewing the English law of implied in law contracts or quasi-contract, one treatise noted that the current basis for indebitatus assumpsit, quantum meruit and quantum valebat could be summarized by one theory:

> "Quasi-contractual claims are, therefore, those which fall within the scope of the actions for money had and received or for money paid, or of *quantum meruit* or *quantum valebat* [as much as it is worth] claims, and which are founded upon the principle of unjust enrichment. . . ." Goff & Jones, LAW OF RESTITUTION 4 (1966).

American cases also recognize this relationship:

> "A prominent characteristic of the concept of quantum meruit is as a device for the prevention of unjust enrichment of one party at the expense of another." In re Taylor's Estate, 132 N.Y.S.2d 686, 689 (1954).

The full spectrum of quasi-contract law, specifically including quantum meruit has apparently been long recognized by one state as grounded in the doctrine of unjust enrichment. Brown *v.* Thornton, 150 Mont. 150 (1967) and cases cited therein.

This interrelationship in restitution theory has not gone unrecognized in Wisconsin. [In two cases] this court recognized that subcontractors may have a basis for recovery in the quasi-contract action of unjust enrichment. In Don Ganser & Assoc., Inc. *v.* MHI, Inc., 31 Wis.2d 212, 216–17 (1966)[, t]he elements of such action were listed as:

> ". . . (1) a benefit conferred upon the defendant by the plaintiff, (2) appreciation by the defendant of the fact of such benefit, and (3) acceptance and retention by the defendant of the benefit, under circumstances such that it would be inequitable to retain the benefit without payment of the value thereof."

. . . Respondent's desire to call their action quantum meruit and to frame their complaint in terms of language from cases following that theory by name does not avoid the clear decisional law that regards unjust enrichment as an element necessary for recovery in these circumstances.

As in *Utschig,* there is also a lack of proof that an *independent* request or invitation for their services was made by Sprague. Quantum meruit as a measure of recovery for an implied in fact contract would demand as much. An owner is not liable on a contract implied by the facts simply because he has received goods or services or knows that services have been rendered. . . .

The respondents' right to recover here rested on the theory denominated in past construction cases as unjust enrichment. . . . [N]o unjust enrichment has occurred here. Payments by Sprague to Keller to cover his work and the work of his subcontractors has not left Sprague enriched. The absence of payment to Seegers is due to Keller's actions.

Although Sprague was also a general contractor as well as owner, this status does not add distinguishment that makes the *Superior Plumbing* rationale inapplicable. The claimant there was a subcontractor once removed from the defendant, as are the Seegers here.

Under the circumstances of this case we conclude that it is inequitable to compel the owner to pay the Seegers after payment had been made to Keller. The owner had a right to rely upon his agreement with Keller. There was also no implied agreement to compensate the Seegers brothers. . . .

NOTE

What if Sprague had not paid Seegers?

Kossian v. American National Insurance Co.

Court of Appeal of California, Fifth District, 1967.
254 Cal. App. 2d 647.

■ STONE, ASSOCIATE JUSTICE. On February 19, 1964, fire destroyed a portion of the Bakersfield Inn, owned by one Reichert. At the time, the property was subject to a first deed of trust in which defendant was the beneficiary. Pursuant to the requirements of the deed of trust, defendant's interest in the property was protected by policies of fire insurance. On March 16, 1964, Reichert, as owner in possession, entered into a written contract with plaintiff whereby plaintiff agreed to clean up and remove the debris from the fire damaged portion of the Inn for the sum of $18,900. Defendant had no knowledge of the execution of the agreement between plaintiff and Reichert.

Plaintiff commenced work in the middle of March 1964, and completed it in early April. During the entire time work was in progress Reichert was in possession of the premises as owner, although defendant caused a notice of Reichert's default under the deed of trust to be filed four days after the contract for demolition was entered into between plaintiff and Reichert. The record does not reflect that plaintiff had actual knowledge of the notice of default until after the work was completed.

Some time after plaintiff had fully performed the contract, Reichert filed a petition in bankruptcy. The trustee in bankruptcy abandoned the premises comprising the Bakersfield Inn, together with any interest in the four fire insurance policies up to the amount of $424,000. Each policy contained a provision insuring against the cost of cleaning up and removing debris caused by fire damage.

Following abandonment of the policies by the trustee in bankruptcy, Reichert and his wife assigned their interest in them to defendant in accordance with the terms of the deed of trust. Defendant submitted proofs of loss, claiming a total of $160,000, including the sum of $18,000 as the estimated cost for removing and cleaning up debris. These claims were rejected by the carriers; negotiations followed; the compromise figure of $135,620 was agreed upon and this amount paid to defendant. We do not have an itemization of the adjusted claims of loss upon which the compromised loss settlement was made, so that the record is not clear as to what part of the $18,900 cost of debris removal defendant received. It is clear, however, that the insurance payment included at least a part of the cost of debris removal and demolition.

Defendant demonstrates, by a careful analysis of the facts, that there was no direct relationship between plaintiff and defendant in regard to either the work performed on the property after the fire or in relation to the fire insurance policies. The contract for debris removal was between plaintiff and Reichert, and defendant did not induce plaintiff, directly or indirectly, to enter into that contract. Plaintiff had no lien against the property resulting from his work, and if he had such a lien it would have been wiped out by defendant's foreclosure of its first deed of trust.

Had the circumstances been simply that defendant, by foreclosure, took the property improved by plaintiff's debris removal, there would be a benefit conferred upon defendant by plaintiff, but no unjust enrichment. It is the additional fact that defendant made a claim to the insurance carriers for the value of work done by plaintiff that is the nub of the case.

Defendant argues that plaintiff was not a party to the insurance contracts, while defendant had a contract right to collect indemnity for losses resulting from the fire, including the debris removal cost. This contract right was embodied in the insurance policies. Defendant relies upon Russell *v.* Williams, 58 Cal.2d 487, where it is said:

> "It is a principle of long standing that a policy of fire insurance does not insure the property covered thereby, but is a personal contract indemnifying the insured against loss resulting from the destruction of or damage to his interest in that property. This principle gives rise to the supplemental rule that, in the absence of a special contract, the proceeds of a fire insurance policy are not a substitute for the property the loss of which is the subject of indemnity."

Defendant says it made no agreement, express or implied, with plaintiff that it would pay for the debris removal or that any part of the insurance proceeds would be applied for that purpose. Therefore, concludes defendant, there being no privity of relationship between it and plaintiff, and no fraud or deceit alleged or proved, defendant has the right to the property benefited by plaintiff's work and labor expended in removing the debris and to the insurance payments as well.

Plaintiff makes no claim to the insurance "fund" upon the ground he relied thereon similar to the reliance of a mechanic or materialman that forms the basis of an equitable claim to a building fund. He relies upon the basic premise that defendant should not be allowed to have the fruits of plaintiff's labor and also the money value of that labor. This, of course, is a simplified pronouncement of the doctrine of unjust enrichment, a theory which can, in some instances, have validity without privity of relationship. The most prevalent; implied-in-fact contract recognized under the doctrine of unjust enrichment is predicated upon a relationship between the parties from which the court infers an intent. However, the doctrine also recognizes an obligation *imposed* by law regardless of the intent of the parties. In these instances there need be no relationship that gives substance to an implied intent basic to the "contract" concept, rather the obligation is imposed because good conscience dictates that under the circumstances the person benefited should make reimbursement.

Plaintiff's claim does not rest upon a quasi contract implied in fact, but upon an equitable obligation imposed by law. It is true that defendant's right to the insurance payment was a contract right embodied in the policies of insurance . . . , nevertheless the indemnity payment was based in part upon a claim of loss that did not exist because plaintiff had already remedied the loss by his work for which he was not paid.

We are cited no California cases that are close aboard, and independent research reveals none. Lack of precedent applicable to the facts peculiar to this case is not surprising, however, as the authors of the Restatement recognize that the essential nature of equity cases concerned with problems of restitution makes definitive precedent unlikely. We are guided by the "Underlying Principles" delineated in the Restatement on Restitution:

> "The rules stated in the Restatement of this Subject depend for their validity upon certain basic assumptions in regard to what is required by justice in the various situations. In this Topic, these are stated in the form of principles. They cannot be stated as rules since either they are too indefinite to be of value in a specific case or, for historical or other reasons, they are not universally applied. They are distinguished from rules in that they are intended only as general guides for the conduct of the courts . . . ."

The governing principle is expressed in the opening sentence of the Restatement on Restitution, as follows:

> "The Restatement of this Subject deals with situations in which one person is accountable to another on the ground that otherwise he would unjustly benefit or the other would unjustly suffer loss."

The question, simply stated, is whether in a jurisdiction that recognizes the equitable doctrine of unjust enrichment one party should be indemnified twice for the same loss, once in labor and materials and again in money, to the detriment (forfeiture) of the party who furnished the labor and materials. We conclude that the doctrine of unjust enrichment is applicable to the facts of this case, and that plaintiff is entitled to reimbursement out of the insurance proceeds paid defendant for work done by plaintiff.

The facts concerning the amount of insurance recovered by defendant and the percentage of the total proof of loss attributable to plaintiff's work are not altogether clear, probably because this is a proceeding for summary judgment before trial of the action. In any event, it is clear that defendant, in addition to taking over the property which plaintiff cleared of debris, also received indemnity insurance payments covering at least part of the cost for clearing that property of debris. The amount can be made certain by a trial on the merits, and if it develops that defendant recovered only a part of the cost for debris removal, this fact does not preclude a partial recovery by plaintiff. We learn from the Restatement [§ 155(1)]:

> "Where a person is entitled to restitution from another because the other, without tortious conduct, has received a benefit, the measure of recovery for the benefit thus received is the value of what was received . . . ."

Thus, to the extent defendant received insurance for debris removal performed by plaintiff, plaintiff should recover. If defendant received less than the value of plaintiff's work, as defendant seems to contend, then plaintiff should recover *pro tanto*. . . .

Earhart v. William Low Co.

Supreme Court of California, 1979.
25 Cal.3d 503.

■ TOBRINER, JUSTICE. In this case we must determine whether a party who expends funds and performs services at the request of another, under the reasonable belief that the requesting party will compensate him for such services, may recover in quantum meruit although the expenditures and services do not directly benefit property owned by the requesting party. . . .

Plaintiff Fayette L. Earhart is the president and owner of Earhart Construction Company. For approximately two months in early 1971, plaintiff and defendant William Low, on behalf of defendant William Low Company, engaged in negotiations for the construction of the Pana Rama Mobile Home Park. These negotiations culminated in a construction contract which was to become binding when defendant obtained the requisite financing to build the park and when plaintiff secured a labor and material or performance bond for the work. Neither condition was ever fulfilled.

The proposed park was to cover a number of acres, some of which defendant owned, and the balance of which were owned by Ervie Pillow. In May 1971 defendant and Pillow entered into an escrow agreement in which Pillow agreed to sell her tract to defendant on the condition that defendant obtain financing for the mobile home park. According to plaintiff, a "special use permit" allowing the construction of a mobile home park on Pillow's land was of particular interest to defendant. Plaintiff claimed that the permit would expire on May 27, 1971, without possibility of renewal, unless work on the property were "diligently under way" by that date.

Plaintiff maintained that on May 25, 1971, defendant telephoned him to inform him that he had secured the necessary financing for the park, and, waiving all conditions to the contract, urged plaintiff to move equipment onto the property and commence work immediately in order to "save" the special use permit. Plaintiff's crew began work at once and continued to work for one week, often in the presence of defendant. On June 1, 1971, plaintiff submitted a progress bill to defendant and at that time learned that defendant had not secured the requisite financing. Defendant refused to pay plaintiff's bill, revealing that in the interim he had signed a construction contract for the park with another firm. . . .

At the conclusion of the trial, the court determined that plaintiff was entitled to recover from defendant on a theory of quantum meruit. . . .

In assessing the amount of the damages to which plaintiff was entitled under quantum meruit, however, the court limited plaintiff's recovery to the reasonable value of the work done on defendant's tract, declining to award damages for the reasonable value of services rendered in construction on the Pillow property. . . . [T]he trial court interpreted this court's decision in Rotea *v.* Izuel, 14 Cal.2d 605 (1939), as precluding plaintiff's recovery with respect to the work on the Pillow property. The court stated in this regard: "[I]t is an established proposition of law in California . . . that you can't get recovery for services furnished to a third person, even though the services were furnished at the request of the defendant. . . . So the plaintiff can't recover for services furnished Mrs. Pillow. . . . [E]ven though the plaintiff renders services or delivers a product, if it is of no value to the defendant, then the defendant doesn't pay for it. All he pays for is the value of what he got, notwithstanding how much it cost the plaintiff to produce it. That's the proper measure in this case." . . .

While the unfair receipt of a tangible benefit to the defendant may have inspired the common law courts to order restitution, the court in *Rotea* need not have interpreted the ancient principle of unjust enrichment so literally. Even under contemporary authorities, the court could have recognized, consistent with the orthodox principle of unjust enrichment, that a defendant who receives the satisfaction of obtaining another person's compliance with the defendant's request to perform services incurs an obligation to pay for labor and materials expended in reliance on that request.

Section 1 of the Restatement of Restitution, which predates the decision in *Rotea,* provides that "[a] person who has been unjustly enriched at the expense of another is required to make restitution to the other." (Rest., Restitution (1937) § 1.) A person is enriched if he has "received a benefit." (*Id.*, com. a., p. 12.) Furthermore, "[a] person confers a benefit upon another if he . . . performs services *beneficial to or at the request of the other*. . . ." (*Id.*, com. b., p. 12.) While the Restatement does not establish that performance of services at the request of another uniformly results in the unjust retention of "benefit," the Restatement recognizes, unlike the decision in *Rotea,* that performance of services at another's behest may itself constitute "benefit" such that an obligation to make restitution may arise. . . .

The determination to protect "justifiable reliance" . . . provides the basis for several parallel contractual doctrines as well. The first of these doctrines rests on the theory that "part performance" of an otherwise invalid contract may satisfy the purposes of the statute of frauds. Thus a court may award damages based on an unenforceable contract if unconscionable injury would result from denying enforcement after one party has been induced to make a serious change of position. Closely allied to the doctrine of part performance is the notion that reliance by one party on an oral contract may "estop" the other from setting up a defense based upon the statute of frauds.

Finally, section 90 of the Restatement of Contracts—the so-called "promissory estoppel" section—provides that reasonably expected reliance may under some circumstances make binding a promise for which nothing has been given or promised in exchange.[9] . . .

In view of the equitable considerations lying at the foundation of these several doctrines . . . , we conclude that compensation for a party's performance should be paid by the person whose request induced the performance. . . .

■ CLARK, JUSTICE, concurring and dissenting. . . . Neither principles of unjust enrichment nor of implied in fact contracts require imposing upon defendant an obligation to pay for improvement to the Pillow property in the circumstances before us.

Unjust enrichment presumes some benefit to the persons unjustly enriched sufficient to warrant implication of a promise to pay. . . .

In Rotea *v.* Izuel, 14 Cal.2d 605 (1939), it was held that an obligation will not be implied in law "where the direct benefit is received by a third party and the only benefit received by the defendant is the incidental benefit which he may find in the satisfaction of obtaining compliance with his request." Absent promise of payment, a person who does no more than request an attorney to consult with a potential client does not incur an obligation to pay the attorney for the consultation.

The same rule should apply where the only benefit obtained by the defendant from the requested performance is substantially similar to the benefit received by the plaintiff from the same act. The hitchhiker should not be held to have promised to pay for his ride in the absence of a promise to pay. He and the person providing the ride receive the same benefit from the ride. A defendant who has solicited bids should not be held to have promised to pay the expenses incurred in preparing the bids unless he has expressly promised to do so. The bid provides substantially

[9] Section 90 provides, "A promise which the promisor should reasonably expect to induce action or forbearance of a definite and substantial character on the part of the promisee and which does induce such action or forbearance is binding if injustice can be avoided only by enforcement of the promise." (Restatement, Contracts (1932) p. 110.)

the same benefit to the one who solicits and the bidder—the opportunity to enter into a contract. Absent express agreement to pay, the potential customer does not obtain a cause of action for services rendered when he accepts the retailer's request to examine his merchandise, nor does the salesman who responds to the potential customer's requests for assistance. Again, the benefits are substantially the same—the opportunity to consummate a transaction.

When the defendant receives benefits in addition to those received by the plaintiff or which are substantially different, unjust enrichment may be remedied through imposition of a duty to pay. But so long as the only benefits received by the defendant from plaintiff's conduct are substantially equivalent to those obtained by the plaintiff, mere compliance with a request is not a sufficient benefit to warrant imposition of such duty absent a promise to pay. Absent agreement to pay, it would be mere speculation to conclude the benefit to the defendant rather than the substantially equivalent benefit to plaintiff was the motivating force for plaintiff's performance.

The improvements made to the defendant company's property inured to the benefit of defendant company, and the trial court properly determined those improvements warranted imposition of a duty to pay their reasonable value. However, the improvements made to the Pillow property did not inure to the use and enjoyment of defendant company but to the owner of that property and recovery was properly denied.

In one respect plaintiff's performance on the Pillow property did confer a benefit to the defendant company which in other circumstances might warrant recovery. Defendant received an advantage comparable to the extension of time to perform a contract or exercise an option. If the use permit had lapsed, the value of defendant company's right to purchase the Pillow property would have been impaired. It is doubtful whether defendant company would have continued its search for financing, and whether potential lenders would still be interested in the project. The fact that defendant company did not ultimately acquire the Pillow property does not mean it failed to receive contractual advantage from plaintiff's activity in preserving the use permit. To the contrary, some benefit was realized through increasing the time for defendant company to obtain financing for its project.

However, plaintiff secured a substantially similar benefit from his performance. Plaintiff had a contract to build the mobile home park for $892,557.86 contingent upon defendant obtaining financing. If the use permit lapsed, it would be unlikely that the transaction would go forward. By commencing work to maintain the permit, thereby increasing the time to obtain financing, plaintiff also increased the likelihood that his contract would be effective. Because the benefits to plaintiff are substantially similar to those to defendant company, there is no unjust enrichment, and no basis for finding an implied in fact promise to pay. . . .

C. RESTITUTION AND CONTRACT

1. FAILED CONTRACTS

Renner v. Kehl

Supreme Court of Arizona, 1986.
150 Ariz. 94.

■ GORDON, VICE CHIEF JUSTICE. . . . In 1981 the petitioners, defendants below, acquired from the State of Arizona agricultural development leases covering 2,262 acres of unimproved desert land near Yuma. The petitioners made no attempt to develop the property themselves, but instead decided to sell their interest in the land. The respondents, plaintiffs below, were residents of the state of Washington interested in the large scale commercial cultivation of jojoba. The respondents and their agent, who was familiar with commercial jojoba development, were shown the petitioners' property and became interested in purchasing it. The property appeared to be ideal for the respondents' purposes; the soil and climate were good and both parties were of the opinion that sufficient water was available beneath the land to sustain jojoba production. The respondents made it clear that they were interested in the property only for jojoba production and required adequate water supplies.

The respondents decided to buy the leases and on June 5, 1981, executed a Real Estate Purchase Contract to that effect. Respondents agreed to pay $222,200 for the leases, and paid petitioners $80,200 as a down payment, the remainder to be paid in annual installments. In November of 1981 respondents began development of the property for jojoba production. As part of the development process the respondents had five test wells drilled, none of which produced water of sufficient quantity or quality for commercial jojoba cultivation. After spending approximately $229,000 developing the land respondents determined that the aquifer underlying the property was inadequate for commercial development of jojoba. At this point the project was abandoned and the respondents sued to rescind the purchase contract. . . .

The court found that the respondents were entitled to rescission based on mutual mistake of fact and failure of consideration, and ordered the respondents to reassign the lease to the petitioners. . . .

The trial court also ordered that petitioners pay the respondents $309,849.84 together with costs and attorney's fees. Of the $309,849.84 awarded to the respondents, $229,649.84 represents reimbursement of the costs borne by the respondents in developing the property for jojoba production. The petitioners challenge the $229,649.84 awarded as an improper grant of "consequential damages."

The court of appeals upheld the full award "[b]ecause the plaintiffs have not received a double recovery in the award of rescission and consequential damages. . . ." The appeals court relied upon Fousel *v.* Ted

Walker Mobile Homes, Inc., 124 Ariz. 126 (App. 1979), for the proposition that rescission can support an award of consequential damages.

In *Fousel* the plaintiffs purchased a mobile home from the defendants, who engaged in a series of misrepresentations which cost the plaintiffs considerable inconvenience and expense. The plaintiffs prevailed upon their claim for fraud and breach of contract and were awarded $2,705.26 in consequential damages and $10,000 in punitive damages. The court of appeals held that the doctrine of election of remedies does not necessarily bar an award of consequential or punitive damages, only "benefit of the bargain" damages. . . . The court quoted from [a prior case] wherein we stated that "[t]here is ample authority that a *defrauded* party may not only receive back the consideration he gave, but also may recover any sums that are necessary to restore him to his position prior to the making of the contract." Jennings *v.* Lee, 105 Ariz. 167, 173 (emphasis added).

In this case there was no breach of contract for fraud. We are dealing with a rescission based upon mutual mistake, which implies freedom from fault on the part of both parties. . . . The reliance of the court of appeals upon *Fousel* was misplaced; we hold that absent proof of breach for fraud or misrepresentation a party who rescinds a contract may not recover consequential damages. . . .

This does not mean, however, that the respondents are entitled only to recover their down payment. When a party rescinds a contract on the ground of mutual mistake he is entitled to restitution for any benefit that he has conferred on the other party by way of part performance or reliance. Restitutionary recoveries are not designed to be compensatory; their justification lies in the avoidance of unjust enrichment on the part of the defendant. Thus the defendant is generally liable for restitution of a benefit that would be unjust for him to keep, even though he gained it honestly. . . .

The first step determining the proper measure of restitution requires that the rescinding party return or offer to return, conditional on restitution, any interest in property that he has received in the bargain. In Arizona this includes reimbursement for the fair market value of the use of the property. . . . Thus the respondents were obliged to return the land to the petitioners in exchange for their down payment, and in addition to pay the petitioners the fair rental value of the land for the duration of their occupancy.

However, to avoid unjust enrichment the petitioners must pay the respondents a sum equal to the amount by which their property has been enhanced in value by the respondents' efforts. . . . Thus the petitioners must pay to the respondents that amount of money which represents the enhanced value of the land due to the respondents' development efforts. In short, the respondents are entitled to their down payment, plus the amount by which their efforts increased the value of the petitioners' property, minus an amount which represents the fair rental value of the land during their occupancy. They are not entitled to the $229,649.84 expended upon development, because that would shift the entire risk of mistake onto the petitioners, which is incompatible with equitable rescission. . . .

NOTES

1. The court said that consequential damages would shift the entire risk of mistake to the sellers. Is it preferable to place the entire risk on the buyers?

2. A few courts have allowed recovery in situations of this kind. For example: Scully employed Angus to move a building. Along the way, the building was destroyed by fire. Neither party was at fault for the fire and the contract did not assign the risk of fire. The court held that both parties were excused from their contractual obligations but Angus could recover for the reasonable value of services rendered in moving the building halfway:

> "[T]he rule may be said to be that where one is to make repairs or do any other work on the house of another under a special contract, and his contract becomes impossible of performance on account of the destruction of the house without any fault on his part, then he may recover for what he has done."

Angus *v.* Scully, 176 Mass. 357, 359 (1900).

Is this a special case?

The Restatement (Third) of Restitution and Unjust Enrichment suggests that compensation for losses may be appropriate in connection with rescission for mistake, impossibility, or frustration of purpose. Comments explain that in the context of unwinding a failed contract, the object of restitution is not simply to prevent unjust enrichment, but more generally to allocate losses in a fair way. See Restatement (Third) of Restitution and Unjust Enrichment § 34, cmt. *d* and Reporter's Note (2011).

Farash v. Sykes Datatronics, Inc.

Court of Appeals of New York, 1983.
59 N.Y.2d 500.

■ CHIEF JUDGE COOKE. Plaintiff claims that he and defendant entered an agreement whereby defendant would lease a building owned by plaintiff, who was to complete its renovation and make certain modifications on an expedited basis. Defendant, however, never signed any contract and never occupied the building. Plaintiff commenced this litigation, and defendant unsuccessfully moved to dismiss for failure to state a cause of action. On appeal, the Appellate Division reversed, with two Justices dissenting in part. For the reasons that follow, we now modify.

Plaintiff pleaded three causes of action in his complaint. The first was to enforce an oral lease for a term longer than one year. This is clearly barred by the Statute of Frauds (General Obligations Law, § 5–703, subd. 2). The third cause of action is premised on the theory that the parties contracted by exchanging promises that plaintiff would perform certain work in his building and defendant would enter into a lease for a term longer than one year. This is nothing more than a contract to enter into a lease; it is also subject to the Statute of Frauds. Hence, the third cause of action was properly dismissed.

Plaintiff's second cause of action, however, is not barred by the Statute of Frauds. It merely seeks to recover for the value of the work performed by plaintiff in reliance on statements by and at the request of defendant. This is not an attempt to enforce an oral lease or an oral agreement to enter a lease, but is in disaffirmance of the void contract and so may be maintained. That defendant did not benefit from plaintiff's efforts does not require dismissal; plaintiff may recover for those efforts that were to his detriment and that thereby placed him in a worse position. "The contract being void and incapable of enforcement in a court of law, the party . . . rendering the services in pursuance thereof, may treat it as a nullity, and recover . . . the value of the services."

The dissent's primary argument is that the second cause of action is equivalent to the third, and so is also barred by the Statute of Frauds. It is true that plaintiff attempts to take the contract outside the statute's scope and render it enforceable by arguing that the work done was unequivocally referable to the oral agreement. This should not operate to prevent recovery under a theory of quasi contract as a contract implied by law, which "is not a contract at all but an obligation imposed by law to do justice even though it is clear that no promise was ever made or intended" (Calamari and Perillo, CONTRACTS [2d ed.], § 1–12, p. 19). Obviously, the party who seeks both to enforce the contract that is unenforceable by virtue of the Statute of Frauds and to recover under a contract implied in law will present contradictory characterizations. This, however, is proper in our courts where pleading alternative theories of relief is accepted. Moreover, the existence of any real promise is unnecessary; plaintiff's attempt to make his acts directly referable to the unenforceable contract simply is irrelevant.

The authorities all recognize that a promisee should be able to recover in the present situation. "[I]f the improvements made by the plaintiff are on land that is not owned by the defendant and in no respect add to his wealth, the plaintiff will not be given judgment for restitution of their value, even though he may have made such improvements in reliance upon the contract that the defendant has broken. For such expenditures as these in reliance on a contract, the plaintiff can get judgment only in the form of damages for consequential injury" (5 Corbin, CONTRACTS, p. 578). Thus, plaintiff may recover for those expenditures he made in reliance on defendant's representations and that he otherwise would not have made. The Restatement provides that an injured party who has not conferred a benefit may not obtain restitution, but he or she may "have an action for damages, including one for recovery based on . . . reliance" (Restatement, Contracts 2d, § 370, Comment *a*). "[T]he injured party has a right to damages based on his reliance interest, including expenditures made in preparation for performance or in performance, less any loss that the party in breach can prove with reasonable certainty the injured party would have suffered had the contract been performed" (Restatement, Contracts 2d, § 349). The Restatement recognizes an action such as is involved here (see Restatement, Contracts 2d §§ 139, 349, Comment *b*). . . .

As stated by Professor Williston (12 Williston, CONTRACTS [3d ed.] pp. 282–284, 286–287):

> "Again, even though the defendant's liability is imposed by law irrespective of the agreement of the parties, and may, therefore, be called quasi contractual, where the defendant is a wrongdoer the plaintiff may well be preferred, and if a complete restoration of the *status quo* or its equivalent is impossible the plaintiff should at least be replaced in as good a position as he originally was in, although the defendant is thereby compelled to pay more than the amount which the plaintiff's performance has benefitted him. . . .
>
> "That is, the law should impose on the wrongdoing defendant a duty to restore the plaintiff's former status, not merely to surrender any enrichment or benefit that he may unjustly hold or have received; although if the market value or, in the absence of a market value, the benefit to the defendant of what has been furnished exceeds the cost or value to the plaintiff, there is no reason why recovery of this excess should not be allowed.
>
> "These different possible situations, as has been said, have often been confused with one another, because the form of action in each of them was identical at common law—general assumpsit on a *quantum meruit or quantum valebat* count; and this tended to induce courts and others to inquire what is the rule of damages under such counts—a question not susceptible of a single answer."

A lesson in this area can be taken from Professors Calamari and Perillo: "The basic aim of restitution is to place the plaintiff in the same economic position as he enjoyed prior to contracting. Thus, unless specific restitution is obtained in Equity, the plaintiff's recovery is for the reasonable value of services rendered, goods delivered, or property conveyed less the reasonable value of any counter-performance received by him. The plaintiff recovers the reasonable value of his performance whether or not the defendant in any economic sense benefitted from the performance. The quasi-contractual concept of benefit continues to be recognized by the rule that the defendant must have received the plaintiff's performance; acts merely preparatory to performance will not justify an action for restitution. 'Receipt,' however, is a legal concept rather than a description of physical fact. If what the plaintiff has done is part of the agreed exchange, it is deemed to be 'received' by the defendant." (Calamari and Perillo, CONTRACTS [2d ed.], § 15–4, p. 574).

We should not be distracted by the manner in which a theory of recovery is titled. On careful consideration, it becomes clear that the commentators do not disagree in result, but only in nomenclature. Whether denominated "acting in reliance" or "restitution," all concur that a promisee who partially performs (*e.g.*, by doing work in a building or at an accelerated pace) at a promisor's request should be allowed to recover the fair and reasonable value of the performance rendered, regardless of the enforceability of the original agreement. . . .

■ JASEN, JUDGE (dissenting). Plaintiff's second cause of action alleges that "[p]laintiff, in reliance on statements made [by] the defendant and at its request, performed work, provided labor and material to the defendant" and that "[d]efendant has failed to compensate the plaintiff for monies and other expenses incurred by the plaintiff in preparing the property at 49 East Avenue to the defendants' needs," causing damage to the defendant in the amount of $400,000. . . .

The majority fails to specify the theory of recovery upon which it bases its conclusion that "plaintiff may recover for those efforts that were to his detriment and that thereby placed him in a worse position." Insofar as this conclusion is based upon quasi contract, it is incorrect for the well-established rule in this State is that in order for a plaintiff to recover under such a cause of action, he must demonstrate that the defendant was unjustly enriched by his efforts. The rule has been clearly set forth by this court and consistently followed: "[a] *quasi* or constructive contract rests upon the equitable principle that a person shall not be allowed to enrich himself unjustly at the expense of another. In truth it is not a contract or promise at all. It is an obligation which the law creates, in the absence of any agreement, when and because the acts of the parties or others have placed in the possession of one person money, or its equivalent, under such circumstances that in equity and good conscience he ought not to retain it, and which *ex aequo et bono* belongs to another." Since as the majority correctly points out, defendant did not benefit from plaintiff's efforts, no recovery under quasi contract may be had.

The "lesson" provided by Professors Calamari and Perillo, cited by the majority, is inapposite to the case before us because section 15–4 of their text deals exclusively with actions based on breach while plaintiff does not allege in his second cause of action that defendant breached any agreement. Additionally, I note that insofar as this statement would allow recovery by the plaintiff under a theory of restitution, even though the defendant has not been benefited by any of plaintiff's efforts, such is not the law in New York. The majority itself concedes this point in stating, "an injured party who has not conferred a benefit may not obtain restitution." Moreover, assuming *arguendo* the accuracy of the legal principle stated by Calamari and Perillo, this principle does not accord relief to the plaintiff in the instant appeal. As the two professors correctly note, "the defendant must have received the plaintiff's performance; acts merely preparatory to performance will not justify an action for restitution." First, defendant received nothing from the plaintiff, as the majority accurately points out. Second, plaintiff's acts in renovating his building were "merely preparatory to performance" of the alleged oral contract whereby plaintiff and defendant agreed to enter into a two-year lease. Thus, even if section 15–4 were applicable, plaintiff would not be entitled to the relief which the majority is offering.

I also fail to see how sections 998 and 1011 of Corbin's treatise and sections 349 and 370 of the Restatement of Contracts, Second, support the majority's position. Corbin's discussion of reliance damages in sections 998 and 1011 (like Calamari and Perillo's) is concerned solely with a remedy available to a plaintiff injured by a defendant who has *breached a contract.* Since there was no such contract entered into by the parties here, and accordingly no breach thereof, those sections of Corbin's text do not even address the issue involved here.

Similarly, the Restatement lends no support to the majority's view. While it is true that section 370 would allow a party to maintain "an action for damages, including one for recovery based on . . . reliance," a reading of the entire section, *including its cite to section 349 as the sole authority for this proposition,* makes clear that such an action is based strictly on a theory of promissory estoppel, a theory which, as is discussed more fully below, has never been asserted by the parties and which this court has heretofore declined to adopt.[i]

The majority also mistakenly relies on a quote from section 349 of the Restatement of Contracts, Second—"[T]he injured party has a right to damages based on his reliance interest, including expenditures made in preparation for performance or in performance, less any loss that the party in *breach* can prove with reasonable certainty the injured party would have suffered had the *contract* been performed" (emphasis supplied). This passage, by its very terms, deals solely with remedies available where a party has breached an existing contract. Plaintiff, however, does not allege in his second cause of action the existence of any contract. Nor does he allege that defendant committed any breach. In the majority's view, plaintiff's second cause of action is not based upon breach of contract, but, rather, "is in disaffirmance of the void contract." Thus, section 349 of the Restatement does not address the situation presented on this appeal and, accordingly, provides no support for the majority's position.

It appears that the majority, in holding that plaintiff can recover the value of his efforts expended in reliance on defendant's alleged statements, is recognizing a cause of action sounding in promissory

---

[i] [Section 370 reads as follows:

"Requirement That Benefit Be Conferred. A party is entitled to restitution under the rules stated in this Restatement only to the extent that he has conferred a benefit on the other party by way of part performance or reliance."]

estoppel. This is implicit in its reference to the Restatement of Contracts, Second, section 139 and section 349, Comment *b,* as support for its conclusion that "[t]he Restatement recognizes an action such as is involved here." Section 139 is quite simply one of the estoppel sections of the Restatement. (See Restatement, Contracts 2d, § 139, Comment *a*.). . . .

While the doctrine of promissory estoppel has been recognized and applied in certain cases, to do so here, where the issue has not been pleaded or addressed in the parties' affidavits and has neither been argued nor briefed, is ill-advised. . . .

In the absence of either a contract requiring defendant to pay for plaintiff's renovation or some evidence that defendant was unjustly enriched, thus allowing plaintiff to recover under a cause of action sounding in quasi contract, defendant should not be held potentially liable to plaintiff for such renovation costs. Accordingly, I would affirm the order of the Appellate Division.

NOTES

1. Did the court allow recovery for benefits conferred, or for losses incurred in reliance on the oral contract?

2. Is the case for allowing a reliance-based claim stronger in *Farash* than in *Renner*?

Bradkin v. Leverton

Court of Appeals of New York, 1970.
26 N.Y.2d 192.

■ CHIEF JUDGE FULD. . . . The complaint recites that the plaintiff, employed by H.L. Federman & Co. [Federman] to find corporations which needed financing, procured for his employer the business of financing Mauchly Associates, Inc. By a letter dated October 25, 1966, Federman acknowledged not only that the plaintiff had earned $10,000 for having arranged $200,000 worth of financing in Mauchly but, in addition, that he was "to receive 10% of [any] net profit" which it (Federman) might realize "[s]hould there be a second financing, or any other financing . . . concerning Mauchly in the year 1967." The complaint further recites that the defendant was an officer, director and nonvoting stockholder of Federman, that he became acquainted with Mauchly only through the plaintiff and that he knew or should have known that the plaintiff was to receive 10% of any profits derived from financing Mauchly. However, the complaint continues, solely through the "business relations between Mauchly and Federman created by the plaintiff," the defendant was enabled, without the plaintiff's knowledge, to "arrange private financing transactions" with Mauchly. The plaintiff, who learned of the defendant's actions later, charges that there was an implied promise by the defendant to pay the plaintiff 10% of his net profit—which amounted to more than

$1,000,000—and that, although "due demand" was made by him, the defendant refused to compensate him "out of the profit from his Mauchly financing." In a second cause of action, the plaintiff, claiming that he is entitled to 10% of the profits realized by the defendant, seeks an accounting. . . .

Although not admitting that the plaintiff introduced Mauchly to Federman or that he learned of Mauchly through the plaintiff in the first instance, the defendant does admit that some time in 1966, and again in January and June, 1967, he or his wife loaned Mauchly more than $200,000 and that he became a director of that corporation. He contends, however, that, even if there had been an agreement between him and the plaintiff, the Statute of Frauds renders it unenforceable since there was no writing; [and] that the complaint fails to state a cause of action since he, as an officer of Federman, was not individually liable under the plaintiff's agreement with Federman.

The court at Special Term granted the defendant's motion and dismissed the complaint. It was its view that, since the plaintiff was, in effect, seeking a "finder's fee," the Statute of Frauds required a writing signed by the defendant and that the letter from Federman did not remove the statute's bar. The Appellate Division affirmed the resulting order of dismissal without opinion. Two justices dissented; concluding that the complaint stated a cause of action in tort, they interpreted it "as alleging both a breach of the contract induced by the defendant and an interference by defendant in the performance of the contract."

We agree with the Appellate Division dissenters that the complaint should be upheld but we read it, as does its draftsman, as stating a cause of action in quasi contract.

Quasi contracts are not contracts at all, although they give rise to obligations more akin to those stemming from contract than from tort. The contract is a mere fiction, a form imposed in order to adapt the case to a given remedy. Briefly stated, a quasi-contractual obligation is one imposed by law where there has been no agreement or expression of assent, by word or act, on the part of either party involved. The law creates it, regardless of the intention of the parties, to assure a just and equitable result. . . .

Although there was no agreement between them, express or implied, the defendant received a benefit from the plaintiff's services under circumstances which, in justice, preclude him from denying an obligation to pay for them. As already noted, the plaintiff had, according to the complaint, introduced Mauchly to Federman and, under his written agreement with Federman, he was to receive from that party, in addition to an introduction fee of $10,000, "10% of [its] net profit" on a "second financing . . . concerning Mauchly in the year 1967." It was solely from this relationship, which the plaintiff had created between Federman and Mauchly, that the defendant's dealings with Mauchly arose. By intruding into the transaction set up by the plaintiff, the defendant made use of his corporate position to promote his own private interests. More specifically, when the plaintiff procured Mauchly for Federman, he fully performed his part of the contract with Federman and thereupon became entitled, without more, to 10% of any profit which that corporation would have realized from any further financing of Mauchly. Since the defendant, an officer and director of Federman, intruded into the transaction and took unto himself the Mauchly financing, he obtained the benefit of the plaintiff's labors and must compensate him for such services. . . .

A contract to pay a finder's fee must, of course, be in writing and, obviously, this requirement may not be avoided by an action for compensation in *quantum meruit.* However, the contract required to be in writing is one between the finder and the principal or employer with whom he has assertedly contracted and from whom he seeks compensation. . . .

Quite manifestly, the purpose of the statute is to protect against fraudulent dealings *between the finder and his employer,* not between the finder and a third party, such as the defendant before us. Since there is no danger of "unfounded and multiple claims for commissions" where a third party is concerned, the Statute of Frauds provides no defense to him. When . . . a finder's contract meets all the requirements of the statute, a third party may not "take over" that contract and then evade his obligation to the finder by relying upon the statute. This is precisely what the present defendant is attempting to do. Federman had promised in writing to pay the plaintiff a finder's fee on any Mauchly financing and, when the defendant took over the corporation's financing arrangements, he assumed its obligation to the plaintiff for commissions. He is not privileged to assert the defense of the statute, which would not have been available to Federman.

In sum, given the facts alleged, it would be against good conscience for the defendant to retain the benefits of the contract which the plaintiff made with the defendant's corporation without compensating the plaintiff for the services he fully performed pursuant to that contract. Accordingly, if the plaintiff proves the allegations of his complaint, he will be entitled to recover from the defendant, as damages, the amount which the defendant's corporation had obligated itself to pay him if there was a "second financing . . . concerning Mauchly." . . .

2. RESTITUTION AS A REMEDY FOR BREACH

Acme Mills & Elevator Co. v. Johnson

Court of Appeals of Kentucky, 1911.
141 Ky. 718.

■ CLAY, C. [In April, 1909, Johnson agreed to deliver 2000 bushels of wheat to Acme Mills at $1.03 per bushel, the wheat to be delivered when Johnson completed his summer threshing. Johnson finished threshing on

July 29, 1909, but failed to deliver wheat to Acme as agreed. The market value of wheat on July 29 was less than $100 per bushel. Acme presented evidence that, after entering into the contract with Acme, Johnson resold the wheat to Liberty Mills for $116 per bushel (and, presumably, delivered the threshed wheat to Liberty).]

In contracts for the delivery of personal property at a fixed time and at a designated place, the vendee is entitled to damages against the vendor for a failure to comply, and the measure of damages is the difference between the contract price and the market price of the property at the place and time of delivery. This principle of law is so well settled, not only in this state, but in all the courts of this country, that it is no longer open to discussion. There is no reason why this rule should not apply to the facts of this case. . . . Appellee was not required by his contract to deliver to appellant any particular wheat. Had he delivered other wheat of like quantity and quality, he would have complied with the contract. When he sold his wheat on July 14th or 15th for a price in excess of the contract price, and therefore failed to deliver to appellant wheat of the quantity and quality contracted for, he took the chances of being mulcted in damages for the breach of the contract. . . .

[I]t was . . . incumbent upon appellant to prove that it had been damaged. . . . As stated before, the evidence overwhelmingly established the fact-indeed, it is practically admitted-that the market price of wheat of the kind and quality contracted to be delivered at the time and place designated in the contract did not exceed $1 per bushel. That being true, appellant, instead of being damaged by the breach of the contract, was actually benefitted to the extent of about three cents per bushel. . . .

NOTES

1. Pursuant to a written contract, Oliver agreed to represent Campbell in a divorce action. Campbell was to pay a fee of $750 after the trial. The trial took 29 days. After the judge announced his intended decision, but before argument on proposed findings of fact and conclusions of law, Campbell discharged Oliver, stating that he would proceed *pro se* and that he refused to pay Oliver more than $450 he had already paid. Oliver then brought an action for restitution seeking $9,550, which, he claimed, represented the reasonable value of his services (less the $450 previously paid by Campbell). The trial court found that the reasonable value of Oliver's services was $5,000, but held that his recovery was limited by the contract. The California Supreme Court agreed. Ordinarily, when a client breaches a contract for legal services, the discharged lawyer may treat the contract as rescinded and sue for restitution of the value of services rendered. However, if the plaintiff has performed his part of the contract in full and the only performance due from the defendant is payment of the agreed price, the contract price sets a limit on recovery. Thus, because Oliver "had performed practically all of the services he was employed to perform when he was discharged," his recovery must be limited to $300. Oliver *v.* Campbell, 43 Cal.2d 298, 306–07 (1954).

2. Restitution is also available to a breaching party (usually as an offset against damages), if that party has conferred benefits on the party suing for breach. In this situation also, restitution is limited by the rate of compensation provided in the contract.

3. The plaintiff's restitution claim in *Acme Mills* was not for benefits conferred by the plaintiff's performance, but for benefits derived from the breach; the court's answer to the claim was no.

The Massachusetts Supreme Judicial Court reached a similar conclusion in Salter *v.* Beal, 321 Mass. 105, 109 (1947). A third-party seller offered Salter a used machine for $25,000. Salter hired Beal, a used machinery dealer, to evaluate the offer. Beal privately appraised the machine at $100,000, but advised Salter to offer $20,000, representing that this was a fair price. After the seller rejected Salter's offer, Beal bought the machine for $28,000.

The court determined that employment for purposes of a single appraisal did not establish a fiduciary relationship between Beal and Salter. In the absence of a fiduciary relation, Salter had no claim "unless possibly for damages for breach of contract, which so far as appears were nominal only. It does not appear that the plaintiffs could have or would have bought the machinery if the defendant Beal had fairly reported its value." *Id.*, 321 Mass. at 109.

With *Acme Mills* and *Salter*, compare the following case.

Ocor Products Corp. v. Walt Disney Productions, Inc.

United States District Court, District of New Hampshire, 1988.
682 F.Supp. 90.

■ DEVINE, CHIEF JUDGE. . . . Ocor, through its PAK 2000 division, manufactures polyethylene bags. Since 1976 plaintiff has been the exclusive importer of a bag with a plastic handle known as the "Model Oscar," designed by a French corporation, Decomatic, S.A. Since 1982 Ocor has held an exclusive license to manufacture and distribute the Model Oscar bag in the United States. The Model Oscar handle is a heavy-duty handle with a snap-style closure across the top of the bag, and the bag is typically resold at retail as a durable shopping bag.

In 1981 David Brown, a sales representative for PAK 2000, solicited an order from Disney for Model Oscar bags to be sold at the soon-to-be-opened EPCOT Center. The parties agreed to the purchase and sale of 300,000 bags. Disney issued purchase orders (called "merchandise orders") on December 9, 1981, January 13, 1982, and February 24, 1982, to purchase the bags in lots of 100,000. The bags were shipped by plaintiff and accepted by defendant.

On December 20, 1983, Disney issued a merchandise order for 100,000 additional bags. On January 3, 1984, the day Ocor received the order, it issued an acknowledgment that divided the order into two shipments, each of 50,000 bags ("PAK 2000 document"). Upon receiving the PAK 2000 document, Danelle Hickman, an assistant buyer for Disney, signed it and returned a copy to Ocor. On the back of the document was a list of conditions of sale and delivery. Provision K (or "§ K"), which is the section in dispute here, stated:

> "All designs which may be submitted in whatever form to the customer, or copies or derivatives of such designs, remain the exclusive property of PAK 2000. It is prohibited to reproduce, use, or remit to third parties such designs, artwork, etc., without our express written consent."

Disney sent a revised merchandise order for the first shipment of 50,000 bags on January 11, 1984, and for the second shipment on July 3, 1984. Plaintiff sent its second acknowledgment form to Disney on July 3, 1984, which contained a Provision K identical to the one set forth above. Ms. Hickman also signed and returned this form.

Prior to the execution of the PAK 2000 documents, Disney had sent a sample of the PAK 2000 bag to Canasa Trading Group ("Canasa"), a Disney subsidiary, to have Canasa search for a foreign supplier of a bag of similar design at less cost. The sample was subsequently submitted to Kutex International ("Kutex"), a Hong Kong agent. Kutex in turn arranged to have a similar bag designed by a Hong Kong manufacturer, a bag which eventually replaced the PAK 2000 Model Oscar bag at EPCOT Center.

Disney placed its first order for the replacement bag on August 14, 1984. The replacement bag has different artwork than the PAK 2000 bag, but has essentially the same handle as the Model Oscar handle. Plaintiff alleges that defendant's actions constitute a breach of Provision K of the PAK 2000 form and that defendant is liable for plaintiff's lost profits or, in the alternative, for unjust enrichment.

[Disney moved for summary judgment. The court first determined that summary judgment for Disney on the plaintiff's claim for lost profits was inappropriate because a jury could reasonably find both that Disney had agreed to the terms of Provision K and that Disney had breached the agreement by ordering substitute bags from the Hong Kong manufacturer.]

Disney also moves for summary judgment on the [plaintiff's] unjust enrichment claim, stating that as a matter of law it has not retained benefits unjustly. In contradiction, Ocor argues that Disney has been unjustly enriched by $114,945, which it alleges is the difference between the cost of the Ocor bag and the cost of the Hong Kong-manufactured bag times the number of Hong Kong bags purchased, or, in the alternative, by $91,466, Ocor's alleged lost profits.

Unjust enrichment is an equitable doctrine which allows recovery when it would be unconscionable for a defendant to retain a benefit wrongfully obtained. A plaintiff is entitled to restitution if he establishes that a defendant was unjustly enriched, either through a wrongful act or by passively accepting a benefit that would be unconscionable to retain. A defendant may be unjustly enriched, even if the plaintiff has not suffered a corresponding loss.

Disney argues that because it was under no contractual obligation to purchase additional Ocor bags, any financial benefit it received from buying replacement bags at a lower price was a benefit which rightfully inured to Disney. This argument misses the essence of the unjust enrichment claim. If Ocor can establish that Disney wrongfully "copied" the Ocor bag design (*i.e.*, in violation of § K), and consequently was able to obtain a bag of the same design for less cost than it would have had to pay to purchase the Ocor bag, then Disney obtained a financial benefit wrongfully and was unjustly enriched, even if Ocor did not suffer a corresponding loss in sales to Disney. Disney therefore has not established as a matter of law that it was not unjustly enriched, and its cross-motion for summary judgment on the unjust enrichment claim must be denied. . . .

NOTE

The Restatement (Third) of Restitution and Unjust Enrichment sides with the court in *Ocor Products* in cases involving what it describes as an "opportunistic" breach. Specifically, Section 39 provides:

> "(1) If a deliberate breach of contract results in profit to the defaulting promisor and the available damage remedy affords inadequate protection to the promisee's contractual entitlement, the promisee has a claim to restitution of the profit realized by the promisor as a result of the breach. Restitution by the rule of this section is an alternative to a remedy in damages.
>
> "(2) A case in which damages afford inadequate protection to the promisee's contractual entitlement is ordinarily one in which damages will not permit the promisee to acquire a full equivalent to the promised performance in a substitute transaction.
>
> "(3) Breach of contract is profitable when it results in gains to the defendant (net of potential liability in damages) greater than the defendant would have realized from performance of the contract. Profits from breach include saved expenditure and consequential gains that the defendant would not have realized but for the breach, as measured by the rules that apply in other cases of disgorgement."

Restatement (Third) of Restitution and Unjust Enrichment § 39 (2011).

D. FIDUCIARY AND CONFIDENTIAL RELATIONS

A fiduciary is required to act on someone else's behalf, and among the duties of a fiduciary are loyalty and good faith. There are a number of different kinds of fiduciary relationships, including trust, guardianship, and partnership. Much of the law governing these fiduciary relationships was developed by the English courts of equity. The equity courts also developed restitutionary responses to breaches of fiduciary duty. To this day, a breach of fiduciary duty remains an important basis for restitution.

Of the cases that follow, the first involves a breach of fiduciary duty, while the following two (*Snepp* and *Sharp*) show how the courts have sometimes extended this basis of liability beyond those who are fiduciaries.

Cook County v. Barrett

Appellate Court of Illinois, 1975.
36 Ill. App. 3d 623.

■ DEMSEY, JUSTICE. . . . The County of Cook filed a complaint and an amended complaint in chancery against former County Clerk, Edward J. Barrett, seeking the declaration of a constructive trust and an accounting for bribes allegedly received by him while he held office. . . .

The County represented that Barrett served as the elected Clerk of Cook County from 1956 through 1970, a position of trust imposing obligations to faithfully perform the duties of office in the interest of the people of Cook County and not for the incumbent's personal gain. . . . Throughout the period of Barrett's tenure, the County Board of Commissioners at various times purchased and rented voting machines for use in elections. The board acted on the basis of contracts and proposals submitted and recommended by Barrett. By virtue of his office and influence with the board, his recommendations were "tantamount to the acceptance" of the proposals tendered by him. During this same time, he was also charged with the responsibility to care for voting machines in County custody which included in discretion to award contracts of insurance on the machines.

Count I charged that Barrett abused his position of trust by employing it to seek secret personal gains from the Shoup Voting Machine Corporation, in that he caused Shoup ". . . to secretly pay him money that constituted fees and/or allowances and/or bribes," as a consequence of which the County paid considerably more money for the voting machines purchased and rented from Shoup than it would have otherwise. It was alleged that these payments from Shoup to Barrett amounted to approximately $180,000 for the years 1967–1970 but were unknown for previous years and a detailed accounting was needed to determine the exact figure for the entire period covered by the complaint. The Plaintiff prayed that Barrett be declared a constructive trustee for the citizens and taxpayers of the County for the amounts received by him from Shoup, and that he be required to account to the County for those sums.

Count II also prayed for a declaration of constructive trust and for an accounting, but arose from a different group of transactions. The remedy was invoked to recover secret payments received by Barrett from Arthur Gallagher & Company, an insurance agency, in connection with his award of insurance contracts on County voting machines to companies represented by Gallagher. As in the first count, it was alleged that the amount of these payments for the period 1956 to 1967 was completely unknown, that it had been approximated for 1967 to 1970 at $6,000, but that a detailed accounting was necessary to discover the exact figure by which the defendant had been unjustly enriched. . . .

Barrett contends that the County is entitled only to fees and allowances which are legally collected, that to allow recovery by a public body of bribes or kickbacks paid to its officers would be against public policy; that the County alleged no damage and suffered none, that no money moved from the County to him, that if any money was paid it was paid by Shoup and Gallagher not by the County, and that since no money moved out of the County treasury it could not have been depleted; that the complaint did not allege that he had been unjustly enriched at the expense of the County or that in the absence of bribery the County would have paid less for voting machines or insurance. . . .

A constructive trust arises not by any agreement or understanding of the parties but by operation of law and is imposed upon grounds of public policy, to prevent a person from holding for his own benefit that which he has gained by reason of a special trust or confidence reposed in him by an innocent party. Stated most succinctly, the purpose of the remedy is to prevent unjust enrichment.

The particular circumstances in which equity will impress a constructive trust are ". . . as numberless as the modes by which property may be obtained through bad faith and unconscientious acts." 4 POMEROY'S EQUITY JURISPRUDENCE (5th Ed.) sec. 1045, p. 97. . . .

At all times and for all the transactions pertinent to the complaint Barrett was the fiduciary of the people of Cook County. As an elected public official he held a position of the highest public trust. In the transactions with Shoup and Gallagher, Barrett acted as the County's agent, negotiating terms of purchase and recommending County action. An agent is fiduciary to his principal and the relation is treated generally the same, and with virtually the same strictness, as that of trustee and beneficiary.

In deciding this appeal, it is not necessary to locate the perimeters of the fiduciary obligations due the public from their elected officials. It is sufficient to recognize that, when such an official acts as agent for the public body in business transactions, he owes to his principal duties of loyalty and good faith at least equal to those required of a private fiduciary in like circumstances. The obligations of a person who occupies the latter category are such that he must not place himself in a position which is adverse to that of his principal during the continuance of the agency. . . .

The remedy for breach of this duty is simple and salutary. Since a fiduciary is bound to act solely for the benefit of his principal, equity will intervene to prevent him from accruing any advantage—however innocently—from transactions conducted in behalf of the principal. So, when a fiduciary, who has acted for his beneficiary or principal, receives a gift, or bonus or commission from a party with whom he has transacted business, that benefit may be recovered from him by the beneficiary of the fiduciary relationship. . . . The Restatement of Restitution, section 197, states:

> "Sec. 197. BONUS OR COMMISSION RECEIVED BY FIDUCIARY.
>
> "Where a fiduciary in violation of his duty to the beneficiary receives or retains a bonus or commission or other profit, he holds what he receives upon a constructive trust for the beneficiary.
>
> "Comment:
>
> "a. Bribes and Commissions. The rule stated in this Section is applicable not only where the fiduciary receives something in the nature of a bribe given him by a third person in order to induce him to violate his duty as fiduciary, but also where something is given to him and received by him in good faith, if it was received for an act done by him in connection with the performance of his duties as fiduciary. . . .
>
> "c. Where no harm to beneficiary. The rule stated in this Section is applicable although the profit received by the fiduciary is not at the expense of the beneficiary. Thus, where an agent to purchase property for his principal acts properly in making the purchase but subsequently receives a bonus from the seller, he holds the money received upon a constructive trust for his principal. The rule stated in this Section . . . is not based on harm done to the beneficiary in the particular case, but rests upon a broad principle of preventing a conflict of opposing interests in the minds of fiduciaries, whose duty it is to act solely for the benefit of their beneficiaries."

. . . The defendant suggests . . . that the County ". . . is not entitled to money which is not legally collected and such money is the property of the person from whom it has been exacted." This contention was invited by the broad language of the complaint, which termed the payments by Shoup and Gallagher "fees and/or allowances and/or bribes." It has been held that where public officers charge greater fees for the performance of ministerial functions than those prescribed by law, retaining the portion wrongfully exacted, the payors are entitled to the return of so much of the fee as is unlawful, and the public body, in the absence of statutory authority requiring that such funds be deposited in the public treasury, has no greater claim to the excess charge than the officer who fraudulently collected it. . . . However, the rule has no pertinence to cases of bribery. The payments alleged in this case came to Barrett personally and were not treated either by the payors or the recipient as fees or allowances due the County. So, Barrett is correct insofar as he contends that the County is not "entitled" to the money, *i.e.* it never held a claim at law on the funds. But that fact furnishes the very reason for the County's resort to equity to claim the money. Barrett errs in his view that Shoup and Gallagher retained a superior right to the funds. We know of no action cognizable at law or equity for the return of illegal payments knowingly and willingly made. . . .

Snepp v. United States

Supreme Court of the United States, 1980.
444 U.S. 507.

■ PER CURIAM. . . . Based on his experiences as a CIA agent, Snepp published a book about certain CIA activities in South Vietnam. Snepp published the account without submitting it to the Agency for prepublication review. As an express condition of his employment with the CIA in 1968, however, Snepp had executed an agreement promising that he would "not . . . publish . . . any information or material relating to the Agency, its activities or intelligence activities generally, either during or after the term of [his] employment . . . without specific prior approval of the Agency." The promise was an integral part of Snepp's concurrent undertaking "not to disclose any classified information relating to the Agency without proper authorization." Thus, Snepp had pledged not to divulge *classified* information and not to publish *any* information without prepublication clearance. The Government brought this suit to enforce Snepp's agreement. It sought a declaration that Snepp had breached the contract, an injunction requiring Snepp to submit future writings for prepublication review, and an order imposing a constructive trust for the Government's benefit on all profits that Snepp might earn from publishing the book in violation of his fiduciary obligations to the Agency.[2]

The District Court found that Snepp had "willfully, deliberately and surreptitiously breached his position of trust with the CIA and the [1968] secrecy agreement" by publishing his book without submitting it for prepublication review. The court also found that Snepp deliberately misled CIA officials into believing that he would submit the book for prepublication clearance. Finally, the court determined as a fact that publication of the book had "caused the United States irreparable harm and loss." The District Court therefore enjoined future breaches of Snepp's agreement and imposed a constructive trust on Snepp's profits.

---

[2] At the time of suit, Snepp already had received about $60,000 in advance payments. His contract with his publisher provides for royalties and other potential profits.

The Court of Appeals accepted the findings of the District Court and agreed that Snepp had breached a valid contract.[3] It specifically affirmed the findings that Snepp's failure to submit his manuscript for prepublication review had inflicted "irreparable harm" on intelligence activities vital to our national security. Thus, the court upheld the injunction against future violations of Snepp's prepublication obligation. The court, however, concluded that the record did not support imposition of a constructive trust. The conclusion rested on the court's perception that Snepp had a First Amendment right to publish unclassified information and the Government's concession—for the purposes of this litigation—that Snepp's book divulged no classified intelligence. In other words, the court thought that Snepp's fiduciary obligation extended only to preserving the confidentiality of classified material. It therefore limited recovery to nominal damages and to the possibility of punitive damages if the Government—in a jury trial—could prove tortious conduct.

Judge Hoffman, sitting by designation, dissented from the refusal to find a constructive trust. The 1968 agreement, he wrote, "was no ordinary contract; it gave life to a fiduciary relationship and invested in Snepp the trust of the CIA." Prepublication clearance was part of Snepp's undertaking to protect confidences associated with his trust. Punitive damages, Judge Hoffman argued, were both a speculative and inappropriate remedy for Snepp's breach. We agree with Judge Hoffman that Snepp breached a fiduciary obligation and that the proceeds of his breach are impressed with a constructive trust.

Snepp's employment with the CIA involved an extremely high degree of trust. In the opening sentence of the agreement that he signed, Snepp explicitly recognized that he was entering a trust relationship. The trust agreement specifically imposed the obligation not to publish *any* information relating to the Agency without submitting the information for clearance. Snepp stipulated at trial that—after undertaking this obligation—he had been "assigned to various positions of trust" and that he had been granted "frequent access to classified information, including information regarding intelligence sources and methods." Snepp published his book about CIA activities on the basis of this background and exposure. He deliberately and surreptitiously violated his obligation to submit all material for prepublication review. Thus, he exposed the

---

[3] The Court of Appeals and the District Court rejected each of Snepp's defenses to the enforcement of his contract. In his petition for certiorari, Snepp relies primarily on the claim that his agreement is unenforceable as a prior restraint on protected speech.

When Snepp accepted employment with the CIA, he voluntarily signed the agreement that expressly obligated him to submit any proposed publication for prior review. . . . Moreover, this Court's cases make clear that—even in the absence of an express agreement—the CIA could have acted to protect substantial government interests by imposing reasonable restrictions on employee activities that in other contexts might be protected by the First Amendment. The Government has a compelling interest in protecting both the secrecy of information important to our national security and the appearance of confidentiality so essential to the effective operation of our foreign intelligence service. The agreement that Snepp signed is a reasonable means for protecting this vital interest.

classified information with which he had been entrusted to the risk of disclosure.

Whether Snepp violated his trust does not depend upon whether his book actually contained classified information. The Government does not deny—as a general principle—Snepp's right to publish unclassified information. Nor does it contend—at this stage of the litigation—that Snepp's book contains classified material. The Government simply claims that, in light of the special trust reposed in him and the agreement that he signed, Snepp should have given the CIA an opportunity to determine whether the material he proposed to publish would compromise classified information or sources. Neither of the Government's concessions undercuts its claim that Snepp's failure to submit to prepublication review was a breach of his trust.

Both the District Court and the Court of Appeals found that a former intelligence agent's publication of unreviewed material relating to intelligence activities can be detrimental to vital national interests even if the published information is unclassified. When a former agent relies on his own judgment about what information is detrimental, he may reveal information that the CIA—with its broader understanding of what may expose classified information and confidential sources—could have identified as harmful. In addition to receiving intelligence from domestically based or controlled sources, the CIA obtains information from the intelligence services of friendly nations and from agents operating in foreign countries. The continued availability of these foreign sources depends upon the CIA's ability to guarantee the security of information that might compromise them and even endanger the personal safety of foreign agents. . . .

In view of this and other evidence in the record, both the District Court and the Court of Appeals recognized that Snepp's breach of his explicit obligation to submit his material—classified or not—for prepublication clearance has irreparably harmed the United States Government.

The decision of the Court of Appeals denies the Government the most appropriate remedy for Snepp's acknowledged wrong. Indeed, as a practical matter, the decision may well leave the Government with no reliable deterrent against similar breaches of security. No one disputes that the actual damages attributable to a publication such as Snepp's generally are unquantifiable. Nominal damages are a hollow alternative, certain to deter no one. The punitive damages recoverable after a jury trial are speculative and unusual. Even if recovered, they may bear no relation to either the Government's irreparable loss or Snepp's unjust gain.

The Government could not pursue the only remedy that the Court of Appeals left it without losing the benefit of the bargain it seeks to enforce. Proof of the tortious conduct necessary to sustain an award of punitive damages might force the Government to disclose some of the very confidences that Snepp promised to protect. The trial of such a suit, before a jury if the defendant so elects, would subject the CIA and its officials to probing discovery into the Agency's highly confidential affairs. . . . When the Government cannot secure its remedy without unacceptable risks, it has no remedy at all.

A constructive trust, on the other hand, protects both the Government and the former agent from unwarranted risks. This remedy is the natural and customary consequence of a breach of trust. It deals fairly with both parties by conforming relief to the dimensions of the wrong. If the agent secures prepublication clearance, he can publish with no fear of liability. If the agent publishes unreviewed material in violation of his fiduciary and contractual obligation, the trust remedy simply requires him to disgorge the benefits of his faithlessness. Since the remedy is swift and sure, it is tailored to deter those who would place sensitive information at risk. And since the remedy reaches only funds attributable to the breach, it cannot saddle the former agent with exemplary damages out of all proportion to his gain. The decision of the Court of Appeals would deprive the Government of this equitable and effective means of protecting intelligence that may contribute to national security. We therefore reverse the judgment of the Court of Appeals in so far as it refused to impose a constructive trust on Snepp's profits, and we remand the case to the Court of Appeals for reinstatement of the full judgment of the District Court. . . .

■ MR. JUSTICE STEVENS, with whom MR. JUSTICE BRENNAN and MR. JUSTICE MARSHALL join, dissenting. . . .

The rule of law the Court announces today is not supported by statute, by the contract, or by the common law. Although Congress has enacted a number of criminal statutes punishing the unauthorized dissemination of certain types of classified information, it has not seen fit to authorize the constructive trust remedy the Court creates today. Nor does either of the contracts Snepp signed with the agency provide for any such remedy in the event of a breach. The Court's per curiam opinion seems to suggest that its result is supported by a blend of the law of trusts and the law of contracts. But neither of these branches of the common law supports the imposition of a constructive trust under the circumstances of this case.

Plainly this is not a typical trust situation in which a settlor has conveyed legal title to certain assets to a trustee for the use and benefit of designated beneficiaries. Rather, it is an employment relationship in which the employee possesses fiduciary obligations arising out of his duty of loyalty to his employer. One of those obligations, long recognized by the common law even in the absence of a written employment agreement, is the duty to protect confidential or "classified" information. If Snepp had breached that obligation, the common law would support the implication of a constructive trust upon the benefits derived from his misuse of confidential information.

But Snepp did not breach his duty to protect confidential information. Rather, he breached a contractual duty, imposed in aid of the basic duty to maintain confidentiality, to obtain prepublication clearance. In order to justify the imposition of a constructive trust, the majority attempts to equate this contractual duty with Snepp's duty not to disclose, labeling them both as "fiduciary." I find nothing in the common law to support such an approach.

Employment agreements often contain covenants designed to ensure in various ways that an employee fully complies with his duty not to disclose or misuse confidential information. One of the most common is a covenant not to compete. Contrary to the majority's approach in this case, the courts have not construed such covenants broadly simply because they support a basic fiduciary duty; nor have they granted sweeping remedies to enforce them. On the contrary, because such covenants are agreements in restraint of an individual's freedom of trade, they are enforceable only if they can survive scrutiny under the "rule of reason." That rule, originally laid down in the seminal case of Mitchel *v.* Reynolds, 1 P.Wms. 181, 24 Eng. Rep. 347 (1711), requires that the covenant be reasonably necessary to protect a legitimate interest of the employer (such as an interest in confidentiality), that the employer's interest not be outweighed by the public interest, and that the covenant not be of any longer duration or wider geographical scope than necessary to protect the employer's interest.

The Court has not persuaded me that a rule of reason analysis should not be applied to Snepp's covenant to submit to prepublication review. Like an ordinary employer, the CIA has a vital interest in protecting certain types of information; at the same time, the CIA employee has a countervailing interest in preserving a wide range of work opportunities (including work as an author) and in protecting his First Amendment rights. The public interest lies in a proper accommodation that will preserve the intelligence mission of the Agency while not abridging the free flow of unclassified information. When the Government seeks to enforce a harsh restriction on the employee's freedom, despite its admission that the interest the agreement was designed to protect—the confidentiality of classified information—has not been compromised, an equity court might well be persuaded that the case is not one in which the covenant should be enforced.

But even assuming that Snepp's covenant to submit to prepublication review should be enforced, the constructive trust imposed by the Court is not an appropriate remedy. If an employee has used his employer's confidential information for his own personal profit, a constructive trust over those profits is obviously an appropriate remedy because the profits are the direct result of the breach. But Snepp admittedly did not use confidential information in his book; nor were the profits from his book in any sense a product of his failure to submit the book for prepublication review. For, even if Snepp had submitted the book to the agency for prepublication review, the Government's censorship authority would surely have been limited to the excision of classified material. In this case, then, it would have been obliged to clear the book for publication in precisely the same form as it now stands. Thus, Snepp has not gained any profits as a result of his breach; the Government, rather than Snepp, will be unjustly enriched if he is required to disgorge profits attributable entirely to his own legitimate activity.

Despite the fact that Snepp has not caused the Government the type of harm that would ordinarily be remedied by the imposition of a constructive trust, the Court attempts to justify a constructive trust remedy on the ground that the Government has suffered *some* harm. The Court states that publication of "unreviewed material" by a former CIA agent "can be detrimental to vital national interests even if the published information is unclassified." . . .

In support of its position that Snepp's book had in fact had such an impact, the Government introduced testimony by the Director of the CIA, Admiral Stansfield Turner, stating that Snepp's book and others like it had jeopardized the CIA's relationship with foreign intelligence services by making them unsure of the Agency's ability to maintain confidentiality. Admiral Turner's truncated testimony does not explain, however, whether these unidentified "other" books actually contained classified information. If so, it is difficult to believe that the publication of a book like Snepp's, which does not reveal classified information, has significantly weakened the Agency's position. Nor does it explain whether the unidentified foreign agencies who have stopped cooperating with the CIA have done so because of a legitimate fear that secrets will be revealed or because they merely disagree with our Government's classification policies.

In any event, to the extent that the Government seeks to punish Snepp for the generalized harm he has caused by failing to submit to prepublication review and to deter others from following in his footsteps, punitive damages is, as the Court of Appeals held, clearly the preferable remedy "since a constructive trust depends on the concept of unjust enrichment rather than deterrence and punishment." . . .

Despite the fact that the Government has specifically stated that the punitive damages remedy is "sufficient" to protect its interests, the Court forges ahead and summarily rejects that remedy on the grounds that (a) it is too speculative and thus would not provide the Government with a "reliable deterrent against similar breaches of security," and (b) it might require the Government to reveal confidential information in court, the Government might forego damages rather than make such disclosures, and the Government might thus be left with "no remedy at all." It seems to me that the Court is foreclosed from relying upon either ground by the Government's acquiescence in the punitive damages remedy. Moreover, the second rationale is entirely speculative and, in this case at least, almost certainly wrong. . . . [U]nder the Court of Appeals' opinion the Government would be entitled to punitive damages simply by proving that Snepp deceived it into believing that he was going to comply with his duty to submit the manuscript for prepublication review and that the Government relied on these misrepresentations to its detriment. I fail to see how such a showing would require the Government to reveal any confidential information or to expose itself to "probing discovery into the Agency's highly confidential affairs." . . .

The uninhibited character of today's exercise in lawmaking is highlighted by the Court's disregard of two venerable principles that favor a more conservative approach to this case.

First, for centuries the English-speaking judiciary refused to grant equitable relief unless the plaintiff could show that his remedy at law was inadequate. Without waiting for an opportunity to appraise the adequacy of the punitive damages remedy in this case, the Court has jumped to the conclusion that equitable relief is necessary.

Second, and of greater importance, the Court seems unaware of the fact that its drastic new remedy has been fashioned to enforce a species of prior restraint on a citizen's right to criticize his government.[17] Inherent in this prior restraint is the risk that the reviewing agency will misuse its authority to delay the publication of a critical work or to persuade an author to modify the contents of his work beyond the demands of secrecy. The character of the covenant as a prior restraint on free speech surely imposes an especially heavy burden on the censor to justify the remedy it seeks. It would take more than the Court has written to persuade me that that burden has been met. . . .

Sharp v. Kosmalski

Court of Appeals of New York, 1976.
40 N.Y.2d 119.

■ GABRIELLI, JUDGE. Plaintiff commenced this action to impose a constructive trust upon property transferred to defendant on the ground that the retention of the property and the subsequent ejection of the plaintiff therefrom was in violation of a relationship of trust and confidence and constituted unjust enrichment. The Trial Judge dismissed plaintiff's complaint and his decision was affirmed without opinion by the Appellate Division.

Upon the death of his wife of 32 years, plaintiff, a 56-year-old dairy farmer whose education did not go beyond the eighth grade, developed a very close relationship with defendant, a school teacher and a woman 16 years his junior. Defendant assisted plaintiff in disposing of his wife's

[17] . . . In view of the national interest in maintaining an effective intelligence service, I am not prepared to say that the restraint is necessarily intolerable in this context. I am, however, prepared to say that, certiorari having been granted, the issue surely should not be resolved in the absence of full briefing and argument.

belongings, performed certain domestic tasks for him such as ironing his shirts and was a frequent companion of the plaintiff. Plaintiff came to depend upon defendant's companionship and, eventually, declared his love for her, proposing marriage to her. Notwithstanding her refusal of his proposal of marriage, defendant continued her association with plaintiff and permitted him to shower her with many gifts, fanning his hope that he could induce defendant to alter her decision concerning his marriage proposal. Defendant was given access to plaintiff's bank account, from which it is not denied that she withdrew substantial amounts of money. Eventually, plaintiff made a will naming defendant as his sole beneficiary and executed a deed naming her a joint owner of his farm. The record reveals that numerous alterations in the way of modernization were made to plaintiff's farmhouse in alleged furtherance of "domestic plans" made by plaintiff and defendant.

In September, 1971, while the renovations were still in progress, plaintiff transferred his remaining joint interest to defendant. At the time of the conveyance, a farm liability policy was issued to plaintiff naming defendant and her daughter as additional insureds. Furthermore, the insurance agent was requested by plaintiff, in the presence of defendant, to change the policy to read "J. Rodney Sharp, life tenant. Jean C. Kosmalski, owner." In February, 1973, the liaison between the parties was abruptly severed as defendant ordered plaintiff to move out of his home and vacate the farm. Defendant took possession of the home, the farm and all the equipment thereon, leaving plaintiff with assets of $300.

Generally, a constructive trust may be imposed "[w]hen property has been acquired in such circumstances that the holder of the legal title may not in good conscience retain the beneficial interest" (Beatty *v.* Guggenheim Exploration Co., 225 NY 380, 386; 1 Scott, TRUSTS [3d ed], § 44.2, p 337; 4 POMEROY'S EQUITY JURISPRUDENCE [5th ed], § 1053, p 119)). In the development of the doctrine of constructive trust as a remedy available to courts of equity, the following four requirements were posited: (1) a confidential or fiduciary relation, (2) a promise, (3) a transfer in reliance thereon and (4) unjust enrichment.

Most frequently, it is the existence of a confidential relationship which triggers the equitable considerations leading to the imposition of a constructive trust. Although no marital or other family relationship is present in this case, such is not essential for the existence of a confidential relation. The record in this case clearly indicates that a relationship of trust and confidence did exist between the parties and, hence, the defendant must be charged with an obligation not to abuse the trust and confidence placed in her by the plaintiff. The disparity in education between the plaintiff and defendant highlights the degree of dependence of the plaintiff upon the trust and honor of the defendant.

Unquestionably, there is a transfer of property here, but the Trial Judge found that the transfer was made "without a promise or

CHAPTER 13

MEASURING RESTITUTION

A. RESTITUTION: LEGAL AND EQUITABLE

When a plaintiff brings a suit that sounds in unjust enrichment and wins, the court will usually award a restitutionary remedy. Some kinds of restitution originated at law, including claims such as "quasi-contract." Other kinds of restitution originated in equity, including remedies such as "constructive trust" and "accounting for profits." As will be discussed below, the differences between legal and equitable restitution remain significant.

1. LEGAL RESTITUTION

In most jurisdictions in the United States, a claim for restitution of money will ordinarily be considered "legal." (Exceptions are discussed momentarily.) The labels used for legal restitution vary from jurisdiction to jurisdiction, and sometimes even within a jurisdiction.

Some cases retain historical terminology such as "indebitatus assumpsit," "general assumpsit," "quantum meruit," "quantum valebat," and "money had and received." See, *e.g.*, Daake *v.* Decks N Such Marine, Inc., 201 So.3d 179 (Fla. App. 2016) (quantum meruit).

Other cases describe legal restitutionary claims simply as "restitution" or "unjust enrichment." See, *e.g.*, Electrical Wholesale Supply Co., Inc. *v.* Fraser, 356 P.3d 254 (Wyo. 2015) (unjust enrichment). This terminology causes confusion, however, because the same terms can be used for equitable remedies and the basis of liability.

Other cases use "quasi-contract" as a general label for legal restitution based on unjust enrichment. See, *e.g.*, Hitachi Systems Corp. *v.* WebMethods Inc., 60 Va. Cir. 79 (Va. Cir. Ct. 2002). That label can also be misunderstood. When plaintiffs sue in unjust enrichment, they are not basing their claim on a contract. Nevertheless, for hundreds of years the common law courts have tended to resolve these claims as if there had been a contract—that is, as if the defendant had promised to pay to the plaintiff the money unjustly held. As one court put it, "Quasi-contracts are not true contracts but are judicially created obligations to do justice. . . . The courts are in accord in stressing that the most significant requirement for recovery in quasi-contract is that the enrichment to the defendant must be unjust; that is, the defendant must receive a true windfall or 'something for nothing.' " Alaska Sales & Service Inc. *v.*

Millet, 735 P.2d 743 (Alaska 1987). As long as one remembers the *quasi* in quasi-contract, it remains a good label.[i]

To be a successful litigator, the essential thing is for you to recognize the range of terminology and learn the usage in your own jurisdiction. Whatever label is used, when a plaintiff prevails on a legal restitutionary claim, the court will award a judgment for a certain amount of money. That judgment resembles an award of damages (except, of course, that it is measured by the defendant's gain and not by the plaintiff's loss). That the restitutionary claim is legal, as opposed to equitable, has several important consequences. These include the possibility of a jury, the lack of various equitable defenses, the lack of equitable enforcement powers such as contempt, and the lack of preferential treatment in bankruptcy.

2. EQUITABLE RESTITUTION

Courts in the United States also award restitutionary remedies that are equitable in the technical sense (*i.e.*, they are derived from courts of equity, not courts of law). These include accounting for profits, constructive trust, equitable lien, and subrogation. With these remedies, there is no jury, and all of the usual constraints and powers of equity apply.

Accounting for profits, also called simply accounting, is a remedy that has an element of discovery or investigation. It lets a court inquire into how a defendant has handled money or property, with the goal being to determine the defendant's gains so they can be paid to the plaintiff (or equitably divided with the plaintiff). Courts give this remedy when there has been a breach of fiduciary duty or when the relevant accounts are so complicated that a jury trial would be impossible.

Constructive trust is a remedy by which a court sets aside the wrongful ownership of property, such as land, a house, a patent, or an identifiable fund of money (*e.g.*, "the Robinsons' bank account"). It is especially useful for correcting the wrongful ownership of "property that has changed form since it left the plaintiff's hands." Ward Farnsworth, RESTITUTION: CIVIL LIABILITY FOR UNJUST ENRICHMENT 119 (2014). When granting a constructive trust, what the court does is declare that the defendant holds the property—and whatever the property can be traced into—on the plaintiff's behalf. The defendant is treated like a trustee for the plaintiff. Then the court requires the defendant to convey the property and proceeds back to the plaintiff, often with conditions about how this is to be done, and sometimes with a set-off for various expenses the defendant has incurred or will incur.

---

[i] Perhaps it would be more apt to use "quasi-contract" for most cases of legal restitution, while still using "money had and received" for cases of mistaken payments, since it is more likely that the parties will have no prior relationship; and "quantum meruit" for cases of services rendered, since it can be useful to emphasize the narrowness of these claims, as discussed in Arthur R. Miller, Common Law Protection for Products of the Mind: An "Idea" Whose Time Has Come, 119 Harv. L. Rev. 703, 777–78 (2006).

Equitable lien is like constructive trust but with one important difference: where constructive trust gives the plaintiff title (or an equitable interest in title), an equitable lien instead gives the plaintiff a security interest in the property. Whenever the property is sold, the plaintiff collects his or her money. A court may require foreclosure immediately.

Subrogation is another remedy used when the plaintiff seeks to recover identifiable property. "But in a typical subrogation case, the defendant has already used the plaintiff's property in order to pay a liability owed to a third party. Subrogation lets the innocent plaintiff step into the shoes of the third party and have the same rights that the third party has (or had) against the defendant." Samuel L. Bray, The System of Equitable Remedies, 63 UCLA L. Rev. 530, 555 (2016).

Thus there are a variety of restitutionary claims and remedies, and each one has its own advantages, disadvantages, and uses. For deciding whether a restitutionary claim or remedy is legal or equitable, the general rule is that an award of money is legal, while restitution of specific property (or an interest in specific property) is equitable.

There are two main exceptions to this general rule. First, a fund of money can be specific property for purposes of a constructive trust. Second, the profits of a misbehaving fiduciary (or person in a confidential relationship) are obviously money, yet they can be recovered with accounting for profits or constructive trust. In addition, note that in some jurisdictions a case of extraordinarily complex financial records can be investigated with an accounting, even if the defendant is not a fiduciary.

Another term sometimes encountered in cases involving restitution is "disgorgement"; it first came into vogue in the late twentieth century. See George P. Roach, A Default Rule of Omnipotence: Implied Jurisdiction and Exaggerated Remedies in Equity for Federal Agencies, 12 Fordham J. Corp. & Financial L. 1, 49 (2007). As a matter of common law and equity, there is no remedy of "disgorgement." Instead, the term is best thought of as a rough synonym for a restitutionary claim or remedy that might on closer inspection be legal (*e.g.*, quasi-contract) or equitable (*e.g.*, accounting for profits).

B. RESTITUTION PRIMARILY IN MONEY

Restitution focuses on gains rather than losses: the objective is to shift benefits that one party has obtained unjustly at another's expense to the party who ought to have them. Benefits, however, can be measured in a number of ways. The Restatement (Third) of Restitution and Unjust Enrichment proposes that, depending on context, the appropriate measure of restitution may be:

"(a) the value of the benefit in advancing the purposes of the recipient;

"(b) the cost to the claimant of conferring the benefit;

"(c) the market value of the benefit; or

"(d) a price the defendant has expressed a willingness to pay, if the defendant's assent may be treated as valid on the question of price."

Restatement (Third) of Restitution and Unjust Enrichment § 49(3) (2011).

The choice of measure depends in large part on the degree to which the recipient was at fault in the transaction. The Restatement recognizes four categories of recipient: innocent recipients, conscious legal wrongdoers, recipients who have unconsciously committed a legal wrong, and recipients who are not legal wrongdoers but nevertheless are responsible in some way for the events leading to enrichment. *Id.* Conscious wrongdoers are also liable for "profits," which encompass not only the value received directly from the claimant, but also "secondary enrichment," including interest, proceeds, or "consequential gains" from further transactions. *Id.* §§ 51, 53.

The cases that follow illustrate some of the problems that can arise in measuring restitution.

Olwell v. Nye & Nissen Co.

Supreme Court of Washington, 1946.
26 Wash.2d 282.

■ MALLERY, JUSTICE. On May 6, 1940, plaintiff, E.L. Olwell, sold and transferred to the defendant corporation his one-half interest in Puget Sound Egg Packers, a Washington corporation having its principal place of business in Tacoma. By the terms of the agreement, the plaintiff was to retain full ownership in an "Eggsact" egg-washing machine, formerly used by Puget Sound Egg Packers. The defendant promised to make it available for delivery to the plaintiff on or before June 15, 1940. It appears that the plaintiff arranged for and had the machine stored in a space adjacent to the premises occupied by the defendant but not covered by its lease. Due to the scarcity of labor immediately after the out-break of the war, defendant's treasurer, without the knowledge or consent of the plaintiff, ordered the egg washer taken out of storage. The machine was put into operation by defendant on May 31, 1941, and thereafter for a period of three years was used approximately one day a week in the regular course of the defendant's business. Plaintiff first discovered this use in January or February of 1945 when he happened to be at the plant on business and heard the machine operating. Thereupon plaintiff offered to sell the machine to defendant for $600 or half of its original cost in 1929. A counter offer of $50 was refused and approximately one month later this action was commenced to recover the reasonable value of defendant's use of the machine, and praying for $25 per month from the commencement of the unauthorized use until the time of trial. A second cause of action was alleged but was not pressed and hence is not here involved. The court entered judgment for plaintiff in the amount of $10 per week for the period of 156 weeks covered by the statute of limitations, or $1,560, and gave the plaintiff his costs.

Defendant has appealed to this court assigning error upon the judgment, upon the trial of the cause on the theory of unjust enrichment, upon the amount of damages, and upon the court's refusal to make a finding as to the value of the machine and in refusing to consider such value in measuring damages.

The theory of the respondent was that the tort of conversion could be "waived" and suit brought in quasi-contract, upon a contract implied in law, to recover, as restitution, the profits which inured to appellant as a result of its wrongful use of the machine. With this the trial court agreed and in its findings of facts found that the use of the machine "resulted in a benefit to the users, in that said use saves the users approximately $1.43 per hour of use as against the expense which would be incurred were eggs to be washed by hand; that said machine was used by Puget Sound Egg Packers and defendant, on an average of one day per week from May of 1941, until February of 1945 at an average saving of $10.00 per each day of use."

In substance, the argument presented by the assignments of error is that the principle of unjust enrichment, or quasi-contract, is not of universal application, but is imposed only in exceptional cases because of special facts and circumstances and in favor of particular persons; that respondent had an adequate remedy in an action at law for replevin or claim and delivery; that any damages awarded to the plaintiff should be based upon the use or rental value of the machine and should bear some reasonable relation to its market value. Appellant therefore contends that the amount of the judgment is excessive.

It is uniformly held that in cases where the defendant *tort feasor* has benefited by his wrong, the plaintiff may elect to "waive the tort" and bring an action in assumpsit for restitution. Such an action arises out of a duty imposed by law devolving upon the defendant to repay an unjust and unmerited enrichment.

It is clear that the saving in labor cost which appellant derived from its use of respondent's machine constituted a benefit. . . .

It is also necessary to show that while appellant benefited from its use of the egg-washing machine, respondent thereby incurred a loss. It is argued by appellant that since the machine was put into storage by respondent, who had no present use for it, and for a period of almost three years did not know that appellant was operating it and since it was not injured by its operation and the appellant never adversely claimed any title to it, nor contested respondent's right of repossession upon the latter's discovery of the wrongful operation, that the respondent was not damaged because he is as well off as if the machine had not been used by appellant.

The very essence of the nature of property is the right to its exclusive use. Without it, no beneficial right remains. However plausible, the appellant cannot be heard to say that his wrongful invasion of the respondent's property right to exclusive use is not a loss compensable in law. To hold otherwise would be subversive of all property rights since his use was admittedly wrongful and without claim of right. The theory of unjust enrichment is applicable in such a case.

We agree with appellant that respondent could have elected a "common garden variety of action," as he calls it, for the recovery of damages. It is also true that except where provided for by statute, punitive damages are not allowed, the basic measure for the recovery of damages in this state being compensation. If, then, respondent had been *limited* to redress *in tort* for damages, as appellant contends, the court below would be in error in refusing to make a finding as to the value of the machine. In such case the award of damages must bear a reasonable relation to the value of the property.

But respondent here had an election. He chose rather to waive his right of action *in tort* and to sue *in assumpsit* on the implied contract. Having so elected, he is entitled to the measure of restoration which accompanies the remedy.

> ". . . If the value of what was received and what was lost were always equal, there would be no substantial problem as to the amount of recovery, since actions of restitution are not punitive. In fact, however, the plaintiff frequently has lost more than the defendant has gained, and sometimes the defendant has gained more than the plaintiff has lost.
>
> "In such cases the measure of restitution is determined with reference to the tortiousness of the defendant's conduct or the negligence or other fault of one or both of the parties in creating the situation giving rise to the right to restitution. If the defendant was tortious in his acquisition of the benefit he is required to pay for what the other has lost although that is more than the recipient benefited. *If he was consciously tortious in acquiring the benefit, he is also deprived of any profit derived from his subsequent dealing with it.* If he was no more at fault than the claimant, he is not required to pay for losses in excess of benefit received by him and he is permitted to retain gains which result from his dealing with the property." (Italics ours) Restatement of Restitution, pp. 595, 596.

Respondent may recover the profit derived by the appellant from the use of the machine.

[The court then reduced the judgment in Olwell's favor to $900, on the ground that $900 was the figure named in Olwell's complaint and the judgment could not exceed the amount initially requested.]

Gaste v. Kaiserman

United States Court of Appeals, Second Circuit, 1988.
863 F.2d 1061.

■ JON O. NEWMAN, CIRCUIT JUDGE. This appeal involves a copyright infringement action against the composer and publisher of the highly successful popular song "Feelings," brought by Louis Gaste, the composer of an obscure French song written nearly 17 years earlier. . . .

In 1956, plaintiff-appellee Gaste, a resident and citizen of France, composed the music to a song entitled "Pour Toi" as part of the score of a motion picture *Le Feu aux Poudres,* which was released in France that same year. Gaste registered the sheet music for the song in the United States Copyright Office in 1957. Neither the movie nor the song, which was published and recorded separately in France, had great success. Worldwide revenues of "Pour Toi" have amounted to less than $15,000.

From France, the scene shifts to Brazil, nearly two decades later. In 1973, the then unheralded and relatively unknown Brazilian singer and composer Morris Kaiserman, known professionally as Morris Albert, composed and recorded the song "Feelings." "Feelings" became a smash hit internationally, winning "gold records" in a number of countries.

Gaste contended at trial that Kaiserman had gained access to Gaste's virtually unknown song through Enrique Lebendiger, the owner of [Fermata Melodies, Inc.], which was Kaiserman's publisher. Gaste's evidence, detailed below in the discussion of access, established that Fermata had had some dealings with Gaste's publishing company, Les Editions Louis Gaste, in the 1950s.

[The court first concluded that Gaste held a valid copyright in the music to the song "Pour Toi," and that there was sufficient evidence to support the jury's finding that Kaiserman had copied Gaste's melody.]

Fermata objects to the damages award of $268,000.[ii] Fermata argues that the award, which is based on its revenues from "Feelings" in the United States, should be reduced to account for the amount of the song's success attributable to the lyrics, independent of the infringing music. Fermata also argues that it is entitled to a reduction for the costs incurred in producing and distributing "Feelings."

We note preliminarily that the jury apparently made some apportionment of profits to account for the contribution of the lyrics and for the expenses incurred by Fermata. The parties agreed that Fermata's gross revenues from "Feelings" for the relevant time period were, in round numbers, $337,000. Although the record is not entirely clear on

[ii] [By "damages," the court means restitution of profits. The Copyright Act provides for recovery of "actual damages suffered by him or her as a result of the infringement, and any profits of the infringer that are attributable to the infringement and are not taken into account in computing the actual damages." 17 U.S.C.A § 504(b) (2004). The award of profits is based on the rightholder's entitlement to the work and its proceeds. Consequently, although liability depends on a finding that the infringer copied the claimant's work, it does not always require proof of conscious misappropriation.]

Kaiserman's revenue, the relevant figure appears to be $265,000.The jury found damages in the amount of $268,000 against Fermata and $233,000 against Kaiserman. Thus, the jury awarded Gaste approximately 80 percent of Fermata's gross revenues from "Feelings," and 88 percent of Kaiserman's revenues.

The District Court instructed the jury that if it made an apportionment for the lyrics, that apportionment would apply equally to Fermata and to Kaiserman. The jury was also told that only Fermata was entitled to reductions to cover the costs it incurred. Therefore, although we cannot be certain of the jury's reasoning absent a special verdict, it seems likely that the jury made a 12 percent reduction for both defendants to account for the lyrics and then made a further reduction of 8 percent for Fermata to account for its costs. With that in mind, we take Fermata's argument to be that the jury did not apportion enough and did not recognize enough of Fermata's costs.

A. *Lyrics.* A successful copyright plaintiff is entitled to recover only those profits that are "attributable to the infringement." 17 U.S.C. § 504(b) (1982). "In establishing the infringer's profits, the copyright owner is required to present proof only of the infringer's gross revenue, and the infringer is required to prove his or her deductible expenses and the elements of profit attributable to factors other than the copyrighted work." *Id.* An infringing defendant is entitled to an apportionment of profits to account for his independent contributions only when "the evidence is sufficient to provide a fair basis of division so as to give the copyright proprietor all the profits that can be deemed to have resulted from the use of what belonged to him." Sheldon *v.* Metro-Goldwyn Pictures Corp., 309 U.S. 390, 402 (1940). Confronted with imprecision in the computation of expenses, a court should err on the side of guaranteeing the plaintiff a full recovery, but want of precision is not a ground for denying apportionment altogether.

There was no dispute at the trial that Kaiserman wrote the lyrics to "Feelings," and that those lyrics were noninfringing. Fermata and Kaiserman argued to the jury that as much as 80 percent of the income from the song should be attributed to the lyrics.

The evidence on the value of the lyrics was decidedly mixed. Kaiserman's expert, Lou Levy, a retired music publisher, testified that while there was no set rule, the normal practice in the record industry when the lyrics and music to a song are written by different artists is to split the royalties 50/50. He said a well-known lyricist or composer could draw a larger share and that a "bad" lyricist might get as little as 15 percent. Levy testified that he "loved" the song "Feelings" and that he believed the title and lyrics were "far better" than the music itself. Nonetheless, he was unable to recall the words to the song on the stand and yet was able to sing the opening tune. He also said that the music and the words were inseparable and refused to estimate any percentage division.

Defendants also argued at trial that the lyrics must have had some effect because "Pour Toi" had virtually no commercial success, while "Feelings" was a smash hit. On the other hand, there was also evidence that "Dis Lui," a French version of "Feelings" with completely different words, also had considerable success. This could indicate either that the French words were also popular or that it was the music that gave the song its appeal.

We note that in ABKCO Music, Inc. *v.* Harrisongs Music, Ltd., 508 F. Supp. 798 (S.D.N.Y. 1981), modified, 722 F.2d 988 (2d Cir. 1983), the District Court determined that three-fourths of the income of the infringing song "My Sweet Lord" was due to the music plagiarized from an earlier hit song, "He's So Fine." The Court deducted 25 percent for the defendant's contribution of the lyrics to "My Sweet Lord" and for the marketability added to the song by the fact that the defendant was former Beatle George Harrison.

Judge Conner, contrasting this case to *ABKCO* and declining to alter the jury's damage award, noted that Kaiserman, a virtual unknown before "Feelings," did not independently add the selling power of a Harrison. On the other hand, Fermata points out that the music to "Pour Toi" did not have the independently confirmed selling power of the music to "He's So Fine," which had been a No. 1 song in its own right.

We find no grounds to reject the jury's decision to apportion no more than 12 percent for the lyrics. As Judge Owen noted in *ABKCO,* "this is not an area susceptible to precise measurement." The jury had an opportunity to judge for itself the independent appeal of the lyrics and the music. The evidence of the varied success of the three songs with the same music—"Feelings," "Pour Toi," and "Dis Lui"—could reasonably have been interpreted as favoring either side. Given this mix of evidence, we cannot say that the jury's decision to rank the lyrics of "Feelings" at the low end of the scale was so unreasonable as to require reversal.

B. *Fermata's Costs.* As noted above, the jury appears to have subtracted approximately 8 percent from Fermata's revenues to account for Fermata's costs related to "Feelings," in addition to the 12 percent deduction for the lyrics. Fermata argues that the jury's verdict was contrary to the evidence. The company claims to have proved various costs that should have reduced the award to zero.

Again, we decline to overturn the jury's verdict. The burden is on the infringer to prove his costs. We note that Fermata's evidence of its costs was sorely lacking in documentation. Such documentary evidence is uniquely within the province of a defendant to produce. When a defendant infringer's own failure to keep records results in uncertainty, all doubt must be resolved in favor of the plaintiff. The jury here did not act unreasonably in rejecting estimates of costs that were not fully documented.

We also reject Fermata's contention that nearly 90 percent of its costs must be attributed to "Feelings" because "Feelings" brought in nearly 90 percent of the company's revenues. In a very similar case, we held that " '[o]verhead' which does not assist in the production of the infringement should not be credited to the infringer; that which does, should be; it is a question of fact in all cases.". . .

Here, Fermata published some 200 songs in addition to "Feelings." It was Fermata's burden to prove that its overhead was nonetheless attributable mainly to "Feelings." The jury, which assessed the credibility of the testimony about Fermata's expenses, was entitled to reject Fermata's evidence. In [a prior case], we held that even when defendants had not been able to establish their costs with precision, they should be able to deduct the minimum amount they in all likelihood spent. The jury's decision to allow Fermata only an 8 percent reduction for its costs is not inconsistent with that rule. . . .

Edwards v. Lee's Administrator

Court of Appeals of Kentucky, 1936.
265 Ky. 418.

■ STITES, JUSTICE. . . . About twenty years ago L. P. Edwards discovered a cave under land belonging to him and his wife, Sally Edwards. The entrance to the cave is on the Edwards land. Edwards named it the "Great Onyx Cave," no doubt because of the rock crystal formations within it which are known as onyx. This cave is located in the cavernous area of Kentucky, and is only about three miles distant from the world-famous Mammoth Cave. Its proximity to Mammoth Cave, which for many years has had an international reputation as an underground wonder, as well as its beautiful formations, led Edwards to embark upon a program of advertising and exploitation for the purpose of bringing visitors to his cave. Circulars were printed and distributed, signs were erected along the roads, persons were employed and stationed along the highways to solicit the patronage of passing travelers, and thus the fame of the Great Onyx Cave spread from year to year, until eventually, and before the beginning of the present litigation, it was a well-known and well-patronized cave. Edwards built a hotel near the mouth of the cave to care for travelers. He improved and widened the footpaths and avenues in the cave, and ultimately secured a stream of tourists who paid entrance fees sufficient not only to cover the cost of operation, but also to yield a substantial revenue in addition thereto. . . . In April, 1928, F. P. Lee, an adjoining landowner, filed this suit against Edwards and the heirs of Sally Edwards, claiming that a portion of the cave was under his land, and praying for damages, for an accounting of the profits which resulted from the operation of the cave, and for an injunction prohibiting Edwards and his associates from further trespassing upon or exhibiting any part of the cave under Lee's land. At the inception of this litigation, Lee undertook to procure a survey of the cave . . . . Edwards sought a writ of prohibition in this court against the circuit judge to prevent the carrying out of the order of survey. The writ was denied. . . . [T]he maxim, "Cujus est solum, ejus est usque ad cœlum et ad infernos" (to whomsoever the soil belongs, he owns also to the sky and to the depths) was considered and applied, and an analogy drawn between trespassing through mining beneath another's land and passing under it through a cave. . . . On final hearing the chancellor stated separately his findings of law and of fact in the following language:

> "The Court finds as a matter of law the plaintiff is entitled to recover of defendants the proportionate part of the net proceeds defendants received from exhibiting Great Onyx Cave from the years 1923 to 1930, inclusive, as the footage of said cave under Lee's land bears to the entire footage of the cave exhibited to the public for fees during the years 1923 to 1930, inclusive, with 6% interest on plaintiff's proportionate part of said fund for each year from the first day of the following year . . . .
>
> "2. The Court finds as a matter of fact there was 6,449.88 feet of said cave exhibited to the public during 1923 to 1930, inclusive, and that 2,048.60 feet of said footage was under Lee's lands making plaintiff entitled to 2048.60/6449.88 or 1/3 of the proceeds. . . ."

Appellants, in their attack here on the measure of damages and its application to the facts adduced, urge: (1) That the appellees had simply a hole in the ground, about 360 feet below the surface, which they could not use and which they could not even enter except by going through the mouth of the cave on Edwards' property; (2) the cave was of no practical use to appellees without an entrance, and there was no one except the appellants on whom they might confer a right of beneficial use; (3) Lee's portion of the cave had no rental value; (4) appellees were not ousted of the physical occupation or use of the property because they did not and could not occupy it; (5) the property has not in any way been injured by the use to which it has been put by appellants, and since this is fundamentally an action for damages arising from trespass, the recovery must be limited to the damages suffered by appellees (in other words, nominal damages) and cannot properly be measured by the benefits accruing to the trespasser from his wrongful use of the property; (6) as a result of the injunction, appellees have their cave in exactly the condition it has always been, handicapped by no greater degree of uselessness than it was before appellants trespassed upon it.

Appellees, on the other hand, argue that this was admittedly a case of willful trespass; that it is not analogous to a situation where a trespasser simply walks across the land of another, for here the trespasser actually used the property of Lee to make a profit for himself; that even if nothing tangible was taken or disturbed in the various trips through Lee's portion of the cave, nevertheless there was a taking of esthetic enjoyment which, under ordinary circumstances, would justify a recovery of the reasonable rental value for the use of the cave; that there being no basis for arriving at reasonable rental values, the chancellor took the only course open to him under the circumstances and properly assessed the damages on the basis of the profits realized from the use of Lee's portion of the cave. Appellees have taken a cross-appeal, however, on the theory that, since the trespass was willful, their damages should be measured by the gross profits realized from the operation of the cave rather than from its net profits. . . .

The proof . . . clearly indicates that the trespasses were willful, and not innocent. . . .

Ordinarily, the measure of recovery in assumpsit for the taking and selling of personal property is the value received by the wrongdoer. On the other hand, where the action is based upon a trespass to land, the recovery has almost invariably been measured by the reasonable rental value of the property. . . . But . . . it is apparent that rental value has been adopted, either consciously or unconsciously, as a convenient yardstick by which to measure the proportion of profit derived by the trespasser directly from the use of the land itself.

[The court then reviewed a variety of cases awarding restitution for unauthorized possession of land and misappropriation of trade names and trade secrets.]

[W]e are led inevitably to the conclusion that the measure of recovery in this case must be the benefits, or net profits, received by the appellants from the use of the property of the appellees. The philosophy of all these decisions is that a wrongdoer shall not be permitted to make a profit from his own wrong. . . . Appellees are not entitled to recover gross profits. They are limited to the benefits accruing to the appellants. . . .

In determining the profits which might fairly be said to arise directly from the use of appellees' segment of the cave, the chancellor considered not only the footage exhibited, but the relative value of the particular points of interest featured in advertising the cave, and their possible appeal in drawing visitors. Of thirty-one scenes or objects in the cave advertised by appellants, twelve were shown to be on appellees' property. Several witnesses say that the underground Lucikovah river, which is under the appellees' land for almost its entire exhibited length, is one of the most attractive features of the cave, if not its leading attraction. Other similar attractions are shown to be located on appellees' property. The chancellor excluded profits received by the appellants from the operation of their hotel, and we think the conclusion that one-third of the net profits received alone from the exhibition of the cave is a fair determination of the direct benefits accruing to the appellants from the use of the appellees' property. . . .

NOTES

1. Why exclude profits from the hotel from the restitution awarded to Lee?

2. Edwards explored the cave, improved it, and successfully advertised it as a tourist attraction. In determining net profits, should he be credited for the value of his services in developing the cave, as well as his out-of-pocket expenses? Should the court allocate a greater portion of net profits to Edwards to reflect the contribution that his development of the cave made to the profits of the enterprise?

3. Alley, a real estate broker, persuaded Ellison, aged 84, to sell Alley an option to purchase Ellison's farm. The price named in the option was $200,000 and the consideration Alley paid for the option was $500. Alley also acted as an advisor to Myers, aged 73, who had recently sold her farm (in a transaction arranged by Alley) to a developer for a hold-out price. Myers needed to reinvest the proceeds of her sale to avoid capital-gain taxation and Alley advised her to purchase Ellison's farm. Alley informed Myers that the price of the farm was $380,000. He then arranged a two-step closing in which Myers paid $380,000 to Alley for the Ellison farm and Alley's option to purchase it; then Alley paid $200,000 to Ellison in exchange for a deed made out to Myers.

In a suit by Ellison against Alley for breach of fiduciary duty, the court ordered Alley to disgorge his $180,000 profit on the transaction. It also refused to allow Alley a credit for the commission he would ordinarily charge for arranging a sale: "To permit the defendants credit for a reasonable commission on the sale of the Ellison property would be no more than offering an undeserved reward for avarice." Ellison *v.* Alley, 842 S.W.2d 605, 608 (Tenn. 1992).

Somerville v. Jacobs

Supreme Court of Appeals of West Virginia, 1969.
153 W. Va. 613.

■ HAYMOND, PRESIDENT. The plaintiffs, W.J. Somerville and Hazel M. Somerville, herein sometimes referred to as the plaintiffs, the owners of Lots 44, 45 and 46 in the Homeland Addition to the city of Parkersburg, in Wood County, believing that they were erecting a warehouse building on Lot 46 which they owned, mistakenly constructed the building on Lot 47 owned by the defendants, William L. Jacobs and Marjorie S. Jacobs, herein sometimes referred to as the defendants. Construction of the building was completed in January 1967 and by deed dated January 14, 1967 the Somervilles conveyed Lots 44, 45 and 46 to the plaintiffs Fred C. Engle and Jimmy C. Pappas who subsequently leased the building to the Parkersburg Coca-Cola Bottling Company, a corporation. Soon after the building was completed but not until then, the defendants learned that the building was on their property and claimed ownership of the building and its fixtures on the theory of annexation. The plaintiffs then instituted this proceeding for equitable relief in the Circuit Court of Wood

County and in their complaint prayed, among other things, for judgment in favor of the Somervilles for $20,500.00 as the value of the improvements made on Lot 47, or, in the alternative, that the defendants be ordered to convey their interest in Lot 47 to the Somervilles for a fair consideration. The Farmers Building and Loan Association, a corporation, the holder of a deed of trust lien upon the land of the defendants, was on motion permitted to intervene and be made a defendant in this proceeding. . . .

By final judgment rendered June 11, 1968, the circuit court required the defendants within 60 days to elect whether they would (1) retain the building and pay W.J. Somerville $17,500.00 or suffer judgment against themselves in his favor in that amount, or (2) convey title to Lot 47 of Homeland Addition to W.J. Somerville for the sum of $2,000.00 cash. . . .

The undisputed facts [are] that the plaintiff W.J. Somerville in placing the warehouse building upon Lot 47 entertained a reasonable belief based on the report of the surveyor that it was Lot 46, which he owned, and that the building was constructed by him because of a reasonable mistake of fact and in the good faith belief that he was constructing a building on his own property and he did not discover his mistake until after the building was completed. It is equally clear that the defendants who spent little if any time in the neighborhood were unaware of the construction of the building until after it was completed and were not at any time or in any way guilty of any fraud or inequitable conduct or of any act that would constitute an estoppel. In short, the narrow issue here is between two innocent parties and the solution of the question requires the application of principles of equity and fair dealing between them.

It is clear that the defendants claim the ownership of the building. Under the common law doctrine of annexation, the improvements passed to them as part of the land. This is conceded by the plaintiffs but they assert that the defendants can not keep and retain it without compensating them for the value of the improvements, and it is clear from the testimony of the defendant William L. Jacobs in his deposition that the defendants intend to keep and retain the improvements and refuse to compensate the plaintiffs for their value. The record does not disclose any express request by the plaintiffs for permission to remove the building from the premises if that could be done without its destruction, which is extremely doubtful as the building was constructed of solid concrete blocks on a concrete slab, and it is reasonably clear, from the claim of the defendants of their ownership of the building and their insistence that certain fixtures which have been removed from the building be replaced, that the defendants will not consent to the removal of the building even if that could be done.

In that situation if the defendants retain the building and refuse to pay any sum as compensation to the plaintiff W.J. Somerville they will be unjustly enriched in the amount of $17,500.00, the agreed value of the building, which is more than eight and one-half times the agreed $2,000.00 value of the lot of the defendants on which it is located, and by the retention of the building by the defendants the plaintiff W.J. Somerville will suffer a total loss of the amount of the value of the building. If, however, the defendants are unable or unwilling to pay for the building which they intend to keep but, in the alternative, would convey the lot upon which the building is constructed to the plaintiff W.J. Somerville upon payment of the sum of $2,000.00, the agreed value of the lot without the improvements, the plaintiffs would not lose the building and the defendants would suffer no financial loss because they would obtain payment for the agreed full value of the lot and the only hardship imposed upon the defendants, if this were required, would be to order them to do something which they are unwilling to do voluntarily. . . . Under the facts and circumstances of this case, if the defendants refuse and are not required to exercise their option either to pay W.J. Somerville the value of the improvements or to convey to him the lot on which they are located upon his payment of the agreed value, the defendants will be unduly and unjustly enriched at the expense of the plaintiff W.J. Somerville who will suffer the complete loss of the warehouse building which by bona fide mistake of fact he constructed upon the land of the defendants. Here, in that situation, to use the language of the Supreme Court of Michigan in Hardy *v.* Burroughs, 251 Mich. 578, "It is not equitable . . . that defendants profit by plaintiffs' innocent mistake, that defendants take all and plaintiffs nothing."

To prevent such unjust enrichment of the defendants, and to do equity between the parties, this Court holds that an improver of land owned by another, who through a reasonable mistake of fact and in good faith erects a building entirely upon the land of the owner, with reasonable belief that such land was owned by the improver, is entitled to recover the value of the improvements from the landowner and to a lien upon such property which may be sold to enforce the payment of such lien, or, in the alternative, to purchase the land so improved upon payment to the landowner of the value of the land less the improvements and such landowner, even though free from any inequitable conduct in connection with the construction of the building upon his land, who, however, retains but refuses to pay for the improvements, must, within a reasonable time, either pay the improver the amount by which the value of his land has been improved or convey such land to the improver upon the payment by the improver to the landowner of the value of the land without the improvements.

It is pertinent to observe that, in cases involving the right to recover for improvements placed by mistake upon land owned by one other than the improver, the solution of the questions involved depends largely upon the circumstances and the equities involved in each particular case. Here, under the facts as stipulated by the parties, the equities which control the decision are clearly in favor of the plaintiffs. . . .

■ CAPLAN, JUDGE, dissenting. . . . In my opinion for the court to permit the plaintiff to force the defendants to sell their property contrary to their wishes is unthinkable and unpardonable. This is nothing less than condemnation of private property by private parties for private use. . . .

I am aware of the doctrine that equity frowns on unjust enrichment. However, contrary to the view expressed by the majority, I am of the opinion that the circumstances of this case do not warrant the application of such doctrine. It clearly is the accepted law that as between two parties in the circumstances of this case he who made the mistake must suffer the hardship rather than he who was without fault.

I would reverse the judgment of the Circuit Court of Wood County and remand the case to that court with directions that the trial court give the defendant, Jacobs, the party without fault, the election of purchasing the building, of selling the property, *or* of requiring the plaintiff to remove the building from defendant's property. . . .

Shick v. Dearmore

Supreme Court of Arkansas, 1969.
246 Ark. 1209.

■ GEORGE ROSE SMITH, JUSTICE. In 1967 the appellee, Ben Dearmore, sold a vacant residential lot to Norbert Nelson, who was to pay for the lot in monthly installments over a period of two years. Nelson took possession of the lot by moving a trailer house to it and began the construction of a permanent dwelling house on the land. Nelson employed the appellant [Shick], a well driller, to drill a water well on the property. Shick successfully completed a well by drilling to a depth of 284 feet and installing 191 feet of pipe. Nelson ran out of money without having paid Dearmore for the lot or Shick for the water well. Nelson abandoned the project and apparently left the state, his whereabouts thereafter being unknown.

Later on it was learned that Nelson and Shick had made a mistake in locating the well, which was actually drilled at a point a few inches past Nelson's boundary line and upon an adjoining lot also owned by Dearmore. . . .

Dearmore knew nothing about the drilling until the well had been completed. At the end of the trial the chancellor apparently ruled in Dearmore's favor but went on to say that Shick might remove the pipe and restore the land as nearly as possible to its original condition. Upon objection, however, the court invited briefs on the question and later rendered a decree holding that the casing installed in the well was a permanent improvement that became part of the realty; so Shick had no right to remove it. This appeal is from that decree. . . .

We are convinced that in a court of equity Shick should be given the right to remove the casing and restore the land to its original condition, if that can be done without damaging the land. Any other holding would allow Dearmore to be unjustly enriched by obtaining a flowing water well to which he has no equitable claim.

The chancellor followed the strict common-law rule in holding that a permanent improvement placed upon another's land by mistake becomes a part of the realty and cannot be removed. Such a rule is obviously unjust when the improvement can be removed without damage to the freehold. . . .

When the Restatement of Restitution was published in 1937 the American Law Institute took the position in § 42 that the harshness of the common-law rule had been mitigated in most states at least to the extent of allowing restitution as a defense or set-off to affirmative relief sought by the landowner. Since then the steady trend of the decisions has been to allow the removal of the improvements in an equitable proceeding whenever that course can be followed without substantial damage to the land. . . .

We are so strongly in favor of the equitable view that has been taken more and more widely in the past several decades that we have no hesitancy in adopting it in the case at hand. Thus the chancellor's immediate reaction at the close of the proof was right—that Shick should be allowed to remove his casing and restore the land to its original condition. It is not entirely clear, however, that such a course can be followed without damage to the land that might fairly be considered to be substantial when compared to the pecuniary loss that Shick would otherwise sustain. Pursuant to our discretionary power to remand a chancery case for further proof, we think it best to remand this cause to give the parties an opportunity to develop the proof upon the point mentioned, with leave to the chancellor to dispose of the matter by an award according to the principles of equity. . . .

■ FOGLEMAN, JUSTICE (dissenting). . . . The majority opinion, based upon the chancellor's finding that this fixture is a permanent improvement, allows appellant to come upon the land and reclaim it. However equitable this result may seem in this case, it amounts to an overruling of a long standing rule of property, *i.e.*, that permanent fixtures become part of the realty and belong to the owner thereof. . . .

NOTES

1. *Somerville* and *Shick* involve restitution in equity rather than law. As these cases indicate, equitable remedies can take a variety of forms, with quite different effects for the parties.

2. Roberts mistakenly drilled a well on Comer's adjacent property. Comer brought an action of ejectment against Roberts, and Roberts counterclaimed for equitable relief. The Oregon Supreme Court affirmed the trial court's decree ordering Comer to transfer to Roberts the one-eleventh of an acre on which the well stood in return for a payment of $500. Comer *v.* Roberts, 252 Or. 189 (1968).

C. CLAIMS TO SPECIFIC PROPERTY: CONSTRUCTIVE TRUSTS AND TRACING

Brown v. Brown

Missouri Court of Appeals, 2005.
152 S.W.3d 911.

■ JOSEPH M. ELLIS, JUDGE. . . . The subject of the lawsuit is approximately twenty acres of rural real estate, on which a modular home, a cabin . . . , a nine-acre lake, and a single-wide trailer are present. The land, which is located about five miles west of Odessa, Missouri, was originally purchased in February 1966 by Catherine [Brown] and her husband, Edward Brown. There were four children of the marriage: John, Pam, Joseph, and Carolyn. When Edward Brown died on June 24, 1988, his interest in the real estate devolved to Catherine, who became the sole record title owner of the property. By warranty deed dated June 12, 1989, Catherine granted the land to Catherine and her son John as joint tenants with right of survivorship. . . . On October 16, 1997, Catherine executed another warranty deed transferring title to her remaining interest in the land to Catherine and her daughter Pam as joint tenants with right of survivorship. . . .

John testified that some time in 1999, he and his mother decided that Pam should be properly added as a third joint tenant with right of survivorship. On August 23, 1999, [Catherine, John, and Pam] visited the Independence, Missouri, law office of Joyce B. Kerber, an attorney, bringing with them a copy of the 1989 and 1997 warranty deeds. . . .

After the meeting of August 23, 1999, Kerber prepared three quitclaim deeds. The first was a quitclaim deed conveying John's interest in the land to Catherine. The second transferred Pam's interest in the land to Catherine, and the third deeded Catherine's interest in the land to Catherine, John, and Pam as joint tenants with right of survivorship. Kerber testified that the first two quitclaim deeds were prepared with the intention of clearing up the prior and conflicting warranty deeds executed by Catherine so the property could then properly be conveyed, via the third quitclaim deed, to Catherine, John, and Pam as joint tenants with right of survivorship. . . .

As misfortune would have it, on November 4, 1999, the Recorder of Deeds recorded the deeds in the reverse order of that intended by Kerber, Catherine, John, and Pam. That is to say, the third quitclaim deed (from Catherine to the three parties jointly) was recorded first, followed by the other two quitclaim deeds (from John to Catherine and from Pam to Catherine) very shortly thereafter. . . . Unbeknownst to John and Pam, the result of the order of the filing of the deeds was that Catherine held the property in fee simple absolute, leaving them no interest in the property whatsoever.

On April 3, 2002, Catherine . . . executed a beneficiary deed purporting to convey the property, upon her death, to each of her four children (Joseph, Carolyn, John, and Pam) as joint tenants with right of survivorship. . . . Considered in conjunction with the effect of the prior quitclaim deeds (including the order in which they were recorded), this would have left John and Pam with one-fourth interests in the property on Catherine's death, rather than one-half interests . . . .

Shortly thereafter, John and Pam discovered what had happened. When Catherine subsequently refused to rectify the mistake by altering or revoking the beneficiary deed, their relationship with her deteriorated. On June 12, 2002, John and Pam filed the present action, seeking a variety of equitable relief, including the imposition of a constructive trust and the cancellation of the beneficiary deed, to rectify the mistake made by Kerber and/or the Lafayette County Recorder of Deeds. . . .

Technically, constructive trusts are not trusts at all, but equitable devices employed by courts of equity. They arise "by operation of law, or, more accurately, by construction of the court, regardless and independently of any actual or presumed intention of the parties to create a trust." Schultz *v.* Schultz, 637 S.W.2d 1, 4 (Mo. banc 1982). "The constructive trust may be defined as the device used by chancery to compel one who unfairly holds a property interest to convey that interest to another to whom it justly belongs." Kerber *v.* Rowe, 348 Mo. 1125 (1941). "In a constructive trust the beneficial interest in the property is from the beginning in the person who has been wronged. The constructive trust arises from the situation in which he is entitled to the remedy of restitution, and it arises as soon as that situation is created." Page *v.* Joplin National Bank & Trust Co., 363 Mo. 1008 (1953).

Thus a court of equity may impose or declare a constructive trust to provide a remedy in cases where one who " 'has acquired property under such circumstances as make it inequitable for him to retain it' " by making him or her a trustee for the person or persons injured thereby. Schultz, 637 S.W.2d at 4. In doing so, the court merely uses the machinery of a trust as a remedial device, even though the actual mechanism used to do so is, in strict contemplation of the law, not a trust. . . .

[C]ontrary to Appellant's argument, it is not necessary that the unjustly enriched party be found to have engaged in legal wrongdoing or have had wrongful or malicious intent. Rather, the touchstone for imposition of a constructive trust is injustice or unfairness, which may take the form or be the product of fraud (actual or constructive), abuse of a fiduciary or confidential relationship, undue influence, or unjust enrichment. . . . [T]he constructive trust is a fluid, flexible device which may be employed to remedy many different types of injustice. . . .

[T]he trial court found that Catherine accidentally received an undivided fee simple interest in the property as a result of a mistake made by attorney Kerber and/or the Lafayette County Recorder of Deeds.

At the moment she received all Respondents' interest in the property and thereby began enjoying an undivided ownership interest in real estate that was not intended to become hers alone, Catherine became subject to a duty to hold the real estate in constructive trust for John and Pam, the equitable co-owners of the property, even though Catherine's acquisition of their ownership interests was not wrongful in and of itself. When Catherine subsequently executed the beneficiary deed, she breached the constructive trust, unjustly depriving John and Pam of a significant portion of their vested present and future interest in the property and unjustly enriching herself in the process. As equity requires that the mistake be remedied by returning the property to its rightful owners, the trial court did not err in imposing a constructive trust. . . .

NOTE

Husband and Wife divorced in August 1996, after six years of marriage. In September, the court entered a decree requiring Husband to pay $200 a week in child and spousal support, beginning September 20. Husband failed to make the September 20 payment. On September 28, he purchased a winning $2 lottery ticket, which paid $4.9 million. Wife sued, claiming that because Husband bought the ticket with money he should have paid to her, the court should impose a constructive trust on the winnings in her favor. The court denied her claim, reasoning that although Husband owed Wife a debt on September 28, he did not hold identifiable property subject to a constructive trust on that date; therefore his lottery winnings were not proceeds of assets held in trust. Ruffin *v.* Ruffin, 2000 WL 198078 (Va. App. 2000) (unpublished opinion).

Costell v. First National Bank of Mobile

Supreme Court of Alabama, 1963.
274 Ala. 606.

■ MERRILL, JUSTICE. This appeal is from a final decree granting relief to complainants, who sought to have a constructive trust declared on two parcels of land. . . .

The theory of the bill is that Margaret Cox, a miserly old lady who distrusted banks, had hidden in her home at the time of her death a large amount of currency, some or all of which was stolen by Irene Hurley, a stenographer for the attorney representing the special administrator, while the attorney, the special administrator and the heirs of the decedent were searching Mrs. Cox's home in the hope of finding any such currency. It is then charged that Irene Hurley passed some of the Cox currency to her uncle, W. C. Lantron, who lived in Texas, and that he used this Cox money in buying two parcels of land in Mobile in April, 1953, some seven months after the death of Mrs. Cox. . . .

All of the evidence that Irene Hurley stole the money was circumstantial, but it was nevertheless cogent. Some of the evidence follows.

Margaret Cox was known by her relatives to have gold, bonds and currency in large denominations hidden somewhere. She had rental property which furnished a good income and she paid all her bills in cash. She had operated a store in her earlier days.

Mrs. Cox died at her home at 4:30 A. M. on September 8, 1934, and the only person with her was Mrs. Roberta Steele, the widow of a nephew of Mrs. Cox. Mrs. Steele had handled the checks and bond coupons for Mrs. Cox for about ten years, cashing them at the bank and giving the cash to Mrs. Cox. She usually got large bills, $100, $50 and $20. Mrs. Cox had $95,000 in bonds, but in April, 1934, some Liberty Bonds were called and Mrs. Steele cashed those and gave her nine $1000 bills. Mrs. Cox kept her currency in a black bag or pocket book. She had several rolls of bills with a string tied around them.

On the morning Mrs. Cox died, Mrs. Steele took the $86,000 in bonds from a hidden drawer and put them in her own bank. That same day, Frank Norden, a nephew of Mrs. Cox, consulted an attorney, told him that money was probably hidden in the house, and the attorney prepared papers to have Norden appointed special administrator. He was so appointed on Saturday and he posted night and day guards outside the house until Monday. On Monday morning he, his three sisters, his attorney and the attorney's secretary, Irene Hurley, entered the house to make a search for hidden money. They found $11,800 in gold coins in the bottom of a wood box by the fireplace. When they took out the wood and turned the box upside down, the gold rolled all over the floor. The coins were piled up in the middle of the bed. They did not find the bonds (Mrs. Steele had them) and they did not find the black bag.

During the search, Irene Hurley said her husband was outside and had never seen that much gold and requested that he be permitted to come in and see it. She was told that he could come to the door of the room and look in. He did so, and Irene handed him a rolled up apron that she had been wearing that day. He took the apron and left. She also brought and carried away a briefcase with her employer's name on it. At this time, Irene Hurley was making $18 per week, was known to be poor, wore inexpensive clothes and her house was in great need of repair.

Shortly after the death of Mrs. Cox, Irene Hurley, her husband and her mother seemed to be much more prosperous. They moved into the house on one of the parcels of land described in the bill, Irene began to flash diamond rings, wear expensive clothes and they had three automobiles. In 1938, Irene and her husband were divorced without any recorded property settlement, but she continued to live well.

In October, 1935, the administrators hired D. N. Harrelson, a private detective, to try to locate the missing currency. He found that Irene Hurley had been spending a considerable amount of money in the seven months following Mrs. Cox's death, that she had moved into a nice home which had been bought by a supposedly rich uncle, W. C. Lantron, from Texas, who claimed to be a millionaire.

Harrelson went to Texas, found that W. C. Lantron looked like a tramp, was living in a two-room shanty in an oil field, was working occasionally for fifty or seventy-five cents a day and his wife "had been on relief." He got Lantron to go with him to the office of the District Attorney in Breckenridge, Texas, and with a deputy sheriff, questioned Lantron. At first, Lantron denied any knowledge of anything concerning Mobile, but he stated orally and in writing that he went to Mobile and purchased a house and lot for $4500, paying $3000 in cash and promising to pay the balance in a few months without an interest charge. He also purchased a lot for $676 cash. All the money was furnished to him by Irene Hurley. Later, Irene came to Breckenridge, where Lantron lived, and they drove to Graham and he went into the First National Bank at Graham and got a certified check for $1500 . . . (the balance due on the house and lot). He paid for this certified check with a $1000 bill and the rest in hundreds and fifties. He said he insisted on going to Graham because he did not want people in Breckenridge to get suspicious over his having that much money. The banker at Graham, the District Attorney and the deputy sheriff testified by deposition in the case. . . .

Later, Lantron answered interrogatories saying that Irene did not furnish the money and that the money was his own. However, he refused to answer over eighty interrogatories on the grounds that the answer would tend to incriminate him, or subject him to criminal prosecution.

Irene Hurley also refused to answer over one hundred interrogatories because "the same calls for testimony that may tend to subject the respondent to criminal prosecution." Her statement, like Lantron's, was in answer to interrogatories and was made under oath. . . .

Of course, Irene Hurley could not acquire title to stolen money, but she could acquire title to the land purchased with the stolen money. . . .

It is a general rule in most jurisdictions that if the funds of one person are wrongfully used by another in the purchase of real estate in his own name, or in the improvement of his real estate, a constructive trust in the property purchased or improved will arise in favor of the one whose money was wrongfully used, whether the relation at the time of the misuse or misapplication of the funds was a fiduciary one, or that of employer and employee, or whether they stood to each other as strangers; and the beneficiary of the trust so raised is entitled to go into equity and compel a conveyance of the legal title to the property to himself, in the hands of either of the wrongdoer, or of a transferee who does not stand as a bona fide purchaser for value. . . .

We hold that the allegations and the proof show that the two parcels of property were purchased with money stolen by Irene Hurley and the court correctly held that a constructive trust arose in the property in favor of the heirs of Margaret Cox, and that they were entitled to the property purchased with the stolen money. . . .

NOTES

1. LaMar Kay was employed as an accountant by The Church of Jesus Christ of Latter-day Saints (also known as the Mormon Church). For two years, he embezzled funds from the Church and placed them in a bank account he maintained under a fictitious name. He wrote checks from this account to purchase a Pontiac Firebird and a Chevrolet Corvette and transferred the titles to both cars to Vickie Jolley. The trial court imposed a constructive trust on both cars in favor of the Church. The Utah Supreme Court affirmed, saying:

> "Inasmuch as [Jolley] is not a bona fide purchaser for value, her defenses in raising the question as to her lack of knowledge of the source of the funds which purchase the automobiles, and her averment that a constructive trust can only be impressed upon the wrongdoing fiduciary or confidant, are of no avail to her. Where one has stolen or embezzled the money or property of another . . . [a] constructive trust may be impressed upon it in his hands; and equity may continue the trust effective against any subsequent transferee, unless transferred to a bona fide purchaser and under circumstances where equity would require a different result."

Corporation of the President of the Church of Jesus Christ of Latter-Day Saints *v.* Jolley, 24 Utah 2d 187, 188–89 (1970).

2. More than a century ago, Dean Ames described the process of "tracing" restitution claims to identifiable property:

> "If a trustee wrongfully sells the trust-*res* or exchanges it for other property, the *cestui que trust* may charge him as a constructive trustee of the money or newly acquired property, or of any subsequent product of either; or, if he prefers, he may enforce an equitable lien to the amount of the misappropriation upon any property in the hands of the wrongdoer, which is the traceable product of the original trust-*res.* If, at the time of relief given, the new property is worth less than the original trust-*res,* the *cestui que trust,* after exhausting his lien, will have a personal claim against the trustee for the difference. If the new property is worth as much as or more than the original trust-*res,* the enforcement of the constructive trust or of the equitable lien will be a full satisfaction of all claims founded on the breach of the express trust. When the value of the new property exceeds that of the original trust, the *cestui que trust,* by enforcing the constructive trust, makes a profit by the trustee's breach of the express trust, and this profit may be very large, as when the trust fund is invested in land or corporate shares which advance rapidly, or, to put the most conspicuous instance of great profit, when the trustee invests trust money in taking out a policy of life insurance which becomes payable soon afterwards by the death of the insured. The *cestui que trust* takes the whole of the insurance money, although ten times as much as the trust money misappropriated. This excess above full compensation is not given to the *cestui que trust* by reason of any

merit on his part. It comes to him as a mere windfall. Public policy demands that the faithless trustee should not retain any advantage derived from his breach of trust. Hence the wholesome rule that whatever a trustee loses in the misuse of the trust fund he loses for himself, and whatever he wins, he wins for the beneficiary."

James B. Ames, Following Misappropriated Property Into Its Product, 19 Harv. L. Rev. 511, 511–512 (1906).

Simonds v. Simonds

Court of Appeals of New York, 1978.
45 N.Y.2d 233.

■ BREITEL, CHIEF JUDGE. Plaintiff Mary Simonds, decedent's first wife, seeks to impress a constructive trust on proceeds of insurance policies on decedent's life. The proceeds had been paid to the named beneficiaries, defendants Reva Simonds, decedent's second wife, and their daughter Gayle. Plaintiff, however, asserts as superior an equitable interest arising out of a provision in her separation agreement with decedent. . . .

On March 9, 1960, decedent Frederick Simonds and his wife of 14 years, plaintiff Mary Simonds, entered into a separation agreement which, on March 31, 1960, was incorporated into an Illinois divorce decree granted to plaintiff on grounds of desertion. The agreement provided, somewhat inartfully: "The husband agrees that he will keep all of the policies of Insurance now in full force and effect on his life. Said policies now being in the sum of $21,000.00 and the Husband further agrees that the Wife shall be the beneficiary of said policies in an amount not less than $7,000.00 and the Husband further agrees that he shall pay any and all premiums necessary to maintain such policies of Insurance and if for any reason any of them now existing the policies shall be cancelled or be caused to lapse, he shall procure additional insurance in an amount equal to the face value of the policies having been cancelled or caused to lapse." Thus, the husband was to maintain, somehow, at least $7,000 of life insurance for the benefit of his first wife as a named beneficiary.

On May 26, 1960, less than two months after the divorce, decedent husband married defendant Reva Simonds. Defendant Gayle Simonds was born to the couple shortly thereafter.

Sometime after the separation agreement was signed, the then existing insurance policies were apparently canceled or permitted to lapse. It does not appear from the record why, how, or when this happened, but the policies were not extant at the time of decedent husband's death on August 1, 1971. In the interim, however, decedent has acquired three other life insurance policies, totaling over $55,000, none of which named plaintiff as a beneficiary. Hence, at the time of decedent's death he had continuously violated the separation agreement by maintaining no life insurance naming the first wife as a beneficiary. . . .

[T]he first wife would of course be entitled to maintain an action for breach against the estate. The estate's insolvency, however, would make such an action fruitless. Thus, the controversy revolves around plaintiff's right, in equity, to recover $7,000 of the insurance proceeds. . . .

Equity arose to soften the impact of legal formalisms; to evolve formalisms narrowing the broad scope of equity is to defeat its essential purpose.

Whatever the legal rights between insurer and insured, the separation agreement vested in the first wife an equitable interest in the insurance policies then in force. An agreement for sufficient consideration, including a separation agreement, to maintain a claimant as a beneficiary of a life insurance policy vests in the claimant an equitable interest in the policies designated. This interest is superior to that of a named beneficiary who has given no consideration, notwithstanding policy provisions permitting the insured to change the designated beneficiary freely. . . .

Obviously, the policies now at issue are not the same policies in existence at the time of the separation agreement. But it has been held that mere substitution of policies, or even substitution of insurance companies, does not defeat the equitable interest of one who has given sufficient consideration for a promise to be maintained as beneficiary under an insurance policy. The persistence of the promisee's equitable interest is all the more evident where the agreement expressly provides for a change in policies, and in effect provides further that the promisee's right shall attach to the new policies.

For a certainty, the first wife's equitable interest would be easier to trace if the new policies were quid pro quo replacements for the original policies. The record does not reveal whether this was so. But inability to trace plaintiff's equitable rights precisely should not require that they not be recognized, much as in the instance of damages difficult to prove. The separation agreement provides nexus between plaintiff's rights and the later acquired policies. The later policies were expressly contemplated by the parties, and it was agreed that plaintiff would have an interest in them. No reason in equity appears for denying plaintiff that interest, so long as no one who has given value for the policies or otherwise suffered a detriment is involved. The second wife's innocence does not offset the wrong by the now deceased husband.

The conclusion is an application of the general rule that equity regards as done that which should have been done. Thus, if an insured, upon lapse or cancellation of insurance, followed by replacement with new insurance, has a contractual obligation to designate a particular person as beneficiary, equity will consider the obligee as a beneficiary.

In this case, then, the first wife's interest in the original policies extended as well to the later acquired policies. The husband, upon lapse or cancellation of the earlier policies, had by virtue of the separation agreement an obligation to name her as beneficiary on the later policies, an obligation enforceable in equity despite the husband's failure to comply with the terms of the separation agreement. Due to the husband's failure to do what he should have done, the first wife acquired not only a right at law to sue his estate for breach of contract, a right now worthless, but also an equitable right in the policies, a right which, upon the husband's death, attached to the proceeds.

And, since the first wife was entitled to $7,000 of the insurance proceeds at the time of the husband's death, she is no less entitled because the proceeds have already been converted by being paid, erroneously, to the named beneficiaries. Her remedy is imposition of a constructive trust. . . .

Unjust enrichment . . . does not require the performance of any wrongful act by the one enriched. Innocent parties may frequently be unjustly enriched. What is required, generally, is that a party hold property "under such circumstances that in equity and good conscience he ought not to retain it" (Miller *v.* Schloss, 218 N.Y. 400, 407). A bona fide purchaser of property upon which a constructive trust would otherwise be imposed takes free of the constructive trust, but a gratuitous donee, however innocent, does not.

The unjust enrichment in this case is manifest. At a time when decedent was, certainly, anxious to remarry, he entered into a separation agreement with his wife of 14 years. As part of the agreement, he promised to maintain $7,000 in life insurance with the first wife as beneficiary. Later he broke his promise, and died with insurance policies naming only the second wife and daughter as beneficiaries. They have collected the proceeds, amounting to more than $55,000, while the first wife has collected nothing. Had the husband kept his promise, the beneficiaries would have collected $7,000 less in proceeds. To that extent, the beneficiaries have been unjustly enriched, and the proceeds should be subjected to a constructive trust. . . .

The issues in this case should not generate significant controversy. The action is in equity, and the equities are clear. True, some courts have decided the issues differently. Those cases, however, rely heavily on formalisms and too little on basic equitable principles, long established in Anglo-American law and in this State and especially relevant when family transactions are involved. "A court of equity in decreeing a constructive trust is bound by no unyielding formula. The equity of the transaction must shape the measure of relief" (Beatty *v.* Guggenheim Exploration Co., 225 N.Y. 380, 389 [Cardozo, J.]). . . .

NOTES

1. Jerome Rogers signed a separation agreement in which he promised to maintain his $15,000 life insurance policy in force, naming his ex-wife Susan as beneficiary. Jerome let the policy lapse. Later, he married Judith; still later, he obtained a $15,000 policy naming Judith as beneficiary. Then he died. The New York Court of Appeals held that Judith held the proceeds of the policy in effect at Jerome's death subject to a constructive trust for Susan. The court noted that, unlike the separation agreement in Simonds *v.* Simonds, the Rogers' separation agreement did not expressly cover future policies. This difference, however, was of no consequence: in either case the agreement to maintain insurance "did not and could not identify a specific *res* as subject to the first wife's superior right." Rogers *v.* Rogers, 63 N.Y.2d 582, 587 (1984). The court explained it decision in favor of Susan as follows:

> "In general, it is necessary to trace one's equitable interest to identifiable property in the hands of the purported constructive trustee. But in view of equity's goal of softening where appropriate the harsh consequences of legal formalisms, in limited situations the tracing requirement may be relaxed."

Id. at 586.

2. Alfred Perry signed a separation agreement with his wife Isobel in which he agreed to substitute his minor children for his mother, Mary, as beneficiaries of a life insurance policy. He kept the policies in place but never made the change. Mary paid the premiums on the policy until Alfred's death, when the proceeds were paid to her. The court held that the settlement agreement "constituted an equitable assignment of the policies for the children's benefit and gave them a vested right to proceeds, subject to be defeated only by proof of a superior right." Perry *v.* Perry, 484 S.W.2d 257, 258 (Mo. 1972). The fact that Mary paid the premiums did not alter the effect of the assignment; however, Mary was entitled to a set-off against the children's claim in the amount of her payments.

Central Trust Co. v. Shepard (In re Shepard)

United States Bankruptcy Court, Middle District of Florida, 1983.
29 B.R. 928.

■ GEORGE L. PROCTOR, BANKRUPTCY JUDGE.

FINDINGS OF FACT

... 2. In mid-November, 1981, Shepard contacted David Milliman, an officer of Central [Trust Company] and told him that he was engaged in a new business venture, JDS Marketing, Inc. ("JDS"), to sell computer programs to consumers at a cost of between $50 and $250.

3. A standard merchant servicing agreement was entered into by Shepard and Central which allowed Shepard to deposit MasterCharge and VISA charge slips into his account and receive instantaneous credit in the face amount of the slips.

4. On November 11, 1981, a checking account was opened at Central in the name of JDS, and within a few days Shepard began depositing charge slips into the account.

5. Between November 19, 1981, and December 7, 1981, a period of about 20 days, Shepard deposited into the account charge slips totaling approximately $274,000.

6. Between November 20, 1981, and December 11, 1981, roughly the same time frame, Shepard withdrew from the account cash totaling approximately $250,000. . . .

8. Ken Morgan, the officer in charge of security at Central, reviewed the JDS records and noted large deposits and large withdrawals, especially one by wire transfer for $150,000 to be picked up in Las Vegas by Shepard on December 4, 1981.

9. Morgan and others under his supervision telephoned several of the persons whose names appeared on the charge slips and discovered that either they had ordered $5 worth of phonograph records pursuant to a newspaper advertisement or that they had ordered nothing from JDS but, at some time previously, had ordered something from Shepard Electronics, Inc., another business owned by and under the control of Shepard.

10. On December 17, 1981, Morgan was advised that the United States Postal Service was investigating Shepard and JDS based on a complaint filed by the New York Times. Morgan learned that Shepard had placed advertisements in the Times and other newspapers of national circulation offering to sell the "top ten record albums in the country" for $5.

11. The advertisements appeared in the newspapers the day before Shepard opened the JDS account, listing a toll-free telephone number through which record orders could be charged to VISA or MasterCharge. The telephone orders were received by an answering service in Omaha, Nebraska with which Shepard had contracted to receive and forward the orders. Upon receipt of the orders, the answering service forwarded them by courier to Shepard in Rochester, New York where he altered the $5 orders (charge slips) to read either $50 or $250. . . .

13. From June, 1981, through December 18, 1981, Shepard employed Mary E. ("Liz") McCormick as a secretary. McCormick is the person who actually made the deposits into the JDS account at Central and in many instances cashed the checks to make the withdrawals.

14. McCormick last saw Shepard on December 7, 1981. After that date, however, and in accordance with Shepard's instructions, McCormick cashed three more checks, each in the amount of $10,000.

15. McCormick put the $30,000 in currency into a filing cabinet in Shepard's home. McCormick last saw the money in the cabinet on

December 18, 1981. To her knowledge, no one other than she had access to the house.

16. On December 22, 1981, United States Postal Inspector Frank Kormann obtained a search warrant authorizing a search of Shepard's home.

17. The premises were searched the same day and among the items recovered was currency in the total amount of $28,440. The currency was still wrapped or "strapped" in the paper wrappers utilized by Central in the normal course of its business.

18. The wrappers had been dated and stamped by Central tellers, who worked at the branch at which Shepard had opened the JDS account, which was the same branch at which McCormick had cashed the last three checks totaling $30,000. The dates on the wrappers, which signify the date a Central teller counted and "strapped" the money, corresponded to the dates on which the checks were cashed. . . .

21. Central has been damaged, to date, by the fraudulent conduct of Shepard in the amount of $239,954.91. Central's loss is computed by taking the total withdrawals ($249,551.50) and subtracting or giving credit for any recoveries made by Central ($9,596.59). The "credit" figure ($9,596.59) is comprised of a few cash deposits made into the JDS account ($762) and of an amount returned to Central by a payee of one of the checks written on the JDS account ($8,834.59).

CONCLUSIONS OF LAW

. . . 5. Under New York law, a constructive trust will be imposed if a person holding title to property is subject to an equitable duty to convey it to another person and he would be unjustly enriched if he were permitted to retain it.

6. The circumstances in which a court will impose a constructive trust include those where the property was obtained by fraud. Based on the fact that Shepard obtained the currency in question as a result of a fraudulent scheme, absent an intervening bankruptcy, Shepard clearly would be charged with an equitable duty to reconvey any interest he may have in the currency to Central.

7. A constructive trust is analogous to an express trust in that a bifurcation of title occurs; bare legal title to the property is held by the possessor of the property while the beneficial interest is held by the person entitled to the property.

8. A constructive trust arises at the time of the occurrence of the events giving rise to the duty to reconvey the property. . . .

10. A person claiming to be the beneficiary under a constructive trust [is] required to trace the trust property and identify it in its original or substituted form. In the instant case, Central has clearly satisfied the tracing requirement.

11. Under the Bankruptcy Code, where a debtor holds only bare legal title to property without any equitable interest, bare legal title is all that becomes property of the estate. In other words, a trustee in bankruptcy succeeds to only such title and rights in property as the debtor had at the time the petition was filed. . . .

13. Although the bankruptcy trustee acquires bare legal title to property imposed with a constructive trust in favor of another, this interest is of no value to the estate and the trustee will be required to reconvey the property to the beneficial owner, subject only to proof under the doctrine of tracing. Shepard acquired the currency pursuant to a fraudulent scheme and therefore held the currency in constructive trust for Central. As a result, the Trustee acquired only bare legal title to the currency while Central retained the beneficial interest. This Court will require the Trustee to reconvey the currency to Central. . . .

NOTES

1. A bankruptcy trustee is charged with marshaling the debtor's non-exempt assets for division among unsecured creditors. The trustee is deemed to have the rights of a creditor with a judgment lien against all assets included in the bankruptcy estate. As the court indicated, the estate includes whatever title or rights in property the debtor owned when the bankruptcy petition was filed. Secured creditors are protected to the extent of the assets securing their claims, but the filing of a bankruptcy petition automatically stays collection proceedings. As a result, they must obtain permission from the court before foreclosing on collateral.

2. Shepard probably did not have many assets for division among his creditors. Why should Central Trust be in a better position than others?

3. Johnson persuaded Osin to convey land to him in exchange for a $30,000 note, falsely representing that he would prepare and record a deed of trust (a form of mortgage) securing the note. Johnson did not prepare and record the deed of trust. After the transaction with Osin, Johnson borrowed money from Perpetual Building Association, giving Perpetual a deed of trust on the land. Several other creditors then obtained judgments against Johnson. Under governing statutes, the judgment creditors automatically acquired judgment liens on all Johnson's assets, including the land.

In a contest among Osin, Perpetual, and Johnson's judgment creditors, the court held that Osin was entitled to a constructive trust on the land. It also held that Perpetual, which lent money to Johnson in exchange for a deed of trust on the land, was in the position of a bona fide purchaser (to the extent of the loan). Consequently, Perpetual's interest in the land was prior to Osin's equitable interest, but Osin's equitable interest was prior to the liens acquired by the Johnson's judgment creditors. The court explained:

> "The logical and rational basis for preferring the bona fide purchaser over the grantor . . . is that as between two innocent parties . . . , [Mrs. Osin] must yield to those who in good faith relied on the state of the record which her negligence allowed to exist. . . .

"The same rationale does not have equal validity when applied to judgment creditors of the fraudulent grantee. A judgment creditor possessing a statutory lien on property does not occupy a position equivalent to that of a purchaser for value and thus 'if the land of the debtor is subject to equities, the judgment creditor's lien is subject to such equities.' 3 Scott, TRUSTS § 308.1, p. 2276 (2d ed. 1956). As a matter of simple ordinary fairness, which is the essence of equity, there is every reason why a defrauded grantor of title should command a higher priority than creditors of the fraudulent grantee since such creditors usually do not rely on the record title in their extension of credit. The equitable considerations dictating the priority of an equitable right over subsequently acquired judgment liens was aptly summarized by this court many years ago:

> '. . . The [constructive trust] claimant . . . has an equity to the specific thing which binds the conscience of his grantor; whilst the judgment creditor, who has advanced nothing on the faith of the specific thing, is entitled only to that which his debtor really has, at the time, or could honestly convey or encumber; his beneficial interest and nothing more.' Hume *v.* Riggs, 12 App. D.C. 355, 367 (1898)."

Osin *v.* Johnson, 243 F.2d 653, 656–57 (D.C. Cir. 1957).

4. Omegas Group and Datacomp entered into a complex and somewhat shady agreement for customizing and re-marketing new IBM computers. In accordance with the agreement, Datacomp ordered computers from Omegas Group, which in turn ordered them from IBM. Omegas ran into financial difficulties that prevented it from placing orders with IBM, but continued to collect payments from Datacomp. Omegas Group then filed a bankruptcy petition. The bankruptcy court determined that the arrangement between Omegas Group and Datacomp was a form of joint venture and that Omegas Group owed Datacomp a duty to disclose its financial difficulties before collecting funds from Datacomp. Accordingly, the bankruptcy court imposed a constructive trust on funds Omegas Group received from Datacomp after Omegas Group realized that it would not be able to comply with the arrangement. In a maverick decision, the Court of Appeals for the Sixth Circuit reversed:

> "[T]he essence of the argument put forth by [Datacomp] goes as follows: 'Judge, due to debtor's fraud (or whatever), our property rights as beneficiaries of the constructive trust arose [before the filing of the bankruptcy petition]. Therefore, we stand not in the position of unsecured creditors, nor even equal to the trustee in the position of judgment creditors, but as the rightful owner of the *res* held in trust. Oh, and by the way, would you mind conferring on us these ownership rights and declaring that they arose prepetition?' This may seem silly phrased in this manner, but it is exactly the argument that most courts have accepted in holding that, due to some prepetition breach or bad act by the debtor, the claimed property or money is subject to a constructive trust and therefore

'did not come into the bankruptcy estate and must be returned to the [debtor].' Sommer *v.* Vermont Real Estate Investment Trust, 25 B.R. 813, 817 (Bankr. D. Vt. 1982); see also City National Bank of Miami *v.* General Coffee Corp., 828 F.2d 699, 704 (11th Cir.1987) ('[W]e agree with the district court that the constructive trust in favor of [claimant] came into existence before the bankruptcy proceedings began.'). . . .

"We think that § 541(d) [the Bankruptcy Code provision defining the property of the bankruptcy estate] simply does not permit a claimant in the position of Datacomp to persuade the bankruptcy court to impose the remedy of constructive trust for alleged fraud committed against it by the debtor in the course of their business dealings, and thus to take ahead of all creditors, and indeed, ahead of the trustee. Because a constructive trust, unlike an express trust, is a remedy, it does not exist until a plaintiff obtains a judicial decision finding him to be entitled to a judgment 'impressing' defendant's property or assets with a constructive trust. Therefore, a creditor's claim of entitlement to a constructive trust is not an "equitable interest" in the debtor's estate existing prepetition, excluded from the estate under § 541(d). . . .

"The equities of bankruptcy are not the equities of the common law. Constructive trusts are anathema to the equities of bankruptcy since they take from the estate, and thus directly from competing creditors, not from the offending debtor. . . .

"To permit a creditor, no matter how badly he was 'had' by the debtor, to lop off a piece of the estate under a constructive trust theory is to permit that creditor to circumvent completely the Code's equitable system of distribution."

XL/Datacomp, Inc. *v.* Wilson (In re Omegas Group, Inc.), 16 F.3d 1443, 1451–53 (6th Cir. 1994).

Carlson Orchards, Inc. v. Linsey (In re Linsey)

Bankruptcy Court, District of Massachusetts, 2003.
296 B.R. 582.

■ JOEL B. ROSENTHAL, BANKRUPTCY JUDGE. . . . [Nina Linsey worked as a bookkeeper for Carlson Orchards. During her 11 months of employment with Carlson, she embezzled more than $100,000 from the company by diverting checks payable to the company and writing extra paychecks to herself. She used some of the embezzled money to buy two cars, a Plymouth Grand Voyager and a Ford pick-up truck, both titled in the name of her husband, David Linsey, and some to purchase services and materials for improvements to the Linsey home, referred to as "the Property." The Linsey Property was subject to a valid homestead exemption.]

Carlson requests imposition of a constructive trust in its favor in the 1999 Plymouth Grand Voyager, the 1995 Ford F–150, and an undivided 32.26% interest in the Property. . . .

[I]n order to obtain a constructive trust over the property of a debtor, a party must (1) show either sufficient wrongdoing by the debtor in acquiring the property or a fiduciary relationship between the party and the debtor, and (2) be able to trace the wrongfully held property. . . . The first of the two requirements is easily met by Nina Linsey's admitted embezzlement. The tracing requirement, however, merits additional discussion.

It is well established that mere commingling of trust property with other property of the debtor does not defeat imposition of a constructive trust. In the case of commingling, however, the claimant bears the further burden of tracing the alleged trust property "specifically and directly" back to the illegal transfers giving rise to the trust. 4 COLLIER ON BANKRUPTCY ¶ 541.11[3] (15th ed. rev. 2000). The normal procedure for tracing trust proceeds which have been commingled in a bank account is by way of the "lowest intermediate balance test." The First Circuit explained the application of that test as follows:

> "Under that test . . . , a court will follow the trust fund and decree restitution from an account where the amount on deposit has at all times since the commingling of the funds equaled or exceeded the amount of the trust fund. Where, however, after the commingling, all the money is withdrawn, the trust fund is treated as lost, even though later deposits are made into the account. Should the amount on deposit be reduced below the amount of the trust fund but not depleted, the claimant is entitled to the lowest intermediate balance in the account. This is based on the fiction that the trustee would withdraw non-trust funds first, retaining as much as possible of the trust fund in the account."

Connecticut General Life Insurance Co. *v.* Universal Insurance Co., 838 F.2d 612, 619 (1st Cir. 1988).

The evidence that Carlson introduced to trace the funds stolen by Nina Linsey included 11 checks written by Nina Linsey. . . .

At trial, it was established that . . . checks payable to Home Depot were for the purchase of new windows and siding for the Property and for the installation of the windows and siding, that the checks payable to Joe Kenney were for landscaping improvements to the Property, and that the checks payable to Barry Electric were for electrical improvements to the Property. It was also established that the checks to David Linsey and Framingham Dodge were payments for the two vehicles. Thus, the checks listed above sufficiently trace the funds from Nina Linsey's bank accounts to the vehicles and home improvements. The Plaintiff, however, still must identify that the funds transferred by these checks are embezzled funds, rather than legitimate funds of Nina Linsey, and therefore subject to the trust.

It is conceded by the Defendants that the two vehicles were purchased with embezzled funds. Thus, Carlson is relieved of his burden of having to prove the funds transferred by the [car-payment] checks . . . were embezzled funds.

As to the remaining checks, the eight "home improvement" checks, Carlson must show that the balance in the account upon which each check was drawn did not dip below the amount of the check during the period of time between the time that embezzled funds were deposited into the account and the time the checks were drawn upon the account. . . .

The Court now turns to tracing the funds for each of the eight home improvement checks, applying the "lowest intermediate balance test": . . .

Check #1029 ($2,034)—Check #1029 was drawn upon the Community Checking Account on April 6, 2001. The balance in the Community Checking Account at that time was $4,849.74. These funds can be traced back to web transfers [of embezzled funds] in the amount of $5,262.24. [Therefore] the full $4,849.74 in the Community Checking Account on April 6, 2001 was subject to a trust and . . . Check #1029, in the amount of $2,034, was drawn upon that trust. . . .

Check #1031 ($600) and . . . Check #1028 ($2300)—Following Check #1029 being drawn upon the Community Checking Account, the balance in that account was $2,655.74. For the reasons discussed, *supra,* this $2,655.74 was subject to the trust. On April 9, 2001 there was another web transfer of $1,600 of trust funds . . . . This brought the amount of the trust (as well as the balance) in the Community Checking Account to $4,255.74. Check #1031 and check #1028 (totaling $2,900) were drawn upon these funds and thus the Court concludes that these checks are subject to the trust. . . .

Check #411 ($600)—Check #411 was drawn upon the Marlborough Account on April 19, 2001. A check in the amount of $2,000 was deposited into the Marlborough Account on April 13, 2001. The balance of the Marlborough Account between April 13 and April 19 at all times exceeded $600 and therefore Check #411 was drawn upon trust funds. . . .

Check #397 ($6,101)—Check #397 was drawn upon the Marlborough Account on June 1, 2001. The balance in the Marlborough Account at that time was $6,121.02. These funds can primarily be traced to a deposit made on May 22, 2001 in the amount of $6,814.01. The balance in the Marlborough Account, however, dipped to $5,522 on May 29, 2001. Although deposits were made into the Marlborough Account in the amount of $1,414.01 on May 30, 2001 and $300 on May 31, 2001, there is no evidence, nor can the Court determine with any precision, that these deposits were embezzled funds. Therefore, applying the "lowest intermediate balance test," the Court concludes that $5,522 of Check #397 was subject to the trust. . . .

Check #1061 ($6,957)—Check #1061 was drawn upon the Community Checking Account on June 7, 2001. Deposits of $2,000 and $6,905.24 were made into that account on May 30, 2001 and May 31, 2001, respectively. The balance in the account was reduced to $5,549.37 on June 5, 2001 but a deposit in the amount of $2,561.03 [presumed to be embezzled funds], on June 6, 2001, brought the total funds subject to the trust to $8,111.40. The balance between June 6, 2001 and the date that check #1061 was drawn upon the Community Checking Account did not dip below the amount of check #1061 ($6,957) and therefore the entire amount of check #1061 was drawn upon trust funds. . . .

Check #699 ($3,000)—Check #699 was drawn upon the Community Checking Account on August 3, 2001. A deposit of $4,500 was made into the Community Checking Account on that same day. Therefore, the entire amount of check #699 was drawn upon trust funds. . . .

Check #151 ($4,400)—Check #151 was drawn upon the Community Checking Account on June 21, 2001. A deposit of $5,615.39 was made into the Community Checking Account on June 19, 2001 and the balance of that account did not dip below the amount of check #151 ($4,400) between June 19 and June 21, 2001. Therefore, the entire amount of check #151 was drawn upon trust funds.

Based on the above, the Court concludes that Carlson has met its burden on tracing $25,413 from funds embezzled by Nina Linsey through Nina Linsey's bank account to improvements made to the Property. Nevertheless, the Defendants argue that the homestead filed by the Debtor in August 1994 should defeat the constructive trust. It is well established, however, that a homestead may not be employed as a shield and defense after fraudulently imposing on others. A homestead exemption does not apply where the homestead was purchased or improved with fraudulently acquired or stolen funds, embezzled funds or trust funds. . . .

The final question before the Court is what is the appropriate remedy. As to the two vehicles, it is admitted that they were purchased with the embezzled funds and thus are subject to a constructive trust in favor of Carlson. As to the improved property, the proper remedy is an equitable lien in favor of Carlson in the amount of $25,413. [Carlson is not entitled to a constructive trust on a fractional share of the property because Linsey] used the commingled funds to improve the property, rather than buy the property.

For the foregoing reasons, a constructive trust in favor of Carlson Orchards is imposed on the 1999 Plymouth Grand Voyager and the 1995 Ford F–150 and those vehicles are ORDERED turned over to Carlson Orchards. An equitable lien in favor of Carlson Orchards in the amount of $25,413 is hereby placed on the property located at 11 Meadowbrook Road, Hudson, Massachusetts. Upon proper filing of a motion for relief from the automatic stay . . . , Carlson Orchards may seek to execute on this Judgment in state court.

NOTES

1. Husband used Wife's funds to build an addition to their home, which was titled in his name. He promised repeatedly to convey a half interest in the property to her, but never did. After they divorced, Wife sued. The North Carolina Supreme Court held that Wife's claim was barred, but also concluded that, if she had sued earlier, she would have been entitled to an equitable lien on the property in the amount of the funds she provided.

> " '[W]here the wife voluntarily delivers her money to the husband, the law presumes that he takes it as trustee for her, and not as a gift. . . .' Etheredge *v.* Cochran, 196 N.C. 681, 682. . . .
>
> "Therefore, defendant had the duty to restore plaintiff her funds. Since she is able to trace the money into the improvements which defendant made on the land, any judgment obtainable would qualify as an equitable lien.
>
> "An equitable lien, or encumbrance, is not an estate in land, nor is it a right which, in itself, may be the basis of a possessory action. It is simply a charge upon the property, which charge subjects the property to the payment of the debt of the creditor in whose favor the charge exists. . . . In other words, an equitable lien, by charging specific property, provides an enforcement of the obligation more effective than that provided for the enforcement of the ordinary money judgment.
>
> " 'An equitable lien arises either from a written contract which shows an intention to charge some particular property with a debt or obligation, or is declared by a court of equity out of the general considerations of right and justice, as applied to the relations of the parties and the circumstances of their dealings." Garrison *v.* Vermont Mills, 154 N.C. 1, 6, modifying on rehearing 152 N.C. 643. . . .
>
> "In the absence of a contract an equitable lien most frequently arises in cases where one person has wrongfully expended, for improvements on his property, the funds of another, but instances of this sort of lien are not confined to such cases."

Fulp *v.* Fulp, 264 N.C. 20, 24–25 (1965).

2. If the recipient of property traceable to an unjust enrichment is innocent (for example, if the recipient obtained the property in good faith as a gift), the court may limit the claimant's remedy to an equitable lien and thus allow the recipient to retain any appreciation or gains from a profitable exchange.

If the recipient is a conscious wrongdoer, the claimant ordinarily may choose between a constructive trust and an equitable lien. The constructive trust typically is more advantageous if the property has appreciated. If, however, the property is worth less than the amount of the claimant's underlying restitution claim, the equitable lien may be more advantageous because it gives the claimant both a lien on traceable property and deficiency claim. In other words, if the traceable property is sold and the sale proceeds are insufficient to cover the underlying restitution claim, then, by analogy to a consensual lien, the claimant can continue to assert a claim to the balance due.

3. Subrogation, as described above (Chapter Twelve, Section E (Subrogation, Indemnity, and Contribution)) is a basis for liability in unjust enrichment: a person who discharges another's debt, and has some good reason to do so, can claim restitution from the debtor in the amount of the discharged debt. When various creditors are competing for the debtor's assets, subrogation has an additional remedial role, allowing the restitution claimant "to assume the same priority position as the holder of the previous encumbrance." Mort *v.* United States, 86 F.3d 890, 893 (9th Cir. 1996).

The case that follows (in which the court refers to remedial subrogation as "subrogation by equitable assignment") is an example.

Equity Savings and Loan Association v. Chicago Title Insurance Co.

Superior Court of New Jersey, Appellate Division, 1983.
190 N.J. Super. 340.

■ BRODY, J.A.D. Harvey Goldberg misused his position as an attorney in arranging the placement of two mortgages on the same property. He falsely represented to each mortgagee that its mortgage was a first lien. Their priorities are at issue in this foreclosure suit.

Goldberg's machinations began while the property was encumbered by a $12,000 first mortgage to Philip Raben and a $40,000 second mortgage to Valley Savings and Loan Association ("Valley"). In order to obtain a $48,000 mortgage loan from Equity Savings and Loan Association ("Equity"), Goldberg secured a subordination of the Raben mortgage but falsely certified to Equity that he had cancelled the Valley mortgage. In fact, he did not pay the Valley mortgage which by virtue of the subordination became the first mortgage on the property. About a year later Goldberg obtained a $54,000 mortgage loan from Spencer Savings and Loan Association ("Spencer") for his corporation Trunc Enterprises, Inc. which by then had acquired title to the property. Goldberg disclosed to Spencer only the Valley mortgage and satisfied it out of the proceeds of the Spencer loan. He concealed the Equity and Raben mortgages. When the truth came out, Chicago Title Insurance Co. ("Chicago") paid Spencer under its policy, took an assignment of the Spencer mortgage and purchased the Raben mortgage. This left the record priorities as follows: Equity, Chicago (Raben) and Chicago (Spencer). The present dispute is between Equity and Chicago. Relying on the state of the record and finding the equities equally balanced, the trial judge concluded that Equity was first. We reverse.

Since part of the proceeds of the Spencer loan was used to satisfy the Valley mortgage, Chicago, Spencer's assignee, stands in the shoes of Valley as though the Valley mortgage had been assigned to Spencer instead of cancelled. A refinancing lender whose security turns out to be defective is subrogated by equitable assignment "to the position of the lender whose lien is discharged by the proceeds of the later loan, there being no prejudice to or justified reliance by a party in adverse interest . . . ." Kaplan *v.* Walker, 164 N.J. Super. 130, 138 (App. Div. 1978); Restatement, Restitution, § 162 at 653 (1937).

The trial judge declined to apply the doctrine of subrogation by equitable assignment because, as he viewed it, there is no equitable reason to give Spencer an advantage over Equity since each was identically defrauded by Goldberg into believing its junior mortgage was first. We disagree. The difference between the two is that while there is no evidence of what Goldberg did with Equity's money, he used part of Spencer's money to cancel Valley's mortgage thereby gratuitously enhancing Equity's security. Since Spencer's money was obtained by fraud (the concealment of the Equity and Raben mortgages), Equity's windfall may be viewed as a product of the money stolen from Spencer. When stolen property or its product can be traced, it must be returned to its true owner. Here the return of Spencer's money is accomplished through application of the doctrine of subrogation by equitable assignment. . . .

The mortgage priorities are therefore as follows: (1) Chicago in the amount it paid to satisfy the Valley mortgage, (2) the Equity mortgage, and (3) the Chicago mortgages. . . .

PART V

ADDITIONAL TOPICS

CHAPTER 14

REMEDIES AGAINST THE GOVERNMENT

As a general rule, the remedies available against a private defendant are also available against a public defendant. These include damages and injunctions, as well as restitutionary remedies such as the constructive trust. Nevertheless, special issues arise when suits are brought against government officers.

In recent decades, federal courts have been wary of imposing substantial damages on state and federal officers, often pointing to concerns about over-deterrence or the potential fiscal burden on a government. At the same time, there has been a growth in the use of injunctions against officers. Neither of these trends—the trend toward less use of damages, and the trend toward more use of injunctions—has been steady, however, and it is unclear what the future will hold.

Under the traditional model, plaintiffs would sue state and federal officers for damages under common law causes of action such as trespass. Where damages would be inadequate, an injunction could be given, but it would be limited to protecting the plaintiffs and their property from expected, and usually imminent, executive action.

Several things have changed with regard to damages. One is the growth of government immunity from state tort law. Another is the rise and fall of *Bivens* claims, which are constitutional claims seeking damages from federal actors. Still another is the enormous increase in qualified immunity that protects state and federal officers from liability.

In addition, there has been a dramatic increase in the scope and incidence of injunctions against the government in the last half-century. One such kind of injunction—a structural injunction, in which a court takes over the management of an institution such as a school system—has ebbed since the high tide of the decade and a half after Brown *v.* Board of Education. Since the 1970s, federal courts have been less willing to issue broad structural injunctions. But the quick resort to injunctions has continued, and a suit for an injunction (with a request for a preliminary injunction pending resolution of the case) is now the default for challenges to a statute or agency rule.

There has thus been major change, over the last two centuries, in the law and practice of remedies against the government. And there may be more change ahead.[i] Whatever happens, for a good litigator,

[i] Nearly every element of the current model of remedies against the government has been the subject of vigorous criticism, whether on grounds of the original understanding of the Constitution, equitable principles, the historic practices of the federal courts, current practices related to indemnification, or incentives for government conduct. See, *e.g.*, James E. Pfander,

Shakespeare was right: "What's past is prologue." Litigators may need to make arguments that draw upon the traditional and current models, and Section A of this chapter equips you to understand them both. Section B considers structural injunctions against government institutions.

A. EXECUTIVE ACTIONS NOT AUTHORIZED BY LAW

1. THE TRADITIONAL MODEL

Little v. Barreme

Supreme Court of the United States, 1804.
2 Cranch 170.

■ MARSHALL, CHIEF JUSTICE, now delivered the opinion of the Court.

The *Flying-Fish* a *Danish* vessel having on board *Danish* and neutral property, was captured on the 2d of *December* 1799, on a voyage from *Jeremie* to *St. Thomas's* by the United States frigate *Boston*, commanded by Captain *Little*, and brought into the port of *Boston*, where she was libelled as an *American* vessel that had violated the non-intercourse law.

The judge before whom the cause was tried, directed a restoration of the vessel and cargo as neutral property, but refused to award damages for the capture and detention, because in his opinion, there was probable cause to suspect the vessel to be *American*.

On an appeal to the circuit court this sentence was reversed, because the *Flying-Fish* was on a voyage *from*, not *to*, a *French* port, and was therefore, had she even been an *American* vessel, not liable to capture on the high seas.

During the hostilities between the *United States* and *France*, an act for the suspension of all intercourse between the two nations was annually passed. That [statute] under which the *Flying-Fish* was condemned, declared every vessel, owned, hired or employed wholly or in part by an *American*, which should be employed in any traffic or commerce with or for any person resident within the jurisdiction or under the authority of the *French* republic, to be forfeited together with her cargo; the one half to accrue to the *United States*, and the other to any

---

CONSTITUTIONAL TORTS AND THE WAR ON TERROR (2017) (qualified immunity); William Baude, Is Qualified Immunity Unlawful?, 106 Cal. L. Rev. (forthcoming 2018) (qualified immunity); Samuel L. Bray, Multiple Chancellors: Reforming the National Injunction, 131 Harv. L. Rev. (forthcoming 2017) (national injunctions); John Harrison, Ex Parte Young, 60 Stan. L. Rev. 989 (2008) (injunctions and sovereign immunity); Marin K. Levy, Judging the Flood of Litigation, 80 U. Chi. L. Rev. 1007 (2013) (floodgates); Joanna C. Schwartz, Police Indemnification, 89 N.Y.U. L. Rev. 885 (2014) (indemnification); and Carlos M. Vázquez & Stephen I. Vladeck, State Law, the Westfall Act, and the Nature of the *Bivens* Question, 161 U. Pa. L. Rev. 509 (2013) (*Bivens* and immunity from suit). Whatever the strength of these criticisms, however, the current model does consist of a number of interconnected elements, and that fact encourages inertia.

person or persons, citizens of the *United States*, who will inform and prosecute for the same.

The 5th section of this act authorises the president of the *United States*, to instruct the commanders of armed vessels, "to stop and examine any ship or vessel of the *United States* on the high sea, which there may be reason to suspect to be engaged in any traffic or commerce contrary to the true tenor of the act, and if upon examination it should appear that such ship or vessel is bound or sailing *to* any port or place within the territory of the *French* republic or her dependencies, it is rendered lawful to seize such vessel, and send her into the *United States* for adjudication." . . .

It was so obvious, that if only vessels sailing to a *French* port could be seized on the high seas, that the law would be very often evaded, that this act of congress appears to have received a different construction from the executive of the *United States*; a construction much better calculated to give it effect.

A copy of this act was transmitted by the secretary of the navy, to the captains of the armed vessels, who were ordered to consider the 5th section as a part of their instructions. The same letter contained the following clause. "A proper discharge of the important duties enjoined on you, arising out of this act, will require the exercise of a sound and an impartial judgment. You are not only to do all that in you lies, to prevent all intercourse, whether direct or circuitous, between the ports of the *United States*, and those of *France* or her dependencies, where the vessels *are apparently as well as really American*, and protected by *American* papers only, but you are to be vigilant that vessels or cargoes really *American*, but covered by *Danish* or other foreign papers, and bound *to* or *from French* ports, do not escape you."

These orders given by the executive under the construction of the act of congress made by the department to which its execution was assigned, enjoin the seizure of *American* vessels sailing from a *French* port. Is the officer who obeys them liable for damages sustained by this misconstruction of the act, or will his orders excuse him? If his instructions afford him no protection, then the law must take its course, and he must pay such damages as are legally awarded against him; if they excuse an act not otherwise excusable, it would then be necessary to inquire whether this is a case in which the probable cause which existed to induce a suspicion that the vessel was *American*, would excuse the captor from damages when the vessel appeared in fact to be neutral.

I confess the first bias of my mind was very strong in favor of the opinion that though the instructions of the executive could not give a right, they might yet excuse from damages. I was much inclined to think that a distinction ought to be taken between acts of civil and those of military officers; and between proceedings within the body of the country and those on the high seas. That implicit obedience which military men usually pay to the orders of their superiors, which indeed is indispensably necessary to every military system, appeared to me strongly to imply the principle that those orders, if not to perform a prohibited act, ought to justify the person whose general duty it is to obey them, and who is placed by the laws of his country in a situation which in general requires that he should obey them. I was strongly inclined to think that where, in consequence of orders from the legitimate authority, a vessel is seized with pure intention, the claim of the injured party for damages would be against that government from which the orders proceeded, and would be a proper subject for negotiation. But I have been convinced that I was mistaken, and I have receded from this first opinion. I acquiesce in that of my brethren, which is, that the instructions cannot change the nature of the transaction, or legalize an act which without those instructions would have been a plain trespass. . . .

Captain *Little* then must be answerable in damages to the owner of this neutral vessel, and as the account taken by order of the circuit court is not objectionable on its face, and has not been excepted to by council before the proper tribunal, this court can receive no objection to it.

There appears then to be no error in the judgment of the circuit court, and it must be affirmed with costs.

NOTES

1. In 1807, Congress enacted a private bill indemnifying Captain Little (*i.e.*, paying his damages). See James E. Pfander & Jonathan L. Hunt, Public Wrongs and Private Bills: Indemnification and Government Accountability in the Early Republic, 85 N.Y.U. L. Rev. 1862, 1902 (2010).

2. In a companion case, the Court stated that: "A public officer entrusted on the high seas to perform a duty deemed necessary by his country, and executing according to the best of his judgment the orders he has received, if he is a victim of any mistake he commits, ought certainly never to be assessed with vindictive or speculative damages." Murray *v.* The Schooner Charming Betsy, 2 Cranch 64 (1804). "Vindictive damages" are roughly equivalent to what would now be called "punitive damages."

American School of Magnetic Healing v. McAnnulty

Supreme Court of the United States, 1902.
187 U.S. 94.

[The postmaster of the city of Nevada, Missouri, withheld the mail from a local corporation, the American School of Magnetic Healing, on the grounds that its business was fraudulent. The American School of Magnetic Healing taught "that the mind of the human race is largely responsible for its ills, and is a perceptible factor in the treating, curing, benefiting, and remedying thereof. It typically received about 3,000 letters per day, including checks and other funds totalling between $1,000 and $1,600 each day. The Postmaster General of the United States then determined that the school was "conducting a scheme or device for obtaining money through the mails by means of false and fraudulent pretenses, representations, and promises," as forbidden by a Lottery Act. The Postmaster General ordered all mail sent to the school to be returned to sender, with the word "fraudulent" stamped or written on the outside. The school then sued in federal district court, alleging that the Postmaster General acted without legal authority and seeking "an injunction to restrain the postmaster from carrying out the order of the Postmaster General." The defendant filed the equivalent of a motion to dismiss (demurrer), succeeding because the district court found no basis for relief in law or equity.]

■ MR. JUSTICE PECKHAM. . . . [The Court first concluded that the Postmaster General's action was not authorized by law, because the relevant "statutes were not intended to cover any case of what the Postmaster General might think to be false opinions, but only cases of actual fraud in fact, in regard to which opinion formed no basis."]

Here it is contended that the Postmaster General has, in a case not covered by the acts of Congress, excluded from the mails letters addressed to the complainants. His right to exclude letters, or to refuse to permit their delivery to persons addressed, must depend upon some law of Congress, and if no such law exists, then he cannot exclude or refuse to deliver them. . . .

The facts, which are here admitted of record, show that the case is not one which, by any construction of those facts, is covered or provided for by the statutes under which the Postmaster General has assumed to act, and his determination that those admitted facts do authorize his action is a clear mistake of law as applied to the admitted facts, and the courts, therefore, must have power in a proper proceeding to grant relief. Otherwise, the individual is left to the absolutely uncontrolled and arbitrary action of a public and administrative officer, whose action is unauthorized by any law, and is in violation of the rights of the individual. Where the action of such an officer is thus unauthorized, he thereby violates the property rights of the person whose letters are withheld.

In our view of these statutes the complainants had the legal right, under the general acts of Congress relating to the mails, to have their letters delivered at the postoffice as directed. They had violated no law which Congress had passed, and their letters contained checks, drafts, money orders, and money itself, all of which were their property as soon as they were deposited in the various postoffices for transmission by mail. They allege, and it is not difficult to see that the allegation is true, that, if such action be persisted in, these complainants will be entirely cut off from all mail facilities, and their business will necessarily be greatly injured, if not wholly destroyed, such business being, so far as the laws of Congress are concerned, legitimate and lawful. In other words, irreparable injury will be done to these complainants by the mistaken act of the Postmaster General in directing the defendant to retain and refuse to deliver letters addressed to them. The Postmaster General's order, being the result of a mistaken view of the law, could not operate as a defense to this action on the part of the defendant, though it might justify his obedience thereto until some action of the court. In such a case as the one before us there is no adequate remedy at law, the injunction to prohibit the further withholding of the mail from complainants being the only remedy at all adequate to the full relief to which the complainants are entitled. Although the Postmaster General had jurisdiction over the subject-matter (assuming the validity of the acts), and therefore it was his duty, upon complaint being made, to decide the question of law whether the case stated was within the statute, yet such decision, being a legal error, does not bind the courts. . . .

[W]e are constrained to reverse the judgment of the circuit court, with instructions to overrule the defendant's demurrer to the amended bill, with leave to answer, and to grant a temporary injunction as applied for by complainants, and to take such further proceedings as may be proper, and not inconsistent with this opinion. In overruling the demurrer, we do not mean to preclude the defendant from showing on the trial, if he can, that the business of complainants, as in fact conducted, amounts to a violation of the statutes as herein construed.

Judgment reversed.

■ MR. JUSTICE WHITE and MR. JUSTICE MCKENNA, believing the judgment should be affirmed, dissented from the foregoing opinion.

Philadelphia Co. v. Stimson

Supreme Court of the United States, 1912.
223 U.S. 605.

■ MR. JUSTICE HUGHES delivered the opinion of the court:

This suit was brought in the supreme court of the District of Columbia to set aside certain harbor lines in the harbor of Pittsburg, Pennsylvania, so far as they encroached upon land owned by the complainant, and to restrain the Secretary of War from causing criminal proceedings to be instituted against the complainant because of the reclamation and occupation of its land outside the prescribed limits. The court of appeals of the District affirmed a decree sustaining a demurrer to the bill, and the complainant appeals.

The allegations of the bill, in substance, are as follows:

The complainant, a corporation of the commonwealth of Pennsylvania, is the owner in fee of "Brunot's island," formerly Chartier's or Hamilton's island, in the Ohio river, in Allegheny county, Pennsylvania. In 1858, a statute was enacted in Pennsylvania, providing for the appointment of commissioners to ascertain and mark the lines of ordinary high and low water in the Allegheny, Monongahela, and Ohio rivers in the vicinity of Pittsburg. The act recited that the lines of land along the shores of the rivers had not been clearly ascertained, and it was important to all persons interested that their several rights and privileges should be defined. After the commissioners' surveys had been completed and the lines located, opportunity was to be afforded in the court by which they were appointed, for any needed corrections; and the map or plan finally determined upon was to be recorded. The statute declared that "the lines so approved shall forever after be deemed, adjudged, and taken firm and stable for the purposes aforesaid." Proceedings were had accordingly and the high- and low-water lines along the shore of Brunot's island were definitely fixed. In consequence the bill asserts that all the land, whether or not under water, inside of the commissioners' lines, became the property of the owners of Brunot's island; and that by virtue of the statute, and the action of the commissioners under it in fixing the high-water line as a permanent boundary, the right of the owners of the island to accretions beyond that line was taken away, while at the same time they were no longer subject to loss or diminution of their land by reason of its submergence "through the avulsion of floods or freshets or through gradual erosion."

Subsequent to the establishment, in 1865, of the state commissioners' line, a considerable portion of the shore of the island, "on the so-called back channel, within the said high-water mark," was washed away from time to time by heavy floods and freshets, so that a large part of the upland was slightly submerged, but not to an extent sufficient to permit of navigation. Some years ago, the United States government, in order to increase the depth of water in the harbor of Pittsburg, caused a dam to be constructed across the Ohio river a short distance below Brunot's island, known as the Davis island dam. And the effect of this dam, says the bill, by the increase of the depth of water in the channel, was to submerge Brunot's island to a far greater extent, and to make the water over the complainant's land navigable "at certain times, and for certain purposes," where it was not navigable before.

In 1895, the Secretary of War, claiming to act under the authority of § 12 of the act of Congress of September 19, 1890, and knowing that the shore of Brunot's island had been washed away by floods and freshets, established a harbor line which ran across the complainant's land within the line of the state commissioners. It is further alleged that although the submerged land was generally covered by water, "it was not ordinarily navigable water," and "has never constituted, nor does it now constitute, a part of the public navigable waters of the United States"; that no authority was conferred by the act of Congress upon the Secretary of War to regulate or interfere with the use of the complainant's land by the establishment of harbor lines upon the same; and that, even if the water over this land was in fact part of the public navigable waters of the United States, without being rendered thus navigable by the construction of the dam, still the Secretary of War had no right so to run the harbor line over the land in question as to deprive the complainant of its use and enjoyment. It was the right of the complainant, the bill avers, to repair the damage caused by floods and freshets, and to reclaim the submerged portion by filling in or wharfing, "keeping at all times within the lines of the part that had been torn away by the violence of the waters."

In 1907, the Secretary of War, claiming authority under § 11 of the act of Congress of March 3, 1899, against the complainant's protest, changed the harbor line. The report of the United States engineer at Pittsburg stated that the conditions of high and low water had not changed since 1895, but as, along a part of the shore of the island, the harbor line of 1895 ran several hundred feet outside high-water mark as it then existed, it seemed advisable to change it so as to coincide with the actual high-water mark. A copy of the report with the order of the Secretary of War, dated February 23, 1907, was annexed to the bill and made a part of it. In this it is stated that the location of the proposed harbor lines was within the bed of the stream as it existed as a physical fact.

The bill further shows that to facilitate the delivery of coal for the operation of its power house on the island, the complainant desired to reclaim a part of it which had been submerged by establishing a coal wharf on the back channel, where both the harbor line of 1895 and that of 1907 "ran some distance landward of the said state commissioners' high-water line." According to the proposed plans, the wharf or pier was to extend over the complainant's land and to cross both of the harbor lines to the state commissioners' line. While these plans were being perfected, the Secretary of War, through his representative, the United States engineer officer at Pittsburg, declared to the complainant that it had no right to build upon its land across either of the harbor lines, and he refused to permit the complainant to reclaim its land or to build its wharf thereon outside the harbor line of 1907. He threatened that if it undertook to do so, he would prevent it and cause the complainant and its employees "to be prosecuted and fined by the authorities of the Federal government" for violations of the acts of Congress of September 19, 1890, and March 3, 1899. It was further charged that if the Secretary of War had authority to fix the original harbor line of 1895, that his power was exhausted by what was then done, and that the harbor line of 1907 was wholly unauthorized.

In consequence of the severe penalties prescribed by the acts of Congress for the construction of buildings, piers, or wharves outside any harbor line established by the Secretary of War, and by reason of the defendant's threats of prosecution in case the complainant carried out its plan of reclamation and the construction of its wharf, the bill avers that the complainant is prevented from making use of its property; that the defendant's action constitutes a taking of its property for public use without just compensation; that it is subjected in its endeavor, so long as the harbor line remains unmodified, to a multiplicity of criminal prosecutions; and that the harbor line is a cloud upon its title. . . .

In demurring to the bill the defendant asserted that it was bad in substance, and also specially assigned the following grounds:

"1. This proceeding is virtually a suit against the United States.

"2. This court has no jurisdiction to restrain the enforcement of a penalty or prosecution for violation of law.

"3. This court has no jurisdiction to restrain the defendant from instituting criminal proceedings against complainant. . . .

First. If the conduct of the defendant constitutes an unwarrantable interference with property of the complainant, its resort to equity for protection is not to be defeated upon the ground that the suit is one against the United States. The exemption of the United States from suit does not protect its officers from personal liability to persons whose rights of property they have wrongfully invaded. Little *v.* Barreme, 2 Cranch, 170. And in case of an injury threatened by his illegal action, the officer cannot claim immunity from injunction process. The principle has frequently been applied with respect to state officers seeking to enforce unconstitutional enactments. Osborn *v.* Bank of United States, 9 Wheat. 738, 843, 868; Ex parte Young, 209 U. S. 123, 159, 160. And it is equally applicable to a Federal officer acting in excess of his authority or under an authority not validly conferred. American School *v.* McAnnulty, 187 U. S. 94.

The complainant did not ask the court to interfere with the official discretion of the Secretary of War, but challenged his authority to do the things of which complaint was made. The suit rests upon the charge of abuse of power, and its merits must be determined accordingly; it is not a suit against the United States.

Second. The second and third grounds of demurrer, specially stated, raise the question as to the jurisdiction of the court to restrain the defendant from instituting criminal proceedings.

A court of equity, said this court in In re Sawyer, 124 U. S. 200, 210, "has no jurisdiction over the prosecution, the punishment, or the pardon of crimes or misdemeanors. . . . To assume such a jurisdiction, or to sustain a bill in equity to restrain or relieve against proceedings for the punishment of offenses, . . . is to invade THE DOMAIN OF THE COURTS OF COMMON LAW, Or of the executive and administrative department of the government." But a distinction obtains when it is found to be essential to the protection of the property rights, as to which the jurisdiction of a court of equity has been invoked, that it should restrain the defendant from instituting criminal actions involving the same legal questions. This is illustrated in the decisions of this court in which officers have been enjoined from bringing criminal proceedings to compel obedience to unconstitutional requirements. In this, there is no attempt to restrain a court from trying persons charged with crime, or the grand jury from the exercise of its functions, but the injunction binds the defendant not to resort to criminal procedure to enforce illegal demands.

It is urged that the statute authorizing the Secretary of War to prevent encroachments upon navigable streams is a valid one, and that the decisions cited do not apply. The validity of the statute is not attacked, because of the assumption that it is not to be construed to contemplate or authorize the alleged deprivation of property. Where the officer is proceeding under an unconstitutional act, its invalidity suffices to show that he is without authority, and it is this absence of lawful power and his abuse of authority in imposing or enforcing, in the name of the state, unwarrantable exactions or restrictions, to the irreparable loss of the complainant, which is the basis of the decree. Ex parte Young, 209 U. S. p. 159. And a similar injury may be inflicted, and there may exist ground for equitable relief, when an officer, insisting that he has the warrant of the statute, is transcending its bounds, and thus unlawfully assuming to exercise the power of government against the individual owner, is guilty of an invasion of private property.

By § 12 of the act of March 3, 1899, it was provided that every person and every corporation which should violate any provision of § 11, relating to the observance of harbor lines, or any rule or regulation made by the Secretary of War in pursuance of that section, should be guilty of a misdemeanor and punished by fine or imprisonment. By § 17 it was made the duty of district attorneys of the United States to prosecute all offenders whenever requested by the Secretary of War. If the complainant's rights, as against the defendant, were as claimed, it was entitled to adequate protection. And, in such case, the remedy might properly embrace the restraining of unfounded prosecutions. . . .

Fourth. Assuming that the court had jurisdiction, we are brought to a consideration of the equity of the bill.

It has been held that the establishment of a general system of harbor lines, for the protection of commerce and navigation, is not of itself an injury to property and cannot be restrained. But it has also been recognized that a different question arises when active measures are taken against an individual proprietor to maintain a location of limits in alleged violation of his private rights, and thus to prevent him from enjoying what is asserted to be the lawful use of his property.

[The Court proceeded to find that the allegations in the complainant's bill, specifically the allegation that soil "was washed away from time to time by heavy floods and freshets," were more in the nature of accretion than avulsion. Because the soil was lost through accretion, that is, gradually, "according to general principles of law the owner would bear the losses caused by the washings of the river."

[As for the construction of the dam, the Court noted that the complainant had purchased the land after the dam was constructed. The question before the Court was whether this subsequent purchaser could get equitable relief, not whether the prior owner had a claim for damages from the diminution in value.

[Finally, the Court considered whether Congress had constitutional authority to instruct the Secretary of War to establish harbor lines to protect the harbor of Pittsburgh, and whether it had in fact instructed the Secretary of War to do so.]

It must be concluded, therefore, that it was competent for Congress to provide for the establishment of the harbor lines in question for the protection of the harbor of Pittsburg. It acted within its constitutional power in authorizing the Secretary of War to fix the lines. That officer did not exhaust his authority in laying the lines first established in 1895, but was entitled to change them, as he did change them in 1907, in order more fully to preserve the river from obstruction. And, in none of the acts complained of, did he exceed the power which had been conferred.

The bill failed to show any ground upon which the complainant was entitled to relief, and it was properly dismissed.

Decree affirmed.

NOTE ON THE TRADITIONAL MODEL OF OFFICER LIABILITY

The three cases just presented offer an overview, for most of U.S. history, of the liability of federal officers for actions not authorized by law. Little *v.* Barreme shows federal officers' liability for trespass in admiralty. American School of Magnetic Healing *v.* McAnnulty shows a circumstance in which a federal court might preliminarily enjoin a federal officer. Philadelphia Co. *v.* Stimson shows the analysis used for deciding whether a federal officer could be enjoined by the courts of the District of Columbia.

In one respect, though, this picture is misleading. Most suits against federal officers were actually brought in state court. A plaintiff would sue a federal officer in state court (*e.g.*, for trespass), the federal officer would raise a defense (*e.g.*, "I was following the law"), and the plaintiff would respond, often by invoking the Fourth Amendment (*e.g.*, "No you weren't following the law, because you were violating the Fourth Amendment"). If the plaintiff prevailed, the jury would award damages against the federal officer. For further discussion, see Telford Taylor, TWO STUDIES IN CONSTITUTIONAL INTERPRETATION (1969); Akhil Reed Amar, Fourth Amendment First Principles, 107 Harv. L. Rev. 757 (1994).

This model of federal officer liability was summarized in the following way by the U.S. Supreme Court in 1963, when it could still be called the governing approach:

> "When it comes to suits for damages for abuse of power, federal officials are usually governed by local law. Federal law, however, supplies the defense, if the conduct complained of was done pursuant to a federally imposed duty, or immunity from suit. Congress could, of course, provide otherwise, but it has not done so. Over the years Congress has considered the problem of state civil and criminal actions against federal officials many times. But no

> general statute making federal officers liable for acts committed 'under color,' but in violation, of their federal authority has been passed. Congress has provided for removal to a federal court of any state action, civil or criminal, against '[a]ny officer of the United States . . . , or person acting under him, for any act under color of such office . . . .' 28 U.S.C. § 1442(a)(1). . . . [I]t is not for us to fill any hiatus Congress has left in this area."

Wheeldin *v.* Wheeler, 373 U.S. 647, 652 (1963).

2. *BIVENS* AND QUALIFIED IMMUNITY

Bivens v. Six Unknown Named Agents of Federal Bureau of Narcotics

Supreme Court of the United States, 1971.
403 U.S. 388.

■ MR. JUSTICE BRENNAN delivered the opinion of the Court.

The Fourth Amendment provides that:

> "The right of the people to be secure in their persons, houses, papers, and effects, against unreasonable searches and seizures, shall not be violated. . . ."

In Bell *v.* Hood, 327 U.S. 678 (1946), we reserved the question whether violation of that command by a federal agent acting under color of his authority gives rise to a cause of action for damages consequent upon his unconstitutional conduct. Today we hold that it does.

This case has its origin in an arrest and search carried out on the morning of November 26, 1965. Petitioner's complaint alleged that on that day respondents, agents of the Federal Bureau of Narcotics acting under claim of federal authority, entered his apartment and arrested him for alleged narcotics violations. The agents manacled petitioner in front of his wife and children, and threatened to arrest the entire family. They searched the apartment from stem to stern. Thereafter, petitioner was taken to the federal courthouse in Brooklyn, where he was interrogated, booked, and subjected to a visual strip search.

On July 7, 1967, petitioner brought suit in Federal District Court. In addition to the allegations above, his complaint asserted that the arrest and search were effected without a warrant, and that unreasonable force was employed in making the arrest; fairly read, it alleges as well that the arrest was made without probable cause. Petitioner claimed to have suffered great humiliation, embarrassment, and mental suffering as a result of the agents' unlawful conduct, and sought $15,000 damages from each of them. The District Court, on respondents' motion, dismissed the complaint on the ground, *inter alia*, that it failed to state a cause of action. The Court of Appeals, one judge concurring specially, affirmed on that basis. We granted certiorari. We reverse.

I

Respondents do not argue that petitioner should be entirely without remedy for an unconstitutional invasion of his rights by federal agents. In respondents' view, however, the rights that petitioner asserts—primarily rights of privacy—are creations of state and not of federal law. Accordingly, they argue, petitioner may obtain money damages to redress invasion of these rights only by an action in tort, under state law, in the state courts. In this scheme the Fourth Amendment would serve merely to limit the extent to which the agents could defend the state law tort suit by asserting that their actions were a valid exercise of federal power: if the agents were shown to have violated the Fourth Amendment, such a defense would be lost to them and they would stand before the state law merely as private individuals. Candidly admitting that it is the policy of the Department of Justice to remove all such suits from the state to the federal courts for decision,[4] respondents nevertheless urge that we uphold dismissal of petitioner's complaint in federal court, and remit him to filing an action in the state courts in order that the case may properly be removed to the federal court for decision on the basis of state law.

We think that respondents' thesis rests upon an unduly restrictive view of the Fourth Amendment's protection against unreasonable searches and seizures by federal agents, a view that has consistently been rejected by this Court. Respondents seek to treat the relationship between a citizen and a federal agent unconstitutionally exercising his authority as no different from the relationship between two private citizens. In so doing, they ignore the fact that power, once granted, does not disappear like a magic gift when it is wrongfully used. An agent acting—albeit unconstitutionally—in the name of the United States possesses a far greater capacity for harm than an individual trespasser exercising no authority other than his own. Accordingly, as our cases make clear, the Fourth Amendment operates as a limitation upon the exercise of federal power regardless of whether the State in whose jurisdiction that power is exercised would prohibit or penalize the identical act if engaged in by a private citizen. It guarantees to citizens of the United States the absolute right to be free from unreasonable searches and seizures carried out by virtue of federal authority. And "where federally protected rights have been invaded, it has been the rule

[4] "[S]ince it is the present policy of the Department of Justice to remove to the federal courts all suits in state courts against federal officers for trespass or false imprisonment, a claim for relief, whether based on state common law or directly on the Fourth Amendment will ultimately be heard in a federal court." Brief for Respondents 13; see 28 U.S.C. § 1442(a). In light of this, it is difficult to understand our Brother BLACKMUN's complaint that our holding today "opens the door for another avalanche of new federal cases." In estimating the magnitude of any such "avalanche," it is worth noting that a survey of comparable actions against state officers under 42 U.S.C. § 1983 found only 53 reported cases in 17 years (1951–1967) that survived a motion to dismiss. Ginger & Bell, Police Misconduct Litigation—Plaintiff's Remedies, 15 Am. Jur. Trials 555, 580–590 (1968). Increasing this figure by 900% to allow for increases in rate and unreported cases, every federal district judge could expect to try one such case every 13 years.

from the beginning that courts will be alert to adjust their remedies so as to grant the necessary relief." Bell *v.* Hood, 327 U.S., at 684.

First. Our cases have long since rejected the notion that the Fourth Amendment proscribes only such conduct as would, if engaged in by private persons, be condemned by state law. . . .

Second. The interests protected by state laws regulating trespass and the invasion of privacy, and those protected by the Fourth Amendment's guarantee against unreasonable searches and seizures, may be inconsistent or even hostile. Thus, we may bar the door against an unwelcome private intruder, or call the police if he persists in seeking entrance. The availability of such alternative means for the protection of privacy may lead the State to restrict imposition of liability for any consequent trespass. A private citizen, asserting no authority other than his own, will not normally be liable in trespass if he demands, and is granted, admission to another's house. But one who demands admission under a claim of federal authority stands in a far different position. The mere invocation of federal power by a federal law enforcement official will normally render futile any attempt to resist an unlawful entry or arrest by resort to the local police; and a claim of authority to enter is likely to unlock the door as well. "In such cases there is no safety for the citizen, except in the protection of the judicial tribunals, for rights which have been invaded by the officers of the government, professing to act in its name. There remains to him but the alternative of resistance, which may amount to crime." United States *v.* Lee, 106 U.S. 196, 219 (1882). Nor is it adequate to answer that state law may take into account the different status of one clothed with the authority of the Federal Government. For just as state law may not authorize federal agents to violate the Fourth Amendment, neither may state law undertake to limit the extent to which federal authority can be exercised. The inevitable consequence of this dual limitation on state power is that the federal question becomes not merely a possible defense to the state law action, but an independent claim both necessary and sufficient to make out the plaintiff's cause of action.

Third. That damages may be obtained for injuries consequent upon a violation of the Fourth Amendment by federal officials should hardly seem a surprising proposition. Historically, damages have been regarded as the ordinary remedy for an invasion of personal interests in liberty. See Nixon *v.* Condon, 286 U.S. 73 (1932); Nixon *v.* Herndon, 273 U.S. 536, 540 (1927); Swafford *v.* Templeton, 185 U.S. 487 (1902); Wiley *v.* Sinkler, 179 U.S. 58 (1900); J. Landynski, SEARCH AND SEIZURE AND THE SUPREME COURT 28 et seq. (1966); N. Lasson, HISTORY AND DEVELOPMENT OF THE FOURTH AMENDMENT TO THE UNITED STATES CONSTITUTION 43 et seq. (1937); Katz, The Jurisprudence of Remedies: Constitutional Legality and the Law of Torts in Bell *v.* Hood, 117 U. Pa. L. Rev. 1, 8–33 (1968). Of course, the Fourth Amendment does not in so many words provide for its enforcement by an award of money damages for the consequences of its violation. But "it is . . . well settled that where legal rights have been invaded, and a federal statute provides for a general right to sue for such invasion, federal courts may use any available remedy to make good the wrong done." Bell *v.* Hood, 327 U.S., at 684. The present case involves no special factors counseling hesitation in the absence of affirmative action by Congress. We are not dealing with a question of "federal fiscal policy," as in United States *v.* Standard Oil Co., 332 U.S. 301, 311 (1947). In that case we refused to infer from the Government-soldier relationship that the United States could recover damages from one who negligently injured a soldier and thereby caused the Government to pay his medical expenses and lose his services during the course of his hospitalization. Noting that Congress was normally quite solicitous where the federal purse was involved, we pointed out that "the United States [was] the party plaintiff to the suit. And the United States has power at any time to create the liability." *Id.*, at 316. Nor are we asked in this case to impose liability upon a congressional employee for actions contrary to no constitutional prohibition, but merely said to be in excess of the authority delegated to him by the Congress. Wheeldin *v.* Wheeler, 373 U.S. 647 (1963). Finally, we cannot accept respondents' formulation of the question as whether the availability of money damages is necessary to enforce the Fourth Amendment. For we have here no explicit congressional declaration that persons injured by a federal officer's violation of the Fourth Amendment may not recover money damages from the agents, but must instead be remitted to another remedy, equally effective in the view of Congress. The question is merely whether petitioner, if he can demonstrate an injury consequent upon the violation by federal agents of his Fourth Amendment rights, is entitled to redress his injury through a particular remedial mechanism normally available in the federal courts. "The very essence of civil liberty certainly consists in the right of every individual to claim the protection of the laws, whenever he receives an injury." Marbury *v.* Madison, 1 Cranch 137, 163 (1803). Having concluded that petitioner's complaint states a cause of action under the Fourth Amendment, we hold that petitioner is entitled to recover money damages for any injuries he has suffered as a result of the agents' violation of the Amendment.

II

In addition to holding that petitioner's complaint had failed to state facts making out a cause of action, the District Court ruled that in any event respondents were immune from liability by virtue of their official position. This question was not passed upon by the Court of Appeals, and accordingly we do not consider it here. The judgment of the Court of Appeals is reversed and the case is remanded for further proceedings consistent with this opinion. . . .

■ MR. JUSTICE HARLAN, concurring in the judgment.

My initial view of this case was that the Court of Appeals was correct in dismissing the complaint, but for reasons stated in this opinion I am now persuaded to the contrary. Accordingly, I join in the judgment of reversal. . . .

In [affirming the District Court's dismissal of the complaint for failure to state a claim for which relief could be granted], Chief Judge Lumbard's opinion reasoned, in essence, that: (1) the framers of the Fourth Amendment did not appear to contemplate a "wholly new federal cause of action founded directly on the Fourth Amendment," and (2) while the federal courts had power under a general grant of jurisdiction to imply a federal remedy for the enforcement of a constitutional right, they should do so only when the absence of alternative remedies renders the constitutional command a "mere form of words." The Government takes essentially the same position here. And two members of the Court add the contention that we lack the constitutional power to accord Bivens a remedy for damages in the absence of congressional action creating "a federal cause of action for damages for an unreasonable search in violation of the Fourth Amendment." Opinion of MR. JUSTICE BLACK; see also opinion of THE CHIEF JUSTICE.

For the reasons set forth below, I am of the opinion that federal courts do have the power to award damages for violation of "constitutionally protected interests" and I agree with the Court that a traditional judicial remedy such as damages is appropriate to the vindication of the personal interests protected by the Fourth Amendment.

I

I turn first to the contention that the constitutional power of federal courts to accord Bivens damages for his claim depends on the passage of a statute creating a "federal cause of action." Although the point is not entirely free of ambiguity, I do not understand either the Government or my dissenting Brothers to maintain that Bivens' contention that he is entitled to be free from the type of official conduct prohibited by the Fourth Amendment depends on a decision by the State in which he resides to accord him a remedy. Such a position would be incompatible with the presumed availability of federal equitable relief, if a proper showing can be made in terms of the ordinary principles governing equitable remedies. However broad a federal court's discretion concerning equitable remedies, it is absolutely clear—at least after Erie R. Co. *v.* Tompkins, 304 U.S. 64 (1938)—that in a nondiversity suit a federal court's power to grant even equitable relief depends on the presence of a substantive right derived from federal law.

Thus the interest which Bivens claims—to be free from official conduct in contravention of the Fourth Amendment—is a federally protected interest. Therefore, the question of judicial *power* to grant Bivens damages is not a problem of the "source" of the "right"; instead, the question is whether the power to authorize damages as a judicial remedy for the vindication of a federal constitutional right is placed by the Constitution itself exclusively in Congress' hands.

II

The contention that the federal courts remedy in the absence of any express for a claimed invasion of his federal constitutional rights until Congress explicitly authorizes the remedy cannot rest on the notion that the decision to grant compensatory relief involves a resolution of policy considerations not susceptible of judicial discernment. Thus, in suits for damages based on violations of federal statutes lacking any express authorization of a damage remedy, this Court has authorized such relief where, in its view, damages are necessary to effectuate the congressional policy underpinning the substantive provisions of the statute. J.I. Case Co. *v.* Borak, 377 U.S. 426 (1964); Tunstall *v.* Brotherhood of Locomotive Firemen & Enginemen, 323 U.S. 210, 213 (1944).

If it is not the nature of the remedy which is thought to render a judgment as to the appropriateness of damages inherently "legislative," then it must be the nature of the legal interest offered as an occasion for invoking otherwise appropriate judicial relief. But I do not think that the fact that the interest is protected by the Constitution rather than statute or common law justifies the assertion that federal courts are powerless to grant damages in the absence of explicit congressional action authorizing the remedy. Initially, I note that it would be at least anomalous to conclude that the federal judiciary—while competent to choose among the range of traditional judicial remedies to implement statutory and common-law policies, and even to generate substantive rules governing primary behavior in furtherance of broadly formulated policies articulated by statute or Constitution—is powerless to accord a damages remedy to vindicate social policies which, by virtue of their inclusion in the Constitution, are aimed predominantly at restraining the Government as an instrument of the popular will.

More importantly, the presumed availability of federal equitable relief against threatened invasions of constitutional interests appears entirely to negate the contention that the status of an interest as constitutionally protected divests federal courts of the power to grant damages absent express congressional authorization. Congress provided specially for the exercise of equitable remedial powers by federal courts, see Act of May 8, 1792, § 2, 1 Stat. 276, in part because of the limited availability of equitable remedies in state courts in the early days of the Republic. See Guaranty Trust Co. *v.* York, 326 U.S. 99, 104–105 (1945). And this Court's decisions make clear that, at least absent congressional restrictions, the scope of equitable remedial discretion is to be determined according to the distinctive historical traditions of equity as an institution, The reach of a federal district court's "inherent equitable powers" is broad indeed, *e.g.*, Swann *v.* Charlotte-Mecklenburg Board of Education, 402 U.S. 1 (1971); nonetheless, the federal judiciary is not empowered to grant equitable relief in the absence of congressional action extending jurisdiction over the subject matter of the suit. See

Textile Workers Union *v.* Lincoln Mills, 353 U.S. 448, 460 (1957) (Burton, J., concurring in result).

If explicit congressional authorization is an absolute prerequisite to the power of a federal court to accord compensatory relief regardless of the necessity or appropriateness of damages as a remedy simply because of the status of a legal interest as constitutionally protected, then it seems to me that explicit congressional authorization is similarly prerequisite to the exercise of equitable remedial discretion in favor of constitutionally protected interests. Conversely, if a general grant of jurisdiction to the federal courts by Congress is thought adequate to empower a federal court to grant equitable relief for all areas of subject-matter jurisdiction enumerated therein, see 28 U.S.C. § 1331(a), then it seems to me that the same statute is sufficient to empower a federal court to grant a traditional remedy at law.6 Of course, the special historical traditions governing the federal equity system, see Sprague *v.* Ticonic National Bank, 307 U.S. 161 (1939), might still bear on the comparative appropriateness of granting equitable relief as opposed to money damages. That possibility, however, relates, not to whether the federal courts have the power to afford one type of remedy as opposed to the other, but rather to the criteria which should govern the exercise of our power. To that question, I now pass.

III

The major thrust of the Government's position is that, where Congress has not expressly authorized a particular remedy, a federal court should exercise its power to accord a traditional form of judicial relief at the behest of a litigant, who claims a constitutionally protected interest has been invaded, only where the remedy is "essential," or "indispensable for vindicating constitutional rights." Brief for Respondents 19, 24. . . .

[I]t seems to me that the range of policy considerations we may take into account is at least as broad as the range of a legislature would consider with respect to an express statutory authorization of a traditional remedy. In this regard I agree with the Court that the appropriateness of according Bivens compensatory relief does not turn simply on the deterrent effect liability will have on federal official conduct. Damages as a traditional form of compensation for invasion of a legally protected interest may be entirely appropriate even if no substantial deterrent effects on future official lawlessness might be thought to result. Bivens, after all, has invoked judicial processes claiming entitlement to compensation for injuries resulting from allegedly lawless official behavior, if those injuries are properly compensable in money damages. I do not think a court of law—vested with the power to accord a remedy—should deny him his relief simply because he cannot show that future lawless conduct will thereby be deterred.

And I think it is clear that Bivens advances a claim of the sort that, if proved, would be properly compensable in damages. The personal interests protected by the Fourth Amendment are those we attempt to capture by the notion of "privacy"; while the Court today properly points out that the type of harm which officials can inflict when they invade protected zones of an individual's life are different from the types of harm private citizens inflict on one another, the experience of judges in dealing with private trespass and false imprisonment claims supports the conclusion that courts of law are capable of making the types of judgment concerning causation and magnitude of injury necessary to accord meaningful compensation for invasion of Fourth Amendment rights.

On the other hand, the limitations on state remedies for violation of common-law rights by private citizens argue in favor of a federal damages remedy. The injuries inflicted by officials acting under color of law, while no less compensable in damages than those inflicted by private parties, are substantially different in kind . . . . Certainly, there is very little to be gained from the standpoint of federalism by preserving different rules of liability for federal officers dependent on the State where the injury occurs.

Putting aside the desirability of leaving the problem of federal official liability to the vagaries of common-law actions, it is apparent that some form of damages is the only possible remedy for someone in Bivens' alleged position. It will be a rare case indeed in which an individual in Bivens' position will be able to obviate the harm by securing injunctive relief from any court. However desirable a direct remedy against the Government might be as a substitute for individual official liability, the sovereign still remains immune to suit. Finally, assuming Bivens' innocence of the crime charged, the "exclusionary rule" is simply irrelevant. For people in Bivens' shoes, it is damages or nothing.

The only substantial policy consideration advanced against recognition of a federal cause of action for violation of Fourth Amendment rights by federal officials is the incremental expenditure of judicial resources that will be necessitated by this class of litigation. There is, however, something ultimately self-defeating about this argument. For if, as the Government contends, damages will rarely be realized by plaintiffs in these cases because of jury hostility, the limited resources of the official concerned, etc., then I am not ready to assume that there will be a significant increase in the expenditure of judicial resources on these claims. Few responsible lawyers and plaintiffs are likely to choose the course of litigation if the statistical chances of success are truly *de minimis*. And I simply cannot agree with my Brother BLACK that the possibility of "frivolous" claims—if defined simply as claims with no legal merit—warrants closing the courthouse doors to people in Bivens' situation. There are other ways, short of that, of coping with frivolous lawsuits.

On the other hand, if—as I believe is the case with respect, at least, to the most flagrant abuses of official power—damages to some degree will be available when the option of litigation is chosen, then the question appears to be how Fourth Amendment interests rank on a scale of social values compared with, for example, the interests of stockholders defrauded by misleading proxies. Judicial resources, I am well aware, are increasingly scarce these days. Nonetheless, when we automatically close the courthouse door solely on this basis, we implicitly express a value judgment on the comparative importance of classes of legally protected interests. And current limitations upon the effective functioning of the courts arising from budgetary inadequacies should not be permitted to stand in the way of the recognition of otherwise sound constitutional principles.

Of course, for a variety of reasons, the remedy may not often be sought. And the countervailing interests in efficient law enforcement of course argue for a protective zone with respect to many types of Fourth Amendment violations. But, while I express no view on the immunity defense offered in the instant case, I deem it proper to venture the thought that at the very least such a remedy would be available for the most flagrant and patently unjustified sorts of police conduct. Although litigants may not often choose to seek relief, it is important, in a civilized society, that the judicial branch of the Nation's government stand ready to afford a remedy in these circumstances. It goes without saying that I intimate no view on the merits of petitioner's underlying claim.

For these reasons, I concur in the judgment of the Court.

■ [The dissenting opinion of MR. CHIEF JUSTICE BURGER is omitted.]

■ MR. JUSTICE BLACK, dissenting.

In my opinion for the Court in Bell *v.* Hood, 327 U.S. 678 (1946), we did as the Court states, reserve the question whether an unreasonable search made by a federal officer in violation of the Fourth Amendment gives the subject of the search a federal cause of action for damages against the officers making the search. There can be no doubt that Congress could create a federal cause of action for damages for an unreasonable search in violation of the Fourth Amendment. Although Congress has created such a federal cause of action against *state* officials acting under color of state law,* it has never created such a cause of action against federal officials. If it wanted to do so, Congress could, of course, create a remedy against federal officials who violate the Fourth Amendment in the performance of their duties. But the point of this case and the fatal weakness in the Court's judgment is that neither Congress nor the State of New York has enacted legislation creating such a right

* "Every person who, under color of any statute, ordinance, regulation, custom, or usage, of any State or Territory, subjects, or causes to be subjected, any citizen of the United States or other person within the jurisdiction thereof to the deprivation of any rights, privileges, or immunities secured by the Constitution and laws, shall be liable to the party injured in an action at law, suit in equity, or other proper proceeding for redress." Rev. Stat. § 1979, 42 U.S.C. § 1983.

of action. For us to do so is, in my judgment, an exercise of power that the Constitution does not give us.

Even if we had the legislative power to create a remedy, there are many reasons why we should decline to create a cause of action where none has existed since the formation of our Government. The courts of the United States as well as those of the States are choked with lawsuits. The number of cases on the docket of this Court have reached an unprecedented volume in recent years. A majority of these cases are brought by citizens with substantial complaints—persons who are physically or economically injured by torts or frauds or governmental infringement of their rights; persons who have been unjustly deprived of their liberty or their property; and persons who have not yet received the equal opportunity in education, employment, and pursuit of happiness that was the dream of our forefathers. Unfortunately, there have also been a growing number of frivolous lawsuits, particularly actions for damages against law enforcement officers whose conduct has been judicially sanctioned by state trial and appellate courts and in many instances even by this Court. My fellow Justices on this Court and our brethren throughout the federal judiciary know only too well the time-consuming task of conscientiously poring over hundreds of thousands of pages of factual allegations of misconduct by police, judicial, and corrections officials. Of course, there are instances of legitimate grievances, but legislators might well desire to devote judicial resources to other problems of a more serious nature.

We sit at the top of a judicial system accused by some of nearing the point of collapse. Many criminal defendants do not receive speedy trials and neither society nor the accused are assured of justice when inordinate delays occur. Citizens must wait years to litigate their private civil suits. Substantial changes in correctional and parole systems demand the attention of the lawmakers and the judiciary. If I were a legislator I might well find these and other needs so pressing as to make me believe that the resources of lawyers and judges should be devoted to them rather than to civil damage actions against officers who generally strive to perform within constitutional bounds. There is also a real danger that such suits might deter officials from the *proper* and honest performance of their duties.

All of these considerations make imperative careful study and weighing of the arguments both for and against the creation of such a remedy under the Fourth Amendment. I would have great difficulty for myself in resolving the competing policies, goals, and priorities in the use of resources, if I thought it were my job to resolve those questions. But that is not my task. The task of evaluating the pros and cons of creating judicial remedies for particular wrongs is a matter for Congress and the legislatures of the States. Congress has not provided that any federal court can entertain a suit against a federal officer for violations of Fourth Amendment rights occurring in the performance of his duties. A strong inference can be drawn from creation of such actions against state officials that Congress does not desire to permit such suits against federal officials. Should the time come when Congress desires such lawsuits, it has before it a model of valid legislation, 42 U.S.C. § 1983, to create a damage remedy against federal officers. Cases could be cited to support the legal proposition which I assert, but it seems to me to be a matter of common understanding that the business of the judiciary is to interpret the laws and not to make them.

I dissent.

■ MR. JUSTICE BLACKMUN, dissenting.

I, too, dissent. I do so largely for the reasons expressed in Chief Judge Lumbard's thoughtful and scholarly opinion for the Court of Appeals. But I also feel that the judicial legislation, which the Court by its opinion today concededly is effectuating, opens the door for another avalanche of new federal cases. Whenever a suspect imagines, or chooses to assert, that a Fourth Amendment right has been violated, he will now immediately sue the federal officer in federal court. This will tend to stultify proper law enforcement and to make the day's labor for the honest and conscientious officer even more onerous and more critical. Why the Court moves in this direction at this time of our history, I do not know. The Fourth Amendment was adopted in 1791, and in all the intervening years neither the Congress nor the Court has seen fit to take this step. I had thought that for the truly aggrieved person other quite adequate remedies have always been available. If not, it is the Congress and not this Court that should act.

Ziglar v. Abbasi

Supreme Court of the United States, 2017.
137 S. Ct. 1843.

■ JUSTICE KENNEDY delivered the opinion of the Court . . . .

After the September 11 terrorist attacks in this country, and in response to the deaths, destruction, and dangers they caused, the United States Government ordered hundreds of illegal aliens to be taken into custody and held. Pending a determination whether a particular detainee had connections to terrorism, the custody, under harsh conditions to be described, continued. In many instances custody lasted for days and weeks, then stretching into months. Later, some of the aliens who had been detained filed suit, leading to the cases now before the Court.

The complaint named as defendants three high executive officers in the Department of Justice and two of the wardens at the facility where the detainees had been held. Most of the claims, alleging various constitutional violations, sought damages under the implied cause of action theory adopted by this Court in Bivens *v.* Six Unknown Federal Narcotics Agents, 403 U.S. 388 (1971). Another claim in the complaint was based upon the statutory cause of action authorized and created by

Congress under Rev. Stat. § 1980, 42 U.S.C. § 1985(3). This statutory cause of action allows damages to persons injured by conspiracies to deprive them of the equal protection of the laws. . . .

[T]he Court of Appeals ruled that the complaint was sufficient for the action to proceed against the named officials who are now before us.

The Court granted certiorari to consider these rulings. The officials who must defend the suit on the merits, under the ruling of the Court of Appeals, are the petitioners here. The former detainees who seek relief under the fourth amended complaint are the respondents. The various claims and theories advanced for recovery, and the grounds asserted for their dismissal as insufficient as a matter of law, will be addressed in turn. . . .

II

The first question to be discussed is whether petitioners can be sued for damages under *Bivens* and the ensuing cases in this Court defining the reach and the limits of that precedent.

A

In 1871, Congress passed a statute that was later codified at Rev. Stat. § 1979, 42 U.S.C. § 1983. It entitles an injured person to money damages if a state official violates his or her constitutional rights. Congress did not create an analogous statute for federal officials. Indeed, in the 100 years leading up to *Bivens*, Congress did not provide a specific damages remedy for plaintiffs whose constitutional rights were violated by agents of the Federal Government.

In 1971, and against this background, this Court decided *Bivens*. The Court held that, even absent statutory authorization, it would enforce a damages remedy to compensate persons injured by federal officers who violated the prohibition against unreasonable search and seizures. The Court acknowledged that the Fourth Amendment does not provide for money damages "in so many words." 403 U.S., at 396. The Court noted, however, that Congress had not foreclosed a damages remedy in "explicit" terms and that no "special factors" suggested that the Judiciary should "hesitat[e]" in the face of congressional silence. *Id.*, at 396–397. The Court, accordingly, held that it could authorize a remedy under general principles of federal jurisdiction.

In the decade that followed, the Court recognized what has come to be called an implied cause of action in two cases involving other constitutional violations. In Davis *v.* Passman, 442 U.S. 228 (1979), an administrative assistant sued a Congressman for firing her because she was a woman. The Court held that the Fifth Amendment Due Process Clause gave her a damages remedy for gender discrimination. And in Carlson *v.* Green, 446 U.S. 14 (1980), a prisoner's estate sued federal jailers for failing to treat the prisoner's asthma. The Court held that the Eighth Amendment Cruel and Unusual Punishments Clause gave him a damages remedy for failure to provide adequate medical treatment.

These three cases—*Bivens*, *Davis*, and *Carlson*—represent the only instances in which the Court has approved of an implied damages remedy under the Constitution itself.

B

To understand *Bivens* and the two other cases implying a damages remedy under the Constitution, it is necessary to understand the prevailing law when they were decided. In the mid-20th century, the Court followed a different approach to recognizing implied causes of action than it follows now. During this "*ancien regime*," Alexander *v.* Sandoval, 532 U.S. 275, 287 (2001), the Court assumed it to be a proper judicial function to "provide such remedies as are necessary to make effective" a statute's purpose, J.I. Case Co. *v.* Borak, 377 U.S. 426, 433 (1964). Thus, as a routine matter with respect to statutes, the Court would imply causes of action not explicit in the statutory text itself. See, *e.g.*, Sullivan *v.* Little Hunting Park, Inc., 396 U.S. 229, 239 (1969) ("The existence of a statutory right implies the existence of all necessary and appropriate remedies").

These statutory decisions were in place when *Bivens* recognized an implied cause of action to remedy a constitutional violation. Against that background, the *Bivens* decision held that courts must "adjust their remedies so as to grant the necessary relief" when "federally protected rights have been invaded." 403 U.S., at 392; see also 403 U.S., at 402 (Harlan, J., concurring) (discussing cases recognizing implied causes of action under federal statutes). In light of this interpretive framework, there was a possibility that "the Court would keep expanding *Bivens* until it became the substantial equivalent of 42 U.S.C. § 1983." Kent, Are Damages Different?: *Bivens* and National Security, 87 S. Cal. L. Rev. 1123, 1139–1140 (2014).

C

Later, the arguments for recognizing implied causes of action for damages began to lose their force. In cases decided after *Bivens*, and after the statutory implied cause-of-action cases that *Bivens* itself relied upon, the Court adopted a far more cautious course before finding implied causes of action. In two principal cases under other statutes, it declined to find an implied cause of action. Later, in Cannon *v.* University of Chicago, 441 U.S. 677 (1979), the Court did allow an implied cause of action; but it cautioned that, where Congress "intends private litigants to have a cause of action," the "far better course" is for Congress to confer that remedy in explicit terms. . . .

The decision to recognize an implied cause of action under a statute involves somewhat different considerations than when the question is whether to recognize an implied cause of action to enforce a provision of the Constitution itself. When Congress enacts a statute, there are specific procedures and times for considering its terms and the proper means for its enforcement. It is logical, then, to assume that Congress will be explicit if it intends to create a private cause of action. With respect to the Constitution, however, there is no single, specific congressional action to consider and interpret.

Even so, it is a significant step under separation-of-powers principles for a court to determine that it has the authority, under the judicial power, to create and enforce a cause of action for damages against federal officials in order to remedy a constitutional violation. When determining whether traditional equitable powers suffice to give necessary constitutional protection—or whether, in addition, a damages remedy is necessary—there are a number of economic and governmental concerns to consider. Claims against federal officials often create substantial costs, in the form of defense and indemnification. Congress, then, has a substantial responsibility to determine whether, and the extent to which, monetary and other liabilities should be imposed upon individual officers and employees of the Federal Government. In addition, the time and administrative costs attendant upon intrusions resulting from the discovery and trial process are significant factors to be considered. . . .

For these and other reasons, the Court's expressed caution as to implied causes of actions under congressional statutes led to similar caution with respect to actions in the *Bivens* context, where the action is implied to enforce the Constitution itself. Indeed, in light of the changes to the Court's general approach to recognizing implied damages remedies, it is possible that the analysis in the Court's three *Bivens* cases might have been different if they were decided today. To be sure, no congressional enactment has disapproved of these decisions. And it must be understood that this opinion is not intended to cast doubt on the continued force, or even the necessity, of *Bivens* in the search-and-seizure context in which it arose. *Bivens* does vindicate the Constitution by allowing some redress for injuries, and it provides instruction and guidance to federal law enforcement officers going forward. The settled law of *Bivens* in this common and recurrent sphere of law enforcement, and the undoubted reliance upon it as a fixed principle in the law, are powerful reasons to retain it in that sphere.

Given the notable change in the Court's approach to recognizing implied causes of action, however, the Court has made clear that expanding the *Bivens* remedy is now a "disfavored" judicial activity. This is in accord with the Court's observation that it has "consistently refused to extend *Bivens* to any new context or new category of defendants." Correctional Services Corp. *v.* Malesko, 534 U.S. 61, 68 (2001). Indeed, the Court has refused to do so for the past 30 years.

For example, the Court declined to create an implied damages remedy in the following cases: a First Amendment suit against a federal employer, a race-discrimination suit against military officers, a substantive due process suit against military officers, a procedural due process suit against Social Security officials, a procedural due process suit against a federal agency for wrongful termination, an Eighth

Amendment suit against a private prison operator, a due process suit against officials from the Bureau of Land Management, and an Eighth Amendment suit against prison guards at a private prison.

When a party seeks to assert an implied cause of action under the Constitution itself, just as when a party seeks to assert an implied cause of action under a federal statute, separation-of-powers principles are or should be central to the analysis. The question is "who should decide" whether to provide for a damages remedy, Congress or the courts?

The answer most often will be Congress. When an issue "involves a host of considerations that must be weighed and appraised," it should be committed to "those who write the laws" rather than "those who interpret them." Bush *v.* Lucas, 462 U.S. 367, 380 (1983). In most instances, the Court's precedents now instruct, the Legislature is in the better position to consider if "the public interest would be served" by imposing a "new substantive legal liability." Schweiker *v.* Chilicky, 487 U.S. 412, 426–427 (1988). As a result, the Court has urged "caution" before "extending *Bivens* remedies into any new context." The Court's precedents now make clear that a *Bivens* remedy will not be available if there are " 'special factors counselling hesitation in the absence of affirmative action by Congress.' " Carlson, 446 U.S., at 18 (quoting *Bivens*, 403 U.S., at 396).

This Court has not defined the phrase "special factors counselling hesitation." The necessary inference, though, is that the inquiry must concentrate on whether the Judiciary is well suited, absent congressional action or instruction, to consider and weigh the costs and benefits of allowing a damages action to proceed. Thus, to be a "special factor counselling hesitation," a factor must cause a court to hesitate before answering that question in the affirmative.

It is not necessarily a judicial function to establish whole categories of cases in which federal officers must defend against personal liability claims in the complex sphere of litigation, with all of its burdens on some and benefits to others. It is true that, if equitable remedies prove insufficient, a damages remedy might be necessary to redress past harm and deter future violations. Yet the decision to recognize a damages remedy requires an assessment of its impact on governmental operations systemwide. Those matters include the burdens on Government employees who are sued personally, as well as the projected costs and consequences to the Government itself when the tort and monetary liability mechanisms of the legal system are used to bring about the proper formulation and implementation of public policies. These and other considerations may make it less probable that Congress would want the Judiciary to entertain a damages suit in a given case.

Sometimes there will be doubt because the case arises in a context in which Congress has designed its regulatory authority in a guarded way, making it less likely that Congress would want the Judiciary to interfere. And sometimes there will be doubt because some other feature of a case—difficult to predict in advance—causes a court to pause before acting without express congressional authorization. In sum, if there are sound reasons to think Congress might doubt the efficacy or necessity of a damages remedy as part of the system for enforcing the law and correcting a wrong, the courts must refrain from creating the remedy in order to respect the role of Congress in determining the nature and extent of federal-court jurisdiction under Article III.

In a related way, if there is an alternative remedial structure present in a certain case, that alone may limit the power of the Judiciary to infer a new *Bivens* cause of action. For if Congress has created "any alternative, existing process for protecting the [injured party's] interest" that itself may "amoun[t] to a convincing reason for the Judicial Branch to refrain from providing a new and freestanding remedy in damages." Wilkie *v.* Robbins, 551 U.S. 537, 550 (2007). . . .

III

[The Court went on to apply the preceding framework to the particular claim before it, concluding that there should be no *Bivens* claim.]

It is of central importance, too, that this is not a case like *Bivens* or *Davis* in which "it is damages or nothing." Bivens, *supra*, at 410 (Harlan, J., concurring in judgment). Unlike the plaintiffs in those cases, respondents do not challenge individual instances of discrimination or law enforcement overreach, which due to their very nature are difficult to address except by way of damages actions after the fact. Respondents instead challenge large-scale policy decisions concerning the conditions of confinement imposed on hundreds of prisoners. To address those kinds of decisions, detainees may seek injunctive relief. And in addition to that, we have left open the question whether they might be able to challenge their confinement conditions via a petition for a writ of habeas corpus.

Indeed, the habeas remedy, if necessity required its use, would have provided a faster and more direct route to relief than a suit for money damages. A successful habeas petition would have required officials to place respondents in less-restrictive conditions immediately; yet this damages suit remains unresolved some 15 years later. (. . .[T]he Court need not determine the scope or availability of the habeas corpus remedy, a question that is not before the Court and has not been briefed or argued.) In sum, respondents had available to them "other alternative forms of judicial relief." Minneci *v.* Pollard, 565 U.S. 118, 124 (2012). And when alternative methods of relief are available, a *Bivens* remedy usually is not.

There is a persisting concern, of course, that absent a *Bivens* remedy there will be insufficient deterrence to prevent officers from violating the Constitution. In circumstances like those presented here, however, the stakes on both sides of the argument are far higher than in past cases the Court has considered. If *Bivens* liability were to be imposed, high officers who face personal liability for damages might refrain from taking urgent and lawful action in a time of crisis. And, as already noted, the costs and difficulties of later litigation might intrude upon and interfere with the proper exercise of their office.

On the other side of the balance, the very fact that some executive actions have the sweeping potential to affect the liberty of so many is a reason to consider proper means to impose restraint and to provide some redress from injury. There is therefore a balance to be struck, in situations like this one, between deterring constitutional violations and freeing high officials to make the lawful decisions necessary to protect the Nation in times of great peril. The proper balance is one for the Congress, not the Judiciary, to undertake. For all of these reasons, the Court of Appeals erred by allowing respondents' detention policy claims to proceed under *Bivens*.

V

One issue remains to be addressed: the claim that petitioners are subject to liability for civil conspiracy under 42 U.S.C. § 1985(3). . . .

The civil-conspiracy prohibition contained in § 1985(3) was enacted as a significant part of the civil rights legislation passed in the aftermath of the Civil War. The statute imposes liability on two or more persons who "conspire . . . for the purpose of depriving . . . any person or class of persons of the equal protection of the laws." § 1985(3). In the instant suit, respondents allege that petitioners violated the statute by "agreeing to implement a policy" under which respondents would be detained in harsh conditions "because of their race, religion, ethnicity, and national origin." Assuming these allegations to be true and well pleaded, the question is whether petitioners are entitled to qualified immunity.

The qualified immunity rule seeks a proper balance between two competing interests. On one hand, damages suits "may offer the only realistic avenue for vindication of constitutional guarantees." Harlow *v.* Fitzgerald, 457 U.S. 800, 814 (1982). "On the other hand, permitting damages suits against government officials can entail substantial social costs, including the risk that fear of personal monetary liability and harassing litigation will unduly inhibit officials in the discharge of their duties." Anderson *v.* Creighton, 483 U.S. 635, 638 (1987). As one means to accommodate these two objectives, the Court has held that Government officials are entitled to qualified immunity with respect to "discretionary functions" performed in their official capacities. *Ibid.* The doctrine of qualified immunity gives officials "breathing room to make reasonable but mistaken judgments about open legal questions." Ashcroft *v.* al-Kidd, 563 U.S. 731, 743 (2011).

The Court's cases provide additional instruction to define and implement that immunity. Whether qualified immunity can be invoked turns on the "objective legal reasonableness" of the official's acts. And reasonableness of official action, in turn, must be "assessed in light of the legal rules that were clearly established at the time [the action] was taken." Anderson, *supra*, at 639. This requirement—that an official loses qualified immunity only for violating clearly established law—protects officials accused of violating "extremely abstract rights."

The Fourth Amendment provides an example of how qualified immunity functions with respect to abstract rights. By its plain terms, the Amendment forbids unreasonable searches and seizures, yet it may be difficult for an officer to know whether a search or seizure will be deemed reasonable given the precise situation encountered. See Saucier *v.* Katz, 533 U.S. 194, 205 (2001) ("It is sometimes difficult for an officer to determine how the relevant legal doctrine, here excessive force, will apply to the factual situation the officer confronts"). For this reason, "[t]he dispositive question is whether the violative nature of particular conduct is clearly established." Mullenix *v.* Luna, 136 S. Ct. 305, 308 (2015) (*per curiam*).

It is not necessary, of course, that "the very action in question has previously been held unlawful." Anderson, *supra*, at 640. That is, an officer might lose qualified immunity even if there is no reported case "directly on point." But "in the light of pre-existing law," the unlawfulness of the officer's conduct "must be apparent." *Id.*, at 640. To subject officers to any broader liability would be to "disrupt the balance that our cases strike between the interests in vindication of citizens' constitutional rights and in public officials' effective performance of their duties." Davis *v.* Scherer, 468 U.S. 183, 195 (1984). For then, both as a practical and legal matter, it would be difficult for officials "reasonably [to] anticipate when their conduct may give rise to liability for damages." *Ibid.*

In light of these concerns, the Court has held that qualified immunity protects "all but the plainly incompetent or those who knowingly violate the law." Malley *v.* Briggs, 475 U.S. 335, 341 (1986). To determine whether a given officer falls into either of those two categories, a court must ask whether it would have been clear to a reasonable officer that the alleged conduct "was unlawful in the situation he confronted." Saucier, *supra*, at 202. If so, then the defendant officer must have been either incompetent or else a knowing violator of the law, and thus not entitled to qualified immunity. If not, however—*i.e.*, if a reasonable officer might not have known for certain that the conduct was unlawful—then the officer is immune from liability.

Under these principles, it must be concluded that reasonable officials in petitioners' positions would not have known, and could not have predicted, that § 1985(3) prohibited their joint consultations and the resulting policies that caused the injuries alleged. . . .

[O]fficials employed by the same governmental department do not conspire when they speak to one another and work together in their official capacities. Whether that contention should prevail need not be decided here. It suffices to say that the question is sufficiently open so that the officials in this suit could not be certain that § 1985(3) was applicable to their discussions and actions. Thus, the law respondents seek to invoke cannot be clearly established. It follows that reasonable officers in petitioners' positions would not have known with any certainty that the alleged agreements were forbidden by law. See Saucier, 533 U.S., at 202. Petitioners are entitled to qualified immunity with respect to the claims under 42 U.S.C. § 1985(3).

■ [JUSTICE SOTOMAYOR, JUSTICE KAGAN, and JUSTICE GORSUCH took no part in the consideration or decision of these cases.]

■ JUSTICE THOMAS, concurring in part and concurring in the judgment. . . .

With respect to respondents' *Bivens* claims, I join the opinion of the Court to the extent it reverses the Second Circuit's ruling. The Court correctly applies our precedents to hold that *Bivens* does not supply a cause of action against petitioners for most of the alleged Fourth and Fifth Amendment violations. . . .

As for respondents' claims under 42 U.S.C. § 1985(3), I join Part V of the Court's opinion, which holds that respondents are entitled to qualified immunity. The Court correctly applies our precedents, which no party has asked us to reconsider. I write separately, however, to note my growing concern with our qualified immunity jurisprudence.

The Civil Rights Act of 1871, of which § 1985(3) and the more frequently litigated § 1983 were originally a part, established causes of action for plaintiffs to seek money damages from Government officers who violated federal law. Although the Act made no mention of defenses or immunities, "we have read it in harmony with general principles of tort immunities and defenses rather than in derogation of them." Malley *v.* Briggs, 475 U.S. 335, 339 (1986). We have done so because "[c]ertain immunities were so well established in 1871 . . . that we presume that Congress would have specifically so provided had it wished to abolish them." Buckley *v.* Fitzsimmons, 509 U.S. 259, 268 (1993). Immunity is thus available under the statute if it was "historically accorded the relevant official" in an analogous situation "at common law," Imbler *v.* Pachtman, 424 U.S. 409, 421 (1976), unless the statute provides some reason to think that Congress did not preserve the defense.

In some contexts, we have conducted the common-law inquiry that the statute requires. For example, we have concluded that legislators and judges are absolutely immune from liability under § 1983 for their official acts because that immunity was well established at common law in 1871. We have similarly looked to the common law in holding that a prosecutor is immune from suits relating to the "judicial phase of the criminal process," although not from suits relating to the prosecutor's advice to police officers.

In developing immunity doctrine for other executive officers, we also started off by applying common-law rules. In *Pierson*, we held that police officers are not absolutely immune from a § 1983 claim arising from an arrest made pursuant to an unconstitutional statute because the common law never granted arresting officers that sort of immunity. Rather, we concluded that police officers could assert "the defense of good faith and probable cause" against the claim for an unconstitutional arrest because that defense was available against the analogous torts of "false arrest and imprisonment" at common law.

In further elaborating the doctrine of qualified immunity for executive officials, however, we have diverged from the historical inquiry mandated by the statute. In the decisions following *Pierson*, we have "completely reformulated qualified immunity along principles not at all embodied in the common law." Anderson *v.* Creighton, 483 U.S. 635, 645 (1987) (discussing Harlow *v.* Fitzgerald, 457 U.S. 800 (1982)). Instead of asking whether the common law in 1871 would have accorded immunity to an officer for a tort analogous to the plaintiff's claim under § 1983, we instead grant immunity to any officer whose conduct "does not violate clearly established statutory or constitutional rights of which a reasonable person would have known." Mullenix *v.* Luna, 136 S. Ct. 305, 308 (2015) (per *curiam*). We apply this "clearly established" standard "across the board" and without regard to "the precise nature of the various officials' duties or the precise character of the particular rights alleged to have been violated." Anderson, *supra*, at 641–643. We have not attempted to locate that standard in the common law as it existed in 1871, however, and some evidence supports the conclusion that common-law immunity as it existed in 1871 looked quite different from our current doctrine. See generally Baude, Is Qualified Immunity Unlawful? 106 Cal. L. Rev. (forthcoming 2018).

Because our analysis is no longer grounded in the common-law backdrop against which Congress enacted the 1871 Act, we are no longer engaged in "interpret [ing] the intent of Congress in enacting" the Act. Malley, *supra*, at 342. Our qualified immunity precedents instead represent precisely the sort of "freewheeling policy choice[s]" that we have previously disclaimed the power to make. Rehberg *v.* Paulk, 566 U.S. 356, 363 (2012); see also Tower, *supra*, at 922–923 ("We do not have a license to establish immunities from" suits brought under the Act "in the interests of what we judge to be sound public policy"). We have acknowledged, in fact, that the "clearly established" standard is designed to "protec[t] the balance between vindication of constitutional rights and government officials' effective performance of their duties." Reichle *v.* Howards, 566 U.S. 658, 664 (2012); Harlow, *supra*, at 807 (explaining that "the recognition of a qualified immunity defense . . . reflected an attempt to balance competing values"). The Constitution assigns this kind of balancing to Congress, not the Courts.

In today's decision, we continue down the path our precedents have marked. We ask "whether it would have been clear to a reasonable officer that the alleged conduct was unlawful in the situation he confronted," rather than whether officers in petitioners' positions would have been accorded immunity at common law in 1871 from claims analogous to respondents'. Even if we ultimately reach a conclusion consistent with the common-law rules prevailing in 1871, it is mere fortuity. Until we shift the focus of our inquiry to whether immunity existed at common law, we will continue to substitute our own policy preferences for the mandates of Congress. In an appropriate case, we should reconsider our qualified immunity jurisprudence.

■ JUSTICE BREYER, with whom JUSTICE GINSBURG joins, dissenting. . . .

It is by now well established that federal law provides damages actions at least in [contexts similar to *Bivens*, *Davis*, and *Carlson*], where claims of constitutional violation arise. Congress has ratified *Bivens* actions, plaintiffs frequently bring them, courts accept them, and scholars defend their importance. See J. Pfander, CONSTITUTIONAL TORTS AND THE WAR ON TERROR (2017) (canvassing the history of *Bivens* and cataloguing cases). Moreover, the courts, in order to avoid deterring federal officials from properly performing their work, have developed safeguards for defendants, including the requirement that plaintiffs plead "plausible" claims, Ashcroft *v.* Iqbal, 556 U.S. 662, 679 (2009), as well as the defense of "qualified immunity," which frees federal officials from both threat of liability and involvement in the lawsuit, unless the plaintiffs establish that officials have violated "clearly established . . . constitutional rights," *id.*, at 672. "[This] Court has been reluctant to extend *Bivens* liability to any new context or new category of defendants." *Id.*, at 675. But the Court has made clear that it would not narrow *Bivens*' existing scope.

The plaintiffs before us today seek damages for unconstitutional conditions of confinement. They alleged that federal officials slammed them against walls, shackled them, exposed them to nonstop lighting, lack of hygiene, and the like, all based upon invidious discrimination and without penological justification. In my view, these claims are well-pleaded, state violations of clearly established law, and fall within the scope of longstanding *Bivens* law. For those reasons, I would affirm the judgment of the Court of Appeals. I shall discuss at some length what I believe is the most important point of disagreement. The Court, in my view, is wrong to hold that permitting a constitutional tort action here would "extend" *Bivens*, applying it in a new context. To the contrary, I fear that the Court's holding would significantly shrink the existing *Bivens* contexts, diminishing the compensatory remedy constitutional tort law now offers to harmed individuals. . . .

I recognize . . . the strongest of the Court's arguments, namely, the fact that plaintiffs' claims concern detention that took place soon after a serious attack on the United States and some of them concern actions of high-level Government officials. While these facts may affect the substantive constitutional questions (*e.g.*, were any of the conditions "legitimate"?) or the scope of the qualified-immunity defense, they do not extinguish the *Bivens* action itself. If I may paraphrase Justice Harlan, concurring in *Bivens*: In wartime as well as in peacetime, "it is important, in a civilized society, that the judicial branch of the Nation's government stand ready to afford a remedy" "for the most flagrant and patently unjustified," unconstitutional "abuses of official power." 403 U.S., at 410–411 (opinion concurring in judgment). . . .

Can we, in respect to actions taken during [wartime], rely exclusively, as the Court seems to suggest, upon injunctive remedies or writs of habeas corpus, their retail equivalent? Complaints seeking that kind of relief typically come during the emergency itself, when emotions are strong, when courts may have too little or inaccurate information, and when courts may well prove particularly reluctant to interfere with even the least well-founded Executive Branch activity. That reluctance may itself set an unfortunate precedent, which, as Justice Jackson pointed out, can "li[e] about like a loaded weapon" awaiting discharge in another case. e Korematsu *v.* United States, 323 U.S. 214, 246 (1944) (dissenting opinion).

A damages action, however, is typically brought after the emergency is over, after emotions have cooled, and at a time when more factual information is available. In such circumstances, courts have more time to exercise such judicial virtues as calm reflection and dispassionate application of the law to the facts. We have applied the Constitution to actions taken during periods of war and national-security emergency. I should think that the wisdom of permitting courts to consider *Bivens* actions, later granting monetary compensation to those wronged at the time, would follow *a fortiori*.

As is well known, Lord Atkins, a British judge, wrote in the midst of World War II that "amid the clash of arms, the laws are not silent. They may be changed, but they speak the same language in war as in peace." Liversidge *v.* Anderson, [1942] A.C. 206 (H.L. 1941) 244. The Court, in my view, should say the same of this *Bivens* action.

With respect, I dissent.

NOTE

1. Writing for the Court, Justice Kennedy stated that: "in the 100 years leading up to *Bivens*, Congress did not provide a specific damages remedy for plaintiffs whose constitutional rights were violated by agents of the Federal Government." That is technically true. Yet federal officers were subject to suits for damages in state court. In the twentieth century, however, there was a huge growth in the immunity doctrines that shield governments and officers from liability, meaning that now it will often be "*Bivens* or nothing."

What inference should be drawn from the growth of immunity doctrines? Consider several possibilities: Federal courts should maintain and expand *Bivens* liability. Congress should enact a Section 1983-like cause of action against federal officers. Courts and legislatures should cut back on immunity doctrines, returning to their traditional scope at common law.

Courts should embrace equitable remedies as the default against federal officers. Congress should curtail the removal of claims against federal officers to federal court. Of these various possibilities, which one(s) should Congress or the federal courts embrace? Which are consistent with the distinct roles of the legislature and judiciary under our constitutional separation of powers?

2. *Ziglar* suggests that the case was not one of "*Bivens* or nothing" because the writ of habeas corpus might have been available to challenge conditions of confinement. For the plaintiffs in the case, of course, the suggestion comes too late. Even for future plaintiffs, though, the suggestion is carefully hedged, because the Court does not actually say the writ would be available. One reason may be that habeas is a legal remedy traditionally requiring the release of the prisoner; it is not as well adapted as an equitable remedy to managing conditions of confinement. Another reason may be that Article I, Section 9 of the U.S. Constitution allows Congress to suspend the writ of habeas corpus "when in Cases of Rebellion or Invasion the public Safety may require it."

3. The three opinions in *Ziglar* take different positions on the judicially created doctrine of qualified immunity. That doctrine is meant to shield state and federal officers from liability unless they act contrary to "clearly established law." Qualified immunity has been developed by the courts and is based on policy rationales, including the supposition that officers will not vigilantly enforce the law if they risk personal liability any time they make a mistake. That supposition has been called into question, however. In a recent study, Professor Joanna Schwartz found that:

> Police officers are virtually always indemnified. Between 2006 and 2011, in forty-four of the country's largest jurisdictions, officers financially contributed to settlements and judgments in just .41% of the approximately 9225 civil rights damages actions resolved in plaintiffs' favor, and their contributions amounted to just .02% of the over $730 million spent by cities, counties, and states in these cases. Officers did not pay a dime of the over $3.9 million awarded in punitive damages. And officers in the thirty-seven small and mid-sized jurisdictions in my study never contributed to settlements or judgments in lawsuits brought against them. Governments satisfied settlements and judgments in police misconduct cases even when indemnification was prohibited by statute or policy. And governments satisfied settlements and judgments in full even when officers were disciplined or terminated by the department or criminally prosecuted for their conduct.
>
> My findings of widespread indemnification undermine assumptions of financial responsibility relied upon in civil rights doctrine. Although the Court's stringent qualified immunity standard rests in part on the concern that individual officers will be overdeterred by the threat of financial liability, actual practice suggests that these officers have nothing reasonably to fear, at least where payouts are concerned.

Joanna C. Schwartz, Police Indemnification, 89 N.Y.U. L. Rev. 885, 890 (2014).

The current scope of qualified immunity is illustrated by the following case.

Buckley v. Haddock

United States Court of Appeals, Eleventh Circuit, 2008.
292 Fed. Appx. 791.

■ EDMONDSON, CHIEF JUDGE: This case involves an excessive-force claim and arises from an encounter between a sheriff's deputy and a motorist who refused to submit to lawful arrest during a traffic stop. Deputy Jonathan Rackard seeks interlocutory review of the district court's decision denying him qualified immunity for the repeated use of a taser in effecting the arrest of Jesse Buckley ("Plaintiff"). Because Deputy Rackard's use of force was not unconstitutionally excessive and, in any event, because the preexisting law at the time did not clearly establish that this use of force was excessive, we reverse the district court's decision and remand the case for dismissal of the federal claims against Deputy Rackard.

I. Background

Rackard, a deputy sheriff in Washington County, Florida, stopped Plaintiff for speeding in March 2004. The traffic stop occurred at night on the side of a two-lane highway that had no street lights. It was dark.

Financially destitute and homeless, Plaintiff became agitated about getting a ticket. Plaintiff began to sob. Despite Deputy Rackard's repeated requests, Plaintiff refused to sign the traffic citation: signing is required by law. See Fla. Stat. § 318.14(2)-(3). Deputy Rackard warned Plaintiff twice that, if he did not sign the citation, he would be arrested. After the second warning, Plaintiff said "arrest me." Without resisting, Plaintiff allowed himself to be handcuffed; he was then still sitting in his vehicle. Now handcuffed, Plaintiff got out of his car.

As the deputy started to walk with Plaintiff to the patrol car, Plaintiff—a 23-year-old young man who weighed 180 pounds and was 6 feet, 2 inches tall—dropped to the ground behind his car, crossed his legs, and continued to sob. Deputy Rackard cautioned Plaintiff about the danger of getting hit by traffic on the nearby road. Plaintiff responded, "My life would be better if I was dead."

Deputy Rackard asked Plaintiff several times to stand up. Plaintiff did not do so. The deputy then attempted to lift Plaintiff to his feet; but Plaintiff remained limp and did not stand. After repeatedly and plainly warning Plaintiff that a taser device would be used (to which Plaintiff shouted, "I don't care anymore—tase me") and after giving Plaintiff some time to comply, the deputy discharged the taser. The taser was used for approximately five seconds in the "stun gun" mode. The deputy applied the taser's electrodes directly to Plaintiff's clothed back and chest. After

Deputy Rackard discharged the taser, he asked Plaintiff again to stand up; but Plaintiff did not comply. Again, the deputy plainly warned Plaintiff that the taser would be used. Plaintiff still did not stand. After some time, Deputy Rackard discharged the taser for another five-second burst. The taser delivers an electrical shock; it hurts.

At this point, Deputy Rackard walked to his patrol car and, by radio, called for backup. Plaintiff remained on the ground. When the deputy returned, he ordered Plaintiff to get up. Again, Deputy Rackard plainly warned Plaintiff that the taser would be used and allowed Plaintiff time to comply. The deputy then attempted a second time to lift Plaintiff to his feet, but to no avail. Plaintiff still did not stand; and the deputy used the taser a third time. Even though Plaintiff continued to resist moving to the patrol car, Deputy Rackard made no more use of the taser.

Once another police officer arrived, Plaintiff promptly relented; and with the assistance of the other officer, Deputy Rackard escorted Plaintiff to the patrol car without incident. Plaintiff suffered sixteen small burn marks on his back from the taser with some scarring (the record does not say whether or not the scars are permanent) and keloid growth around some of the burns. Plaintiff also claims that he suffered emotional injury from the incident: He says that he now finds it difficult to trust police officers and to ask for their assistance.

Plaintiff brought this section 1983 suit against Deputy Rackard in his individual capacity, alleging that the deputy used excessive force in violation of the Fourth Amendment. Deputy Rackard moved for summary judgment on the basis of qualified immunity, which the district court denied.

II. Discussion

A. Excessive Force Claim

That the right to make an arrest "necessarily carries with it the right to use some degree of physical coercion or threat thereof to effect it" is well established. Graham *v.* Connor, 490 U.S. 386 (1989).

For excessive force claims, "objective reasonableness" is the test. But we have noted some secondary factors to consider: "(1) the need for the application of force, (2) the relationship between the need and amount of force used, and (3) the extent of the injury inflicted." Draper *v.* Reynolds, 369 F.3d 1270, 1277–78 (11th Cir. 2004). The nature and degree of force needed is measured by such factors as "the severity of the crime at issue, whether the suspect poses an immediate threat to the safety of the officers or others, and whether he is actively resisting arrest or attempting to evade arrest by flight." Graham, 109 S. Ct. at 1872. . . .

In the light of the undisputed facts established in the record, we conclude that Defendant's use of force in this particular situation was not outside the range of reasonable conduct under the Fourth Amendment. Of particular importance are three facts. First, the incident occurred at night on the side of a highway with considerable passing traffic. Second, the deputy could not complete the arrest—that is, truly control Plaintiff—because Plaintiff was resisting. Third, the deputy resorted to using the taser only after trying to persuade Plaintiff to cease resisting, after attempting to lift Plaintiff, and after repeatedly and plainly warning Plaintiff that a taser would be used and then giving Plaintiff some time to comply.

Although, as the district court observed, the underlying offense of refusing to sign a traffic citation was relatively minor, we nevertheless credit the government with a significant interest in enforcing the law on its own terms, rather than on terms set by the arrestee. The government has an interest in arrests being completed efficiently and without waste of limited resources: police time and energy that may be needed elsewhere at any moment. Even though Plaintiff was handcuffed, he still refused repeatedly to comply with the most minimal of police instructions-that is, to stand up and to walk to the patrol car. That Plaintiff was resisting arrest weighs in the deputy's favor. In addition, to the extent that the incident occurred beside an active highway at night, we also credit the government's interest in the safety of Deputy Rackard, Plaintiff, and even passing motorists: a legitimate interest to be advanced by putting Plaintiff in the patrol car. See Pennsylvania *v.* Mimms, 434 U.S. 106 (1977) (acknowledging that the "hazard of accidental injury from passing traffic" may be "appreciable" in some situations). Deputy Rackard warned Plaintiff early on that they should not remain exposed alongside the highway for fear of being hit by a passing vehicle.

Against these important governmental interests weigh the nature and quality of the intrusion on Plaintiff's Fourth Amendment interests. Plaintiff alleges that he sustained, as a result of Deputy Rackard's acts, emotional injury as well as sixteen small taser burns, which caused some scarring and keloid growth. Although Plaintiff's injuries are not insignificant, neither are they severe. Plaintiff points to no evidence in the record that the deputy's use of the taser caused any second-order physical injuries; nor has Plaintiff pointed to evidence that the burns he did sustain required medical attention. Accordingly, we regard the deputy's use of the taser in this particular case as—at most—moderate, non-lethal force. See Sanders *v.* City of Fresno, 551 F. Supp. 2d 1149, 1168 (E.D. Cal. 2008) (viewing "the use of a Taser as an intermediate or medium, though not insignificant, quantum of force").

While conceding that a single use of the taser might arguably have been reasonable, the district court nevertheless concluded (and Plaintiff argues) that the other applications of the taser were grossly disproportionate and unnecessary, especially given that the arrest had been "fully secured" and given that backup was en route to assist in moving Plaintiff to the patrol car.

We disagree. Never was Plaintiff fully secured until after the second officer arrived. The district court's suggestion that Plaintiff had been fully secured because he was handcuffed is mistaken: Plaintiff was not bound at the feet (so, he could both run and kick), he was moving around on the ground alongside a busy road, and he would not comply with the deputy's repeated instructions to stand up and to move to the patrol car where Plaintiff could be confined. An objectively reasonable police officer could rightly believe that force was therefore necessary to secure the non-compliant Plaintiff in the patrol car and thereby complete the arrest.

We also reject the district court's rationale that had Deputy Rackard "simply waited for back up, two officers could have lifted [Plaintiff] and carried him to the car without any application of force." A single officer in the deputy's situation confronting a non-compliant arrestee like Plaintiff need not-as a matter of federal constitutional law-wait idly for backup to arrive to complete an otherwise lawful arrest that the officer has started.

The federal courts must not dictate through their interpretation of the Constitution how the police should allocate their limited resources. In most circumstances where an arrestee is resisting, a single officer can constitutionally effectuate an otherwise lawful arrest by resorting to the use of moderate, nonlethal force. No constitutional basis exists for requiring two or more officers to make routine arrests, even if deploying more officers might result in less force actually being used.

That an officer has requested more police assistance does not make the use of force before reinforcements arrive unreasonable. For instance, that the deputy called for backup after his second use of the taser does not render the third use unreasonable or excessive because the facts and circumstances that justified the first use still apply: that is, Plaintiff continued to resist arrest, the deputy and Plaintiff's safety while on the side of a highway at night was still at risk (not to mention the safety of other motorists), and the use of the taser itself was moderate, non-lethal force. . . .

B. Qualified Immunity

Although we conclude that the Constitution was not violated at all, we will also decide about immunity. Even if some of the deputy's use of force was excessive under the Fourth Amendment, we conclude nevertheless that he is entitled to qualified immunity because he—given the circumstances he was facing—violated no already clearly established federal right.

In their individual capacities, government officials are entitled to immunity from suit "unless the law preexisting [their] supposedly wrongful act was already established to such a high degree that every objectively reasonable official standing in [their] place would be on notice that what the defendant official was doing would be clearly unlawful given the circumstances." Pace *v.* Capobianco, 283 F.3d 1275, 1282 (11th Cir. 2002).

We have pointed out before that "[g]overnment officials are not required to err on the side of caution." Marsh *v.* Butler County, 268 F.3d 1014, 1030 n. 8 (11th Cir. 2001) (*en banc*); see also Saucier *v.* Katz, 533 U.S. 194 (2001) ("The concern of the immunity inquiry is to acknowledge that reasonable mistakes can be made as to the legal constraints on particular police conduct. . . . If the officer's mistake as to what the law requires is reasonable, however, the officer is entitled to the immunity defense."). As a consequence, qualified immunity does protect "all but the plainly incompetent or those who knowingly violate the law." Malley *v.* Briggs, 475 U.S. 335 (1986).

With these principles in mind, Plaintiff must demonstrate that, from the preexisting law, the deputy had "fair and clear notice" that the deputy's conduct would break federal law. To show that the law was clearly established in a case like this "where the applicable legal standard is a highly general one, such as 'reasonableness,' preexisting caselaw that has applied general law to specific circumstances will almost always be necessary to draw a line that is capable of giving fair and clear notice that an official's conduct will violate federal law." Thomas *v.* Roberts, 323 F.3d 950, 954 (11th Cir. 2003). If an earlier case is "fairly distinguishable from the circumstances facing a government official," then that case cannot "clearly establish the law for the circumstances facing that government official." Vinyard *v.* Wilson, 311 F.3d 1340, 1352 (11th Cir. 2002).

Neither Plaintiff nor the district court has cited case-law establishing that Deputy Rackard's use of the taser was clearly unlawful. Both rely on Lee *v.* Ferraro, 284 F.3d 1188 (11th Cir. 2002), in which this Court denied qualified immunity to a defendant police officer on an excessive force claim. In *Lee*, the facts showed that the officer pulled over a young woman during the afternoon rush hour for a minor traffic violation, forced her out of her car, handcuffed her, and led her to the back of the car where the officer slammed her head against the car's trunk and kept spreading her legs with his foot. Construing the facts in the light most favorable to the woman, the *Lee* panel stressed that she *did not resist* the officer at any time during the incident.

The district court thought the present case was "analogous," concluding that—like the facts in *Lee*—the crime here was minor, Plaintiff posed no threat to the deputy or anyone else, and Plaintiff "never actively resisted or attempted to evade arrest by flight." The district court, as well as Plaintiff in his brief, placed considerable stress on the fact that Plaintiff had already been handcuffed, that Plaintiff resisted only passively, and that the deputy used the taser more than once.

We regard *Lee* as easily distinguishable from the facts and circumstances of this case. At best, *Lee* decides only that no officer can use force against an arrestee who is already handcuffed and who is resisting arrest in no way. But unlike *Lee*, where the court stressed that the arrestee did not resist at any time during the arrest, here Plaintiff did resist: for example, he physically dropped to the ground, repeatedly refused to comply with the deputy's reasonable orders (even after being warned that a taser would be used), and made no effort to stand when the deputy attempted on two occasions physically to lift Plaintiff to his feet. The use of force in *Lee* was wholly uncalled for; *Lee* decides nothing about the gamut of options for force usage in the circumstances of arrestee intransigence. The circumstances that call on police to use some intermediate force—between no force and deadly force—remain the cases where the law of excessive force is most ambiguous. It will probably always be so, considering the limitless set of potential different fact combinations and the necessity of allowing for flexible responses from the police.

Lee does not control this case. More important for qualified immunity purposes, an objectively reasonable police officer could have believed that additional facts present here but not present in *Lee*—for instance, that Plaintiff was resisting arrest on a roadside at night and that the deputy plainly warned Plaintiff before using the taser—might "make a difference" about whether the conduct in the present case would violate federal law. Therefore, whatever fair and clear warning about unconstitutional force that *Lee* (or any other decisional law that has been drawn to our attention) gives does not reach the factual particularities of this case. Furthermore, the force used here did not approach being so excessive as obviously to violate the Fourth Amendment on its face. Cf., *e.g.*, Priester *v.* City of Riviera Beach, 208 F.3d 919 (11th Cir. 2000) (denying qualified immunity—in the absence of controlling judicial precedent—where defendant police officers ordered dog to attack a compliant, non-resisting arrestee). At the very least, therefore, Deputy Rackard is entitled to qualified immunity.

III. Conclusion

Plaintiff resisted arrest. Given this circumstance in the context of all the other facts, Deputy Rackard's gradual use of force, culminating with his repeated (but limited) use of a taser, to move Plaintiff to the patrol car was not unconstitutionally excessive. In addition, even if Plaintiff could establish that some of the deputy's use of force violated the Fourth Amendment, the deputy still would be entitled to qualified immunity because the applicable law at the time did not clearly establish that the deputy's conduct—given the circumstances—was unconstitutional. Accordingly, the district court erred in denying Deputy Rackard's motion for summary judgment.

Reversed and Remanded.

■ DUBINA, CIRCUIT JUDGE, concurring specially: Although I believe that Deputy Rackard's conduct of applying the taser on the third occasion violated the Constitution, nevertheless, I agree with Chief Judge Edmondson that such violation was not clearly established. Accordingly, I agree that we should reverse the district court's denial of summary judgment based on qualified immunity.

■ MARTIN, DISTRICT JUDGE, dissenting: I respectfully dissent from the judgment in this case. I write to express my view that the Fourth Amendment forbids an officer from discharging repeated bursts of electricity into an already handcuffed misdemeanant—who is sitting still beside a rural road and unwilling to move—simply to goad him into standing up. I also conclude that at the time of the incident, Deputy Rackard was on fair notice that his conduct was unconstitutional. Not only did Deputy Rackard unnecessarily discharge his taser gun against Mr. Buckley three times, but each time he did so, he repeatedly prodded Mr. Buckley's body with the stun gun's live electrodes—inflicting additional pain and leaving Mr. Buckley with sixteen burn scars. Because our law clearly establishes such conduct as unconstitutional, I would affirm the district court's denial of qualified immunity and allow this action to proceed.

I.

A video captured the events in question, and I suggest it be published together with this opinion. Because the factual details are important to the required analysis, I will supplement those included in Chief Judge Edmondson's opinion, stated in a light most favorable to Mr. Buckley.

After Deputy Rackard handcuffed Mr. Buckley, he voluntarily got out of his car and walked with Deputy Rackard to the back of the car, but he then collapsed into a sitting position on the grass beside the road. The road was, by Deputy Rackard's description, "desolate" and "out in the middle of no where." There was scant traffic. Mr. Buckley sat motionless with one leg crossed, leaning forward and sobbing.

After observing Mr. Buckley collapse and after attempting to persuade him to stand, Deputy Rackard turned away from Mr. Buckley and walked to his police car to communicate his status over the police radio. For thirty-five seconds, Mr. Buckley sat unattended. When Deputy Rackard returned and first attempted to lift Mr. Buckley, Buckley remained limp. Deputy Rackard partially lifted Mr. Buckley and dragged him several feet away from the road. Mr. Buckley remained limp and uncooperative as he was dropped to the ground. Deputy Rackard again unsuccessfully attempted to persuade Mr. Buckley to stand up, and the following conversation transpired:

> Deputy Rackard: [I'm] going to tase you. Do you understand me?
>
> Mr. Buckley: [Crying] Go ahead.
>
> Deputy Rackard: Buckley, get up ok?
>
> Mr. Buckley: [Crying]
>
> Deputy Rackard: [Places taser on Mr. Buckley's back.] I'm fixing to tase you. Get off the ground, ok?
>
> Mr. Buckley: [Crying] I don't care anymore. Tase me. [Sound of taser.]

(Buckley Video at 8:01:25.)

As the taser was applied that first time, Mr. Buckley cried out and fell forward from his seated position, with his chest on the ground, his knees bent and his legs folded underneath him. Mr. Buckley squirmed on the ground in response to the taser, but Deputy Rackard followed Mr. Buckley's movement, attempting to maintain the taser gun's contact with Mr. Buckley's back. When Deputy Rackard lost contact with Mr. Buckley's body, he immediately replaced the taser on him. Mr. Buckley unfolded his legs and lurched forward onto the right side of his body. The clicking of the taser gun continued and Deputy Rackard removed the gun from Mr. Buckley's back, pinned it briefly against his chest, and then returned it to his back. Deputy Rackard continued holding the taser gun against Mr. Buckley's back until it completed its five-second discharge.

Upon completion of the first discharge, Mr. Buckley laid flat with his chest and face on the ground and his hands still cuffed behind his back, crying. Three seconds passed, and Deputy Rackard ordered Mr. Buckley to stand up, threatening again to shoot him with the taser gun. Though Mr. Buckley had been responsive and defiant before, he did not respond to Deputy Rackard's second warning.

Deputy Rackard again discharged the taser into Mr. Buckley's back, just twenty seconds after he had completed his first five-second discharge. This second tase also lasted five seconds. In response to the taser, Mr. Buckley flipped over onto his back, causing the taser gun to lose contact with his body. Deputy Rackard quickly re-pinned it onto Mr. Buckley's chest, and in response, Mr. Buckley jerked forward. As with the first tase, Deputy Rackard followed Mr. Buckley's movements in attempt to continue the contact between the taser and Mr. Buckley's body. Deputy Rackard replaced the nodes of the taser onto Mr. Buckley's back, lost contact, then lodged the taser gun a final time into Mr. Buckley's back, holding it steady until it completed its discharge.

After the second discharge, Deputy Rackard stood up silently, turned away from Mr. Buckley, and returned to his police vehicle, leaving Mr. Buckley unattended on the side of the road for the second time. He returned approximately thirty seconds later and again ordered Mr. Buckley to stand up. Mr. Buckley sat cross-legged, leaning forward and still crying. He offered no response to Deputy Rackard. After again attempting to lift Mr. Buckley, Deputy Rackard pressed the taser gun against Buckley's back, warned Buckley, and discharged it a third time.

The final discharge caused Mr. Buckley again to lurch forward onto his side. As Deputy Rackard had before, he followed the movement of Mr. Buckley's body with the taser gun. He lost contact with Mr. Buckley's body at least four times, and each time re-pinned the taser against Mr. Buckley onto different areas of Mr. Buckley's chest and back.

After the final discharge, Deputy Rackard left Mr. Buckley for the third time and returned to his police car. He announced over the radio that the "subject's in custody; not wanting—refusing to come to the car." He approached Mr. Buckley briefly and again returned to his patrol car, leaving Mr. Buckley unattended for the fourth time during the encounter. Less than three minutes later—and five minutes from the time Deputy Rackard first tased Mr. Buckley—a second officer arrived on the scene. The two officers easily lifted Mr. Buckley off the ground and escorted him away. This action followed.

II.

The first question, as instructed by Saucier *v.* Katz, 533 U.S. 194, 201 (2001), is whether Deputy Rackard used excessive force. This is not a case about whether an officer may use a taser gun to subdue an unruly or dangerous individual. Rather, the question in the case is whether a taser gun may be used repeatedly against a peaceful individual as a pain-compliance device—that is, as an electric prod—to force him to comply with an order to move.

Like the district court below, I conclude that the repeated and sustained use of the taser gun for the sole purpose of coercing Mr. Buckley to move was unreasonable under the circumstances and thus violated the Fourth Amendment.

[Judge Martin based this conclusion on the minor crimes for which Mr. Buckley was arrested, the lack of immediate threat he posed, and the fact that he did not try to flee or "actively resist arrest." The use of the taser, Judge Martin concluded, "was a wholly disproportionate response to the need to remove Mr. Buckley from the roadside and transport him to the police station."]

In sum, I conclude that no reasonable officer could have believed that the force used by Deputy Rackard was necessary in response to the situation at hand. Accordingly, under the first prong of *Saucier*, I would hold that Mr. Buckley has brought forth sufficient evidence to state a Fourth Amendment violation against Deputy Rackard.

III.

I would also find, under the second prong of *Saucier*, that the law was clearly established at the time of the incident that Deputy Rackard's conduct was unconstitutional. Whatever the debatability of employing a single, controlled electric shock against a non-compliant individual to coerce him into movement, in this case Deputy Rackard repeatedly prodded Mr. Buckley's body which maximized the level of pain he experienced. In light of the repeated and continuous nature of the force used against Mr. Buckley, the substantial pain and bodily injury that resulted, and the absence of any arguable justification, I have no difficulty in concluding that no particularized preexisting case law was necessary for it to be clearly established that Deputy Rackard's conduct was unconstitutional. Deputy Rackard's use of force was so grossly disproportionate to the need for force that no reasonable officer would have believed such conduct was legal. See Lee, 284 F.3d at 1198–99 (holding that qualified immunity should be denied where an officer's conduct "lies so obviously at the very core of what the Fourth Amendment prohibits that the unlawfulness of the conduct was readily apparent to the official, notwithstanding the lack of case law"); Hope *v.* Pelzer, 536 U.S. 730, 745 (2002) (denying qualified immunity for "obvious cruelty" despite lack of factually similar prior precedent); Priester *v.* City of Riviera Beach, 208 F.3d 919, 926 (11th Cir. 2000) ("It would create perverse incentives indeed if a qualified immunity defense could succeed against those types of claims that have not previously arisen because the behavior alleged is so egregious that no like case is on the books.").

Accordingly, I would affirm the district court's denial of qualified immunity.

B. STRUCTURAL REMEDIES FOR CONSTITUTIONAL VIOLATIONS

Swann v. Charlotte-Mecklenburg Board of Education

United States District Court, Western District of North Carolina, 1970.
318 F. Supp. 786.

■ MCMILLAN, DISTRICT JUDGE.

I. SUMMARY.

Pursuant to the mandates of the Supreme Court of the United States and the Fourth Circuit Court of Appeals, further hearings (eight days of them) have been conducted July 15–24, 1970, regarding methods for desegregation of the public schools of Charlotte and Mecklenburg County, North Carolina, and the known plans for desegregation of the elementary schools have been reconsidered. . . .

II. BRIEF HISTORY OF PROCEEDINGS.

On April 23, 1969, after lengthy hearings and research, an order was entered that the defendants submit a plan for the desegregation of the schools of Charlotte and Mecklenburg County, North Carolina, to be predominantly effective in the fall of 1969, and to be completed by the fall of 1970. Among other things the court found that under North Carolina law there is no "freedom of choice" to attend any school; that the Board of Education has the total control over the assignment of students to schools; and that residence has never created a right to attend a particular school. It was further found that all the black and predominantly black schools of this school system are illegally segregated. The November 7, 1969 opinion contained detailed guidelines for desegregating this particular group of schools, and included the following findings:

> "The black schools are for the most part in black residential areas. However, that does not make their segregation

> constitutionally benign. In previous opinions the facts respecting their *locations*, their *controlled size* and their *population* have already been found. Briefly summarized, these facts are that the present location of white schools in white areas and of black schools in black areas is the result of a varied group of elements of public and private action, all deriving their basic strength originally from public law or state or local governmental action. These elements include among others the legal separation of the races in schools, school busses, public accommodations and housing; racial restrictions in deeds to land; zoning ordinances; city planning; urban renewal; location of public low rent housing; and the actions of the present School Board and others, before and since 1954, in locating and controlling the capacity of schools so that there would usually be black schools handy to black neighborhoods and white schools for white neighborhoods. There is so much state action embedded in and shaping these events that the resulting segregation is not innocent or '*de facto*,' and the resulting schools are not 'unitary' or desegregated."

Segregation of black children into black schools is *not* because of residential patterns, but because of assignment and other policies of the School Board, including the call upon segregated housing and school site selection to lend respectability to those policies.

(There is appended hereto an 18-page exhibit listing approximately 65 sections of the General Statutes of North Carolina and 2 sections of its Constitution under which the segregation of the black race in North Carolina has been the policy of our Constitution and the letter of our statutes for many years. Many of these provisions were repealed by the 1969 General Assembly, but most of them were still on the books when the April 23, 1969 opinion was written.)

A consultant, Dr. John A. Finger, Jr., 1969, was appointed by the court in December, 1969, to draw a desegregation plan after it became apparent that the defendants had no such plan and had not resolved to prepare one which would desegregate the schools. . . . [T]he court appointed consultant prepared plans for the desegregation of all the black schools. Faced with the imminent existence of valid desegration plans, the Board then went to work and prepared some plans of its own.

This court approved the Board's plan for senior high schools (with one minor change); it gave the School Board a choice of several plans or procedures as choice of several plans or procedures as to junior high schools; and it disapproved the Board's plan for elementary schools, because it left half the black children in black schools, and ordered into effect one of the plans designed by the consultant, Dr. Finger, for desegregation of the elementary schools.

[There were further proceedings in the District Court and the Court of Appeals, and the North Carolina General Assembly enacted an "anti-bussing law" that was held to be unconstitutional in part. When the Court of Appeals considered the District Court's order requiring integration, it largely affirmed, though "[i]t expressly disapproved the Board's plan for elementary schools because it left half the black elementary children in 'black' schools, and it remanded the matter for the school board to prepare a new plan using all reasonable means of desegregation, and for the district court to reconsider the assignment of elementary pupils under a theory of 'reasonableness.'" The Supreme Court granted a petition for a writ of certiorari, and it reinstated the judgment of the district court pending further proceedings.]

At the July 15–July 24 hearings the defendants announced that:

> (a) Faculties have been assigned for all schools according to the February 5, 1970 order, so that when schools open in September all faculties will have about 75% white teachers and about 25% black teachers;
>
> (b) The senior high schools will be desegregated this fall in accordance with the plan previously approved by the district court and by the Circuit Court;
>
> (c) The junior high schools will be desegregated this fall in accordance with the plan previously approved by the district court and by the Circuit Court; and
>
> (d) As to elementary schools the majority of the defendants have no official plan and no plan of action for desegregation except the plan, previously rejected by both district court and the Circuit Court, which would leave half the black elementary children in segregated schools.

Since the schools board has refused to obey the Circuit Court's instructions to file a new elementary plan by June 30, 1970, it might, were this an ordinary case, have no standing to be heard further. However, the case affects numerous people who, though not Board members, are entitled to have the matter further considered as fully and fairly as possible.

This court has tried to follow faithfully the orders of the Supreme Court and the Circuit Court. This presents some unique problems; the Circuit Court's "reasonableness" order is vague; the Supreme Court's order allowing certiorari is cryptic, and raises and leaves unanswered several major questions; neither order is a clear guide for this court. However, this court believes that, regardless of the Board's continued default, this court's duty is to reconsider the elementary desegregation problem in view of the questions whether the methods previously required by the court are reasonable and whether the Board has exhausted all reasonable methods available to it.

III. THE EXTENT OF CONTINUED SEGREGATION—AND ITS RESULTS.

The schools are still segregated as described in this court's memorandum opinion of November 7, 1969. Over 9,000 black children attend schools that are 100% black. Two-thirds (16,000) of the black children still attend racially identifiable "black" schools. Fifty-seven schools are "white" and twenty-five are predominantly "black."

The tangible results of segregation continue to be apparent from the 1969–70 Stanford Achievement Tests in Paragraph Meaning and Arithmetic, given during the sixth month of school, for grades 3, 6, 8 and 10. In "black" schools third graders perform at first grade or early second grade levels, while their contemporaries at "white" schools perform at levels generally from one to two grades higher. Sixth graders in black schools (Double Oaks and Bruns Avenue, for example) perform at third grade levels while their contemporaries at Olde Providence, Pinewood, Lansdowne and Myers Park perform at seventh or eighth grade levels. In the eighth grade we see Piedmont Junior High students reading at early fifth grade levels while their contemporaries at McClintock and Alexander Graham read at early ninth grade levels. . . .

Of factors affecting educational progress of black children, segregation appears to be *the factor under control of the state* which still constitutes the greatest deterrent to achievement.

IV. THE LEGAL BASIS FOR DESEGREGATION.

A. *Segregated public schools are unconstitutional.*—Desegregation is based on the Constitution as interpreted in Brown *v.* Board of Education, 347 U.S. 483 (1954), where the Supreme Court said:

> "Segregation of white and colored children in public schools has a detrimental effect upon the colored children. The impact is greater when it has the sanction of the law; for the policy of separating the races is usually interpreted as denoting the inferiority of the Negro group. A sense of inferiority affects the motivation of a child to learn. *Segregation with the sanction of law, therefore, has a tendency to [retard] the educational and mental development of Negro children and to deprive them of some of the benefits they would receive in a racial[ly] integrated school system.* . . .
>
> "We conclude that in the field of public education the doctrine of 'separate but equal' has no place. *Separate educational facilities are inherently unequal.* . . ." (Emphasis added.)

Green *v.* County School Board of New Kent County, 391 U.S. 430 (1968) placed upon school boards the burden

> " . . . to come forward with a plan that promises realistically to work, and promises realistically to work *now*," [and]

"... to convert promptly to a system without a 'white' school and a 'Negro', school, *but just schools.*" (Emphasis added.)

The principal difference between New Kent County, Virginia, and Mecklenburg County, North Carolina, is that in New Kent County the number of children being denied access to equal education was only 740, whereas in Mecklenburg that number exceeds 16,000. If *Brown* and [other cases] are confined to small counties and to "easy" situations, the constitutional right is indeed an illusory one. A black child in urban Charlotte whose education is being crippled by unlawful segregation is just as much entitled to relief as his contemporary on a Virginia farm.

B. *"Racial balance" is not required by this court.*—The November 7, 1969 order expressly contemplated wide variations in permissible school population; and the February 5, 1970 order approved plans for the schools with pupil populations varying from 3% at Bain Elementary to 41% at Cornelius. This is not racial balance but racial diversity. The purpose is not some fictitious "mix," but the compliance of this school system with the Constitution by eliminating the racial characteristics of its schools.

C. *"Bussing" is still an irrelevant issue.*—. . . The state authorities have announced intention and promulgated rules to comply with [a court order] by providing transport on the usual basis for *all* city children who live over 1½ miles from school. . . .

D. *This is a local case in a local court—a lawsuit—to test the constitutional rights of local people.*—The *principles* which outlaw racial discrimination in public schools certainly are of nationwide application, but the *facts* and results may vary from case to case. This is a local suit involving actions of the State of North Carolina and its local governments and agencies. The facts about the development of black Charlotte may not be the facts of the development of black Chicago or black Denver or New York or Baltimore. Some other court will have to pass on that problem. The decision of the case involves local history, local statutes, local geography, local demography, local state history including half a century of bus transportation, local zoning, local school boards—in other words, local and individual merits.

This court has not ruled, and does not rule that "racial balance" is required under the Constitution; nor that all black schools in all cities are unlawful; nor that all school boards must bus children or violate the Constitution; nor that the particular order entered in this case would be correct in other circumstances not before this court.

The orders of this court have been confined to the only area they can properly embrace, and that is *the rights of the particular parties represented in this case, on the particular facts and history of this case.*

E. *The issue is not the validity of a "system," but the rights of individual people.*—If the rights of citizens are infringed by the system, the infringement is not excused because in the abstract the system may appear valid. "Separate but equal" for a long time was thought to be a valid system but when it was finally admitted that individual rights were denied by the valid system, the system gave way to the rights of individuals.

F. *The Issue Is One Of Constitutional Law—Not Politics.*—At the hearings the defendants offered public opinion polls and testimony that parents don't like "bussing," and that this attitude produces an adverse educational effect upon the minds of the children. The court has excluded such evidence, and must continue to proceed unaffected, if possible, by this and other types of political pressure and public opinion. . . .

To yield to public clamor, however, is to corrupt the judicial process and to turn the effective operation of courts over to political activism and to the temporary local opinion makers. This a court must not do.

In the long run, it is true, a majority of the people will have their way. The majority must be a majority of the pertinent voting group. As our slave-owning grandfathers of the South learned in 1865, the pertinent voting group on constitutional matters includes the people and their elected representatives from the nation at large, not just the South, and not just Mecklenburg County. Methods exist to amend the Constitution. If the Constitution is amended or the higher courts rule so as to allow continued segregation in the local public schools, this court will have to be governed by such amendment or decisions. In the meanwhile, the duty of this and other courts is to seek to follow the Constitution in the light of the existing rulings of the Supreme Court, and under the belief that the constitutional rights of people should not be swept away by temporary local or national public opinion or political manipulation.

Civil rights are seldom threatened except by majorities. One whose actions reflect accepted local opinion seldom needs to call upon the Constitution. It is axiomatic that persons claiming constitutional protection are often, for the time being, out of phase with the accepted "right" thinking of their local community. If in such circumstances courts look to public opinion or to political intervention by any other branch of the government instead of to the more stable bulwarks of the Constitution itself, we lose our government of laws and are back to the government of man, unfettered by law, which our forefathers sought to avoid. . . .

G. *The duty to desegregate schools does not depend upon the Coleman report, nor on any particular racial proportion of students.*—The essence of the *Brown* decision is that segregation implies inferiority, reduces incentive, reduces morale, reduces opportunity for association and breadth of experience, and that the segregated education itself is inherently unequal. The tests which show the poor performance of segregated children are evidence showing one result of segregation. Segregation would not become lawful, however, if all children scored equally on the tests.

Nor does the validity of *Brown* depend upon whether the system contains ideal proportions of black and white students. The Charlotte-Mecklenburg system does contain a theoretical "ideal" 70–30 proportion of white and black students. This has some bearing upon the reasonableness of any particular local plan or part of such plan. However, it does not give rise to any legitimate contention that *Brown* may be ignored where you cannot have at least 60% or 70% white children in a school. The HEW plan providing for 57% black students in a group of schools may well be constitutional in some other system, though unconstitutional in Mecklenburg where a school 57% black is immediately racially identifiable as a "black" school.

V. THE REASONABLENESS OF THE SPECIFIC METHODS AND THE OVERALL PLANS AVAILABLE TO DESEGREGATE THE BLACK CHARLOTTE SCHOOLS.

A. *The facts under which any question of "reasonableness" must be judged.*—From the lengthy and largely repetitious testimony at the July 15–24 hearings, and from previous evidence, the following facts bearing on "reasonableness" are found:

1. In North Carolina the school bus has been used for half a century to transport children to *segregated consolidated* schools. Last year 610,000 children, comprising nearly 55% of the state's public school population, were transported daily on school busses. With the 1970 extension of transportation to inner-city children, the average daily school bus population of North Carolina this September will reach perhaps three-fifths of all public school children. . . .

10. There is no black residential area in this school system which is so large that the students can not be afforded a desegregated education by reasonable means. The additional length of travel required to implement the best available plans for desegregating the system is less than the average distance of bus transportation now being provided elementary children under existing bus practices, and the travel times are less than times required by existing bus routes. . . .

30. No capital outlay will be needed to supply busses for the 1970–71 school year. The state is ready and willing to lend the few busses the Board may need; replacements can be bought after actual need has been determined under operating conditions. . . .

32. . . . The longest bus routes in the entire county are the routes by which four and five-year-old kindergarten children are transported to child development centers. The Pineville Child Development Center has one bus, No. 297, which travels over 79 miles a day on one round trip with four and five-year-old children. . . . The Bain Elementary School has a bus route, No. 115, which travels over 61 miles on one round trip each day, requiring two hours in the morning and two hours in the afternoon with elementary children. Routes to numerous elementary schools are very long in miles and time. The more than 10,000 children in grades one

through six who have been riding school busses all these years and who now ride at an average travel time of an hour and a quarter each way are not shown to have had their education damaged by the experience.

Educationally it appears unreasonable to postpone desegregation of small children until later grades. The only concrete evidence of an educational nature in the whole hearing which rose above the level of opinion is the Stanford Achievement Tests which show that the performance gap, which show that the noticeable in the first grade, has become several grades wide by the time the segregated black child reaches the sixth grade. The lasting effects of segregation are minimized if it is eliminated at an early age. . . .

35. The defendants have plenty of money, plenty of know-how plenty of busses on hand or available upon request, and plenty of capacity to implement the court ordered plan or the minority plan or any combination of the various plans. Their contentions to the contrary, and their five million dollar "estimates," when heard against the actual facts, border on fantasy!

B. *Reasonableness of methods.*—. . . The end in view is the desegregation of the schools. The methods available include the following: (1) consolidation of schools (which began fifty years or more ago, and for which the school bus has been the "ordinary or usual," as well as the necessary tool; (2) assignment of pupils; (3) school bussing; (4) non-contiguous zoning (before *Brown*, no black child was allowed to attend the nearest school if it happened to be white); (5) restructuring of grades in schools; (6) rezoning; (7) pairing, clustering and grouping of schools; (8) use of satellite zones; (9) freedom of choice, with appropriate restrictions; and (10) closing of schools.

All of these methods have been approved as legal by the Fourth Circuit Court of Appeals and by other courts. They work; singly and in combination they can work to accomplish the reassignment of children to eliminate assignment of children to eliminate they accomplish the end in view, and if they have been in use for half a century, they certainly qualify as "reasonable" methods. They are "appropriate to the end in view"; they desegregate the schools in a practical way.

C. *The various plans.*—

1. *The 5/4 Majority Board Plan.*—The original Board plan was rejected by this court and by the Circuit Court. The School Board has not obeyed the order of the Circuit Court of Appeals to file a new plan, and has not drafted nor attempted to draft another plan. The Board majority have not explored other methods of desegregation as directed by the Circuit Court (pairing, clustering, grouping, non-contiguous zoning, re-arranging grade structures), except to discuss these matters among themselves and to offer lengthy testimony rationalizing the non-use of alternative methods. Although parts of the disapproved Board plan could be used in a current plan, the Board plan as originally proposed is still

inadequate because it leaves half the black elementary students still attending black schools. The court does not find it to be reasonable.

2. *The HEW plan.*—This plan proposes to adopt the basic zoning program of parts of the Board majority plan, and then to re-zone some of the black schools with some white schools, mostly in low and middle income areas, and by clustering, pairing, grouping and transportation, to produce a substantial desegregation of most of the black schools. The faults of the plan are obvious. It leaves two schools (Double Oaks and Oaklawn) completely black; it leaves more than a score of other schools completely white; it would withdraw from numerous white schools the black students who were transported to those schools during the 1969–70 school year. . . .

3. *The court order of February 5, 1970, including the Finger Plan.*—This order directs the desegregation of the schools. It offers the Finger plan as one way to do it, and encourages the Board to use its own resources to develop something better. As to the Finger elementary plan itself, the court, after eight days of further evidence and extensive further study, still finds it to be a reasonable method or collection of methods for solving the problem. The plan was designed by a qualified educator. It was drafted with technical assistance of the school staff. It does the complete job. It has a clear pupil assignment plan. It preserves a sound grade structure; it is adaptable to ungraded experimentation; it can be implemented piecemeal, in sections or by clusters of schools if necessary; it embraces local knowledge; it can be implemented immediately. It uses all reasonable methods of desegregation. It takes proper advantage of traffic movement and school capacity. It passes all tests of reasonableness.

4. *The 4/5 Minority Board Plan.*—This plan was presented intelligently and clearly by Dr. Carlton Watkins, its chief drafter, one of a 4/5 minority of the Board. It was spared any aggressive attack by Board witnesses or counsel. It is home grown. It was conceived and drafted by four members of the local Board. It uses all the techniques of the Finger plan. It desegregates all the schools. Like the Finger plan, it involves all communities of the county. It appears to the court that it can be implemented with somewhat shorter travel distances for school busses, though perhaps a few more children might have to ride school busses than under the Finger plan. . . . The principal fault of the minority plan is its present lack of a system of pupil assignment. Board witnesses were not willing to admit it outright, but the court has the very definite impression that they could draft a pupil assignment plan and put the minority plan into effect this fall if so directed by the Board.

5. *An earlier draft of the Finger plan.*—This draft . . . would require less transportation than any other plan before the court, and for shorter distances. It would have to be implemented all at once, and it does not involve all of the county in its scope. From the standpoint of economics it may be the cheapest plan available. From the standpoint of avoidance of

tendencies toward resegregation and from the standpoint of total community-involvement in the total community plan it is not on a par with the minority plan nor the final Finger plan. It is, however, like the minority plan and the final Finger plan ordered by the court, a "reasonable" plan.

VI. A RESERVATION CONCERNING REASONABLENESS VERSUS CONSTITUTIONAL RIGHTS.

Reasonable remedies should always be sought. Practical rather than burdensome methods are properly required. On facts reported above, the methods required by this order are reasonable. However, if a constitutional right has been denied, this court believes that it is the constitutional right that should prevail against the cry of "unreasonableness." If a home has been illegally searched and evidence seized, the evidence is suppressed. If a defendant in a drunk driving case "takes the Fifth" and puts the state to its proof, the state has to prove its case without any testimony from him. The unreasonableness of putting the state to some expense can not be weighed against nor prevail over the privilege against self-incrimination or the right of people to be secure in their homes. If, as this court and the Circuit Court have held, the rights of children are being denied, the cost and inconvenience of restoring those rights is no reason under the Constitution for continuing to deny them. Griffin *v.* County School Board of Prince Edward County, *supra.*

ORDER

1. Pursuant to the June 29, 1970 mandate of the Supreme Court of the United States, this court's order of February 5, 1970 will remain in effect pending these proceedings and except as modified herein or by later order of this or a higher court.

2. The action of the Board in making faculty assignments in accordance with the order of February 5, 1970 is approved.

3. The action of the Board in making pupil assignments and other arrangements to operate the senior high schools in accordance with this court's order of February 5, 1970 is approved.

4. The action of the Board in making pupil assignments and other arrangements to operate the junior high schools in accordance with this court's order of February 5, 1970 is approved.

5. Numbered paragraphs 10 and 11 of the February 5, 1970 order of this court are amended by inserting the words "cumulative" and "substantially" at the appropriate points in each paragraph so that the two paragraphs will read as follows:

> "10. That 'freedom of choice' or 'freedom of transfer' may not be allowed by the Board if the cumulative effect of any given transfer of group of transfers is to increase substantially the

degree of segregation in the school from which the transfer is requested or in the school to which the transfer is desired.

"11. That the Board retain its statutory power and duty to make assignments of pupils for administrative reasons, with or without requests from parents. Administrative transfers shall not be made if the cumulative result of such transfers is to restore or substantially increase the degree of segregation in either the transferor or the transferee school."

6. As to the elementary schools:

(a) The order entered by this court on February 5, 1970 having been subjected to three weeks of review under the reasonableness test is expressly found to be reasonable, and the School Board are directed to put the court ordered plan of desegregation into effect at the opening of school in the fall of 1970, unless they avail themselves of some of the options indicated herein.

(b) The plan for elementary school desegregation proposed by a 4/5 minority of the School Board (the Watkins plan) has been examined and is found to be reasonable, as far as it goes. It is, however, incomplete because it contains no plan for pupil assignment. The School Board are authorized to prepare an appropriate pupil assignment plan and use the minority plan for elementary school desegregation instead of the comparable portions of the plan previously ordered by the court, if they so elect.

(c) The School Board, if they so elect, may use portions of the minority plan and portions of the court ordered plan, bearing in mind that the most important single element in the order of this court on February 5, 1970 is paragraph 16, reading as follows:

"16. The duty imposed by the law and by this order is the desegregation of schools and the maintenance of that condition. The *plans* discussed in this order, whether prepared by Board and staff or by outside consultants, such as computer expert, Mr. John W. Weil, or Dr. John A. Finger, Jr., are *illustrations of means or partial means to that end*. The defendants are encouraged to use their full 'know-how' and resources to attain the results above described, and thus to achieve the constitutional end by any means at their disposal. The test is not the method or plan, but the *results*."

(d) The Board are free to incorporate into any plan they may make whatever portions of the work of the Department of Health, Education and Welfare staff, or such parts of the original partial Finger plan (Plaintiffs' Exhibit 10), which are consistent with their duty to carry out the order to desegregate the schools.

(e) If the Board elect to carry out the Finger plan, they are authorized, if they find it advisable, to close Double Oaks school and reassign its pupils in accordance with the general purposes of the February 5, 1970 order.

(f) The Board are directed to file a written report with this court on or before noon on Friday, August 7, 1970, indicating what plan or combination of plans they have voted to use.

(g) The Board are again reminded, as they were reminded during the July 15, 1970 hearings, that since the 29th day of June, 1970, they have been and still are subject to the order of the Supreme Court, which reinstated this court's February 5, 1970 order pending these proceedings, and that this court will be under some duty to measure the Board's performance against what they could have done starting on June 29, 1970.

7. The following portion of this order is taken in modified form from the recommendations in the proposed plan of the Department of Health, Education and Welfare. It has been included in part in orders of district courts to various school systems, such as the school system in Dorchester County, South Carolina. It is included in this order not with any idea of impairing or affecting any party's right of appeal, but with the thought that this community has a difficult job of implementing a major desegregation program and that just as in the case of Greenville, South Carolina, whose schools were desegregated before any final word came from the Supreme Court, it will take leadership to do the job. Some of these suggestions of the Department of Health, Education and Welfare are therefore incorporated in this order as follows, for such aid as they may be in working through the difficult administrative and community problems which must be overcome:

SUGGESTIONS FOR PLAN IMPLEMENTATION

Successful implementation of desegregation plans largely depends upon local leadership and good faith in complying with mandates of the Courts and the laws upon which the Courts act. The following suggestions are offered to assist local officials in planning for implementation of desegregational orders.

Community.

1. The Superintendent and Board of Education should frankly and fully inform all citizens of the community about the legal requirements for school desegregation and their plans for complying with these legal requirements.
2. The Board of Education should issue a public statement clearly setting forth its intention to abide by the law and comply with orders of the Court in an effective and educationally responsible manner.
3. School officials should seek and encourage support and understanding of the press and community organizations representing both races.

4. The Board of Education, or some other appropriate governmental unit, should establish a bi-racial advisory committee to advise the Board of Education and its staff throughout the implementation of the desegregation plan. Such committee should seek to open up community understanding and communication, to assist the Board in interpreting legal and educational requirements to the public.
5. The Superintendent should actively seek greater involvement of parents of both races through school meetings, newsletters, an active and bi-racial P.T.A., class meetings, parent conferences, and through home visits by school personnel.
6. The Superintendent and Board of Education should regularly report to the community on progress in implementing the desegregation plan.

School Personnel.

1. The Superintendent should provide all personnel copies of the desegregation plan and arrange for meetings where the personnel will have an opportunity to hear it explained.
2. The Board of Education should issue a policy statement setting forth in clear terms the procedures it will follow in reassignment of the personnel.
3. Assignments of staff for the school year should be made as quickly as possible with appropriate followings by school principals to assure both welcome and support for personnel new to each school: Invitations to visit school before the new school year begins should be offered.
4. The Superintendent should see that a special orientation program is planned and carried out for both the professional and non-professional staffs (including bus drivers, cafeteria workers, secretaries and custodians) preparatory to the new school year. He should make every effort to familiarize new and reassigned staff with facilities, services, and building policies, and prepare them to carry out their important role in a constructive manner. The Superintendent should direct each principal to see that each teacher new to a school is assigned for help and guidance to a teacher previously assigned to that school. Such teachers should have an opportunity to meet before the school year actually begins.
5. The Superintendent should arrange an in-service training program during the school year to assist personnel in resolving difficulties and improving instruction throughout the implementation period. Help in doing this is available from the St. Augustine College in Raleigh, North Carolina.

8. The Clerk is directed to serve copies of this order on the members of the School Board individually, and upon all other parties by sending copies by certified mail to their counsel of record.

9. Subject to further orders from higher courts, jurisdiction is retained, and the attention of the parties is called to pages 27 and 28 of the order of the Fourth Circuit Court of Appeals respecting the duties of the court and the parties with regard to any desired modification of the plan or of this order. . . .

NOTE

On August 7, 1970, the board agreed to "acquiesce" in the Finger Plan, pending subsequent appeals. The next year the Supreme Court affirmed the District Court's order in Swann *v.* Charlotte-Mecklenburg Board of Education, 402 U.S. 1, stating that:

> "The objective today remains to eliminate from the public schools all vestiges of state-imposed segregation. Segregation was the evil struck down by *Brown I* as contrary to the equal protection guarantees of the Constitution. That was the violation sought to be corrected by the remedial measures of *Brown II*. That was the basis for the holding in Green that school authorities are "clearly charged with the affirmative duty to take whatever steps might be necessary to convert to a unitary system in which racial discrimination would be eliminated root and branch." 391 U.S., at 437–438.
>
> "If school authorities fail in their affirmative obligations under these holdings, judicial authority may be invoked. Once a right and a violation have been shown, the scope of a district court's equitable powers to remedy past wrongs is broad, for breadth and flexibility are inherent in equitable remedies.
>
> " 'The essence of equity jurisdiction has been the power of the Chancellor to do equity and to mould each decree to the necessities of the particular case. Flexibility rather than rigidity has distinguished it. The qualities of mercy and practicality have made equity the instrument for nice adjustment and reconciliation between the public interest and private needs as well as between competing private claims.' Hecht Co. *v.* Bowles, 321 U.S. 321, 329–330, cited in Brown II, *supra*, 349 U.S., at 300.
>
> "This allocation of responsibility once made, the Court attempted from time to time to provide some guidelines for the exercise of the district judge's discretion and for the reviewing function of the courts of appeals. However, a school desegregation case does not differ fundamentally from other cases involving the framing of equitable remedies to repair the denial of a constitutional right. The task is to correct, by a balancing of the individual and collective interests, the condition that offends the Constitution.
>
> "In seeking to define even in broad and general terms how far this remedial power extends it is important to remember that judicial powers may be exercised only on the basis of a constitutional violation. Remedial judicial authority does not put

judges automatically in the shoes of school authorities whose powers are plenary. Judicial authority enters only when local authority defaults."

Id. at 15–16.

Milliken v. Bradley[ii]

Supreme Court of the United States, 1974.
418 U.S. 717.

■ MR. CHIEF JUSTICE BURGER delivered the opinion of the Court.

We granted certiorari in these consolidated cases to determine whether a federal court may impose a multidistrict, areawide remedy to a single-district de jure segregation problem absent any finding that the other included school districts have failed to operate unitary school systems within their districts, absent any claim or finding that the boundary lines of any affected school district were established with the purpose of fostering racial segregation in public schools, absent any finding that the included districts committed acts which effected segregation within the other districts, and absent a meaningful opportunity for the included neighboring school districts to present evidence or be heard on the propriety of a multidistrict remedy or on the question of constitutional violations by those neighboring districts.

I

The action was commenced in August 1970 by the respondents, the Detroit Branch of the National Association for the Advancement of Colored People and individual parents and students, on behalf of a class later defined by order of the United States District Court for the Eastern District of Michigan, dated February 16, 1971, to included "all school children in the City of Detroit, Michigan, and all Detroit resident parents who have children of school age." The named defendants in the District Court included the Governor of Michigan, the Attorney General, the State Board of Education, the State Superintendent of Public Instruction, the Board of Education of the city of Detroit, its members, the city's and its former superintendent of schools. The State of Michigan as such is not a party to this litigation and references to the State must be read as references to the public officials, state and local, through whom the State is alleged to have acted. In their complaint respondents attacked the constitutionality of a statute of the State of Michigan known as Act 48 of the 1970 Legislature on the ground that it put the State of Michigan in the position of unconstitutionally interfering with the execution and operation of a voluntary plan of partial high school desegregation, known as the April 7, 1970, Plan, which had been adopted by the Detroit Board of Education to be effective beginning with the fall 1970 semester. The complaint also alleged that the Detroit Public School System was and is

---

[ii] This decision is called *Milliken I*, because the case returned to the Supreme Court.

segregated on the basis of race as a result of the official policies and actions of the defendants and their predecessors in office, and called for the implementation of a plan that would eliminate "the racial identity of every school in the [Detroit] system and . . . maintain now and hereafter a unitary, nonracial school system." . . .

The trial of the issue of segregation in the Detroit school system began on April 6, 1971, and continued through July 22, 1971, consuming some 41 trial days. On September 27, 1971, the District Court issued its findings and conclusions on the issue of segregation, finding that "Governmental actions and inaction at all levels, federal, state and local, have combined, with those of private organizations, such as loaning institutions and real estate associations and brokerage firms, to establish and to maintain the pattern of residential segregation throughout the Detroit metropolitan area." . . .

The District Court found that the Detroit Board of Education created and maintained optional attendance zones[3] within Detroit neighborhoods undergoing racial transition and between high school attendance areas of opposite predominant racial compositions. These zones, the court found, had the "natural, probable, foreseeable and actual effect" of allowing white pupils to escape identifiably Negro schools. . . .

The District Court found that in the operation of its school transportation program, which was designed to relieve overcrowding, the Detroit Board had admittedly bused Negro Detroit pupils to predominantly Negro schools which were beyond or away from closer white schools with available space. This practice was found to have continued in recent years despite the Detroit Board's avowed policy, adopted in 1967, of utilizing transportation to increase desegregation:

> "With one exception (necessitated by the burning of a white school), defendant Board has never bused white children to predominantly black schools. The Board has not bused white pupils to black schools despite the enormous amount of space available in inner-city schools. There were 22,961 vacant seats in schools 90% or more black."

With respect to the Detroit Board of Education's practices in school construction, the District Court found that Detroit school construction generally tended to have a segregative effect with the great majority of schools being built in either overwhelmingly all-Negro or all-white neighborhoods so that the new schools opened as predominantly one-race schools. Thus, of the 14 schools which opened for use in 1970–1971, 11 opened over 90% Negro and one opened less than 10% Negro.

The District Court also found that the State of Michigan had committed several constitutional violations with respect to the exercise of its general responsibility for, and supervision of, public education. The

[3] Optional zones, sometimes referred to as dual zones or dual overlapping zones, provide pupils living within certain areas a choice of attendance at one of two high schools.

State, for example, was found to have failed, until the 1971 Session of the Michigan Legislature, to provide authorization or funds for the transportation of pupils within Detroit regardless of their poverty or distance from the school to which they were assigned; during this same period the State provided many neighboring, mostly white, suburban districts the full range of state-supported transportation.

The District Court found that the State, through Act 48, acted to "impede, delay and minimize racial integration in Detroit schools." The first sentence of § 12 of Act 48 was designed to delay the April 7, 1970, desegregation plan originally adopted by the Detroit Board.[iii] . . .

Turning to the question of an appropriate remedy for these several constitutional violations, . . . [o]n March 28, 1972, the District Court issued its findings and conclusions on the three Detroit-only plans submitted by the city Board and the respondents. It found that the best of the three plans "would make the Detroit school system more identifiably Black . . . thereby increasing the flight of Whites from the city and the system." From this the court concluded that the plan "would not accomplish desegregation . . . within the corporate geographical limits of the city." Accordingly, the District Court held that it "must look beyond the limits of the Detroit school district for a solution to the problem" . . . .

[T]he District Court conducted hearings on a metropolitan plan. . . . [O]n June 14, 1972, the District Court issued its ruling on the "desegregation area" and related findings and conclusions. The court acknowledged at the outset that it had "taken no proofs with respect to the establishment of the boundaries of the 86 public school districts in the counties [in the Detroit area], nor on the issue of whether, with the exclusion of the city of Detroit school districts, such school districts have committed acts of de jure segregation." Nevertheless, the court designated 53 of the 85 suburban school districts plus Detroit as the "desegregation area" and appointed a panel to prepare and submit "an effective desegregation plan" for the Detroit schools that would encompass the entire desegregation area. The plan was to be based on 15 clusters, each containing part of the Detroit system and two or more suburban districts, and was to "achieve the greatest degree of actual desegregation to the end that, upon implementation, no school, grade or classroom [would be] substantially disproportionate to the overall pupil racial composition."

On July 11, 1972, and in accordance with a recommendation by the court-appointed desegregation panel, the District Court ordered the Detroit Board of Education to purchase or lease "at least" 295 school

[iii] [The first sentence of Section 12 read as follows: "The implementation of any attendance provisions for the 1970–71 school year determined by any first class school district board *shall be delayed* pending the date of commencement of functions by the first class school district boards established under the provisions of this amendatory act but such provision shall not impair the right of any such board to determine and implement prior to such date such changes in attendance provisions as are mandated by practical necessity. . ." (emphasis added).]

buses for the purpose of providing transportation under an interim plan to be developed for the 1972–1973 school year. The costs of this acquisition were to be borne by the state defendants.

[A divided Court of Appeals affirmed the District Court's findings as to constitutional violations, and it concluded that the metropolitan-wide remedy was "within the equity power of the District Court." It remanded for the District Court to join all of the affected suburban school districts as parties and give them an opportunity to be heard, and it vacated the portion of the order that required the purchase of school buses.]

II

. . . The target of the *Brown* holding was clear and forthright: the elimination of state-mandated or deliberately maintained dual school systems with certain schools for Negro pupils and others for white pupils. This duality and racial segregation were held to violate the Constitution in the cases subsequent to 1954 . . .

In Brown *v.* Board of Education, 349 U.S. 294 (1955) (*Brown II*), the Court's first encounter with the problem of remedies in school desegregation cases, the Court noted:

> "In fashioning and effectuating the decrees, the courts will be guided by equitable principles. Traditionally, equity has been characterized by a practical flexibility in shaping its remedies and by a facility for adjusting and reconciling public and private needs." Id., at 300.

In further refining the remedial process, *Swann* held, the task is to correct, by a balancing of the individual and collective interests, "the condition that offends the Constitution." A federal remedial power may be exercised "only on the basis of a constitutional violation" and, "[a]s with any equity case, the nature of the violation determines the scope of the remedy." Swann *v.* Charlotte-Mecklenburg Board of Education, 402 U.S. 1, 16 (1971).

Proceeding from these basic principles, we first note that in the District Court the complainants sought a remedy aimed at the *condition* alleged to offend the Constitution—the segregation within the Detroit City School District. The court acted on this theory of the case and in its initial ruling on the "Desegregation Area" stated:

> "The task before this court, therefore, is now, and . . . has always been, now to desegregate the Detroit public schools."

Thereafter, however, the District Court abruptly rejected the proposed Detroit-only plans . . . . [T]he court reasoned [that] it was imperative to "look beyond the limits of the Detroit school district for a solution to the problem of segregation in the Detroit public schools . . ." since "[s]chool district lines are simply matters of political convenience and may not be used to deny constitutional rights." Accordingly, the District Court proceeded to redefine the relevant area to include areas of predominantly white pupil population in order to ensure that "upon implementation, no school, grade or classroom [would be] substantially disproportionate to the overall pupil racial composition" of the entire metropolitan area. . . .

[T]he District Court's approach to what constituted "actual desegregation" raises the fundamental question, not presented in *Swann*, as to the circumstances in which a federal court may order desegregation relief that embraces more than a single school district. The court's analytical starting point was its conclusion that school district lines are no more than arbitrary lines on a map drawn "for political convenience." Boundary lines may be bridged where there has been a constitutional violation calling for interdistrict relief, but the notion that school district lines may be casually ignored or treated as a mere administrative convenience is contrary to the history of public education in our country. No single tradition in public education is more deeply rooted than local control over the operation of schools; local autonomy has long been thought essential both to the maintenance of community concern and support for public schools and to quality of the educational process. . . .

The metropolitan remedy would require, in effect, consolidation of 54 independent school districts historically administered as separate units into a vast new super school district. Entirely apart from the logistical and other serious problems attending large-scale transportation of students, the consolidation would give rise to an array of other problems in financing and operating this new school system. Some of the more obvious questions would be: What would be the status and authority of the present popularly elected school boards? Would the children of Detroit be within the jurisdiction and operating control of a school board elected by the parents and residents of other districts? What board or boards would levy taxes for school operations in these 54 districts constituting the consolidated metropolitan area? What provisions could be made for assuring substantial equality in tax levies among the 54 districts, if this were deemed requisite? What provisions would be made for financing? Would the validity of long-term bonds be jeopardized unless approved by all of the component districts as well as the State? What body would determine that portion of the curricula now left to the discretion of local school boards? Who would establish attendance zones, purchase school equipment, locate and construct new schools, and indeed attend to all the myriad day-to-day decisions that are necessary to school operations affecting potentially more than three-quarters of a million pupils?

It may be suggested that all of these vital operational problems are yet to be resolved by the District Court, and that this is the purpose of the Court of Appeals' proposed remand. But it is obvious from the scope of the interdistrict remedy itself that absent a complete restructuring of the laws of Michigan relating to school districts the District Court will become first, a *de facto* "legislative authority" to resolve these complex questions, and then the "school superintendent" for the entire area. This is a task which few, if any, judges are qualified to perform and one which would deprive the people of control of schools through their elected representatives.

Of course, no state law is above the Constitution. School district lines and the present laws with respect to local control, are not sacrosanct and if they conflict with the Fourteenth Amendment federal courts have a duty to prescribe appropriate remedies. But our prior holdings have been confined to violations and remedies within a single school district. We therefore turn to address, for the first time, the validity of a remedy mandating cross-district or interdistrict consolidation to remedy a condition of segregation found to exist in only one district.

The controlling principle consistently expounded in our holdings is that the scope of the remedy is determined by the nature and extent of the constitutional violation. Swann, 402 U.S., at 16. Before the boundaries of separate and autonomous school districts may be set aside by consolidating the separate units for remedial purposes or by imposing a cross-district remedy, it must first be shown that there has been a constitutional violation within one district that produces a significant segregative effect in another district. Specifically, it must be shown that racially discriminatory acts of the state or local school districts, or of a single school district have been a substantial cause of interdistrict segregation. Thus an interdistrict remedy might be in order where the racially discriminatory acts of one or more school districts caused racial segregation in an adjacent district, or where district lines have been deliberately drawn on the basis of race. In such circumstances an interdistrict remedy would be appropriate to eliminate the interdistrict segregation directly caused by the constitutional violation. Conversely, without an interdistrict violation and interdistrict effect, there is no constitutional wrong calling for an interdistrict remedy.

The record before us, voluminous as it is, contains evidence of *de jure* segregated conditions only in the Detroit schools; indeed, that was the theory on which the litigation was initially based and on which the District Court took evidence. With no showing of significant violation by the 53 outlying school districts and no evidence of any interdistrict violation or effect, the court went beyond the original theory of the case as framed by the pleadings and mandated a metropolitan area remedy. To approve the remedy ordered by the court would impose on the outlying districts, not shown to have committed any constitutional violation, a wholly impermissible remedy based on a standard not hinted at in *Brown I* and *II* or any holding of this Court.

In dissent, MR. JUSTICE WHITE and MR. JUSTICE MARSHALL undertake to demonstrate that agencies having statewide authority participated in maintaining the dual school system found to exist in Detroit. They are apparently of the view that once such participation is shown, the District Court should have a relatively free hand to reconstruct school districts outside of Detroit in fashioning relief. Our assumption, *arguendo*, that state agencies did participate in the maintenance of the Detroit system, should make it clear that it is not on this point that we part company. The difference between us arises instead from established doctrine laid down by our cases. *Brown*, *Green*, *Swann*, *Scotland Neck*, and *Emporia* each addressed the issue of constitutional wrong in terms of an established geographic and administrative school system populated by both Negro and white children. In such a context, terms such as "unitary" and "dual" systems, and "racially identifiable schools," have meaning, and the necessary federal authority to remedy the constitutional wrong is firmly established. But the remedy is necessarily designed, as all remedies are, to restore the victims of discriminatory conduct to the position they would have occupied in the absence of such conduct. Disparate treatment of white and Negro students occurred within the Detroit school system, and not elsewhere, and on this record the remedy must be limited to that system.

The constitutional right of the Negro respondents residing in Detroit is to attend a unitary school system in that district. Unless petitioners drew the district lines in a discriminatory fashion, or arranged for white students residing in the Detroit district to attend schools in Oakland and Macomb Counties, they were under no constitutional duty to make provisions for Negro students to do so. The view of the dissenters, that the existence of a dual system in *Detroit* can be made the basis for a decree requiring cross-district transportation of pupils, cannot be supported on the grounds that it represents merely the devising of a suitably flexible remedy for the violation of rights already established by our prior decisions. It can be supported only by drastic expansion of the constitutional right itself, an expansion without any support in either constitutional principle or precedent.

III

We recognize that the six-volume record presently under consideration contains language and some specific incidental findings thought by the District Court to afford a basis for interdistrict relief. However, these comparatively isolated findings and brief comments concern only one possible interdistrict violation and are found in the context of a proceeding that, as the District Court conceded, included no proof of segregation practiced by any of the 85 suburban school districts surrounding Detroit. . . .

IV

. . . We conclude that the relief ordered by the District Court and affirmed by the Court of Appeals was based upon an erroneous standard and was unsupported by record evidence that acts of the outlying districts effected the discrimination found to exist in the schools of Detroit. Accordingly, the judgment of the Court of Appeals is reversed and the case is remanded for further proceedings consistent with this opinion leading to prompt formulation of a decree directed to eliminating the segregation found to exist in Detroit city schools, a remedy which has been delayed since 1970.

Reversed and remanded.

■ MR. JUSTICE STEWART, concurring.

. . . [The] finding of a violation of the Equal Protection Clause was upheld by the Court of Appeals, and is accepted by this Court today. In the present posture of the case, therefore, the Court does not deal with questions of substantive constitutional law. The basic issue now before the Court concerns, rather, the appropriate exercise of federal equity jurisdiction.[1] . . .

The courts were in error for the simple reason that the remedy they thought necessary was not commensurate with the constitutional violation found. . . . [I]n this case the Court of Appeals approved the concept of a remedial decree that would go beyond the boundaries of the district where the constitutional violation was found, and include schools and schoolchildren in many other school districts that have presumptively been administered in complete accord with the Constitution. . . .

This is not to say, however, that an interdistrict remedy of the sort approved by the Court of Appeals would not be proper, or even necessary, in other factual situations. Were it to be shown, for example, that state officials had contributed to the separation of the races by drawing or redrawing school district lines, by transfer of school units between districts, or by purposeful racially discriminatory use of state housing or zoning laws, then a decree calling for transfer of pupils across district lines or for restructuring of district lines might well be appropriate.

In this case, however, no such interdistrict violation was shown. Indeed, no evidence at all concerning the administration of schools outside the city of Detroit was presented other than the fact that these schools contained a higher proportion of white pupils than did the schools within the city. Since the mere fact of different racial compositions in contiguous districts does not itself imply or constitute a violation of the Equal Protection Clause in the absence of a showing that such disparity was imposed, fostered, or encouraged by the State or its political subdivisions, it follows that no interdistrict violation was shown in this case. The formulation of an inter-district remedy was thus simply not responsive to the factual record before the District Court and was an abuse of that court's equitable powers. . . .

---

[1] As this Court stated in Brown *v.* Board of Education, 349 U.S. 294, 300: "[E]quity has been characterized by a practical flexibility in shaping its remedies and by a facility for adjusting and reconciling public and private needs. These [school desegregation] cases call for the exercise of these traditional attributes of equity power."

■ MR. JUSTICE DOUGLAS, dissenting.

. . . The issue is not whether there should be racial balance but whether the State's use of various devices that end up with black schools and white schools brought the Equal Protection Clause into effect. Given the State's control over the educational system in Michigan, the fact that the black schools are in one district and the white schools are in another is not controlling—either constitutionally or equitably.[13] No specific plan has yet been adopted. We are still at an interlocutory stage of a long drawn-out judicial effort at school desegregation. It is conceivable that ghettos develop on their own without any hint of state action. But since Michigan by one device or another has over the years created black school districts and white school districts, the task of equity is to provide a unitary system for the affected area where, as here, the State washes its hands of its own creations.

■ MR. JUSTICE WHITE, with whom MR. JUSTICE DOUGLAS, MR. JUSTICE BRENNAN, and MR. JUSTICE MARSHALL join, dissenting.

The District Court and the Court of Appeals found that over a long period of years those in charge of the Michigan public schools engaged in various practices calculated to effect the segregation of the Detroit school system. The Court does not question these findings, nor could it reasonably do so. Neither does it question the obligation of the federal courts to devise a feasible and effective remedy. But it promptly cripples the ability of the judiciary to perform this task, which is of fundamental importance to our constitutional system, by fashioning a strict rule that remedies in school cases must stop at the school district line unless certain other conditions are met. As applied here, the remedy for unquestioned violations of the protection rights of Detroit's Negroes by the Detroit School Board and the State of Michigan must be totally confined to the limits of the school district and may not reach into adjoining or surrounding districts unless and until it is proved there has been some sort of "interdistrict violation"—unless unconstitutional actions of the Detroit School Board have had a segregative impact on other districts, or unless the segregated condition of the Detroit schools has itself been influenced by segregative practices in those surrounding districts into which it is proposed to extend the remedy.

Regretfully, and for several reasons, I can join neither the Court's judgment nor its opinion. The core of my disagreement is that deliberate acts of segregation and their consequences will go unremedied, not because a remedy would be infeasible or unreasonable in terms of the usual criteria governing school desegregation cases, but because an effective remedy would cause what the Court considers to be undue administrative inconvenience to the State. The result is that the State of

[13] MR. JUSTICE STEWART indicates that equitable factors weigh in favor of local school control and the avoidance of administrative difficulty given the lack of an "interdistrict" violation. It would seem to me that the equities are stronger in favor of the children of Detroit who have been deprived of their constitutional right to equal treatment by the State of Michigan.

Michigan, the entity at which the Fourteenth Amendment is directed, has successfully insulated itself from its duty to provide effective desegregation remedies by vesting sufficient power over its public schools in its local school districts. If this is the case in Michigan, it will be the case in most States.

There are undoubted practical as well as legal limits to the remedial powers of federal courts in school desegregation cases. The Court has made it clear that the achievement of any particular degree of racial balance in the school system is not required by the Constitution; nor may it be the primary focus of a court in devising an acceptable remedy for *de jure* segregation. A variety of procedures and techniques are available to a district court engrossed in fashioning remedies in a case such as this; but the courts must keep in mind that they are dealing with the process of *educating* the young, including the very young. The task is not to devise a system of pains and penalties to punish constitutional violations brought to light. Rather, it is to desegregate an *educational* system in which the races have been kept apart, without, at the same time, losing sight of the central *educational* function of the schools.

Viewed in this light, remedies calling for school zoning, pairing, and pupil assignments, become more and more suspect as they require that schoolchildren spend more and more time in buses going to and from school and that more and more educational dollars be diverted to transportation systems. Manifestly, these considerations are of immediate and urgent concern when the issue is the desegregation of a city school system where residential patterns are predominantly segregated and the respective areas occupied by blacks and whites are heavily populated and geographically extensive. Thus, if one postulates a metropolitan school system covering a sufficiently large area, with the population evenly divided between whites and Negroes and with the races occupying identifiable residential areas, there will be very real practical limits on the extent to which racially identifiable schools can be eliminated within the school district. It is also apparent that the larger the proportion of Negroes in the area, the more difficult it would be to avoid having a substantial number of all-black or nearly all-black schools.

The Detroit school district is both large and heavily populated. It covers 139.6 square miles, encircles two entirely separate cities and school districts, and surrounds a third city on three sides. Also, whites and Negroes live in identifiable areas in the city. The 1970 public school enrollment in the city school district totaled 289,763 and was 63.6% Negro and 34.8% white. If "racial balance" were achieved in every school in the district, each school would be approximately 64% Negro. A remedy confined to the district could achieve no more desegregation. Furthermore, the proposed intracity remedies were beset with practical problems. None of the plans limited to the school district was satisfactory to the District Court. The most promising proposal, submitted by respondents, who were the plaintiffs in the District Court, would "leave many of its schools 75 to 90 per cent Black." Transportation on a "vast scale" would be required; 900 buses would have to be purchased for the transportation of pupils who are not now bused. . . .

The District Court therefore considered extending its remedy of the suburbs. After hearings, it concluded that a much more effective desegregation plan could be implemented if the suburban districts were included. In proceeding to design its plan on the basis that student bus rides to and from school should not exceed 40 minutes each way as a general matter, the court's express finding was that "[f]or all the reasons stated heretofore—including time, distance, and transportation factors—desegregation within the area described is physically easier and more practicable and feasible, than desegregation efforts limited to the corporate geographic limits of the city of Detroit." . . .

[T]he Court leaves unchallenged the District Court's conclusion that a plan including the suburbs would be physically easier and more practical and feasible than a Detroit-only plan. Whereas the most promising Detroit-only plan, for example, would have entailed the purchase of 900 buses, the metropolitan plan would involve the acquisition of no more than 350 new vehicles. . . .

Until today, the permissible contours of the equitable authority of the district courts to remedy the unlawful establishment of a dual school system have been extensive, adaptable, and fully responsive to the ultimate goal of achieving "the greatest possible degree of actual desegregation." There are indeed limitations on the equity powers of the federal judiciary, but until now the Court had not accepted the proposition that effective enforcement of the Fourteenth Amendment could be limited by political or administrative boundary lines demarcated by the very State responsible for the constitutional violation and for the disestablishment of the dual system. Until now the Court has instead looked to practical considerations in effectuating a desegregation decree, such as excessive distance, transportation time, and hazards to the safety of the schoolchildren involved in a proposed plan. . . .

Finally, I remain wholly unpersuaded by the Court's assertion that "the remedy is necessarily designed, as all remedies are, to restore the victims of discriminatory conduct to the position they would have occupied in the absence of such conduct." In the first place, under this premise the Court's judgment is itself infirm; for had the Detroit school system not followed an official policy of segregation throughout the 1950's and 1960's, Negroes and whites would have been going to school together. There would have been no, or at least not as many, recognizable Negro schools and no, or at least not as many, white schools, but "just schools," and neither Negroes nor whites would have suffered from the effects of segregated education, will all its shortcomings. Surely the Court's remedy will not restore to the Negro community, stigmatized as it was by the dual school system, what it would have enjoyed over all or most of this period if the remedy is confined to present-day Detroit; for the maximum remedy available within that area will leave many of the schools almost totally black, and the system itself will be predominantly black and will become increasingly so. Moreover, when a State has engaged in acts of official segregation over a lengthy period of time, as in the case before us, it is unrealistic to suppose that the children who were victims of the State's unconstitutional conduct could now be provided the benefits of which they were wrongfully deprived. Nor can the benefits which accrue to school systems in which schoolchildren have not been officially segregated, and to the communities supporting such school systems, be fully and immediately restored after a substantial period of unlawful segregation. . . .

■ MR. JUSTICE MARSHALL, with whom MR. JUSTICE DOUGLAS, MR. JUSTICE BRENNAN, and MR. JUSTICE WHITE join, dissenting.

. . . The great irony of the Court's opinion and, in my view, its most serious analytical flaw may be gleaned from its concluding sentence, in which the Court remands for "prompt formulation of a decree directed to eliminating the segregation found to exist in Detroit city schools, a remedy which has been delayed since 1970." The majority, however, seems to have forgotten the District Court's explicit finding that a Detroit-only decree, the only remedy permitted under today's decision, "would not accomplish desegregation." . . .

Having concluded . . . that the school system in the city of Detroit was a *de jure* segregated system and that the State of Michigan had the affirmative duty to remedy that condition of segregation, the District Court then turned to the difficult task of devising an effective remedy. It bears repeating that the District Court's focus at this stage of the litigation remained what it had been at the beginning—the condition of segregation within the Detroit city schools. . . .

The Court also misstates the basis for the District Court's order by suggesting that since the only segregation proved at trial was within the Detroit school system, any relief which extended beyond the jurisdiction of the Detroit Board of Education would be inappropriate because it would impose a remedy on outlying districts "not shown to have committed any constitutional violation." The essential foundation of interdistrict relief in this case was not to correct conditions within outlying districts which themselves engaged in purposeful segregation. Instead, interdistrict relief was seen as a necessary part of any meaningful effort by the State of Michigan to remedy the state-caused segregation within the city of Detroit. . . .

[S]everal factors in this case coalesce to support the District Court's ruling that it was the State of Michigan itself, not simply the Detroit Board of Education, which bore the obligation of curing the condition of segregation within the Detroit city schools. The actions of the State itself directly contributed to Detroit's segregation. Under the Fourteenth Amendment, the State is ultimately responsible for the actions of its local agencies. And, finally, given the structure of Michigan's educational system, Detroit's segregation cannot be viewed as the problem of an independent and separate entity. Michigan operates a single statewide system of education, a substantial part of which was shown to be segregated in this case.

What action, then, could the District Court require the State to take in order to cure Detroit's condition of segregation? Our prior cases have not minced words as to what steps responsible officials and agencies must take in order to remedy segregation in the public schools. Not only must distinctions on the basis of race be terminated for the future, but school officials are also "clearly charged with the affirmative duty to take whatever steps might be necessary to convert to a unitary system in which racial discrimination would be eliminated root and branch." Green *v.* County School Board of New Kent County, 391 U.S. 430, 437–438 (1968). Negro students are not only entitled to neutral nondiscriminatory treatment in the future. They must receive "what *Brown II* promised them: a school system in which all vestiges of enforced racial segregation have been eliminated." Wright *v.* Council of the City of Emporia, 407 U.S. 451, 463 (1972). These remedial standards are fully applicable not only to school districts where a dual system was compelled by statute, but also where, as here, a dual system was the product of purposeful and intentional state action. . . .

Under a Detroit-only decree, Detroit's schools will clearly remain racially identifiable in comparison with neighboring schools in the metropolitan community. Schools with 65% and more Negro students will stand in sharp and obvious contrast to schools in neighboring districts with less than 2% Negro enrollment. Negro students will continue to perceive their schools as segregated educational facilities and this perception will only be increased when whites react to a Detroit-only decree by fleeing to the suburbs to avoid integration. School district lines, however innocently drawn, will surely be perceived as fences to separate the races when, under a Detroit-only decree, white parents withdraw their children from the Detroit city schools and move to the suburbs in order to continue them in all-white schools. The message of this action will not escape the Negro children in the city of Detroit. It will be of scant significance to Negro children who have for years been confined by de jure acts of segregation to a growing core of all-Negro schools surrounded by a ring of all-white schools that the new dividing line between the races is the school district boundary.

Nor can it be said that the State is free from any responsibility for the disparity between the racial makeup of Detroit and its surrounding suburbs. The State's creation, through *de jure* acts of segregation, of a growing core of all-Negro schools inevitably acted as a magnet to attract Negroes to the areas served by such schools and to deter them from settling either in other areas of the city or in the suburbs. By the same token, the growing core of all-Negro schools inevitably helped drive whites to other areas of the city or to the suburbs. . . . The rippling effects on residential patterns caused by purposeful acts of segregation do not automatically subside at the school district border. With rare exceptions, these effects naturally spread through all the residential neighborhoods within a metropolitan area.

The State must also bear part of the blame for the white flight to the suburbs which would be forthcoming from a Detroit-only decree and would render such a remedy ineffective. Having created a system where whites and Negroes were intentionally kept apart so that they could not become accustomed to learning together, the State is responsible for the fact that many whites will react to the dismantling of that segregated system by attempting to flee to the suburbs. Indeed, by limiting the District Court to a Detroit-only remedy and allowing that flight to the suburbs to succeed, the Court today allows the State to profit from its own wrong and to perpetuate for years to come the separation of the races it achieved in the past by purposeful state action.

The majority asserts, however, that involvement of outlying districts would do violence to the accepted principle that "the nature of the violation determines the scope of the remedy." Swann, *supra*, 402 U.S., at 16. Not only is the majority's attempt to find in this single phrase the answer to the complex and difficult questions presented in this case hopelessly simplistic, but more important, the Court reads these words in a manner which perverts their obvious meaning. The nature of a violation determines the scope of the remedy simply because the function of any remedy is to cure the violation to which it is addressed. In school segregation cases, as in other equitable causes, a remedy which effectively cures the violation is what is required. No more is necessary, but we can tolerate no less. To read this principle as barring a district court from imposing the only effective remedy for past segregation and remitting the court to a patently ineffective alternative is, in my view, to turn a simple commonsense rule into a cruel and meaningless paradox. Ironically, by ruling out an interdistrict remedy, the only relief which promises to cure segregation in the Detroit public schools, the majority flouts the very principle on which it purports to rely. . . .

One final set of problems remains to be considered. We recognized in *Brown II*, and have re-emphasized ever since, that in fashioning relief in desegregation cases, "the courts will be guided by equitable principles. Traditionally, equity has been characterized by a practical flexibility in shaping its remedies and by a facility for adjusting and reconciling public and private needs." Brown II, 349 U.S., at 300.

Though not resting its holding on this point, the majority suggests that various equitable considerations militate against interdistrict relief. The Court, for example, refers to financing and administrative problems, the logistical problems attending large-scale transportation of students, and the prospect of the District Court's becoming a "*de facto* 'legislative authority'" and "'school superintendent' for the entire area." The entangling web of problems woven by the Court, however, appears on further consideration to be constructed of the flimsiest of threads. . . .

Desegregation is not and was never expected to be an easy task. Racial attitudes ingrained in our Nation's childhood and adolescence are not quickly thrown aside in its middle years. But just as the inconvenience of some cannot be allowed to stand in the way of the rights of others, so public opposition, no matter how strident, cannot be permitted to divert this Court from the enforcement of the constitutional principles at issue in this case. Today's holding, I fear, is more a reflection of a perceived public mood that we have gone far enough in enforcing the Constitution's guarantee of equal justice than it is the product of neutral principles of law. In the short run, it may seem to be the easier course to allow our great metropolitan areas to be divided up each into two cities—one white, the other black—but it is a course, I predict, our people will ultimately regret. I dissent.

NOTES

1. In what ways does the District Court order in Milliken *v.* Bradley go further than the District Court order in *Swann*, above?

2. One question the justices confront is what the goal should be of the constitutional remedy. Another question is what the limiting principles should be, the principles for where a court will stop in its pursuit of the goal. How do the justices in the majority and the justices in the dissent answer these questions? Which of their limiting principles are based in the law of equity? Further discussion of structural injunctions can be found in Chapter Six, Section D (Injunctions and Federalism).

3. Milliken *v.* Bradley is widely considered to be a pivot in the Supreme Court's post-*Brown* cases from broader to narrower relief in school desegregation cases. Residential segregation continued to increase in U.S. cities and suburbs. Although *de jure* racial segregation was abolished, the combined effect of (a) widespread residential segregation and (b) the use of only intra-district remedies was that many public schools continued to be *de facto* segregated along racial lines.

City of Los Angeles v. Lyons

Supreme Court of theUnited States, 1983.
461 U.S. 95.

■ JUSTICE WHITE delivered the opinion of the Court.

The issue here is whether respondent Lyons satisfied the prerequisites for seeking injunctive relief in the federal district court.

I

This case began on February 7, 1977, when respondent, Adolph Lyons, filed a complaint for damages, injunction, and declaratory relief in the United States District Court for the Central District of California.

The defendants were the City of Los Angeles and four of its police officers. The complaint alleged that on October 6, 1976, at 2 a.m., Lyons was stopped by the defendant officers for a traffic or vehicle code violation and that although Lyons offered no resistance or threat whatsoever, the officers, without provocation or justification, seized Lyons and applied a "chokehold"—either the "bar arm control" hold or the "carotid-artery control" hold or both—rendering him unconscious and causing damage to his larynx. Counts I through IV of the complaint sought damages against the officers and the City. Count V, with which we are principally concerned here, sought a preliminary and permanent injunction against the City barring the use of the control holds. That count alleged that the city's police officers, "pursuant to the authorization, instruction and encouragement of defendant City of Los Angeles, regularly and routinely apply these choke holds in innumerable situations where they are not threatened by the use of any deadly force whatsoever," that numerous persons have been injured as the result of the application of the chokeholds, that Lyons and others similarly situated are threatened with irreparable injury in the form of bodily injury and loss of life, and that Lyons "justifiably fears that any contact he has with Los Angeles police officers may result in his being choked and strangled to death without provocation, justification or other legal excuse." Lyons alleged the threatened impairment of rights protected by the First, Fourth, Eighth and Fourteenth Amendments. Injunctive relief was sought against the use of the control holds "except in situations where the proposed victim of said control reasonably appears to be threatening the immediate use of deadly force." Count VI sought declaratory relief against the City, *i.e.*, a judgment that use of the chokeholds absent the threat of immediate use of deadly force is a *per se* violation of various constitutional rights.

The District Court, by order, granted the City's motion for partial judgment on the pleadings and entered judgment for the City on Count V and VI. The Court of Appeals reversed the judgment for the City on Count V and VI, holding over the Citys objection that despite our decisions in O'Shea *v.* Littleton, 414 U.S. 488 (1974), and Rizzo *v.* Goode, 423 U.S. 362 (1976), Lyons had standing to seek relief against the application of the chokeholds. The Court of Appeals held that there was a sufficient likelihood that Lyons would again be stopped and subjected to the unlawful use of force to constitute a case or controversy and to warrant the issuance of an injunction, if the injunction was otherwise authorized. We denied certiorari.

On remand, Lyons applied for a preliminary injunction. Lyons pressed only the Count V claim at this point. The motion was heard on affidavits, depositions and government records. The District Court found that Lyons had been stopped for a traffic infringement and that without provocation or legal justification the officers involved had applied a "department-authorized chokehold which resulted in injuries to the plaintiff." The court further found that the department authorizes the use of the holds in situations where no one is threatened by death or grievous bodily harm, that officers are insufficiently trained, that the use of the holds involves a high risk of injury or death as then employed, and that their continued use in situations where neither death nor serious bodily injury is threatened "is unconscionable in a civilized society." The court concluded that such use violated Lyons' substantive due process rights under the Fourteenth Amendment. A preliminary injunction was entered enjoining "the use of both the carotid-artery and bar arm holds under circumstances which do not threaten death or serious bodily injury." An improved training program and regular reporting and record keeping were also ordered.[3] The Court of Appeals affirmed in a brief *per curiam* opinion stating that the District Court had not abused its discretion in entering a preliminary injunction. We granted certiorari, and now reverse.

III

It goes without saying that those who seek to invoke the jurisdiction of the federal courts must satisfy the threshhold requirement imposed by Article III of the Constitution by alleging an actual case or controversy. Plaintiffs must demonstrate a "personal stake in the outcome" in order to "assure that concrete adverseness which sharpens the presentation of issues" necessary for the proper resolution of constitutional questions. Baker *v.* Carr, 369 U.S. 186, 204 (1962). Abstract injury is not enough. The plaintiff must show that he "has sustained or is immediately in danger of sustaining some direct injury" as the result of the challenged official conduct and the injury or threat of injury must be both "real and immediate," not "conjectural" or "hypothetical."

In O'Shea *v.* Littleton, 414 U.S. 488 (1974), we dealt with a case brought by a class of plaintiffs claiming that they had been subjected to discriminatory enforcement of the criminal law. Among other things, a county magistrate and judge were accused of discriminatory conduct in various respects, such as sentencing members of plaintiff's class more harshly than other defendants. The Court of Appeals reversed the dismissal of the suit by the District Court, ruling that if the allegations were proved, an appropriate injunction could be entered.

We reversed for failure of the complaint to allege a case or controversy. Although it was claimed in that case that particular members of the plaintiff class had actually suffered from the alleged unconstitutional practices, we observed that "[p]ast exposure to illegal conduct does not in itself show a present case or controversy regarding injunctive relief . . . if unaccompanied by any continuing, present adverse effects." Past wrongs were evidence bearing on "whether there is a real

[3] By its terms, the injunction was to continue in force until the court approved the training program to be presented to it. It is fair to assume that such approval would not be given if the program did not confine the use of the strangleholds to those situations in which their use, in the view of the District Court, would be constitutional. Because of successive stays entered by the Court of Appeals and by this Court, the injunction has not gone into effect.

and immediate threat of repeated injury." But the prospect of future injury rested "on the likelihood that [plaintiffs] will again be arrested for and charged with violations of the criminal law and will again be subjected to bond proceedings, trial, or sentencing before petitioners." The most that could be said for plaintiffs' standing was "that *if* [plaintiffs] proceed to violate an unchallenged law and *if* they are charged, held to answer, and tried in any proceedings before petitioners, they will be subjected to the discriminatory practices that petitioners are alleged to have followed." We could not find a case or controversy in those circumstances: the threat to the plaintiffs was not "sufficiently real and immediate to show an existing controversy simply because they anticipate violating lawful criminal statutes and being tried for their offenses. . . ." It was to be assumed "that [plaintiffs] will conduct their activities within the law and so avoid prosecution and conviction as well as exposure to the challenged course of conduct said to be followed by petitioners."

We further observed [in *O'Shea*] that case or controversy considerations "obviously shade into those determining whether the complaint states a sound basis for equitable relief," and went on to hold that even if the complaint presented an existing case or controversy, an adequate basis for equitable relief against petitioners had not been demonstrated:

> "[Plaintiffs] have failed, moreover, to establish the basic requisites of the issuance of equitable relief in these circumstances—the likelihood of substantial and immediate irreparable injury, and the inadequacy of remedies at law. We have already canvassed the necessarily conjectural nature of the threatened injury to which [plaintiffs] are allegedly subjected. And if any of the [plaintiffs] are ever prosecuted and face trial, or if they are illegally sentenced, there are available state and federal procedures which could provide relief from the wrongful conduct alleged." 414 U.S., at 502.

Another relevant decision for present purposes is Rizzo *v.* Goode, 423 U.S. 362 (1976), a case in which plaintiffs alleged widespread illegal and unconstitutional police conduct aimed at minority citizens and against City residents in general. The Court reiterated the holding in *O'Shea* that past wrongs do not in themselves amount to that real and immediate threat of injury necessary to make out a case or controversy. The claim of injury rested upon "what one or a small, unnamed minority of policemen might do to them in the future because of that unknown policeman's perception" of departmental procedures. 423 U.S., at 372. This hypothesis was "even more attenuated than those allegations of future injury found insufficient in *O'Shea* to warrant [the] invocation of federal jurisdiction." The Court also held that plaintiffs' showing at trial of a relatively few instances of violations by individual police officers, without any showing of a deliberate policy on behalf of the named defendants, did not provide a basis for equitable relief. . . .

IV

No extension of *O'Shea* and *Rizzo* is necessary to hold that respondent Lyons has failed to demonstrate a case or controversy with the City that would justify the equitable relief sought. Lyons' standing to seek the injunction requested depended on whether he was likely to suffer future injury from the use of the chokeholds by police officers. Count V of the complaint alleged the traffic stop and choking incident five months before. That Lyons may have been illegally choked by the police on October 6, 1976, while presumably affording Lyons standing to claim damages against the individual officers and perhaps against the City, does nothing to establish a real and immediate threat that he would again be stopped for a traffic violation, or for any other offense, by an officer or officers who would illegally choke him into unconsciousness without any provocation or resistance on his part. The additional allegation in the complaint that the police in Los Angeles routinely apply chokeholds in situations where they are not threatened by the use of deadly force falls far short of the allegations that would be necessary to establish a case or controversy between these parties.

In order to establish an actual controversy in this case, Lyons would have had not only to allege that he would have another encounter with the police but also to make the incredible assertion either, (1) that *all* police officers in Los Angeles *always* choke any citizen with whom they happen to have an encounter, whether for the purpose of arrest, issuing a citation or for questioning or, (2) that the City ordered or authorized police officers to act in such manner. Although Count V alleged that the City authorized the use of the control holds in situations where deadly force was not threatened, it did not indicate why Lyons might be realistically threatened by police officers who acted within the strictures of the City's policy. If, for example, chokeholds were authorized to be used only to counter resistance to an arrest by a suspect, or to thwart an effort to escape, any future threat to Lyons from the City's policy or from the conduct of police officers would be no more real than the possibility that he would again have an encounter with the police and that either he would illegally resist arrest or detention or the officers would disobey their instructions and again render him unconscious without any provocation.

Under *O'Shea* and *Rizzo*, these allegations were an insufficient basis to provide a federal court with jurisdiction to entertain Count V of the complaint.[8] This was apparently the conclusion of the District Court in

---

[8] . . . Lyons alleged that he feared he would be choked in any future encounter with the police. The reasonableness of Lyons' fear is dependent upon the likelihood of a recurrence of the allegedly unlawful conduct. It is the *reality* of the threat of repeated injury that is relevant to the standing inquiry, not the plaintiff's subjective apprehensions. The emotional consequences of a prior act simply are not a sufficient basis for an injunction absent a real and immediate

dismissing Lyons' claim for injunctive relief. Although the District Court acted without opinion or findings, the Court of Appeals interpreted its action as based on lack of standing, *i.e.*, that under *O'Shea* and *Rizzo*, Lyons must be held to have made an "insufficient showing that the police were likely to do this to the plaintiff again." For several reasons—each of them infirm, in our view—the Court of Appeals thought reliance on *O'Shea* and *Rizzo* was misplaced and reversed the District Court.

First, the Court of Appeals thought that Lyons was more immediately threatened than the plaintiffs in those cases since, according to the Court of Appeals, Lyons need only be stopped for a minor traffic violation to be subject to the strangleholds. But even assuming that Lyons would again be stopped for a traffic or other violation in the reasonably near future, it is untenable to assert, and the complaint made no such allegation, that strangleholds are applied by the Los Angeles police to every citizen who is stopped or arrested regardless of the conduct of the person stopped. We cannot agree that the "odds" that Lyons would not only again be stopped for a traffic violation but would also be subjected to a chokehold without any provocation whatsoever are sufficient to make out a federal case for equitable relief. We note that five months elapsed between October 6, 1976, and the filing of the complaint, yet there was no allegation of further unfortunate encounters between Lyons and the police.

Of course, it may be that among the countless encounters between the police and the citizens of a great city such as Los Angeles, there will be certain instances in which strangleholds will be illegally applied and injury and death unconstitutionally inflicted on the victim. As we have said, however, it is no more than conjecture to suggest that in every instance of a traffic stop, arrest, or other encounter between the police and a citizen, the police will act unconstitutionally and inflict injury without provocation or legal excuse. And it is surely no more than speculation to assert either that Lyons himself will again be involved in one of those unfortunate instances, or that he will be arrested in the future and provoke the use of a chokehold by resisting arrest, attempting to escape, or threatening deadly force or serious bodily injury.

Second, the Court of Appeals viewed *O'Shea* and *Rizzo* as cases in which the plaintiffs sought "massive structural" relief against the local law enforcement systems and therefore that the holdings in those cases were inapposite to cases such as this where the plaintiff, according to the Court of Appeals, seeks to enjoin only an "established," "sanctioned" police practice assertedly violative of constitutional rights. *O'Shea* and *Rizzo*, however, cannot be so easily confined to their facts. If Lyons has made no showing that he is realistically threatened by a repetition of his experience of October, 1976, then he has not met the requirements for seeking an injunction in a federal court, whether the injunction

threat of future injury by the defendant. Of course, emotional upset is a relevant consideration in a damages action.

contemplates intrusive structural relief or the cessation of a discrete practice.

The Court of Appeals also asserted that Lyons "had a live and active claim" against the City "if only for a period of a few seconds" while the stranglehold was being applied to him and that for two reasons the claim had not become moot so as to disentitle Lyons to injunctive relief: First, because under normal rules of equity, a case does not become moot merely because the complained of conduct has ceased; and second, because Lyons' claim is "capable of repetition but evading review" and therefore should be heard. We agree that Lyons had a live controversy with the City. Indeed, he still has a claim for damages against the City that appears to meet all Article III requirements. Nevertheless, the issue here is not whether that claim has become moot but whether Lyons meets the preconditions for asserting an injunctive claim in a federal forum. The equitable doctrine that cessation of the challenged conduct does not bar an injunction is of little help in this respect, for Lyons' lack of standing does not rest on the termination of the police practice but on the speculative nature of his claim that he will again experience injury as the result of that practice even if continued.

The rule that a claim does not become moot where it is capable of repetition, yet evades review, is likewise inapposite. Lyons' claim that he was illegally strangled remains to be litigated in his suit for damages; in no sense does that claim "evade" review. Furthermore, the capable-of-repetition doctrine applies only in exceptional situations, and generally only where the named plaintiff can make a reasonable showing that he will again be subjected to the alleged illegality. As we have indicated, Lyons has not made this demonstration.

The record and findings made on remand do not improve Lyons' position with respect to standing. The District Court, having been reversed, did not expressly address Lyons' standing to seek injunctive relief, although the City was careful to preserve its position on this question. There was no finding that Lyons faced a real and immediate threat of again being illegally choked. The City's policy was described as authorizing the use of the strangleholds "under circumstances where no one is threatened with death or grievous bodily harm." That policy was not further described, but the record before the court contained the department's existing policy with respect to the employment of chokeholds. Nothing in that policy, contained in a Police Department manual, suggests that the chokeholds, or other kinds of force for that matter, are authorized absent some resistance or other provocation by the arrestee or other suspect. On the contrary, police officers were instructed to use chokeholds only when lesser degrees of force do not suffice and then only "to gain control of a suspect who is violently resisting the officer or trying to escape."

Our conclusion is that the Court of Appeals failed to heed *O'Shea*, *Rizzo*, and other relevant authority, and that the District Court was quite right in dismissing Count V.

V

Lyons fares no better if it be assumed that his pending damages suit affords him Article III standing to seek an injunction as a remedy for the claim arising out of the October 1976 events. The equitable remedy is unavailable absent a showing of irreparable injury, a requirement that cannot be met where there is no showing of any real or immediate threat that the plaintiff will be wronged again—a "likelihood of substantial and immediate irreparable injury." O'Shea *v.* Littleton, 414 U.S., at 502. The speculative nature of Lyons' claim of future injury requires a finding that this prerequisite of equitable relief has not been fulfilled.

Nor will the injury that Lyons allegedly suffered in 1976 go unrecompensed; for that injury, he has an adequate remedy at law. Contrary to the view of the Court of Appeals, it is not at all "difficult" under our holding "to see how anyone can ever challenge police or similar administrative practices." 615 F.2d, at 1250. The legality of the violence to which Lyons claims he was once subjected is at issue in his suit for damages and can be determined there.

Absent a sufficient likelihood that he will again be wronged in a similar way, Lyons is no more entitled to an injunction than any other citizen of Los Angeles; and a federal court may not entertain a claim by any or all citizens who no more than assert that certain practices of law enforcement officers are unconstitutional. This is not to suggest that such undifferentiated claims should not be taken seriously by local authorities. Indeed, the interest of an alert and interested citizen is an essential element of an effective and fair government, whether on the local, state or national level. A federal court, however, is not the proper forum to press such claims unless the requirements for entry and the prerequisites for injunctive relief are satisfied.

We decline the invitation to slight the preconditions for equitable relief; for as we have held, recognition of the need for a proper balance between state and federal authority counsels restraint in the issuance of injunctions against state officers engaged in the administration of the states' criminal laws in the absence of irreparable injury which is both great and immediate. O'Shea, 414 U.S., at 499; Younger *v.* Harris, 401 U.S. 37, 46 (1971). Mitchum *v.* Foster, 407 U.S. 225 (1972) held that suits brought under 42 U.S.C. § 1983 are exempt from the flat ban against the issuance of injunctions directed at state court proceedings, 28 U.S.C. § 2283. But this holding did not displace the normal principles of equity, comity and federalism that should inform the judgment of federal courts when asked to oversee state law enforcement authorities. In exercising their equitable powers federal courts must recognize "[t]he special delicacy of the adjustment to be preserved between federal equitable power and State administration of its own law." Stefanelli *v.* Minard, 342

U.S. 117, 120 (1951); O'Shea *v.* Littleton, 414 U.S., at 500. The Court of Appeals failed to apply these factors properly and therefore erred in finding that the District Court had not abused its discretion in entering an injunction in this case.

As we noted in *O'Shea*, 414 U.S., at 503, withholding injunctive relief does not mean that the "federal law will exercise no deterrent effect in these circumstances." If Lyons has suffered an injury barred by the Federal Constitution, he has a remedy for damages under § 1983. Furthermore, those who deliberately deprive a citizen of his constitutional rights risk conviction under the federal criminal laws.

Beyond these considerations the state courts need not impose the same standing or remedial requirements that govern federal court proceedings. The individual states may permit their courts to use injunctions to oversee the conduct of law enforcement authorities on a continuing basis. But this is not the role of a federal court absent far more justification than Lyons has proffered in this case.

The judgment of the Court of Appeals is accordingly

Reversed.

■ JUSTICE MARSHALL, with whom JUSTICE BRENNAN, JUSTICE BLACKMUN and JUSTICE STEVENS join, dissenting.

. . . The Court's decision removes an entire class of constitutional violations from the equitable powers of a federal court. It immunizes from prospective equitable relief any policy that authorizes persistent deprivations of constitutional rights as long as no individual can establish with substantial certainty that he will be injured, or injured again, in the future. THE CHIEF JUSTICE asked in Bivens *v.* Six Unknown Federal Narcotics Agents, 403 U.S. 388, 419 (1971) (dissenting opinion), "what would be the judicial response to a police order authorizing 'shoot to kill' with respect to every fugitive?" His answer was that it would be "easy to predict our collective wrath and outrage." We now learn that wrath and outrage cannot be translated into an order to cease the unconstitutional practice, but only an award of damages to those who are victimized by the practice and live to sue and to the survivors of those who are not so fortunate. Under the view expressed by the majority today, if the police adopt a policy of "shoot to kill," or a policy of shooting one out of ten suspects, the federal courts will be powerless to enjoin its continuation. The federal judicial power is now limited to levying a toll for such a systematic constitutional violation.

CHAPTER 15

PUNITIVE DAMAGES

A. TORTS

Taylor v. Superior Court

Supreme Court of California, 1979.
24 Cal.3d 890.

▪ RICHARDSON, JUSTICE. We consider whether punitive damages are recoverable in a personal injury action brought against an intoxicated driver. . . .

Section 3294 of the Civil Code authorizes the recovery of punitive damages in noncontract cases "where the defendant has been guilty of oppression, fraud, or malice, express or implied . . . ." As we recently explained, "This has long been interpreted to mean that malice in fact, as opposed to malice implied by law, is required. The malice in fact, referred to . . . as animus malus, may be proved under section 3294 either expressly (by direct evidence probative on the existence of hatred or ill will) or by implication (by indirect evidence from which the jury may draw inferences)."

Other authorities have amplified the foregoing principle. Thus it has been held that the "malice" required by section 3294 "implies an act conceived in a spirit of mischief or with criminal indifference towards the obligations owed to others." In Dean Prosser's words: "Where the defendant's wrongdoing has been intentional and deliberate, and has the character of outrage frequently associated with crime, all but a few courts have permitted the jury to award in the tort action 'punitive' or 'exemplary' damages . . . . [¶] Something more than the mere commission of a tort is always required for punitive damages. There must be circumstances of aggravation or outrage, such as spite or 'malice,' or a fraudulent or evil motive on the part of the defendant, *or such a conscious and deliberate disregard of the interests of others that his conduct may be called wilful or wanton*." (W. Prosser, LAW OF TORTS (4th ed. 1971) § 2, at pp. 9–10, italics added.)

Defendant's successful demurrer to the complaint herein was based upon plaintiff's failure to allege any actual intent of defendant to harm plaintiff or others. Is this an essential element of a claim for punitive damages? As indicated by Dean Prosser, courts have not limited the availability of punitive damages to cases in which such an intent has been shown. As we ourselves have recently observed, in order to justify the imposition of punitive damages the defendant ". . . must act with the intent to vex, injure, or annoy, *or with a conscious disregard of the plaintiff's rights.*" (Italics added; Neal *v.* Farmers Insurance Exchange, 21 Cal.3d 910, 922 (1978).)

The *Searle* court, speaking through Justice Friedman, after reviewing many of the earlier decisions, concluded that "The phrase *conscious disregard* is sometimes used to describe the highly culpable state of mind which justifies an exemplary award. . . . [¶] We suggest *conscious disregard of safety* as an appropriate description of the *animus malus* which may justify an exemplary damage award when nondeliberate injury is alleged." The *Searle* court likewise rejected suggestions in earlier cases that mere *reckless* disregard or misconduct would be sufficient to sustain an award of punitive damages, because "The central spirit of the exemplary damage statute, the demand for evil motive, is violated by an award founded upon recklessness alone."

We concur with the *Searle* observation that a conscious disregard of the safety of others may constitute malice within the meaning of section 3294 of the Civil Code. In order to justify an award of punitive damages on this basis, the plaintiff must establish that the defendant was aware of the probable dangerous consequences of his conduct, and that he wilfully and deliberately failed to avoid those consequences.

Relying on Gombos *v.* Ashe, 158 Cal. App. 2d 517 (1958), defendant asserts that historically the act of driving while intoxicated has never been considered "malice" under section 3294. In *Gombos,* plaintiff has alleged that defendant drove his car in a "highly reckless manner with absolute disregard and callous indifference to the rights and safety" of others, in that he became "knowingly and wilfully intoxicated" despite his knowledge that his intoxication "rendered him physically unfit" to drive safely. Despite these allegations, the court held that ". . . it is quite apparent that such facts fall short of alleging malice in fact, express or implied. One who becomes intoxicated, knowing that he intends to drive his automobile on the highway, is of course negligent, and perhaps grossly negligent. It is a reckless and wrongful and illegal thing to do. But it is not a malicious act."

Plaintiff seeks to distinguish *Gombos* by stressing the additional allegations in the present complaint which include defendant's history of alcoholism, his prior arrests and convictions for drunk driving, his prior accident attributable to his intoxication, and his acceptance of employment involving the transportation of alcoholic beverages. Certainly, the foregoing allegations may reasonably be said to confirm defendant's awareness of his inability to operate a motor vehicle safely while intoxicated. Yet the essence of the *Gombos* and present complaints remains the same: Defendant became intoxicated and thereafter drove a car while in that condition, despite his knowledge of the safety hazard he created thereby. This is the essential gravamen of the complaint, and while a history of prior arrests, convictions and mishaps may heighten the probability and foreseeability of an accident, we do not deem these aggravating factors essential prerequisites to the assessment of punitive damages in drunk driving cases.

We note that when *Gombos* was decided it was unclear whether, as a general principle, an award of punitive damages could be based upon a finding of defendant's conscious disregard of the safety of others. In the evolution of this area of tort law during the ensuing 20 years it has now become generally accepted that such a finding is sufficient. Examining the pleadings before us, we have no difficulty concluding that they contain sufficient allegations upon which it may reasonably be concluded that defendant consciously disregarded the safety of others. There is a very commonly understood risk which attends every motor vehicle driver who is intoxicated. One who wilfully consumes alcoholic beverages to the point of intoxication, knowing that he thereafter must operate a motor vehicle, thereby combining sharply impaired physical and mental faculties with a vehicle capable of great force and speed, reasonably may be held to exhibit a conscious disregard of the safety of others. The effect may be lethal whether or not the driver had a prior history of drunk driving incidents.

The allowance of punitive damages in such cases may well be appropriate because of another reason, namely, to deter similar future conduct, the "incalculable cost" of which is well documented. Section 3294 expressly provides that punitive damages may be recovered "for the sake of example." The applicable principle was well expressed in a recent Oregon case upholding an award of punitive damages against a drunken driver, "the fact of common knowledge that the drinking driver is the cause of so many of the more serious automobile accidents is strong evidence in itself to support the need for *all possible means of deterring* persons from driving automobiles after drinking, including exposure to awards of punitive damages in the event of accidents." (Harrell *v.* Ames, 265 Or. 183, 190 (1973), italics added.) According to a recent annotation, the *Harrell* case represents the view of a substantial majority of those courts of other states which have considered the matter. We think it also represents the better reasoned view. . . .

▪ [The opinion concurring and dissenting by CHIEF JUSTICE BIRD is omitted.]

▪ CLARK, JUSTICE, dissenting. I share the majority's dismay at the carnage on our highways. And if today's decision would significantly reduce the number of accidents involving drunk drivers, the majority might be justified in changing the law relating to punitive damage. However, today's decision clearly will not reduce the number of drunk drivers on our highways. We should therefore adhere to the traditional rule . . . that driving while intoxicated does not establish the malice essential to an award of punitive damages. . . .

The reasons for hesitancy in awarding punitive damages are obvious. First, the plaintiff is fully compensated for injury by compensatory damages. An additional award or fine from the defendant may constitute unjust enrichment. Unlike fines paid into the public treasury for public use, we may assume fines paid to private persons will not be similarly used.

Second, civil law is concerned with vindicating rights and compensating persons for harm suffered when those rights are invaded. Criminal law is concerned with punishing wrongdoers. In our tripartite system of government, the Legislature prescribes punishment for criminal conduct. Ordinarily, the Legislature specifies the range of criminal punishment, and it is for trial judges or administrative specialists to determine the appropriate punishment within that range.

Punitive damage is awarded in the context of a civil trial. While the Legislature has provided punitive damage may be awarded in certain civil cases, it has not created standards to guide the jury in determining when such awards are justified. Consequently, punitive damage may be awarded at whim. Upon deciding to grant punitive damage, little if any guidance is given the jury as to the appropriate size of the award. Moreover, when the defendant's conduct also constitutes a crime for which he has been or will be punished, the punitive award constitutes double punishment—potentially in excess of the maximum punishment specified in the Penal Code and a dubious exception to the prohibition against multiple punishment.

Third, punitive damage trials interfere with policies governing trial procedures. Punishment ordinarily serves as a deterrent to future conduct. As Justice Peters pointed out, if the plaintiff can place punitive damages in issue, it means "that the plaintiffs can offer evidence of the financial status of the defendant. This would convert personal injury cases where intoxication or wilful misconduct are involved from the trial of a negligence case into a field day in which the financial standing of the defendant would become a major issue." (Gombos *v.* Ashe, *supra*, 158 Cal. App. 2d at p. 258.)

In addition, the trier of fact assessing deterrence should be advised whether the compensatory award will come out of the defendant's pocket—thereby reducing his assets—or whether it will be paid by a liability insurer. But "Section 1155 of the Evidence Code provides that evidence of insurance is inadmissible to prove negligence or wrongdoing. The obvious purpose of the provision is to prevent the prejudicial use of evidence of liability insurance in an action against an insured." (Royal Globe Insurance Co. *v.* Superior Court, 23 Cal.3d 880, 891 (1979).) It is apparent that to permit punitive damages in accident cases will distract the trier of fact from its liability function, interfering with sound policies governing trial procedures.

Fourth, although situations do exist where punitive awards have a substantial deterrent effect, others exist in which deterrence is marginal at best. Because restitution only requires a wrongdoer give up his unjustified gains, compensatory damage will not always constitute deterrence. If the conduct while clearly wrongful is not criminal, a punitive award may be necessary to deter. Otherwise persons contemplating the wrongful conduct may feel they are in a no-lose situation, only gaining by the wrongful conduct.

On the other hand, deterrent effect of a punitive award may be minimal or marginal where the conduct already constitutes a crime and the criminal statute is regularly and effectively enforced. Deterrence by punitive award is also marginal where wrongful conduct is as likely to result in injury to the wrongdoer as to others.

In addition, if application of punitive award depends upon a fortuitous rather than an intended consequence of wrongful conduct, potential wrongdoers will not be deterred. They will simply assume the unintended consequence will not occur. This consideration has particular relevance to the instant case because the majority seek to deter drunk driving by enhancing penalty only when an accident occurs. Drunk drivers not involved in accidents—comprising the vast majority—are not subject to the penalty. . . .

Fifth, the prevalence of liability insurance in our society requires that any evaluation of punitive damage in accident cases, especially in the context of deterrence, must consider the insurance factor.

Under the traditional view, an award of punitive damage nullifies all insurance coverage. An insurer is not liable for loss intentionally caused by the insured, and any contract providing for liability is void as being against public policy. When an insured commits an intentional injury, he cannot require his insurer to indemnify him for either punitive or compensatory damage paid under a judgment. Because punitive damage is recoverable only for malicious or other intentional injury, a punitive award traditionally exonerated the insurance company from coverage. . . .

The practical significance of the majority's opinion is not that juries may assess punitive damage in accident cases involving drunk driving, but rather the undesirable result the liability insurers will now avoid all coverage in such cases. While a few victims injured by wealthy drunk drivers will receive both compensatory and punitive damages, the many unfortunately injured by drivers without assets will be unable to recover even compensatory damages from insurers.

Because wary plaintiffs are unlikely to jeopardize carrier coverage for compensatory damage, they will not seek punitive damage unless the defendant is either wealthy or uninsured. For this reason, the deterrent effect as to insured drivers who are not wealthy is further diluted. . . .

NOTES ON STANDARDS FOR PUNITIVE DAMAGES

1. Following the decision in *Taylor*, the California legislature amended Section 3294 by deleting the words "express or implied" and adding a definition of malice that includes "despicable conduct which is carried on by the defendant with conscious disregard of the rights or safety of others."

Cal. Civ. Code § 3294(c)(1) (1997). Courts have treated this amendment as a confirmation of *Taylor*, which continues to be cited.

2. Tuttle was injured in a car accident caused by Raymond. Raymond was speeding at the time and had just run a red light. A jury awarded Tuttle $50,000 in compensatory damages and $22,000 in punitive damages. The Supreme Court of Maine overturned the award and held that "punitive damages are available based upon tortious conduct only if the defendant acted with malice":

> "It is generally accepted that mere negligence cannot support an award of punitive damages. . . .
>
> "Whatever qualitative difference exists between mere negligence and 'gross' negligence, it is insufficient to justify allowing punitive damages based upon the latter class of conduct. 'Gross' negligence simply covers too broad and too vague an area of behavior, resulting in an unfair and inefficient use of the doctrine of punitive damages. A similar problem exists with allowing punitive damages based merely upon 'reckless' conduct. . . .
>
> "We therefore hold that punitive damages are available based upon tortious conduct only if the defendant acted with malice.
>
> "This requirement of malice will be most obviously satisfied by a showing of 'express' or 'actual' malice. Such malice exists where the defendant's tortious conduct is motivated by ill will toward the plaintiff. Punitive damages will also be available, however, where deliberate conduct by the defendant, although motivated by something other than ill will toward any particular party, is so outrageous that malice toward a person injured as a result of that conduct can be implied. We emphasize that, for the purpose of assessing punitive damages, such 'implied' or 'legal' malice will *not* be established by the defendant's mere reckless disregard of the circumstances."

Tuttle *v.* Raymond, 494 A.2d 1353, 1361 (Me. 1985).

3. Approving an award of punitive damages for malicious prosecution, the New York Court of Appeals made the following statements:

> "A necessary element of the cause of action for malicious prosecution is 'actual malice' or 'malice in fact.' The 'actual malice' element of a malicious prosecution action does not require a plaintiff to prove that the defendant was motivated by spite or hatred, although it will of course be satisfied by such proof. Rather, it means that the defendant must have commenced the prior criminal proceeding due to a wrong or improper motive, something other than a desire to see the ends of justice served. . . .
>
> "[A] finding of liability for malicious prosecution precludes a determination as a matter of law that punitive damages are improper, for the actual malice necessary to support an action for malicious prosecution also serves to justify an award of exemplary damages. . . .

> "This is not to say, of course, that exemplary damages must be awarded in every such action, for the trier of facts is not required to make such an award simply because it may do so. Whether to award punitive damages in a particular case, as well as the amount of such damages, if any, are primarily questions which reside in the sound discretion of the original trier of the facts, in this case the jury, and such an award is not lightly to be disturbed. . . ."

Nardelli *v.* Stamberg, 44 N.Y.2d 500, 503 (1978).

Grimshaw v. Ford Motor Co.

California Court of Appeals, 1981.
119 Cal. App. 3d 757.

■ TAMURA, ACTING PRESIDING JUSTICE. . . .

The Accident:

In November 1971, the Grays purchased a new 1972 Pinto hatchback manufactured by Ford in October 1971. . . .

On May 28, 1972, Mrs. Gray, accompanied by 13-year-old Richard Grimshaw, set out in the Pinto from Anaheim for Barstow to meet Mr. Gray. The Pinto was then six months old and had been driven approximately 3,000 miles. Mrs. Gray stopped in San Bernardino for gasoline, got back onto the freeway (Interstate 15) and proceeded toward her destination at 60–65 miles per hour. As she approached the Route 30 off-ramp where traffic was congested, she moved from the outer fast lane to the middle lane of the freeway. Shortly after this lane change, the Pinto suddenly stalled and coasted to a halt in the middle lane. . . . [T]he driver of a 1962 Ford Galaxie was unable to avoid colliding with the Pinto. . . .

At the moment of impact, the Pinto caught fire and its interior was engulfed in flames. According to plaintiffs' expert, the impact of the Galaxie had driven the Pinto's gas tank forward and caused it to be punctured by the flange or one of the bolts on the differential housing so that fuel sprayed from the punctured tank and entered the passenger compartment through gaps resulting from the separation of the rear wheel well sections from the floor pan. By the time the Pinto came to rest after the collision, both occupants had sustained serious burns. When they emerged from the vehicle, their clothing was almost completely burned off. Mrs. Gray died a few days later of congestive heart failure as a result of the burns. Grimshaw managed to survive but only through heroic medical measures. He has undergone numerous and extensive surgeries and skin grafts and must undergo additional surgeries over the next 10 years. He lost portions of several fingers on his left hand and portions of his left ear, while his face required many skin grafts from various portions of his body. . . .

[Grimshaw and the heirs of Mrs. Gray sued Ford. Grimshaw was awarded $2,526,000 compensatory damages and $125 million punitive damages. The punitive damages award was later reduced by the trial court to $3.5 million through remittitur. Mrs. Gray's heirs were awarded $559,680 for wrongful death; punitive damages were not available under the applicable wrongful death statute.]

Design of the Pinto Fuel System:

In 1968, Ford began designing a new subcompact automobile which ultimately became the Pinto. Mr. Iacocca, then a Ford Vice President, conceived the project and was its moving force. Ford's objective was to build a car at or below 2,000 pounds to sell for no more than $2,000.

Ordinarily marketing surveys and preliminary engineering studies precede the styling of a new automobile line. Pinto, however, was a rush project, so that styling preceded engineering and dictated engineering design to a greater degree than usual. Among the engineering decisions dictated by styling was the placement of the fuel tank. It was then the preferred practice in Europe and Japan to locate the gas tank over the rear axle in subcompacts because a small vehicle has less "crush space" between the rear axle and the bumper than larger cars. The Pinto's styling, however, required the tank to be placed behind the rear axle leaving only 9 or 10 inches of "crush space" far less than in any other American automobile or Ford overseas subcompact. In addition, the Pinto was designed so that its bumper was little more than a chrome strip, less substantial than the bumper of any other American car produced then or later. The Pinto's rear structure also lacked reinforcing members known as "hat sections" (2 longitudinal side members) and horizontal cross-members running between them such as were found in cars of larger unitized construction and in all automobiles produced by Ford's overseas operations. The absence of the reinforcing members rendered the Pinto less crush resistant than other vehicles. Finally, the differential housing selected for the Pinto had an exposed flange and a line of exposed bolt heads. These protrusions were sufficient to puncture a gas tank driven forward against the differential upon rear impact.

Crash Tests:

. . . [Pinto] prototypes as well as two production Pintos were crash tested by Ford to determine, among other things, the integrity of the fuel system in rear-end accidents. Ford also conducted the tests to see if the Pinto as designed would meet a proposed federal regulation requiring all automobiles manufactured in 1972 to be able to withstand a 20-mile-per-hour fixed barrier impact without significant fuel spillage and all automobiles manufactured after January 1, 1973, to withstand a 30-mile-per-hour fixed barrier impact without significant fuel spillage.

The crash tests revealed that the Pinto's fuel system as designed could not meet the 20-mile-per-hour proposed standard. . . .

The Cost To Remedy Design Deficiencies:

. . . The vulnerability of the production Pinto's fuel tank at speeds of 20 and 30-miles-per-hour fixed barrier tests could have been remedied by inexpensive "fixes," but Ford produced and sold the Pinto to the public without doing anything to remedy the defects. Design changes that would have enhanced the integrity of the fuel tank system at relatively little cost per car included the following: Longitudinal side members and cross members at $2.40 and $1.80, respectively; a single shock absorbent "flak suit" to protect the tank at $4; a tank within a tank and placement of the tank over the axle at $5.08 to $5.79; a nylon bladder within the tank at $5.25 to $8; placement of the tank over the axle surrounded with a protective barrier at a cost of $9.95 per car; substitution of a rear axle with a smooth differential housing at a cost of $2.10; imposition of a protective shield between the differential housing and the tank at $2.35; improvement and reenforcement of the bumper at $2.60; addition of eight inches of crush space a cost of $6.40. Equipping the car with a reinforced rear structure, smooth axle, improved bumper and additional crush space at a total cost of $15.30 would have made the fuel tank safe in a 34 to 38-mile-per-hour rear end collision by a vehicle the size of the Ford Galaxie. If, in addition to the foregoing, a bladder or tank within a tank were used or if the tank were protected with a shield, it would have been safe in a 40 to 45-mile-per-hour rear impact. If the tank had been located over the rear axle, it would have been safe in a rear impact at 50 miles per hour or more.

Management's Decision To Go Forward With Knowledge Of Defects:

. . . The Pinto crash tests results had been forwarded up the chain of command to the ultimate decision-makers and were known to the Ford officials who decided to go forward with production.

Harley Copp, a former Ford engineer and executive in charge of the crash testing program, testified that the highest level of Ford's management made the decision to go forward with the production of the Pinto, knowing that the gas tank was vulnerable to puncture and rupture at low rear impact speeds creating a significant risk of death or injury from fire and knowing that "fixes" were feasible at nominal cost. He testified that management's decision was based on the cost savings which would inure from omitting or delaying the "fixes." . . .

Punitive Damages

The concept of punitive damages is rooted in the English common law and is a settled principle of the common law of this country. . . . When our laws were codified in 1872, the doctrine was incorporated in Civil Code section 3294, which at the time of trial read: "In an action for the breach of an obligation not arising from contract, where the defendant has been guilty of oppression, fraud, or malice, express or implied, the plaintiff, in addition to the actual damages, may recover damages for the sake of example and by way of punishing the defendant."[11]

---

[11] . . . "(c) As used in this section, the following definitions shall apply:

Ford argues that "malice" as used in section 3294 . . . requires animus malus or evil motive an intention to injure the person harmed and that the term is therefore conceptually incompatible with an unintentional tort such as the manufacture and marketing of a defectively designed product. This contention runs counter to our decisional law. . . . California cases . . . have interpreted the term "malice" as used in section 3294 to include, not only a malicious intention to injure the specific person harmed, but conduct evincing "a conscious disregard of the probability that the actor's conduct will result in injury to others." (Dawes *v.* Superior Court, 111 Cal. App. 3d 82, 88, hg. Den. (Dec. 17, 1980). . . .

In Taylor *v.* Superior Court, our high court's most recent pronouncement on the subject of punitive damages, the court observed that . . . "[i]n order to justify an award of punitive damages on this basis, the plaintiff must establish that the defendant was aware of the probable dangerous consequences of his conduct, and that he wilfully and deliberately failed to avoid those consequences." . . .

The interpretation of the word "malice" as used in section 3294 to encompass conduct evincing callous and conscious disregard of public safety by those who manufacture and market mass produced articles is consonant with and furthers the objectives of punitive damages. The primary purposes of punitive damages are punishment and deterrence of like conduct by the wrongdoer and others. In the traditional noncommercial intentional tort, compensatory damages alone may serve as an effective deterrent against future wrongful conduct but in commerce related torts, the manufacturer may find it more profitable to treat compensatory damages as a part of the cost of doing business rather than to remedy the defect. Governmental safety standards and the criminal law have failed to provide adequate consumer protection against the manufacture and distribution of defective products. Punitive damages thus remain as the most effective remedy for consumer protection against defectively designed mass produced articles. They provide a motive for private individuals to enforce rules of law and enable them to recoup the expenses of doing so which can be considerable and not otherwise recoverable. . . .

Through the results of the crash tests Ford knew that the Pinto's fuel tank and rear structure would expose consumers to serious injury or death in a 20 to 30 mile-per-hour collision. There was evidence that Ford could have corrected the hazardous design defects at minimal cost but

---

"(1) Malice' means conduct which is intended by the defendant to cause injury to the plaintiff or conduct which is carried on by the defendant with a conscious disregard of the rights or safety of others.

"(2) 'Oppression' means subjecting a person to cruel and unjust hardship in conscious disregard of that person's rights.

"(3) 'Fraud' means an intentional misrepresentation, deceit, or concealment of a material fact known to the defendant with the intention on the part of the defendant of thereby depriving a person of property or legal rights or otherwise causing injury."

decided to defer correction of the shortcomings by engaging in a cost-benefit analysis balancing human lives and limbs against corporate profits. Ford's institutional mentality was shown to be one of callous indifference to public safety. There was substantial evidence that Ford's conduct constituted "conscious disregard" of the probability of injury to members of the consuming public. . . .

In its instructions to the jury, the trial court defined malice as follows: " 'Malice' means a motive and willingness to vex, harass, annoy or injure another person. Malice may be inferred from acts and conduct, such as by showing that the defendant's conduct was wilful, intentional, and done in conscious disregard of its possible results." The court also instructed the jury that plaintiff Grimshaw had the burden of proving "[t]hat the defendant acted with malice which may be inferred from defendant's conduct if the conduct was wilful, intentional and done in conscious disregard of its possible result."

On appeal, Ford contends that the phrase "conscious disregard of its possible results" used in the two instructions would permit a plaintiff to impugn almost every design decision as made in conscious disregard of some perceivable risk because safer alternative designs are almost always a possibility. Ford argues that to instruct the jury so that they might find "malice" if any such "possibility" existed was erroneous; it maintains that an instruction on "malice" in products liability must contain the phrase "conscious disregard of (the probability/a high probability) of injury to others," in order to preclude prejudicial error. . . .

We agree with Ford . . . that to be as accurate as possible, the rule should be expressed in terms of probability of injury rather than possibility. . . .

Ford has failed to demonstrate prejudice from the claimed defect in the instructions on malice. When the instructions are read as a whole, the jury could not possibly have interpreted the words "conscious disregard of its possible results" to extend to the innocent conduct depicted by Ford. The term "motive and willingness . . . to injure" and the words "wilful," "intentional," and "conscious disregard" signify animus malus or evil motive. . . . The jury was instructed that Ford was not required under the law to produce either the safest possible vehicle or one which was incapable of producing injury. The instructions on malice manifestly referred to conduct constituting conscious and callous disregard of a substantial likelihood of injury to others and not to innocent conduct by the manufacturer. Further, plaintiffs made no attempt in their arguments to the jury to give the instructions on malice the interpretation to which Ford says they are susceptible. Plaintiffs did not argue possibility of injury; they argued that injury was a virtual certainty and that Ford's management knew it from the results of the crash tests. Thus, the instructions on malice, even assuming them to have been erroneous because the word "possible" was used instead of "probable," did not constitute prejudicial error. . . .

Ford's final contention is that the amount of punitive damages awarded, even as reduced by the trial court, was so excessive that a new trial on that issue must be granted. Ford argues that its conduct was less reprehensible than those for which punitive damages have been awarded in California in the past; that the 3 1/2 million dollar award is many times over the highest award for such damages ever upheld in California; and that the award exceeds maximum civil penalties that may be enforced under federal or state statutes against a manufacturer for marketing a defective automobile. We are unpersuaded.

In determining whether an award of punitive damages is excessive, comparison of the amount awarded with other awards in other cases is not a valid consideration. Nor does "[t]he fact that an award may set a precedent by its size" in and of itself render it suspect; whether the award was excessive must be assessed by examining the circumstances of the particular case. In deciding whether an award is excessive as a matter of law or was so grossly disproportionate as to raise the presumption that it was the product of passion or prejudice, the following factors should be weighed: The degree of reprehensibility of defendant's conduct, the wealth of the defendant, the amount of compensatory damages, and an amount which would serve as a deterrent effect on like conduct by defendant and others who may be so inclined. Applying the foregoing criteria to the instant case, the punitive damage award as reduced by the trial court was well within reason.

In assessing the propriety of a punitive damage award, as in assessing the propriety of any other judicial ruling based upon factual determinations, the evidence must be viewed in the light most favorable to the judgment. Viewing the record thusly in the instant case, the conduct of Ford's management was reprehensible in the extreme. It exhibited a conscious and callous disregard of public safety in order to maximize corporate profits. Ford's self-evaluation of its conduct is based on a review of the evidence most favorable to it instead of on the basis of the evidence most favorable to the judgment. Unlike malicious conduct directed toward a single specific individual, Ford's tortious conduct endangered the lives of thousands of Pinto purchasers. Weighed against the factor of reprehensibility, the punitive damage award as reduced by the trial judge was not excessive.

Nor was the reduced award excessive taking into account defendant's wealth and the size of the compensatory award. Ford's net worth was 7.7 billion dollars and its income after taxes for 1976 was over 983 million dollars. The punitive award was approximately .005% of Ford's net worth and approximately .03% of its 1976 net income. The ratio of the punitive damages to compensatory damages was approximately 1.4 to one. Significantly, Ford does not quarrel with the amount of the compensatory award to Grimshaw.

Nor was the size of the award excessive in light of its deterrent purpose. An award which is so small that it can be simply written off as a part of the cost of doing business would have no deterrent effect. An award which affects the company's pricing of its product and thereby affects its competitive advantage would serve as a deterrent. The award in question was far from excessive as a deterrent against future wrongful conduct by Ford and others.

Ford complains that the punitive award is far greater than the maximum penalty that may be imposed under California or federal law prohibiting the sale of defective automobiles or other products. For example, Ford notes that California statutes provide a maximum fine of only $50 for the first offense and $100 for a second offense for a dealer who sells an automobile that fails to conform to federal safety laws or is not equipped with required lights or brakes; that a manufacturer who sells brake fluid in this state failing to meet statutory standards is subject to a maximum of only $50; and that the maximum penalty that may be imposed under federal law for violation of automobile safety standards is $1,000 per vehicle up to a maximum of $800,000 for any related series of offenses. It is precisely because monetary penalties under government regulations prescribing business standards or the criminal law are so inadequate and ineffective as deterrents against a manufacturer and distributor of mass produced defective products that punitive damages must be of sufficient amount to discourage such practices. Instead of showing that the punitive damage award was excessive, the comparison between the award and the maximum penalties under state and federal statutes and regulations governing automotive safety demonstrates the propriety of the amount of punitive damages awarded.

Grimshaw's Appeal

Grimshaw has appealed from the order conditionally granting Ford a new trial on the issue of punitive damages and from the amended judgment entered pursuant to that order.

Grimshaw contends that the new trial order is erroneous because (1) the punitive damages awarded by the jury were not excessive as a matter of law, (2) the specification of reasons was inadequate; and (3) the court abused its discretion in cutting the award so drastically. For reasons to be stated, we have concluded that the contentions lack merit.

The court prefaced its specification of reasons with a recitation of the judicially established guidelines for determining whether a punitive award is excessive. The court then observed that there was evidence in the record (referring to Exhibit 125) which might provide a possible rational basis for the 125 million dollar jury verdict which would dispel any presumption of passion or prejudice,[17] adding, however, that the court was not suggesting that the amount was warranted "or that the

[17] Exhibit 125 was the report by Ford engineers showing savings which would be realized by deferring design changes to the fuel system of Ford automobiles to meet the proposed governmental standards on the integrity of the fuel systems.

jury did utilize Exhibit 125, or any other exhibits, and if they did, that they were justified in so doing." The court then noted, based on the fact that Ford's net worth was 7.7 billion and its profits during the last quarter of the year referred to in the financial statement introduced into evidence were more than twice the punitive award, that the award was not disproportionate to Ford's net assets or to its profit generating capacity. The court noted, however, that the amount of the punitive award was 44 times the compensatory award, the court stated that while it did not consider that ratio alone to be controlling because aggravating circumstances may justify a ratio as high as the one represented by the jury verdict, it reasoned that the ratio coupled with the amount by which the punitive exceeded the compensatory damages (over 122 million dollars) rendered the jury's punitive award excessive as a matter of law.

Grimshaw contends that the court erred in determining that the ratio of punitive to compensatory damages rendered the punitive excessive as a matter of law. The trial court, however, did not base its decision solely on the ratio of punitive to compensatory. It took into account the ratio, the "aggravating circumstances" (the degree of reprehensibility), the wealth of the defendant and its profit generating capacity, the magnitude of the punitive award, including the amount by which it exceeded the compensatory. Those were proper considerations for determining whether the award was excessive as a matter of law. . . . [W]e find no abuse of discretion. . . .

Finally, while the trial judge may not have taken into account Ford's potential liability for punitive damages in other cases involving the same tortious conduct in reducing the award, it is a factor we may consider in passing on the request to increase the award. Considering such potential liability, we find the amount as reduced by the trial judge to be reasonable and just. We therefore decline the invitation to modify the judgment by reducing the amount of the remittitur.

NOTES

1. Beginning in the 1980s, a number of state legislatures acted to limit punitive damage awards. Consider the following statutes:

(a) N.H. Rev. Stat. Ann. § 507:16 (West 1986).

> "PUNITIVE DAMAGES OUTLAWED.
>
> "No punitive damages shall be awarded in any action, unless otherwise provided by statute."

(b) Va. Code Ann. § 8.01–38.1 (West 1987).

> "Limitation on recovery of punitive damages.
>
> ". . . In no event shall the total amount awarded for punitive damages exceed $350,000. The jury shall not be advised of the limitation prescribed by this section. However, if a jury returns a verdict for punitive damages in excess of the maximum amount specified in this section, the judge shall reduce the

award and enter judgment for such damages in the maximum amount provided by this section."

(c) Fla. Stat. Ann. § 768.73 (West 1999).

"PUNITIVE DAMAGES; LIMITATION.

"(1)(a) Except as provided in paragraphs (b) and (c), an award of punitive damages may not exceed the greater of:

"1. Three times the amount of compensatory damages awarded to each claimant entitled thereto, consistent with the remaining provisions of this section; or

"2. The sum of $500,000.

"(b) Where the fact finder determines that the wrongful conduct proven under this section was motivated solely by unreasonable financial gain and determines that the unreasonably dangerous nature of the conduct, together with the high likelihood of injury resulting from the conduct, was actually known by the managing agent, director, officer, or other person responsible for making policy decisions on behalf of the defendant, it may award an amount of punitive damages not to exceed the greater of:

"1. Four times the amount of compensatory damages awarded to each claimant entitled thereto, consistent with the remaining provisions of this section; or

"2. The sum of $2 million.

"(c) Where the fact finder determines that at the time of injury the defendant had a specific intent to harm the claimant and determines that the defendant's conduct did in fact harm the claimant, there shall be no cap on punitive damages.

"(d) This subsection is not intended to prohibit an appropriate court from . . . determining the reasonableness of an award of punitive damages that is less than three times the amount of compensatory damages.

"(2)(a) Except as provided in paragraph (b), punitive damages may not be awarded against a defendant in a civil action if that defendant establishes, before trial, that punitive damages have previously been awarded against that defendant in any state or federal court in any action alleging harm from the same act or single course of conduct for which the claimant seeks compensatory damages. . . .

"(b) In subsequent civil actions involving the same act or single course of conduct for which punitive damages have already been awarded, if the court determines by clear and convincing evidence that the amount of prior punitive damages awarded was insufficient to punish that defendant's behavior, the court may permit a jury to consider awarding subsequent punitive damages. . . ."

2. The Kentucky Supreme Court invalidated a tort-reform statute requiring proof of "subjective awareness" that conduct will result in harm to support recovery of punitive damages. The court reasoned that the common law standard for punitive damages in Kentucky, which predated the state constitution, was a standard of gross negligence; therefore the statute violated plaintiffs' "jural right" to punitive awards in tort cases. Williams *v.* Wilson, 972 S.W.2d 260 (1998).

3. Salla, a zone manager responsible for eight convenience stores owned by Ultramar, wrongfully fired White. White sued Ultramar and a jury awarded $42,000 in compensatory damages and $300,000 in punitive damages. A California statute provided that an employer is liable for punitive damages only if the employer had

> "advance knowledge of the unfitness of the employee and employed him or her with a conscious disregard of the rights or safety of others or authorized or ratified the wrongful conduct for which the damages are awarded or was personally guilty of oppression, fraud, or malice. With respect to a corporate employer, the advance knowledge and conscious disregard, authorization, ratification or act of oppression, fraud, or malice must be on the part of an officer, director, or managing agent of the corporation."

The California Supreme Court held that the term "managing agent" includes employees who have "substantial discretionary authority over significant aspects of" the business, and that Salla fit this description. White *v.* Ultramar, 21 Cal.4th 563 (1999), citing Cal. Civ. Code Ann. § 3294(b) (1980).

4. The United States Supreme Court, which has jurisdiction over punitive damages awarded in admiralty cases, has divided on the question whether a corporation can be held liable for punitive damages based on acts of managers that contravene clearly stated formal policies of the corporation. Exxon Shipping Co. *v.* Baker, 554 U.S. 471, 482–84 (2008). As a result, it left standing a ruling by the Ninth Circuit that Exxon was liable.

5. An employee of Norfolk & Western Railway caused an accident. The victims sued both the employee and Norfolk & Western and obtained an award of $67,000 in compensatory damages and $200,000 in punitive damages. The employee was found to have acted willfully; Norfolk & Western was not.

Norfolk & Western paid the judgment and sought reimbursement from its insurance company, based on a policy covering "all sums . . . the insured shall become legally obligated to pay as damages." The court gave judgment for Norfolk & Western, saying:

> "Since the strong underlying purpose of the punitive damage award is to deter, the availability of insurance may totally undo the public policy of the state. . . .
>
> "The rule against shifting the impact of a punitive damage award has an exception, however. An employer may be held liable for a punitive damage award against his agent when the agent acted within the scope of his employment. . . .

> "There is . . . a distinction . . . in Indiana law between liability for punitive damages directly imposed and such liability when vicariously imposed. The former situation arises [when] the corporation itself is found to have acted maliciously or oppressively. The latter situation arises when the corporation, without itself being guilty of willful misconduct, is held to respond in damages for the intentional tort of its agent. In the former case, it would contravene public policy to allow the corporation to shift to an insurer the deterrent award imposed on account of the corporation's own wrongful acts; in the latter case, it would not be inconsistent with public policy to allow the corporation to shift to an insurer the punitive damage award when that award is placed upon the corporation solely as a matter of vicarious liability. . . .
>
> "In this case it is quite clear that the insured was only vicariously liable. . . .
>
> "Accordingly, under Indiana law it is not contrary to public policy for Norfolk & Western to shift the punitive damage award to its liability insurer. . . ."

Norfolk and Western Railway Co. *v.* Hartford Accident and Indemnity Co., 420 F. Supp. 92, 95–98 (N.D. Ind. 1976).

6. It is a long-standing rule that punitive damages are not permissible in equity. As one court said,

> "There is no impediment to prevent a court of equity from decreeing full and exact justice to all parties. Now, full restitution has been made to the complainant, and she has been made whole. It would ill comport with the principles of equity for the court to visit upon the defendants a sort of punishment to the pecuniary profit of the complainant and consequent loss of the defendants. A court of equity is a court of conscience, but not a forum of vengeance. It will make restitution, but not reprisals. It will fill full the measure of compensation, but will not overflow it with vindictive damages."

Bush *v.* Gaffney, 84 S.W.2d 759, 764 (Tex. Civ. App. 1935). Where the courts of law and of equity have been merged, the rule still operates in many jurisdictions to bar punitive damages as to equitable claims (*e.g.*, claims for breach of fiduciary duty). In other jurisdictions, no distinction is made between law and equity for purposes of punitive damages. See, *e.g.*, I. H. P. Corp. *v.* 210 Central Park South Corp., 12 N.Y.2d 329 (1963), which is reprinted in Chapter Eight, Section D (Damages in Combination with Injunctive Relief).

For discussion of the traditional rule and its reasons, see the leading Australian case of Harris *v.* Digital Pulse Pty. Ltd. (2003) 56 NSWLR 298 (NSWCA), and Samuel L. Bray, Punitive Damages Against Trustees?, in RESEARCH HANDBOOK ON FIDUCIARY LAW (Gordon Smith & Andrew Gold eds., forthcoming 2018).

Smith v. Wade

Supreme Court of the United States, 1983.
461 U.S. 30.

■ JUSTICE BRENNAN delivered the opinion of the Court. . . .

The petitioner, William H. Smith, is a guard at Algoa Reformatory, a unit of the Missouri Division of Corrections for youthful first offenders. The respondent, Daniel R. Wade, was assigned to Algoa as an inmate in 1976. In the summer of 1976 Wade voluntarily checked into Algoa's protective custody unit. Because of disciplinary violations during his stay in protective custody, Wade was given a short term in punitive segregation and then transferred to administrative segregation. On the evening of Wade's first day in administrative segregation, he was placed in a cell with another inmate. Later, when Smith came on duty in Wade's dormitory, he placed a third inmate in Wade's cell. According to Wade's testimony, his cellmates harassed, beat, and sexually assaulted him.

Wade brought suit under 42 U.S.C. § 1983 against Smith and four other guards and correctional officials, alleging that his Eighth Amendment rights had been violated. At trial his evidence showed that he had placed himself in protective custody because of prior incidents of violence against him by other inmates. The third prisoner whom Smith added to the cell had been placed in administrative segregation for fighting. Smith had made no effort to find out whether another cell was available; in fact there was another cell in the same dormitory with only one occupant. Further, only a few weeks earlier, another inmate had been beaten to death in the same dormitory during the same shift, while Smith had been on duty. Wade asserted that Smith and the other defendants knew or should have known that an assault against him was likely under the circumstances. . . .

The district judge also charged the jury that it could award punitive damages on a proper showing:

> ". . . If you find the issues in favor of the plaintiff, and if the conduct of one or more of the defendants is shown to be *a reckless or callous disregard of, or indifference to, the rights or safety of others,* then you may assess punitive or exemplary damages in addition to any award of actual damages. . . ."

The jury . . . found Smith liable . . . and awarded $25,000 in compensatory damages and $5,000 in punitive damages. . . .

Section 1983 is derived from § 1 of the Civil Rights Act of 1871. It was intended to create "a species of tort liability" in favor of persons deprived of federally secured rights. We noted in Carey *v.* Piphus, 435 U.S. 247 (1978), that there was little in the section's legislative history concerning the damages recoverable for this tort liability. In the absence of more specific guidance, we looked first to the common law of torts (both modern and as of 1871), with such modification or adaptation as might be necessary to carry out the purpose and policy of the statute. . . .

Smith correctly concedes that "punitive damages are available in a 'proper' § 1983 action. . . ." . . .

Smith . . . attacks the instruction that punitive damages could be awarded on a finding of reckless or callous disregard of or indifference to Wade's rights or safety. Instead, he contends that the proper test is one of actual malicious intent—"ill will, spite, or intent to injure." He offers two arguments for this position: first, that actual intent is the proper standard for punitive damages in all cases under § 1983; and second, that even if intent is not always required, it should be required here because the threshold for punitive damages should always be higher than that for liability in the first instance. We address these in turn. . . .

Perhaps not surprisingly, there was significant variation (both terminological and substantive) among American jurisdictions in the latter nineteenth century on the precise standard to be applied in awarding punitive damages—variation that was exacerbated by the ambiguity and slipperiness of such common terms as "malice" and "gross negligence." Most of the confusion, however, seems to have been over the degree of negligence, recklessness, carelessness, or culpable indifference that should be required—not over whether actual intent was essential. On the contrary, the rule in a large majority of jurisdictions was that punitive damages . . . could be awarded without a showing of actual ill will, spite, or intent to injure. . . .

The same rule applies today. The Restatement (Second) of Torts (1977), for example, states: "Punitive damages may be awarded for conduct that is outrageous, because of the defendant's evil motive *or his reckless indifference to the rights of others.*" *Id.*, § 908(2) (emphasis added). . . .

The remaining question is whether the policies and purposes of § 1983 itself require a departure from the rules of tort common law. As a general matter, we discern no reason why a person whose federally guaranteed rights have been violated should be granted a more restrictive remedy than a person asserting an ordinary tort cause of action. . . .

Smith's argument, which he offers in several forms, is that an actual intent standard is preferable to a recklessness standard because it is less vague. . . . [D]eterrence, he contends, cannot be achieved unless the standard of conduct sought to be deterred is stated with sufficient clarity to enable potential defendants to conform to the law and to avoid the proposed sanction. Recklessness or callous indifference, he argues, is too uncertain a standard to achieve deterrence rationally and fairly. A prison guard, for example, can be expected to know whether he is acting with actual ill will or intent to injure, but not whether he is being reckless or callously indifferent.

Smith's argument, if valid, would apply to ordinary tort cases as easily as to § 1983 suits; hence, it hardly presents an argument for adopting a different rule under § 1983. In any event, the argument is unpersuasive. While, *arguendo,* an intent standard may be easier to understand and apply to particular situations than a recklessness standard, we are not persuaded that a recklessness standard is too vague to be fair or useful. . . .

More fundamentally, . . . Smith seems to assume that prison guards and other state officials look mainly to the standard for punitive damages in shaping their conduct. We question the premise; we assume, and hope, that most officials are guided primarily by the underlying standards of federal substantive law—both out of devotion to duty, and in the interest of avoiding liability for compensatory damages. At any rate, the conscientious officer who desires clear guidance on how to do his job and avoid lawsuits can and should look to the standard for actionability in the first instance. The need for exceptional clarity in the standard for punitive damages arises only if one assumes that there are substantial numbers of officers who will not be deterred by compensatory damages; only such officers will seek to guide their conduct by the punitive damages standard. The presence of such officers constitutes a powerful argument *against* raising the threshold for punitive damages. . . .

We hold that a jury may be permitted to assess punitive damages in an action under § 1983 when the defendant's conduct is shown to be motivated by evil motive or intent, or when it involves reckless or callous indifference to the federally protected rights of others. We further hold that this threshold applies even when the underlying standard of liability for compensatory damages is one of recklessness. Because the jury instructions in this case are in accord with this rule, the judgment of the Court of Appeals is

Affirmed.

■ JUSTICE REHNQUIST, with whom THE CHIEF JUSTICE and JUSTICE POWELL join, dissenting. . . .

[T]he doctrine of punitive damages permits the award of "damages" beyond even the most generous and expansive conception of actual injury to the plaintiff. This anomaly is rationalized principally on three grounds. First, punitive damages "are assessed for the avowed purpose of visiting *a punishment* upon the defendant." C. McCormick, LAW OF DAMAGES 275 (1935) (emphasis added). Second, the doctrine is rationalized on the ground that it deters persons from violating the rights of others. Third, punitive damages are justified as a "bounty" that encourages private lawsuits seeking to assert legal rights.

Despite these attempted justifications, the doctrine of punitive damages has been vigorously criticized throughout the Nation's history. Countless cases remark that such damages have never been "a favorite in the law." The year after § 1983 was enacted, the New Hampshire Supreme Court declared, "The idea of [punitive damages] is wrong. It is a monstrous heresy. It is an unsightly and unhealthy excrescence, deforming the symmetry of the body of the law." Fay *v.* Parker, 53 N.H. 342, 382 (1872). Such remarks reflect a number of deeply held reservations regarding punitive damages, which can only be briefly summarized here.

Punitive damages are generally seen as a windfall to plaintiffs, who are entitled to receive full compensation for their injuries—but no more. Even assuming that a punitive "fine" should be imposed after a civil trial, the penalty should go to the state, not to the plaintiff—who by hypothesis is fully compensated. Moreover, although punitive damages are "quasi-criminal," their imposition is unaccompanied by the types of safeguards present in criminal proceedings. This absence of safeguards is exacerbated by the fact that punitive damages are frequently based upon the caprice and prejudice of jurors. We observed in Electrical Workers *v.* Foust, 442 U.S. 42 (1979), that "punitive damages may be employed to punish unpopular defendants," and noted elsewhere that "juries assess punitive damages in wholly unpredictable amounts bearing no necessary relation to the harm caused." Finally, the alleged deterrence achieved by punitive damage awards is likely outweighed by the costs—such as the encouragement of unnecessary litigation and the chilling of desirable conduct—flowing from the rule, at least when the standards on which the awards are based are ill-defined. . . .

[The] distinction between acts that are intentionally harmful and those that are very negligent, or unreasonable, involves a basic difference of kind, not just a variation of degree. The former typically demands inquiry into the actor's subjective motive and purpose, while the latter ordinarily requires only an objective determination of the relative risks and advantages accruing to society from particular behavior. . . .

[A] careful examination of the decisions available to the members of the 42d Congress reveals a portrait different in important respects from that painted by the Court. While a few jurisdictions may have adopted a more lenient, if less precise, standard of recklessness, the majority's claim that the prevailing standard in 1871 was one of recklessness simply cannot be sustained. The decisions of this Court, which were likely well-known to federal legislators, supported an *animus* requirement. . . .

An intent requirement, unlike a recklessness standard, is logically consistent with the underlying justification for *punitive* damages. It is a fundamental principal of American law that penal consequences generally ought to be imposed only where there has been some sort of wrongful *animus* creating the type of culpability warranting this treatment. . . . Given that punitive damages are meant to punish, it is difficult to believe that Congress would have departed from the "instinctive," "universal and persistent" linkage in our law between punishment and wrongful intent. . . .

It is anomalous, and counter to deep-rooted legal principles and common-sense notions, to punish persons who meant no harm, and to award a windfall, in the form of punitive damages, to someone who already has been fully compensated. These peculiarities ought to be carefully limited—not expanded to every case where a jury may think a defendant was too careless, particularly where a vaguely-defined, elastic standard like "reckless indifference" gives free reign to the biases and prejudices of juries. In short, there are persuasive reasons not to create a new punitive damages remedy unless it is clear that Congress so intended.

This argument is particularly powerful in a case like this, where the uncertainty resulting from largely random awards of punitive damages will have serious effects upon the performance by state and local officers of their official duties. . . . After the Court's decision, governmental officials will be subjected to the possibility of damage awards unlimited by any harm they may have caused or the fact they acted with unquestioned good faith: when swift action is demanded, their thoughts likely will be on personal financial consequences that may result from their conduct—but whose limits they cannot predict—and not upon their official duties. It would have been difficult for the Court to have fashioned a more effective Damoclean sword than the open-ended, standardless and unpredictable liability it creates today.

Moreover, notwithstanding the Court's inability to discern them, there are important distinctions between a right to damages under § 1983 and a similar right under state tort law. A leading rationale seized upon by proponents of punitive damages to justify the doctrine is that "the award is . . . a covert response to the legal system's overt refusal to provide financing for litigation." Yet, 42 U.S.C. § 1988 provides not just a "covert response" to plaintiffs' litigation expenses but an explicit provision for an award to the prevailing party in a § 1983 action of "a reasonable attorney's fee as part of the costs." By permitting punitive damages *as well as* attorney's fees, § 1983 plaintiffs, unlike state tort law plaintiffs, get not just one windfall but two—one for them, and one for their lawyer. This difference between the incentives that are present in state tort actions, and those in § 1983 actions, makes the Court's reliance upon the standard for punitive damages in the former entirely inapposite: in fashioning a new financial lure to litigate under § 1983 the Court does not act in a vacuum, but, by adding to existing incentives, creates an imbalance of inducements to litigate that may have serious consequences.

The staggering effect of § 1983 claims upon the workload of the federal courts has been decried time and again. The torrent of frivolous claims under that section threatens to incapacitate the judicial system's resolution of claims where true injustice is involved; those claims which truly warrant redress are in a very real danger of being lost in a sea of meritless suits. Yet, apparently oblivious to this, the Court today reads into the silent, inhospitable terms of § 1983 a remedy that is designed to serve as a "bounty" to encourage private litigation. . . .

When federal courts enforce punitive damage awards against local officials they intrude into sensitive areas of sovereignty of coordinate branches of our nation, thus implicating the most basic values of our system of federalism. Moreover, by yet further distorting the incentives that exist for litigating claims against local officials in federal court, as opposed to state courts, the Court's decision makes it even more difficult for state courts to attempt to conform the conduct of state officials to the Constitution.

■ [The dissenting opinion of JUSTICE O'CONNOR is omitted.]

NOTE

The Civil Rights Act of 1991 added to Title VII of the Civil Rights Act an express provision for punitive damages, in language that closely tracks the majority's holding in Smith *v.* Wade. However, the meaning of this language has been disputed. Liability for compensatory damages for discrimination depends on a finding of intentional discrimination, and, despite the Court's statements in Smith *v.* Wade, a number of circuit courts have required some additional element of egregiousness to justify punitive damages in Title VII cases. *E.g.*, Ngo *v.* Reno Hilton Resort Corp., 140 F.3d 1299, *as modified*, 156 F.3d 988 (9th Cir. 1998).

Smith v. Whitaker

Supreme Court of New Jersey, 1999.
160 N.J. 221.

■ STEIN, J. . . . On January 4, 1990, Helen V. Robbins, a sixty-year-old widow, was killed when her 1979 Lincoln Town Car was hit by a 36,000-pound oil truck owned by defendant Coastal Oil Company of New York (Coastal) and driven by defendant Alan L. Whitaker, Jr. (Whitaker). . . . Due to maladjusted brakes, Whitaker was unable to stop the truck as he approached the intersection even though he was "standing" on the brakes. The truck crossed the intersection, struck Robbins's automobile, and "overtopped" it. A state trooper responded to the scene within approximately five minutes of the accident. The trooper observed that Robbins did not appear to be breathing and that she appeared to be unconscious. Robbins was transported to a nearby hospital, where she was pronounced dead.

In June 1990, Harold E. Smith, the . . . executor of Robbins's estate, filed an action against Whitaker and Coastal pursuant to the Wrongful Death Act and the Survivor's Act. . . .

[Evidence] showed that one month prior to the accident the State Police, after inspecting Whitaker's vehicle, had cited Coastal with numerous safety violations, including two "out-of-service" conditions that indicated the vehicle would not be considered safe to operate until those conditions were corrected. . . . Evidence also was presented that in the weeks leading up to the accident both Whitaker and Coastal were aware that the brakes were not working properly. An inspection at the time of the accident revealed that both rear brakes were so far out of adjustment as to render the vehicle unsafe to drive. Finally, the evidence suggested that Coastal provided no instruction or training for its drivers regarding proper brake safety or maintenance and that Coastal simply ignored regulatory record-keeping requirements regarding its vehicle maintenance.

[In a bifurcated trial, two juries awarded compensatory damages of $44,117 under the Wrongful Death Act and punitive damages of $1,250,000 under the Survivor's Act.]

Although [wrongful death actions and survival actions] arise from the identical occurrence, *i.e.,* the death of the plaintiff, they serve different purposes and are designed to provide a remedy to different parties. "The fundamental purpose of a wrongful death action is to compensate survivors for the pecuniary losses they suffer because of the tortious conduct of others." Alexander *v.* Whitman, 114 F.3d 1392, 1398 (3d Cir. 1997). . . .

[C]ourts interpreting the [Wrongful Death] Act have consistently held that it permits recovery only of a survivor's calculable economic loss and that the Act does not support an award of punitive damages. . . .

The Survivor's Act, in contrast to the Wrongful Death Act, contains no express limitation on the types of damages recoverable under the statute. . . .

As a rule, a claim for punitive damages may lie only where there is a valid underlying cause of action. . . .

As Coastal notes, the primary damages recoverable in a survival action sounding in tort are for the decedent's pain and suffering between the time of injury and death. Damages for pain and suffering are permitted only for pain and suffering that is conscious. . . .

When the value of a real legal injury cannot be measured in money, a plaintiff who has been substantially harmed may not be able to establish an entitlement to compensatory damages. . . .

[P]unitive damages awarded on a "free-standing" basis, *i.e.,* without an award of compensatory damages in the underlying action, ordinarily must be premised on a valid judgment for, at a minimum, nominal damages. . . .

In the unique context of a survival action, we do not view the absence of a compensatory damage award as necessarily fatal to the assertion of plaintiff's claim for punitive damages. . . . [P]laintiff's failure to establish compensatory damages arises not from the absence of any appreciable injury to Robbins, but from the fact that her instantaneous death precluded any damages award for pain and suffering.

We recognize that an award of at least nominal damages ordinarily is required to sustain a punitive damages award. Even where a plaintiff has suffered a harm inestimable in terms of dollars and cents, an award of nominal damages serves to confirm the jury's finding that plaintiff has suffered a harm cognizable at law. That deficiency is not significant in these circumstances, however, where the elements of causation and defendant's negligence were established in the related wrongful death action. . . .

Accordingly, where all of the essential elements of a punitive damages claim are established, such a claim may be sustained without proof of pain and suffering.

We also conclude that the recent amendments to the Punitive Damages Act, requiring an award of compensatory damages as a predicate for a punitive damages award, are inapplicable to a survival action where the decedent was killed instantly. . . . [T]he statutory requirement indicates a valid legislative attempt to curtail suits seeking redress for allegedly malicious conduct that causes no substantial injury. . . . We do not believe . . . that the Legislature could have intended to bar a claim for punitive damages where, as here, a party suffered the grievous and, indeed, ultimate injury of death, because of the fortuitous circumstance that the victim died instantly. . . .

■ [The concurring opinion of JUSTICE GARIBALDI is omitted.]

NOTE

Lois and Harvey Jacque owned a 170-acre farm. Steenberg Homes, Inc., contracted to sell and deliver a mobile home to neighbors of the Jacques. Steenberg asked the Jacques for permission to cut across their land to deliver the mobile home, which would save Steenberg the cost of navigating a snow-covered private road. The Jacques, an elderly couple who had previously lost property to adverse possession, repeatedly and adamantly refused, telling Steenberg to "follow the road, that is what the road is for." Steenberg proceeded to cut across the Jacques property anyway. A sheriff came to the scene and issued a $30 fine, the criminal penalty for intentional trespass.

The Jacques sued Steenberg for trespass. A jury awarded $1 in nominal damages and $100,000 in punitive damages. Steenberg objected, citing the established Wisconsin rule that nominal damages will not support an award of punitive damages. The Wisconsin Supreme Court upheld the Jacques' award, making an exception to the established rule for cases of trespass. The court recited a hypothetical posed in a nineteenth century English decision, Merest *v.* Harvey, 128 Eng. Rep. 761 (Court of Common Pleas 1814):

> "Suppose a gentleman has a paved walk in his paddock, before his window, and that a man intrudes and walks up and down before the window of his house, and looks in while the owner is at dinner, is the trespasser permitted to say 'here is a halfpenny for you which is the full extent of the mischief I have done.' Would that be a compensation? I cannot say that it would be."

Jacque *v.* Steenberg Homes, Inc., 209 Wis. 2d 605, 616 (1997). The Wisconsin court continued:

"Thus, . . . in certain situations of trespass, the actual harm is not in the damage done to the land, which may be minimal, but in the loss of the individual's right to exclude others from his or her property and . . . this right may be punished by a large damage award despite the lack of measurable harm. . . .

"Society [also] has an interest in punishing and deterring intentional trespassers beyond that of protecting the interests of the individual landowner. Society has an interest in preserving the integrity of the legal system. Private landowners should feel confident that wrongdoers who trespass upon their land will be appropriately punished. When landowners have confidence in the legal system, they are less likely to resort to "self-help" remedies. . . .

"People expect wrongdoers to be appropriately punished. Punitive damages have the effect of bringing to punishment types of conduct that, though oppressive and hurtful to the individual, almost invariably go unpunished by the public prosecutor. The $30 forfeiture was certainly not an appropriate punishment for Steenberg's egregious trespass in the eyes of the Jacques. It was more akin to Merest's 'halfpenny.' . . . Steenberg Homes plowed a path across the Jacques' land and dragged the mobile home across that path, in the face of the Jacques' adamant refusal. A $30 forfeiture and a $1 nominal damage award are unlikely to restrain Steenberg Homes from similar conduct in the future. An appropriate punitive damage award probably will."

Id. at 616–621.

B. CONTRACTS

Miller Brewing Co. v. Best Beers of Bloomington, Inc.

Supreme Court of Indiana, 1993.
608 N.E.2d 975.

■ KRAHULIK, JUSTICE. [Miller terminated its distributorship agreement with Best Beers on flimsy grounds and transferred the distributorship to another wholesaler, which undertook to sell only Miller products. Best Beers brought suit under an Indiana statute (Ind. Code Ann. § 7.1–5–5–9 (West 1982)) making it unlawful to terminate a beer distributorship "unfairly and without due regard for the equities of the other party." A jury found for Best Beers and awarded compensatory damages of $397,852 and punitive damages of $1,989,260.]

Miller next attacks Best Beer's entitlement to punitive damages. . . .

Opinions of this Court have consistently stated the general rule that punitive damages are not allowed in a breach of contract action. . . .

The notion that in some instances punitive damages are available for a breach of contract appears to have begun in Vernon Fire & Casualty *v.* Sharp, 264 Ind. 599 (1976). In that case, plaintiff sued his insurer for breach of an insurance contract, and the jury awarded compensatory damages for the breach. Plaintiff also alleged tortious conduct on part of the insurer for refusing to pay policy proceeds admittedly due, and was awarded punitive damages. . . . The Court acknowledged . . . the widely-recognized principle that where the conduct of the breaching party independently establishes the elements of a common law tort, and where the proven tort is of the kind for which punitive damages are allowed, then punitive damages may be awarded. In such a case, however, the punitive damages are awarded for the tort, and not for the breach of contract. . . .

In spite of its conclusion that the plaintiff had established the elements of fraud as an independent tort, the majority proceeded to opine that the requirement of an independent tort was not very compelling "when it appears from the evidence as a whole that a serious wrong, tortious in nature, has been committed, but the wrong does not conveniently fit the confines of a pre-determined tort" and where "the public interest will be served by the deterrent effect punitive damages will have upon future conduct of the wrongdoer and parties similarly situated." Such language has been cited in subsequent Indiana cases addressing the availability of punitive damages in a breach of contract action. . . .

A rule that requires establishment of an independent tort furthers the public interest in recognizing the existence of *bona fide* business disputes and separating them from breaches of contract achieved in a tortious manner. As we [have previously stated], breaches of contract "will almost invariably be regarded by the complaining party as oppressive if not outright fraudulent." Travelers Indemnity Co. *v.* Armstrong, 442 N.E.2d 349, 364 (1982). "The public interest cannot be served by any policy that deters resort to the courts for the determination of bona fide business disputes," *id.* at 363, or prohibits one party to a contract from exercising his common law rights to breach a contract and pay a rightful amount of compensatory damages. Unlike torts, where the duty is owed to all and a broad measure of damages is available, contract obligations are owed only to the parties to the contract and damages are limited to those reasonably within the expectations of the parties when the contract is made. Vernon Fire, 264 Ind. at 607. . . . [A]s the Court of Appeals noted in [an earlier case], "it is not our prerogative to reopen the floodgates of punitive damages in contract cases . . . and let all disputes and quarrels over broken contracts and disappointed business ventures become the subject of acrimonious litigation over punitive damages.". . .

We hold that in order to recover punitive damages in a lawsuit founded upon a breach of contract, the plaintiff must plead and prove the existence of an independent tort of the kind for which Indiana law recognizes that punitive damages may be awarded. . . .

Best Beers does not seriously contend that there was sufficient evidence of an independent tort upon which punitive damages could have been awarded, but merely asserts that the above evidence is clear and convincing evidence of a "serious wrong tortious in nature." As discussed above, such evidence is insufficient to support an award of punitive damages in a breach of contract case. At best, such evidence establishes that Miller wrongfully terminated the contract, for which Best Beers was awarded compensatory damages. . . .

■ DICKSON, JUSTICE, dissenting. In Vernon Fire & Casualty Insurance Co. *v.* Sharp, this Court recognized two exceptions to the general rule that punitive damages are not recoverable in a contract action. The first arises when conduct of the breaching party not only constitutes breach of contract but also independently establishes the elements of a common law tort. The second occurs when the evidence reveals that a serious wrong, tortious in nature, has been committed, although the wrong "does not conveniently fit the confines of a pre-determined tort."

Judicial response to the *Vernon* exceptions has been both positive and widespread. . . .

The Court of Appeals, in a case somewhat similar to that before us, determined that conduct by a brewing company, while failing to meet the common law elements of tort, nevertheless was sufficiently tort-like to sustain an award of punitive damages. The brewer's breach of a distribution contract, allegedly precipitated by the distributor's refusal to adopt internal management controls required by the brewer, was found to be tortiously oppressive conduct. The court observed that punitive damages properly served the public interest inasmuch as the brewer's conduct contravened principles of free market economy which could ultimately manifest itself in higher prices for consumers. . . .

Today, . . . the majority abruptly seeks to modify *Vernon* and its progeny by relegating to dicta the exception permitting punitive damages where a contract breach attended by egregiously culpable conduct falls short of an independently actionable tort. However attractive it may be to limit an award of punitive damages to such bright-line situations, reprehensible behavior often defies strict tort categorization and should not go undeterred merely because it fails to completely conform to the precise contours of pre-existing tort classifications.

The majority speculates that recovery of punitive damages under the second *Vernon* exception would "reopen" the floodgates of punitive damages in contract cases. I disagree. The gates have already been open for the 17 years since *Vernon*, and neither catastrophe nor havoc has resulted. Twin restraints of case law and statutory enactment are clearly in place. Punitive damages are appropriate only upon clear and convincing evidence showing that the defendant "acted with malice, fraud, gross negligence or oppressiveness" and that such conduct "was not the result of a mistake of fact or law, honest error o[f] judgment, overzealousness, mere negligence, or human failing." Moreover, Ind.

Code § 34–4–34–2 (governing punitive damages) emphasizes that facts supporting punitive damages must be established by "clear and convincing evidence." . . .

Vernon's flexible and responsive application of the law to category-resistant dimensions of human behavior represents an enlightened approach to the infinite variations that elude rigid doctrinal formulations. Experience has shown this approach to be wise, effective, balanced, and just. It should not now be discarded.

NOTE

In E.I. DuPont de Nemours & Co. *v.* Pressman, 679 A.2d 436 (Del. 1996), a wrongful discharge case, the Delaware Supreme Court rejected a claim for punitive damages as a remedy for willful breach of contract. It commented that the goal of contract remedies is to compensate for lost expectancy, then added that:

> "Traditional contract doctrine is also supported by the more recent theory of efficient breach. The theory holds that properly calculated expectation damages increase economic efficiency by giving 'the other party an incentive to break the contract if, but only if, he gains enough from the breach that he can compensate the injured party for his losses and still retain some of the benefits from the breach.' Restatement (Second) of Contracts, Reporter's Note to Introductory Note to ch. 16, Remedies. . . . Punitive damages would increase the amount of damages in excess of the promisee's expectation interest and lead to inefficient results."

Id. at 445–46.

C. CONSTITUTIONAL LIMITS ON PUNITIVE DAMAGES

BMW of North America, Inc. v. Gore

Supreme Court of the United States, 1996.
517 U.S. 559.

■ JUSTICE STEVENS delivered the opinion of the Court. . . .

In January 1990, Dr. Ira Gore, Jr. (respondent), purchased a black BMW sports sedan for $40,750.88 from an authorized BMW dealer in Birmingham, Alabama. After driving the car for approximately nine months, and without noticing any flaws in its appearance, Dr. Gore took the car to "Slick Finish," an independent detailer, to make it look "snazzier than it normally would appear." Mr. Slick, the proprietor, detected evidence that the car had been repainted.[3] Convinced that he had been cheated, Dr. Gore brought suit against petitioner BMW of

[3] The top, hood, trunk, and quarter panels of Dr. Gore's car were repainted at BMW's vehicle preparation center in Brunswick, Georgia. The parties presumed that the damage was caused by exposure to acid rain during transit between the manufacturing plant in Germany and the preparation center.

North America (BMW), the American distributor of BMW automobiles . . . The complaint prayed for $500,000 in compensatory and punitive damages, and costs.

At trial, BMW acknowledged that it had adopted a nationwide policy in 1983 concerning cars that were damaged in the course of manufacture or transportation. If the cost of repairing the damage exceeded 3 percent of the car's suggested retail price, the car was placed in company service for a period of time and then sold as used. If the repair cost did not exceed 3 percent of the suggested retail price, however, the car was sold as new without advising the dealer that any repairs had been made. Because the $601.37 cost of repainting Dr. Gore's car was only about 1.5 percent of its suggested retail price, BMW did not disclose the damage or repair to the Birmingham dealer. . . .

To support his claim for punitive damages, Dr. Gore introduced evidence that since 1983 BMW had sold 983 refinished cars as new, including 14 in Alabama, without disclosing that the cars had been repainted before sale at a cost of more than $300 per vehicle. Using [an] actual damage estimate of $4,000 per vehicle, Dr. Gore argued that a punitive award of $4 million would provide an appropriate penalty for selling approximately 1,000 cars for more than they were worth. . . .

The jury returned a verdict finding BMW liable for compensatory damages of $4,000. In addition, the jury assessed $4 million in punitive damages, based on a determination that the nondisclosure policy constituted "gross, oppressive or malicious" fraud.

BMW filed a post-trial motion to set aside the punitive damages award. The company introduced evidence to establish that its nondisclosure policy was consistent with the laws of roughly 25 States defining the disclosure obligations of automobile manufacturers, distributors, and dealers. The most stringent of these statutes required disclosure of repairs costing more than 3 percent of the suggested retail price; none mandated disclosure of less costly repairs. Relying on these statutes, BMW contended that its conduct was lawful in these States and therefore could not provide the basis for an award of punitive damages.

BMW also drew the court's attention to the fact that its nondisclosure policy had never been adjudged unlawful before this action was filed. Just months before Dr. Gore's case went to trial, the jury in a similar lawsuit filed by another Alabama BMW purchaser found that BMW's failure to disclose paint repair constituted fraud. Before the judgment in this case, BMW changed its policy by taking steps to avoid the sale of any refinished vehicles in Alabama and two other States. When the $4 million verdict was returned in this case, BMW promptly instituted a nationwide policy of full disclosure of all repairs, no matter how minor. . . .

The trial judge denied BMW's post-trial motion, holding, inter alia, that the award was not excessive. On appeal, the Alabama Supreme

Court also rejected BMW's claim that the award exceeded the constitutionally permissible amount. . . .

The Alabama Supreme Court did . . . rule in BMW's favor on one critical point: The court found that the jury improperly computed the amount of punitive damages by multiplying Dr. Gore's compensatory damages by the number of similar sales in other jurisdictions. Having found the verdict tainted, the court held that "a constitutionally reasonable punitive damages award in this case is $2,000,000," and therefore ordered a remittitur in that amount. The court's discussion of the amount of its remitted award expressly disclaimed any reliance on "acts that occurred in other jurisdictions"; instead, the court explained that it had used a "comparative analysis" that considered Alabama cases, "along with cases from other jurisdictions, involving the sale of an automobile where the seller misrepresented the condition of the vehicle and the jury awarded punitive damages to the purchaser." . . .

Punitive damages may properly be imposed to further a State's legitimate interests in punishing unlawful conduct and deterring its repetition. In our federal system, States necessarily have considerable flexibility in determining the level of punitive damages that they will allow in different classes of cases and in any particular case. Most States that authorize exemplary damages afford the jury similar latitude, requiring only that the damages awarded be reasonably necessary to vindicate the State's legitimate interests in punishment and deterrence. Only when an award can fairly be categorized as "grossly excessive" in relation to these interests does it enter the zone of arbitrariness that violates the Due Process Clause of the Fourteenth Amendment. Cf. TXO Production Corp. *v.* Alliance Resources Corp., 509 U.S. 443, 456 (1993). . . .

No one doubts that a State may protect its citizens by prohibiting deceptive trade practices and by requiring automobile distributors to disclose presale repairs that affect the value of a new car. But the States need not, and in fact do not, provide such protection in a uniform manner. . . .

We think it follows from these principles of state sovereignty and comity that a State may not impose economic sanctions on violators of its laws with the intent of changing the tortfeasors' lawful conduct in other States. Before this Court Dr. Gore argued that the large punitive damages award was necessary to induce BMW to change the nationwide policy that it adopted in 1983. But by attempting to alter BMW's nationwide policy, Alabama would be infringing on the policy choices of other States. To avoid such encroachment, the economic penalties that a State such as Alabama inflicts on those who transgress its laws, whether the penalties take the form of legislatively authorized fines or judicially imposed punitive damages, must be supported by the State's interest in protecting its own consumers and its own economy. Alabama may insist that BMW adhere to a particular disclosure policy in that State. Alabama does not have the power, however, to punish BMW for conduct that was lawful where it occurred and that had no impact on Alabama or its residents. Nor may Alabama impose sanctions on BMW in order to deter conduct that is lawful in other jurisdictions.

In this case, we accept the Alabama Supreme Court's interpretation of the jury verdict as reflecting a computation of the amount of punitive damages "based in large part on conduct that happened in other jurisdictions." . . . The award must be analyzed in the light of [conduct that occurred in Alabama[21]], with consideration given only to the interests of Alabama consumers, rather than those of the entire Nation. When the scope of the interest in punishment and deterrence that an Alabama court may appropriately consider is properly limited, it is apparent—for reasons that we shall now address—that this award is grossly excessive.

Elementary notions of fairness enshrined in our constitutional jurisprudence dictate that a person receive fair notice not only of the conduct that will subject him to punishment, but also of the severity of the penalty that a State may impose. Three guideposts, each of which indicates that BMW did not receive adequate notice of the magnitude of the sanction that Alabama might impose for adhering to the nondisclosure policy adopted in 1983, lead us to the conclusion that the $2 million award against BMW is grossly excessive: the degree of reprehensibility of the nondisclosure; the disparity between the harm or potential harm suffered by Dr. Gore and his punitive damages award; and the difference between this remedy and the civil penalties authorized or imposed in comparable cases. . . .

Degree of Reprehensibility

. . . In this case, none of the aggravating factors associated with particularly reprehensible conduct is present. The harm BMW inflicted on Dr. Gore was purely economic in nature. . . .

Dr. Gore contends that BMW's conduct was particularly reprehensible because nondisclosure of the repairs to his car formed part of a nationwide pattern of tortious conduct. Certainly, evidence that a defendant has repeatedly engaged in prohibited conduct while knowing or suspecting that it was unlawful would provide relevant support for an argument that strong medicine is required to cure the defendant's disrespect for the law. Our holdings that a recidivist may be punished more severely than a first offender recognize that repeated misconduct is more reprehensible than an individual instance of malfeasance. . . .

A review of the text of [non-disclosure statutes in other states] the statutes, however, persuades us that in the absence of a state-court determination to the contrary, a corporate executive could reasonably interpret the disclosure requirements as establishing safe harbors. . . .

[21] Of course, . . . evidence describing out-of-state transactions . . . may be relevant to the determination of the degree of reprehensibility of the defendant's conduct.

Perhaps the statutes may also be interpreted in another way. We simply emphasize that the record contains no evidence that BMW's decision to follow a disclosure policy that coincided with the strictest extant state statute was sufficiently reprehensible to justify a $2 million award of punitive damages. . . .

There is no evidence that BMW acted in bad faith when it sought to establish the appropriate line between presumptively minor damage and damage requiring disclosure to purchasers. . . . In this regard, it is also significant that there is no evidence that BMW persisted in a course of conduct after it had been adjudged unlawful on even one occasion, let alone repeated occasions.

Finally, the record in this case discloses no deliberate false statements, acts of affirmative misconduct, or concealment of evidence of improper motive . . . .

Ratio

The second and perhaps most commonly cited indicium of an unreasonable or excessive punitive damages award is its ratio to the actual harm inflicted on the plaintiff. The principle that exemplary damages must bear a "reasonable relationship" to compensatory damages has a long pedigree. . . .

The $2 million in punitive damages awarded to Dr. Gore by the Alabama Supreme Court is 500 times the amount of his actual harm as determined by the jury. . . .

Of course, we have consistently rejected the notion that the constitutional line is marked by a simple mathematical formula, even one that compares actual and potential damages to the punitive award. Indeed, low awards of compensatory damages may properly support a higher ratio than high compensatory awards, if, for example, a particularly egregious act has resulted in only a small amount of economic damages. A higher ratio may also be justified in cases in which the injury is hard to detect or the monetary value of noneconomic harm might have been difficult to determine. . . . When the ratio is a breathtaking 500 to 1, however, the award must surely "raise a suspicious judicial eyebrow." TXO, 509 U.S., at 481 (O'Connor, J., dissenting).

Sanctions for Comparable Misconduct

Comparing the punitive damages award and the civil or criminal penalties that could be imposed for comparable misconduct provides a third indicium of excessiveness. As JUSTICE O'CONNOR has correctly observed, a reviewing court engaged in determining whether an award of punitive damages is excessive should "accord 'substantial deference' to legislative judgments concerning appropriate sanctions for the conduct at issue." Browning-Ferris Industries of Vermont, Inc. *v.* Kelco Disposal, Inc., 492 U.S. 257, 301 (1989) (opinion concurring in part and dissenting in part). . . .

The maximum civil penalty authorized by the Alabama Legislature for a violation of its Deceptive Trade Practices Act is $2,000; other States authorize more severe sanctions, with the maxima ranging from $5,000 to $10,000. . . .

The fact that a multimillion dollar penalty prompted a change in policy sheds no light on the question whether a lesser deterrent would have adequately protected the interests of Alabama consumers. . . .

The fact that BMW is a large corporation rather than an impecunious individual does not diminish its entitlement to fair notice of the demands that the several States impose on the conduct of its business. . . .

■ [The concurring opinion of JUSTICE BREYER is omitted.]

■ JUSTICE SCALIA, with whom JUSTICE THOMAS joins, dissenting.

Today we see the latest manifestation of this Court's recent and increasingly insistent "concern about punitive damages that 'run wild' " Pacific Mutual Life Insurance Co. *v.* Haslip, 499 U.S. 1, 18 (1991). Since the Constitution does not make that concern any of our business, the Court's activities in this area are an unjustified incursion into the province of state governments. . . .

[A] state trial procedure that commits the decision whether to impose punitive damages, and the amount, to the discretion of the jury, subject to some judicial review for "reasonableness," furnishes a defendant with all the process that is "due." I do not regard the Fourteenth Amendment's Due Process Clause as a secret repository of substantive guarantees against "unfairness"—neither the unfairness of an excessive civil compensatory award, nor the unfairness of an "unreasonable" punitive award. . . .

One might understand the Court's eagerness to enter this field, rather than leave it with the state legislatures, if it had something useful to say. In fact, however, its opinion provides virtually no guidance to legislatures, and to state and federal courts, as to what a "constitutionally proper" level of punitive damages might be. . . .

[T]he Court identifies "[t]hree guideposts" that lead it to the conclusion that the award in this case is excessive: degree of reprehensibility, ratio between punitive award and plaintiff's actual harm, and legislative sanctions provided for comparable misconduct. The legal significance of these "guideposts" is nowhere explored, but their necessary effect is to establish federal standards governing the hitherto exclusively state law of damages. . . .

The relationship between judicial application of the new "guideposts" and jury findings poses a real problem for the Court, since as a matter of logic there is no more justification for ignoring the jury's determination as to how reprehensible petitioner's conduct was (*i.e.*, how much it deserves to be punished), than there is for ignoring its determination that it was reprehensible at all (*i.e.*, that the wrong was willful and punitive damages are therefore recoverable). . . . The elevation of "fairness" in punishment to a principle of "substantive due process" means that every punitive award unreasonably imposed is unconstitutional; such an award is by definition excessive, since it attaches a penalty to conduct undeserving of punishment. Indeed, if the Court is correct, it must be that every claim that a state jury's award of compensatory damages is "unreasonable" (because not supported by the evidence) amounts to an assertion of constitutional injury. And the same would be true for determinations of liability. By today's logic, every dispute as to evidentiary sufficiency in a state civil suit poses a question of constitutional moment, subject to review in this Court. That is a stupefying proposition. . . .

■ JUSTICE GINSBURG with whom THE CHIEF JUSTICE joins, dissenting.

The Court, I am convinced, unnecessarily and unwisely ventures into territory traditionally within the States' domain, and does so in the face of reform measures recently adopted or currently under consideration in legislative arenas. . . .

The respect due the Alabama Supreme Court requires that we strip from this case a false issue: No impermissible "extraterritoriality" infects the judgment before us; the excessiveness of the award is the sole issue genuinely presented. . . .

[T]he Alabama Supreme Court . . . concluded that, considering only acts in Alabama, $2 million was "a constitutionally reasonable punitive damages award."

Alabama's Supreme Court reports that it "thoroughly and painstakingly" reviewed the jury's award, according to principles set out in its own pathmarking decisions and in this Court's opinions . . . . Alabama's highest court could have displayed its labor pains more visibly, but its judgment is nonetheless entitled to a presumption of legitimacy. . . .

[This] decision leads us further into territory traditionally within the States' domain, and commits the Court, now and again, to correct "misapplication of a properly stated rule of law." . . .

In contrast to habeas corpus review under 28 U.S.C. § 2254, the Court will work at this business alone. It will not be aided by the federal district courts and courts of appeals. It will be the only federal court policing the area. The Court's readiness to superintend state-court punitive damages awards is all the more puzzling in view of the Court's longstanding reluctance to countenance review, even by courts of appeals, of the size of verdicts returned by juries in federal district court proceedings. . . .

NOTES ON CONSTITUTIONAL REVIEW OF PUNITIVE DAMAGES

1. In Browning-Ferris Industries of Vermont, Inc. *v.* Kelco Disposal, Inc., 492 U.S. 257 (1989), the Court had held that the Excessive Fines Clause of the Eighth Amendment does not apply to awards of punitive damages in cases between private parties.

2. In Cooper Industries, Inc. *v.* Leatherman Tool Group, Inc., 532 U.S. 424 (2001), the Court held that federal courts of appeal reviewing federal district court decisions upholding punitive damages awards by federal juries should apply a de novo standard of review. The standard of review for state court decisions was not before the Court.

State Farm Mutual Automobile Insurance Co. v. Campbell

Supreme Court of the United States, 2003.
538 U.S. 408.

■ JUSTICE KENNEDY delivered the opinion of the Court. . . .

In 1981, Curtis Campbell (Campbell) was driving with his wife, Inez Preece Campbell, in Cache County, Utah. He decided to pass six vans traveling ahead of them on a two-lane highway. Todd Ospital was driving a small car approaching from the opposite direction. To avoid a head-on collision with Campbell, who by then was driving on the wrong side of the highway and toward oncoming traffic, Ospital swerved onto the shoulder, lost control of his automobile, and collided with a vehicle driven by Robert G. Slusher. Ospital was killed, and Slusher was rendered permanently disabled. The Campbells escaped unscathed.

In the ensuing wrongful death and tort action, Campbell insisted he was not at fault. Early investigations did support differing conclusions as to who caused the accident, but "a consensus was reached early on by the investigators and witnesses that Mr. Campbell's unsafe pass had indeed caused the crash." Campbell's insurance company, petitioner State Farm Mutual Automobile Insurance Company (State Farm), nonetheless decided to contest liability and declined offers by Slusher and Ospital's estate (Ospital) to settle the claims for the policy limit of $50,000 ($25,000 per claimant). State Farm also ignored the advice of one of its own investigators and took the case to trial, assuring the Campbells that "their assets were safe, that they had no liability for the accident, that [State Farm] would represent their interests, and that they did not need to procure separate counsel." To the contrary, a jury determined that Campbell was 100 percent at fault, and a judgment was returned for $185,849, far more than the amount offered in settlement.

At first State Farm refused to cover the $135,849 in excess liability. Its counsel made this clear to the Campbells: "You may want to put for sale signs on your property to get things moving." Nor was State Farm willing to post a supersedeas bond to allow Campbell to appeal the judgment against him. Campbell obtained his own counsel to appeal the verdict. During the pendency of the appeal, in late 1984, Slusher, Ospital, and the Campbells reached an agreement whereby Slusher and Ospital agreed not to seek satisfaction of their claims against the Campbells. In exchange the Campbells agreed to pursue a bad faith action against State Farm and to be represented by Slusher's and Ospital's attorneys. The Campbells also agreed that Slusher and Ospital would have a right to play a part in all major decisions concerning the bad-faith action. No settlement could be concluded without Slusher's and Ospital's approval, and Slusher and Ospital would receive 90 percent of any verdict against State Farm.

In 1989, the Utah Supreme Court denied Campbell's appeal in the wrongful-death and tort actions. State Farm then paid the entire judgment, including the amounts in excess of the policy limits. The Campbells nonetheless filed a complaint against State Farm alleging bad faith, fraud, and intentional infliction of emotional distress. . . .

The jury awarded the Campbells $2.6 million in compensatory damages and $145 million in punitive damages, which the trial court reduced to $1 million and $25 million respectively.

The Utah Supreme Court . . . reinstated the $145 million punitive damages award. . . .

Under the principles outlined in BMW of North America, Inc. *v.* Gore, this case is neither close nor difficult. It was error to reinstate the jury's $145 million punitive damages award. . . .

We have instructed courts to determine the reprehensibility of a defendant by considering whether: the harm caused was physical as opposed to economic; the tortious conduct evinced an indifference to or a reckless disregard of the health or safety of others; the target of the conduct had financial vulnerability; the conduct involved repeated actions or was an isolated incident; and the harm was the result of intentional malice, trickery, or deceit, or mere accident. . . .

Applying these factors in the instant case, we must acknowledge that State Farm's handling of the claims against the Campbells merits no praise. The trial court found that State Farm's employees altered the company's records to make Campbell appear less culpable. State Farm disregarded the overwhelming likelihood of liability and the near-certain probability that, by taking the case to trial, a judgment in excess of the policy limits would be awarded. State Farm amplified the harm by at first assuring the Campbells their assets would be safe from any verdict and by later telling them, postjudgment, to put a for-sale sign on their house. While we do not suggest there was error in awarding punitive damages based upon State Farm's conduct toward the Campbells, a more modest punishment for this reprehensible conduct could have satisfied the State's legitimate objectives, and the Utah courts should have gone no further.

This case, instead, was used as a platform to expose, and punish, the perceived deficiencies of State Farm's operations throughout the country. The Utah Supreme Court's opinion makes explicit that State Farm was being condemned for its nationwide policies rather than for the conduct directed toward the Campbells. . . .

A State cannot punish a defendant for conduct that may have been lawful where it occurred. Nor, as a general rule, does a State have a legitimate concern in imposing punitive damages to punish a defendant for unlawful acts committed outside of the State's jurisdiction. . . .

For a more fundamental reason, however, the Utah courts erred in relying upon this and other evidence: The courts awarded punitive damages to punish and deter conduct that bore no relation to the Campbells' harm. A defendant's dissimilar acts, independent from the acts upon which liability was premised, may not serve as the basis for punitive damages. A defendant should be punished for the conduct that harmed the plaintiff, not for being an unsavory individual or business. . . . Punishment on these bases creates the possibility of multiple punitive damages awards for the same conduct; for in the usual case nonparties are not bound by the judgment some other plaintiff obtains. . . .

Although "[o]ur holdings that a recidivist may be punished more severely than a first offender recognize that repeated misconduct is more reprehensible than an individual instance of malfeasance," in the context of civil actions courts must ensure the conduct in question replicates the prior transgressions. TXO Production Corp. *v.* Alliance Resources Corp., 509 U.S. 443, 462, n.28 (1993) (noting that courts should look to "the existence and frequency of similar past conduct").

Turning to the second *Gore* guidepost, we . . . decline again to impose a bright-line ratio which a punitive damages award cannot exceed. Our jurisprudence and the principles it has now established demonstrate, however, that, in practice, few awards exceeding a single-digit ratio between punitive and compensatory damages, to a significant degree, will satisfy due process. . . .

[R]atios greater than those we have previously upheld may comport with due process where "a particularly egregious act has resulted in only a small amount of economic damages." BMW of North America, Inc. *v.* Gore, 517 U.S. 559, 582 (1996). The converse is also true, however. When compensatory damages are substantial, then a lesser ratio, perhaps only equal to compensatory damages, can reach the outermost limit of the due process guarantee. . . .

In sum, courts must ensure that the measure of punishment is both reasonable and proportionate to the amount of harm to the plaintiff and to the general damages recovered. In the context of this case, we have no doubt that there is a presumption against an award that has a 145-to-1 ratio. . . .

The Utah Supreme Court sought to justify the massive award by pointing to State Farm's purported failure to report a prior $100 million punitive damages award in Texas to its corporate headquarters; the fact that State Farm's policies have affected numerous Utah consumers; the fact that State Farm will only be punished in one out of every 50,000 cases as a matter of statistical probability; and State Farm's enormous wealth. . . . The failure of the company to report the Texas award is out-of-state conduct that, if the conduct were similar, might have had some bearing on the degree of reprehensibility . . . . Here, it was dissimilar, and of . . . marginal relevance . . . .

The remaining premises for the Utah Supreme Court's decision bear no relation to the award's reasonableness or proportionality to the harm. . . . The wealth of a defendant cannot justify an otherwise unconstitutional punitive damages award. . . .

The third guidepost in *Gore* is the disparity between the punitive damages award and the "civil penalties authorized or imposed in comparable cases." . . . [The Utah Supreme Court noted that various civil and criminal penalties might have been imposed on State Farm for fraud, including $10,000 for each fraudulent act, suspension of its license to conduct business in Utah, disgorgement of profits, and imprisonment.] The existence of a criminal penalty does have bearing on the seriousness with which a State views the wrongful action. When used to determine the dollar amount of the award, however, the criminal penalty has less utility. Great care must be taken to avoid use of the civil process to assess criminal penalties that can be imposed only after the heightened protections of a criminal trial have been observed . . . .

The judgment of the Utah Supreme Court is reversed, and the case is remanded for further proceedings not inconsistent with this opinion.

■ [The dissenting opinions of JUSTICE SCALIA and JUSTICE THOMAS are omitted.]

■ JUSTICE GINSBURG, dissenting. . . . [O]n the key criterion "reprehensibility," there is a good deal more to the story than the Court's abbreviated account tells.

Ample evidence allowed the jury to find that State Farm's treatment of the Campbells typified its "Performance, Planning and Review" (PP & R) program; implemented by top management in 1979, the program had "the explicit objective of using the claims-adjustment process as a profit center." "[T]he Campbells presented considerable evidence," the trial court noted, documenting "that the PP & R program . . . has functioned, and continues to function, as an unlawful scheme . . . to deny benefits owed consumers by paying out less than fair value in order to meet preset, arbitrary payout targets designed to enhance corporate profits." . . .

Evidence the jury could credit demonstrated that the PP & R program regularly and adversely affected Utah residents. Ray Summers, "the adjuster who handled the Campbell case and who was a State Farm employee in Utah for almost twenty years," described several methods used by State Farm to deny claimants fair benefits, for example, "falsifying or withholding of evidence in claim files." A common tactic, Summers recounted, was to "unjustly attac[k] the character, reputation and credibility of a claimant and mak[e] notations to that effect in the claim file to create prejudice in the event the claim ever came before a jury." State Farm manager Bob Noxon, Summers testified, resorted to a tactic of this order in the Campbell case when he "instruct[ed] Summers to write in the file that Todd Ospital (who was killed in the accident) was speeding because he was on his way to see a pregnant girlfriend." In truth, "[t]here was no pregnant girlfriend." . . .

Regarding liability for verdicts in excess of policy limits, the trial court referred to a State Farm document titled the "Excess Liability Handbook"; written before the Campbell accident, the handbook instructed adjusters to pad files with "self-serving" documents, and to leave critical items out of files, for example, evaluations of the insured's exposure. Divisional superintendent Bill Brown used the handbook to train Utah employees. While overseeing the Campbell case, Brown ordered adjuster Summers to change the portions of his report indicating that Mr. Campbell was likely at fault and that the settlement cost was correspondingly high. The Campbells' case, according to expert testimony the trial court recited, "was a classic example of State Farm's application of the improper practices taught in the Excess Liability Handbook."

The trial court further determined that the jury could find State Farm's policy "deliberately crafted" to prey on consumers who would be unlikely to defend themselves. In this regard, the trial court noted the testimony of several former State Farm employees affirming that they were trained to target "the weakest of the herd"—"the elderly, the poor, and other consumers who are least knowledgeable about their rights and thus most vulnerable to trickery or deceit, or who have little money and hence have no real alternative but to accept an inadequate offer to settle a claim at much less than fair value."

The Campbells themselves could be placed within the "weakest of the herd" category. The couple appeared economically vulnerable and emotionally fragile. At the time of State Farm's wrongful conduct, "Mr. Campbell had residuary effects from a stroke and Parkinson's disease." . . .

Evidence of out-of-state conduct, the Court acknowledges, may be "probative [even if the conduct is lawful in the State where it occurred] when it demonstrates the deliberateness and culpability of the defendant's action in the State where it is tortious . . . ." "Other acts" evidence concerning practices both in and out of State was introduced in this case to show just such "deliberateness" and "culpability." Viewed in this light, there surely was "a nexus" between much of the "other acts" evidence and "the specific harm suffered by [the Campbells]." . . .

NOTES

1. On remand, the Utah Supreme Court concluded "that a 9-to-1 ratio between compensatory and punitive damages, yielding a $9,018,780.75 punitive damages award, serves Utah's legitimate goals of deterrence and retribution within the limits of due process." Campbell *v.* State Farm Mutual Automobile Insurance Co., 98 P.3d 409, 418 (Utah 2004).

2. Jesse Williams, a heavy smoker of Marlboros, died of a smoking-related illness. His widow sued Phillip Morris, alleging that it had falsely and knowingly led him to believe that cigarettes were safe. The plaintiff's arguments to the jury made reference to the effects of Phillip Morris's advertising on other Oregonians and to the many other smokers (1 in 10) likely to die from smoking related illness. The jury awarded compensatory damages of $821,000 and punitive damages of $79.5 million.

The U.S. Supreme Court held the award of punitive damages invalid. Justice Breyer wrote:

> "[T]he Constitution's Due Process Clause forbids a State to use a punitive damages award to punish a defendant for injury that it inflicts upon nonparties or those whom they directly represent . . . . [A] defendant threatened with punishment for injuring a nonparty victim has no opportunity to defend against the charge, by showing, for example in a case such as this, that the other victim was not entitled to damages because he or she knew that smoking was dangerous or did not rely upon the defendant's statements to the contrary.
>
> "For another, to permit punishment for injuring a nonparty victim would add a near standardless dimension to the punitive damages equation. How many such victims are there? How seriously were they injured? . . .
>
> "Evidence of actual harm to nonparties can help to show that the conduct that harmed the plaintiff also posed a substantial risk of harm to the general public, and so was particularly reprehensible . . . . Yet for the reasons given above, a jury may not go further than this and use a punitive damages verdict to punish a defendant directly on account of harms it is alleged to have visited on nonparties. . . .
>
> "How can we know whether a jury, in taking account of harm caused others under the rubric of reprehensibility, also seeks to *punish* the defendant for having caused injury to others? Our answer is that state courts cannot authorize procedures that create an unreasonable and unnecessary risk of any such confusion occurring. In particular, we believe that where the risk of that misunderstanding is a significant one—because, for instance, of the sort of evidence that was introduced at trial or the kinds of argument the plaintiff made to the jury—a court, upon request, must protect against that risk."

Philip Morris USA *v.* Williams, 549 U.S. 346, 353–57 (2007).

Justice Stevens dissented, saying that:

> "[T]he majority relies on a distinction between taking third-party harm into account in order to assess the reprehensibility of the defendant's conduct—which is permitted—and doing so in order to punish the defendant 'directly'—which is forbidden. This nuance eludes me. When a jury increases a punitive damages award because injuries to third parties enhanced the reprehensibility of the defendant's conduct, the jury is by definition punishing the defendant—directly—for third-party harm. A murderer who kills his victim by throwing a bomb that injures dozens of bystanders should be punished more severely than one who harms no one other than his intended victim. Similarly, there is no reason why the measure of the appropriate punishment for engaging in a campaign of deceit in distributing a poisonous and addictive substance to thousands of cigarette smokers statewide should not include consideration of the harm to those "bystanders" as well as the harm to the individual plaintiff."

Id. at 360 (Stevens, J., dissenting).

On remand, the Oregon Court reinstated the $79.5 million award on technical procedural grounds. Williams *v.* Philip Morris, Inc., 344 Or. 45 (2008), *cert. dismissed*, 556 U.S. 178 (2009).

3. On March 23, 1989, in an icy sea off the coast of Alaska, Captain Joseph Hazelwood, a known alcoholic who had drunk at least five double vodkas that evening, abandoned the bridge of the 900-foot oil tanker *Exxon Valdez*. The two crew members left in charge, neither of whom was licensed to navigate the ship, missed a turn. The ship ran aground, spilling eleven million gallons of oil into the Prince William Sound.

Commercial fishermen and native Alaskans who lost their livelihoods as a result of the environmental disaster than ensued brought a class action against Exxon under federal admiralty law. Exxon paid about $500 million in compensatory damages to the plaintiffs. The jury also awarded $5 billion in punitive damages, which the Court of Appeals for the Ninth Circuit remitted to $2.5 billion. The United States Supreme Court vacated the award and remanded with instructions that the ratio of punitive to compensatory damages should not exceed a maximum of 1:1. In doing so, the Court noted that it was not interpreting the Due Process Clauses but was instead exercising its broader authority to fashion admiralty law in the manner of a common law court. Justice Souter wrote:

> "A survey of the literature reveals that discretion to award punitive damages has not mass-produced runaway awards, and although some studies show the dollar amounts of punitive-damages awards growing over time, even in real terms, by most accounts the median ratio of punitive to compensatory awards has remained less than 1:1. Nor do the data substantiate a marked increase in the percentage of cases with punitive awards over the past several decades. The figures thus show an overall restraint and suggest that in many instances a high ratio of punitive to

compensatory damages is substantially greater than necessary to punish or deter.

"The real problem, it seems, is the stark unpredictability of punitive awards. Courts of law are concerned with fairness as consistency, and evidence that the median ratio of punitive to compensatory awards falls within a reasonable zone, or that punitive awards are infrequent, fails to tell us whether the spread between high and low individual awards is acceptable. The available data suggest it is not. A recent comprehensive study of punitive damages awarded by juries in state civil trials found a median ratio of punitive to compensatory awards of just 0.62:1, but a mean ratio of 2.90:1 and a standard deviation of 13.81. Theodore Eisenberg, et al., Juries, Judges, and Punitive Damages: Empirical Analyses Using the Civil Justice Survey of State Courts 1992, 1996, and 2001 Data, 3 J. Empirical Legal Studies 263, 269 (2006). Even to those of us unsophisticated in statistics, the thrust of these figures is clear: the spread is great, and the outlier cases subject defendants to punitive damages that dwarf the corresponding compensatories. The distribution of awards is narrower, but still remarkable, among punitive damages assessed by judges: the median ratio is 0.66:1, the mean ratio is 1.60:1, and the standard deviation is 4.54. . . .

"Starting with the premise of a punitive-damages regime, these ranges of variation might be acceptable or even desirable if they resulted from judges' and juries' refining their judgments to reach a generally accepted optimal level of penalty and deterrence in cases involving a wide range of circumstances, while producing fairly consistent results in cases with similar facts. But anecdotal evidence suggests that nothing of that sort is going on, . . . [and we] are aware of no scholarly work pointing to consistency across punitive awards in cases involving similar claims and circumstances. . . .

"Our review of punitive damages today, then, considers not their intersection with the Constitution, but the desirability of regulating them as a common law remedy for which responsibility lies with this Court as a source of judge-made law in the absence of statute. Whatever may be the constitutional significance of the unpredictability of high punitive awards, this feature of happenstance is in tension with the function of the awards as punitive, just because of the implication of unfairness that an eccentrically high punitive verdict carries in a system whose commonly held notion of law rests on a sense of fairness in dealing with one another. . . .

"[Examples of criteria for judicial review of punitive damages awards set out in state statutes and judicial decisions, and our experience with federal sentencing guidelines] leave us skeptical that verbal formulations, superimposed on general jury instructions, are the best insurance against unpredictable outliers. . . .

"[O]ur better judgment is that eliminating unpredictable outlying punitive awards . . . will probably have to take the form . . . of quantified limits. One option would be to follow the States that set a hard dollar cap on punitive damages . . . . The trouble is . . . that there is no 'standard' tort or contract injury . . . .

"The more promising alternative is to leave the effects of inflation to the jury or judge who assesses the value of actual loss, by pegging punitive to compensatory damages using a ratio or maximum multiple. . . . [T]he potential relevance of the ratio between compensatory and punitive damages is indisputable, being a central feature in our due process analysis. . . .

"There is . . . evidence of an accepted limit of reasonable civil penalty, however, in several studies mentioned before, showing the median ratio of punitive to compensatory verdicts, reflecting what juries and judges have considered reasonable across many hundreds of punitive awards. . . .

"These studies cover cases of the most as well as the least blameworthy conduct triggering punitive liability, from malice and avarice, down to recklessness, and even gross negligence in some jurisdictions. The data put the median ratio for the entire gamut of circumstances at less than 1:1, meaning that the compensatory award exceeds the punitive award in most cases. In a well-functioning system, we would expect that awards at the median or lower would roughly express jurors' sense of reasonable penalties in cases with no earmarks of exceptional blameworthiness within the punishable spectrum (cases like this one, without intentional or malicious conduct, and without behavior driven primarily by desire for gain, for example) and cases (again like this one) without the modest economic harm or odds of detection that have opened the door to higher awards. . . . On these assumptions, a median ratio of punitive to compensatory damages of about 0.65:1 probably marks the line near which cases like this one largely should be grouped. Accordingly, given the need to protect against the possibility (and the disruptive cost to the legal system) of awards that are unpredictable and unnecessary, either for deterrence or for measured retribution, we consider that a 1:1 ratio, which is above the median award, is a fair upper limit in such maritime cases."

Exxon Shipping Co. *v.* Baker, 554 U.S. 471 (2008).

4. Notice that in *State Farm*, the Court said that "[t]he wealth of a defendant cannot justify an otherwise unconstitutional punitive damages award," 538 U.S. at 427. Traditionally, however, state courts have often permitted, and sometimes required, juries to consider the defendant's wealth in assessing punitive damages. That continues to be the practice in some jurisdictions. See, *e.g.*, Soto *v.* BorgWarner Morse TEC Inc., 239 Cal. App. 4th 165, 191–92 (2015), as modified (Aug. 20, 2015), review denied (Oct. 28,

2015): "The purposes of punitive damages are to punish the defendant for the conduct that harmed the plaintiff and deter the commission of future wrongful acts. It follows that the wealthier the wrongdoing defendant, the larger the award of exemplary damages need be in order to accomplish the statutory objective[s]."

5. Professors Polinsky and Shavell, in their analysis of punitive damages, propose an optimal formula for punitive damage awards, as follows: "the total damages imposed on an injurer should equal the harm [done] multiplied by the reciprocal of the probability that the injury will be found liable when he ought to be." Further, "it follows . . . that, if damages are raised above the magnitude given by our formula when corporations are relatively wealthy, those corporations will be led to take excessive precautions." A. Mitchell Polinsky & Steven Shavell, Punitive Damages: An Economic Analysis, 111 Harv. L. Rev. 869, 889, 911 (1998). Another analysis concludes that punitive damages should take into account defendant wealth, in order to ensure that wealthy defendants take a socially optimal amount of care. C. Y. Cyrus Chu & Chen-Ying Huang, On the Definition and Efficiency of Punitive Damages, 24 Int'l Rev. L. & Econ. 241 (2004). Chu and Huang do not express a conclusion about corporate defendants because of principal–agent complications.

6. A different view is expressed by Professor Benjamin Zipursky. He argues that: "When a court awards punitive damages in a tort action, the state is not itself delivering a punishment; it is empowering a private tort plaintiff to be punitive. . . . The plaintiff who is seeking punitive damages because of the defendant's willful wronging of her is suing in her own right, not on behalf of the state." Benjamin C. Zipursky, *Palsgraf*, Punitive Damages, and Preemption, 125 Harv. L. Rev. 1757, 1779 (2012). On this view, what leads courts to apply the Due Process Clause to punitive damages is the mistaken notion that punitive damages are a form of state regulatory action, a remedy given to a plaintiff acting who is acting as a private attorney general.

FURTHER NOTES ON EMPIRICAL RESEARCH ON PUNITIVE DAMAGES

1. Punitive Damages Award Levels

A. Trend Over Time

The NCSC-BJS data described in Chapter Four, above, also provide a summary of punitive damages awards over time in state court trials. Table 1 shows, for cases with punitive awards at trial, and for the counties in the Civil Justice Survey, the mean and median punitive awards in jury and judge trials.

Table 1. Mean and Median Punitive Award 1991 to 2005, State Court Trials

Year	Mean	Median	N	Mean	Median	N
	Punitive award, juries			Punitive award, judges		
1991	748,674	69,601	177	data on judge trials not collected		
1996	2,418,073	64,657	121	743,114	39,057	55
2001	6,979,674	82,708	155	168,761	55,138	48
2005	2,967,017	147,000	141	251,063	37,514	45
Total	3,241,247	82,708	594	407,227	46,885	148

Note. Amounts are in 2005 dollars.

B. Speculation About Punitive Damages Award Levels

Much speculation exists about how juries determine the level of punitive damages awards. Theodore Olson, who would later be Solicitor General of the United States, wrote the following in 1989:

> No matter what the official legal formulation in any state, whether the standard is described as malice or fraud or reckless conduct or gross negligence, in practice the jury can and will award whatever the plaintiff's lawyer can justify in a powerful closing argument.
>
> Juries are remarkably ill-equipped for that task because they sit in only one case, hear evidence only in that case, and are then given very vague guidance with which to form a judgment. They do not know what punishments are meted out for similar acts or for other improper acts. They therefore pick numbers out of a hat. Our legal system has never accepted this kind of situational justice.

This kind of rhetoric may be what the *Exxon Shipping Co.* Court was referring to when it stated "American punitive damages have been the target of audible criticism in recent decades . . . but the most recent studies tend to undercut much of it. . . . [D]iscretion to award punitive damages has not mass-produced runaway awards . . . ."

C. The Relation Between Punitive and Compensatory Damages

Since the NCSC-BJS Civil Justice Survey data described above provide information about both compensatory and punitive damages awarded at trial, one can use those data to explore the relation between punitive and compensatory damages. Table 2 shows the ratio of punitive to compensatory damages for the years of the Civil Justice Survey, subdivided by jury and judge trials. Similar information, which was reported in the Journal of Empirical Legal Studies article cited by the Court, likely was what the Court had in mind when it noted that the median ratio was around 1:1.

Table 2. Punitive Compensatory Ratio 1991 to 2005, State Court Trials

Year	Mean	Median	N	Mean	Median	N
	Punitive/compensatory ratio, juries			Punitive/compensatory ratio, judges		
1991	2.1	0.8	173	data on judges not gathered		
1996	4.6	0.5	119	1.2	0.6	54
2001	8.3	0.6	150	1.8	0.7	48
2005	2.9	1.0	136	1.3	0.9	42
Total	4.4	0.7	578	1.5	0.7	144

Figure 1 shows for each year of the survey the relation between the punitive award in a case and the compensatory award I the same case. Does the figure support Mr. Olson's assertion that punitive damages numbers are being picked out of a hat?

Figure 1. Punitive-Compensatory Relation, 1991 to 2005, State Courts

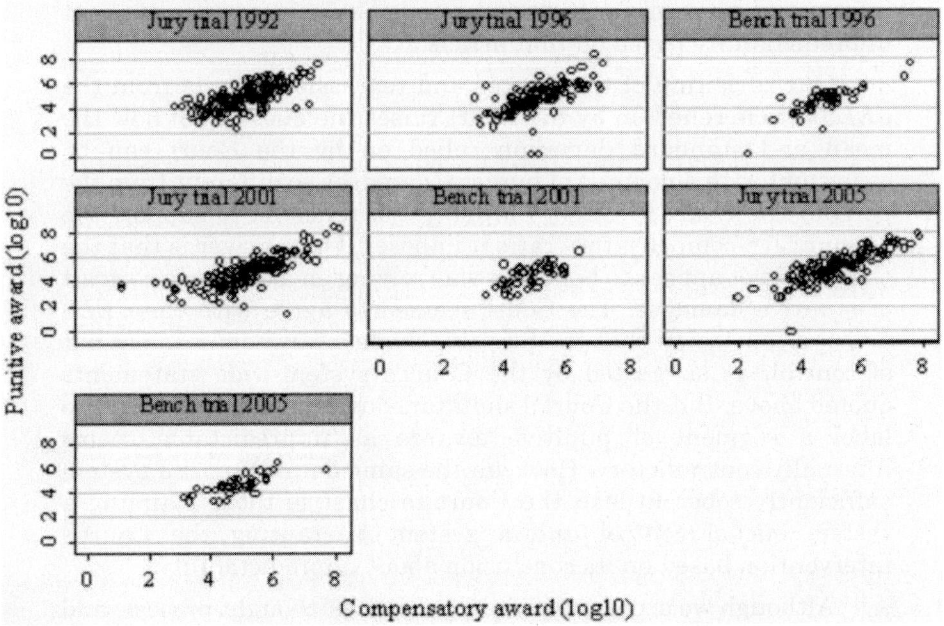

D. *Exxon Shipping Co.*'s Treatment of the Punitive-Compensatory Relation

Although the Court relied on the mean and standard deviation of the punitive-compensatory ratio to suggest a systemic problem with punitive damages awards, Figure 1 visually suggests a highly explicable pattern between punitive and compensatory awards. The Court's use of the mean and standard deviation of the punitive-compensatory ratio has led to criticism of the Court's use of data in *Exxon Shipping Co.* Consider the following discussion from Theodore Eisenberg, Michael Heise, & Martin T.

Wells, Variability in Punitive Damages: Empirically Assessing Exxon Shipping Co. v. Baker, 166 J. Institutional & Theoretical Econ. 5 (2010):

> As the compensatory award increases, so does the punitive award and it does so in a linear fashion in log-transformed dollars. Moreover, the figures show that the pattern is similar for both judges and juries. If lay juries generated awards that were too unpredictable, the figures suggest that the juries were no more unpredictable than professional judges. One's eye provides the essential linear relation between punitive and compensatory awards. And more formal regression analysis confirms the visual story.
>
> Not only do the figures show regularity in the punitive-compensatory relation, they show substantially more variation in that relation for low compensatory awards. The scatterplots in [Figure 1] show that for compensatory awards less than $10,000 (4 on the x-axis in the log 10 units used), there is little pattern to the punitive compensatory relation. The graphs and regression models in the *JELS* article that the Supreme Court relied on both provided information that might have tempered the Court's concern about unpredictability based on that article.
>
> Our revisiting of the figures and regression results from the *JELS* article relied on by the Court raises the question of how the mean and standard deviation relied on by the Court can be consistent with a portrait of punitive damages so different from the portrait the Court in *Exxon Shipping Co.* relied on to support the 1:1 punitive-compensatory ratio it imposed. One answer is that the Court did not appear to believe it was relying on a different portrait of punitive damages. The Court seemed to agree with the *JELS* article's conclusion that the punitive damages system was not out of control, as suggested by the Court's system-wide statements quoted above. But the Court's simultaneous reliance on the data to label a segment of punitive awards as unpredictable seems internally contradictory. How can the same data support a system sufficiently sober to lead the Court to chastise those claiming a system out of control *and* a system warranting the Court's intervention based on its conclusion about unpredictability?
>
> Although we are not privy to the Justices' thought process, and therefore cannot fully resolve the opinion's seeming internal contradiction, we believe we can provide some statistical insight into why the mean and standard deviation relied on by the Court do not support its concern about unpredictability. The short answer is that the detailed analysis in the *JELS* article more fully accounted for the relation between punitive and compensatory damages than did the summary statistics in [the table] that the Court relied on, while seemingly ignoring the rest of the *JELS* article that related to this issue. The key additional factor explored throughout the article was the importance of the level of the compensatory award. To show the importance of the compensatory

award level in assessing the mean and standard deviation relied on by the Court, Table [3] presents relevant summary statistics for jury cases with punitive and compensatory damages, but now stratified by the level of compensatory awards in the *JELS* article data.

Table 3. Stratifying the Punitive-Compensatory Ratio in Jury Trials by the Size of the Compensatory Award (Using the BJS data relied on in *Exxon Shipping Co.*)

Compensatory award range	Median punitive-compensatory ratio	Mean punitive-compensatory ratio	Punitive-compensatory standard deviation	Number of cases in award range
$0 to 999	24.69	101.47	175.44	11
$1k to 9,999	1.00	9.64	39.37	43
$10k to 99,999	0.56	1.68	3.58	162
$100k to 999,999	0.55	1.62	3.32	151
$1m to 9,999,999	0.42	1.46	3.71	57
$10m to <$100m	0.57	1.12	1.31	13
$100m or more	2.41	2.41	–	1

Notes. "k"=$1,000; "m"=$1 million. All amounts are in dollars inflation adjusted to 2001. Source. Bureau of Justice Statistics.

Table [3] suggests that all of the high mean and standard deviation that concerned the Court comes from cases with compensatory awards of less than $10,000. For cases with compensatory awards of less than $1,000, the table's fourth column shows that the punitive-compensatory ratio standard deviation was 175.44; for cases with compensatory awards from $1,000 to $9,999, the standard deviation was 39.37. But the standard deviation dramatically decreased for cases with compensatory awards of $10,000 or more and did not exceed 3.58 for any group of these compensatory awards. For cases with larger awards the mean ratio and its standard deviation were quite stable.

E. Blockbuster Punitive Awards

Large punitive awards, such as those in *Exxon Shipping Co.*, have been the subject of separate analysis.[i] With horror stories about punitive damages' high frequency and lack of relation to compensatory awards discredited, one of the last empirical frontiers is large punitive awards. It no longer is the mass of punitive awards that is said to be so troublesome. Rather it is the relative handful of extreme awards.

---

[i] This part of the note is based on Theodore Eisenberg & Martin T. Wells, The Significant Association Between Punitive and Compensatory Damages in Blockbuster Cases: A Methodological Primer, 3 J. Empirical Legal Studies 169 (2006).

Joni Hersch and W. Kip Viscusi (H-V) gathered data on the largest punitive damages awards, those in excess of $100 million. Joni Hersch & W. Kip Viscusi, Punitive Damages: How Judges and Juries Perform 33 J. Legal Stud. 1 (2004). Their analysis claimed that these "blockbuster" punitive damages awards bear no relation to compensatory awards. They studied the relation between punitive and compensatory awards in 63 tried cases decided from January 1985 to June 2003. The cases were collected using "a detailed search to identify all cases for which there were punitive damages of at least $100 million." During the same time period they found three bench trials resulting in a punitive damages award in excess of $100 million. Contrary to findings in several other data sets, H-V report no meaningful relation between punitive awards and compensatory awards in the same case. "Analysis of these very large awards indicates that they bear no statistical relation to the compensatory awards."

But traditional statistical methods, applied somewhat more rigorously than H-V apply them, reveal a reasonably strong association between punitive and compensatory damages, even in blockbuster cases. The core results can be summarized in Figure 2.[ii] Circles in the top and bottom parts of the figure indicate values obtained from statistical regression models that attempt to model the amount of the punitive award (the y-axes) as a function of the amount of the compensatory award (the x-axes). The x's in the figure indicate observed values: that is, each x represents an actual punitive and compensatory award in a case with a punitive award of at least $100 million. The text in the figure ("tobacco," "*Engle*" (a tobacco case), and "*Exxon*") designates specific cases. Each tobacco case is labeled. The straight lines in the figures represent the best-fitting regression lines that try to model the relation between the punitive award and the compensatory award.

A simple visual way to assess the models is to observe how close the predicted values (the circles) and the regression lines are to the actual values (the x's). The H-V analysis is shown in the bottom graph in the figure. It shows how poorly the H-V model fits the data and especially the tobacco cases. The predicted values in the bottom graph nowhere come close to the observed values. The top graph in the figure, which accounts for the distinctive nature of tobacco cases (high punitive awards per dollar of compensatory award) captures reasonably well the central tendencies in both the tobacco cases' awards and in the awards and in other cases. It is not surprising that the H-V model has such low explanatory power. It is poorly specified to fit the data. Their conclusion that there is no significant relation between large punitive awards and compensatory awards appears to be incorrect.

[ii] The top figure is based on a regression model that includes a dummy variable for tobacco and employs a skewness minimizing transformation that helps account for the arbitrarily selected floor of $100 million in the dependent variable in the H-V data. The lines in the top figure represent the best-fitting lines for the tobacco cases (tobacco dummy variable = 1 in the regression model) and non-tobacco cases (tobacco dummy variable = 0 in the regression model). The line in the bottom figure is for all cases combined and is based on a H-V model used to support the claim of no significant association between punitive and compensatory awards.

Figure 2. Comparison of Fit of Models
Eisenberg-Wells (top figure) & Hersch-Viscusi (bottom figure)

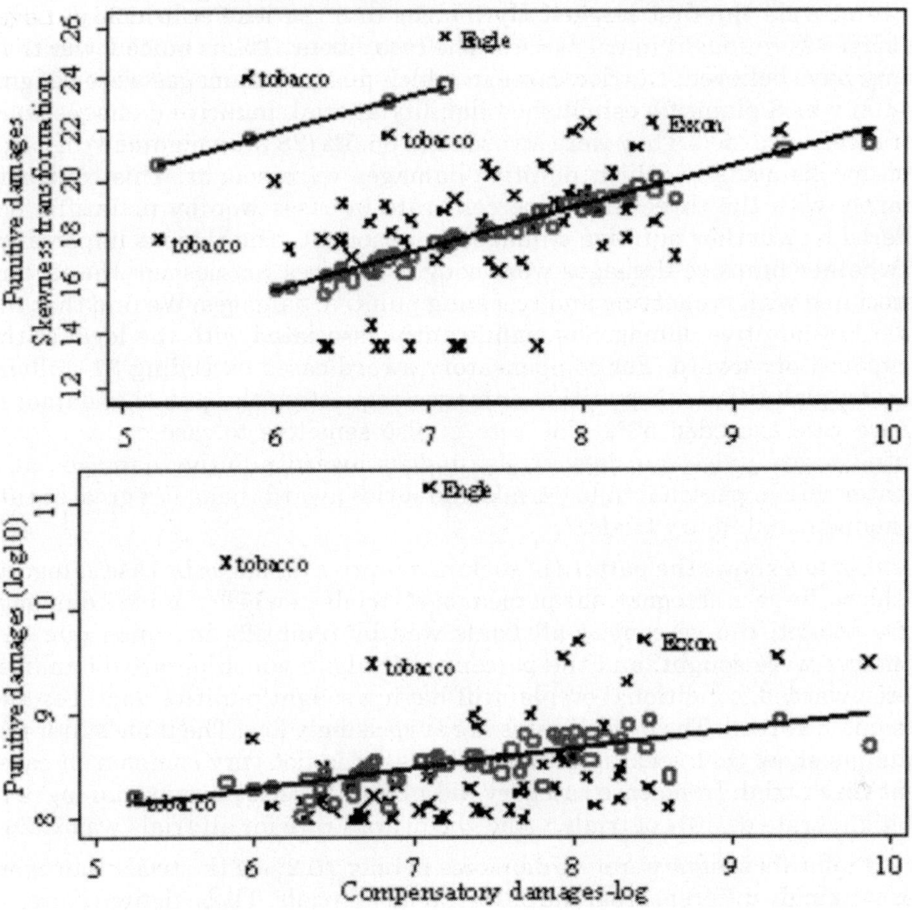

In later work, Viscusi effectively acknowledged the strong association between punitive and compensatory awards in blockbuster cases. Alison F. Del Rossi & W. Kip Viscusi, The Changing Landscape of Blockbuster Punitive Damages Awards, 12 Am. L. & Econ. Rev. 116 (2010).

2. Note on the Existence of Punitive Damages Awards[iii]

A limitation of most prior punitive damages studies is the absence of information about whether punitive damages were requested. An important data set from the National Center for State Courts (NCSC) and the Bureau of Justice Statistics (BJS) allows fuller exploration of whether punitive damages will be awarded. The data set, which consists of civil trials concluded in 156 counties in 2005, is the fourth in the NCSC-BJS series of Civil Justice Surveys dating back to cases terminated in 1991–92. In the 2005 iteration, the survey added a variable that recorded whether punitive damages were sought.

[iii] This note is based on Theodore Eisenberg, Michael Heise, Nicole L. Waters, & Martin T. Wells, The Decision to Award Punitive Damages, 2 J. Legal Analysis 577 (2010).

This single additional variable has opened the curtain on the rate at which punitive damages are awarded to an unprecedented extent. It enables us to provide the first large-study insight into the rate at which punitive damages were sought in tried cases. The rate, about 10%, is much lower than many have believed. In tried cases in which punitive damages were sought, and in which plaintiffs established liability at trial, punitive damages were not rarely awarded. They were awarded in 35.5% (28.5% weighted[iv]) of cases won by plaintiffs in which punitive damages were sought. This contrasts sharply with the three to five percent rate in cases won by plaintiffs, not filtered by whether punitive damages were sought. The obvious importance of whether punitive damages were sought requires reassessing the factors associated with requesting and receiving punitive damages. We find that the award of punitive damages is significantly associated with the level of the compensatory award. For compensatory award cases exceeding $1 million, won by plaintiffs with punitive damages requested, the punitive damages award rate exceeded 50%. The rate is also sensitive to case category and varies across judge and jury trials. Judges award punitive damages at a greater rate in personal injury trials and juries award them at a greater rate in nonpersonal injury trials.

Table 4 shows the pattern of seeking punitive damages by case category. It shows, by case category, the percent of all trials in which punitive damages were sought, the percent of all trials won by plaintiffs in which punitive damages were sought, and the percent of trials in which punitive damages were awarded, conditional on plaintiff having sought punitive damages and prevailed at trial. The overall rates are surprisingly low. The table's first two columns show that seeking punitive damages is not very common in cases that reach trial. In no case category did plaintiffs seek punitive damages in as high a rate as 40% of trials.[v] And the overall rate for all trials was 9.0%.

Plaintiffs sought punitive damages in only 10.2% of the trials they won, not strikingly different from the 9.0% rate in all trials. These figures increase to 11.5% and 13.1%, respectively, if one use probability weights to account for the different numbers of cases represented by the large and small county samples. The rate is somewhat depressed by the large motor vehicle category. Excluding motor vehicle cases, plaintiffs sought punitive damages in 398 of 2,768 trials they won, or 14.4%, which increases to 17.6% if one accounts for the sample design using probability weights. The table shows substantial heterogeneity across case categories. If one separates judge and jury trials, plaintiffs sought punitive damages in 9.3% (11.0% weighted) of judge-tried cases they won and 10.6% (14.1% weighted) of jury-tried cases they won.

[iv] Weighted results refer to rates that account for the sample design, which overrsampled cases from large counties relative to cases from smaller counties.

[v] The rate slightly exceeded 40% for "Employment discrimination" and "Intentional tort/tortious interference" when the data are weighted to reflect the differential sampling of large and small counties.

Table 4. Rates of Seeking and Obtaining Punitive Damages, by Case Category

Case category	All trials: Percent with punitives sought	N	Trials won by plaintiffs: Percent with punitives sought	N	Trials won by plaintiffs, punitives sought: Percent with punitive award	N
Slander, libel, defamation	38.9%	54	55.2%	29	60.0%	15
Employment – discrimination	32.8%	131	41.3%	63	25.0%	24
Intentional/tortious interference	32.4%	74	33.3%	48	43.8%	16
Conversion	26.9%	78	26.1%	46	66.7%	12
Employment – other	25.7%	183	26.0%	100	38.5%	26
False arrest / imprisonment	25.0%	24	0.0%	6	—	0
Fraud	24.8%	479	30.9%	278	39.3%	84
Intentional tort	23.6%	259	32.0%	128	65.8%	38
Other/unknown real property	20.6%	34	—	0	—	0
Partnership dispute	18.6%	43	24.2%	33	37.5%	8
Other/unknown contract/commercial	18.1%	94	22.0%	59	38.5%	13
Buyer plaintiff (contract)	13.9%	631	16.4%	384	27.4%	62
Title or boundary dispute	12.9%	171	—	0	—	0
Animal attack	12.5%	48	16.7%	36	0.0%	6
Malpractice - other prof'l	11.7%	77	8.1%	37	33.3%	3
Prod. liability – asbestos	11.3%	53	7.1%	28	100.0%	1
Prod liability – other	10.7%	122	2.6%	39	0.0%	1
Other negilgent act/unknown tort	9.9%	202	10.6%	104	36.4%	11
Rental/lease agreement	8.2%	184	7.2%	125	44.4%	9
Subrogation	7.4%	27	11.8%	17	50.0%	2
Malpractice - medical/dental	5.9%	972	7.4%	203	30.8%	13
Seller plaintiff (contract)	5.3%	873	4.8%	642	20.0%	30
Motor vehicle tort	3.3%	2,931	3.7%	1,778	20.3%	64
Premises liability	2.7%	853	2.9%	341	20.0%	10
Eminent domain/condemnation	0.0%	73	—	0	—	0
Mortgage foreclosure	0.0%	31	0.0%	22	—	0
Total	9.0%	8,701	10.2%	4,546	35.5%	448

Note. Table shows the rate at which punitive damages were sought in all trials, the rate at which punitive damages were sought in trials won by plaintiffs, and the rate at which punitive damages were obtained in trials won by plaintiffs in which punitive damages were sought. Source. NCSC-BJS 2005 Civil Justice Survey.

Table 5 shows, now subdivided by locale, the same information as Table 4, the rate at which punitive damages were sought for all trials, the rate at which they were sought in plaintiff wins, and the rate at which they were awarded when plaintiffs won at trial. The table treats as a single locale the 110 smaller counties not in the core Civil Justice Survey group of 46 large counties.

Both the mean and the median seeking rates, across the 47 locales, are less than 10% of all trials. In two counties (Santa Clara and Fulton), both with relatively few trials, the rate exceeded 30%. In seven additional counties, the rate exceeded 20%. Four of those counties, Los Angeles, San Francisco, Franklin, and Fairfax, had more than 100 trials. In 21 counties, the rate was less than 5% but three of these counties are in states that preclude or substantially constrain the award punitive damages.

Table 5. Rates of Seeking and Obtaining Punitive Damages, by Locale

	All trials		Trials won by plaintiffs		Trials won by plaintiffs, punitives sought	
Site	% with punitives sought	N	% with punitives sought	N	% with punitive award	N
Maricopa, AZ	10.3%	252	14.7%	116	23.5%	17
Pima, AZ	5.1%	79	6.5%	46	33.3%	3
Alameda, CA	16.1%	174	19.6%	97	52.6%	19
Contra Costa, CA	22.2%	27	33.3%	9	33.3%	3
Fresno, CA	1.9%	52	2.9%	35	0.0%	1

Table 5. Rates of Seeking and Obtaining Punitive Damages, by Locale

	All trials		Trials won by plaintiffs		Trials won by plaintiffs, punitives sought	
Site	% with punitives sought	N	% with punitives sought	N	% with punitive award	N
Los Angeles, CA	27.2%	379	32.3%	186	28.8%	59
Orange, CA	19.5%	272	24.8%	129	31.3%	32
San Bernardino, CA	17.4%	69	15.4%	39	0.0%	6
San Francisco, CA	21.7%	120	19.0%	63	41.7%	12
Santa Clara, CA	31.5%	54	36.0%	25	44.4%	9
Ventura, CA	15.4%	78	11.4%	35	75.0%	4
Fairfield, CT	6.9%	72	2.1%	48	100.0%	1
Hartford, CT	7.6%	79	4.5%	44	0.0%	2
Dade, FL	5.1%	195	4.2%	119	60.0%	5
Orange, FL	2.9%	70	5.6%	36	0.0%	1
Palm Beach, FL	1.7%	116	2.7%	73	50.0%	2
Fulton, GA	32.5%	40	45.5%	22	20.0%	10
Honolulu, HI	22.2%	18	30.0%	10	0.0%	3
Cook, IL	1.8%	675	2.7%	365	50.0%	10
DuPage, IL	12.3%	81	13.2%	53	42.9%	7
Marion, IN	1.6%	127	2.4%	85	0.0%	2
Jefferson, KY	5.5%	110	13.3%	45	50.0%	6
Essex, MA	1.8%	56	6.3%	16	100.0%	1
Middlesex, MA	2.0%	99	0.0%	27	—	0
Suffolk, MA	0.8%	121	2.8%	36	100.0%	1
Worcester, MA	0.0%	73	0.0%	18	—	0
Oakland, MI	2.0%	149	1.4%	74	—	0
Wayne, MI	0.0%	179	0.0%	69	—	0
Hennepin, MN	3.4%	179	5.3%	95	33.3%	3
St. Louis, MO	15.7%	140	13.4%	82	54.5%	11
Bergen, NJ	6.2%	161	7.0%	57	0.0%	4
Essex, NJ	3.0%	134	3.3%	61	50.0%	2
Middlesex, NJ	3.7%	219	3.7%	81	33.3%	3

Table 5. Rates of Seeking and Obtaining Punitive Damages, by Locale

	All trials		Trials won by plaintiffs		Trials won by plaintiffs, punitives sought	
Site	% with punitives sought	N	% with punitives sought	N	% with punitive award	N
New York, NY	4.7%	340	4.4%	160	16.7%	6
Cuyahoga, OH	5.7%	227	4.8%	124	83.3%	6
Franklin, OH	29.8%	131	20.4%	93	44.4%	18
Allegheny, PA	2.7%	220	4.3%	115	100.0%	3
Philadelphia, PA	4.1%	610	4.5%	356	18.8%	16
Bexar, TX	23.7%	76	39.4%	33	46.2%	13
Dallas, TX	3.0%	203	2.4%	84	50.0%	2
Harris, TX	4.3%	506	5.7%	261	66.7%	15
Fairfax, VA	20.9%	163	22.8%	101	43.5%	23
King, WA	1.5%	199	1.6%	127	0.0%	2
Milwaukee, WI	3.8%	131	2.5%	79	100.0%	2
Mecklenburg, NC	17.9%	39	11.5%	26	0.0%	3
El Paso, TX	7.7%	39	11.1%	27	66.7%	3
Total large counties	8.2%	7,533	9.3%	3,882	38.5%	351
smaller counties (110)	14.1%	1,168	15.4%	664	24.7%	97
Total	9.0%	8,701	10.2%	4,546	35.5%	448

Note. Table shows the rate at which punitive damages were sought in all trials, the rate at which punitive damages were sought in trials won by plaintiffs, and the rate at which punitive damages were obtained in trials won by plaintiffs in which punitive damages were sought. Source. NCSC-BJS 2005 Civil Justice Survey.

The last two columns in Tables 4 and 5 show that, in trials won by plaintiffs in which they sought punitive damages, the overall rate at which punitive damages were awarded was 35.5%. Accounting for the differential sampling of large and small counties yields an overall rate of 28.5%. These rates differ substantially from rates based on punitive awards in trials won by plaintiffs that do not account for whether punitive damages were sought. Since the tables' middle two numerical columns show punitive requests in only about 10% of plaintiff trial wins, failure to account for whether punitive damages were sought could be viewed as misstating the punitive damages award rate—the rate at which they are awarded when sought—by about a factor of 10.

Mathias v. Accor Economy Lodging, Inc.

United States Court of Appeals, Seventh Circuit, 2003.
347 F.3d 672.

■ POSNER, CIRCUIT JUDGE. The plaintiffs brought this diversity suit governed by Illinois law against affiliated entities . . . that own and operate the "Motel 6" chain of hotels and motels. One of these hotels . . . is in downtown Chicago. The plaintiffs, a brother and sister, were guests there and were bitten by bedbugs, which are making a comeback in the U.S. as a consequence of more conservative use of pesticides. The plaintiffs claim that in allowing guests to be attacked by bedbugs in a motel that charges upwards of $100 a day for a room and would not like to be mistaken for a flophouse, the defendant was guilty of "willful and wanton conduct" and thus under Illinois law is liable for punitive as well as compensatory damages. The jury agreed and awarded each plaintiff $186,000 in punitive damages though only $5,000 in compensatory damages. The defendant appeals, complaining primarily about the punitive-damages award. . . .

The defendant argues that at worst it is guilty of simple negligence, and if this is right the plaintiffs were not entitled by Illinois law to any award of punitive damages. It also complains that the award was excessive—indeed that any award in excess of $20,000 to each plaintiff would deprive the defendant of its property without due process of law. The first complaint has no possible merit, as the evidence of gross negligence, indeed of recklessness in the strong sense of an unjustifiable failure to avoid a *known* risk, was amply shown. In 1998, EcoLab, the extermination service that the motel used, discovered bedbugs in several rooms in the motel and recommended that it be hired to spray every room, for which it would charge the motel only $500; the motel refused. The next year, bedbugs were again discovered in a room but EcoLab was asked to spray just that room. The motel tried to negotiate "a building sweep [by EcoLab] free of charge," but, not surprisingly, the negotiation failed. By the spring of 2000, the motel's manager "started noticing that there were refunds being given by my desk clerks and reports coming back from the guests that there were ticks in the rooms and bugs in the rooms that were biting." She looked in some of the rooms and discovered bedbugs. The defendant asks us to disregard her testimony as that of a disgruntled ex-employee, but of course her credibility was for the jury, not the defendant, to determine.

Further incidents of guests being bitten by insects and demanding and receiving refunds led the manager to recommend to her superior in the company that the motel be closed while every room was sprayed, but this was refused. This superior, a district manager, was a management-level employee of the defendant, and his knowledge of the risk and failure to take effective steps either to eliminate it or to warn the motel's guests are imputed to his employer for purposes of determining whether the employer should be liable for punitive damages. . . .

The infestation continued and began to reach farcical proportions, as when a guest, after complaining of having been bitten repeatedly by insects while asleep in his room in the hotel, was moved to another room only to discover insects there; and within 18 minutes of being moved to a third room he discovered insects in that room as well and had to be moved still again. (Odd that at that point he didn't flee the motel.) By July, the motel's management was acknowledging to EcoLab that there was a "major problem with bed bugs" and that all that was being done about it was "chasing them from room to room." Desk clerks were instructed to call the "bedbugs" "ticks," apparently on the theory that customers would be less alarmed, though in fact ticks are more dangerous than bedbugs because they spread Lyme Disease and Rocky Mountain Spotted Fever. Rooms that the motel had placed on "Do not rent, bugs in room" status nevertheless were rented.

It was in November that the plaintiffs checked into the motel. They were given Room 504, even though the motel had classified the room as "DO NOT RENT UNTIL TREATED," and it had not been treated. Indeed, that night 190 of the hotel's 191 rooms were occupied, even though a number of them had been placed on the same don't-rent status as Room 504. One of the defendant's motions in limine that the judge denied was to exclude evidence concerning all other rooms—a good example of the frivolous character of the motions and of the defendant's pertinacious defense of them on appeal.

Although bedbug bites are not as serious as the bites of some other insects, they are painful and unsightly. Motel 6 could not have rented any rooms at the prices it charged had it informed guests that the risk of being bitten by bedbugs was appreciable. Its failure either to warn guests or to take effective measures to eliminate the bedbugs amounted to fraud and probably to battery as well .... There was, in short, sufficient evidence of "willful and wanton conduct" within the meaning that the Illinois courts assign to the term to permit an award of punitive damages in this case.

But in what amount? In arguing that $20,000 was the maximum amount of punitive damages that a jury could constitutionally have awarded each plaintiff, the defendant points to the U.S. Supreme Court's recent statement that "few awards [of punitive damages] exceeding a single-digit ratio between punitive and compensatory damages, to a significant degree, will satisfy due process." State Farm Mutual Automobile Insurance Co. *v.* Campbell, 538 U.S. 408 (2003). The Court went on to suggest that "four times the amount of compensatory damages might be close to the line of constitutional impropriety." *Id.*, citing Pacific Mutual Life Insurance Co. *v.* Haslip, 499 U.S. 1, 23–24 (1991), and BMW of North America, Inc. *v.* Gore, 517 U.S. 559, 581 (1996). The ratio of punitive to compensatory damages determined by the jury was, in contrast, 37.2 to 1.

The Supreme Court did not, however, lay down a 4-to-1 or single-digit-ratio rule-it said merely that "there is a presumption against an award that has a 145-to-1 ratio"—and it would be unreasonable to do so. We must consider why punitive damages are awarded and why the Court has decided that due process requires that such awards be limited. The second question is easier to answer than the first. The term "punitive damages" implies punishment, and a standard principle of penal theory is that "the punishment should fit the crime" in the sense of being proportional to the wrongfulness of the defendant's action, though the principle is modified when the probability of detection is very low (a familiar example is the heavy fines for littering) or the crime is potentially lucrative (as in the case of trafficking in illegal drugs). Hence, with these qualifications, which in fact will figure in our analysis of this case, punitive damages should be proportional to the wrongfulness of the defendant's actions.

Another penal precept is that a defendant should have reasonable notice of the sanction for unlawful acts, so that he can make a rational determination of how to act; and so there have to be reasonably clear standards for determining the amount of punitive damages for particular wrongs.

And a third precept, the core of the Aristotelian notion of corrective justice, and more broadly of the principle of the rule of law, is that sanctions should be based on the wrong done rather than on the status of the defendant; a person is punished for what he does, not for who he is, even if the who is a huge corporation.

What follows from these principles, however, is that punitive damages should be admeasured by standards or rules rather than in a completely ad hoc manner, and this does not tell us what the maximum ratio of punitive to compensatory damages should be in a particular case. To determine that, we have to consider why punitive damages are awarded in the first place.

England's common law courts first confirmed their authority to award punitive damages in the eighteenth century, see Dorsey D. Ellis, Jr., "Fairness and Efficiency in the Law of Punitive Damages," 56 S. Cal. L. Rev. 1, 12–20 (1982), at a time when the institutional structure of criminal law enforcement was primitive and it made sense to leave certain minor crimes to be dealt with by the civil law. And still today one function of punitive-damages awards is to relieve the pressures on an overloaded system of criminal justice by providing a civil alternative to criminal prosecution of minor crimes. An example is deliberately spitting in a person's face, a criminal assault but because minor readily deterrable by the levying of what amounts to a civil fine through a suit for damages for the tort of battery. Compensatory damages would not do the trick in such a case, and this for three reasons: because they are difficult to determine in the case of acts that inflict largely dignitary harms; because in the spitting case they would be too slight to give the victim an incentive to sue, and he might decide instead to respond with violence—and an age-old purpose of the law of torts is to provide a substitute for violent retaliation against wrongful injury—and because to limit the plaintiff to compensatory damages would enable the defendant to commit the offensive act with impunity provided that he was willing to pay, and again there would be a danger that his act would incite a breach of the peace by his victim.

When punitive damages are sought for billion-dollar oil spills and other huge economic injuries, the considerations that we have just canvassed fade. As the Court emphasized in *Campbell,* the fact that the plaintiffs in that case had been awarded very substantial compensatory damages—$1 million for a dispute over insurance coverage—greatly reduced the need for giving them a huge award of punitive damages ($145 million) as well in order to provide an effective remedy. Our case is closer to the spitting case. The defendant's behavior was outrageous but the compensable harm done was slight and at the same time difficult to quantify because a large element of it was emotional. And the defendant may well have profited from its misconduct because by concealing the infestation it was able to keep renting rooms. Refunds were frequent but may have cost less than the cost of closing the hotel for a thorough fumigation. The hotel's attempt to pass off the bedbugs as ticks, which some guests might ignorantly have thought less unhealthful, may have postponed the instituting of litigation to rectify the hotel's misconduct. The award of punitive damages in this case thus serves the additional purpose of limiting the defendant's ability to profit from its fraud by escaping detection and (private) prosecution. If a tortfeasor is "caught" only half the time he commits torts, then when he is caught he should be punished twice as heavily in order to make up for the times he gets away.

Finally, if the total stakes in the case were capped at $50,000 (2 x [$5,000 + $20,000]), the plaintiffs might well have had difficulty financing this lawsuit. It is here that the defendant's aggregate net worth of $1.6 billion becomes relevant. A defendant's wealth is not a sufficient basis for awarding punitive damages. That would be discriminatory and would violate the rule of law, as we explained earlier, by making punishment depend on status rather than conduct. Where wealth in the sense of resources enters is in enabling the defendant to mount an extremely aggressive defense against suits such as this and by doing so to make litigating against it very costly, which in turn may make it difficult for the plaintiffs to find a lawyer willing to handle their case, involving as it does only modest stakes, for the usual 33–40 percent contingent fee.

In other words, the defendant is investing in developing a reputation intended to deter plaintiffs. It is difficult otherwise to explain the great stubbornness with which it has defended this case, making a host of frivolous evidentiary arguments despite the very modest stakes even when the punitive damages awarded by the jury are included.

As a detail (the parties having made nothing of the point), we note that "net worth" is not the correct measure of a corporation's resources. It is an accounting artifact that reflects the allocation of ownership between equity and debt claimants. A firm financed largely by equity investors has a large "net worth" (= the value of the equity claims), while the identical firm financed largely by debt may have only a small net worth because accountants treat debt as a liability.

All things considered, we cannot say that the award of punitive damages was excessive, albeit the precise number chosen by the jury was arbitrary. It is probably not a coincidence that $5,000 + $186,000 = $191,000/191 = $1,000: *i.e.*, $1,000 per room in the hotel. But as there are no punitive-damages guidelines, corresponding to the federal and state sentencing guidelines, it is inevitable that the specific amount of punitive damages awarded whether by a judge or by a jury will be arbitrary. (Which is perhaps why the plaintiffs' lawyer did not suggest a number to the jury.) The judicial function is to police a range, not a point. . . .

Owens-Corning Fiberglas Corp. v. Malone

Supreme Court of Texas, 1998.
972 S.W.2d 35.

■ BAKER, JUSTICE, delivered the opinion of the Court.

[For approximately 30 years, Owens-Corning Fiberglas Corporation (OCF) manufactured and marketed Kaylo, an insulation product containing asbestos. In 1972, it removed asbestos from Kaylo after it became evident that exposure to asbestos dust caused mesothelioma, a deadly cancer of the lining of the chest, and other lung diseases. Evidence indicated that OCF knew of the dangers of asbestos long before it discontinued its use but concealed this information from the public.

[The portion of the court's opinion reprinted here responds to OCF's appeal of a judgment for $1.6 million in compensatory damages and $3.7 million in punitive damages, rendered after a consolidated trial of four individual claims.]

OCF argues that continued punitive damage awards for the same course of conduct violate substantive due process because the punishment and deterrence objectives underlying punitive damages have already been achieved by previous punitive damage awards for that course of conduct. OCF contends that because no legitimate purpose is served by additional punitive damage awards against it for manufacturing and distributing Kaylo, continued punitive damage awards, including the ones here, are irrational and arbitrary in violation of the Due Process Clause.

Answering this constitutional argument is no easy task. . . . Of the many courts that have faced this challenge, only one has expressly held that multiple awards of punitive damages for the same conduct violate a defendant's due process rights. Other courts faced with this argument have rejected it for five principal reasons.

First, courts have rejected due process challenges to multiple punitive damage awards by holding that procedural safeguards provide all the protection that is necessary. However, we believe that courts must consider multiple punitive damage awards for the same conduct against a party's substantive due process rights. . . .

Second, some courts have rejected substantive due process challenges out of parochial concerns. These courts reason that a court-imposed limit on punitive damage awards will only affect claimants within their own jurisdiction, prejudicing those claimants and only providing minimal or arbitrary relief to defendants.

Third, courts have rejected OCF's argument to avoid what those courts perceive as inequitable results. . . .

Erecting a constitutional barrier to additional punitive damages awards against a particular defendant for the same course of conduct may, to some extent, allow only those plaintiffs who win the "race to the courthouse" to recover punitive damages. However, punitive damages are not designed to compensate individuals, but are only intended to punish tortious conduct and to deter its repetition. Therefore, when engaging in a substantive due process analysis of multiple punitive damage awards for the same conduct, courts should focus on the defendant's due process rights and whether the twin aims of punishment and deterrence have been adequately served rather than on plaintiffs' remedies.

Fourth, some courts have decided that no single court is capable of crafting an acceptable solution to the national problem of multiple punitive damages in mass tort litigation, and have suggested that legislative action is the answer.

It may be that a truly uniform solution can only be fashioned by either the Supreme Court or Congress. Nevertheless, the difficulty or enormity of the task does not grant us leave to avoid OCF's properly preserved due process challenge under applicable constitutional principles and to ensure that its due process rights are not violated. . . .

Finally, courts have rejected due process challenges to multiple punitive damage awards not because such challenges are necessarily unsound as a matter of constitutional law, but because the defendant failed to preserve error on the issue, there was not an adequate record to show a due process violation, or, whatever limits due process may impose on multiple punitive damage awards, that limit clearly was not surpassed on the facts presented.

Although we recognize that other courts have struggled with the issue and have discussed valid reasons for rejecting OCF's due process challenge, we join the courts and commentators that have acknowledged that repeatedly imposing punitive damages on the same defendant for the same course of wrongful conduct may implicate substantive due process constraints. . . .

[A] successful substantive due process challenge under an aggregate punitive damages award theory, that such a challenge can properly be evaluated only if the defendant develops a sufficient record. In a posttrial review to decide whether a punitive damages award, when aggregated with previously paid punitive damage awards for the same course of conduct, is unconstitutionally excessive, trial courts may consider evidence beyond what is admissible during the trial. After the trial, the danger of unfair prejudice, confusion of the issues, or misleading the jury no longer exists. . . .

First, and most important, a court should give considerable weight to the degree of reprehensibility of the defendant's conduct. . . . [T]he court of appeals upheld the trial court's judgment finding that OCF's conduct demonstrated indifference to the health and safety of others for many years. This finding weighs in favor of allowing additional punitive damages awards against OCF. . . .

Second, a court should examine the profitability of the wrongful conduct. The $3 million in punitive damage awards previously paid by OCF[7] is double the amount of profits OCF claims it earned from its Kaylo sales. Punitive damages, however, are not necessarily confined to the amount of profits. Where evidence shows that product sales resulted in widespread and devastating injuries and little profit in relation to the seller's overall financial condition, merely taking away that profit may or may not impose much punishment on the seller. . . . [B]ecause Kaylo sales approximated only 2 percent of OCF's total sales, and an even smaller percentage of its total profits, "Kaylo profits do not provide an accurate indication of the likely punitive impact of a punitive damage award against OCF." Thus, the evidence about the profits, or lack thereof, from OCF's Kaylo sales does not support OCF's due process argument.

Third, because courts should ensure that punitive damage awards do not exceed an amount necessary to accomplish society's goals of punishment and deterrence, a court should examine the defendant's financial position. Here, the trial court and the court of appeals . . . determined that OCF's financial position is not so precarious that further punitive damages awards against it should be disallowed. We agree. The evidence reveals that OCF is a solvent, healthy company. In 1993, shortly before this case was tried, OCF reported to its shareholders that "[a]t the end of 1991, our company was valued by the market at $932 million; 12 months later, the market value of the company was in excess of $1.5 billion, an increase of 60%!" Moreover, in March 1993, OCF reported to

[7] At oral argument, OCF pointed out that since the trial court rendered judgment here, at least $14 million in punitive damages has been levied against it in other cases involving Kaylo. Also, in its briefing, OCF indicated that "[t]ens of millions of dollars in punitive damages already have been awarded against Owens-Corning for the company's involvement with Kaylo." However, these awards do not factor into our analysis because they are not part of the trial court record. Consequently, there is no proof that these awards have actually been paid.

the SEC that "the additional uninsured and unreserved costs which may arise out of pending personal injury and property damages asbestos claims and additional similar asbestos claims filed in the future will not have a materially adverse effect on the Company's financial position." Thus, we cannot say that the prior paid punitive damage awards against OCF, combined with the punitive damage awards here, have exceeded the goals of punishment and deterrence.

OCF has not shown that the aggregate punitive damage awards against it have exceeded the "twin goals of punishment and deterrence underlying such awards" to constitute a violation of its substantive due process rights. . . .

CHAPTER 16

REMEDIAL DEFENSES

There are several ways in which defenses might properly be characterized as remedial. First, the defense may be based on a background rule that prevents the plaintiff from seeking relief although the substantive doctrinal requirements for legal liability are met. Statutes of limitations belong in this category. The defense of estoppel also fits this description: the plaintiff has a valid claim on the merits, but has acted in a way that makes it unfair to assert the claim.

Second, the defense may bar some, but not all, of the remedies normally available for violation of the plaintiff's substantive right. The most common examples are equitable defenses, meaning defenses that operate to deny the plaintiff equitable remedies, but not legal remedies.

The following materials illustrate both types of remedial defenses.

A. GENERALLY APPLICABLE REMEDIAL DEFENSES

1. STATUTES OF LIMITATIONS

A typical statute of limitations provides that certain types of claims are barred if they are not filed within a designated time after the cause of action first accrued. In an ordinary case, the cause of action accrues at the time of injury, although there are situations in which the time of the defendant's injurious act is not the same as the time the plaintiff suffers harm. The statute may also spell out "tolling" rules that delay the beginning of the limitations period. In addition, courts may invoke "equitable" tolling rules or interpret the statute in ways that soften the impact of the statute in certain circumstances.

In addition to statutes of limitation, there is a special defense about timeliness that can be raised against equitable claims. It is the defense of laches, and is discussed below in Section B (Equitable Defenses).

In re Swine Flu Products Liability Litigation

United States Court of Appeals, Ninth Circuit, 1985.
764 F.2d 637.

■ FARRIS, CIRCUIT JUDGE. Monte Sanborn appeals the grant of summary judgment in the District Court of Idaho, Callister, J., in which the district court found that Sanborn's wrongful death claim was time-barred. Sanborn had brought a Federal Tort Claims Act wrongful death and survival action against the United States and Wyeth Laboratories, the administrator and the manufacturer of the swine flu vaccine which allegedly resulted in the death of Sanborn's wife. The district court dismissed both claims as time-barred; Sanborn appeals only the wrongful death claim.

Sanborn's wife Edna was vaccinated under the National Swine Flu Immunization Program in Idaho on or about December 12, 1976. The United States suspended the immunization program on December 16, 1976, after reports in the medical literature indicated a link between the vaccine and Guillain-Barre Syndrome, a rare neurological disease. Mrs. Sanborn died on January 4, 1977; an autopsy did not reveal the cause of death.

Apart from a single post-autopsy consultation with Dr. Donndelinger, the county coroner who supervised the autopsy, Sanborn took no steps to discover the cause of his wife's death until August 1979, when he then read a magazine article describing a link between the swine flu vaccination and GBS. In January 1980, he read a second article in his local newspaper describing a suit brought by a woman who had allegedly contracted GBS after receiving the swine flu vaccine. On May 2, 1980, Sanborn filed an administrative claim with the U.S. Public Health Service; he subsequently brought suit in federal district court.

The district court dismissed Sanborn's claim on two grounds. The court held that a FTCA wrongful death claim "accrues" on the date of death .... Alternatively, the court found that even if the medical malpractice "discovery rule" governed, Sanborn's claim was barred for failure to bring suit within two years of the time that he knew, or in the exercise of reasonable diligence should have known, of his wife's injuries and their cause. . . .

We first decide whether Sanborn's claim "accrued" 1) at the time of his wife's death, or 2) at the time when he discovered, or in the exercise of reasonable diligence should have discovered, both the injury and the cause of his wife's death. There is general agreement that a medical malpractice claim does not accrue under the FTCA until the plaintiff discovers, or reasonably should have discovered, his injury and its causes. . . .

In all of these cases applying the discovery rule, the traditional tort rule that a claim accrues at the time of injury has been supplanted because "the nature of the tort itself and the character of the injury will frequently prevent knowledge of what is wrong, so that the plaintiff is forced to rely upon what he is told by the physician." United States *v.* Kubrick, 444 U.S. 111, 120 n. 7 (1979). . . . [I]t is not until he learns of both the fact of injury and its cause that the malpractice plaintiff falls "on the same footing as any negligence plaintiff." Davis *v.* United States, 642 F.2d 328, 330–331 (9th Cir. 1981).

The rationale of the medical malpractice discovery rule is fully applicable to Sanborn's wrongful death claim. On the date of Mrs. Sanborn's death the medical and general communities were still ascertaining whether a GBS victim even had any rights against the manufacturer and administrator of the swine flu vaccine. We do not ignore the traditional concerns that a claim be time-barred when "evidence has been lost, memories have faded, and witnesses have disappeared." Order of Railroad Telegraphers *v.* Railway Express Agency, 321 U.S. 342, 349 (1944). But under these facts, fundamental fairness concerns must prevail. . . .

The dispositive issue becomes whether Sanborn knew or should have reasonably discovered the cause of his wife's death prior to May 2, 1978—two years before he actually filed an administrative claim with the government. . . . Because there is no evidence that Sanborn actually knew of the cause, the government's statute of limitations defense ultimately turns on whether Sanborn failed to exercise due diligence. "[W]hat constitutes due diligence is necessarily a case-by-case determination. For example, mere temporal proximity of the negligent act to the illness is not alone determinative." Mann *v.* A.H. Robins Co., 741 F.2d 79, 82 n.2 (5th Cir. 1984) (applying Texas law in Dalkon Shield case).

The question whether Sanborn should have reasonably discovered the cause of his wife's death will turn on two issues of fact. . . .

A. Press reports in the general community.

The government notes that reports appeared in the medical literature in late 1976 and early 1977 connecting swine flu vaccinations with neurological problems, and that the vaccination program itself was suspended approximately one week after Mrs. Sanborn was inoculated. The suspension of the program was reported widely in the press, including in the December 17 and 18, 1976 issues of the Idaho *Statesman,* a newspaper servicing Sanborn's community. The government argues that because of these press reports, Sanborn should have "reasonably known" of the cause of his wife's death.

There are two difficulties with holding Sanborn, as a matter of law, to the alleged general community awareness. First, no record has yet been developed to indicate the extent to which Sanborn's immediate community in fact was made aware of the causal connection between the vaccine and GBS-like symptoms. Although Dr. Gabrielson, who treated Mrs. Sanborn while she was alive, was aware in early 1977 that the vaccination program had been suspended because of a possible connection to neurological disease, the county coroner himself was apparently sufficiently oblivious to the dangers of the vaccine that he did not advise Sanborn, when directly asked in February 1977, of a possible link to Mrs. Sanborn's death. The record reflects a genuine dispute over a material fact: the extent of community knowledge during the period Sanborn could properly have brought suit.

Even if the facts indisputably demonstrate some community awareness of the dangers underlying the swine flu program, we have recently held that a series of press releases, accompanied by "Dear

Doctor" letters to over 200,000 physicians, did not put a plaintiff who had suffered injuries arising out of her use of the Dalkon Shield intrauterine device on notice for purposes of the discovery rule. See Allen *v.* A.H. Robins, 752 F.2d 1365, 1370–71 (9th Cir. 1985). We instead found accrual on the date when the plaintiff viewed a "60 Minutes" program which discussed the Dalkon Shield's dangers. Sanborn cannot be held accountable as a matter of law for press accounts in late 1976 or 1977. See also McGowan *v.* University of Scranton, 759 F.2d 287, 303 (3d Cir. 1985) (reversing grant of summary judgment when unclear whether press reports on "toxic shock syndrome" should reasonably have led to plaintiff's discovery of cause of her infection); O'Brien *v.* Eli Lilly & Co., 668 F.2d 704, 710 (3d Cir. 1982) (claim accrued when plaintiff actually read articles indicating link of diethylstilbestrol to cancer). Additional fact-finding is necessary to determine whether the general community awareness was sufficient to find that Sanborn should reasonably have known of the cause of his wife's death.

B. The county coroner's assurances.

Sanborn avers that when he asked the county coroner whether the swine flu vaccine could have contributed to his wife's death, the coroner—who had not personally performed the autopsy—told him that any symptoms would have appeared immediately after the inoculation and would not have been delayed as long as they had been in Mrs. Sanborn's case. Furthermore, the coroner suggested that Mrs. Sanborn's long history of tranquilizer use, her weakened heart, and a possible viral infection led to her death. Sanborn argues that a "reasonable person" would have been discouraged, as he was, from inquiring any further; the government contends that a reasonable person would have consulted other medical or legal personnel, particularly when the autopsy did not disclose the cause of death.

Several circuits have suggested that "where a claimant is given a 'credible explanation' of his condition not pointing to malpractice, he may not be found to have failed to exercise reasonable diligence because he did not earlier pursue his claim." Exnicious *v.* United States, 563 F.2d 418, 421 (10th Cir. 1977). Whether Sanborn acted reasonably in failing to make additional inquiries is a genuine issue of material fact.

The government also argues that the coroner was never informed of Mrs. Sanborn's symptoms and thus could not have been expected to connect them with the vaccine. This contention merely underscores the existence of the issue. Whether Sanborn had reason to know that the coroner was ignorant of Mrs. Sanborn's physical condition and withheld discussion of her symptoms, or whether Sanborn merely relied on the knowledge which one would naturally presume the coroner to possess in discussing a particular autopsy, is an issue that can only be resolved after additional fact-finding.[2]

It is disputable whether Sanborn should reasonably have discovered the causal connection between the vaccine and his wife's death. Because this issue is one of fact for the jury, summary judgment should not have been granted. . . .

NOTE

Jane Doe was a student in a parochial high school from 1967 to 1971; Jane Roe was a student in the same school from 1968 to 1972. In 1994, Doe and Roe sued the school and its chaplain, charging the chaplain with, among other things, rape, battery, and forced prostitution. They argued that the running of the statute of limitations should be based on the discovery rule, which Maryland courts had adopted in various contexts. They claimed further that they did not discover the cause of action until 1992, when they began to recover "repressed memories" of the abuse in the course of therapy. The court affirmed summary judgment in favor of the defendants:

> "We find that the critical question to the determination of the applicability of the discovery rule to lost memory cases is whether there is a difference between forgetting and repression. It is crystal clear that in a suit in which a plaintiff 'forgot' and later 'remembered' the existence of a cause of action beyond the 3-year limitations period, that suit would be time-barred. Dismissal of such a case reflects our judgment that the potential plaintiff had 'slumbered on his rights,' should have known of his cause of action, and was blameworthy. To permit a forgetful plaintiff to maintain an action would vitiate the statute of limitations and deny repose for all defendants.
>
> "Plaintiffs in this case, however, claim that in order to avoid the pain associated with recalling the abuse they suffered, their memories were 'repressed," not merely 'forgotten,' and later 'recovered,' rather than 'remembered.' They argue that this difference renders them 'blamelessly ignorant' and excuses their failure to file suit in a timely manner. . . .
>
> "First, the adversaries of repression stress that there is no empirical, scientific evidence to support the claims that repression exists. The studies purporting to validate repression theory are justly criticized as unscientific, unrepresentative, and biased. . . .
>
> "Second, critics of repression theory point out that the scientific, and specifically, the psychological community has not

---

2 The government also argues that because Dr. Gabrielson, who treated Mrs. Sanborn prior to her death, was aware of a possible link between GBS and neurological disease, Sanborn "should have" questioned Dr. Gabrielson, since he would then have learned the probable cause of his wife's death. This argument misconstrues the "should have reasonably known" standard, which looks not to the likelihood that a plaintiff would in fact have discovered the cause of his injury if he had only inquired, but instead focuses on whether the plaintiff could reasonably have been expected to make the inquiry in the first place.

embraced repression theory, and that, in fact, serious disagreement exists. . . .

"Finally, critics of repression theory argue that the 'refreshing' or 'recovery' of 'repressed' memories is more complicated than repression proponents would have us believe. This argument takes two forms: (1) that memories refreshed with the assistance of a mental health professional are subject to manipulations reflecting the biases of the treating professional; and (2) that a repressed memory cannot be retrieved whole and intact from the cold storage of repression. . . .

"After reviewing the arguments on both sides of the issue, we are unconvinced that repression exists as a phenomenon separate and apart from the normal process of forgetting. Because we find these two processes to be indistinguishable scientifically, it follows that they should be treated the same legally. Therefore we hold that the mental process of repression of memories of past sexual abuse does not activate the discovery rule. The plaintiffs' suits are thus barred by the statute of limitations. If the General Assembly should wish to rewrite the law, that is its prerogative and responsibility."

Doe *v.* Maskell, 342 Md. 684, 691–96 (1996).

Addison v. State

Supreme Court of California, 1978.
21 Cal.3d 313.

■ RICHARDSON, JUSTICE. . . . The [California] Tort Claims Act describes the specific steps which must be taken before a civil action for money or damages may be brought against a public entity. First, plaintiff must present a claim to the appropriate agency within 100 days after accrual of the cause of action. Thereafter, the agency has 45 days within which to accept or reject the claim. If the claim is rejected in writing, plaintiff has six months thereafter within which to bring a court action. It has been held that "The prescribed statutes of limitations for commencement of actions against the state are mandatory and must be strictly complied with. . . ." (Chase *v.* State of California, 67 Cal. App. 3d 808, 812 (1977).) As will appear, however, occasionally and in special situations, the foregoing statutory procedure does not preclude application of the equitable tolling doctrine, the purpose of which is to soften the harsh impact of technical rules which might otherwise prevent a good faith litigant from having a day in court. . . .

Plaintiffs, whose business was the sale of automobiles at auction, were investigated by state and county officials for allegedly fraudulent practices in the conduct of these sales. On March 11, 1975, officers of the Department of Motor Vehicles and the deputy district attorney of Santa Clara County allegedly entered plaintiffs' place of business in San Jose and, pursuant to a search warrant, seized numerous records. . . . Defendants publicized this raid and made available to the news media the contents of the warrant and supporting affidavits. Plaintiffs assert that defendants' action was improper and constituted defamation, abuse of process, and conversion.

Plaintiffs filed timely damage claims with both the state and county pursuant to the provisions of the Tort Claims Act referred to above. These claims were rejected . . . . Each letter of rejection included the admonition required by the act that: "WARNING. . . you have only six (6) months from the date (of service of this notice) to file a *court action* on this claim."

Three and one-half months later, on September 11, 1975, plaintiffs filed a complaint in the United States District Court, Northern District of California, alleging both a federal civil rights violation and, on the basis of the federal court's pendent jurisdiction, the state law causes of action for defamation, conversion, and abuse of process for which claims had been filed and rejected. On November 26, 1975, defendants moved to dismiss this action for lack of jurisdiction. On February 9, 1976, plaintiffs, anticipating an adverse ruling on the motion, filed their complaint in the present Santa Clara County action. The federal court granted the motion to dismiss on February 17, 1976, after determining that a federal civil rights action would not lie against public entities. Having dismissed the federal causes of action, the court decided not to retain the state causes of action and dismissed them, allegedly without prejudice to refiling in state court.

It is fundamental that the primary purpose of statutes of limitation is to prevent the assertion of stale claims by plaintiffs who have failed to file their action until evidence is no longer fresh and witnesses are no longer available. . . . The statutes, accordingly, serve a distinct public purpose, preventing the assertion of demands which through the unexcused lapse of time, have been rendered difficult or impossible to defend. However, courts have adhered to a general policy which favors relieving plaintiff from the bar of a limitations statute when, possessing several legal remedies he, reasonably and in good faith, pursues one designed to lessen the extent of his injuries or damage.

[I]n Elkins *v.* Derby, 12 Cal.3d 410 (1974), we unanimously held that the statute of limitations on a personal injury action is tolled while plaintiff asserts a workers' compensation remedy against defendant. In such a case, we noted, defendant can claim no substantial prejudice, having received timely notice of possible tort liability upon filing of the compensation claim, and having ample opportunity to gather defense evidence in the event a court action ultimately is filed. We also noted the long settled rule that whenever exhaustion of administrative remedies is a prerequisite to a civil action the running of the limitations period is suspended during the administrative proceedings and we stated that "regardless of whether the exhaustion of one remedy is a prerequisite to the pursuit of another, if the defendant is not prejudiced thereby, the running of the limitations period is tolled '[w]hen an injured person has several legal remedies and, reasonably and in good faith, pursues one.' "

Similarly, in Bollinger *v.* National Fire Insurance Co., 25 Cal.2d 399 (1944), plaintiff had filed in a timely manner a previous action against an insurer but the action had been improperly dismissed as premature under the terms of the insurance policy. Plaintiff promptly filed a new action, but by then the period of limitations had run. Nevertheless, we allowed the action, based upon the broad policy which is implicit in Code of Civil Procedure . . . , permitting the plaintiff to file a new action within one year if a judgment in his favor is reversed on appeal.

The rule announced in *Bollinger* is a general equitable one which operates independently of the literal wording of the Code of Civil Procedure. As we observed in that case: "[T]his court is not powerless to formulate rules of procedure where justice demands it. Indeed, it has shown itself ready to adapt rules of procedure to serve the ends of justice where technical forfeitures would unjustifiably prevent a trial on the merits."

As demonstrated by *Bollinger* and *Elkins,* application of the doctrine of equitable tolling requires timely notice, and lack of prejudice, to the defendant, and reasonable and good faith conduct on the part of the plaintiff. These elements seemingly are present here. As noted, the federal court, without prejudice, declined to assert jurisdiction over a timely filed state law cause of action and plaintiffs thereafter promptly asserted that cause in the proper state court. . . .

Furthermore, since the federal court action was timely filed, defendants were notified of the action and had the opportunity to begin gathering their evidence and preparing their defense. No prejudice to defendants is shown, for plaintiffs' state court action was filed within one week of the dismissal of the federal suit. To apply the doctrine of equitable tolling in this case, in our view, satisfies the policy underlying the statute of limitations without ignoring the competing policy of avoiding technical and unjust forfeitures. . . .

As with other general equitable principles, application of the equitable tolling doctrine requires a balancing of the injustice to the plaintiff occasioned by the bar of his claim against the effect upon the important public interest or policy expressed by the Tort Claims Act limitations statute.

In our view, the balance in this case must be struck in plaintiffs' favor. If the tolling doctrine were not applied, plaintiffs would be denied a hearing on the merits of their claim. The doctrine's application, on the other hand, should not substantially undermine the policy of prompt resolution of claims. As we have noted, plaintiffs filed their state court action within nine months after their right to sue arose and by reason of the federal suit, defendants were fully notified within the six-month statutory period of plaintiffs' claims and their intent to litigate. Defendants were informed at all times of the nature of plaintiffs' claims. Any delay resulting from plaintiffs' original erroneous choice of forum was minimal. . . .

NOTES

1. Lewis retained Bartlett, a sole practitioner, to represent her in a personal injury action. Bartlett began settlement negotiations, marking March 16, the day before the expiration of the statute of limitations applicable to Lewis's action, on his calendar as the date for filing a complaint. On March 12, Bartlett was hit by a car outside the Orange County courthouse and rendered unconscious. He regained consciousness on March 22 but continued to suffer from amnesia. Bartlett discovered his mistake on April 26 and filed Lewis's complaint the following day (41 days late). The court applied the doctrine of equitable tolling to allow Lewis's action to proceed. Lewis *v.* Superior Court, 175 Cal. App. 3d 366 (1985).

Courts also may toll statutes of limitations when the defendant has concealed the cause of action or is otherwise estopped from relying on the time bar. Estoppel is discussed the next section of this chapter.

2. The federal statute of limitations for tax refunds is not subject to equitable tolling. United States *v.* Brockamp, 519 U.S. 347 (1997).

2. ESTOPPEL

Barry v. Donnelly

United States Court of Appeals, Fourth Circuit, 1986.
781 F.2d 1040.

■ JAMES DICKSON PHILLIPS, CIRCUIT JUDGE. In this declaratory judgment action, Honoria and William Donnelly appeal from a summary judgment declaring that they are barred by the Virginia statute of limitations from suing to recover from Ellen Barry, a close family friend and alleged bailee, a painting by Mrs. Donnelly's father, Gerald Murphy. Because we conclude that there are genuine issues of fact material to the Donnellys' claim that Ellen Barry should be precluded from asserting the statute of limitations under the doctrine of equitable estoppel, we vacate the district court's order and remand for further proceedings.

Gerald Murphy and his wife, Sara, lived in Paris during the 1920s and counted, among their friends, many of the principal artists and writers of that era, including Picasso, Hemingway, and Fitzgerald. Although his work was not at that time particularly well known, Murphy was himself a serious painter. Since his death in 1964, his paintings have become very valuable.

In 1964, Gerald Murphy brought his painting entitled "Cocktail" to the Washington, D.C., apartment of Ellen Barry, an old and dear friend of the Murphy family. According to Honoria Donnelly, Murphy contemplated that Barry would use and enjoy the painting for as long as she liked, but that she would ultimately return the artwork to his family. Barry maintains that the painting was a gift.

The painting has remained in Ellen Barry's possession and over the years she has loaned it to various museums, each time identifying the work as from the collection of Mrs. Phillip Barry. In October of 1978, Ellen Barry wrote to Honoria Donnelly requesting, for purposes of her "records and insurance," a written confirmation that the painting had been a gift from Gerald Murphy. In March of 1979, Mrs. Donnelly, who now resides in Virginia, responded with a letter indicating that she understood the arrangement to be merely a loan and suggesting that, in order to avoid future estate tax problems, the parties "put something in writing" to this effect.

Honoria Donnelly's letter referred to a conversation that the parties agree transpired sometime previously, probably during 1965, in which Barry indicated that she would eventually give or bequeath the painting to the Donnellys for their son, John. Accordingly, around this time, Mrs. Barry tagged the back of the painting with instructions to "Give to Honoria Donnelly for John Donnelly." The parties disagree, however, as to whether this promise was later reaffirmed by Ellen Barry in discussions that ensued following the correspondence of 1978–79. Thus, Honoria Donnelly claims that notwithstanding Ellen Barry's 1978 assertion of ownership, Barry later confirmed that she would ultimately return the painting to the Donnellys. According to Mrs. Barry, on the other hand, there was no further discussion concerning the disposition of the painting after 1965.

On June 12, 1979, Ellen Barry wrote once more to Honoria Donnelly, again insisting that Gerald Murphy intended the painting as a gift and not as a loan for an indefinite term. According to Honoria Donnelly, it was not until 1983 that she learned that Ellen Barry no longer intended to give or bequeath the work to the Donnellys for their son, John.

On December 5, 1984, Ellen Barry, invoking diversity jurisdiction, sought a declaratory judgment pursuant to 28 U.S.C. § 2201, to resolve this controversy, in which she claims entitlement to the painting as a gift or, alternatively, assuming that the painting was merely loaned, by the running of Virginia's five-year statute of limitations on actions to recover property. Solely for purposes of her motion for summary judgment, Ellen Barry conceded the Donnellys' characterization of the transaction as a bailment as well as their claim that Barry renewed her promise to return the painting even after her assertions of ownership in 1978–79.

The district court granted summary judgment in favor of Barry, holding that her letter of October 1978 was an act inconsistent with the asserted bailment and therefore triggered the applicable Virginia statute of limitations. The court characterized Barry's representations that she would return the painting as merely "a promise to do something in the future" rather than fraud sufficient to toll the statute of limitations. Apparently considering that under controlling state law only fraud could have that effect, the court therefore concluded that on the undisputed facts the statute barred any claim by the Donnellys so that Barry was entitled to judgment as a matter of law . . . .

Assuming, as the district court found, that on the summary judgment record the undisputed evidence revealed no conduct amounting to fraud, this did not entitle Barry to judgment as a matter of law. Under Virginia law, one may be estopped to plead the bar of a statute of limitations by conduct short of fraud, under the general doctrine of equitable estoppel. City of Bedford *v.* James Leffel & Co., 558 F.2d 216, 217–18 (4th Cir. 1977). Under that doctrine, estoppel occurs where "the aggrieved party reasonably relied on the words and conduct of the person to be estopped in allowing the limitations period to expire." *Id.* at 218. As applied to the statute of limitations, the "central premise is that one cannot justly or equitably lull his adversary into a false sense of security, and thereby cause his adversary to subject his claim to the bar of the statute [of limitations], and then be permitted to plead the very delay caused by his course of conduct as a defense to the action when brought." *Id.* at 218.

While equitable estoppel in both its general applications as well as in its special application to statutes of limitations pleas frequently involves fraud or deceit and is "most clearly applicable" when it does, "deceit is not an essential element of estoppel" in either its general or special applications under Virginia law. *Id.* at 218. The essential elements of equitable estoppel, in both its general applications and in its special application to statutes of limitation pleas under Virginia law are . . . : "absent a showing of fraud and deception, . . . a representation, reliance, a change of position, and detriment." T . . . *v.* T . . ., 224 S.E.2d 148, 152 (Va. 1976). . . .

[W]e hold that whether Barry reaffirmed her promise to return the painting after her assertion of ownership in 197879, and whether, if she did, the Donnellys reasonably relied upon that reaffirmation in failing to sue within the limitations period are issues requiring resolution by trial. . . .

NOTES ON ESTOPPEL

1. Estoppel, like the laches defense discussed in Section B, originated in the Court of Chancery as a defense to equitable relief. Over time, however, it worked its way into the common law and now, in most jurisdictions, it applies as a defense to any kind of claim. Estoppel's movement from equity into law is not unique. "There exist numerous examples of the readiness of the common law courts to [render recourse to Chancery pointless by providing common law analogues to equitable doctrines], for though the doctrinal proposition is that equity follows the law, historically the tendency has frequently been the reverse." A. W. B. Simpson, A HISTORY OF THE COMMON LAW OF CONTRACT: THE RISE OF THE ACTION OF ASSUMPSIT 280 (1987).

2. As the court indicated in Barry *v.* Donnelly, estoppel is not limited to cases involving statutes of limitations. Parties can be estopped to assert rights of all kinds, and the courts' formulations of the doctrine vary from case

to case. Courts frequently refer to misrepresentation as the basis for estoppel, but the doctrine is considerably broader than the tort of misrepresentation.

A case on the borderline of the estoppel doctrine is First Federal Savings & Loan Association of Toledo *v.* Perry's Landing, Inc., 11 Ohio App. 3d 135 (1983). A bank loan officer made "equivocal" statements to a borrower about the likelihood of enforcement of a due-on-sale clause in a mortgage loan agreement. When a sale later occurred, the bank delayed for several months, then decided to enforce the clause and foreclose the mortgage. The Ohio Court of Appeals adopted a broad definition of estoppel, but held that the bank was not estopped from foreclosing in the circumstances of the case:

> "No single formulation of the equitable doctrine of estoppel is applicable to every case, and in applying estoppel, each case must be considered on its own facts. . . .
>
> "First Federal would have us hold that a knowingly false representation or concealment of material fact is the essential element of estoppel. That element, however, is more properly a decisive ingredient of misrepresentation, not estoppel, and we decline so to hold. . . .
>
> "The concept of estoppel has its roots in ethical premises and is the legal expression of normative policies that equity jurisprudence has fostered and developed over the centuries. In essence, the expression of estoppel in the form of a rule is that one party will not be permitted to deny that which, by his words, his acts, or his silence (when there was an obligation to speak), he has induced a second party reasonably and in good faith to assume and rely upon to that party's prejudice or pecuniary disadvantage. Distillable from the foregoing rule are the following four essential elements.
>
> "First, there must be something in the nature of a *representation* by words, acts, or silence. The representation must be factual, not promissory, or else the elements and analysis appropriate to a *promissory* estoppel context may apply. The facts underlying the representation must be *known* to the party at the time he makes it, or at least the circumstances must be such that he is necessarily chargeable with knowledge of them. In addition, if silence is involved, it amounts to a representation only if the circumstances were such that the law recognized a duty to speak. Second, the representation must communicate some fact or state of affairs in a *misleading* way. Third, the representation must induce actual reliance by the second party, and such reliance must be *reasonable under the circumstances and made in good faith.* Fourth, the relying party would suffer prejudice or pecuniary disadvantage if the party whose representation was relied upon were not estopped or precluded from asserting an otherwise valid right in contradiction to his earlier representation. . . .

> "The mortgage agreements in this case were negotiated by experienced businessmen, and the record reveals no unconscionable conduct on First Federal's part in reaching the terms of those agreements. Furthermore, it is not at all clear that Waldvogel's statements were misleading or were intended to induce appellee to act in reliance on them. Appellee's reliance cannot be said to have been reasonable or in good faith if based upon ambiguous or uncertain statements."

Id. at 144–47.

Gilbert v. Gilbert

Superior Court of New Jersey, Chancery Division, 1960.
61 N.J. Super. 476.

■ WICK, J.S.C. This is a motion to dismiss the complaint for failure to state a claim upon which relief can be granted.

The facts, as presented by the complaint, are as follows: The plaintiff met John E. Gilbert in 1949 and, after some acquaintance with him, he sought to persuade her to marry him, but she refused to do so unless he would make a suitable property settlement on her prior to the marriage. He thus offered to provide her with a home of her own and a housekeeper and plaintiff accepted this offer with the proviso that the agreement be reduced to writing and signed by them. They fixed September 10, 1949 as the date of the marriage. On August 27, 1949, she having become insistent that she would not marry him unless a written agreement was executed, he, in order to further induce the marriage, executed a will (a copy of which is attached to the complaint) in which he left her certain real property, a Buick automobile and one-third of whatever cash he had in the bank. In reliance on the provisions of the will for her benefit and his representations that it would be his last will, she entered into the marriage on September 10, 1949. In October or November of 1949 he made a further will which, as she is advised and believes, left her his entire estate. On October 27, 1950 he executed a further will leaving his entire estate to his children, Margaret E. Gilbert and John E. Gilbert, Jr. This is the last will he left on his death on March 1, 1960. She has filed a caveat with the Surrogate of Burlington County against the probate of that will and the admissibility of that will to probate has not yet been adjudicated.

She seeks judgment that the execution of that will by him was a breach of their antenuptial agreement and a fraud; the probate of that will would constitute a breach of the antenuptial agreement and perpetrate a fraud on her; the will of August 27, 1949 was irrevocable without her consent except by a will more favorable to her and is valid and entitled to probate; she is the owner of the property that was to be left to her under either the will of August 27, 1949, or that of October or November, 1949; the probate of the will of October 27, 1950 would create a cloud on her title to the real and personal property which is hers under the earlier two wills. She would further have the probate of the October 27, 1950 will restrained. . . .

The breach of an antenuptial agreement is not such a fraud as will prevent the application of the statute of frauds. It has also been decided that mere breach of the further agreement to reduce the antenuptial agreement to writing is not such a fraud as will prevent the application of the statute. In Alexander *v.* Alexander, 96 N.J. Eq. 10, 124 A. 523 (Ch. 1924) it is stated by Leaming, V.C., as follows:

> "Fraud, alone, will deny the intervention of the statute. Equity at all times will lend its aid to defeat a fraud, notwithstanding the statute of frauds. But the fraud against which equity will relieve in this class of cases, notwithstanding the statute, is not the mere moral wrong of repudiating a contract actually entered into, which, by reason of the statute, a party is not bound to perform for want of its being in writing. The fraud must be inherent in the transaction, such as a false representation that a contemplated written agreement has been executed pursuant to the parol agreement, or other similar artifices. . . . 2 STORY EQUITY JURISPRUDENCE (13th ed.) . . . "

It might be said that the line of distinction developed by the . . . authorities is that an assurance with a subsequent change of mind is a mere moral wrong while an assurance with a present intention never to follow through with it is a fraud which will prevent the application of the statute. This, certainly, is a correct statement of the two different situations. However, there is further involved, as is implicit in the principles quoted above, the problem of what is sufficient proof of the fraudulent intention. That is, may the court, upon mere proof that there was an assurance and a later breach of it raise the inference that this was not a mere change of mind, but a deliberate plan. It seems to me that the . . . authorities . . . require something more. . . .

In [Green *v.* Green, 34 Kan. 740 (1886),] the husband was induced into the marriage upon the representation by the wife that she owned a 160-acre farm and that its proceeds should go to their support after they were married so long as they lived, and then to her children. They were married on August 31, 1882. However, on August 30, 1882, she had executed, without his knowledge, deeds conveying her farm to her children. After the marriage she controlled and rented the farm in her own name, but he received none of the proceeds. The deeds were delivered to the children on March 5, 1884. She deserted her husband, whether before or after delivery of the deeds does not appear. In [Peek *v.* Peek, 77 Cal. 106 (1888),] the wife married the husband on the assurance that he would, on or before the marriage, make a conveyance to her of certain real property. On the day before the marriage he told her he was going to have the deeds drawn, but returned in a few minutes saying that it could not be done that day. The next morning he again said he would have the deeds drawn but returned saying that they were too busy at the court house, but that he would have it done as soon as practicable. She accordingly married him that night. That very same morning, however, when he was making excuses, he had a deed executed conveying the property to his son by a former marriage.

These cases . . . appear consistent with the proposition laid down by Story and Leaming. In both, the fraud is evidenced by more than the mere assurance and subsequent breach, rather there is positive evidence of the fraudulent purpose. . . .

It is thus apparent that the complaint fails to allege or demonstrate a fraud that will prevent the application of the statute. Nothing appears more than a subsequent breach of the several interrelated promises. There is no allegation that the reduction of the agreement to writing was prevented by the contrivance or artifice of the husband similar to or in the nature of those indicated by the authorities above.

The plaintiff further argues that the execution of the will in pursuance of the antenuptial agreement followed by the marriage constitutes such part performance as to take the case out of the statute. . . . This, however, would not appear to be the law in New Jersey. . . .

White v. Production Credit Association of Alma

Court of Appeals of Michigan, 1977.
76 Mich. App. 191.

■ R.B. BURNS, JUDGE. . . . Plaintiff is a cattle farmer who has been buying, raising, and selling feeder cattle since 1960. The business requires periodic financing to cover basic operating expenses and the purchase of cattle. Defendant is a federally-chartered lending institution.

In the fall of 1970, James Orr, a representative of defendant, represented to plaintiff that defendant could and would provide exclusive financial assistance to plaintiff. Plaintiff accepted Orr's offer, submitted a financial statement and a loan application for $128,000. The loan was approved within two days.

Due to drought and other problems, 1970 was a poor year for plaintiff. He and Orr discussed the feasibility of irrigation and both agreed that it would be the answer to plaintiff's problem. According to plaintiff, defendant agreed to finance the irrigation project and provide financing for the balance of plaintiff's operation, including the purchase of cattle each year, for a period of 7 to 10 years, the time period anticipated to pay off the irrigation equipment loan. This irrigation loan was to be repaid in seven equal installments.

Plaintiff agreed to maintain a herd of approximately 500 cattle each year. As security for the financing, plaintiff agreed to deliver mortgages and security agreements to defendant covering all of the farm's real estate and fixtures, all crops, both present and future, all livestock on hand and to be acquired, and all machinery and equipment, including the irrigation system.

Defendant advanced the long-term loan for the irrigation project and plaintiff executed the security agreements.

Within five months, and seven months before the first payment was due, defendant reversed its position and wrote to plaintiff requesting he refinance the irrigation loan with another institution. Plaintiff was unable to acquire another source to refinance the irrigation project. Defendant then refused to loan plaintiff money to finance the purchase of cattle for the 1972 and the 1973 seasons. Plaintiff was unable to secure other financing because all of his security was pledged to defendant. Orr admitted at trial that the only reason defendant did not finance plaintiff's cattle operations for the years 1972 and 1973 was that plaintiff did not refinance the long-term irrigation project with another lending institution.

After numerous attempts, plaintiff finally obtained FHA refinancing in March, 1974, and the obligation to defendant was paid in full, including over $25,000 in interest. During the 2-year period, plaintiff was unable to purchase any cattle due to lack of financing. Testimony established that plaintiff lost $85,304 in 1972 and $34,445 in 1973.

These damages were essentially unchallenged and the jury returned a verdict for plaintiff of $100,000.

At the close of plaintiff's opening statement, defendant moved for a summary judgment on the basis that the alleged oral contract was within the statute of frauds because it could not have been completed within one year.

Plaintiff's attorney argued that the statute did not apply because the defendant was estopped to assert the statute as the plaintiff had relied on the oral contract to his detriment.

The doctrine of equitable estoppel is set forth in 3 Williston, CONTRACTS (3d ed.), § 533A, p. 796:

> "Where one has acted to his detriment solely in reliance on an oral agreement, an estoppel may be raised to defeat the defense of the Statute of Frauds."

. . . In the instant case the plaintiff relied upon the defendant's promise, installed an irrigation system and granted defendant a security interest in all of his collateral, to his detriment. It was proper for the trial judge to apply the doctrine. . . .

Office of Personnel Management v. Richmond

Supreme Court of the United States, 1990.
496 U.S. 414.

■ JUSTICE KENNEDY delivered the opinion of the Court.

This case presents the question whether erroneous oral and written advice given by a Government employee to a benefit claimant may give rise to estoppel against the Government, and so entitle the claimant to a monetary payment not otherwise permitted by law. We hold that payments of money from the Federal Treasury are limited to those authorized by statute, and we reverse the contrary holding of the Court of Appeals.

Not wishing to exceed a statutory limit on earnings that would disqualify him from a disability annuity, respondent Charles Richmond sought advice from a federal employee and received erroneous information. As a result he earned more than permitted by the eligibility requirements of the relevant statute and lost six months of benefits. Respondent now claims that the erroneous and unauthorized advice should give rise to equitable estoppel against the Government, and that we should order payment of the benefits contrary to the statutory terms. Even on the assumption that much equity subsists in respondent's claim, we cannot agree with him or the Court of Appeals that we have authority to order the payment he seeks.

Respondent was a welder at the Navy Public Works Center in San Diego, California. He left this position in 1981 after petitioner, the Office of Personnel Management (OPM), approved his application for a disability retirement. OPM determined that respondent's impaired eyesight prevented him from performing his job and made him eligible for a disability annuity under 5 U.S.C. § 8337(a). Section 8337(a) provides this benefit for disabled federal employees who have completed five years of service. The statute directs, however, that the entitlement to disability payments will end if the retired employee is "restored to an earning capacity fairly comparable to the current rate of pay of the position occupied at the time of retirement."

The statutory rules for restoration of earning capacity are central to this case. Prior to 1982, an individual was deemed restored to earning capacity, and so rendered ineligible for a disability annuity, if

> "in *each of 2 succeeding calendar years* the income of the annuitant from wages or self-employment . . . equals at least 80 percent of the current rate of pay of the position occupied immediately before retirement." 5 U.S.C. § 8337(d) (1976 ed.).

The provision was amended in 1982 . . . to change the measuring period for restoration of earning capacity from two years to one:

> "Earning capacity is deemed restored if *in any calendar year* the income of the annuitant from wages or self-employment

> or both equals at least 80 percent of the current rate of pay of the position occupied immediately before retirement." 5 U.S.C. § 8337(d).

After taking disability retirement for his vision impairment, respondent undertook part-time employment as a school bus driver. From 1982 to 1985, respondent earned an average of $12,494 in this job, leaving him under the 80% limit for entitlement to continued annuity payments. In 1986, however, he had an opportunity to earn extra money by working overtime. Respondent asked an Employee Relations Specialist at the Navy Public Works Center's Civilian Personnel Department for information about how much he could earn without exceeding the 80% eligibility limit. Relying upon the terms of the repealed pre-1982 statute, under which respondent could retain the annuity unless his income exceeded the 80% limit in *two* consecutive years, the specialist gave respondent incorrect advice. The specialist also gave respondent a copy of Attachment 4 to Federal Personnel Manual Letter 831–64, published by petitioner OPM, which also stated the former 2-year eligibility rule. The OPM form was correct when written in 1981; but when given to respondent, the form was out of date and therefore inaccurate. Respondent returned to the Navy in January 1987, and again was advised in error that eligibility would be determined under the old 2-year rule.

After receiving the erroneous information, respondent concluded that he could take on the extra work as a school bus driver in 1986 while still receiving full disability benefits for impaired vision so long as he kept his income for the previous and following years below the statutory level. He earned $19,936 during 1986, exceeding the statutory eligibility limit. OPM discontinued respondent's disability annuity on June 30, 1987. The annuity was restored on January 1, 1988, since respondent did not earn more than allowed by the statute in 1987. Respondent thus lost his disability payments for a 6-month period, for a total amount of $3,993.

Respondent appealed the denial of benefits to the Merit Systems Protection Board (MSPB). He argued that the erroneous advice given him by the Navy personnel should estop OPM and bar its finding him ineligible for benefits under the statute. The MSPB rejected this argument, noting that the officials who misinformed respondent were from the Navy, not OPM. The MSPB observed that, "[h]ad [respondent] directed his request for information to the OPM, presumably, he would have learned of the change in the law." The MSPB held that "OPM cannot be estopped from enforcing a statutorily imposed requirement for retirement eligibility." The MSPB denied respondent's petition for review, and respondent appealed to the Court of Appeals for the Federal Circuit.

A divided panel of the Court of Appeals reversed, accepting respondent's contention that the misinformation from Navy personnel estopped the Government, and that the estoppel required payment of disability benefits despite the statutory provision to the contrary. . . .

From our earliest cases, we have recognized that equitable estoppel will not lie against the Government as against private litigants. . . .

Despite the clarity of these earlier decisions, dicta in our more recent cases have suggested the possibility that there might be some situation in which estoppel against the Government could be appropriate. . . .

The language in our decisions has spawned numerous claims for equitable estoppel in the lower courts. . . .

As it has in the past, the Government asks us to adopt "a flat rule that estoppel may not in any circumstances run against the Government." The Government bases its broad rule first upon the doctrine of sovereign immunity. Noting that the "United States, as sovereign, is immune from suit save as it consents to be sued," the Government asserts that the courts are without jurisdiction to entertain a suit to compel the Government to act contrary to a statute, no matter what the context or circumstances. The Government advances as a second basis for this rule the doctrine of separation of powers. The Government contends that to recognize estoppel based on the misrepresentations of Executive Branch officials would give those misrepresentations the force of law, and thereby invade the legislative province reserved to Congress. This rationale, too, supports the Government's contention that estoppel may never justify an order requiring executive action contrary to a relevant statute, no matter what statute or what facts are involved.

We have recognized before that the "arguments the Government advances for the rule are substantial." And we agree that this case should be decided under a clearer form of analysis than "we will know an estoppel when we see one." But it remains true that we need not embrace a rule that no estoppel will lie against the Government in any case in order to decide this case. We leave for another day whether an estoppel claim could ever succeed against the Government. A narrower ground of decision is sufficient to address the type of suit presented here, a claim for payment of money from the Public Treasury contrary to a statutory appropriation.

The Appropriations Clause of the Constitution, Art. I, § 9, cl. 7, provides that: "No Money shall be drawn from the Treasury, but in Consequence of Appropriations made by Law." For the particular type of claim at issue here, a claim for money from the Federal Treasury, the Clause provides an explicit rule of decision. Money may be paid out only through an appropriation made by law; in other words, the payment of money from the Treasury must be authorized by a statute. All parties here agree that the award respondent seeks would be in direct contravention of the federal statute upon which his ultimate claim to the funds must rest. . . . The benefits respondent claims were not "provided by" the relevant provision of the subchapter; rather, they were specifically denied. It follows that Congress has appropriated no money for the payment of the benefits respondent seeks, and the Constitution prohibits that any money "be drawn from the Treasury" to pay them. . . .

[O]ur cases denying estoppel are animated by the same concerns that prompted the Framers to include the Appropriations Clause in the Constitution. . . .

The obvious practical consideration . . . for adherence to the requirement of the Clause is the necessity, existing now as much as at the time the Constitution was ratified, of preventing fraud and corruption. We have long ago accepted this ground as a reason that claims for estoppel cannot be entertained where public money is at stake, refusing to "introduce a rule against an abuse, of which, by improper collusions, it would be very difficult for the public to protect itself." But the Clause has a more fundamental and comprehensive purpose, of direct relevance to the case before us. It is to assure that public funds will be spent according to the letter of the difficult judgments reached by Congress as to the common good, and not according to the individual favor of Government agents or the individual pleas of litigants.

Extended to its logical conclusion, operation of estoppel against the Government in the context of payment of money from the Treasury could in fact render the Appropriations Clause a nullity. If agents of the Executive were able, by their unauthorized oral or written statements to citizens, to obligate the Treasury for the payment of funds, the control over public funds that the Clause reposes in Congress in effect could be transferred to the Executive. If, for example, the President or Executive Branch officials were displeased with a new restriction on benefits imposed by Congress to ease burdens on the fisc (such as the restriction imposed by the statutory change in this case) and sought to evade them, agency officials could advise citizens that the restrictions were inapplicable. Estoppel would give this advice the practical force of law, in violation of the Constitution.

It may be argued that a rule against estoppel could have the opposite result, that the Executive might frustrate congressional intent to appropriate benefits by instructing its agents to give claimants erroneous advice that would deprive them of the benefits. But Congress may always exercise its power to expand recoveries for those who rely on mistaken advice should it choose to do so. In numerous other contexts where Congress has been concerned at the possibility of significant detrimental reliance on the erroneous advice of Government agents, it has provided appropriate legislative relief.

One example is of particular relevance. In Schweiker *v.* Hansen, 450 U.S. 785 (1981), we rejected an estoppel claim made by a Social Security claimant who failed to file a timely written application for benefits as required by the relevant statute. Congress then addressed such situations in the Budget Reconciliation Act of 1989 [which preserves claimants' eligibility in cases of this kind]. The equities are the same whether executive officials' erroneous advice has the effect of frustrating congressional intent to withhold funds or to pay them. In the absence of estoppel for money claims, Congress has ready means to see that payments are made to those who rely on erroneous Government advice. Judicial adoption of estoppel based on agency misinformation would, on the other hand, vest authority in these agents that Congress would be powerless to constrain.

[The Court also discussed the Congressional practice of enacting special legislation to address hard cases no covered by the Federal Torts Claims Act.]

Respondent would have us ignore these obstacles on the ground that estoppel against the Government would have beneficial effects. But we are unwilling to "tamper with these established principles because it might be thought that they should be responsive to a particular conception of enlightened governmental policy." And respondent's attempts to justify estoppel on grounds of public policy are suspect on their own terms. Even short of collusion by individual officers or improper Executive attempts to frustrate legislative policy, acceptance of estoppel claims for Government funds could have pernicious effects. It ignores reality to expect that the Government will be able to "secure perfect performance from its hundreds of thousands of employees scattered throughout the continent." Hansen *v.* Harris, 619 F.2d 942, 954 (2d Cir. 1980) (Friendly, J., dissenting), rev'd *sub nom.* Schweiker *v.* Hansen, 450 U.S. 785 (1981). To open the door to estoppel claims would only invite endless litigation over both real and imagined claims of misinformation by disgruntled citizens, imposing an unpredictable drain on the public fisc. Even if most claims were rejected in the end, the burden of defending such estoppel claims would itself be substantial.

Also questionable is the suggestion that if the Government is not bound by its agents' statements, then citizens will not trust them, and will instead seek private advice from lawyers, accountants, and others, creating wasteful expenses. Although mistakes occur, we may assume with confidence that Government agents attempt conscientious performance of their duties, and in most cases provide free and valuable information to those who seek advice about Government programs. A rule of estoppel might create not more reliable advice, but less advice. The natural consequence of a rule that made the Government liable for the statements of its agents would be a decision to cut back and impose strict controls upon Government provision of information in order to limit liability. Not only would valuable informational programs be lost to the public, but the greatest impact of this loss would fall on those of limited means, who can least afford the alternative of private advice. The inevitable fact of occasional individual hardship cannot undermine the interest of the citizenry as a whole in the ready availability of Government information. The rationale of the Appropriations Clause is that if individual hardships are to be remedied by payment of Government funds, it must be at the instance of Congress.

Respondent points to no authority in precedent or history for the type of claim he advances today. Whether there are any extreme circumstances that might support estoppel in a case not involving payment from the Treasury is a matter we need not address. As for monetary claims, it is enough to say that this Court has never upheld an assertion of estoppel against the Government by a claimant seeking public funds. In this context there can be no estoppel, for courts cannot estop the Constitution. The judgment of the Court of Appeals is

Reversed.

■ [The concurring opinion of JUSTICE WHITE is omitted.]

■ JUSTICE STEVENS, concurring in the judgment.... Payments of pension benefits to retired and disabled federal servants are made "in Consequence of Appropriations made by Law" even if in particular cases they are the product of a mistaken interpretation of a statute or regulation. The Constitution contemplates appropriations that cover programs—not individual appropriations for individual payments. The Court's creative reliance on constitutional text is nothing but a red herring.

The dispute in this case is not about whether an appropriation has been made; it is instead about what rules govern administration of an appropriation that has been made. . . . [Justice Stevens then suggested that the Court should not adopt an absolute rule against estoppel of the government.]

■ JUSTICE MARSHALL, with whom JUSTICE BRENNAN joins, dissenting. . . .

Significant policy concerns would of course be implicated by an indiscriminate use of estoppel against the Government. But estoppel is an equitable doctrine. As such, it can be tailored to the circumstances of particular cases, ensuring that fundamental injustices are avoided without seriously endangering the smooth operation of statutory schemes. In this case, the Federal Circuit undertook a thorough examination of the circumstances and concluded that denying Richmond his pension simply because he followed the Government's advice would be fundamentally unjust. . . .

3. CHANGE OF POSITION AS A DEFENSE TO LIABILITY IN RESTITUTION

Woolsey v. Nationwide Insurance Co.

United States District Court, Western District of Arkansas, 1988.
697 F. Supp. 1053.

■ MORRIS SHEPPARD ARNOLD, DISTRICT JUDGE. [The Kings' son was seriously injured in an automobile accident and died three days later. The son's insurance policy, issued by Nationwide, provided benefits for collision loss and for personal injuries, including medical expenses and death benefits. At the Kings' request, Nationwide paid the death and collision benefits, totaling about $15,000, to the Kings. This was a mistake; according to the policy and applicable statutes, the benefits were payable to the son's personal representative.

[After receiving the payment from Nationwide, the Kings spent about $10,000 to pay funeral expenses and some medical bills not covered by the policy. Later the personal representative sued Nationwide, claiming the benefits paid to the Kings. Nationwide cross-claimed for restitution from the Kings. At this point, the time period for claims against the estate had run, so the Kings were no longer able to seek restitution from the estate in the event they were found liable to Nationwide.

[The court first determined that Nationwide was liable to the son's personal representative for the amounts mistakenly paid to the Kings.]

Defendant asserts . . . that if it is liable to [the personal representative] on the collision and death benefits portions of the relevant policy then it is entitled to restitution from the parents of the money mistakenly paid them. Defendant showed at trial that it made these payments thinking that it was obligated to do so and under the assumption that no estate would ever be opened. Arkansas law adheres to the familiar rule that a person who pays money on account of a mistake of fact is entitled to restitution . . . .

The parents, however, assert as a defense to this restitutionary claim the fact that their position has changed since the original payment so as to make repayment to the defendant inequitable. The parents have shown that they have already spent all the money paid them for collision loss and death benefits. They cannot exactly account for the money, but they did prove that they spent $8,859.00 on their son's funeral and paid $1,135.00 of his medical bills; and Mrs. King testified that they would not have been able to afford to spend these sums but for the insurance payments because they were destitute at the time of their son's death. In other words, the parents assert as a defense that they have changed their position by spending money that they would not have otherwise spent and that there are no physical assets to which these expenditures can be traced. The question is whether these facts are sufficient to defeat the restitutionary claim of the defendant. . . .

Since change of circumstances is an affirmative defense to a restitutionary claim, the burden is on the parents to show that they would not have incurred any of the expenses paid by the insurance money unless they had received that money. While this is a matter of some difficulty, the court, after hearing the testimony of the parents, is of the view, and finds, that all or substantially all of the money paid by the defendant was spent by the parents in ways that the parents would not have otherwise spent money because they were destitute. . . .

NOTES

1. What would happen if the parents were not destitute?

2. The change-of-position defense is a form of estoppel. In Heckler *v.* Community Health Service of Crawford County, Inc., 467 U.S. 51 (1984), a non-profit health clinic received $71,480 in federal funds to provide health services to Medicare beneficiaries. Under applicable regulations, the payment was erroneous. After discovering the mistake, the government sued for restitution of the money paid. The clinic argued in response that it had changed its position by expending the funds to provide services.

The Court rejected the clinic's defense. It cited the line of cases in which it had refused to allow estoppel claims against the government, but ultimately decided that, in any event, the clinic had not made out a valid defense:

> "Estoppel is an equitable doctrine invoked to avoid injustice in particular cases. While a hallmark of the doctrine is its flexible application, certain principles are tolerably clear:
>
>> 'If one person makes a definite misrepresentation of fact to another person having reason to believe that the other will rely upon it and the other in reasonable reliance upon it does an act . . . the first person is not entitled . . .
>>
>> '(b) to regain property or its value that the other acquired by the act, if the other in reliance upon the misrepresentation and before discovery of the truth has so changed his position that it would be unjust to deprive him of that which he thus acquired.' Restatement (Second) of Torts § 894(1) (1979).
>
> "Thus, the party claiming the estoppel must have relied on its adversary's conduct 'in such a manner as to change his position for the worse.'[9] . . .
>
> "In this case the consequences of the Government's misconduct were not entirely adverse. Respondent did receive an immediate benefit as a result of the double reimbursement. Its detriment is the inability to retain money that it should never have received in

[9] 3 J. Pomeroy, EQUITY JURISPRUDENCE § 805, p. 192 (S. Symons ed. 1941).

the first place. . . . [R]espondent lost no rights but merely was induced to do something which could be corrected at a later time.

"There is no doubt that respondent will be adversely affected by the Government's recoupment of the funds that it has already spent. It will surely have to curtail its operations and may even be forced to seek relief from its debts through bankruptcy. However, there is no finding as to the extent of the likely curtailment in the volume of services provided by respondent, much less that respondent will reduce its activities below the level that obtained when it was first advised that the double reimbursement was proper. Respondent may need an extended period of repayment or other modifications in the recoupment process if it is to continue to operate, but questions concerning the Government's method of enforcing collection are not before us. The question is whether the Government has entirely forfeited its right to the money.

"A for-profit corporation could hardly base an estoppel on the fact that the Government wrongfully allowed it the interest-free use of taxpayers' money for a period of two or three years, enabling it to expand its operation. No more can respondent claim any right to expand its services to levels greater than those it would have provided had the error never occurred. Curtailment of operation does not justify an estoppel when—by respondent's own account—the expansion of its operation was achieved through unlawful access to governmental funds. . . .

"Thus, assuming estoppel can ever be appropriately applied against the Government, it cannot be said that the detriment respondent faces is so severe or has been imposed in such an unfair way that petitioner ought to be estopped from enforcing the law in this case."

Id. at 59–66.

B. EQUITABLE DEFENSES

Certain defenses are "equitable" in the sense that they preclude the plaintiff from requesting equitable relief but do not provide a complete defense against liability.[i] In a merged court, the consequence is that the court may deny an equitable remedy, such as an injunction, but allow the plaintiff to recover damages.

Equitable defenses are traced back to the days when equitable relief was available only in equity courts, and Chancellors felt freer than common law judges to invoke moral standards in support of their decisions. In a merged court, it may seem odd that one form of remedy should operate on a higher moral plane than another. Yet courts continue to make this distinction among remedies. The distinction can be justified on functional grounds, for equitable remedies tend to require more

[i] Note, however, that an equitable defense may bar liability completely where the substantive body of law is equitable (*e.g.*, fiduciary law).

intensive commitments from the court, and they tend to be more vulnerable to misuse by litigants (as when a plaintiff uses an injunction to "hold up" a defendant, exacting an excessive settlement).

1. LACHES

Environmental Defense Fund, Inc. v. Alexander

United States Court of Appeals, Fifth Circuit, 1980.
614 F.2d 474.

■ ALVIN B. RUBIN, CIRCUIT JUDGE. This attempt to halt the construction of a federally financed waterway because the width of the waterway exceeds the size authorized by Congress was dismissed by the district court on the basis that it was barred by laches—delay in presenting the claim resulting in prejudice to the defendants. . . .

The headwater of this litigation commenced to flow forty years ago when the Army Corps of Engineers presented Congress with a preliminary design for the proposed Tennessee-Tombigbee Waterway. The design was reviewed and modified in a report submitted to Congress in 1946. In that year Congress authorized construction of the waterway in accordance with the plans presented to it. . . .

Shortly after authorizing construction, Congress decided that the waterway was not economically feasible, and for some time it did not appropriate any funds for construction. However, studies continued. In June, 1966, in response to a request by Congress for restudy of the economic desirability of the project, the Corps of Engineers recommended that the proposed plan be modified to provide for a 300-foot channel (for convenience we refer to this as the 300-foot channel although this is its minimum width at its bottom). . . .

On May 18, 1967, the Association of American Railroads, on behalf of the L & N Railroad Company and other railroad companies in the waterway area, submitted a report to the Senate Appropriations Committee specifically suggesting the need for a reevaluation of the project authorization because of the increase in the project's width from 170 feet to 300 feet. Subsequently, the Appropriations Committees recommended appropriation of construction funds for the waterway with the increased bottom width. During the budget hearings for fiscal year 1971, representatives of appellants L & N Railroad and Committee for Leaving the Environment of America Natural (CLEAN) appeared before the House and Senate Appropriations Committees to oppose funding of the waterway.

Congress appropriated construction funds of $1 million for fiscal year 1971 and $6 million for fiscal year 1972. CLEAN and the Environmental Defense Fund (EDF) filed suit to enjoin the construction of the waterway in 1971. . . . Actual construction of the waterway began in 1972. Ultimately, the 1971 suit was dismissed by the court, and construction proceeded.

In November, 1976, this suit was filed, again seeking to enjoin construction. Plaintiffs alleged that the project under construction differed substantially from the project authorized by Congress and would have a greater impact on the environment and economic conditions of the surrounding areas, violating both statutory limitations and administrative regulations. . . . Over a year later, on January 30, 1978, an amended complaint was filed questioning, for the first time, the authority of the Corps to build a 300-foot channel.

When this suit was filed, the Corps had spent $36,000,000 out of a total estimated cost of $604,000,000 for channels and canals. By January 30, 1978, when the amended complaint was filed, it estimates it had completed 18% of the total project and spent over $265,000,000. After filing the lack of authority claims, the plaintiffs made no effort to obtain immediate injunctive relief and thus halt the further expenditure of funds or work on the project.

The Corps is now obligated on outstanding construction contracts in the amount of $864,302,200. If the project is restricted to a 170-foot channel, some of these funds may be recouped by sale of the unnecessary right of way and by renegotiation of contracts. Those who question authority to proceed urge that a substantial part of the $864 million could be saved if the project were restricted to 170 feet. In response to inquiry by this court concerning amounts spent for construction, the Corps estimates that by September 30, 1978, $408,651,600 had been spent for construction and $616,007,156 has been spent to the present. The opponents of the waterway state that the following sums have been spent on actual project construction:

As of September 30, 1976: $93,314,300.

As of September 30, 1977: $176,324,100.

As of September 30, 1978: $286,862,900. . . .

The district judge did not decide whether the Secretary was authorized to increase the width of the channel because he concluded that the challenge was barred by laches. Deciding only that issue, he directed entry of a final judgment . . . .

What is sought here is an injunction, an equitable form of relief. The doctrine of laches was developed by chancellors of equity to prevent the assertion of stale claims and to remedy an injustice that sometimes arose from the existence of the separate system of equity: when an equitable remedy was sought, the statute of limitations that ordinarily would apply to a legal right was inapplicable.

The doctrine was eventually adopted by common law courts and, following the merger of law and equity, became part of the general body of rules governing relief in the federal court system. Its interpretation in equity courts was not uniform; at times the courts required a showing of prejudice to the defendants, at other times the chancellor applied it if a plaintiff had unreasonably delayed the assertion of his claim whether or not the defendant had been prejudiced. One basic principle has, however, been consistently followed: equitable remedies are not available if granting the remedy would be inequitable to the defendant because of the plaintiff's long delay.

Today, three independent criteria must be met before laches can be invoked to bar litigation. "The defendant must show: (1) a delay in asserting a right or claim; (2) that the delay was not excusable; and (3) that there was undue prejudice to the party against whom the claim is asserted." Save Our Wetlands, Inc. *v.* United States Army Corps of Engineers, 549 F.2d 1021, 1026 (5th Cir. 1977). Whether laches bars an action in a given case depends upon the circumstances of that case and is "a question primarily addressed to the discretion of the trial court." Gardner *v.* Panama Railroad Co., 342 U.S. 29, 30 (1951).

As we have recently said, the applicability of the doctrine of laches to environmental litigation is no longer open to doubt. It is equally applicable to suits questioning public authority to act.

The record, which we have already summarized, amply supports the district judge's finding that on November 3, 1966, about a decade before the suit was filed, the Corps gave public notice of its recommendation to expand the width of the canal together with an invitation to the public to submit written comments. . . .

There is also ample evidence that the waterway opponents who appear in this suit were aware of this change: the 1967 opposition to a 300-foot channel by the Association of American Railroads, in part on L & N RR's behalf; the opposition to funding of the 300-foot channel project by CLEAN and EDF in Congress; and the suit to halt construction in 1971. The present waterway opponents did not challenge that decision until 1978, eleven years later. Even if we assume the challenge to have been effective when the complaint was filed in 1976, the delay was nine years. If we accept the contention that appellants remained blissfully ignorant of the increased dimensions throughout the congressional hearings on the waterway and despite the public attention the project received, they were aware of the width increase no later than 1971, when they sought to enjoin construction and stipulated to that width. This suit was not filed until five years thereafter, and the issue of authority to make the width increase was not injected until two years later.

Mere neglect to challenge action is not sufficient to establish laches in any case. When government action is involved, members of the public are entitled to assume that public officials will act in accordance with law. Therefore, apart from the question of prejudice, which we will discuss later, the government must show that those whom it seeks to bar by invoking laches were or should have been aware of the questionable nature of the governmental activity. The waterway opponents in this case had an adequate indication that the Secretary of the Army had unilaterally expanded the width of the canal beyond its statutorily authorized channel width. This was enough to alert them to the claim that the authorities were not acting legally. . . .

Because there is no evidence of any excuse for the lengthy delay, we next consider the final prerequisite to laches: prejudice. Measuring prejudice entails balancing equities. . . . [W]e are required to consider the expenditures made by the defendants against the benefits claimed if their efforts were halted. Environmental concerns are not presented to us; therefore . . . detriment to the environment cannot be a factor in our balance; the benefits we must weigh that could accrue by arresting work can be only those arising from the claimed vindication of congressional authority.

The amounts expended may be large in absolute terms but this does not tilt the scales if it represents a relatively small percentage of the total expenditures anticipated. See, *e.g.*, Ecology Center of Louisiana, Inc. *v.* Coleman, 515 F.2d 860 (5th Cir. 1975) ($1 million had been spent out of a total estimated cost of $667 million). Here by the most conservative estimates, between $176 million and $286 million had been spent before the no-authority claim was asserted. This represented about 11% of the total project cost, far more than the 1/6 of 1% expended in *Coleman.* Vast amounts of soil had been excavated, locks had been built, and local authorities had constructed bridges. Reshaping the project would not only entail waste of much of those expenditures but also the outlay of additional funds to narrow the channel; moreover, there is substantial evidence that the narrower channel would be economically impractical and would never have been constructed. . . .

Laches is a clement doctrine. It assures that old grievances will some day be laid to rest, that litigation will be decided on the basis of evidence that remains reasonably accessible and that those against whom claims are presented will not be unduly prejudiced by delay in asserting them. Inevitably it means that some potentially meritorious demands will not be entertained. But there is justice too in an end to conflict and in the quiet of peace. The district court concluded that the day for battle on the authorization issue had come and gone and that the question should now be laid to rest unheard. Finding his factual premises supported by the record and his conclusions of law correct, we AFFIRM his judgment.

NOTES ON LACHES

1. As the court noted, the English Chancellors first developed the doctrine of laches as a way to limit the time for bringing bills in equity. Statutes of limitations applied only to actions in the common law courts, but the Chancellors applied analogous limitations under the heading of "laches." Most, if not all, American states eventually enacted statutes of limitations covering suits in equity. Nevertheless, the doctrine of laches remains important because it enables the court to narrow or entirely withhold

equitable relief when the plaintiff has delayed for a time shorter than the statutory period.

2. The modern doctrine of laches requires proof of both an unreasonable delay by the plaintiff and resulting prejudice to the defendant. Thus, it is closely analogous to estoppel. Laches applies specifically to equitable relief, although claims for damages may be barred in similar circumstances on the ground of estoppel.

3. In Groesbeck *v.* Morgan, 206 N.Y. 385, 389–90 (1912), the New York Court of Appeals reversed a decree of specific performance on the basis of laches, saying:

> "No doctrine of equity jurisprudence is better settled than the rule that specific performance is not a strict legal right and is never granted when the lapse of time renders such relief inequitable in its consequences. In determining whether such delay is fatal in the domain of equity, regard must always be had to the peculiar circumstances of each case. . . . [A] purchaser seeking specific performance must be 'ready, desirous, prompt and eager.' The vendee in the present contract manifested none of these attributes. He allowed nearly five years to elapse after he became aware that the defendant had acquired an unincumbered title before he instituted the present suit. No excuse is offered for the delay, while the effect of it now is to make the defendant convey to the plaintiff land which has increased in value by many thousands of dollars. . . . 'He cannot be suffered to lie by and speculate on the rise of the estate.' "

Did the defendant suffer prejudice as a result of the delay?

4. In two cases, one in patent law and one in copyright law, the Supreme Court of the United States has considered whether the doctrine of laches should have its traditional scope. In Petrella *v.* Metro-Goldwyn-Mayer, Inc., 134 S. Ct. 1962 (2014), in an opinion by Justice Ginsburg, the Court held:

> "(1) that laches is available as a defense, notwithstanding the statute of limitations; (2) that laches is a defense only to claims for equitable remedies; (3) that laches can either knock out an equitable remedy entirely or shape its scope; (4) that only in extraordinary circumstances may laches bar equitable relief entirely; and (5) that laches is available only to shorten the statutory time period but not to extend it. In reaching these conclusions, the Court noted that laches had been 'developed by courts of equity.' It insisted that the adoption of the Federal Rules of Civil Procedure did not change 'the substantive and remedial principles' applied by the federal courts, including the principle that laches was available only against claims for equitable relief. The Court described its approach as traditional: it was 'adher[ing]' to the 'understandings, past and present, of the essentially gap-filling, not legislation-overriding, office of laches.' "

Samuel L. Bray, The Supreme Court and the New Equity, 68 Vand. L. Rev. 997, 1035–36 (2015). *Petrella* was a copyright decision. The Court concluded that laches had the same scope in patent law in SCA Hygiene Products Aktiebolag *v.* First Quality Baby Products, LLC, 137 S. Ct. 954 (2017).

2. UNCLEAN HANDS

Carmen v. Fox Film Corp.

United States Court of Appeals, Second Circuit, 1920.
269 F. 928.

[Jewel Carmen was a movie actress residing in California. On July 31, 1917, while still a minor, she executed a contract with two motion picture companies. The William Fox Vaudeville Company agreed to employ her for six months, with an option in the company to extend the employment for successive periods of six months until October 17, 1919. The salary began at $125 per week and increased to $200 per week, with an additional consideration of $650 for each option. After October 17, 1919, the Fox Film Corporation agreed to employ her for one year at $175 per week; with options to continue the employment for another year. If she exercised the options, her salary would gradually be increased to $250 per week.

[Several years before the expiration of these two agreements, the plaintiff received a telegram from Frank A. Kenney, the president of the Frank A. Keeney Pictures Corporation, asking whether she was available for employment. She replied that she was free. Keeney sent her a contract, which she executed on March 28, 1918, a few months before she turned 21, the age of majority in California. The contract provided for her exclusive appearance in motion pictures with the Keeney Corporation for two years commencing July 15, 1918, with options to continue the employment for four more years. The weekly compensation was to begin at $450 and rise $50 each six months until July, 1923, when she would receive $1000 every week.

[At the time this contract was made, Keeney had no knowledge that the plaintiff had contracts with the Fox companies extending beyond the beginning of his proposed contract. He testified at trial that he would not have made the contract if he had known the facts. On July 13, 1918, the plaintiff came of age; two days later she repudiated the Fox contracts on the ground that she had signed them during her minority. Fox insisted on her performance and threatened Keeney with suit if it assisted her breach by employing her. On September 19, 1918, the various motion picture companies made an agreement, whereby Keeney promised to refrain from using the plaintiff's services pending the determination of the rights of the respective parties, and the Fox promised to indemnify Keeney from any damage it might suffer through any action the plaintiff might bring against it. After this, Keeney refused to employ Carmen.

[Carmen sued Fox in the District Court for the Southern District of New York, seeking a declaration that the contracts she made during her minority were void and an injunction restraining Fox from asserting that the contracts were valid and from interfering with her contractual relations. The trial judge granted the injunction.]

■ ROGERS, CIRCUIT JUDGE. . . . [T]he conduct of the plaintiff has been such as entitles her to no relief in this court. According to her own allegations in her complaint, she was a minor when she entered into the contract with Keeney, and she misled him into making the contract by representing that she was free to make it, when in fact she was morally not free to make the contract, and there was doubt whether she was legally free to make it. If the contracts with defendants were valid, she was under a legal and moral obligation not to make the contract with the Keeney corporation. And if the contracts were voidable because of her infancy, then, while she was under no legal obligation to recognize them, she was under a moral obligation to abide by them, and good faith required her to continue to render the services she had agreed to give. In either case her action in repudiating her pledged word was misconduct of which no person of honor and conscience would have been guilty. That no action could be brought against her at law because of what she did does not alter the moral character of her act. And when she comes into a court of conscience and asks its affirmative aid to assist her in carrying into effect the inequitable arrangement into which she unfaithfully entered, the appeal falls on deaf ears. One who comes into equity must come with clean hands, and her hands are not clean. The testimony discloses that reliance cannot be placed upon her agreements which the law does not oblige her to keep, and that for a money gain to herself she unscrupulously disregarded her express contracts.

In Story's EQUITY JURISPRUDENCE (14th Ed.) vol. 1, Sec. 99, the rule is laid down as follows:

> "Equity imperatively demands of suitors in courts fair dealing and righteous conduct with reference to the matters concerning which they seek relief. He who has acted in bad faith, resorted to trickery and deception, or been guilty of fraud, injustice, or unfairness will appeal in vain to a court of conscience, even though in his wrongdoing he may have kept himself strictly 'within the law.' Misconduct which will bar relief in a court of equity need not necessarily be of such a nature as to be punishable as a crime or to constitute the basis of a legal action. Under this maxim, any willful act in regard to the matter in litigation, which would be condemned and pronounced wrongful by honest and fair-minded men, will be sufficient to make the hands of the applicant unclean. Both courts and text-writers have repeatedly spoken upon this subject in no uncertain language."

. . . The maxim that one who comes into equity must come with clean hands expresses rather a principle of inaction than one of action. It means that equity will refuse its aid in any manner to one seeking its active interposition if he has been guilty either of unlawful or inequitable conduct respecting the subject-matter of the litigation.

An illustration of the maxim is found in the attitude of courts of equity in the matter of specific performance. A court of equity always refuses specific performance of a contract which has been obtained by the plaintiff by sharp and unscrupulous practices, by over-reaching, by concealment of important facts, even though not actually fraudulent. The contract may be a legal one, against which no defense could be set up at law, and one which a court of equity would not cancel. But if it has been procured by unconscientious means a court of equity refuses specific performance.

The right which one seeks to enforce in a court of equity must be one which in and of itself appeals to the conscience of a chancellor. Mr. Justice Brewer, speaking for the court in Deweese *v.* Reinhard, 165 U.S. 386, 390, said:

> "A court of equity acts only when and as conscience commands, and if the conduct of the plaintiff be offensive to the dictates of natural justice, then, whatever may be the rights he possesses and whatever use he may make of them in a court of law, he will be held remediless in a court of equity."

. . . In 1816 a case came before Vice Chancellor Plumer, Cory *v.* Gerteken, 2 Maddox, 40, in which an infant who was nearly of age prevailed upon his trustees to transfer to him certain stock to which he was entitled on coming of age, and represented to them that they ran no risk in doing it. After coming of age he assigned his rights to an assignee, and suit was brought against the trustees on the ground that payment to an infant was bad. The bill was dismissed and the Vice Chancellor said:

> "The concealment of his infancy, under such circumstances, certainly was a fraud, and precludes him, or his assigns, who stand precisely in his situation, from calling for a repayment."

The fact that a contract has been dishonestly or dishonorably obtained is a bar to relief in equity. . . .

NOTES

1. Carmen subsequently sued Fox Film Corp. for damages in tort. In Carmen *v.* Fox Film Corp., 204 App. Div. 776 (N.Y. App. Div. 1923), the court held that the dismissal of her bill in equity was no bar to her legal action, because the dismissal was not an adjudication on the merits of her cause of action for tort. The jury awarded her $43,500 and $17,182 more in interest.

2. One should not be misled by the successful outcome of Carmen's lawsuit. It has long been recognized that frequently "a defeat because of the defense in equity is in fact final, regardless of theoretical reservations" that

there may be a recovery "at law." John P. Frank & John Endicott, Defenses in Equity and "Legal Rights," 14 La. L. Rev. 380, 389 (1954). For additional discussion of the practical significance of equitable defenses, see Ralph A. Newman, The Renaissance of Good Faith in Contracting in Anglo-American Law, 54 Cornell L. Rev. 553 (1969) and Edward Yorio, A Defense of Equitable Defenses, 51 Ohio St. L.J. 1201 (1990).

Claire v. Rue de Paris, Inc.

Supreme Court of Georgia, 1977.
239 Ga. 191.

■ BOWLES, JUSTICE. . . . [P]laintiff in the court below filed identical petitions in Fulton Superior Court against the respective defendants, alleging in each that he is a shareholder in each of the defendant corporations, owning 33⅓ per cent of all outstanding shares. Each complaint says that the acts of those in control of each corporation are illegal and/or fraudulent and the corporations and the plaintiff will suffer irreparable injury unless a dissolution is ordered. He alleges that the corporation assets are being misapplied and/or wasted. . . . He seeks to recover attorney fees and by way of relief, asks that an injunction issue enjoining the officers and directors of each corporation from disposing of the corporate assets, [and] that each corporation be dissolved . . . .

[In response to a motion for summary judgment,] plaintiff filed with the court four affidavits. One affiant said he had personally purchased and consumed on the premises of the Rue de Paris Restaurant alcoholic beverages on Sunday. Another said as a bartender he had been personally instructed by an owner of the Rue de Paris Restaurant how to mix water with alcoholic beverages sold and served at the restaurant and had been instructed to serve "watered down" alcoholic beverages to patrons. Another affiant declared that he had seen alcoholic beverages served on Sunday at Rue de Paris of Buckhead, Inc. and that he had been served alcoholic beverages on Sundays by employees of Rue de Paris of Buckhead, Inc. Another affiant confirmed that he had purchased and consumed on the premises of the Rue de Paris Restaurant alcoholic beverages on Sundays. Another confirmed that she had been employed by the defendants as a bookkeeper from the date of incorporation until June, 1975. She swore that during that period cash sales were regularly voided on the cash register and the proceeds therefrom were not reflected on defendants' accounting statements or tax returns as income; and that this practice was instituted on the express instructions of Aaron Alembik, an officer and director of defendants; that cash so withheld from defendants' income was received by the current officers of the corporation; and that the accounting records of the defendants after the termination of plaintiff's services led the witness to believe that the practice was continuing and that the shareholders were being damaged thereby.

The deposition of the plaintiff showed that . . . he took money from the cash register for his friends to drink; that the three of them, witness, and the other two principals, took $50.00 a week cash out of the business; and that he also charged personal expenses such as long distance telephone calls to Europe and flowers for his wife to the company for which no reimbursement was made. He testified that he had an agreement with the other owners to take home food and liquor for personal consumption, and he also gave to a personal friend a case of wine because "we did not have it on the inventory, anyway." He admitted receiving money from liquor sales the bartender did not account for on the register. . . .

Plaintiff's complaint in each case seeks equitable relief. . . . He readily admits that he has personally taken money from the business. He also admits he took food and beverages from the business. He, therefore, comes into court with unclean hands and must be denied the relief he seeks. The defendants need not invoke the clean hands maxim as the court will apply it of its own accord.

The rule is firmly established that ". . . where stockholders in a corporation participate in the performance of an act, or acquiesce in and ratify the same, they are estopped to complain thereof in equity." Bloodworth *v.* Bloodworth, 225 Ga. 379 (1969). This applies to derivative shareholder claims as well as direct actions against corporations.

Under the " 'clean hands' maxim, 'whenever a party, who, as actor, seeks to set the judicial machinery in motion and obtain some remedy, has violated conscience, or good faith, or other equitable principle, in his prior conduct, then the doors of the court will be shut against him in limine; the court will refuse to interfere on his behalf, to acknowledge his right, or to award him any remedy.' " Smith *v.* Nix, 206 Ga. 403 (1950) and many cases there cited.

It would contravene the principles of equity and good conscience to allow a director and stockholder to complain about the acts of the other directors of the corporation in taking money from the business, when the moving party himself readily admits that he had acted in concert with the managing officers in doing the very same thing. Additionally, where a plaintiff readily admits that he has personally taken money and properties of the corporation for his personal use his hands are "unclean" within the meaning of the term, and they are not made clean by his removal from office and subsequently filing suit against the corporation asking dissolution. . . .

McCune v. Brown

Arkansas Court of Appeals, 1983.
8 Ark. App. 51.

■ CLONINGER, JUDGE. On August 28, 1981, appellee, W.G. Brown, Sr., filed a complaint in equity against the appellant, Billie Jean McCune, seeking a temporary restraining order to keep appellant from removing any of the contents of a safety deposit box leased to her at Worthen Bank & Trust Company in Little Rock, Arkansas. The contents of the box consisted of 650 gold Krugerrands, 13 Mexican pesos and one double eagle gold piece valued at approximately $250,000. The gold was placed in appellant's safety deposit box on December 12, 1978, at a time when appellee was involved in a divorce proceeding with his wife. Appellee admitted at trial that he had transferred the gold to appellant, his daughter, in an attempt to defeat his ex-wife's rights to the property.

The chancellor held that appellee had proved his right to possession of the gold and therefore was entitled to it . . . . The chancellor found that appellee had not made a completed gift of the gold and further held that appellee was not estopped from asserting his claim to the gold. . . .

[The court affirmed the chancellor's finding that Brown, Sr. did not intend a gift to Billie Jean. The following discussion pertains to Billie Jean's defense that Brown, Sr. had unclean hands (which the court equated with estoppel).]

As appellant points out, this case is very similar to a recent case decided by this court, Melvin *v.* Melvin, 270 Ark. 522 (Ark. App. 1980). In *Melvin,* the chancellor made a property division in a divorce proceeding whereby he awarded the husband a Winnebago motor home. On appeal the wife argued that the Winnebago was not marital property which the chancellor could divide because it was a gift to her before marriage. The chancellor had found that the transfer of title to the Winnebago to his present wife was solely an attempt to keep his former wife from receiving it in an earlier divorce proceeding. The chancellor further found that the general understanding at the time of the transfer was that it would be transferred back to the husband at some time subsequent to the divorce.

On appeal, the Arkansas Court of Appeals found that the evidence supported the court's finding that the husband intended no gift of the Winnebago to his present wife. However, the court further found that the husband was estopped from asserting any claim to the Winnebago. The court recognized that the transfer was made to preclude any possible claim by appellee's former wife. The court analogized this situation to one in which a husband conveys property to his wife in order to defraud his creditors. A conveyance made to defraud creditors is still good between the parties. [The transferor] does not come into court with clean hands.

We agree with appellant that the facts of this case are very similar to the facts in *Melvin*. However, we find that the *Melvin* case is in conflict with previous cases decided by the Arkansas Supreme Court in the application of the clean hands maxim. In Batesville Truck Line, Inc. *v.* Martin, 219 Ark. 603 (1951), the Arkansas Supreme Court held that the clean hands doctrine must, in order to defeat a suit, have an immediate and necessary relation to the equity which the complainant seeks to enforce against the defendant. Further, the party complaining of the wrong must have been injured thereby to justify the application of the principle of unclean hands. The purpose of the maxim is to secure justice and equity, and not to aid one in an effort to acquire property to which he has no right.

In *Batesville Truck Line, Inc.*, a transit permit was granted by the Public Service Commission to a dummy corporation formed by appellee, Clay Martin, and appellant, Gilbert F. Tugwell. Martin's name was withheld from the P.S.C. proceedings because otherwise the permit would have been denied. Tugwell later refused to transfer to Martin any of the stock. Martin brought this lawsuit to require appellant to specifically perform a contract to transfer to Martin 50% of the corporate stock of Batesville Truck Line, Inc. The corporation and its stockholders, including Tugwell, were made parties defendant. The trial resulted in a decree in appellee's favor which directed Tugwell and his wife to transfer the stock to Clay Martin. Tugwell's plea of "unclean hands" against Martin was denied for the reason that Tugwell participated in the fraud on the Commission. . . .

Recently, the Arkansas Supreme Court has taken the position that it will balance the equities between the parties in the application of the clean hands doctrine, and if the policy against permitting unjust enrichment of the transferee is outweighed by the policy against giving relief to a person who has entered into an illegal transaction then the property owner's conduct is not so reprehensible that he should lose the property.

In the instant case, we find that there was evidence to support the chancellor's decision that appellee was not estopped from asserting his interest in the gold. We hold that this case is governed by the rule stated in *Batesville Truck Line,* and to the extent that Melvin *v.* Melvin, is in conflict, that case is overruled. In order to justify application of the clean hands maxim, appellant must prove that she was somehow injured thereby. Further, a chancellor may balance the equities between the parties in determining whether or not to apply the maxim.

Here, the evidence strongly suggests that appellant knew why the gold was being transferred to her. Although she testified that appellee had made an unconditional gift of the gold to her, the chancellor chose to believe appellee and his witnesses who testified that the gold was transferred to appellant for the purpose of keeping it from his former wife and appellant understood that the gold was to be transferred back to him some time after the divorce. . . . We find no error in the chancellor's ruling on this issue. . . .

NOTES ON UNCLEAN HANDS

1. Jacob Landau conveyed real property to his son Alfred, without consideration, in order to avoid the claims of his (Jacob's) creditors. Fraudulent conveyance statutes allow creditors to reclaim transfers of this

kind from the transferee, but Jacob's creditors never discovered the conveyance. After Jacob's debts were discharged in bankruptcy proceedings, Alfred reconveyed the property to Jacob, without consideration. Later, Jacob brought an action to quiet his title to the property against any possible claim by Alfred. Alfred, no longer so compliant, opposed the decree on the ground that Jacob's hands were not clean. The New York Court of Appeals upheld a decree quieting Jacob's title. The court said:

> "[W]e are reminded by the late Professor Zechariah Chafee that moral indignation against the plaintiff must operate, not in a vacuum, but in harmony with other important purposes and functions of the substantive law involved. As he criticized the application of the unclean hands doctrine in a situation similar to that here present, 'This ethical attitude seems entirely out of place. What ought to count is the strong social policy in favor of making the land records furnish an accurate map of the ownership of all land in the community. Whatever A's old misdeeds, he *is* the lawful owner of this lot and the records ought to show this fact. The existing record falsely makes R owner. It may mislead scores of honest citizens—people who have strong reasons for wishing to buy the lot, such as creditors of A, creditors of R, or lawyers drawing deeds of adjoining lots who are anxious to insert an accurate description. What is the sense of perpetuating an erroneous land record in order to penalize A for past misdeeds by causing him inconvenience? Better regard his dirty hands as washed during the lapse of twenty years rather than mess up the recording system.' (Chafee, SOME PROBLEMS OF EQUITY, 21–22 [1950].)"

Seagirt Realty Corp. *v.* Chazanof, 13 N.Y.2d 282, 287 (1963). Two dissenting judges believed that the court should not grant relief to Landau.

2. Heller & Merz Co.'s bluing (a coloring agent used on fabrics) had long been known to the public under the names of "American Ball Blue" and "American Wash Blue." The Shavers adopted the same names for their bluing, and Heller & Merz obtained an injunction against use of the names. This ruling was affirmed on appeal. In response to the argument that the plaintiff had unclean hands because it had recently been manufacturing and selling other brands, "Germania" and "Bavarian" Ball Blue, in boxes falsely simulating foreign products, the court said:

> "The principle that 'he who comes into equity must do so with clean hands' . . . does not repel all sinners from courts of equity, nor does it disqualify any complainant from obtaining relief there who has not dealt unjustly in the very transaction concerning which he complains. The iniquity which will repel him must have an immediate and necessary relation to the equity for which he sues. There is no evidence that the appellee has been guilty of any injustice, fraud, or wrong in acquiring the good will of its business in the American ball blue and the American wash blue, which is the subject of this suit, or in its relations with the appellants, and relief cannot be denied to it because it may have been wicked in

> other transactions which affect neither the appellants nor the equity here under consideration."

Shaver *v.* Heller & Merz Co., 108 Fed. 821, 834 (8th Cir. 1901).

3. American University, a fraudulent institution for instruction in chiropractic treatment, falsely stated in its advertising that it had a professional staff of teachers with a consulting staff of practitioners, and gave the incomes of some of its graduates, of whom none actually existed. Wood, a discharged employee who had assisted in these frauds, was using American's lists of actual and prospective students to organize an equally fraudulent school of his own, and to conduct a campaign to destroy American's business. The trial judge granted American's request for injunctive relief. This decision was reversed by the appellate court, and its judgment was affirmed by the state supreme court.

> "[A]s a general rule it is required that the wrongdoing or fraud of the complainant, to bar him from relief on the ground that he comes with unclean hands, must be connected with the subject of the litigation and have some relation to the rights of the parties arising out of the transaction. That rule is not applicable to the facts in this record. It is true the fraud and wrongdoing of complainant did not affect the private rights of defendants, and afforded no justification in morals for their seeking to profit by exposing them, but on the ground of the public interest and policy we do not think complainant's grievance is of a character to be redressed in a court of equity. The misrepresentations of complainant in the conduct of its business affected the public, and it would seem a strange thing if a court of conscience should be required to protect a suitor in the commission of a fraud upon the public.
>
> "A court of equity is a court of conscience and will exercise its extraordinary powers only to enforce the requirements of conscience. It is no part of its function to aid a litigant in the promotion of a fraud upon the public."

American University *v.* Wood, 294 Ill. 186, 195 (1920).

4. The equitable doctrine of unclean hands has a legal counterpart, commonly known as the *in pari delicto* defense, which is applicable to damage claims as well as claims for equitable relief. *In pari delicto* is narrower than unclean hands, in that it depends on a finding that the plaintiff acted not only unfairly, but also illegally in connection with the claim. It typically comes into play when the parties were involved in a common illegal activity, then began to argue among themselves.

An example is Bateman Eichler, Hill Richards, Inc. *v.* Berner, 472 U.S. 299 (1985), in which investors brought a securities fraud action against corporate insiders who had disclosed what they pretended was private information about the prospects of mining venture. The insiders defended on the ground that the plaintiff investors were *in pari delicto*, because they traded on the supposed inside information, in violation of securities laws. The Supreme Court indicated that the *in pari delicto* defense should be limited to cases in which the parties bear a similar degree of fault and the underlying policies of the laws involved will not be harmed by barring relief. Because the defendant insiders were more culpable than the plaintiff investors and the policies of the securities laws favored private actions to enforce anti-fraud provisions, the Court permitted the plaintiffs to proceed.

3. SPECIAL INSTANCES OF FRAUD AND MISTAKE

Defenses to contractual obligation based on fraud and mistake were first recognized in equity, as grounds for a decree enjoining the equity defendant from suing at law to enforce the contract or for rescission. Over time, the law courts recognized standard forms of fraud and mistake as defenses or as grounds for informal rescission. In certain borderline types of fraud and mistake, however, courts may recognize a defense to specific performance without recognizing a full defense to contractual obligation. Some examples follow. Are they justified?

Kelly v. Central Pacific Railroad Co.

Supreme Court of California, 1888.
74 Cal. 557.

[The defendant, which held title to land along its railroad, offered tracts for sale with a "preference" to be given to persons currently occupying the land. Kelly falsely represented to the defendant's land agent that he was the occupant of a certain tract, knowing that in fact another person, Cole, was inhabiting the land. Accordingly, the land agent agreed to convey to Kelly. Upon learning of the deception, the agent tendered back Kelly's down payment, but Kelly refused to accept the money and instead sued for specific performance of the contract to convey the lands. Cole intervened and requested that the land be conveyed to him at the same price. The lower court ordered that Kelly should convey the land to Cole and Kelly appealed.]

■ HAYNE, C. . . . The point made on Kelly's appeal is, that the false representation was not productive of injury to the railroad company, and the argument is that there was no injury, because, in the first place, it was under no obligation to convey to Cole,—the promise contained in the circular being merely that "preference will *generally* be given to settlers" . . .—and because, in the second place, the company was willing to convey, and will convey, the land to Cole for the same price that it agreed to convey it to Kelly, and hence could not be injured pecuniarily. . . .

[W]e think there are two answers to the argument for the appellant.

First. Assuming the correctness of appellant's major proposition,—viz., that in order to defeat a suit for specific performance on the ground of fraud, the fraud must be productive of injury,—it is not necessary that the injury should result *to the vendor*. It is sufficient if it would result to third persons. It is upon this principle that the relief is refused, where the thing to be done would operate as a fraud upon the public. . . . So upon the same principle, the relief is refused where the agreement was in fraud of the rights of creditors, or in fraud of the rights of other parties. . . . The court will not make itself an instrument to carry out the fraud, whether the person to be injured be a party to the contract or not. It will not assist the plaintiff to get the benefit of the intervenor's labor and improvements upon the tract in controversy.

Second. But we do not think that in order to defeat a suit for the specific performance of a contract to convey land, upon the ground of fraud, the fraud must be productive of damage either to the vendor or to third persons. If the misrepresentation was intentional, and made for the purpose of deceiving the vendor, and the vendor relies upon it, and was deceived by it, and would not have entered into the contract but for the fact that he was so deceived, then we think a court of equity will not enforce the contract, whether it be accompanied by damage or not. So far as this kind of suit is concerned, such a misrepresentation is material although not accompanied by damage. . . .

It is perfectly true . . . that an action at law cannot be maintained for fraud unless accompanied by damage. It is also true . . . that a court of equity will not set aside a contract obtained through fraud unless it be productive of injury. But it is not true that this applies to suits for specific performance. It is well settled that a court of equity may refuse specific performance of a contract which it would not set aside.

Although the court will refuse to destroy the contract, it will not further in any way the fraudulent design. In such cases, by an application of the maxim, that he who comes into equity must come with clean hands, the court is enabled to give greater effect to the principles of morality than can be done in ordinary cases. . . . And it is evident that such must be the rule. To say otherwise is to place suits for specific performance on the same level with actions at law . . . .

In the present case the false and fraudulent representation of plaintiff was the inducing cause of the contract. This is apparent from the fact that so soon as the company discovered the fraud which had been practiced upon it, it repudiated the contract. And it is expressly found that "the land agent, but for such deception, would not have awarded said south half of northeast quarter to said Kelly, but would have awarded it to said Cole." This state of facts well illustrates the wisdom of the doctrine which does not insist upon measuring everything by the standard of damage, but so far as can be done, allows parties to determine what is for their own interests, and to contract or refuse to contract accordingly. It is evident from the circulars contained in the record that it was the policy of the company to encourage the settlement of its vast tracts of unoccupied land. To carry out this policy it offered special inducements to settlers. It ought to be allowed to fulfill its promises to those who have relied upon its good faith. It is not for one who falsely pretends to be entitled to the benefit of those promises to say that it is all the same to the company because he pays the same price as the other would. The case is one where the vendor has special motives for selling to one person at a price which it would not accept from another. . . .

[Kelly's] case against the company, therefore, fails. And this being so, he cannot inquire into the correctness of the decree directing the company to convey to the intervenor. For if he is not entitled to the specific thing, it is of no consequence to him what becomes of it, and he cannot concern himself with that question. . . .

Panco v. Rogers

Superior Court of New Jersey, Chancery Division, 1952.
19 N.J. Super. 12.

■ HANEMAN, J.S.C. The plaintiffs herein seek the rescission of a written agreement to sell real estate, upon the ground of mutual mistake. The defendant seeks specific performance of said agreement, by way of counterclaim. The alleged mistake lies in the consideration to be paid for the conveyance of the realty, plaintiffs alleging that it should have been $12,500 and defendant alleging it should have been $5,500, as expressed in said agreement.

I find the following facts in connection herewith:

> John Panco, a man of some 77 years of age, had been the owner of the realty here involved since 1913, the purchase of which was his only transaction involving real estate until that now under consideration. Being a carpenter by trade, he had, by his own efforts, constructed the home there situated. He had had very little formal schooling and was, at the time of the execution of the agreement, quite deaf.

In the fore part of the year 1951 the plaintiffs had decided to sell the premises here involved and to move to Florida. In furtherance of such a plan, with the aid of their daughter, Alice Panco, they prepared an advertisement which was inserted in the *Philadelphia Inquirer,* and placed a sign in the window of the house, advertising said property for sale. In response to these advertisements, several prospective purchasers arrived at the premises, but none accepted at the asking price of $12,500. The defendant, who lived in the neighborhood, came to the property on or about May 15, 1951. He was escorted through the property by the plaintiff Mary Panco, in the absence of her husband, John Panco. Mary Panco is apparently of foreign extraction and speaks with an accent. Upon inquiring the price, defendant alleges that he was advised by Mary Panco that it was $5,500. The plaintiff Mary Panco denies the price as so stated, but alleges that the price asked was $12,500. The said defendant brought his intended bride to examine the premises upon the following Thursday. Upon this occasion there was no further discussion of price. On the succeeding Tuesday, May 22, 1951, the defendant, as per arrangements made the preceding night, took John Panco to his, defendant's, attorney, where the agreement was prepared. The plaintiff,

John Panco, took very little vocal part in the discussion at the attorney's office. . . .

The defendant, after the agreement had been signed by him and John Panco, drove the latter to his home, where the signature of Mary Panco was obtained. That evening, when Alice Panco returned home from work, the plaintiffs for the first time, upon her explanation, understood that the agreement called for a consideration of $5,500. John Panco insisted that the $5,500 related to a part payment on account of the purchase price of $12,500. They immediately contacted a son-in-law of the plaintiffs who, in turn, contacted the defendant. A conference ensued at plaintiff's residence. Although plaintiffs contend that the defendant agreed to cancel the transaction, the defendant states that he did not definitely agree to do so. The plaintiffs then offered to repay to the defendant not only his deposit, but whatever expenses he had been put to, including attorney's fees. This offer they still make.

The testimony satisfies me that the property here involved is worth considerably in excess of $5,500, and is worth at least $10,000, and that the plaintiffs had established their sale price at $12,500 and believed that they were obtaining $12,500. . . .

I am satisfied that there was a mutual mistake in the parol negotiations, *i.e.*, the defendant conceived that he was purchasing the property for $5,500 and the plaintiffs that they were selling at $12,500. It is understandable that such an error might have arisen when it is noted that Mary Panco, the only person with whom the defendant discussed price before the preparation of the agreement, speaks with an accent.

Insofar as the provisions of the final written agreement are concerned, there was a unilateral mistake, *i.e.*, the defendant knew that the agreement provided for a sales price of $5,500 and the plaintiffs believed that the agreement provided for $12,500.

Normally, rescission cannot be enforced on account of the mistake of one party only, which the other party did not share and where such other party was not guilty of fraud, undue influence, concealment or bad faith and would not derive any unconscionable advantage from the enforcement of the contract. . . .

Considering all of the essential elements concerned, I find that although the plaintiffs are free of such negligence as would prevent them from relief, and acted promptly, and that the defendant can be restored to his original position, that there was no actual fraud, undue influence or concealment on the part of the defendant, and hence the plaintiffs may not have a rescission of the contract.

However, insofar as the affirmative relief demanded by the defendant is concerned, the specific performance of the contract, such an application is addressed to the sound discretion of a court of equity, which may grant or deny, as the circumstances of the case warrant. Upon an application for specific performance the court must be satisfied that the claim is fair, reasonable and just, and in judging of its fairness, the court will look not only at the terms of the contract itself, but at all of the surrounding circumstances, including the relations of the parties.

One seeking a specific performance may, upon a proper finding, be relegated to his remedy at law. A decree of specific performance will never be made unless substantial justice is done thereby, but the parties will be left to their remedies at law.

Although inadequacy of price is not in and of itself a sufficient ground for refusing specific performance, it may be so gross as to shock the conscience of the court and amount to conclusive and decisive evidence of fraud in the transaction, even in the absence of affirmative proof of fraud or misrepresentation. Actual proof of fraud is, under those circumstances, not necessary. . . .

Where the enforcement of a contract for the sale of land would be harsh, oppressive or manifestly unjust to one of the parties thereto, its specific performance will not be decreed, but the parties will be left to their remedy at law. To succeed in a suit for specific performance, the court must be satisfied that the claim is fair, reasonable and equal in all its parts, and to so determine. The court will look not merely at the terms of the agreement but at the relation of the parties and the surrounding circumstances as well. . . .

The question is not what must the court do, but what should it do, in view of the circumstances, to further justice.

Therefore, taking into consideration all of the elements of this case, including the age, lack of education and deafness of John Panco, the foreign extraction of his wife, the original mistake as to the consideration, the manner in which the contract was prepared, and the attendant circumstances, the price, which I find inadequate, and as well the fact that a refusal to direct specific performance will result in no damage to defendant except the loss of a bargain, it is here held that a judgment of specific performance would be harsh, oppressive, unjust, inequitable and unfair to the plaintiffs; and defendant's counterclaim will as well be dismissed. . . .

Double AA Corp. v. Newland & Co.

Supreme Court of Montana, 1995.
273 Mont. 486.

■ TRIEWEILER, JUSTICE. . . . The ranch, which is the subject of the dispute, formerly belonged to Raymond George. Raymond died in 1974 and, as provided in his will, left the ranch in a testamentary trust for his family. His daughter Maxine was designated the trustee. The trust provided that his wife, Olga George, would receive income from the trust for her life and that the George children held remainder interests as follows: Maxine George—three-ninths, as well as a first option to purchase from the other remaindermen; Leo George—two-ninths; Kenneth George—two-ninths; and Shirley Bragg—two-ninths. Maxine died in 1980, and . . . Shirley Bragg became the trustee following Maxine's death.

On December 13, 1989, Double AA Corporation, a Delaware Corporation whose sole shareholders are Charles Allmon and Gwen Allmon, agreed with Shirley Bragg, who at that time was the trustee of the Raymond W. George trust, to purchase the George family's ranch in the Paradise Valley south of Livingston. Shirley agreed on behalf of the trust to convey the property, and a substantial deposit was transferred. [As required for sale of property held in a testamentary trust, Shirley petitioned for and received judicial approval for the sale. Then, prior to the closing, Shirley wrote Charles Allmon a letter informing him that she wished to rescind the transaction, based on a mistake about taxes. Allmon refused, and Double AA filed this action for specific performance.]

At trial, Shirley testified that in 1988 she had received advice from Wes Johnson, a financial planner for Investment Diversified Services (IDS), that if the trust did not sell the ranch there would be tax consequences in an amount between $200,000 and $300,000 at the time of Olga's death. Olga was nearly 90 years old when Shirley received this advice. Wes Johnson admitted he had little knowledge about taxes and was not qualified to render tax advice. He also testified that he was paid on a commission basis, and as a result felt pressure to locate investors for IDS. He encouraged that the ranch be sold and the proceeds be invested with IDS. Shirley testified that she reluctantly agreed to sell because of Johnson's tax advice. . . .

Shirley [also] testified that the erroneous information she had received from Johnson was confirmed by Legal Tech, a Billings accounting firm. However, she was informed in November 1990 that Olga's death would not result in any immediate tax consequences. Instead, she learned that capital gains tax in the amount of $400,000 would be due upon sale of the ranch to Double AA. She testified that the attorney who represented her prior to the sale had not advised her that Johnson's advice was incorrect. There was also contradicted testimony that her previous attorney was to receive a percentage of the broker's commission which was to be paid by Double AA. . . .

> "*A bill in equity for specific performance is an appeal to the conscience of the court, and generally, in such a proceeding, the inquiry must be whether, in equity and good conscience, the court should specifically enforce the contract.* Accordingly, specific performance will be granted when it is apparent from a view of all the circumstances of the particular case that it will serve the ends of justice, and it will be withheld when, from a like view, it appears that it will produce hardships or injustice to either party. . . ."

Seifert *v.* Seifert, 568 P.2d 155, 157 (Mont. 1977) (quoting 81 C.J.S. *Specific Performance* § 3). . . .

In determining whether a contract should be specifically enforced, courts look at the contract, as well as the relationship of the parties, and will determine if the contract to be enforced is fair and reasonable.[1] Factors courts consider include execution of a contract under circumstances unfavorable to the defendant because of lack of advice, and the difference in the parties' business experience and knowledge. . . .

The District Court made specific findings, which are supported by substantial evidence, in relation to the above-listed equitable considerations and statutes. The court found: (1) Double AA knew, or should have known, before the sale, that Shirley misapprehended facts material to the contract and Shirley testified she told Charles that she felt pressured to sell because of her erroneous belief regarding the potential tax liability; (2) Shirley was a victim of mistaken information and inaccurate advice. The "mistaken fact [regarding taxes] more than anything else was the reason Shirley consented to [the] sale [of] the George family ranch"; (3) Charles and Shirley had extremely divergent backgrounds in business transactions. Charles was a well-known professional investor, had experience in multi-million dollar transactions, and had extensive education, background, and experience in business. To the contrary, Shirley was a somewhat unsophisticated trustee who was neither prepared for her position as trustee nor educated in business nor business transactions, negotiations, or taxes.

Finally, the court found that the land was not unique to Double AA. Charles testified that the ranch was no more unique than land that he already had except that it was contiguous with property he owned in the Paradise Valley. The court found that the loss would impose a greater hardship on the George Family Trust than Double AA because Shirley's decision to sell was a direct result of the incorrect tax advice, and the ranch had been in the George family for over 100 years.

Based on its findings, the court concluded that, in light of the circumstances surrounding the execution of the contract, specific performance was not appropriate because the contract was not fair, just, and reasonable, and Shirley's assent was based on a mistake or misapprehension. . . .

While a misapprehension or mistake regarding taxes is insufficient to avoid a contract, such a misunderstanding or mistake, in light of the surrounding circumstances, may be a sufficient reason to deny specific performance as an equitable remedy.

---

[1] In *In re George Trust* [an appeal of the prior decision approving Shirley's sale of the property], we upheld the District Court's finding that Double AA's offer of $1,300,000, along with the other benefits, was fair and reasonable. . . .

[However,] we did not address whether it would be fair and reasonable to specifically enforce the contract.

Moreover, we have upheld the denial of specific performance where the defendant relied on advice from her attorney which produced factual and legal misapprehensions. . . .

Based on the equitable principles and statutory criteria set forth above, evidence in the record, and the District Court's findings, including the parties' unequal positions and the mistaken information on which the trustee relied, we hold that the District Court did not abuse its discretion. . . .

4. UNDUE HARDSHIP

Patel v. Ali

Chancery Division, 1984.
[1984] Ch. 283.

■ GOULDING, J. read the following judgment. . . .

The circumstances of [this] case are unusual and it has caused me some anxiety. The argument for the defendant, as it has been eloquently presented on paper and by her counsel, necessarily arouses so much sympathy that I felt for a long time that any exercise of discretionary jurisdiction in her favour would probably be unfair to her opponents, just because of the force of such sympathy.

The material facts are not in dispute and can be shortly stated. In the year 1979 the defendant was living in the property with her husband, Mr. Ali. They occupied it as their matrimonial home. Another couple, Mr. and Mrs. Nazir Ahmed, were also living in the house. Mr. Ahmed is the second defendant to the action. The property was freehold and was registered in the name of Mr. Ahmed and the defendant, who claim to be not only legally but beneficially entitled thereto. On 31 July 1979 the contract was entered into between both defendants as vendors and the plaintiffs, Mr. and Mrs. Patel, as purchasers. The price was £24,000, the contractual completion date 28 August 1979.

The performance of the contract has been subject—and this is a circumstance which, to my mind, is of the greatest importance in the case—to a quite extraordinary delay, for which neither side on this appeal has sought to blame the other. The causes of the delay have not been explored in detail in the evidence, but it appears that a great deal of it can be put down to two difficulties. In the first place, the trustee in bankruptcy of Mr. Ali has made claim to a beneficial interest in the property. . . . [This impediment was finally resolved by a bankruptcy court order allowing the sale to proceed, with the understanding that the trustee could continue to press his claims against proceeds of the sale.] The second cause of delay, so it is said, was a succession of difficulties experienced by the plaintiffs in effecting service of proceedings on Mr. Ahmed, who has returned to Pakistan. . . .

Meanwhile, the circumstances of the defendant had changed disastrously. At the date of the contract she had one child who was still a baby; and, so far as she knew, she was in good health. She was about 23 years old. She spoke and still speaks, in the words of her solicitor's affidavit, "virtually no English at all." In the summer of 1980 she was found to have a bone cancer in her right thigh. On 24 July 1980, that is three days after the order of Fox J. in the bankruptcy proceedings, her right leg was amputated at the hip joint. She was then in an advanced state of pregnancy and gave birth to her second child on 31 August 1980. In the spring of 1981 her husband went to prison and remained there until mid-summer 1982. After his release she became pregnant again and her third child was born in August 1983.

The defendant has been fitted with an artificial leg. She is able to walk about the house and dress herself, but not to do shopping, and she needs help with household duties and with the children. She is greatly dependent on friends and relations to enable her to keep her home going and to look after her children, especially on her sister who, I was told, lives only a few doors away, and on a friendly neighbour, Mrs. Dhillon.

It is in these circumstances that the defendant asks the court to refuse specific performance of the contract and to leave the plaintiffs to their remedy in damages. Her advisers recognise that the court must be satisfied that the legal remedy will be effective, and there is evidence that sympathetic persons in the Muslim Community in which she lives are willing to put up money for that purpose.

That the hardship to the defendant of enforced removal from the property would be great is, on the evidence, beyond doubt. Any accommodation which the local authority could immediately provide for the defendant is likely to deprive her of the daily assistance on which she relies, or at least greatly to diminish it. The move would necessarily cause much more severe disturbance to the lives of the children, now aged five years, three years and four or five months, than a family removal does in ordinary cases, and might even make it impossible for the defendant to keep them with her, handicapped as she is by her physical disability.

The hardship which would be caused to the plaintiffs if specific performance were refused and adequate pecuniary compensation were available is not, so far as the evidence reveals, greater than what is necessarily involved in being disappointed of the purchase after so long a delay. Since the contractual date for completion in 1979 the plaintiffs have lived in accommodation rented from their local authority, Brent London Borough Council.

It is not in dispute that, like other equitable relief, the specific performance of contracts is a discretionary remedy; but, in the ordinary case of a sale of land or buildings, the court normally grants it as of course and withholds it only on proof of special facts. The textbooks and reported decisions have long recognised hardship as one ground on which, in a proper case, a purchaser or vendor may be refused specific performance and be left to his right to damages for breach of contract at law. . . . [In] the majority of cases, the hardship which moves the court to refuse specific performance is either a hardship existing at the date of the contract or a hardship due in some way to the plaintiff. . . . It is sufficient for me to cite a passage from FRY ON SPECIFIC PERFORMANCE, 6th ed. (1921), p. 199:

> "It is a well-established doctrine that the court will not enforce the specific performance of a contract, the result of which would be to impose great hardship on either of the parties to it; and this although the party seeking specific performance may be free from the least impropriety of conduct. The question of the hardship of a contract is generally to be judged of at the time at which it is entered into: if it be then fair and just and not productive of hardship, it will be immaterial that it may, by the force of subsequent circumstances or change of events, have become less beneficial to one party, except where these subsequent events have been in some way due to the party who seeks the performance of the contract. For whatever contingencies may attach to a contract, or be involved in the performance of either part, have been taken upon themselves by the parties to it. It has been determined that the reasonableness of a contract is to be judged of at the time it is entered into, and not by the light of subsequent events, and we have already seen that the same principle applies in considering the fairness of a contract."

However, the principle so stated cannot be erected into a fixed limitation of the court's equitable jurisdiction. . . . [T]he court has sometimes refused specific performance because of a change of circumstances supervening after the making of the contract and not in any way attributable to the plaintiff. One such case is . . . Webb *v.* Direct London and Portsmouth Railway Co., 1 De.G.M. & G. 521 (1852), where the Court of Appeal refused specifically to enforce a purchase of land by the company after it had abandoned its proposed enterprise of constructing a railway from Epsom to Portsmouth. Similar in principle are the cases where the court has refused injunctions to compel specific performance of restrictive covenants by reason of a change in the character of the neighbourhood, even where the plaintiff and his predecessors in title have in no way contributed thereto. Thus, I am satisfied that the court's discretion is wide enough, in an otherwise proper case, to refuse specific performance on the ground of hardship subsequent to the contract and not caused by the plaintiff.

Another limitation suggested by [plaintiffs' counsel] was that, in the reported cases, as he said, hardship successfully relied on has always related to the subject matter of the contract and has not been just a personal hardship of the defendant. Certainly, mere pecuniary difficulties, whether of purchaser or of vendor, afford no excuse from performance of a contract. In a wider sense than that, I do not think the suggested universal proposition can be sustained. In *Webb's* case, the hardship in no way affected the title to the property or its physical condition. It was a hardship to the railway company to be compelled to pay for land it could never use, just as it is a hardship to the defendant here to be compelled to convey a house she cannot now well do without.

The important and true principle, in my view, is that only in extraordinary and persuasive circumstances can hardship supply an excuse for resisting performance of a contract for the sale of immovable property. A person of full capacity who sells or buys a house takes the risk of hardship to himself and his dependents, whether arising from existing facts or unexpectedly supervening in the interval before completion. This is where, to my mind, great importance attaches to the immense delay in the present case, not attributable to the defendant's conduct. Even after issue of the writ, she could not complete, if she had wanted to, without the concurrence of the absent Mr. Ahmed. Thus, in a sense, she can say she is being asked to do what she never bargained for, namely to complete the sale after more than four years, after all the unforeseeable changes that such a period entails. I think that in this way she can fairly assert that specific performance would inflict upon her "a hardship amounting to injustice. . . ." Equitable relief may, in my view, be refused because of an unforeseen change of circumstances not amounting to legal frustration . . . .

In the end, I am satisfied that it is within the court's discretion to accede to the defendant's prayer if satisfied that it is just to do so. And, on the whole, looking at the position of both sides after the long unpredictable delay for which neither seeks to make the other responsible, I am of opinion that it *is* just to leave the plaintiffs to their remedy in damages if that can indeed be effective. . . .

I will direct that, if within a specified period . . . a certain sum is paid into court to the credit of the action, or otherwise secured to the satisfaction of the plaintiffs, then the master's order will be discharged. Instead, an inquiry will be ordered what damage the plaintiffs have suffered by reason of the breach of contract by Mr. Ahmed and the defendant. The defendant will be ordered to pay the amount found due on the inquiry and the plaintiffs' taxed costs of the action, including this appeal, the costs of the inquiry being reserved. I have heard argument regarding the sum to be paid in, and I fix it at £10,000. If the money is not provided by the date specified, the appeal is to stand dismissed with costs. . . .

NOTES ON UNCONSCIONABIILITY

1. The Wentzes, who were farmers, agreed to sell the Campbell Soup Company their output of Chantenay red carrots for prices ranging from $23–$30 per ton. The contract was a form agreement written by Campbell, which provided, among other things, that if Campbell was unable to use the carrots

due to an act of god or a strike at Campbell, Campbell was excused from paying; in that case the Wentzes could resell their carrots to someone else *if* they obtained Campbell's consent. If an act of god or a strike at Campbell prevented the Wentzes from delivering carrots, the Wentzes were excused from performing but could not resell their carrots to someone else. The contract also contained a liquidated damages clause, providing for damages of $50 per acre of carrots if the Wentzes breached the agreement. An unexpected carrot shortage drove the market price of Chantenay red carrots to $90 per ton (a difference that far exceeded the liquidated damages named in the contract). The Wentzes breached, and Campbell sued for specific performance.

The court determined that, although carrots are a fungible commodity in ordinary circumstances, the carrot shortage made damages an inadequate remedy. Therefore, specific performance was presumptively available. However, the court found the contract too one-sided for equitable enforcement:

> "The provision of the contract which we think is the hardest is paragraph 9. . . . Campbell is excused from accepting carrots under certain circumstances. But even under such circumstances the grower, while he cannot say Campbell is liable for failure to take the carrots, is not permitted to sell them elsewhere unless Campbell agrees. This is the kind of provision which the late Francis H. Bohlen would call 'carrying a good joke too far.' . . .[ii]
>
> "We are not suggesting that the contract is illegal. Nor are we suggesting any excuse for the grower in this case who has deliberately broken an agreement entered into with Campbell. We do think, however, that a party who has offered and succeeded in getting an agreement as tough as this one is, should not come to a chancellor and ask court help in the enforcement of its terms."

Campbell Soup Co. *v.* Wentz, 172 F.2d 80, 83 (3rd Cir. 1948).

2. Section 2–302 of the Uniform Commercial Code provides as follows:

"Unconscionable Contract or Clause.

> "(1) If the court as a matter of law finds the contract or any term of the contract to have been unconscionable at the time it was made the court may refuse to enforce the contract, or it may enforce the remainder of the contract without the unconscionable term, or it may so limit the application of any unconscionable term as to avoid any unconscionable result.
>
> "(2) If it is claimed or appears to the court that the contract or any term thereof may be unconscionable the parties shall be afforded a reasonable opportunity to present evidence as to its commercial setting, purpose and effect to aid the court in making the determination."

[ii] [Francis H. Bohlen taught at the University of Pennsylvania Law School from 1898 to 1938 and was the Reporter for the first Restatement of Torts.]

Comment 1 to this section states that the "principle is one of the prevention of oppression and unfair surprise and not of disturbance of allocation of risks because of superior bargaining power."

5. INADEQUATE CONSIDERATION

Jefferys v. Jefferys

Chancery, 1841.
41 Eng. Rep. 443.

A father having, by a voluntary settlement, conveyed certain freehold and covenanted to surrender certain copyhold estates to trustees in trust for the benefit of his daughters, afterwards devised part of the same estates to his widow, who, after his death, was admitted to some of the copyholds. A suit having been instituted by the daughters to have the trusts of the settlement carried into effect, and to compel the widow to surrender the copyholds to which she had been admitted, a decree was made for carrying into effect the trusts as far as they related to the freeholds, the Plaintiff's title to them being complete; but as to the copyholds, the bill was dismissed, with costs.

By articles of agreement, dated the 25th of July 1834, and made between John Jefferys of the one part, and Bowden and Thorn of the other part, John Jefferys, after reciting that he was desirous of making some certain and irrevocable provision for the support and maintenance of his daughters Martha, Charlotte, and Sarah Jefferys, covenanted with [made a sealed promise to] Bowden and Thorn, as trustees, forthwith to settle all his real estate to the same uses, ends, intents, and purposes as were expressed in his will, dated the 25th of May 1834; and, accordingly, he executed certain indentures [deeds] of lease and release[iii] of the 16th and 17th of September 1834, whereby, in consideration of the natural love and affection which he had for his three daughters, and for divers other good causes and considerations, he conveyed certain freehold hereditaments, subject to the incumbrances affecting the same, and covenanted to surrender certain copyhold hereditaments, to Bowden and Thorn, upon trust, out of the rents and profits thereof to pay to him an annuity of 80*l.* for his life; and after his death to sell the freehold and copyhold hereditaments, and out of the monies arising therefrom to pay off certain incumbrances, and to stand possessed of the residue of such monies, upon certain trusts, for the benefit of his three daughters.

By the will of Sarah Jefferys, who died in April 1835, all her interest under the settlement became vested in her two sisters. John Jefferys never surrendered the copyholds, pursuant to the covenant. In September 1836, he died, having, by will, dated the 18th of August 1836, given part of the before-mentioned freehold and copyhold estates to his wife Isabella, who was, shortly after his death, admitted to part of the copyhold estates.

In July 1837 this bill was filed by Martha and Charlotte Jefferys against Isabella Jefferys and Bowden and Thorn, praying that the trusts

---

[iii] [An indenture of lease and release was a conveyance used to avoid the Statute of Uses.]

of the indenture of the 17th September 1834 might be carried into execution; and that Isabella Jefferys might be decreed to surrender the copyholds, to which she had been admitted, to Bowden and Thorn, as trustees of that indenture.

By the will of Martha Jefferys, who died in April 1838, all her interest under the settlement became vested in her sister Charlotte Jefferys, the surviving Plaintiff; and Isabella Jefferys having, since the filing of the bill, married one Abraham Peacock, a bill of revivor and supplement was filed by the surviving Plaintiff. . . .

■ THE LORD CHANCELLOR [COTTENHAM]. The title of the Plaintiffs to the freehold is complete; and they may have a decree for carrying the settlement into effect so far as the freeholds are concerned. With respect to the copyholds, I have no doubt that the Court will not execute a voluntary [*i.e.*, gratuitous] contract; and my impression is, that the principle of the Court to withhold its assistance from a volunteer applies equally, whether he seeks to have the benefit of a contract, a covenant, or a settlement. As, however, the decision in [a prior case] is entitled to the highest consideration, I will not dispose of this case absolutely, without looking at a former case, in which I had occasion to refer to that decision. Unless I alter the opinion I have expressed, the bill must be dismissed with costs, so far as the copyholds are concerned. . . .

Seymour v. Delancey

Chancery Court of New York, 1822.
6 Johns. Ch. Rep. 222.
Court for the Trial of Impeachments and the Correction of Errors of New York, 1824.
3 Cow. 445.

■ THE CHANCELLOR [KENT]. The question in this case is, whether it be fit and proper, under all the circumstances, to decree a specific performance of the contract of sale.

The main objection to the exercise of this power of the Court, in the present case, is the great inadequacy of price which the plaintiff was to allow for the two farms, of which he seeks title.

By the articles of agreement, Thomas Ellison, the ancestor of the defendants, was to convey, by the first of June, 1820, two farms, lying in the towns of Montgomery and Wallkill, in Orange county, and containing, in the whole, 763 acres of land, and the plaintiff was to give, in exchange, the one equal undivided third part of two lots of land, in the village of Newburgh. The agreement was executed on the 14th of January, 1820, and, by the terms of it, each party was at liberty to take possession of the estate to be conveyed to him, and to receive the profits to his own use; and it is in proof, that each party did enter into possession, on the execution of the agreement.

The witnesses differ greatly in their estimates of the value of these respective pieces of land. . . . It is impossible to be precise in ascertaining the difference in value between the lands of the two parties, but I am satisfied, that at the date of the agreement, the village lots were not worth half the value of the country farms; and we should make an ample advance of the one, and an ample diminution of the other, in value, if we were to fix the one third of the Newburgh lots at 6,000 dollars, and the farms at 12,000 dollars.

The question then recurs, is it the dictate of sound legal discretion, that this agreement should be specifically carried into execution by the authority of this Court? It is an application to sound discretion. . . . A Court of equity must be satisfied, that the claim for a deed is fair and just, and reasonable, and the contract equal in all its parts, and founded on an adequate consideration, before it will interpose with this extraordinary assistance. If there be any well founded objection on any of these grounds, the practice of the Court is to leave the party to his remedy at law for a compensation in damages. . . .

The doctrine involved in this inquiry has been repeatedly brought into discussion since the time of Lord Eldon . . . . [I]n these later cases, there is a doubt thrown over the question, whether inadequacy of price alone, though not so great as to be evidence of fraud, will be sufficient, in any case, and without any other ingredient, as infirmity of mind, surprise, &c., to withhold the decree for a specific performance. But, after so much recognition of the general doctrine, that equity will not enforce hard, or unreasonable, or unequal bargains, but rather leave them to a jury at law, to mitigate or apportion the damages, as the justice of the case shall appear; . . . I do not perceive the necessity or even the propriety of that doubt and distrust, if not disapprobation, which Lord Eldon and the Master of the Rolls, have been pleased to express. . . .

I conclude, then, that inadequacy of price may, of itself, and without fraud or other ingredient, be sufficient to stay the application of the power of this Court to *enforce* a specific performance of a private contract to sell land; though it may be true, as the Lord Ch. Baron [Eyre] said, in Griffith *v.* Spratley [1 Cox Eq. 383], that mere inadequacy of price, independent of other circumstances, is not sufficient to *set aside* the transaction. In the present case, the inadequacy is so great as to give the character of hardship, unreasonableness and inequality to the contract, and to render it discreet and proper, under the established principles of the Court, to refuse to decree a specific performance, and to leave the plaintiff to seek his compensation in damages at law.

The civil law went far beyond the English law on this subject, and a contract for the sale of land was rescinded by judicial authority, though made in good faith, if the price was below half the value. . . . This was the law in France before the revolution. Though by the Napoleon Code, the ratio is fixed at 7–12ths below the real value.

If it were to be granted that an inadequacy, great as that in the present case, was not sufficient to stay the powers of the Court, without the weight of some additional ingredient, we have that ingredient in this case.

Ellison, the ancestor of the defendants, was, in the last year or two of his life, rendered, for a considerable part of his time, unfit for business, by habitual intoxication. His mind must have felt the pernicious effects of that habit, and have lost its original strength, when he made the bargain in question. The proof is abundantly sufficient to render the fact of his competency to contract, with the requisite judgment, doubtful. One of the witnesses says, that for the greater part of the last two years of his life, he was incompetent. The answer sets up this defence, in terms sufficiently intelligible to admit the proof, and to prevent the objection of surprise. It states, that for some time previous to his death, he was occasionally incapable of attending to business. The contract was made in January, and he died in August, 1820; and this language is, perhaps, as direct and explicit as children could have been inclined to use, and it was, no doubt, well understood by the plaintiff, for the habitual intoxication of Ellison appears to have been a matter of public notoriety in the village of Newburgh. This fact adds greatly to the force of the considerations growing out of the inadequacy of the price, and is clearly sufficient, within the view of all the cases, to render it highly discreet and just to refuse the aid of the Court to a specific performance of so hard and so extravagant a bargain, gained from a habitual drunkard, in the last year of his life, and just before his infirmities had begun to incapacitate him entirely for business.

There is another circumstance in the case which ought to be taken into consideration, when the plaintiff comes here seeking a specific performance. He was not in a condition to give a good title to the village lots, either when he contracted, or when the deeds were to be exchanged, or at the time of the death of Ellison. The lots were under mortgage for 5000 dollars, which I consider as their full value, and that mortgage was not redeemed until after Ellison's death. The plaintiff was in default on the first of June, 1820. He ought to have shown himself able and ready to convey on that day. One of his witnesses, who is a physician, says, that Ellison, from June to within a week of his death, was competent in mind to do business. The plaintiff shows no sufficient excuse for his want of readiness and ability; and I cannot but persuade myself, after having examined most of the English cases, that the united force of the circumstances of this case would have overcome the scruples of the most cautious mind that has ever investigated and expressed any opinion on the subject, and that a bill with so much fact against the equity of the claim, has never been sustained. . . .

I am, consequently, of opinion, that the bill be dismissed, without costs. . . .

[The plaintiff appealed to the Court for the Trial of Impeachments and the Correction of Errors. This court consisted of the Lieutenant-Governor, the Chancellor, the Chief Justice and the two Associate

Justices of the Supreme Court, and the 32 members of the state Senate. Kent had retired as Chancellor prior to the hearing of the appeal, and had been succeeded by Nathan Sanford, who, however, took no part in the hearing or decision of the appeal. Neither of the Associate Justices of the Supreme Court took part in the decision, one (Woolworth, J.) because he had not heard the argument, the other (Sutherland, J.) because of illness. By a vote of 14–10, the high court reversed Chancellor Kent's decision. The opinion of the Court for the Trial of Impeachments and the Correction of Errors of New York follows.]

■ SUDAM, SENATOR. . . . In reviewing this part of the case, it will be the duty of the Court to investigate the evidence as to the value of the Newburgh lots, and the farms to be exchanged for them. Should they arrive at the conclusion that *mere inadequacy* in value, where there is *no fraud, misrepresentation, imposition, or concealment of facts, is of itself sufficient to avoid the contract,* it will save a great deal of the labor and investigation which might otherwise be required. I admit, however, that where the inadequacy of price in a contract is so flagrant and palpable as to convince a man at the first blush, that one of the contracting parties had been imposed on by some false pretence, such a contract ought not to be enforced by this, or any other Court of Equity. It is not to be denied, that it is the settled doctrine of the Court of Chancery, that it will not carry into effect, specifically, a contract where the inadequacy of price amounts to conclusive evidence of fraud. . . .

There is no question so well calculated to generate a variety of opinion, as that which regards the value of a village lot, or a farm in the country; and unless the disproportion should be gross and palpable, it would be very difficult to estimate how much more had been given by A. for a lot than the price at which B. would value it. . . .

Upon the whole, I am of opinion, that there is not in the present case such an inadequacy of price, as, of itself, amounts to conclusive evidence of fraud; that the contract between the appellant and Ellison, in his lifetime, was entered into with a full knowledge of all the circumstances by Ellison, and after much deliberation; and that it is fair in all its parts; and that the respondents ought to be compelled specifically to carry it into effect. . . .

McKinnon v. Benedict

Supreme Court of Wisconsin, 1968.
38 Wis.2d 607.

This is an appeal from a judgment of the county court of Vilas county for damages for a trespass on the property owned by Roderick W. McKinnon and Dorothy D. McKinnon, and from an injunction which restrained the defendants, Roy A. Benedict, Jr., and Evelyn M. Benedict, from operating a trailer park and campsite on certain resort property located in Vilas county. The Benedicts have appealed from this judgment.

The Benedict property is approximately an 80-acre tract located on the shores of Mamie Lake, one of the chain of Cisco Lakes, on the Michigan-Wisconsin border. It is operated as a resort known as Bent's Camp. The Benedict property is completely surrounded by the McKinnon tract of approximately 1,170 acres. The McKinnons have lived on Mamie Lake since 1925, although at the present time they reside there only during the summer months and during the Christmas holidays. During the remainder of the year, the McKinnons reside in Arizona, where Roderick McKinnon is an investment counsellor. He is a member of the Wisconsin State Bar and at various times practiced law with the Milwaukee firms of Miller, Mack & Fairchild and Whyte, Hirschboeck, Minahan, Harding & Harland. During World War II, he was in intelligence work for the United States government. He served with the United States State Department and was, at one time, vice president of Cleaver-Brooks Company.

Until 1961, Bent's Camp was operated by a Mr. and Mrs. L.L. Dorsey. This property, although abutting Mamie Lake, is divided by county trunk B. The resort area is located near the lakeshore to the northeast of county trunk B and consists of 14 cabins and a main lodge. The area of Bent's Camp southwest of county trunk B is a small, undeveloped parcel of timberland. During 1960 the Dorseys were interested in selling the property. Their agent, one Handlos, located the Benedicts as prospective buyers. They, however, were in need of financial assistance to make the purchase, and they were referred to Roderick W. McKinnon, who agreed to loan the Benedicts the sum of $5,000 as a partial down payment. This loan was made on the basis of an understanding that the Benedicts would continue to operate Bent's Camp as an American plan family resort. On August 31, 1960, McKinnon wrote a letter to the Benedicts incorporating the terms on which the advance was made:

"Dear Roy:

"It is my understanding that in consideration of my advancing you $5000, for use as a downpayment on Bent's Camp we agree between one another as follows:

"(1) You and Mrs. Benedict will sign a non-interest bearing note for $5000, due January 1, 1961, and a first mortgage on your cottage in Gogebic County, Michigan. If you should sell this property or your property in Wheaton, Illinois prior to the time the note is paid, you will pay the note out of the proceeds.

"(2) As soon as convenient after your acquisition of Bent's Camp, we will sign a recordable agreement providing that for a period of 25 years no trees will be cut between my land and Bent's Camp, nor between Bent's Camp and County Highway 'B' nor will any improvements be constructed or placed closer to my property than the present buildings. This restriction will have no application to any of your land lying west of County

> Trunk 'B' nor to your separate 40-acre 'woodlot.' If you wish, we will supply trees to be planted in this area at no cost to you.
>
> "(3) In the event you desire, we will from time to time designate certain trees or certain areas on our property where you may cut fire wood at no cost to you.
>
> "(4) I will help you try to reach a satisfactory solution concerning the lease held by Mrs. J. Stuart Vair. I will also try to generate business for your camp and to otherwise assist you in getting the operation well organized.
>
> "If the foregoing meets with your approval, will you and Mrs. Benedict please sign below and return one copy for my files."

The approval was signed by both of the Benedicts, and the letter was returned to McKinnon. Thereafter, the Benedicts executed a note in the sum of $5,000 and a mortgage on their cottage property in Michigan. The promised $5,000 was shortly thereafter transmitted and used as a down payment. The loan was paid in full in the spring of 1961. The Benedicts thus had the use of the $5,000 from early September, 1960, to April, 1961, a period of about seven months. The Benedicts purchased the property from the Dorseys on a land contract at a price of $60,000. That land contract provided that, while the Benedicts continued to be obligated to the Dorseys under the terms of the contract, they would replace all personal property so as to maintain it in substantially the same state as at the time of the agreement. They also agreed that no timber would be cut except for firewood without the written consent of the Dorseys and that the premises were to be operated substantially in the same manner as they had been operated by the Dorseys in the previous years.

At the time the land contract was executed, Bent's Camp consisted of 14 cottages, only five of which could be used for resort purposes. Between 1961 and 1964, the Benedicts invested $20,000 in cottages, installing bathrooms and kitchens so that all of the cabins were habitable. Roy Benedict testified that during the period between 1961 and 1964, the income from the operations of the American Plan resort substantially decreased and that it became increasingly difficult to make the land-contract payments.

One of the conditions of the letter of August 31, 1960, was that McKinnon would attempt to reach a satisfactory solution concerning the lease held by Mrs. J. Stuart Vair. The record shows that Mrs. Vair held a fifty-year lease on one of the cabins at an annual rental of $5 per year. The record reveals only one attempt, and that unsuccessful, on the part of McKinnon to "reach a satisfactory solution." The agreement also provided that McKinnon would try to generate business for the camp and otherwise assist in getting the operation well organized. The record indicates no attempt whatsoever on the part of McKinnon to get the operation "well organized." There was evidence that at least one small group had spent a few days at Bent's Camp at the suggestion of McKinnon, but it is apparent that the amount of business generated by him was almost nil.

Because of financial pressures, the Benedicts, in the fall of 1964, decided to add to a trailer park and facilities for a tent camp. A trailer park was laid out just to the northeast of county trunk B. In the fall of 1964, Roy Benedict bulldozed the hills in that area and installed sewer, water, and electric facilities for 18 trailers at a cost of approximately $8,000. In the spring of 1965 work was commenced on a campsite on a hill located to the south of the cottages and across the bay from the McKinnon property. The Benedicts have invested to date approximately $1,200 on this campsite, most of which was expended for grading.

In June of 1965, McKinnon wrote to Benedict stating:

> "I have heard indirectly that you are making some fairly major changes in the operation of Bent's Camp.
>
> "Although I do not know the exact nature of the changes, I am confident that you and Ev will bear in mind our agreement of August 31, 1960 . . . . I enclose a photostatic copy."

When the McKinnons returned to Wisconsin in June of 1965, they became aware of the nature of the work done by Benedict and immediately commenced suit to enjoin defendants "from the acts done or being done and uses to be made or being made" of the property. The McKinnons relied not only on the agreement of August 31, 1960, but also alleged the violation of county zoning and trailer ordinances and alleged a trespass across a point of land, wholly surrounded by the Benedict property, which was owned by McKinnon.

After a trial before the court, the trial judge found for the plaintiffs in accordance with the demands of the complaint enjoining the defendants from further bulldozing or hill leveling and from conducting on the premises a trailer park or a mobile home camp. The renting of any portion of the land for trailers or campers was prohibited by the judgment, and the Benedicts were restrained from using the premises for any other purpose than as an American Plan summer resort until August 31, 1985. It is from this judgment the defendants appeal.

■ HEFFERNAN, JUSTICE. . . . We are . . . not confronted with the question of damages that may result from the breach of this contract and confine ourselves solely to the right of the plaintiffs to invoke the equitable remedy of specific performance, in this case the enjoining of the defendants from the breach of the contract. . . .

[The Restatement of Contracts § 367] cites three bases for a court of equity refusing specific performance of a contract. They are:

> "(a) the consideration for it is grossly inadequate or its terms are otherwise unfair, or

> "(b) its enforcement will cause unreasonable or disproportionate hardship or loss to the defendant or to third persons, or
>
> "(c) it was induced by some sharp practice, misrepresentation, or mistake."

. . . These, of course, are ancient principles of equity . . . .

Coupled with the general equitable principle that contracts that are oppressive will not be enforced in equity is the principle of public policy that restrictions on the use of land "are not favored in the law," and that restrictions and prohibitions as to the use of real estate should be resolved, if a doubt exists, in favor of the free use of the property. . . .

The bargain between the McKinnons and the Benedicts has proved to be a harsh one indeed. If the terms of the agreement of August 31, 1960, are to be enforced literally, the Benedicts have for a period of twenty-five years stripped themselves of the right to make an optimum and lawful use of their property. The agreement provides that no improvements can be constructed closer to the McKinnon property than those buildings and improvements that were in existence in 1960. . . .

There was clear testimony that Benedict found difficulty in meeting his land-contract obligations, and his efforts to construct a campsite and trailer camp were motivated by the desire to put the resort on a more stable financial basis. While it is understandable that McKinnon may object to the erection of a trailer park and a campsite on adjacent property, nevertheless, they are legal and proper uses, assuming that they conform with the ordinances and statutes and do not constitute a nuisance; and any contract that seeks to prohibit them on a neighbor's property must be supported by consideration that has some relationship to the detriment to be sustained by the property owner whose uses are thus curtailed.

The great hardship sought to be imposed upon the Benedicts is apparent. What was the consideration in exchange for this deprivation of use? The only monetary consideration was the granting of a $5,000 loan, interest free, for a period of seven months. The value of this money for that period of time, if taken at the same interest rate as the 5 percent used on the balance of the land contract, is approximately $145; and it should be noted that this was not an unsecured loan, since McKinnon took a mortgage on the cottage property of the Benedicts in Michigan. In addition, McKinnon stated that he would "help you try" to reach a solution of the problem posed by Mrs. Vair's occupancy of one of the cottages on a fifty-year lease at $5 per year. His one attempt, as stated above, was a failure; and McKinnon's promise to generate business resulted in an occupancy by only one group for less than a week. For this pittance and these feeble attempts to help with the operational problems of the camp, the Benedicts have sacrificed their right to make lawful and reasonable use of their property.

In oral argument it was pointed out that the value of the $5,000 loan could not be measured in terms of the interest value of the money, since, without this advance, Benedict would have been unable to purchase the camp at all. To our mind, this is evidence of the fact that Benedict was not able to deal at arm's length with McKinnon, for his need for these funds was obviously so great that he was willing to enter into a contract that results in gross inequities. Lord Chancellor Northington said "necessitous men are not, truly speaking, free men." Vernon *v.* Bethell, 2 Eden 110, 113 (1762).

We find that the inadequacy of consideration is so gross as to be unconscionable and a bar to the plaintiffs' invocation of the extraordinary equitable powers of the court.

While there is no doubt that there are benefits from this agreement to McKinnon, they are more than outweighed by the oppressive terms that would be imposed upon the Benedicts. McKinnon testified that he and his wife spend only the summer months on their property. Undoubtedly, these are the months when it is most important that there be no disruption of the natural beauty or the quiet and pleasant enjoyment of the property, nevertheless, there was testimony that the trailer camp could not be seen from the McKinnon home, nor could the campsite be seen during the summer months of the year, when the leaves were on the trees. Thus, the detriment of which the McKinnons complain, that would be cognizable in an equity action, is minimal, while the damage done to the Benedicts is severe.

Considering all the factors—the inadequacy of the consideration, the small benefit that would be accorded the McKinnons, and the oppressive conditions imposed upon the Benedicts—we conclude that this contract failed to meet the test of reasonableness that is the *sine qua non* of the enforcement of rights in an action in equity. . . .

A fair reading of the transcript indicates no sharp practice, dishonesty, or overreaching on the part of McKinnon. However, there was a wide disparity between the business experience of the parties. McKinnon was a man of stature in the legal field, an investment counsellor, a former officer of a major corporation, and had held posts of responsibility with the United States government, while, insofar as the record shows, Benedict was a retail jeweler and a man of limited financial ability. He no doubt overvalued the promises of McKinnon to assist in getting the operation "well organized" and to solve the lease problem and to "generate business." These factors, in view of Benedict's financial inability to enter into an arms-length transaction, may be explanatory of the reason for the agreement, but the agreement viewed even as of the time of its execution was unfair and based upon inadequate consideration. We, therefore, have no hesitancy in denying the plaintiffs the equitable remedy of injunction. . . .

C. EQUITABLE LIMITS ON ENFORCEMENT OF CONTRACTS

In addition to recognizing special defenses to equitable relief, courts sometimes invoke equitable principles to limit enforcement of private legal arrangements. In a merged legal system, these principles can be regarded as substantive rules of law. Yet, their origins lie in equity and courts continue to view them as discretionary considerations rather than fixed limits on contract enforcement. Some examples follow.

1. BREACH OF FIDUCIARY DUTY

Firebaugh v. Hanback

Supreme Court of Virginia, 1994.
247 Va. 519.

■ POFF, SENIOR JUSTICE. We awarded this appeal to consider whether two real estate agents who had entered into a contract to purchase real estate owned by their principal were entitled to specific performance of that contract. We will uphold the chancellor's judgment denying the prayer of the purchasers' bill of complaint.

The chancellor based his decision on a finding that the agents breached the fiduciary duty they owed to their principal. We will summarize the evidence underlying that finding as it was adduced in hearings conducted by a commissioner in chancery.

Eugene D. Lunsford, a licensed real estate agent associated with Real Estate III, solicited a listing agreement for his firm from Edwin Murray Hanback and John C. Richards, Trustees for Ye Old Hunters Club (the club). In its original form dated April 2, 1990, the agreement listed for sale "126.669 acres located on the East side of Route 600 South of Deerfield." Lunsford mailed a copy of that form to Quinlan H. Hancock, one of the five members of the club. In a letter to Lunsford, Hancock returned what he identified as a "modified listing agreement which is necessary under the circumstances." The description of the property was modified by a handwritten note to read "126.669 acres plus or minus," and the date of the document was changed to May 15, 1990.

The evidence showed that, following an appraisal performed on site by Richard C. Firebaugh, the club had acquired the property in 1973. The deed, which reserved life estates to the grantors and the survivor, described the property as "120.80 acres, more or less, this being a sale in gross and not by the acre, and being . . . a tract formerly containing 193.80 acres, more or less." Lunsford had obtained the information required to draft the listing agreement by examining that deed and the county tax records. Those records showed that the club had paid all annual assessments against property identified as containing 126.669 acres.

In September 1990, Lunsford enclosed in a letter to Hancock a written offer to purchase signed by Raymond R. Wittekind and Margaret B. Wittekind. As drafted the offer identified the property as "126 acres more or less" but provided:

> "Seller to provide purchaser at closing with boundary survey not more than 10 years old. If not available Purchaser and Seller to equally share the cost of a new survey. Deviations in acreage in excess of 10 acres shall increase the purchase price by $500 per acre for overage and decrease the price by $500 per acre for underage."

In a letter to Lunsford dated September 11, 1990, Hancock returned the document, executed as a contract by Hanback and Richards, but in a modified form. The language concerning a survey and its effect upon the purchase price was stricken and the deletions were initialed by the trustees of the club. In his letter, Hancock stated that he could "only represent that the acreage is the same as when we acquired it" and that the "executed contract" was "for the sale of the . . . farm in an 'as is' condition." Hancock explained at the hearing that "what I mean by that [language] is just exactly what was there" and that he had "communicated" that meaning to Lunsford "[m]any, many times."

The Wittekinds signed a counter offer at a higher price, and Lunsford submitted it to the club. Hancock testified that this offer "was rejected by the members because it had a provision that deviation in acreage from 126 acres of five acres or more . . . shall result in a price adjustment." Further, he stated that he "again, explained to Mr. Lunsford . . . the fact that we were selling the farm as such, without regard to acreage."

In a telephone conversation conducted with Hancock in November 1990, Lunsford relayed a third offer at a still higher price submitted by the Wittekinds. As appears from the exhibit introduced at the hearing, the document contained similar language concerning a survey and acreage deviation price changes as that included in the two prior Wittekind offers, and the club rejected that offer as well.

Lunsford testified that the cause of the failure to obtain a final contract with the Wittekinds was "not being able to get a release signed on [the life estate]" and that Hancock had "said he and the Hunt Club would pay half of [the cost of a survey]." Asked if he had discussed such a solution with Lunsford, Hancock replied, "Absolutely not."

In December 1990, Lunsford referred to trustees of the club an offer made by a third party. That offer described the property as "126 acres, Map #40–46" and contained no language concerning a survey or acreage deviation. The club rejected that offer but only because it contained a provision for deferred payment of a portion of the purchase price.

The listing agreement the club executed in May 1990 with Real Estate III expired on December 31, 1990. Lunsford prepared an extension agreement dated January 1, 1991. His description of the property failed to include the words "plus or minus" which Hancock had added to the original draft of the listing agreement. Lunsford acknowledged at the hearing that he had signed the names of the trustees of the club to the extension agreement without their permission.

Lunsford left Real Estate III and joined Richard C. Firebaugh in the firm of Dick Firebaugh Real Estate, Inc. Lunsford explained to Firebaugh the reasons he had been unsuccessful in his attempts to negotiate a sale of the club's farm. At Lunsford's invitation, the club executed a listing agreement with his new firm. After taking a view of the farm, Firebaugh and Lunsford became interested in acquiring the property themselves.

Lunsford testified that he and Firebaugh "discussed the writing of the contract" and that "he told me what to put on the contract." Lunsford's wife filled in the blank spaces on the printed form as he instructed. Lunsford testified that "Mr. Firebaugh looked at it, was not happy with it, changed some of the things on it" and that "[w]e redid it at least once, maybe twice."

As submitted to the club, the contract, dated April 20, 1991, defined the term "real property" as "the land, and all improvements thereon . . . described as . . . 126 acres, more or less." The contract further provided that the "[p]roperty is being purchased in 'as is' condition unless otherwise noted," fixed the purchase price at $110,000, and waived the broker's commission.

The trustees executed the contract in that form. Hancock testified that his understanding was that the club was selling "exactly what we got from [the prior owners], regardless of what it was," and that he assumed that the closing attorney would insert a provision in the deed identifying the transaction as a sale in gross.

Lunsford and Firebaugh construed the language of the contract differently. Lunsford testified that "had we been buying the property by the gross, I would have put [it] in [the contract]." Reaffirming his earlier testimony, Hancock said that he intended the "as is" language to address the acreage as well as the condition of the premises and that the subject of the sale was to be "something close to the acreage that's in the contract." Hancock added that the purchasers' interpretation of the language of the contract was not communicated to the trustees of the club before they signed the document.

After the trustees signed, the purchasers employed Robert E. Funk to conduct a survey. Funk reported that his preliminary calculations showed that the farm contained only 89.5 acres, and the purchasers did not close the sale on the date scheduled. The purchasers' attorney advised the club by letter that there was a "deficiency in acreage of 36.5 acres" and that Firebaugh and Lunsford were prepared to close at a later date at an "abated purchase price of $90,967.8."

The club refused a tender of a cashier's check for that amount, and the purchasers filed a bill of complaint asking the court to "order the Defendants specifically to perform the contract and . . . order an abatement in the purchase price of $19,032.20. . . ." . . .

Our review of the record shows that the purchasers intended the contract they drafted and revised to be a contract of sale by the acre rather than a sale in gross; that the purchasers were aware that the sellers, who had repeatedly rejected other contract offers containing explicit provisions for a survey and a sale by the acre, intended to execute nothing other than a contract of sale in gross; and that the purchasers failed to advise the sellers of their interpretation of the language they had chosen until the trustees of the club had executed what they thought was a contract of sale in gross. . . .

As a fiduciary,

> "a broker owes his principal the duty to use utmost fidelity to him and must disclose to him all facts within the broker's knowledge which may be material to the transaction, or which might influence the principal in deciding upon a course of action."

Burruss *v.* Green Auction Co., 228 Va. 6, 10 (1984).

As a general rule, it is true, as the purchasers say, that

> "[w]hen the seller is unable to convey the entire estate in the land that he has contracted to sell, the buyer may compel the seller to convey whatever estate he may have and the buyer will be allowed an abatement of the purchase price to compensate him for the deficiency in title."

Hawks *v.* Sparks, 204 Va. 717, 720 (1963).

However, we have recognized exceptions to the general rule.

> "[S]pecific performance of a contract is not a matter of right, but rests in the discretion of the trial court to be granted or refused according to established principles and the facts of each case."

Id. Thus, we have denied specific performance of contracts executed under a mutual mistake of fact.

"[H]e who asks equity must do equity, and he who comes into equity must come with clean hands." Walker *v.* Henderson, 151 Va. 913, 927–28 (1928) (decree awarding real estate vendee specific performance reversed). The court in *Walker* explained that "[f]ailure to communicate facts material under the circumstances, or conduct leading to misapprehension, may influence a court to refuse specific performance." Reaffirming this principle, we have recently held that a court of equity may be justified in applying the "clean hands" doctrine against a litigant who fails to communicate material facts, even when he owes no fiduciary duty to do so.

As we have said, Firebaugh and Lunsford had a fiduciary relationship with the club. We are of opinion that the record fully supports the chancellor's conclusion that the purchasers breached their fiduciary duties and, applying the "clean hands" doctrine, we hold that a correct application of the law supports the chancellor's decision that the purchasers "are not entitled to specific performance of the contract . . . [or] to enforce it according to the original terms and conditions." . . .

NOTE ON FIDUCIARY DUTIES

Chancellor Kent made the following remarks on the subject of fiduciary duty:

> "[H]uman laws are not so perfect as the dictates of conscience; and the sphere of morality is more enlarged than the limits of civil jurisdiction. There are many duties that belong to the class of imperfect obligations, which are binding on conscience, but which human laws do not, and cannot undertake directly to enforce. But when the aid of a court of equity is sought, to carry into execution such a contract, then the principles of ethics have a more extensive sway; and a purchase, made with such a reservation of superior knowledge, would be of too sharp a character to be aided and forwarded in its execution by the powers of the Court of Chancery. . . . It is a rule in equity, that all the material facts must be known to both parties, to render the agreement fair and just in all its parts; and it is against all the principles of equity, that one party, knowing a material ingredient in an agreement, should be permitted to suppress it, and still call for specific performance."

2 James Kent, COMMENTARIES ON AMERICAN LAW *490–91 (12th ed., O.W. Holmes, Jr., ed., 1873).

Kent also noted that:

> "Cicero de Officiis states the case of a corn-merchant of Alexandria arriving at Rhodes in a time of great scarcity, with a cargo of grain, and with knowledge that a number of other vessels, with similar cargoes, had already sailed from Alexandria for Rhodes, and which he had passed on the voyage. He then puts the question, whether the Alexandrian merchant was bound in conscience to inform the buyers of that fact, or to keep silence, and sell his wheat for an extravagant price; and he answers it by saying, that, in his opinion, good faith would require of a just and candid man, a frank disclosure of the fact."

Id. *491 n. (d).

2. FORFEITURE

J.N.A. Realty Corp. v. Cross Bay Chelsea, Inc.

Court of Appeals of New York, 1977.
42 N.Y.2d 392.

■ WACHTLER, JUDGE. J.N.A. Realty Corp., the owner of a building in Howard Beach, commenced this proceeding to recover possession of the premises claiming that the lease has expired. The lease grants the tenant, Cross Bay Chelsea, Inc., an option to renew and although the notice was sent, through negligence or inadvertence, it was not sent within the time prescribed in the lease. The landlord seeks to enforce the letter of the agreement. The tenant asks for equity to relieve it from a forfeiture.

The Civil Court, after trial, held that the tenant was entitled to equitable relief. The Appellate Term affirmed, without opinion, but the Appellate Division, after granting leave reversed and granted the petition. The tenant has appealed to this court.

Two primary questions are raised on the appeal. First, will the tenant suffer a forfeiture if the landlord is permitted to enforce the letter of the agreement. Secondly, if there will be a forfeiture, may a court of equity grant the tenant relief when the forfeiture would result from the tenant's own neglect or inadvertence.

At the trial it was shown that J.N.A. Realty Corp. (hereafter JNA) originally leased the premises to Victor Palermo and Sylvester Vascellero for a 10-year term commencing on January 1, 1964. Paragraph 58 of the lease, which was attached as part of 12-page rider, granted the tenants an option to renew for a 10-year term provided "that Tenant shall notify the landlord in writing by registered or certified mail six (6) months prior to the last day of the term of the lease that tenant desires such renewal." The tenants opened a restaurant on the premises. In February, 1964 they formed the Foro Romano Corp. (Foro) and assigned the lease to the corporation.

By December of 1967 the restaurant was operating at a loss and Foro decided to close it down and offer it for sale or lease. In March, 1968 Foro entered into a contract with Cross Bay Chelsea, Inc. (hereafter Chelsea), to sell the restaurant and assign the lease. As a condition of the sale Foro was required to obtain a modification of the option to renew so that Chelsea would have the right to renew the lease for an additional term of 24 years.

The closing took place in June of 1968. First JNA modified the option and consented to the assignment. The modification, which consists of a separate document to be attached to the lease, states: "the Tenant shall have a right to renew this lease for a further period of Twenty-Four (24) years, instead of Ten (10) years, from the expiration of the original term of said lease . . . . All other provisions of Paragraph #58 in said lease, . . . shall remain in full force and effect, except as hereinabove modified." Foro then assigned the lease and sold its interest in the restaurant to Chelsea for $155,000. The bill of sale states that "the value of the fixtures and chattels included in this sale is the sum of $40,000 and that the remainder of the purchase price is the value of the leasehold and possession of the restaurant premises." At that point five and one-half years remained on the original term of the lease.

In the summer of 1968 Chelsea reopened the restaurant. JNA's president, Nicholas Arena, admitted on the stand that . . . throughout the term of the tenancy he was "most assuredly" aware of the time limitation on the option. In fact there is some indication in the record that JNA had previously used this device in an attempt to evict another tenant. Nevertheless it was not until November 12, 1973 that JNA took any action to inform the tenant that the option had lapsed. Then it sent a letter noting that the date had passed and, the letter states, "not having heard from you as prescribed by paragraph #58 in our lease we must assume you will vacate the premises" at the expiration of the original term, January 1, 1974. By letter dated November 16, 1973 Chelsea, through its attorney, sent written notice of intention to renew the option which, of course, JNA refused to honor.

At the trial Chelsea's principals claimed that they were not aware of the time limitation because they had never received a copy of paragraph 58 of the rider. They had received a copy of the modification but they had assumed that it gave them an absolute right to retain the tenancy for 24 years after the expiration of the original term. However, at the trial and later at the Appellate Division, it was found that Chelsea had knowledge of, or at least was "chargeable with notice" of, the time limitation in the rider and thus was negligent in failing to renew within the time prescribed. . . .

It is a settled principle of law that a notice exercising an option is ineffective if it is not given within the time specified. "At law, of course, time is always of the essence of the contract" (De Funiak, MODERN EQUITY, § 80, p. 223). Thus the tenant had no legal right to exercise the option when it did, but to say that is simply to pose the issue; it does not resolve it. Of course the tenant would not be asking for equitable relief if it could establish its rights at law.

The major obstacle to obtaining equitable relief in these cases is that default on an option usually does not result in a forfeiture. The reason is that the option itself does not create any interest in the property, and no rights accrue until the condition precedent has been met by giving notice within the time specified. Thus equity will not intervene because the loss of the option does not ordinarily result in the forfeiture of any vested rights. . . .

But when a tenant in possession under an existing lease has neglected to exercise an option to renew, he might suffer a forfeiture if he has made valuable improvements on the property. . . . [I]t has been noted that "although the tenant has no legal interest in the renewal period until the required notice is given, yet an equitable interest is recognized and protected against forfeiture in some cases where the tenant has in good faith made improvements of a substantial character, intending to renew the lease, if the landlord is not harmed by the delay in the giving of the notice and the lessee would sustain substantial loss in case the lease were not renewed" (2 Pomeroy, EQUITY JURISPRUDENCE (5th ed.), § 453b, p. 296). . . .

A tenant or mortgagor should not be denied equitable relief from the consequences of his own neglect or inadvertence if a forfeiture would result. The rule applies even though the tenant or mortgagor, by his inadvertence, has neglected to perform an affirmative duty and thus breached a covenant in the agreement.

On occasion the court has cautioned that equitable relief would be denied where there has been a willful or gross neglect, but it has been reluctant to employ the sanction when a forfeiture would result. . . .

Here, as noted, the tenant has made a considerable investment in improvements on the premises—$40,000 at the time of purchase, and an additional $15,000 during the tenancy. In addition, if the location is lost, the restaurant would undoubtedly lose a considerable amount of its customer good will. The tenant was at fault, but not in a culpable sense. It was, as Cardozo says, "mere venial inattention." There would be a forfeiture and the gravity of the loss is certainly out of all proportion to the gravity of the fault. Thus, under the circumstances of this case, the tenant would be entitled to equitable relief if there is no prejudice to the landlord.

However, it is not clear from the record whether JNA would be prejudiced if the tenant is relieved of its default. . . . This . . . must be resolved at a new trial. . . .

■ BREITEL, CHIEF JUDGE (dissenting). . . . Had an honest mistake or similar "excusable fault," as opposed to what is undoubtedly mere carelessness, occasioned the tenant's tardiness, absent prejudice to the landlord, equitable relief would be available. At issue, instead, is the availability of equitable relief where the only excuse for the commercial tenant's dilatory failure to exercise its option to renew is sheer carelessness.

Enough has been said to uncover a common situation. Experienced and even hardened businessmen at cross-purposes over the renewal of a valuable lease term seek on the one hand to stand by the written agreement, and on the other, to loosen the applicable rules to receive *ad hoc* adjustment of equities and relief from economic detriment. The landlord wants a higher return. The tenant wants to keep the old bargain. Which of the profit-seeking parties in this particular case should prevail as a matter of morals is not within the province of the courts. The well-settled doctrine is that with respect to options, whether they be lease renewal options, options to purchase real or personal property, or stock options, time is of the essence. The exceptions, namely, estoppel, fraud, mistake, accident, or overreaching, are few. Commercial stability and certainty are paramount, and always the dangers of unsolvable issues of fact and speculative manipulation (as with stock options) are to be avoided.

The landlord should be awarded possession of the premises in accordance with the undisputed language and manifested intention of the written lease, its 12-page rider, and modification. It does not suffice that the tenant may suffer an economic detriment in losing the renewal period. Nor does it suffice that the delay in giving notice may have caused the landlord no "prejudice," other than loss of the opportunity to relet the property or renegotiate the terms of a lease on a fresh basis. Once an option to renew a lease has been conditioned upon the tenant's giving timely notice, the commercial lessee should not be heard to complain that through carelessness a valued asset has been lost, anymore than one would allow the landlord to complain of the economic detriment to him in agreeing to an improvident option to renew. . . .

NOTE ON RELIEF FROM FORFEITURE

With *J.N.A. Realty*, compare Graf *v.* Hope Building Corp., 254 N.Y. 1 (1930), reprinted in Chapter One, above.

CHAPTER 17

WINDING UP

The merits of the case have been determined. The parties' basic rights to relief have been fixed. A number of problems nonetheless remain, of which this chapter addresses two. First: if the judgment includes a monetary award, how can the plaintiff collect? Collection is a complicated subject, much affected by local law. The materials included here cover only a few basic collection problems.

Second, there is the matter of attorneys' fees: who should pay for the litigation? In the federal courts and most state courts, the default rule is that each party to a lawsuit pays its own costs of litigation. The difficulties lie in the many exceptions to this rule.

A. A BRIEF LOOK AT THE PROCESS OF COLLECTING MONEY JUDGMENTS

Simmons v. Simmons

Superior Court of Pennsylvania, 1986.
356 Pa. Super. 32.

■ BECK, JUDGE. . . . Appellee-wife Linda Simmons acquired against appellant-husband Edward Simmons a judgment for $3024.60 representing child support arrearages. To enforce the judgment, wife obtained the issuance of a writ of execution which directed the sheriff of York County to seize certain items of husband's personal property. The sheriff accordingly seized husband's specified personalty which was subsequently sold at a sheriff's sale. At the sale, wife purchased husband's pop-up camper and Bronco II vehicle for $89.34, the sheriff's costs in the execution procedure.

As a result of the sheriff's sale, wife obtained the camper and Bronco II subject to the claims of the credit company which had lent husband the purchase money for those items and, apparently, had a security interest in them. After the sheriff's sale, the camper and Bronco II were taken by the credit company in payment of the balance of the purchase money loans made to husband. Due to the sheriff's sale of the camper and Bronco II to wife, husband requested that wife have the judgment against him marked satisfied. Wife refused to do so. . . .

Under the Pennsylvania Rules of Civil Procedure, a judgment for support arrearages is enforceable by execution upon the judgment. To initiate the execution process, the judgment creditor files a praecipe for a writ of execution with the prothonotary of the county where the judgment for support arrearages has been entered. The prothonotary then issues a writ of execution which contains a notice to the judgment debtor and instructions to the county sheriff concerning the execution. The notice advises the judgment debtor that his property may be taken through the execution process in an attempt to have the judgment against him satisfied. In addition, the notice explains that some of the judgment debtor's property may be exempt from seizure. Finally, the notice informs the judgment debtor that he has a right to present a legal defense to prevent the seizure of his property.

The instructions to the sheriff direct the sheriff to levy upon the judgment debtor's property specified in the writ and to sell the judgment debtor's interest therein. In the context of an execution upon a judgment, a levy consists of a sheriff's actual or constructive seizure of the judgment debtor's property. "The levy is an assertion of title by the sheriff, amounting at least to a legal divestiture of the possession of the [judgment debtor], and such as would subject the officer making it to an action of trespass, but for the protection of the execution." Duncan's Appeal, 37 Pa. 500, 502 (1860).

Therefore, to make a valid levy on a judgment debtor's tangible personal property, the sheriff must prevent the judgment debtor's immediate enjoyment of the property by either assuming exclusive, physical possession of the personalty or openly exercising power or control over the personalty. A sheriff's levy on the judgment debtor's property listed in the writ of execution constitutes service of the writ upon the judgment debtor where, as in the case sub judice, the writ directs the sheriff to levy upon only tangible personalty.

After at least six days' prior public notice, levied upon personalty adequate in amount to satisfy the judgment, interest and likely execution costs may be sold by the sheriff at a public sale. The judgment/execution creditor must "pay to the sheriff all costs, charges and expenses incident to the execution, the maintenance of the lien of the execution and the preservation of the [levied upon] property. . . ." Pa. R.C.P. No. 3138.

If the judgment/execution creditor or any other creditor entitled to share the proceeds of the sheriff's sale purchases the property offered at the sale, the sheriff must "accept on account of the purchase price the receipt of the purchaser up to the amount of the proceeds to which [the creditor] is entitled." Pa. R. C. P. No. 3133. . . . The proceeds of the sale, if any, are distributed in accordance with Pa. R. C. P. Nos. 3136 and 3137. Thereafter, the sheriff must make a return to the prothonotary who issued the writ of execution and must include in the return any schedule of distribution that was utilized.

Following the sheriff's sale, a judgment debtor may, in writing, request that a judgment creditor who has received satisfaction of a judgment enter satisfaction in the prothonotary's office where the judgment is outstanding. . . .

At the sheriff's sale in the case sub judice, wife purchased the levied upon Bronco II and camper for $89.34 representing the execution costs.

But in buying at the sheriff's sale, wife obtained only that interest in the Bronco II and camper which husband had. Accordingly, wife acquired the Bronco II and camper subject to the secured interests of the credit company which had lent husband the purchase money for those items. Because the secured interests of the credit company had priority over wife's execution lien based on the judgment for support arrearages, the credit company took possession of the Bronco II and camper in payment of the outstanding balance of its purchase money loans to husband. Hence, the sheriff's sale did not produce any proceeds which could be applied to payment of wife's judgment against husband, and the trial court properly refused to hold that the sheriff's sale had either partially or fully discharged wife's judgment for support arrearages. . . .

Citibank, N.A. v. Prime Motor Inns Ltd. Partnership

Court of Appeals of New York, 2002.
98 N.Y.2d 743.

■ MEMORANDUM. . . . In 1993, Citibank secured a $5.3 million judgment against Martin W. Field. Four years later, Joseph and Tremayne Selig obtained a judgment against Field in the amount of $19.5 million. Thereafter, Prime Motor Inns L.P. (PMI) offered to pay Field $500,000 to abandon his proxy fight for ownership of PMI's hotels, subject to the approval of the PMI partners. Before the partnership vote, Field executed an instrument entitled "Collateral Assignment" which assigned to Joseph Selig "all sums due and to become due" under the PMI settlement "as security for the payment" of his judgment. Citibank levied upon the $500,000 shortly before Selig filed a UCC–1 statement in New Jersey. After the partners of PMI approved the payment to Field, Citibank initiated this turnover proceeding. Supreme Court and the Appellate Division determined that the Field assignment to Selig was a security interest and that Citibank had a superior right as a lien creditor.

We agree with the courts below that Field provided Selig with a security interest in the settlement payment, which was subject to the perfection and priority rules of the Uniform Commercial Code. Citibank properly levied upon the $500,000 before Selig perfected his security interest and thereby established its superior right to the settlement proceeds.

Murdock Acceptance Corp. v. Woodham

Supreme Court of Mississippi, 1968.
208 So.2d 56.

■ RODGERS, JUSTICE. . . . Parks Auto Sales in Newton, Mississippi was owned and operated by T. C. Parks, husband of Mrs. Myrtle W. Parks. There appear of record in the Chancery Clerk's Office of Newton County several instruments, each of which is what is known as a "Statement of Trust Receipt Financing." One of these instruments was filed in each year consecutively from 1961 through 1964. Each was signed by the appellant, Murdock Acceptance Corporation, as "entruster" and by Parks Auto Sales by T. C. Parks as "trustee."

The appellee, Mrs. Maymie Woodham, obtained a judgment against T. C. Parks and Mrs. T. C. Parks, and this judgment was enrolled September 15, 1964. . . . Mr. Parks died intestate July 11, 1965, and no administration was had on his estate. Mrs. Parks, without any change in the appearance of the business, took possession and control of "Parks Auto Sales" . . . .

Mrs. Parks, on August 16, 1965, executed a power of attorney naming two of Murdock's employees as attorneys in fact for "Parks Auto Sales," and granting them the power of attorney to execute in favor of Murdock trust receipts and notes covering motor vehicles delivered to Mrs. Parks. She delivered this power of attorney to Murdock Acceptance Corporation. One of these attorneys in fact, Adelyn W. Farr, executed a trust receipt on September 28, 1965, naming Murdock as "entruster" and Parks Auto Sales as "trustee." This trust receipt covered three of the automobiles upon which levy was made. A similar instrument was executed October 23, 1965, which included the other three automobiles involved in this controversy. . . . None of the trust receipts was recorded.

On December 14, 1965, a writ of execution on the appellee's enrolled judgment was issued at the request of the appellee. At nine o'clock the following morning, December 15, a statement of financing was filed naming Murdock as entruster and "Parks Auto Sales by Mrs. Myrtle W. Parks" as trustee. At eleven o'clock that same morning, the sheriff of Newton County, acting under the writ of execution, advised Mrs. Parks that he was making levy of execution on the six automobiles involved. He did not take possession of the vehicles nor place any sort of notice on them, but he did advise Mrs. Parks not to dispose of them in any manner.

This case involves the right of Murdock Acceptance Corporation to claim the automobiles levied upon by virtue of the financing statements of record, which, it is contended, give Murdock prior right, title, and claim to the automobiles. The trial court's judgment was in favor of the judgment creditor, Mrs. Woodham.

It is apparent that Parks Auto Sales and Murdock Acceptance Corporation were engaged in trust receipt financing, more commonly known as "floor planning." This method involves a secured transaction by which the borrower (designated as "trustee") signs a statement to the effect that he will hold the goods given into his possession in trust for the lender (designated as the "entruster") and shall have the right to dispose of them to others for the sole purpose of repaying the loan. This statement is known as a trust receipt. As a security device in sales financing, the trust receipt has become widely used in financing dealer purchases of everything from automobiles to appliances.

The law applicable to trust receipts financing has been modified and compiled by the Uniform Trust Receipts Act. Under the common law, the entruster's security interest was protected against all but an innocent purchaser without recording a document evidencing this interest. To avoid the problem of having "secret liens," the Uniform Trust Receipts Act requires a notice or statement to be filed with the proper authority. . . . The law permits one statement filed in accordance with the act to do for all trust receipt transactions covering the goods described in the statement between the entruster and the trustee entered into during a period from thirty days preceding the filing to one year following the date of filing. In other words, the recorded statement is notice that the parties are engaged in this method of financing the purchase of the particular goods. The entruster's security interest in goods which are the subject of a trust receipt transaction during a year following the filing of the statement is protected against all but a buyer in the ordinary course of trade. The security interest in goods subject to a trust receipt is also protected for a period of thirty days without a statement being filed. After this thirty day period has passed without a statement having been filed, the security interest of the entruster is void against a creditor who then acquires a lien by levy, provided the creditor had no actual knowledge of entruster's interest. . . .

Appellee points out that the statements of financing filed in the chancery clerk's office were allegedly improperly indexed under the name of the finance company, Murdock Acceptance Corporation, rather than under the name of the dealer, Parks, and therefore did not constitute notice to her. However, . . . [t]he statements were recorded; and, although the clerk improperly indexed the instruments, constructive notice to the appellee was implied. It is also the rule in this state as announced by this Court that one may "safely repose on the presumption that the recording officer has done his duty" and is under no duty to see that an instrument is properly recorded. Bank of Lexington *v.* Cooper, 115 Miss. 782 (1917).

The filing of the financing statement by appellant on December 15, 1965, did not protect Murdock Acceptance Corporation's interest in the automobiles which were subject to the trust receipts dated September 28 and October 23 of that year, unless it can be said that the filing of that statement occurred prior to appellee's becoming a lien creditor. Appellant contends that appellee did not actually become a lien creditor until eleven o'clock on the morning of December 15 and the proof shows the statement of financing was filed at nine o'clock that same morning. However, the record also shows that appellee secured the issuance of process on December 14. Section 5080–08(2)(a) provides as follows:

> "Where a creditor secures the issuance of process which within a reasonable time after such issuance results in attachment of a levy on the goods, he is deemed to have become a lien creditor as of the date of the issuance of process."

The appellee requested the issuance of process the day before filing occurred; therefore, if there were a valid attachment or levy on the automobiles, this section would operate to place the appellee within the provisions of section 5080–08.

Appellant contends that the levy of execution was not valid, because the sheriff did not take possession of the goods as required by section 1905 of the Code. In the case of Industries Sales Corporation *v.* Reliance Manufacturing Company, 243 Miss. 463 (1962), which also involved a trust receipt financing arrangement, this Court held that constructive possession was sufficient.

> ". . . In order for there to be a valid levy, the officer must assume dominion and control over the property, but the seizure may be either actual or constructive. An officer levying an execution on chattels is not required to physically take them with him, if he reduces them to his possession and control. The levy is not vitiated by leaving the chattels in the possession of the debtor."

Id. at 467.

In the instant case, the sheriff took the motor serial numbers of the automobiles and advised Mrs. Parks not to sell or dispose of them in any manner. He took constructive possession of the automobiles. Therefore the levy of execution was valid.

Appellee became a lien creditor on December 14; and thus the financing statement filed December 15, 1965, is ineffectual to protect appellant's security interest in the particular automobiles. . . .

B. ATTORNEYS' FEES

Alyeska Pipeline Service Co. v. Wilderness Society

Supreme Court of the United States, 1975.
421 U.S. 240.

■ MR. JUSTICE WHITE delivered the opinion of the Court.

This litigation was initiated by respondents Wilderness Society, Environmental Defense Fund, Inc., and Friends of the Earth in an attempt to prevent the issuance of permits by the Secretary of the Interior which were required for the construction of the trans-Alaska oil pipeline. The Court of Appeals awarded attorneys' fees to respondents against petitioner Alyeska Pipeline Service Co. based upon the court's equitable powers and the theory that respondents were entitled to fees because they were performing the services of a "private attorney general." . . . We reverse.

A major oil field was discovered in the North Slope of Alaska in 1968. In June 1969, the oil companies constituting the consortium owning Alyeska submitted an application to the Department of the Interior for rights-of-way for a pipeline that would transport oil from the North Slope across land in Alaska owned by the United States, a major part of the transport system which would carry the oil to its ultimate markets in the lower 48 States. A special interdepartmental task force studied the proposal and reported to the President. An amended application was submitted in December 1969, which requested a 54-foot right-of-way, along with applications for "special land use permits" asking for additional space alongside the right-of-way and for the construction of a road along one segment of the pipeline.

Respondents brought this suit in March 1970, and sought declaratory and injunctive relief against the Secretary of the Interior on the grounds that he intended to issue the right-of-way and special land-use permits in violation of § 28 of the Mineral Leasing Act of 1920 and without compliance with the National Environmental Policy Act of 1969 (NEPA). On the basis of both the Mineral Leasing Act and the NEPA, the District Court granted a preliminary injunction against issuance of the right-of-way and permits.

Subsequently the State of Alaska and petitioner Alyeska were allowed to intervene. On March 20, 1972, the Interior Department released a six-volume Environmental Impact Statement and a three-volume Economic and Security Analysis. After a period of time set aside for public comment, the Secretary announced that the requested permits would be granted to Alyeska. Both the Mineral Leasing Act and the NEPA issues were at that point fully briefed and argued before the District Court. That court then decided to dissolve the preliminary injunction, to deny the permanent injunction, and to dismiss the complaint.

Upon appeal, the Court of Appeals for the District of Columbia Circuit reversed, basing its decision solely on the Mineral Leasing Act. Finding that the NEPA issues were very complex and important, that deciding them was not necessary at that time since pipeline construction would be enjoined as a result of the violation of the Mineral Leasing Act, that they involved issues of fact still in dispute, and that it was desirable to expedite its decision as much as possible, the Court of Appeals declined to decide the merits of respondents' NEPA contentions which had been rejected by the District Court. . . .

Congress then enacted legislation which amended the Mineral Leasing Act to allow the granting of the permits sought by Alyeska and declared that no further action under the NEPA was necessary before construction of the pipeline could proceed. . . .

With the merits of the litigation effectively terminated by this legislation, the Court of Appeals turned to the questions involved in respondents' request for an award of attorneys' fees. Since there was no applicable statutory authorization for such an award, the court proceeded to consider whether the requested fee award fell within any of the exceptions to the general "American rule" that the prevailing party may not recover attorneys' fees as costs or otherwise. The exception for an award against a party who had acted in bad faith was inapposite, since the position taken by the federal and state parties and Alyeska "was manifestly reasonable and assumed in good faith . . . ." Application of the "common benefit" exception which spreads the cost of litigation to those persons benefiting from it would "stretch it totally outside its basic rationale . . . ." The Court of Appeals nevertheless held that respondents had acted to vindicate "important statutory rights of all citizens . . . "; had ensured that the governmental system functioned properly; and were entitled to attorneys' fees lest the great cost of litigation of this kind, particularly against well-financed defendants such as Alyeska, deter private parties desiring to see the laws protecting the environment properly enforced. Title 28 U.S.C. § 2412 was thought to bar taxing any attorneys' fees against the United States, and it was also deemed inappropriate to burden the State of Alaska with any part of the award.[16] But Alyeska, the Court of Appeals held, could fairly be required to pay one-half of the full award to which respondents were entitled for having performed the functions of a private attorney general. . . .

In the United States, the prevailing litigant is ordinarily not entitled to collect a reasonable attorneys' fee from the loser. We are asked to fashion a far-reaching exception to this "American Rule"; but having considered its origin and development, we are convinced that it would be inappropriate for the Judiciary, without legislative guidance, to reallocate the burdens of litigation in the manner and to the extent urged by respondents and approved by the Court of Appeals.

At common law, costs were not allowed; but for centuries in England there has been statutory authorization to award costs, including attorneys' fees. Although the matter is in the discretion of the court, counsel fees are regularly allowed to the prevailing party.

During the first years of the federal-court system, Congress provided through legislation that the federal courts were to follow the practice with respect to awarding attorneys' fees of the courts of the States in which the federal courts were located, with the exception of district courts under admiralty and maritime jurisdiction which were to follow a specific fee schedule. Those statutes, by 1800, had either expired or been repealed.

In 1796, this Court appears to have ruled that the Judiciary itself would not create a general rule, independent of any statute, allowing awards of attorneys' fees in federal courts. . . . This Court has consistently adhered to that early holding.

[16] In the circumstances of this case it would be inappropriate to tax fees against appellee State of Alaska. The State voluntarily participated in this suit, in effect to present to the court a different version of the public interest implications of the trans-Alaska pipeline. Taxing attorneys' fees against Alaska would in our view undermine rather than further the goal of ensuring adequate spokesmen for public interests.

The practice after 1799 and until 1853 continued as before, that is, with the federal courts referring to the state rules governing awards of counsel fees .... By legislation in 1842, Congress did give this Court authority to prescribe the items and amounts of costs which could be taxed in federal courts but the Court took no action under this statutory mandate.

In 1853, Congress undertook to standardize the costs allowable in federal litigation. In support of the proposed legislation, it was asserted that there was great diversity in practice among the courts and that losing litigants were being unfairly saddled with exorbitant fees for the victor's attorney. The result was a far-reaching Act specifying in detail the nature and amount of the taxable items of cost in the federal courts. One of its purposes was to limit allowances for attorneys' fees that were to be charged to the losing parties. Although the Act disclaimed any intention to limit the amount of fees that an attorney and his client might agree upon between themselves, counsel fees collectible from the losing party were expressly limited to the amounts stated in the Act ....

Although, as will be seen, Congress has made specific provision for attorneys' fees under certain federal statutes, it has not changed the general statutory rule that allowances for counsel fees are limited to the sums specified by the costs statute. The 1853 Act was . . . included in the Revised Code of 1948 as 28 U.S.C. §§ 1920 and 1923(a). Under § 1920, a court may tax as costs the various items specified, including the "docket fees" under § 1923(a). . . .

To be sure, the fee statutes have been construed to allow, in limited circumstances, a reasonable attorneys' fee to the prevailing party in excess of the small sums permitted by § 1923. In Trustees *v.* Greenough, 105 U.S. 527 (1882), the 1853 Act was read as not interfering with the historic power of equity to permit the trustee of a fund or property, or a party preserving or recovering a fund for the benefit of others in addition to himself, to recover his costs, including his attorneys' fees, from the fund or property itself or directly from the other parties enjoying the benefit. That rule has been consistently followed. Also, a court may assess attorneys' fees for the "willful disobedience of a court order . . . as part of the fine to be levied on the defendant," or when the losing party has "acted in bad faith, vexatiously, wantonly, or for oppressive reasons . . . ." F. D. Rich Co. *v.* United States ex rel. Industrial Lumber Co., 417 U.S. 116, 129 (1974). These exceptions are unquestionably assertions of inherent power in the courts to allow attorneys' fees in particular situations, unless forbidden by Congress, but none of the exceptions is involved here.[31] The Court of Appeals expressly disclaimed reliance on any of them.

---

[31] A very different situation is presented when a federal court sits in a diversity case. "[I]n an ordinary diversity case where the state law does not run counter to a valid federal statute or rule of court, and usually it will not, state law denying the right to attorneys' fees or giving a

Congress has not repudiated the judicially fashioned exceptions to the general rule against allowing substantial attorneys' fees; but neither has it retracted, repealed, or modified the limitations on taxable fees contained in the 1853 statute and its successors. Nor has it extended any roving authority to the Judiciary to allow counsel fees as costs or otherwise whenever the courts might deem them warranted. What Congress has done, however, while fully recognizing and accepting the general rule, is to make specific and explicit provisions for the allowance of attorneys' fees under selected statutes granting or protecting various federal rights. These statutory allowances are now available in a variety of circumstances, but they also differ considerably among themselves. Under the antitrust laws, for instance, allowance of attorneys' fees to a plaintiff awarded treble damages is mandatory. In patent litigation, in contrast, "[t]he court, in *exceptional* cases, *may* award reasonable attorney fees to the prevailing party." 35 U.S.C. § 285 (emphasis added). Under Title II of the Civil Rights Act of 1964, the prevailing party is entitled to attorneys' fees, at the discretion of the court, but we have held that Congress intended that the award should be made to the successful plaintiff absent exceptional circumstances. Under this scheme of things, it is apparent that the circumstances under which attorneys' fees are to be awarded and the range of discretion of the courts in making those awards are matters for Congress to determine.

It is true that under some, if not most, of the statutes providing for the allowance of reasonable fees, Congress has opted to rely heavily on private enforcement to implement public policy and to allow counsel fees so as to encourage private litigation. . . . But congressional utilization of the private-attorney-general concept can in no sense be construed as a grant of authority to the Judiciary to jettison the traditional rule against nonstatutory allowances to the prevailing party and to award attorneys' fees whenever the courts deem the public policy furthered by a particular statute important enough to warrant the award.

Congress itself presumably has the power and judgment to pick and choose among its statutes and to allow attorneys' fees under some, but not others. But it would be difficult, indeed, for the courts, without legislative guidance, to consider some statutes important and others unimportant and to allow attorneys' fees only in connection with the former. . . . Moreover, should courts, if they were to embark on the course urged by respondents, opt for awards to the prevailing party, whether plaintiff or defendant, or only to the prevailing plaintiff? Should awards be discretionary or mandatory? Would there be a presumption operating for or against them in the ordinary case?

As exemplified by this case itself, it is also evident that the rational application of the private-attorney-general rule would immediately collide with the express provision of 28 U.S.C. § 2412. Except as

right thereto, which reflects a substantial policy of the state should be followed." 6 J. Moore, FEDERAL PRACTICE 54.77(2), pp. 1712–1713 (2d ed. 1974). . . .

otherwise provided by statute, that section permits costs to be taxed against the United States, "but not including the fees and expenses of attorneys" . . . .

We need labor the matter no further. It appears to us that the rule suggested here and adopted by the Court of Appeals would make major inroads on a policy matter that Congress has reserved for itself. Since the approach taken by Congress to this issue has been to carve out specific exceptions to a general rule that federal courts cannot award attorneys' fees beyond the limits of 28 U.S.C. § 1923, those courts are not free to fashion drastic new rules with respect to the allowance of attorneys' fees to the prevailing party in federal litigation or to pick and choose among plaintiffs and the statutes under which they sue and to award fees in some cases but not in others, depending upon the courts' assessment of the importance of the public policies involved in particular cases. Nor should the federal courts purport to adopt on their own initiative a rule awarding attorneys' fees based on the private-attorney-general approach when such judicial rule will operate only against private parties and not against the Government.

We do not purport to assess the merits or demerits of the "American Rule" with respect to the allowance of attorneys' fees. It has been criticized in recent years, and courts have been urged to find exceptions to it. It is also apparent from our national experience that the encouragement of private action to implement public policy has been viewed as desirable in a variety of circumstances. But the rule followed in our courts with respect to attorneys' fees has survived. It is deeply rooted in our history and in congressional policy; and it is not for us to invade the legislature's province by redistributing litigation costs in the manner suggested by respondents and followed by the Court of Appeals.

The decision below must therefore be reversed. . . .

■ MR. JUSTICE DOUGLAS and MR. JUSTICE POWELL took no part in the consideration or decision of this.

■ [The dissenting opinion of MR. JUSTICE BRENNAN is omitted.]

■ MR. JUSTICE MARSHALL, dissenting.

In reversing the award of attorneys' fees to the respondent environmentalist groups, the Court today disavows the well-established power of federal equity courts to award attorneys' fees when the interests of justice so require. . . .

The statutory analysis aside, the Court points to the difficulties in formulating a "private attorney general" exception that will not swallow the American Rule. I do not find the problem as vexing as the majority does. In fact, the guidelines to the proper application of the private-attorney-general rationale have been suggested in several of our recent cases, both under statutory attorneys' fee provisions and under the common-benefit exception. . . .

The reasonable cost of the plaintiff's representation should be placed upon the defendant if (1) the important right being protected is one actually or necessarily shared by the general public or some class thereof; (2) the plaintiff's pecuniary interest in the outcome, if any, would not normally justify incurring the cost of counsel; and (3) shifting that cost to the defendant would effectively place it on a class that benefits from the litigation.

There is hardly room for doubt that the first of these criteria is met in the present case. Significant public benefits are derived from citizen litigation to vindicate expressions of congressional or constitutional policy. As a result of this litigation, respondents forced Congress to revise the Mineral Leasing Act of 1920 rather than permit its continued evasion. The 1973 amendments impose more stringent safety and liability standards, and they require Alyeska to pay fair market value for the right-of-way and to bear the costs of applying for the permit and monitoring the right-of-way.

Although the NEPA issues were not actually decided, the lawsuit served as a catalyst to ensure a thorough analysis of the pipeline's environmental impact. . . .

The second criterion is equally well satisfied in this case. Respondents' willingness to undertake this litigation was largely altruistic. . . .

Respondents' claim also fulfills the third criterion, for Alyeska is the proper party to bear and spread the cost of this litigation undertaken in the interest of the general public. The Department of the Interior, of course, bears legal responsibility for adopting a position later determined to be unlawful. And, since the class of beneficiaries from the outcome of this litigation is probably coextensive with the class of United States citizens, the Government should in fairness bear the costs of respondents' representation. But, the Court of Appeals concluded that it could not impose attorneys' fees on the United States, because in its view the statute providing for assessment of costs against the Government, 28 U.S.C. § 2412, permits the award of ordinary court costs, "but [does] not includ[e] the fees and expenses of attorneys." . . .

Alyeska, as a consortium of oil companies that do business in 49 States and account for some 20% of the national oil market, would indeed be able to redistribute the additional cost to the general public. In my view the ability to pass the cost forward to the consuming public warrants an award here. The decision to bypass Congress and avoid analysis of the environmental consequences of the pipeline was made in the first instance by Alyeska's principals and not the Secretary of the Interior. The award does not punish the consortium for these actions but recognizes that it is an effective substitute for the public beneficiaries who successfully challenged these actions. . . .

NOTE ON THE PRIVATE ATTORNEY GENERAL DOCTRINE

As the Court indicated in footnote 31, when the plaintiff's substantive claim is based on state law, claims for attorney's fees are also governed by state law. In Serrano *v.* Priest, 20 Cal. 3d 25 (1977), the California Supreme Court approved an award of attorneys' fees on a "private attorney general" theory. A number of other state courts have joined California. See, *e.g.*, Brown *v.* State, 565 So.2d 585 (Ala. 1990); Arnold *v.* Arizona Department of Health Services, 160 Ariz. 593 (1989); Montanans for the Responsible Use of the School Trust *v.* State, 296 Mont. 402 (1999); Claremont School District *v.* Governor, 144 N.H. 590 (1999); Deras *v.* Myers, 272 Or. 47 (1975); Stewart *v.* Utah Public Service Commission, 885 P.2d 759 (Utah 1994).

Fogerty v. Fantasy, Inc.

Supreme Court of the United States, 1994.
510 U.S. 517.

■ CHIEF JUSTICE REHNQUIST delivered the opinion of the Court.

The Copyright Act of 1976, 17 U.S.C. § 505, provides in relevant part that in any copyright infringement action "the court may . . . award a reasonable attorney's fee to the prevailing party as part of the costs." The question presented in this case is what standards should inform a court's decision to award attorney's fees to a prevailing defendant in a copyright infringement action—a question that has produced conflicting views in the Courts of Appeals.

Petitioner John Fogerty is a successful musician, who, in the late 1960's, was the lead singer and songwriter of a popular music group known as "Creedence Clearwater Revival." In 1970, he wrote a song entitled "Run Through the Jungle" and sold the exclusive publishing rights to predecessors-in-interest of respondent Fantasy, Inc., who later obtained the copyright by assignment. The music group disbanded in 1972 and Fogerty subsequently published under another recording label. In 1985, he published and registered a copyright to a song entitled "The Old Man Down the Road," which was released on an album distributed by Warner Brothers Records, Inc. Respondent Fantasy, Inc., sued Fogerty, Warner Brothers, and affiliated companies, in District Court, alleging that "The Old Man Down the Road" was merely "Run Through the Jungle" with new words. The copyright infringement claim went to trial and a jury returned a verdict in favor of Fogerty.

After his successful defense of the action, Fogerty moved for reasonable attorney's fees pursuant to 17 U.S.C. § 505. The District Court denied the motion, finding that Fantasy's infringement suit was not brought frivolously or in bad faith as required by circuit precedent for an award of attorney's fees to a successful defendant. The Court of Appeals affirmed, and declined to abandon the existing Ninth Circuit standard for awarding attorney's fees which treats successful plaintiffs and successful defendants differently. Under that standard, commonly termed the "dual" standard, prevailing plaintiffs are generally awarded attorney's fees as a matter of course, while prevailing defendants must show that the original suit was frivolous or brought in bad faith. In contrast, some courts of appeals follow the so-called "evenhanded" approach in which no distinction is made between prevailing plaintiffs and prevailing defendants. . . .

We reverse. . . .

[R]espondent contends that our decision in Christiansburg Garment Co. *v.* EEOC, 434 U.S. 412 (1978), in which we construed virtually identical language, supports a differentiation in treatment between plaintiffs and defendants.

Christiansburg construed the language of Title VII of the Civil Rights Act of 1964, which in relevant part provided that the court "in its discretion, may allow the prevailing party . . . a reasonable attorney's fee as part of the costs . . . ." We had earlier held, interpreting the cognate provision of Title II of that Act, that a prevailing plaintiff "should ordinarily recover an attorney's fee unless some special circumstances would render such an award unjust." Newman *v.* Piggie Park Enterprises, Inc., 390 U.S. 400, 402 (1968). This decision was based on what we found to be the important policy objectives of the Civil Rights statutes, and the intent of Congress to achieve such objectives through the use of plaintiffs as "private attorney[s] general." In *Christiansburg*, we determined that the same policy considerations were not at work in the case of a prevailing civil rights defendant. We noted that a Title VII plaintiff, like a Title II plaintiff, is "the chosen instrument of Congress to vindicate 'a policy that Congress considered of the highest priority.' " We also relied on the admittedly sparse legislative history to indicate that different standards were to be applied to successful plaintiffs than to successful defendants. . . .

The goals and objectives of the two Acts are . . . not completely similar. . . . The primary objective of the Copyright Act is to encourage the production of original literary, artistic, and musical expression for the good of the public. . . . [I]t has been noted that "[e]ntities which sue for copyright infringement as plaintiffs can run the gamut from corporate behemoths to starving artists; the same is true of prospective copyright infringement defendants." Cohen *v.* Virginia Electric & Power Co., 617 F. Supp. 619, 622–623 (E.D. Va. 1985). . . .

While it is true that one of the goals of the Copyright Act is to discourage infringement, it is by no means the only goal of that Act. In the first place, it is by no means always the case that the plaintiff in an infringement action is the only holder of a copyright; often times, defendants hold copyrights too, as exemplified in the case at hand. . . .

Because copyright law ultimately serves the purpose of enriching the general public through access to creative works, it is peculiarly important that the boundaries of copyright law be demarcated as clearly as possible.

To that end, defendants who seek to advance a variety of meritorious copyright defenses should be encouraged to litigate them to the same extent that plaintiffs are encouraged to litigate meritorious claims of infringement. In the case before us, the successful defense of "The Old Man Down the Road" increased public exposure to a musical work that could, as a result, lead to further creative pieces. Thus a successful defense of a copyright infringement action may further the policies of the Copyright Act every bit as much as a successful prosecution of an infringement claim by the holder of a copyright. . . .

We now turn to petitioner's argument that § 505 was intended to adopt the "British Rule." Petitioner argues that, consistent with the neutral language of § 505, both prevailing plaintiffs and defendants should be awarded attorney's fees as a matter of course, absent exceptional circumstances. . . .

First, . . . [t]he statute says that "the court may also award a reasonable attorney's fee to the prevailing party as part of the costs." The word "may" clearly connotes discretion. . . .

Second, we are mindful that Congress legislates against the strong background of the American Rule. Unlike Britain where counsel fees are regularly awarded to the prevailing party, it is the general rule in this country that unless Congress provides otherwise, parties are to bear their own attorney's fees. While § 505 is one situation in which Congress has modified the American Rule to allow an award of attorney's fees in the court's discretion, we find it impossible to believe that Congress, without more, intended to adopt the British Rule. Such a bold departure from traditional practice would have surely drawn more explicit statutory language and legislative comment. . . .

Thus we reject both the "dual standard" adopted by several of the Courts of Appeals and petitioner's claim that § 505 enacted the British Rule for automatic recovery of attorney's fees by the prevailing party. Prevailing plaintiffs and prevailing defendants are to be treated alike, but attorney's fees are to be awarded to prevailing parties only as a matter of the court's discretion. "There is no precise rule or formula for making these determinations," but instead equitable discretion should be exercised "in light of the considerations we have identified." Hensley *v.* Eckerhart, 461 U.S. 424, 436–437 (1983). Because the Court of Appeals erroneously held petitioner, the prevailing defendant, to a more stringent standard than that applicable to a prevailing plaintiff, its judgment is reversed and the case is remanded for further proceedings consistent with this opinion.

■ [The concurring opinion of JUSTICE THOMAS is omitted.]

NOTES ON PREVAILING PARTIES

1. Section 1988 and many other fee shifting provisions authorize fee awards to "prevailing parties." Gagne, a recipient of benefits under

Connecticut's Aid to Families With Dependent Children program, brought a suit alleging that the state's AFDC regulations did not conform to federal requirements. The parties negotiated a settlement agreement in which the state program administrator agreed to make the changes requested by Gagne, and the District Court entered a consent decree. Gagne then claimed attorneys' fees under § 1988. The Supreme Court allowed the claim, stating that "Nothing in the language of § 1988 conditions the District Court's power to award fees on full litigation of the issues or on a judicial determination that the plaintiff's rights have been violated." Maher *v.* Gagne, 448 U.S. 122, 129 (1980).

2. A teachers' union brought suit against a school district, challenging the district's policy against discussion of union activity with or among teachers during school days. The Court of Appeals for the Fifth Circuit determined that the district's prohibition against union contacts with teachers during school days was constitutional, but that the prohibition of discussion among teachers violated the teachers' First Amendment Rights. The Fifth Circuit then denied the union's fee claim, reasoning that although the union had prevailed on a secondary issue, it had not prevailed on the "central issue" in the case.

The Supreme Court rejected the "central issue" test and allowed the fee claim, stating that:

> "If the plaintiff has succeeded on 'any significant issue in litigation which achieve[d] some of the benefit the parties sought in bringing suit' the plaintiff has crossed the threshold to a fee award of some kind. . . . The touchstone of the prevailing party inquiry must be the material alteration of the legal relationship of the parties in a manner which Congress sought to promote in the fee statute. Where such a change has occurred, the degree of the plaintiff's overall success goes to the reasonableness of the award . . . , not to the availability of a fee award *vel non.*"

Texas State Teachers Association *v.* Garland Independent School District, 489 U.S. 782, 791–92 (1989).

3. West Virginia law disqualified persons who were not capable of "self-preservation" in dangerous situations from living in assisted care facilities. Buckhannon Board and Care Home, Inc. sued the state health department claiming that the self-preservation requirement violated the anti-discrimination provisions of the federal Fair Housing Act. While the suit was pending, the state legislature enacted bills eliminating the requirement. Buckhannon claimed fees under § 1988, on the ground that its lawsuit had served as the "catalyst" for legislative change. The Supreme Court rejected the catalyst theory and denied Buckhannon's fee claim:

> "A defendant's voluntary change in conduct, although perhaps accomplishing what the plaintiff sought to achieve by the lawsuit, lacks the necessary judicial *imprimatur* on the change."

Buckhannon Board and Care Home, Inc. *v.* West Virginia Department of Health and Human Resources, 532 U.S. 598, 605 (2001).

Four dissenters argued that the catalyst theory "is a key component of the fee-shifting statutes Congress adopted to advance enforcement of civil rights." *Id.* at 623 (Ginsburg, J., dissenting).

Perdue v. Kenny

Supreme Court of the United States, 2010.
559 U.S. 542.

■ JUSTICE ALITO delivered the opinion of the Court.

This case presents the question whether the calculation of an attorney's fee, under federal fee-shifting statutes, based on the "lodestar," *i.e.,* the number of hours worked multiplied by the prevailing hourly rates, may be increased due to superior performance and results. We have stated in previous cases that such an increase is permitted in extraordinary circumstances, and we reaffirm that rule. But as we have also said in prior cases, there is a strong presumption that the lodestar is sufficient; factors subsumed in the lodestar calculation cannot be used as a ground for increasing an award above the lodestar; and a party seeking fees has the burden of identifying a factor that the lodestar does not adequately take into account and proving with specificity that an enhanced fee is justified. Because the District Court did not apply these standards, we reverse the decision below and remand for further proceedings consistent with this opinion.

Respondents (plaintiffs below) are children in the Georgia foster-care system and their next friends. They filed this class action on behalf of 3,000 children in foster care and named as defendants the Governor of Georgia and various state officials (petitioners in this case). Claiming that deficiencies in the foster-care system in two counties near Atlanta violated their federal and state constitutional and statutory rights, respondents sought injunctive and declaratory relief, as well as attorney's fees and expenses.

The United States District Court for the Northern District of Georgia eventually referred the case to mediation, where the parties entered into a consent decree, which the District Court approved. The consent decree resolved all pending issues other than the fees that respondents' attorneys were entitled to receive under 42 U.S.C. § 1988.

Respondents submitted a request for more than $14 million in attorney's fees. Half of that amount was based on their calculation of the lodestar-roughly 30,000 hours multiplied by hourly rates of $200 to $495 for attorneys and $75 to $150 for non-attorneys. In support of their fee request, respondents submitted affidavits asserting that these rates were within the range of prevailing market rates for legal services in the relevant market.

The other half of the amount that respondents sought represented a fee enhancement for superior work and results. . . .

The District Court awarded fees of approximately $10.5 million. . . . [It first calculated a lodestar award of approximately $6 million.]

The court then enhanced [the lodestar] award by 75%, concluding that the lodestar calculation did not take into account "(1) the fact that class counsel were required to advance case expenses of $1.7 million over a three-year period with no on[-]going reimbursement, (2) the fact that class counsel were not paid on an on-going basis as the work was being performed, and (3) the fact that class counsel's ability to recover a fee and expense reimbursement were completely contingent on the outcome of the case." The court stated that respondents' attorneys had exhibited "a higher degree of skill, commitment, dedication, and professionalism . . . than the Court has seen displayed by the attorneys in any other case during its 27 years on the bench." The court also commented that the results obtained were "extraordinary" and added that "[a]fter 58 years as a practicing attorney and federal judge, the Court is unaware of any other case in which a plaintiff class has achieved such a favorable result on such a comprehensive scale." The enhancement resulted in an additional $4.5 million fee award. . . .

The general rule in our legal system is that each party must pay its own attorney's fees and expenses, but Congress enacted 42 U.S.C. § 1988 in order to ensure that federal rights are adequately enforced. Section 1988 provides that a prevailing party in certain civil rights actions may recover "a reasonable attorney's fee as part of the costs."[3] Unfortunately, the statute does not explain what Congress meant by a "reasonable" fee, and therefore the task of identifying an appropriate methodology for determining a "reasonable" fee was left for the courts.

One possible method was set out in Johnson *v.* Georgia Highway Express, Inc., 488 F.2d 714, 717–719 (5th Cir. 1974), which listed 12 factors that a court should consider in determining a reasonable fee.[4] This method, however, "gave very little actual guidance to district courts. Setting attorney's fees by reference to a series of sometimes subjective factors placed unlimited discretion in trial judges and produced disparate results." Pennsylvania *v.* Delaware Valley Citizens' Council for Clean Air, 478 U.S. 546 (1986) (*Delaware Valley I*).

An alternative, the lodestar approach, . . . "achieved dominance in the federal courts" after our decision in Hensley *v.* Eckerhart, 461 U.S. 424 (1983). . . .

---

[3] Virtually identical language appears in many of the federal fee-shifting statutes.

[4] These factors were: "(1) the time and labor required; (2) the novelty and difficulty of the questions; (3) the skill requisite to perform the legal service properly; (4) the preclusion of employment by the attorney due to the acceptance of the case; (5) the customary fee; (6) whether the fee is fixed or contingent; (7) time limitations imposed by the client or the circumstances; (8) the amount involved and the results obtained; (9) the experience, reputation, and ability of the attorneys; (10) the 'undesirability' of the case; (11) the nature and length of the professional relationship with the client; and (12) awards in similar cases." Hensley *v.* Eckerhart, 461 U.S. 424, 430 n. 3 (1983).

Although the lodestar method is not perfect, it has several important virtues. First, in accordance with our understanding of the aim of fee-shifting statutes, the lodestar looks to "the prevailing market rates in the relevant community." Blum *v.* Stenson, 465 U.S. 886, 895 (1984). Developed after the practice of hourly billing had become widespread, the lodestar method produces an award that *roughly* approximates the fee that the prevailing attorney would have received if he or she had been representing a paying client who was billed by the hour in a comparable case. Second, the lodestar method is readily administrable, and unlike the *Johnson* approach, the lodestar calculation is "objective" and thus cabins the discretion of trial judges, permits meaningful judicial review, and produces reasonably predictable results.

Our prior decisions concerning the federal fee-shifting statutes have established six important rules that lead to our decision in this case.

First, a "reasonable" fee is a fee that is sufficient to induce a capable attorney to undertake the representation of a meritorious civil rights case. Section 1988's aim is to enforce the covered civil rights statutes, not to provide "a form of economic relief to improve the financial lot of attorneys." Delaware Valley I, *supra*, at 565.

Second, the lodestar method yields a fee that is presumptively sufficient to achieve this objective.

Third, although we have never sustained an enhancement of a lodestar amount for performance, we have repeatedly said that enhancements may be awarded in "rare" and "exceptional" circumstances.

Fourth, we have noted that "the lodestar figure includes most, if not all, of the relevant factors constituting a 'reasonable' attorney's fee," and have held that an enhancement may not be awarded based on a factor that is subsumed in the lodestar calculation. We have thus held that the novelty and complexity of a case generally may not be used as a ground for an enhancement because these factors "presumably [are] fully reflected in the number of billable hours recorded by counsel." We have also held that the quality of an attorney's performance generally should not be used to adjust the lodestar "[b]ecause consideration concerning the quality of a prevailing party's counsel's representation are reflected in the reasonable hourly rate." Delaware Valley I, *supra*, at 566.

Fifth, the burden of proving that an enhancement is necessary must be borne by the fee applicant.

Finally, a fee applicant seeking an enhancement must produce "specific evidence" that supports the award. Blum, 465 U.S., at 899, 901. This requirement is essential if the lodestar method is to realize one of its chief virtues, *i.e.,* providing a calculation that is objective and capable of being reviewed on appeal.

In light of what we have said in prior cases, we reject any contention that a fee determined by the lodestar method may not be enhanced in any situation. The lodestar method was never intended to be conclusive in all circumstances. Instead, there is a "strong presumption" that the lodestar figure is reasonable, but that presumption may be overcome in those rare circumstances in which the lodestar does not adequately take into account a factor that may properly be considered in determining a reasonable fee.

In this case, we are asked to decide whether either the quality of an attorney's performance or the results obtained are factors that may properly provide a basis for an enhancement. We treat these two factors as one. When a plaintiff's attorney achieves results that are more favorable than would have been predicted based on the governing law and the available evidence, the outcome may be attributable to superior performance and commitment of resources by plaintiff's counsel. Or the outcome may result from inferior performance by defense counsel, unanticipated defense concessions, unexpectedly favorable rulings by the court, an unexpectedly sympathetic jury, or simple luck. Since none of these latter causes can justify an enhanced award, superior results are relevant only to the extent it can be shown that they are the result of superior attorney performance. Thus, we need only consider whether superior attorney performance can justify an enhancement. And in light of the principles derived from our prior cases, we inquire whether there are circumstances in which superior attorney performance is not adequately taken into account in the lodestar calculation. We conclude that there are a few such circumstances but that these circumstances are indeed "rare" and "exceptional," and require specific evidence that the lodestar fee would not have been "adequate to attract competent counsel."

First, an enhancement may be appropriate where the method used in determining the hourly rate employed in the lodestar calculation does not adequately measure the attorney's true market value, as demonstrated in part during the litigation.[5] This may occur if the hourly rate is determined by a formula that takes into account only a single factor (such as years since admission to the bar) or perhaps only a few similar factors. In such a case, an enhancement may be appropriate so that an attorney is compensated at the rate that the attorney would receive in cases not governed by the federal fee-shifting statutes. But in order to provide a calculation that is objective and reviewable, the trial judge should adjust the attorney's hourly rate in accordance with specific proof linking the attorney's ability to a prevailing market rate.

Second, an enhancement may be appropriate if the attorney's performance includes an extraordinary outlay of expenses and the litigation is exceptionally protracted. [W]hen an attorney agrees to

---

[5] Respondents correctly note that an attorney's "brilliant insights and critical maneuvers sometimes matter far more than hours worked or years of experience." But as we said in Blum *v.* Stenson, 465 U.S. 886, 898 (1984), "[i]n those cases, the special skill and experience of counsel should be reflected in the reasonableness of the hourly rates."

represent a civil rights plaintiff who cannot afford to pay the attorney, the attorney presumably understands that no reimbursement is likely to be received until the successful resolution of the case, and therefore enhancements to compensate for delay in reimbursement for expenses must be reserved for unusual cases. In such exceptional cases, however, an enhancement may be allowed, but the amount of the enhancement must be calculated using a method that is reasonable, objective, and capable of being reviewed on appeal, such as by applying a standard rate of interest to the qualifying outlays of expenses.

Third, there may be extraordinary circumstances in which an attorney's performance involves exceptional delay in the payment of fees. An attorney who expects to be compensated under § 1988 presumably understands that payment of fees will generally not come until the end of the case, if at all. Compensation for this delay is generally made "either by basing the award on current rates or by adjusting the fee based on historical rates to reflect its present value." Missouri *v.* Jenkins, 491 U.S. 274, 282 (1989). But we do not rule out the possibility that an enhancement may be appropriate where an attorney assumes these costs in the face of unanticipated delay, particularly where the delay is unjustifiably caused by the defense. In such a case, however, the enhancement should be calculated by applying a method similar to that described above in connection with exceptional delay in obtaining reimbursement for expenses.

We reject the suggestion that it is appropriate to grant performance enhancements on the ground that departures from hourly billing are becoming more common. As we have noted, the lodestar was adopted in part because it provides a rough approximation of general billing practices, and accordingly, if hourly billing becomes unusual, an alternative to the lodestar method may have to be found. However, neither respondents nor their *amici* contend that that day has arrived. . . .

We are told that, under an increasingly popular arrangement, attorneys are paid at a reduced hourly rate but receive a bonus if certain specified results are obtained, and this practice is analogized to the award of an enhancement such as the one in this case. The analogy, however, is flawed. An attorney who agrees, at the outset of the representation, to a *reduced hourly rate* in exchange for the opportunity to earn a performance bonus is in a position far different from an attorney in a § 1988 case who is compensated at the *full prevailing rate* and then seeks a performance enhancement in addition to the lodestar amount after the litigation has concluded. . . .

In the present case, the District Court did not provide proper justification for the large enhancement that it awarded. . . .

[T]he effect of the enhancement was to increase the top rate for the attorneys to more than $866 per hour, and the District Court did not point to anything in the record that shows that this is an appropriate figure for the relevant market.

The District Court pointed to the fact that respondents' counsel had to make extraordinary outlays for expenses and had to wait for reimbursement, but the court did not calculate the amount of the enhancement that is attributable to this factor. Similarly, the District Court noted that respondents' counsel did not receive fees on an ongoing basis while the case was pending, but the court did not sufficiently link this factor to proof in the record that the delay here was outside the normal range expected by attorneys who rely on § 1988 for the payment of their fees or quantify the disparity. Nor did the court provide a calculation of the cost to counsel of any extraordinary and unwarranted delay. And the court's reliance on the contingency of the outcome contravenes our holding in Burlington *v.* Dague, 505 U.S. 557 (1992).

Finally, insofar as the District Court relied on a comparison of the performance of counsel in this case with the performance of counsel in unnamed prior cases, the District Court did not employ a methodology that permitted meaningful appellate review. . . .

Determining a "reasonable attorney's fee" is a matter that is committed to the sound discretion of a trial judge, see 42 U.S.C. § 1988 (permitting court, "in its discretion," to award fees), but the judge's discretion is not unlimited. It is essential that the judge provide a reasonably specific explanation for all aspects of a fee determination, including any award of an enhancement. Unless such an explanation is given, adequate appellate review is not feasible, and without such review, widely disparate awards may be made, and awards may be influenced (or at least, may appear to be influenced) by a judge's subjective opinion regarding particular attorneys or the importance of the case. In addition, in future cases, defendants contemplating the possibility of settlement will have no way to estimate the likelihood of having to pay a potentially huge enhancement.

Section 1988 serves an important public purpose by making it possible for persons without means to bring suit to vindicate their rights. But unjustified enhancements that serve only to enrich attorneys are not consistent with the statute's aim. In many cases, attorney's fees awarded under § 1988 are not paid by the individuals responsible for the constitutional or statutory violations on which the judgment is based. Instead, the fees are paid in effect by state and local taxpayers, and because state and local governments have limited budgets, money that is used to pay attorney's fees is money that cannot be used for programs that provide vital public services. . . .

■ [The concurring opinions of JUSTICE KENNEDY and JUSTICE THOMAS are omitted.]

■ JUSTICE BREYER, with whom JUSTICE STEVENS, JUSTICE GINSBURG, and JUSTICE SOTOMAYOR join, concurring in part and dissenting in part. . . .

This case well illustrates why our tiered and functionally specialized judicial system places the task of determining an attorney's fee award primarily in the district court's hands. The plaintiffs' lawyers spent eight years investigating the underlying facts, developing the initial complaint, conducting court proceedings, and working out final relief. The District Court's docket, with over 600 entries, consists of more than 18,000 pages. Transcripts of hearings and depositions, along with other documents, have produced a record that fills 20 large boxes. Neither we, nor an appellate panel, can easily read that entire record. Nor should we attempt to second-guess a district judge who is aware of the many intangible matters that the written page cannot reflect. . . .

[T]he record indicates that the lawyers' objective in this case was unusually important and fully consistent with the central objectives of the basic federal civil-rights statute, 42 U.S.C. § 1983. Moreover, the problem the attorneys faced demanded an exceptionally high degree of skill and effort. Specifically, these lawyers and their clients sought to have the State of Georgia reform its entire foster-care system—a system that much in the record describes as well below the level of minimal constitutional acceptability. The record contains investigative reports, mostly prepared by Georgia's own Office of the Child Advocate, which show, for example, the following:

- The State's foster-care system was unable to provide essential medical and mental health services; children consequently and unnecessarily suffered illness and life long medical disabilities, such as permanent hearing loss, due to failures on the part of the State to administer basic care and antibiotics.
- Understaffing and improper staffing placed children in the care of individuals with dangerous criminal records; children were physically assaulted by the staff, locked outside of the shelters at night as punishment, and abused in other ways.
- The shelters themselves were "unsanitary and dilapidated," "unclean," infested with rats, "overcrowded," unsafe, and "out of control."
- Due to improper supervision and other deficiencies at the shelters, 20% of the children abused drugs; some also became victims of child prostitution.
- Systemic failures also caused vulnerable children to suffer regular beatings and sexual abuse, including rape, at the hands of more aggressive shelter residents.

- Not surprisingly, many children-upwards of 5 per day and over 750 per year-tried to escape these conditions; others tried to commit suicide.

. . . The upshot is that the plaintiffs' attorneys did what the child advocate could not do: They initiated this lawsuit. They thereby assumed the role of "a 'private attorney general' " by filling an enforcement void in the State's own legal system, a function "that Congress considered of the highest priority," Newman *v.* Piggie Park Enterprises, Inc., 390 U.S. 400, 402 (1968), and "meant to promote in enacting § 1988," Texas State Teachers Association *v.* Garland Independent School District, 489 U.S. 782, 793 (1989). . . .

NOTES ON FEES FOR NONLAWYERS

1. In Kay *v.* Ehrler, 499 U.S. 432 (1991), the Supreme Court held that an attorney who represented himself in a successful civil rights action should not be awarded a "reasonable attorney's fee as part of the costs" under 42 U.S.C. 1988. The Court said:

> "A rule that authorizes awards of counsel fees to pro se litigants—even if limited to those who are members of the bar—would create a disincentive to employ counsel whenever such a plaintiff considered himself competent to litigate on his own behalf. The statutory policy of furthering the successful prosecution of meritorious claims is better served by a rule that creates an incentive to retain counsel in every such case."

Id. at 437.

2. In Missouri *v.* Jenkins, 491 U.S. 274 (1989), the Court ruled that the "reasonable attorney's fee" recoverable under Section 1988 includes separately billed paralegal and law clerk time.

> "Clearly, a 'reasonable attorney's fee' cannot have been meant to compensate only work performed personally by members of the bar. Rather, the term must refer to a reasonable fee for the work product of an attorney. Thus, the fee must take into account the work not only of attorneys, but also of secretaries, messengers, librarians, janitors, and others whose labor contributes to the work product for which an attorney bills her client; and it must also take account of other expenses and profit. The parties have suggested no reason why the work of [law clerks and] paralegals should not be similarly compensated, nor can we think of any. We thus take as our starting point the self-evident proposition that the 'reasonable attorney's fee' provided for by statute should compensate the work of [law clerks and] paralegals, as well as that of attorneys."

Id. at 285.

City of Riverside v. Rivera

Supreme Court of the United States, 1986.
477 U.S. 561.

■ JUSTICE BRENNAN announced the judgment of the Court and delivered an opinion in which JUSTICE MARSHALL, JUSTICE BLACKMUN, and JUSTICE STEVENS join.

The issue presented in this case is whether an award of attorney's fees under 42 U.S.C. § 1988 is *per se* "unreasonable" within the meaning of the statute if it exceeds the amount of damages recovered by the plaintiff in the underlying civil rights action.

Respondents, eight Chicano individuals, attended a party on the evening of August 1, 1975, at the Riverside, California, home of respondents Santos and Jennie Rivera. A large number of unidentified police officers, acting without a warrant, broke up the party using tear gas and, as found by the District Court, "unnecessary physical force." Many of the guests, including four of the respondents, were arrested. The District Court later found that "[t]he party was not creating a disturbance in the community at the time of the break-in." Criminal charges against the arrestees were ultimately dismissed for lack of probable cause.

On June 4, 1976, respondents sued the city of Riverside, its chief of police, and 30 individual police officers under 42 U.S.C. §§ 1981, 1983, 1985(3), and 1986 for allegedly violating their First, Fourth, and Fourteenth Amendment rights. The complaint, which also alleged numerous state-law claims, sought damages, and declaratory and injunctive relief. . . . The jury returned a total of 37 individual verdicts in favor of the respondents and against the city and five individual officers, finding 11 violations of § 1983, four instances of false arrest and imprisonment, and 22 instances of negligence. Respondents were awarded $33,350 in compensatory and punitive damages: $13,300 for their federal claims, and $20,050 for their state-law claims.

Respondents also sought attorney's fees and costs under § 1988. They requested compensation for 1,946.75 hours expended by their two attorneys at a rate of $125 per hour, and for 84.5 hours expended by law clerks at a rate of $25.00 per hour, a total of $245,456.25. The District Court found both the hours and rates reasonable, and awarded respondents $245,456.25 in attorney's fees. . . .

Petitioners, joined by the Solicitor General as *amicus curiae,* maintain that [the] lodestar approach is inappropriate in civil rights cases where a plaintiff recovers only monetary damages. In these cases, so the argument goes, use of the lodestar may result in fees that exceed the amount of damages recovered and that are therefore unreasonable. Likening such cases to private tort actions, petitioners and the Solicitor General submit that attorney's fees in such cases should be proportionate to the amount of damages a plaintiff recovers. Specifically, they suggest that fee awards in damages cases should be modeled upon the contingent fee arrangements commonly used in personal injury litigation. In this case, assuming a 33% contingency rate, this would entitle respondents to recover approximately $11,000 in attorney's fees.

The amount of damages a plaintiff recovers is certainly relevant to the amount of attorney's fees to be awarded under § 1988. It is, however, only one of many factors that a court should consider in calculating an award of attorney's fees. We reject the proposition that fee awards under § 1988 should necessarily be proportionate to the amount of damages a civil rights plaintiff actually recovers.

As an initial matter, we reject the notion that a civil rights action for damages constitutes nothing more than a private tort suit benefiting only the individual plaintiffs whose rights were violated. Unlike most private tort litigants, a civil rights plaintiff seeks to vindicate important civil and constitutional rights that cannot be valued solely in monetary terms. And, Congress has determined that "the public as a whole has an interest in the vindication of the rights conferred by the statutes enumerated in § 1988, over and above the value of a civil rights remedy to a particular plaintiff. . . ." Hensley *v.* Eckerhart, 461 U.S. 424, 444, n.4 (1983) (BRENNAN, J., concurring in part and dissenting in part). . . .

Congress enacted § 1988 specifically because it found that the private market for legal services failed to provide many victims of civil rights violations with effective access to the judicial process. These victims ordinarily cannot afford to purchase legal services at the rates set by the private market. Moreover, the contingent fee arrangements that make legal services available to many victims of personal injuries would often not encourage lawyers to accept civil rights cases, which frequently involve substantial expenditures of time and effort but produce only small monetary recoveries. . . .

In order to ensure that lawyers would be willing to represent persons with legitimate civil rights grievances, Congress determined that it would be necessary to compensate lawyers for all time reasonably expended on a case.

This case illustrates why the enforcement of civil rights laws cannot be entrusted to private-sector fee arrangements. The District Court observed that "[g]iven the nature of this lawsuit and the type of defense presented, many attorneys in the community would have been reluctant to institute and to continue to prosecute this action." The court concluded, moreover, that "[c]ounsel for plaintiffs achieved excellent results for their clients, and their accomplishment in this case was outstanding. The amount of time expended by counsel in conducting this litigation was reasonable and reflected sound legal judgment under the circumstances." Nevertheless, petitioners suggest that respondents' counsel should be compensated for only a small fraction of the actual time spent litigating the case. In light of the difficult nature of the issues presented by this lawsuit and the low pecuniary value of the many of the rights respondents sought to vindicate, it is highly unlikely that the prospect of a fee equal to a fraction of the damages respondents might recover would have been sufficient to attract competent counsel. Moreover, since counsel might not have found it economically feasible to expend the amount of time respondents' counsel found necessary to litigate the case properly, it is even less likely that counsel would have achieved the excellent results that respondents' counsel obtained here. Thus, had respondents had to rely on private-sector fee arrangements, they might well have been unable to obtain redress for their grievances. It is precisely for this reason that Congress enacted § 1988. . . .

[T]here already exists a wide range of safeguards designed to protect civil rights defendants against the possibility of excessive fee awards. Both the House and Senate Reports identify standards for courts to follow in awarding and calculating attorney's fees; these standards are designed to insure that attorneys are compensated only for time *reasonably expended* on a case. The district court has the discretion to deny fees to prevailing plaintiffs under special circumstances, and to award attorney's fees against plaintiffs who litigate frivolous or vexatious claims. . . . We believe that these safeguards adequately protect against the possibility that § 1988 might produce a "windfall" to civil rights attorneys. . . .

■ JUSTICE POWELL, concurring in the judgment. I join only the Court's judgment. . . . For me affirmance—quite simply—is required by the District Court's detailed findings of fact, which were approved by the Court of Appeals. On its face, the fee award seems unreasonable. But I find no basis for this Court to reject the findings made and approved by the courts below. . . .

Where recovery of private damages is the purpose of a civil rights litigation, a district court, in fixing fees, is obligated to give primary consideration to the amount of damages awarded as compared to the amount sought. In some civil rights cases, however, the court may consider the vindication of constitutional rights in addition to the amount of damages recovered. In this case, for example, the District Court made an explicit finding that the "public interest" had been served by the jury's verdict that the warrantless entry was lawless and unconstitutional. Although the finding of a Fourth Amendment violation hardly can be considered a new constitutional ruling, in the special circumstances of this case, the vindication of the asserted Fourth Amendment right may well have served a public interest, supporting the amount of the fees awarded.[3] As the District Court put it, there were allegations that the police misconduct was "motivated by a general hostility to the Chicano community in the area. . . ." The record also contained evidence of racial slurs by some of the police. . . .

---

[3] It probably will be the rare case in which an award of *private damages* can be said to benefit the public interest to an extent that would justify the disproportionality between damages and fees reflected in this case.

■ CHIEF JUSTICE BURGER, dissenting. I join JUSTICE REHNQUIST's dissenting opinion. I write only to add that it would be difficult to find a better example of legal nonsense than the fixing of attorney's fees by a judge at $245,456.25 for the recovery of $33,350 damages.

The two attorneys receiving this nearly quarter-million-dollar fee graduated from law school in 1973 and 1974; they brought this action in 1975, which resulted in the $33,350 jury award in 1980. Their total professional experience when this litigation began consisted of Gerald Lopez' 1-year service as a law clerk to a judge and Roy Cazares' two years' experience as a trial attorney in the Defenders' Program of San Diego County. For their services the District Court found that an hourly rate of $125 per hour was reasonable.

Can anyone doubt that no private party would ever have dreamed of paying these two novice attorneys $125 per hour in 1975, which, considering inflation, would represent perhaps something more nearly a $250 per hour rate today? For example . . . , would any private litigant be willing to pay a total of $17,875 simply for preparation of a pretrial order? . . .

■ JUSTICE REHNQUIST, with whom THE CHIEF JUSTICE, JUSTICE WHITE, and JUSTICE O'CONNOR, join, dissenting. . . .

I see no escape from the conclusion that the District Court's finding that respondents' attorneys "reasonably" spent 1,946.75 hours to recover a money judgment of $33,350 is clearly erroneous, and that therefore the District Court's award of $245,456.25 in attorney's fees to respondents should be reversed. The Court's affirmance of the fee award . . . turns § 1988 into a relief act for lawyers. . . .

In the context of § 1988, there would obviously be some exceptions to the general rules of "billing judgment" . . . but none of these exceptions are applicable here. If the litigation is unnecessarily prolonged by the bad-faith conduct of the defendants, or if the litigation produces significant, identifiable benefits for persons other than the plaintiffs, then the purpose of Congress in authorizing attorney's fees under § 1988 should allow a larger award of attorney's fees than would be "reasonable" where the only relief is the recovery of monetary damages by individual plaintiffs. Nor do we deal here with a case such as Carey *v.* Piphus, 435 U.S. 247 (1978), in which the deprivation of a constitutional right necessarily results in only nominal pecuniary damages. Here, respondents successfully claimed both compensatory and punitive damages for false arrest and imprisonment, negligence, and violations of their constitutional rights under the Fourth and Fourteenth Amendments, and the jury assessed damages as juries do in such cases. In short, this case shares none of the special aspects of certain civil rights litigation which the plurality suggests . . . would justify an award of attorney's fees totally divorced from the amount of damages awarded by the jury. . . .

Goodrich v. E.F. Hutton Group, Inc.

Supreme Court of Delaware, 1996.
681 A.2d 1039.

■ HOLLAND, JUSTICE. . . . Goodrich . . . was certified as the class representative in an action against . . . E.F. Hutton. . . . The Court of Chancery approved a proposed settlement of this class action . . . . It also awarded attorney's fees in an amount "equal to one-third of the gross amount paid out to claimants not to exceed $515,000, plus interest on the amount paid as a fee. . . ." . . .

Goodrich argues that the Court of Chancery either committed legal error, or abused its discretion, in awarding and disbursing attorney's fees as a percentage of the gross amount paid out to class members. . . .

This is one of those relatively rare cases in which it was necessary to appoint an attorney "to uphold the side of a question that no party before the Court is willing to advocate." Maurer *v.* International Re-Insurance Corp., 95 A.2d 827, 831 (Del. 1953). Such an advocate is properly paid from the fund at issue. . . .

This Court has concluded that the Court of Chancery properly applied established equitable precepts. . . .

Goodrich commenced this action on November 27, 1985 on behalf of a class of customers of E.F. Hutton who had received funds from E.F. Hutton. The funds were received during the period since July 1, 1980. The funds were paid by means of checks drawn on accounts maintained in banks located more than 500 miles from the E.F. Hutton office in which the customer transacted business. The complaint charged E.F. Hutton with a wrongful scheme to delay or withhold funds from its customers in order to gain the interest-free use of the money during the period of delayed payment. This conduct was alleged . . . to have constituted . . . a breach of fiduciary duty to the customers. . . .

On May 11, 1995, the parties submitted a Stipulation of Settlement (the "Settlement") to the Court of Chancery. Under the terms of the Settlement, E.F. Hutton agreed to pay $3.3 million into an interest-bearing escrow account. . . .

According to the Settlement, the escrow account would be drawn upon to pay attorney's fees for the class, the costs of notice to the class, and the costs of settlement administration not to exceed $600,000, up to a combined limit of $1.1 million. With respect to the balance of the funds in the escrow account (at least $2.2 million), the Settlement provided for payment to class members. . . .

[To obtain a payment from the fund, class members were required to list and document checks received from E.F. Hutton.] To the extent class members did not claim funds available in the escrow account, the Settlement established that such remaining funds were to be "returned to Defendant Hutton or its designee." . . .

The Court of Chancery decided to award to Goodrich's attorneys a fee of 33 1/3% of the total amount actually paid out to class members, up to a limit of $515,000 [about 16% of the 3.3 million paid into escrow]. . . . [I]f class members submitted claims amounting to only $1,545,000 of the $2.2 million potentially distributable, counsel for the class would receive [the maximum award of] $515,000 in fees. . . .

Pursuant to the American Rule, prevailing litigants are responsible for the payment of their own attorney's fees. The American Rule has two general categories of exceptions: fee-shifting statutes and equitable doctrines.

In this case, Goodrich invoked the most venerable equitable exception to the American Rule: the "common fund" doctrine (sometimes called the "equitable fund" doctrine or the "fund-in-court" doctrine). . . .

The common fund doctrine is founded on the equitable principle that those who have profited from litigation should share its costs. Boeing Co. *v.* Van Gemert, 444 U.S. 472, 478 (1980). . . . Jurisdiction over the fund enables a court to prevent such inequity by assessing fees out of the entire fund, spreading the burden proportionately among those benefitted. Accordingly, the doctrine provides that "a litigant or a lawyer who recovers a common fund for the benefit of persons other than himself or his client is entitled to a reasonable attorney's fee from the fund as a whole." *Id.*

Class action suits which result in the recovery of money exemplify the classic creation of a common fund. . . .

If the settlement of a class action is approved and has provided for a monetary recovery, the common fund doctrine permits an attorney to independently request an award of fees from that same settlement fund. At that point, "the plaintiffs' attorney's role changes from one of fiduciary for the clients to that of a claimant against the fund created for the clients' benefit." This divergence of interests requires a court to continue its "third-party" role in reviewing common fund fee applications. "[T]here is often no one to argue for the interests of the class," because class members with small claims often do not file objections to proposed settlements and fee applications. Rawlings *v.* Prudential-Bache Properties, Inc., 9 F.3d 513, 516 (6th Cir. 1993). The defendant who contributed to the fund also will usually have no interest in how the fund is divided between the class and the plaintiff's attorney.

The equitable nature of awarding attorney's fees from a common fund requires a court to exercise broad discretion by applying a reasonableness standard. The appropriate method a court should use to determine a reasonable attorney's fee to be awarded from a common fund has been the subject of considerable debate. Originally, fees were calculated and awarded as a reasonable percentage of the common fund. . . .

In the 1970s, courts began to use the "lodestar" approach to calculate fee awards in common fund cases. That method requires a court to calculate the product of an attorney's reasonable hours expended on the litigation and reasonable hourly rate to arrive at the "lodestar." That lodestar calculation can then be adjusted, through application of a "multiplier" or fee enhancer, to account for additional factors, *e.g.*, the contingent nature of the case and the quality of an attorney's work. . . .

In the 1980s, [various] events led to a reconsideration of the lodestar method of calculating common fund fee awards. . . .

At the present time, the majority of federal courts use a reasonable percentage of the fund method when making attorney fee awards in common fund cases. . . .[9]

Federal common fund attorney's fee jurisprudence is not binding upon the Court of Chancery or this Court. Nevertheless, its history is didactic. . . .

The Court of Chancery concluded . . . that it would not be desirable to adopt . . . a *per se* rule that awarded attorney's fees as a percentage in relation to the maximum common fund available, without regard to the benefits actually realized by class members. . . .

The condition precedent to invoking the common fund doctrine is a demonstration that a common benefit has been conferred. The Court of Chancery expressed concern about whether the common fund was an accurate quantification of the actual benefit that had been conferred in this case. By conditioning the award of attorney's fees upon the claims actually submitted, the Court of Chancery exercised its discretion equitably, to correlate the attorneys' compensation with the structure of the settlement benefits the attorneys had negotiated for the class. . . .

The adoption of a mandatory methodology or particular mathematical model for determining attorney's fees in common fund cases would be the antithesis of the equitable principles from which the concept of such awards originated. New mechanical guidelines are neither appropriate nor needed for the Court of Chancery. . . .

NOTES ON COMMON FUNDS FEES

1. The common fund method approved in *Goodrich* often provides more flexibility than does the approach to the lodestar set forth in Perdue *v.* Kenny in statutory fee-shifting cases, with its presumption against enhancement based on novelty and complexity. In cases that settle, courts often employ the common fund method notwithstanding the presence of a relevant fee-shifting statute. "The Circuits generally have concluded that common fund principles [may] govern, however, where a fee shifting case settles before judgment." Nilsen *v.* York County, 400 F. Supp. 2d 266, 271

[9] The D.C. Circuit and the Eleventh Circuit require the use of the percentage method in common fund cases. At least five other circuits leave it to the trial court's discretion to choose between the lodestar and percentage methods in common fund cases.

n.12 (D. Me. 2005), citing Staton *v.* Boeing Co., 327 F.3d 938, 967–68 (9th Cir. 2003); Brytus *v.* Spang & Co., 203 F.3d 238, 246–47 (3d Cir. 2000); Florin *v.* Nationsbank, 34 F.3d 560, 564 (7th Cir. 1994); Suffolk *v.* Long Island Lighting Co., 907 F.2d 1295, 1327 (2d Cir. 1990). A Federal Judicial Center report notes the use of common fund principles in settled cases brought under fee-shifting statutes. Alan Hirsch & Diane Sheehey, Federal Judicial Center, AWARDING ATTORNEYS' FEES AND MANAGING FEE LITIGATION 69 (2005) ("[T]he fact that a fee-shifting statute applies to a particular case does not preclude recovery from a common fund. No courts have held to the contrary.").

2. The amount of fees in common fund recoveries can be explored as a function of the amount of the class recovery, time, locale, case category, and risk. The material that follows describe empirical research on each of these questions.

A. Class Action Attorney Fees and Class Recovery Amounts

In common fund cases, the dominant method for calculating counsel's compensation is to award a percentage of the fund. Figure 1 shows scatterplots of the fee amount and class recovery for two time periods, 1993 to 2002 and 2003 to 2008, represented by Figures 1a and 1b. Figure 1c shows the relation for the time periods combined and Figure 1d shows the relation for cases with recoveries greater than or equal to $100 million. The scales have been transformed into log10 units to address the bunching of cases at the lower end of the recovery scale that would occur in a linear dollar scale. Units of log10 can easily be interpreted because the log10 scale is simply based on powers of ten (for example, a value of 9 on a log10 scale is equal to $1 billion, or one followed by nine zeros). Amounts in Figure 1 and subsequent figures and tables in this Note are in 2008 inflation adjusted dollars.

Figures 1a and 1b show the strong, linear relation between the fee and the amount of the class recovery. They also show that the pattern is virtually unchanged over a 16 year period. The linear correlation coefficient for the relation between fee and recovery exceeds 0.94 (out of a maximum theoretical correlation coefficient of 1.00) for each time period and the slope of the relationships appears constant for the two time periods. The relation between fees and class recoveries can also be observed when all the data are combined, as shown in Figure 1c. In both the separate and combined data sets, the size of the class recovery swamps all other influences on the size of the fee. Figure 1d, which is limited to large cases, also shows a strong linear relation between fee and recovery. For these 109 cases, the linear correlation coefficient remains high 0.77 and is highly statistically significant ($p<0.0001$).

Figure 1. Fee as a Function of Recovery

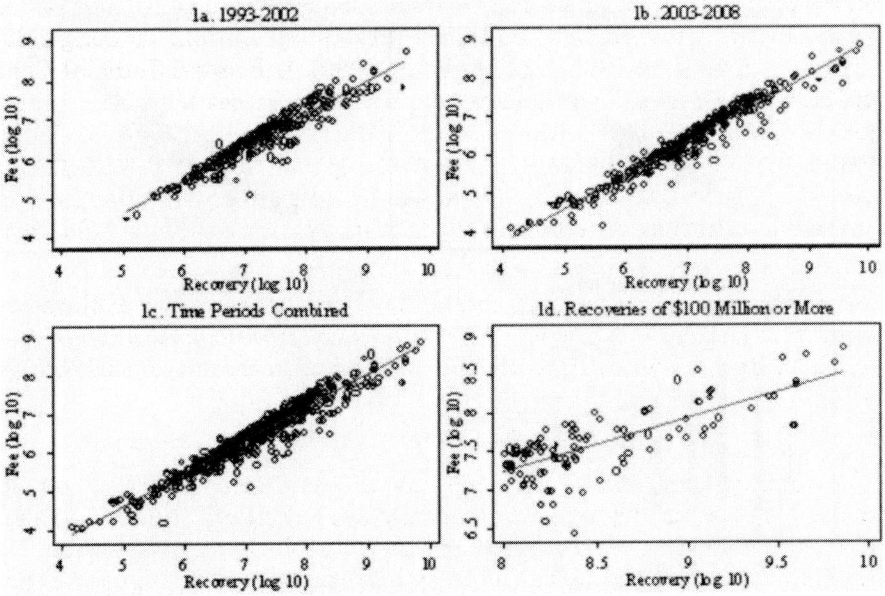

The strong association between fee and recovery has been repeatedly demonstrated in articles on which part of this Note is based. Theodore Eisenberg & Geoffrey P. Miller, Attorneys' Fees and Expenses in Class Action Settlements: 1993–2008, 7 J. Empirical Legal Studies 248 (2010); Theodore Eisenberg & Geoffrey P. Miller, Attorney Fees in Class Action Settlements: An Empirical Study, 1 J. Empirical Legal Studies 27 (2004); Brian Fitzpatrick, An Empirical Study of Class Action Settlements and Their Fee Awards, 7 J. Empirical Legal Studies 811 (2010).

Figure 2 further supports the primacy of the recovery amount as the explanation for the fee award. For ease of comparison, Figure 2a reproduces the combined time period data from Figure 1c. Figures 2b and 2c show that neither the hours claimed nor the age of a case are as strongly associated with the fee amount as is the class recovery amount.

Figure 2. Fee as a Function of Recovery, Hours, and Age 2003-2008

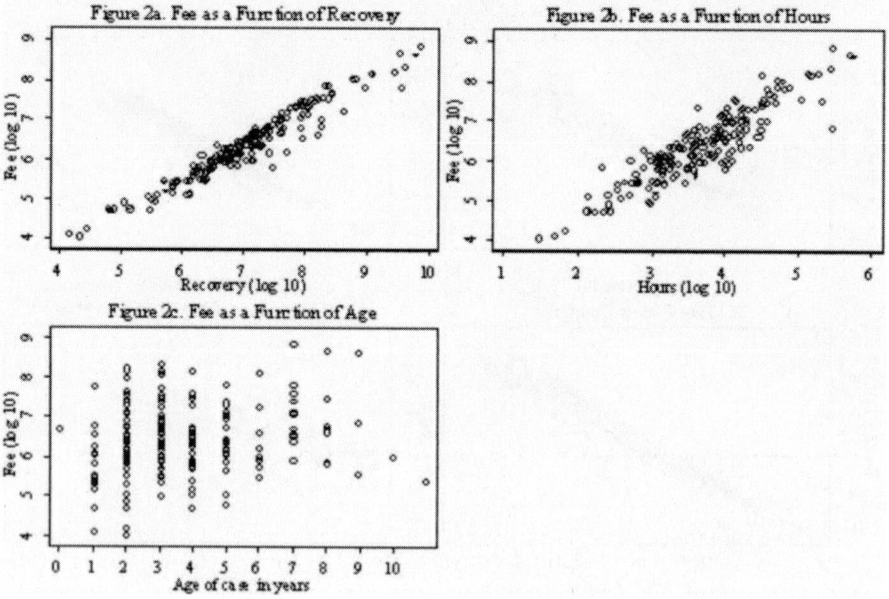

The data also reveal that the level of both class recoveries and attorney fees have not varied substantially over time. As Figure 3 shows, these amounts have shown no distinct time trend for most of 16 years. Inflation-adjusted recoveries and fees through 2007 were at levels not significantly different from where they were in 1993 and in fact are lower in inflation-adjusted dollars. In 2008, a noticeable drop in mean and median recoveries and fees occurred. The difference in class recovery medians between 2008 and all earlier years combined is statistically significant at $p=0.002$, and the difference in fees between 2008 and earlier years is significant at $p=0.0003$. The difference in the median ratio of fee to recovery (ratio of the logs) did not significantly differ between 2008 and earlier years ($p=0.517$).

Figure 3. Class Recovery & Attorney Fee Over Time Mean & Median

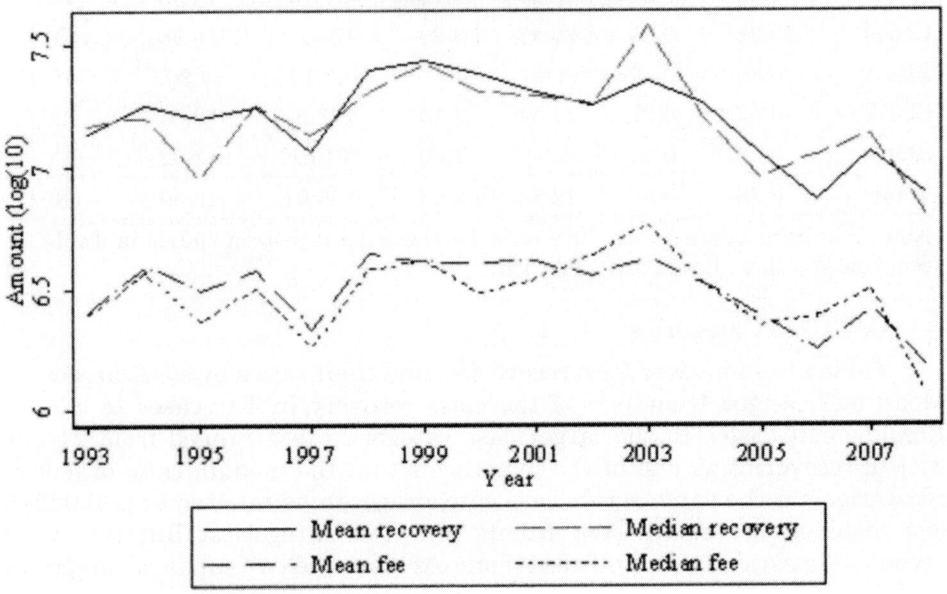

B. Fees Across Locales

Table 1 shows summary statistics about fees and recoveries by locale. The mean fee to recovery ratio was 0.23, or 23% of the class award, but this percent varies by recovery size, as shown in Figure 5 below. The mean fee was $12.8 million and the median was $2.3 million. The mean class recovery was $116.0 million and the median was $12.5 million.

Table 1. Fee and Class Recoveries, by Locale, 1993–2008

	Mean ratio	Median ratio	Mean fee	Median fee	Mean gross recovery	Median gross recovery	Number of cases
Appellate court	0.19	0.20	5.89	2.15	57.86	13.37	25
CDCA	0.25	0.25	3.93	2.75	16.30	19.90	10
DDC	0.22	0.22	16.69	2.14	134.79	13.00	18
DMA	0.16	0.15	11.50	7.00	118.55	81.00	10
DMN	0.25	0.27	8.77	4.75	40.99	14.25	16
DNJ	0.21	0.22	32.26	7.80	503.42	36.88	35
EDCA	0.26	0.25	0.40	0.12	3.26	0.54	12
EDLA	0.26	0.23	7.79	1.77	43.53	8.61	13
EDMI	0.22	0.20	6.56	1.34	34.80	11.75	17
EDNY	0.32	0.25	11.33	2.38	142.42	9.03	26
EDPA	0.28	0.29	12.66	1.51	75.79	6.88	70
MDFL	0.21	0.21	3.64	2.66	18.23	14.87	12

NDCA	0.26	0.25	4.44	2.00	24.06	9.25	47
NDIL	0.24	0.24	12.14	2.75	51.45	12.50	29
Other	0.24	0.25	20.47	3.25	154.98	16.38	161
SDCA	0.26	0.25	4.66	1.14	63.12	4.90	10
SDNY	0.22	0.22	11.54	2.13	127.97	12.85	103
State	0.20	0.20	5.94	2.00	61.61	12.32	75
Total	0.23	0.24	12.84	2.33	116.01	12.50	689

Note. Standard abbreviations are used for the federal district courts in Table 1.
Sources: Westlaw, LexisNexis, PACER.

C. Case Categories

Table 2 summarizes fees, recoveries, and their ratios by case categories. Mean fees ranged from 11% of the class recovery in Tax cases to 27% in Employment cases. In the larger case categories fees ranged from 21% to 27% of recoveries. A test of the hypothesis that the median ratio of fees to recoveries are the same across case categories can be rejected at $p<0.022$, if one includes the small Civil Rights and Tax categories. But the effect becomes statistically insignificant if one excludes the two smallest categories ($p=0.222$).

Table 2. Fee and Class Recoveries, by Case Category, 1993–2008

	Mean ratio	Median ratio	Mean fee	Median fee	Mean gross recovery	Median gross recovery	Number of cases
Antitrust	0.22	0.23	21.02	9.15	163.48	39.36	71
Civil Rights	0.24	0.23	4.10	1.52	16.53	7.48	18
Consumer	0.25	0.20	10.04	1.70	128.42	9.33	125
Corporate	0.21	0.19	3.35	1.12	16.51	9.86	30
Employment	0.27	0.25	2.43	0.75	12.28	3.00	55
ERISA	0.23	0.25	6.61	3.46	29.54	14.00	43
Securities	0.23	0.25	14.78	2.52	141.96	12.50	268
Tax Refund/ Tax	0.11	0.06	12.96	5.50	188.01	60.07	8
Tort	0.21	0.20	30.15	6.63	254.60	25.86	29
Other	0.23	0.25	13.59	2.00	61.86	10.75	42
Total	0.23	0.24	12.84	2.33	116.01	12.50	689

Sources: Westlaw, LexisNexis, PACER.

Figure 4 shows the core relation between fee amount and class recovery by case category. It shows that relation through separate scatterplots for each of ten case categories. The pattern is consistent across categories. Every category shows the same basic relation between fee and recovery.

Figure 4. Fee and Recovery by Case Category, 1993-2008

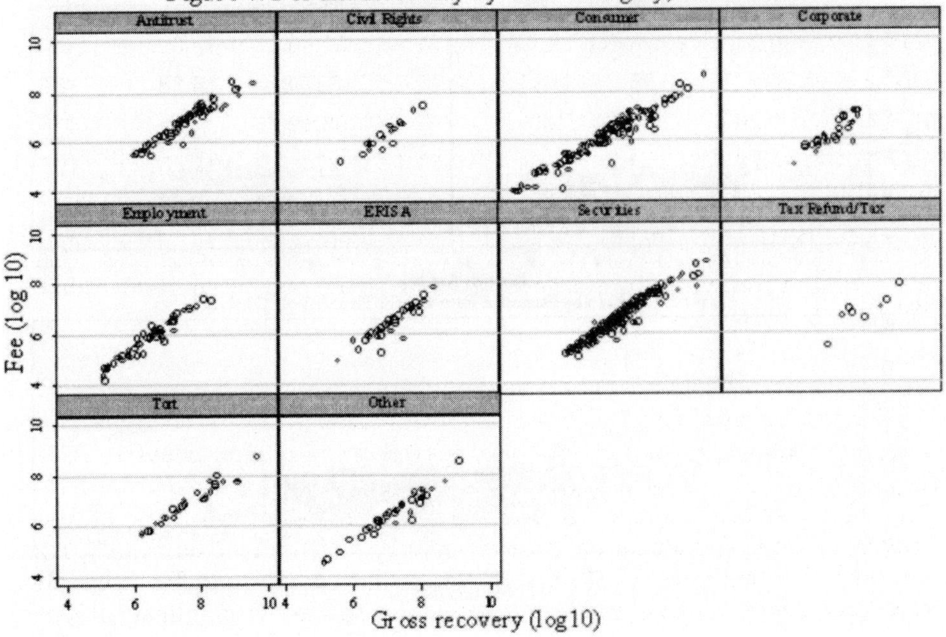

D. Scaling Effect

The existence of a scaling effect—the fee percent decreases as class recovery increases—is central to justifying aggregate litigation such as class actions. Plaintiffs' ability to aggregate into classes that reduce the percentage of recovery devoted to fees should be a hallmark of a well-functioning class action system. As Figure 5 shows, a substantial scaling effect existed in the 2003–2008 period, as well as in the earlier 1993–2002 period. The linear correlation coefficient for 2003–2008 was –0.57 and for 1993–2002 was –0.50, both statistically significant at $p<0.0001$. The lines in the figure show the best-fitting regression line for each data subset and Figure 5a shows the regression line for the combined data set.

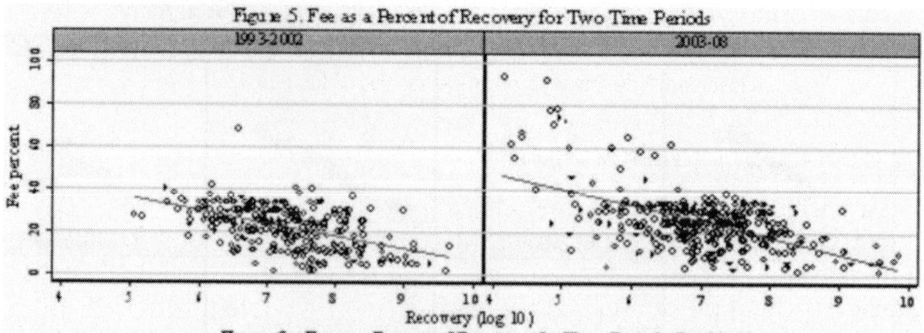

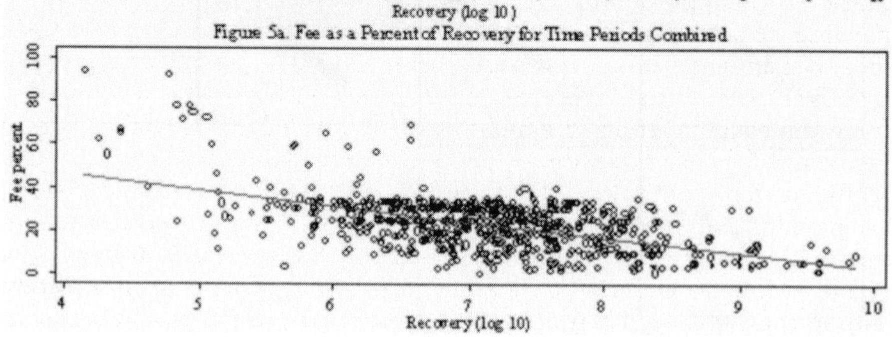

E. Risk

Standards applied to attorney fees uniformly indicate that greater risk warrants an increased fee. *E.g.*, Goldberger *v.* Integrated Resources, Inc., 209 F.3d 43, 50 (2d Cir. 2000). Table 3 reports, by case category, the mean fee percent separately for high risk and other cases. It confirms that courts systematically reward risk. For every case category except Antitrust and Other, mean fee percents were higher in high risk cases than in other cases. The difference within categories was statistically significant only for the large Securities category (t-test significance level =0.006).

Table 3. Fee Percent, by Risk Level

	High risk		Low/medium risk	
	N	Fee %	N	Fee %
Antitrust	9	20.1	62	22.2
Civil Rights	4	29.3	13	23.2
Consumer	14	31.3	110	24.7
Corporate	4	23.4	26	20.8
Employment	4	35.1	51	26.2
ERISA	5	24.6	38	23.2
Securities	45	26.4	217	22.7
Tax Refund/Tax	–	–	8	10.8
Tort	8	25.1	21	19.0
Other	13	22.1	29	23.9

Total	106	26.1	575	23.1

Sources: Westlaw, LexisNexis, PACER.

NOTE ON CONTINGENCY FEES

In both common fund cases and statutory fee-shifting cases, attorneys typically represent clients on a contingent basis. Attorneys do not receive compensation unless the client recovers and this method of financing litigation is the topic of much discussion. It has been noted that "The folklore regarding contingency fees produces sharply contrasting images. On the one hand, contingency fees represent the average person's 'key to the courthouse.' Individuals who would otherwise be left with no recourse can pursue the compensation to which they are entitled. At the other extreme, contingency fees are the source of all evil in the civil justice system: chasing ambulances for clients, creating expectations that every little injury deserves large payments in compensation, and filing inflated and fraudulent claims." Herbert M. Kritzer, The Wages of Risk: the Returns of Contingency Fee Legal Practice, 47 DePaul L. Rev. 267, 268 (1998). One central question is whether contingency fee practice produces better economic returns than hourly practice. Kritzer finds that lawyers who take cases on a contingency fee basis "can expect to do somewhat better than they do on their hourly fee cases." *Id.* at 303.

Chambers v. NASCO, Inc.

Supreme Court of the United States, 1991.
501 U.S. 32.

■ JUSTICE WHITE delivered the opinion of the Court.

This case requires us to explore the scope of the inherent power of a federal court to sanction a litigant for bad-faith conduct. Specifically, we are asked to determine whether the District Court, sitting in diversity, properly invoked its inherent power in assessing as a sanction for a party's bad-faith conduct attorney's fees and related expenses paid by the party's opponent to its attorneys. We hold that the District Court acted within its discretion, and we therefore affirm the judgment of the Court of Appeals.

This case began as a simple action for specific performance of a contract, but it did not remain so. Petitioner G. Russell Chambers was the sole shareholder and director of Calcasieu Television and Radio, Inc.: (CTR), which operated television station KPLC-TV in Lake Charles, Louisiana. On August 9, 1983, Chambers, acting both in his individual capacity and on behalf of CTR, entered into a purchase agreement to sell the station's facilities and broadcast license to respondent NASCO, Inc., for a purchase price of $18 million. The agreement was not recorded in the parishes in which the two properties housing the station's facilities were located. Consummation of the agreement was subject to the approval of the Federal Communications Commission (FCC); both parties were obligated to file the necessary documents with the FCC no later than September 23, 1983. By late August, however, Chambers had changed his mind and tried to talk NASCO out of consummating the sale. NASCO refused. On September 23, Chambers, through counsel, informed NASCO that he would not file the necessary papers with the FCC.

NASCO decided to take legal action. On Friday, October 14, 1983, NASCO's counsel informed counsel for Chambers and CTR that NASCO would file suit the following Monday in the United States District Court for the Western District of Louisiana, seeking specific performance of the agreement, as well as a temporary restraining order (TRO) to prevent the alienation or encumbrance of the properties at issue. NASCO provided this notice in accordance with Federal Rule of Civil Procedure 65 and Rule 11 of the District Court's Local Rules (now Rule 10), both of which are designed to give a defendant in a TRO application notice of the hearing and an opportunity to be heard.

The reaction of Chambers and his attorney, A.J. Gray III, was later described by the District Court as having "emasculated and frustrated the purposes of these rules and the powers of [the District] Court by utilizing this notice to prevent NASCO's access to the remedy of specific performance." On Sunday, October 16, 1983, the pair acted to place the properties at issue beyond the reach of the District Court by means of the Louisiana Public Records Doctrine. Because the purchase agreement had never been recorded, they determined that if the properties were sold to a third party, and if the deeds were recorded before the issuance of a TRO, the District Court would lack jurisdiction over the properties.

To this end, Chambers and Gray created a trust, with Chambers' sister as trustee and Chambers' three adult children as beneficiaries. The pair then directed the president of CTR, who later became Chambers' wife, to execute warranty deeds conveying the two tracts at issue to the trust for a recited consideration of $1.4 million. Early Monday morning, the deeds were recorded. The trustee, as purchaser, had not signed the deeds; none of the consideration had been paid; and CTR remained in possession of the properties. Later that morning, NASCO's counsel appeared in the District Court to file the complaint and seek the TRO. With NASCO's counsel present, the District Judge telephoned Gray. Despite the judge's queries concerning the possibility that CTR was negotiating to sell the properties to a third person, Gray made no mention of the recordation of the deeds earlier that morning. That afternoon, Chambers met with his sister and had her sign the trust documents and a $1.4 million note to CTR. The next morning, Gray informed the District Court by letter of the recordation of the deeds the day before and admitted that he had intentionally withheld the information from the court.

Within the next few days, Chambers' attorneys prepared a leaseback agreement from the trustee to CTR, so that CTR could remain in possession of the properties and continue to operate the station. The following week, the District Court granted a preliminary injunction against Chambers and CTR and entered a second TRO to prevent the trustee from alienating or encumbering the properties. At that hearing, the District Judge warned that Gray's and Chambers' conduct had been unethical.

Despite this early warning, Chambers, often acting through his attorneys, continued to abuse the judicial process. In November 1983, in defiance of the preliminary injunction, he refused to allow NASCO to inspect CTR's corporate records. The ensuing civil contempt proceedings resulted in the assessment of a $25,000 fine against Chambers personally. Two subsequent appeals from the contempt order were dismissed for lack of a final judgment.

Undeterred, Chambers proceeded with "a series of meritless motions and pleadings and delaying actions." These actions triggered further warnings from the court. At one point, acting *sua sponte,* the District Judge called a status conference to find out why bankers were being deposed. When informed by Chambers' counsel that the purpose was to learn whether NASCO could afford to pay for the station, the court canceled the depositions consistent with its authority under Federal Rule of Civil Procedure 26(g).

At the status conference nine days before the April 1985 trial date, the District Judge again warned counsel that further misconduct would not be tolerated. Finally, on the eve of trial, Chambers and CTR stipulated that the purchase agreement was enforceable and that Chambers had breached the agreement on September 23, 1983, by failing to file the necessary papers with the FCC. At trial, the only defense presented by Chambers was the Public Records Doctrine.

In the interlude between the trial and the entry of judgment during which the District Court prepared its opinion, Chambers sought to render the purchase agreement meaningless by seeking permission from the FCC to build a new transmission tower for the station and to relocate the transmission facilities to that site, which was not covered by the agreement. Only after NASCO sought contempt sanctions did Chambers withdraw the application.

The District Court entered judgment on the merits in NASCO's favor, finding that the transfer of the properties to the trust was a simulated sale and that the deeds purporting to convey the property were "null, void, and of no effect." Chambers' motions, filed in the District Court, the Court of Appeals, and this Court, to stay the judgment pending appeal were denied. Undeterred, Chambers convinced CTR officials to file formal oppositions to NASCO's pending application for FCC approval of the transfer of the station's license, in contravention of both the District Court's injunctive orders and its judgment on the merits. NASCO then sought contempt sanctions for a third time, and the oppositions were withdrawn.

When Chambers refused to prepare to close the sale, NASCO again sought the court's help. A hearing was set for July 16, 1986, to determine whether certain equipment was to be included in the sale. At the beginning of the hearing, the court informed Chambers' new attorney, Edwin A. McCabe, that further sanctionable conduct would not be tolerated. When the hearing was recessed for several days, Chambers, without notice to the court or NASCO, removed from service at the station all of the equipment at issue, forcing the District Court to order that the equipment be returned to service.

Immediately following oral argument on Chambers' appeal from the District Court's judgment on the merits, the Court of Appeals, ruling from the bench, found the appeal frivolous. The court imposed appellate sanctions in the form of attorney's fees and double costs, pursuant to Federal Rule of Appellate Procedure 38, and remanded the case to the District Court with orders to fix the amount of appellate sanctions and to determine whether further sanctions should be imposed for the manner in which the litigation had been conducted.

On remand, NASCO moved for sanctions, invoking the District Court's inherent power, Fed. Rule Civ. Proc. 11, and 28 U.S.C. § 1927. After full briefing and a hearing, the District Court determined that sanctions were appropriate "for the manner in which this proceeding was conducted in the district court from October 14, 1983, the time that plaintiff gave notice of its intention to file suit to this date." At the end of an extensive opinion recounting what it deemed to have been sanctionable conduct during this period, the court imposed sanctions against Chambers in the form of attorney's fees and expenses totaling $996,644.65, which represented the entire amount of NASCO's litigation costs paid to its attorneys. In so doing, the court rejected Chambers' argument that he had merely followed the advice of counsel, labeling him "the strategist" behind a scheme devised "first, to deprive this Court of jurisdiction and, second, to devise a plan of obstruction, delay, harassment, and expense sufficient to reduce NASCO to a condition of exhausted compliance."

In imposing the sanctions, the District Court first considered Federal Rule of Civil Procedure 11. It noted that the alleged sanctionable conduct was that Chambers and the other defendants had "(1) attempted to deprive this Court of jurisdiction by acts of fraud, nearly all of which were performed outside the confines of this Court, (2) filed false and frivolous pleadings, and (3) attempted, by other tactics of delay, oppression, harassment and massive expense to reduce plaintiff to exhausted compliance." The court recognized that the conduct in the first and third categories could not be reached by Rule 11, which governs only papers filed with a court. As for the second category, the court explained that the falsity of the pleadings at issue did not become apparent until after the trial on the merits, so that it would have been impossible to assess sanctions at the time the papers were filed. Consequently, the

District Court deemed Rule 11 "insufficient" for its purposes. The court likewise declined to impose sanctions under § 1927, both because the statute applies only to attorneys, and therefore would not reach Chambers, and because the statute was not broad enough to reach "acts which degrade the judicial system," including "attempts to deprive the Court of jurisdiction, fraud, misleading and lying to the Court." The court therefore relied on its inherent power in imposing sanctions . . . .

It has long been understood that "[c]ertain implied powers must necessarily result to our Courts of justice from the nature of their institution," powers "which cannot be dispensed with in a Court, because they are necessary to the exercise of all others." For this reason, "Courts of justice are universally acknowledged to be vested, by their very creation, with power to impose silence, respect, and decorum, in their presence, and submission to their lawful mandates." These powers are "governed not by rule or statute but by the control necessarily vested in courts to manage their own affairs so as to achieve the orderly and expeditious disposition of cases." . . .

Because of their very potency, inherent powers must be exercised with restraint and discretion. A primary aspect of that discretion is the ability to fashion an appropriate sanction for conduct which abuses the judicial process. . . . [O]utright dismissal of a lawsuit, which we [have] upheld . . . , is a particularly severe sanction, yet is within the court's discretion. Consequently, the "less severe sanction" of an assessment of attorney's fees is undoubtedly within a court's inherent power as well.

Indeed, "[t]here are ample grounds for recognizing . . . that in narrowly defined circumstances federal courts have inherent power to assess attorney's fees against counsel," Roadway Express, Inc. *v.* Piper, 447 U.S. 752, 765 (1980), even though the so-called "American Rule" prohibits fee-shifting in most cases. See Alyeska Pipeline Service Co. *v.* Wilderness Society, 421 U.S. 240, 259 (1975). . . .

[M]ost relevant here, a court may assess attorney's fees when a party has "acted in bad faith, vexatiously, wantonly, or for oppressive reasons." *Id.*, at 258–259. In this regard, if a court finds "that fraud has been practiced upon it, or that the very temple of justice has been defiled," it may assess attorney's fees against the responsible party, Universal Oil Products Co. *v.* Root Refining Co., 328 U.S. 575, 580 (1946), as it may when a party "shows bad faith by delaying or disrupting the litigation or by hampering enforcement of a court order," Hutto *v.* Finney, 437 U.S. 678, 689, n.14 (1978). The imposition of sanctions in this instance transcends a court's equitable power concerning relations between the parties and reaches a court's inherent power to police itself, thus serving the dual purpose of "vindicat[ing] judicial authority without resort to the more drastic sanctions available for contempt of court and mak[ing] the prevailing party whole for expenses caused by his opponent's obstinacy." *Ibid.*

We discern no basis for holding that the sanctioning scheme of the statute and the rules displaces the inherent power to impose sanctions for the bad-faith conduct described above. . . .

[W]hen there is bad-faith conduct in the course of litigation that could be adequately sanctioned under the rules, the court ordinarily should rely on the rules rather than the inherent power. But if in the informed discretion of the court, neither the statute nor the rules are up to the task, the court may safely rely on its inherent power. . . .

We likewise do not find that the District Court's reliance on the inherent power thwarted the purposes of the other sanctioning mechanisms. Although the dissent makes much of the fact that Rule 11 and Rule 26(g) "are cast in mandatory terms," the mandate of these provisions extends only to *whether* a court must impose sanctions, not to *which* sanction it must impose. . . .

Under Louisiana law, there can be no punitive damages for breach of contract, even when a party has acted in bad faith in breaching the agreement. Indeed, "as a general rule attorney's fees are not allowed a successful litigant in Louisiana except where authorized by statute or by contract." Rutherford *v.* Impson, 366 So.2d 944, 947 (La. App. 1978). It is clear, though, that this general rule focuses on the award of attorney's fees because of a party's success on the underlying claim. . . . This substantive state policy is not implicated here, where sanctions were imposed for conduct during the litigation.

Here the District Court did not attempt to sanction petitioner for breach of contract, but rather imposed sanctions for the fraud he perpetrated on the court and the bad faith he displayed toward both his adversary and the court throughout the course of the litigation. . . .

Second, Chambers claims that the fact that the entire amount of fees was awarded means that the District Court failed to tailor the sanction to the particular wrong. As NASCO points out, however, the District Court concluded that full attorney's fees were warranted due to the frequency and severity of Chambers' abuses of the judicial system and the resulting need to ensure that such abuses were not repeated.[20] Indeed, the court found Chambers' actions were "part of [a] sordid scheme of deliberate misuse of the judicial process" designed "to defeat NASCO's claim by harassment, repeated and endless delay, mountainous expense and waste of financial resources." It was within the court's discretion to vindicate itself and compensate NASCO by requiring Chambers to pay for all attorney's fees. . . .

Chambers challenges the District Court's imposition of sanctions for conduct before other tribunals, including the FCC, the Court of Appeals,

---

[20] In particular, Chambers challenges the assessment of attorney's fees in connection with NASCO's claim for delay damages and with the closing of the sale. As NASCO points out, however, Chambers' bad-faith conduct in the course of the litigation caused the delay for which damages were sought and greatly complicated the closing of the sale, through the cloud on the title caused by the fraudulent transfer.

and this Court, asserting that a court may sanction only conduct occurring in its presence. Our cases are to the contrary, however. As long as a party receives an appropriate hearing, as did Chambers, the party may be sanctioned for abuses of process occurring beyond the courtroom, such as disobeying the court's orders. Here, for example, Chambers' attempt to gain the FCC's permission to build a new transmission tower was in direct contravention of the District Court's orders to maintain the status quo pending the outcome of the litigation, and was therefore within the scope of the District Court's sanctioning power. . . .

■ [The dissenting opinion of JUSTICE SCALIA is omitted.]

■ JUSTICE KENNEDY, with whom THE CHIEF JUSTICE and JUSTICE SOUTER join, dissenting.

Today's decision effects a vast expansion of the power of federal courts, unauthorized by rule or statute. I have no doubt petitioner engaged in sanctionable conduct that warrants severe corrective measures. But our outrage at his conduct should not obscure the boundaries of settled legal categories.

With all respect, I submit the Court commits two fundamental errors. First, it permits the exercise of inherent sanctioning powers without prior recourse to controlling rules and statutes, thereby abrogating to federal courts Congress' power to regulate fees and costs. Second, the Court upholds the wholesale shift of respondent's attorney's fees to petitioner, even though the District Court opinion reveals that petitioner was sanctioned at least in part for his so-called bad-faith breach of contract. The extension of inherent authority to sanction a party's prelitigation conduct subverts the American Rule and turns the *Erie* doctrine upside down by punishing petitioner's primary conduct contrary to Louisiana law. Because I believe the proper exercise of inherent powers requires exhaustion of express sanctioning provisions and much greater caution in their application to redress prelitigation conduct, I dissent. . . .

Inherent powers are the exception, not the rule, and their assertion requires special justification in each case. . . .

Inherent powers can be exercised only when necessary, and there is no necessity if a rule or statute provides a basis for sanctions. . . .

[T]he Federal Rules of Civil Procedure are "as binding as any statute duly enacted by Congress, and federal courts have no more discretion to disregard the Rule[s'] mandate than they do to disregard constitutional or statutory provisions." Bank of Nova Scotia *v.* United States, 487 U.S. 250, 255 (1988). See also Fed. Rule Civ. Proc. 1 (Federal Rules "*govern* the procedure in the United States district courts in *all* suits of a civil nature") (emphasis added). . . .

The Federal Rules establish explicit standards for, and explicit checks against, the exercise of judicial authority. . . . These definite standards give litigants notice of proscribed conduct and make possible meaningful review for misuse of discretion—review which focuses on the misapplication of legal standards.

By contrast, courts apply inherent powers without specific definitional or procedural limits. . . . This standardless exercise of judicial power may appear innocuous in this litigation between commercial actors. But the same unchecked power also can be applied to chill the advocacy of litigants attempting to vindicate all other important federal rights. . . .

By allowing exclusive resort to inherent authority whenever "conduct sanctionable under the rules was intertwined within conduct that only the inherent power could address," the Court encourages all courts in the federal system to find bad-faith misconduct in order to eliminate the need to rely on specific textual provisions. This will ensure the uncertain development of the meaning and scope of these express sanctioning provisions by encouraging their disuse, and will defeat, at least in the area of sanctions, Congress' central goal in enacting the Federal Rules—"uniformity in the federal courts." Hanna *v.* Plumer, 380 U.S. 460, 472 (1965). . . .

NOTE

In certain contexts, an award of fees is appropriate as a form of compensation for substantive wrongdoing. Examples include malicious prosecution and false arrest.

Brandt was injured and made a claim against Standard Insurance. Standard denied the claim in bad faith. Brandt brought an action (1) to obtain the benefits due and (2) for damages for breach of the insurers' implied duty of good faith. The court awarded attorney's fees to Brandt:

> "When an insurer's tortious conduct reasonably compels the insured to retain an attorney to obtain the benefits due under a policy, it follows that the insurer should be liable in a tort action for that expense. The attorney's fees are an economic loss—damages—proximately caused by the tort. These fees must be distinguished from recovery of attorney's fees *qua* attorney's fees, such as those attributable to the bringing of the bad faith action itself. What we consider here is attorney's fees that are recoverable as damages resulting from a tort in the same way that medical fees would be part of the damages in a personal injury action. . . .
>
> "The fees recoverable, however, may not exceed the amount attributable to the attorney's efforts to obtain the rejected payment due on the insurance contract. Fees attributable to obtaining any portion of the plaintiff's award which exceeds the amount due under the policy are not recoverable."

Brandt *v.* Superior Court, 37 Cal. 3rd 813, 817, 819 (1985).

In re Estate of Szorek

Illinois Court of Appeals, 1990.
194 Ill. App. 3d 750.

■ PRESIDING JUSTICE LAPORTA delivered the modified opinion of the court . . . .

Walter Szorek died intestate on March 20, 1987 . . . . Prior to his death and at the direction of Szorek plaintiff transferred approximately $72,000 of Szorek's funds then on deposit in a Fairfield Savings and Loan account to a certificate of deposit with defendant Liberty Savings and Loan Association. The certificate of deposit account was opened on February 6, 1987, in the names of Walter Szorek and plaintiff as joint tenants with right of survivorship.

Upon Szorek's death, . . . plaintiff attempted to collect the funds from defendant as surviving joint tenant[. She] was advised by an officer of defendant association that because of a discrepancy of Szorek's date of birth on the signature card and his date of birth on the death certificate, they would not pay the funds to her.

Within weeks of Szorek's death the public administrator opened a probate estate and was appointed administrator by the court. [The public administrator claimed the certificate of deposit as an asset of the estate and filed an action to recover the amount of the certificate from the defendant bank, on behalf of unknown heirs of Szorek. Plaintiff then filed a declaratory judgment action asserting her right to the funds as surviving joint tenant. The defendant filed a counterclaim in interpleader to resolve the controversy over ownership, and the actions were consolidated.] . . .

Following a hearing . . . , the trial judge ordered defendant to turn over the entire account balance plus accrued interest to plaintiff except for the sum of $3,500 reserved pending a hearing on defendant's petition for fees and costs. On July 19, 1988, the trial judge awarded defendant the sum of $3,757.39 for attorney fees ($3,647) and costs ($110.39) to be paid from the funds reserved and the balance to be paid by plaintiff. . . .

We first consider the agreement entered into by the parties when the account was created. . . .

Upon deposit of Szorek's funds, defendant required plaintiff and Szorek to execute signature cards as part of its customary process in opening a certificate of deposit account. The language of the signature card states in pertinent part: . . .

> "The undersigned agree that this account is subject to and is to be administered in accordance with the rules established by the Board of Directors for the account established herewith, and acknowledge receipt of a copy of said rules."

Also part of the record is defendant's disclosure statement for certificates of deposit which contains this language:

> "Account Rules and Regulations for Savings and Certificate of Deposit. By signing the signature card associated with your Liberty Savings savings account and a variety of certificates of deposit, you, the account holder, have agreed that your account be bound by this agreement, now in force and to such other rules as may be changed and adopted hereafter. . . .
>
> "8. Death or Incompetence: The Association may prohibit or restrict withdrawals upon being notified of the death or incompetence of an account holder until all the obligations according to this Agreement and the law have been met. . . .
>
> "11. Expenses and Charges: All expenses incurred by the Association relative to this account on account of summons, subpoena, garnishment, citation, attachment, levy or any other proceedings affecting this account, including court costs and attorney's fees, shall be charged to the account holder . . . .
>
> "In the event the institution becomes a party to any legal proceedings between you and third persons, or between account holders, it is agreed that the account holders will pay, compensate and reimburse all liability, costs, charges and expenses, including attorney's fees and court costs, incurred by the Institution as a result of such proceedings."

Plaintiff argues that the printed language of the signature card was an adhesion contract, standardized and offered to the depositor without any realistic opportunity to bargain or to do anything other than acquiesce to its specified terms. While the depositor plaintiff here was asked to sign the association's standardized form of agreement to open the account, she did not object to its terms, and, of course, she could have elected to invest the funds elsewhere and sought other terms. Having chosen to open this account plaintiff agreed to all of its terms.

Plaintiff next argues . . . that the signature card was virtually unreadable, and she was unaware that the so-called agreement provided that defendant was entitled to recover litigation attorney fees and costs from the depositor should the account be legally challenged in a court of law. . . .

[P]laintiff's responses to questions about events following her visit to the defendant association to open the account disclosed that she signed the card there and then took the bank book, signature cards and "papers" to Szorek and left them for his signature and to be mailed by him to the defendant. She clearly had the opportunity at that time to read its terms with any assistance needed if she so desired.

We next consider whether plaintiff had knowledge of the rules and regulations by which the account would be administered. . . . The signature card signed by plaintiff acknowledges her receipt of a copy of the rules.

Where required by the specific terms of a written contract expenses and attorney fees are recoverable. Where the language of a contract is clear and unambiguous it must be given full effect. . . .

[P]laintiff made no statement under oath either in her pleadings or by her testimony regarding whether she had received the disclosure statement. We must therefore accept her signed acknowledgement on the signature card that she received a copy of the rules.

The record also reveals that from 1979 to 1987 plaintiff was employed by Fairfield Savings and Loan Association and while so employed she dealt with customer deposits and accounts on a daily basis. Because of her eight years of bank experience and her familiarity with bank account documents, we find plaintiff's disclaimer of any knowledge that by executing the signature card she as the depositor agreed to reimburse defendant for attorney fees and litigation costs to be unpersuasive.

We next consider whether defendant acted properly in refusing to pay the account proceeds over to the plaintiff as the surviving joint tenant upon her demand following Szorek's death. . . .

[P]laintiff presented Szorek's death certificate which contained two items of information different from that on the signature card. The death certificate showed his date of birth to be July 17, 1907, and his residence as 1734 N. Paulina, Chicago, Illinois, whereas the account showed the date of birth as March 15, 1923, and his residence as 3659 N. Spaulding Street, Chicago, Illinois. Plaintiff also acknowledged, and the proof of heirship in the probate proceedings confirms, that she was not Szorek's daughter although the signature card listed her as his daughter. She furnished the erroneous information to the bank. . . .

Faced with the challenge of adverse claims on the funds defendant had the duty not only to respond to the citation and declaratory judgment actions, but to file a counterclaim in interpleader to resolve the ownership controversy, as it did. Defendant was indifferent as to the success of either plaintiff or administrator and was obligated and willing to pay the money to the one found by the court to be entitled to it; having filed its counterclaim in interpleader, defendant has fulfilled its duty with regard to the funds. . . .

[P]laintiff argues that an award of attorney fees to defendant was not appropriate because defendant was the unsuccessful litigant here. . . .

We find that defendant was neither the successful nor unsuccessful litigant here, but rather merely held funds for the benefit of an appropriate payee. By its agreement with the depositors and by all statutory requirements imposed by the legislature for the defendant's administering of the certificate of deposit funds defendant was required to pay the funds to the party legally entitled to them, and only after compliance with all legal requirements and resolution of disputed claims. . . .

NOTE

California Civil Code § 1717 provides:

> "ACTION ON CONTRACT; AWARD OF ATTORNEY'S FEES AND COSTS; PREVAILING PARTY; DEPOSIT OF AMOUNTS IN INSURED, INTEREST-BEARING ACCOUNT; DAMAGES NOT BASED ON CONTRACT
>
> "(a) In any action on a contract, where the contract specifically provides that attorney's fees and costs, which are incurred to enforce that contract, shall be awarded either to one of the parties or to the prevailing party, then the party who is determined to be the party prevailing on the contract, whether he or she is the party specified in the contract or not, shall be entitled to reasonable attorney's fees in addition to other costs. . . .
>
> "Attorney's fees provided for by this section shall not be subject to waiver by the parties to any contract which is entered into after the effective date of this section."

Rosenberg v. Levin

Supreme Court of Florida, 1982.
409 So.2d 1016.

■ OVERTON, JUSTICE. . . . Levin hired Rosenberg and Pomerantz to perform legal services pursuant to a letter agreement which provided for a $10,000 fixed fee, plus a contingent fee equal to fifty percent of all amounts recovered in excess of $600,000. Levin later discharged Rosenberg and Pomerantz without cause before the legal controversy was resolved and subsequently settled the matter for a net recovery of $500,000. Rosenberg and Pomerantz sued for fees based on a "quantum meruit" evaluation of their services. After lengthy testimony, the trial judge concluded that quantum meruit was indeed the appropriate basis for compensation and awarded Rosenberg and Pomerantz $55,000. . . .

The traditional contract rule adopted by a number of jurisdictions holds that an attorney discharged without cause may recover damages for breach of contract under traditional contract principles. The measure of damages is usually the full contract price, although some courts deduct a fair allowance for services and expenses not expended by the discharged attorney in performing the balance of the contract. Some jurisdictions following the contract rule also permit an alternative recovery based on quantum meruit so that an attorney can elect between recovery based on the contract or the reasonable value of the performed services.

Support for the traditional contract theory is based on: (1) the full contract price is arguably the most rational measure of damages since it reflects the value that the parties placed on the services; (2) charging the full fee prevents the client from profiting from his own breach of contract;

and (3) the contract rule is said to avoid the difficult problem of setting a value on an attorney's partially completed legal work.

To avoid restricting a client's freedom to discharge his attorney, a number of jurisdictions in recent years have held that an attorney discharged without cause can recover only the reasonable value services rendered prior to discharge. This rule was first announced in Martin *v.* Camp, 219 N.Y. 170 (1916), where the New York Court of Appeals held that a discharged attorney could not sue his client for damages for breach of contract unless the attorney had completed performance of the contract. The New York court established quantum meruit recovery for the attorney on the theory that the client does not breach the contract by discharging the attorney. Rather, the court reasoned, there is an implied condition in every attorney-client contract that the client may discharge the attorney at any time with or without cause. With this right as part of the contract, traditional contract principles are applied to allow quantum meruit recovery on the basis of services performed to date. Under the New York rule, the attorney's cause of action accrues immediately upon his discharge by the client, under the reasoning that it is unfair to make the attorney's right to compensation dependent on the performance of a successor over whom he has no control.

The California Supreme Court, in Fracasse *v.* Brent, 6 Cal. 3d 784 (1972), also adopted a quantum meruit rule. That court carefully analyzed those factors which distinguish the attorney-client relationship from other employment situations and concluded that a discharged attorney should be limited to a quantum meruit recovery in order to strike a proper balance between the client's right to discharge his attorney without undue restriction and the attorney's right to fair compensation for work performed. The *Fracasse* court sought both to provide clients greater freedom in substituting counsel and to promote confidence in the legal profession while protecting society's interest in the attorney-client relationship.

Contrary to the New York rule, however, the California court also held that an attorney's cause of action for quantum meruit does not accrue until the happening of the contingency, that is, the client's recovery. If no recovery is forthcoming, the attorney is denied compensation. The California court offered two reasons in support of its position. First, the result obtained and the amount involved, two important factors in determining the reasonableness of a fee, cannot be ascertained until the occurrence of the contingency. Second, the client may be of limited means and it would be unduly burdensome to force him to pay a fee if there was no recovery. The court stated that: "[S]ince the attorney agreed initially to take his chances on recovering any fee whatever, we believe that the fact that the success of the litigation is no longer under his control is insufficient to justify imposing a new and more onerous burden on the client." *Id.*, at 792.

The third rule is an extension of the second that limits quantum meruit recovery to the maximum fee set in the contract. This limitation is believed necessary to provide client freedom to substitute attorneys without economic penalty. Without such a limitation, a client's right to discharge an attorney may be illusory and the client may in effect be penalized for exercising a right.

The Tennessee Court of Appeals, in Chambliss, Bahner & Crawford *v.* Luther, 531 S.W.2d 108 (Tenn. Ct. App. 1975), expressed the need for limitation on quantum meruit recovery . . . :

> "To adopt the rule advanced by Plaintiff would, in our view, encourage attorneys less keenly aware of their professional responsibilities than Attorney Chambliss, . . . to induce clients to lose confidence in them in cases where the reasonable value of their services has exceeded the original fee and thereby, upon being discharged, reap a greater benefit than that for which they had bargained."

. . . It is our opinion that it is in the best interest of clients and the legal profession as a whole that we adopt the modified quantum meruit rule which limits recovery to the maximum amount of the contract fee in all premature discharge cases involving both fixed and contingency employment contracts. The attorney-client relationship is one of special trust and confidence. The client must rely entirely on the good faith efforts of the attorney in representing his interests. This reliance requires that the client have complete confidence in the integrity and ability of the attorney and that absolute fairness and candor characterize all dealings between them. These considerations dictate that clients be given greater freedom to change legal representatives than might be tolerated in other employment relationships. We approve the philosophy that there is an overriding need to allow clients freedom to substitute attorneys without economic penalty as a means of accomplishing the broad objective of fostering public confidence in the legal profession. Failure to limit quantum meruit recovery defeats the policy against penalizing the client for exercising his right to discharge. However, attorneys should not be penalized either and should have the opportunity to recover for services performed.

Accordingly, we hold that an attorney employed under a valid contract who is discharged without cause before the contingency has occurred or before the client's matters have concluded can recover only the reasonable value of his services rendered prior to discharge, limited by the maximum contract fee. We reject both the traditional contract rule and the quantum meruit rule that allow recovery in excess of the maximum contract price because both have a chilling effect on the client's power to discharge an attorney. Under the contract rule in a contingent fee situation, both the discharged attorney and the second attorney may receive a substantial percentage of the client's final recovery. Under the unlimited quantum meruit rule, it is possible, as the instant case illustrates, for the attorney to receive a fee greater than he bargained for under the terms of his contract. Both these results are unacceptable to us.

We further follow the California view that in contingency fee cases, the cause of action for quantum meruit arises only upon the successful occurrence of the contingency. If the client fails in his recovery, the discharged attorney will similarly fail and recover nothing. We recognize that deferring the commencement of a cause of action until the occurrence of the contingency is a view not uniformly accepted. Deferral, however, supports our goal to preserve the client's freedom to discharge, and any resulting harm to the attorney is minimal because the attorney would not have benefited earlier until the contingency's occurrence. There should, of course, be a presumption of regularity and competence in the performance of the services by a successor attorney.

In computing the reasonable value of the discharged attorney's services, the trial court can consider the totality of the circumstances surrounding the professional relationship between the attorney and client. Factors such as time, the recovery sought, the skill demanded, the results obtained, and the attorney-client contract itself will necessarily be relevant considerations. . . .

NOTES

1. Blanchard was awarded $10,000 for a beating unconstitutionally inflicted upon him by a police officer. The trial court granted him $7,500 in attorney's fees, but the Court of Appeals reduced that award to $4,000, the amount to which the lawyer was entitled under a contingency fee agreement with Blanchard. The appellate court's decision was based upon its view that a contingency fee agreement sets a ceiling on the fee recoverable under Section 1988.

The Supreme Court reversed. Blanchard *v.* Bergeron, 489 U.S. 87 (1989). In the Court's view, the statute "contemplates reasonable compensation . . . for the time and effort expended by the attorney for the prevailing plaintiff, no more and no less." Even if Blanchard's fee contract had induced his lawyer to handle the case without any expectation of further recovery under Section 1988, the statute ensures access of civil rights plaintiffs to competent legal assistance by requiring every losing defendant to pay every "prevailing" plaintiff a fee that a judge deems reasonable. Hence, even lawyers who are willing to handle civil rights cases on a *pro bono* basis are entitled to attorneys' fees under Section 1988. A contrary result might lead to "an undesirable emphasis . . . on the importance of the recovery of damages" in these cases.

2. Venegas charged police officers with violating his civil rights by falsely arresting him and lying at his trial. He hired Mitchell to represent him in his civil suit. Their contract set Mitchell's fee at 40% of the gross amount of any recovery. The contract also stated that Venegas would not waive any statutory right to recover attorneys' fees and that any statutory

recovery would reduce the amount owed under the contingent fee agreement on a dollar-for-dollar basis.

After Venegas won a judgment of $2,800,000, the trial court assessed Mitchell's statutory fee at $75,000. It also decided that Mitchell's claim was not limited to the statutory award, and that the contract set a reasonable fee. The Supreme Court affirmed, stating that "§ 1988 controls what the losing defendant must pay, not what the prevailing plaintiff must pay his lawyer." Venegas *v.* Mitchell, 495 U.S. 82, 90 (1990).

INDEX

References are to Pages